# BUSINESS POLICY
## Strategy Formation and Management Action

# McGRAW-HILL SERIES IN MANAGEMENT
## Keith Davis and Fred Luthans, Consulting Editors

# BUSINESS POLICY

## Strategy Formation and Management Action SECOND EDITION

WILLIAM F. GLUECK
College of Business and Public Administration
University of Missouri, Columbia

McGraw-Hill Book Company
NEW YORK  ST. LOUIS  SAN FRANCISCO  AUCKLAND  DÜSSELDORF
JOHANNESBURG  KUALA LUMPUR  LONDON  MEXICO  MONTREAL
NEW DELHI  PANAMA  PARIS  SÃO PAULO  SINGAPORE  SYDNEY
TOKYO  TORONTO

To Nancy

Bill, Lisa, David, and Melissa

BUSINESS POLICY: Strategy Formation and
Management Action

1 2 3 4 5 6 7 8 9 0  K P K P  7 8 3 2 1 0 9 8 7 6

Library of Congress Cataloging in Publication Data

Glueck, William F
  Business policy.

  (McGraw-Hill series in management)
  Includes bibliographies.
  1. Industrial management.   2. Industrial
management—Case studies.   I. Title.
HD31.G56   1976        658.4        75–30819
ISBN 0–07–023514–7

This book was set in Times Roman by Kingsport
Press, Inc. The editors were William J. Kane and
Matthew Cahill; the designer was Betty Binns;
the production supervisor was Judi Allen.
New drawings were done by Vantage Art, Inc.
Kingsport Press, Inc., was printer and binder.

# Contents

---

\* Disguised cases

# Preface

The second edition of this text, like the first, is designed to meet the needs of students of strategic planning and strategic management. The book itself contains three parts: text, readings, and cases. The *text* attempts to summarize the state of the art of business policy and strategic planning. It would be impossible to give all the references available. No doubt I have overlooked some important ones, but I have tried to review the work of most theorists, practitioners, and researchers in the field.

In comparison to the first edition, the *text has been thoroughly rewritten.* Some of the new features are:

**1** A conceptual model is used to tie the material together.

**2** Frequently used concepts are defined and displayed so that they can be easily located by the reader.

**3** Where appropriate, major findings have been summarized in propositional form.

**4** Important research studies are displayed for reading convenience.

In comparison to the previous edition, the *readings* section has been shortened, owing to the sharp increase in printing costs. Currently, there are eight readings, six of which are new. These readings were included because of their importance and their resistance to accurate summarization. Also, many of them are not readily available in all libraries.

The *case* section now includes a note about the case method. Only two of the twenty-three cases in the first edition are reprinted. There is an additional case in this edition, besides two industry notes. The new cases are up to date and include 1974 and sometimes 1975 data. Only seven cases are disguised. The remaining seventeen concern well-known companies whose products and services are of interest to most students.

Several new features in the case section are:

**1** Industry comparisons. For example, One-Day and Ideal Sheen are laundries, St. John's and St. Luke's are hospitals, Seven-Up and Dr Pepper are soft drink firms, Parkview and Seattle are in the arts, and Lacasse and Shuckman are similar industries. There is also one case oriented to the auto industry.

**2** Cases from nonbusiness sectors: arts (Parkview Symphony and Seattle Opera), health care (St. John's Hospital, St. Luke's Hospital), and cooperatives.

**3** A greater proportion of service industries in view of the shift in employment in that direction. Eleven of the twenty-four cases are service-related.

**4** Division of the cases into sections which parallel the text portion.

**5** One case, AMMCO, is available in film (from Northwestern University School of Management, attention of Dr. Ram Charan) as well as in the text.

**6** Two cases, St. John's Hospital and Hawaii Best, have later parts available in the Instructor's Manual for longitudinal analysis.

No book is the product of one author. Obviously, I am thankful to the authors of the research cited in the book. I also wish to thank the following writers for permission to reprint their articles: Robert Buchele (University of Hawaii), Arnold Cooper et al. (Purdue University), E. G. Malmlow (B&S Corporation, Zurich), Henry Mintzberg (McGill University), Dan Schendel et al. (Purdue University), Sidney Schoeffler et al. (Harvard Business School), and Donald Thain (University of Western Ontario).

I also wish to acknowledge those who wrote a portion of the cases contained in the book: Ichak Adizes and Marcia Blaine (University of California, Los Angeles), Archibald Cameron (Hawker Siddley, Ltd.), Ram Charan (Northwestern University), Sally Coltrin (Virginia Polytechnic Institute and State University), Richard Grimes (University of Texas) and William A. Russell, Charles Hofer (Northwestern University) and John Bringhurst, Walter Newsom (Mississippi State University), Paul Rabinowitz, Donald Scotten and Jeffrey Susbauer (Cleveland State University), and Richard Stover (Missouri Division of Corrections). Of course neither these cases nor my own would be possible without the cooperation of the enterprises studied. We thank them for their help. I also wish to thank Karl Stoeckel and John Scorah, who served as assistants for part of the book.

Finally, I wish to thank the following reviewers who gave helpful comments on the manuscript: Charles Hofer, Northwestern University; Harvey Hegarty, Indiana University; Lawrence Jauch, Kansas State University; Gene Newport, University of Alabama at Birmingham; Fred Luthans, University of Nebraska at Lincoln; and Robert Paul, University of Missouri at Columbia.

*William F. Glueck*

# Text
# and
# readings

## CHAPTER 1

# An invitation to strategic planning

## LEARNING OBJECTIVES

**1** To learn what the strategic planning process is

**2** To understand why strategic planning takes place

This is a book about business policy: the strategic planning process in businesses and other institutions in a developed society.

The book contains three types of material. The first is the textual material which describes what we know about business policy and strategy. Then there are some readings. These are essays (usually by other writers) which are included because they are important—so important that they are not summarized in the text alone. Finally, there are cases. The cases are descriptions of businesses, a few hospitals, some arts organizations, and cooperatives. The cases provide the reader with an opportunity to analyze the strategic planning of real organizations and prescribe improvements for them. The cases look at all aspects of the company that seem important to understanding the business as a whole. More will be said about case analysis in a short note at the beginning of the case section of the book. Understanding a company's strategy and effectiveness is not easy. It requires that you look at how the company has come to grips with the challenges and opportunities facing it. It requires you to make judgments about whether the business or hospital or co-op is well run and how to improve it. This is a challenging job—the job of top managers of divisions or companies. It will provide you with a new understanding of how companies succeed or fail.

## What is strategic planning?

After having mentioned business policy or strategic planning several times so far, it seems important to define the terms so that later uses will be clear. Business policy, long-range planning, strategic planning, and strategic management are terms which may have as many definitions as there are experts [1].[1] For all practical purposes, they mean the same thing. Strategic planning is the term that will be used in this book. There are many excellent definitions [2], and many experts have contributed to the understanding of these terms.

The objectives are the basic economic and social purposes for which the enterprise exists. For a business, examples of objectives are rate of return on investment and serving the public by offering

---

[1] Footnotes will not be used in this book. The authorities drawn on for a section are listed as references at the end of each chapter.

excellent airline service. For a hospital, an example is the offering of quality patient care to victims of heart disease at a minimum cost.

Strategy is the *means* used to achieve the ends (objectives). A strategy is not just any plan, however. A strategy is a plan that is unified: it ties all the parts of the enterprise together. A strategy is comprehensive: it covers all major aspects of the enterprise. A strategy is integrated: all the parts of the plan are compatible with each other and fit together well. Perhaps the managers in Figure 1–1 have hit on a great new strategy. Both Dr Pepper and 7UP companies are included as case studies in this book. Their managements assure me they have rejected the strategy for their companies. At any point in time, top managers examine the firm in its environment and try to plan their strategies for better results. Thus when William McCune took over as Polaroid's president in 1975, he tried to prepare a strategic plan to meet the challenges of increasing costs, declining profits, and the probable entry of Kodak into Polaroid's market.

Another way to describe strategic planning in more detail than this definition is to model the process. Figure 1–2 is the model of strategic planning used in this book. Each of the elements of the model is examined later in the book. The objectives are the ends the firm seeks to achieve. These are defined and interpreted by the top managers of the firm. The strategic planning process is normally performed by the top managers, although in some large enterprises, a planning staff may perform some of the detailed analysis for the top managers to save them time. In decentralized enterprises the strategists include division managers. Strategic planning is a continuous process, adapting to changing circumstances. Its output is not a document or plan, but rather a managerial philosophy. To say strategic planning is a process rather than a series of steps is not mere shifting of words. Witte and others have shown that there are *no* steps to decision making such as strategic planning. But we discuss steps separately because you cannot discuss a continuous process. The "steps" are interrelated and take place simultaneously.

### STRATEGIC PLANNING IN THE NOT-FOR-PROFIT AND PUBLIC SECTORS [3]

Probably the first major institutions engaged in strategic planning were the military organizations. Earlier works on business strategy used many terms developed by such military theorists as von Clausewitz. It is generally recognized that much of the success of the great generals of history was due to their strategic planning. Generals such as Alexander the Great, Julius Caesar, Basil the Great, Napoleon, the Duke of Wellington, and Patton probably would not

*"Think of it, gentlemen—not only do we stop
polluting our waters but we produce
seventy–million gallons a year of the best soft
drink you've ever tasted!"*

**FIGURE 1–1** ■ Drawing by Erikson; copyright Playboy, 1969. Reproduced by special permission.

be known to you without the strategic planning done by themselves and their staffs.

Other institutions rise or fall partly because of their weaknesses or effectiveness of the strategies. There are no more Whig or Federalist political parties. Some unions such as the Knights of Labor and the IWW did not succeed. Governments and government agencies come and go. The Tennessee Valley Authority prospered because of good strategy, as Selznick has shown. And James Webb was an excellent strategist for NASA. More or better strategic planning may have saved some and advanced the fortunes of others. East has shown how strategic planning can be quite similar in business and government.

Some formal church organizations are in financial troubles and may cease to exist. Adair's study of the Church of England indicates how it might reach its objectives by better strategic planning. Higher education is another sector which badly needs strategic planning. Reimnetz, Clark, and Hosmer have examined this. Clark attributes the past successes of Swarthmore, Antioch, and Reed Colleges to the strategic planning of these institutions. Hosmer shows that three new schools of administration failed because of poor strategic planning. It is my belief that many colleges and universities will close their

**5**

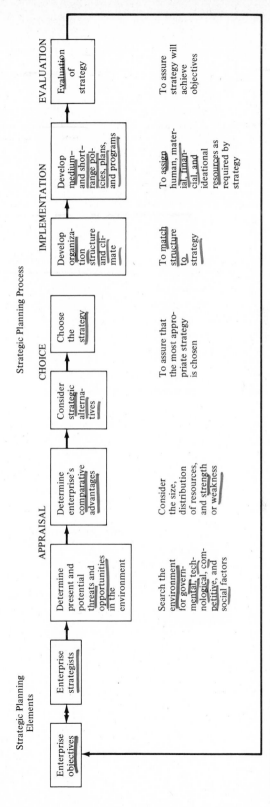

**FIGURE 1–2** ■ A model of strategic planning.

doors and others will barely survive in the next 10 years unless they develop an effective strategy.

Douglas Mankin, Richard Grimes, and I have examined how health care facilities such as hospitals perform strategic planning. These studies extend over a 5-year period and will provide some insights.

Cases that focus on the operations of several nonbusiness sectors (hospitals, consumer co-ops, arts organizations such as symphonies) have been included in this book. These allow you to apply the tools of strategic planning across several sectors. Because you do not know now which kinds of organizations you will work for in the course of your career, it is useful for you to be exposed to many sectors.

## Why strategic planning? [4]

Most of us want to know why we should continue looking at a topic before we go on. There are lots of things we can do with our time besides reading a book or learning about a particular subject. This section will give you some reasons for learning more about strategic planning.

All kinds of reasons can be given by executives and researchers as to why firms (and other institutions) should engage in business policy or strategic planning. Only a few will be listed here.

**1** *The conditions of most businesses change so fast that strategic planning is the only way to anticipate future problems and opportunities.* Much will be said in this book about changes business faces and how these changes have increased dramatically in the last half-century. Of course, the amount of change and the severity of it is not equal in all businesses. Perhaps you know what a washboard is. Your grandmother washed your parents' clothes on one. Several companies make them in 1976. Obviously, the environment facing American Washboard is not as fast-changing as that facing IBM. Strategic planning allows a firm's top executives to anticipate change and provide direction and control for the enterprise. It will also allow the firm to innovate in time to take advantage of new opportunities in the environment and reduce its risk because it anticipated the future. It also helps assure full exploitation of opportunities.

**2** *Strategic planning provides all the employees with clear goals and directions to the future of the enterprise.* Most people perform better (in quality and quantity) if they know what is expected to be done and where the enterprise is going. This also helps reduce conflict. Effective strategic planning points the way for the employees to follow. It provides a strong incentive to employees and management to achieve company objectives. It also serves as the basis for management control and evaluation.

**3** *Businesses which perform strategic planning are more effective than those which do not, and their employees are more satisfied.* This reason has been advanced by many experts for a long time. For example, in the first article published in the *Harvard Business Review* in 1922, Harvard's Dean Wallace Donham in effect made this argument. He contended that unless business systematized its decision making, business decisions were little different from gambling decisions. Strategic planning is one way to systematize the most important of business decisions. Now business involves great risk taking. But strategic planning attempts to provide data so that reasonable and informed gambles can be made when necessary.

Successful companies are successful for many reasons: adequate resources, good people, luck, good products and services, and so on. This is not to say

■ **THE ANSOFF STUDY**

Igor Ansoff and his associates looked at 93 companies which had made important strategic decisions about mergers and acquisitions during the period 1946–1965. They wanted to see if those companies that had planned the mergers in a strategic planning sense were more successful than those companies that did not. The study found that those doing strategic planning outperformed the nonplanners on all financial and sales measures such as earnings growth, asset growth, stock price growth, sales growth, earnings-per-share growth, and others. Besides performing better, the companies that used strategic planning were able to predict the outcomes of their planning much better than the nonplanners.

■ **THE EASTLACK AND McDONALD STUDY**

Eastlack and McDonald studied 211 companies. (Of these, 105 were from the *Fortune* 500's largest companies and the other half from a random sample of presidents of companies who read *Harvard Business Review*.) They concluded that chief executive officers who involved themselves in strategic planning headed the fastest-growing companies.

■ **THE STAGNER STUDY**

Stagner studied 217 top executives in 109 large American firms. Among his findings were the following: Where strategic planning took place using a top management committee, the firms had the largest profit as a percentage of capital. Where meetings involved a discussion of strategy among all top executives, where they carefully considered the decisions with regard to cost and profit, and where they kept a record of the decisions, the firms had the largest profit as a percentage of sales.

■ **PIMS PROJECT**

Schoeffler, Buzzell, and Heany report on an in-depth study of 57 large corporations that engage in 620 different businesses. These men have been gathering data on how such factors as share of market, investment intensity, and corporate diversity affect return on investment or profitability. Their data are so consistent as to indicate that by using them and similar institutional data, strategic planning can pay off very well indeed. This study appears as a reading in Chapter 6.

■ **THUNE AND HOUSE STUDY**

These researchers studied 18 matched pairs of medium- to large-size companies in the petroleum, food, drug, steel, chemical, and machinery industries. One firm of about the same size and growth rate did not use strategic planning; the other did. Thune and House observed the results for 7 years after the one company in each pair initiated strategic planning. They found that the firms which had formal strategic planning significantly outperformed their own past results and those of the nonplanners on most measures of success such as return on equity, earnings-per-share growth, return on investment. On no measure of success did the planners underperform the nonplanners.

■ **THE HEROLD STUDY**

Herold observed the performance of Thune and House's pairs of companies in the drug and chemical industries for 4 years after their study was completed. In those 4 years, the companies with formal strategic planning continued to outperform the nonplanners. In fact, the planners increased the margin of performance improvement over the nonplanners.

---

that strategic planning is all you need to make a success of your business career. But there have been several studies (see page 7) which show that firms that plan their strategies are more effective [5].

These are not the only studies which give indications of the value of strategic planning. Recent sophisticated investigations by Hatten and Kirchoff give us hope that strategic planning can isolate the key factors in an industry and thus help a firm plan its strategy more effectively. The studies do not *prove* that strategic planning leads invariably to success. A few studies have questioned this. When Najjar asked 94 small Ohio firms' executives about strategic planning, the companies who planned did not necessarily *think* they were more successful. Najjar did not look at the *actual* performance to find out, though. And Rue and Fulmer found that some service industry firms who were nonplanners outperformed the planners. It really is impossible to *prove* that strategic planning always pays. To do that, you would have to hold constant all kinds of variables which the "real world" does not allow us to hold constant. But what these studies should tell you is that strategic planning looks as if it is worth learning about. I contend that Proposition 1–1 is true.

Because of the studies about strategic planning, many businesses make sure it is a part of their management development programs. The American Assembly of Collegiate Schools of Business strongly suggest that accredited schools of business teach strategic planning. They do this because they tend to accept these research studies. They also do so because they believe that persons exposed to strategic planning will develop a breadth of understanding of the general manager. Strategic planning focuses on business problems, not just functional problems such as marketing or financial problems. By simulating applications of strategic planning such as cases and games, business policy or strategic planning helps build your knowledge of management and develops the attitudes necessary to be a successful business generalist and practitioner. It should also help in learning how to assess a business to determine if one prefers to be employed by it or to purchase its stock.


## A final distinction and a preview

As we progress through this book, you will be exposed to several kinds of material. Two of them are called normative and descriptive studies. *Normative* studies report what the manager or researcher feels strategic planning or one

---

**PROPOSITION** ■ Businesses which develop formal strategic planning systems will be more ef-
**1–1** fective in achieving their objectives than those which do not.

---

of its parts *should be. Descriptive* studies report on what the manager or researcher *actually found happening* during strategic planning.

The fact is that we know little about how many organizations do strategic planning. But what we do know has increased greatly in the last 10 years and is increasing rapidly at present [6].

The normative and descriptive studies will be clearly identified and their findings will be examined and evaluated.

In the chapters that follow, we shall now examine in more detail the strategic planning process and important issues about strategic planning. Chapter 2 discusses the key elements of strategic planning: the strategic decision makers, how decisions are reached in business, and the decision outcomes (objectives). Then the strategic planning process is described beginning with Chapter 3.

## References

**[1]** A list of some of the definers includes:

Ackoff, Russell: *A Concept of Corporate Planning,* New York: Wiley, 1970.

Anshen, Melvin, and William Guth: "Strategies for Research in Policy Formulation," *Journal of Business,* **46** (3): 1973.

Drucker, Peter: "Entrepreneurship in Business Enterprise," *Journal of Business Policy,* **1** (1): 1970.

Egerton, Henry C., and James K. Brown: *Planning and the Chief Executive,* New York: Conference Board, 1972.

Hussey, E.: *Introducing Corporate Planning,* Oxford, U.K.: Pergamon, 1971.

Newman, William: "Selecting a Company Strategy," *Journal of Business Policy,* **2** (2): 1971/72.

Schendel, Dan, and Kenneth Hatten: "Business Policy or Strategic Management?" *Proceedings, Academy of Management,* 1972.

Taylor, Bernard: "Introducing Strategic Management," *Long Range Planning,* September 1973.

Thomas, S. Denis: "Educational Objectives for Business Policy," *Journal of Business Policy,* **2** (3): 1972.

**[2]** The following had direct influence on the definition used in this book:

Ansoff, H. Igor: *Corporate Strategy,* New York: McGraw-Hill, 1965.

Cohen, Kalman, and Richard Cyert: "Strategy: Formulation, Implementation, and Monitoring," *Journal of Business,* **46** (4): 1973.

Grinyer, Peter: "The Anatomy of Business Strategic Planning Reconsidered," *Journal of Management Studies,* **8** (2): 1971.

Steiner, George: "Comprehensive Managerial Planning," chap. 12 in J. McGuire (ed.), *Contemporary Management,* Englewood Cliffs, N.J.: Prentice-Hall, 1974.

Witte, Eberhard: "Field Research on Complex Decision Making Process: The Phase Theorem," *International Studies of Management and Organization,* **2**: 1972.

**[3]** Adair, John: "Formulating Strategy for the Church of England," *Journal of Business Policy,* **3** (4): 1973.

Clark, Burton: "Belief and Loyalty in College Organization," *Journal of Higher Education,* **46** (6): June 1971.

East, R. J.: "Comparison of Strategic Planning in Large Corporations and Government," *Long Range Planning,* **5** (2): 1972.

Hosmer, LaRue: "Academic Strategy," unpublished D.B.A. thesis, Harvard Business School, 1972.

Reimnetz, Charles: "Testing a Planning and Control Model in Non Profit Organizations," *Academy of Management Journal,* March 1972.

Selznick, Phillip: *TVA & the Grassroots,* Berkeley: University of California Press, 1949.

**[4]** Ansoff, H. Igor: *Corporate Strategy,* New York: McGraw-Hill, 1965, chap. 1.

————: "Strategy as a Tool for Coping with Change," *Journal of Business Policy,* **1** (4): 3–7, Summer 1971.

Donham, Wallace B.: "Essential Groundwork for a Broad Executive Theory," *Harvard Business Review,* **1** (1): 1–10, October 1922.

Drucker, Peter: *Management,* New York: Harper & Row, 1973, chap. 61.

Nanus, Burt, and Robert Coffey: "Future Oriented Business Education," *California Management Review,* **15** (4): 28–34, Summer 1973.

**[5]** Ansoff, H. Igor, et al.: *Acquisition Behavior of U.S. Manufacturing Firms, 1946–65,* Nashville, Tenn.: Vanderbilt University Press, 1971.

Eastlack, Joseph, Jr., and Philip McDonald: "CEO's Role in Corporate Growth," *Harvard Business Review,* pp. 150–163, May–June 1970.

Hatten, Kenneth: "Strategy, Profits, and Beer," *Proceedings, Academy of Management,* 1975.

Herold, David: "Long Range Planning and Organizational Performance: A Cross Validation Study," *Academy of Management Review,* pp. 91–102, March 1972.

Kirchoff, Bruce: "Empirical Analysis of the Strategic Factors Contributing to Return on Investment," *Proceedings, Academy of Management,* 1975.

Najjar, Mohamed: "Planning in Small Manufacturing Companies," unpublished Ph.D. thesis, Ohio State University, 1966.

Rue, Leslie, and Robert Fulmer: "Is Long Range Planning Profitable?" *Proceedings, Academy of Management,* 1972.

Schoeffler, Sidney, Robert Buzzell, and Donald Heany: "Impact of Strategic Planning on Profit Performance," *Harvard Business Review,* pp. 137–145, March–April 1974.

Stagner, Ross: "Corporate Decision Making," *Journal of Applied Psychology,* **53** (1): 1–13, February 1969.

Thune, Stanley, and Robert House: "Where Long Range Planning Pays Off," *Business Horizons,* pp. 81–87, August 1970.

**[6]** Some good summaries of recent research in strategic planning are:

Hofer, Charles: "Research on Strategic Planning: A Summary of Past Studies and Suggestions for Future Efforts," *Proceedings, Academy of Management,* 1973.

————: "Research on a Contingency Theory of Strategic Behavior: Issues and Methods," *Proceedings, Midwest Academy of Management,* 1974.

————: "Toward a Contingency Theory of Strategic Behavior," *Proceedings, Academy of Management,* 1974.

Taylor, Bernard: "The Future Development of Corporate Strategy," *Journal of Business Policy,* **2**(2): 1972.

## CHAPTER 2

# Basic elements of strategic planning

**1** To get a better understanding of who strategic planners are

**2** To understand how managers make decisions in real organizations

**3** To learn what organizational objectives are, how they are formed, changed, and have impact on the strategic planning process

In our initial chapter, a model of the strategic planning was presented. This is reproduced as Figure 2–1. The highlighted portion indicates that this chapter will focus on the basic elements involved in strategic planning: the decision makers, how they make decisions, and how enterprise objectives fit into strategic planning.

## Decision makers and their jobs [1]

Three groups of individuals come to mind when we think of those who make strategic planning decisions: boards, top managers of companies and/or divisions, and corporate planning staffs.

The ultimate authority of most institutions rests in a board. In universities, the board is called board of regents, board of curators, and other titles. In business, boards are usually called boards of directors.

In theory, boards are composed of knowledgeable individuals who can pass judgment on management's decisions. The National Industrial Conference Board's study of 753 corporations found that boards of industrial firms generally have from 9 to 11 members, whereas bank boards typically have as many as 24. They found that there has been a trend toward outside domination of boards, and that by 1962, 63 percent of industrial firms surveyed had boards with a majority of outside members. Eighty-five percent of the financial firms surveyed also had outside boards. Ninety percent of the manufacturing firms surveyed elected directors for 1-year terms.

Boards can emphasize one or several of these six duties more than the others. For example, if the corporation is closely held, the board may be stockholder-oriented and emphasize roles 2 and 3.

If outside contacts are important for the success of the corporation, then the board may emphasize role 5. The board may consist primarily of outsiders (nonmanagers). If outside contacts are not important, the board may be primarily composed of insiders (managers) and it may stress role 4. Desfosses and Smith found that 57.5 percent of large company directors are insiders. There are legal restrictions on interlocking directors, and these may limit the choices a management has to develop its board.

Pfeffer studied the boards of 80 large and medium-sized U.S. nonfinancial corporations. He found that businesses tended to use their boards as

11

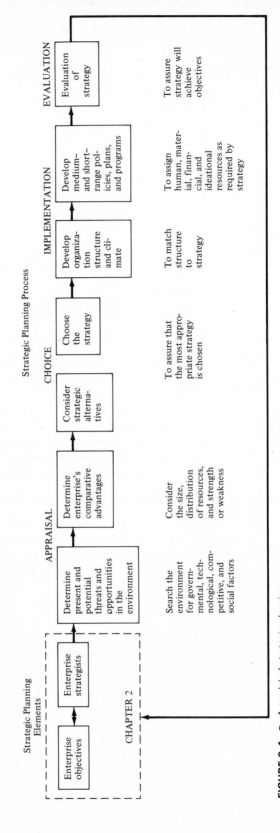

**FIGURE 2–1** ■ A model of strategic planning.

a way to tie themselves to other needed organizations, for example, banks. He found that the larger the company, the larger the board. He also found that the more the firm needed outside capital and the more it was regulated, the greater was the percentage of outside directors.

So much for the theory of boards. Most studies of the boards find that they are not effective in fulfilling their duties. Studies by Drucker and Mace summarize the findings to support this statement (see page 14).

Mace found these roles because boards are the creatures of the top managements who nominate persons for board membership. The stockholders simply ratify their choices.

Recent events may change this. Directors are legally liable for inadequate performance. Several legal cases such as *Escott v. Bar Chris Construction Corp.* (283 F. Supp. 643; S.D.N.Y. 1968) and Penn Central have led to suits and litigation. One suit against the directors of a Beverly Hills bank charged the 24 directors and top managers with mismanagement, and the plaintiffs sought $350 million in damages. One result is that directors are taking out more liability insurance for themselves. One insurance company said this had increased 900 percent in the last 5 years and $63 million claims against the insurance were being processed in 1 year. Another response is that more executives are refusing directorships. And the Securities and Exchange Commission has stepped in requiring boards to be changed. For example, the SEC has required Mattel to put more outsiders on the board.

IMPROVE THE BOARD OF DIRECTORS?

Obviously if no one will serve on the board, we shall have no boards. So various persons have made suggestions for improving the operations of boards.

What Drucker calls the functioning board or sub-board has been called a corporate audit committee of the boards. Mautz and Neumann found few of these operating in industry in 1970. By 1974, the *Wall Street Journal* reported that its study found 80 percent of the 1130 companies responding had audit committees of outside directors. The idea is for the board to have an information source available to it *independent* of management to protect itself and better serve as directors.

■ **PETER DRUCKER'S OBSERVATIONS**
Peter Drucker has been on boards and has studied them for years. His comments on boards can be summarized as follows: Regardless of their composition and legal position anywhere in the world, boards do not function as they are said to function (as supervisors of management).

Drucker supports his statement by observing that invariably when there is a corporate disaster, the board seems to be the last to know it. This is so, he argues, because to perform effectively, the board requires full-time people. Yet the board typically meets quarterly for a few days each time. And Drucker believes boards are not effective because management *does not* want them to be effective.

■ **MYLES MACE'S STUDY**
Myles Mace has studied boards for years. He is the author of several books on the subject and he too has personal experience on many boards. With regard to boards of large and medium-sized firms, his studies found that the outside directors played the following roles:

**1** Outside directors are advisers to the company president. They do not make significant decisions.

**2** The outside members do serve as some sort of discipline for the company president, requiring him to explain his behavior quarterly.

**3** In crises, boards occasionally do make decisions.

**4** Boards do not establish corporate objectives, form policies, or do strategic planning. Management does this.

**5** Boards do not ask probing or discerning questions. They ratify decisions already made.

**6** Boards do not choose top managers. Except in crisis situations, they ratify the choices of the management.

---

The audit focuses on management's quality, the corporation's relationship to society, internal operations of the company, or whatever the board desires it to do. The committee of the board meets with executives of the company, the certified public accountants, or whomever they wish.

This instrument like many others will become what the board and top management want it to be: strong or weak, useful or useless. In summary, boards of directors do not engage in strategic planning. They ratify the strategic plans made by top managers, except in times of extreme crisis.

TOP MANAGERS [2]

Various perceptions exist of what a top executive, such as a president, is really like. These hardworking individuals are venerated by some and harpooned by others.

There is not the space to describe in detail what an executive is like psychologically or sociologically. The focus of this section will be how a top manager

RESEARCH ■ **DRUCKER'S SUGGESTIONS**
STUDY **1** Split the board into (a) a public or community relations board which deals with outside "publics," (b) a functioning board to review, counsel, and advise and if necessary remove management. There is no reason why both of these cannot be legally one board as long as the duties are separated.

**2** Put the right people on boards. Do *not* include former managers of the firm or those who sell things to the board such as lawyers, consultants, or suppliers. What is really needed is full-time professional directors who are independent of management and will serve for a maximum of 5 years.

is involved in strategic planning activity. As you learned in the discussion about boards of directors above, the top managers make the strategic decisions in most effective organizations. As Myles Mace has said: "Effective corporate planning is not possible without the personal involvement and leadership of the chief operating executive."

And Harry Henshel, president of Bulova Watch Company, says in his article "The President Stands Alone" that no one will make risky strategic decisions if the president does not take the lead in strategic planning. Henshel describes how he had to make three risky decisions to get Bulova moving again:

**1** To produce a new type of watch to take market leadership: the Accutron

**2** To challenge Timex with a low-priced quality watch: the Caravelle

**3** To broaden the marketing channels beyond traditional jewelers

He argues that none of these were popular, all of them were necessary, and without presidential action, Bulova would have continued their steep decline.

This and other evidence tends to suggest that top managers should be selected for their strategic planning abilities.

In decentralized organizations, sometimes strategic planning decisions are delegated for a division's business sector to division vice presidents (or presidents). These individuals are described by Uyterhoeven. They must satisfy their superiors in their strategic planning activities.

To really understand how strategic planning decisions take place, it is vital that we review what the top managers' jobs are really like [3]. There are lots of articles and books around describing *in general* what a manager does. Most of these describe a manager as a planner, organizer, controller, etc. This is inadequate as a job description. It is more of a *normative* narrative: what a manager should do. There have been some good studies of what a manager actually does. The researchers learned by observing and recording the executive's activities or by asking the executive to record in diaries or question-

DEFINITION ■ TOP MANAGERS
The *top managers* are those chief operating officers whose responsibility it is to make the major decisions for the firms. Normally they are the inside members of the board of directors. They may be called president, vice president, or administrator, or have other titles, depending on the institutions' history.

naires what he or she does. The best of these studies are in reference 3 and include the works of Carlson, Burns, Bates and Sykes, Beishon and Palmer, Heller, Stewart, Wilkie and Young, Horne and Lupton, Stogdill, Mahoney, Luijk, and Mintzberg. A summary of Mintzberg's findings is in the readings section of this chapter. Most of these studies portray an executive working under intense pressure, at a rapid pace with many interruptions. Many studies show that the executive has no more than 9 minutes between interruptions. The executive is interrupted primarily by verbal stimuli: telephone calls and visits from people or to people. The executive prefers to focus on action on present problems.

Not all the studies found as many interruptions. For example, Wilkie and Young studied owners of small furniture and lumber businesses. These managers spent more time alone and with fewer interruptions. There may be major differences between executives focusing primarily on functions such as marketing, as Perrow hints.

What does all this have to do with strategic planning? Some implications are as follows:

**1** To the extent that the research done thus far is representative of most top executives, there is inadequate time for other than superficial strategic planning.

**2** These work patterns could be the result of the job itself or of executive preferences for *action*.

**3** If significant strategic planning is to take place, there are several options: *(a)* redesign the executive job to include blocks of time to synthesize information to make rational and thoughtful decisions as opposed to superficial decisions, *(b)* use staff planners to do detailed data gathering to provide the executive with a more scientific basis for significant strategic planning.

Many of the writers [4] who forecast the future argue that one of these options just described will take place in the future. Table 2–1 is one such prediction.

Psychologists have spent a half-century documenting that there are significant differences between people on a variety of characteristics. Much of the evidence to date indicates that those who rise to top management tend to be *action*-oriented rather than contemplation-oriented. This need not be so in the future—not for all executives. But because this appears to be so at present, it is obvious why it is so difficult to introduce strategic planning in many companies.

### CORPORATE PLANNING STAFFS

As just discussed, some firms, mostly large and complex firms, have provided their chief executives with strategic planning staffs. Such a staff can participate in many aspects of the strategic planning process: it can perform environmental appraisal studies, it can study the firm to assess its strengths and weaknesses, it can generate some strategic alternatives and research their feasibility, and it can aid in implementing the strategy chosen in organization and policies. But all the evidence indicates that such a staff rarely, if ever, seriously participates in the strategic choice process. This is the *crucial* job of the top executive and the staff serves as the executive's research and follow-through team. There

**TABLE 2–1 ■ CHANGING CHARACTERISTICS OF GENERAL MANAGEMENT**

| Firm of today | Firm of the future |
|---|---|
| *Archetype requirements* | |
| Leader | Leader |
| Administrator-planner | Administrative planner |
| Entrepreneur | Extrapolative planner |
| | Entrepreneur |
| | Statesman |
| | System architect |
| *Timing priorities among archetype needs* | |
| Sequential | Simultaneous |
| *Contents of decisions* | |
| Operating issues, corporate policies | Strategy formulation, design of systems for strategy implementation |
| Exploitation of firm's current position | Innovation in patterns of firm's products, markets, and technology |
| Economic, technological, national intraindustry perspective | Economic, sociopolitical, technological, multinational, multi-industry perspective |
| *Decision process* | |
| Emphasis on historical experience, judgment, past programs for solving familiar problems | Emphasis on anticipation, rational analysis, pervasive use of specialist experts, techniques for coping with novel decision situations |
| Personnel-intensive process | Technology-intensive process |
| *Information for decisions* | |
| Formal information systems for internal performance history | Formal systems for anticipatory, external environment information |
| One-way, top-down flow of information | Interactive, two-way communication channels linking managers and other professionals with knowledge workers |
| Computer systems emphasizing volume and fast response information for general management | Computer systems emphasizing richness, flexibility, and accessibility of information for general management |
| Emphasis on periodic operations plans, capital and operating expenditure budgets | Emphasis on continuous planning, covering operations, projects, systems resource development |
| | Control based on cost-benefits forecasts |
| *Organizational design criteria* | |
| Continuous emphasis on efficiency, productivity in utilizing current resources and organization | Simultaneous continuous emphasis on efficiency, productivity, and innovation |
| Periodic emphasis on innovation in product-market patterns, technologies | |
| Emphasis on economies of scale | Emphasis on flexible, adaptive response |
| Emphasis on best assignment of task within organizational structure | Emphasis on best design of an ad hoc organization to perform a given task |

is a fairly large number of studies describing the kinds of persons serving on such a staff, the companies with such a staff, and the duties performed as just described by the staff [5]. *Business Week* in 1975 indicated that because of fast-changing conditions, some top managers were asking their corporate planning staffs to provide more information and recommendations. But, at their most powerful, the staff merely assists the chief executive. In some corporations where strategic planning is well developed (for example, General Electric), it takes place simultaneously at headquarters and divisions.

Proposition 2–1 is not meant to indicate that corporate planners do not perform useful functions or that to become a corporate planner is not a rewarding career. What it emphasizes is that the strategic decisions are made *by top management.*

## Realistic decision making [6]

Life has many decision opportunities for us. Much of our time is spent in
making decisions or choices. Some are not important: What shall I have for
lunch today? Should I drink a cola or an uncola at break time? Some are
important: Should I go to college or not? Should I marry Sam or Tom (Sally
or Teddy)? Should I marry at all? This book focuses on one special kind of
decision: strategic planning. In many ways strategic planning is like the serious
decisions just mentioned. Before one can fully understand one species of
decisions (strategic decisions), one needs to understand the genus: decision
making. Thus, the second key element of strategic planning is realistic decision
making. The next few pages will review for you *very briefly* what we know
about how people make decisions. This will help you evaluate strategic planning decisions better.

The description of decision making which follows is from many sources,
but one of the best I have found is that of MacCrimmon; I have followed his
analysis fairly closely.

A decision is made by a decision maker in a decision environment. This
environment is strongly influenced by the beliefs and values of the decision
maker, as will be discussed in the objectives section of the book.

There are various theories about how people make decisions. The main
theories will be briefly mentioned.

This theory is the oldest decision theory. It has been criticized because:

**1** The decision maker is often not a unique actor, but part of a multiparty decision situation.

**2** Decision makers are not rational enough or informed enough to consider all alternatives or know all the consequences. And information is costly.

**3** Decision makers make decisions with more than a maximization of objectives in mind. Besides, the objectives may change.

**4** Really this theory is *normative;* real decision makers do not make decisions this way.

*(B)* **Behavioral theory of decision making**

**1** The decision maker is an individual with needs, drives, and inclinations that are different from those of other decision makers involved in the process.

**2** The decision maker has limited knowledge of alternatives and the consequences of the decision.

**3** The organization in which the decision maker works limits the choices available to him or her.

**4** The decision maker does not seek to maximize outcomes, but he or she chooses the first *satisfactory* alternative he finds which fits his values.

Although this theory more closely fits the reality of decision making that most of us have seen, it has not received as much research support as is desirable. The developers of this theory, Herbert Simon, Richard Cyert, and James March, stated their theory and few have tried to prove or disprove it.

*(C)* **The political theory**

**1** Decision making is a process, not an act such as a single choice.

**2** Decisions are arrived at by considering some alternatives which are very close to the present way of doing things.

**3** The decision maker considers only a limited number of consequences: the most relevant and easiest to predict.

**4** Decisions are made when the several people involved in the process agree they have found a solution. They do this by mutual adjustment and negotiation following the rules of the game: the way decisions have been made in the organizations in the past.

---

The political theory has been developed primarily by Lindblom, Richard Nenstadt, and G. Allison. This approach, which Lindblom has called "incremental adjustment" or "disjointed incrementalism" or "muddling through," is not only the way decisions are made, they argue, but is the *best* way. This approach tends to support the observation that most of us have made: It is hard to move people off the dead center of where we are now.

Again, this "political theory" has not received as much "scientific" support as desirable. But a combination of the last two theories is a lot closer to the reality of decision making than the "rational" theory.

Every day, we have numerous things on our minds and a considerable amount to do. What does it take to arrive at a decision? MacCrimmon says it takes four conditions for decision making to start.

**1** *A gap must exist between desired state and existing state.* First, there must be a gap between level of objective achievement desired or expected and what we are achieving. Thus, if our objective was to achieve a market share of 10 percent and we are getting only 2 percent, there is a gap.

**2** *The gap must be large enough to be noticeable and thus perceived as deserving attention.* Some theorists refer to minimum thresholds before threats, opportunities, or gaps receive attention. If we are achieving 9½ percent market share, we may not notice the gap and thus no decision will be forthcoming.

**3** *The decision maker must be motivated to reduce the gap.* There are multiple objectives to our organization. Before a decision maker is motivated to make a decision, the gap must be a gap in a significant objective.

**4** *The decision maker must believe that she or he can do something about the gap.* If the decision maker believes the gap is beyond the control of himself, herself, or the organization, decision making will not take place. Thus, if a gap is a sales decline in corn, and the decline is caused by inadequate rain to grow the corn, the decision maker may not try to deal with the sales decline.

Once a problem is perceived as a gap, the decision maker begins to generate alternative solutions. The decision maker can choose routine methods of alternative generation (for example, looking at what the organization did before in such cases) or creative approaches. The latter can use such techniques as brainstorming, the morphological approach, relational algorithms, or synectics.

To help make the choice, the decision maker may gather information. The approaches used here can vary from conservative focusing on nearby persons and organizations to focused gambling. How much information is sought and from where depends on how the decision maker sees the problem. If it is a simple problem with which he or she has experience, little new information will be gathered. If it is quite different, then more information from unique sources might be sought.

The choice is based on the criteria chosen: the decision outcomes or objectives. These will be discussed in the next section.

## Decision outcomes: objectives

The third basic element in the strategic planning process is the ends sought by the process and the organization: the organizational objectives [7].

All organizations had objectives when they started. The original objective may be the current objective or the objective may have changed.

Is it easy to determine what an enterprise's objectives are? Not always. Most

*Organizational objectives* are those ends which the organization seeks to achieve by its existence and operations.

organizations have many objectives. Ideally, an analyst can categorize these into superior or ultimate objectives and secondary objectives. But the objectives change from pressures inside and outside the enterprise, as we shall see. The objectives can be very concretely spelled out or can be very vague. Many organizations drift along with little or no clear direction from objectives.

Rhenman divides objectives into two categories: External-institutional objectives—those which define the impact of the organization on its environment; and internal objectives—those which define how much is expected of the resources the organization has. An external objective might be to provide the cheapest life insurance to as many persons as possible; an internal objective might be to increase the return on investment to 6 percent per year. Rhenman then divides organizations into four types as shown in Table 2–2.

The marginal organization is one without formal objectives in mind. It usually is a small firm which has recently started and is simply trying to survive. If successful, it usually moves on to become a corporation (in Rhenman's sense, not the legal sense).

The appendix organization is one formed by another organization to serve the founding organization's purposes. So, it has external objectives, but no internal ones. Usually, this organization strives to become an "institution."

The corporation (not in the legal sense now, this is just Rhenman's title) has developed its internal objectives but has only a vague sense of its external purposes. The institution is an organization with a fully developed set of formal objectives. All four of these exist. So all four sets of possibilities about objectives exist too.

## WHY DO ORGANIZATIONS HAVE OBJECTIVES? [8]

It is not easy to formulate objectives, as we shall see. So why bother? There are at least three reasons why formal objectives are important:

1 Objectives define the organization in its environment.

2 Objectives help coordinate decisions and decision makers.

3 Objectives provide performance standards.

Most organizations need to justify their existence, that is, to make themselves legitimate in the eyes of governments, customers, and society at large.

### TABLE 2–2 ▪ ORGANIZATIONS AND OBJECTIVES: RHENMAN

|  | Without internal objectives | With internal objectives |
|---|---|---|
| **Without external objectives** | Marginal organization | Corporation (not legal sense) |
| **With external objectives** | Appendix organization | Institution |

By stating objectives, they also attract people to work for the organization who identify with the objectives. Thus, objectives define the enterprise. James Thompson tells us that organizations develop a set of objectives which define its domain and claim a sector of products or services offered and population served.

Second, stated objectives direct the attention of employees to desirable standards of behavior. They may reduce conflict in decision making if all employees know what the objectives are. They become constraints on decisions, as Simon has argued.

Finally, objectives provide the ultimate standard by which the organization judges itself successful, very successful, or unsuccessful. Without objectives, the organization has no basis for evaluating its success.

### HOW ARE OBJECTIVES FORMULATED? [9]

Objectives are formulated by the top managers of firms. These executives do not choose objectives in a vacuum. Their choices are affected by three factors.

1  The realities of the external environment and external power relationships
2  The realities of the enterprise's resources and internal power relationships
3  The value systems of the top executives

It should be made clear here that not all persons accept these conditions as important to how objectives are formed. Two simpler theories have been advanced. Traditional economists have suggested that the firm's objectives are simply the objectives of the entrepreneur or top manager. Chester Barnard believed that objectives were formed when a consensus about what the objectives were arose from the employees. This is a sort of "trickle up theory."

In the theory discussed here, it is asserted that top managers set the objectives and that there are several influencing factors. The first is *forces in the environment.* The managers may wish to maximize profits, but must modify this objective because of governmental regulations regarding pollution controls, excess profits tax, antitrust, consumer labeling, and others. Trade unions may require higher than market rates of wages, featherbedding requirements, fringe benefits, more holidays, and others. Competitors may sell other products or services at unrealistically low prices and spend excessive amounts on advertising. Suppliers may become monopolized and charge outrageous prices.

The second factor restraining the top managers is the internal resources of the firm. If the enterprise is American Telephone and Telegraph, it may be able to deal on more equal terms with big government, big labor, or big suppliers than Sally's Speedy Laundry can. So this conditions the objectives chosen.

Running through both these factors are the political realities of the management relative to other groups involved. Does the management have full support of the stockholders? Paul Smucker has the support of the Smucker family stockholders to emphasize quality as an objective for his preserves firm, for example. Has the management developed the support of employees and key employee groups like the professional employees' lower and middle management? If so, the management can set higher objectives that employees will help achieve. Or the management can act to force employees to meet the objectives and receive support from owners if they wish to establish drastic sanctions to assure success.

The third factor influencing choice of objectives is the *values and preferences of the managers* [10]. These are the values that managers have developed from their education, experience, and the information they receive in their jobs. So each manager's values are his or her own. But enterprises with strong value systems or ideologies will attract and retain managers whose values are similar. These values are essentially a set of attitudes about what is good or bad, desirable or undesirable.

In their most general description, values are classified as follows:

Theoretical: an orientation toward truth and knowledge
Economic: an orientation toward what is useful
Aesthetic: an orientation toward form and harmony
Social: an orientation toward people
Political: an orientation toward power
Religious: an orientation toward unity in the universe

Most studies show that executives show stronger inclination toward economic, theoretical, and political values than the other three.

But other values may relate more specifically to the choice of objectives than these general values. Below are listed the extremes of values.

Values toward various groups in the strategic situation:

| Very combative | 1 | Very passive |
|---|---|---|
| Very innovative | 2 | Noninnovative |
| Dynamic | 3 | Stable |
| Risk-oriented | 4 | Risk-aversive |
| Quality | 5 | Quantity |
| Autocratic | 6 | Participative |
| Enemy *TO ENV* | 7 | Friend *TO ENV.* |
| Caveat emptor | 8 | Socially responsible |
| Individual decision | 9 | Collective decision |

**1** For example, some executives believe that to be successful, a firm must attack in the marketplace. Others believe you "go along to get along."

**2** Some executives believe that to succeed, a firm must innovate. Others prefer to "let others make the mistakes first."

**3** Some executives prefer fast-changing, dynamic environments, others stable quiet sectors.

**4** Some executives know that to "win big, you must take big risks." Others comment, "Risk runs both ways."

**5** Some executives believe one is successful by producing quality. Others go for volume.

**6** Some executives believe one treats employees so they know who is boss. Others believe cooperation comes from participative style.

**7** Some executives view the government and consumers, unions, and other groups in society as enemies. Others believe cooperation is possible and desirable.

**8** Many executives believe their firms should be socially responsible. Others feel they are there to make a buck and let the buyer beware.

**9** Some executives believe that two or more heads are better than one. Others feel they are paid to make the decisions.

■ **PROTHRO'S STUDY (1920s)**
1 The business elite are superior to other men in ability.

2 The test of ability is competitive earnings.

3 Material or economic progress is the important goal.

4 Social stability is necessary.

5 Popular or majority control is dangerous.

6 Individualism must be preserved.

■ **SUTTON ET AL.'S STUDY (Late 1940s)**
1 The same six as Prothro.

2 Businessmen exist to serve the public's needs.

3 Opportunity for advancement must be provided for all achieving executives.

■ **ENGLAND STUDY; LUSK AND OLIVER STUDY (1960s and 1970s)**
1 My company is an important entity.

2 My customers should be served well.

3 Ability should be rewarded.

4 High productivity is what counts.

5 Profit maximization is a major objective.

6 Organizational efficiency is a major objective.

The list could go on. But it is easy to see how one set of executives with certain values would be inclined to emphasize one set of objectives, another group another set of objectives.

There have been a few studies of what values most business executives hold at any point in time. Various studies have listed the values business executives seemed to have at several points in time (see above).

In a replication of England's study, Raymond Lee found significantly different values held by Japanese and Korean managers and American managers.

Khandwalla studied 103 Canadian firms and their environment. Executives completed executive-values questionnaires. He also examined the firms' effectiveness. Grossly oversimplifying a comprehensive and detailed study, he found that in effective firms executives' values matched the needs of their environment. I condensed his multidimensional categories into two extremes and present them on page 25.

Thus, in successful firms, the managers had values which were functional considering their environment. We can summarize Khandwalla's findings, as shown in Proposition 2–2.

Specifically, then, how do decision makers choose objectives? They are not set by managers alone. They do not wait for a consensus to filter up to the top. They are set by a process like that described by Cyert and March, and

■ **KHANDWALLA'S FINDINGS ABOUT VALUES AND ENVIRONMENTS**

**Environment 1** | **Values**

Higher-technology firms (high R&D) | Flexibility
Higher rates of technological change | Lack of formality
High competitive pressure | Risk taking
High pressure from political, social, | Innovation-oriented attitude
  and other outside forces | Need for rational-systematic planning
Unpredictable, dynamic environments | Planning

**Environment 2**

Low-technology firms
Low rate of technological change | Formality and order by procedures
Lower competitive pressure | Risk aversion
Less outside pressure | Innovation-aversion attitude
Stable and safe environments | "Seat-of-the-pants" planning

---

**PROPOSITION
2–2**
■ In successful firms, managerial values will match the characteristics of the firms' environments.

---

by Lindblom. They result from the managers' trying to satisfy the needs of all groups involved with the enterprise. These coalitions of interests—stock-holders, employees, suppliers, customers, and others—have sometimes con-flicting objectives. Managers as the strongest group in the coalition try to reconcile these conflicts. Management cannot settle them once and for all. There is quasiresolution of conflict. They "bargain" with the various groups and try to produce a set of objectives which can satisfy the groups at that time.

Management does not begin to set objectives from scratch each year. They begin from the most recent set of objectives. These may have been set by strong leaders in the past. The leaders consider incremental changes from the present set, given the current environment and current demands of the conflicting groups. The managers have developed aspiration levels of what the objectives ought to be in a future period. In theory, managers could use indifference curves to compute the tradeoffs between two objectives. But, by muddling through, they set the current set of objectives to satisfy as many of the demands and their wishes as they can. Proposition 2–3 summarizes some of the points just made.

Organizational objectives change as a result of:

1 Increased demands from coalition groups that make up the enterprise.

2 Change of the aspiration levels of managers. They may begin to extrapolate past

---

**PROPOSITION
2–3**
■ Objectives are formed for an organization when its top managers react to com-plex interplay of the demands of groups in the environment and inside the firm. The managers incrementally adjust the objectives considering these demands and their own values and aspirations.

---

**THOMPSON**

■ Objectives change frequently in firms whose task environment and technology are volatile.

achievements and say the enterprise can do more. Or they look at what relevant competitors or other enterprises have achieved and decide to match or achieve these levels.

**3** Finally, crisis. Sills describes the crisis at the National Foundation for Infantile Paralysis when a cure was found for the disease. NASA went through a crisis when men were placed on the moon. When such an achievement or crisis arises, objectives must be changed, and in successful organizations, they are changed.

James Thompson's predication is given in Proposition 2–4.

Objectives change when executives perceive a gap between desired ends and the current achievement level.

### STATED OBJECTIVES OF ENTERPRISES [11]

There have been some studies of what objectives enterprises say they have for their organizations. It is important, in interpreting this research and in listening to business executives talk about objectives, to distinguish between official objectives and operative objectives.

Sometimes, the two types of objectives are the same. Oftentimes, you must examine the behavior of firms to see which are which.

Which objectives do businesses pursue then? At one time, it was thought that the businesses existed mainly or solely to maximize profits. This was a doctrine of traditional economists: a normative objective. But even prominent economists such as Baumol, Williamson, and Grabowski and Mueller have argued that this is not so. In fact, the evidence is clear to support Proposition 2–5.

There have been several studies of the objectives which business firms pursue. Table 2–3 summarizes the findings of the two major studies. Dent studied 145 businesses in the 1950s. As you will note, many potential objectives are not ranked at all. Profit is the leading objective, but not the only one. Next mentioned was public service in the form of good products or services and employee welfare. Dent also found that large businesses stressed public service more than small businesses. Firms that were unionized stressed em-

---

**DEFINITION**  ■ OFFICIAL AND OPERATIVE OBJECTIVES

*Official* objectives are those vague, general objectives which firms say they seek on official occasions, as in annual reports, in public statements by top management, and in the company charter.

*Operative* objectives are those ends sought through actual behavior of the organization (modified Perrow).

ployee welfare more than nonunionized firms. Also, if the firm had more
white-collar workers, they were less profit-oriented than the heavily blue-collar
firms. Finally Dent points out that more successful firms focused *outward:* to
stress meeting competition and producing good products. Less successful firms
focused on internal efficiency.

England studied over 1000 executives in the mid-1960s. He did not find the

TABLE 2–3 • OBJECTIVES BUSINESS ACTUALLY PURSUES

| Potential objectives | Dent study | England study |
|---|---|---|
| Maximize net profit over a short period | a | a |
| Maximize the company's net assets and reserves | | |
| Maximize net profit over a long period | a | a |
| Maximize the dividends for the shareholders | c | |
| Maximize the company's prestige | | |
| Be influential in local community decisions | | |
| Survive | | |
| Maximize the rate of innovation of products or service | | |
| Be of service to the community | c | c |
| Be the leading innovator in the industry | | b |
| Be a socially responsible company | c | c |
| Provide high rewards and benefits to the employees | a | c |
| Create a friendly and pleasant workplace | a | c |
| Have satisfied employees | a | c |
| Prevent unionization or further unionization | | |
| Provide income or jobs for owning family members | | |
| Keep government out of this business | | |
| Keep tax payments to a minimum | | |
| Maximize the market share | | |
| Maximize the company's rate of growth | b | b |
| Increase sales growth | | |
| Provide the best-quality products or services possible | a | |
| Be a market leader, e.g., first in market with new products or services | b | b |
| Have the most satisfied customers | | |
| Be the most efficient firm in the industry | c | a |
| Run a stable organization | b | b |

a Most important third of objectives ranked.
b Middle third of objectives ranked.
c Least important third of objectives ranked.

*"In my book, fulfilling oneself and making
money hand over fist are synonymous."*

differences in goal rankings based on organizational differences that Dent
found. His differences were explainable as individual differences.

In comparing the two studies, we see only a few major differences, and some
of these are due to the fact that the two researchers *did not provide the
executives with the same list of objectives.* The major differences are these:
Dent's executives ranked employee welfare objectives considerably higher
than the later England study. England's executives put much more emphasis
on efficiency than Dent's executives did. There appears to be remarkable
consistency in objectives considering time differences, sample differences, and
objective differences given the executives.

### WHAT ABOUT SOCIAL RESPONSIBILITY? [12]

The literature has been filled with articles and books the last few years indicating that business executives ought to be or are making social responsibility
a major objective of their enterprises. Social responsibility is defined quite
broadly and includes everything from production of safe products to giving
profits to welfare organizations or the arts. Business schools are offering
courses variously titled but usually called business and society or the social
responsibility of business. Checklists and social audits have been drawn up
presumably for managers to measure themselves against.

Few advocates of swashbuckling "screw the public: let's maximize profits"
are heard these days. But Milton Friedman maintains his position that businesses exist to produce products or offer services at lowest cost. It is the role
of government and/or voluntary organizations to take care of social needs with
funds from taxes or gifts from business.

As the Dent and England studies indicate, business executives tend to agree
more with Friedman than the social responsibility ethic. Some business execu-

tives always were more socially responsible than others. They had stronger religious or moral values. A glance at the newspapers indicates that not all executives have strong moral and legal values. The list of firms fined for illegal political gifts include Goodyear, Ashland Oil, Gulf Oil, Phillips Petroleum, American Airlines, Braniff Airlines, W. T. Grant, 3M, and several divisions of AT&T. Many others are compelled by researchers like Ralph Nader, pressure groups, and the government to modify their objectives to include some elements of social responsibility in their set of objectives. But much of it seems to be lip service. As some elements of the coalition press for social responsibility, the executives give some response. But most of the evidence we have indicates that social responsibility is not a major objective of most businesses. Nor is it likely to be in the foreseeable future. At best, it appears to modify the standard objectives listed earlier.

## Objectives, strategies, and missions: some overlap

I have tried to maintain a fairly clear-cut separation in definitions. Objectives are the ends, strategies the means to the ends. But some companies do not help this because they sometimes mix the two. One example is a firm that lists as one of its objectives the serving of a particular product or service market. For example, American Telephone and Telegraph at one point listed as one of its major objectives the provision of quality telephone service at low cost for all the people. Another firm might list as an objective the provision of high-quality metal toys to pre-teen-age children. If listed as an objective, this kind of statement of objective *overlaps* general objectives and the corporate strategy. For it spells out as an *end* some of the *means* of achieving that end. Thus we have a condition where strategy moves into objectives.

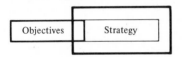

This is not the problem with conglomerate firms. Richard Hanna's study [13] of Litton, Bangor Punta, and Indian Head found the strategy less specific than most. The strategy consisted only of general financial, growth, and organizational guidelines.

But as discussed early in this book, it is impossible to separate the stages of the strategic planning process *clearly* in a firm. We can do it only in theory for ease of presentation.

## Objectives: general and specific [14]

Rhenman and I both pointed out that many, usually smaller organizations have not formulated objectives at all. When firms do so, they seem to move through a series of steps in the kinds of objectives they devise, as shown below.

1  No formal objectives

2  Formulation of general objectives, usually not in written form

**3** Formulation of general, written objectives

**4** Formulation of specific objectives

**5** Formulating and ranking of specific objectives

Once an administrator is aware of the desirability of objectives, he begins to formulate them. If you ask the top management what their objectives are, you might be given them *in general.* You will not find them in writing anywhere.

The next step is to get the objectives in writing, appearing perhaps in annual reports. By then, the firm is fairly large and formalized (stage 2 or 3 at least in stages of development theory as will be discussed later in the book).

The hurdle that appears at step 4 is to get the executives to specify the objective, for example, from: "increase return on investment" with greater detail "increase return on investment to 6 percent."

The final and most difficult step is to ask management to compute tradeoffs between objectives. This requires them to say: ROI is more important than market share, market share is more important than satisfied employees. This step is found only in the most sophisticated of firms—perhaps in less than 1 percent of firms in the United States and Canada.

There are various techniques for moving the firm through these steps. One of the more popular at present is the management-by-objectives technique. MBO tries to develop a company philosophy requiring top management to proceed through step 5 in formulating objectives. Then middle and lower management are expected to translate these objectives into specific targets at their level to better assure the achievement of the objectives. More will be said about MBO in the implementation chapter. Schaffer recommends that the objectives with the highest priorities should be short-run measurable goals. Eilon makes two propositions (2–6 and 2–7) that apply here.

Unspecific objectives allow less effective management to get by with lower performance longer. So they fight them too.

## Objectives and the strategic planning process [15]

In summary, objectives are the beginning and ending point of the strategic planning process. Figure 2–1 was reproduced at the beginning of the chapter to reemphasize how objectives fit into the process. By glancing at the figure again, it can be seen that objectives precede the strategic planning process. It is very difficult to formulate strategies if you do not know where you are going. Then the process begins: analysis of environment and internal resources; consideration of alternative strategies; choice of strategy; implementation of

*Eilon*

**PROPOSITION 2–6** ■ As time goes on, objectives tend to get more specific.

**PROPOSITION 2–7** ■ Management tends to resist this specificity because it tends to reduce its flexibility.

strategy. If the process is effective, the objectives will be reached, and then new and probably higher objectives will be set. If the objectives were unrealistically high or if unforeseen changes in the environment arise, the objectives might have to be incrementally lowered. In both cases, reformulation of the objectives can be viewed as the end of the previous cycle of strategic planning. This is shown on the figure by the linkage between the end of the process and objectives.

Objectives will become a meaningful part of the strategic planning process only if top management formulates them well and institutionalizes them, communicates them, and reinforces them throughout the corporation. The strategic planning process will be successful to the extent that top management participates in formulating the objectives and that these objectives reflect the values of management and the realities of the organization's situation. Now that we know a little more about the basic elements—the decision makers, the decision-making process, and the decision outcomes: enterprise objectives— Chapter 3 starts the discussion of the strategic planning process itself. We will begin with the analysis of the firm's environmental opportunities and threats.

## References

[1] Bacon, Jeremy: *Corporate Directorship Practices,* Studies in Business Policy 125, New York: The Conference Board, 1967.

Desfosses, Louis, and Ephraim Smith: "Corporate Director under Fire," *California Management Review,* **15** (2): Winter 1972.

Drucker, Peter: *Management,* New York: Harper & Row, 1974, chap. 52.

Estes, Robert: "Outside Directors: More Vulnerable than Ever," *Harvard Business Review,* January–February 1973.

Groobey, John: "Making the Board of Directors More Effective," *California Management Review,* **16** (3): Spring 1974.

Mace, Myles: *Directors: Myth and Reality,* Cambridge, Mass.: Harvard University Press, 1971.

Mautz, R., and F. Neumann: "The Effective Corporate Audit Committee," *Harvard Business Review,* November–December 1970.

Mueller, Robert: *Board Life,* New York: Amacom, 1974.

Pfeffer, Jeffrey: "Size and Composition of Corporate Boards of Directors," *Administrative Science Quarterly,* **17** (2): June 1972.

Vanderwicken, Peter: "Change Invades the Boardroom," *Fortune,* May 1972.

Wilde, Frazar, and Richard Vancil: "Performance Audits by Outside Directors," *Harvard Business Review,* July–August 1972.

Zald, Mayer: "The Power and Functions of Boards of Directors," *American Journal of Sociology,* July 1969.

[2] Ackerman, Robert: "Organization and the Investment Process: A Comparative Study," unpublished D.B.A. thesis, Harvard Business School, 1968.

Ansoff, H. Igor: "Toward a Strategic Theory of Firms," in *Business Strategy,* London: Penguin, 1970.

Henshel, Harry: "The President Stands Alone," *Harvard Business Review,* September–October 1971.

Mace, Myles: "The President and Corporate Planning," *Harvard Business Review,* January–February 1965.

McMurry, Robert: "Power and the Ambitious Executive," *Harvard Business Review,* November–December 1973.

Uyterhoeven, Hugo: "General Managers in the Middle," *Harvard Business Review,* March–April 1972.

**[3]**  Bates, James, and A. Sykes: "Aspects of Managerial Efficiency," *Journal of Industrial Economics,* **10** (3): July 1962.

Beishon, R., and A. Palmer: "Studying Managerial Behavior," *International Studies of Management and Organization,* **2** (1): Spring 1972.

Haas, John A., et al.: "Actual vs. Ideal Time Allocation Reported by Managers," *Personnel Psychology,* **22:** 1969.

Heller, Frank: "Research on Five Styles of Managerial Decision Making," *International Studies of Management and Organization,* **2** (1): Spring 1972.

Mintzberg, Henry: "Managerial Work: Analyses from Observation," *Management Science,* **18** (2): October 1971.

————: *The Nature of Managerial Work,* New York: Harper & Row, 1973.

Stewart, Rosemary: "Studies of Managerial Jobs: Methodologies and Profiles," *International Studies of Management and Organization,* **2** (1): Spring 1972.

Wilkie, Roy, and James Young: "Managerial Behavior in the Furniture and Timber Industries," *International Studies of Management and Organization,* **2** (1): Spring 1972.

**[4]**  Anshen, Melvin: "The Management of Ideas," *Harvard Business Review,* July–August 1969.

Ansoff, H. Igor, and Richard Brandenburg: "The General Manager of the Future," *California Management Review,* **11** (3): Spring 1969.

*Business Week:* "Piercing Future Fog in the Executive Suite," April 28, 1975.

Katz, Robert: "Skills of an Effective Administrator," *Harvard Business Review,* **33** (1): 1955.

Miner, John: "The Real Crunch in Managerial Manpower," *Harvard Business Review,* November–December 1973.

**[5]**  Athreya, Mrityunjay: "Guidelines for the Effectiveness of Long Range Planning Process," unpublished D.B.A. thesis, Harvard University, 1970.

Chambers, John, et al.: "Catalytic Agent for Effective Planning," *Harvard Business Review,* January–February 1971.

Denning, Basil: "Organizing the Corporate Planning Function," *Long Range Planning,* **1** (4): 1969.

Dobbie, John: "Guides to a Foundation for Strategic Planning in Large Firms," *Proceedings, Academy of Management,* 1974.

Ewing, David W.: *The Human Side of Planning,* New York: Macmillan, 1969.

Litschert, Robert: "The Structure of Long Range Planning Groups," *Academy of Management Journal,* **14** (1): March 1971.

Mason, R. Hal: "Developing a Planning Organization," *Business Horizons,* August 1969.

Mason, Richard: "A Dialectical Approach to Strategic Planning," *Management Science,* **15** (8): April 1969.

Pettigrew, Andrew: "Strategic Aspects of the Management of Specialist Activity," Working Paper, European Institute for Advanced Studies in Management, 1974.

Ringbakk, K. A.: "Organized Planning in Major U.S. Companies," *Long Range Planning,* **2** (2): December 1969.

————: "The Corporate Planning Life Cycle: An International Point of View," *Long Range Planning,* **5** (3): 1972.

Steiner, George: "The Rise of the Corporate Planner," *Harvard Business Review,* September–October 1970.

Taylor, Bernard, and Peter Irving: "Organized Planning in Major U.K. Companies," *Long Range Planning,* **3** (4): June 1971.

**[6]** Ansoff, H. Igor: *Corporate Strategy,* New York: McGraw-Hill, 1965, especially chaps. 1, 2.

Grémion, Catherine: "Toward a New Theory of Decision Making?" *Sociologie du Travail,* **11:** October–December 1969.

MacCrimmon, Kenneth: "Managerial Decision Making," in Joseph McGuire (ed.), *Contemporary Management,* Englewood Cliffs, N.J.: Prentice-Hall, 1974.

Schlarbaum, Gary, and George Racette: "Measuring Risk: Some Theoretical and Empirical Issues," *Journal of Business Research,* **2** (3): July 1974.

**[7]** Dror, Y.: "Prolegomena to Policy Sciences," *Policy Sciences,* **1** (1): 1970.

Peters, Lynn, and Thomas Wotruba: "Goals and Directions: Two Aspects of Business Policy," *Northwest Business Management,* **4** (3): Spring 1967.

Rhenman, Eric: *Organization Theory for Long Range Planning,* New York: Wiley, 1973.

**[8]** Simon, Herbert: "On the Concept of Organizational Goals," *Administrative Science Quarterly,* **9** (1): 1964.

Thompson, James: *Organizations in Action,* New York: McGraw-Hill, 1967.

**[9]** Cyert, Richard, and James March: *A Behavioral Theory of the Firm,* Englewood Cliffs, N.J.: Prentice-Hall, 1963, pp. 29–43.

Eilon, Samuel: "Goals and Constraints," *Journal of Management Studies,* **8** (3): October 1971.

Hickson, D. J., et al.: "A Strategic Contingencies Theory of Intraorganizational Power," *Administrative Science Quarterly,* **16** (2): June 1971.

MacCrimmon, Kenneth: "Managerial Decision Making," op. cit.

Sills, David: *The Volunteers,* Glencoe, Ill.: Free Press, 1957, pp. 253–268.

**[10]** Bernthal, Wilmar: "Value Perspectives in Management Decisions," *Academy of Management Journal,* 1962.

Cyert, Richard, and James March: *A Behavioral Theory of the Firm,* op. cit.

Eastlack, Joseph, Jr., and Phillip McDonald: "CEO's Role in Corporate Growth," *Harvard Business Review,* May–June 1970.

Eels, Richard, and Clarence Walton: *Conceptual Foundations of Business,* Homewood, Ill.: Richard D. Irwin, 1974, chap. 19.

England, George: "Personal Value Systems of American Managers," *Academy of Management Journal,* March 1967.

Khandwalla, Pradip: "Style of Management and Environment: Some Findings," *Administrative Science Quarterly,* in press.

Lee, Raymond, and George England: "Organizational Goals and Expected Behavior among American, Japanese, and Korean Managers," *Academy of Management Journal,* **14** (4): December 1971.

Lodge, George: "Top Priority: Renovating Our Ideology," *Harvard Business Review,* September–October 1970.

Lusk, Edward, and Bruce Oliver: "American Managers' Personal Value Systems Revisited," *Academy of Management Journal,* September 1974.

Prothro, James: *The Dollar Decade,* Baton Rouge: Louisiana State University Press, 1954.

Reimann, Bernard: "The Public Philosophy of Organizations," *Academy of Management Journal,* **17** (3): September 1974.

Sutton, Francis, et al.: *The American Business Creed,* Cambridge, Mass.: Harvard University Press, 1956.

**[11]** Baumol, William: *Business Behavior, Value, and Growth,* New York: Harcourt, Brace & World, 1966.

Denning, B. W.: "The Integration of Business Studies at the Conceptual Level," *Journal of Management Studies,* **5** (1): February 1968.

Dent, James: "Organizational Correlates of the Goals of Business Managers," *Personnel Psychology,* **12** (3): 1959.

England, George: "Organizational Goals and Expected Behavior of American Managers," *Academy of Management Journal,* June 1967.

Grabowski, Henry, and Dennis Mueller: "Managerial and Stockholder Welfare Models of Firm Expenditures," *Review of Economics and Statistics,* **52:** 9–24, 1972.

Perrow, Charles: "The Analysis of Goals in Complex Organizations," *American Sociological Review,* **26:** 854–866, 1961.

Saunders, Charles: "Setting Organizational Objectives," *Journal of Business Policy,* **3** (4): 1973.

Williamson, Oliver: *The Economics of Discretionary Behavior,* Englewood Cliffs, N.J.: Prentice-Hall, 1963.

**[12]** Ackerman, Robert: "How Companies Respond to Social Demands," *Harvard Business Review,* July–August 1973.

Adams, Kenneth: "The Impact of Changing Social Value," *Journal of Business Policy,* **3** (4): 1973.

Adizes, Ichak, and J. Fred Weston: "Comparative Models of Social Responsibility," *Academy of Management Journal,* **16** (1): March 1973.

Andrews, Kenneth: "Can the Best Corporations Be Made Moral?" *Harvard Business Review,* May–June 1973.

Bauer, Raymond, and Don Fenn, Jr.: "What is a Corporate Social Audit?" *Harvard Business Review,* January–February 1973.

Bradshaw, T. F.: "Corporate Social Reform: An Executive's Viewpoint," *California Management Review,* **15** (4): Summer 1973.

Carrol, Archie: "Corporate Social Responsibility: Its Managerial Impact and Implications," *Journal of Business Research,* **2** (1): January 1974.

Davis, Keith: "The Case for and against Business Assumption of Social Responsibilities," *Academy of Management Journal,* **16** (2): June 1973.

Friedman, Milton: "The Social Responsibility of Business Is to Increase Its Profits," *New York Times Magazine,* September 13, 1970.

Shocker, Allan, and S. Prakash Sethi: "An Approach to Incorporating Societal Preferences in Developing Corporate Action Strategies," *California Management Review,* **15** (4): Summer 1973.

Steiner, George: "Social Policies for Business," *California Management Review,* **15** (2): 1972.

Votaw, Dow: "Corporate Social Reform: An Educator's View-Point," *California Management Review,* **15** (4): Summer 1973.

Webley, Simon: "Business Policy and Business Ethics," *Journal of Business Policy,* **3** (3): Spring 1973.

[13] Hanna, Richard: "The Concept of Corporate Strategy in Multi-Industry Companies," unpublished D.B.A. thesis, Harvard Business School, 1968.

[14] Eilon, Samuel: "Goals and Constraints," op. cit.

Howell, Robert: "Managing by Objectives: A Three Stage System," *Business Horizons,* February 1970.

Schaffer, Robert: "Putting Action into Planning," *Harvard Business Review,* November–December 1967.

Tosi, Henry, et al.: "Setting Goals in Management by Objectives," *California Management Review,* Summer 1970.

[15] Guth, William: "Formulating Organizational Objective Strategy: A Systematic Approach," *Journal of Business Policy,* **2** (1): 1972.

——— and Renato Tagiuri: "Personal Values and Corporate Strategy," *Harvard Business Review,* September–October 1965.

# A new look at the chief executive's job*

Henry Mintzberg

Ask what a chief executive does and you will likely be told that he "plans," "organizes," "coordinates," and "controls." In fact, these four words date back to 1916, when Henry Fayol first described the executive's job. How useful are they? Consider the following sequence of activities, drawn from the actual work of chief executives: So what?

As he enters his office at 8:23, the president's secretary motions for him to pick up the telephone. "Jerry, there was a bad fire in the plant last night, about $30,000 damage. We should be back in operation by Wednesday. Thought you should know."

At 8:45, a Mr. Jamison is ushered into the president's office. They discuss Mr. Jamison's retirement plans and his cottage in New Hampshire. The president presents a plaque to him commemorating his thirty-two years with the organization.

Mail processing follows: An innocent-looking letter, signed by a Detroit lawyer, reads, "A group of us in Detroit has decided not to buy any of your products because you used that anti-flag, anti-American pinko, Bill Lindell, on your Thursday night TV show." The president dictates a restrained reply.

A 10:00 meeting is scheduled with a professional staffer. He claims that his superior, a high-ranking vice-president of the organization, mistreats his staff, and that if the man is not fired, they will all walk out. As soon as the meeting ends, the manager rearranges his schedule to investigate the claim and to react to this crisis.

Which of these activities should we call planning, and which organizing, coordinating, and controlling? Indeed, what do words such as "coordinating" and "planning" mean in the context of real activity? In fact, these four words do not describe management work at all, but only certain of its vague objectives. They are convenient abstractions that we use to label our ignorance of the manager's job.

Over the years, a number of researchers have undertaken systematic studies of the work of managers, usually by having them fill out diaries or by actually observing them while they worked. Their studies, few of them widely reported, have focused on managers at all levels of the hierarchy and in every type of organization—Swedish managing directors; British presidents, middle managers, and foremen; American corporate and governmental chief executives; hospital administrators; foremen; street gang leaders; and many others. From an anal-

* Reprinted by permission of the publisher from *Organizational Dynamics,* Winter 1973. Copyright © 1973 by AMACOM, a division of American Management Associations.

ysis of this research, and from my own detailed examination of the ways in which five chief executives spent their working time, a picture of the top executive's job emerges that is entirely different from the classical view of managerial work.

## Ten basic managerial roles

In the study of the chief executives of five middle- to large-size American organizations (a consulting firm, a consumer goods manufacturer, a technology firm, a hospital, and a school system), I recorded all the activities that each performed during one week of intensive observation—a total of 368 verbal contacts and 890 pieces of mail during the five weeks. I then analyzed the reason for their participation in each, and developed from this analysis a framework of ten basic roles to describe their jobs.

(A)   The ten roles fall into three groupings. The "interpersonal" roles, of which there are three, describe aspects of the manager's work that involve interpersonal contact for its own sake. *Figurehead,* the simplest of roles, describes the manager as a symbol, required by the status of his office, to carry out a variety of social, legal, and ceremonial duties. He must preside at formal dinners, greet visiting dignitaries, sign various government forms, and make himself available to the important customers who believe that they merit the attention of the chief executive.

The *leader* role describes the manager's interpersonal relationship with his own subordinates, his need to hire, train, and motivate them. As leader, the manager must essentially bring their needs in accord with those of his organization.

The *liaison* role focuses on the manager's interpersonal dealings with people outside of his own organization. He spends a considerable amount of his time developing a network of high-status contacts in which information and favors are traded for mutual benefit. The chief executive joins boards of directors, attends trade conferences, performs public service work all as part of his liaison role.

(B)   A second set of roles, again three in number, describe the activities the manager performs primarily to process information. In the *monitor* role, he continually seeks and receives information about his organization in order to understand his milieu thoroughly. Much of this information is privileged; he alone receives it because of the contacts he develops in his liaison role and because of his status in the leader role. In the *disseminator* role the manager shares some of this privileged information with his subordinates, and in the *spokesman* role he informs outsiders about the progress of his organization.

(C)   The last four roles describe the decision-making activities of the manager. As *entrepreneur* the manager takes responsibility for bringing about change in his organization. He looks for problems and opportunities, and he initiates projects to deal with them. As *disturbance handler,* the manager must take charge when his organization faces a major disturbance or crisis—the loss of a key executive, a strike, the destruction of a facility.

As *resource allocator,* the manager decides who will get what in his organization. He schedules his own time according to his priorities; he designs his organization, in effect deciding who will do what; and he authorizes all its important decisions. No major action can be taken without his approval, for he must take responsibility for it. Finally, as *negotiator* the manager takes charge whenever his organization must enter into crucial negotiations with other parties. His presence is required because he has the information and the authority to make the "real-time" decisions that difficult negotiations require.

Perhaps the most significant feature of these ten roles is that they are inseparable—they form a "Gestalt," an integrated whole. In effect, status, as manifested in the interpersonal roles, brings information to the chief executive, and it is this information (together with the status) that enables him to perform the decision-making roles effectively. This description appears to hold true for all chief executives—in my study, for example, a school superintendent in a stable milieu and a company president in a highly competitive consumer goods industry.

We do find, however, that different chief executives emphasize different roles. For example, the liaison role appears to be more important in service industries than in manufacturing—the president of a consulting firm feels obliged to spend substantial time with his firm's clients. The presidents of small companies pay less attention to the figurehead role and other formal activities; they are more wrapped up in their firm's operating problems and many spend a lot of time handling disturbances.

It is also interesting to note the difference between production managers, sales managers, and managers of staff groups. As it happens, each appears to concentrate on one set of roles. Production managers are most concerned with maintaining the workflow; they give their greatest attention to the decisional roles, especially disturbance handler and negotiator. In contrast, the sales manager is typically more extroverted. He spends much of his time in communication with clients and subordinates, and the interpersonal roles—liaison, leader, and figurehead—are most important to his job. Staff managers are experts as well as managers; they focus on the informational roles in an attempt to develop their expertise and to disseminate the expert advice of their specialists to those who need it.

In general, we can delineate different types of managerial jobs. For example, "contact man" managers spend much time with outsiders, "entrepreneurs" focus on change and growth, "real-time" managers focus on day-to-day workflow problems, "team" managers are primarily concerned with leadership, and "new" managers spend most of their time developing contacts and trying to get information about a new job and a new milieu. But despite the obvious need for managers to focus on the particular roles most important to their particular jobs, all ten roles are a basic part of all senior managers' jobs. The relationships between interpersonal contact, information processing, and decision making are absolutely inseparable in the manager's work.

## Major findings about the chief executive's job

These ten roles suggest a number of key characteristics of the chief executive's job. In addition, studies of how these men operate—of the frequency and duration of meetings, their use of the mails, their pattern of activities over the work day—suggest a number of other characteristics of their work. I describe nine important characteristics below.

**1** *The chief executive must serve as the key linking device between his organization and its environment.* In the liaison role the manager develops his high-status contacts, and in the spokesman and negotiator roles he deals with his organization's public. In effect, he uses his status in the maintenance of prime links with outsiders. This is not a grandiose task. It involves frequent, occasionally mundane, contact with all kinds of people—taking a big customer out to dinner, telling a congressional hearing why his firm acted as it did, negotiating with the workers over a major grievance, asking a friend to help in securing a contact.

**2** *The chief executive is the nerve center of key information in his organization.* Consider the words of Richard Neustadt, who in his book *Presidential Power* analyzed the activities of three U.S. Presidents:

The essence of Roosevelt's technique for information-gathering was competition. "He would call you in," one of his aides once told me, "and he'd ask you to get the story on some complicated business, and you'd come back after a couple of days of hard labor and present the juicy morsel you'd uncovered under a stone somewhere, and then you'd find out he knew all about it, along with something else you didn't know. Where he got his information from he wouldn't mention, usually, but after he had done this to you once or twice you got damn careful about *your* information."

Now compare this with the comments of George Homans on a study of street gang leaders:

Since interaction flowed toward (the leaders), they were better informed about the problems and desires of group members than were any of the followers and therefore better able to decide on an appropriate course of action. Since they were in close touch with other gang leaders, they were also better informed than their followers about conditions in Cornerville at large. Moreover, in their position at the focus of the chains of interaction, they were better able than any follower to pass on to the group the decisions which had been reached.

At two extremes in the leadership spectrum, we can see a common bond. In both cases, the leaders are nerve centers of key organizational information. External information comes through the liaison role, and internal information, through the leader role. In effect, his position provides the manager with privileged information, and this information in turn provides him with much of his power. Note also that both quotes suggest that the manager's information system is not a formal one. In fact, there is considerable evidence that most of the manager's important information comes not from any official MIS but from the contacts and information channels he himself sets up. His brain, not the computer, is the data bank of key information in the organization.

**3** *The chief executive must take full charge of his organization's strategy-making system.* The four decision-making roles suggest that the chief executive runs the strategy-making system in his organization—the system by which important decisions are made and integrated. The president has unique authority and information, and no other member of his organization can take responsibility for these decisions. Decisions related to crises, problems, and major opportunities must be overseen and integrated by the chief executive.

**4** *The chief executive performs much work at an unrelenting pace.* The first three points suggest the great responsibility that every chief executive assumes. He must run three complex systems in his organization—liaison, information processing, and strategy-making. This burden forces him to adopt an immense workload. Studies of chief executives find that they seldom stop working. Their evening activities are usually work related, and they seldom appear able to put their concern for their work aside. During office hours, the pace of work is hectic and, should free time become available, an ever-present pile of mail or an eager subordinate will quickly usurp it. This is not a job for reflection and relaxation. It is an openended job, with no tangible mileposts where the incumbent can stop and say, "Now my work is finished." The president must always keep going, never sure when he has succeeded, never sure when his whole organization might come down around him because of some miscalculation. Hence, he is a man with a perpetual preoccupation.

**5** *The chief executive's work is characterized by brevity, discontinuity, and variety.* No matter what he is doing, the chief executive is plagued by what he might do and what he must do. Hence, he becomes conditioned by his pace and workload. He tries to keep all his activities brief, actively encouraging interruption in his work in order to maintain the rapid pace and the flow of information; he seeks variety in his work, again to maintain the pace. Studies of managerial activities highlight a surprising fragmentation

### ANALYSIS OF THE CHRONOLOGY RECORD
#### Based on five weeks of observation

| Category | Composite | Mgr. A | Mgr. B | Mgr. C | Mgr. D | Mgr. E |
|---|---|---|---|---|---|---|
| Total hours worked | 202 hrs | 28[a] | 36 | 45 | 53 | 40 |
| Hours in travel to outside meetings (not included) | 18 hrs | 5.4 | 7.1 | 4.5 | 0.3 | 0.3 |
| Hours of evening meetings (included) | 24 hrs | — | 3 | 3 | 7 | 11 |
| Total amount of mail | 890 pieces | 161 | 165 | 230 | 222 | 112[b] |
| Average amount of mail processed per day | 36 pieces | 32 | 33 | 46 | 44 | 22[b] |
| Total number of activities | 547 | 101 | 86 | 96 | 160 | 104 |
| **Desk work** | | | | | | |
| Number of sessions | 179 | 36 | 31 | 25 | 54 | 33 |
| Time on desk work | 44 hrs | 10.6 | 8.3 | 8.3 | 10.7 | 6.4 |
| Average duration | 15 min | 18 | 16 | 20[c] | 12 | 12 |
| Proportion of time | 22% | 38% | 23% | 18% | 20% | 16% |
| **Telephone calls**[d] | | | | | | |
| Number of calls | 133 | 27 | 27 | 30 | 22 | 27 |
| Time on telephone | 13 hrs | 2.4 | 3.2 | 3.0 | 1.9 | 2.4 |
| Average duration | 6 min | 5 | 7 | 6 | 5 | 5 |
| Proportion of time | 6% | 9% | 9% | 7% | 4% | 6% |
| **Scheduled meetings** | | | | | | |
| Number of meetings | 105 | 16 | 14 | 27 | 18 | 30 |
| Time in meetings | 120 hrs | 10.6 | 20.6 | 29.1 | 29.5 | 29.8 |
| Average duration | 68 min | 40 | 88 | 65 | 98 | 60 |
| Proportion of time | 59% | 38% | 57% | 65% | 55% | 75% |
| **Unscheduled meetings** | | | | | | |
| Number of meetings | 101 | 10 | 14 | 10 | 55 | 12 |
| Time in meetings | 20 hrs | 1.7 | 3.5 | 4.0 | 9.6 | 1.2 |
| Average duration | 12 min | 10 | 15 | 24 | 10 | 6 |
| Proportion of time | 10% | 6% | 10% | 9% | 18% | 3% |
| **Tours** | | | | | | |
| Number of tours | 29 | 12 | — | 4 | 11 | 2 |
| Time on tours | 5 hrs | 2.9 | — | 0.5 | 1.5 | 0.2 |
| Average duration | 11 min | 14 | — | 8 | 8 | 6 |
| Proportion of time | 3% | 10% | 0% | 1% | 3% | 1% |
| Proportion of activities lasting less than 9 min | 49% | 44% | 40% | 45% | 56% | 51% |
| Proportion lasting longer than 60 min | 10% | 5% | 12% | 13% | 9% | 12% |

[a] It was decided to exclude a seven-hour trip that manager A took to Washington in connection with congressional hearings.
[b] Manager E commented that his mail was significantly lighter at the time of observation—the last week of classes.
[c] Manager C spent Saturday processing much of his mail. He was largely uninterrupted, spending one 3.1 hour session and one 0.7 hour session. Excluding these, the average duration of his desk work sessions would have been 12 minutes.
[d] Telephone calls screened or made by the secretary were excluded.

of work. In my study, the five chief executives averaged 36 written and 10 verbal contacts each day, almost every one dealing with a distinct issue. The significant issues were interspersed with trivial ones, requiring the managers to shift moods quickly and frequently. Fully half of the activities I observed were completed in less than nine minutes, and only one-tenth took more than one hour! (See the table on page 40 for a detailed breakdown.) One study of a Swedish managing director found that only 12 times in 35 days did he work undisturbed in his office for more than 22 minutes! The top manager is encouraged by the realities of the job to make decisions abruptly, to maintain the hectic pace, to avoid wasting time.

6   *Chief executives gravitate to the more active, more concrete elements in their work*. In their work habits, they show strong preference for activities that are current, specific, and well-defined, and those that are nonroutine. As examples, in my study they gave little attention to routine operating reports; relatively few of their meetings were regularly scheduled; little of their time was devoted to open-ended touring; and almost never was a chief executive observed partaking in general, abstract discussion. As Neustadt noted in his study of three U.S. Presidents:

It is not information of a general sort that helps a President see personal stakes; not summaries, not surveys, not the *bland amalgams*. Rather . . . it is the odds and ends of *tangible detail* that pieced together in his mind illuminate the underside of issues put before him.

The chief executive is certainly not a planner in the accepted sense of that term. The pressures of the job simply do not allow for reflection. Rather the job breeds adaptive information manipulators, men who work in an environment of stimulus-response and who prefer live action.

7   *Chief executives demonstrate a preference for the verbal media*.   Communication is the manager's work and his prime tools are five media—mail, telephone calls, unscheduled meetings, scheduled meetings, and tours. The first is a written form of communication, the last is observational, and the other three are verbal, involving different aspects of interpersonal contact. Virtually every study of managerial time allocation emphasizes the surprisingly large amount of time managers spend in verbal contact—talking and listening. Some 75 percent of the time of the five chief executives in my study was spent in verbal activities, the bulk of that in scheduled meetings. Top managers appear to dislike processing mail and reading. It is a slow, dull medium, containing little actionable material, and it doesn't fit in accordance with the stimulus-response nature of their work. In my study, I found that 87 percent of the chief executives' mail did not deal with issues of "live action." The tour provides the manager with an opportunity to observe activity firsthand; surprisingly, touring accounted for only 3 percent of the manager's time in my study and only 10 percent in a study of Swedish chief executives. Evidently, this activity is not specific and well defined enough for most managers. Telephone calls and meetings consume the bulk of the top manager's time; this is where the action of his managerial work is found.

8   *The prime occupational hazard of the chief executive's job is superficiality*.   To summarize the previous points, the key problem facing the chief executive is that every pressure of his job drives him to be superficial. He is driven to overwork, to adapt an unrelenting pace, to fragment his work, to be abrupt, to avoid relaxed, reflective activities, to favor verbal communication over reading. Every pressure tells him to get it done quickly, not to probe, to avoid getting deeply involved. All this is reflected most clearly in the chief executive's "dilemma of delegation." He is forced to carry a great workload, yet he cannot easily delegate responsibility for his tasks. To delegate, he must send along the necessary information, but because so much of his information is in his memory, it takes much time to disseminate it. Hence, the top manager is often faced with the dilemma of doing it himself and adding to his workload or of delegating the task knowing it will be done by someone less informed than he. And so he comes under this immense pressure, and so superficiality becomes his prime occupational hazard.

**9** *There is no science in managerial work.* Careful study of chief executive's activities demonstrate that there is as yet no science in their work. That is to say, managers do not work according to procedures that have been prescribed by scientific analysis. Indeed, except for using the telephone, the airplane, and the dictating machine, it would appear that the top manager of today is indistinguishable from his historical counterparts. He may seek different information, but he gets much of it in the same way—from word of mouth. He may make decisions dealing with modern technology, but he uses the same intuitive (that is, nonexplicit) procedures in making them. Even the computer, which has had such a great impact on other kinds of organizational work, has apparently done little to alter the working methods of the top manager.

The management scientist, despite his accomplishments in the fields of production and data processing, has done virtually nothing to change the senior manager's basic working habits. The reason for all this is simply that we do not understand the intricate details of the top manager's job—the mental processes (or programs) he uses. And if we do not understand the job, how can we improve it or, for that matter, teach it in the classroom? Hence, despite all the talk about management science and despite all our investment in business school education, we must admit that we cannot really teach the essence of management. The job remains in the realm of intuitive thinking, and the world is full of highly successful top managers who have never spent one day in a management course.

## Five points for more effective managing

There are no simple solutions to the dilemmas and problems facing the senior manager in his job. But these can be alleviated if he fully understands them and manages with a conscious recognition of them. Thus, introspection—to develop a better understanding of the job and its problems—is, in my view, the crucial ingredient for better managing. Five points that can lead to such an understanding and improvement are outlined below.

**1** *Share privileged information.* The chief executive must recognize that he is the nerve center of important organizational information. He must further recognize that the power to make effective decisions stems directly from having this information. Hence, if the senior manager cannot effectively disseminate his information to his subordinates, he will be hesitant to delegate much of his work, and he will therefore be seriously overworked. The difficulty, of course, is that because so much of the information is verbal, it takes much time to disseminate it. Written reports can be copied and circulated, verbal information cannot. Only the few subordinates who have frequent verbal contact with the chief executive really find out what is going on.

The top manager must make a concentrated effort to inform his subordinates—to tell them of the trade gossip, the anger of a big customer, the pressures brought to bear by a consumer group, his ideas for future development of product lines. Somehow he must document his information, take it out of his memory, and put it on paper—so that it can be shared with others. In effect, he should debrief himself periodically. Many effective managers now do this; many others could benefit from the practice.

One objection to this proposal might be that some information is confidential and documenting it might expose it to the wrong people. But the risks of exposure must be weighed against the significant advantages of having a well-informed group of subordinates who can make effective, and compatible, decisions.

**2** *Deal consciously with superficiality.* As noted above, it is too easy for the chief executive to operate on a continually superficial level, so that all issues are dealt with abruptly, as if none needs much attention. A top manager who is continually conscious of this problem will be able to alleviate it substantially. He will consider when he can act and when he must await further information, when he should take a decision in one large step and when it should be serialized over a period of time to allow for digestion, when he can move alone and when he must rely on the word of a subordinate. He will try to gain access to in-depth reports of issues, either by reading them himself or by accepting the advice of experts. In particular, I believe that the management scientist has not been used sufficiently to analyze policy issues. The manager can improve the quality of his decisions significantly by getting the unbiased opinion of someone who has the time, skill, and inclination to do broad, basic analysis.

**3** *Gain control of time.* Effective top managers appear to gain control of their own time in two ways. First, they make the most of their obligations. Managers must spend so much of their time discharging obligations that if they were to view them as just that, they would have little time to make effective changes. To an important extent, therefore, success derives from turning to their own advantage those things they must do. The shrewd top manager treats the chaos of a crisis as an opportunity to make some necessary changes. A mutiny in a department may be the opportunity to effect a needed reorganization; a drop in sales is a chance to overcome opposition to the dropping of old product lines. He uses a ceremonial speech as an opportunity to lobby for a cause; every time he meets a subordinate, no matter what the reason, he encourages him in his work; and every time he must meet an outsider, he tries to extract some useful information.

Second, the top manager must free himself from obligations to devote enough time to those issues that he (and perhaps no one else) believes should be attended to. The manager must seek a balance between change and stability in his organization. He is responsible for ensuring both that his organization produces today's goods and services efficiently and that it adapts to tomorrow's new environment. But the pressures of today's production may leave no time for tomorrow's changes. Between the mail, the callers, and the crises, not to mention the ever-hovering subordinates waiting for a free moment, the passive manager will find no free time to address the major, but not pressing, issues.

"Free" time is made, not found, in the top manager's job. The manager must force it into his schedule. Many managers suffer from a "diary complex"—what does not get scheduled does not get done. Trying to keep some time open for contemplation or for general "planning" will not work. The top manager is not a planner in a reflective sense, and no amount of admonition in the literature will make him so. His milieu is one of stimulus-response. He must schedule these specific things he wants to do; then he will be obliged to do them. If he wishes to innovate, he must initiate a project and involve others who will report back to him; if he wishes to tour facilities, he must commit himself so that others expect him to do so. Then, he will serve his own organization's broader ends while continuing to manage as he must.

**4** *See the comprehensive picture in terms of its details.* The top manager faces a kind of jigsaw puzzle. Always working with small pieces, he must never forget the whole picture. The manager must inform himself by piecing together tangible details—the action by a competitor, the new interest rate, the conflict between two executives, the new process technology, the depletion of a natural resource. The danger, however, is that in his search for tangible detail, the manager may be unable to see the broad issues. He may be unable to abstract himself from the details of the present, or he may not be able to reconcile the new details with his old, broad views. A government leader may operate with a model of the economy that is no longer valid; a company president may operate with an outmoded model of what motivates his workers. The top manager must expose himself directly to the models of specialists from time to time, not necessarily to accept their view of reality, but at least to compare it with his own.

**5** *Use the management scientist.* The main message of this paper is that top managers have the information and the authority to make effective decisions, but they often lack the time and the concentration that complex issues require. Alternately, the management scientist—planner, operations researcher, information systems expert, and so on—has the time to concentrate and the techniques of analysis, but lacks the authority and the information. Hence, there exists what I have elsewhere called a "planning dilemma." An effective relationship between top manager and management scientist will require a concerted effort on the part of both parties. The senior manager will have to help the management scientist to understand his work and his problems; he will have to make more room in his decision-making processes for inputs from systematic, comprehensive investigation; and, most important, he will have to transmit his crucial, verbal information to the analyst.

For his part, the management scientist will have to better understand the complex dynamic factors of the top manager's job—the crises, the need for timing and delays, the inherent ambiguity of strategic decisions. He will have to learn to forego elegance in his techniques—strategy issues require clever, systematic analysis, but few of them are well-structured enough to allow for the use of sophisticated techniques. The top manager needs someone with time and a clear head, not a grab bag of fancy tricks.

There are a number of areas where manager and analyst can cooperate. In the design of information systems, for example, the top manager has traditionally been provided with precisely the kind of information he does not seek or need—routine, historical, quantitative information. Hence, top managers design their own informal information systems. But the analyst can put together the kind of formal systems senior managers need—as soon as he seriously studies what information they actually use, and as soon as he recognizes that the computer need not be the heart of the manager's information system. In fact, the senior manager has great need for an in-between MIS—formal and systematic, but not quantitative or computerized. Analysts would collect and feed to the top manager some of the intelligence information he needs—the events of the trade, significant changes in the organization, relevant actions by the government, new ideas of competitors, and so on. Some of this information is privileged, available only to the manager. But some is not, and it should be collected by specialists.

In the area of strategy making, there are numerous fruitful opportunities for manager-analyst cooperation. Cost benefit or return on investment analysis has not been used nearly enough to analyze complex strategy issues. A properly oriented, well-informed team of management scientists could do much good here. In the area of long-range planning, we have read too much about a simple, static process. Senior managers need adaptive plans that reflect their need to time moves and to shift parameters in midstream. They need contingency plans to deal with devastating events that may or may not occur. And when faced with a crisis or a high-pressure situation, the top manager can use a team of analysts who are prepared to do a quick-and-dirty analysis—to feed him with the analysis of the situation and the broad perspective of the issue while it is still alive.

The payoff from manager-management scientist cooperation can be immense, provided both parties can learn to work together. Such cooperation can finally lead us out of the vacuum in management thought that continues to plague us in this age of sophisticated technology.

## Selected bibliography

Readers interested in more depth on the issues covered in this article and in an extensive review of the literature on the manager's job, can see my book, *The Nature of Managerial Work* (published in 1973 by Harper and Row). This book also analyzes the unique features of different types of managerial jobs and discusses at length the role of management science at the policy level.

Three books particularly influenced me in my study. *Managerial Behavior* by Leonard Sayles (McGraw-Hill, 1964) presents a penetrating analysis of the complex pressures facing middle managers, while *Presidential Power* by Richard Neustadt (New

American Library, 1964) does the same for the U.S. Presidency. In particular, Neustadt analyzes the use of power by Presidents Roosevelt, Truman, and Eisenhower. In *Managers and their Jobs,* Rosemary Stewart presents the results of a study, using the diary method, of the work of 160 senior and middle managers in Britain. Each of these three books successfully dispels traditional notions of the manager's work.

A further complement to these views is the work of Charles Lindblom of Yale University, even though his books concern decision-making rather than managerial work. His books should be considered required reading for any executive who feels the need for another opinion on how policies really are formulated in organizations. Lindblom writes about government, but businessmen will have little difficulty recognizing their own behavior here. Executives will find *The Policy-Making Process* (Prentice-Hall, 1968) the most readable of Lindblom's works.

Finally, a provocative article by H. E. Wrapp, entitled "Good Managers Don't Make Policy Decisions" (*Harvard Business Review,* September-October, 1967) is easy and relevant reading for all chief executives.

# Environmental appraisal and analysis

### LEARNING OBJECTIVES

**1** To learn the techniques available to managers for environmental analysis and prediction

**?** **2** To understand the factors in the environment managers should examine and how to prepare an environmental threat and opportunities profile

**3** To review the techniques *actually* used by managers to appraise the environment

**4** To learn how managers *actually* search the environment and choose the factors to focus their strategic planning on

In this chapter, the discussion of the strategic planning process begins. Specifically, Chapter 3 focuses on the appraisal and analysis of the environment as highlighted in Figure 3–1.

The top manager and, where applicable, his or her corporate planning staff and subordinates keep an eye on what is going on in the marketplace and the industry to see what opportunities or threats await them.

Managers need to search the environment to (1) determine what factors in the environment present *threats* to the company's present strategy and objectives accomplishment, and (2) determine what factors in the environment present *opportunities* for greater accomplishment of objectives by adjusting the company's strategy.

The strategic planning literature is filled with cases of companies that violated the previous tenets and declined. Disregard for changes in technology, the government, or the population has led to significant long-run impact on the businesses. Let us consider a few cases:

**1** For years, the major type of life insurance sold was "ordinary life." In this insurance a policy is paid for over a fixed period of years, has a cash value, and is designed to be protection for the policy holder's family *and* to be an investment. Then came the inflation from the 1960s onward. Term life insurance caught on.

**2** Aramco was a large firm in Saudi Arabia owned primarily by American firms to produce crude oil. The Saudi government nationalized the firm.

**3** Recent large increases in the sales of soft drinks and beverages have been influenced by the popularity of nonreturnable containers. Some governmental bodies are passing laws against these containers.

**4** In 1948, some of the largest firms in the United States were Paramount, Warner Brothers, and MGM. Enter the television networks: CBS, NBC, and ABC.

**5** Dictaphone had the dictation market pretty much to itself and a few foreign manufacturers. Then IBM, a computer manufacturer, entered their business.

**6** Many persons made a good living running diaper service companies. Suddenly Procter and Gamble brought out Pampers and others joined the parade.

**7** Not so long ago, copies were made by typing stencils. These were put on duplicating machines made by firms like A. B. Dick and Company. Xerox, IBM, and others came along with a new product which captured the market from the stencils.

**8** For years, the ethical drug manufacturers went about their business. Then they were attacked by consumer

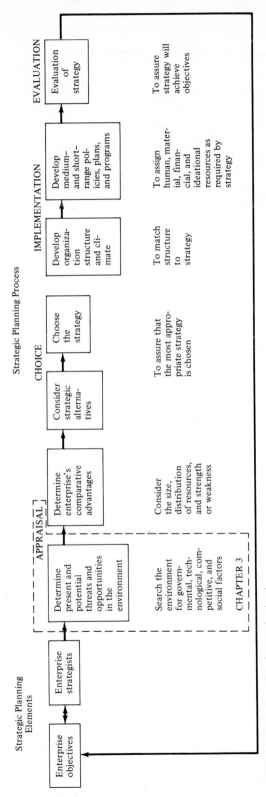

**FIGURE 3–1** ■ A model of strategic planning.

**DEFINITION** ■ ENVIRONMENTAL APPRAISAL AND ANALYSIS

*Environmental appraisal* is the process by which strategic planners monitor the economic, governmental, supplier, technological, and market settings to determine opportunities and threats to their enterprise.

*Environmental analysis* consists of decisions made to react to, anticipate, or ignore environmental cues.

groups, government agencies, and medical groups for: (*a*) being a threat to the public health because of inadequate chemical investigation of new drugs; using misleading promotional activities; and producing dangerous or ineffective products; and (*b*) having excessively high prices resulting in high profits by misuse of patents and brand names (Randall [1]).

Often a company becomes convinced it is almost invincible and need not examine what is happening in the marketplace. When the company ceases to adjust the environment to its strategy or does not react to the demands of the environment by changing its strategy, the results are lessened achievement of corporate objectives.

It is also vital that a company have a thorough understanding of the environment before making changes in the strategy that includes entering new markets. Figure 3–2 highlights this point.

With regard to Proposition 3–2, Anthony Down's research is based on what happened to government departments. But the impressionistic evidence supports Propositions 3–1 and 3–2.

This chapter will describe the techniques which can be used for environmental search and analysis and the factors which some experts feel should be examined. The chapter concludes with how the search and analysis actually take place.


## Techniques for environmental search and analysis

For strategic planners to analyze adequately the threats and opportunities in the environment, they can use three search techniques (see page 49).


###  INFORMATION GATHERING

Executives can learn about the environment by gathering *verbal and written* information.

**PROPOSITION** ■ A firm whose strategy fits the needs of the firm's environment will be more ef-
**3–1** fective.

**PROPOSITION** ■ The major causes of growth, decline, and other large-scale changes in firms
**3–2** are factors in the environment, not internal developments (modified Downs [1]).

*"You know, Mother, you could be waiting for a ship that may never come in."*

FIGURE 3–2 ■ Environmental analysis and success. Drawing by Weber; © 1973 The New Yorker Magazine, Inc.

*Verbal* information is that which we learn by hearing it. This information can be gathered informally or formally (in such experiences as meetings and conferences).

*Sources* of verbal information include:

1  Such media as radio and television

2  Enterprises' employees such as peers, subordinates, and superiors

3  Others outside the enterprise including: (*a*) enterprise customers; (*b*) persons in the industry channels (for example, wholesalers, brokers); (*c*) enterprise suppliers; (*d*) competitors and their employees; (*e*) financial executives such as bankers, stockbrokers, stock analysts; (*f*) consultants; (*g*) government and university employees.

*Written* information is what we learn by reading. Carbonnel and Dorrance [2] have done an excellent job listing some of the best sources of written information available for these aspects of environmental information. They list the specific publications executives could look at. I list only the types of publications available.

## 2) SPYING

A second source of information, usually used to gather information about potential or actual competitors, is spying. The top executive (or more likely

---

DEFINITION ■ ENVIRONMENTAL SEARCH TECHNIQUES
Environmental search is accomplished through the use of three techniques:

1  Information gathering

2  Spying

3  Forecasting

---

1 **Economic and industry information**
   (*a*) U.S. Department of Commerce
      (1) Bureau of the Census, such as *Survey of Manufacturers; Statistical Abstract*
      (2) Office of Business Economics, such as *Survey of Current Business*
      (3) Bureau of Economic Analysis, such as *Business Conditions Digest*
      (4) Business and Defense Services Administration, such as *U.S. Industrial Outlook*
   (*b*) Council of Economic Advisers: economic indicators
   (*c*) Securities and Exchange Commission: quarterly reports of finance and capital expenditures
   (*d*) St. Louis Federal Reserve Board: economic statistics
   (*e*) Conference Board: research and statistical reports
   (*f*) Trade association publications: research and statistical reports

2 **International economic information**
   (*a*) U.S. Department of Commerce: *Guide to Foreign Trade Statistics and others*
   (*b*) OECD: *Economic Outlook and Main Economic Indicators*
   (*c*) United Nations: *Statistical Yearbook*
   (*d*) OIT: *Yearbook of Labour Statistics*
   (*e*) Business International
   (*f*) St. Louis Federal Reserve Bank: reports

3 **Commodity and resource information**
   (*a*) U.S. Department of the Interior: *Minerals Yearbook; Geological Survey*
   (*b*) U.S. Department of Agriculture: *Agricultural Abstract*
   (*c*) Federal Power Commission: *Statistics of Utilities*
   (*d*) Institute publications (for example, American Petroleum Institute)

4 **Technological and scientific information**
   (*a*) National Science Foundation: *Annual Report*
   (*b*) *Research and Development Directors*

5 **Company-oriented information**
   (*a*) Company annual reports
   (*b*) Securities and Exchange Commission, Form 10-K
   (*c*) Journals: *Fortune* Directory, *Wall Street Transcript, Barrons, Forbes, Dun's,* etc.
   (*d*) Investment services and directories: Dun & Bradstreet, Standard and Poors, *Value Line,* Moody's, Starch Marketing, etc.
   (*e*) Trade association publications

---

a middle-level executive encouraged however surreptitiously by a top executive) employs an individual or individuals to determine trade secrets. The spy can be an employee of the competitor, a supplier or customer of the competitor, or a "professional" spy.

The third method available is to prepare (or have prepared for you) formal forecasts about the future for the company or industry. The forecast can focus on any aspect of the future as it affects the company: technological, demographic, market, and other factors.

There are essentially three types of formal forecasting methods used at present:

1  Qualitative techniques

2  Historical comparison and projection

3  Causal models

The first method, qualitative techniques, uses experts to estimate the future. In expert estimation, an individual or several individuals considered knowledgeable are asked to forecast the future. This can be done an individual at a time, or the more formal Delphi method can be used. All kinds of experts can be used. I am not sure that palmists are used, but they might have been.

The second method, historical comparison and projection, plots current trends and extrapolates them into the future through various methods from graphs to computers.

The third approach is to model the environmental factors with company factors. Techniques in this third category include regression models, econometric models, and input-output models.

Forecasting techniques have had mixed results in terms of successful predictions of the future. As the very volatile shifts in materials prices and business cycle indicators in 1972–1974 show, it is not easy to forecast the future.

## Environmental factors: a normative list

Having discussed several of the techniques that executives could use to search and analyze the environment, we move on to *what* in the environment *should be* looked at.

Many analysts have provided managers with lists of factors they ought to examine if they wish to do a good job of strategic planning. I have attempted to summarize these factors. Table 3–1 provides you with a list of the environmental characteristics which many experts believe executives *should* be considering in their environmental analyses.

DEFINITION ■ ENVIRONMENTAL FACTORS
*Environmental factors* are those characteristics external to the enterprise which experts feel the executives should monitor. These characteristics are:

General environmental factors

Supplier factors

Market factors

**TABLE 3-1 ■ FACTORS TO BE CONSIDERED IN ENVIRONMENTAL ANALYSIS**

| General environmental factors | Changes in governmental structure<br>Major new governmental restrictions on operations of your company or industry<br>Major political or community pressure affecting your company or industry<br>Major changes in the ethical values or social environment affecting your business<br>Major pressure by consumer groups affecting your company or industry<br>Changes in economy or economic policy affecting your company or industry<br>Changes in distribution of wealth in the society affecting the demand for your product or services<br>Population changes affecting demand for your products or services |
|---|---|
| Supplier factors | Major changes in availability of major raw materials, subassemblies, etc.<br>Major changes in price and conditions affecting major raw materials or subassemblies, etc.<br>Additional entry of major potential supplies of significant raw materials or subassembly needs<br>Exit of major supplier of significant raw material or subassembly needs<br>Technological breakthrough affecting equipment or system of delivery of products or service offered by company |
| Market factors | Major new products or services introduced into industry<br>Major shifts in the pricing structure of products or services<br>Major shifts in the demand for your products or services<br>Major shifts in the consumer preferences about your products or services<br>Major new competitors entering your industry<br>Major changes in the product life cycle for your industry |

## GENERAL ENVIRONMENTAL FACTORS [4]

There are many factors in the political or governmental, demographic and general economic environment which a top manager must observe. By observing the general environmental factors, the enterprise can anticipate threats or opportunities and thus derive a comparative advantage over competitors.

Probably the most pervasive environmental influence is governmental policy. Federal, state (or provincial in Canada), and local governments influence the enterprise not just by their taxing powers. In addition to taxation, governmental bodies can have three kinds of influence on an enterprise: (1) direct competition with the firm, (2) protecting and/or stimulating its growth, and (3) regulating (that is, limiting) it or its industry.

*Governmental competition* From their beginnings, the United States and Canadian governments have performed certain services and produced certain products which put them in competition with firms. Safeway Stores have to compete with U.S. military commissaries, and Canadian Pacific Railways must compete with the Canadian National Railroad.

A firm competing in these industries or other industries likely to be involved must consider what government "firms," with no requirement for profit and no tax payments, could do in the industry.

*Governmental protection or subsidies* The government can support or encourage industries as well as compete with them. They can do this by substantial purchases of a firm's products or services, by providing direct subsidies or indirect protection (patents, tariffs), or by providing finances through cost-plus or research funds. Examples of companies affected in these ways are defense companies, mining companies (especially silver and nickel), and transportation companies (especially shipbuilding, waterways, and short-hop airlines). Again, you should ask yourself: Is the company subsidized or likely to receive support in the future? Some possible examples might include support for oceanography, pollution, mass transit, housing, private vocational training firms, and minority-group-owned businesses and others.

*Governmental regulation*  In addition to competing with or subsidizing firms, the government regulates certain aspects of all firms' operations and many aspects of industrywide operation. They can and do regulate factors such as entry (atomic energy), exit, merger (antitrust), location (defense, regional development), product standards (for safety, wholesomeness), prices and profits (especially in subsidized industries and utilities, but also others through the FTC), labor relations and policies, and other aspects of operations such as taxes, pollution controls, and social responsibility (hiring the hard-core unemployed, minority-group hiring).

The amount and extent of governmental regulations vary widely, of course. The finance industry (banks, insurance, stock market) is closely regulated, and so is the utility industry. Other industries such as airwaves media, pharmaceuticals, defense, atomic energy, and food are strongly influenced. Others such as toys, personal service, and clothing are affected very little. The news is full of stories of how environmental regulation has become increasingly strict. Look at what has happened to the Reserve Mining Company in Silver Bay, Minnesota, because of its dumping of fluids into Lake Superior. And Procter and Gamble has been questioned about the safety of Sure deodorant. Microwave oven sales have been affected by government questions about their safety.

Another factor a top manager tries to keep up with is demographic changes. These are broad characteristics of the population that affect the firm because its customers and employees are being changed. One factor is the size and location of the population. A population shift from cities to suburbs, for example, affects some businesses. American and Canadian people are becoming better-educated, resulting in better-skilled employees and more demanding and discriminating customers. Incomes per family are increasing in absolute and real terms, allowing the firm's customers to buy more of the better goods and services. More women work than ever before, adding to total family income and giving more stability to income when one of the breadwinners leaves a job, becomes ill, or for some other reason cannot work.

Modes of transportation also affect firms. If air freight becomes less expensive, for example, it can change certain businesses. The rapidly completed interstate highway system has increased the speed of truck transportation and has affected other businesses.

But perhaps more important than this, the values and norms of the American and Canadian people change over time. Attitudes toward the importance of work and the desirability or need for goods and services have changed, and attitudes toward behavior at work also have changed. Moreover, increasing education and the all-pervasive influence of powerful media, especially television, have accelerated the speed and impact of these changes.

Finally, the condition of the economy at a given time influences an enterprise's strategy. What was possible in prosperity years like 1963 and 1972 may not be possible in recession or depression years like 1932, 1958, and 1974, and if inflation is to accelerate, quick decisions must be made to offset it.

Top management must assess the impact that these broad social changes

TABLE 3–2 ■ RESEARCH AND DEVELOPMENT EXPENDITURES BY INDUSTRY

**A** Expenditures for research and development per employee

| SIC used | 1961 dollars | 1961 rank | 1968 dollars | 1968 rank | Percent change from 1961 to 1968 | Rank of percent change |
|---|---|---|---|---|---|---|
| Food and kindred products | 140 | 19.5 | 230 | 17.5 | 64 | 2 |
| Textiles and apparel | 90 | 22 | 90 | 21.5 | 0 | 21.5 |
| Lumber, wood products, and furniture | 110 | 21 | 90 | 21.5 | −18 | 16 |
| Paper and allied products | 160 | 18 | 200 | 19 | 25 | 11 |
| Industrial chemicals | 1,420 | 5 | 1,450 | 5 | 2 | 19.5 |
| Drugs and medicines | 1,430 | 4 | 1,980 | 2 | 38 | 6 |
| Other chemicals | 970 | 8 | 990 | 9 | 2 | 19.5 |
| Petroleum refining and extracting | 580 | 11 | 810 | 10 | 40 | 5 |
| Rubber products | 500 | 12 | 630 | 12 | 26 | 10 |
| Stone, clay, and glass products | 350 | 13.5 | 430 | 14 | 23 | 12 |
| Primary ferrous products | 140 | 19.5 | 180 | 20 | 29 | 9 |
| Nonferrous and other metal products | 270 | 15.5 | 330 | 15.5 | 22 | 13.5 |
| Fabricated metal products | 270 | 15.5 | 330 | 15.5 | 22 | 13.5 |
| Machinery | 810 | 9 | 1,080 | 8 | 33 | 8 |
| Communication equipment and electrical components | 1,890 | 2 | 1,900 | 3 | 0 | 21.5 |
| Other electrical equipment | 1,600 | 3 | 1,860 | 4 | 16 | 17 |
| Motor vehicle and other transportation equipment | 670 | 10 | 1,180 | 7 | 46 | 4 |
| Aircraft and missiles | 4,470 | 1 | 4,640 | 1 | 4 | 18 |
| Scientific and mechanical measuring instruments | 1,410 | 6 | 640 | 11 | −55 | 3 |
| Optical, surgical, photo, and other instruments | 1,120 | 7 | 1,330 | 6 | 19 | 15 |
| Other manufacturing industries | 350 | 13.5 | 230 | 17.5 | 34 | 7 |
| Nonmanufacturing industries | 180 | 17 | 480 | 13 | 167 | 1 |

have had and are likely to have on their products and/or services and employees. Are the firm's products likely to become obsolete because of these changes in migration, incomes, education, or value (for example, cigarettes, certain farm and small-town products, services, or retail outlets, lard, heavy clothing, and automobiles)? Because of environmental problems and value changes are products with great potential just "taking off" (for example, mass-transit facilities, pollution-control devices, marijuana cigarettes, noise-control mechanisms, "new towns")? These are some of the questions a firm must ask itself to attempt to assess the potential impact of social changes on its products and/or services and employees.

## SUPPLIER FACTORS

A second set of factors in the environment will be called supplier factors. First, the firm must keep track of changes in the availability and prices of raw materials or subassemblies it needs. Consider the major shifts in the prices

| | 1961 percent of sales | 1961 rank | 1968 percent of sales | 1968 rank | Percent change from 1961 to 1968 | Rank of percent change |
|---|---|---|---|---|---|---|
| Food and kindred products | 0.4 | 20.5 | 0.4 | 20.5 | 0 | 19 |
| Textiles and apparel | 0.5 | 19 | 0.5 | 19 | 0 | 19 |
| Lumber, wood products, and furniture | 0.6 | 18 | 0.4 | 20.5 | −33 | 6 |
| Paper and allied products | 0.7 | 16.5 | 0.7 | 16.5 | 0 | 19 |
| Industrial chemicals | 5.2 | 6 | 4.1 | 7 | −17 | 11.5 |
| Drugs and medicines | 4.3 | 7 | 6.8 | 5 | 58 | 1 |
| Other chemicals | 2.8 | 10 | 2.3 | 11 | −18 | 10 |
| Petroleum refining and extracting | 1.0 | 15 | 1.0 | 14.5 | 0 | 19 |
| Rubber products | 2.2 | 11 | 3.3 | 9 | 50 | 3.5 |
| Stone, clay, and glass products | 1.5 | 12 | 1.9 | 12 | 27 | 7 |
| Primary ferrous products | 0.7 | 16.5 | 0.7 | 16.5 | 0 | 19 |
| Nonferrous and other metal products | 1.2 | 14 | 1.0 | 14.5 | −17 | 11.5 |
| Fabricated metal products | 1.4 | 13 | 1.3 | 13 | − 7 | 14 |
| Machinery | 4.2 | 8 | 4.4 | 6 | 5 | 15.5 |
| Communication equipment and electrical components | 12.7 | 2 | 9.6 | 2 | −24 | 8 |
| Other electrical equipment | 8.0 | 3 | 7.6 | 3 | − 5 | 15.5 |
| Motor vehicle and other transportation equipment | 4.0 | 9 | 3.2 | 10 | −20 | 9 |
| Aircraft and missiles | 23.5 | 1 | 10.8 | 1 | −54 | 2 |
| Scientific and mechanical measuring instruments | 6.0 | 5 | 3.8 | 8 | −37 | 5 |
| Optical, surgical, photo, and other instruments | 6.1 | 4 | 7.0 | 4 | 15 | 13 |
| Other manufacturing industries | 0.4 | 20.5 | 0.6 | 18 | 50 | 3.5 |
| Nonmanufacturing industries | — | — | — | — | — | — |

*Source:* Compiled from National Science Foundation: *Research and Development in Industry,* yearly report (5640 March 1971, NS1.22:IN2/968).

of wheat, sugar, and petroleum from 1973 to 1974. Some of the rises were due to weather factors (wheat). Other increases were caused by changes in the supplier organization. Just as the OPEC nations joined to raise the price of oil, so other suppliers could affect the prices of goods and/or services needed by the organization (see Lucado).

The second major area of supplier factors is technological change. A technological change can allow new products or services to be offered by the enterprise. Or it can lead to new operating procedures to change the way of doing business. Examples of possible or actual product-service breakthroughs include transistors, lasers, and efficient batteries for electric cars. The change in production methods in the printing industry by the use of computerized typesetting is an example of operating procedures. Cooper describes what happened in five industries when industry executives ignored technological changes (reading at the end of this chapter). Of course, the technological information available need not be the latest breakthrough. For as Fronko has observed, "One company's cast-off technology is another company's opportunity."

Not all sectors of the economy are likely to be equally affected by technological change. Some sectors are more volatile than others. There are few good measures of likely volatility. One is the amount of research and development spent by an industry. One would expect that the more it spends, the more likely there is to be change coming. Table 3–2 gives one recent ranking of such industries. Government expenditures for research and development are not shown in Table 3–2. As we shall see, it is one thing to know that a technological change has taken place. It is another to determine if the change will have a major impact on your industry and your company.

## MARKET FACTORS

An executive must keep his eye on several variables in the market environment. The first is the competitive structure of the industry. What is the structure now? What has been the trend in the last 10 years? One way to categorize the competitive environment of the industry is as follows:

1 One firm controls 50 percent or more of sales.

2 Four or five firms control 50 percent or more of sales

3 Nine or ten firms control 50 percent or more of sales

4 No firm controls more than 10 percent of sales.

If your firm controls 5 percent of industry sales, your strategic posture differs depending on your competitive environment. For example:

| Industry structure | You with your 5 percent of sales |
|---|---|
| 1 Monopoly | Weak |
| 2 Oligopoly | Moderate: probably a "second tier" or middle-sized firm |
| 3 Monopolistic competition | Strong: one of the industry leaders |
| 4 Competition | Strong, perhaps an industry leader |

A second variable is where the products or services are in the life cycle. Is the product's demand growing rapidly? Flat? Declining? One cannot base the strategy only on our sales. Industry sales must be examined.

What is the status of new products in the industry? Is your firm a market leader here? Or a follower? Do your competitors have complete lines with many new products, and do you have a short line of mostly mature products?

An assessment of the environment can be made on a profile as shown in Table 3–3 for the Reiter Company.

It is obvious that a small glove manufacturer like Reiter has less concern with governmental restrictions than American Telephone and Telegraph Company. The profile is designed to highlight threats and opportunities which

DEFINITION ■ ENVIRONMENTAL THREAT AND OPPORTUNITIES PROFILE
The *environmental threat and opportunities profile* is a systematic evaluation of environmental factors weighted by the significance of each factor for the company.

| Factors | Weighting of factor[a] | | | | Significance to Reiter[b] |
|---|---|---|---|---|---|
| | Strong + | + | − | Strong − | |
| **General factors** | | | | | |
| Government restrictions | | ✓ | | | 0 |
| Consumer pressure | | ✓ | | | 0 |
| Economic changes | | ✓ | | | + |
| Wealth changes | | ✓ | | | + |
| Population changes | | ✓ | | | 0 |
| **Supplier factors** | | | | | |
| Raw materials | ✓ | | | | ++ |
| Pricing of raw materials | ✓ | | | | +++ |
| Number of suppliers | | | ✓ | | 0 |
| Technological breakthrough | | ✓ | | | ++ |
| **Market factors** | | | | | |
| New products | | ✓ | | | + |
| Pricing structure | ✓ | | | | ++ |
| Demand | ✓ | | | | +++ |
| Consumer preferences | ✓ | | | | ++ |
| New competitors | | ✓ | | | + |
| Product life cycle | | ✓ | | | 0 |

[a] Weighting indicates the degree to which the factor evaluated is an advantage or disadvantage to Reiter.
[b] Significance is coded as follows: 0 = neutral; − = negative; the more minuses, the more negative; + = positive; the more pluses, the more positive. Significance indicates the degree to which the weighted factor has or will have strategic impact on the firm.

are significant for the focal company. This profile is matched with the strategic advantage profile as described in Chapter 4.

These then are *some* of the factors in the environment which top managers are urged to scan. Not all can be listed. The details of each factor have been discussed under other subject headings like economics, marketing, purchasing, political science, and sociology. We move now to a brief look at some tools of scanning which managers actually use to search the environment for information about it.

## Actual techniques used for environmental search and analysis

In an earlier part of this chapter, the environmental search techniques available to executives were described. This section reviews the techniques actually used.

**DEFINITION** ■ ACTUAL TECHNIQUES USED FOR ENVIRONMENTAL SEARCH AND ANALYSIS
The actual techniques used for search and analysis are those methods of information gathering, spying, and forecasting which executives use in examining the environment as determined by research.

There have been several studies of how managers search the environment as part of the strategic planning process. The first study to be examined is that of Aguilar. He studied 41 firms in the chemical industry in the United States and Europe by means of a questionnaire and 5 of these 41 by case study. Some of the findings of Aguilar's study are:

**RESEARCH STUDY** ■ **AGUILAR'S FINDINGS**

**1** Verbal sources of information are much more important than written sources. Seventy-five percent of information cited by executives was in verbal form.

**2** The higher the executive in the organization, the more important verbal sources became.

**3** Of the written sources used, the most important were newspapers (two-thirds), then trade publications, then internal company reports.

**4** The major sources of verbal information are subordinates, then friends in the industry, and very infrequently superiors.

**5** Information received from outside an organization is usually unsolicited.

**6** Information received from inside the organization is usually solicited by the executive.

**7** Information received from outside tends to have a greater impact on the decision maker than inside information.

**8** The outside sources used varied according to the job of the manager. Thus, marketing managers talked more to customers.

**9** The larger the company, the greater the reliance on inside sources of verbal information.

He found that executives change scanning modes when the present mode fails. The mode varies according to the magnitude of the problem, to whether it is seen as a problem that is definable, and to other factors. Warren Keegan used Aguilar's approach to study how executives in 13 multinational firms searched the environment. His findings replicate Aguilar's findings.

A third study was done by Robert Collings. Collings examined how 137 executives in 49 investment companies in New York and Boston searched the environment for important or strategic information. He interviewed the executives and did in-depth case studies at one small, one large, and two medium-sized firms. On many points, his findings agree with Aguilar's.

**RESEARCH STUDY** ■ **COLLINGS'S FINDINGS**

**1** The more sources of information used by an executive to scan the environment, the more effective was his or her environmental analysis.

**2** Managers used more sources from outside the company than inside it. (Most of Collings's firms were smaller than Aguilar's.)

**3** Managers used primarily verbal sources of information, not written sources.

**4** The *least* useful sources of information were superiors, meetings, reports, and studies.

**5** The lower the level of executive, the more the use of written sources of information.

**6** The larger the firm, the more the use of inside sources (verbal and written).

**7** The larger the firm, the broader and the more specific and longer the time frame of the search of the environment.

---

A fourth study provides information about how 1211 executives said they gather information *about their competitors.* Wall's respondents, all readers of the *Harvard Business Review,* found the following:

---

RESEARCH STUDY ■ **WALL'S FINDINGS**
**1** The most frequently used sources of information about competitors were the following (in order):
(*a*) Company salespeople
(*b*) Published sources
(*c*) Professional and personal contacts with competitors
(*d*) Customers

**2** Other less frequently used sources were (in order):
(*a*) Formal market research
(*b*) Middlemen (brokers, wholesalers, etc.)
(*c*) Process-product analysis of competitors' products
(*d*) Suppliers

**3** Least frequently used sources were:
(*a*) Competitors' employees
(*b*) Advertising agencies and consultants

---

Taylor studied 79 managers in a heavy manufacturing firm. In examining differences in processing information in decision making, he found that older managers took longer to make decisions because they sought more information before making decisions. The older executives evaluated the information more accurately, were less confident about their decisions, and were more flexible in altering their decisions if the environment changed. Finally, a few large firms, such as Atlantic Richfield and Dow Chemical, are setting up staff groups whose main focus is environmental analysis and information gathering.

---

**PROPOSITION 3–3** ■ Most top managers gather information about the environment verbally primarily from subordinates and friends or acquaintances in the industry.

---

Proposition 3–3 summarizes some of the findings about how executives actually gather information for their environmental search and analysis.

### SPYING [6]

A second potential tool for environmental analysis is spying by a firm on its competitors or other sources in industry.

We know very little about the actual spying activities of firms. Juicy tidbits, usually as a result of a suit, sometimes reach the press. Jerry Wall describes the results of his study of over 1200 executives who read the *Harvard Business Review.* He received 1211 usable replies. He asked the executives about the extent of spying (in 1973) and compared his findings with a similar study in 1959. Thirty-four percent of Wall's respondents said they believed spying had increased in the last 10 years; another 34 percent believed the level was the same. Twenty-three percent said they did not know, and 9 percent believed it never existed or had declined.

Only 8 percent of the respondents indicated their firms had formal departments which regularly gather information on competitors. Wall concluded that in general spying has not increased dramatically since 1959. Spying appeared to occur most frequently in defense and space industries.

### FORECASTING AND MODELING [7]

Various research studies have indicated that in *larger* firms in the United States, Canada, and Europe, formal forecasting of future events goes on. Usually, this forecasting is done by staff specialists in such departments as economic analysis, market research, and corporate planning. In medium-size and smaller firms, it is rare to find formal forecasting activities.

The forecasters project future trends in the economy, technology, products, and other factors. They do this qualitatively or quantitatively, using such techniques as mathematical trend models or single equation econometric models and other tools.

The question is this: Does the top management use the data provided? In a word, no. The findings of Collings, Aquilar, and Keegan support this. Thurston has studied one variety of these forecasters: technological forecasters. He has found that there is little or no interconnection between technological forecasting and corporate strategy and that at present, top managers do not use these forecasts in making strategic decisions. Perhaps because the forecasters are far from top management in status, they have to send the decision makers their recommendations in writing. And we all know now that most top managers rely primarily on verbal sources of information for these decisions. This may also be true because line managers can be very good forecasters on their own, as Copeland and Marioni and Vancil showed.

With regard to modeling, in 1975 Thomas Naylor reported that of 346 large corporations surveyed, three-fourths had developed corporate models of their businesses. These computer models deal with many variables but typically focus on 8 to 12 crucial variables for their industry, for example, consumer spending on nondurables, interest rates, and rate of inflation. Dow Chemical uses 140 separate cost inputs alone to its model. In addition, the firms often check their results against the results of other models. They attempt to use these models as inputs to their plans. But the models cannot predict unexpected events, and thus many business executives are unenthusiastic. A. J. Ashe, vice president of B. F. Goodrich Company, said: "Econometric models have gone to pot because of the inability to quantify variables going into a model. If you are forecasting the replacement tire market, you have to go back and decide how many miles will be driven, driving patterns, etc. My problem is that the relationships never stay the same."

## Information actually sought by managers [8]

Now that we know *how* strategic decision makers seek information, let us look at *what* information the executives actually look for. Table 3–1 provided you with a list of environmental factors managers could look for. Four studies have examined what executives actually examine. Three of these studies are summarized in Table 3–4.

These studies appear to conclude that executives seek first to learn about market tidings, which include information on market potential, competitors' strengths and marketing plans, pricing, and customer information. After determining market tidings, the next most important environmental information set is technological tidings, which include information on new products, processes, technology, costs of production, and patent and licensing data.

## The Glueck-*Fortune* study

Recently I have undertaken a research project which may provide some clues to executives for searching the environment. *Fortune* has published case studies since 1930 describing what has been happening to large firms during the period. About half of these case studies are sketchy and the other half are reasonably complete. I have examined a random sample of 358 of the 630 complete studies. Some associates and this author analyzed the contents of these cases. We determined which challenges the companies were facing, which responses to the challenges they used, and whether they were successful or not in their response. The initial work in this area was done by Hofer [9], who looked at some of the companies described in the 1960s in *Fortune* as well as some in 1970 and 1971.

Examining companies over a 45-year period provides an opportunity to see how the challenges change over those years and in different economic conditions (recession, prosperity, etc.).

TABLE 3–4 ■ PERCENTAGE OF EXECUTIVES WHO RATED THE FACTORS AS IMPORTANT IN RESEARCH STUDIES

| Factor | Aguilar | Collings | Wall |
|---|---|---|---|
| General environmental | 8% | 5% | Least important |
| Supplier | 10% | 15% | Next most important |
| Market | 75% | 60% | Most important |
| Other | 7% | 20% | |

The 358 companies come from many industries:

| | |
|---|---|
| Consumer goods manufacturing | 34.6% |
| Industrial goods | 31.0 |
| Construction, mining, and oil | 8.9 |
| Retail, wholesale, and trade | 8.1 |
| Conglomerates | 8.1 |
| Transportation | 6.1 |
| Other (advertising, media, publications, banking, insurance, personal services) | 3.2 |
| | 100.0% |

Essentially, the cases were content-analyzed and coded for the challenges facing the company on the basis of the categories in Table 3–1. If the challenge was mentioned, it was tabulated. Then if the challenge was described in detail and the company indicated it was an *important* challenge, it was rank-ordered in importance from first to fifth. The following challenges were listed most frequently.

1 General environmental challenges, 573. Index of 71.6.

2 Market challenges, 402. Index of 68.0.

3 Supplier challenges, 163. Index of 32.6.

In the study, general environmental challenges were most important, followed by market challenges. Supplier challenges are far behind. An index was computed because the lists of factors were not of the same length and general environment had more chances of being mentioned. The most frequently *mentioned* specific challenges were:

1 Changes in the economy or economic policy   161

2 New product introduced by the company   116

3 New product introduced by a competitor   101

4 Major new government restrictions   67

5 Major shifts in consumer preferences for the company's product or services   65

Next, the challenges were tabulated by the state of the economy at the time of the case (recession, depression, etc.). These were the findings:

1 General economic conditions are of most concern in recovery, then recessionary periods.

2 Supplier conditions are never of great concern, but are of some concern in depression and recovery, the least in prosperity.

3 Market conditions are of the greatest concern in recovery periods.

4 In depression, the factors of greatest concern are (in this order):
(*a*) General economic conditions
(*b*) New products introduced by competitors
(*c*) Shifts in pricing structure of products
(*d*) Changes in prices by suppliers

5 In recovery, the factors of greatest concern (in this order) are:
(*a*) General economic conditions
(*b*) New products introduced by the company
(*c*) Changes in technology of process and products
(*d*) New products introduced by competitors

6 In recession, the factors of greatest concern are:
(*a*) General economic conditions

(*b*)   Governmental restrictions
(*c*)   New products introduced by competitors
(*d*)   Changes in the distribution of wealth affecting the company
(*e*)   New products introduced by the company
(*f*)   Major shifts in consumer preferences about products

7   In prosperity, the factors of greatest concern are:
(*a*)   General economic conditions
(*b*)   New products introduced by the company
(*c*)   New products introduced by competitors
(*d*)   New governmental restrictions
(*e*)   Major shifts in consumer preferences about products

What appears to happen is that the economy is always the greatest concern. Concern with new products is also high. Companies are most concerned with new product introductions by competitors in bad times like depression. Pricing is a major factor primarily in depression.

When we examined how concern for the challenges had changed *over time,* the following was found:

1930s:   Economic changes, competitors' new products, company new products, changes in wealth

1940s:   Economic changes, governmental restrictions, supplier availability

1950s:   New company products, competitors' new products, economic changes

1960s:   New company products, competitors' new products, changing consumer ideas about products, economic changes, governmental restrictions

1970s:   Governmental restrictions, economic changes

Notice how the economy was the greatest concern in the thirties and forties, then dropped back, and reappeared near the top of the list in the seventies. The forties were a special period with supplier problems and governmental restrictions. Governmental restrictions reappear as the primary problem in the seventies, having reappeared late in the sixties. New products were the primary concern of the fifties and sixties.

Finally, we examined how the challenges were viewed by different industries. Taking the most important two or three challenges as faced by each industry, we see the following percentages of the firms concerned with these challenges:

Consumer goods     42 percent each for general economy, new company products, and competitors' new products

Industrial goods     50 percent with general economy; 40 percent new company products; 35 percent competitors' new products

Construction, etc.     47 percent with general economy; 37 percent each with supplier availability and supplier price

Defense and space     50 percent general economy; $33\frac{1}{3}$ percent with government restrictions

Retail and wholesale     44 percent general economy; 31 percent each with consumer ideas about product and changes in wealth of customers

Transportation and utilities     73 percent with general economy; 54 percent with government restrictions

Conglomerate     44 percent economic conditions; 41 percent new company products

All industries are concerned with the economy. But beyond that the differences come. New products are the concern of the consumer goods, conglomerate, and industrial groups. Government restrictions are the concern of transportation and utilities and of defense and space. Construction is concerned with supply problems.

In conclusion, my research indicates much greater concern with economic conditions than Aguilar found. Beyond that, marketing challenges predominate in many (but not all) industries. Much more research is needed to find out more about the factors that executives actually analyze in the environment.

Thus far in the chapter, we have reviewed techniques managers could use to search the environment and which ones they do use. And we have examined the kinds of information they could look at and which kinds they do look at. This brings us to a crucial question: How and when do executives decide to act upon information they learn about from the environment?

## Decision making on environmental information [10]

This section will describe how managers make decisions on whether to search the environment, and what, if anything, the decision maker does about the information received in action terms.

Managers can be, if they let themselves, bombarded with information from the environment. They are faced with choices on what information to continue to examine and whether they should act upon that information.

When Du Pont announced it was marketing Corfam, a leather substitute for such products as shoes, what should the leather companies have done? Du Pont is a large and successful company. How should they have reacted? In fact, a few years later Du Pont got out of the Corfam business. Others entered it then. But what should the leather companies do now?

The tobacco companies faced a real threat with the surgeon general's report 10 years ago. Should they have gotten out of the business? In fact, by 1974, sales increases in cigarettes matched the pre-surgeon-general period.

What should discount retailers do about the entrance of catalog discount retailers? Ignore them? Come out with their own? What should stockbrokers do about the increasing direct entrance of some banks into their business?

If companies ignore threats, they can become less than growth companies. Look at Curtiss-Wright in the airplane industry, Baldwin Locomotives in the railroad industry, the ink pen firms in the writing instrument industry. It is all very well for analysts to tell managers they should observe the environment and act upon its data. But how? And when? And as Braybrooke and Lindblom showed (citing Bruner's research), it is impossible to scan the complete environment. Executives must focus the scanning.

You may recall MacCrimmon's definition of the process: *A decision is a choice made by a decision maker in a decision environment.*

The environment of the decision affects the decision. There are at least six items which can affect the decision. These can be called dimensions of environmental analysis.

1  The attitudes and experiences of the strategic planners
2  The age of the enterprise

3 Size and power of the enterprise

4 Technology and volatility of the enterprise's environment

5 Geographic dimension of the enterprise

6 The business(es) the firm is in or could be in

## MANAGERIAL ATTITUDE DIMENSION

The first dimension is managerial attitudes toward the environment. The kind of person the decision maker is affects whether search is initiated, how intensively, and whether action follows. The attitudes that the decision maker has toward the possible impact of the environment are crucial to these decisions. The executives develop these attitudes from their past experiences.

Nystrom, in analyzing why some organizations stagnate, contrasts executives who have closed cognitive styles with those who have global styles. The latter look at the total environment as important to monitor. The former tend to lead stagnant organizations. They focus on a very narrow part of the environment and tend to overemphasize details instead of the "big picture." It seems that managers of stagnant enterprises have a general attitude of self-satisfaction with past accomplishments. They do not compare themselves to other companies—just their own. Cooper, in looking at the identification and appraisal of major technological change, comes to a similar conclusion. He points out that major technological change usually originates outside the current industry group. So, if a manager focuses narrowly, he or she will miss the major threat. These men and women have "closed" minds in Rokeach's sense of the term and tend to be present- rather than future-oriented.

And Dill makes the point that successful managers must now more than ever search the environment for kibitzers such as consumer and governmental groups who more and more are influencing how firms operate.

Aguilar's findings can be rephrased as Proposition 3–4, which is similar to Braybrooke and Lindblom's findings about politicians.

Before you criticize those managers, think back to the last time you had a job. Theoretically, you could be laid off at any time. Yet you did not start looking for another job until the layoffs actually began to happen. Managers are similar. First, it is hard to know what to look for in the environment, or how hard to look.

But, there are probably other reasons than that it is hard to do to explain why managers do not search the environment as much as they "should." First of all, they have lots of things to do: meet customers, promote people, lots of ordinary tasks. And ordinary short-run tasks have a way of filling up the day. Simon called this phenomenon the "Gresham's law of planning": present pressing duties drive out long-run consideration. But there is still more to it *GLUECK* than that. I believe the explanation to be as follows: Managers prefer to act and think about the present short-run problems (as opposed to strategic plan-

---

**PROPOSITION 3–4** ■ Most managers *react* to environmental change. They do not anticipate or plan for it.

---

ning process including environmental analysis) because (1) that is what they have *learned* to do as junior managers, and (2) this behavior has been reinforced by feedback and reward or punishment over their whole career.

A junior-level marketing executive is rewarded for today's and this week's sales, not sales forecasting. A junior-level operations executive is rewarded for getting today's work out, not planning a plant addition for 5 years from now. The junior accountant must get statements out on time if he or she wishes to be rewarded.

If the whole career learning is based on speedy feedback and reward for short-run results, the executives carry these behavior patterns into senior management positions.

This fact affects the whole strategic planning process. Environmental analysis carries a special burden as well. The environment often brings change. It is widely observed that people resist change. This is not just perversity. We spend our time and ego building present procedures and ways of doing things. To change these is to experience in a small way death and predeath, retirement. If the old ways must change, the "old" executives can be threatened. I believe that executives go through four stages in the awareness and acceptance of change from the environment.

1  Denial that the change has taken place or is important to the firm

2  Anger that this force is changing their way of doing business; defense of present practices

3  Depression about the impact of the change on their business

4  Resignation to the change and beginnings of adaptation

It would appear that the more quickly the executive moves from stage 1 to stage 4 in reaction to a change, the more effective will be the strategic response to the change.

These stages are modifications of the four psychological stages psychiatrists observe in terminally ill patients. Alfred Gross has developed a four-stage typology. The stages are (1) blindness, (2) destroying the competitor, (3) direct confrontation and overcompensation, and (4) adjustment and adaptation.

## THE AGE DIMENSION

The second dimension is that of *time* measured by the age of the enterprise and especially the experience in the industry of its top management. If the enterprise is new and the executives are inexperienced, they will not really know where to focus. If the executives are experienced and the enterprise has a history of relative successes and failures, they will have developed some ideas of which factors have been most important to watch *in the past*.

---

**PROPOSITION 3–5**  ■  The older the enterprise and the more experienced the executive, the narrower the focus of the search of the environment.

---

## SIZE AND POWER DIMENSION

The third dimension is the *power* of the enterprise relative to elements in the environment. The less dependent (or more powerful) the enterprise, the less it will focus on that part of the environment in which they exert power.

Propositions 3–6 to 3–9 make the point that the enterprise examines the critical factors in the environment and tends to spend less time and energy examining them when the enterprise has leverage or when it lacks dependence.

## TECHNOLOGY-VOLATILITY DIMENSION

The fourth dimension is the relative *volatility* of the technological environment in which the enterprise operates.

The technological environment has two sides:

1 Technology affecting the operations of the company

2 Technology affecting the products or services the enterprise offers

One or both of these can be volatile at any point in time. The environment can be more or less volatile, measured by:

1 The frequency of change in the environment

2 The amount or degree of the change in the environment

3 The irregularity or unpredictability of the change in the environment

Again, the environment can be volatile in one or all three of these measures of volatility.

---

**PROPOSITION 3–6** ■ The more powerful the enterprise relative to its competitors, the less it will focus on the competitive sector of the environment.

---

**PROPOSITION 3–7** ■ The less dependent the enterprise is on one or a few customers, the less it will focus on the customer sector of the environment.

---

**PROPOSITION 3–8** ■ The less dependent the enterprise is on the government for subsidy and the less regulated the enterprise is, the less it will focus its environmental analysis on the political sector of the environment.

---

**PROPOSITION 3–9** ■ The less dependent the enterprise is on one or a few supplies, the less it will focus its environmental analysis on the supplier sector.

---

**PROPOSITION 3–10** ■ The greater the volatility of the technological environment, the more the managers must focus on the technological sector of the environment.

---

Emery and Trist have described four types of environments which combine the power and volatility dimensions (see below).

Following the analysis thus far, the most environmental analysis should take place in turbulent fields, the least in placid, randomized fields. Managers in placid, clustered environment should focus their environmental analysis on the competitors. In disturbed, reactive environments, the managers should focus mostly on the oligopolistic leaders and secondarily on the technological environment.

## THE GEOGRAPHIC DIMENSION [11]

The fifth dimension which helps a manager to focus environmental monitoring is *geography*.

Firms which operate a cement business in the southern United States have less reason to examine the national and international environment for changes in the environment [11].

There is a large amount of literature about the potentials of doing business internationally. In fact, for many a firm its major growth in the last decade has come because it became a multinational firm. If this choice is made, changes in exchange rates, laws of other countries and U.S. and Canadian export policies, governmental changes abroad, joint ownership strategies, and similar factors need to be examined and monitored closely. If the firm is not a multinational, these data become much less relevant.

There is a great deal of evidence that if the firm is a multinational, strategic planning is very important for its success [12].

## THE BUSINESS COMPLEXITY DIMENSION

The final dimension influencing environmental search and analysis is how the company defines its business or market scope. If it is defined narrowly, the

RESEARCH
STUDY

■ **EMERY AND TRIST'S ENVIRONMENTS**

**1** *Placid, randomized:* Less volatile technology and no really powerful competitors (somewhat like economists' pure competition)

**2** *Placid, clustered:* Less volatile technology and some leading competitors (like monopolistic competition)

**3** *Disturbed, reactive:* Moderately volatile technology and definite industry leaders (oligopoly)

**4** *Turbulent:* Very volatile technology and unpredictable competitive conditions

PROPOSITION
3–11

■ The more restricted the geographic area in which the firm operates, the less widely it must reach the environment.

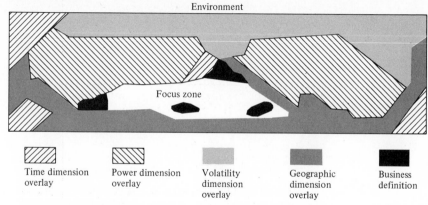

Focus zone

Time dimension overlay

Power dimension overlay

Volatility dimension overlay

Geographic dimension overlay

Business definition

**FIGURE 3–3** ■ How the dimensions become overlays to environmental search and analysis.

executives tend to focus narrowly. If the firm is a conglomerate (or wishes to be), its area of search should be much broader.

## Executives and environmental focusing

It is impossible in the limited time available to search every aspect of the environment and use all the tools to look at every factor in the environment. Executives must narrow the list of factors down and concentrate on this shorter list. In effect, what happens is that executives block out parts of the environment from their view. Five dimensions of environmental analysis become overlays that perform the blocking function. (The sixth, their attitudes, affects the blocking indirectly.)

The concept of the dimensions as overlays is diagrammed in Figure 3–3. The executive tends to search and analyze only the "focus zone." For his experience overlay blanks out some area, the power overlay another area, the geographic and volatility overlays still more areas. If any of these dimensions change in importance, the focus zone could increase or decrease accordingly. This analysis is consistent with Cyert and March's problemistic search and uncertainty avoidance and with Braybrooke and Lindblom's analysis.

## Environmental decision making and strategic planning

This chapter has reviewed the tools of environmental analysis executives should and do use, the factors executives should and do use, and some ideas about how executives decide whether they will act upon environmental information. This section will summarize some final points and briefly lead us into the next chapter. No serious environmental search will be made unless:

**1** The executives perceive the gap between present accomplishment and desired accomplishment.

**2** The executives focus on the problem area.

*"As Bob Dylan said, you don't have to be a weather man
to tell which way the wind is blowing."*

**FIGURE 3–4** ▪ Drawing by Lorenz; © 1973 The New Yorker Magazine, Inc.

**3** There is motivation to reduce the gap.

**4** Executives see the company as able to do something.

If the executives are as self-satisfied as those in Figure 3–4, it may in fact take a *crisis* to induce them to make decisions on environmental threats or opportunities. Only then do they (1) see the gap; (2) see it as a problem; (3) have motivation to close the gap (self-survival) and take action.

Even here is an interesting question: How bad must things get before a crisis is perceived? Consider 1974–1975. It was one of the worst years in the history of the casualty insurance business. Auto sales for 1974 were down 22 percent and dropping lower in early 1975.

We do not know how bad things must get for the executives to define a crisis situation. Which of the following is a crisis?

| | | | | | | | |
|---|---|---|---|---|---|---|---|
| Sales down | 1% | 5% | 10% | 15% | 20% | 25% | 30% etc. |
| Profits down | 1% | 5% | 10% | 15% | 20% | 25% | 30% etc. |
| Combination of both down | 1% | 5% | 10% | 15% | 20% | 25% | 30% etc. |

Thus the *crucial* variable in environmental analysis and action on those data is executive attitudes and expectations in good times and bad.

Environmental analysis is a crucial part of the strategic planning process. If the environment is ignored or quasi-ignored by strategic decision makers, the process cannot be as effective as it would be if they *tried* to anticipate what is coming. Usually the lead time is *long,* not overnight. As Cooper points out, diesel locomotives were first built in 1924 and received a lot of publicity. It was in 1934 that General Motors produced its first diesel, and the Baldwin and Lima Companies never did leave the steam locomotive field 20 years after sales of steam had been dropping and diesel sales were increasing yearly.

To the extent that the firm focuses its analysis *primarily* internally in all but the most stable sectors of the economy, its strategic planning process will be less effective. Environmental analysis is discussed separately for convenience. You recognize that it interrelates with objectives formation, alternative generation, and other aspects of strategic planning.

Next we turn to analysis of the internal strengths and weaknesses of the firm. This is the subject of Chapter 4.

## References

[1] Downs, Anthony: *Inside Bureaucracy,* Boston: Little, Brown, 1967.

Randall, Frederich: "Corporate Strategies in the Drug Industry," unpublished D.B.A. thesis, Harvard Business School, 1972.

[2] Carbonnel, François de, and Roy Dorrance: "Information Sources for Planning Decisions," *California Management Review,* 15(4): Summer 1973.

[3] Ansoff, H. Igor: "The Future of the Firm," in *Business Strategy,* London: Penguin, 1970.

Chambers, John, et al.: "How to Choose the Right Forecasting Technique," *Harvard Business Review,* July–August 1971.

Copeland, Ronald, and Robert Marioni: "Executive's Forecasts of Earnings per Share versus Forecasts of Naive Models," *Journal of Business,* 45(4): 1972.

Coyle, R. G.: "Systems Dynamics: An Approach to Policy Formulation," *Journal of Business Policy,* 3(3): 1973.

Dory, John, and Robert Lord: "Does T. F. Really Work?" *Harvard Business Review,* November–December 1970.

Farmer, Richard: "Looking Back at Looking Forward," *Business Horizons,* February 1973.

Fogler, H. Russell: "A Pattern Recognition Model for Forecasting," *Management Science,* 20(8): 1974.

Hatten, Kenneth, and Mary Piccoli: "An Evaluation of Technological Forecasting Method by Computer Based Simulation," *Proceedings, Academy of Management,* 1973.

Jantsch, Erich: "Forecasting and Systems Approach," *Management Science,* 19(12): 1973.

Kahn, Herman, and A. Wiener: *The Next Thirty-Three Years,* New York: Macmillan, 1967.

Makridakis, Spyros, and Steven Wheelwright: "Integrating Forecasting and Planning," *Long Range Planning,* September 1973.

Thompson, James D.: "Technology Polity and Societal Development," *Administrative Service Quarterly,* pp. 6–21, 1973.

Thurston, Phillip: "Make TF Serve Corporate Planning," *Harvard Business Review,* September–October 1971.

Ways, Max: "Tomorrow's Management," *Fortune,* 74(1): 1966.

Weston, Frederick, Jr.: "Operations Research Techniques Relevant to Corporate Planning Function Practices," *Academy of Management Journal,* **16**(3): 1973.

Yurchak, W. Russel, and Elmer Bratt: "The Duality between Long Term Planning and Forecasting," *Business Economics,* Summer 1968.

[4] Cannon, J. Thomas: "Auditing the Competitive Environment," in *Business Strategy and Policy,* New York: Harcourt, Brace & World, 1968, pp. 84–102.

Cooper, Arnold: "Strategic Responses to Technological Threats," *Proceedings, Academy of Management,* 1973.

Copisaro, Alcon: "The Future Impact of Technology on Management," chap. 24 of *The Arts of Top Management: A McKinsey Anthology,* New York: McGraw-Hill, 1971.

Denning, Basil: "Strategic Environmental Appraisal," *Long Range Planning,* pp. 22–27, March 1973.

Fronko, Edward: "One Company's Cast Off Technology Is Another Company's Opportunity," *Innovation,* **23**: August 1971.

Henry, Harold: "Policy and Planning Impacts of Environmental Protection in Major Corporations," *Proceedings, Academy of Management,* 1973.

Jacoby, Neil: *Corporate Power and Social Responsibility,* New York: Macmillan, 1973.

Monsen, R. Joseph: *Business and the Changing Environment,* New York: McGraw-Hill, 1973.

Pfeffer, Jeffrey: "Interorganizational Influence and Managerial Attitudes," *Academy of Management Journal,* September 1972.

Sethi, S. Prakash: *Up against the Corporate Wall,* Englewood Cliffs, N.J.: Prentice-Hall, 1974.

Yoshihara, Hideki: "Toward a Comprehensive Concept of Strategy Adapted Behavior of Firms," International Conference on Strategic Management, Vanderbilt University, May 1973.

[5] Aguilar, Francis: *Scanning the Business Environment,* New York: Macmillan, 1967.

Collings, Robert: "Scanning the Environment for Strategic Information," unpublished D.B.A. thesis, Harvard Business School, 1968.

Keegan, Warren: "Scanning the International Business Environment," unpublished D.B.A. thesis, Harvard Business School, 1967.

Taylor, Ronald: "Age and Experience as Determinants of Managerial Information Processing and Decision Making Performance," *Academy of Management Journal,* **18**(1): 1975.

Wall, Jerry: "What the Competition Is Doing: Your Need to Know," *Harvard Business Review,* November–December 1974.

[6] Wall, Jerry: ibid.

[7] Copeland, Ronald, and Robert Marioni: op. cit.

Vancil, Richard: "The Accuracy of Long Range Planning," *Harvard Business Review,* September–October 1970.

[8] Aguilar, Francis: op. cit.

Collings, Robert: op. cit.

Wall, Jerry: op. cit.

[9] Hofer, Charles R.: "Some Preliminary Research on Patterns of Strategic Behavior," *Proceedings, Academy of Management,* 1973.

[10] Aguilar, Francis: op. cit.

Cooper, Arnold: "Identifying, Appraising and Reacting to Major Technological Change," *Proceedings of Winter Conference of American Marketing Association,* December 1967.

Dill, William: "Strategic Management in a Kibitzer's World," New York: New York University, 1974. (Mimeographed.)

Emery, F. E., and E. L. Trist: "The Causal Texture of Organizational Environments," *Human Relations,* **18:** 1963.

Gross, Alfred: "Adapting to Competitive Change," *MSU Business Topics,* **18**(1): Winter 1970.

MacCrimmon, Kenneth: "Managerial Decision Making," in J. McGuire (ed.), *Contemporary Management,* Englewood Cliffs, N.J.: Prentice-Hall, 1974.

Mintzberg, Henry: "The Myth of MIS," *California Management Review,* **15**(1): Fall 1972.

————: "Impediments to the Use of Management Information," Montreal: McGill University, 1974. (Mimeographed.)

Nystrom, Harry: "Cognitive Style in Management and Reaction to Organizational Stagnation," Sweden: University of Uppsala, 1974. (Mimeographed.)

[11] The vast literature on multinational strategies includes:

Bradley, Gene, and Edward Bursk: "Multinationalism and the 29th Day," *Harvard Business Review,* January–February 1972.

Eels, Richard: *Global Corporations,* New York: Interbook Incorporated, 1972.

Litvak, I. A., and C. J. Maule: "Branch Plant Entrepreneurship," *Business Quarterly,* Spring 1972.

Lorange, Peter: "Formal Planning in Multinational Corporations," *Columbia Journal of World Business,* Summer 1973.

Rapp, William: "Strategy Formulation and International Competition," *Columbia Journal of World Business,* Summer 1973.

Schwendiman, John: *Strategic and Long Range Planning for the Multinational Corporation,* New York: Praeger, 1971.

Sethi, S. Prakash, and Jangdish Sheth: *Multinational Business Operations: Long Range Planning, Organization and Management,* Pacific Palisades: Goodyear, 1973.

Simmonds, K.: "Building a Global Strategy," in *International Business and Multinational Enterprise,* Homewood, Ill.: Richard D. Irwin, 1973.

Vaupel, James, and Joan Curhan: *The Making of Multinational Enterprise,* Cambridge, Mass.: Harvard Business School, 1969.

———— and ————: *The World's Multinational Enterprises,* Cambridge: Harvard Business School, 1973.

Wilkins, Mira: *The Emergence of Multinational Enterprise,* Cambridge, Mass.: Harvard University Press, 1970.

Yoshino, M. Y.: "International Business: What Is the Best Strategy?" *Business Quarterly,* Fall 1966.

[12] The evidence is scattered through the literature. Some of the references which touch on this are:

Fouraker, Lawrence, and John Stopford: "Organizational Structure and the Multinational Strategy," *Administrative Science Quarterly,* pp. 47–64, June 1968.

Frenko, Lawrence: "Strategy and Structure — Frustration = the Experiences of European Firms in America," *Business Quarterly,* Autumn 1972.

Hussey, D. E.: "Strategic Planning for International Business," *Long Range Planning,* **5**(2): 1972.

Rose, Sanford: "The Rewarding Strategies of Mulitnationalism," *Fortune,* September 15, 1968.

Schollhamner, Hans: "Long Range Planning in Multinational Firms," *Columbia Journal of World Business,* September–October 1971.

# Strategic responses to technological threats

A. Cooper
E. Demuzzio
K. Hatten
E. Hicks
D. Tock

Of the various kinds of environmental change, few are more pervasive or important than technological change. This paper is concerned with major technological innovations of the kind which may create new industries and transform existing ones.

Most previous research on technological innovation has been concerned with innovators, including the sources of innovation and the determinants of successful innovations. This research is concerned with major technological innovations from the viewpoint of firms in traditional industries which appear threatened. A current example would be those suppliers to the automobile industry who appear threatened by the advent of the Wankel engine.

Major technological innovations often seem to originate outside traditional industries and to invade them, thereby confronting the traditional firms with threats which strike at the heart of their competitive positions. Producers of kerosene lamps, passenger liners, steam radiators, hardwood flooring, motion pictures, and buggy whips all have had to contend with such threats. Few environmental changes can have such important strategic implications.

## The scope of the research

This paper presents preliminary results of empirical research relating to five industries in which a new technology challenged an older, established technology. The industries and the new technological innovations were as follows:

1  The steam locomotive industry and the diesel-electric locomotive

2  The vacuum tube industry and the transistor

3  The fountain pen industry and the ball-point pen

4  The producers of boilers for fossil fuel power plants and nuclear power plants

5  The safety razor and the electric razor

Within each of these traditional industries, examination centered upon certain firms. Two steam locomotive producers, four vacuum tube companies, five fountain pen firms, two producers of power plant boilers, and two safety razor companies were studied in depth.

Reprinted by permission of Dr. Arnold Cooper, Purdue University.

## TABLE 1 ■ TRADITIONAL INDUSTRIES STUDIED

| | Locomotives | Vacuum (receiving) tubes | Fountain pens | Safety razors | Fossil-fuel boilers |
|---|---|---|---|---|---|
| | American Locomotive Co. Baldwin Locomotive Works | Columbia Broadcasting System (CBS) Radio Corp. of America (RCA) Raytheon Mfg. Co. Sylvania Electric Products, Inc. | Esterbrook Pen Co. Eversharp, Inc. Parker Pen Co. Sheaffer Pen Co. Waterman Pen Co. | American Safety Razor Corp. Gillette Safety Razor Co. | Babcock & Wilcox Co. Combustion Engineering, Inc. |
| Sales decline immediately after new technology introduced? | No | No | a | No | No |
| Sales eventually begin long-term decline? | Yes | Yes | Yes | No | No |
| Time from introduction of new technology until sales of new technology exceeded old | 2 years[b] | 11 years | 9 years | 25 years[c] | Not during the 20 years since first sale |
| New markets created by new technology? | No | Yes | Yes | No | No |
| New technology limited in application or crude at first? | Yes | Yes | Yes | Yes | Yes |
| New technology applied sequentially to submarkets? | Yes | Yes | Yes[d] | No | No |
| First commercial introduction by a firm in traditional industry? | No[e] | Yes | No | No | No[f] |
| First commercial introduction by a new firm? | No | No | Yes | Yes | No |
| Old firms participate in new technology? | Yes | Yes | Yes (4 of 5) | Yes (briefly) | Yes |
| Acquisition a means of participating in new technology? | No | Raytheon—Yes | Parker—Yes | Gillette—Yes[g] | No |
| Old technology improved after new technology was introduced? | Yes | Yes | Yes | Yes | Yes |
| Traditional firms involved in improving old technology and in entering new technology? | Yes | Yes | Yes (4 of 5) | Yes (participation in electric razors short-lived) | Yes |
| Attempt to establish barriers to new technology? | No | No | No | No | No |

[a] Data were not found to indicate whether sales of fountain pens declined in the year the ball-point pen was introduced.
[b] Although the first diesel-electric switcher locomotive was introduced in 1924, the product remained on virtually an experimental basis until 1934, when General Motors introduced the first main line diesel-electric locomotive. Available sales data relate to units sold rather than sales dollars, but it appears that diesel-electric sales exceeded steam locomotive sales by 1936. Subsequently, steam locomotive unit sales exceeded diesel-electric unit sales during World War II, but steam locomotive sales dropped sharply after the war.
[c] During 1956–1958, electric razor sales exceeded sales of razor blades. However, subsequently, razor blades regained a sales lead and have maintained it to the time of the study.
[d] The pen market is segmented by price. Initially, the ball-point pen was relatively expensive.
[e] The first main line diesel-electric was introduced by General Motors, a firm which never made steam locomotives.
[f] The first nuclear power plant was developed by Westinghouse, a firm with a strong position in turbines. However, in this study the traditional industry was regarded as the production of boilers for fossil-fuel power plants.
[g] Gillette acquired Braun A.G. and thereby entered the overseas market for electric razors. Gillette has not reentered the U.S. market since 1938, when its internally developed electric razor was introduced and subsequently withdrawn.

We shall address ourselves to two broad questions:

**1** What were the patterns of substitution of the new technology for the old one and what was the ultimate impact of the new technology? What factors affected these patterns?

**2** What were the strategies adopted in threatened industries? What strategies were associated with high and low performance?

The findings are tentative, being based on the study of only fifteen firms in five industries. In some instances the data are fragmentary; in particular, information about the strategies and performance of smaller firms in the traditional industries often are not readily available. An additional difficulty is that the processes being examined are complex and the situations studied vary along a variety of dimensions.

## New technology competing with old

It is clear that, at any time, many businesses are confronted with a host of external technological threats. For instance, producers of components for fossil fuel power plants have had to appraise not only the very imminent threat of nuclear power plants, but also a number of more remote technological threats, including solar power, fuel cells, magnetohydrodynamics, and direct thermoelectric production of electricity. Suppliers of automobile engine components face the threat not only of the Wankel engine, but also of steam and electrically powered automobiles.

It is clear that many technological threats do not have a substantial impact, at least in the short run. Many of the electric power generation technologies mentioned above have, to date, been confined primarily to the laboratory. Innovations such as the preservation of food by irradiation, the "picturephone," and the leather substitute Corfam have all had only limited impact on established industries.

It is also clear that surviving past technological threats does not confer future immunity. In 1934, when General Motors introduced the first main line diesel-electric locomotive, the producers of steam locomotives could look back upon two earlier threats which they had survived—the electric locomotive and, in the decade of the 1920s, passenger cars with individual gasoline-powered engines. Both of these prior threats captured only small segments of the American locomotive market. There was no indication that the next threat, the diesel-electric, would destroy the traditional industry within 15 years.

This paper has little to say about the host of threats which may or may not develop. This research is concerned with major technological innovations which, in fact, had substantial impact.

## Sales of the new and old technologies

In the five industries studied, the following patterns of substitution occurred:

**1** After the introduction of the new technology, the sales of the old technology did not *immediately* decline. In fact, the sales continued to expand.[1]

**2** In some instances, despite growth in sales of the new technology, sales of the old technology continued to expand for the entire period studied. Sales of fossil fuel power plants grew by more than 100 percent in the years after the first nuclear power plant was sold, and safety razor sales have grown more than 800 percent since the first electric razor was introduced in 1931.

**3** When sales of the old technology did decline, the time period from first commercial introduction to the time when dollar sales of the new technology exceeded dollar sales of the old ranged from 2 to 11 years.

---

[1] In one industry, fountain pens, data were not available to indicate whether a sales decline occurred in the year when the new technology, ball-point pens, was introduced.

From the above findings, it is clear that new technology does not capture markets "overnight." Substantial sales opportunities may exist in the old technology for extended periods. It may be difficult for management in the traditional firms to judge the eventual impact, but at least there is usually time to develop a new strategy.

**4** The new technology often created new markets which were not available to the old technology. Although the initial ball-point pens were expensive, low-priced pens were later developed which opened up a new market—the "throw-away" pen. It was also estimated that 50 percent of the applications for the transistor were in equipment made possible only by the invention of the transistor.

**5** The new technology was expensive and relatively crude at first. Often, its initial shortcomings led observers to believe it would find only limited applications. Early electric razors were described as "claw-footed." Although the first ball-point pens wrote under water, they blotted, skipped, and stopped writing on paper and even leaked in your pocket; after an initial "fad" phase, public disenchantment set in and sales dropped dramatically. The first transistors were expensive and sharply limited in regard to frequency, power capabilities, and temperature tolerance; some observers thought they would never find more than limited application.

**6** The new technology often invaded the traditional industry by capturing sequentially a series of submarkets. The new technology, crude as it was, often had performance advantages for certain applications. Some submarkets were insulated from competition for extended periods. General Motors' diesel-electric locomotive first invaded the submarket for passenger locomotives, subsequently the submarket for switcher locomotives, and then freight locomotives—the major submarket accounting for about 75 percent of industry sales. The transistor found early application in hearing aids and "pocket radios," but not in radar systems and television.

From these findings, it is clear that judgments about the potential of new technology are difficult. Initial shortcomings are no insurance that the technology will not be a threat. The fact that it initially finds application in only a few submarkets does not mean that its application will always be limited.

It is clear that some market segments in a traditional industry are threatened earlier and to a greater extent than others. Firms whose strategies involve emphasis on less-threatened segments may enjoy extended sales in the old technology. In the vacuum tube industry, replacement sales continued strong and some types of tubes such as high-power tubes have not come under direct competition from solid-state devices 21 years after the introduction of the transistor.

## Appraising the potential of new technologies

In appraising the potential of a new technology, it would be a mistake to wait until decline in sales of the old technology "triggered" the need for appraisal of the threat. By then, much of the lead time may have passed. It is necessary to appraise the new, threatening technology when it is still relatively crude. In doing this, one should identify the critical attributes of that technology and the barrier problems blocking or slowing improvement of those attributes. Whether these problems will be overcome depends upon the fundamental laws of nature involved and the effort being applied by the innovating organizations.

It is not enough simply to judge that someday a new technology will replace an old one. Rates of penetration are critical. When the Baldwin Locomotive

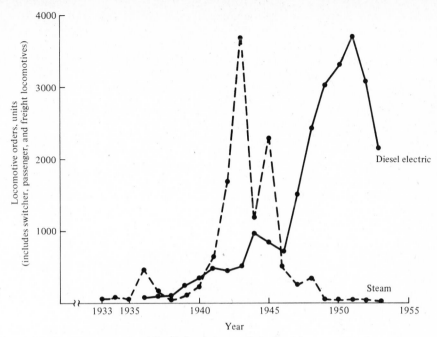

**FIGURE 1** ■ Steam locomotive orders and diesel electric locomotives shipped.

Works was founded in 1831, it would have been of little value to tell the founders that someday their principal product would be obsolete. However, when Sylvania introduced a new line of vacuum tubes for computers in 1957, the rapid rate of improvement of transistors then taking place was extremely relevant.

Data on the use of the old and new technologies in each of the five industries are given in Figures 1 to 5. One might have expected S-shaped growth curves, in which, if the new technology passed the old, it would subsequently widen or at least maintain its advantage.

1 S-shaped growth patterns did sometimes exist, but a variety of factors caused variations in the sales of both the old and new technologies:

(*a*) War-time conditions sometimes dislocated markets and suppliers. During World War II supplies were not allocated for the production of the electric razor, and the millions of young men then coming of shaving age did not have a choice between the old and new technologies. In locomotives, World War II also seemed to help sales of the old technology. General Motors was limited to the production of freight locomotives. American Locomotive Company and Baldwin Locomotive Works received orders for thousands of steam switcher locomotives, more than they had received for the entire decade of the 1930s.

(*b*) With the ball-point pen, there was an initial "fad" phase of sales. Production went from no units in 1944 to 150 million units in 1946 to less than 10 million units in 1948. In 1950 the product returned to the market in improved form and subsequently enjoyed enormous growth.

(*c*) When technological change was rapid, the new technology was sometimes being replaced by a still newer one. Thus, the transistor was in the process of replacing the vacuum tube when it in turn began to be replaced by integrated circuits. The ball-point pen was facing competition from a still newer technology, the felt-tip marker.

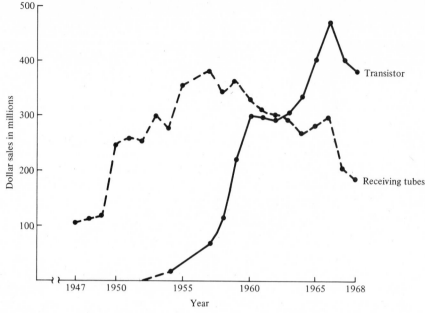

**FIGURE 2** ■ Receiving tube and transistor sales. A receiving tube is a type of vacuum tube which amplifies.

## Alternative strategies

If it appears that a new technology may have a substantial impact on a traditional industry, what are alternative strategies which firms in the threatened industry might follow?

Fundamentally, management might choose to participate or not to participate in the new technology. In deciding not to participate, several specific kinds of actions might be elected: (1) do nothing; (2) engage in vigorous scanning activity including formal intelligence activities to keep informed on new developments in the competing technology; (3) seek to hold back the new threat—to fight it through public relations and legal efforts; (4) increase flexibility, so as to be able to move in response to subsequent developments in the new technology; (5) avoid the threat through decreasing dependence on the most threatened submarkets; (6) expand work on the improvement of the existing technology.

A firm might, however, choose to participate in the new technology. Of course, the degree of commitment might vary widely, ranging from a token involvement, such as defensive R&D, to seeking to become a leader in the new technology through major and immediate commitments. Major dimensions of a strategy involving participation in the new technology include decisions about the magnitude of commitments to the new technology, the timing of those commitments, and the extent of reliance on internal development versus acquisitions.

In the five industries studied, we can identify the strategies adopted by threatened firms and draw limited conclusions about the implications of these strategies. The study has focused upon the more prominent firms in the tradi-

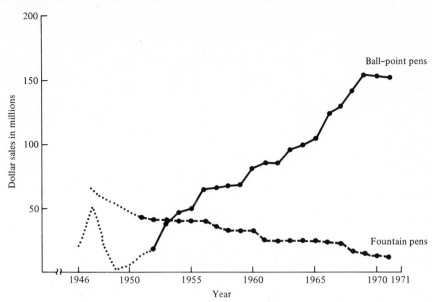

**FIGURE 3** ■ Writing instrument sales. For years prior to 1951 for fountain pens and 1952 for ball-point pens, industry sales data are estimated.

tional industries so that conclusions relating to the smaller firms are sketchy. One difficulty is the problem of judging success over time. Sometimes firms which are unquestionably successful in the short run, such as Raytheon in the infant transistor industry, subsequently are unsuccessful. Recognizing these limitations, we can note the following patterns of innovation and response:

**1** The first commercial introduction of the new technology often was made by a firm outside the traditional industry. One might have expected that the traditional firms would have been the "logical" sources of industry innovation because of their strong customer relationships, well-developed channels of distribution, and organizations oriented toward serving those industries. However, in three of the five industries studied, the pioneers were companies with no previous relationship with the customers of the traditional industry.

**2** In two of the three industries in which capital requirements were low, new firms were the first to introduce the new technology. The first electric razor was introduced by Schick, a new firm, and the first ball-point pen by Reynolds, also a new firm. In the other industry with low capital barriers to entry, transistors, new firms were not first, but were later among the most important competitors. The cost of entering the nuclear power field has been very great, undoubtedly in excess of $100 million. With the diesel-electric locomotive, General Motors made an initial investment in manufacturing plant alone of $6 million.

## Participation in the new technology

**3** Of the fifteen companies studied, all but one made at least some effort to participate in the new technology. (The exception was Esterbrook, a small producer of medium-priced fountain pens, which never introduced a ball-point pen. It did subsequently

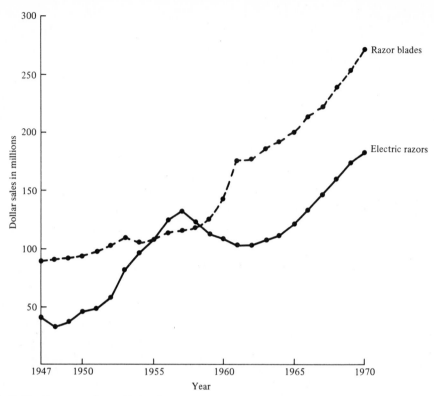

**FIGURE 4** ▪ Electric razor and razor blade sales.

merge in 1967 with Venus, a pencil and ball-point pen manufacturer.) Two firms made only token commitments to the new technology, and these were both producers of safety razors—Gillette and American Safety Razor. They both introduced electric razors about 1938, but then withdrew their products, apparently, in part, owing to patent barriers. All of the other twelve firms made major efforts to establish positions in the new technology.

**4** Firms with small market shares in the old technology usually were not successful in establishing positions in the new technology. In locomotives, the five smallest producers never made the transition to diesel-electrics. The hundreds of small razor blade firms never had successful electric razors. The companies with minor shares of the power plant boiler market never even tried to enter the nuclear power field.

## Nature of participation

**5** The timing of participation in the new technology varied widely among the traditional firms. Vacuum tube producers, Raytheon and RCA, were among the first to enter the transistor market, and Eversharp produced a ball-point pen within 6 months of its introduction by Reynolds. By contrast, Parker introduced a ball-point pen 9 years after its first commercial introduction, and Baldwin Locomotive introduced its first passenger diesel-electric 12 years after General Motors. No consistent relationship was observed between the timing of participation in the new technology by traditional firms and their subsequent success.

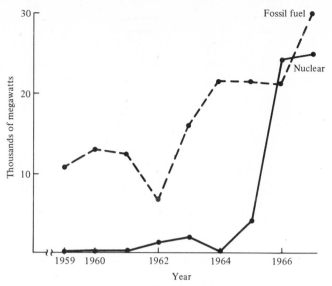

**FIGURE 5** ■ Utility orders for electric generating equipment.

6 Only three of the fifteen traditional firms used acquisition as a means of participating in the new technology. Parker acquired Eversharp as a means of successfully entering the low-priced ball-point pen market after having first developed a high-priced ball-point pen. Gillette successfully entered the overseas electric razor field by acquiring Braun A. G. Raytheon, having previously made major commitments to germanium transistors, acquired Rheem Semiconductor as a means of entering the silicon transistor field. Interestingly, two successful innovators, General Motors and BIC, also used acquisitions. General Motors' acqustions of two small firms, Winton Engine and Electro-Motive Company, provided a foothold in diesel and railroad technologies, and BIC's acquisition of Waterman apparently provided it with channels of distribution in the American market.

7 When the new technology was still undergoing rapid change, a strategy of making early and major commitments to the new technology was often unsuccessful. All of the entrants in the "first cycle" of the ball-point pen suffered when the public reacted against the extreme crudeness of the early products. Those vacuum tube producers who made major investments in early transistor technology were at a competitive disadvantage to later entrants who emphasized more advanced technology.

## Emphasis on the old technology

8 In every industry studied, the old technology continued to be improved and reached its highest stage of development after the new technology was introduced. For instance, the efficiency of fossil fuel power plants was improved approximately 10 percent in the years after the first order was placed for a nuclear power plant. The same occurred in other industries; for instance, the smallest and most reliable vacuum tubes ever produced were developed after the introduction of the transistor.

9 All 15 companies studied appeared to continue to make heavy commitments to the improvement of the old technology. None adopted a strategy of early withdrawal from the old technology in order to concentrate on the new.

**10**   Most of the firms studied followed a strategy of dividing their resources, so as to participate in a major way in both the old and the new technologies. For instance, American Locomotive developed both an advanced turbine-powered steam locomotive and diesel-electric locomotives. CBS and Raytheon developed new lines of vacuum tubes and also made major investments in R&D and production facilities for transistors. This strategy appeared to be unsuccessful more often than successful.

**11**   Although barriers to the diffusion of the new technologies existed, none of the traditional firms studied visibly attempted to create or strengthen the barriers to the new technology.

**12**   There was only one instance in which a firm outside the traditional industry which had pioneered the new technology subsequently entered the old technology also. BIC, a firm which had achieved great success in France with a low-priced ball-point pen, acquired Waterman, a fountain pen producer which had not been successful with its ball-point pen. BIC-Waterman was quite successful in America with a low-priced ball-point pen, but the fountain pen product line was discontinued 4 years after the acquisition.

## Overall performance

**13**   Sometimes, the new technology presented severe competitive challenges for all participants for a period of time. The nuclear-power field involved very heavy investments for many years by all participants before the first profits were shown. In the "first cycle" of ball-point pen sales, the industry profits and losses are not publicly available. However, the precipitous sales decline which occurred within 2 years of the product's introduction drove from the market most of the 200 new firms, as well as the traditional companies with ball-point pens.

**14**   In those industries studied in which the old technology enjoyed growing sales, safety razors and fossil fuel power plants, the traditional firms studied were able to maintain their competitive positions and do well.

**15**   Many of the most successful firms in the new technology had never participated in the old technology. In industries in which capital barriers to entry were not great, new firms were among the most successful. Examples of new firms were Papermate in ball-point pens, Fairchild Semiconductor in transistors, and Schick in electric razors.

**16**   Overall, the traditional firms examined in this study were not very successful in participating in the new technology. Of the twelve firms studied which made major commitments to the new technology, only one, Parker in pens, appeared to enjoy long-term success as an independent firm participating in the new technology.

## Commentary

It is interesting that the traditional firms continued to make substantial commitments to the old technology, even when sales had already begun to decline from the competitive pressure of the new technology. Possibly, this demonstrated, in part, how difficult it is to change the patterns of resource allocation in an established organization. Decisions about allocating resources to old and new technologies within the organization are loaded with implications for the decision makers; not only are old product lines threatened, but also old skills and positions of influence.

It is also interesting to speculate about why most of the traditional firms were relatively unsuccessful in establishing strong competitive positions in the new technologies. Clearly, in several of the industries studied resource limitations were not the major factor, inasmuch as a number of new companies were relatively successful. This may be an indication of the relative difficulty of changing successfully organizational strategy. The skills, the attitudes, and the assumptions which undergird successful strategy in a traditional technology may require modification in both major and subtle ways to bring about equivalent success in the new technology. Apparently, many organizations find this difficult to do.

## CHAPTER 4

# Appraising the strategic advantages of the firm

This chapter discusses the other half of the appraisal process, as Figure 4–1 indicates. At the same time as an executive examines the opportunities and threats from the environment, he or she must know the strengths and weaknesses the firm has to meet these challenges or threats. Thus the executive can match the two in the development and choice of a strategy. At various times, the process about to be described has been called profiling the organization, the management or capability or resource audit, internal company analysis, comparative advantage analysis, and strategic advantage analysis. These terms are roughly comparable, but the term and definition shown two pages following will be used.

Consider two auto firms: General Motors and American Motors. You work for American Motors. Considering GM's massive resources, strong dealer organization, and other strengths, can AMC compete directly and in the same market with similar products as GM has *effectively*? If you are AMC, you analyze your strengths and try to move into product-service markets not served well by GM and in which you have advantages.

Every firm has some advantages over others. Small firms can move faster and can serve customers and markets which large firms cannot serve as profitably. Some firms have excellent production facilities but are less strong in marketing. Some enterprises have well-known brands but have sluggish research and development departments. Strategic advantage analysis tries to determine where the firm can operate most effectively.

When I decided to write a business policy book, it was because I was not satisfied with many books then available. The best-selling books came from the pens of Harvard Business School professors. The books generally consisted of 30 or so cases. It was not my strategic advantage to write another casebook like theirs. That was their strategic advantage, for Harvard has been known as the "case" school for 50 years. So, I wrote a book that included text, readings, and cases and tried to reach a market I felt they were not reaching.

This chapter does two more things:

**1** Indicates the factors which should be examined to determine where the firm's strategic advantages lie

**2** Describes how companies have determined their strategic advantage and which factors concern them most

**86**

87

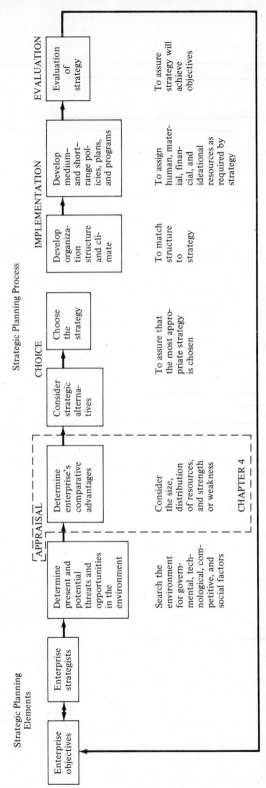

**FIGURE 4–1** ■ A model of strategic planning.

Appraising the firm's strategic advantages is the process by which executives analyze the firm's material, financial, ideational, and other resources to determine where the firm has significant strengths so that it can exploit the opportunities and meet the threats of the environment.

PROPOSITION 4–1 ▪ A firm whose strategy fits its environment, considering its strategic advantages, will be more effective than one which does not.

## Strategic advantage factors [1]

To analyze a firm's strengths and weaknesses adequately, executives need a frame of reference or checklist of factors to examine. A *complete* list might involve thousands of items. I have prepared Tables 4–1, 4–2, 4–3, and 4–4 as beginning guides of the most likely factors to begin the analysis with. (See also the reading by Robert Buchele at the end of this chapter.)

Each factor listed is analyzed with the most appropriate tool available. Thus financial factors might be analyzed through the use of earnings, debt, and turnover ratios.

The output of this analysis is the *strategic advantage profile*. Effective development of the profile requires two steps:

1 Give weight to the factor: Does the company possess a strong advantage, some advantage; is it a weakness or a strong weakness?

2 Determine whether the strength or weakness is of strategic importance. It is obvious that not all factors are equally significant in all industries at all times. Thus, effective lobbying (Table 4–4, number 10) is a much more significant factor in regulated industries like insurance and airlines than in less regulated industries like hardware, lumber, furniture, and writing instruments. This step indicates whether the strength or weakness will have a major impact for the focal enterprise.

A sample strategic advantage profile is given in Table 4–5 for the Reiter Company, a small manufacturer of gloves and similar products located in the midwestern United States. The case was contained in the first edition of my book as a disguised company.

In effect, what this profile does is give a visual representation of what the company is as it has developed from past strategic decisions and interaction with its environment. A close look at the profile shows us:

1 How the company has competed with its competitors and how it can lead from strengths in future competition

DEFINITION ▪ STRATEGIC ADVANTAGE PROFILE
The strategic advantage profile is a systematic evaluation of the enterprise's strategic advantage factors *weighted* by the significance of each factor for the company in its environment.

**TABLE 4–1 ■ STRATEGIC ADVANTAGE FACTORS: MARKETING**

**1** Competitive structure and market share: To what extent has the firm established a strong market share in the total market or its key submarkets?

**2** Efficient and effective market research system

**3** The product mix: quality of products and services

**4** Product-services line: completeness and new product leadership, and product mix; phase of life cycle the main products are in

**5** Efficient and effective channels of distribution and geographic coverage, including international efforts

**6** Pricing strategy for products and services

**7** Efficient and effective sales force: close ties with key customers. How vulnerable are we in terms of concentration of sales to a few customers?

**8** Effective advertising: Has it established the company's product-brand image to develop loyal customers?

**9** Efficient and effective marketing promotion and packaging

**10** Efficient and effective service after purchase

**11** Efficient and effective evaluation of marketing policies

---

**TABLE 4–2 ■ STRATEGIC ADVANTAGE FACTORS: OPERATIONS**

**1** Raw materials cost

**2** Raw materials availability

**3** Efficient and effective inventory control systems

**4** Efficient and effective facilities: Are they productive? Is the facilities' capacity overutilized, underutilized, given the current demand?

**5** Degree of vertical integration of operations

**6** Efficient and effective management information systems

**7** Efficient and effective equipment for production and/or for office

**8** Strategic location of facilities and offices

**9** Efficient and effective operations procedures: production design, scheduling, output, and quality control

**10** Lower total costs of operations compared to competitors

**11** Efficient and effective research and development unit: basic and applied research

**12** Patents and similar legal protection for products, processes, and similar trade secrets

---

**TABLE 4–3 ■ STRATEGIC ADVANTAGE FACTORS: FINANCE AND ACCOUNTING**

**1** Low cost of capital relative to industry and competitors because of stock price and dividend policy

**2** Effective capital structure, allowing flexibility in raising additional capital as needed; financial leverage

**3** Amicable relations with owners and stockholders

**4** Advantageous tax conditions

**5** Barriers to new entry because of size of resources needed

**6** Efficient and effective financial planning, working capital, and capital budgeting procedures

**7** Efficient and effective accounting systems for cost, budget and profit planning, and auditing procedures

---

TABLE 4–4 ■ STRATEGIC ADVANTAGE FACTORS: PERSONNEL AND MANAGEMENT

1   High-quality employees and managers

2   Comparative costs of labor

3   Effective relations with trade unions

4   Efficient and effective personnel relations policies: staffing, appraisal and promotion, training and development, and compensation and benefits

5   Corporate image and prestige

6   Effective organization structure and climate

7   Company size relative to industry

8   Strategic planning system

9   Enterprise's record for reaching objectives: How consistent has it been? How well does it do compared to similar enterprises?

10   Influence with regulatory and governmental bodies

11   Balanced functional experience and track record of top management: Are replacements trained and ready to take over? Do the top managers work well together as a team?

---

TABLE 4–5 ■ STRATEGIC ADVANTAGE PROFILE FOR REITER

| Factor | Weighting of factor[a] | | | | Significance to Reiter[b] |
|---|---|---|---|---|---|
| | Strong + | + | − | Strong − | |
| **Marketing** | | | | | |
| Total market share | | ✓ | | | 0 |
| Strength in submarkets | | ✓ | | | + |
| Product-service line and service | ✓ | | | | + |
| Channels of distribution | | | ✓ | | − |
| Pricing | | ✓ | | | 0 |
| **Operations** | | | | | |
| Raw materials | ✓ | | | | + |
| Facilities | | | | ✓ | − − |
| MIS | ✓ | | | | 0 |
| Costs of operation | | | ✓ | | − |
| Inventory control | | | | ✓ | − − |
| **Finance and accounting** | | | | | |
| Accounting systems | | | | ✓ | − |
| Stockholder relations | | | | ✓ | − − − − − |
| Tax conditions | | | | ✓ | − |
| Financial strength | ✓ | | | | ++ |
| Financial management | | | | ✓ | 0 |
| **Personnel and management** | | | | | |
| High-quality employees | | ✓ | | | 0 |
| Personnel relations | | | ✓ | | 0 |
| Company size relative to competitor | | | ✓ | | 0 |
| Record of reaching objectives | | | | ✓ | 0 |
| Top management amicability | | | | ✓ | − − − − − |
| Top management training and depth | | | | ✓ | − − − − − |
| Profitability: consistent | | | ✓ | | − |

[a] Weighting indicates the degree to which the factor evaluated is an advantage or disadvantage.
[b] Significance is coded as follows: 0 = neutral; − = negative, and the more minuses the more negative; + = positive, and the more pluses the more positive. Significance indicates degree to which the weighted factor has or will have *strategic impact* for the firm.

**2** What business it has been in: product and service, geographically and in other ways and which ones it should be in

The analyst should also compare how high the firm has set its sights as far as objectives are concerned. Then, used properly, this profile allows the strategic planner to match the environmental threat and opportunities profile (Chapter 3) with it. Thus the top manager can better select the strategy from a series of alternatives and better implement that strategy.

## Some research on strategic advantages

It should be obvious by now that the previous section is *normative;* a statement of idealized formal analysis of strategic advantages.

Very little is known about how many enterprises actually *formally* examine their strategic advantages. The author's and other researchers' impressionistic research indicates that most effective top managers know their strategic advantages. How formally they use this information as an input in strategic decision making is still not well researched.

One piece of research in this area was done by Stevenson [2]. He studied how managers defined a company's strengths and weaknesses. He studied two concentrically diversified firms—one primarily in paper, the other in the ink industry. He also interviewed executives in four other firms. One hundred and ninety-one executives were interviewed at all levels of the two firms. Stevenson also examined written documents in the firms. His research sought to answer three questions:

**1** What capabilities of a firm are identified as a strength or weakness?

**2** What criteria do executives use to rank a capability as a strength or weakness?

**3** What information does an executive use to make the judgments in questions 1 and 2 above?

---

**RESEARCH STUDY**

■ **STEVENSON'S FINDINGS**

**1** *What capabilities are identified as strengths or weaknesses?* The factors rated were organizational (management), personnel, marketing, technical (operating), and financial.

(*a*) *Overall,* factors mentioned as strengths or weaknesses were: marketing (26.7 percent), organization (22 percent), technical operations (22 percent), personnel (21.5 percent), and financial (7.9 percent).

(*b*) Executives at different levels listed factors as strengths or weaknesses *significantly differently.* Thus:

(1) At top management levels, the factors considered most important (in order were) organizational (42.4 percent), personnel (32.9 percent), financial (15.3 percent).

(2) Divisional or middle level: marketing (52.5 percent), personnel (17.5 percent), technical (operations) (15 percent).

(3) Lower level: operations (53.8 percent), marketing (33.8 percent).

(*c*) Some factors tended to be mentioned as strengths more than weaknesses; these were marketing and personnel. The organizational, financial, and technical factors were mentioned more frequently as weaknesses than strengths. Factors that are people-related such as judgment tended to be regarded as strengths. Inanimate objects such as facilities were mentioned more often as weaknesses.

(*d*) The definition of whether a factor is a strength or weakness was influenced by the company, its history, and level of job he or she holds.

(*e*) The higher the job, the more factors an executive mentioned as a strength or weakness.

**2** *Criteria for judging strengths and weaknesses* Three criteria were used by the managers:

(*a*) Attributes: when a factor was listed as a strength or weakness without describing a measurement.

(*b*) Efficiency measures: when a factor was described as productive in terms of converting inputs to outputs.

(*c*) Effectiveness measures: when a factor was described as contributing to accomplishing *corporate objectives*.

(1) Some factors were consistently listed as measured by *attributes*. These were reputation, experience and attitudes of personnel, breadth of product line, growth pattern of the firm or industry, and organization form.

(2) Some factors were consistently listed as measured by *efficiency*. These were number of employees, facilities, standard procedures, and production techniques.

(3) Some factors were listed as measured by *effectiveness*. These were top management interest and skill, control system, technical skills of employees, sales force, knowing customer needs, product quality and customer service, product development, basic research, and financial size.

(4) Strengths and weaknesses can be assessed using three measures: historical (compared to own past results); competitive (compared to accomplishments of competitors); normative (what they ought to be). Strengths were assessed by historical measures; weaknesses by normative measures.

(5) Top-level factors were assessed with historical and normative measures. Competitive measures were used on lower-level problems.

(6) Efficiency and effectiveness are compared with competitive and normative measures.

(7) Organization and personnel are assessed by historical measures; markets and technical factors by competitive measures; financial factors by multiple assessments.

**3** *Information used to assess strengths and weaknesses* Information for assessment was derived from sources inside or external to the firm. It could be received from formal channels, such as documents and meetings, or informal means such as statements.

(*a*) The executives used information from external and internal sources to assess the strengths and weaknesses of their firms. 52.7 percent were external, 47.3 percent internal.

(*b*) Of the external sources (52.7 percent), 31 percent were personal observations, 21 percent were noncustomer outside sources such as industry data. External sources provided data about competitors' industry performance.

(c) Of the internal sources (47.3 percent), 31.7 percent came from formal channels, mostly company documents. The rest were from statements by superiors and subordinates. Internal sources focused on company factors.
(d) The higher the level of the executive, the more formal channels become an important source of assessment.
(e) Some factors were harder to acquire assessment information on; these were research and development, organization structure and climate, and top management skills and interests.

Stevenson's findings are interesting. They are reported in some detail because his study is the best one known to the author on the topic. How his findings would differ had he used a larger sample, smaller firms, single product line firms, or conglomerates, or firms in other industries is not known at this time.

## Glueck-*Fortune* study

It was described in Chapter 3 how this author analyzed a random sample of 358 *Fortune* articles about large firms written between 1930 and 1974.

One thing examined was the factors executives considered serious *weaknesses* or *problems* in a strategic advantage sense. The weaknesses-problem areas were (and this obviously is not a comprehensive list):

1 Excess of production capacity
2 Shortage of production capacity
3 Excess of cash and finances
4 Shortage of cash and finances
5 Excess of capacity: distribution
6 Shortage of capacity: distribution
7 Excess of personnel
8 Shortage of personnel
9 Increase in employee unionization
10 Top management problems or change in top management
11 Ownership problems or change
12 Takeover bid or threat to ownership

Tables 4–6, 4–7, 4–8, and 4–9 provide the data analyzing the perceived strategic disadvantages as seen in 358 companies over a 44-year period.

As Table 4–6 indicates, the most *frequently* perceived strategic disadvantages overall are (in this order): top management problems or change, financial shortages, ownership changes or takeover bid, and production overcapacity.

Table 4–7 reveals that the disadvantages do not appear equally frequently in phases of the business cycle. The most significant disadvantage was top management problem or change, which appears more frequently (as a percentage) in the extremes of the cycle (depression and prosperity) than at the other times. Takeover bids are three times as likely in recovery periods as in depres-

| | Number seeing the disadvantage | Ranking of importance | | | | | Index of importance[a] |
|---|---|---|---|---|---|---|---|
| | | Most important | Second | Third | Fourth | Fifth | |
| Change in ownership | 28 | 6 | 5 | 5 | 6 | 6 | 2.96 |
| Takeover bid or merger | 34 | 11 | 13 | 8 | 2 | 0 | 4.26 |
| Change in top management | 92 | 26 | 21 | 27 | 11 | 7 | 3.52 |
| Increase in employee unionization | 9 | 2 | 1 | 3 | 3 | 0 | 3.22 |
| Excess of personnel | 12 | 3 | 4 | 3 | 1 | 1 | 3.58 |
| Shortage of personnel | 11 | 4 | 0 | 4 | 2 | 1 | 3.36 |
| Excess of capacity— distribution | 10 | 2 | 4 | 3 | 1 | 0 | 3.70 |
| Shortage of capacity— distribution | 11 | 1 | 2 | 5 | 2 | 1 | 3.00 |
| Excess of cash | 8 | 4 | 3 | 0 | 1 | 0 | 4.25 |
| Shortage of cash | 39 | 13 | 10 | 9 | 6 | 1 | 3.41 |
| Excess of capacity— production | 33 | 5 | 15 | 5 | 3 | 5 | 3.36 |
| Shortage of capacity— production | 15 | 5 | 0 | 1 | 5 | 4 | 2.80 |

[a] Computed as follows: Number ranking as most important X 5, plus next most important X 4 . . . plus least important X 1 divided by N.

sion and twice as likely in recession and prosperity as in depression. Ownership changes are twice as likely in recovery as in depression. Unionization problems are ten times as great in recovery as in depression. Cash shortages are twice as likely in depression as in prosperity.

Table 4–8 indicates how the disadvantages have appeared over the years. One (change in top management) is a persistent problem. Two others (excess and shortage of production capacity) have declined over the years.

A number of disadvantages peaked in one period. Thus shortage of cash was far worse in the 1930s. Excess cash was a problem of the sixties. Excess distribution was a problem of the thirties.

Ownership changes did not take place in the fifties and there were no

| Disadvantage | Depression | Recovery | Recession | Prosperity |
|---|---|---|---|---|
| Change in ownership | 1 | 8 | 8 | 13 |
| Takeover bid or merger | 1 | 12 | 10 | 21 |
| Change in top management | 5 | 19 | 26 | 54 |
| Increase in employee unionization | 0 | 7 | 4 | 3 |
| Excess of personnel | 1 | 2 | 4 | 6 |
| Shortage of personnel | 0 | 2 | 3 | 9 |
| Excess of capacity— distribution | 2 | 3 | 6 | 2 |
| Shortage of capacity— distribution | 0 | 3 | 3 | 8 |
| Excess of cash | 0 | 0 | 2 | 6 |
| Shortage of cash | 4 | 5 | 16 | 17 |
| Excess of capacity— production | 3 | 5 | 9 | 18 |
| Shortage of capacity— production | 1 | 5 | 1 | 12 |
| | $N=18$ | $N=71$ | $N=92$ | $N=169$ |

**TABLE 4-8 ■ STRATEGIC DISADVANTAGES OF 358 COMPANIES (1930–1974) BY TIME PERIODS**

| Disadvantages | 1930s | 1940s | 1950s | 1960s | 1970s |
|---|---|---|---|---|---|
| Change in ownership | 8 | 5 | 2 | 8 | 7 |
| Takeover bid or merger | 16 | 1 | 11 | 8 | 8 |
| Change in top management | 21 | 14 | 23 | 29 | 17 |
| Increase in employee unionization | 9 | 1 | 2 | 2 | 0 |
| Excess of personnel | 1 | 1 | 2 | 4 | 5 |
| Shortage of personnel | 2 | 5 | 6 | 0 | 1 |
| Excess of capacity— distribution | 6 | 1 | 3 | 0 | 2 |
| Shortage of capacity— distribution | 5 | 1 | 3 | 4 | 0 |
| Excess of cash | 0 | 0 | 1 | 7 | 0 |
| Shortage of cash | 12 | 4 | 8 | 8 | 9 |
| Excess of capacity— production | 9 | 4 | 11 | 6 | 4 |
| Shortage of capacity— production | 5 | 5 | 5 | 3 | 0 |
| | $N=94$ | $N=42$ | $N=77$ | $N=79$ | $N=53$ |

takeover bids in the forties. Unionization was seen as a problem of the thirties. Shortages of personnel were disadvantages of the forties and fifties.

Table 4–9 indicates how the strategic disadvantages were distributed by the type of business a firm was in. In construction, mining, and oil, no one disadvantage appeared often. In consumer goods and transportation, only one challenge appeared in one-fourth or more of the companies: top management problems. This was also a major problem with industrial goods, but another was a shortage of cash.

As interesting as the Stevenson research is and as potentially useful his and my studies might be, the subject of strategic advantage analysis is in its infant stage and so no propositions will be suggested.

**TABLE 4-9 ■ STRATEGIC DISADVANTAGES OF 358 COMPANIES (1930–1974) BY INDUSTRIAL CATEGORY**

| Disadvantages | Consumer goods | Industrial goods | Construction, mining, oil | Retail and wholesale trade | Transportation, public | Other |
|---|---|---|---|---|---|---|
| Change in ownership | 9 | 10 | 3 | 2 | 1 | 5 |
| Takeover bid or merger | 13 | 18 | 3 | 0 | 3 | 7 |
| Change in top management | 39 | 27 | 4 | 9 | 8 | 17 |
| Increase in employee unionization | 8 | 4 | 0 | 1 | 1 | 0 |
| Excess of personnel | 3 | 2 | 0 | 1 | 4 | 3 |
| Shortage of personnel | 5 | 3 | 2 | 1 | 2 | 1 |
| Excess of capacity— distribution | 5 | 5 | 0 | 1 | 2 | 0 |
| Shortage of capacity— distribution | 6 | 6 | 0 | 1 | 1 | 0 |
| Excess of cash | 3 | 3 | 0 | 1 | 0 | 1 |
| Shortage of cash | 6 | 20 | 2 | 2 | 7 | 5 |
| Excess of capacity— production | 11 | 11 | 2 | 4 | 6 | 1 |
| Shortage of capacity— production | 5 | 7 | 3 | 0 | 1 | 3 |
| | $N=113$ | $N=116$ | $N=19$ | $N=23$ | $N=36$ | $N=43$ |

## Strategic planning and strategic advantage analysis

The section of Chapter 3 which describes how decisions are made on the data generated by environmental analysis applies to strategic advantage data as well. As was indicated at the start of this chapter, strategic advantage analysis is the other half of the appraisal process. Having appraised both external and internal factors and having profiled the environment and the firm by environmental threat and opportunities profile and strategic advantage profile, the decision maker is in a better position to move on to the next stage in the strategic planning process (discussed in Chapter 5): generation of alternative strategies and consideration of these alternative strategies.

## References

[1] Ansoff, H. Igor: *Corporate Strategy*, New York: McGraw-Hill, 1965, chap. 5.

[2] Pitts, Robert: "The Role of 'Distinctive Competence' in Selection of Product-Market Strategy and Organization Design," Pennsylvania State University, 1975. (Mimeographed.)

Stevenson, Howard: "Defining Corporate Strengths and Weaknesses," unpublished D.B.A. thesis, Harvard Business School, 1968.

Warren, E. Kirby: "The Capability Inventory: Its Role in Long Range Planning," *Management of Personnel Quarterly*, 3(4): Winter 1965.

# How to evaluate a firm*

Robert B. Buchele

The sharp drops in earnings and even losses recently suffered by many so-called growth companies, whose stocks had been bid so high, have cast doubts upon the adequacy of the established methods which are used by investment specialists to evaluate companies.

Equally dramatic but less evident have been the serious declines of numerous companies shortly after having been rated as "excellently managed" by the best known of the evaluation systems using a list of factors covering numerous aspects of corporate management.

What has happened to render these evaluation systems so inadequate? What lessons can be learned by persons whose work requires them to do overall evaluations of companies—investors, acquisition specialists, consultants, long-range planners, and chief executives? Finally, what are the requirements for a system for evaluating firms that will function reliably under today's conditions?

After all, the decline of even blue chip companies is not a new phenomenon. To quote from an unpublished paper recently presented by Ora C. Roehl at a management conference at UCLA:

The Brookings Institution sometime ago made a study of the 100 top businesses in the USA in the early 1900s, and they found that after 40 years only 36 were still among the leaders.

We all look at the Dow-Jones industrial average practically every day and we know the companies that are a part of the Average today—from Allied Chemical, Aluminum Company of America, and American Can to U.S. Steel, Westinghouse, and Woolworth. But, as we go back in time a bit, we find names that once were important enough to be a part of the Average and which we have heard of, such as Hudson Motors, Famous Players-Lasky, and Baldwin Locomotive. It is not long, however, before we run into one-time business leaders whose names are strange to us, such as Central Leather, U.S. Cordage Company, Pacific Mail, American Cotton Oil Company, and one with a nostalgic sort of name, The Distilling and Cattle Feeding Company.[1]

What is new, however, is the current pace of such events. Stemming, in part, from the rise of industrial research expenditures from less than $200 million in 1930 to an estimated $12.4 billion in 1960,[2] the pace of industrial change has been accelerating for many years. It is now so rapid that firms can rise or fall more quickly than ever before.

* Reprinted by permission from Robert B. Buchele, "How to Evaluate a Firm," *California Management Review,* Fall 1962, pp. 5–17.

Sophisticated technologies are spreading to many industries; in addition, as we shall see in this article, various management techniques contribute to the quickening pace of change. In consequence, the rapid rate of change now affects a great many American firms rather than just that minority known as "growth" companies.

## Present evaluation methods

### FINANCIAL ANALYSIS

This method typically consists of studying a "spread" of profit and loss figures, operating statements and balance sheet ratios for the past 5 or 10 years. The underlying assumption is that the future performance of a company can be reliably projected from trends in these data. The reasoning is that these data represent the "proof of the pudding." If they're sound, the company as a whole, particularly its top management, must be sound, for a competent top management will keep a firm healthy.

Through the years this method has worked well because the basic assumption has been reasonably valid. Despite the fact that some blue chip companies have failed, it is still reasonably valid for the large firms who are thoroughly entrenched in their markets and who make substantial investments in executive development, in market development, and in any technology that promises to threaten one of their market positions.

However, the assumption is becoming less safe, especially in connection with medium-sized and small firms, as the pace of industrial change steadily accelerates. Thus, a firm whose financial record is unimpressive may be on the verge of a technological breakthrough that will send its profits rocketing ahead; conversely, a company that looks good in financial analyses may be doomed because it is being by-passed technologically or marketing-wise or because rigor mortis has taken over the executive offices.

In practice, the financial-analysis method is often supplemented by market research in the form of interviews with leading customers, by interviews with the firm's top executives, and by consultation with scientists capable of evaluating technological capabilities and trends. Although these supplementary activities help, financial analysis still is neither adequately comprehensive nor adequately oriented to the future.

Thus, this type of market research can yield some insights into the effectiveness of past and present performance but is too superficial to tell much about the future. The interviews with top executives can be more misleading than informative simply because they are conducted by financial people inexperienced in management, marketing, or technology.[3] The use of scientists is a commendable step forward. However, it provides help in only one and possibly two of the many areas essential to a thorough evaluation.

### KEY FACTOR RATINGS

Systems more comprehensive than the financial-analysis method have been developed, mainly by consultants seeking to understand firms' overall strengths and weaknesses in order to be able to prescribe for them. Such

The evaluator must also be able to distinguish between creative market research and pedestrian fact-gathering that plods along a year too late to help management conquer the future. Only when market research secures fresh quantitative data on future markets can management integrate market development with product development.

## Manufacturing

Next area to be studied is production. Questions to be asked include:

*Manufacturing*   What is the nature of the manufacturing processes, the facilities and the skills—are they appropriate to today's competition? How flexible are they—will they be or can they be made appropriate to tomorrow's competition?

What is the quality of the manufacturing management in terms of planning and controlling work schedule-wise, cost-wise, and quality-wise? Is there evidence of an industrial engineering capability that steadily improves products and methods? Does manufacturing management effectively perform its part of the process of achieving new products?

The answers to these questions call mainly for conventional type analysis which need not be commented upon here. This is not to say that there are not now, as always, new and better techniques being developed in the manufacturing field. Certainly an alert manufacturing management will use such progressive techniques as "value engineering" to simplify product designs and, thus, reduce costs; and it will use electronic data processing and other modern industrial engineering methods of controlling the work pace and other cost elements.

But, basically, manufacturing management still is, and long has been, evaluated on the basis of performance schedule-wise, cost- and quality-wise, and techniques for such evaluations are among the oldest and best-developed tools of management consultants and others concerned with industrial engineering.

The quickening pace of technological change does, however, require special attention to the ability of the engineering and manufacturing departments to cooperate effectively in bringing new products into production and in utilizing new processes. Also, it requires special caution with respect to firms with heavy investments in inflexible capital equipment because such investments might be susceptible to almost sudden obsolesence.

## Summary on R&D and operations

To make the most of information acquired about a firm's operating departments and R&D, it is advantageous at this point to pull all this sometimes diffuse information together into a sight summary that pulls the whole picture of operations into focus. Questions running along lines such as these help clarify it:

*The overall picture*   Is this a complete, integrated, balanced operation; or have certain strong personalities emphasized some functions and neglected others?

What is the quality of performance of key R&D and operating executives; do they understand the fundamental processes of management, namely planning, controlling, organizing, staffing, and directing? Are plans and controls in each department inadequate, adequate, or overdeveloped into a "paperwork mill"?

Is there throughout the departments a habit of steady progress in reducing overhead, lowering breakeven points and improving quality?

Are all departments future-minded; do they cooperate effectively in developing worthy new products geared to meet the customer's future needs?

Finance is the third area of a corporation which should be analyzed carefully in appraising its present and future development. In this connection, both the men handling a company's finances and the figures on the balance sheet should be studied. Beginning inquiries could be:

*Financial analysis* What main strength and weaknesses of the firm emerge from analysis of the trends in the traditional financial data: earnings ratios (to sales, to tangible net worth, to working capital) and earnings-per-share; debt ratios (current and acid tests, to tangible net worth, to working capital, to inventory); inventory turnover; cash flow; and the capitalization structure?

What do the trends in the basic financial facts indicate as to the firm's prospects for growth in sales volume and rate of earnings? Does "quality of earnings" warrant compounding of the earnings rate?

Although this reading has already pointed out limitations of financial analysis standing alone as a method of evaluating firms, its importance as one of the key elements of an evaluation should never be overlooked. Because financial analysis has been so important for so long, its techniques have been well developed. Therefore, it is not necessary to discuss them here.

One concept concerning "growth" companies, however, does require comment. The technique of evaluating a growth firm on the basis of an assumption that it will "plow back" its earnings and thereby achieve a compounded rate of increase in earnings per share is of questionable validity. By compounding earnings on a straight-line (or uninterrupted) basis, financial analysts arrive at estimates of future earnings that justify stock prices from 40 to 100 times present earnings per share.

## No firm progresses evenly

The concept of straight-line progress just doesn't square with the facts of life as observed by students of management. Especially in small and medium-sized companies, progress typically occurs in a saw-tooth, rather than a straight-line pattern. This phenomenon is based partly on the existence of business cycles and partly on the fact the firms are affected by the strengths and limitations of humans in key positions. There are stages in which the typical growing firm requires managerial talents greater than—or, possibly, only different from—those talents essential to its start.

At these critical periods the earnings per share may slow down or even turn into losses. Such events devastate the compounding process; if one compounds a more realistic 5 to 10 percent rate of growth per year, the result is far less sensational than is secured by compounding a 20 to 25 percent rate. It is exceedingly rare that a firm achieves the higher percentages for any sustained period; Litton Industries and IBM appear to be the exceptions that prove the rule. The reference to quality of earnings is meant to shed light on the sustainability of the rate of improvements in earnings. Here the evaluator must distinguish between continuous, sustainable improvement and isolated events (such as a single acquisition or securing an especially favorable contract) or cyclical events (a period of high profitability certain to be followed by a corresponding low).

## The money men

Figures alone don't tell the complete financial story of a firm. Its money management must be rated and this involves an evaluation of both policies and men, not only those in the financial division but also the men in charge of planning and top management. You need to know their attitudes about . . . the following:

*Financial management*   Is there a sound program for steadily increasing return on investment? Do the long-range financial plans indicate that management understands the costs of capital and how to make money work hard?

Have balance sheets and operating statements been realistically projected for a number of years into the future?

Is there careful cash planning and strong controls that help the operating departments lower breakeven points? Are capital expenditures inadequate, adequate, or excessive with respect to insuring future operating efficiency? Are capital investment decisions based on thorough calculations?

Does management have the respect of the financial community? Is the firm knowledgeable and aggressive in tax administration?

Although many financial departments function only as record-keepers and rules-enforcers, some play a truly creative role. Financial management can today contribute as much or more to improvement in earnings per share as can any other part of management.[11] In fact, in recent years bold use of the newer forms of financing have in many cases contributed as much to the rapid rise of companies as have technological innovations. And, alas, bold but unwise financing has ruined many a promising young company.

The questions here are designed to help the evaluator discover whether or not the financial people are vigorously contributing in a number of ways to the steady improvement of earnings currently and in the long run.

## Rating top management

All study of management invariably and understandably leads to a searching examination of the top management men. Here there are pitfalls for the unwary. The analyst must first identify the true top management before he can examine their performance record. Things, in terms of who actually runs the show, are not always what they seem on the organization chart. So key topics are:

*Top management and its record*   What person or group constitutes top management? Has present top management been responsible for profit-and-loss results of the past few years?

The problem is to determine the individual or group of individuals who contribute directly and regularly to those decisions that shape the basic nature of this business and significantly affect profit and loss results. This usually cannot be determined reliably by direct questions to persons in key positions; few men are objective about themselves on these matters.

## Watch them work

Rare is the top executive who will admit that he is a one-man rule type; rare is the vice-president or department head who will admit that he is a highly paid errand boy. Accordingly, direct observation of management at work is needed. Some additional information can also be gained through examination of minutes of meetings and files of memos.

After top management has been identified, the evaluator must ask whether this management has had time to prove itself one way or the other. The criterion is whether or not major decisions and programs put forth by this top management have come to fruition. It is not simply a matter of looking at profit and loss figures for a few years. We all know that in certain situations factors other than top management capability (for example, an inherited product line that is unusually strong) can produce good profits for a number of years.

Next we consider the key topics:

*Top management and the future*  What are top management's chief characteristics? How adequate or inadequate is this type of management for coping with the challenges of the future?

Will the present type and quality of top management continue, or will it deteriorate? Will it improve? Or will it change its basic character?

We must ask how and why top management has achieved the results that it has achieved so that we can judge how adequate it will be for meeting tomorrow's challenges. Exploring the how and why gets the evaluator into the subject of types of management and their effects on profitability—the thorniest area of contemporary management theory. Over the past 20 years a tremendous literature has accumulated on such subjects as participative leadership, autocratic versus bureaucratic versus democratic types of management, and related subjects.

Some writers have claimed or implied great virtues for participative-democratic methods; others have attacked such methods as wasteful and ineffective, wholly inappropriate in industrial life and have advocated "benevolent autocracy." The confusion recently reached a zenith with the almost simultaneous publication of conflicting views by eminent professors from the same university.[12]

Industrial psychologists and sociologists have provided valuable insights into management practices and their effects upon profitability. Although a skilled social scientist could contribute importantly to the evaluation of a firm's top management, there is a more direct way of evaluating top management's capability for coping with future challenges.

The direct method is to determine how top management has in the past coped with the future. This technique is based on the idea that management is essentially the process of planning to achieve certain goals and, then, controlling activities so that the goals are actually attained. It is in the processes of planning and controlling that top management does its major decision making. Since planning and controlling are the heart of the managerial process, it is in these activities that top management most fully reveals its vital characteristics.

The evaluator can probe deeply into the content of the firm's past and current long-range and short-range plans, into the methods by which the plans are formulated, and into the controls used to bring those plans to fruition. This technique gets away, to a considerable extent, from subjective judgments; it deals with such facts as what was planned, how it was planned and what actually happened.

Fortunately, these activities can be studied without great difficulty and by persons who do not have formal training in the behavioral sciences. A simple yet highly informative procedure is to compare succeeding sets of old long-range plans with one another, with present plans and with actual events.

## Do their plans work?

First, a firm that is effectively tomorrow-minded will have long-range plans. These may not be neatly bound in a cover labeled "long-range plans"; however, they will exist either in minutes of meetings, in memos, in reports to stockholders or in other places. Second, the old plans will contain evidence as to whether top management truly has studied the future to determine and anticipate the nature of the opportunities and threats that will inevitably arise.

Third, the old plans will contain evidence of the nature and quality of the solutions developed for meeting the challenges of the future—how creative, aggressive and realistic management has been in initiative matters such as selecting R&D programs, establishing diversification strategy and program, developing new markets, planning the organizational changes needed to keep fit for new tasks, and effectively utilizing advanced techniques (e.g., operations research, automation) when feasible.

Special attention to initiative matters will indicate whether or not top management is creative and aggressive enough to keep up with an accelerating rate of change.

Fourth, comparison of succeeding sets of plans will indicate whether consistent progress has been made or top management is recklessly aggressive in that it undertakes unrealistic, ill-conceived, unachievable plans.

The same technique can be applied to short-range plans such as annual budgets, sales forecasts and special developmental programs of many types. This study will indicate whether or not forecasts are typically accurate, whether or not plans typically are successfully completed, whether or not new products are developed on schedule, and whether or not they are supported by marketing, finance, and management programs ready to go at the right time. Again, as in the case of long-range plans, the inquiry will reveal whether decision making is mature or immature. Has management made profitability a habit, or just a subject of wishful thinking?

A management that knows how to bring plans to fruition builds into every plan a set of controls designed to give early warning of problems and an indication that corrective action is needed. Examination of the controls and the ways in which they are used will indicate whether or not top management is on top of its problems or vice versa.

## Who makes the plans?

Investigation of the methods by which plans are formulated and control is exercised will reveal a great deal about whether top management is autocratic, bureaucratic or democratic. This inquiry holds more than academic interest; the extent to which lower levels of management contribute to the formulation of plans and the extent to which they are held accountable for results will tell much about the firm's down-the-line strength.

## Executive turnover

Also, these factors are particularly important indicators of whether top management will retain its vigor, will improve, or will deteriorate. Thus, they indicate whether or not top management is making sincere efforts to recruit and develop middle management that will become a new and better generation of top management. Other insights into whether management is bringing in too little or too much new blood can be gained by examining age patterns and statistics on turnover in executive ranks, by reviewing formal executive development efforts and by interviews with some of the men.

## Yardstick to gauge growth factors

In summary, the technique of probing deeply into the firm's actual plans and controls and methods of planning and control can yield abundant evidence to indicate whether or not top management has the characteristics of a growth firm. These characteristics have been set forth in a major study by Stanford Research Institute of the factors that usually distinguish growth from non-growth firms. They are as follows:

Amnity for growth fields

Organized programs to seek and promote new opportunities

Proven competitive abilities in present lines of business

Courageous and energetic managements, willing to make carefully calculated risks

Luck

Incidentally, this study found that high growth companies had twice the earning power of low-growth companies, while maintaining four times the growth rate.[13]

## The board of directors

Rounding out the top management of every corporation is an enigmatic, unpublicized group of men about whom a competent analyst should be most curious. They are the Board of Directors. Questions such as these should be asked about them: What influence and/or control does the Board of Directors exercise? What are the capabilities of its members? What are their motivations?

In my experience one of the most frequent and serious errors of small and medium-sized firms is failure to have and use effectively a strong Board of Directors. Too often the entrepreneurial types who start firms disdain help until they are in deep trouble.

Especially in firms headed by a scientist or a supersalesman, a strong and active Board can be invaluable in helping make up for the top executives' lack of rounded managerial training and experience. Except in a few unusual situations, a board must be an "outside," or nonemployee, Board to be strong.

## Dummies or policy makers

To be active and helpful, an "outside" Board must have some motivation, either financial or the psychic motivation involved in being confronted with real problems and being able to contribute to their solution. Examination of files and minutes of Board meetings will reveal whether or not there is a good flow of information to the outside directors and a contribution by them to the solution of significant problems.

## Adding up the facts

With all the data in about the four vital areas of a firm, products and competition, operations and R&D, finance, and top management, the analyst ends his task by posing one more set of questions which might be called *summary and evaluation strategy*. They should run something like this:

What other factors (use a checklist)[14] can assume major importance in this particular situation?

Of all the factors studied, which, if any, is overriding in this particular situation? Which factors are of major importance because they govern other factors?

What are the basic facts of life about the economics and competition of this industry now and over the next decade? In view of this firm's particular strengths and weaknesses, what are the odds that it will succeed and at what level of success, in this industry? What are the prospects of its succeeding by diversifying out of its industry?

## Determining other vital factors

There is a purpose behind every evaluation study. That purpose or the particular nature of the firm and its industry might place importance upon any of an almost infinite number of factors. Accordingly, the evaluator must thoughtfully run through a checklist containing such considerations as: personnel management practices (e.g., labor relations, profit sharing, compensation levels), valuation questions (e.g., valuation of fixed or real assets or inventory or unique assets), geographical location as related to labor markets, taxes, cost of distribution, seasonality factors, in-process or impending litigation, or any matter footnoted in the financial reports so that the auditing firm is, in effect, warning of an unusual circumstance.

The purpose of a particular evaluation study often will determine which factor, if any, is overriding. Logically, the quality of top management should usually be the overriding factor. By definition a highly competent top management group can solve the other problems such as securing competent scientists and other personnel, developing new products, getting financing, etc. However, there may be an investment or acquisition situation in which the product line, for example, is the overriding factor because it is so obsolete that even the finest management could not effect a recovery within existing time and financial parameters.

## Matching buyer and acquisition

If the evaluation is being done to help decide the advisability of an acquisition, many additional considerations come into play. The problem is one of matching the acquiring and acquired firms; many firms have acquired grief rather than growth because they have neglected this point. At one extreme, acquisition of one healthy company by another may be unwise because the two are so different that the acquirer may mismanage the acquired company. At the other extreme, it may be wise for one unhealthy company to acquire another unhealthy one if the strengths of one remedy the weaknesses of the other, and vice versa.

## The character of the company

The acquirer must precisely define his objectives in acquiring. Also, he must carefully consider the "character," or "climate," of the other firm in relation to his own. The subject of "company character" has not been well developed in management practice or in literature. Nevertheless, a consideration of the "character" of the two companies is highly relevant, and the outline presented in this article will help the evaluator consider some of the more obvious elements of "company character" such as the nature of its engineering and manufacturing skills, the type of distribution channels and marketing skills required, the type of managerial leadership practiced and top management's aggressiveness and the quality of its decisions in initiative matters.

In sum, the evaluation of a firm requires a clinical judgment of the highest order. The purposes of the evaluation study set the criteria for the judgment. Except in a few instances in which conditions are highly stable, the day is rapidly passing when simple financial analyses, or even financial analyses supplemented by a few interviews and judgments of scientists will suffice for evaluation of a firm.

# References and notes

**1** "Evaluating Your Company's Future," Unpublished paper presented at the Fourth Annual Management Conference, UCLA Executive Program Association, Los Angeles, Oct. 20, 1960, p. 2.

**2** Data from the National Science Foundation, in: *Research Management,* vol. III, no. 3, Autumn 1960, p. 129.

**3** Lee Dake explains in detail a case in which a financial analyst and a management consultant arrived at opposite conclusions about a firm's prospects in "Are Analysts' Techniques Adequate for Growth Stocks?" *The Financial Analysts Journal,* vol. 16, no. 6, 1960, pp. 45–49. Dake's thesis can be confirmed many times over in the present author's experience. Particularly distressing was the case where a persuasive but incompetent chief executive persuaded three investment firms to recommend his stock less than six months before declaration of losses exceeding the firm's tangible net worth!

**4** The factors are: (*a*) economic function, (*b*) corporate structure, (*c*) health of earnings, (*d*) services to stockholders, (*e*) research and development, (*f*) directorate analysis, (*g*) fiscal policies, (*h*) production efficiency, (*i*) sales vigor, (*j*) executive evaluation. The factors and their uses are explained in detail in a series of ten reports: *The Management Audit Series,* New York: The American Institute of Management, starting in 1953.

**5** Most dramatic was the case of the Douglas Aircraft Company whose "excellently managed" rating for 1957–1959 was followed by staggering losses in late '59 and '60. Among numerous other examples that can be cited are the 1957 ratings of Olin Mathiesen Chemical Co. and Allis-Chalmers Manufacturing Company, both of which, soon after receiving "excellently managed" ratings, suffered serious declines that have openly been discussed in business magazines. For the ratings, see *Manual of Excellent Managements,* New York: The American Institute of Management, 1957. For accounts of the travails of these firms see *Business Week,* Apr. 15, 1961, pp. 147–149 and Apr. 9, 1960, p. 79.

**6** "Industrial Administration through the Eyes of an Investment Company," *Appraising Managerial Assets—Policies, Practices, and Organization,* General Management Series #151, New York: American Management Association, 1950. The new emphasis is suggested in a postscript to a reprint published in 1960 by the Keystone Custodian Funds, Inc., Boston, Mass.: 1960, p. 13. Professor Schell suggested increased emphasis on tax administration, too. The original factors were: (*a*) breadth and variety of viewpoint in administration, (*b*) vigor and versatility in operating management, (*c*) clarity and definiteness of long-term objectives, (*d*) vigilance in matters of organization, (*e*) dependence upon far-reaching plans, (*f*) maintenance of integrated controls, (*g*) upkeep in harmony with an advancing art, (*h*) improvement as a normal expectancy, (*i*) creativeness through high morale, (*j*) effectiveness of managerial attitudes, (*k*) resources for consistently distinguished leadership in a specific industry.

**7** For an illustration and discussion of use of life-cycle curves, see C. Wilson Randle, "Selecting the Research Program: A Top Management Function," *California Management Review,* vol. II, no. 2, 1960, pp. 10–11.

**8** The Bell and Howell methods are described in two articles: "How to Coordinate Executives," *Business Week,* Sept. 12, 1953, pp. 130 ff., and "How to Plan Profits Five Years Ahead," *Nation's Business,* Oct., 1955, p. 38.

**9** An invaluable review of this literature up to early 1957 is given in Albert H. Rubenstein, "Looking Around: Guide to R&D," *Harvard Business Review,* vol. 35, no. 3, 1957, pp. 133 ff. Among the most pertinent articles since Rubenstein's review are: Ora C. Roehl, "The Investment Analyst's Evaluation of Industrial Research Capabilities," *Research Management,* vol. 3, no. 3, 1960, pp. 127 ff.; Maurice Nelles, "Changing the World Changers," a paper presented at the Ninth Annual Management Conference, The Graduate School of Business Administration, University of Chicago, Mar. 1, 1961; C. Wilson Randle, "Problems of R&D Management," *Harvard Business Review,* vol. 37, no. 1, 1959, pp. 128 ff.; James B. Quinn, "How to Evaluate Research Output," *Harvard Business Review,* vol. 38, no. 2, 1960, pp. 69 ff.; and "Long-range Planning of Industrial Research," *Harvard Business Review,* vol. 39, no. 4, 1961, pp. 88 ff.

**10** H. Igor Ansoff, "Strategies for Diversification," *Harvard Business Review,* September–October, 1957.

**11** For an exposition of this thought as applied to large firms, see "The New Power of the Financial Executive," *Fortune,* vol. 65, no. 1, 1962, pp. 81 ff. See also the new text by J. Fred Weston, *Managerial Finance,* New York: Holt, 1962.

**12** Rensis Likert, reporting on a decade of social science research into patterns of management makes a case for participative management in *New Patterns of Management,* New York: McGraw-Hill, 1961. George Odiorne, reporting on studies of successful managements, warns strongly against the views of social scientists and makes a case for the more traditional, somewhat autocratic, business leader in *How Managers Make Things Happen,* New York: Prentice-Hall, 1961. Both authors are professors at the University of Michigan.

**13** *Environmental Change and Corporate Strategy,* Menlo Park, Calif.: Stanford Research Institute, 1960, p. 8. A more recent report on this continuing research project is given by Robert B. Young, "Keys to Corporate Growth," *Harvard Business Review,* vol. 39, no. 6, 1961, pp. 51–62. Young concludes: "In short, the odds for corporate growth are highest when the top executives of a firm treat their future planning as a practical decision-making challenge requiring personal participation, and direct their planning efforts toward the origins of opportunity itself. Such an approach can make the difference between having constantly to adapt to day to day crises and enjoying profitable future growth."

**14** For one such checklist, see Robert G. Sproul, Jr., "Sizing Up New Acquisitions," *Management Review,* vol. 49, no. 1, 1960, pp. 80–82.

## CHAPTER 5

# Considering alternative strategies [1]

### LEARNING OBJECTIVES

**1** To understand why firms consider several alternative strategies prior to strategic choice

**2** To learn how the alternatives are generated

**3** To review the major strategic alternatives firms use

**4** To understand which alternatives are best for various situations

Let us now assume that you as the strategic planner have thoroughly considered and analyzed the environment for opportunities and threats. You have prepared the environmental threat and opportunities profile (Chapter 3). You have done a good job assessing the enterprise's strengths and weaknesses. You have prepared the strategic advantage profile (Chapter 4).

As indicated in Figure 5–1, you have completed the appraisal phase of the strategic planning process and are ready to begin the choice phase. This phase consists of two steps:

**1** The generation of a reasonable number of strategic alternatives that will help fill the gaps or take advantage of the opportunities as a result of matching the environmental threat and opportunities profile with the strategic advantage profile (Chapter 5)

**2** The choice of the best strategy to fill the gap or exploit the opportunity (Chapter 6)

This chapter looks at how the strategic decision makers generate alternative strategies to fill the gaps found when comparing the results of the two profiles and the firm's objectives. This can be framed in terms of product groups or whole systems of products.

First, we shall discuss various aspects of the alternatives examined:

Active or passive alternatives

Flexible or programmed alternatives

Business definitions and alternatives

Then the chapter looks at the four grand strategies which firms consider as alternatives:

Stability

Combination

Growth

Retrenchment

and the various substrategies that are variations on these grand strategies.

### ACTIVE OR PASSIVE ALTERNATIVES [2]

Strategic planners can generate active or passive strategic alternatives.

Barnard [2], Bonis [2], and Bell [3] have described how firms face environments which differ and therefore give some clues as to whether active or

**116**

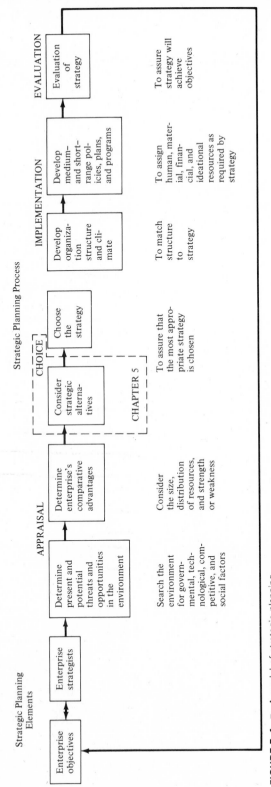

**FIGURE 5-1** ■ A model of strategic planning.

DEFINITION ■ ACTIVE AND PASSIVE STRATEGIES

An *active or offensive strategy* is one in which the strategic planners move the organization *before* they are forced to react to environmental threats or opportunities.

A *passive or defensive strategy* is one whose major characteristic is to react to environmental pressures only when forced to do so by circumstances.

---

passive alternatives make sense for a firm. In general, large and dominant firms will be effective if they develop active strategic alternatives in their major market segments. Small firms will survive if they have passive strategies toward the large firms' major market and active strategies toward market segments ignored by the dominant firm(s) and which they can develop.

Obviously, firms can develop strategies which are offensive with regard to one part of the environment, passive toward others. In fact, a crucial characteristic determining the choice of active or passive strategies may be the relative size of the firm in its market.

## CONTINGENCY-FLEXIBLE AND PROGRAMMED STRATEGIES [4]

A programmed strategy is possible when environmental conditions for it are right. McCaskey contrasted these conditions with those necessary for contingency-flexible strategies.

McCaskey believes that programmed planning is suitable for stable environments with people who prefer well-defined roles. The flexible strategy is suitable for unstable environments with people who prefer variety and stimulation. Conditions change rapidly. Since 1972 large firms have chosen their strategies but also have developed plans "B," "C," and "D" on a "what if" basis. If the "what if" comes to be, plan B becomes the strategy. As *Business Week* reported,

This year [1975] a lot of "worst case" contingency plans came off the shelf. Mead Corp. has three short-term contingency plans—A, B, and C, standing for aggressive, basic,

---

DEFINITION ■ PROGRAMMED STRATEGY

A *programmed strategy* is one which is planned in such a detailed and integrated way as to make it difficult to change, once the strategy has begun to be implemented.

---

DEFINITION ■ FLEXIBLE-CONTINGENCY STRATEGY

A *flexible strategy* is one which allows for shifts in the thrust of the plan when conditions warrant it.

A *contingency approach* to strategy requires the planner to choose the preferred strategy given the best estimate of conditions and other strategic choices.

---

and conservative. Mead's basic B plan, formulated last October, was scrapped very early. "We even felt our C plan was too optimistic," says Vice-Chairman William W. Womack, who is in charge of strategy. "We tore everything up and asked for a new ABC, and our current B plan is even lower than our earlier C plan." Mead's new B plan, drawn in January, projects sales of $1.4-billion in 1975, down from the earlier B plan projection of $1.7-billion.

So planners are literally obliged to stress flexibility, which means multiple contingency plans, rather than a single forward plan, and more frequent revisions. It is not a very satisfactory solution, but as James E. Matheson, director of the Decision Analysis Group at Stanford Research Institute, says, "it is one way of coping with uncertainty." Henry M. Boettinger, corporate planning director at American Telephone & Telegraph Co., calls it "pulsing your way into the future."

Most writers argue that moderately flexible strategies are the most effective. But that is easier to advocate than pull off. In 1973–1974, the environment gave special problems to the auto industry. The energy crisis appeared to dictate a shift to compact cars. General Motors and others began to convert their factories to this strategy about the time that the crisis disappeared from motorists' minds and the motorists then began buying regular-sized cars again. Once the equipment is purchased and plans are drawn to shift to compact cars, it is hard for a capital-intensive firm like General Motors to be flexible. Contingency strategies would have required several fallback strategies when conditions worsened.

---

RESEARCH STUDY ■ **ENVIRONMENTAL CONDITIONS FOR FLEXIBLE AND PROGRAMMED STRATEGIES** [McCaskey]

| Programmed strategies | Flexible strategies |
|---|---|
| *Characteristics* | |
| Teleological, directed toward external goals. | Directional, moving from internal preferences. |
| Goals are specific and measurable. | Domain is sometimes hard to define. |
| Rational, analytic. | Intuitive, use unquantifiable elements. |
| Focused, narrowed perception of task. | Broad perception of task. |
| Lower requirement to process novel information. | Greater need to process novel information. |
| More efficient use of energy. | Possible redundancy, false leads. |
| Separate planning and acting phases. | Planning and acting not separate phases. |
| *Contingent upon* | |
| People who prefer well-defined tasks. | People who prefer variety, change, and complexity. |
| Tasks and industries that are quantifiable and relatively stable. | Tasks and industries not amenable to quantification and which are rapidly changing. |
| Mechanistic organization forms, "closed" systems. | Organic organization forms, "open" systems. |
| "Tightening up the ship" phase of a project. | "Unfreezing" phase of a project. |

---

At this point in the strategic planning process, the decision maker is clear on what the environment has to offer and where the firm's strengths and weaknesses lie. The strategic planner has decided on how flexible and aggressive the firm can be. The question now becomes: What can I do? The answers to that question become the alternative strategies you consider.

You do not consider alternatives out in the wild blue yonder. You begin to consider alternatives which:

1  You know about

2  You think will work

3  Are not major breaks with the past (unless you have clearly diagnosed the situation as desperate, life and death)

So the alternatives you consider are incremental steps, usually small incremental steps from your present pace and business. MacCrimmon points out that you can choose them by trying to:

1  Work forward from the present to the future.

2  Picture the future state and see how you can get there from where you are now.

Normative decision theorists will tell you to "consider all alternatives." This is impossible because:

1  You do not know all of them and cannot know all of them. You are not omniscient.

2  It would take too much time and energy and so, if the situation appears to need moderate changes, you probably consider a few strategies that make minor adjustments from your present strategy. If the situation appears to be serious or quite different from situations you have faced before, you consider creative, brainstorming alternatives.

Why consider strategic alternatives at all? Why not just accept the first strategy that pops into the decision maker's mind? This is the opposite of the normative statement: Consider *all* alternatives. I suppose it is possible that the decision maker is so bright that he or she *intuitively* and *always* picks the right strategy for the circumstances. But surely you have had the experience of having a problem and having "the answer" pop into your mind. It was "the answer" before you thought it over and talked it over and realized there were serious shortcomings to the answer. Always trying to generate several reasonable alternatives allows systematic comparison of the tradeoffs, strengths, and weaknesses of both. Thus the choice is likely to be a much better choice.

## The central strategic alternative: business definition [6]

The central factor examined at the beginning of consideration of strategy is the business the firm is in or wants to be in.

For smaller firms, this business definition is simple enough. One describes the product or service category served by the firm. This is true for many medium-sized organizations as well. A majority of large firms are involved in multiple businesses. So their business definition is more complex.

Joe's Bar is in one business; Joe's Bar and Grill is in two. American Motors furnishes surface transportation. General Motors does that, as well as offering appliances and other products.

Some firms are in so many businesses that it is hard if not impossible to describe the "business" they are in. Hanna's study of three conglomerates (Litton, Indian Head, and Bangor Punta) found that their strategy making did not involve delineating specific product-service businesses at all. Their "definition of business" involved only the specifications in detail of the corporate objectives in terms of growth rates, financial policies to guide their acquisition of funds and firms, and organizational policies. But most enterprises' strategic alternatives revolve around changes in the business the enterprise is currently in and in the efficiency and effectiveness by which they achieve their corporate objectives in their chosen business sector.

Thus the central strategic alternatives that strategic planners always consider are the following:

**1** Should we stay in the same business(es)?

**2** Should we get out of this business entirely or some subparts of it by merging, liquidating, or selling off part of it?

**3** Should we do a more efficient or effective job in the business we are in in a slimmed-down way?

**4** Should we try to grow in this business by: (*a*) Increasing our present business? (*b*) Acquiring similar businesses?

**5** Should we try to grow primarily in other businesses?

**6** Should we do alternatives 2 *and* 4a?

These strategic alternatives will be described now. If alternative 1 is answered "yes," the choice is a stability strategy. If alternative 1 is answered "no" and alternative 2 or 3 is accepted, the strategy is retrenchment. Alternatives 4 and 5 are called growth strategies, and alternative 6 is called combination strategy.

### FOUR ALTERNATIVE STRATEGIES [7]

We now discuss the grand strategies from which a strategic planner chooses his alternative. There are all kinds of ways to classify strategies. My four-way classification is given in Table 5–1. The table also points out the relative frequency of use of the alternatives, when they are effective, and the substrategy varieties available. Each grand strategy will now be described and analyzed.

## Stability strategy [8]

A slogan for this strategy might be "Maintain Present Course: Steady as It Goes." Since writing the first edition, I have tried to think up a different name for this strategy. I have found when managers or students describe a company which fits this strategy, and I label it "stability," they react by denying this.

**TABLE 5-1 ■ STRATEGIC ALTERNATIVES**

| Grand strategy | Substrategies | Frequency of use | Effectiveness |
|---|---|---|---|
| Stability | | *Most frequent* strategy | **1** When industry is mature **2** When environment is slow in changing **3** When firm is successful now |
| Combination | **1** Combine two or more grand strategies simultaneously **2** Combine two or more grand strategies in sequence | **1** Used mainly by large firms **2** Used more often than retrenchment | **1** In periods of economic transition (recession, recovery) **2** In periods of change in main product-service life cycle |
| Growth | **1** Internal concentric conglomerate **2** External (merger) concentric conglomerate **3** Vertical integration | Second most frequent strategy | **1** Successful if early in life cycle **2** Mixed success **3** Usually not very successful |
| Retrenchment | **1** Functional improvement-cost cutting **2** Captive company **3** Liquidation or sell-out | *Least frequent* strategy | **1** Mixed success **2** Mixed success **3** Last resort |

They suggest it is really combination strategy or "moderate" growth strategy. This is probably because in the United States and Canada, a strong value is growth. Expressions like "you must grow or die" abound. Yet there is nothing wrong with a stability strategy. It can be and is effective. Since we are in fact entering a period of lessened resources and lower population growth (in the United States and Canada, anyway), it may be the most rational strategy.

Katz's contention is given in Proposition 5–1.

**DEFINITION ■ STABILITY STRATEGY**

A *stability strategy* is one that an enterprise pursues when:

**1** It continues to serve the public in the same or very similar sectors as defined in its business definition.

**2** It continues to pursue the same or similar objectives, adjusting the level of achievement about the same percentage each year as it has achieved in the past.

**3** Its main strategic decisions focus on incremental improvement of functional performance.

**PROPOSITION ■** In an effective stability strategy, companies will concentrate their resources
**5–1** where the company presently has or can rapidly develop a meaningful competitive advantage in the narrowest possible product-market scope consistent with the firm's resources and market requirements.

A stability strategy sometimes is thought to be a do-nothing strategy. Often it is that. Yet it can be and is a consciously chosen strategy by many enterprises.

The author believes that stability is the strategy pursued by most firms at any one point in time. This is hard to prove, however. Stability is not the kind of strategy that makes news. Just as it is news to say 1 million are unemployed and it is not news to write 85 million are employed, so articles and research usually do not focus on stability strategies. Later in the chapter, my research will *not* support this contention. But it is based on *Fortune* cases, and *Fortune* gets many more readers by describing a major growth or cutback program than by writing about how Apex Wire is doing what it has always done.

## WHY A STABILITY STRATEGY?

Except when an enterprise starts out, a strategic planner has a natural beginning point for consideration of strategic alternatives: what we have been doing. A stability strategy is chosen for a number of reasons. Here are a few.

1   The firm is doing well or perceives itself as doing well. Management is not always sure what combination of decisions is responsible for this. So, "we continue the way we always have around here."

2   A stability strategy is less risky. A high percentage of changes fail—whether we are talking about new products or new ways of doing things. So conditions must be really bad to take the additional risk. The larger the firm and the more successful it has been, the greater is the resistance to the risk.

3   Managers prefer action to thought. A stability strategy can evolve because the executives never get around to considering any other alternatives. Many firms pursuing a stability strategy do so unconsciously. They react to forces in the environment and will change strategies only in extraordinary times.

4   It is easier and more comfortable for all concerned to pursue stability strategy. No disruptions in routines take place.

5   The firm is acquiring a large enough market share to subject it to pressure from the government with regard to antitrust.

6   The firm needs a breathing spell. It has grown so fast that it must stabilize for a while or it will become inefficient and unmanageable. Its costs may have gotten out of hand, especially if it appears that hard times are coming.

Stability strategies are implemented by "steady as it goes" approaches to decisions on the level of objectives sought; few major functional changes are made in product-service line, channels, production capacity; it will involve no major changes in vertical integration. A stability strategy may lead to defensive moves such as legal-patent moves to reduce competition. Stability usually involves keeping track of new developments to make sure the stability strategy continues to make sense.

---

**PROPOSITION 5–2** ▪ As firms get older, they become more conservative and are more likely to pursue a stability strategy.

---

Stability strategies can be implemented for firms or parts of firms in combination with other strategies.

The stability strategy is the best one for a firm that is doing well in an industry with a future and when the environment is not excessively volatile. This means that for most industries and companies a stability strategy is effective.


## Combination strategy

A slogan that describes the combination strategy is "Fit different strategies to different environments."

In combination strategies, the decision makers consciously apply several grand strategies to different parts of the firm or to different future phases in time. The logical possibilities are:

1   Stability in some divisions, growth in others

2   Stability in some divisions, retrenchment in others

3   Retrenchment in some divisions, growth in others

4   All three grand strategies in different divisions of the companies

The same logical possibilities exist in time-phased combinations, but the number of possibilities is greater. Thus with regard to stability strategies, the possibilities are:

1   Stability, then growth for the company or division

2   Growth, then stability for the company or division

3   Retrenchment, then stability for the company or division

4   Stability, then retrenchment for the company or division

Although possibility 4 seems a less likely combination, obviously the number of combinations is large, especially if the substrategies of growth and retrenchment become alternatives.

Most large firms such as *Fortune's* 500 largest industrials are probably the most frequent users of combination strategies. Even here, it is the multi-industry firm that is most likely to use them. The medium-sized firm that is multi-industry-based is also a likely user.

---

**DEFINITION** ■ COMBINATION STRATEGY
A *combination strategy* is a strategy that an enterprise pursues when:

**1** Its main strategic decisions focus on the conscious use of several grand strategies (stability, growth, retrenchment) at the same time in several divisions of the company; or it plans to use several grand strategies at different future times.

**2** Its objectives and business sector served may be the same or change depending on how it applies the grand strategies of growth and retrenchment.

---

A combination strategy is not an easy one to use. It is much easier to keep a firm in one set of values or one strategy at a time. But when a company faces many environments and these environments are changing at different rates, and its products are in different stages of the life cycle, it is easy to visualize conditions under which a combination strategy makes sense. In the case of the simultaneous combination strategy (several grand strategies at the same point in time), Proposition 5–3 serves as a hypothesis.

Thus, it is probable that when the economy is humming along (as in 1965), most industries are doing well. Therefore, the grand strategy might be growth. But at the start of recession, some industries begin to hurt and others are still doing well. Thus a combination strategy makes sense for a multi-industry firm at that time.

In the case of time-phased combination strategies, several scenarios come to mind. For example, a firm realizes some of its main product lines are beyond the optimum in the product life cycle and it is not worth the investment to "prop the product up." The firm may choose to retrench in this area with growth in the new product area. In effect, this is what Textron did, getting out of textiles and into lots of other products. Pet Milk severely reduced its investment in the milk business with a view toward growth in other food products (Musselman apple products) and other businesses (Stuckey's restaurants), and this is what W. R. Grace has done since 1945. Then the firm was in Latin American businesses (sugar, textiles, paper) and steamships. J. Peter Grace felt they had to retrench these businesses and grow in others. So now Grace is involved in chemicals, fertilizers, containers, and other businesses. Polaroid appears to be following a combination strategy as Martin describes it in 1975.

All strategies can be effective. The question is: When is a combination strategy most likely to be effective? What should have become clearer in the section just finished is that combination strategies are most likely to be effective for *larger firms* which are *multi-industry* firms in periods of *economic transition* or periods of *product-service transition* in the life cycle.

The combination strategy is the best one for a firm whose divisions have uneven performance or future potential.

## Growth strategies [9]

A stability strategy was the most talked and written about in the 1930s and 1940s. Growth strategies were the talk of the 1950s and 1960s. A look at the references for this section will confirm this. Recent shortages of food and natural resources and movements such as zero population growth and the

---

**PROPOSITION 5–3** ■ Simultaneous combination strategies are most likely to be effective in times of business cycle change; for example, they are more likely to be effective in recovery and recession than in the heights of prosperity or the depths of recession.

---

environmentalist movements may affect the values of managers and the societal conditions in such a way that growth may not be as popular a strategy in the late 1970s and 1980s as it was in the 1950s and 1960s. Only time will tell.

The theme of the growth strategy is: "To do what we have been doing the way we have been doing it is to commit suicide now or in the future."

## WHY DO COMPANIES FOLLOW GROWTH STRATEGIES?

After reading the list of reasons for following the stability strategy, it may be hard to imagine reasons for adopting a growth strategy. For *stability* has a number of things going for it:

1 Less risk in the short run

2 Inertia

3 Past experience of the firm

The reasons given for adopting a *growth* strategy are:

1 In volatile industries, a stability strategy can mean short-run success, long-range death. So growth is necessary for survival.

2 Many executives equate growth with effectiveness.

3 Some believe that society benefits from growth strategies.

4 The best explanation for growth strategies, however, seems to be managerial motivation. It is true that risk is less with a stability strategy, but so are the rewards financially and otherwise. There are many managers who wish to be remembered—to leave a monument to themselves in the workplace. Who remembers the executive who stood at the helm for 5 years "steady as it goes?" Troughton claims growth strategies result from the power needs of many executives. I would point out that the recognition needs are strong in these executives too. Thus these needs or drives encourage some executives to gamble and choose a grand strategy of growth. A growth company also becomes better known and may attract better management.

There are of course special problems with growth strategies. For example, there is the finding by Weinberg that as growth rates accelerate, profitability declines. *Dun's Review* exposed the "crisis of the $100 million company" as a result of growth. Growth requires a particular management style and ideology as Worchester argued. Cash crisis can develop, and Drucker finds that

---

**DEFINITION** ■ GROWTH STRATEGY
A *growth strategy* is one that an enterprise pursues when it increases its level of objectives upward in a significant increment, much higher than an extrapolation of its past achievement level. The most frequent increase indicating a growth strategy is to raise the market share and/or sales objective upward significantly.

---

**PROPOSITION 5-4** ■ In highly competitive, volatile industries, firms that do not plan for growth will not survive.

---

high-growth companies faced identity crises and lots of problems of adjustment.

In fact, Drucker refers to the 1950s and 1960s as a "growth craze" period.

Still, for many managers, there is only one way to go: growth. There are many growth substrategies. They will be discussed now.

## THE GROW-TO-SELL-OUT STRATEGY

Many entrepreneurs plan from the start of their business to make it a growth company, and when it gets to the fast growth rate apex of the product life cycle, they will sell out (usually for stock) to a larger firm. Typically, they take the proceeds in stock (for tax purposes), staying on as consultants for some years (3 to 5). They usually agree not to compete with the acquiring firm for a period. This can maximize their return and allow them to retire early or build up another firm to be sold out. Many entrepreneurs have done this. This strategy has not been studied in any depth. But this is not a particular *way* to grow. The growth will now be examined.

## INTERNAL GROWTH: PRESENT PRODUCT-SERVICE LINE [10]

The first way in which a firm can grow is to increase the sales, profits, and market share of the current product-service line faster than it has been increasing them in the past. This is most probably the most frequently used growth strategy.

This can be accomplished in at least five ways:

**1** Expand sales by increasing primary demand and encouraging new uses for the present products or services in the same area, with the same customers, pricing, and products, and with the present organizational arrangement. Kotler has called this an intensive growth or integrative growth strategy. He argues that this strategy is effective for firms with small market shares whether the product is in high-growth stage or maturity stage of the life cycle.

**2** Expand sales of the product or service into additional sectors of the economy.

**3** Expand sales of the product or service into additional geographic areas.

**4** Expand sales of the product or service by introducing new pricing strategies.

**5** Expand sales of the product or service by introducing minor modifications in the product or service to new segments of the markets. Examples include new sizes, private labeling or brand labeling, and others.

There are other variations of these approaches. And many companies have been very successful by following this strategy. Some examples are W. K. Kellogg (cereals), William Wrigley (chewing gum), many petroleum companies such as Clark, Ashland, the metals companies such as Anaconda, tire firms like Goodyear, the photography companies such as Eastman Kodak. Four research studies have shown how and when internal growth with present products is an effective strategy. A research study by Gutman found internal growth with present products as a very effective growth strategy. He studied 53 of the 150 firms in 1954–1958 whose *growth rate* was twice the rate of growth of the gross national product during the period.

■ **GUTMAN'S FINDINGS (1954–1958)**
The firms with the highest growth rates acted thus:

**1** They chose industries whose sales increased more rapidly than the economy as a whole.

**2** They chose the subsectors and submarkets within the industries which grew more rapidly than the industry and *concentrated* on these sectors, not the whole industry.

**3** They entered the subsector earlier than competing firms.

**4** More than 80 percent of the growth firms introduced new products for current customers.

**5** About 40 percent introduced new products for new consumers. Only about 7 percent tried to sell existing products to new customers.

**6** Two-thirds of the high-growth firms sold their products outside the United States.

**7** Those whose growth included mergers did not outperform those that grew entirely from internal methods.

---

Chevalier and Catry studied three U.S. industries which are in the mature stages of the product life cycle, where it is difficult for one company to influence market share, and where technology is not too volatile: auto manufacturing, biscuit and cookie manufacturing, and cement manufacturing. They found relative market share correlated with relative profits. From these and other studies of growth strategies they have these recommendations:

---

■ **CHEVALIER AND CATRY'S EFFECTIVENESS GUIDES**
**1** The first guide is to focus on products whose markets are growing. Never focus on slow-growth products unless there is technical or market know-how you can learn to apply to more promising markets. Or enter these markets only if you can produce a much simpler, much cheaper model when the dominant firms are not innovating.

**2** It is better to be a big fish in a small pond if the pond (market segment) is growing. Get out of small nongrowth markets. Don't be a follower.

**3** Choose feasible markets to compete in. Don't try to compete against larger firms with strong brand loyalty (in consumer goods) or large firms with strong financial capacity (industrial goods).

**4** In growing markets, it is easier to grow by combining push for primary demand with secondary demand push. Small firms with limited cash resources and market share should ignore primary demand. Major emphasis on secondary demand is optional when the objective is limited market share in a very competitive market.

---

RESEARCH
STUDY

**■ FRUHAN'S EFFECTIVENESS GUIDES**

Before a firm sets a growth goal in terms of market share, it must consider two questions:

**1** Does the company have adequate financial resources to increase its market share? GE and RCA did not when they tried to increase their computer market share, so they left the industry with major losses. Chrysler and American Motors do not have adequate financial resources to increase their market share in autos.

**2** Will the government allow the firm to acquire its market share the way it chooses to? Winn-Dixie, by concentrating on the Southeast and with moderate merger rate, was successful. National Tea did not develop large market share anywhere and merged too often and thus was stopped short of its objectives with disastrous results. The CAB prevented the larger carriers from increasing their number of flights at the expense of smaller carriers and thus the latter have done better.

**3** If these criteria are not met, larger market share makes no sense.

RESEARCH
STUDY

**■ BOSTON CONSULTING GROUP'S EFFECTIVENESS GUIDES**

**1** Get the biggest market share you can as early as you can.

**2** Initially, the products will be sold below cost, but then as volume builds, costs must be lowered. With the largest market share, this should be easy to do.

**3** Hold costs and prices down. This will reduce the attractiveness of entrance to the market.

---

Thus Chevalier and Catry found that a firm can grow effectively internally, but some internal growth methods were more effective than others.

Another study of internal growth of firms in the maturity or saturation phase of the product life cycle is that of Fruhan. He studied the relationship between market share and profitability in nine computer firms, three auto firms, three food chains, and eleven airlines over a 4- to 6-year period.

The Boston Consulting Group has studied 24 products in seven industries longitudinally: electric power, consumer durables, plastics, consumer nondurables, petroleum, nonferrous metals, and electrical parts. Their focus was on the cost-to-price relationship. Their results suggest the above growth strategy for internal growth.

Firms which followed these steps in this order were most effective. Other guidelines for effectiveness are in the reading by Schoeffler et al. in Chapter 6. A study by Stanford Research Institute found:

PROPOSITION
5–5

**■** Firms which have the most effective growth strategies grow from a base of proven competitive abilities in present lines of business, organize divisions or departments to promote new opportunity in growth fields, and take moderate risks.

■ DIVERSIFICATION AND CONGLOMERATION

A growth strategy is a *diversification* strategy if, in adding new products or services, the strategic planners choose those products or services that are in different SIC codes but are similar to the present product-service line in one of several ways: technology, production, marketing channels, customers [11].

A growth strategy is a *conglomerate* strategy if the new products or services added are not significantly related to the present product-service line in technology, production, marketing channels, or customers [12].

A second strategy of internal growth is to expand by adding new products or new product lines which are different from previous product lines.

Kotler points out that there are three ways to enter new products' markets: joint development (with a company already in the line), internal development, and acquisition or merger. This section focuses on internal development.

These types of new product-service strategies can overlap, but when IBM added typewriters and dictating equipment to its other office products (computers), it was diversifying. Some firms add products and services which have little or no relationship to each other and thus follow conglomerate strategy. An example of this is ITT. At its height, it operated telephone companies (here and abroad), Continental Baking (bread), Sheraton (hotels), Levitt & Sons (home builders), Avis (car rental), Canteen (vending), Hartford Insurance, and Grinnel (insurance).

So the two terms denote the *degree* of difference in the new products offered. Firms can become diversified by internal or external diversification (mergers). They can diversify internally by use of a standard organization or new ventures organization. The latter is receiving a lot of attention lately.

There are built-in preferences for the present product lines in most companies. This is true for the same reasons as those given for the preference for stability strategy. So many, especially larger, firms have created new venture or new product teams or suborganizations. Their job is to seek out and develop new products or services for the firm. Firms such as Dow Chemical, Monsanto, Du Pont, General Electric, Cabot, American Can, Union Carbide, International Paper, Boise Cascade, Norfolk & Western, 3M, Celanese, Lever, and Albright & Wilson have used this approach. Susbauer surveyed 210 of America's largest firms and found 70 percent claiming to use this approach. Fourteen percent of medium-sized firms being surveyed also claimed to use it.

A variation is the joint development project. For example, Johnson & Johnson is working with a smaller firm, Damon, to produce medical instruments. Ford is working with Thermo Electron for possible joint development of the steam-engine car.

### WHY DO FIRMS DIVERSIFY?

There are no doubt many reasons for executives to choose a growth-diversification strategy; a good summary of them is given by Drucker. As will be seen later, Drucker opposes "excessive" diversification.

**■ DRUCKER'S REASONS FOR DIVERSIFICATION**

**1 Internal pressures**

(*a*) Psychologically, people get tired of doing the same things over and over again. They also believe diversification will help them avoid the danger of overspecialization.

(*b*) Diversification is seen as a way to balance the vulnerabilities due to one's own wrong size.

(*c*) Diversification is seen as a way to convert present internal cost centers into revenue producers.

**2 External pressures (more important than internal pressures)**

(*a*) The economy (or market) the firm is operating in appears too small and confined to allow growth.

(*b*) The firm's technology, research, and development turn up products which appear to have promise.

(*c*) Tax legislation encourages reinvestment in research and development instead of dividends, and this leads to new products often as a base for diversification.

---

Diversification is not a new strategy. Steiner points out that in the sixteenth century, the House of Fugger was in banking, textiles, spices, copper, silver, and finance all over Europe. The East India Company (eighteenth century) was quite diversified.

Chandler describes how specialization (one product or product line) growth has declined relative to diversification for years in Europe, Japan, and the United States, and Gort has pointed out that less than 1 percent of establishments were diversified (operated in more than one industry group); but this 1 percent employed 38 percent of the working people in the United States. The diversified firms were concentrated in rapid-growth industries, with high increases in labor productivity and a high ratio of technical employees to all employees. Gort believed firms diversified because they felt it was easier than trying to increase primary demand or market share.

Some firms have wanted to diversify so badly that they have fought legal battles to do so. Thus the large meat-packers accepted a consent decree in 1920 not to diversify. In 1974, the companies (Swift Division of Esmark; Armour Division of Greyhound; Cudahy, a division of General Host) were given the right to enter 75 previously barred businesses.

DIVERSIFICATION STRATEGIES

There are several directions which firms can follow in a diversification strategy. These are shown in Table 5–2. Essentially, firms can diversify in a concentric way—close to present product service lines—or quite differently from present product lines in marketing and/or technological ways (conglomerate diversification).

Ansoff and Malmlow (reprinted in this book) have described systematic ways to diversify in their works cited in the references for this chapter. And

**TABLE 5-2 ■ A DIVERSIFICATION MATRIX**

|  | Internal development | External purchase (merger) |
|---|---|---|
| *Horizontal diversification* | | |
| **Market** | | |
| Concentric | Develop products or services that serve similar customers in similar markets. | Purchase products or services, companies that serve similar customers in similar markets. |
| Conglomerate | Develop products and services that are different from present product line and/or markets. | Purchase products or services, companies that serve different customers and/or markets. |
| **Technology** | | |
| Concentric | Develop products that use technologies similar to present line. | Purchase firms which utilize technologies similar to present line. |
| Conglomerate | Develop products that use technologies different from present line. | Purchase firm using technologies different from present line. |
| *Vertical diversification* | | |
| Forward | Develop outlets for sale of current products and related products (or different products: *conglomerate*) to consumer. | Purchase outlets for sale of products to consumer. |
| Backward | Develop own supplier division to cover present materials or different materials (conglomerate). | Purchase suppliers of raw materials. |

Ansoff has prescribed how to analyze the diversification decision. Ansoff's contention is given in Proposition 5–6.

There have been very few studies on the effectiveness of internal diversification strategies of growth. Most traditional economists such as Schall are dubious of the value of diversification to firm effectiveness. Rumelt's study of the relationship of diversification to firm effectiveness is the best one in the area. But he does not separate out those who diversified internally from those who diversified by merger. His study will be discussed below under external growth.

EFFECTIVENESS OF EXTERNAL-INTERNAL GROWTH

Another growth strategy is a joint venture or joint development form of growth. Thus Ford is working with Thermo Electron Corporation for the possible development of a steam car (see "A Pollution-free Car?" case later

---

**PROPOSITION 5-6** ■ Internal growth and development tend to take priority over diversification from within, unless the latter is supported, stimulated, and directed by top management.

---

FIGURE 5–2 ■ Drawing by H. Martin; © The New Yorker Magazine, Inc.

in this volume). Another joint venture is the engine proposal put forth by Volkswagen and American Motors. But to my knowledge, there has been no scientific study of this growth strategy.

### EXTERNAL GROWTH: HORIZONTAL AND CONCENTRIC MERGERS [13]

Thus far in this section, the emphasis has been growth from *within* a company. But companies also grow externally by acquiring other firms or parts of firms which they feel would add to their effectiveness. External growth has become increasingly popular. There are a number of terms used for external growth: acquisitions, mergers (one company loses its identity), consolidations (both companies lose identity and a new company arises). But one term will be used for all these: mergers.

Mergers take place within one country or across national borders. Thus Unilever and Shell resulted from mergers of British and Dutch firms and Agfa-Gevaert resulted from a Belgian-German merger.

---

**DEFINITION** ■ MERGERS: HORIZONTAL AND CONCENTRIC
A *merger* is combination of two or more businesses in which one acquires the assets and liabilities of the other in exchange for stock or cash; or both companies are dissolved and asserts and liabilities are combined and new stock is issued.

A *horizontal* merger is a combination of two or more firms in the same business and aspects of the production process.

A *concentric* merger is a combination of two or more firms in similar businesses.

---

Of course horizontal and concentric mergers are not completely clear-cut. Typical examples of horizontal mergers are the Free Press and Macmillan (two book publishers), Pure Oil and Sun Oil, Motorola TV and Sony TV, and the proposed merger of Pan American Airways and American Airlines. American Motors resulted from horizontal mergers of Nash Motors and Hudson Motors.

Concentric mergers take place when firms in *generally* similar business merge. General Foods resulted from the combination of such firms as Post Cereals, Maxwell House Coffee, Jello, and cake mix and other food products. They did not merge two gelatin firms, or two coffee firms, but several food companies which share similar marketing channels. Pet, Beatrice, Borden, and Carnation also in the food business are the results of concentric mergers.

## WHY MERGERS TAKE PLACE

There are many reasons why a firm may desire to merge. They can be grouped under buyer's motives and seller's motives.

RESEARCH
STUDY ■ **BUYER'S MOTIVES FOR MERGING**

**1** To increase the company's stock value. In the past, often mergers led to increases in the stock price and/or price-earnings ratio.

**2** To increase the growth rate of the firm faster than present internal growth.

**3** To make a good investment: to purchase a unit which makes a better use of funds than plowing the same funds into internal growth.

**4** To improve the stability of a firm's earnings and sales; this is done by acquiring firms whose earnings and sales complement our firm's peaks and valleys.

**5** To balance or fill out the product line.

**6** To diversify the product line when the life cycle of our products has peaked.

**7** To reduce competition by purchasing a competitor.

**8** To acquire a needed resource quickly; for example, high-quality technology or highly innovative management.

**9** For tax reasons: to purchase a firm with prior tax losses which will offset our current or future earnings.

**10** To increase efficiency and profitability, especially if there is synergy between the two companies. Synergy exists when the strengths of two companies more than offset their joint weaknesses: the $2 + 2 = 5$ effect.

*Sales synergy* arising from many products using the same salespersons, warehouses, channels, advertising.

*Investment synergy* arising from many products using the same plant, inventories, R&D, or machinery.

*Operating synergy* arising from many products resulting in higher utilization of facilities, personnel, and spreading of overhead. This usually is maximized in horizontal mergers.

*Management synergy* arising from management experience in handling problems in one industry that helps to solve problems in another industry.

Synergy can be negative too, and Lorange points out that in most mergers, at least one and possibly more of these factors can be negative. In theory, the concept of synergy is appealing. It should be pointed out that there has been little or no systematic proof that synergy actually exists.

---

**RESEARCH** ■ **SELLER'S MOTIVES FOR MERGING**
**STUDY**  **1**  To increase the value of the owners' stock and investment in the firm.

**2**  To increase the firm's growth rate by receiving more resources from the acquiring company.

**3**  To acquire the resources to stabilize operations and make them more efficient.

**4**  For tax reasons: if the firm is owned by a family or individual, it helps deal with estate tax problems.

**5**  To help diversify the owning family's holdings beyond the present firm.

**6**  To deal with top management problems such as management succession for an entrepreneur, then top management, dissension in top management.

---

As can be seen from examining the two lists, there are a number of "matching" reasons; when there are enough matches, mergers are more likely to take place.

## HOW COMPANIES MERGE

Before a successful merger can take place, there must be sound planning, as Ansoff and his associates showed.

Willard Rockwell, Jr., who has been personally involved in a number of mergers, gives these "ten commandments" on acquiring a company:

---

**RESEARCH** ■ **ROCKWELL'S TEN COMMANDMENTS ON HOW TO MERGE**
**STUDY**
"Must" factors

**1**  Pinpoint and spell out the merger objectives, especially earnings objectives.

**2**  Specify substantial gains for the stockholders of both companies.

**3**  Be able to convince yourself that the acquired company's management is—or else can be made—competent.

**4** Certify the existence of important dovetailing resources—but do not expect perfection.

### Other key considerations

**5** Spark the merger program with the chief executive's involvement.

**6** Clearly define the business you are in (for example, bicycles or transportation).

**7** Take a depth sounding of strengths, weaknesses, and other key performance factors—the target acquisition company's and your own.

**8** Create a climate of mutual trust by anticipating problems and discussing them early with the other company.

**9** Do not let "caveman" advances jeopardize the courtship. Do not threaten the management that is to be acquired.

**10** Most important of these latter six rules, make people your no. 1 consideration in structuring your assimilation plan.

---

In effect, Rockwell is suggesting that the firm plan the merger well by profiling the two companies and comparing them. Thus, you could prepare strategic advantage profiles and environmental threat and opportunities profiles for both companies and systematically compare them. Thus he advocates good strategic planning (commandments 1, 4, 6, 7). In essence, he also believes that crucial to merger success are the human and financial considerations. Neisheim has modeled the acquisition process. He describes how to fight off a merger attempt.

## HUMAN AND LEGAL CONSIDERATIONS

Although some of the literature might give you the impression that merging is primarily a financial question, more evidence is arising that Proposition 5–7 is correct.

For example, Ebeid examined one form of mergers: the cash tender offer approach. He studied 117 of such offers over a 17-year period. He really was looking to see whether there were more successful ways of bidding, stock market times, and similar characteristics. One of his major conclusions was that the merger offer was most likely to fail when the management of the target firm opposed the merger offer. This made the merger more costly if it was consummated. But more important, it was less likely to be consummated.

---

**PROPOSITION 5–7** ■ Mergers fail to come to be and fail after consummation more frequently for human reasons than any other reason.

---

The psychologist Levinson has studied merger failures. His major conclusion was:

There are many reasons for merger, including psychological reasons. Many mergers have been disappointing in their results and painful to their participants. These failures have been attributed largely to rational financial, economic, and managerial problems.

I contend that some psychological reasons for merger not only constitute a major, if unrecognized, force toward merger, but that they also constitute the basis for many, if not most, disappointments and failures. At least those that have turned sour, or have the most dangerous potential for turning sour, are those that arise out of some neurotic wish to become big by voraciously gobbling up others, or out of obsolescence.

Such mergers flounder because of the hidden assumptions the senior partner makes, and the condescending attitudes toward the junior organization which then follow. These result in efforts at manipulation and control which, in turn produce (*a*) disillusionment and the feeling of desertion on the part of the junior organization, and (*b*) disappointment, loss of personnel, and declining profitability for the dominant organization.

Many of the human problems develop when the executives of the acquiring company seem threatening to the target company and they fear they will have to leave the firm.

A second question to consider is: Will the relevant government body approve the merger? In the United States, the Antitrust Division of the Justice Department might get involved. In the United Kingdom and the Common Market, there are monopolies commissions. Canada also has a "watchdog" to examine multinational mergers and other mergers.

As will be shown later in the chapter, the most frequent result of mergers is *diminished performance*. Rockwell found most executives dissatisfied with results of their mergers, and so there is good reason for government to try to reduce mergers (Scherer). Companies who do wish to merge need to determine if the relevant government agencies are likely to intervene and try to prevent the merger.

EXTERNAL GROWTH: CONGLOMERATE MERGERS [13]

Conglomerate mergers take place mostly for the same reasons as horizontal or concentric mergers. The exceptions are buyer's reason 5 (to balance or fill out the product line) and buyer's reason 7 (to reduce competition by purchasing a competitor). In fact, legal considerations, especially antitrust reasons, were an additional reason given for the development of conglomerate mergers.

Conglomerate mergers were some of the most discussed mergers in the 1960s. A series of firms became well known during this period. The best known at the height of the publicity about them were featured in a cover story in *Time* (September 8, 1967). These were ITT [whose leader's (Harold Geneen's) face graced the cover], Gulf and Western, Textron, and Ling-Temco-Vought. *For-*

---

**DEFINITION** ■ CONGLOMERATE MERGER
A *conglomerate merger* is a combination of two or more firms in businesses which are not closely related by technology or production processes or markets.

---

**1** Conglomerates' central offices are much smaller than diversified majors'. Usually they have no staff officials (for example, research and development).

**2** Conglomerates tend to place most major operating decisions at decentralized divisional levels. This is often because the central office has no one expert in making operating decisions in that business.

**3** Thus division managers are autonomous as long as the division "delivers."

**4** Diversified majors have better opportunity for synergy than conglomerates.

---

*tune* (May 15, 1969) trumpeted ten whose "impressive earnings records cannot be explained away as just financial trickery. These ten were LTV, Textron, Ogden, Indian Head, Gulf and Western, Walter Kidde, Litton, ITT, Bangor Punta, and City Investing. Since those heady days, many of these firms have fallen on hard times. There have been many apologists or advocates of conglomerates (Attiyeh, Berg, Judelson, Markham, Vance). Winslow and Drucker have been two of the main critics of conglomerates.

Berg has clarified some of the differences between diversified majors (several industry firms) and conglomerates.

Berg defined a conglomerate company as a firm which has at least five or six divisions which sell different products principally to markets rather than to each other. (If they sell privately to each other, they are integrated firms.) Berg says that conglomerates diversified quickly, primarily through mergers, and usually into product-service lines unrelated to their prior business. By "diversified majors," Berg means firms which developed their diversification over a long period of time primarily through internal growth into products or services related to their prior business. Examples of diversified majors given by Berg are Koppers, Borg Warner, and International Harvester. Berg says conglomerate management style is different.

Berg and other "advocates" of conglomerates believe that by placing responsibility where it belongs—at the divisional level—conglomerates can evaluate the performance better and not become involved in operating decisions which prevent top management from performing the strategic planning and evaluation functions.

Conglomerates grew quickly primarily by purchasing other companies for stock when a conglomerate's stock was at a much higher P/E than the target company's stock. Thus the conglomerate growth rate would remain large because of mergers and sometimes because of internal growth as well.

EFFECTIVENESS OF EXTERNAL GROWTH STRATEGIES

Two studies which focus on when mergers are effective will be reviewed now.

Kitching studied 22 firms that merged over a number of years and examined 69 of the 181 mergers of 20 of the companies in the period studied (1960–1965).

■ **KITCHING'S FINDINGS**

**1**   Nearly half the mergers (45 percent of the sample) were of the fashiona- ble conglomerate type. Horizontal acquisitions were the next most common (25 percent), followed by concentric technology (14 percent), concentric marketing (13 percent), and vertical integration (3 percent). There is a rela- tively high risk of failure in concentric acquisitions, and a relatively low one in horizontal mergers.

**2**   A "size mismatch" (where the acquired company's sales were less than 2 percent of the parent company's sales volume before the merger) occurs in 84 percent of the acquisitions considered failures.

**3**   In 81 percent of the failures, the organizational format (either the report- ing relationships established after the merger or the extent of autonomy al- lowed) is disturbed at least once after the acquisition is first brought into the new "family."

**4**   Theoretically, synergy in mergers should be greatest where production facilities are combined, because economies of scale are possible. Combina- tions based on technology (process know-how and R&D transfer), market- ing, organization (personnel economies and productivity increases), and fi- nance (additional and lower-cost capital) should be of diminishing value, in that order. According to top managers, however, the ease with which syn- ergy is actually released occurs in the reverse order; that is, synergy is most easily accomplished where financial resources are pooled, and it is most dif- ficult to achieve where production facilities are combined. Furthermore, the dollar payoff is actually lowest on the average, where production and tech- nological resources are put together; highest, where financial resources are combined.

**5**   Failure rates vary by types of merger:

| Acquisition type | Percent of total | Percent of failures |
|---|---|---|
| Vertical integration | 3 | 0 |
| Horizontal | 25 | 11 |
| Concentric marketing | 13 | 26 |
| Concentric technology | 14 | 21 |
| Conglomerate | 45 | 42 |

In addition, Kitching believes that a major reason for failure is lack of planning before mergers with the result that two managements which sepa- rately could manage two firms were unable to manage the combined firm effectively.

Drucker agrees strongly with Kitching, especially his fifth point. He says:

Never was the belief in diversification [especially diversification by merger] as a panacea more widely held than in the 1950's and 1960's. Yet the success stories of these years were not the businesses that diversified [by mergers] let alone the conglomerates. They were businesses with one central product or product line, one central market, one central technology.

The examples he gives are: IBM, Xerox, Sony, Honda, Toyota, Fiat, Volkswa- gen, Pilkington Glass (England), Atlas, Copco (Swedish drilling firm), Sears,

**TABLE 5-3 ■ ESTIMATED PERCENTAGE OF FIRMS IN EACH STRATEGIC CATEGORY**

| Strategic category | 1949 | 1959 | 1969 |
|---|---|---|---|
| *Major classes* | | | |
| Single business[a] | 34.5 | 16.2 | 6.2 |
| Dominant business[b] | 35.4 | 37.3 | 29.2 |
| Related business[c] | 26.7 | 40.0 | 45.2 |
| Unrelated business[d] | 3.4 | 6.5 | 19.4 |
| *Minor classes* | | | |
| Single business[a] | 34.5 | 16.2 | 6.2 |
| Dominant vertical (integrated)[b] | 15.7 | 14.8 | 15.6 |
| Dominant constrained (tied to prior business)[b] | 18.0 | 16.0 | 7.1 |
| Dominant linked (diversified with some ties to prior business) | 0.9 | 3.8 | 5.6 |
| Dominant unrelated (diversified position is unrelated to dominant)[b] | 0.9 | 2.6 | 0.9 |
| Related constrained (related closely to past business)[c] | 18.8 | 29.1 | 21.6 |
| Related linked (diversification linked to past business to some degree)[c] | 7.9 | 10.9 | 23.6 |
| Unrelated passive conglomerate[d] | 3.4 | 5.3 | 8.5 |
| Acquisitive conglomerate[d] | 0.0 | 1.2 | 10.9 |
| Number of firms used to derive the estimates | 189 | 207 | 183 |

[a] 95 percent or more of business in one end product business.
[b] 70 to 94 percent of business in one end product business.
[c] Less than 70 percent in one end product business, and diversification primarily in concentrically related products.
[d] Less than 70 percent in one end product business and diversification unrelated to primary product group.

Marks and Spencer (British retailer), Enskilda Bank (Sweden), Prentice-Hall, Eastman Kodak, GM, and Swiss pharmaceutical firms.

The other study is that of Rumelt. He examined the performance from 1949 to 1969 of 250 large United States firms in a very sophisticated research project. He was interested in the relation between types of growth and performance. First he classified the firms into strategic categories at various points in recent years as shown in Table 5–3. A summary of Rumelt's findings regarding growth and performance is included.

Propositions 5–8, 5–9, and 5–10 summarize the results of the major research studies on mergers.

---

**RESEARCH STUDY** ■ **GROWTH AND PERFORMANCE** [RUMELT]

Although performance varied within each category (for example, single business), subgroups did perform differently. The *worst* performers were vertically integrated (dominant vertical) and unrelated passive. The *highest* performers were dominant constrained and related constrained. The *average* performers were related linked and acquisitive conglomerate.

---

**PROPOSITION 5–8** ■ In general, merged companies have grown less than the sum of the growth rates of the separate companies.

---

**PROPOSITION**
**5-9**

**PROPOSITION** ■ In general, the stockholders of the merging firm are worse off than if the firm
**5-9** had not been merged.

**PROPOSITION** ■ In general, horizontal and concentric mergers were more effective than con-
**5-10** glomerate mergers for their stockholders.

Of course, someone usually benefits from mergers. The usual group to benefit is the executive group heading the acquiring firm. Salaries tend to be correlated with firm size. So their salaries and power are greater. The losers have been the stockholders of the acquiring firm. Many times the employees of the acquired firm also are worse off: they lose their jobs or get shuffled about. The merger brokers also get fat fees. Studies by Samuels, Reid, Hogarty, Lynch, Stich, and others support Propositions 5-8, 5-9, and 5-10. Lev and Mandelker are not quite as critical of mergers as the others. In general, though, joint earnings are lower and joint stock prices are lower, for most mergers. It is obvious that not all mergers fail; many studies cited by Reid indicate 75 percent of merged firms are worse off than unmerged firms. But mergers look like an easy way to grow and look dramatic and decisive as well.

### VERTICAL INTEGRATION AS A GROWTH STRATEGY [14]

The final growth strategy is vertical integration.

Examples of vertical integration include the following. Holiday Inns integrated backward when it created a supplies division and began producing furniture and distributing items like cleaning supplies and food for its inns. Ashland Oil could integrate forward if it decided to sell all its output of gasoline through its own service stations instead of most of it through distributors. Seven-Up vertically integrated backward when it bought its flavor supplier and then the lemon groves which provided the raw materials for the flavor company and Seven-Up. Falstaff could integrate forward by buying its distributors and then buying beer outlets such as bars or beverage outlets. Webster describes the vertical integration strategy of Exxon from 1911 to 1963.

Several theorists have speculated about why firms follow a vertical integration strategy.

**DEFINITION** ■ VERTICAL INTEGRATION
*Vertical integration* is a growth strategy which is characterized by the extension of the firm's business definition in two possible directions from the present.

A *backward* integration strategy has the firm entering the business of supplying some of the firm's present inputs.

A *forward* integration strategy moves the firm into the business of distribution of the output of the firm by entering the channels closer to the ultimate consumer.

Vertical integration can take place by internal growth or external growth (merger).

Scott believes that growth in volume but not complexity will lead to more capital-intensive production and distribution. This leads to vertical integration. Thompson holds that firms with long linked technologies will be more effective if they grow through vertical integration. Thompson also believes that firms with intensive technologies will be more effective if they grow by incorporating the object worked on.

Williamson points out that economists have not studied vertical integration very much but are suspicious of it. Perhaps, he argues, that is because economists tend to assume that the supplier market is operating well. This may not be the case and so firms may wish to improve the continuity and quality of supply by vertically integrating. But, as Williamson points out, this can have anticompetitive effects by causing more barriers to entry.

Vertical integration has not been a frequently used strategy.

### GROWTH STRATEGIES: A SUMMARY [15]

The preceding section has described various types of growth strategies, the extent of the use, and why they are used. There are many of them. Table 5–4 summarizes the growth strategies which the J. M. Smucker Company, manufacturer of fruit products such as jams, jellies, and ice cream toppings, could use. This may help you tie the strategies together better.

## Retrenchment strategies [16]

A slogan to characterize the retrenchment strategy might be: "Slow Down and Catch Your Breath: We've Got to Do Better." This strategy is probably the least frequently used strategy of all those discussed.

**TABLE 5–4 ■ POTENTIAL GROWTH STRATEGIES FOR THE J. M. SMUCKER COMPANY**

| | Internal | External | Integrated plan |
|---|---|---|---|
| **Vertical** | | | |
| Forward | Build Smucker stores to sell products in | Acquire or merge with XYZ stores | Develop firm either vertically or horizontally |
| Backward | Develop Smucker's orchards, glassworks, box factories, etc. | Acquire or merge with ABC orchards, etc. | |
| **Horizontal** | | | |
| Similar products | Develop Smucker's peanut butter, honey, and similar goods | Acquire or merge with Sioux Bee Honey, Jumbo Peanut Butter, etc. | Develop a concentrically diversified firm |
| Different products added | Develop products similar to the present line, such as fruit, fruit candy | Acquire or merge with firms that fit company's personality | Develop a concentrically diversified firm |
| No product scope defined (conglomerate) | Develop and market products which fit corporate image | Acquire or merge with firms that fit firm's image | Develop a conglomerate multi-industry firm |

A *retrenchment strategy* is one that an enterprise pursues when it decides to improve its performance in reaching its objectives by:

1 Focusing on functional improvement, especially reduction of costs

2 Reducing the number of functions it performs by becoming a captive company

3 Reducing the number of the products and markets it serves up to and including liquidation of the business

## WHY A RETRENCHMENT STRATEGY?

This strategy is the hardest to follow; it goes against the grain of most strategic planners. It implies failure. Just as most business executives hate to cut prices, they hate a retrenchment strategy. Why do they follow it then? A few reasons are:

1 The firm is not doing well or perceives itself as doing poorly.

2 The firm has not met its objectives by following one of the three other strategies and there is pressure to improve performance, from stockholders, customers, or others. It is the strategy of last resort.

## ARE RETRENCHMENT STRATEGIES EFFECTIVE?

Any strategy, if chosen at the right time and implemented properly, will be effective. The retrenchment strategy is the best one for the firm which has tried everything, has made some mistakes, and is now ready to do something about it. The more serious the crisis, the more serious the retrenchment strategy needs to be. For minor crises, cutback in costs and operations will do. For moderate crises, divestiture of some divisions or units may be necessary. For serious crises, a captive company strategy or even liquidation may be necessary. Rucker found its strategy of divestment from its prior conglomerate strategy to single-industry strategy in the mid-1970s very effective.

## CUTBACK AND TURNAROUND STRATEGY

One strategy a firm can take when it hits hard times is to try to make itself more efficient in everything it does. The firm may be facing stable or declining sales or profits. Eisenberg has suggested some ways to reduce administrative costs, increase production and sales efficiency, and make better use of cash and other financial resources by improving research and development and checking computer costs and similar approaches to budget cutting. Usually personnel are reduced by attrition, or in more serious cases, by percentage cuts. Perhaps the product line is shortened and more emphasis is put on the profitable products. Maybe advertising and sales promotion are reduced. The company may trim its customer list to save transportation and sales costs. Inventory may be more closely controlled. Cheaper materials may be used. The strategy may become: hold the present business but cut the costs. Schendel and his associates have described some effective examples of turnarounds in the reading at the end of this chapter.

Personnel cuts can be especially traumatic and in the long run may cost the company money if later on new employees have to be hired and trained.

Some recent examples illustrate a cutback strategy. W. T. Grant (opening in 1905) grew to 1182 stores by 1973. From 1969 to 1973, it opened 376 new stores—15 new ones in one day. By 1974, costs were rising and profits dropping. Grant's president decided to reduce its operations to the best 900 stores and cut capital spending by 90 percent. This retrenchment was designed to improve performance. Later, Grant took the next step: divested itself of its stake in Zeller to raise money. National Tea Company, the large grocery chain, went through a similar reduction in 1973–1974. In 1974–1975, Teledyne took drastic steps to save its Argonaut Insurance unit. In 1971, Goodyear deliberately reduced many of its products for the same purpose. In some divisions, 20 percent of the products were reduced. In a similar move, Du Pont eliminated Corfam after an investment of $100 million.

A&P in 1975 perceived itself in such trouble that it cut back one-third of its stores, including whole regions like the Texas division.

The *Wall Street Journal* was full of stories of firms cutting back to prevent a situation bad enough to require a turnaround strategy. Thus Singer, Allied Stores, Greyhound, Evans Products, and others were involved in cost cutting to improve profits and operations.

Effective managers-owners choose a cutback strategy when their growth, combination, or stability strategy is perceived threatened by short-run environmental pressures. It is considered to be only a temporary strategy by effective managers-owners.

Firms which do not adopt a cutback strategy when environmental pressures call for it could become pathological and be forced into captive company or liquidation strategy.

The cutback strategy is a typical reaction to difficult or bad times. Most firms react to adversity with this strategy, usually expecting it to be a short-run strategy, and then shift to one of the other three strategies. It will be interesting to see what turnaround strategy will be effective at Pan American Airways.


### DIVESTMENT STRATEGY

In a cutback strategy, the firm eliminates costs or products to improve efficiency. In a divestment strategy, the firm decides to get out of certain lines of business and sells off units, divisions, or autonomous companies. Some of the best-known divestitures recently have been:

RCA's sale of its computer business

General Electric's sale of its computer and phonograph business

Motorola's sale of its television business

Continental Telephone's sale of its data services businesses

Westinghouse's sale of its appliances division and mail-order business

Union Carbide's sale of semiconductor components

And the list could be quite long. Vignola found that divestment increased 70 percent from 1971 to 1972.

There are a number of reasons why a firm might desire to divest. Several of these are:

1  Inadequate market share or sales growth

2  Lower profit than other divisions

3  Technological change requiring more resources than the company is willing to commit

4  Antitrust requirements such as Procter and Gamble's Clorox case or ITT's Avis and Automatic Canteen cases

With the exception of the fourth reason the conditions in Proposition 5–11 apply.

Davis suggests that a divestiture committee follow the decision process in Figure 5–3 to make this decision.

Vignola provides sensible advice on what to do before divestment. In effect he suggests the preparation of the environmental threat and opportunities profile and strategic advantage profile for each division. He describes the technical decisions to be made to price and sell the unit off if the decision is made to divest.

Gilmore closely examined the divestment decision in three large firms. He tried to see whether the decisions were made "rationally" or even behaviorally as Cyert and March or Bower suggested.

Again, we contrast the normative position (divest when it makes financial sense) with the reality. The CEOs hate to admit a mistake; they believe the division will turn around if given just a little more time and good luck, and so they put off making a decision. So divestment committees should be aware of the tendency to put off divestment decisions if the CEO had earlier ties with the division.

---

**PROPOSITION 5–11**  ■ When financial return from a unit drops below the minimally required level for a reasonable period of time, the unit should be divested.

---

**RESEARCH STUDY**  ■ **GILMORE'S FINDINGS ON DIVESTITURES**

1  When chief executives received recommendations to divest products or divisions which they had commitments because of their previous decisions, they put the decision off.

2  The board of directors appointed new chief executive officers after normal retirement of the previous CEO with the understanding that he would divest.

3  The new CEO, unrestrained by prior personal commitments, values, etc., and by the board's expectations, divested the divisions for rational economic reasons.

---

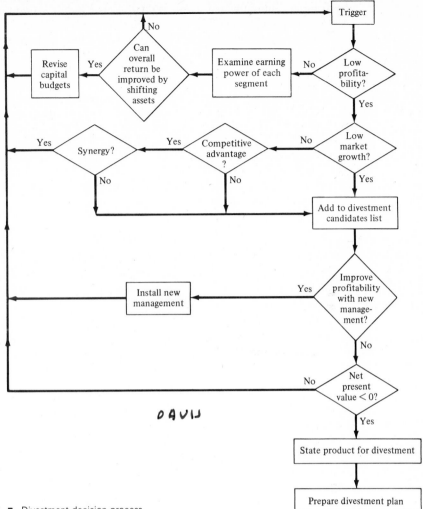

FIGURE 5–3 ■ Divestment decision process.

### CAPTIVE COMPANY STRATEGY

A third strategy which can be seen as a retrenchment strategy is to become the captive of your present or potentially largest customer. In effect, when you become captive, your captor makes many decisions for you. Perhaps these decisions include product design, production control, and quality control. The captor negotiates the price of the goods usually from a position of strength.

A captive company may retrench into this position intentionally or unintentionally. Many captives are firms that supply well-known retailers (such as Sears, Safeway, Kroger) or produce part of the line of well-known brands. For example, Foulds produces most of its pasta output for Kraft. Whirlpool produces most of its output as Sears's Kenmore appliances.

Among large firms that are captives are I. D. Packing, Hempe Manufacturing, and Kellwood Company. A case on Kellwood is contained in this book.

The captive negotiates the price with the captor, assuring itself of adequate return much in the way a public utility and the public service commission of a state relate. The captive becomes closely tied to the results of its major purchaser, and this can be risky. Still it is a way to assure adequate profitability, especially if the company competes with much bigger companies that can spend large amounts on advertising and marketing. Most captive companies are not well known, but they can be large.

This strategy requires a management that is able to develop good long-term relationships with its major customer. In a way, it is a strategy that can be as risky as doing most of your business with the military. But if the contractual relationship is a good one, the firm can prosper and hedge against the loss of business by developing its own line, as Whirlpool is doing very successfully now. Still, many executives intuitively like to be relatively independent and this strategy may be unrewarding to them. It may be one of the few choices a firm has at times, however.

As you will see in analyzing Kellwood, not all captives become captives by retrenchment. Kellwood was formed to strengthen 15 of Sears's suppliers. Effective managers-owners choose a captive company strategy because of (1) inability or unwillingness to strengthen the marketing function or (2) the perception that this strategy is the best means to achieve financial strength. It will be rationalized as a security strategy but is in fact risky and costly to prestige and independence needs of the manager.

## LIQUIDATION STRATEGY

The ultimate retrenchment, at least in the present business, is to *sell out*. Of course, firms sell out for reasons other than retrenchment. Someone is willing to pay much more for the business than the executives think it is worth, and there are suitable (or even better) alternative investments or businesses to use the funds in. Or the executives may feel the business is at its peak and has nowhere to go but down, and so they decide to get out. They may be tired or old, or both, or they may be inefficient and know it (or become convinced of it). The firm may be spinning its wheels and getting nowhere for lack of resources or many other reasons. Buyers may be willing to buy even extremely poorly run businesses for tax losses, or they may believe they can "turn the business around." But selling the firm is one strategy that can and in some cases must be considered.

Some firms and executives seem unable to take this step, even when it would be desirable. If work has been a central life interest to the executive, it can seem psychologically like selling an old friend to sell the business. A particular business can "get in your blood," and without it, life would have little or no meaning to many executives. To others, as long as there is "action," one business or another will do. Again, the values of the executives can be crucial in this choice.

Some recent examples of liquidation or sell-out strategy include:

Rolls Royce Ltd. (England)

Halcyon the Great (Canada)

Simon Cigar (Canada)

Royal Castle System

**PROPOSITION**
**5–12**
■ An effective manager-owner will sell the company when its present liquidation value is more than the discounted present flow of the firm's future flow of income (modified normative economic theory model).

A variation of liquidation is to liquidate a division.

Richard Hexter points out that selling a company is an investment decision whose objective should be to increase the value of the owner's equity in the future. He points out that although many firms have acquisition departments, he knows none with a department of divestiture or a director of being acquired.

Frequently, Hexter contends, the decision to sell is hasty, ill thought out, and dependent on the first buyer who offers or who the top executive feels will treat them "right." Once the decision to sell out is made, the company should decide what the company is worth on the basis of its tangible assets, its management, its products, and all intangible assets. Hexter suggests that the skillful company wishing to sell will select buyers as carefully as merger-bound companies seek acquisition. They will evaluate offers in the same way as considering a merger: they will discount the future flow of funds to present value. Effective managers-owners choose to sell out or terminate business under three conditions: (1) when they perceive their firm as unable to compete; (2) when they choose to leave the business for personal reasons such as retirement; and (3) when they perceive their opportunities are better in another business.

In theory, Proposition 5–12 is true.

We have no detailed studies of selling out firms. But if Gilmore's findings are accurate, how much more likely are presidents to do all they can to prevent selling out except when they want to retire or see better opportunities elsewhere.

## Strategic alternatives and strategic planning

This chapter has described what strategic alternatives are available to firms. It tells which ones are used most frequently and when each is most likely to be effective.

Again, we learned that managers consider a limited number of alternatives, usually the closest to the present strategic choice. Considering major shifts takes place only when the firm feels severely threatened by the environment.

In Chapter 6, we will review how the manager chooses *the* strategy from the alternatives developed as a result of the strategic alternative generation process just described here.

## References

[1] Ansoff, H. Igor, and John Stewart: "Strategies for Technology Based Business," *Harvard Business Review,* **45** (6): November–December 1967.

Donaldson, Gordon: *Strategy for Financial Mobility,* Cambridge, Mass.: Harvard University Press, 1969.

Gibson, R. E.: "The Strategy of Corporate Research and Development," *California Management Review,* Fall 1966.

Schwartz, Eli, and J. Richard Aronson: "Some Surrogate Evidence in Support of the Concept of Optimal Financial Structure," *Journal of Finance,* 1967.

Skinner, Wickham: "Manufacturing: Missing Link in Corporate Strategy," *Harvard Business Review,* **47** (3): May–June 1969.

[2] Barnard, Chester: *The Functions of the Executive,* Cambridge, Mass.: Harvard University Press, 1938.

Bonis, Jean: "Organization and Environment," *International Studies of Management and Organization,* **2** (3): 314–343, Fall 1972.

[3] Bell, Gerald: "Organizations and External Environment," in J. McGuire (ed.), *Contemporary Management,* Englewood Cliffs, N.J.: Prentice-Hall, 1974.

Sales, Arnaud: "The Firm and Control of Its Environment," *International Studies of Management and Organization,* **2** (3): 230–257, Fall 1972.

[4] McCaskey, Michael: "A Contingency Approach to Planning," *Academy of Management Journal,* **17** (2): 281–291, June 1974.

[5] MacCrimmon, Kenneth: "Managerial Decision Making," in J. McGuire (ed.), *Contemporary Management,* Englewood Cliffs, N.J.: Prentice-Hall, 1974.

[6] Hanna, Richard: "The Concept of Corporate Strategy in Multi-Industry Companies," unpublished D.B.A. dissertation, Harvard Business School, 1968.

Kami, Michael: "Business Planning as Business Opportunity," in Peter Drucker (ed.), *Preparing Tomorrow's Business Leaders Today,* Englewood Cliffs, N.J.: Prentice-Hall, 1969.

[7] Hutchins, John: "Recent Contributions to Business History: The United States," *Journal of Economic History,* **19:** March 1959.

[8] Cooper, Arnold, et al.: "Strategic Responses to Technological Threats," *Proceedings, Academy of Management,* 1973.

Katz, Robert: *Management of the Total Enterprise,* Englewood Cliffs, N.J.: Prentice-Hall, 1971.

[9] Some references on growth in general include:

Drucker, Peter: *Management,* New York: Harper & Row, 1974, chap. 60.

Guth, William: "The Growth and Profitability of the Firm: A Managerial Explanation," *Journal of Business Policy,* **2** (3): Spring 1972.

Hall, William: "Strategic Planning, Product Innovation and the Theory of the Firm," *Journal of Business Policy,* **3** (3): Spring 1973.

McGuire, Joseph: *Factors Affecting the Growth of Manufacturing Firms,* Seattle: University of Washington Bureau of Business Research, 1963.

Mueller, Dennis: "A Life Cycle Theory of the Firm," *Journal of Industrial Economics,* **20** (3): July 1972.

Tilles, Seymour: "Developmental Models and Corporate Growth," *California Management Review,* **6** (3): Spring 1964.

Troughton, F.: "Growth & Organization in Business: Their Roots in Nature," *Management International Review,* **2/3:** 1970.

Worchester, Robert: "Planning for Growth in Leading U.S. Firms," *Long Range Planning,* **2** (3): 1970.

**[10]** Argenti, John: *Systematic Corporate Planning,* New York: Halstead Press, Wiley, 1974, chap. 13.

Chevalier, Michel: "The Strategy Spectre behind Your Market Share," *European Business,* Summer 1974.

—— and Bernard Catry: "Don't Misuse Your Market Share Goal," *European Business,* pp. 43–50, Winter–Spring 1974.

Copulsky, William, and Herbert McNulty: *Entrepreneurship and the Corporation,* New York: Amacom, 1974.

Fruhan, William, Jr.: *The Fight for Competitive Advantage: A Study of U.S. Domestic Trunk Airlines,* Cambridge, Mass.: Harvard University Press, 1972.

——: "Pyrrhic Victories in Fights for Market Share," *Harvard Business Review,* September–October 1972.

Gutman, Peter: "Strategies for Growth," *California Management Review,* **6** (4): Summer 1964.

Hake, Bruno: *Hazards of Growth,* London: Longmans, 1974, chap. 5.

Hanan, Mark: "Corporate Growth through Venture Management," *Harvard Business Review,* January–February 1969.

——: "Corporate Growth through Internal Spinoffs," *Harvard Business Review,* November–December 1969.

Litschert, Robert: "Some Characteristics of Long Range Planning: An Industry Study," *Academy of Management Journal,* September 1968.

——: *Perspectives on Experience,* Boston: Boston Consulting Group, 1970.

Roberts, Edward, and Alan Frohman: "Internal Entrepreneurship: Strategy for Growth," *Business Quarterly,* Spring 1972.

Susbauer, Jeffrey: "Some Empirical and Theoretical Implication of Internal Entrepreneurship Programs," *Proceedings, Midwest Business Administration Association,* April 1972.

**[11]** Ansoff, H. Igor: *Corporate Strategy,* New York: McGraw-Hill, 1965.

——: "Toward a Strategic Theory of the Firm," in *Business Strategy,* London: Penguin, 1970.

Bright, Willard: "Alternative Strategies for Diversification," *Research Management,* July 1969.

Chandler, Alfred, Jr., and Herman Daems: "The Rise of Managerial Capitalism and Its Impact on Investment Strategy in the Western World and Japan," Working Paper, European Institute for Advanced Studies in Management, 1974.

Didricksen, Jon: "The Development of Diversified and Conglomerate Firms in the United States 1920–1970," *Business History Review,* **46** (2): Summer 1972.

Drucker, Peter: *Management,* op. cit., chaps. 56, 57.

Hake, Bruno: "Strategies for Diversification," *Long Range Planning,* **5** (2): 1972.

——: *Hazards of Growth,* op. cit.

Mason, R. S.: "Product Diversification and the Small Firm," *Journal of Business Policy,* **3** (3): Spring 1973.

Steiner, George: "Why and How to Diversify," *California Management Review,* **6** (4): Summer 1964.

**[12]** Boulden, James: "Merger Negotiations: A Decision Model," *Business Horizons,* **12** (1): 1969.

*California Management Review,* **16** (4): Summer 1974. Issue devoted to antitrust.

Caves, Richard: *American Industry's Structure, Conduct, and Performance,* Englewood Cliffs, N.J.: Prentice-Hall, 1967.

Chandler, Alfred, Jr.: "The Structure of American Industry in the Twentieth Century," *Business History Review,* **43** (3): Autumn 1969.

Copulsky, William, and Herbert McNulty: *Entrepreneurship and the Corporation,* op. cit., chap. 6.

Davis, Richard: "Compatibility in Corporate Marriages," *Harvard Business Review,* **46** (4): July–August 1968.

Ebeid, Fred: "The Interfirm Corporate Cash Tender Offer: Operating, Market and Bid Characteristics of Target Firms," unpublished Ph.D. thesis, University of Illinois, 1974.

Handy, John: "How to Face Being Taken Over," *Harvard Business Review,* November–December 1969.

Hastings, Robert: "In the Wake of a Merger: The Human Trauma," *Business Horizons,* June 1970.

Levinson, Harry: "A Psychologist Diagnoses Merger Failures," *Harvard Business Review,* March–April 1970.

Lorange, Peter: "A Note on Merger Analysis," Intercollegiate Case Clearinghouse no. 9–272–693, Harvard Business School, 1972.

————: "A Note on Merger Negotiations," Intercollegiate Case Clearinghouse no. 9–272–692, Harvard Business School, 1972.

MacDougal, Gary, and Fred Malek: "Master Plan for Merger Negotiations," *Harvard Business Review,* January–February 1970.

Mazzolini, Renato: "European Mergers Are Fine . . . without the Europeans," *European Business,* Summer 1974.

Reum, W. Robert, and Thomas Steele III: "Contingency Payouts Cut Acquisition Risks," *Harvard Business Review,* March–April 1970.

Rockwell, Willard, Jr.: "How to Acquire a Company," *Harvard Business Review,* **46** (5): September–October 1968.

Samuels, J. M. (ed.): *Readings on Mergers and Takeovers,* New York: St. Martin's, 1972.

Scherer, F. M.: *Industrial Market Structure and Economic Performance,* Chicago: Rand McNally, 1970, especially chaps. 9, 11, 12, 17, 19–22.

Searby, Frederich: "Control Post Merger Change," *Harvard Business Review,* September–October 1969.

Smalter, Donald, and Roderic Lavely: "P/E Analysis on Acquisition Strategy," *Harvard Business Review,* **44** (6): November–December 1966.

Spurgeon, I. N.: "Diversification by Acquisition: The Problem of Price/Earnings Ratio Disparity," *Journal of Business Policy,* **1** (3): 1970.

Wittnebert, Fred: "Bigness vs. Profitability," *Harvard Business Review,* January–February 1970.

**[13]** Attiyeh, Robert: "Where Next for Conglomerates?" *Business Horizons,* Dec. 1969.

Berg, Norman: "Strategic Planning in Conglomerate Companies," *Harvard Business Review,* May–June 1965.

————: "What's Different about Conglomerate Management?" *Harvard Business Review,* November–December 1969.

Drucker, Peter: *Management,* op. cit., especially chaps. 56, 57.

"Fortune:" *The Conglomerate Commotion,* New York: Viking, 1970.

Lynch, Harry: *Financial Performance of Conglomerates,* Cambridge, Mass.: Harvard Business School, 1971.

Markham, Jesse: *Conglomerate Enterprise and Public Policy,* Cambridge, Mass.: Harvard University Press, 1973.

Simkowitz, Michael, and Robert Monroe: "A Discriminate Analysis Function for Conglomerate Targets," *Southern Journal of Business,* **6** (3): November 1971.

Stone, David: *An Economic Approach to Planning the Conglomerate of the 70's,* Princeton: Auerbach, 1970.

Vance, Stanley: "The Management of Multi Industry Corporations," *Proceedings, Academy of Management,* 1969.

————: *Managers in the Conglomerate Era,* New York: Wiley, Interscience, 1971.

Winslow, John: *Conglomerates Unlimited,* Bloomington: Indiana University Press, 1973.

**[14]** Webster, Frederick: "A Model of Vertical Integration Strategy," *California Management Review,* **10** (2): 1967.

Williamson, Oliver: "The Vertical Integration of Production: Market Failure Considerations," *American Economic Review,* May 1971.

**[15]** Ansoff, H. Igor, et al.: *Acquisition Behavior of U.S. Manufacturing Firms 1946–1965,* Nashville, Tenn.: Vanderbilt University Press, 1971.

Hogarty, Thomas: "The Profitability of Corporate Mergers," *Journal of Business,* **43** (3): 317–327, 1970.

Kitching, John: "Why Do Mergers Miscarry?" *Harvard Business Review,* **45** (6): 84–101, November–December 1967.

Lev, Baruch, and Gershon Mandelker: "The Microeconomic Consequences of Corporate Mergers," *Journal of Business,* **45** (1): 85–104, January 1972.

Lintner, John: "Expectations, Mergers, and Equilibrium in Purely Competitive Securities Markets," *American Economic Review,* pp. 101–112, May 1971.

Reid, Samuel: "Is the Merger the Best Way to Grow?" *Business Horizons,* **12** (1): 41–50, 1969.

Rumelt, Richard: *Strategy, Structure, and Economic Performance,* Boston: Harvard Business School, 1974.

Samuels, J. M.: "The Success or Failure of Mergers and Takeovers," in J. M. Samuels, (ed.), *Readings on Mergers and Takeovers,* op. cit.

Schall, Lawrence: "Asset Valuation, Firm Investment, and Firm Diversification," *Journal of Business,* **45** (1): 11–28, January 1972.

Scherer, F. M.: *Industrial Market Structure and Economic Performance,* op. cit.

Schoeffler, Sidney, et al.: "Impact of Strategic Planning on Profit Performance," *Harvard Business Review,* pp. 137–145, March–April 1974.

Stich, Robert: "Have U.S. Mergers Been Profitable?" *Management International Review,* **14** (2/3): 33–40, 1974.

Weston, J. Fred, and S. K. Mansinghka: "Tests of the Efficiency of Performance of Conglomerate Firms," *Journal of Finance,* September 1971.

**[16]** Bettauer, Arthur: "Strategy for Divestments," *Harvard Business Review,* March–April 1967.

Davis, James: "The Strategic Divestment Decision," *Long Range Planning,* pp. 15–18, February 1974.

Franko, Edward: "One Company's Cast Off Technology Is Another Company's Opportunity," *Innovation,* **23:** 52–59, August 1971.

Eisenberg, Joseph: *Turnaround Management,* New York: McGraw-Hill, 1972.

Gilmore, Stuart: "The Divestment Decision Process," unpublished D.B.A. dissertation, Harvard Business School, 1973.

Hayes, Robert: "New Emphasis on Divestment Opportunities," *Harvard Business Review,* pp. 55–64, July–August 1972.

Hexter, Richard: "How to Sell Your Company," *Harvard Business Review,* **46** (5): 71–77, September–October 1968.

Vignola, Leonard: *Strategic Divestment,* New York: Amacona, 1974.

Wallender, Harvey, III: "A Planned Approach to Divestment," *Columbia Journal of World Business,* **8** (1): 33–37, Spring 1973.

# A systematic approach to diversification*

E. G. Malmlow

## Diversification as a planned strategy

Corporate strategic planning[1] includes the generation or thorough revision of:

*The purpose* of the corporation—a written statement describing the company as it should evolve during the next 5–10 years;

*The strategies*—a set of decisions as to how to produce the consequent changes from the existing situation, especially how to allocate available resources among the various actions needed;

*The strategic goals*—a list of specific, measurable results to be attained from year to year during the period planned for; and

*The development projects*—all programmed for the controlled implementation of the chosen strategies.

The strategies and their development projects aim at a whole range of changes. Included are (a) strategies and projects for those changes in the existing business which will require considerable resources, such as major efficiency improvements in some areas, expansion in certain markets, renewal of old product lines, weeding out of unprofitable products, and disposition of undesirable parts of the business, and (b) strategies and projects for diversification into new lines of business, through either internal research and development (R & D) efforts or acquisitions of companies already active in such different businesses, or suitable combinations of these two lines of action, for example R & D efforts organized in coalitions with other enterprises. Figure 1 shows this structure of the strategic plan, and the interrelationships between its component parts. In Figure 2 the same classes of strategies have been grouped in a simple product-market matrix. In the discussion that follows, the diversification strategies and projects are given special attention.

*The strategic planning process* as now developed and well proven in practice comprises an integrated set of structured tasks. One of these tasks is to determine the financial potential of the corporation for the coming years as a realistic growth rate that may actually be achieved. This analysis results in the choice of financially important strategies and a projection of the funds which will become available for investments for each year ahead. By comparing

* Reprinted by permission from *Long Range Planning,* **6** (4): December 1973, pp. 2–12. Copyright © 1973 by Pergamon Press Ltd.

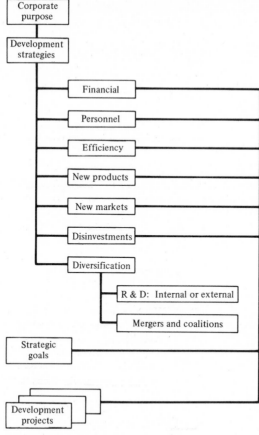

**FIGURE 1** ■ Structure of the corporate strategic plan.

these investment volumes with the needs estimated for all the already existing investment ideas, the financial situation immediately becomes clear. In most cases one easily finds well-defended uses for all the money to become available during the first 2, possibly 3 years ahead. But then there is normally a widening investment gap between the cash to become available and any profitable uses of that cash. Figure 3 illustrates this planning situation which, when faced by the top management planning team, automatically leads to some pertinent and crucial questions. Must one not immediately start some serious work on creating enough new ideas for the further development of the corporation? Should they be for higher efficiency, for more of the same products, for better products, or perhaps for different lines of business? In practically all cases in the author's experience, top management has decided also to initiate or strengthen the diversification strategy of the corporation, and to start active work on its implementation by means of a project to search for and develop opportunities for new lines of business.

Let it be said, to be sure, that many organizations have decided to diversify without having gone through the logical planning process presumed here. The acquisition route has been especially popular in such cases. But the contention here is none the less that the chances for a successful outcome are considerably

| Market \ Product | Present | New |
|---|---|---|
| Present | Efficiency disinvestment | New products |
| New | New markets | Diversification |

**FIGURE 2** ■ Product-market matrix.

increased when the diversification decision is an organic part of a comprehensive strategic plan. Only then does the project receive the widespread support from within the organization which it requires, only then are the directions in which to look given at the outset, and only then are the investment volumes to aim at properly balanced with the various expansion opportunities into new products and new markets, and clearly stated for several years ahead.

## Organization of diversification projects

The first major effort to move from a strategic decision all the way to a recommendation for the corporation to enter a new line of business is always best organized under the aegis of an *ad hoc* task force. A member of the top management team should be appointed leader of the project, and the other members of the group should represent different vital functions among which marketing and production at least are mandatory.

The project work is divided into two phases: an idea phase, and then an information, analysis, and entry strategy phase. During the idea phase the task force should undertake much of the project work itself in group meetings, individually between meetings, and in the form of interviews with other members of the organization. The result from this phase is a set of promising clusters of ideas, which should be investigated further during the second phase. For each such idea cluster a study leader is appointed to direct the relevant work.

During the information phase, the task force acts as a steering body for the work now delegated to the study leaders. The result will be a set of recommendations from the study leaders, either to enter a new line of business or to abandon the investigated business area. Positive recommendations are accompanied by suggested entry strategies and estimates of investment needs and profitability.

Because of the uncertainty of success and because management wishes to retain organizational flexibility when it comes to a decision to enter a new line of business, all team members make their contributions to the project on a

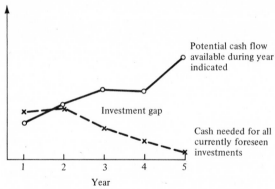

FIGURE 3 ■ Investment gap analysis—a unique and powerful planning tool.

part-time basis. They must therefore delegate more of their normal work to others during the project time period. Those who serve as study leaders do not all consider this arrangement a happy solution, it must be admitted, because they become so interested in their studies that they would wish to spend all their time on the new project. But when faced with the only realistic alternatives, they too agree with the chosen organizational method. It works out rather well in practice.

The total time needed for a typical effort of this kind is 3 to 4 months for the idea phase and 8 to 9 months for the information phase. This schedule also makes it possible to start a project when the strategies have all been decided upon as part of the planning work one year, and then have the resulting recommendations submitted in time for the strategy decision meetings during the following year.

Already then the objective may be reached of having more promising investment opportunities to choose from then there are funds available during as many as 3 or 4 years ahead. Then a new major diversification project can wait one more year. If the objective mentioned has not been reached, on the other hand, a new project will be organized at once.

## The idea phase

New business opportunities derive from needs in the market, which can be served by the corporation. These needs change as a result of emerging new technologies, social and political developments, and variations in customer attitudes and preferences. Thus, all searches for new opportunities must start in the business environment, with special attention to any observable novel trends and exceptional growth areas. The product life cycle concept is of course intimately involved in this observation, and it goes without saying that diversification into an already mature market will hold a very limited promise of success because of the already depressed profit margins and the vigorous defense of the market shares held by the already established firms.

Furthermore, a diversification decision will have a much better chance for

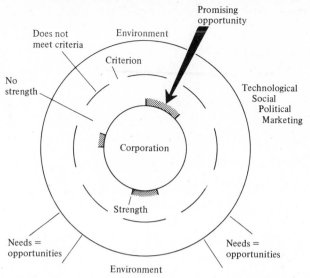

**FIGURE 4** ■ Selection of promising opportunities.

a good outcome if the corporation in its new line of business can utilize and build on some already existing strength(s). Only in that way will the diversifying corporation be in a better competitive situation than just any newcomer having discovered the same opportunity but having to start from the very beginning in all respects.

Finally, there is a set of conditions which must be reasonably well satisfied, if the diversification opportunity is to be considered good enough to warrant further investigation during the second phase of the project. The strategic plan and all the discussions held during the planning process serve as a natural and logical base for the establishment of this list of conditions or criteria.

Thus, if an opportunity discovered in the business environment passes the criteria screen and at the same time utilizes an existing corporate strength, then the opportunity can be considered a promising one. In Figure 4 an attempt is made to illustrate schematically this interplay between sources of new business opportunities, corporate strengths, and diversification criteria.

The diversification task force starts with the *list of criteria and a review of the corporate strengths.* A one-day discussion is normally sufficient in practice. The resulting lists are of course different for different organizations, but experience has shown the following entries to be typical for manufacturing industries:

*Criteria* (figures for 2–6 to be agreed upon)

1   Acceptable product groups or functions
2   Minimum sales volume within 5 years
3   Minimum projected growth rate in the market
4   Maximum investment for purposeful entry
5   Minimum profitability
6   Maximum time needed from decision to first order

In addition, there may be such criteria listed in individual companies as for example:

7   Acceptable geographical markets

8   Allowable kinds and volume of needed R&D

9   Acceptable licence arrangements

10  Maximum allowable influence on physical environment

11  Minimum estimated time for product line to reach maturity

12  Maximum numbers of skilled workers to be needed

*Corporate strengths* (general illustration only)

1   Financial situation solid

2   Ownership structure allows growth

3   Marketing experience and good customer relations in given areas

4   Production flexibility in some plants

5   Well developed management systems of certain kinds

6   Experienced R&D personnel in special sciences

7   Some raw materials inexpensively and safely available

8   Transportation facilities developed

9   Sub-deliveries of semi-finished parts easily obtainable

10  Management cadre well educated and motivated

With these lists completed, they are documented and filed for use later on, when the list of opportunities has been developed. This latter task is divided into two steps: the generation and listing of single ideas, identified by means of catchwords; and the grouping of these ideas into clusters, consisting of ideas which are related and which, when taken together, represent an opportunity for a new line of business.

In actual projects there has been a need discovered for a clarification at this point. First, there is often a remaining confusion between the new products search as it is normally carried on continuously by the company and the search for new lines of business or diversification as discussed here. Reference to Figure 2 helps to explain that new products are developed essentially for the present markets in order to keep the existing business competitive. This work is normally carried out by the R&D department of the existing organization, or of a division thereof, in close cooperation with its marketing people. Any clustering of ideas is normally not needed in that connection. Secondly, and this cause for confusion is to some extent related to the first, a few of the participants in the idea search hold back some of their thoughts because the company does not have the people, the plant, and the marketing organization immediately foreseen as needed. When the existence of any such confusion is perceived it must be carefully explained that if such competences already existed this could only mean that the corporation were already in the business being contemplated. But here, in this project, the search is for new businesses, and thus these competences—excepting listed strengths—are, by definition, not to be expected.

The *generation and listing of separate ideas* is done by members of the task force working as a group and individually in group interview meetings with a number of other members of the organization known often to have suggestions and to be creative. Several techniques have been tried in practice, but the two found easiest to explain and consequently most productive are the so-called brainstorming and 'staircase' methods.

*Brainstorming* is such a well-known technique that there is very little need for elaboration here. Suffice it to say that the session leader from the very beginning must bear down strictly on any utterances of judgments about offered ideas. After only a few such interventions the team will perform as intended, letting the associations flow freely.

The method which is here called the *staircase technique* starts with a viable part of the existing business and then hypothetically adds in one step at a time what is needed to enter a series of related businesses. Team work is organized, and the forthcoming ideas are entered on a blackboard or large sheet of paper for everyone to see. Each time a new step has been added to the staircase, this step hypothetically becomes the 'existing' business. After a while the team concludes that the new ideas generated are too outlandish for the purpose to be served. Then a new start is made with the actually existing business, and the staircase is built in another direction on the board. This is repeated several times, and it happens that two or even three staircases—sequences of ideas—converge on the same landing. This reinforces to some extent the idea recorded there.

The technique has been found to fire the imagination, and just one extract from an actual project will be sufficient as an illustration. The start was made with the existing line of packaging from plastic film materials. The staircase is here shown going downwards only a few steps:

Plastic film extrusion

Plastic tubing extrusion

Farm and garden watersprinkling installations

Electric installations with plastic conduits

Plastic insulated electric wires

Brainstorming and staircase building and, if preferred, other techniques are utilized first by the task force itself, and then in a number of additional sessions with a task force member as leader. Typically, hundreds of different ideas are recorded within a few weeks and assembled centrally by the task force.

As the second step towards a list of opportunities, the single *ideas are to be grouped into related clusters*. This work is done in a meeting with the task force during which the members use their knowledge of the business and apply their judgment directly. The procedure is about as follows:

1  The complete list is studied by each member of the task force. Note that no single ideas are to be evaluated at this stage.

2  A number of the ideas in the list really are ideas for product improvements or innovations within the existing business. These are divorced from the diversification project, listed separately under the appropriate profit center or functional department headings, and later turned over to the managers of these corporate units for use according to their own judgments.

3  A number of tentative cluster headings are produced, based on the impressions received by the task force members during their review of the total list as mentioned under point (1) above.

**4**  The single ideas are sorted one by one under the tentative headings. During the process, the exact wordings of the headings are changed to better ones, and sometimes whole groups of ideas are broken out and given separate names.

Typically, some 10–20 clusters are formed, each representing a new business opportunity. For each one *a first rather quick survey* is to be made by someone within the organization who at some previous time has had some connection with the business indicated by the name of the cluster or who has a background which enables him quickly to grasp the implications of the generated opportunity.

During this first survey, information is to be gathered and organized about:

**1**  The total volume of the now existing market in the geographical area indicated

**2**  The growth rate in this market

**3**  The currently active competitors

**4**  The needs in the market which could be served by this corporation, if it decides to enter

This task should not be allowed to absorb more than a month or so, if the overall project schedule is to be kept to an acceptable length. Therefore, only readily available information is to be assembled and evaluated. Interviews with persons from outside the corporation are generally very productive, in addition to the standard reviews of any specialized literature about the subject. Written reports are submitted to the task force with time for study in advance of the final meeting to be held within the idea phase of the project.

During this meeting *the three elements: opportunities, criteria, and strengths are matched* against each other, keeping the concept illustrated in Figure 4 in mind. The criteria and strengths are numbered and listed vertically, for example. Then the opportunities each receive a column and the columns are placed side by side, horizontally. The opportunities are now discussed one at a time by the task force, moving down the list of criteria and strengths. For an outside advisor, these discussions reveal an impressive amount of relevant information in addition to the information gathered during the separate surveys. Each conclusion finally evaluates an opportunity with regard to each criterion and each strength, and a check mark is entered to serve the memory about the discussion and its result. In practice, a simple code system consisting of a plus (+), zero (0), and (−) has been found most suitable. Thus plus of course notes that the criterion is met or the strength utilized, and a minus notes that this is not so. A zero is used to memorize that one does not really know yet, or that the point is not really too important for this particular opportunity. Table 1 illustrates a typical outcome of this evaluation effort, taken from an actual project.

A word of warning must be entered here. The temptation exists, surely, to translate each separate judgment into a number like grades on a scale from 0 to 10, for example, and then to add these numbers down for each opportunity to form a total number, indicating its relative worth. This temptation must be resisted, however, because the different criteria and strengths all have different weights, and furthermore these weights vary with the opportunity being discussed. It must be repeated that the indicators plus, zero, and minus, are there to serve the memory only of all the factors brought out during the meeting.

TABLE 1 ■ EVALUATION OF OPPORTUNITIES

| Opportunity no. | | 1 | 2 | 3 | 4 | 5 | 6 | 7 | 8 | 9 | 10 | 11 | 12 | 13 | 14 |
|---|---|---|---|---|---|---|---|---|---|---|---|---|---|---|---|
| **Criterion no.** | 1 | + | + | + | 0 | + | + | + | + | 0 | + | + | + | 0 | 0 |
| | 2 | + | + | + | + | + | 0 | − | − | + | + | + | + | + | + |
| | 3 | + | + | + | + | + | + | − | − | + | + | 0 | + | + | + |
| | 4 | 0 | + | + | + | 0 | + | − | − | 0 | 0 | 0 | + | + | + |
| | 5 | + | + | + | + | + | + | − | + | − | + | − | + | + | + |
| | 6 | − | + | + | 0 | + | 0 | − | + | 0 | + | 0 | − | + | + |
| | 7 | + | − | 0 | 0 | + | 0 | + | 0 | 0 | + | + | + | 0 | + |
| **Strength no.** | 1 | + | + | + | 0 | 0 | + | + | + | + | + | + | + | 0 | + |
| | 2 | 0 | 0 | 0 | 0 | + | 0 | 0 | 0 | 0 | + | + | + | 0 | + |
| | 3 | + | 0 | + | 0 | 0 | 0 | 0 | + | 0 | + | 0 | + | 0 | + |
| | 4 | + | + | + | 0 | + | + | + | + | + | + | + | + | 0 | 0 |
| | 5 | 0 | 0 | 0 | 0 | 0 | 0 | 0 | 0 | + | 0 | 0 | 0 | + | 0 |
| | 6 | 0 | 0 | 0 | 0 | 0 | 0 | + | 0 | + | 0 | + | 0 | 0 | 0 |
| | 7 | + | 0 | + | 0 | 0 | 0 | + | 0 | 0 | 0 | 0 | 0 | 0 | 0 |
| | 8 | 0 | + | 0 | + | 0 | 0 | 0 | 0 | 0 | + | + | + | 0 | 0 |
| | 9 | + | 0 | 0 | 0 | 0 | 0 | 0 | + | 0 | 0 | 0 | 0 | 0 | 0 |
| | 10 | + | 0 | 0 | 0 | 0 | + | 0 | 0 | 0 | 0 | 0 | 0 | 0 | 0 |
| | 11 | + | 0 | + | + | 0 | + | + | + | 0 | + | 0 | + | 0 | + |
| | 12 | + | 0 | + | 0 | 0 | 0 | 0 | + | 0 | + | 0 | + | 0 | + |

Finally, each opportunity is evaluated as a whole and given a rank in view of all the information and judgment now available to the task force in its meeting. Depending on the foreseen resources to become available for the study of each opportunity during the second project phase to follow, a number of *the most promising opportunities are selected* for further work. Typically, the number varies between four and eight in practice. These are then recommended to the top management planning team in a report from the now completed idea phase, wherein also a summary review is given of the approaches used and the results obtained in each step of the process. The report is presented to the planning team by its member in charge of this project. In this actual case, opportunities Nos. 1, 2, 3, 6, 9 and 14 were selected singly, and Nos. 10 and 12 combined into one and also selected for a total of seven opportunities. Opportunities Nos. 5 and 11 are kept on a waiting list and may be investigated later.

## The information phase

Many corporations have jumped directly from the idea phase to a decision to try and enter one or more of the most promising lines of new business. The results, certainly, have been widely scattered between the extremes of utter failure to a satisfactory degree of ultimate success. Here, it is strongly suggested instead, that each opportunity approved by top management for more work be investigated further, before any major investments are decided upon. The purpose of the study to be made during this second phase of the project is to learn enough about the contemplated new business to produce a reasonably solid foundation for a recommendation to proceed or not to proceed.

The expenses incurred during this phase are always minor in comparison to the benefits. If the effort leads to a positive recommendation, the work must be considered a necessary first task anyway, and if the final recommendation is to stay away from the business in question, the savings are very large indeed.

The time to be spent on this phase, however, is a more difficult question. On the one hand, the more thorough the study the better will be the foundation for the recommendation. On the other hand, the rate of change and the pressures from competition is such nowadays, that high speed of response to uncovered opportunities becomes an increasingly powerful competitive tool. Obviously, a compromise has to be made, and currently the period of 8–9 months allowable between the end of the idea phase and the next strategy planning meeting appears to be a good choice.

Although in practice the different tasks to be carried out do overlap each other, it is useful to divide the effort into the following steps:

1  Assembly of information
2  Analyses and projections
3  Choice of business role for the corporation
4  Development of effective entry strategies
5  Investments and profitability
6  Recommendations

Organizationally, the appointed study leaders may form work groups in order to share the load with other experienced people in the company. The project task force calls all study leaders to project meetings every 4–6 weeks. During these meetings each study leader reports on work done since the last meeting, participates in a general discussion about his study and its problems, and presents his plan for the work to be done before the next meeting. An outside advisor may work during one day or less individually with each study leader before each such general project meeting with the task force, which now acts as a steering body.

Each study leader is expected to use an average of half his working time on the project. In practice, they normally become so interested and absorbed by the new task, that they also give a considerable amount of their own time during extended periods. Some good-natured conflicts with their line supervisor may occur here and there; if needed, these are to be resolved by some member of the task force who is organizationally placed in a position to mediate. After all, this type of conflict must always be expected when the organization totally is well motivated.

During the first meeting of the task force with all the study leaders, a review is made of the work to be done in the successive steps. The contents of such a review and the ensuing discussions is given in the sections which follow.

The start is made with the *assembly of information.* The areas to cover concern (*a*) the market, (*b*) methods of distribution, (*c*) the technologies—both products and processes—and (*d*) the competition from other firms and other products or processes serving the same market needs.

All time aspects are to be considered: the past, the present, and the future. Statistical information is assembled from past years and brought forward to the present, and in many actual cases other researchers have made projections into the future, which can be applied if the primary sources of the used data can be traced.

As sources for information, use is of course first made of all available literature. Reference from one article leads to a series of others. Conferences and exhibitions often contain applicable, useful information. Sometimes, plant visits are also arranged in this connection. Branch organizations assemble information continually, which at times is made freely available.

In addition, direct interviews with persons inside and outside the company, having some expert knowledge about the area under study, are extremely useful. Especially the interviews with outside experts tend to throw new light on the whole situation. By talking to not only end users but also to retailers, distributors, wholesalers, importers, exporters, parts suppliers, raw material suppliers, community representatives, tax authorities, regulatory bodies, and so forth, a rather well verified total picture eventually emerges of the current situation, of some of its history, and of the outlook. One simply starts with someone believed at the outset to possess some useful insight, he will then suggest other names, and the list soon mushrooms. For each first project of this type in a corporation, there has to be expected a certain hesitancy if not a built-in psychological resistance to this type of activity. However, already after the first couple of interviews by a study leader, all his doubts about it disappear.

The *analysis and projection* step is concentrated on (*a*) the size of the market and its most probable development, (*b*) the prices paid up to now and the outlook for future years, (*c*) the alternative methods in use for distribution and any possible innovations in connection with a new entry into the business, and (*d*) the strongest competitors active now, those to be expected, and any ideas as to what their actions might be when they are faced with the attempted entry also by this corporation.

The forecasting techniques to be used are normally well known within the corporation; if not, references to suitable literature about the subject suffices. The most popular methods might be briefly explained in the first meeting. The other points (*b*)–(*d*) are self-explanatory.

The choice of *the business role* follows logically as the next step. During the information assembly and the analysis and projection steps the study leaders have built in their minds a rather firm idea about their respective areas of study. Now the study leader lists all observed needs in the environmental market, considering any niches in the market and any new emerging technologies. Alternative roles are outlined, and each alternative is evaluated against the criteria and strengths already listed at the beginning of the idea phase. The study leaders did not take part in the work during the idea phase, their information is now so much better than it was then, and thus they are able to make a renewed, impartial evaluation and choice between the generated alternatives. On this basis they make their recommendation to the task force in a general project meeting. Following discussion there, the final, specific role is chosen.

The development of effective *entry strategies* is an even more creative task. The study leader places himself hypothetically in the role of general manager for the new line of business and considers every step which he has to take in order to establish his business. All functions are considered; marketing, production, and administration, and for each both time and money are required. Network planning becomes the standard tool, and the critical path determines the total time needed from a decision to go ahead to the moment when the first orders can be expected. Again, if this planning technique is not sufficiently well known within the corporation, the advisor takes the time needed to explain and demonstrate it during his sessions with the individual study leaders.

The start is made with the market share to be acquired during the first years. In a rapidly growing market the entry strategy may well be to go after no more than the actual growth, leaving the competitors with their existing sales volumes or only a low growth. In this way a price war may be effectively avoided for several years. The resulting goals for the market share to be aimed at by the corporation may still appear quite ambitious.

Based on these sales goals, the necessary increases of corporate resources of various kinds are then determined. Existing strengths are utilized to the fullest extent possible, but even so additional men, machines, and materials are needed, and completely new plants may be required. Fundamentally, the days are long past, when one could make a small beginning, see how it goes, and use self-generated funds for gradual expansion. In the present business environment a new entry must be well planned, forceful, and irrevocable—at least in the eyes of competition—in order to be successful.

Next, the marketing methods to be used are selected. Only a wide enough scope warrants the needed, very expensive mass media methods mandatory for consumer products, and only a technically well-trained sales force can handle industrial accounts competently enough. The time needed for the marketing preparations may be quite as long as that on the production side, a fact which is too often overlooked.

Administration work for the new line of business normally does not present any other problems than that the study leaders lack personal experience with these matters. The members of the task force and the outside advisor easily make up for this common deficiency.

At this point the total strategy can be reduced to a set of activities, organized in a time schedule, and the foreseen investments are noted for each relevant time period following a decision to proceed at 'time zero'. Of course, the plan may for certain entries include such steps as acquisition of other companies, joint ventures, or coalitions with other enterprises for certain tasks. Then, these entry strategies depend on the successful conclusions of the foreseen negotiations. But normally it is still too early to divulge the corporation's interest in this field to any other company. It is then desirable to develop alternative strategies to be used if the negotiations are not successful. Such alternative routes also strengthen the negotiation position, because the other party almost always has experience enough to sense any situation where such alternatives do not as yet exist. It goes without saying, that acquisitions, etc., are here nothing more than sub-strategies to the diversification strategy. They are means to an end, but no ends in themselves.

Finally, an organizational arrangement for the new line of business is evolved. The solutions range in practice from a rather simple addition to an already existing profit center, through the set up of a new profit center within the corporation, to the organization of a new corporate subsidiary company. A subsidiary becomes an attractive arrangement as soon as any form of joint venture is aimed at, and the majority holding has a tendency to go to the company which took the initiative.

Total *investments and profitability* estimates can now be made. The total cash needed for all types of activities, until the first year of a positive contribution, is compiled for the initial years in question. The needed working capital is included also for the build-up period, if any. These cash flows out represent the investment.

Next, the number of years to be used for the profitability calculations are

# TABLE 2 ■ RISK ANALYSIS INPUT DATA

| | 74 | 75 | 76 | 77 | 78 |
|---|---|---|---|---|---|
| **1 Total market (ton)** | | | | | |
| | 290,000 | 320,000 | 350,000 | 390,000 | 430,000 |
| | 305,000 | 345,000 | 390,000 | 440,000 | 500,000 |
| | 350,000 | 425,000 | 510,000 | 620,000 | 740,000 |
| | 380,000 | 480,000 | 590,000 | 750,000 | 930,000 |
| Probability (per cent) | | | | | |
| | 30 | 30 | 30 | 30 | 30 |
| | 50 | 50 | 50 | 50 | 50 |
| | 20 | 20 | 20 | 20 | 20 |
| **2 Market share (per cent)** | | | | | |
| | 0.50 | 0.50 | 0.40 | 0.40 | 0.40 |
| | 0.55 | 0.55 | 0.50 | 0.50 | 0.50 |
| | 0.65 | 0.65 | 0.60 | 0.60 | 0.60 |
| | 0.70 | 0.70 | 0.70 | 0.70 | 0.70 |
| Probability (per cent) | | | | | |
| | 25 | 25 | 25 | 25 | 25 |
| | 50 | 50 | 50 | 50 | 50 |
| | 25 | 25 | 25 | 25 | 25 |
| **3 Price per unit (T.Sw.Fr./ton)** | | | | | |
| | 5,95 | 6,35 | 6,85 | 7,30 | 7,80 |
| | 7,00 | 7,45 | 8,00 | 8,55 | 9,15 |
| | 8,60 | 9,20 | 9,85 | 10,50 | 11,25 |
| | 9,15 | 9,80 | 10,50 | 11,20 | 12,00 |
| Probability (per cent) | | | | | |
| | 70 | 60 | 50 | 50 | 50 |
| | 20 | 30 | 40 | 40 | 40 |
| | 10 | 10 | 10 | 10 | 10 |
| **4 Cost of raw materials (T.Sw.Fr./ton)** | | | | | |
| | 3,80 | 4,00 | 4,20 | 4,40 | 4,60 |
| | 4,00 | 4,30 | 4,65 | 5,00 | 5,40 |
| | 4,40 | 4,90 | 5,55 | 6,25 | 7,10 |
| | 4,60 | 5,20 | 6,00 | 6,90 | 8,00 |
| Probability (per cent) | | | | | |
| | 10 | 10 | 10 | 10 | 10 |
| | 80 | 80 | 80 | 80 | 80 |
| | 10 | 10 | 10 | 10 | 10 |
| **5 Production costs (T.Sw.Fr./ton)** | | | | | |
| | 0,27 | 0,25 | 0,23 | 0,21 | 0,19 |
| | 0,28 | 0,27 | 0,25 | 0,24 | 0,22 |
| | 0,31 | 0,31 | 0,30 | 0,30 | 0,29 |
| | 0,32 | 0,33 | 0,33 | 0,33 | 0,33 |
| Probability (per cent) | | | | | |
| | 15 | 15 | 15 | 15 | 15 |
| | 50 | 50 | 50 | 50 | 50 |
| | 35 | 35 | 35 | 35 | 35 |
| **6 Marketing costs (T.Sw.Fr./ton)** | | | | | |
| | 0,35 | 0,38 | 0,41 | 0,45 | 0,49 |
| | 0,37 | 0,40 | 0,45 | 0,50 | 0,54 |
| | 0,42 | 0,47 | 0,55 | 0,65 | 0,73 |
| | 0,45 | 0,53 | 0,63 | 0,74 | 0,88 |
| Probability (per cent) | | | | | |
| | 40 | 30 | 30 | 30 | 30 |
| | 40 | 50 | 50 | 50 | 50 |
| | 20 | 20 | 20 | 20 | 20 |

**165** ■ A systematic approach to diversification

TABLE 2 ■ RISK ANALYSIS INPUT DATA (*continued*)

| | 72 | 73 | 74 | 75 | 76 | 77 | 78 |
|---|---|---|---|---|---|---|---|
| **7 Overhead costs (T.Sw.Fr.)** | | | | | | | |
| | 120 | 250 | 480 | 530 | 590 | 640 | 710 |
| | 125 | 290 | 505 | 570 | 645 | 730 | 820 |
| | 150 | 370 | 550 | 650 | 765 | 900 | 1065 |
| | 170 | 410 | 575 | 690 | 830 | 1000 | 1200 |
| **Probability (per cent)** | | | | | | | |
| | 10 | 10 | 20 | 20 | 20 | 20 | 20 |
| | 70 | 60 | 50 | 50 | 50 | 50 | 50 |
| | 20 | 30 | 30 | 30 | 30 | 30 | 30 |
| **8 Investments (T.Sw.Fr.)** | | | | | | | |
| | 2700 | 2400 | 3300 | | | | |
| | 2600 | 2450 | 3350 | | | | |
| | 2850 | 2750 | 3450 | | | | |
| | 2100 | 3000 | 3500 | | | | |
| **Probability (per cent)** | | | | | | | |
| | 10 | 10 | 10 | | | | |
| | 60 | 60 | 60 | | | | |
| | 30 | 30 | 30 | | | | |

determined, based on the reasoning which is spelled out in the reports. Practice varies between corporations, but it is fair to say that in industry a period of 10 years is common whenever the economic life of the investments to be made is not even shorter.

Thereupon the following data for each year within the period are assembled from the information, analyses, projections, and entry strategies now at hand:

1  Total market potential within chosen geographic area

2  The market share aimed at

3  Net price per unit

4  Raw materials cost per unit

5  Production cost per unit

6  Marketing costs per unit

7  Overhead total

8  Investments total

From these data, the profitability is calculated according to the standards set up in the corporation for investment proposals. The pay-back period, the net present value index at a set discount rate, and the internal rate of return are three useful measures to use, for example.

For the large investments required for diversification, a risk analysis with the aid of a computer is to be recommended. Then, for each of the eight input data above, uncertainty ranges are estimated on the basis of the best judgment available, and subjective probabilities are assigned to each range. Normally, only one range on each side of the most probable one is used; any further refinement has no foundation in available information. Table 2 shows the figures from an actual case, although the unit of currency used, Swiss francs, does not necessarily mean that the case is taken from that country. For each year, there are four figures, setting the boundaries for the three ranges. The three probability figures below apply to these ranges.

The computer printouts for pay-back, net present value index, and internal

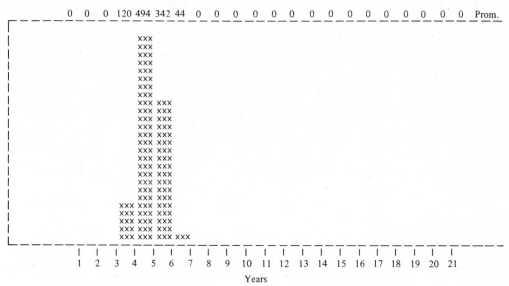

Probability

```
         0   0   0  120 494 342  44   0   0   0   0   0   0   0   0   0   0   0   0   0   0   0  Prom.
      ┌ ─ ─ ─ ─ ─ ─ ─ ─ ─ ─ ─ ─ ─ ─ ─ ─ ─ ─ ─ ─ ─ ─ ─ ─ ─ ─ ─ ─ ─ ─ ─ ─ ─ ─ ─ ─ ─ ┐
      |              xxx
      |              xxx
      |              xxx
      |              xxx
      |              xxx
      |              xxx
      |              xxx
      |              xxx
      |              xxx xxx
      |              xxx xxx
      |              xxx xxx
      |              xxx xxx
      |              xxx xxx
      |              xxx xxx
      |              xxx xxx
      |              xxx xxx
      |              xxx xxx
      |              xxx xxx
      |              xxx xxx
      |              xxx xxx
      |          xxx xxx xxx
      |          xxx xxx xxx
      |          xxx xxx xxx
      |          xxx xxx xxx
      └ ─ ─ ─ ─ ─xxx xxx xxx xxx─ ─ ─ ─ ─ ─ ─ ─ ─ ─ ─ ─ ─ ─ ─ ─ ─ ─ ─ ─ ─ ─ ─ ─
          |  |  |  |  |  |  |  |  |  |  |  |  |  |  |  |  |  |  |  |  |
          1  2  3  4  5  6  7  8  9  10 11 12 13 14 15 16 17 18 19 20 21
```

Years

**FIGURE 5** ■ Pay-back 5·32 years.

rate of return are reproduced in Figures 5–7. Especially the uncertainty range for the internal rate of return (IRR) is interesting. The probability curve is the result of 500 simulations by the computer of the IRR calculations, where-under the input figures within the ranges given are being used randomly, but with an overall frequency which corresponds to the input probabilities given. The results vary from 20 to 70 per cent before interest and taxes.

Different opportunities of course result in differing profitability ranges, and when the most probable center values happen to come close to each other, a choice—if one is necessary—becomes difficult.

For this reason, and there are others, the profitability analysis can be taken one step further by means of a translation into 'utility'. First, the attitude towards risk on the part of the decision maker is investigated by means of a series of preformulated questions posed during a couple of personal interviews a month or so apart. At least two interview sessions are needed to test the consistency of the answers. The questions are different in the two interviews of course.

The results from the interviews are analysed on the basis of an arbitrary utility scale, for example, − 100 to + 100, and with an IRR scale on which is plotted the minimum value needed to cover the corporate long term debt portion of all investments. At this IRR-value, the returns will cover interest and amortization of the debt, but the owners will receive no return on their equity portion. This particular consideration is not to be forgotten. In the same case example as already used above the curve for the decision maker's risk attitude is the one shown in Figure 8. The final step consists of a summation of the utilities from all the IRR ranges, weighted by means of the probabilities for each range.

Thus, 22.5 per cent IRR has a utility of 66 in Figure 8, and the probability from Figure 7 is 3 per cent. This gives $66 \times 0.03 = 1.98$ utility units—and so

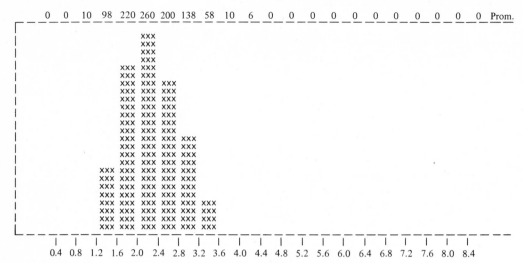

**FIGURE 6** ■ Net present value index 2·30: NPV (returns)/NPV (investments).

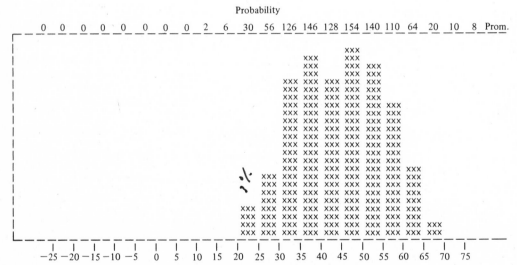

**FIGURE 7** ■ Internal rate of return 45·08: NPV (returns) ≡ NPV (investments).

forth. When all utilities are added together, the total is read off from the vertical axis to the curve and down to a single value for IRR. This value can be termed as the IRR, discounted for the risk attitude. It is generally lower than the center value by some 4–10 per cent, and the end result can be used for comparisons with other projects.

However, there are other uncertainties in a project of this type. There may be uncertainties about delivery times for pieces of machinery, or even uncertainties about the proper functioning in spite of any guarantees. The market

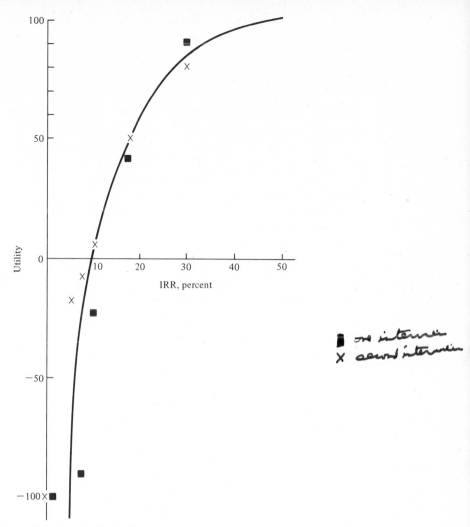

**FIGURE 8** ■ Case example of risk attitude curve.

aimed for may suddenly be invaded by another newcomer, or there may be a wild strike against the building contractor. These uncertainties are usually not reducable to uncertainties in the input data as discussed above, but they must be carefully considered and reported to the top management together with other vital information.

Finally, the study leaders arrive at their personal *recommendations* about their respective projects. These conclude the written reports to the steering body, and the total result is presented and discussed in a final general meeting. Thereupon the task force alone works out its report, covering all the studies, and adds its views to the recommendations from the study leaders. The total result is then presented to the top management team by the member who served as leader for the task force.

The top management team usually discusses the recommendations and the information behind them in connection with the strategy discussions for the total corporation, whereby the new lines become integral parts of the total strategic plan.

## Renewed diversification projects

During renewed efforts, there is a need to organize for a continuous inflow of ideas from the environment. This can be done by establishing an 'idea bank', known to all members of the organization. Also, the responsibility to follow up on the magazines specializing in news about innovations, for example, can be permanently delegated to selected managers. Any time they find an interesting item, they send a copy to the idea bank. The ideas themselves may not be directly useful, but they do cause associations and new combinations and thus enhance the creativity within the corporation.

## Reference

1  See, for example, E. G. Malmlow, Corporate Strategic Planning in Practice, *Long Range Planning*, Vol. 5, No. 3, pp. 2–9 (September 1972).

# Corporate turnaround strategies*

Dan Schendel
G. Richard Patton
James Riggs

Most business firms at some time suffer declines in their fortunes. Some die, while others recover and go on, perhaps to another crisis. This paper examines those circumstances that accompany decline, recovery, and survival—a turnaround in performance. Before there can be a turnaround, there first must be a downturn so the paper also explores whether there are patterns of management actions and performance in both the decline and the upturn phases of turnaround situations. If such patterns exist and can be identified, management should be able to spot downturns early and take effective corrective action.

We break management actions into two broad classes: (1) those dealing with the efficient conduct of the firm's existing business, and (2) those dealing with the question of what business the firm is in. The first class of actions shall be variously referred to here as efficiency actions, operating decisions, operations management, or tactical actions. All these relate to maximizing the efficiency of resource usage. The second class of actions will also encompass several different terms: effectiveness actions, strategic decisions, or strategic management, all of which deal with the question of what business the firm is in, what products it offers, and to what markets. In more homely terms, the first class deals with whether the "game plan" itself is being properly executed, while the second class asks whether the "game plan" is the proper one. Clearly, both classes of management actions or decisions can be taken during turnaround situations.

This paper is concerned with one main topic. Little is known about how management (or circumstances—we call them environmental events) turns declining firms into healthy ones. We try to shed some light on this obviously important matter by studying what managers actually do when faced with a decline in earnings, and what effects these actions have on the firms' performances. A detailed methodology for studying this question was developed.[1] This paper concentrates on the results obtained.

---

* Reprinted by permission of Dr. Daniel Schendel, Purdue University.
[1] See Dan Schendel, G. R. Patton, and J. Riggs, "Corporate Turnaround Strategies," Krannert Institute for Research in the Behavioral, Economic and Management Sciences, Paper No. 486, January 1975, for a working version of the paper which discusses a number of these methodological issues.

Probably the main objective of management is to steadily improve net income earned, that is, to achieve growth of profits. To capture this primary objective, a net income growth decision rule was used to identify turnarounds:[2]

Downturn phase: 4 years of a decline in net income as normalized by GNP growth.

Upturn phase: 4 years of an increase in net income with allowance for a possible 2-year deviation between the downturn and upturn phase. Again, net income was normalized by GNP growth.

Thus, if growth in net income was less than GNP growth, the firm was in a decline, even though there may have been absolute growth in the size of net income. Similarly, during the upturn phase, net income growth had to exceed the growth rate of GNP. The firm had to perform better than the general economy. Figure 1 illustrates the two possible income patterns.

Note that to be included in the sample the firm must meet these specifications for 8 or more years. This long time span is used because the downturn time span has to be long enough to assure that there is indeed some problem with the company, that it has not simply made a minor mistake with short-run impact. Likewise, a fairly long upturn time span gives confidence that the firm's fortunes have in fact been reversed; its earnings really are turning up. A tactical maneuver could possibly improve earnings for 1 or 2 years while leaving a fundamental strategic problem unsolved and festering. This should show up as a renewed downturn within the 4-year period.

Second, such a long period is required to ensure that any strategic and tactical moves taken have time to work themselves out and have an impact on the firm's earnings. A major diversification may take several years to have an impact. For example, construction of a major plant may require two or more years of planning and construction. The 8-year period permits all but the lengthiest of such actions and their changes to be observed over the period of decline, formulation of turnaround strategy, implementation, and early effectiveness.

Sixty-eight of the 1800 firms on Standard and Poor's Compustat tape fit our net earnings turnaround criteria. Fifty-four firms had income patterns like that shown in Figure 1(a), and fourteen were like Figure 1(b). The average length of downturn was 5.18 years, with a range from the minimum of 4 years, up to 10 years. The average length of the upturn phase was 7.65 years, with a range of 4 to 16 years.

The original sample of 68 firms was cut to 54 to eliminate foreign-based firms, service and retailing firms, and in general those firms for which few data were available.[3] Such companies as Household Finance, Kresge, and Distillers Corp.–Seagrams were eliminated for these various reasons. After this elimination, there remained a viable cross section of industries as shown in Table 1. Only 3 four-digit industry codes contained more than two turnaround firms. The major exception comes in the integrated domestic oil companies, where

---

[2] Other measures were used to define turnaround (i.e., return on assets and earnings per share), but the samples they generated were not as satisfactory, for various reasons, as that generated using net income.

[3] We were trying to get at least one point of commonality—in this case a manufacturing orientation—across all firms.

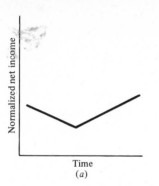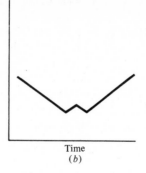

**FIGURE 1** ■ Depiction of turnaround situations.

five firms were found. It is significant that there is only one industry with multiple turnarounds in it. This indicates that the sample selection procedure is not simply mapping industry cyclical swings. The firms chosen actually *were* doing less well than their competitors during the downturn phase, and their managers were thus faced with the need to turn their companies around, relative not only to GNP growth, but also to others in the same industry.

Table 2 gives the turnaround years, assets, sales, income, and employee sizes of the sample firms. A wide range of small to very large firms is represented. Included are such firms as Greyhound, Alcoa, Shell Oil, RCA, Coca-Cola, Heileman Brewers, Ceco Corp., Koehring, and Rath Packing Co.

### CLASSIFICATION OF TURNAROUND FIRMS

If one makes the reasonable assumption that performance results from both management actions and external, noncontrollable events, it is then possible to further classify the firms in a way useful to the study of strategic behavior. If management actions can be identified and broken into strategic and operating decisions, and if noncontrollable events can be so classified, and if performance across the downturn and upturn phases can be associated with such actions and events, then it should be possible to say even more about strategies useful to turning firms around and, indeed, it may be possible to say something about causes of declines as well. In particular then, a classification such as that in Table 3 is required. This four-cell matrix would classify the turnaround firms in terms of whether the downturn was associated with predominantly strategic or operating actions and events. To build such a matrix classification

TABLE 1 ■ INDUSTRY CLASSIFICATION OF TURNAROUND FIRMS

**1** Number of four-digit SIC industries represented: 40

**2** Number of firms per four-digit industry:

Firms:   1  2  3  4
Cases:  30  7  2  1

**3** Number of two-digit SIC industries represented: 17

**4** Number of firms per two-digit industry:

Firms:  1  2  3  4  5  (or more)
Cases:  5  4  1  3  2    2

**TABLE 2 ■ SAMPLE CHARACTERISTICS**

| 1 | Turnaround year | 1957 | 1958 | 1959 | 1960 | 1961 | 1962 | 1963 | 1964 | 1965 | 1966 |
|---|---|---|---|---|---|---|---|---|---|---|---|
| | Frequency of turnaround | 4 | 5 | 13 | 8 | 15 | 15 | 4 | 3 | 0 | 1 |
| 2 | Average asset size (millions): | $362.9 | | | | | | | | | |
| | Range: | $15.3–$2076.2 | | | | | | | | | |
| 3 | Average sales (millions): | $399.1 | | | | | | | | | |
| | Range: | $16.1–$1954.5 | | | | | | | | | |
| 4 | Average income (millions): | $18.19 | | | | | | | | | |
| | Range: | $0.3–$140.4 | | | | | | | | | |
| 5 | Average number of employees: | 18,730 | | | | | | | | | |
| | Range: | 600–110,000 | | | | | | | | | |

of the sample requires a history of management actions and events significant to the firm over a minimum 8-year time period.

Classification of actions and noncontrollable events into strategic and operating categories was guided by the distinctions drawn between those two areas by Ansoff (1965), Chandler (1962), and Schendel and Hatten (1972). The specific strategic causes of declines or cures leading to upturn were examined in terms of the major dimensions of strategy:

The basic goals and objectives of the business

The product-market matches chosen on which to compete

The major patterns of resource allocation (indicating how management wishes to grow and the basis for its competitive advantage)

The major operating policies (especially functional area policies)

Major environmental assumptions made

Operating decisions are those intended to implement strategic decisions and are those actions dealing with resource usage. Despite the emphasis given operations management by managers, and management theory, performance decline or even failure does occur because the firm is inefficient, because its day-to-day operations are inadequate, or because the right thing is being done, but it is not being done well enough.

With the use of this general distinction between strategic and operating actions and events (more specific, detailed criteria based on these distinctions were used as classification guidelines), the actions reported in the literature[4]

---

[4] Unfortunately, it is not feasible to do field studies to gather primary data on a sample of the size we are using. Moreover, such data would have to cover lengthy historical periods. The information used here was taken from such sources as annual reports, the *Wall Street Transcript*, the *Wall Street Journal, Business Week,* etc.

**TABLE 3 ■ CLASSIFICATION OF MANAGEMENT ACTIONS IN TURN-AROUND SITUATIONS**

| | Upturn | | |
|---|---|---|---|
| Downturn | Strategic | Operating | Total |
| Strategic | SS | SO | $S_d$ |
| Operating | OS | OO | $O_d$ |
| Total | $S_u$ | $O_u$ | |

**TABLE 4**

| | Upturn | | |
|---|---|---|---|
| Downturn | Strategic | Operating | Total |
| Strategic | 9 | 6 | 15 |
| Operating | 16 | 23 | 39 |
| Total | 25 | 29 | 54 |

were classified into these two categories during both the downturn and upturn phases. After classifying the actions and events as strategic or operating, we determined whether there was an association between management actions and events and the performance decline and those actions that may have led to the upturn.

The method used to classify firms gave equal weight to all actions and used a simple majority rule to decide whether the downturn cause and upturn cure were strategic or operating in nature.[5] This decision rule gave a matrix breakdown as shown in Table 4.

## Downturn phase

Downturn can be attributed to events that management cannot control or, in some cases, to events that are difficult to anticipate and to which it is difficult to adapt. Recession is an example of such an event. Also, downturn can be attributed to management actions (or inactions) as well. Both controllable events (management actions or decisions) and noncontrollable events (environmental change) are of interest as possible causes of downturn.

### DOWNTURN CHARACTERISTICS

Content analysis of the chronology of management actions and environmental events during downturn suggests that there are several major categories into which the actions and events can be classified. While it is not possible to attribute causal relationships, the literature suggests that inferential relationships can be drawn between the strategic and operating problems listed and poor firm performance.

The events themselves can be grouped into seven general classes:

1 Lower price levels

2 Recessions

3 Strikes and labor problems

4 Lower profit margins

5 Increased competition

6 Raw material supply problems and cost increases

7 Managerial difficulties

---

[5] Several different decision rules were used to classify firms, including one based on multidimensional scaling methods. There were some differences in classification, but there was insufficient disagreement to report here. Perhaps the most interesting result of this sensitivity study was the promise that multidimensional scaling methods can be used for work of this kind.

*Lower price levels*  One of the most common environmental events was price pressures resulting in lower selling prices for end products. Reasons for price drops were twofold. First, many firms lowered prices in an attempt to introduce their products to a new market and to gain acceptance for their products on a price basis over more conventional products and materials. Plastic material manufacturers were a prime example as they lowered prices trying to gain acceptance of plastics over more conventional materials such as wood, paper, etc. The second reason was a response to competitors' lowering prices as an attempt to ward off introduction of lower-priced, substitute materials. In all, 23 firms suffered from lowering of selling prices during the downturn phase.

*Recession*  About a third of the firms noted that they were adversely affected by the 1954, 1956, and 1960 recessions and general economic slowdowns. Firms engaged in heavy manufacturing and capital goods industries were particularly affected. It can be argued that since these firms performed poorly relative to other firms facing the same economic conditions, this was really a "signal" of a deeper strategic problem, for example, lack of product and market diversification. Indeed, most of these firms used some form of diversification as a cure and guarded against this problem occurring again in the future. Closely related to this cause was the temporary decline in demand experienced by 17 firms, a decline not necessarily related to recession periods. In most cases this decline was caused by economic slowdown or cuts in government spending. The above argument about an underlying strategic problem and cure also applies here.

*Strikes*  Major strikes had a deep economic effect on 17 firms. This was due primarily to (1) lost production, (2) changing to other suppliers, and (3) increased costs due to high wage settlements. Frequently, these strikes continued for several months and, in some cases, more than a year.

*Lower profit margins*  Several firms suffered from low profit margins due to excessive production costs, outdated equipment, and failure to adopt new production methods. This inefficient use of resources was a serious problem for 19 firms.

*Increased competition*  Increased competition, particularly foreign competition, was another major event associated with downturn. There appeared to be two forms of increased competitive pressure. The first was increased competition from producers of the same product. This took three forms: (1) foreign competitors with price (cost) structure advantages, (2) competitors with shipping and sales advantages due to geographic location, and (3) competitors with technological advantages. For example, Cleveland Cliffs Iron Ore Corp. suffered increased foreign competition due to higher-quality and lower-cost foreign ores. As a result, Cleveland Cliffs was forced to develop new, higher-quality ore reserves and develop new production techniques, a costly process.

The second cause of increased competition was substitution of a new technology or new product for another one, for example, plastics for metals, aluminum for tin.

*Raw material supply*  Many corporations (17) experienced problems with raw material supplies. There were frequent mentions of costly supply strikes, price increases, and quality problems.

*Managerial difficulties*  Although it is not frequently reported directly in the literature, one could infer from the number of top management changes that managerial incompetence was frequently blamed for poor performance.

Although the literature cited only 6 firms, 39 firms made major changes in top management personnel. Unfortunately, these important internal managerial affairs were impossible to discern from the general literature used. However, their importance to turnaround is probably very great.

## STRATEGIC AND OPERATIONS DIFFERENCES—DOWNTURN

Using the majority decision rule, the turnaround sample was broken into the matrix shown in Table 4, in which 15 firms were assigned to the strategic downturn category and 39 to the operations class. In an attempt to identify differences between these downturn classes, eight performance and resource allocation variables were studied for statistically significant differences in percentage change. Table 5 gives the results.

The strategic group of firms showed a decrease in debt, and decreases in net income and employees, while showing increases in sales, R&D, assets, and capital expenditures. The operations group showed a positive growth for all variables except net income and employees. There were only three variables; debt, capital expenditures, and assets, where there were significant differences between strategic and operations groups.

It appears that the strategic group was spending relatively more on R&D and capital expenditures, perhaps trying to overcome major competitive difficulties, while the operations group was trying to solve problems of inefficiency. When compared to the upturn phase, growth rates in all categories are substantially lower for both groups.

## Upturn phase

During the upturn phase of the turnaround, events and management actions are beginning to act as cures for the decline. It is useful here, as earlier with downturns, to suggest that the cures can be related to both management actions and to noncontrollable environmental events, such as a recovery of the economy from recession.

**TABLE 5 ■ MEAN PERCENTAGE GROWTH RATES IN SELECTED PERFORMANCE RESULTS FOR TURNAROUND SITUATIONS**

| | Downturn | | Upturn | | Turnaround | |
|---|---|---|---|---|---|---|
| | Strategic | Operations | Strategic | Operations | Down | Up |
| Debt | −15.06%[a] | 21.85%[a] | 9.8% | 24.75% | $58.7M[b] | $74.6M[b] |
| Capital expenditures | 15.60%[a] | 1.75%[a] | 94.67% | 104.07% | $27.7M[b] | $37.8M[b] |
| R&D | 28.67% | 11.75% | 17.60% | 19.37% | $14.01 | $16.8 |
| EPS ($) | $1.88 | $2.04 | $2.11 | $2.70 | $1.97 | $2.41 |
| Net income | −20.43% | −23.50% | 150.49% | 113.77% | −22.5%[a] | 133.3%[a] |
| Sales | 7.94% | 6.12% | 42.06% | 50.66% | 6.55%[a] | 46.44%[a] |
| Employees | −0.15% | −3.74% | 27.58% | 18.17% | −2.65%[a] | 22.69%[a] |
| Assets | 15.75%[a] | 26.19%[a] | 34.85% | 52.76% | 19.44[a] | 43.57[a] |

[a] Significant difference at 99 percent level.
[b] Significant difference at 95 percent level.

While an attempt is made to associate actions and events with results and to speak of cures, associations between action patterns and results are only that. These relationships may not be causal.

## UPTURN CHARACTERISTICS

An analysis of the environmental events and managerial actions suggests seven major areas into which they can be classified:

1 Major plant expenditures
2 Increased emphasis on a functional area
3 Efficiency actions
4 Diversification
5 Vertical integration
6 Divestiture
7 Top management changes

*Major plant expenditures* The most common cures were major plant expenditures with 37 firms engaged in some form of this solution. In many cases, this took the form of plant modernization in order to increase efficiency and reduce operating costs, not necessarily to increase capacity. In many cases new plants were built or existing ones expanded to increase capacity. This action was frequently dependent to some degree on other actions, such as increased advertising or expansion of the same basic product line.

*Functional area emphasis* Another major action taken was increased emphasis on a particular functional area, doing the same thing but doing it more efficiently, often on a larger scale. This was particularly evident in increased emphasis on R&D in order to improve product quality or broaden a product line and in increased attention to marketing and advertising. Most of the firms commenting on their R&D expenditures indicated that efforts were directed toward short-run objectives, such as improvements of current products, not to longer-run basic research.

*Efficiency* Thirty-one firms cited efficiency moves and cost-saving steps as contributing to profit improvement. This included new equipment expenditures, general "belt tightening" (including firings), tighter raw material control, and increased emphasis on budgeting and cost control. Only three firms utilized a cutback in capital expenditures.

*Diversification* Dominant among strategic actions were diversification moves with 48 firms utilizing this strategic alternative. There were two major forms of diversification cited: product and geographic. Product diversification was divided between internal development (22 cases), through acquisition (29 cases), and joint ventures with other firms (5 cases). Geographic diversification was divided between domestic (6 cases) and foreign (21 cases).

*Vertical integration* Vertical integration was cited by only 2 firms. While this is a major strategic action, it apparently was little used by this sample.

Since most (32) of the firms studied turned around between 1959 and 1963, a time during which conglomerates were first becoming popular, the product diversification may have reflected the times. However, there is an extremely high coincidence of diversification and turnaround, indicating both a more aggressive stance and willingness to accept managerial challenges, and a recognition of the desirability of reducing market risk by broadening the company's product line and/or customer base.

*Divestment* Divestment, the elimination of divisions or whole product lines, is the opposite of diversification and was used by 16 companies. Explanations were generally that the divested products did not fit with the new image or definition of the companies. This indicates a trend toward defining the corporate image and a fundamental rethinking of the corporation's position and purpose which took place during some companies' downturn periods. Frequently, these spin-offs brought in cash which also benefited the companies, and in some cases it appears that the spin-offs stopped cash outflows, an immediate benefit of the strategic move.

*Top management changes* Not surprisingly, one of the more common strategic actions involves changes in upper management, whether putting current managers in new positions (most common being to raise the president to chairman and to promote or bring in a new president), or bringing in entirely new managers or management teams. With 39 firms listing major management changes it seems likely that some firms' lack of success could be attributed to stagnant management or management incapable of coping with adverse conditions. It was typical for the new management to inaugurate significant changes in marketing emphasis, R&D expenditures, modernization of facilities, or other items which appear to be associated with turnarounds. These moves could, of course, have been made by the previous management, but they were not, typically, indicating stagnation or complacency. Since many of the statements in the literature used were made by the new management, it is not clear to what extent previous management had been "victims" or "scapegoats." Closely related to this was the action of corporate reorganization. In 13 firms, decentralization (establishment of profit centers) occurred, while in 10 firms centralization (consolidation of management decision making) occurred.

The management factor, both operationally and strategically, has to be a significant causal factor in turnaround situations. Unfortunately, the nature of this research did not permit its incorporation and refinement to the degree its importance warrants.

### STRATEGIC AND OPERATIONS DIFFERENCES—UPTURN

The majority rule matrix (Table 4) showed a grouping of 25 firms using strategic "cures" for downturn, with 29 utilizing operations or tactical actions and decisions. These two groups were studied for differences in performance and resource allocation results in terms of the eight variables presented in Table 5.

All variables showed higher growth rates, for both the strategic and operations groups, than were typical of the downturn phase. There were, however, no significant differences in mean growth rates between the strategic and operations group on any of the eight variables.

### DOWNTURN-UPTURN COMPARISON

As indicated in the turnaround column of Table 5, statistically significant differences exist in the sizes of performance measures and resource allocation measures for six of the eight variables used. R&D and EPS do not show a significant difference, but here, as in the other six variables, the direction of change is toward improvement in every measure. Truly the sample did turn around as these measures strongly indicate.

One of the major purposes of this study was to relate turnarounds to strategic or operations causes and cures. While it is clear that the sample firms did turn around, it is not clear that turnaround can be related to the strategic and operating actions and events identified for each firm and then used to classify them.

Up to this point the cells of the matrix of Table 3 have not been examined. These cells combine both the downturn and upturn phases of the turnaround situation and yield four different groupings:

1   Strategic causes for downturn/strategic cures for upturn (SS)

2   Strategic causes for downturn/operating cures for upturn (SO)

3   Operating causes for downturn/strategic cures for upturn (OS)

4   Operating causes for downturn/operating cures for upturn (OO)

SS   This first category is a natural pattern in that if fundamental parts of the strategy have gone sour, then it is reasonable that new strategies be formulated that can return the firm to a growth position. The pattern of resource allocation and of recovery in performance measures should be consistent with an SS pattern.

SO   This is an inconsistent pattern and when it exists, turnaround should not be as sound, if it occurs at all, as in the SS case. The firm is presumably doing the wrong things, no matter how efficiently it is doing them.

OS   This pattern is a sound one and can arise under a variety of circumstances, including fundamental dissatisfaction with existing performance or the conclusion that operations difficulties result from inappropriate strategy rather than inefficiencies.

OO   This is also a natural pattern of action and was predominant in the turnaround sample. Where there is no difficulty with the existing strategy, but where performance is less than desired, this pattern should be a natural one.

Tests of mean differences between these four classifications revealed a significant difference only between SS and SO for the use of debt during turnaround, it being used to a greater extent in SS than SO. In none of the other seven variables tested (listed in Table 5) were there significant differences.

The division of downturn causes and upturn cures into strategic and operations actions and events has conceptual appeal. Why the classification did not result in more statistically significant differences may be due more to the secondary data used than to a shortcoming in the concept itself. Further study and richer data would be desirable before conclusions can be reached on the usefulness of the classification concept.

## Conclusions

This study of 54 firms that suffered declines and then turned their poor performance around has tried to relate the downturn and upturn phases of turnaround to strategic actions and noncontrollable environmental events. While statistically significant differences were found between strategic and operations actions and events for the downturn phase, none were found for the upturn phase. For the overall downturn-upturn cell groupings only limited significance was found.

The sample studied did show clear evidence of a turnaround in performance. All performance and resource allocation measures supported this. As for the "causes" of downturn, seven event and action patterns singly or in combination appeared most frequently associated with decline: (1) lowered price levels, (2) recessions, (3) strikes and labor problems, (4) lowered profit margins, (5) increased competition, (6) raw material supply problems and cost increases, and (7) managerial problems.

The most frequently cited elements of strategic cures were (1) introduction of new management, and by implication alterations in strategy, (2) diversification, both internally through product development and externally through acquisition, and (3) divestment of failing or poorly performing product lines and divisions. Greater efficiency through operations management moves was also widely used to turn decline back into growth. Actions especially prominent were steps to gain increased production efficiency, and general cost-cutting and improved budgeting practices.

The research is currently being extended to include a matched sample study: one firm that turns around and a matched firm that continues in prolonged stagnation or decline. More emphasis is being placed on the long-term performance pattern rather than a strict monotonic change in performance, and the care in matching should permit the noncontrollable environmental events to be evaluated for their impact on turnarounds.

## References

Altman, Edward, J.: "Financial Ratios, Discriminant Analysis and the Prediction of Corporate Bankruptcy," *Journal of Finance*, **XXIII** (4): September 1968.

Ansoff, H. I.: *Corporate Strategy*, New York: McGraw-Hill, 1965.

Beaver, William H.: "Financial Ratios as Predictors of Failure," *Journal of Accounting Research*, **2:** 71–127, 1966.

Brooks, J. N.: *The Fate of the Edsel and Other Business Adventures*, New York: Harper and Row, 1963.

Chandler, A. D.: *Strategy and Structure*, Cambridge, Mass: M.I.T. Press, 1962.

Fishbein, Martin: "A Behavior Theory Approach to the Relations between Beliefs about an Object and the Attitude toward the Object," in M. Fishbein (ed.), *Readings in Attribute Theory and Management*, New York: Wiley, 1967, pp. 389–399.

Green, P. E., and F. J. Carmone: *Multidimensional Scaling*, Boston: Allyn and Bacon, 1970, p. 143.

Green, P. E., and U. R. Rao: *Applied Multidimensional Scaling*, New York: Holt, Rinehart, and Winston, 1972, pp. 199, 200.

Hofer, Charles W.: "Some Preliminary Research on Patterns of Strategic Behavior," *Academy of Management Proceedings*, Thirty-third Annual Meeting, August 19–22, 1973.

Mintzberg, Henry: "Research on Strategy-Making," *Academy of Management Proceedings*, Thirty-second Annual Meeting, August 13–16, 1972.

Ross, J. E., and M. J. Kami: *Corporate Management in Crisis,* Englewood Cliffs, N. J.: Prentice-Hall, 1973.

Schendel, D. E., and K. J. Hatten: "Business Policy or Strategic Management: A Broader View for an Emerging Discipline," *Academy of Management Proceedings,* Thirty-second Annual Meeting, August 13–16, 1972.

# Choosing the strategy

Figure 6–1 reminds us again that with this chapter we complete the choice phase of the strategic planning process.

The top managers can do this by selecting the most crucial factors from the strategic advantage profile and the environmental threat and opportunities profile and systematically comparing them with each strategic alternative.

In Chapter 3, I derived an environmental threat and opportunities profile; in Chapter 4 the strategic advantages profile was given. For the Reiter Company Table 6–1 provides the kind of analysis necessary for strategic choice for the top managers. Briefly, Reiter is a small manufacturer of work gloves and hats and also owns a wholesaling company for these products for part of the area. Reiter is competitive and profitable. The focal executive is a young man who inherited the business suddenly when his father died. At one point his father and uncle ran the business, but the uncle had started a competing business. The uncle took over Reiter's presidency too for a while until the new boss was ready to run the business. The uncle is at once a strength (he is very good at buying the raw materials—a crucial factor), but he also sends all new business to his company. The wholesaling division is only marginally profitable. The son is considering: more of the same (A); cutting back on the wholesaler and growing later, using some of the money to buy the uncle out (B) (the uncle holds a chunk of Reiter's stock); or he could sell off the wholesaler and buy the uncle out now (C). But then he loses the uncle's expertise.

The choice process involves systematically considering how each strategy would affect each critical factor (in Table 6–1, variable 1 is the most crucial factor) until the best strategy is chosen. Ziemer and Maycock give an example of the rating process among alternatives.

This choice can be made by the top executive alone or in conjunction with other top executives, sometimes with the advice of staff specialists intuitively or formally in a meeting. Proposition 6–1 from Stagner's study indicates how larger firms might wish to proceed.

"Formal" in Proposition 6–1 does not mean with the use of models of the management science type. Schoeffler and his associates give us some data on the effectiveness of strategic choices in the reading at the end of this chapter. Hall [1] found these were not being used to make strategic choices in spite of exhortation for modeling by many authors.

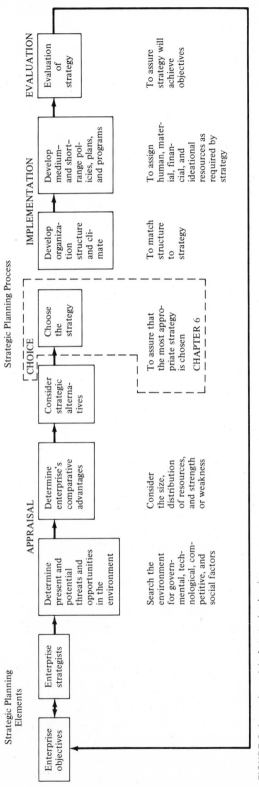

**184**

**FIGURE 6–1** ■ A model of strategic planning.

■ STRATEGIC CHOICE [2]

Strategic choice is the decision which selects from among the alternatives considered the strategy which will best meet the enterprise's objectives. The choice involves selection of criteria, evaluation of the alternatives against these criteria, and the actual selection.

■ Effective companies hold formal meetings, involving all or most of top management, to make strategic choices and to record the criteria used.

## Strategic choice criteria

The ultimate measure by which the top managers choose a particular strategy is whether it meets the criteria of the top management. The ultimate criteria are the extent to which the strategic alternative helps the enterprise meet its *objectives*. Mintzberg, in the article reprinted at the end of this chapter, describes three different strategic choice patterns. Four factors influence how the top executives view these criteria and the choice:

1 Managerial perceptions of external dependence
2 Managerial attitudes toward risk
3 Managerial awareness of past enterprise strategies
4 Managerial power relationships and organization structure

## Managerial perceptions of external dependence [3]

What should be clear now is that managers do not think alike about strategic choice (Lundberg; McKenney and Keen; Nyström). They operate in different environments (Khandwalla) but perceive the same environments differently.

TABLE 6–1 ■ STRATEGIC CHOICE FOR REITER COMPANY

| Crucial environmental variables[a] | Crucial internal variables[b] | Strategic alternatives |
|---|---|---|
| **3** Advantageous purchasing of raw materials<br><br>**4** Strong demand for gloves at present prices | **1** Poor top management amiability and stockholder relations<br><br>**2** Few well-trained managers<br><br>**5** Strong financial position<br><br>**6** Good product line and strong position in the market | Stability<br><br>Combination: cutback, then growth<br><br>Combination: divestment, then growth |

[a] From environmental threat and opportunities profile.
[b] From strategic advantage profile.

**185** ■ Choosing the strategy

Their freedom of choice is not unlimited. Propositions 6–2, 6–3, and 6–4 specify some of the limits:

---

**PROPOSITION 6–2**  ■ The strategic choice is limited by the extent to which the firm is dependent for its survival on owners, competitors, customers, the government, and the community.

---

**PROPOSITION 6–3**  ■ The more dependent the firm, the less flexibility it has in strategic choice except in crisis conditions.

**1** The more dependent the firm is on a few owners (or a family), the less flexible it is in its strategic choice.

**2** The more dependent the firm is on its competitors, the less it will be able to choose an aggressive strategy. (*Dependent* is defined as relatively weak in competitive struggle.)

**3** The more dependent the firm is for its success and survival on a few customers, the more responsive the effective firm will be to their wishes.

**4** The more dependent the firm is on the government and community, the less responsive it will be to market conditions and owners' desires.

---

**PROPOSITION 6–4**  ■ The strategic choice is affected by the relative volatility of market sector the firm chooses to operate in. The more volatile the sector, the more flexible the strategic response needs to be in effective organizations.

---

These propositions discuss dependence as if it were an objectively measurable phenomenon. It is. General Motors is much more powerful in the auto business in the United States than American Motors is. But in addition to the *objective* phenomena are the *subjective* views of the decision makers. Facts do not speak for themselves. Executives interpret these facts. Two firms of equal power (objectively measured in the environment) can be headed by executives who see the firms differently. One firm's executives can see their firm as weak, the other as strong (relatively). Thus the weights they put on the strategic alternatives can vary.

## 2) Managerial attitudes toward risk [4]

A second filter on the choice is how much risk the firm, its stockholders, and management feel comfortable with. Wilson, an executive of the large British firm GKN, has described how even after risky decisions are made, there are two steps forward, one back in the process of risk taking.

General Electric's vice president Reuben Gutoff described his company's attitude towards risk in 1975:

A decade ago, our venture activity was pretty well tied up with major corporate ventures of very large size: nuclear, commercial jet engines, and computers. In line

**TABLE 6–2 ■ RISK ATTITUDES AND STRATEGIC CHOICE**

| Managerial attitudes toward risk | Probable choice filters |
|---|---|
| **1** Risk is necessary for success. | High risk projects are acceptable or desirable. |
| **2** Risk is a fact of life and some risk is desirable. | Balance high with low risk choices (bet hedging). |
| **3** High risk is what destroys enterprises and needs to be minimized. | Risk aversion: risky projects are rejected. |

with trying to reduce the risk exposure of the company and at the same time not lose any of the entrepreneurship, we have moved towards more organically grown, smaller in size, larger in number ventures (taking risks in bite sizes).

Managerial attitudes toward risk vary from comfort if not exhilaration with high risk to strong risk aversion. The risk averters probably view the firm as very weak and will accept only defensive strategies with very low risks. Three polar conditions with regard to risk can be conceived (Table 6–2).

Thus, insofar as they influence managerial attitudes, the risk attitudes of the managers and stockholders will eliminate some strategic alternatives and highlight others.

## 3) Managerial awareness of past enterprise strategies [5]

Henry Mintzberg attempted to learn about the strategic choice process by examining the strategic choices *over time* of several major strategic changes:

Volkswagen's strategy from 1934 to 1969
United States' strategy in Vietnam, 1950–1968

After a thorough analysis of these and other strategic choices, he concluded:

---

**RESEARCH STUDY** ■ **MINTZBERG'S 1972 CONCLUSIONS**

**1** Present strategy evolves from a past strategy developed by a powerful leader. This unique and tightly integrated strategy (a gestalt strategy) is a major influence on later strategic choices.

**2** Then the strategy becomes programmed, and bureaucratic momentum keeps it going. Mintzberg calls this the push-pull phenomenon: the original decision maker pushes the strategy, then lower management pulls it along.

**3** When this strategy begins to fail because of changing conditions, the enterprise grafts new substrategies onto the old and only later gropes for a new strategy. (In other words, a stability strategy is tried.)

**4** As the environment changes even more, the enterprise begins to consider seriously the retrenchment, combination, or growth strategies previously suggested by a few executives and ignored at the time.

---

Past strategies are the beginning point of the choice and may eliminate some choices as a result.

## 4) Managerial power relationships [6]

Those with experience know that the power relationships are a key reality in organizational life. In many enterprises, if the top manager begins to advocate one alternative, it is soon unanimous. In others, cliques develop and if one clique begins to support one, the other opposes it.

Sometimes, personalities get involved in the choice: whom the boss likes and respects has a lot to do with which choice is made. And sometimes if "mistakes" are made, the powerful can shift blame to lower-level executives.

No one doubts that power or politics influences decisions, including strategic decisions. The question is: How often is power the crucial factor or a factor in these decisions?

There is not a lot of evidence, but two studies give us some ideas on this. Mintzberg studied 25 strategic decisions. He found that when politics was a factor, it slowed the decision-making process down. He also found that in 8 of the 25 decisions, power or politics was a crucial factor. It was a less important factor in all the other decisions as well. Mintzberg also analyzed how the power relationships were exercised.

---

**RESEARCH STUDY**

■ **MINTZBERG'S 1974 FINDINGS**

**1** There were three ways in which strategic choices were made: judgment, bargaining, and analysis. In judgment, a single individual makes a choice in his own mind (the word *judgment* is used here simply as a label for subconscious decision processes); in bargaining, selection is made by a group of decision makers with conflicting objectives (each exercising judgment); and in analysis, factual data are brought to bear systematically on the evaluation process, generally by staff experts as opposed to managers (choice, by judgment or bargaining, following analysis).

**2** Mintzberg proposes several hypotheses about when each way was used:

---

**PROPOSITION 6–5**

■ The more centralized the responsibility for the decision made, the less documented and quantitative the data available for selection; and the greater the time pressures, the greater the tendency to use judgment.

---

Mintzberg believes judgment is affected by the kinds of variables I labeled attitudes toward past strategy, risk, external dependence, the power realities, and their lack of knowledge.

---

**PROPOSITION 6–6**

■ Bargaining is used when the power for making the decision is divided within the organization, and the issue under consideration is contentious.

---

Here the choice is also affected by the same variables as in judgment, but now it is more complex because there are more decision makers.

PROPOSITION
6-7 ■ The greater the a priori agreement on objectives (and responsibility for selection), the greater the availability of documented and quantitative data and staff specialists; and the larger the relative commitment of resources, the greater the tendency to use analysis.

Mintzberg found analyses were used mostly in larger organizations in *significant* (costly) decisions. Decisions made using analysis were twice as quick as those made using judgment. But the analysis was filtered through the same variables of management attitudes.

**3** Finally Mintzberg found that managers prefer to use judgment or bargaining (not analysis) though they sometimes tried to hide the fact that they did not prefer analysis.

Once again, we find a tendency to prefer action and intuition to systematic analysis in strategic decision making. Finally, Guth studied how a billion-dollar United States corporation adapted its strategy structure to environmental threats over a 4-year period. He found that the decisions were significantly influenced by interpersonal relations and power relationships of the top managers. These studies give us some ideas about the relative impact of power on strategic choice decisions.

### IMPACT OF LOWER-LEVEL MANAGERS ON STRATEGIC CHOICE [6]

Of course, top managers make the strategic choices. But earlier choices made by their subordinates limit the choices usually considered. For example, Bower studied the strategic decisions made in a very large corporation. He found that executives on different levels affect the process in such a way that the final choice does not consider all alternatives. Table 6–3 summarizes his finding. His finding was that a lot of the filtering and choices were made at lower levels before they got to the top levels.

Jules Schwartz tested Bower's findings on Digital Equipment and Texas Instruments Companies. He examined four risky strategic decisions regarding product innovation. He found Bower's model accurate and concluded that lower-level management helped prepare proposals for choice and helped evaluate the risks. The evaluations tended to influence the choices suggested to top management that were less risky, incremental choices, rather than risky, breakthrough choices. *sub - risk adverse*

Eugene Carter studied six acquisition decisions and other strategic decisions at a firm of medium to small size. He also focused on how many persons at many levels influenced the proposals the president eventually made a choice on. His findings were:

RESEARCH ■ CARTER'S FINDINGS
STUDY

**1** Lower-level managers tend to suggest choices that are likely to be accepted and to withhold suggestions that have little chance of approval; where possible, choices are adapted to fit the objectives.

**2** Different departments evaluated choices differently and in their own interest when commenting on a proposed strategic choice.

**3** The greater the uncertainty of outcome in the total environment of the organization, the greater the number of criteria (goals) which will be sought to guide the strategic choice decisions.

**4** The number of criteria (goals) considered in appraising a choice is directly related to the degree of uncertainty in the project's forecasts, where the hierarchy of criteria is determined by mapping of certainty versus uncertainty.

The considerable research that has been reviewed here warrants a summary of how it appears the choice is made.

## Summary: Choice process

The choice of a strategy is not a routine or easy decision. As Braybrooke and Lindblom state:

When a person sets out to make a choice, he [or she] embarks on a course of mental activity more circuitous, more complex, more subtle, and perhaps more idiosyncratic than he [or she] perceives. . . . Dodging in and out of the unconscious, moving back and forth, from concrete to abstract, trying chance here and system there, soaring, jumping, backtracking, crawling, sometimes freezing on point like a bird dog, he [or she] exploits mental processes that are only slowly yielding to observation and systematic description.

Strategic choice, like all decisions, is made in the context of the decision maker and the decision situation. The manager's attitude toward risk, and his or her feelings about where the enterprise fits, blocks out certain choices from view. In 1910 John Dewey asserted:

We do not approach any problem with a wholly naive mind; we approach it with certain

TABLE 6–3 ■ BOWER'S FINDINGS AFFECTING STRATEGIC CHOICE AND RESOURCE ALLOCATION

| Level | Phase | Definition | Impetus | Determination of structural context |
|---|---|---|---|---|
| Corporate group | Corporate | . . . | . . . | Primary determinant |
| Division | Integrating | . . . | Primary determinant | |
| Area product group | Initiating | Primary determinant | | |

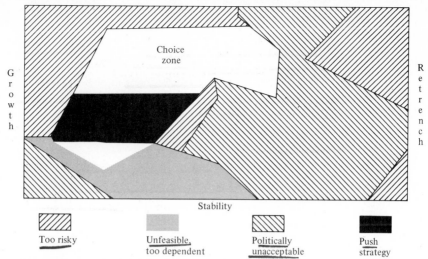

FIGURE 6–2 ■ Overlays for strategic choice.

acquired habitual modes of understanding, with a certain store of previously evolved meanings or at least of experiences from which meanings may be educed.

Unable to follow the "rational model" of choice because of a lack of ability, lack of costly information, or fast-changing conditions, the strategic planner focuses on choices from alternatives which change the status quo by increments. The planner ranks the few incremental choices within what I call the choice zone in Figure 6–2. This figure represents the small choice zone after ignoring the risky, unfeasible, and unacceptable zones. The choice follows the pattern in Table 6–4 and "Glueck's Choice Process."

General Electric recently formulated its decision-making approach—called the "stoplight strategy." The strategy enables GE to evaluate such factors as the value of a patent or the impact of social change.

TABLE 6–4 ■ INCREMENTAL STRATEGIC CHOICE

| Step | Choice | Strategy | |
|------|--------|----------|--|
| 5 | 6 | Retrenchment | 6D liquidation<br>6C captive company<br>6B divestment<br>6A cutback |
| 4 | 5 | Growth with retrenchment | 5C captive company<br>5B divestment<br>5A cutback |
| 3 | 4 | Growth (A–F as 3A–F) | |
| 2 | 3 | Combination: Stability with | 3F external growth: conglomerate<br>3E external growth: concentric<br>3D external growth: horizontal<br>3C internal growth: new products (conglomerate)<br>3B internal growth: new products (concentric)<br>3A internal growth: present products |
| 1 | 2<br>1 | Stability: functional change<br>Stability: more of the same | |

**A** Compare first the present strategy (stability) with an incremental functional change staying with present grand strategy.

**B** If A appears unable to meet the gaps in objectives, compare the stability (functional change) strategy with combination strategy of stability plus horizontal-concentric growth.

**C** If B appears insufficient, compare combination strategy (stability and growth) to growth.

**D** If C is insufficient, compare combinations (growth with retrenchment).

**E** If D is insufficient, compare D with retrenchment.

**F** In sum, the decision maker considers choices closest to the present and incrementally moves from the most preferred strategies to the least preferred. The decision maker stops when it appears the gap is met. Table 6–4 portrays the steps.

*See prior page*

## Contingency strategies

In more developed strategic planning, top managers make their choice of strategy. But they also prepare alternative strategies if conditions should change. When conditions change sufficiently, consideration of the contingency strategy is triggered. *Business Week* reported in 1975:

> Instead of relying on a single corporate plan with perhaps one or two variations, top management at more and more companies is now getting a whole battery of contingency plans and alternate scenarios. "We shoot for alternative plans that can deal with either/or eventualities," says George J. Prendergast, in charge of planning at chemical giant E. I. du Pont de Nemours & Co.
>
> Companies are reviewing and revising plans more frequently in line with changing conditions. Instead of the old five-year plan that might have been updated annually, plans are often updated quarterly, monthly, or even weekly. Arizona Public Service Co. last year adopted a "dynamic" budget that looks ahead two years but is rolled over every month. At Ralston Purina Co., a 1% change in the price of a prime commodity kicks off a change in the company's cost models and the whole corporate plan may change accordingly.
>
> In the end, of course, that puts more pressure on top management, which must operate with an eye to numerous plans instead of being able to follow a single scenario. At Exxon Corp., for instance, most-probable-case forecasts have been replaced by less definitive "envelopes" that include a range of possibilities. Says Brice A. Sachs, deputy corporate planning manager: "Today you still have to have a game plan. How do you get to that? Top management judgment and intuition. We don't really pin some things down anymore. There's a lot more thrown at the management."

## Strategic choices actually made [7]

Now that we understand a bit more about *how* the strategic choice is made, this section will review some information on which strategies have been chosen most frequently in the past. The objective of this section is to build a data bank of past choices under varying conditions to guide the future choices of business executives.

Charles Hofer (1973) reported the results of his analysis of managers' strategic choices in *Fortune* case studies in 1960–1965. Some of his conclusions were:

---

**RESEARCH STUDY** ■ **HOFER'S FINDINGS, 1960–1965 CASES**

**1**   Different types of challenges lead to different strategies.

**2**   When environmental opportunities are large and/or when there are excess resources, firms tried to increase the scope of present operations.

**3**   When conditions opposite to condition 2 existed, firms cut back and made changes in functional strategies or chose conglomerate diversification.

**4**   The most frequent strategies were development of new products for existing markets and increased penetration of existing products in existing markets.

**5**   The least frequent strategies used were forward vertical integration and internal diversification.

---

Hofer then began to look at how firms responded with strategic decisions at various phases of the life cycle. Hofer's preliminary hypotheses as a result of these analyses are Propositions 6–8 to 6–12. Hofer developed the propositions in further detail for use of strategic planners.

---

**RESEARCH STUDY** ■ **HOFER'S STRATEGIC PROPOSITIONS**

**6–8**   The most fundamental variable in determining an appropriate competitive strategy is the stage of the product life cycle.

**6–9**   Major changes in business strategy are usually required during three stages of the life cycle: introduction, maturity, and decline.

**6–10**   In the introductory stage of the life cycle, the major determinants of competitive business strategy are the newness of the product, the rate of technological change in product design, the needs of the buyer, and the frequency with which the product is purchased.

**6–11**   In the maturity stage of the life cycle, the major determinants of competitive business strategy are the nature of buyer needs, the degree of product differentiation, the rate of technological change in process design, the degree of market segmentation, the ratio of distribution costs to manufacturing value added, and the frequency with which the product is purchased.

The secondary determinants of competitive business strategy during the maturity phase of the product life cycle vary depending on the degree of product differentiation and the nature of the buyer's needs as indicated in the following proposition.

**6–12** In the decline stage of the life cycle, the major determinants of competitive business strategy are buyer loyalty, the degree of product differentiation, the price elasticity of demand, the company's share of market and product quality, and marginal plant size.

---

My analysis of the strategic choices of executives of 358 *Fortune* companies over 45 years extended Hofer's work.

I found the following strategies and frequencies in the companies' choices:

Growth 54.4 percent

Combination 28.7 percent

Stability 9.2 percent

Retrenchment 7.5 percent

When we look closely at how the strategic choices varied by economic period, and remembering the overall distribution in all periods, we see:

**1** Retrenchment, the least popular strategy, almost equals the growth strategy in depression periods, but is about one-fourth of growth strategies in good times, one-half in recession, and one-third in recovery.

**2** Stability strategy, second from bottom in popularity, is chosen more than half as often as growth in depression and prosperity, two-thirds as often as growth in recovery, and is least popular (about one-third) in recession.

**3** Combination strategies are the most popular in prosperity when they equal one-third of growth. They are less popular in other periods.

**4** Growth is the most popular in prosperity of course (more than 50 percent), but it is chosen about as often in recession and recovery. It drops to about one-third in depression strategies.

On the basis of the overall distribution of the strategies, it is interesting to note that the emphasis in strategic choices has changed over time. Combination strategies have become more popular, and by the 1960s they were about 20 percent of strategies. Early 1970 saw a decline in combination choices to 10 percent. Growth was a consistent 40 percent of choices over the years. Stability has held at about 20 percent, and retrenchment has gone up and down from as low as 10 percent (1940s) to as high as 25 percent (1970s).

The choices vary by industry type. Growth is consistently high (40 to 55 percent) but highest in conglomerate and the "other" category, lowest in industrial goods. With combination strategies, conglomerate and others were the highest, industrial goods the lowest as with growth (varying from a high of 10 percent, low of 5 percent). With stability, the percentage varied from 33⅓ percent (construction, mining, and oil) to a low of 10 percent (conglomerate and other); the lows were 7½ percent for consumer goods and industrial goods.

When I looked at which strategies were most effective, I found that combination strategies and stability strategies were effective about half the time. Retrenchment was more than twice as likely to be a failure as a success whereas growth was much more likely to be a success than a failure.

Before ending this section, I must admit these data do not support my proposition in Chapter 5 that the most frequently followed strategies are (in order) stability, combination, growth, and retrenchment.

I believe this did not prove out because *Fortune* does not write many cases on small and medium-sized firms and is less likely to write a story of a stability strategy; it lacks drama.

## Choice and the strategic planning process [8]

Just before the summary of the chapter, I would like to give you Robert Katz's advice on strategic choice.

Robert Katz, without telling us how he arrived at his conclusions, says that his years of observations of strategic choice lead him to give top managers these guidelines on which alternative to choose:

---

RESEARCH STUDY

■ **KATZ'S ADVICE ON STRATEGIC CHOICE**

**1** Always lead from strength: choose the alternative that maximizes present strengths.

**2** Concentrate resources where the company has (or could develop readily) a meaningful competitive advantage and ignore small products with small market shares.

**3** Small companies should be as inconspicuous as possible, but should choose products or markets neglected by the large companies.

**4** Small companies' major strategic advantage is to move quickly into new opportunities.

---

This chapter has focused on the height of the drama of strategic planning: the actual choice of the strategy. It is the most exciting and least understood. It stands at the center of strategic planning. Failure of a firm can result if the manager cannot make a choice. It is really what he is paid for. In fact, choice, analysis, and implementation overlap and can be separated only in our minds. We still have a lot to learn about conditions under which strategic choices are made. Miller has made a start on researching this, but it is likely to be years before we have definite answers.

Chapter 7 focuses on how the choice must translate into action through implementation.

## References

**[1]** Gilmore, Frank, and Richard Brandenberg: "Anatomy of Corporate Planning," *Harvard Business Review,* pp. 61–69, November–December 1962.

Hall, William: "Strategic Planning Models: Are Top Managers Really Finding Them Useful?" *Journal of Business Policy,* **3** (2): 33–42, Winter 1973.

Mason, R. Hal, et al.: "Corporate Strategy: A Point of View," *California Management Review,* **13** (3): 5–12, Spring 1971.

Sellstedt, B.: "Some Quantitative Methods in Strategic Planning," European Institute for Advanced Studies in Management, mimeograph, 1974.

Wynne, Bayard, and Peter Newsted: "Aumenting Man's Judgment with Interactive Computer Systems," Working Paper, University of Wisconsin-Milwaukee, 1974.

[2] Stagner, Ross: "Corporate Decision Making," *Journal of Applied Psychology,* 53 (1): 1–13, February 1969.

Ziemer, D. R., and P. D. Maycock: "A Framework for Strategic Analysis," *Long Range Planning,* pp. 6–17, June 1973.

[3] Khandwalla, Pradip: "Style of Management and Environment: Some Findings," Working Paper, Montreal: McGill University, 1974.

Lundberg, Olof, and Max Richards: "A Relationship between Cognitive Style and Complex Decision Making; Implications for Business Policy," *Proceedings, Academy of Management,* 1972.

McKenney, James, and Peter Keen: "How Managers' Minds Work," *Harvard Business Review,* pp. 79–90, May–June 1974.

Nyström, Harry: "Uncertainty, Information and Organizational Decision Making: A Cognitive Approach," *Swedish Journal of Economics,* **76:** 131–139, 1974.

[4] Hetrick, James: "A Formal Model for Long Range Planning: Assessment of Opportunity and Risk," *Long Range Planning,* 1 (4): 54–65, 1968.

Wilson, A. C. B.: "Human and Organization Problems in Corporate Planning," *Long Range Planning,* 5: 67–71, March 1972.

[5] Guth, William: "Towards a Social System Theory of Corporate Strategy," *Journal of Business,* Spring 1976.

Mintzberg, Henry: "Research on Strategy Making," *Proceedings, Academy of Management,* 1972.

———— et al.: "The Structure of Unstructured Decisions," Montreal: McGill University, 1974. (Mimeograph.)

[6] Bower, Joseph: *Managing the Resource Allocation Process,* Cambridge, Mass.: Harvard University Press, 1970.

Carter, E. Eugene: "The Behavioral Theory of the Firm and Top Level Corporate Decisions," *Administrative Science Quarterly,* 16 (4): 413–428, 1971.

Gilmore, Frank: "Overcoming the Perils of Advocacy in Corporate Planning," *California Management Review,* 15 (3): 127–137, Spring 1973.

McMurry, Robert: "Power and the Ambitious Executive," *Harvard Business Review,* pp. 140–145, November–December 1973.

Pettigrew, Andrew: "Information Control as a Power Resource," *Sociology,* 6 (2): May 1972.

Schwartz, Jules: "The Decision to Innovate," unpublished D.B.A. thesis, Harvard Business School, 1973.

Wheelwright, Steven: "An Experimental Analysis of Strategic Planning Procedures," *Journal of Business Policy,* 3 (3): 61–74, Spring 1973.

Zaleznik, Abraham: "Power and Politics in Organizational Life," *Harvard Business Review,* pp. 47–60, May–June 1970.

[7] Hofer, Charles: "Some Preliminary Research on Patterns of Strategic Behavior," *Proceedings, Academy of Management,* 1973.

————: "Toward a Strategic Theory of the Firm," *Proceedings, Academy of Management,* 1974.

[8] Katz, Robert: *Management of the Total Enterprise,* Englewood Cliffs, N.J.: Prentice-Hall, 1971.

Miller, Dan: "Towards Contingency Theory of Strategy Formulation," *Proceedings, Academy of Management,* August 1975.

# Strategy-making in three modes

## Henry Mintzberg

How do organizations make important decisions and link them together to form strategies? So far, we have little systematic evidence about this important process, known in business as *strategy-making* and in government as *policy-making*. The literature of management and public administration is, however, replete with general views on the subject. These fall into three distinct groupings or "modes." In the *entrepreneurial* mode, found in the writings of some of the classical economists and of many contemporary management writers, one strong leader takes bold, risky actions on behalf of his organization. Conversely, in the *adaptive* mode, described by a number of students of business and governmental decision-making, the organization adapts in small, disjointed steps to a difficult environment. Finally, the proponents of management science and policy science describe the *planning* mode, in which formal analysis is used to plan explicit, integrated strategies for the future.

I shall begin by describing each mode as its proponents do, in simple terms and distinct from the other two. Considered in this way, each may appear to be a naive reflection of the complex reality of strategy-making. But taken as a set of three, as I shall do in subsequent sections, to be combined and alternated by managers acting under different conditions, these modes constitute a realistic and useful description of the strategy-making process. To illustrate this point, I shall cite studies of the strategy-making behaviors of a number of very different kinds of organizations—hotels, hospitals, car dealerships, modeling agencies, airports, radio stations, and so on. Finally, I shall discuss some important implications for strategic planning.

## The entrepreneurial mode

The entrepreneur was first discussed by early economists as that individual who founded enterprises. His roles were essentially those of innovation, of dealing with uncertainty, and of brokerage. The entrepreneur found capital which he brought together with marketing opportunity to form, in the words of Joseph Schumpeter, the well known Harvard economist, "new combinations."

Reprinted by permission from *California Management Review,* Winter 1973, pp. 44–53.

In a recent book called *The Organization Makers,* Orvis Collins and David Moore present a fascinating picture of those independent entrepreneurs, based on a study of 150 of them. The authors trace the lives of these men from childhood, through formal and informal education, to the steps they took to create their enterprises. Data from psychological tests reinforce their analysis. What emerges are pictures of tough, pragmatic men driven from early childhood by a powerful need for achievement and independence. At some point in his life, each entrepreneur faced disruption ("role deterioration"), and it was here that he set out on his own:

What sets them apart is that during this time of role deterioration they interwove their dilemmas into the projection of a business. In moments of crisis, they did not seek a situation of security. They went on into deeper insecurity . . .[1]

A number of management writers view the entrepreneurial mode of strategy-making not only in terms of creating new firms but in terms of the running of ongoing enterprises. Typical of these is Peter Drucker, who writes in a recent article:

Central to business enterprise is . . . the entrepreneurial act, an act of economic risk-taking. And business enterprise is an entrepreneurial institution . . . Entrepreneurship is thus central to function, work and performance of the executive in business.[2]

What are the chief characteristics of the entrepreneurial mode of strategy-making as described by economists and management writers? We can delineate four:

**1** In the entrepreneurial mode, strategy-making is dominated by the active search for new opportunities.

The entrepreneurial organization focuses on opportunities; problems are secondary. Drucker writes: "Entrepreneurship requires that the few available good people be deployed on opportunities rather than frittered away on 'solving problems'."[3] Furthermore, the orientation is always active rather than passive. Robert McNamara, when he was Secretary of Defense, stressed the active role for the government administrator:

I think that the role of public manager is very similar to the role of a private manager; in each case he has the option of following one of two major alternative courses of action. He can either act as a judge or a leader. In the former case, he sits and waits until subordinates bring to him problems for solution, or alternatives for choice. In the latter case, he immerses himself in the operations of the business or the governmental activity . . .

I have always believed in and endeavored to follow the active leadership role as opposed to the passive judicial role.[4]

**2** In the entrepreneurial organization, power is centralized in the hands of the chief executive.

Collins and Moore write of the founder-entrepreneur: "The entrepreneurial personality . . . is characterized by an unwillingness to 'submit' to authority, an inability to work with it, and a consequent need to escape from it."[5] In the entrepreneurial mode, power rests with one man capable of committing the organization to bold courses of action. He rules by fiat, relying on personal power and sometimes on charisma. Consider this description of an Egyptian firm:

The great majority of Egyptian-owned private establishments . . . are organized closer to the pattern of the Abboud enterprises. Here the manager is a dominant individual who extends his personal control over all phases of the business. There is no charted plan of organization, no formalized procedure for selection and development of managerial personnel, no publicized system of wage and salary classifications.

. . . authority is associated exclusively with an individual . . .

Abboud is the kind of person most people have in mind when they discuss the successful Egyptian entrepreneur.[6]

But while there may be "no charted plan of organization," typically one finds instead that strategy is guided by the entrepreneur's own vision of direction for his organization—his personalized plan of attack. Drucker writes:

Every one of the great business builders we know of—from the Medici and the founders of the Bank of England down to IBM's Thomas Watson in our days—had a definite idea, indeed a clear 'theory of the business' which informed his actions and decisions.[7]

3  Strategy-making in the entrepreneurial mode is characterized by dramatic leaps forward in the face of uncertainty.

Strategy moves forward in the entrepreneurial organization by the taking of large, bold decisions. The chief executive seeks out and thrives in conditions of uncertainty, where his organization can make dramatic gains. The entrepreneurial mode is probably most alive in the popular business magazines such as *Fortune* and *Forbes* which each month devote a number of articles to the bold actions of manager-entrepreneurs. The theme that runs through these articles is what has been referred to as the "bold stroke," the courageous move that succeeds against all the odds and all the advice.

4  Growth is the dominant goal of the entrepreneurial organization

According to psychologist David McClelland, the entrepreneur is motivated above all by his need for achievement. Since his organization's goals are simply the extension of his own, we can conclude that the dominant goal of the organization operating in the entrepreneurial mode is growth, the most tangible manifestation of achievement. *Fortune* magazine came to this conclusion in a 1956 article about the Young Presidents' Organization entitled "The Entrepreneurial Ego":

Most of the young presidents have the urge to build rather than manipulate. 'Expansion is a sort of disease with us,' says one president. 'Let's face it,' says another. 'We're empire builders. The tremendous compulsion and obsession is not to make money, but to build an empire.' The opportunity to keep on pushing ahead is, indeed, the principal advantage offered by the entrepreneurial life.[8]

In summary, we can conclude that the organization operating in the entrepreneurial mode suggests by its actions that the environment is malleable, a force to be confronted and controlled.


## The adaptive mode

The view of strategy-making as an adaptive process has gained considerable popularity since the publication of two complimentary books in 1963. Charles

Lindblom and David Braybrooke wrote *A Strategy of Decision* about policy-making in the public sector, while Richard Cyert and James March published *A Behavioral Theory of the Firm* based on empirical studies of decision-making.

Lindblom first called this approach "the science of 'muddling through'," later "disjointed incrementalism."[9] The term "adaptive" is chosen here for its simplicity. As described by Lindblom, the adaptive policy-maker accepts as given a powerful status quo and the lack of clear objectives. His decisions are basically remedial in nature, and he proceeds in small steps, never moving too far from the given status quo. In this way, the policy-maker comes to terms with his complex environment.

Cyert and March's strategy-maker, although working in the business firm, operates in much the same fashion. Again, his world is complex and he must find the means to cope with it. Cyert and March suggest that he does so in a number of ways. He consciously seeks to avoid uncertainty, sometimes solving pressing problems instead of developing long-run strategies, other times "negotiating" with the environment (for example, establishing cartels). Furthermore, because the organization is controlled by a coalition of disparate interests, the strategy-maker must make his decisions so as to reduce conflicts. He does this by attending to conflicting goals sequentially, ignoring the inconsistencies:

Just as the political organization is likely to resolve conflicting pressures to 'go left' and 'go right' by first doing one and then the other, the business firm is likely to resolve conflicting pressures to 'smooth production' and 'satisfy customers' by first doing one and then the other.[10]

Four major characteristics distinguish the adaptive mode of strategy-making:

**1** Clear goals do not exist in the adaptive organization; strategy-making reflects a division of power among members of a complex coalition.

The adaptive organization is caught in a complex web of political forces. Unions, managers, owners, lobby groups, government agencies, and so on, each with their own needs, seek to influence decisions. There is no one central source of power, no one simple goal. The goal system of the organization is characterized by bargaining among these groups, with each winning some issues and losing others. Hence, the organization attends to a whole array of goals sequentially, ignoring the inconsistencies among them. The organization cannot make decisions to "maximize" any one goal such as profit or growth; rather it must seek solutions to its problems that are good enough, that satisfy the constraints.

**2** In the adaptive mode, the strategy-making process is characterized by the "reactive" solution to existing problems rather than the "proactive" search for new opportunities.

The adaptive organization works in a difficult environment that imposes many problems and crises. Little time remains to search out opportunities. And even if there were time, the lack of clear goals in the organization would preclude a proactive approach:

. . . if [the strategy-makers] cannot decide with any precision the state of affairs they want to achieve, they can at least specify the state of affairs from which they want to escape. They deal more confidently with what is wrong than with what in the future may or may not be right.[11]

Furthermore, the adaptive organization seeks conditions of certainty wherever possible, otherwise it seeks to reduce existing uncertainties. It establishes cartels to ensure markets, negotiates long-term purchasing arrangements to stabilize sources of supply, and so on.

**3**  The adaptive organization makes its decisions in incremental, serial steps.

Because its environment is complex, the adaptive organization finds that feedback is a crucial ingredient in strategy-making. It cannot take large decisions for fear of venturing too far into the unknown. The strategy-maker focuses first on what is familiar, considering the convenient alternatives and the ones that differ only slightly from the status quo. Hence, the organization moves forward in incremental steps, laid end to end in serial fashion so that feedback can be received and the course adjusted as it moves along. As Lindblom notes, ". . . policy-making is typically a never-ending process of successive steps in which continual nibbling is a substitute for a good bite." [12]

**4**  Disjointed decisions are characteristic of the adaptive organization.

Decisions cannot be easily interrelated in the adaptive mode. The demands on the organization are diverse, and no manager has the mental capacity to reconcile all of them. Sometimes it is simply easier and less expensive to make decisions in disjointed fashion so that each is treated independently and little attention is paid to problems of coordination. Strategy-making is fragmented, but at least the strategy-maker remains flexible, free to adapt to the needs of the moment. Lindblom provides us with an apt summary of the adaptive mode:

Man has had to be devilishly inventive to cope with the staggering difficulties he faces. His analytical methods cannot be restricted to tidy scholarly procedures. The piece-mealing, remedial incrementalist or satisficer may not look like an heroic figure. He is nevertheless a shrewd, resourceful problem-solver who is wrestling bravely with a universe that he is wise enough to know is too big for him. [13]

## The planning mode

In a recent book, Russell Ackoff isolates the three chief characteristics of the planning mode:

**1**  Planning is something we do in advance of taking action; that is, it is *anticipatory decision-making*. . . .

**2**  Planning is required when the future state that we desire involves a set of interdependent decisions; that is, a *system of decisions*. . . .

**3**  Planning is a process that is directed toward producing one or more future states which are desired and which are not expected to occur unless something is done. [14]

Formal planning demands rationality in the economist's sense of the term—the systematic attainment of goals stated in precise, quantitative terms. The key actor in the process is the analyst, who uses his scientific techniques to develop formal, comprehensive plans.

The literature of planning is vast, and is growing rapidly. Much of the early writing concerned "operational planning"—the projecting of various budgets based on the given strategies of the organization. More recently, attention has turned to the planning of organizational strategies themselves, the more significant and long-range concerns of senior managers. Two techniques have received particular attention—strategic planning in business and planning-programming-budgeting system (PPBS) in government.

George Steiner has written what up to this point is the definitive book on business planning, entitled *Top Management Planning*. The general prescriptive flavor of the planning literature is found throughout this book. For example, "Plans can and should be to the fullest possible extent objective, factual, logical, and realistic in establishing objectives and devising means to attain them." [15] Steiner outlines a stepwise procedure for business planning which begins with three studies: (1) fundamental organizational socioeconomic purpose, (2) values of top management, and (3) evaluation of external and internal opportunities and problems, and company strengths and weaknesses. Strategic plans are then devised, and these lead to the formulation of medium-range programs and short-range plans. In Steiner's opinion, comprehensive planning is important because it simulates the future, applies the systems approach, prevents piecemeal decision-making, provides a common decision-making framework throughout the company, and so on.

In PPBS, the focus is on the budget rather than the general plan (although a budget is, of course, one type of plan). The steps in the process are, by now, well known—the determination of overall governmental goals and objectives, the generation of program proposals to achieve these, the evaluation of these proposals in terms of costs and benefits, the choice of a group of proposals that will satisfy the objectives while not overextending the resources, and the translation of these into five-year and one-year budgets for implementation.

We can delineate three essential features of the planning mode:

**1** In the planning mode, the analyst plays a major role in strategy-making.

The analyst or planner works alongside the manager, and assumes major responsibility for much of the strategy-making process. His role is to apply the techniques of management science and policy analysis to the design of long-range strategies. A U.S. Senator notes the reasons for this:

I am convinced that we never will get the kind of policy planning we need if we expect the top-level officers to participate actively in the planning process. They simply do not have the time, and in any event they rarely have the outlook or the talents of the good planner. They cannot explore issues deeply and systematically. They cannot argue the advantages and disadvantages at length in the kind of give-and-take essential if one is to reach a solid understanding with others on points of agreement and disagreement. [16]

**2** The planning mode focuses on systematic analysis, particularly in the assessment of the costs and benefits of competing proposals.

Formal planning involves both the active search for new opportunities and the solution of existing problems. The process is always systematic and structured. As one business planner wrote recently:

No doubt much of top-level management is unscientific. But by applying a systematic, structured approach to these problems, we have a better basis for analyzing them. We may identify more specifically the challenges and needs in the situation and see how they are interrelated. [17]

Formal planning follows a stepwise procedure in which particular attention is paid to the cost-benefit evaluation of proposals, where the planning methodology is best developed. The planner tests proposals for feasibility, determines their efficiency (or economic value), and relates them to each other. The planner deals best with conditions known to the management scientist as "risk"—where the uncertainty can be expressed in statistical terms. Conditions of certainty require no planning; those of pure uncertainty cannot be subjected to analysis.

**3** The planning mode is characterized above all by the integration of decisions and strategies.

Ackoff notes that "the principal complexity in planning derives from the interrelatedness of decisions rather than from the decisions themselves."[18] But this interrelatedness is the key element in planning. An organization plans in the belief that decisions made together in one systematic process will be less likely to conflict and more likely to complement each other than if they were made independently. For example, planning can ensure that the decision to acquire a new firm complements (or at least does not conflict with) the decision to expand the product line of an existing division. Thus, strategic planning is a process whereby an organization's strategy is designed essentially at one point in time in a comprehensive process (all major decisions made are interrelated). Because of this, planning forces the organization to think of global strategies and to develop an explicit sense of strategic direction.

To conclude the planning mode is oriented to systematic, comprehensive analysis and is used in the belief that formal analysis can provide an understanding of the environment sufficient to influence it.

The upper part of Table I presents in summary form the characteristics of the three modes of strategy-making, while Figure 1 depicts these three modes in graphic form. The first figure shows the taking of bold steps consistent with the entrepreneur's general vision of direction. In the second figure, we see a purely adaptive organization taking incremental steps in reaction to environ-

**TABLE I ■ CHARACTERISTICS AND CONDITIONS OF THE THREE MODES**

|  | Entrepre-neurial mode | Adaptive mode | Planning mode |
|---|---|---|---|
| *Characteristic* |  |  |  |
| Motive for decisions | Proactive | Reactive | Proactive & reactive |
| Goals of organization | Growth | Indeterminate | Efficiency & growth |
| Evaluation of proposals | Judgemental | Judgemental | Analytical |
| Choices made by | Entrepreneur | Bargaining | Management |
| Decision horizon | Long term | Short term | Long term |
| Preferred environment | Uncertainty | Certainty | Risk |
| Decision linkages | Loosely coupled | Disjointed | Integrated |
| Flexibility of mode | Flexible | Adaptive | Constrained |
| Size of moves | Bold decisions | Incremental steps | Global strategies |
| Vision of direction | General | None | Specific |
| *Condition for use* |  |  |  |
| Source of power | Entrepreneur | Divided | Management |
| Objectives of organization | Operational | Nonoperational | Operational |
| Organizational environment | Yielding | Complex, dynamic | Predictable, stable |
| Status of organization | Young, small or strong leadership | Established | Large |

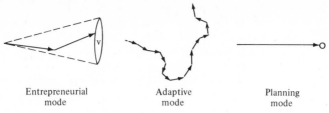

| Entrepreneurial | Adaptive | Planning |
| mode | mode | mode |

**FIGURE 1** ■ Paths of the three modes.

mental forces, while the third figure indicates a precise plan with a specific, unalterable path to one clear end point.

## The determination of mode

What conditions drive an organization to favor one mode of strategy-making over the others? We may delineate a number of characteristics of the organization itself, such as its size and the nature of its leadership, and features of its environment, such as competition and stability. These are discussed below and are summarized in the lower portion of Table I.

The *entrepreneurial* mode requires that strategy-making authority rest with one powerful individual. The environment must be yielding, the organization oriented toward growth, the strategy able to shift boldly at the whim of the entrepreneur. Clearly, these conditions are most typical of organizations that are small and/or young. Their sunk costs are low and they have little to lose by acting boldly. Young organizations in particular have set few precedents for themselves and have made few commitments. The way is open for them to bunch a number of key decisions at an early stage and take them in entrepreneurial fashion. This behavior may also be characteristic of the organization in trouble—it has little to lose by acting boldly, indeed this may be its only hope. In a study of the Montreal radio industry, one student concluded that the less successful stations were predisposed to adopt an entrepreneurial approach in order to catch up and displace the leader (whose behavior was primarily adaptive).

To satisfy the condition of centralized power, the organization must be either a business firm (often with the owner as chief executive), or an institutional or governmental body with a powerful leader who has a strong mandate. The entrepreneurial mode is often found with charismatic leadership. Charles de Gaulle could have been characterized as an entrepreneur at the head of government.

Use of the *adaptive* mode suggests that the organization faces a complex, rapidly changing environment and a divided coalition of influencer forces. Goals cannot be agreed upon unless they are in "motherhood" form and non-operational (they cannot be quantified). Here we have a clear description of the large established organization with great sunk costs and many controlling groups holding each other in check. This is typical of most universities, of many large hospitals, of a surprising number of large corporations, and of many governments, especially those in minority positions or composed of coalitions of divergent groups. Indeed, the American system of government has been expressly designed to create conditions of divided power, and it is, therefore, not surprising that Charles Lindblom, the chief proponent of the adaptive approach, is a student of the U.S. public policy-making process.

In order to rely on the *planning* mode, an organization must be large enough to afford the costs of formal analysis, it must have goals that are operational, and it must face an environment that is reasonably predictable and stable. (This last point inevitably raises the comment that planning is most necessary when the environment is difficult to understand. This may be true, but the costs of analyzing a complex environment may be prohibitive and the results may be discouraging. As one Latin American chief executive commented: "Planning is great. But how can you plan—let alone plan long-term—if you don't know what kind of government you'll have next year?" [19])

The above conditions suggest that formal comprehensive planning will generally be found in business firms of reasonable size that do not face severe and unpredictable competition and in government agencies that have clear, apolitical mandates. NASA of the 1960s is a prime example of extended use of the planning mode in government. Its goal was precise and operational, its funding predictable, its mission essentially apolitical in execution. The communist form of government with its five year plan is another good example. The power system is hierarchical, goals can be made operational, the home environment can be controlled and made more or less stable and predictable (at least as long as the crops are good).

## Mixing the modes

What is the relationship between our three abstractions and strategy-making reality? Clearly, few organizations can rely on a pure mode. More likely, an organization will find some combination of the three that reflects its own needs. Management students at McGill University have examined a number of business and public organizations according to these three modes, and they have uncovered a variety of ways in which organizations mix these modes. I shall discuss four combinations below, citing examples from these studies to illustrate each.

**Combination 1:** *Mixing the pure modes*   As we have seen, the literature tends to delineate three modes which are quite distinct in their characteristics. This trichotomy provides a convenient starting point for analysis; however, we cannot preclude the existence of other modes that mix their characteristics. Indeed, studies have revealed various combinations of the modes. We have, for example, found a number of adaptive entrepreneurs. One owned a car dealership. Reluctant to delegate authority but unable to achieve further growth without doing so, he was content to hold power absolutely, like the entrepreneur, but to avoid risk and move in incremental steps, like the adaptive strategy-maker.

We can find the two other combinations of the pure modes as well. In entrepreneurial planning, the organization takes bold, decisive steps in terms of a systematic plan for growth, while in adaptive planning the organization reaches a specific goal through a flexible path. Herbert Simon describes an example of adaptive planning found in nature:

We watch an ant make his laborious way across a wind- and wave-molded beach. He moves ahead, angles to the right to ease his climb up a steep dunelet, detours around a pebble, stops for a moment to exchange information with a compatriot. Thus he makes his weaving, halting way back to his home. . . . [His path] has an underlying sense of direction, of aiming toward a goal. . . . He has a general sense of where home lies, but he cannot foresee all the obstacles between. He must adapt his course repeatedly to the difficulties he encounters . . .[20]

**Combination 2:** *Mixing modes by function* Within single organizations, we have found different modes in different functional areas. One group of students carefully studied all departments of a large downtown hotel, and found evidence of all three modes. Where operations were largely routinized and predictable, as in housekeeping and the front office, the planning mode was used. In marketing, where there was room for imagination and bolder action, the hotel tended to act in an entrepreneurial fashion, while in the personnel department, which faced a complicated labor market, the mode was clearly adaptive.

Another group studied a modeling agency and found that in the area of fashion it was forced (as were all its competitors) to adapt to the dictates of the hautes couturieres of Paris, while it was free to be entrepreneurial or to plan in the areas of marketing and operations. Clearly, different parts of an organization can employ those modes which best fit their particular situations.

**Combination 3:** *Mixing modes between parent and subunit* Neil Withers, a member of a group studying the Montreal International Airport (which comes under the purview of the Canadian Department of Transport), became interested in the relationship between a parent organization and its subunit (a division, a subsidiary, an agency, and so on). The question he addressed was: If the parent uses a particular mode, what limitations does that impose on the subunit (assuming, of course, that there is not enough decentralization to allow the subunit to operate independently)? Withers considers all nine possible combinations in which each could use one of the three modes, and he draws some interesting conclusions.

Figure 2 shows the use of the adaptive mode by both parent and subunit—a situation Withers refers to as "muddling through times two." In this case, the subunit merely follows the path of the parent, adapting to its incremental moves, and following a slightly more varied and lagged path. Withers concludes that the adaptive mode is, in fact, always an acceptable one for the subunit, no matter what the mode of the parent.

Withers believes "entrepreneurial duets"—whereby both parent and subunit employ the entrepreneurial mode—to be "the worst possible combination." The subunit is subjected not only to its own bold moves but to the unexpected bold moves of the parent. The disruption may prove intolerable. One is led to conclude that no centralized organization is big enough for two entrepreneurs. Sooner or later one must make a bold, unexpected move that interferes with the other. (In contrast, another group described a decentralized social work agency where strategy-making was largely in the hands of the social workers. They were all entrepreneurs, acting independently to initiate original programs and seeking approval from the main office whose behavior was described as adaptive.)

Finally, Withers considers the conditions under which the subunit can plan. Figure 3 shows a situation where the subunit plans while the parent organization adapts. The subunit at time $t_1$ anticipates the trend of the parent's strategy and plans accordingly.

Up to time $t_2$ no difficulties are incurred, and the subunit continues to extrapolate. But soon the parent's direction begins to change, and the subunit finds itself in conflict with the parent. According to Withers, "The use of

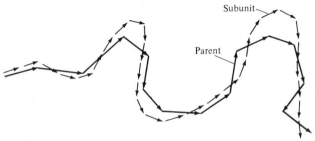

FIGURE 2 ■ Muddling through times two.

planning in this uncertainty may not yield sufficiently improved results over [adapting] to justify the cost of planning and the long-term commitment of resources." Withers concludes that subunit planning will work only if the parent plans and if the two planning centers are properly coordinated.

**Combination 4:** *Mixing modes by stage of development* A number of writers have described the growth of organizations in terms of three or four basic stages—generally corresponding to a life cycle beginning with youth and ending with maturity. It appears that we can characterize the various stages by the mode of strategy-making employed.

Generally, the young organization is entrepreneurial—it has few committed resources, it stands to lose little and to gain much by taking bold steps, leadership tends to be charismatic, and there is much spirit associated with its mission. This is the period of expansion and growth. But each new strategic decision commits additional resources, and gradually the organization locks itself into specific strategies, bureaucratic structures, and demanding pressure groups. The adaptive mode sets in. For example, one group of students studied a Montreal hospital which began in a most entrepreneurial fashion, with dramatic innovations in design and operation. Some time later, when the hospital was established, the provincial government took over increasing control of its budgets and by the time of the study these students felt that the adaptive mode was most descriptive of this organization's strategy-making behavior.

The adaptive mode may signal the final stage of maturity, or the conditions may be such that an organization can attempt to regenerate itself through a new period of entrepreneurship. In fact, it appears that the way to turn around a large, adaptive organization requiring major change is to bring in an entrepreneurial leader. Only by consolidating power in the hands of one strong newcomer will it be possible to override the established factions and the entrenched attitudes.

Some organizations appear to develop cyclical patterns in which periods of entrepreneurship are alternated with periods of adaptiveness. They make a set of bold changes in order to grow, then settle down to a period of stability in which the changes are consolidated, later embark on a new period of growth, and so on. Perhaps in some cases these follow economic cycles—an entrepreneurial mode in an expanding economy, an adaptive mode during recession.

Some time ago, I interviewed the president of a hotel chain who traced his firm's strategy through to the third distinct cycle of change and consolidation. The first stage of growth, as a real estate firm, involved the purchase of a number of older downtown hotels as property investments. Later, realizing

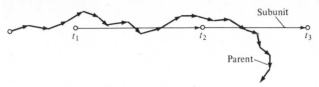

**FIGURE 3** ■ Planning in an adaptive environment.

the potential of investments, the firm entered a period of consolidation in which the properties were developed into an efficient hotel chain. Having reached this point after some years, a second wave of entrepreneurial growth began. First the firm became public in order to obtain expansion capital and then it entered into a major expansion program involving primarily the construction of a chain of modern motor hotels. Toward the end of the program, the firm found that its financial resources were overextended, partly due to higher expansion costs than anticipated. Again growth was halted while the firm consolidated its new units, concentrating on making them efficient, and waiting until its financial reserves were sufficient to begin to grow again. About three years later, at the time of the interview, cycle three has just begun, this time with the emphasis on the construction of larger downtown hotels.

Such an approach to strategy-making may, in fact, be a sensible one. It proceeds on the assumption that it is better to keep the modes distinct, concentrating fully on one mode at a time rather than mixing them and having to reconcile the different styles of strategy-making.

Other organizations, as they mature, tend to use the planning mode—the development of new strategies by controlled, orderly change. As these organizations grow large, they commit more and more of their staff resources to planning. Indeed, this is the thesis of John Kenneth Galbraith who claims, in *The New Industrial State,* that large business firms are controlled by the planners (the "technostructure") who use their techniques to enable the firms in turn to control their markets.

Our studies have not covered these large firms, but analyses of the strategy-making behaviors of a diverse array of smaller organizations—airlines, brokerage firms, universities, race tracks, cultural centers—suggest that virtually all start in the entrepreneurial mode, most later shift to an adaptive mode, and some move on to planning or back to entrepreneurship in their maturity.

## Implications for strategic planning

What can we conclude from this description of strategy-making? One point merits special emphases. *Planning is not a panacea for the problems of strategy-making.* As obvious as this seems, there is little recognition of it in planning books or by planners. Instead, one finds a focus on abstract, simple models of the planning process that take no cognizance of the other two modes of strategy-making. Little wonder then that one finds so much frustration among formal planners. Rather than seeking panaceas, we should recognize that the mode used must fit the situation. An unpredictable environment suggests use of the adaptive mode just as the presence of a powerful leader may enable the organization to best achieve its goals through the entrepreneurial mode.

Some situations require no planning, others only limited planning. Often the planning mode can be used only when mixed with the others. Most important, planners must recognize the need for the manager to remain partially in the adaptive mode at all times. Crises and unexpected events are an important part of every strategy-maker's reality. Conventional planning requires operational goals which managers cannot always provide (the coalition may simply not agree on anything specific). Furthermore, it must be recognized that good planning is expensive, it often requires unrealistic stability in the environment, and, above all, it is the least flexible of the strategy-making modes. All this is not to conclude that planning is useless; rather, it suggests that the planner must become more realistic about the limitations of his science.

Often there is a need to redesign the formal planning process. Adaptive planning would differ from conventional planning in a number of important respects. The plans would be flexible so that the manager could adjust as the future unfolded itself. He would be able to time his moves accordingly—to begin construction on the new plant when interest rates fall, to reorganize the structure after certain executives retire. The plans would also provide for different options—alternate locations for a new plant depending on impending state legislation, different possible acquisition strategies depending on the success of recent acquisitions, and so on. In other words, like the path of the ant described earlier, strategic plans would specify end points and perhaps alternate routes, but they would also leave the manager with the flexibility necessary to react to his dynamic environment.

In addition, the planner could draw up a series of contingency plans to help the manager deal with any one of a number of possible events that could have a sudden, devastating effect on the organization. He could also be prepared to "plan in the real-time," that is, to apply his analytical techniques quickly for the manager who faces an unforeseen crisis. By preparing in this way, planners can more closely adapt themselves to the realities of strategy-making.

## References

1  O. Collins and D. G. Moore, *The Organization Makers* (New York: Appleton, Century, Crofts, 1970), p. 134.

2  P. F. Drucker, "Entrepreneurship in the Business Enterprise," *Journal of Business Policy* (1:1, 1970), p. 10.

3  *Ibid.,* p. 10.

4  Quoted in C. J. Hitch, *Decision-making for Defense* (Berkeley: University of California Press, 1967).

5  Collins and Moore, *op. cit.,* p. 45.

6  F. Harbison and C. A. Myers, *Management in the Industrial World* (New York: McGraw-Hill, 1959), pp. 40–41.

7  Drucker, *op. cit.,* p. 5.

8  S. Klaw, "The Entrepreneurial Ego," *Fortune* (August 1956), p. 143.

9  See C. E. Lindblom, "The Science of 'Muddling Through,' " *Public Administration Review* (19, 1959), pp. 79–88; C. E. Lindblom and David Braybrooke, *A Strategy of*

*Decision* (New York: Free Press, 1963); C. E. Lindblom, *The Intelligence of Democracy* (New York: Free Press, 1965); and C. E. Lindblom, *The Policy-making Process* (Englewood Cliffs, N.J.: Prentice-Hall, 1968).

**10**  R. M. Cyert and J. G. March, *A Behavioral Theory of the Firm* (Englewood Cliffs, N.J.: Prentice-Hall, 1963), p. 118.

**11**  Lindblom, *op. cit.* (1968), p. 25.

**12**  *Ibid.,* p. 25.

**13**  Lindblom, *op. cit.* (1968), p. 27.

**14**  R. L. Ackoff, *A Concept of Corporate Planning* (New York: Wiley Interscience, 1970), pp. 2–5.

**15**  G. A. Steiner, *Top Management Planning* (New York: Macmillan, 1969), p. 20.

**16**  Quoted in R. N. Anthony, *Planning and Control Systems: A Framework for Analysis* (Boston: Harvard Graduate School of Business Administration, 1965), p. 46–47.

**17**  M. F. Cantley, "A Long-Range Planning Case Study," *OR Quarterly* (20, 1969), pp. 7–20.

**18**  R. L. Ackoff, *op. cit.,* p. 3.

**19**  Quoted by H. Stieglitz, *The Chief Executive and His Job* (New York: National Industrial Conference Board, Personnel Policy Study Number 214, 1969), pp. 46–47.

**20**  H. A. Simon, *The Sciences of the Artificial* (Cambridge, Mass.: MIT Press, 1969), pp. 23–24.

# Impact of strategic planning on profit performance

Sidney Schoeffler, Robert D. Buzzell, and Donald F. Heany

What rate of return on investment (ROI) is "normal" in a given type of business, under given market and industry conditions? What factors explain differences in typical levels of ROI among various kinds of businesses?

How will ROI in a specific business be affected by a change in the strategy employed? By a change in competitive activity?

Many corporate presidents and planning directors wish they had more reliable answers to these kinds of questions, for they are at the heart of strategic planning in the modern corporation. Consider some of the ways in which these questions arise:

*Forecasting profits* In a diversified company, the usual practice is for business plans to be prepared by each product division or other operating unit. These plans are then reviewed by corporate executives, often with the assistance of corporate staff specialists. Among the key elements of each unit's plan are, of course, estimates of investment requirements and profits for future periods.

Often these forecasts are simply projections of local experience. But when market conditions are expected to change, or when a change in strategy is contemplated, how reliable is the past as a guide to the future?

*Allocating resources* A major purpose of reviewing divisional plans at the corporate level is to make effective allocations of capital, manpower, and other scarce resources among divisions. Often the capital appropriation requests of the divisions add up to more than headquarters can provide.

The problem, then, is one of emphasis: Which products and markets promise the greatest returns? Here, especially, the profit estimates supplied by divisional managers are likely to be of doubtful reliability, since each division is in the position of pleading its own case.

*Measuring management performance* Closely related to the problem of forecasting profits is the need to evaluate actual profit results. Suppose Division A earns 30% on its investment (pretax), while Division B achieves an ROI of only 15%. Is A's management twice as effective as B's, and should it be rewarded accordingly?

Executives of Division B would no doubt object to this. They would attribute differences in ROI to differences in conditions such as market growth rate and strength of competition. Perhaps they are right. What corporate management would like, in this situation, is some way of determining what level of ROI is reasonable or "normal" for different operating units under given circumstances.

*Appraising new business proposals* Still another common problem in strategic planning is that of estimating ROI in a prospective new business which is being considered for either internal development or acquisition. When the business is new to the company, actual experience, by definition, cannot be consulted. Even when entry is proposed via acquisition, the current performance of the existing business may be of doubtful reliability as a guide to its future.

The common thread running through the four types of strategic planning situations just described is the need for some means of estimating return on investment in a given business, under given industry and market conditions, following a given strategy. Every experienced business executive and corporate planner knows that ROI varies enormously from one business to another and from year to year in an individual division or product line. How can these variations be explained and predicted?

Some answers to these questions are beginning to emerge from a unique research project called PIMS—a study of actual experiences of hundreds of businesses which is aimed at measuring the profit impact of market strategies. Building on work that has been under way at the General Electric Company for more than 10 years (see Exhibit I), the PIMS project is a sharing of experience among 57 major North American corporations.

PIMS was organized in early 1972 as a project of the Marketing Science Institute, a nonprofit research organization associated with the Harvard Business School. The project was established as a cooperative venture, with HBS faculty members and research assistants working alongside planning specialists from industry. (Industry personnel did not, of course, have access to any of the data supplied by other companies.) The project is now organizing its third yearlong phase.

This article is a progress report on Phases I and II of the PIMS project. In it, we shall describe how the study has been carried out and summarize some of the major findings of the first two years' work.


## PIMS profit models

In Phase I of PIMS, 36 corporations supplied information on some 350 businesses. The information included descriptions of industry and market characteristics, as well as selected operating results and balance sheet figures for the years 1970 and 1971.

(All financial data were submitted to PIMS in "scaled" form—that is, actual dollar amounts were multiplied by a scaling factor, such as .5. This procedure served to ensure both the confidentiality of the original data and the relationships among the figures.)

The primary purpose of Phase I was to establish the feasibility of obtaining reasonably comparable data from a large number of diverse companies. Although differences in accounting systems and terminology did pose problems, the project was successful: profit results were explained and predicted

■ **GE'S SEARCH FOR ANSWERS**

The current effort to find better ways to explain and predict operating performance began back in 1960, as an internal project at the General Electric Company.

Fred J. Borch, then GE's vice-president of marketing services, called in Jack McKitterick, his director of market research, and pointed out what today is generally accepted as an axiom: as the market share of a business goes up, so do operating economies. Borch asked McKitterick to survey any relevant published research and the experience of other businessmen with respect to this relationship. If the relationship were valid, executives might have an important clue as to how to improve operating results.

Equally important, Borch wanted to find a handle for GE's growing "manageability" problem. Sales were already at the $4 billion level. By 1970, they were likely to be $8 billion to $9 billion. How could corporate officers like himself stay in touch with so many diverse businesses, ranging all the way from turbine generators to toasters?

After months of exploration, McKitterick became convinced that the best way to address the question was to do some basic pioneering work on the apparent causes of GE's own successes and failures. Borch agreed and authorized a major research project to probe for "laws of the market place." Project PROM (profitability optimization model) was organized under the direction of coauthor Sidney Schoeffler.

After five years of intensive research and testing, Project PROM produced a computer-based model that captured the major factors which explain a great deal of the variability in return on investment. Since this model reflects data from diverse markets and industries, it is often referred to as a "cross-sectional" model—as contrasted to a time-series model based on data over a series of years for a single business.

With the help of this model, GE could estimate the "average" level of profit or investment or cash flow that went with various combinations of the success determinants. The model did not and could not predict the "precise" ROI of any one of GE's businesses in a given year.

When Borch became GE's chief executive officer in 1964, he found the PROM model to be (a) a tool for detecting high-risk strategic moves, (b) a rich source of questions for the review of strategies proposed by divisional managers, and (c) a means of computing the differential between the entire company's financial goals and the expected aggregate earnings of its components. (If the model predicted a shortfall, it could then be used to display the future implications of "belt tightening," component by component.)

In addition to making extensive use of the model himself, Borch also encouraged his group executives and division managers to use it. He supported follow-on research to improve the coverage and predictive powers of the early models.

Today, cross-sectional models are standard elements of GE's corporate planning system.

with considerable accuracy. Moreover, the principal results of GE's earlier work were confirmed. By and large, the same factors that influenced ROI in GE businesses also showed up in the analysis of profitability among the 36 diverse corporations.

Thus, in late 1972, MSI agreed to sponsor a second, enlarged phase of the PIMS project. This time, 57 companies enlisted in the study and supplied more extensive information, covering the years 1970–1972, for 620 businesses. Analysis of this data base over the past several months has led to the current set of PIMS profit models. For the composition of our sample of businesses, see Exhibit I.

### EXPLAINING ROI

The models we and our associates have developed are designed to answer two basic questions: What factors influence profitability in a business—and how much? How does ROI change in response to changes in strategy and in market conditions?

In building quantitative models to explain ROI and changes in ROI, we have drawn on economic theory and on the opinions and beliefs of experienced executives. Economic theory suggests, for example, that different "market structures"—i.e., the number and relative size of competitors—will lead to different profit levels. Business experience indicates that product quality—a factor that has received little attention from economists—is also related to ROI.

Whatever economic theory or businessmen's opinions may suggest, however, the ultimate test of whether and how a given factor is related to profitability is an empirical one. To make such a test, we have constructed an equation that explains more than 80% of the variation in profitability among the 620 businesses in the PIMS data base.

This profit level equation includes more than 60 terms composed of various combinations of 37 basic factors. As might be expected, profitability is related to many different factors. Some of the most important ones are listed and defined in Exhibit II.

#### EXHIBIT I ■ PIMS SAMPLE OF INDIVIDUAL BUSINESSES*

| | |
|---|---|
| Number of companies | 57 |
| Number of businesses | 620* |
| *Type of company* | *Percent of total* |
| Consumer product manufacturers | 19.8% |
| Capital equipment manufacturers | 15.6 |
| Raw materials producers | 11.9 |
| Components manufacturers | 24.1 |
| Supplies manufacturers | 16.5 |
| Service and distribution | 12.1 |
| Total | 100.0% |

* The data presented in Exhibits III-X are based on analyses of 521 businesses. Since the time these analyses were made, information has been received on an additional 99 businesses.

EXHIBIT II ■ ROI AND KEY PROFIT INFLUENCES

**Return on investment (ROI)** The ratio of net, pretax operating income to average investment. Operating income is what is available after deduction of allocated corporate overhead expenses but before deduction of any financial charges on assets employed. "Investment" equals equity plus long-term debt, or, equivalently, total assets employed minus current liabilities attributed to the business.

**Market share** The ratio of dollar sales by a business, in a given time period, to total sales by all competitors in the same market. The "market" includes all of the products or services, customer types, and geographic areas that are directly related to the activities of the business. For example, it includes all products and services that are competitive with those sold by the business.

**Product (service) quality** The quality of each participating company's offerings, appraised in the following terms: What was the percentage of sales of products or services from each business in each year which were superior to those of competitors? What was the percentage of equivalent products? Inferior products? The measure used in Exhibit IV and Exhibit V is the percentage "superior" minus the percentage "inferior."

**Marketing expenditures** Total costs for sales force, advertising, sales promotion, marketing research, and marketing administration. The figures do not include costs of physical distribution.

**R&D expenditures** Total costs of product development and process improvement, including those costs incurred by corporate-level units which can be directly attributed to the individual business.

**Investment intensity** Ratio of total investment to sales.

**Corporate diversity** An index which reflects (1) the number of different 4-digit Standard Industrial Classification industries in which a corporation operates, (2) the percentage of total corporate employment in each industry, and (3) the degree of similarity or difference among the industries in which it participates.

---

The PIMS profit level equation and a separate equation which predicts changes in ROI have been used to construct separate reports for each business in the data pool. These reports "diagnose" the factors influencing ROI in a business, given all of its specific characteristics such as its market, competitive position, capital intensity, and so on.

Because every business is, in some respects, unique, these diagnostic reports vary enormously. But by comparing businesses that are similar in terms of one or more basic profit-influencing factors with businesses that have different characteristics, we can identify some general patterns or relationships.

For example, we can determine an average relationship between market share and profitability by comparing average levels of ROI for groups of businesses with different market shares. This is the approach we have used in subsequent sections of this article.

## Profit determinants

As we mentioned a moment ago, our profit model includes 37 distinct factors which, in various combinations, are significantly related to profitability. However, we shall limit our discussion to just three major determinants of return on investment revealed by our analysis of the PIMS data base—namely, market share, investment intensity, and company factors.

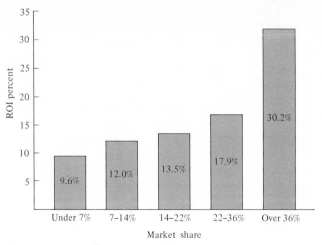

**EXHIBIT III** ■ Relationship of market share to profitability.

## MARKET SHARE

Our analyses give strong support to the proposition that market share is indeed a major influence on profitability. As shown in Exhibit III, ROI goes up steadily as market share increases. On the average, businesses with market shares above 36% earned more than three times as much, relative to investment, as businesses with less than 7% share of their respective markets. (Each of the five market share categories shown in this exhibit represents approximately one fifth of the sample.)

The relationship between market share and profitability has been widely discussed since the inception of Project PROM at General Electric, when the idea was relatively novel. But how and why market share affects profitability is not fully understood as yet.

Our findings suggest that businesses with relatively large market shares tend to have above-average rates of investment turnover, particularly working capital. Also, the ratio of marketing expense to sales is generally lower for high-share businesses than for those with small market shares. These differences are indications of economies of scale that may go along with strong market positions.

However, much remains to be done, both in exploring the connection between market share and ROI and in determining how the relationship varies for different types of businesses or for different market conditions.

Whatever the reasons, the data in Exhibit III clearly show that it is very profitable to have a high share of market. Beyond this, the PIMS profit model sheds some light on how market share and other factors work together to influence ROI.

Consider, for example, the impact of both market share and product quality on ROI, as shown in Exhibit IV. In this exhibit, and in several others that follow, we have divided the PIMS sample of businesses into three approximately equal groups on the basis of each of two factors. The percentages for each of the nine subgroups shown include between 40 and 70 businesses.

EXHIBIT IV ■ EFFECT OF MARKET SHARE AND PRODUCT QUALITY ON ROI

| Market share | Product quality | | |
|---|---|---|---|
| | Inferior | Average | Superior |
| Under 12% | 4.5% | 10.4% | 17.4% |
| 12%–26% | 11.0 | 18.1 | 18.1 |
| Over 26% | 19.5 | 21.9 | 28.3 |

The best of all possible worlds is to have both high market share and superior quality: businesses in this category averaged 28.3% return on investment. But even when quality was relatively inferior, average ROI for high-share businesses was a respectable 19.5%. On the other hand, superior-quality producers with weak market positions earned an average 17.4% on investment, which suggests that quality can partially offset low share.

It should be noted that product quality and market share usually, but by no means always, go together. The percent distribution of the three market share groups, in terms of quality levels, was as follows:

| Percent of businesses with | Market share | | |
|---|---|---|---|
| | Under 12% | 12%–26% | Over 26% |
| Inferior quality | 47% | 33% | 20% |
| Average quality | 30 | 36 | 30 |
| Superior quality | 23 | 31 | 50 |
| Number of businesses | 169 | 176 | 176 |

While it is not surprising that both market share and relative quality influence ROI, in the short term there may be relatively little that management can do to change these factors. Are some strategies more profitable than others, given the basic competitive position of a business? Analysis of the results achieved by the businesses in the PIMS sample suggests that some guidelines can, indeed, be formulated for businesses in different positions.

Consider, for example, the data in Part A of Exhibit V. Here, as in Exhibit IV, the sample has been divided into three roughly equal groups, this time in terms of (a) relative quality, and (b) the ratio of marketing expenditures to sales.

When quality is relatively low—exactly equivalent to competition or somewhat inferior—there is a strong negative relationship between marketing expenditures and ROI. In effect, these figures confirm the old adage that "it doesn't pay to promote a poor product."

ROI is somewhat diminished by a high level of marketing expenditure for businesses with "average" or "superior" relative product quality—but not nearly to the same extent as for competitors with lower-quality products. This might suggest, further, that sellers of higher-quality products or services could inflict severe short-term penalties on weaker competitors by escalating the level of marketing costs in an industry—and that lower-quality producers should avoid such confrontations like the plague.

EXHIBIT V ■ IMPACT OF EXPENDITURES ON PRODUCT QUALITY AND MARKET SHARE

**A   High marketing expenditures damage profitability when quality is low**

| | Ratio of marketing expenditures to sales | | |
|---|---|---|---|
| Product quality | Low under 6% | Average 6%–11% | High over 11% |
| Inferior | 15.4% | 14.8% | 2.7% |
| Average | 17.8 | 16.9 | 14.2 |
| Superior | 25.2 | 25.5 | 19.8 |

**B   High R&D spending hurts profitability when market position is weak but increases ROI when market share is high**

| | Ratio of R&D costs to sales | | |
|---|---|---|---|
| Market share | Low under 1.4% | Average 1.4%–3.0% | High over 3.0% |
| Under 12% | 11.4% | 9.8% | 4.9% |
| 12%–26% | 13.8 | 16.7 | 17.0 |
| Over 26% | 22.3 | 23.1 | 26.3 |

Another clue to how profit influences vary, depending on competitive position, is given in Part B of Exhibit V. This shows, for businesses in the same market share categories as in Exhibit IV, the relationship of ROI to R&D spending levels. When market share is high, average ROI is highest when R&D spending is also high—above 3% of sales.

These figures do not, of course, show which is cause and which is effect; possibly businesses that are highly profitable—for whatever reason—are inclined to invest more of their earnings in research. Most likely, the positive relationship between ROI and R&D spending reflects both this kind of "reverse causation" and a positive impact, in the other direction, of R&D on profits.

When market share is low, the relationship between R&D and profitability is exactly the reverse of that experienced by those with strong positions. The higher the level of R&D spending, the lower profits were, on the average. Here, there appears to be little doubt about cause and effect: low profits would be very unlikely to lead to high R&D spending.

We should emphasize, however, that these data represent short-term effects. Since the PIMS participants supplied information only for a three-year period, it may well be that Part B of Exhibit V reflects a "transitional" cost of innovation. Some support can be given for this interpretation: among businesses with low market shares, ROI was higher (11.6%) when new products comprised a relatively high proportion of total sales than when new products represented only a small fraction of sales (average ROI, 5.3%).

Thus, when and if R&D spending is successfully converted into new products, it can pay off. But the most profitable course of all, for businesses with weak market positions, may be to seek new products without investing in research and development—via imitation, for instance.

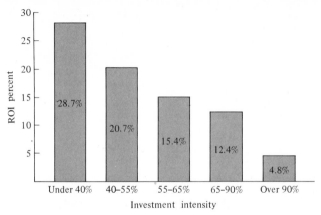

**EXHIBIT VI** ■ Relationship of investment intensity to profitability.

### INVESTMENT INTENSITY

Apart from market share and product quality, the most important determinant of return on investment that was revealed by our analysis of the PIMS data pool is investment intensity, which is simply the ratio of total investment to sales.

Exhibit VI shows the overall relationship between ROI and investment intensity: the higher the ratio of investment to sales, the lower ROI tends to be. Apparently businesses with high investment intensities are not able to achieve profit margins sufficient to offset the greater amounts of investment they require to sustain a given volume of sales. We suspect that a prime reason for this may be the heavy emphasis placed on achieving high volume, and thus high capacity utilization, in investment-intensive industries.

Since both market share and investment intensity are major determinants of profitability, it is not surprising that the combination of the two factors accounts for a substantial portion of total variation in ROI. As shown in Exhibit VII, average ROI for businesses that enjoyed both a high market share and a low degree of investment intensity was 34.6%—more than 17 times the average return earned by the unfortunate businesses with high investment intensity and small market share.

In most cases, the basic level of investment intensity required for a given business is probably not subject to much control by management. The amount of capital required to support a specified amount of sales is determined primarily by the technology of the business and by traditional terms of trade.

**EXHIBIT VII** ■ **LOW MARKET SHARE PLUS HIGH INVESTMENT IN-TENSITY EQUALS DISASTER**

| Investment intensity | Market share | | |
|---|---|---|---|
| | Under 12% | 12%–26% | Over 26% |
| Under 45% | 21.2% | 26.9% | 34.6% |
| 45%–71% | 8.6 | 13.1 | 26.2 |
| Over 71% | 2.0 | 6.7 | 15.7 |

However, very often management does have some choices that affect investment intensity—such as the degree of mechanization or computer utilization. Our data indicate that these types of investments should be carefully controlled if market position is weak. Beyond this, what can managers do about investment intensity? Is a business that requires a high investment/sales ratio simply doomed to exist with low rates of return?

Comparison of various groups of businesses within the investment-intensive category shows that some strategies are likely to be more profitable than others. Consider, for example, the data in Exhibit VIII. Among businesses in the highest investment/sales group, ROI was strongly—and negatively— related to the level of marketing expenditures. For businesses with low investment intensity, the relationship of ROI to marketing expenditures was quite different: average profitability was actually higher when marketing expenditures were "moderate" in relation to sales than when they were low.

Similar comparisons of subgroups within the PIMS sample show that when investment intensity is high (a) high levels of R&D spending depress earnings sharply, at least in the short run, and (b) high labor productivity is vital to profitability. (The average return for businesses with high investment intensity and low productivity—measured by sales per employee—was a negative 1% of investment.)

### COMPANY FACTORS

A third category of profit determinants revealed by the PIMS project consists of characteristics of the company that owns a business. Even when all of the characteristics of two businesses are identical, our analysis suggests that their profit results may vary if they belong to corporations that differ in terms of size, diversity, and other factors.

Exhibit IX shows average ROI levels for businesses belonging to companies that are in "low," "average," and "high" sales categories, and that have different degrees of corporate diversity. The range of corporate size represented in the PIMS sample is, of course, limited: "small" companies are those with annual sales volume under $750 million. Within this range, ROI at the business level was highest for the largest companies and lowest for those in the "average" group.

The explanation for this, we believe, is that the large corporations benefit from economies of scale, while the smaller companies gain some advantages from greater flexibility. Those in the middle are neither fish nor fowl, and consequently they earn the lowest rates of return.

The relationship between business-level ROI and corporate diversity is simi-

**EXHIBIT VIII ■ HIGH MARKETING EXPENDITURES DAMAGE ROI IN INVESTMENT-INTENSIVE BUSINESSES**

| | Ratio of marketing expenditures to sales | | |
|---|---|---|---|
| Investment intensity | Under 6% | 6%–11% | Over 11% |
| Under 45% | 29.3% | 31.7% | 22.0% |
| 45%–71% | 17.6 | 13.2 | 18.3 |
| Over 71% | 10.9 | 10.1 | 3.9 |

**EXHIBIT IX ■ ROI VARIES WITH SIZE AND DIVERSITY OF PARENT COMPANY**

| | Total company sales (in millions) | | |
|---|---|---|---|
| | Low<br>Under $750 | Average<br>$750–$1,500 | High<br>Over $1,500 |
| **Average ROI** | 15.8% | 12.5% | 21.7% |

| | Degree of diversity | | |
|---|---|---|---|
| | Low | Average | High |
| **Average ROI** | 16.1% | 12.9% | 22.1% |

lar to that based on company size. On the average, ROI was practically identical for businesses belonging to highly diversified corporations and for those operated by nondiversified companies. Presumably, the diversified corporations achieve good results through effectiveness as "generalists."

At the other extreme, profitability reflects the advantages of corporate specialization. The lowest levels of ROI are for the middle group, which benefits from neither. (These and other observed relationships between ROI and company characteristics are tentative findings, of course, because of the limited number of companies included in our sample.)

Our final example of a relationship between ROI and a combination of factors serves to illustrate further how company characteristics affect profitability. In Exhibit X, we show average levels of ROI for businesses that have different market shares and that belong to different company size groups.

As in earlier exhibits, the positive impact of a high market share is apparent. But, in addition, the data indicate that larger companies derive greater advantages from strong market positions than smaller companies do. This probably reflects the ability of larger companies to provide adequate support for strong positions, in terms of management personnel and funds for marketing or R&D.

On the other hand, smaller companies do slightly better than large ones in businesses with low market shares. This lends support to the belief that the relatively small companies derive some advantages from flexibility.

## Applying the findings

The corporate applications of the PIMS findings are many and varied. These include aid in profit forecasting for individual business units, measuring management performance, and appraising new business opportunities.

As part of the PIMS project, reports are prepared for each business, showing

**EXHIBIT X ■ LARGE COMPANIES BENEFIT MOST FROM STRONG MARKET POSITIONS**

| Company sales<br>(in millions) | Market share | | |
|---|---|---|---|
| | Under 12% | 12%–26% | Over 26% |
| Under $750 | 14.5% | 13.7% | 19.6% |
| $750–$1,500 | 6.8 | 15.0 | 25.0 |
| Over $1,500 | 12.0 | 17.8 | 29.4 |

how its expected level of ROI is influenced by each of the 37 distinct factors included in the profit model. The result of this kind of analysis is what we call a "PAR" return on investment for a business, given its market and industry environment, its competitive position, its capital structure, and so on.

Some of the participating companies are beginning to put the findings to work by using the PAR reports as a standard of performance for individual divisions. For example, if actual ROI is substantially above the PAR level, this is an indication that divisional management is performing well. The excess of actual over PAR reflects gains made by current tactical superiority, since the factors considered in calculating PAR are largely aspects of the strategic position of the business.

Apart from management performance, special circumstances may cause actual ROI to fall above or below PAR. For instance, the effects of patents and trade secrets are not reflected in the profit model. Subject to this qualification, we believe that PAR or expected profit levels derived from the PIMS model—or from a similar analysis of actual experiences under different conditions—can serve as a meaningful standard for evaluating actual results. Certainly, this kind of standard is preferable to the simple interdivisional comparisons used to judge divisional profits in many large companies today.

Potentially, the most valuable application of the PIMS findings will come from using them to estimate the effects of strategic changes. Each participating corporation has recently received a second set of reports which show how ROI in a given business could be expected to change, both in the short and long term, if modifications were made in its strategic position.

It is too soon to tell how accurate those estimates will be. But it is clear already that many of the managers and planners have obtained valuable insights into the reasons for past performance and the most fruitful directions for change.

## Summing up

The PIMS project has demonstrated the feasibility and the benefits to be realized when companies pool their experiences. Information on strategic actions, market and industry situations, and results achieved can be organized into a multipurpose data base, and analysis of this data base has yielded useful general findings. Executives of the participating companies are beginning to utilize these results in the development and appraisal of strategic plans for individual business units.

Beyond the current benefits, we can also speculate on the broader impact that the approach represented by PIMS may have on the functioning of the private enterprise economy.

Competition is at the heart of our economic system. Will the process of competition become more effective or less effective if PIMS-type information becomes increasingly available? Is the answer the same if we judge effectiveness by some index of "social benefit," rather than by the health and profitability of individual businesses?

It seems entirely probable that the answers are: *more effective* and *yes*.

While competition has been one of the mainsprings for the dynamic growth of the U.S. economy, the great wastage of competition is increasingly retarding our national productivity. Can we maintain the benefits while reducing the drag of the wastage?

Research on multicompany data may enable us to accomplish just that, by helping individual competitors to lessen the frequency and scale of their competitive mistakes. The pooled record of business successes and failures, analyzed in PIMS-type fashion, can identify the courses of action that simply have no plausible promise at all, whether for the company or the customer or anyone else. It can also identify the other courses of action that have a good probability of yielding viable results. Competitors can therefore concentrate their energies on the higher-yield actions, and not dissipate their resources on quixotic ventures and forlorn causes.

Business is not a zero-sum game, where one man's gain is inevitably another man's loss. Sometimes most everyone wins, and sometimes most everyone loses. The systematic comparative study of ongoing experience can help maximize the frequency of the first outcome and minimize the second.

# Implementing the strategy

**1** To understand why enterprises must implement the chosen strategy

**2** To learn how a manager implements a strategy organizationally

**3** To review how a manager involves people in implementation

**4** To understand how implementation includes the development of policies and specific functional decisions

**5** To learn about stages of development theories and how these might help a manager know how to implement a specific strategy

Some of you may think the strategic planning process ended with Chapter 6. The top manager(s) made the strategic choice. Now the enterprise knows how it is going to achieve its objectives.

Figure 7–1 reminds us that we are not through yet. The choice does not mean that the enterprise will follow the decision. No. The employees must be informed of the choice. The resources of the enterprise must be allocated to reinforce the choice. Other policies and decisions must be made consistent with the choice. This process we call implementation.

It involves two related yet different processes:

**1** Organizational implementation of strategic choice

**2** Policy implementation of strategic choice

## Organizational implementation [1]

The first step in implementation is the examination of the enterprise's organizational structure and climate to be sure that this resource is set up to help make the strategy work. I cannot give you all the findings of the disciplines of organization theory and organizational behavior in the few pages left here. I will try to highlight some of the relevant concepts. In essence, the top manager looks at the organization now and says: Do we have the right organization for our strategy?

The effective organizer tries to group duties into meaningful subunits while avoiding duplication of efforts or excessive specialization which can lead to boredom or tunnel vision in the enterprise's executives.

Ansoff and Brandenburg, among others, have shown how four types of organization styles have developed in the business sector: functional, divisional, adaptive, and innovative. Of course, in the smallest enterprises, it is hard to determine much of an organization other than boss and employees. (See Figure 7–2 for graphic presentation.) As the enterprise develops, and more and more employees are added, the first type of organization which arises is the functional. That is, the boss groups his or her employees by the type of work the enterprise does: operations or manufacturing (things), accounting and finance (money), personnel (people), research and development (ideas, new ways of doing things), and environmental relations (marketing, public relations, etc.). This structure is believed to maximize the economies of scale and specialization.

226

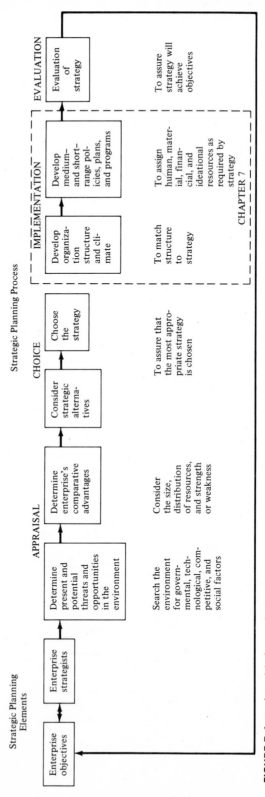

**FIGURE 7-1** ■ A model of strategic planning.

Implementation is the process by which the top managers assure that the strategic choice is communicated to the enterprise. The process involves also the organization of people and resources to reinforce the choice. Finally, implementation involves the development of consistent functional policies which will reinforce the strategic choice.

Organization is the dividing up of the work among groups and individuals (division of labor) and making sure the subparts are linked together to assure that they will work together effectively (coordination).

If the enterprise grows by expanding the variety of operations it performs, then another level of management is inserted above the functional and we have a divisional structure (or multidivisional). It is thought this structure maximizes coordination of the subunits and increases the speed of response to changes in the environment. This level is as far as most enterprises evolve. Some very complex organizations can take one or both of two more steps. The first is the adaptive organization. In firms whose products change frequently and are short-lived (especially defense firms), still another layer was inserted between divisional managers and functional groups. These were project development and project implementation managers to achieve even speedier responses and better coordination. These project groups are temporary and are scrapped when the project is completed.

The second step, the most advanced organization, is innovative organization. As Ansoff and Brandenburg explain it, fast-changing enterprises divide themselves into current business groups and innovation groups. The innovators invent and pretest products or services. Once the products or services are ready for the marketplace, they are transferred to the current business units. Again, this amounts to creating a current business division (for example, toys, tents) and innovation divisions parallel to the current business division. This form tries to combine the best features of the functional, divisional, and adaptive forms of organization.

## Frequency of use of organization structures [2]

Most small enterprises just starting out begin with the primitive structure. They are too busy surviving to spend much time on the niceties of organization.

The largest number of organizations follow the functional style of organizing. This was true of all business organizations that got beyond starting stage, but it is no longer true of the largest organizations. A series of studies of the Harvard Business School has shown how use of the functional style has declined in the United States, Europe, and Japan. For example, Wrigley found that by 1967, 86 percent of the *Fortune* 500 used divisional form. Ninety percent of large firms with multinational sales also used divisional form. Ru-

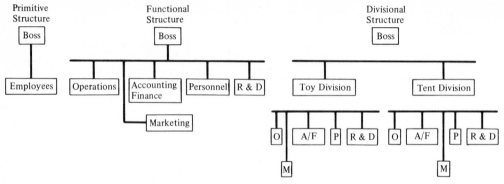

**FIGURE 7-2** ■ Evolution of organization structures.

Rumelt's studies of large United States corporations in 1969 concluded that 20.4 percent used functional organization, 2.4 percent holding companies, 1.5 percent geographic, and 75.5 percent divisional (product divisional) form.

Table 7–1 summarizes the findings of the Harvard studies. A glance at Table 7–1 indicates a major shift toward divisional organization form. Holding companies are popular in Europe because of ownership concentration in fewer hands. Wrigley's study and the other studies conclude that the shift to divisional organizations is a result of the businesses' diversification to end reliance on a single product or product line. Wrigley's findings conclude:

---

**PROPOSITION 7-1** ■ As firms move from single product to dominant product to concentric to conglomerate diversification, they will, if effective, move from functional to divisional organization structure.

---

So as this shift takes place—single product → dominant product → concentric diversification → conglomerate diversification—it is more and more probable that the functional form is replaced by divisional form and maybe the adaptive form.

These findings verify the seminal findings of Chandler in 1962, which are stated in Proposition 7–2.

**TABLE 7-1** ■ **PERCENTAGE OF LARGE FIRMS USING DIFFERENT ORGANIZATIONAL FORMS, 1950–1973**

| Organiza-<br>tional form | United States | | Germany | | | United Kingdom | | France | | | Italy | | | Japan |
|---|---|---|---|---|---|---|---|---|---|---|---|---|---|---|
| | 1950 | 1969 | 1950 | 1960 | 1970 | 1950 | 1970 | 1950 | 1960 | 1970 | 1950 | 1960 | 1970 | 1973 |
| Functional | 75 | 17 | 79 | 70 | 38 | 47.5 | 12.5 | 84 | 61 | 34 | 64 | 65 | 36 | 22 |
| Divisional | 15 | 80 | 5 | 15 | 50 | 2.5 | 57.5 | 6 | 21 | 54 | 8 | 7 | 48 | 78[a] |
| Holding<br>company | 10[b] | 3[b] | 15 | 14 | 12 | 25 | 12.5 | 10 | 18 | 12 | 28 | 28 | 16 | |
| Other | . . . | . . . | 1 | 1 | . . . | 25 | 17.5 | | | | | | | |

[a] Twenty percent of Japanese firms with divisional organizations use functional form for the largest product line and divisional organization for other products and overseas.
[b] Includes geographic organization form in United States figures.

▪ Strategic change without structural adjustment leads to economic inefficiency.

Chandler found that when firms shifted their strategies to diversification, they had to change their organization form to divisional form. The stimulus for these shifts came from the environment, Chandler observed. Rhenman found, in studying Swedish firms, that organization problems result from inability or unwillingness to adapt the organization forms after such changes too.

One should not conclude that all effective businesses need divisional organization forms. These studies were based on *large firms,* not medium- or small-size firms.

## Which organization form is best? [3]

A lot of energy, blood, sweat, and tears was spent trying to find the "best" organization for all business. The results of all this research can be summarized as follows: An organization whose strategy has been implemented with the right organization form for its characteristics will be more effective than an organization which does not fit its characteristics. There is no one "right" way to organize. The best organization is one which fits the organization's (1) size, (2) volatility, (3) complexity, (4) personnel characteristics, and (5) dependence on the environment.

Specifically how should one adapt the structure to those characteristics? Ansoff and Brandenburg propose:

**PROPOSITION 7–3** ▪ Organizations whose strategy is to operate in a stable environment and which are small and have a single product or market will be more effective with a functional organization.

**PROPOSITION 7–4** ▪ Organizations which operate in a moderately dynamic environment, are large, and have diversified concentrically from a single product or market will be more effective with a divisional organization.

**PROPOSITION 7–5** ▪ Organizations which operate in a dynamic environment, are large, have businesses which are technologically intense, and, where the economies of scale are not important, have severely limited time duration of projects or products will be most effective in adaptive organization structure.

**PROPOSITION 7–6** ▪ Organizations which operate in a dynamic environment, are large, and, where economies of scale are important, have intensive technologies and marketing, and in which a large percentage of budget goes to innovation, will be more effective in innovative organization structure.

Walker and Lorsch studied two plants with identical external characteristics: one which was organized functionally, the other divisionally. They concluded:

The functionally oriented plant had more trouble coordinating its parts, less open communications, and was successful in stable production situations. It was less successful in improving plant capabilities, but had high satisfaction and little stress.

The division organization was more effective in coordination and communication, less effective in stable production, but more effective in improving plant capabilities. There was more stress and less satisfaction than at the functional plant.

This result, and many others that could be cited, should lead you to realize that all organization forms work; the key is to match the organization form with the characteristic of the environment.

In general, remember that functional organizations work best in stable environments, with less need for cross-department coordination and communication and less need for innovation. The shorter the product service line, the better the functional form works.

Divisional organizations work best in changing environments which require faster adaptation, more coordination and communication, and innovation. The more complex the product-service line, the more divisional (or even adaptive or innovative) forms work.

## Organization climate and leadership [4]

After the manager is sure the organization structure or form is right, the next step is to make sure the right people are in the right jobs to implement the strategy.

Of course, the process of examining *every* person in every job is not suggested here. What I am talking about is this: Who are in the leadership jobs? Do they have the right characteristics to make the strategy work?

Managers have many characteristics, but the most crucial ones to consider here are:

Education

Experience

Leadership style or organization climate

Some jobs require specific education. The head of R&D normally is technically trained. The controller normally has training in accounting or is a CPA.

Experience is another crucial variable. If the firm is a single product firm and the environment is not changing fast (for example, some metals companies), then an executive with his or her total experience with one firm in one function (marketing) might do fine. If the strategy requires a major shift from the present strategy, then someone with wider experience, preferably in the field we are shifting to, might be desirable.

The final issue, and usually the most crucial personnel issue, is: Can the executive effectively lead the division and relate well to peers, superiors, and subordinates with his or her present style? Can he or she change the leadership style?

It is impossible again for me to review the whole field of leadership and organization climate. But a few guidelines might help here.

Khandwalla has carefully studied more than a hundred large Canadian firms over several years. He has shown that the managerial style (a combination of leadership style and managerial ideologies and values) has an important impact on strategic effectiveness. He describes eight styles (see Table 7–2). None of these eight are better than any of the others. The key is to match a style or set of styles to the right environmental circumstances. Khandwalla says:

These styles often occur in various combinations. One rather effective combination is of the technocratic style with a non-autocratic, participative, human relations oriented style, and conversely, of the seat-of-the-pants judgments oriented style with an autocratic, non participative style. Another effective combination is of the risk taking, growth and innovation oriented style with the organic, seat-of-the-pants judgments oriented, and autocratic styles, and conversely of the adaptively conservative style with the mechanistic, technocratic, and non autocratic styles.

[Remember] the task environment is an important source of forces that should enter into a consideration of what management style to adopt. There is a greater probability, for example, that in a dynamic, competitive environment the risk taking and organic styles will lead to better organizational performance than the conservative and mechanistic styles. Conversely, the mechanistic and the conservative styles have a better chance of succeeding in a non-competitive, stable, static, predictable environment than the organic and risk taking styles. The seat-of-the-pants judgments oriented style has little chance of succeeding in a technologically sophisticated, research and development oriented environment as compared to the technocratic style.

Secondly, the adoption of any particular style usually has many organizational consequences. For example, the adoption of a risk taking, growth oriented style is likely to lead to inter-departmental conflicts, possibly because head-long growth leaves little time for careful planning and scheduling of interdepartmental activities. The use of the autocratic style may lead to poor collaboration between different personnel. Thus, knowing what may be the consequences of the use of a particular style can help the designer take remedial action, such as special scheduling groups to keep track of coordination between different departments in an organization adopting a risk taking style, the possible use of careful selection procedures and indoctrination (as in the defence forces) to minimize resistance to an autocratic use of power. . . . As the wise have all along maintained, there are many paths to Shangri La. Each path, however, must make sense, depending upon the contour of the landscape, the weather, and the personal characteristics of the traveller. This is no less true of the organization.

Trooboff has shown that climate has an important effect on strategic effectiveness. On the basis of his (and other) research I believe Proposition 7–7 is correct.

Effective organizations have the right managers in the key spots. They have developed the organizations to fit the strategy they plan to pursue. They reinforce the strategy and structure with the right climate of managerial values and leadership styles.

---

**PROPOSITION 7–7** ■ Organizations whose strategies are implemented with matching organization or managerial climate will be more effective than those whose are not.

---

TABLE 7–2 ■ EIGHT MANAGEMENT STYLES

| Style | Environment | Organization policies and pattern |
|---|---|---|
| **1** Organic | A Few government regulations<br>B Heterogeneous environment<br>C Competitive industry<br>D Innovative in new products or services | A Risk-taking investment policy<br>B Little formalization of decision making<br>C Personal experience and common sense the basis for decision making<br>D Internal training of executives and up-or-out personnel policies |
| **2** Participative | A Many legal, social, political constraints<br>B Heterogeneous environment<br>C Large organizations<br>D High labor productivity | A High objectives, especially in employee-morale<br>B Decentralized decision making, supported by much management development and management incentive systems<br>C Divisional organization form<br>D Coordination by use of SOPs and participation schemes<br>*Outcomes*<br>A Perceived the company to be outstanding performer<br>B Perceived selves as able to collaborate and solve company problems |
| **3** Innovative, risk-taking | A Young organizations<br>B Risky and dynamic unpredictable environment<br>C Competitive industry<br>D Innovative in processes and new products or services | A Participation schemes used to induce organizational change<br>B Formalized decision making (use of forecasts, budgeting, planning)<br>C Aggressive personnel policies tied to personnel incentives<br>D Strong value for systematic strategic planning for growth<br>*Outcomes*<br>A Rapid growth, with uneven profit performance<br>B Interdepartmental conflict |
| **4** Rational comprehensive | A Many legal, social, political, and economic constraints in the environment<br>B High technology environment with high R&D | A High objectives in morale area<br>B Formalized decision making, especially by groups<br>C Strong value for systematic strategic planning<br>D Formalized organization: SOPs and specialization<br>*Outcomes*<br>A Perceived the company to be outstanding performer<br>B Perceived selves as able to collaborate and solve company problems |
| **5** Mechanistic | A Much government regulation<br>B Homogeneous environment<br>C Stable technology<br>D No competition | A Risk-aversive in decisions<br>B Formalization of decision making<br>C Personal experience and training seen as the basis for decision making |
| **6** Autocratic | A Homogeneous environment<br>B Stagnant technology | A Low performance goals, especially on morale, participation<br>*Outcomes*<br>A Perceived the company to be poor performer<br>B Perceived the company as unable to solve company problems |
| **7** Conservative adaptive | A Older companies<br>B Stable technology with shrinking sales in predictable environment<br>C Little competition and safe environment | A Informal decision making<br>B Unaggressive personnel policies<br>C Low performance goals<br>D Little use of participation and involvement schemes |

**TABLE 7–2** *(continued)*

| Style | Environment | Organization policies and pattern |
|---|---|---|
| | | *Outcomes* |
| | | A  Steady performance (little fluctuation) with little interdepartment conflict |
| | | B  Slow growth or stagnation |
| **8**  Seat-of-the-pants | A  Few legal, social, political, or economic constraints<br>B  Low technology industry | A  Informal decision making<br>B  Individual decision making based on authority of the position |
| | | *Outcomes* |
| | | A  Perceived company as poor performer |
| | | B  Perceived company as unable to collaborate or solve problems |

## Policy implementation of strategic choice [5]

Earlier in the chapter, it was pointed out that organizational implementation is only one half of the implementation phase. The other half is the development of policies, plans, programs, and procedures to flesh out the bare bones of the strategic choice.

Thus, let us say the choice was a combination strategy: retrenchment in one division, growth in another. But retrench how much? how? in which parts? And growth: how much? where? and how? What policies in marketing, finance, and personnel must be developed to assure that the strategic choice becomes reality?

At this point, I could go into a long-winded hairsplitting set of definitions: plans, policies, procedures. But I am not interested in that. What is needed is a set of decisions to:

1  Spell out precisely how the strategic choice will come to be.

2  Set up a follow-up mechanism to make sure the strategic choice and policy decisions will take place. President Truman said to an associate just before he left office: "Poor Ike [Dwight Eisenhower]! He'll sit there in the oval office and issue orders and nothing will happen."

That a choice has been made does not mean the subordinates:

1  Know what they are supposed to do

2  Willingly implement the decision

As Rhenman points out, it is important for management to institutionalize these decisions by clarifying and communicating them and having people in key spots who will carry them out.

This is what policy implementation is all about. One creates policies which are decisional guides to action and these make the strategies chosen work. Policies provide the means of carrying out strategic decisions. The critical element, the major analytical exercise involved in implementation and policy making is the ability to factor the grand strategy into policies that are compatible, workable, and not just "theoretically sound." It is not enough for managers to decide to change the strategy. What comes next is at least as important: How do we get there, when, and how efficiently? This a manager does by preparing tactical plans and policies to implement the grand strategy. For example, let us say the strategic choice was to diversify. Now the policy maker must decide what to diversify into, when to diversify, how much money will be needed, where the money will come from, what changes are needed in marketing, production, and other practices and policies to make diversification work.

The amount of policy making in the formal sense will vary with size and complexity of the firm. If it is a small firm or a simple business, a few policies will suffice. Larger and more complex firms find that books of policies on every major aspect of the firm—marketing, finance, operations, personnel, and so forth—are necessary. For the competitive advantage of the large firm is its power, not its speed. That is where the smaller firm or decentralized division excels.

Having discussed what policy decisions are and why we make them, we take up the next question: What do we make policy decisions about? Well, companies have policies about every major aspect of the firm (operations, finance, marketing, etc.), as well as general management.

One way to decide what policies are needed is to review the checklist or outline you had in Chapters 3 and 4 and remedy the problem you found and plan an integrated approach to reach your strategy.

The minimal policies which must be developed are the key functional decisions necessary in the following areas [6]:

1  Operations
2  Finance and accounting
3  Personnel
4  Marketing and logistics
5  Research and development

Thus, if the choice was to grow, significant policy decisions, like those in the following list, must be made.

1  *Operations*
Can we handle added business with our present facilities and a number of shifts?
Must we add equipment, facilities, shifts? Where?
Can we become more efficient by better scheduling?
What is the firm's inventory safety level? How many suppliers should it need for purchases of major supplies?
What level of productivity and costs should the firm seek to realize?
How much emphasis should there be on quality control?
How far ahead should we schedule production? Guarantee delivery?
Are we going to be operations or production leaders with the latest equipment and methods?

2  *Finance and accounting*
Where will we get added funds to grow: internally or externally?
If externally, how? Where?
What will the growth do to our cash flow?
What accounting systems and policies do we use (for example, LIFO or FIFO)?
What capital structure policy do we pursue? No debt or heavily levered structure? With regard to ownership? With regard to bonds?
How much cash and other assets do we keep on hand?

3  *Personnel*
Will we have an adequate work force?
How much hiring and retraining are necessary?

What types of individuals do we need to recruit: college graduates? Minority groups? How do we recruit: advertise or personal contact?

Methods for selection: informal interviews or very sophisticated testing?

Standards and methods for promotion: from within, seniority, etc.

Payment, incentive plans, benefits, labor relations policies, etc.

Satisfaction level desired on attitude survey.

**4** *Marketing*

Specifically which products or services will be expanded? How? Present or new products?

Which channels will be used to market these products or services? Will we use exclusive dealerships? Multiple channels?

How will we promote these products or services? Is it our policy to use large amounts of TV advertising or no advertising? Heavy personal selling expenses or none? Price competition or nonprice competition?

Do we have an adequate sales force?

What distribution policies do we have? Guaranteed delivery within 3 days? Minimum shipments?

Do we need new warehousing or transportation methods?

**5** *Research and development*

What new projects are necessary to support the growth?

Should we contract some of this out?

How much should we spend on R&D?

These and many other examples of functional policies are needed to implement the grand strategy. Your ability to formulate these will be a good indication of your practical ability to make the strategy work.

It should be clear by now that Proposition 7–8 is accurate.

The items cited in reference 6 give more details on specific functional strategies to implement the strategic choice made.

There is a time dimension in policy formation process. Some policy decisions can be made and implemented immediately (for example, change from LIFO to FIFO, hiring unskilled workers). Others take long lead time to come to fruition (for example, research and development, building new plants). Thus in effect, the enterprise creates a cascade of policies.

|  | Strategic choice |
|---|---|
| >3 years | Long-range policies, plans, programs |
| 1 to 3 years | Medium-range policies, plans, programs |
| <1 year | Short-range policies, plans, programs |

The longer-range policies do affect medium- and short-range decisions.

## Tools of implementation [7]

Effective implementation requires development of policies and mechanisms of control and follow-up. Various tools have been used to determine if "down

**PROPOSITION 7–8** ■ Enterprises which prepare detailed implementation policies and plans for strategic choices will be more effective than those which do not.

the line" deviations from the strategic choice occur. When they do, close control and/or revision of the choice may be required.

One such tool is management by objectives (MBO). That is, take the objectives determined before the strategic planning process. Then interpret these objectives (ends) in terms of the strategic choice (the means to these ends). Then for each subunit of the enterprise, develop a set of objectives which reflect the strategic choices made. Thus a growth strategy by internal development is operationalized as shown in Table 7–3 for a division manager. This is a first cut and further refinement will be needed. Each strategy, set of objectives, and enterprise situation is different.

But the key is to make sure that the strategic choice receives thoughtful follow-through of policy, plan, and procedures to make the strategy a success at all levels down to the smallest unit in the enterprise.

Follow-through requires an effective information system. It requires a reward system which leads to accurate and complete feedback in time to act upon the data.

Good implementation will help assure that the strategic choice will help achieve the enterprise objectives.

## Stages of development theories and strategic planning [8]

We have just finished talking about how when a strategy is chosen, it needs to be implemented organizationally and with functional policies. But these subjects were discussed separately. A group of theorists called "stages of development theorists" have tried to create a theory which will help business executives predict what organization structure and policy changes need to be made as the firm grows larger and more complex. One of these theories (Thain's) has been reprinted at the end of this chapter; you can read and discuss it in detail. As a basis for comparison, a summary of several other interpretations of a stages of development theory is provided here.

TABLE 7–3 ■ PERFORMANCE PLANS FOR A DIVISION MANAGER

**1** *Divisional sales growth of 12 percent*
Large metal toys increased at 8 percent, market share expected 18 percent
Small plastic toys increased by 9 percent, market share expected 26 percent
Introduce inflatable toys line, sales expected 100,000 units

**2** *Increase overall profit by 6 percent*

**3** *Reduce operating costs 2 percent*
Lower inventory levels by 4 percent
Lower overtime by 3 percent
Lower training costs 1 percent
Lower turnover of employees 3 percent

**4** *Reduce financial costs 4 percent*
Improve management of cash
Cut bank loan interest costs by 3 percent
Speed collection of receivables by 2 days on average

**TABLE 7–4 ■ CANNON'S STAGES OF DEVELOPMENT**

| Characteristic | I Entrepreneurial | II Functional development | III Decentralization | IV Staff proliferation | V Recentralization |
|---|---|---|---|---|---|
| Strategic decisions | Made mostly by top man | Made more and more by other managers | May have "loss of control" | Corporate staff assists in decisions | Corporate management makes the decisions |
| Organization structure | Informal operations | Specialization based on functions | To cope with problems of functionalization By industry or product divisions | Corporate staff assists the chief executive | Similar to stage II |
| Communication and climate | From leader down; informal communication | Internal communication is important, is difficult | . . . | Conservatism may result in slower communications | |
| Control system | Minimal need for coordination and control | Concerned with everyday situations | Problems with control | May be problems between line and staff | Tightening of control |

The broadest description is that of J. Thomas Cannon, whose theory is summarized in Table 7–4. As Cannon sees it, the predominant characteristic of companies in stage I is that of a "top man" whose leadership is felt throughout the company. Although there may be certain key persons helping to make strategic decisions, the leader will largely do this himself or herself. As volume grows, specialization becomes necessary, and there is functional delegation and thus movement into stage II. If firms become too preoccupied with functional success and with dealing in day-to-day activities, they may be motivated to move into stage III. However, this stage presents new problems, namely, those of resource allocation, duplication of efforts, and control. While stages IV and V represent solutions to the problems of decentralization, they also represent a movement back to stages I and II. There is the chief executive assisted by corporate staff, and there are problems similar to functional development present, only on a larger scale.

Cannon does not contend that companies move through these stages in sequence, or that they move through all the stages. It is not clear how and why firms decentralize or why they go through these stages. What Cannon does say is that if the firm is in stage II, the organizational characteristic of specialization by function is present (and the other characteristics he gives, as shown in Table 7–4).

Several "stage theories" (Scott, Thain, Salter) developed as a direct result of Chandler's book *Strategy and Structure*. As a result of his longitudinal studies of 50 to 70 large firms from 1901 to 1948, Chandler concluded that as these firms changed their strategy, they implemented a new structure, especially the effective firms.

Chandler observed that four different types of structural arrangements developed over the years. He hypothesized that each must have resulted from different types of growth. His hypothesis was that structure (organizational implementation) follows strategy and the most complex type of structure is a result of interactions of several basic strategies. He contended that:

1 Expansion of volume led to creation of administrative office to handle one *function* in a local area.

2 Growth through geographic dispersion led to need for departmental structure and headquarters to administer several functional field units.

3 Decision to add new functions led to central office and multidepartment structure.

Chandler did not try to develop a stages of development theory. He focused on large firms which were no doubt already in stage II or III of the stages described by Cannon. His purpose was to demonstrate the dependent relationship of structural adaptation to strategic change, although his description does provide insights into the stages of development theory. But he did trace the development of three stages at least in general terms. In stage I, the Entrepreneurial phase where the emphasis is on gathering resources to develop the business, the entrepreneur is the key decision maker and influence on everything from product line to organizational style.

The second stage emphasizes the resource allocation process becoming more efficient. It also is characterized by the market development of product lines and perhaps vertical integration. The final stage concentrated on by Chandler is decentralized multidivisional firm (Cannon's stage III).

The last theory to be commented on here is that of Bruce Scott. He has observed historical and developmental trends in firms for some years. He argues that firms develop through three stages, with two transitions between the stages. Stage I is the informally organized, single unit, single product firm. Stage II is the functionally organized, integrated, single product line firm. Stage III is the multidimensional, diversified firm. Each stage has a cluster of managerial characteristics associated with it. These amount to different ways of managing.

Briefly, his model places emphasis on three related factors—the product-market scope, the channels of distribution, and the internal pattern of transactions for the product flow. Organizational characteristics are closely related to these three factors. However, it seems that the choice of one pattern of product flow transactions rather than a different pattern has the greatest impact upon the other organizational characteristics.

The patterns of internal-external transactions are:

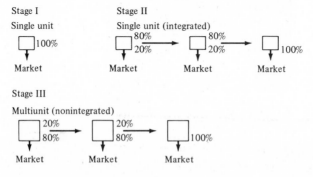

Scott has formulated the following set of propositions which operationalize his model:

**1**  Companies tend to add activities as they grow and age, either within their present line or within new lines of business.

**2**  As the above occurs, there will be a tendency to add specialized subunits.

**3**  More complex administrative problems will result from adding specialized subunits.

**4**  It appears that these administrative problems have been dealt with in a similar manner by different industries.

**5**  There is a closer relationship between the pattern of transactions involved in the product flow and the administrative problems and the technology.

**6**  Stages I, II, and III of the model of corporate development represent basic ways of handling the administrative problems.

**7**  If there is a sufficient increase in a company's activities, the firm will go through a I, II, III stage sequence, reaching II as a result of integration and III as a result of diversification.

**8**  If a company only slightly increases the scope of its activities, over time a more integrated form of organization will result.

He concludes that companies have developed in comparable ways as a result of dealing with similar administrative problems. Thus, it is possible to identify stages which can be used as a *predictive device* in analyzing a firm's future developmental problems. His model has received some support from Tuason and Wrigley.

## An evaluation of stages theories

The stages theories have real potential for helping managers to implement their strategic choices. Before managers can do so, however, several problems must be solved.

First, the inconsistencies between the theorists must be cleared up. How many stages are there: three, four, or five? The theories need also to be consistent in their prediction of management or leadership, objectives, product life, etc. They are not consistent now.

Second, the theorists must give us better guidelines for how long a stage is expected to last, how big a firm is likely to be in stage I of each industry, and similar guidelines.

Finally, the stage theorists need to give us more evidence that if we follow their theories and use their implementation suggestions, the firms will be be better off. That evidence is lacking now.

## Strategic planning and implementation

This chapter has reviewed how the implementation phase of the strategic planning process fits the process and why it is important. It should be remembered that implementation should be considered at the time of choice as well. Chapter 8 completes our discussion of the strategic planning process.

# References

**[1]** Ansoff, H. Igor: "Corporate Structure Present and Future," Working Paper, European Institute for Advanced Studies in Management, 1974.

———— and Richard Brandenburg: "A Language for Organizational Design," *Management Science,* **17** (12): B-717–731, August 1971.

Radosevich, H. Raymond: "Strategic Implications for Organizational Design," International Conference on Strategic Management, Vanderbilt University, 1973. (Mimeograph.)

Starr, Steven: "Organization for Diversity," unpublished D.B.A. thesis, Harvard Business School, 1969.

**[2]** Chandler, Alfred, Jr.: *Strategy and Structure,* Cambridge: M.I.T. Press, 1962.

———— and Herman Daems: "The Rise of Managerial Capitalism and Its Impact on Investment Strategy in the Western World and Japan," Working Paper, European Institute for Advanced Studies in Management, 1974.

Channon, Derek: "The Strategy and Structure of British Enterprise," unpublished D.B.A. thesis, Harvard Business School, 1971.

Dyas, Gareth: "The Strategy and Structure of French Enterprise," unpublished D.B.A. Thesis, Harvard Business School, 1972.

Pavan, Robert: "The Strategy and Structure of Italian Enterprise," unpublished D.B.A. thesis, Harvard Business School, 1972.

Rhenman, Eric: *Organization Theory for Longe Range Planning,* New York: Wiley Interscience, 1973.

Rumelt, Richard: *Strategy, Structure, and Economic Performance,* Cambridge, Mass.: Harvard University Press, 1974.

Thanheiser, Hernz: "Strategy and Structure of German Enterprise," unpublished D.B.A. thesis, Harvard Business School, 1972.

Wrigley, Leonard: "Divisional Autonomy and Diversification," unpublished D.B.A. thesis, Harvard Business School, 1970.

**[3]** Ansoff, H. Igor, and Richard Brandenburg: op. cit.

Child, John: "Organization Structure, Environment, and Performance: The Role of Strategic Choice," London Graduate School of Business Studies, 1970. (Mimeograph.)

————: "Organization, Management, and Adaptiveness," University of Aston, 1974. (Mimeograph.)

Newman, William: "Strategy and Management Structure," *Proceedings, Academy of Management,* 1971.

**[4]** Khandwalla, Pradip: "Environment and Its Impact on Organization," *International Studies of Management and Organization,* pp. 292–313, Fall 1972.

————: "Effect of Competition on the Structure of Top Management Control," *Academy of Management Journal,* **16** (2): 285–295, June 1973.

————: "Viable and Effective Organizational Designs of Firms," *Academy of Management Journal,* **16** (3): 481–495, September 1973.

————: "Style of Management and Environment: Some Findings," Montreal: McGill University, 1974. (Mimeograph.)

Trooboff, Stevan: "Organizational Climate and Performance," unpublished D.B.A. thesis, Harvard Business School, 1972.

[5] Boulden, James, and Ephraim McLean: "An Executive's Guide to Computer Based Planning," *California Management Review,* **17** (1): 58–67, Fall 1974.

Gummesson, Evert: "Organizing for Strategic Management: A Conceptual Model," *Long Range Planning,* pp. 13–18, April 1974.

Rhenman, Eric: op. cit.

[6] Donaldson, Gordon: *Strategy for Financial Mobility,* Cambridge, Mass.: Harvard University Press, 1969.

Gibson, R. E.: "The Strategy of Corporate Research and Development," *California Management Review,* pp. 33–42, Fall 1966.

Skinner, Wickham: "Manufacturing: Missing Link in Corporate Strategy," *Harvard Business Review,* **47** (3): 136–145, May–June 1969.

Smallwood, John: "The Product Life Cycle: A Key to Strategic Marketing Planning," *MSU Business Topics,* pp. 29–36, Winter 1973.

[7] Howell, Robert: "Management by Objectives: A Three Stage System," *Business Horizons,* pp. 41–45, February 1970.

Newman, William: *Constructive Control,* Englewood Cliffs, N.J.: Prentice-Hall, 1975.

Tosi, Henry, et al.: "Setting Goals in Management by Objectives," *California Management Review,* pp. 70–78, Summer 1970.

[8] Ansoff, H. Igor, and Richard Brandenburg: op. cit.

Cannon, J. Thomas: *Business Strategy and Policy,* New York: Harcourt, Brace & World, 1968, pp. 523–538.

Chandler, Alfred, Jr.: op. cit.

Delaney, William: "The Development and Decline of Patrimonial and Bureaucratic Administration," *Administrative Science Quarterly,* **7** (4): 458–501, March 1963.

Filley, A. C.: "A Theory of Small Business and Divisional Growth," unpublished Ph.D. thesis, Ohio State University, 1962.

Glueck, William: "An Evaluation of the Stages of Corporate Development in Business Policy," *Proceedings, Midwest Academy of Management,* 1974.

Hutchins, John: "Business History, Entrepreneurial History and Business Administration," *Journal of Economic History,* **18**: 453–466, 1958.

Liebenstein, Harvey: *Economic Theory and Organizational Analysis,* New York: Harper, 1960.

McGuire, Joseph: *Factors Affecting the Growth of Manufacturing Firms,* Seattle: Bureau of Business Research, University of Washington, 1963.

Penrose, Edith: *The Theory of the Growth of the Firm,* New York: Wiley, 1959.

Rostow, Walt: *The Stages of Economic Growth,* New York: Cambridge University Press, 1960.

Salter, Malcolm: "Stages of Corporate Development," *Journal of Business Policy,* **1** (1): 23–37, 1970.

Scott, Bruce: *Stages of Corporate Development—Part I and II,* Harvard Business School, 1970. (Mimeograph.)

Tuason, Romy: "Corporate Life Cycle and Evaluation of Corporate Strategy," *Proceedings, Academy of Management,* August 1973.

Wall, Jerry: "Industrial Espionage in American Firms," Ph.D. dissertation, University of Missouri, 1974.

Weinshall, Theodore: "The Organization as a Total System in Business Policy," International Seminar for Teachers of Business Policy, Irish Management Institute, July 1971. (Mimeograph.)

# Stages of corporate development

## Donald H. Thain

With increasing pressures for growth and diversification, top managers, long-range planners, and consultants are confronted with many problems in regard to corporate and organizational development. Attempts to solve these key problems, integrally related to the formulation and implementation of corporate strategy, confront top managers with many basic issues:

Is growth and/or diversification desirable?

How do companies grow?

What are the basic stages of evolution in corporate development?

How can one tell what stage of development a company is in?

What are the particular problems and opportunities, strengths and vulnerabilities of each stage?

What are the key factors that management should emphasize at the different stages of development?

How can management plan the transition from one stage to the next?

Is growth to a conglomerate structure via internal product development, mergers and/or acquisitions desirable?

One of the most practical and powerful tools to assist in answering such questions and in identifying and analyzing problems of corporate growth and diversification is the concept of stages of corporate development. [Whereas the idea of stages or chapters in the development of industrial enterprises has been used by others (see, e.g., Alfred D. Chandler, *Strategy and Structure*[1]), this particular version of the concept of organizational development was, to the best of my knowledge, first used explicitly in teaching business policy by Professors Christensen and Scott of the Harvard Business School.]

Several teachers of General Management and others have found this concept to be helpful in understanding and dealing with problems of corporate growth and organizational change in teaching, research and consulting. It also provides an overview that enables practitioners and students to integrate many other related ideas from fields such as human relations, organizational behavior, marketing, control, and finance into a framework relevant to the general management problems of planning and executing corporate strategy.

Reprinted by permission from *Business Quarterly,* Winter 1969, pp. 33–45.

# The stages of corporate development concept

The stages of corporate development concept can be briefly described as follows: As companies that are relatively successful grow larger in size and scope, they experience a number of fairly obvious changes:

1  Sales, expenditures, gross profits and investments increase

2  The numbers of employees increase

3  Resources increase

4  Activities and functions increase in size, scope and number

5  Operating and management problems increase in size, complexity and risk

6  Operating and managerial specialization increases

7  Product lines increase either vertically (diversification in the same industry) or horizontally (diversification into different industries)

8  The number and specialization of organizational subunits increase

This evolution of companies from small and simple to large and complex tends to be marked by three main stages of development as shown in Table 1 (see also Exhibit 1).

One unit means an internally independent, unified product-market business operation. This "nondiversified," "single" product or service unit buys, sells, and operates on its own; it constitutes a single profit center; its operating results are logically represented by one profit and loss statement and its financial condition by one balance sheet.

Although all companies can be classified on this spectrum as to their stage of corporate development, not all are "pure" examples of any one of the stages: That is, many are in a phase of transition from Stage I to II or from II to III.

In the rest of this reading we shall explain this concept in greater detail and describe and comment on some of the problems that it raises not only for top management but also for industry and government planners.

### STAGE I

Except for the few that were founded "ready made" with substantial resources and a top management team, all companies began in Stage I. Many of the great names from the business hall of fame—Henry Ford, John D. Rockefeller, Timothy Eaton, Andrew Carnegie, and the Krupps—were, for a period at least, Stage I company managers.

The major characteristic of the Stage I company is that it is primarily a "one man show." With the exception of perhaps a few shares doled out to directors, relatives or long-time, key employees, he maintains absolute ownership and control. The company's strengths, vulnerabilities and resources are closely

TABLE 1 ■ MAIN STAGES OF CORPORATE DEVELOPMENT

| Small and simple | Transitional | Large and complex |
|---|---|---|
| *Stage I* | *Stage II* | *Stage III* |
| One unit: "one man show" | One unit: functionally specialized group | Multiunit: general office and decentralized divisions |

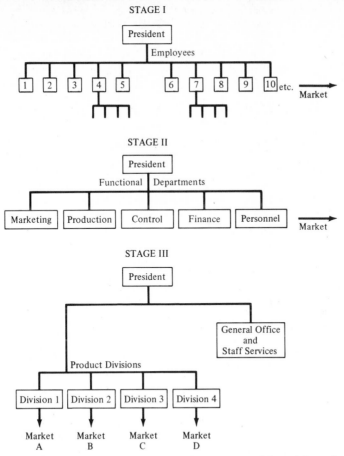

**EXHIBIT 1** ■ Typical organization charts of corporate development of Stage I, Stage II, and Stage III companies.

correlated with his personality, ability, style of management, and personal financial situation. He makes all the important decisions, relying on sales, production and office supervisors only to the extent necessary to see that his unilateral decisions are carried out. The organization chart is usually very simple; most employees report directly to the owner-manager with the exception of those whose work is supervised more or less by others with more seniority or experience.

Because of its tightly limited resources, the Stage I company must rely heavily on support from outside factors such as suppliers, sales agents, bankers, accountants and lawyers. The Stage I owner-manager tends to be a notoriously authoritarian, short-term operator. Because he can't afford back-up managers and staff, he is the proverbial "jack of all trades" and must spend most of his time tending to daily operations and constantly recurring crises, many of which could bring his venture to a sudden, sad ending. It is no accident that nearly all bankruptcies occur in Stage I companies. Although his flexibility for decision making and organizational change may be great, the constraints resulting from lack of resources and narrow vistas impose severe limitations on his scope for action.

In the functional areas of the Stage I company, the major emphasis must be on operating. In marketing the push is on sales, in production, on turning out products to meet shipping schedules, in control, on keeping information for a simple accounting system frequently run by an outside accountant, in finance, on liquidity and working with a banker as necessary, in personnel, on hiring people, usually on short notice to fill holes in the staff. As one Stage I manager defined it, "Management here is just attending to one darn problem after another."

Although many Stage I managers are happy with their lot as "independent businessmen," when the attraction of "being my own boss" wears off, their many problems and vulnerabilities become apparent. His company is never more than a heart beat away from crisis and perhaps disaster. I have been involved in at least two substantial Stage I businesses with a net worth of $200,000 to $400,000 that, except for a few hard assets, were practically worthless overnight as a result of the deaths of their owners. Decisions, frequently dictated by lack of resources, are highly vulnerable to uncontrollable changes by customers and outside suppliers. Unfortunately, the Stage I owner-manager is frequently his own worst enemy. Compelled to work long hours, constantly burdened by the total responsibility of a vulnerable enterprise, unable to manage, plan, and organize, he succumbs to a Stage I managerial style—short-term thinking, operating orientation, swamped by detail, inability to delegate, playing his cards close to his chest and unwilling, perhaps for good reason, to place his confidence in others. This Stage I operating syndrome, as much as anything else, may lead to his undoing.

In spite of all the problems and risks, if all goes well, the Stage I company may prosper to the point where sales, profits, and resources increase and a reasonable degree of stability is gained. Obviously, some Stage I managers are highly successful in terms of income, capital gains, independence, local status, and the rewards related to self-actualization. I have known several Stage I owner-managers who, for good reason, would not exchange positions with anyone.

If the Stage I company owner can sell and earn enough to support the extra overhead costs, can promote or hire other managers, and can adjust his personal style to work "with" others, he may build a management team that enables him to reach the point of corporate development that marks the transition to Stage II.

STAGE II

The distinguishing characteristic of Stage II is that it is a one-unit enterprise run by a team of managers with functionally specialized responsibilities. In other words, when the subtle transition has been made from management by one man to management by a group, the company has made it to Stage II! Although we tend to think of marketing, production, control, finance, and personnel as being the major functions of the business (see Exhibit 1), this breakdown may vary widely depending on the size and scope of the company. In a small, simple, newly developed Stage II company the functional team might be limited—perhaps only the president, a sales manager, and a production manager. In a large, highly developed, complex Stage II company the group might include marketing, production, engineering, control, finance, personnel, labor relations, long-range planning, and public relations. In addition each of these functional units might be further subdivided: For example, marketing might include departments for sales, advertising, brand management, and marketing research. In other firms such as banks or steel companies, the traditional functional groupings might be subunits that more effectively relate to the particular operating problems of the business. In a large integrated oil company, for example, the functional specialization might be exploration, drilling, pipelines, transportation, refining, and marketing. The hallmark of the Stage II organization is that in spite of the variety of functional subunits and the sometimes labored and artificial attempts to make them into performance or profit centers, they really stand or fall together in that they are built around one business, for example, banking or aluminum, and must combine to sell primarily to one end-market, such as petroleum or steel. [It is interesting to note two particular organizational developments that have been tried by many companies to break down large Stage II organizations, e.g., oil, steel, or soap companies, into meaningful performance centers. The first was to divide such large companies into separate units that perform major operating tasks. When such operating units are required to rely on each other as suppliers or customers without the possibility of substantial outside buying and/or selling, they really constitute one overall integrated unit. Thus, even though a steel company might call its mining, transportation, blast furnace, converting, and marketing operations separate divisions, they tend to stand or fall together, and would thus constitute subunits of a Stage II company.]

[The brand management type organization is a second attempt to divide large Stage II companies into meaningful subunits for management purposes. However, the brand management or related product breakdown has been unsatisfactory in several respects because of the difficulty of dividing overlapping functions and defining authority and responsibility in a way that makes performance measurement accurate and meaningful.]

The size, scope, and resources of Stage II companies vary widely—some of the largest companies in the world in industries such as steel, oil, and agricultural implements are basically Stage II. Ownership is usually public but may be private or personal. The great strength of a Stage II company lies in its concentration and specialization in one field. Its great vulnerability is that all its eggs are in one basket. Stage II companies tend to be strong in solving functional and product problems and weak in coping with basic market changes and the general management problems related to strategic change.

Nearly all Stage II companies are much less reliant on external factors than Stage I companies. They are also much less vulnerable to failure or bankruptcy. Stage II companies usually have some "managers" (as contrasted with Stage I operators) and enough depth in resources that they can afford some planning.

Some Stage II companies, for good reasons, remain concentrated in one field which fully challenges their resources and abilities. They grow by expansion of present marketing and production activities and diversification through backward or forward integration into closely related products or services. However, many Stage II companies seeking growth, profitability and security and realizing that they are vulnerable to the life cycle of one product as the Stage I company is to the life cycle of one man, attempt to diversify. If diversification via internal product development, merger or acquisition works out, additional product subunits will emerge and, if these are successful in

| Key factors in management process | Stage I | Stage II | Stage III |
|---|---|---|---|
| **1** Size up: major problems | Survival and growth, dealing with short-term operating problems | Growth, rationalization, and expansion of resources, providing for adequate attention to product problems | Trusteeship in management and investment and control of large, increasing, and diversified resources. Also, important to diagnose and take action on problems at division level |
| **2** Objectives | Personal and subjective | Profits and meeting functionally oriented budgets and performance targets | ROI, profits, earnings per share |
| **3** Strategy | Implicit and personal; exploitation of immediate opportunities seen by owner-manager | Functionally oriented moves restricted to "one product" scope; exploitation of one basic product or service field | Growth and product diversification; exploitation of general business opportunities |
| **4** Organization: major characteristic of structure | One unit "one man show" | One unit functionally specialized group | Multiunit general staff office and decentralized operating divisions |
| **5 a.** Measurement and control | Personal, subjective, control based on simple accounting system and daily communication and observation | Control grows beyond one man, assessment of functional operations necessary, structured control systems evolve | Complex formal system geared to comparative assessment of performance measures, indicating problems and opportunities and assessing management ability of division managers |
| **5 b.** Key performance indicators | Personal criteria, relationships with owner, operating efficiency, ability to solve operating problems | Functional and internal criteria such as sales, performance compared to budget, size of empire, status in group, personal relationships, etc. | More impersonal application of comparisons such as profits, ROI, P/E ratio, sales, market share, productivity, product leadership, personnel development, employee attitudes, public responsibility |
| **6** Reward-punishment system | Informal, personal, subjective, used to maintain control and divide small pool of resources to provide personal incentives for key performers | More structured, usually based to a greater extent on agreed policies as opposed to personal opinion and relationships | Allotment by "due process" of a wide variety of different rewards and punishments on a formal and systematic basis. Company-wide policies usually apply to many different classes of managers and workers with few major exceptions for individual cases |

developing into independent units, the company can make the transition to Stage III.

STAGE III

The hallmark of the Stage III company is a general office with ultimate control over multiple operating divisions, each similar to a Stage II company. Al-

| Key function | Stage I | Stage II | Stage III |
|---|---|---|---|
| Major emphasis | Usually an operating orientation as opposed to product or functional emphasis | Functional orientation | Investment trusteeship, orientation in president's office, functional orientation in staff and product orientation in line |
| Marketing | Major marketing problem is generating sales, usually only one or small number of employees involved | Specialization develops in advertising, sales promotion, marketing research, etc. | Marketing functions become well developed and extremely complex with specialization in a wide variety of marketing functions by product or product line and geographical area |
| Production | Usually a simple, efficient factory operation geared to turn out maximum production with minimum investment | Production operations become more specialized, production management improves with attendent increases in overhead | Complex production function and product specialization usually accompanied by extensive engineering, research and development studies and careful consideration of vertical integration and make or buy problems |
| Measurement and control | Simple accounting system usually supervised by outside accountant | Accounting system becomes more complex with emphasis on cost accounting and simple statistical techniques, control system is adapted to functional decisions and problems | Complex accounting, control and mathematical decision-making tools supervised by functional specialists and emphasizing product profitability and capital investment decisions |
| Finance | Almost nonexistent except to work with banker as necessary | More sophisticated forecasting and cash budgeting techniques used for purpose of planning capital needs and reducing cost of capital | Complex problems of portfolio management aimed at increasing return on invested capital in all divisions and overall |
| Personnel | Handled on a personal basis by owner-manager | Additional functional specialization and evolution of formal policies for hiring, firing, training, and promoting | Development of considerable sophistication both in special head office staff department and in division line operating departments in regard to hiring and training personnel necessary to perpetuate the company complex "manpower planning" approach often utilized |

though the general offices may vary widely in size, organization, power and operating control, their central functions are investment trusteeship, supervision, control and evaluation of division managers and operations, staff advice and further diversification. As investment trustees, managing a "portfolio" of enterprises, they carry out the process of capital budgeting for the corporation as a whole. The cash flows from the divisions are remitted to the general office for reinvestment in the most necessary or highest payoff projects to be found across the company or outside. If a division cannot produce a profit above the required minimum rate of return, it is sold, liquidated, or otherwise disposed of.

Supervision of division operations is carried out primarily by reviewing plans and forecasts, evaluating results and working with the division managers and their staffs to insure their development and performance especially as measured by sales, profits and return on investment.

Staff advice or management consulting is "made available" to operating divisions sometimes by a large, highly qualified group that also provides a talent pool of potential line managers.

Since the emphasis is on finding and developing profit opportunities, most Stage III companies are also staffed and organized to pursue further diversification aggressively and systematically both internally via research and development and product development and externally via mergers and acquisitions.

The successful Stage III company has many strengths that can make it a formidable international economic unit. Its ownership is almost always public and its resources are tremendous—for practical purposes, almost unlimited. Companies such as General Motors have power and resources that dwarf even those of many small countries. In large Stage III companies resources seldom, if ever, limit decisions; it is strategic decisions and concepts of scope and control that limit resources. It can be relatively independent of outside resources. Large cash flows, management depth, functional specialization and market diversification make its vulnerability to bankruptcy practically zero. It has great powers to regroup and survive even in the event of such a serious crisis as the complete failure of an entire product division.

Perhaps the most significant weakness of the gigantic Stage III company is that its organization is so large and complex that it tends to become relatively inflexible. Organizational restraints are necessarily great, defense of the "status quo" becomes built in, and a time-consuming, bureaucratic approach complete with formal and informal administration by "due process" becomes institutionalized. So many checks and balances become operative that significant change may be beyond the power or control of any one man or small group. As one large Stage III company division manager put it to me: "This company has so many boards and committees that it would take us 6 months to get approval to buy ten dollar bills at a buck a piece." Some of these problems of organizational inflexibility, the "dinosaur factor," are, of course, a function of size and apply equally, if not more, to very large Stage II companies.

At this point the reader may be wondering: What is the difference between a Stage III company and a conglomerate? Although there is no strict definition of a *conglomerate*, the term usually implies a divisionalized company that has grown rapidly and diversified widely especially by acquisitions and mergers as well as by internal growth. If so, then all conglomerates are Stage III companies, but a Stage III company is not necessarily a conglomerate, that is, a Stage III company may develop slowly and without mergers and acquisitions.

One common problem in analyzing Stage III or conglomerate type companies is confusion as to the approach and tactics of management. As I see it there are at least four different product-expansion approaches or philosophies expounded by the top managers in such companies. Some Stage III companies such as DuPont adopt what might be termed a *conservative* approach in regard to expansion and addition of new products—they favor diversification and the addition of new divisions but seldom, if ever, seek opportunities that do not evolve directly from present operations. Another group follows an *open-minded* approach as practiced at Westinghouse. Top management does not rule out new and very different product-market opportunities if they make good sense and appear to be related. Other conglomerates, for example, Litton Industries, pursuing an aggressive approach single out acquisition possibilities and attempt to acquire them, apparently backing off if there is considerable overt resistance from incumbent management. Finally, what I could call the *aggressive-attacking* approach is practiced by conglomerates such as Hunt Foods and Industries Inc., headed by Norton Simon, who will bite at almost any attractive company in which management looks slack or vulnerable. Their specialty is financial wheeling and dealing, shaking things up, getting rid of dead wood, and redeploying assets presumably for the benefit of the shareholders.

Depending on one's point of view, the aggressive or aggressive-attacker type thinking may be a "breath of fresh air" or a lot of "dangerous thinking that should be investigated."

A great danger of conglomerates, already recognized by governments and financiers, is that they can provide great power to men whose tactics, motives, and sense of responsibility may leave a lot to be desired. (This is also true of large Stage I or II companies, as well.) There is also in some Stage III companies the tendency to push performance so hard that managers are forced to "play the numbers game," that is, to manipulate return on investment and other performance indicators to show continuous improvement.

Although moral judgments can and should be made of any manager's behavior, it is important that the student of corporate development does not confuse the philosophy of motives of management with the realities, strengths and weaknesses of the basic organization structure.

Since the Stage III corporate organization structure can probably be expanded indefinitely, it is interesting parenthetically to pose the question: What, if anything, lies beyond Stage III? Observation of current trends in regard to national economic planning in Canada and other countries suggests that a possible Stage IV may be the informal but systematic liaising of major companies and industries with government in an organization and communication framework for the formulation and implementation of national economic strategy. In fact it may be argued that the lack of an adequate Stage IV organization structure and concept of development is a major current problem in Canada and many other countries. Needless to say, the problems and managerial challenges involved will be tremendous.

*DuPont: A classic example of the stages of corporate development*  It is interesting and worthwhile to use the stages of corporate development concept in analyzing actual companies to understand their strategic problems and to learn how and why they develop. One of the clearest examples of corporate development through the three stages is found in the DuPont Company.[1] The fortunes of the DuPont Company came to a low ebb in the crisis of 1902 caused by the sudden death by pneumonia of president Eugene DuPont. "At the time of Eugene DuPont's death, the company and the [gunpowder] industry were being managed just as they had been for more than a generation. The DuPont Company itself administered only a few black powder plants and a smokeless powder works . . . until 1902 it remained a family enterprise. As one DuPont noted: 'The business was entirely managed by the senior partner . . . the head of the firm was the *ex officio* head of the family.' This method of operation was anything but effective and efficient. As president, Eugene DuPont and his predecessors "may have controlled their properties but hardly administered them. . . ." "The lack of administrative control is suggested by the fact that Henry DuPont [Eugene's predecessor] carried on single-handedly from a one room office . . . most of the business of his company. He wrote nearly all of the business correspondence himself in longhand."[2]

In the confusion following Eugene DuPont's death the remaining partners concluded that there was no qualified successor and decided to sell the company to an "ancient and friendly competitor."[3]

Young and energetic Alfred DuPont, who refused to accept this possibility, joined with two cousins, Coleman and Pierre, to buy the company from the elder DuPonts. Their first move was to reorganize the company into a functionally specialized group of top managers who "embarked on the strategy of consolidation and centralization." This reorganization, of course, marked the transition of DuPont to Stage II.

Under the central control of a basic Stage II organization, consolidation of gunpowder operations, professional management, capital budgeting, and planning were all emphasized. Perhaps the key turning point in the history of DuPont came as a result of the tremendous expansion to supply the 1914–1918 war demand for gunpowder. Output, sales, assets, plants, employment, and profits all mushroomed suddenly and unexpectedly. This mushrooming growth was also accompanied by backward, forward, and horizontal integration. Toward the end of the war the pressures of excess plant capacity in postwar reconversion intensified the modest efforts at diversification begun as early as 1903. Diversification policy, firmed up in 1917 and implemented soon after, rapidly changed the nature of the DuPont business. The mounting management problems, resulting from substantial diversification, so overwhelmed the centralized functional organized top management group that they lost effective control. After several attempts to strengthen the central office, some managers realized that they needed a new and different pattern of organization. Although the company was still experiencing many operating difficulties, the proposal to reorganize around product divisions suggested by a group of younger managers was repeatedly rejected by top management who thought the solution lay in making the old Stage II organization work better. Finally with the crisis and losses of 1921, perhaps the worst year in DuPont's history, the multidivisional, Stage III structure was finally accepted. Implemented in 1921, and improved in operation over the next few years, the Stage III organization is still in existence in DuPont and has served ever since as a model for the multidivisional or conglomerate organization introduced in many other large companies. Thus we have a clear record, almost to the exact day, of how and why DuPont made the transition from Stage I to II and then from II to III.

*Key management problems of Stages I, II, and III* One of the highest payoff uses of the stages concept is to red flag some of the basic strategic problems common to companies at different stages of development. Research and consulting in a wide variety of companies has convinced me that there are six key factors in the process of general management:

1  Sizing up the company—environment situation and defining problems and opportunities

2  Setting objectives

**3** Formulating strategy

**4** Organizing

**5** Measuring and controlling performance

**6** Designing and implementing a reward-punishment system to influence motivation and performance

Studying these factors in companies in different stages of development, we note *major* differences in the process which are given in Table 4 (see also Table 2).

There are also major differences in the management of the basic functions—marketing, production, control, finance and personnel as the company evolves. These tendencies are indicated in some detail in Table 4.

Comparative analysis clearly indicates that the major challenges both in regard to the functions and the process to management are different in each stage of development. The key skills necessary to be an outstanding general manager also differ in each stage, shifting from short-term operating ability in Stage I to product-functional emphasis in Stage II and broad management abilities in investment trusteeship, diversification and management supervision and development in Stage III. It is not surprising that many top managers who are relatively successful in one stage may find their style and approach uncomfortable, if not inappropriate, in another stage.

*Problems of transition* Many interesting examples of a wide variety of problems in managing corporate development through the transition between stages could be cited. While organizational change may be the most obvious symptom of transition, market opportunity and corporate strategy should always take precedence. For top management, especially the president or chief operating executive, the transition requires basic changes in approach and behavior. As a company evolves, his primary role must change from that of a one-man show, entrepreneur (Stage I) to product specialist, an "oilman" or a "steel man" (Stage II) to an investment trustee. "I'm here to use resources to make money for our shareholders" (Stage III). The president's management style, relationships, skills, and approach must change fundamentally to cope with the new roles necessarily arising from transition to a new stage.

Some companies have failed or stagnated because top management could not evolve from Stage I to II or from II to III. Others, such as the Singer Manufacturing Company, forced by foreign competition and stagnation to diversify, have struggled to make the transition apparently without a clear concept of what exactly they were trying to do. General Motors, one of the

**TABLE 4** ■ **FUNCTIONS OF GENERAL MANAGEMENT**

| Key factor | Stage I | Stage II | Stage III |
|---|---|---|---|
| **1** Size-up<br>**2** Objectives<br>**3** Strategy<br>**4** Organization<br>**5** Measurement and control<br>**6** Reward-punishment system | Emphasis is on the personal approach to each management function. Major problems are lack of functional expertise and broad management experience and necessary concentration on "fire fighting" operations necessary for survival. | Emphasis is on the functional approach and a one product service, market or technology approach. Major weakness is attachment to one product life cycle and lack of strategic product-market options for investment and resource utilization. | Management problems and opportunities related to diversification and multi-subunits. Great strength and resources but many problems in regard to planning, control, and integration. |

first and largest Stage III companies, was formed by the visionary William C. Durant who followed a strategy of consolidation and integration. The financial crisis of 1920 revealed that General Motors was really a noncoordinated string of Stage I companies whose collective lack of control, planning and organization had brought them to the brink of disaster. The company was rescued by DuPont capital and management and the great abilities of Alfred P. Sloan who, among other moves, installed the basic Stage II type functional controls necessary to keep inventories, accounts receivable, and production in line with sales.

Another example of a very different type of problem is that of the Solartron Electric Group Limited. In the late 1950s Solartron made the transition from Stage II to III only to have to reverse itself and reorganize back to Stage II because it could not generate the business and scope necessary to support an expensive, cumbersome and ineffective Stage III organization.

Another interesting problem of managing corporate development is found in the case of the Ford Motor Company. Henry Ford will be recorded in business history as the innovative president and owner of one of the largest Stage I type companies. His personal inability to advance beyond a Stage I managerial style constituted a severe handicap to Ford in the competitive race with General Motors.

*The drive for corporate development*   The drive for corporate growth and development is almost continuous and universal because it is fueled by some very high powered motivators common to managers around the world.

To any observer, with even a passing involvement in corporate development, it is fairly obvious that companies grow and diversify, acquire and merge with other companies primarily because managers want to. Why? As I see it, for several reasons.

One of the most obvious reasons why managers push for development is that it makes them look smart and they gain in income, capital gains, approval, and status because their company is larger, more profitable, more widely known, and this is duly noted by the board of directors, shareholders, and the investment community.

There is little doubt that as Galbraith and others have alleged,[4] nearly all managers have a basic drive for security—to survive and to reduce their fear of the unknown. One of the obvious routes to increased security is to sell more customers, add new products, develop new markets, acquire more and better production facilities, build a stronger financial base, have a larger, deeper, and more skilled organization, and so on.

Another basic reason that top men have for developing the corporation is to gain power, the ability to influence behavior in one's favor. Most managers seem to understand—either implicitly and instinctively or explicitly in a frankly Machiavellian sense—that the bigger and more secure their base of operations, the greater the resources at their command, the greater their power.

Another common and important reason for corporate development is fear of decline and failure of present operations. In my experience the most frequently encountered motivator for development to Stage III is poor and declining profit prospects in a Stage II company's operations. Management is really fighting a rear guard action against the threatened decline or failure of a major part of the company.

The need for challenge and emotional involvement in exciting activity and playing "the performance game" is another basic motivator that drives many other managers to plan and implement corporate development. Although there are many other internal and external reasons for development from Stage I to II and from II to III, these appear to be the main fundamental drives. Obviously, these come from deep inside the manager. It is very doubtful that they could ever be stopped.

*The blocks to corporate development* If it is true that there is all this fundamental drive for corporate development, why is corporate development limited to the extent that it is? The operative forces for and against development represent a synthesis of the interaction of motivation and blocks and forces of attraction and forces of resistance. In a free enterprise society these countervailing forces form a very complex and subtle equilibrium subject to change from a variety of pressures such as changes in personal taxes, monetary and fiscal policy, business laws, and regulations, national economic planning, and so on. Some of the major internal and external blocks to development are briefly summarized below in outline form.

### I   Internal blocks to development

**A**   *Stages I to II*

1   Lack of ambition and drive

2   Personal reasons of owner-manager for avoiding change in status quo

3   Lack of operating efficiency

4   Lack of quantity and quality of operating personnel

5   Lack of resources such as borrowing power, plant, and equipment, salesmen, etc.

6   Product problems and weaknesses

7   Lack of planning and organizational ability

**B**   *Stages II to III*

1   Unwillingness to take the risks involved

2   Management resistance to change for a variety of reasons including old age, aversion to risk taking, desire to protect personal empires, etc.

3   Personal reasons among managers for defending the status quo

4   Lack of control system related to appraisal of investment of decentralized operations

5   Lack of budgetary control ability

6   Organizational inflexibility

7   Lack of management vision to see opportunities for expansion

8   Lack of management development, i.e., not enough managers to handle expansion

9   Management turnover and loss of promising young managers

10   Lack of ability to formulate and implement strategy that makes company relevant to changing conditions

11   Refusal to delegate power and authority for diversification

### II   External blocks to development

**A**   *Stages I to II*

1   Unfavorable economic conditions

2   Lack of market growth

3   Tight money or lack of an underwriter who will assist the company "to go public"

4   Labor shortages in quality and quantity

5   Technological obsolescence of product

**B**   *Stages II to III*

1   Unfavorable economic, political, technological and social conditions, and/or trends

2   Lack of access to financial or management resources

3   Overly conservative accountants, lawyers, investment bankers, etc.

4   Lack of domestic markets necessary to support large diversified corporation

5   "The conservative mentality," e.g., cultural contentment with the status quo and lack of desire to grow and develop

*Strategies for development*   The most straightforward strategic problems in regard to corporate development are those of the Stage I manager. His strategy (timed sequence of conditional moves) must be simply to put his head down and drive straight forward to increase sales and generate enough cash flow to carry the overhead cost of supporting a management team—maybe only two, three, or four members—but still risky and expensive relative to his profit and loss statement and balance sheet. He must then switch from the role of player to coach, delegating operating responsibility and developing, challenging, encouraging, measuring and rewarding and punishing his top management group. Then, as growth permits he can add needed management specialists to the team and rationalize the operation around a sensible equilibrium relating market potential, sales force size, product line, economic lot size, production facilities, extent of integration and financial structure and resources.

Corporate development for the Stage II company can in general take one or both of two routes: (1) expansion through the present product line or (2) diversification by adding new product divisions. Therefore, depending on prospects for the company's basic product-market niche, resources, distinctive competences, management ability, and motivation and perceived market opportunities, the Stage II president can plan moves: (a) to increase growth and penetration in present product markets or (b) to enter new businesses. Strategy (a) is based on moves to compete more effectively so that the company can increase present shares in static or declining markets or hold present shares in growing markets and/or moving to integrate backward or forward into closely related products and activities.

Strategy (b) requires that the company exercise the make or buy option and get into new, nonrelated products via the internal route—research and development, new product development and marketing—or the external route—acquisition of product-market niches that can be more favorably purchased than developed.

The options for growth in a Stage III company are to expand through present product divisions or to develop and/or acquire new product divisions. In most respects such decisions are similar to those confronting the Stage II company except that the Stage III company should be much more experienced and skilled in approaching and solving the many problems involved.

*The problems of development*   Acceptance and use of the stages of organizational development concept does not imply that corporate development must necessarily occur or that transition through the stages is any royal route to a Stage III corporate Utopia. I have observed many problems related to corporate development that give one cause to stop and think before recommending it generally. One of the most interesting ways of analyzing problems of development is to classify them as to whether they are related to moving from Stage I to II or II to III too soon or too late. A brief summary of the most frequently observed problems classified in this way follows:

**I  Problems when transition is premature**

**A**  *Stage I to II*

1  Loss of control by owner-manager

2  Overhead and fixed costs too high to be supported by sales volume

3  Over extension of resources, especially working capital, plant, and management

4  Bankruptcy or failure

**B**  *Stage II to III*

1  Excessive conflict between functional and product oriented managers

2  Unmanageable complexity

3  Unreasonably high overhead costs

4  Major functional weaknesses in product divisions

5  Lack of control over divisions

6  Inability to compete because resources have been spread too thin

7  Competitive vulnerability to companies with strong functional or product excellence

8  Lack of functional specialization

9  Diversification beyond resource and management capability

10  Excessive and uncontrolled risks

11  Loss of confidence in top management

**II  Problems when transition is too late**

**A**  *Stage I to II*

1  "Static psychology" and management

2  Permanent loss of opportunities for expansion

3  Management frustration

4  Loss of promising employees

5  Vulnerability in regard to survival and growth

**B**  *Stage II to III*

1  Lack of needed diversification and growth

2  Management turnover due to disillusion and inability to match development opportunities in company with personal expectations of managers

3  Loss of management development opportunities

4  Frustration of top and middle managers

**5** Unmanageably complex product management problems, e.g., lack of attention to promising products or problem products

**6** Excessive power appropriated by "empire building" functional managers

Most of the problems noted in the outline can be serious, to say the least. The key to avoiding them is to plan logically the evolution of corporate and organization development with great emphasis on proper timing of any transition from Stage I to II or II to III.

## Conclusions

There are three basic stages of corporate and organizational development—Stages I, II and III, as described in the outline.

Powerful, fundamental drives motivate most managers to develop their companies. This development requires the evolutionary growth and development of the entire internal system of the company.

In evolving from small and simple to large and complex, companies usually make two major transitions in stage of corporate and organizational development—from Stage I to II and from II to III.

The major problems of Stage I and II companies are their reliance on one man and one main product-market niche, respectively.

The major advantages of the Stage III company are its built in mobility of capital, management, and technology, and in most cases, its international outlook and flexibility to pursue profit opportunities in whatever businesses they may be found around the world.

In general, corporate development is poorly planned and managers encounter many problems in making the transition between stages. Many of these difficulties result from not adequately understanding the different problems and functions of management that are particularly related to each of the three stages of development and making the transition too early or too late.

Although there is no evidence of any limit to the size of corporations, there are many basic limits to the rate of growth, evolution and transition between stages of development.

One of the most useful methods for integrating many of the functional and strategic problems of corporate planning—both long and short range—is to relate them to the key factors and questions implied by a stage of development oriented analysis of problems and opportunities.

## References

**1** Alfred D. Chandler, *Strategy and Structure,* Cambridge: M.I.T., 1962.

**2** Ibid., Chap. 2.

**3** Loc. cit.

**4** J. K. Galbraith, *The New Industrial Stage,* Houghton Mifflin, Boston, 1967, p. 167.

# Evaluating the strategy

We have come to the last phase of the strategic planning process: evaluation, as emphasized in Figure 8–1.

Evaluation, as seen in Figure 8–2, is the process by which the managers compare the results of the strategy (the means) with the level of achievement of the objectives (the ends). Of course, the objectives may not be met because the choice was not implemented. Or it may be because the strategy chosen was not working. Successful executives are like physicians when they are treating illnesses. They look at the symptoms and make the most probable diagnosis. From this, they prescribe the best procedure or medicine for their diagnosis. The diagnosis results from the appraisal and choice phase of the strategic planning process. The prescription is the implementation. If the prescription does not work, they may change it (a different emphasis in implementation). If this still does not work, they may then believe they made the wrong diagnosis (strategic choice) and then they make another diagnosis. Just as a physician does not give up if the first choice does not work, so the strategic planner makes another choice as the general did in Figure 8–2. His strategy did not work. He had developed a feedback system (he watched) and compared his strategy with the objective (taking the castle) and concluded the strategy had failed. But he was ready, no doubt, with a plan B.

The evaluation process requires:

**1** The motivation to evaluate

**2** A feedback system to provide the data for evaluation

**3** Criteria for evaluation

**4** Decisions about the outcome of the strategic evaluation

## The motivation to evaluate [1]

Before evaluation will take place, the top managers must want to evaluate the performance. This motivation develops if they realize the strategy can fail and if they are rewarded for their performance relative to objectives.

Most experienced managers have had failure experiences. Too many failures can stunt a manager's career and may make him or her so cautious that few creative decisions are made. But no failures can be equally dangerous. The human being can readily

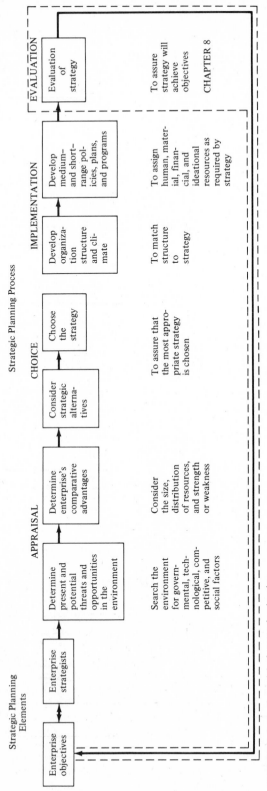

**FIGURE 8–1** ■ A model of strategic planning.

> Evaluation of strategy is that phase of the strategic planning process in which the top managers determine whether their strategic choice in its implemented form is meeting the objectives of the enterprise.

believe he or she is omniscient when the history includes no failures and when he or she is surrounded by admiring assistants. Some failures remind us that we need to evaluate whether our strategies are working. One can think of many examples in political history of failures that resulted from unwillingness to evaluate the strategy: the British experience in the Crimean and Boer Wars, and in India, and the United States' experiences in Vietnam in some campaigns. Businesses can fail for lack of evaluation, too. Cooper (reprinted in Chapter 3) describes Baldwin and Lima Steam Locomotive Companies on the diesel engine question, for example. The divestment decisions described in Chapter 5 showed that the decision makers refused to evaluate the strategy. Their successors made the divestment decision. Perhaps insurance companies are not really evaluating the "whole life" strategy with little but inflation since 1920.

The second half of the motivation to evaluate is whether managers are rewarded directly for performance. If reward were to follow only high performance relative to meeting objectives, the managers would be motivated to evaluate their strategies. However many times this is advocated, there is little evidence that, except in emergency times, there is this *direct* tie. Scientific and impressionistic evidence shows that rewards such as raises and promotions continue even when performance is lacking. Too often, this is because the executives themselves make recommendations on their own salaries and promotions to the board for themselves and each other. To the extent that the chief operating officer and his associates are held to performance before reward, they will be more motivated to evaluate the strategy as the effective means to accomplishing objectives or as the ineffective means.

## 2) Feedback for evaluation

The second requirement for evaluation is information in usable form to evaluate the strategy. This in turn requires an effective management information system and honest and complete reporting of the results of the strategy. Of course, at many enterprises, the top managers do not want to hear bad news. So they hear what they want to hear until it is too late.

The enterprise must encourage complete and accurate reporting so that top managers can react to reversals and reinforce successes.

A crucial issue here is the timing of the evaluation: When should the managers evaluate the results? The ideal answer is that top management should be alerted when significant deviation from budgeted objective results occurs (positive or negative). Each management must define its management by exception criteria (what is a significant deviation?).

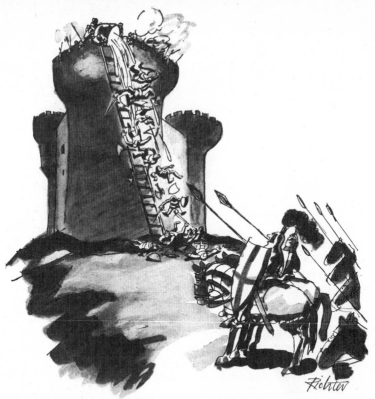

*"So much for Plan A."*

**FIGURE 8–2** ■ Evaluation of strategy. Drawing by Richter; copyright © 1974 The New Yorker Magazine, Inc.

## Criteria for evaluation [2]

Strategies need to be evaluated early after the implementation period to make sure that the strategy is working and then periodically later to see that it is still working.

Seymour Tilles provides us with several criteria to evaluate strategy early after the implementation phase is completed.

**RESEARCH STUDY** ■ **TILLES'S EVALUATION CRITERIA**

**1** *Internal consistency:* Each policy implementation of the strategy fits an integrated pattern.

**2** *Consistency with the environment:* Each policy fits the current demands of the environment.

**3** *Appropriateness, given the enterprise's resources:* Was the strategy implemented in a way which uses the critical resources most effectively?

**4** *Acceptability degree of risk:* Given the values of the management toward risk, does the strategy fit their preferences?

**5** _Appropriateness of time horizon:_ Does the strategic implementation include appropriate time goals?

**6** _Workability:_ Does it achieve the enterprise objectives?

---

Criteria 1 to 6 are qualitative measures of how well the strategy was implemented and is evaluated just after implementation. Workability is the long-run evaluation criterion, quantitative in nature; it will be discussed shortly.

Argenti has a set of criteria similar to Tilles's but he adds:

Does the strategy rely on weaknesses or do anything to reduce them?

Does it exploit major opportunities?

Does it avoid, reduce, or mitigate the major threats? If not, are there adequate contingency plans?

Again, these are qualitative criteria to be applied just after implementation is complete. It should be obvious that the crucial variable in the choice and application of criteria is managerial values toward risk, toward level of objectives achievement, and others.

## Quantitative criteria of evaluation [3]

As Figure 8–1 indicates, evaluation involves relating the results of the strategy with the objectives set at the beginning of the process. So, long-run evaluation blends with the formation of objectives, especially when one is comparing quantitative criteria of accomplishments with quantitative objectives.

In attempting to evaluate the effectiveness of corporate strategy quantitatively, you can see how the firm has done compared to its own history, or compared to its competitors on such factors as:

Net profit

Stock price

Dividend rates

Earnings per share

Return on capital

Return on equity

Market share

Growth in sales

Days lost per employee as a result of strikes

Production costs and efficiency

Distribution costs and efficiency

Employee turnover, absenteeism, and satisfaction indexes

The list of quantitative criteria can be long. The problem is that managers interpret the results themselves. So it probably makes sense to go to _unbiased_ sources. If you are interested in large companies, there are several sources to check.

**1** Compustat will provide you with *financial* results over the past 10 years (or sometimes longer) for large companies.

**2** *Dun's Review* publishes, usually in its November issue, its "Ratio of Manufacturing." This gives you a quantitative guide to how a firm is doing financially in the manufacturing sector.

In addition, *Dun's Review* describes, usually in the same issues, "The U.S.'s Ten Best Run Companies." This provides an unbiased overall view of some usually large companies.

**3** *Fortune* magazine, in its May and June issues, publishes the Fortune 1000 largest manufacturers and the Fortune 50s: the 50 largest retailers, transportation, utilities, banks, insurance companies, and diversified financial corporations. At that time, it also ranks the best and worst performers on financial aspects of the business such as return to investors, sales, profits, sales per dollar of stockholders' equity, etc.

**4** Probably the best unbiased overall evaluation, again usually of the largest corporations, is in the January 1 issue of *Forbes*. The issue is called "The Annual Report on American Industry." *Forbes* ranks the firms totally and by industry on financial factors such as earnings growth, value, and profitability (such as return on equity and return on invested growth). It also ranks the firms on sales and earnings growth, stock market performance, and comparable companies and industries. Finally, it provides "Yardsticks of Managerial Performance." In these, *Forbes* combines all these indexes and rates the firms for the year, longitudinally, and assigns overall ratings to them.

There are no magic numbers to assign evaluation figures to. But these outside assessments can help managements evaluate their performance and thus their strategic performance in an other than qualitative manner. Argenti has shown how techniques such as sensitivity tests, risk analysis, outcome matrixes, models, and simulation can help evaluate results and the strategies.

Qualitative factors are terribly important. Rensis Likert and others have shown how companies can make their short-run financial results look better by firing people (reducing people inventory); this may cost the company much in the long run. In the past, investments to reduce pollution might have reduced short-run performance ratios. So neither qualitative nor quantitative criteria alone will do in evaluation. A combination of both is necessary for effective evaluation of enterprises and the strategies.

Steiner tried to determine if there were specific strategic factors most important to success and thus worth evaluating. He did a study for the Financial

**TABLE 8–1 ■ FACTORS MOST LIKELY TO LEAD TO FUTURE STRATEGIC SUCCESS (STEINER)**

**1** Attract and maintain high-quality top management

**2** Develop future managers for domestic operations

**3** Motivate sufficient managerial drive for profits

**4** Assure better judgment, creativity, and imagination in decision making at top management levels

**5** Perceive new needs and opportunities for products

**6** Develop a better long-range planning program

**7** Improve service to customers

**8** Provide a competitive return to stockholders

**9** Maximize the value of stockholder investment

**10** Develop better a willingness to take risks with commensurate returns in what appears to be excellent new business opportunities to achieve growth objectives

Executives Research Foundation to find out and asked them to rank 71 factors which contributed to success.

The factors that the executives felt were most important to success of a company's strategy, and thus should be evaluated most closely, are given in Table 8–1.

There was relatively little disagreement among different functional executives in various industries and companies of different size. If Steiner is right, the crucial aspects of the strategy that need to be evaluated are:

Management quality and development

Environmental appraisal, especially market tidings

Financial return

## Evaluation and strategic planning process

In summary, evaluation is the final phase of the strategic planning process and its linkage to the beginning phase. The process is not unidirectional; it is a continuous process. An evaluation, if not performed, can be the missing link in the strategic planning process. See Proposition 8–1.

## Strategic planning in retrospect

We have now come through all the phases of the strategic planning process. I have treated the phases as if they were separate and distinct. This is necessary to examine each one at a time. As I warned you earlier, the phases overlap and blend together in the real world of work. They cannot be separated in actual strategic planning, as Witte showed.

I have tried to give you the reasons why strategic planning makes good sense if managers really are interested in effectiveness. But the *irony,* the *supreme irony,* is that to perform other than superficially, the managers must do what they have never been rewarded for doing before: take time out from daily pressures and rewards, step back and look at where the enterprise is now and what it is in for tomorrow. Then anticipate future events and take steps to do something about them.

Strategic planning requires the executives to formalize objectives and formally assess what is up and coming from the environment. It requires them to figure out formally where their firm's strengths and weaknesses are. Next, they are asked not to jump at the first solution that comes to mind, but to compare several choices systematically. Then they must choose the best one, implement it, and take time to evaluate and make changes, if necessary, in the choice. This is hard work and requires executives of strong motivation like Frank and Ernest in Figure 8–3.

---

**PROPOSITION 8–1**  ■ Firms which systematically evaluate the results of strategic choice and implementation will be more effective than those which do not.

---

These steps can be taken in many different ways. What has been presented here is a formal, normative way of going about strategic planning. But in every case, I have also tried to present you with the evidence of how most executives go about strategic planning.

In the long run, I would still contend that our enterprises and societies would be better off if strategic planning were formalized. I cited some of this evidence to support that belief in Chapter 1.

In any case, it is hoped that the presentation of strategic planning in the book will contribute to the understanding of the need for strategic planning, how it is done, and how it could be done to help improve organizational effectiveness.


## References

[1] Glueck, William F.: *Personnel: A Diagnostic Approach,* Dallas: Business Publications, Inc., 1974, especially chaps. 2, 3, 12, 13.

Pitts, Robert: "Variable Incentive Compensation for Division General Managers in Diversified Companies," unpublished D.B.A. thesis, Harvard Business School, 1970.

Prasad, S. B.: "Top Management Compensation and Corporate Performance," *Academy of Management Journal,* **17** (3): 554–558, September 1974.

[2] Argenti, John: *Systematic Corporate Planning,* New York: Wiley, 1974, chap 14.

Ferguson, Charles: *Measuring Corporate Strategy,* Homewood, Ill.: Dow Jones-Irwin, 1974, especially chap. 6.

Price, James: "The Study of Organizational Effectiveness," *Sociological Quarterly,* **13**: 3–15, Winter 1972.

Tilles, Seymour: "How to Evaluate Corporate Strategy," *Harvard Business Review,* **41** (4): 111–121, 1963.

[3] Argenti, John: op. cit., chap. 14.

Likert, Rensis: *The Human Organization,* New York: McGraw-Hill, 1968.

Steiner, George: *Strategic Factors in Business Success,* New York: Financial Executive Research Foundation, 1969.

# A note on the case method

This note is designed to introduce you to the case method, its purpose, and methodology.

## What is a case?

A case is a written description of an enterprise (such as a business, industry, hospital, arts organization). The case usually contains information about many facets of the enterprise: its history, external environment, and internal operations. The cases used in this book are multifaceted, containing material on many aspects of the operations.

Cases are based on material gathered about real organizations. Most of the cases in this book are undisguised; that is, their real names are used. There are some disguised cases. These companies wished to remain anonymous, and so their names and locations were changed. This does not change the reality of their challenges and problems.

## Are cases complete?

There is no such thing as a *complete* case study. The amount of detail required would make the case too long to read and too detailed to analyze. One reaction that frequently is heard is: "I don't have enough information." In reality, the manager *never* has enough information because:

1   It is not available.
2   It is not available at this time.
3   To acquire the information is too costly.

What does the manager do then? The manager makes the necessary decisions based on the information at hand and after making reasonable assumptions about the unknowns. So, with cases, you must work with the information you have and make reasonable assumptions. The data in the case contain enough information for the analyst to examine and determine what the crucial factors are that confront the management at the time.

## Is all the case information important?

When you get your mail, some of it is important, some useless, some of minor interest. At work, managers are bombarded with information. It too consists of a mix of the relevant, the partially relevant, and the useless. So it is with cases. When the case writer gathers information, some of it will become crucial to analysis. Other pieces of information are not especially useful. Since you are training to be a manager, it is your job to do the manager's job: separate the wheat from the chaff.

## Why are cases used in administrative training?

Case studies allow a different kind of learning to take place. It is close to a learn-by-doing approach. Cases are intended to simulate the reality of the manager's job. The material in the case provides the data for analysis and decision making. They become the laboratory materials for applying what we have learned about how to be effective business executives or administrators.

Cases require you to make decisions about the situations presented and to defend those decisions with your peers. Just as in real decision making you will need to persuade your peers and superiors that your analysis and solution are the best, these communication and interpersonal skills are vital to success in management. Cases provide you the opportunity to improve these skills too.

## What roles do students and instructors play in the case method?

Typically, the instructor serves a role different from that of lecturer. He or she encourages the students to analyze problems and recommend solutions. The instructor questions, criticizes, and encourages the students' peers to do the same.

The student can play several roles. Several standard roles are the board chairman, the president, and a consultant. I prefer the consultant's role. Thus the student can analyze and recommend what should be done, given the nature of the problem and the nature of the top executives. If the student feels that the suggestion he or she would like to make is likely to be unacceptable to the president, the student should discuss both solutions.

## How to prepare a case

There are a large number of possible approaches to case preparation. This is one that has worked for me.

**1** Read the case and make notes about major problem areas you pick up as you read through it. List the objectives of the enterprise. Put the case aside for a while.

**2** Read the case again. This time prepare the environmental threat and opportunities and strategic advantage profiles. This will require analysis of the data (Chapters 3, 4).

**3** Prepare a list, rank-ordered in terms of importance of the major opportunities and problems. Prepare a list of alternative strategies (Chapter 5).

**4** Analyze the alternatives in terms of the problems and opportunities and make a choice (Chapter 6).

**5** Implement the strategy (Chapter 7).

**6** Make sure the choice meets the objectives of the enterprise (Chapter 8).

# CASES

# Enterprise objectives and strategic planning

# One-Day Laundry Company[1]

## William F. Glueck

The One-Day Laundry Company recently surpassed its chief competitor to become the largest laundry and dry-cleaning company in Syracuse, New York. Only 4 years ago, the company was merely one of many neighborhood dry-cleaners in the Syracuse area, and was about seventh or eighth in size. The rapid growth began when the company changed hands in 1966.

The company was founded by Charles W. Brown in 1932. Located in the downtown section of Syracuse, the firm quickly gained a reputation for quality work and friendly service. The business was profitable and provided a comfortable living for Mr. Brown and his family for many years. About a year before the owner's death in 1955, he followed the trend to move to the suburbs and relocated the plant near an older, middle-class neighborhood. His widow ran the business for the next 10 years, until she was forced to sell it because of ill health. Richard W. Silsby and Roger L. Swain purchased the business in the summer of 1966.

Mr. Silsby, a native of Ohio, graduated from Michigan University with a degree in personnel management in 1963. From 1963 to 1965 he was the manager of a dry-cleaning company in Syracuse. Silsby saw the advertisement to sell the One-Day Laundry in the newspaper and was immediately interested. He felt that the potential for a dry-cleaning business in the Syracuse area was a promising one, and also saw this as a chance to be his own boss. Mr. Silsby was able to persuade Mr. Swain, whom he met at a civic club, to leave his job with a state agency and form a partnership to purchase One-Day. Mr. Swain is 32 years old and has a degree in accounting.

The new owners decided to expand operations rapidly by borrowing heavily and reinvesting all profits for the next 5 years. During the first year of operations one dry-cleaning plant and one combination dry-cleaning and laundry plant were purchased. Three dry-cleaning plants were added in 1968 and one more in 1969. Two combination dry-cleaning and laundry plants were added in 1969. In addition, five pickup stations were established. Gross sales increased from $90,000 in 1966 to over $750,000 in 1969.

---

[1] This is a disguised case. That is, the facts in it are based on a real company. But the names of the persons involved, the location, and the quantitative data have been changed because the company requested it. It serves no useful purpose to try to determine which company is the "real" company.

Mr. Silsby is operations manager and director. He supervises purchasing, advertising, production, personnel, and transportation. He spends most of his time troubleshooting, traveling to various plants. Mr. Swain serves as treasurer, accountant, and finance officer. Since he spends most of his time at the main plant, he also acts as manager of that plant.

## How One-Day operates

Plant 1 is the original facility and is used for laundry, dry cleaning, and clothes storage. It is located in a deteriorating neighborhood on a heavily traveled street. The area has been the subject of much local criticism due to its high concentration of businesses and generally inadequate parking space. There is room for three cars in One-Day's parking area. Curb service is featured.

Plant 2 is a dry-cleaning plant located near Syracuse University and close to a number of apartment buildings. It is a modern building on a main traffic route. Parking is adequate.

Plant 3 was the first plant built by the partnership. It has both dry-cleaning and laundry facilities, and contains the cold-storage vault used by the whole company. It is a physically attractive building located on a commercial street next to a middle-class neighborhood and close to a number of high-income apartments.

The fourth plant is a dry-cleaning establishment located in the same building as a self-service laundry (not owned by the company). The neighborhood contains rather cheap houses and includes a large primary-secondary educational complex. Parking is shared with a grocery store. On the day the case writer visited the outlet, there was a great deal of litter strewn both inside the building and on the parking lot. On this and a subsequent visit, the attendant was very slow in appearing.

Plants 5, 6, and 8 are all dry-cleaning plants located in newer, middle-class suburban areas. In all cases, the buildings are less than 5 years old and are well maintained. Plant 7 is a combination dry-cleaning and laundry unit in an old and somewhat aristocratic neighborhood.

The ninth unit is in the process of being built. It is One-Day's first venture into the northwest section of Syracuse, an area which consists of luxury housing and some lake shore apartments. The new facility will be a combination of dry cleaning and laundry.

The five pickup stations are located in areas where customers do not have ready access to any of One-Day's main facilities. Most are located in neighborhood shopping centers. In each instance, these stations share the same building with coin-operated laundries owned by another firm. One attendant takes care of both facilities.

One-Day Laundry is a full-service company, serving the laundry, dry-cleaning, and clothes storage (both normal storage and cold storage for furs) needs of their customers. These services are available at all stations. If the receiving station does not have the facilities to perform the desired work, the items are transferred to another station and then returned to the original station for pickup. One-hour service is available for all dry cleaning. Laundry is on an "in-by-nine, out-by-five" basis. In most areas of the city, laundry accounts for about 30 percent of the business. Near the university, however, it amounts to nearly 60 percent of the total volume. "Instant" curb service is advertised. A study showed that the average time spent by a customer at a drive-in facility is 2 minutes.

The full cycle for dry-cleaning operations includes the actual dry-cleaning and drying process, steam pressing (pants, coats, and dresses), steam finishing (pants), clothes wrapping, racking, and delivery.

In the laundry, clothes are marked, and then washed and dried. Shirts, pants, and dresses undergo both a preliminary and a final steam pressing. Sheets are pressed only once. After an item has been pressed, it is folded or packaged for delivery.

The equipment for a laundry facility consists of a boiler and compressor to supply steam, washing machines, a dryer (although most clothes are ironed wet), three or four types of ironers, a packaging rack, and a repair area. The dry-cleaning equipment includes a dry-cleaning machine, a dryer, a number of semiautomatic ironers, a packaging rack, and a repair station. With the exception of the original plant, the equipment is fairly new and modern in design. The equipment in the old plant is less efficient and has caused some maintenance problems. Mr. Silsby stated that labor is the major production cost in this industry, and that they are using automated equipment wherever possible. He added that he subscribed to an industry periodical, and that he closely followed any recommendations on how to improve efficiency.

The design of the work areas in most of the plants is generally good from the standpoint of efficiency. Storage areas are inadequate, however. For example, the passageways at some of the plants are cluttered with large drums of detergent. There are no plans to expand existing facilities although they are presently operating at 80 to 90 percent capacity. Management would rather build new plants to meet future needs than expand old ones, as they feel that small plants are more efficient.

## One-Day's market

Mr. Silsby said that as far as he can predict, One-Day Laundry will limit its marketing area to Syracuse. Syracuse, which is the fourth largest city in New York, is located midway between Albany and Buffalo. The city contains a wide variety of medium and light industry, with products such as machinery, metal products, paper products, auto parts, and clothing. The town also has four colleges, including Syracuse University. It is not a rapidly growing community. In fact, the population actually declined from 220,000 in 1950 to 216,000 in 1960. Many seem to be moving from Syracuse to other metropolitan areas in the state.

One-Day serves many types of persons in the community, and management has tried to vary its promotion accordingly. For example, an appeal is made to the town's established residents with advertising slogans such as "Serving You with Quality for Over 35 Years," and "We Care—and Have Cared for Over 35 Years." On the other hand, ads are placed in a student newspaper emphasizing the growth and progressiveness of the company. Members of the football team sometimes pose for these ads. Some advertising is aimed at the town's wealthier residents, giving assurance that expensive clothes will be handled competently, and explaining in detail the elaborate precautions taken in clothes and fur storage. Delivery service is furnished to a small number of customers who live in the town's most exclusive residential area. Delivery service is not provided to other customers.

One-Day advertises on radio, on television, and in the newspapers. Radio advertising consists of spots on the 7:30 morning and 6:15 evening weather reports of a local station. Sixty-second television commercials are placed on an eleven o'clock news program on Sunday and Monday nights. It is estimated that 85,000 people watch this program. Ads are placed in a major newspaper every few days although management does not feel that this has yielded worthwhile results. Mr. Silsby said that at one time they tried a direct-mail campaign, but did not find it very effective. Mr. Silsby writes all of the company's advertising copy and delivers the television advertisements himself. The total advertising budget is $1600 a month. An independent organization estimates that 168,000 people are being reached by the advertising campaign. Occasionally, one of Mr. Silsby's children delivers the television commercials.

One-Day's prices are comparable to those of competitors in the area, with one exception. A fast-growing chain, Styler Cleaning and Laundry, is underselling all the others. Mr. Silsby commented, "They're wearing out their equipment, but they're not making any money. I don't think they can keep offering such low prices for very long." He admitted, however, that he was surprised that they had been able to keep prices low for as long as they had. Styler dropped prices to a level about 10 to 15 percent below the prevailing rates in late 1968 and has not raised them since. Styler is now the second largest of the three major chains in the area.

The One-Day marketing concept contends that all dry cleaning and laundry are basically the same. "We're selling service, and nothing else," said Mr. Silsby.

There's not much difference in quality from one outfit to the next. Even if there is a difference, people are not apt to notice it. What they do notice, however, are things like how fast they are waited on, whether or not they can get a nearby parking place, how friendly the people behind the counter are, and whether or not the ashtrays have been emptied recently. It's the little things that really make the difference.

Mr. Silsby said that persons employed to work behind the counter are carefully selected on the basis of appearance and personality. Many college students are hired part-time for this job.

## Personnel

Mr. Silsby does all the hiring and firing. In reference to hiring policies, he said, "My first impression of a person usually determines whether or not he gets hired. I look at his personal appearance, personality, interest in the job, and whether or not he's got a wine bottle in his pocket." All references are checked, and no applications are taken over the phone. The company does not discriminate racially, and this is reflected by the fact that nearly one-third of the work force is black.

Labor turnover, a serious problem in most cleaning businesses, is no problem to One-Day. Management feels that this is largely due to the fact that their pay scales are above the area average for the industry. The major job categories and hourly wages are as follows:

| | | |
|---|---|---|
| 1 | Laundry pressers | $1.40 per hour |
| 2 | Dry-cleaning pressers | $1.80 to $2.10 per hour |
| 3 | Dry-cleaning operators | $2.20 to $2.60 per hour |
| 4 | Checkers | $1.70 per hour |
| 5 | Laundry markers | $1.40 per hour |
| 6 | Front personnel | $1.40 per hour |
| 7 | Managers of outlets | $100 per week, plus 3 percent of sales |

Mr. Silsby said that each worker is guaranteed a minimum weekly wage of $50, regardless of how many hours he or she has worked. Time and a half is given for all time over 45 hours.

Fringe benefits include a "surprise" cake given on an employee's birthday, cokes sold at cost, with free cokes during rush periods, a 50 percent discount on all work, and a 1-week vacation. In addition, a $5 award is given to all employees when no garments are lost in a given month. This is awarded for most months.

Promotion, like hiring, is based on Silsby's personal evaluation of the employee. Mr. Silsby emphasized that qualified employees who have the desire to "better themselves" have the opportunity to work up in the organization. Part of the 135-member work force comes to work at 7 A.M. and works until 4 P.M., whereas the others work from 8 A.M. until 5 P.M. Only the dry-cleaning staff works on Saturday, working from 8 until 11 A.M. There are two coffee breaks per day, one at 10 A.M. and the other at 3 P.M.

Most training is done on the job. Many applicants have had previous experience in the production end of the business, and an effort is made to hire these individuals. If their past experience has been limited or specialized, they are rotated through a number of jobs so that they will be able to work wherever needed. There is no educational requirement for production workers. The front workers, who are often high school or college students, do not normally have prior experience. Mr. Silsby trains them personally, emphasizing the importance of good customer relations.

There are no written personnel policies. Mr. Silsby has a number of informal policies that reflect several precepts which are especially dear to him. These include:

1 Never ask of a man what you would not do yourself.

2 The success of the company depends on the worker, and workers produce in a direct relationship to the way management treats them.

3 Employees are people, and they bring their personal troubles to work with them. Help the employees solve their problems, and they work better. (Mr. Silsby has been known to cosign notes, secure legal aid, and perform other services for his employees.)

4 The workers are sensitive to changes in production processes and management. It is better to explain things than to have the employees come to the wrong conclusions.

Mr. Silsby pointed out that the employees have a strong sense of identification with the company, and that this would tend to thwart any attempts at unionization. Many cleaners in the area, including One-Day's two largest competitors, are unionized.

One-Day has no centralized personnel records. Records for each employee are kept at the plant in which he works for a period of 1 year.

## Financing at One-Day

The company has relied upon debt to provide the funds for its rapid expansion. All new locations are 100 percent debt-financed with 5-year notes. It costs the company about $35,000 to set up a dry-cleaning plant, and about $75,000 to build and equip a full-service plant. Everything needed to start a facility is financed with a "package" note at the company's bank. Pickup stations are leased. Mr. Swain said that the break-even points for pickup stations, dry-cleaning plants, and full-service plants are $400 per month, $4000 per month, and $8500 per month, respectively.

Short-term debt is occasionally used to finance inventory. Mr. Swain said that he never used a budget, but he prepared trial balances monthly. Balance sheet and income statements are prepared semiannually. Depreciation is figured on a straight-line basis which assumes an 8-year life for all machinery and equipment.

Mr. Swain said that he was worried that the financial structure of the company was becoming debt-heavy. "I'm not certain that we can continue to expand indefinitely using long-term debt as a source of funds," he said. "The way I see it, we're driving ourselves up against a wall as far as future financing is concerned. The more we go into debt, the higher interest rates we must pay to offset the increased risk." He continued:

This also limits the possibility of future equity financing, since investors would not be willing to pay as much for the stock because of the risk factor. No, I'm becoming more and more convinced that we should start a franchising operation.

He went on to describe the details concerning a franchise plan which he has been "playing around with." Under this plan, the original partnership would act more or less as a holding company, owning two-thirds of the new plants and providing "professional services" for a fee. The franchise holder would put up $10,000 of his own money. Seven thousand of this would pay for the franchise, $2000 would go into "paid-in-surplus," and $1000 would go into "paid-in-equity." He would then be entitled to draw $11,000 in salary plus one-third of net profits. The controlling partnership would pay two-thirds of expenses and take two-thirds of the profits. For 5 percent of sales, the parent company would furnish advertising and bookkeeping services. Laundry service would be provided to plants having only dry-cleaning facilities at a 25 percent discount.

"I think that in the long run this arrangement would work out best for us," Mr. Swain concluded.

I've talked it over with Dick, but he's not willing to go along with the idea at the present time. He's concerned that we might lose control over the operation, and that it would be difficult to maintain our quality image. I feel just the opposite about this. It's becoming virtually impossible for two men to personally supervise the entire chain. Why, we're spending almost all of our time traveling from one unit to another as it is. Right now, we're placing an enormous reliance on the individual plant manager. If they owned a piece of the action, they would work even harder to increase sales.

The two partners are still arguing over the possibility of a franchise operation.

# Appendix

**TABLE 1 ■ ONE-DAY COMPANY, INCOME STATEMENT**
### For years ending December 31, 1967 to 1969

| Financial statement | 1967 | 1968 | 1969 |
|---|---|---|---|
| Net sales | 223,200 | 460,800 | 750,600 |
| Cost of sales | 129,456 | 249,754 | 399,319 |
| Gross profit | 93,744 | 211,046 | 351,281 |
| All other expenses net | 84,905 | 194,918 | 328,763 |
| Profit before taxes | 8,839 | 16,128 | 22,518 |
| Income taxes | 1,607 | 3,779 | 5,929 |
| Net profit or loss | 7,232 | 12,349 | 16,589 |

**TABLE 2 ■ ONE-DAY COMPANY, BALANCE SHEET STATEMENT**
### For years ending December 31, 1967 to 1969

| Financial statement | 1967 | 1968 | 1969 |
|---|---|---|---|
| *Assets* | | | |
| Cash | 15,948 | 24,735 | 47,211 |
| Receivables net | 22,244 | 44,329 | 54,622 |
| Inventory net | 8,542 | 13,880 | 21,614 |
| All other | 7,204 | 9,483 | 11,454 |
| Total current | 53,938 | 92,427 | 134,901 |
| Fixed assets net | 172,816 | 258,545 | 386,929 |
| All other | 17,821 | 21,118 | 21,151 |
| Total noncurrent | 190,637 | 279,663 | 408,080 |
| Total assets | 244,575 | 372,090 | 542,981 |
| *Liabilities* | | | |
| Due to banks | 27,834 | 40,702 | 59,061 |
| Due to trade | 17,221 | 34,261 | 53,293 |
| Income taxes | 1,603 | 3,712 | 5,929 |
| All other | 6,454 | 9,210 | 14,431 |
| Total current | 53,112 | 87,885 | 132,714 |
| Long-term debt | 169,809 | 261,218 | 387,157 |
| Total debt | 222,921 | 349,103 | 519,871 |
| *Equity* | | | |
| R. W. Silsby | 10,000 | 10,000 | 10,000 |
| R. L. Swain | 10,000 | 10,000 | 10,000 |
| Earned surplus | 1,654 | 2,987 | 3,110 |
| Total liabilities and equity | 244,575 | 372,090 | 542,981 |

# Ideal Sheen Cleaners, Inc.

## Donald Scotton and Jeffrey Susbauer

*"My experiences at a very early age caused me to develop a deep-seated fear of poverty. Job opportunities were seldom available. I decided in 1939 that my greatest chance for success involved the establishment and operation of my own business, and it was recognized that to avoid being poor through the successful operation of my business, I would have to consider hard work and education as every day requirements."*

William E. Miller, Sr.,
President, Ideal Sheen Cleaners, Inc.

## Background of the business founder

Mr. William E. Miller, Sr., was a native of Cleveland, Ohio, and had lived in the inner city all of his 58 years. He grew up in the black portion of the community, was educated there, formed and ran his business there, and continued to live there after some financial success was achieved.[1] He graduated from East Technical High School in the early 1930s.

Like many youths, Bill Miller pursued a series of part-time jobs while he was in high school, including several in drugstores. After he was married, he was employed in an automobile tire shop as a tire changer. Because of the continued business depression of the mid-1930s, he lost his job. His father had worked for Swift and Company's local meat-packing plant for more than 30 years; and the father was able to help the son get a job there. This job was in the hide cellar. The hides from slaughtered animals were preserved and stored in the hide cellar. The work consisted of salting and stacking the hides for a period of time until they were cured. When the hides were to be removed from the cellar for further processing, it was necessary to pound off the salt on a bench ladder. Next, the hides were rolled for shipment. Finally, there was the task of shoveling away the residual wet salt. This was an exceedingly hard laboring job.

In addition, employment was uncertain. Periodic layoffs occurred, and it became more difficult to find steady employment to support his wife and child. The futility of his situation was expressed as follows: "I felt so worthless. Here I was—a man with a wife and one baby—and I could not keep a job." So he obtained a job with WPA (the federal Works Project Administration). This employment lasted for 18 months. As indicated by Mr. Miller, there was a limit to the amount of time a person could work on the WPA. During that period, he worked at the city zoo on construction projects that involved bricklaying, assisting stonemasons, and performing other manual labor. He said, "I did not feel like I was getting anywhere. I saw no future. . . . I finally decided that I was not going to make it at jobs. I was not going to find a decent job because I had no training. The only answer seemed to be to go into business for myself."

---

[1] For further information on black business, see Allison Jennings et al., "Note on Black Business in the U.S.," *Intercollegiate Case Clearing House,* 9–371–123.

His wife's father was in the laundry business. The father-in-law was a "jobber," that is, an independent businessman who conducted his own laundry routes and had a wholesale laundry wash and press the garments at 60 percent of the retail price. Mr. Miller reported, "That was what I decided I was going to do. So I went out and hocked what little furniture we had and got $50 from a loan company."

## Six phases of the enterprise

Mr. Miller became an independent businessman in 1939 when he organized a laundry route. The second phase of his business progress occurred in 1944 when he purchased an existing cleaning and tailor shop. The third phase was that of business expansion during the 1950s. A fourth occurred between 1960 and 1969. Growth and crisis from 1969 to 1973 characterized the fifth phase. The sixth phase was a planning period to offset the crisis. Each of these phases of this business life cycle is discussed below.

### PHASE 1: THE LAUNDRY ROUTE

This business was started in 1939. The self-employed laundry route operator established his route, solicited business from householders, made pickups and deliveries to customers, and had the cleaning and pressing done by one of several wholesale laundries. Capital requirements for the enterprise were small. A vehicle was needed to make deliveries and pickups to customers and the commercial laundry. Funds were required to cover the interim from payment to the commercial laundry until collections were made from the route customers. Other funds were needed to support the Miller family until business revenues were predictable. Less than $200 was invested, of which $50 was obtained from a loan shark.

The area served was known as the Central Section of the inner city. It was a black neighborhood, and the business was named the Harlem Laundry. This name was painted on the truck, and the hard work of knocking on doors began. In 1939 most people did their laundry at home; and there was keen competition for the business of those who did send it out. It was extremely difficult to get business. The proprietor became aware that he was not relating to people. He felt uncomfortable in trying to sell his service. He knew that he was not "getting across to them." At this point, Mr. Miller decided to buy a book about which he had heard—Dale Carnegie's *How to Win Friends and Influence People*. He considered this to be the turning point in his early business career. The lessons learned from Carnegie were effective. The business began to grow.

The workday began early in the morning and lasted until nine or ten o'clock every night. Sixty percent of the retail sales dollar went to the wholesale laundry, and the Harlem Laundry received the remaining forty percent. In addition, some customers wanted the combined service of damp wash and pressing, so Mrs. Miller performed the pressing service in their home. A third source of income was established shortly after the business was opened. A source was found that would perform job or wholesale dry cleaning. As in the arrangement for laundering, the Harlem Laundry paid 60 percent of every retail dollar to the wholesale dry cleaner and retained 40 percent.

By 1941, the firm's average income was in excess of $125 per week; and the Miller family purchased a home for $7200. A commercial bank owned the house in question and was concerned about the effect of integrating the block, as well as the ability of the prospective purchaser to meet the payments. This purchase was made possible through the personal endorsement of an influential black realtor, Mr. Robert Riffe. He enjoyed the reputation of having never had a house repossessed that was sold by him.

### PHASE 2: PURCHASE OF A DRY-CLEANING AND TAILOR SHOP

In 1943, a local dry-cleaning and tailor shop became available for purchase. Mr. Miller indicated that he did not want to personally run a dry-cleaning and laundry route the rest of his life. He also felt the insecurity of pursuing his living as a self-employed route man which depended upon his being on the route daily. Illness or other personal misfortunes could eliminate his income.

An attempt was made to borrow sufficient capital from a commercial bank to make the purchase; however, the loan was not forthcoming from such a source. The only choice, again, was a loan shark. One thousand dollars was needed, and the terms were as follows: (1) a 2-year note was signed in the amount of $1500 at the interest rate of 6 percent, (2) renewals were extended but at an unstated penalty, and (3) a second mortgage on his home had to be given as collateral on the note. When this agreement was executed, the $1000 was transferred to Mr. Miller for the purchase of the business.

The new business was taken over, and for the first time there was an identifiable business establishment. The firm assumed the name of the establishment purchased, Avenue Cleaners. The business purchased was identified as a "press shop." It had no dry-cleaning equipment. The garments were sent out to a wholesale cleaner on the usual arrangement of 60 percent for the wholesaler and 40 percent for the retailer. The store fixtures were minimal. The equipment consisted of two manually operated pressing machines. Mr. Miller did not continue the full-time tailoring service which had been performed by the previous owner. A part-time tailor was employed to make simple garment repairs and alterations. The services offered were (1) dry-cleaning and laundry routes, (2) over-the-counter dry-cleaning and laundry services at the store, (3) pressing, and (4) limited garment repairing. Mrs. Miller operated the store while her husband conducted the route services.

Unexpected problems arose. It was extremely difficult to find a reliable presser. In 1948, the building owner wanted to take over the store space for his own use. There was no lease transferred to Mr. Miller when he purchased the business. A new location was found on the same street a few blocks away. When the move was made, it was decided to close out the laundry business. This decision was made because of the declining importance of the laundry service. More families were doing laundry at home, and the decision was a partial response to the difficulty of finding reliable pressers to finish damp wash. Finally, this decision was made in an effort to give Mrs. Miller more free time from the business to care for her home and family.

The business had grown within the scope mentioned above. The personnel usually consisted of Mr. and Mrs. Miller, one or two persons to press garments, and a part-time tailor. This was a period of operational and financial consolidation for the owner. At the same time, he was learning more about his industry and saw the advantage of owning dry-cleaning equipment rather than jobbing it out to other cleaners.

### PHASE 3: EXPANSION IN THE 1950s

In 1952 the decision was made to purchase a dry-cleaning machine. Although retail sales were average, about $500 per week, 60 percent of the dry-cleaning revenue went to the wholesale dry cleaner. Mr. Miller's take-home pay in 1952 was less than the $125 per week he averaged in 1942 when he had the laundry and dry-cleaning route.

The purchase of dry-cleaning equipment was viewed as beneficial, because the 60 percent of the cleaning revenue paid to the wholesaler would be retained. Another reason for purchasing the machinery was that it could be used to attract more business. At that time, customers preferred to do business with a shop that cleaned garments on the premises. They liked to see the cleaning process, and the cleaning machine was placed near the front of the store for easy viewing; and another reason for purchase of the machine was quicker service.

Financing presented its usual challenge. Commercial bank loans were still not available. The usual criteria for a loan could not be met although the business had been in operation as a retail establishment for 9 years. To the best of the proprietor's knowledge, his business was not rated for financial and credit strength by Dun & Bradstreet, Inc. There was no option other than to seek the services of the loan shark. A note was signed for $750 at the legal rate of interest, but only $500 was transferred for the purchase of the machine. The difference of $250 was the lender's required incentive for making the loan.

Although increased revenues were realized, the added machinery also increased the following expenses: loan payments, cleaning supplies, utilities, and salary for an added employee. Business profits did not increase during the first 2 years. Seasonality of the business in summer and winter months also had an effect.

It became apparent that the increased volume made use of manual pressing equipment less possible. The finishing work could not be performed as rapidly as was required. Also, there was a chronic problem of keeping pressers on the job. They were often alcoholics and otherwise unstable. They were not predictable and often failed to report for work. The solution was reached in 1955 when "button-pushed and air-operated" pressing machines were purchased. This made it possible to hire only women.

In 1956 the store next door became available to provide room for expansion to accommodate the new machinery. The usual leasehold improvements were required; and the floors had to be reinforced and supported from below to support the heavy equipment. Additional water and drainage pipe and electrical conduits were installed.

Again, a loan was needed. For the first time in his business career, the owner was able to receive a $2000 loan from a commercial bank. His financial statements did not reveal sufficient strength, but the loan was made on the cosignature of Mr. Robertt Riffe. He was the realtor who had assisted the

Millers in arranging for the purchase and financing of their home in 1941. This set the pattern for future loans, but Mr. Miller was eager to qualify for commercial loans without a cosigner.

### PHASE 4: EXPANSION IN THE 1960s

In 1960 a third store, contiguous to the second store, was taken over to provide adequate storage for finished garments awaiting delivery by the two route men. The firm was incorporated as the Ideal Sheen Cleaners, Inc., in 1963. At this time, Mr. Elmer Whiting, certified public accountant, who represented the firm, arranged for the establishment of a regular line of credit with a commercial bank. Then loans could be obtained upon financial strength of the company rather than cosigners.

In 1965, an additional expansion was planned. Property located 18 blocks away on the same street was purchased in 1968. It consisted of a lot and building formerly used for a fast food operation. The previous owner had become bankrupt, and favorable purchase terms and financing were available from the Shaker Savings Association who held the property. Plans were made to convert the property into an up-to-date cleaning plant and use the old location for a shirt laundry.

Unfortunately, the architecture firm's estimated costs were low, and the construction costs exceeded the $28,000 addition planned by $30,000. That coupled with the original building and land cost of $30,000 necessitated a second loan. A third loan was obtained from a commercial bank to finance new equipment. The plan to convert the old business location of three adjoining stores into a shirt laundry was carried out.

### PHASE 5: GROWTH AND CRISIS

Sales volume and profits continued to grow in fiscal 1968 and 1969 as shown in Table 1. However, certain changes were identified; and it was seen that 1970 would not be a profitable year. The plant expansion which became effective in October 1969 was not utilized at more than 50 percent of capacity during the following 2 years. This situation was not viewed as a casual event.

Several reasons for the crisis were present. One was that the sales potential for the existing way of doing business of the Central Section of the inner city had probably been reached. Another reason was the rapidly spreading trend of wash-and-wear clothing. Emphasis was on easy-to-care-for and do-it-yourself garments. Still another reason was the prolonged trend for the casual look that minimized the need for well-cared-for clothes. A final reason for the decline in profits was the opening of a retail outlet in 1972 to pick up and deliver dry cleaning to the Federal Building in Cleveland. The federal government had encouraged minority businesses to operate in federal buildings. This was done by the Ideal Sheen Cleaners, Inc.; but in June 1973, after 11 months of operations, the firm made arrangements to close the operation. Two thousand dollars had been invested in opening the store, and over $3000 in cost of operations had been incurred. Because of lack of promotion by the sponsor and a realization that dry cleaning was not brought to work by employees in an office, the venture was judged to be a failure.

**TABLE 1 ■ IDEAL SHEEN CLEANERS, INC., CONSOLIDATED PROFIT AND LOSS STATEMENTS**
For fiscal years ending June 30, 1968 to 1972

|  | 1968 | 1969 | 1970 | 1971 | 1972 |
|---|---|---|---|---|---|
| Net sales | $151,000 | $184,400 | $244,400 | $262,800 | $236,700 |
| Cost of production | 71,300 | 82,300 | 139,800 | 128,200 | 116,900 |
| Gross profit from operations | 79,700 | 102,100 | 104,600 | 134,600 | 119,800 |
| Expenses: | | | | | |
| Sales and delivery | 48,500 | 58,000 | 73,300 | 78,800 | 71,700 |
| Administrative | 19,200 | 27,700 | 31,300 | 30,000 | 39,100 |
| Total | 67,700 | 85,700 | 104,600 | 108,800 | 110,800 |
| Operating income | 12,000 | 16,400 | 0 | 25,800 | 9,000 |
| Other income | (600) | 1,400 | 1,400 | 1,300 | 200 |
| Less other expenses | 3,600 | 3,000 | 10,000 | 21,200 | 18,900 |
| Net other income | (4,200) | (1,600) | (8,600) | (19,900) | (18,700) |
| Net profit before taxes | 7,800 | 14,800 | (8,600) | 5,900 | (9,700) |
| Reserve for income taxes | 1,700 | 2,800 | . . . | . . . | . . . |
| Net profit after taxes | $6,100 | $12,000 | $(8,600) | $5,900 | $(9,700) |

Mr. Miller recognized that his firm was at a critical point in its business life cycle. The alternatives were to (1) accept a decline in growth and profits and eventually close down or (2) seek new ways to revitalize the business. The latter option required drastic changes in the concept of doing business, the market to be served, the services, and the internal operations.


PHASE 6: PLANS TO OFFSET BUSINESS MATURITY AND MARKET CHANGE

The focus for the plan occurred in 1971; however, earlier action to expand and adjust services had the effect of removing the firm from a narrow activity of just operating dry-cleaning and laundry routes as a sales-service type of business. Diversification of the services and market penetration were pursued as business strategies to aid in developing and maintaining the firm.

Another continuing action was participation in trade association activities. Mr. Miller was a member of the National Institute of Dry Cleaning since 1952 and its successor, the International Fabricare Institute. This latter institute was formed in 1972 by the joining of the National Institute of Dry Cleaning and the American Institute of Laundry. Over the years, he learned of dry-cleaning trends and developments through associations with members and attendance at meetings of the groups.

Indicative of the changing trend in dry cleaning was an incident that took place during the 1972 annual convention of the International Fabricare Institute held at Atlantic City. One of the speakers asked each person in the audience to introduce himself and shake hands with each of the two persons beside him. When this was done, the speaker indicated that this was appropriate, because one of three would be out of business and not at the convention the following year. Mr. Miller attended the 1973 convention in Chicago and attested that the speaker was correct.

The Ideal Sheen Cleaners, Inc., participated in two surveys run by Dwyier Associates of Arlington, Virginia, in 1970 and 1971. There were approximately 10 cleaners representing geographical sections of the United States invited to participate and finance the studies. The Cleveland firm's share of the cost was approximately $600 for each survey. The results indicated that the needs and desires of customers had changed over the years, and that businesses such as Ideal Cleaners must concentrate on developing additional services and updating internal processes and operations to compete in a market that was being softened by wash and wear garments and do-it-yourself dry-cleaning trends. It was also discovered that supposed loyalty to the dry cleaner did not exist among his customers. Over 50 percent used more than one cleaner. The customer might use more than one dry cleaner because of price variations and differences in services offered such as carpet cleaning in one shop and not in another.

The efforts to offset business maturity in a changing environment were summarized as follows: (1) expansion of the services, (2) development of the existing market, (3) expansion into new markets, and (4) processing plant expansion. These are described below.

*Expansion of services* Five service expansions were planned to provide customers with convenience and needs consistent with those revealed in the surveys mentioned above, information received in meetings of the International Fabricare Institute, and a mail survey of the Ideal Cleaners' customers.

**1** *Cleaning by the pound* This service was offered in recognition of the fact that there are different categories of dry cleaning. For example, a man's suit required more processing than a child's winter snowsuit. The former required cleaning and pressing; the latter required only cleaning. Those cleaners who offered the service permitted customers to bring large amounts of garments and other household fabrics for cleaning only at a special price. The customer was charged a rate per pound rather than a price per garment or piece.

Although this service had been available for several years, the Ideal Cleaners had not promoted it. In 1972, an active promotion was instituted so that existing and new customers would use this firm as a one-stop dry cleaner and not take different categories of cleaning to several firms.

**2** *Easy-care service* This service was begun in December 1972 in response to the need that not all garments required the same pressing and finishing process. Permanent-press garments did not require the same amount of pressing as others, nor was pressing required for garments such as children's snowsuits. The Easy-Care service was devised to reduce the finishing process and, in so doing, reduce the price by 40 percent to the customer. This handling involved standard dry cleaning and then use of a steam tunnel machine rather than pressing. The steam tunnel process removed wrinkles from garments; and it was estimated that at least 30 percent of the garments being dry-cleaned could be so processed; the remainder required a minimum of "touch-up" pressing.

**3** *Carpet and upholstery cleaning* This service was investigated in 1972 through study of the surveys mentioned above, information received from the trade association, and inquiry into the local market. Mr. Miller arranged for the purchase of equipment from the International Equipment Company of Denver. He participated in a 1-week training program in Denver. The training consisted of experience in operating and repairing the machines, use and knowledge of cleaning chemicals, and marketing techniques to aid in communicating and selling the service. The service was placed in operation in the spring of 1973.

**4** *Drapery cleaning* There was an untapped demand for drapery cleaning, and plans were under way in the spring of 1973 to provide the service. It was not feasible to promote it without a further expansion of the processing plant. In addition, financing was required for additional machinery, land, and buildings. This plan was dependent upon a total plan for financing as discussed below.

**5** *Coin-operated laundry* Plans were also under way to add a coin-operated laundry service at the firm's main plant. Customer traffic at the main plant for the purpose of leaving and picking up dry cleaning was supportive of this venture. The surveys reaffirmed the close affinity of laundry and dry-cleaning services, as well as a strong demand for coin-operated laundry facilities in central city retail cleaning establishments. Again, this plan could not be implemented until plant expansion and financing were arranged.

*Penetration of existing market* Plans for adding services were intended to develop the existing market through deeper penetration. They were also intended to be useful for expanding into new markets. Supportive of the effort to draw more business from the existing market were plans to:

**1** *Sell more to existing customers* This was to be achieved by additional training for the driver-salespersons who operated the routes and counter personnel who received the "walk-in" business. Indicative of the additional training was information received by Mr. Miller in his week's training at Denver about the cleaning and care of carpets and upholstered items. Training in cleaning processes was also a planned part of the indoctrination for existing and new drivers and over-the-counter salespeople. A part-time employee was hired to call existing customers before the route salesperson came. This resulted in the customers' having sufficient time to consider which garments should be cleaned or laundered. The impact was larger sales and time savings for route salespersons.

**2** *Attract new customers* New emphasis was to be devoted to methods for locating prospective customers and presenting the merits of the Ideal Cleaners' variety of quality services. It was anticipated that the owner would assume primary responsibility for this action.

**3** *Increase the number of routes* Consideration was also given to the likelihood that the new services would make it feasible to increase the number of driver-salespersons working in the present market. Action was to be delayed until new services and sales training activities had been in operation long enough to have an effect.

*Expansion into new markets* These plans included the opening of new sales routes in the eastern suburbs and a retail outlet in a new apartment complex being built in downtown Cleveland. Priority was given to the development of the retail outlet in Park Centre.

Park Centre was part of the effort to revitalize downtown Cleveland. It was under construction in the summer of 1973; however, approximately 160 of the planned 1000 apartments were completed and occupied. The choices ranged from efficiency to three-bedroom apartments, with two penthouses on top of each of two towers. Rentals ranged from approximately $150 to $500 per month, excluding the penthouses. The twin tower buildings were 23 stories tall. Parking, laundry, and storage facilities were available, and a 75-store shopping mall occupied the first three levels. The retail stores were to be operating by fall, 1973. On top of the shopping mall and garage at the fourth-floor level between the two towers was a landscaped rooftop recreational terrace. This facility also included a rooftop building which included a swimming pool, gymnasium, billiard rooms, party rooms, saunas, etc.

Across the street to the south were the Chesterfield Apartments, erected about 8 years earlier as the first attempt to revitalize the downtown as a good residential area. This facility housed 414 apartments and one of the better downtown restaurants. To the east was a nearly completed apartment building for the elderly which contained 265 living units. Next door to the Chesterfield Apartments was a hotel which was being remodeled into 199 apartments for the elderly. Although two of those facilities were for senior citizens, the other three attracted a large group of young professionals and families without children. Other buildings had been erected in this immediate area within the past 6 years. A minipark had been opened directly to the west of Park Centre. All these facilities gave credence to a belief that a vital residential area was being developed.

Mr. Miller signed a 10-year lease in the spring of 1973 with Park Centre for a retail outlet for Ideal Sheen Cleaners, Inc. He estimated that there were at least 4000 units of housing (apartments) in downtown Cleveland from which he could draw business. The estimated potential of $200,000 annual sales was made for his business. It was his belief that this volume could be achieved within 4 or 5 years. In addition to 1972 sales volume of $236,700, this addition from a new market area seemed quite attractive. Of further encouragement was information contained in the last published *Cost Percentages Bulletin* (July 1968) of the National Institute of Dry Cleaning which showed that a retail outlet similar to the planned Park Centre produced an average net profit before taxes of 20.7 percent of net sales.

The terms of the lease contained the following:

**1** For the first 30 months, the base rent would be $800 per month plus 10 percent of all sales volume over $84,000 annually.

**2** After 30 months, the base rent would be $1000 per month plus 10 percent of all sales volume over $100,000 annually.

**3** Other features were estimated to cost about $100 per month and included:

(*a*) Payment for air conditioning, heat, and utilities on a metered basis.

(*b*) Payment of a pro rata share of maintenance for the common area of the mall.

(*c*) Mandatory membership in the Mall Merchants Association for purposes of joint advertising and promotion of the mall.

So that business at Park Centre could be developed as rapidly as possible, arrangements were made to set up a temporary retail cleaning shop in the Centre's community laundry room that was provided for tenants who wanted to do their own laundry and drying with coin-operated equipment. A luxurious lounge was adjacent to the laundry room for tenants to relax in while the machines were operating. The temporary store opened in June in the lounge and was to operate there until Mr. Miller's store in the shopping mall was to be opened in September 1973. He manned the store personally to become acquainted with the 160 residents and new ones as they moved into the buildings. New tenants were given a coupon offer good for the free cleaning of a suit or equivalent value for other services. The full range of services were available: dry cleaning, shirt laundry, easy-care dry cleaning, carpet and upholstery cleaning, and cleaning by the pound.

Although Mr. Miller operated the temporary quarters in Park Centre during June 1973, he was aware that he could not continue this activity. His other management responsibilities made it mandatory for him to provide more time to the overall direction of the business. He asked the authors of this case study to arrange for students on the Cooperative Education Program of the Cleveland State University to enter training to take over the operation of the Park Centre retail outlet. It was his intention to prepare four women students to operate the outlet. Scheduling was to be arranged for the store to be open 12 hours per day, 6 days per week. Two students would operate the store on schedules of 6 hours per day each for one university quarter session, while the other two were attending classes at the university. At the end of each instructional quarter, the two students on duty at the shop would return for a quarter at the university, and the other two would operate the shop.

In summary, it was planned that the Park Centre retail outlet would appeal to a new market that was emerging in the downtown area. The full set of services were to be available. These were believed to be of equal, and possibly greater, importance to this clientele as compared to the old Central City Market. An additional amenity was visualized as attractive and retentive of customers—a 1-hour cleaning service to be performed on the premises. This would require machinery not common to retail "pickup and delivery" counter operations. Research revealed that less than 10 percent of the business would be done on this basis. Therefore, it would not consume much of the store operator's time, nor would it require the addition of personnel. It was simply an extra, a red-carpet treatment, for customers who might have an emergency need for unusual service.

To support the plan specified above, an additional plant and equipment would be needed. Land was available for purchase next door to the dry-cleaning processing plant. The existing plant had 3300 square feet of space, and it was determined that an additional 4000 square feet was required to operate the planned business volume successfully. This would include the coin-operated laundry, space to clean rugs, carpets, and upholstered furniture, added machinery for traditional dry cleaning, and a transfer of the firm's office from the shirt laundry located about 20 blocks away. In addition, considerable equipment would be required.

This combined expansion was anticipated to cost approximately $191,000 as follows:

| | |
|---|---:|
| Plant: land, building, and leasehold improvements | $ 97,000 |
| Equipment: plant, carpet, and laundromat | 67,000 |
| Park Centre: leasehold improvements and equipment | 27,000 |
| Total | $191,000 |

## Financing the expansion

In anticipation of obtaining loans, the financial information for the 5 years 1968–1972 was examined; and the estimated cash flows, 1973, 1974, and 1975, were prepared. (See Tables 1, 2, and 3.) Mr. Miller made preliminary contact with the Shaker Savings Association about the possibility of financing the land, building, and leasehold expansion through the United States Small Business Administration "502 Loan Program." It was his understanding that if the loan were approved, the bank could loan 50 percent, the Small Business Administration would loan 40 percent, and a local development company would provide the remaining 10 percent. Local development companies were specified as an integral part in Section 502 of the Small Business Investment Act of 1958, as amended. Figure 1, extracted from the pamphlet *Loans to Local Development Companies,* United States Small Business Administration, February 1972, was examined to obtain an overview of the 502 Loan Program.

It appeared that the savings association was receptive to such a loan because

**TABLE 2 ■ IDEAL SHEEN CLEANERS, INC., CONSOLIDATED BALANCE SHEETS**
For fiscal years ending June 30, 1968 to 1972

| | 1968 | 1969 | 1970 | 1971 | 1972 |
|---|---|---|---|---|---|
| *Assets* | | | | | |
| **Current assets** | | | | | |
| Cash on hand | $ 6,800.00 | $ 7,600.00 | $ 1,400.00 | $ 8,700.00 | $ 8,900.00 |
| Notes receivable | 2,200.00 | 0 | 0 | | |
| Accounts receivable | 9,700.00 | 10,200.00 | 9,000.00 | 7,800.00 | 8,200.00 |
| Finished clothes | 10,900.00 | 14,300.00 | 21,300.00 | 19,700.00 | 32,000.00 |
| Other | 4,800.00 | 6,100.00 | 15,000.00 | 24,600.00 | 29,500.00 |
| Total | 34,400.00 | 38,200.00 | 46,700.00 | 60,800.00 | 78,600.00 |
| **Fixed assets** | 51,500.00 | 117,100.00 | 212,800.00 | 219,200.00 | 227,800.00 |
| Less reserve for depreciation | 10,600.00 | 18,200.00 | 33,100.00 | 48,500.00 | 61,500.00 |
| Total | 40,900.00 | 98,900.00 | 179,700.00 | 170,700.00 | 166,300.00 |
| **Other assets** | 14,600.00 | 12,300.00 | 24,500.00 | 6,100.00 | 6,100.00 |
| Total assets | $89,900.00 | $149,400.00 | $250,900.00 | $237,600.00 | $251,000.00 |
| *Liabilities* | | | | | |
| **Current liabilities** | | | | | |
| Accounts payable | $11,000.00 | $ 10,500.00 | $ 29,900.00 | $ 27,200.00 | $ 16,600.00 |
| Notes payable | 18,500.00 | 21,900.00 | 37,900.00 | 12,600.00 | 8,400.00 |
| Miscellaneous taxes payable | 9,000.00 | 8,600.00 | 18,100.00 | 11,100.00 | 23,800.00 |
| Other | 2,700.00 | 3,500.00 | 5,100.00 | 5,300.00 | 3,900.00 |
| Total | 41,200.00 | 44,500.00 | 91,000.00 | 56,200.00 | 52,700.00 |
| **Fixed liabilities** | | | | | |
| Long-term notes | 20,700.00 | 62,100.00 | 128,100.00 | 87,800.00 | 108,600.00 |
| Mortgage payable | 0 | 0 | 0 | 50,000.00 | 49,100.00 |
| Reserve for income tax | 1,800.00 | 2,800.00 | 0 | | |
| Loans from stockholders | 0 | 0 | 1,000.00 | 8,900.00 | 15,700.00 |
| Total | 22,500.00 | 64,900.00 | 129,100.00 | 146,700.00 | 173,400.00 |
| **Net worth** | | | | | |
| Capital stock | 8,000.00 | 8,000.00 | 8,000.00 | 8,000.00 | 8,000.00 |
| Earned surplus | 18,200.00 | 32,000.00 | 22,800.00 | 26,700.00 | 16,900.00 |
| Total | 26,200.00 | 40,000.00 | 30,800.00 | 34,700.00 | 24,900.00 |
| Total liabilities and net worth | $89,900.00 | $149,400.00 | $250,900.00 | $237,600.00 | $251,000.00 |

it held the mortgage on the existing property. Lending banks were given the preference of a first mortgage on the property under provisions of the SBA 502 Program.

It was also Mr. Miller's understanding that he would have to seek the remainder of the funds for the equipment from other sources. He was considering the possibility of receiving the loan from a commercial bank and a local MESBIC (Minority Enterprise Small Business Investment Corporation). These investment corporations were made possible under the Small Business Administration Act of 1958 and under the first specialized application of the Small Business Investment Corporation for minority enterprise in 1968. Their origins and operations were discussed in *MESBIC's and Minority Enterprise:*

TABLE 3 ■ IDEAL SHEEN CLEANERS, INC., COMBINED CASH FLOW PROJECTIONS

| | 1973 1st Quarter | 1973 2d Quarter | 1973 3d Quarter | 1973 4th Quarter | 1974 | 1975 |
|---|---|---|---|---|---|---|
| **Income** | | | | | | |
| E. 101 plant | $54,000.00 | $68,200.00 | $62,000.00 | $65,000.00 | $275,000.00 | $300,000.00 |
| Carpet and drapes | | | 14,000.00 | 18,000.00 | 78,000.00 | 87,000.00 |
| Laundromat | | | 9,000.00 | 36,000.00 | 42,000.00 |
| Park Centre | | | | | 75,000.00 | 83,000.00 |
| Total income | 54,000.00 | 68,200.00 | 76,000.00 | 92,000.00 | 464,000.00 | 512,000.00 |
| Production expenses | 21,000.00 | 27,200.00 | 24,600.00 | 32,450.00 | 162,200.00 | 176,900.00 |
| Depreciation (existing) | 3,300.00 | 3,300.00 | 3,300.00 | 3,300.00 | 13,200.00 | 13,200.00 |
| Depreciation (new) | | | 525.00 | 3,975.00 | 20,436.00 | 20,436.00 |
| Sales and distribution | 15,900.00 | 19,800.00 | 16,000.00 | 17,500.00 | 98,550.00 | 110,300.00 |
| Advertising and promotion | 1,600.00 | 2,000.00 | 2,650.00 | 2,800.00 | 17,850.00 | 19,600.00 |
| Office and administrative | 5,400.00 | 5,400.00 | 5,400.00 | 6,000.00 | 30,000.00 | 30,000.00 |
| Sublet services | 3,000.00 | 3,500.00 | 3,800.00 | 3,500.00 | 14,000.00 | 15,000.00 |
| Interest (existing) | 3,300.00 | 3,300.00 | 3,300.00 | 3,300.00 | 13,000.00 | 13,000.00 |
| Interest (new) | | | | | 13,942.00 | 12,900.00 |
| Total expenses | 53,500.00 | 64,500.00 | 59,575.00 | 72,825.00 | 383,178.00 | 411,336.00 |
| Net profit before taxes | 500.00 | 3,700.00 | 16,425.00 | 19,175.00 | 80,822.00 | 100,664.00 |
| Provision for federal income taxes | 0 | 0 | 0 | 0 | 0 | 41,500.00 |
| Net income | 500.00 | 3,700.00 | 16,425.00 | 19,175.00 | 80,822.00 | 59,164.00 |
| **Cash flow statement** | | | | | | |
| Net income after taxes | 500.00 | 3,700.00 | 16,425.00 | 19,175.00 | 80,822.00 | 59,164.00 |
| Depreciation | 3,300.00 | 3,300.00 | 3,825.00 | 7,275.00 | 34,236.00 | 34,236.00 |
| Interest | 3,300.00 | 3,300.00 | 3,300.00 | 3,300.00 | 26,942.00 | 25,900.00 |
| Total | 7,100.00 | 10,300.00 | 23,550.00 | 29,750.00 | 142,000.00 | 119,300.00 |
| **Debt amortization** | | | | | | |
| Existing debt | 8,100.00 | 8,100.00 | 8,100.00 | 8,100.00 | 32,400.00 | 32,400.00 |
| Bank | | | | 3,745.00 | 14,965.00 | 14,965.00 |
| SBA-502 | | | | 2,407.00 | 9,628.00 | 9,628.00 |
| LDC | | | | 748.00 | 2,993.00 | 2,993.00 |
| Total | $ 8,100.00 | $ 8,100.00 | $ 8,100.00 | $15,000.00 | $ 59,986.00 | $ 59,986.00 |

*A New Way for Corporations to Assist Minority Enterprise,* United States Department of Commerce, Office of Minority Business Enterprise, December 1970.

Mr. Miller's proposed "financing package" accompanied the cash flow projection as shown in Table 4. He was optimistic that his plan for revitalizing and expanding his business would work. He was equally optimistic that his past record as a businessman would enable him to receive the financing required.

## An entrepreneur's philosophy for minority business success

He believed firmly that a man must be dissatisfied with the status quo and uncertainty of working for others. His desire to overcome poverty was recognized as a strong factor in business success. Along with these personal motivations was the necessity to have empathy for others, particularly the underprivileged who were the majority of customers for the minority business. A sense of mission existed and was focused from a lecture that he heard at a local university many years ago. The lecturer said that "it was not possible for a person to have empathy for the poor, unless he, too, had been poor. He could have pity for the underprivileged, but not empathy unless he had shared the same status." Mr. Miller's philosophy was that minority business executives,

Individuals interested in developing the community

Invest in

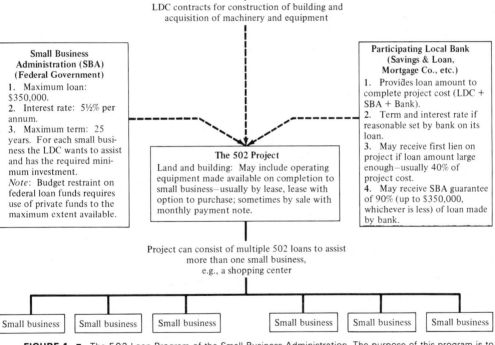

**The Local Development Company (LDC)**

The LDC borrows the "502" money from SBA and the local bank(s), and then, when the project is completed, leases or sells to the small business owner.

1. Must be a corporation with a minimum of 25 stockholders or members.
2. 75% of the stockholders or members must live or do business in the LDC's area of operation—the community, city, or county.
3. Usually invests a minimum of 20% of the cost of the project—usually dollars, but may include assets. SBA and local banks lend the 80% to the LDC.
4. Small business beneficiary may put up 25% of the LDC investment (voluntary, not required).
5. LDC can be organized either for profit or nonprofit. If for profit its rate of return net to stockholders should approximate the average rate of interest paid in financing the project.

LDC contracts for construction of building and acquisition of machinery and equipment

**Small Business Administration (SBA) (Federal Government)**

1. Maximum loan: $350,000.
2. Interest rate: 5½% per annum.
3. Maximum term: 25 years. For each small business the LDC wants to assist and has the required minimum investment.
*Note*: Budget restraint on federal loan funds requires use of private funds to the maximum extent available.

**The 502 Project**

Land and building: May include operating equipment made available on completion to small business—usually by lease, lease with option to purchase; sometimes by sale with monthly payment note.

**Participating Local Bank (Savings & Loan, Mortgage Co., etc.)**

1. Provides loan amount to complete project cost (LDC + SBA + Bank).
2. Term and interest rate if reasonable set by bank on its loan.
3. May receive first lien on project if loan amount large enough—usually 40% of project cost.
4. May receive SBA guarantee of 90% (up to $350,000, whichever is less) of loan made by bank.

Project can consist of multiple 502 loans to assist more than one small business, e.g., a shopping center

| Small business | Small business | Small business | Small business | Small business | Small business |

**FIGURE 1** ■ The 502 Loan Program of the Small Business Administration. The purpose of this program is to encourage growth and prosperity in a community by making available low-interest, long-term loans to local development companies for the purchase of land, the construction, expansion, or remodeling of buildings, and the purchase of operating machinery and equipment for use therein by a small business owner.

**TABLE 4 ■ IDEAL SHEEN CLEANERS, INC., PROPOSED FINANCING FOR BUSINESS EXPANSION, JUNE 1973**

| Loan purpose and source | Loan | Annual amortization |
|---|---|---|
| **Land, building, and leasehold improvements** | | |
| Bank, 15 years, 8½% | $ 48,500 | $ 5,731 |
| Small Business Administration, 25 years, 5½% | 38,800 | 2,859 |
| Loan Development Corp., 25 years, 8½% | 9,700 | 1,146 |
| | 97,000 | 9,736 |
| **Equipment, 10-year life** | | |
| Bank, 10 years, 8½% | 24,000 | 3,571 |
| Small Business Administration, 10 years, 5½% | 19,200 | 2,500 |
| Loan Development Corp., 10 years, 8½% | 4,800 | 714 |
| | 48,000 | 6,785 |
| **Equipment, 5-year life** | | |
| Bank, 5 years, 8½% | 23,000 | 5,663 |
| Small Business Administration, 5 years, 8½% | 18,400 | 4,269 |
| Loan Development Corp., 5 years, 8½% | 4,600 | 1,133 |
| | 46,000 | 11,065 |
| Total | $191,000 | $27,586 |

like himself, were obligated to provide a real service to their customers and encourage them to achieve recognition and economic security.

It was his opinion that there was no shortcut to success. The basic desire to operate one's own business must exist. Hard work over an entire career was a necessary ingredient. Education was a must. Mr. Miller attended night classes for several years at Fenn College, the predecessor of the Cleveland State University, to learn about business practice and its underpinning of cultural subjects. His education has been a continuous process through the media of university lectures and business management programs. In a similar manner he continued to learn about techniques, processes, and business practice through meetings with his trade associations.

He was proud that his two sons had grown up in the business. Both were in their mid-thirties and had progressed well in the firm. It was his belief that he could not give them a business to inherit; rather, he could give them an opportunity to operate a business. The business was not an asset that would produce an automatic profit. It could provide them only with a vehicle for sound business conduct.

Finally, Mr. Miller believed firmly that experience was the backbone for successful operation and survival. Step-by-step learning of business conduct over time was requisite. Although he was influential in encouraging and financing minority business executives, he believed that it was a disservice to attempt to make an "instant businessman" through some of the minority financing programs mentioned above. He had observed that some excellent tradespeople, such as tile installers, carpenters, and bricklayers, had been "put in business over night," and they had no knowledge about running a business. Their failures were tragic but anticipated.

# Two consumer co-ops

## Richard Stover*

Two small stores were opened by young people who felt that certain services should be offered in their community. The student council of the local university formed a corporation to provide services for the student body. One of these services was to be a bookstore. The Small Book Store was opened because the students believed they were being taken advantage of by the two existing bookstores: an independently owned bookstore and one owned by the university. According to state law, the university bookstore cannot offer lower prices than the independent store. In the eyes of the students, this represented a monopoly on the price of textbooks. The independent bookstore set prices for the textbooks, and the university bookstore matched them.

The Food Co-op was started to provide food for a group of people living in a house and their friends. In 1971 the co-op formed a partnership, allowing anyone to join it. The group had decided to offer the community the opportunity to purchase health foods at low prices. These people saw themselves as part of the community and thought they would be living there for quite a while. They felt the local grocery stores were charging high prices for food that was well-packaged and well-preserved, but lacked many of the original vitamins and minerals. They wanted to offer an alternative.

Both groups were composed of young people who did not have any previous education or experience in business management. The Small Book Store had hired a management consultant, but his reports merely pointed out problems with no discussion of possible solutions. Also, neither store had initiated a system of accounting when forming their cooperatives.

The Small Book Store started with a $10,000 loan from the student council and $500 from the sale of corporate stock to the board of directors. With these funds, they planned to purchase records and use the profits from record sales to finance the bookstore.

## The food cooperative

The Food Co-op originated when nine persons decided to provide themselves and their friends with quality foods at low prices. The nine persons were vegetarians, and they wanted food which was organically grown (without insecticides) and high in protein.

* Prepared under the supervision of Professor William F. Glueck.

In January of 1972, the Food Co-op rented a room in a building situated in the downtown business district of a college town. They had been told by many people that there was a need for a store which carried such foods as wild rice, soybeans, grains, and fresh fruits. The members of the co-op decided to charge a $3 membership fee and require each member to work 1 hour a month at the store. This was to help generate capital and provide the co-op with lower overhead, since they would not have to hire part-time help.

The most direct form of competition for the co-op came from a specialty foods store. Although the store dealt in the same line of organic foods, it sold the products already packaged. The co-op buys in bulk and will package orders as they come in from the customers. At that time, the grocery stores did not offer any organic foods for sale.

### THE FOOD CO-OP'S ORGANIZATION

The co-op is managed by two coordinators—women in their early twenties. They earn $50 per month for spending most of a 6-day week at the co-op. They have had no time off in the last 6 months. The coordinators volunteer for the job and are ratified by the membership. At various times, there have been from one to three coordinators. The coordinators are of course partners in the co-op. They run the cash register and go through the inventory to see what and how much of each product needs to be reordered. Decisions on order quantity are made on the basis of past orders and how the coordinators feel the product is selling. New products may be added at the suggestion of shoppers or members of the co-op. The coordinators also report to the partners on how well the store is doing from receipts and invoices. Neither coordinator has had any previous experience or education in business management. One of the coordinators said she was becoming tense, nervous, and angry too easily from job pressure. Their lack of experience and help is beginning to wear the coordinators down. The expansion of the co-op with the same level of help is not helping the situation. If one of the women were to quit, a replacement will be needed. As far as can be determined, there is no one with the time that would do the work. The only method for finding a new coordinator is to ask the partners to find a volunteer who is willing to do the job. One coordinator said she kept going only because she believed very strongly in the cooperative movement.

The other partners volunteer their time as needed. No jobs are assigned. They help out at the time they come in to do their volunteer work.

Policy for the store is set at the monthly meetings, the first Wednesday of each month. The coordinators take an active though not a dominant role in the monthly meetings. The purpose of the meeting was defined: "to reach a consensus of the partners on major problems facing the co-op." Normally, 30 to 40 people are said to attend the meeting. Legally, there are 600 partners. At one recent meeting, the case writer took notes. There were 11 persons present. The main topic of the meeting was whether or not to pay a plumber $175 to install a walk-in freezer which had been purchased for $50. The members felt they needed the walk-in to store food in the summer. There were several questions and points of conflict concerning the walk-in. One person suggested that they have the plumber do the hardest work, and he could finish the work, saving money by not having such a high labor bill. There were several problems with this. First, the plumber had commented that he liked to finish jobs he started because if something went wrong, it might not be his fault and yet he would receive the blame. And the landlord did not want them to "foul up" the plumbing in his building. The second problem was the board of health. The inspector had told the co-op that he would inspect the walk-in *after* it was completed to determine whether or not it was acceptable. Because the cash balance was not up to date, no one knew for sure if they had enough cash to pay the plumber. Someone also brought up that they should look for a way to make the walk-in portable so they could take it with them if the co-op moved.

The conversation then centered on the possibility of moving the Food Co-op to a new location. Some members felt they needed more space and should be on the ground floor to make deliveries easier. They also felt they should move away from the "profit-oriented" atmosphere of the downtown business district. Lack of money and the fact that many people would be leaving the town for the summer were given as reasons for not moving. The Crafts Co-op next door to the Food Co-op had decided to go out of business, and this would create room for expansion of the co-op. The additional rent was $100 per month.

Air conditioning was a topic discussed briefly. The loft over the co-op had been air-conditioned the previous year and was used to store nuts and dried fruits. Air conditioning the main room was discarded because of the high cost involved. The building is old and has many cracks in it. The door to the co-op would be opened quite often and make it hard to keep the room cool. It was decided that air conditioning was a luxury rather than a necessity.

### OPERATING THE CO-OP

The co-op is located in the middle of the downtown business district. It is on the second floor above a shoe store. The second floor is shared with a crafts co-op and a cooperative radio station. The co-op pays $50 a month rent plus utilities. The building has plaster walls and a rough wooden floor. The shelves are made of wood that was found by or given to the members. The co-op has two open refrigerator cases for fruits and two closed ones for milk and cheeses. In the packaging room there is an old scale which was donated by a member. On top of a wooden counter there is a cash register which works, cost $19, and is at least 35 years old. The co-op had purchased several barrels to store food in, but the local board of health inspector said they could not be used. When talking to other merchants in the area, the people at the co-op learned from two different sources that for a "fee" they would have little opposition from the inspector. Recently one of their refrigerators leaked water down into the store below. If there had been any damage, the co-op would not have had the cash to pay for it and still maintain normal operations.

The co-op tries to keep overhead as low as possible. They are very careful about what they buy. The coordinators want to be sure that what they buy will be sold. During their first year, they acquired equipment valued at $616. These are a cash register, walk-in freezer, scale, two open refrigerators, and two closed refrigerators. The only people who receive a salary are the two coordinators, who are paid $50 a month. They each spend about 40 hours a week in the co-op. When the coordinators spend money, they look for ways to reduce the cost and alternative methods which may be cheaper but just as effective. An example of this is the discussion of the walk-in installation. Also, the co-op people are willing to sacrifice space and appearance in their building in return for lower rent.

The co-op carries five types of food. These are (1) bulk spices such as basil leaves and cinnamon, which are repackaged for sale; (2) stone-ground products (for example, wheat flour) and grains such as barley and rice; (3) milk and cheese products; (4) fruits, both fresh and dried; (5) peanuts and peanut products.

The first order given by the co-op was to Arrow Head Mills in Hereford, Texas. They ordered about $200 worth of stone-ground products, peanut products, beans, and seeds. A week later they ordered $100 worth of dried fruits and nuts from Organic Foods and Gardens in California. Food sales have been steadily rising for a year and a half. Orders of approximately $300 were placed every 3 weeks in the beginning of the co-op operation. In 1973 orders average from $300 to $400 and are placed every 2 weeks. Sales for the 1972 year were $24,000, and in the first 3 months of 1973 they were $10,000. Because of the shipping cost, most products are now ordered from Great Plains in Kansas City. Nuts and dried fruits are still ordered from Organic Foods and Gardens. Deliveries are made on Tuesday the week after an order is sent out. An independent truck driver carries the food for 1 cent a pound. The co-op offers to pay anyone who is coming from Kansas City 1 cent a pound for transporting food ordered.

Every product has a 20 percent markup regardless of how large or small it is or how fast it sells. This policy is mostly to help simplify the work of the coordinators. Prices are posted on the wall for grains, seeds, beans, and spices; fruits are marked by small cardboard signs because the purchase price fluctuates more on these items. Pricing the products is easy because they are bought on price-per-pound basis and the markup is computed directly from the invoice.

Members of the co-op receive a 10 percent discount on the price of all foods, leaving only an 8 percent actual markup. Presently there are 600 people listed as members of the co-op, but many of these have moved or graduated and left town. Out of twenty-one customers in a 2-hour period observed by the case writer, only seven were members of the co-op. The co-op does not believe in advertising. No brands are advertised in the store. They seek products whose labels discuss possible uses of the item. They do not advertise to get new customers because they believe this will just raise costs. They believe they offer a community service, and word of mouth advertising should suffice. The co-op is publishing a pamphlet to discuss its purpose and the products offered.


FINANCES AND ACCOUNTING AT FOOD CO-OP

The people of the Food Co-op have been conservative with their money and for a good reason. The Food Co-op started with an initial cash outlay of $750 in loans and $200 from a benefit concert given to raise money for the co-op. All of this went into inventory and the first month's rent ($50). Operating cash was provided by personal loans from members until the co-op could build up its inventory. Figure 1 shows the cash balance in 1972.

The books are set up on an accrual basis, and all entries are made by volunteer accountants (members). This has caused some problems, but not a lack of consistency. There are very simple and obvious titles for the entries

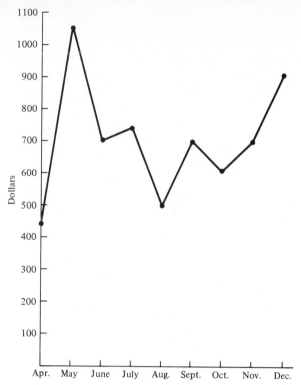

**FIGURE 1** ■ Food cooperative's cash balance, 1972.

in the books. Purchases are recorded as they are received, and sales are kept in a daily journal by the coordinators. The main trouble with the accounting system is that it usually is not current; that is, the books are not complete until a period is ended. At the present time, all journal entries are made, but the books have not been balanced and statements have not been made for the past 5 months. A major fault of their present method is that they have no way of finding the current cash balance. They realize that there is a difference between the actual balance and that of the bank's monthly statement, but they never know how much of a difference there is between the two. The co-op now has a volunteer to get the books balanced and up to date. At the last meeting, it was proposed that the co-op hire a part-time accountant (for $50 per month). This measure was put off till the next meeting because of the low attendance.

The present volunteer accountant suggested that the co-op have itself declared a not-for-profit corporation. Legally, the co-op is a partnership with 600 partners. The co-op owes $500 in state and federal taxes on the $1100 profit from 1972. If the co-op can become a not-for-profit corporation within 90 days after April 15, 1973, they will not have to pay the taxes.

### THE FUTURE

The Food Co-op believes it can prosper by voluntary cooperation. Evidence of this is that it is helping to start another independent co-op in a town 100 miles to the south of the city. Since the co-op here buys in large quantities, they sell part of their orders to the southern co-op at cost plus shipping fees. This is in line with the co-op policy of developing community relationships. They want to enable people to buy food of better quality than can be found in most grocery stores or supermarkets. They are having some trouble with the southern co-op. Their orders are becoming so large that the truck driver has said he will have to change the delivery date because he cannot haul all his other orders and the increasing orders of the Food Co-op. Some people at the local co-op feel that the southern co-op should start making its own orders. Their orders are large enough that they can purchase food in the 50- to 75-pound quantities in which Great Plains orders come. The Food Co-op is also helping a group of people in a town 65 miles north of town to start a co-op of its own. The partners believe that the future is bright at Food Co-op.

## The Small Book Store

About the same time as the Food Co-op began, and in the same college town, the student council at the university loaned the Small Book Store $10,000 to begin operations. The board of directors purchased $500 of corporate stock to help it get started. The Small Book Store started in October of 1970 as part of a corporation formed by the university student council. The corporation had as its purpose the offering of services such as sales of textbooks and school supplies at prices lower than those of the two existing bookstores. The corporation intended to use their bookstore as a basis for any operations which they thought would benefit the student population. The theme was SBS—The Nonprofit Experience.

The store was run by a board of directors consisting of stockholders of the corporation. Voting was based on the number of shares of stock owned. The board was composed of student council members owning equal numbers of shares. None of the board members had had any previous experience in running a business, and none were business majors at this time. The primary qualification of the board members was organizing ability. All were members of the student council and/or officers and active in campus politics. Because of the pressure of schoolwork and campus politics, the directors gave little of their time to the store's operations.

The term for the board of directors was 3 years, but no members stayed that long. The board employed a management consultant early in the store's history. The consultant presented a report which identified problems but offered no solutions. So far as is known, the board took no action as a result of the report.

The day-to-day operations of the store were run by a manager. The manager is not a member of the board nor is she a stockholder. At the board meeting attended by the case writer, the manager took no part in discussion and was not asked at any time about the business. The board members based their discussion on financial reports from the accountant. The duties of the manager are given in Table 1. The present manager is a 19-year-old girl who had worked in the store for 1 year before becoming manager. There had been four earlier managers, each lasting about 6 months. She supervised student part-time help.

**TABLE 1**

**Responsibilities of the manager**
The manager shall have sole authority in the following matters:

1 Hiring, supervising, and compensating employees

2 Fixing of employee schedules and store hours

3 Ordering of merchandise in line with the store's current inventory

4 Purchasing of supplies necessary for the optimum efficiency of the store

5 Paying all bills encumbered during the faithful execution of business

6 Reporting regularly to the board of directors on the financial status of the store and any changes in operations that have been performed

7 Assuring the store is in businesslike condition during store hours and no losses occur owing to negligence of any employees

8 Performing the general functions of policy making and managing associated with an ongoing business

**Responsibilities of the sales consultant**

1 Reordering of current record and tape stock to eliminate shortages

2 Obtaining new records and tapes when deemed advisable

3 Keeping the diversity and specialization of the record and tape stock at a level of optimum sales

4 Providing special sales and advising advertising aides on the level and content of advertising with the approval of the manager

**The board reserves the following authority**

1 To hire, set compensation for, and dismiss the manager and sales consultant

2 To set maximum employee wages and advertising costs for a given period

3 To negotiate and enter into contracts in relation to the store and its operation

4 To assign the manager and/or sales consultant to specific tasks of the board's choosing, but not necessarily without further compensation

5 To alter or expand the function and direction of the store

6 To offer criticism and advice as to the store's operation

7 To oversee the store's records and require the keeping of adequate records

They had to be replaced an average of about three times a year. Three different accountants had worked for the store over the last 2½ years. The case writer believes the manager knew more about the store than the board of directors.

OPERATIONS AT SBS

In the beginning, the store located itself in a small building adjacent to the campus. The first stock purchased was records bought on consignment. The profits made from record sales were to be used to buy books and supplies for the next year. The store moved in October of 1972 because the building, which was rented, was to be torn down. The store moved from a building with a $225 a month rent to one with a $250 a month rent. There were many discussions of high overhead, but no suggestions were mentioned in the minutes of the corporation meetings held during this period to find a less expensive building.

The records were bought on consignment by a sales consultant who dealt only with purchases of records. By 1972 the consultant was no longer used and the manager ordered them. Records were supposed to be the money-maker to keep the store going so the books and school supplies could be sold at a lower price. Because the store never had the cash to purchase records, they had to buy them on consignment. The record business in the town was very competitive. There were three chain stores dealing almost exclusively in records. Many of the department stores also handle records. One of the chain stores will match any price in town on new records. All these stores can buy records at lower prices than the SBS, who buy on consignment. There was a $2,147.26 profit recorded for the first year. This figure is slightly inflated because the cost of goods sold was calculated by adding up payments to the record dealer. This did not reflect the actual cost because not all the records had been paid for at the time the income and balance sheets were prepared.

As a service to students, and in an effort to make the undertaking profitable, the store entered the rental refrigerator business in March 1971. Originally, the store rented the refrigerators to the students for $35 per year, $22.50 per semester, or $17.50 for the summer. Each student was required to pay a $15 deposit and a $2 delivery fee. In July of 1972 the rent of refrigerators was raised to $40 a year and the deposit was lowered to $10 for students. Nonstudents were charged $45 a year with a $15 deposit. Also, in July the corporation switched companies which supplied refrigerators. The first company had had slow deliveries and other problems. The loss of 40 refrigerators out of approximately 1100 rented in 2 years hurt profits, but part of this was deferred by applying the rental paid to the company as part of the price of the lost refrigerators. The cost of the refrigerators is not known, and the loss was not covered in the accounting records. For some reason, the refrigerators were accounted for in a different manner from the rest of the business. Only the refrigerators are under the cash basis of accounting; all the rest are on an accrual basis. On a yearly basis, refrigerators were the most profitable part of the corporation. Net profit was $3800 for the 1971–1972 school year and $2300 for the 1972–1973 school year. The figures for the 1972–1973 period were available because of the cash basis of accounting, and only the cost of trucks for delivery and storage cost were charged as an expense. There was no store overhead charged to the refrigerator account. Later books and other items were added to the product line.

The $250 a month rent was paid for a modern store near the university campus, but one block farther from the university than the original building. It was much larger and more modern than the older building. The board was very impressed with the new location.

Store hours had been 9 until 9. In early 1971, in order to reduce overhead, the hours were shortened to 10 until 8.

When they moved to the new store, the manager felt new equipment was desirable. One such purchase was a new cash register for $612. This exceeded the $500 limit set by the board, but it was accepted by them.

The board was concerned about overhead in 1971. They authorized an increase in salaries from $600 to $700 per month, including $200 per year for the president of the board of directors. A statement was issued asking for voluntary student help in the store's time of need. Little help was forthcoming.

In March 1971, the store's record supplier noted a shortage of $1300 in inventory. This was thought to be the result of shoplifting. Part of the supplier's records were returned in September 1971 because the store manager felt they were being overstocked by salespeople. By the end of 1972, there was almost a $4000 shortage in inventory, which was noted in the accounting books as part of a footnote.

## PRICING POLICY

The board's original price policy concerning books was a 20 percent markup—5 percent below the price of the larger bookstores. In December 1972, the manager of the store said one of the major problems of the store was the lack of a pricing policy. First of all, she stated it was not consistent. Some books were priced a dollar below list while others were a dollar above list price. Second, there was no formal price schedule available to work from. Also, since the store was not making the money from records that had been anticipated, she thought the books should be priced to cover overhead. At a board meeting, the manager told the board that at the present markup they were making money until you counted store overhead and shipping cost. The manager discussed in some detail what overhead was and tried to convince the board that a store must put a price on goods that at least covers the expenses of the store. The board did not move on pricing policy.

Advertising was usually the first item cut back when the board felt it should try to cut cost. Some months they spent $200 for advertising, and others they spent nothing. Most advertising was done through the student newspaper and one of several local radio stations, whose programs appeal to young people. They did have two interesting ideas to gain student support. One was offering 10 percent off paperbacks to people with student ID cards. The other was a $1 discount on the purchase price of a record to people holding a contract for a refrigerator rented from the corporation.

After a bleak year and close to a $2000 loss for the second year, a committee was set up to gain student support for the store. Donations were asked for, and ads were run telling the students that the store needed money. A book pool was started in December 1972 and was used as a source of cash to help the bookstore. The bookstore was to receive 10 percent of the sale price of each book sold by the book pool. None of these measures brought in the amount of cash the corporation needed to keep the store in operation.

## FINANCING THE SBS

Several financial statements are given in Tables 2 and 3. As the store got into difficulties, it hoped for donations of $5000 from students to help it out. The store received donations of $716. In September 1971, the SBS borrowed $2500 from a local bank. In November 1971, the store paid the student council $2000 back on its interest-free note. The council had put pressure on the store to make some returns on its loan. In December 1972, the store tried unsuccessfully to borrow $10,000 from the bank. Cash balances varied widely but were lower in 1972 than earlier. The store rarely had available current statements. No budgets or similar controls were ever set up. Balance sheets and income statements for missing periods could not be found by the management when asked for. The board required the reporting of financial status by the manager, although before February 1971 they had no accountant or accounting system. The first accounting statements were prepared by an auditing firm. The accounting procedures since then have lacked continuity.

TABLE 2 ■ INCOME STATEMENTS FOR SBS, 1970–1973

| | Oct. 17, 1970–<br>Jan. 31, 1971 | Mar. 31, 1971–<br>Feb. 19, 1972 | Jan. 31, 1973–<br>Mar. 31, 1973 |
|---|---|---|---|
| **Sales** | $26,893.69 | $95,157.60 | $8,914.89 |
|    Less sales returns | . . . | 815.86 | 97.96 |
|    Beginning inventory | 20,830.35 | 978.80 | 8,917.55 |
|    Purchases | 150.16 | 88,625.90 | 7,412.58 |
|    Goods available for sale | 20,980.51 | 89,604.70 | 16,330.13 |
|    less ending inventory | | 6,574.53 | 9,943.63 |
|    Cost of goods sold | 20,980.51 | 83,030.17 | 6,386.50 |
|       Gross profit on sales | $5,913.18 | $11,311.57 | $2,430.43 |
| **Sales expenses** | | | |
|    Advertising | $ 146.00 | $ 1,866.31 | $ 505.11 |
|    Incidental supplies | 287.58 | 164.94 | 129.11 |
|    Salary[a] and wages | 1,433.45 | 8,419.62 | 1,541.27 |
|    Employment taxes[b] | 87.79 | 410.41 | 320.00 |
| **Other expenses** | | | |
|    Building maintenance | 113.04 | 170.75 | |
|    Utilities | 87.14 | 375.00 | 77.70 |
|    Rent | 740.00 | 2,163.56 | 500.00 |
|    Insurance | 45.70 | 121.50 | |
|    Organizational ex-<br>     penses[c] | 110.22 | | |
|    Legal expenses | . . . | 529.15 | 48.00 |
|    Depreciation | . . . | 154.18 | |
|    Amortization | . . . | 95.19 | |
|       Total expenses | $3,050.92 | $14,470.61 | $3,121.19 |
| **Rental revenue on re-<br>frigerators** | | 17,798.50 | |
|    Related expenses: | | | |
|      Storage | | 402.00 | |
|      Rented trucks | | 191.97 | |
|      Leases | | 13,365.85 | |
|      Total | | $13,959.82 | 150.00 |
|    Income from refrig-<br>     erator rental | | $ 3,838.68 | |
|    Income (loss) from<br>     operations | $2,862.26 | 678.64 | (690.76) |
|    Less estimated fed-<br>     eral income tax | 715.00 | 148.30 | |
|    Net income[d] (loss) | $2,147.26 | $ 530.34 | $ (540.76) |

[a] No salaries paid for work during October; donated services not accounted for in this statement.
[b] Liability under FUTA and State Unemployment uncertain.
[c] Organizational expense includes costs of incorporation, attorney's fees, and other initial expenses; one-fourth charged against this period, the remainder to be written off monthly until November 30, 1971.
[d] Cost of records sold determined by payments to supplier of goods on consignment; there may be some amount payable for records actually sold in this period.

## RESOLUTION OF SBS'S PROBLEMS

The board decided to close the store in May 1973. Reasons given were decline in sales, lack of profits, too much time of the board expended, rising overhead, and lack of support of student body. It was suggested that the corporation continue the refrigerator rental and a book pool at the start of semesters. It was suggested that they operate this out of a university office and hire a

## TABLE 3 ■ SBS BALANCE SHEET, 1971–1973

| | Jan. 31, 1971 | Feb. 19, 1972 | 1973[a] |
|---|---|---|---|
| *Assets* | | | |
| **Current assets** | | | |
| Cash | $1,969.96 | $ 9,340.22 | |
| Petty cash | 10.28 | . . . | |
| Savings certificate | . . . | 3,000.00 | |
| Accounts receivable | 3.09 | 220.01 | |
| Inventory | 1,859.31 | 6,574.53 | |
| Prepaid insurance | 116.30 | 41.50 | |
| Prepaid utilities | 17.78 | . . . | |
| Prepaid rent | . . . | 88.10 | |
| Total current assets | 3,976.72 | 19,264.36 | |
| **Fixed assets** | | | |
| Building fixtures[b] | 189.41 | 951.47 | |
| Unamortized organizational expenses | 335.82 | 190.39 | |
| Total fixed assets | 525.23 | 1,141.86 | |
| Total assets | $4,501.95 | $20,406.22 | |
| *Liabilities and equity* | | | |
| **Liabilities** | | | |
| Accounts payable | $ 160.89 | $ 2,901.48 | $ 6,886.54[c] |
| Sales taxes payable | 122.75 | 1,079.47 | 1,098.71 |
| Income tax payable | 715.00 | 148.30 | |
| Federal withholding taxes payable | 70.65 | 59.30 | 1,697.70 |
| State withholding tax payable | .67 | 4.85 | |
| Accrued wages payable | . . . | 248.00 | 88.59 |
| Refrigerator deposits | . . . | 8,400.00 | 6,185.00 |
| Total liabilities | 1,069.96 | 12,841.40 | 15,956.54 |
| **Equity** | | | |
| Capital stock[d] | 500.00 | 1,460.00 | 1,460.00 |
| Donated capital | 716.90 | 4,801.37 | 4,945.85 |
| Retained earnings | 2,147.26 | 1,303.45 | (183.65) |
| Total equity | 3,364.16 | 7,564.82 | 6,222.50 |
| Total liabilities and equity | $4,434.12 | $20,406.22 | $22,178.74 |

[a] Data for assets lost by SBS.
[b] Depreciated value.
[c] Includes operating expenses payable ($330.02) and Xerox payable ($2092.45).
[d] Capital stock outstanding consists of 100 shares—par value $5 each, total authorized capital stock is 1000 shares.

secretary part time ($150 per month). They were not satisfied with the services of the university secretary provided free to their corporation.

The corporation had hired at least two management consultants who attended board meetings, but the case writer could find out little of their activities. It seems one of the more obvious sources of help could have been the Business School. Since the corporation was created for the students, they may have been able to enlist the aid of some professor and/or graduate student. They did not do so.

Several problems were brought up in closing the store, but the members of the board felt they would not be much trouble. They had to break contracts with the Xerox Corporation and the records distributor and on the building they are leasing. Also, they must try to sell their record inventory.

## Appendix

A brief summary of Robert Briscoe, "Traders and Idealists: A Study of the Dilemmas of Consumer Co-operatives," unpublished D.B.A. thesis, Harvard Business School, 1971.

Dr. Briscoe's thesis was research designed to answer a number of questions. But one central question was: Why have consumer cooperative businesses been so successful in other lands (Iceland, Finland, Sweden) and not as successful in the United States? To try to answer this question, he decided to examine the cooperative's beliefs about what a co-op is for and how the co-op reconciles the social ideals with the reality of running a business. Briscoe chose to visit 12 consumer co-ops, mostly in New England and the Midwest, some successful (tripled their growth in 12 years) and some unsuccessful (less than doubled sales in 12 years), to see what differences there might be. He interviewed 52 managers of the co-ops.

The major conclusions of Briscoe's research are as follows:

**1** Eighty percent of the managers and directors of the co-ops studied believed that the values of co-ops (for example, democratic management) were incompatible with success in running a business.

**2** He found further that the less successful co-ops' managers and directors expressed these beliefs more frequently than the more successful ones. He says the less successful co-op managers are more likely to believe that the co-op is morally superior, and consequently, should resist change; that the co-op is intrinsically inferior as a business and is therefore unable to change; that there are no feasible and legitimate means to advance the organization's business activities and that there are no inspiring, practicable goals to aim for.

**3** Co-ops with a high proportion of members who see this conflict as serious inhibit the co-op's growth. This is so because they did not focus on realistic growth goals and when asked for opportunities for growth in service, could not mention any. Even managers/directors of the faster-growing co-ops suggested new opportunities for the co-op.

**4** The more successful co-ops have found ways to deal with the dilemmas of the conflict in values. They did this in various ways. They educated their members about the values of co-ops, encouraged participation in decision making, perhaps through representative methods, and were willing to meet competitive prices even if this reduced the patronage refunds to the members.

Although the study is based on a small sample, perhaps it provides some insights into the challenging operations of consumer cooperatives in the United States.

# St. John's Hospital

## John Bringhurst and Charles W. Hofer*

"You can go on making short-range moves here and there, but the time comes when you have to consider the long-range direction of the hospital. You need to determine where you are, what the community needs, and where you *should* be going." This was the thinking of Sister Macrina Ryan as she reflected on her decision to hire an outside consultant to assist in long-range planning for St. John's Hospital in October 1972.

Sister Macrina had been the administrator at St. John's for the previous 7 years. She received her undergraduate training in personnel after which she worked for 2 years in a Cheyenne hospital and 11 years at St. Joseph's Hospital in Denver. While at St. Joseph's she gained experience in both the business office and the personnel department. Before coming to St. John's, she had completed the Hospital Executive Development program offered by St. Louis University. After 6 years at St. John's, she was offered an opportunity for advancement to a larger hospital operated by the Sisterhood. She declined to apply for the position, though, because she needed more time to complete her work at St. John's.

Sister Macrina's administration at St. John's had been marked by several significant changes in both the physical plant and the medical services of the hospital. A number of important issues faced St. John's which required resolution by the end of 1972, however. In attempting to deal with them she felt the need for some independent, outside counsel. Therefore, after gaining the approval of the board of trustees in Leavenworth, Kansas, and discussing the matter with the president of the lay advisory board in Helena, she hired the Medical Planning Associates (henceforth referred to as MPA), a consulting firm based in Malibu, California, to make a comprehensive study of the hospital's capabilities and the health needs of the Helena community. MPA's contract also called for the development of a long-range plan for St. John's based on the results of these studies.

## St. John's history

St. John's, which was organized in 1870 by the Sisters of Charity of Leavenworth, Kansas, was the first

---

* This case was prepared under the preceptorial guidance of Mr. Gerald Leavitt. Editorial assistance was provided by William R. Sandberg, research assistant. Case material of the Northwestern Graduate School of Management is prepared as a basis for class discussion. Cases are not designed to present illustrations of either effective or ineffective handling of administrative problems. Copyright © by Northwestern University, 1973.

**303**

private hospital in the territory of Montana. It had its beginnings in a small frame building located in a tiny mining settlement which eventually became the capital of the state. In the early years of its existence, the hospital's patients were mostly miners, prospectors, and lumbermen. Soon charity patients from Lewis and Clark, Meagher, and Jefferson Counties were added to its patient load. In 1873, a small building behind the hospital became the first mental hospital in Montana. It offered care for psychiatric patients until its abandonment when the state established its own mental health institution in 1877. After the coming of the Northern Pacific Railroad in 1883, the original frame building became inadequate and was replaced by a larger brick and stone structure. This building was damaged beyond repair in the earthquakes of 1935. While a new building was being erected, St. John's utilized the facilities of the Montana Children's Home—now Shodair Hospital. The new unit, which was still the core of the hospital in 1972, was completed in 1939. Since then St. John's has expanded its facilities twice more. Specifically, a new cafeteria and kitchen were added in 1958, and in 1965 the hospital's north and south wings were completed. The north wing contained 10 medical-surgical private rooms, a labor and delivery unit, an x-ray department, and a general storeroom. The south wing consisted of a laundry, the boiler room, physical therapy, the dental room, and the chaplain's quarters. In addition, the south wing had rooms for 25 patients and also housed facilities for extended-care patients. (See Figure 1 for a layout of St. John's facilities in October 1972.)

In 1968, St. John's maternity department was closed temporarily to provide space for medical-surgical patients while the latter area was being refurbished. This renovation also involved conversion of the Sisters' living quarters into a medical records department and a modern coronary intensive-care unit. After a little more than a year without maternity facilities, during which time St. Peter's Community Hospital handled the maternity patient load in Helena, St. John's board of trustees decided not to reopen the department. The trustees believed that this action would eliminate "one of the most expensive examples of duplication and under-utilization of services in Helena."[1] More specifically, they felt their decision would reduce losses for both St. John's, which would be freed of a perennial deficit operation, and St. Peter's, which would gain maternity patients with little or no increase in overhead costs. Additional benefits to St. John's were expected to result from the use of the newly available rooms for additional medical and surgical bed space.

St. John's also established the first school of nursing in Montana. When the earthquakes of 1935 destroyed the school building, the hospital's nursing students were transferred to other schools to complete their training. The nursing school was reopened in 1940 and continued full-scale operations until 1965. At that time, because of financial losses incurred by the school and changing requirements in the field of nursing, the board of trustees decided to close the school. Nursing training at St. John's ceased in 1968 with the graduation of the class which had entered in 1965.

## Hospitals and health services in Helena

The city of Helena, which had a population of approximately 26,000, was served by three hospitals in 1972. St. John's and the Shodair Crippled Chil-

---

[1] From a memorandum of November 26, 1969, from Sister Macrina to the medical staff.

**FIGURE 1** ■ Layout of St. John's Hospital.

dren's Hospital were located in the downtown area, and St. Peter's Community Hospital was on the extreme east side of town. In addition, a Veterans Administration Hospital was located at Fort Harrison, a military post about 6 miles west of Helena. However, it served only armed forces veterans, most of whom were not from the Helena area. (See Figure 2 for a map indicating the locations of the three Helena hospitals.)

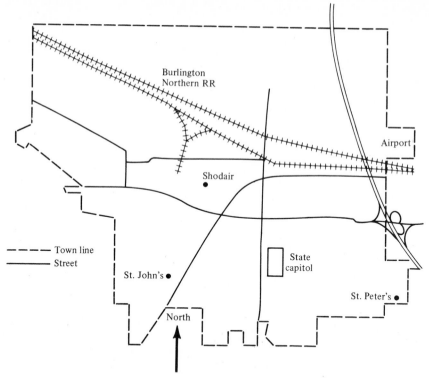

**FIGURE 2** ■ Location of hospitals in Helena, Montana.

St. Peter's Community Hospital was established in 1887. It expanded to a new location in 1924 and in 1968 moved into a modern new facility at its present location. This facility had space for 111 beds, most of which were used for medical-surgical, pediatric, and maternity services. The completion of St. Peter's new building had reduced the utilization of St. John's, in the opinion of many St. John's administrators. Specifically, they pointed out that the average occupancy rate and the total number of ancillary services demanded at St. John's began to decline following the completion of St. Peter's new facility—a trend which continued through 1972. (See Figures 3, 4, and 5 for utilization statistics for St. John's.)

Shodair Crippled Children's Hospital was originally established as a residence for homeless children. The hospital, which was built as an addition to the home in 1937, was a focal point in the community during the polio epidemic of the fifties. With the widespread adoption of Salk and Sabin vaccines, however, Shodair's census declined to the point where its 45-bed capacity averaged less than 40 percent occupancy in the 1970s.

Although the 160 beds of the Veterans Administration Hospital were filled largely with patients from outside the community,[2] it nevertheless offered some competition to the other three Helena area hospitals and thus added to

---

[2] During the 1970s, approximately 20 percent of the VA Hospital's patients were from the Helena area.

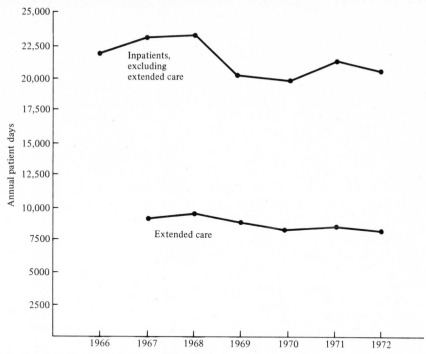

**FIGURE 3** ■ St. John's Hospital patient days, 1966–1972. From St. John's Hospital records.

the surplus bed space problem which these hospitals faced in the 1970s. Specifically, with the exception of the VA Hospital, which often had an admissions waiting list, all the hospitals in the Helena area operated in dangerously low occupancy levels in the early 1970s. For instance, in 1971, St. John's average occupancy was 72 percent, St. Peter's average was 64 percent, and Shodair's was only 37 percent. Moreover, in 1972, St. John's average occupancy dropped to just under 58 percent while St. Peter's and Shodair's averages remained close to their 1971 levels. (See Table 1 for various operating statistics on all four hospitals in the greater Helena area.)

On a national basis, an occupancy rate of 80 to 90 percent was usually considered desirable in the early 1970s although most hospitals also tried to hold some beds open for emergency patients. Thus, by comparison with this standard, there were on average about 60 excess hospital beds in the greater Helena area in mid-1972. Because of this overbedding, considerable competition existed among the city's three private hospitals. The competition was keenest, however, between St. John's and St. Peter's because of the similar types of services offered by the two institutions. For instance, Sister Macrina observed: "If one hospital purchased a new piece of equipment, there was often pressure from physicians, patients, and personnel of the other hospital to purchase the same kind of equipment or something better." Helena's physicians were in a particularly strong position in respect to the city's hospitals because they could strongly affect a hospital's financial stability by referring their patients elsewhere. Such gambits enabled these physicians to exert considerable leverage on the policies of all three hospitals in the early 1970s.

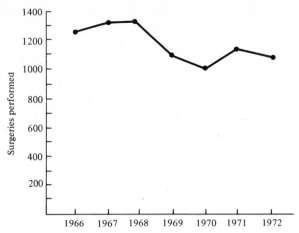

**FIGURE 4** ■ Surgeries performed at St. John's Hospital. From St. John's Hospital records.

## St. John's present situation

Competition from other hospitals was only one of the issues confronting Sister Macrina, however. In the spring of 1972, St. John's received the results of a fire and safety survey by the State Department of Health and Environmental Sciences. Among the deficiencies noted in the survey were some requiring extensive renovations of the main building to comply with new fire standards. For example, one of the required renovations was the installation of a fire warning and sprinkler system in the older portion of the building.[3] Although no exact estimates of the cost of all the required renovations had been made by the end of June, it appeared that these costs might well be greater than the value of the hospital sections which were affected.[4] Since the portion of the hospital which required renovation was 35 years old, Sister Macrina questioned the wisdom of making such extensive and expensive renovations. On the other hand, it was difficult to entertain any thoughts of building a separate new facility when about 40 percent of the existing building was less than 5 years old.

Another issue facing Sister Macrina was the question of whether to renovate St. John's emergency room, which was somewhat outdated and inconveniently located. Like most other hospitals across the country, St. John's had experienced a dramatic increase in demand for outpatient services in recent years. With industry forecasts predicting a continuation of this trend, Sister Macrina was considering the modification of the emergency room and the surgery department to facilitate an increased outpatient workload. To serve both an outpatient clinic and an emergency room, the existing emergency room would have to be extensively remodeled.[5] On the other hand, only minor

---

[3] The portion affected was one-third of the total floor space in St. John's main building. See Figure 1 for a layout of St. John's physical plant.

[4] One of the major reasons for the anticipated high cost of renovations was that St. John's facility had been designed to be earthquake proof when it was constructed in 1935.

[5] No estimates of the costs of a new emergency room had been made by October 1972.

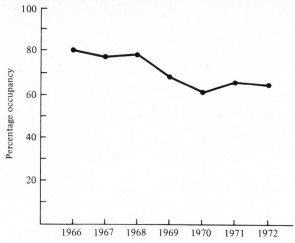

**FIGURE 5** ■ Occupancy rates at St. John's Hospital. From St. John's Hospital records.

alterations would be required to develop the capability for outpatient surgery within the present surgery department.[6] The new requirement for fire protection safety complicated this type of expansionary planning, however, since both surgery and the emergency room were located in the older portion of the hospital.

Another decision facing Sister Macrina involved the sale of certain buildings

---

[6] No cost estimates for any of these options had been obtained by October 1972.

**TABLE 1** ■ **UTILIZATION, EMPLOYMENT, AND PAYROLL DATA OF HELENA AREA HOSPITALS IN 1971 AND 1972**

| | St. John's | | St. Peter's | | Shodair | | Veterans Administration | |
|---|---|---|---|---|---|---|---|---|
| | 1971 | 1972 | 1971 | 1972 | 1971 | 1972 | 1971 | 1972 |
| Number of beds[a] | 114 | 112 | 111 | 111 | 45 | 32 | 160 | 160 |
| Admissions[b] | 3064 | 2950 | 4147 | 4278 | 1119 | 1115 | 2240 | 2315 |
| Average daily census[c] | 82 | 65 | 71 | 72 | 15 | 13 | 139 | 139 |
| Percentage occupancy[d] | 71.9 | 57.5 | 64.0 | 64.9 | 36.6 | 40.6 | 86.9 | 86.9 |
| Personnel[e] | 219[f] | 218[f] | 224[f] | 246[f] | 77 | 80 | 242 | 250 |
| Payroll expense (000)[g] | $1273[h] | $1322[h] | $1452 | $1485 | $331 | $336 | $2366 | $2624 |
| Total expense (000)[g] | $2010 | $2259 | $2684 | $2822 | $517 | $773 | $3501 | $3956 |

[a] As of September 30, 197__. Does not include bassinets for newborn infants.
[b] Number of patients accepted for inpatient service during 12-month period ending September 30, 197__. Does not include newborn.
[c] Average number of inpatients each day during 12-month period ending September 30, 197__. Does not include newborn.
[d] Ratio of census to average number of beds maintained during 12-month period ending September 30, 197__.
[e] Excludes trainees, private nurses, and volunteers. Statistics stated as full-time equivalents.
[f] According to Sister Macrina, a possible explanation for St. John's having a lower ratio of personnel to patients than St. Peter's lay in the difference between the two hospitals' plants: St. John's had a compact, four-story building whereas St. Peter's had a rambling, two-level structure with larger distances between departments.
[g] For the fiscal year ending September 30, 197__.
[h] St. John's paid the Motherhouse a sum equal to the salaries that civilian workers would receive if they filled the Sisters' positions. These sums are included in the payroll expense totals for St. John's.
*Note:* September 30 does not coincide with the end of St. John's fiscal year.
*Source:* AHA *Guide to the Health Care Field,* 1972 and 1973 ed., The American Hospital Association.

and properties owned by the hospital. Specifically, the Model Cities and urban renewal programs of Helena had been negotiating with the hospital over the purchase of St. John's property west of Warren Street. While the city had appraised the property at $20,000, St. John's lay advisory board believed that it was worth twice that amount and was in the process of obtaining their own appraisal.

In addition, the hospital was considering the sale of Immaculata Hall, which was adjacent to the hospital. In recent years, this building had been used as a residence for the Sisters who served at St. John's, as a meeting hall for the hospital, and for storage. It had also been used to house student nurses up to 1968. Over the last decade, however, its occupancy had decreased to the point where the lay advisory board no longer felt it was economical for the hospital to keep the building.[7] The board considered $85,000 a fair price for the structure together with the former school of nursing[8] and the land immediately adjacent to both buildings. The board also believed that the price would rise to $125,000 if the rest of the block were included in the offer. By the end of October, they had been approached by two interested parties. Nonetheless, even though St. John's could use the cash generated by the sale of these assets, Sister Macrina felt consideration also had to be given to possible future expansion needs of St. John's before a final decision was reached.

Another issue which Sister Macrina discussed with the MPA consultants was the question of the services which should be offered at St. John's. This issue was especially important since one possible answer to the problem of competition in an overbedded community such as Helena would be for the different hospitals to specialize in one or more services. For instance, since there had never been enough demand for maternity services in the greater Helena community for two hospitals to efficiently operate obstetric departments, St. John's had closed its maternity service in 1968 and conceded the entire volume to St. Peter's as discussed earlier. Similarly, St. John's elected to close its special pediatric department in order to eliminate the duplication of services when Shodair Children's Hospital's expansion in 1969 enabled it to meet the community's needs for pediatric care. Furthermore, even though St. Peter's continued to operate its pediatric department, its 12-bed ward was generally less than 50 percent occupied and was reportedly operating at a small deficit. Sister Macrina felt that this was a good indication that St. John's should remain out of pediatric services.

The more important question in her opinion, though, was whether St. John's should eliminate other services in areas of duplication or expand their services in areas not adequately covered at present in Helena. For instance, in addition to its general medical-surgical services, St. John's Hospital operated a high-quality extended-care unit for long-term patients.[9] Although the price to the public for these extended-care services was almost double that of most nursing homes in the area, many residents of Helena apparently felt that the extra cost

---

[7] Including Sister Macrina, only seven Sisters were serving at St. John's in October 1972.

[8] The former school of nursing building was being used as apartments and shops in 1972, as indicated in Figure 1.

[9] Extended care was an intermediate stage for patients who could get along with less extensive nursing care than usually required in a hospital but were not yet independent enough for a nursing home. Consequently the cost for such a unit was below what hospitals would normally charge and greater than what nursing homes typically charged. A majority of St. John's extended-care cases came from Helena itself.

was justified by the quality of nursing care available. Moreover, Sister Macrina felt that the fact that the unit was always nearly full and had a sizable waiting list was further evidence that there was sufficient demand for such a unit.

The possibility of offering some completely new specialty beyond those presently offered by St. John's and the other hospitals in Helena was particularly appealing to Sister Macrina since such services might increase the draw of patients from areas outside Helena. For example, a specialized burn center might attract a large number of patients from the greater Northwest since the nearest existing burn center was in Austin, Texas, and that unit drew patients from the entire western half of the United States. Another possibility was the establishment of a special stroke ward as there were no other specialty units for stroke patients in Helena at the time. Although the demand for such a facility was difficult to estimate, there were enough stroke victims in the area that local hospital administrators occasionally discussed the possibility of such a unit among themselves. Still another alternative would be to combine a stroke ward with the present extended-care facility at St. John's to create a geriatric specialty hospital. Supporting this option was the degree to which St. John's was already involved in service to Medicare patients. Although no statistics had been gathered, it was believed by some of St. John's administrators that the older people of the community generally preferred St. John's Hospital to St. Peter's.

There were, of course, other ways in which St. John's might specialize, such as becoming a rehabilitation hospital or a self-care nursing facility, both of which had been mentioned by Helena health officials as areas requiring consideration. No studies of the demand for such facilities in Helena had ever been made, though. Moreover, any such alternative would have to be considered in light of the potential difficulty of bringing a specialty medical staff to this remote community in west central Montana. Thus, while some doctors in the Helena area believed that remoteness would not be a factor as long as the patient demand was there, others felt that the long, hard winters would be a deterrent to an influx of specialized physicians. In sum, one of the big questions for St. John's involved the kinds of services it should offer in order to best meet the needs of the community. (See Table 2 for a listing of the services offered by Helena's three private hospitals in 1972.)

The most drastic response to the problem of competition would be for St. John's to close its doors. Even though such an idea was unpalatable to a large number of the hospital employees and also to many people in the area, it was generally conceded that a 50-bed addition to St. Peter's Hospital could handle the present patient load at St. John's with the exception of the extended-care patients.[10] Furthermore, such a move might provide a significant reduction in cost to the community since ancillary services, such as the x-ray units, the laboratory, and surgery, were not being fully utilized at either hospital.[11] Thus, while the purpose of the MPA study was to assist in long-range planning for St. John's, Sister Macrina felt that the needs of the Helena community were probably the most important factor to be considered in the study. Conse-

---

[10] Construction costs per bed for new hospitals averaged between $20,000 and $30,000 in 1972.
[11] Both St. John's and St. Peter's were self-sufficient in laboratory services. Shodair, although smaller, was also adequate for all of the hospital's normal tests. The VA Hospital contracted with St. John's for some lab services, but these were also available and underutilized at St. Peter's.

TABLE 2 ■ HOSPITAL SERVICES AVAILABLE IN HELENA (SEPTEMBER 1972)

| Service[a] | St. John's | St. Peter's | Shodair | VA |
|---|---|---|---|---|
| Postoperative recovery room | Yes | Yes | Yes | Yes |
| Intensive-care unit | Yes | Yes | No | No |
| Pharmacy | Yes | Yes | Yes | Yes |
| X-ray therapy | No | Yes | No | No |
| Cobalt therapy | No | Yes | No | No |
| Radium therapy | No | Yes | No | No |
| Diagnostic radioisotope | No | Yes | No | No |
| Therapeutic radioisotope | No | Yes | No | No |
| Histopathology laboratory | Yes | Yes | No | Yes |
| Blood bank | Yes | Yes | No | Yes |
| Inhalation therapy | Yes | Yes | Yes | No |
| Extended-care unit | Yes | No | No | No |
| Inpatient renal dialysis | No | Yes | No | No |
| Outpatient renal dialysis | No | Yes | No | No |
| Physical therapy | Yes | Yes | Yes | Yes |
| Clinical psychologist | No | No | Yes | No |
| Outpatient department | No | No | No | Yes |
| Emergency department | Yes | Yes | Yes | Yes |
| Social work department | Yes | No | Yes | Yes |
| Genetic counseling | No | Yes | No | No |
| Inpatient abortions | No | Yes | No | No |
| Dental department | Yes | No | No | Yes |
| Speech therapy | Yes | No | Yes | No |
| Hospital auxiliary | Yes | No | Yes | No |
| Volunteer services | Yes | No | No | Yes |

[a] Services are defined in the American Hospital Association's *Uniform Hospital Definition.*
*Source:* The AHA *Guide to the Health Care Field,* 1973.

quently, she believed the possibility of closing operations altogether had to be considered as a realistic alternative.

## Financial and other considerations

In 1972, St. John's Hospital was considered to be financially sound. Like most nonprofit hospitals, the cost-revenue picture showed the hospital to be operating close to its break-even point. Since charitable contributions for St. John's, as well as for most other area hospitals, had declined to an insignificant level in recent years, operating losses in any particular year had to be balanced by gains in other years. During the past 3 years, St. John's had averaged an annual net loss of 0.18 percent on annual revenues which averaged $2.1 million.[12] (See Tables 3 and 4 for St. John's income statements and balance sheets.)

Many of the other factors which needed to be considered in any long-range plan were social, political, and economic in origin. One of the most important of these was the national health insurance legislation which was pending in Congress. Because of the many and varied packages which Congress was considering, it was extremely difficult to anticipate the scope, form, or type of national health insurance that might ultimately be adopted. Yet, because of the tremendous impact which any resulting legislation might have on the health care system, it was difficult to ignore the issue. For instance, an increase in the government's involvement in health care seemed sure to entail more

---

[12] According to figures compiled for the Internal Revenue Service.

TABLE 3 ▪ ST. JOHN'S HOSPITAL INCOME STATEMENTS (1967–1972)

| | 1967 | 1968 | 1969 | 1970 | 1971 | 1972 |
|---|---|---|---|---|---|---|
| **Revenues** | | | | | | |
| Revenues from patients | | | | | | |
|   Daily patient care | $785,299 | $879,177 | $1,019,526 | $1,090,527 | $1,260,093 | $1,290,043 |
|   Departmental services | 598,258 | 691,037 | 759,408 | 797,573 | 938,959 | 1,077,428 |
| Gross patient revenues | $1,383,557 | $1,570,214 | $1,778,934 | $1,888,100 | $2,199,052 | $2,367,471 |
| Deductions from gross revenues | | | | | | |
|   Provision for uncollectibles | $84,125 | $63,461 | $79,937 | $87,984 | $85,627 | $57,314 |
|   Contractual discounts | 67,640 | 32,078 | 16,479 | 23,835 | 89,353 | 79,400 |
|   Other adjustments[a] | 21,806 | 10,534 | 4,637 | 2,298 | 504 | 0 |
| Total deductions from gross revenues | $173,571 | $106,073 | $101,053 | $114,117 | $175,484 | $136,714 |
| Revenues from patients | $1,209,986 | $1,464,141 | $1,677,881 | $1,773,983 | $2,023,568 | $2,230,757 |
| Cafeteria and recovery of expenses | 59,938 | 53,985 | 52,615 | 51,840 | 52,091 | 50,813 |
| Grants | 8,713 | 24,930 | 13,161 | 9,853 | | |
|   Total operating revenues | $1,278,637 | $1,543,056 | $1,743,657 | $1,835,676 | $2,075,659 | $2,281,570 |
| **Expenses** | | | | | | |
| Salaries and wages | $749,176 | $996,192 | $1,085,109 | $1,197,130 | $1,237,192 | $1,321,761 |
| Supplies and expenses | 430,455 | 532,951 | 575,741 | 636,745 | 727,777 | 829,607 |
| Depreciation | 59,945 | 107,975 | 113,870 | 83,466 | 96,927 | 107,464 |
|   Total operating expenses | $1,239,576 | $1,637,118 | $1,774,720 | $1,917,341 | $2,061,896 | $2,258,832 |
| Net revenue from operations | $39,061 | $(64,062) | $(30,063) | $(81,665) | $13,763 | $22,738 |
| **Nonoperating revenue** | | | | | | |
| Interest income | 0 | 4,679 | 4,970 | 18,552 | 6,871 | 7,927 |
| Net revenues | $39,061 | $(59,383) | $(25,093) | $(63,113) | $20,634 | $30,665 |

[a] Discounts from St. John's standard rates resulted from contractual agreements with commercial insurers and nonprofit third-party payers and from differences between full costs and allowable costs for Medicare reimbursements. The treatment of such deductions was consistent with accepted hospital accounting procedures.
*Source:* St. John's Hospital annual audits, 1968–1972.

control over how federal funds were to be spent. Regardless of the form of any legislation adopted, one likely target for government control would be the area of hospital planning. Thus, it was quite possible that the future directions open to St. John's after the enactment of such legislation might be determined by some regional public planning agency rather than by the hospital. On the other hand, Sister Macrina felt she would have to make a decision about St. John's scope of operations within the next 6 months. Even if this were done before any legislation was passed, however, an unwise choice might restrict the amount of federal revenues the hospital could receive in the future.

Further complications were created by the federal government's wage-price freeze and subsequent Phase II requirements. St. John's had been in need of a small price increase to cover operating losses when price controls had been imposed in August 1972. Phase II, however, negated practically any plans for an increase in prices. This was particularly critical since extensive renovations of any buildings or expansion of any services would require far greater financial reserves than St. John's had available in October 1972.

Other variables which the MPA consultants would have to take into consideration in developing their recommendations were the demographic trends of the greater Helena area, possible changes in the region's ratio of population to hospital beds, and the availability of medical personnel in the community.

TABLE 4 ■ ST. JOHN'S HOSPITAL BALANCE SHEETS

## Years ending May 31[a]

| | 1967 | 1968 | 1969 | 1970 | 1971 | 1972 |
|---|---|---|---|---|---|---|
| **Assets** | | | | | | |
| Cash | $73,561 | $45,718 | $6,148 | $8,497 | $52,852 | $61,227 |
| Accounts receivable from patients[b] | 368,589 | 345,152 | 429,678 | 352,034 | 391,022 | 435,134 |
| Receivable from third-party agencies | 1,015 | 66,334 | 89,009 | 71,642 | 21,000 | 25,153 |
| Inventories, at cost | 35,839 | 43,854 | 51,670 | 51,625 | 54,721 | 65,479 |
| Prepaid expenses | 1,337 | 1,060 | 511 | 1,136 | 1,474 | 1,664 |
| Total | $480,341 | $502,118 | $577,016 | $484,934 | $521,069 | $588,657 |
| Land, building, and equipment, less depreciation | $1,402,741 | $1,517,091 | $1,562,152 | $1,616,529 | $1,553,992 | $1,475,660 |
| Plant improvement and replacement funds: | | | | | | |
| Cash | $98,414 | $145,434 | $65,345 | $14,372 | $21,460 | $89,571 |
| Certificates of deposit | 0 | 0 | 0 | 0 | 100,000 | 102,547 |
| Investments, at cost | 112 | 112 | 112 | 88,000 | 0 | 0 |
| Interest receivable | 0 | 1,059 | 0 | 2,093 | 877 | 1,414 |
| Total | $98,526 | $146,605 | $65,457 | $104,465 | $122,337 | $193,532 |
| Temporary fund cash | 2,077 | 360 | 331 | 0 | 0 | 0 |
| Total assets | $1,983,685 | $2,166,174 | $2,204,956 | $2,205,928 | $2,197,398 | $2,257,849 |
| **Liabilities** | | | | | | |
| Portion due of note payable to Motherhouse | $0 | $12,000 | $18,000 | $18,000 | $41,800 | $41,800 |
| Accounts payable | 36,519 | 51,569 | 25,981 | 36,569 | 38,989 | 53,304 |
| Accrued payroll | 33,088 | 14,745 | 19,600 | 24,760 | 29,475 | 39,233 |
| Acrued Sister's salaries | 0 | 0 | 12,286 | 12,286 | 0 | 0 |
| Other accrued liabilities | 10,355 | 3,616 | 6,726 | 38,425 | 22,338 | 19,727 |
| Accrued interest | 0 | 8,030 | 8,335 | 0 | 0 | 0 |
| Medicare financing payable | 18,000 | 15,000 | 15,000 | 46,994 | 44,298 | 49,811 |
| Payable to third-party agencies | 0 | 0 | 0 | 0 | 3,000 | 10,000 |
| Retainage and construction costs payable | 0 | 0 | 35,471 | 13,381 | 0 | 0 |
| Total current liabilities | $97,962 | $104,960 | $141,399 | $190,415 | $179,900 | $213,875 |
| Deferred contractual adjustment[c] | $0 | $30,506 | $45,506 | $59,506 | $76,395 | $90,000 |
| Note payable to Motherhouse, less current portion | $515,658 | $491,633 | $483,633 | $485,033 | $438,720 | $403,920 |
| Fund balances: | | | | | | |
| Operating fund | $216,442 | $218,089 | $281,025 | $104,953 | $150,524 | $184,726 |
| Plant fund | 1,151,546 | 1,320,626 | 1,253,062 | 1,366,021 | 1,351,859 | 1,365,328 |
| | $1,367,988 | $1,538,715 | $1,534,087 | $1,470,974 | $1,502,383 | $1,550,054 |
| Temporary fund: | | | | | | |
| Due to operating fund | $1,015 | $0 | $0 | $0 | $0 | $0 |
| Fund balance | 1,062 | 360 | 331 | 0 | 0 | 0 |
| Total liabilities | $1,983,685 | $2,166,174 | $2,204,956 | $2,205,928 | $2,197,398 | $2,257,849 |

[a] May 31 marked the end of the fiscal year for the eight hospitals and all schools, colleges, and other institutions operated by the Sisters of Charity of Leavenworth.
[b] Less allowance for uncollectibles and contractual discounts. These two items totaled $185,000 in 1967, $148,367 in 1968, $144,713 in 1969, $135,492 in 1970, $96,683 in 1971, and $160,000 in 1972.
[c] See note a, Table 3.
Source: St. John's Hospital annual audits, 1968–1972.

Overall, the population of Helena was projected to grow by 13 percent (1973)[13] to 32 percent (1970) between 1970 and 1980, depending on the assumptions made with respect to birth and death rates[14] and migration trends. Under the same assumptions, the population of Lewis and Clark county as a whole was forecast to grow by 19 percent (1973) to 27 percent (1970) during the same period. (See Tables 5 and 6 for more detailed demographic data for the greater Helena area.) The factor primarily responsible for the differences between the 1970 and 1973 forecasts was the rapid drop that occurred in average family size in the early 1970s. During this same interval, there were also some changes in national migration trends. Most demographers felt that Helena was not likely to benefit from these trends, however, because the poor rail and road transportation through the area did not encourage a buildup of industry in that part of the state, especially since other nearby

[13] The numbers within the parentheses refer to the date of the forecast.
[14] Both birth and death rates are, in turn, influenced by several other variables. Birth rates, for example, are dependent on the age distribution of the population, the net rate of family formation, the average family size, and the percentage of out-of-wedlock births. Death rates are primarily influenced by the age distribution of the population and the age-conditional mortality rates for the area in question.

**TABLE 5 ■ POPULATION RECORDS AND PROJECTIONS, LEWIS AND CLARK COUNTY, MONTANA**

|  | Actual | | | | Projected | |
|---|---|---|---|---|---|---|
|  | 1960 | 1964 | 1968 | 1970 | 1975 | 1980 |
| City of Helena | 20,227 | 23,000 | 24,395 | 25,850 | 29,750 | 34,200 |
| Rest of county | 7,779 | not available | | 8,014 | none made | 8,900 |
| Total county | 28,006 | not available | | 33,864 | | 43,100 |

Sources: 1960 and 1970 actual: U.S. Census.
1964 and 1968 actual: Lewis and Clark County records.
1975 and 1980 projections: 1970 Lewis and Clark County forecasts.

**TABLE 6 ■ THE POPULATION AGE DISTRIBUTION FOR LEWIS AND CLARK COUNTY, MONTANA**

|  | Actual | | | | Projected | |
|---|---|---|---|---|---|---|
|  | 1960 | | 1970 | | 1980[a] | |
| Age | Male | Female | Male | Female | Male | Female |
| 0–9 | 3,099 | 2,959 | 3,203 | 3,049 | 3,940 | 3,776 |
| 10–19 | 2,321 | 2,574 | 3,392 | 3,574 | 3,494 | 3,689 |
| 20–29 | 1,428 | 1,592 | 1,976 | 2,294 | 2,905 | 3,184 |
| 30–39 | 1,754 | 1,794 | 1,802 | 1,848 | 2,502 | 2,664 |
| 40–49 | 1,761 | 1,874 | 1,858 | 1,933 | 1,913 | 1,994 |
| 50–59 | 1,481 | 1,379 | 1,762 | 1,919 | 1,853 | 1,981 |
| 60–69 | 1,077 | 1,100 | 1,182 | 1,284 | 1,407 | 1,786 |
| 70–79 | 620 | 723 | 657 | 835 | 731 | 982 |
| 80 and over | 184 | 276 | 260 | 453 | 350 | 515 |
| Total | 13,725 | 14,271 | 16,092 | 17,189 | 19,095 | 20,571 |

[a] Assumptions: Continued 1960–1970 migration trends.
Source: Information Systems Bureau, Department of Intergovernmental Relations, U.S. Government, 1973.

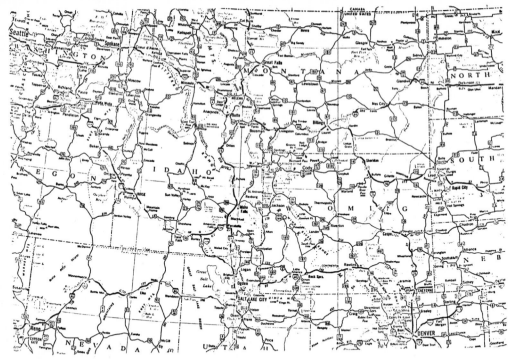

**FIGURE 6** ▪ The greater Pacific Northwest.

**TABLE 7** ▪ **BED-POPULATION RATIOS, BY STATE, 1950 AND 1960**
Beds per 1000 population

| State area | 1950 | 1960 | State area | 1950 | 1960 |
|---|---|---|---|---|---|
| Alabama | 1.9 | 2.5 | Nebraska | 4.0 | 3.9 |
| Arizona | 3.3 | 2.5 | Nevada | 4.1 | 3.3 |
| Arkansas | 1.8 | 2.7 | New Hampshire | 3.9 | 3.7 |
| California | 3.6 | 3.0 | New Jersey | 2.9 | 2.9 |
| Colorado | 3.7 | 3.8 | New Mexico | 2.7 | 2.6 |
| Connecticut | 3.3 | 3.4 | New York | 3.5 | 3.6 |
| Delaware | 3.1 | 2.9 | North Carolina | 2.5 | 2.8 |
| D.C.-Maryland-Virginia | 3.5 | 3.3 | North Dakota | 3.9 | 4.6 |
| Florida | 2.5 | 2.7 | Ohio | 3.1 | 3.3 |
| Georgia | 2.2 | 3.0 | Oklahoma | 3.0 | 3.6 |
| Idaho | 3.0 | 2.8 | Oregon | 3.5 | 3.1 |
| Illinois | 3.7 | 3.8 | Pennsylvania | 3.2 | 3.7 |
| Indiana | 3.2 | 3.3 | Rhode Island | 3.1 | 3.6 |
| Iowa | 3.9 | 3.7 | South Carolina | 2.7 | 3.2 |
| Kansas | 3.7 | 3.7 | South Dakota | 3.9 | 3.8 |
| Kentucky | 2.1 | 3.1 | Tennessee | 2.1 | 2.8 |
| Louisiana | 2.5 | 2.8 | Texas | 2.8 | 3.1 |
| Maine | 3.1 | 3.8 | Utah | 2.5 | 2.8 |
| Massachusetts | 3.9 | 3.7 | Vermont | 4.0 | 4.1 |
| Michigan | 2.7 | 3.1 | Washington | 3.4 | 3.2 |
| Minnesota | 3.9 | 4.0 | West Virginia | 2.7 | 4.0 |
| Mississippi | 1.7 | 2.6 | Wisconsin | 3.6 | 4.1 |
| Missouri | 3.1 | 3.6 | Wyoming | 3.4 | 4.1 |
| Montana | 4.0 | 4.3 | | | |

*Source:* American Hospital Association.

# TABLE 8 ■ PHYSICIANS AND DENTISTS SERVING ON STAFFS OF HELENA HOSPITALS

| | 1964 | 1968 | 1971 | 1972 |
|---|---|---|---|---|
| *Physicians* | | | | |
| **Age category** | | | | |
| 30–39 | | 10 | 9 | 11 |
| 40–49 | | 19 | 20 | 20 |
| 50–59 | | 10 | 9 | 9 |
| 60 and over | | 4 | 5 | 6 |
| **Classification** | | | | |
| Active | 32 | 40 | 36 | 41 |
| Courtesy | 10 | 3 | 7 | 4 |
| Inactive | 0 | 0 | 3 | 0 |
| **Privileges** | | | | |
| Anesthesiology | | 2 | 2 | 2 |
| Dermatology | | 0 | 1 | 1 |
| Eye, ear, nose, and throat | | 1 | 2 | 2 |
| General practice | | 19 | 15 | 12 |
| General surgery | | 9 | 7 | 4 |
| Internal medicine | | 5 | 4 | 5 |
| Neurology | | 0 | 0 | 1 |
| OB gynecology | | 2 | 2 | 2 |
| Ophthalmology | | 1 | 3 | 4 |
| Orthopedics | | 2 | 2 | 3 |
| Pathology | | 1 | 1 | 3 |
| Pediatrics | | 4 | 4 | 4 |
| Radiology | | 2 | 3 | 4 |
| Urology | | 0 | 1 | 1 |
| Total physicians on hospital staffs | 42 | 43 | 43 | 45 |
| *Dentists* | | | | |
| **Age category** | | | | |
| 30–39 | | 6 | 6 | 2 |
| 40–49 | | 4 | 4 | 3 |
| 50–59 | | 1 | 0 | 3 |
| 60 and over | | 3 | 4 | 1 |
| **Classification** | | | | |
| Active | 0 | 0 | 0 | 0 |
| Courtesy | 2 | 14 | 14 | 9 |
| Inactive | 0 | 0 | 0 | 0 |
| Total dentists on hospital staffs | 2 | 14 | 14 | 9 |
| **Total physicians and dentists on hospital staff** | 44 | 57 | 57 | 54 |

*Source:* St. John's Hospital records.

cities such as Great Falls and Bozeman had excellent transportation networks. (See Figure 6 for a map of the region.)

Under almost all sets of assumptions, though, the number of persons over 60 was forecast to increase at a rate more than 20 percent higher than that for the area's population as a whole. Thus, if past illness ratios and the medical procedures for dealing with them remained unchanged, the demand for geriatric services would increase by 23 percent or more by 1980.

On the other hand, the ratio of population to hospital beds for Helena in 1972 was substantially higher than the nationwide median of 3.5 beds per 1000 persons. The latter ratio could only be regarded as a "ball-park" figure, though, since it varied widely among different communities according to their locations. For instance, Alabama had a ratio of 2.5/1000 in 1970 while North Dakota had a ratio of 4.6/1000 the same year. (See Table 7 for a listing by state for 1950 and 1960.) Among the factors which influenced it were the age and wealth of the area's population, the degree to which outpatient facilities were used, and the geographic characteristics of the area. In the latter regard, St. John's received some of its patients from the outlying areas of Lewis and Clark County, as well as approximately 13 percent of its case load from outside the county.[15]

In terms of availability of medical personnel, there was only a moderate increase in the number of physicians in the greater Helena area between 1964 and 1972, as is indicated in Table 8. There was, however, a noticeable trend away from general practice and general surgery toward more specialized fields of medicine. In addition, there was a general shortage of nursing personnel in the area—a condition which had been aggravated by the closing of St. John's nursing school in 1968.

A final, but important set of considerations in any decision on St. John's future were the goals of the Motherhouse of the Sisters of Charity. In the past, the policy of the Sisterhood had been to concentrate on providing general acute care through community-based hospitals in any community they entered. Once in a community, though, they adapted their facilities to the overall medical needs of the community insofar as those needs were unmet by other organizations and were within the financial resources of the Sisterhood. Given the range of services offered by St. Peter's and Shodair, Sister Macrina felt that the Motherhouse might not approve a plan for a major modification in St. John's mission unless she could demonstrate that such modifications were required to meet some aspects of the community's medical needs that St. Peter's or Shodair would not be able to provide, or that the costs of such modifications would be low, or that the necessary capital could be raised in the community or repaid relatively quickly.

As she described St. John's situation to the MPA consultants, Sister Macrina reflected on the fact that the factors influencing long-range planning at St. John's were numerous and difficult to access. Nonetheless, long-range objectives and policies would have to be made in order to give some direction to the hospital's future operations. Thus, the major question facing Sister Macrina and the MPA consultants was: "What should these objectives and policies be?"

---

[15] In 1972, St. John's admissions were distributed among three geographic sources: 86.9 percent from Lewis and Clark County, 11.3 percent from adjoining counties, and 1.7 percent from other areas.

# Ashland Oil, Inc.

## William F. Glueck

One of the fastest-growing firms in the United States is Ashland Oil, Inc.[1] The firm's corporate headquarters is in Russel, Kentucky, a suburb of Ashland, a small eastern Kentucky river town.

Table 1 provides data from *Fortune* 500 rankings that indicate how far Ashland has come in the last few years. Yes, Ashland, not a giant in the petroleum industry, but a giant in total industry, has come a long way from Swiss Oil Company, Ashland's predecessor, which was incorporated in 1918. It was not until 1936 that Swiss Oil and Ashland Refining Company were consolidated to Ashland Oil and Refining Company. The present company name was adopted in 1970.

The company has grown internally, but it has gone through a series of mergers as well. Several of the major mergers which occurred from 1930 to 1972 are given in Table 2.

Ashland organized itself (1974) as shown in Figure 1.

As of 1972, *Moody's Industrial Manual* reported the following principal subsidiaries of Ashland Oil.

**Consolidated Subsidiaries[2]**

Arkhola Sand & Gravel Co.

Ashland Exports, Inc.

Ashland Oil Canada Ltd. (86 percent owned)

Ashland Oil Enterprises, Inc.

Ashland Oil Finance N.V. (Netherlands)

Ashland Oil Purchasing Co.

Ashland Oil & Refining Co. N.V. (Holland)

Ashland Oil and Transportation Co.

Ashland Overseas Finance Corp.

Ashland Pipe Line Co.

Barnes Transportation Co., Inc.

Barrus Construction Co.

Barrus Ready Mix Concrete Co.

W. B. Bennett Paving & Materials Co. Ltd. (Can.)

Canadian Ashland Exploration Ltd.

---

[1] To put this case study into historical perspective, refer to two works which outline the history of Ashland Oil. For the period prior to 1957, see Joseph Massie, *Blazer and Ashland Oil* (Lexington: University of Kentucky Press, 1960); see also Otto Scott, *The Exception: The Story of Ashland Oil and Refining Company* (New York: McGraw-Hill, 1968). The later volume brings the history up to 1967.

[2] As of September 30, 1972, Ashland Oil owned 100 percent interest (except where noted).

**319**

**TABLE 1 ■ ASHLAND OIL'S RANKING IN SALES, ASSETS, INCOME, AND EMPLOYEES, 1965–1973**

| Year | Sales and rank | | Assets and rank | | Net income and rank | | Employees Number | Rank |
|------|------|------|------|------|------|------|------|------|
| 1973 | 2,052,821,000 | 75 | 1,637,252,000 | 93 | 85,219,000 | 97 | 25,000 | 177 |
| 1972 | 1,780,003,000 | 70 | 1,275,002,000 | 93 | 68,309,000 | 87 | 22,700 | 179 |
| 1971 | 1,614,026,000 | 70 | 1,030,181,000 | 111 | 23,805,000 | 196 | 22,000 | 178 |
| 1970 | 1,407,166,000 | 79 | 999,880,000 | 110 | 37,769,000 | 129 | 21,500 | 181 |
| 1969 | 1,151,499,000 | 101 | 846,412,000 | 117 | 52,343,000 | 107 | 18,500 | 208 |
| 1968 | 1,068,663,000 | 92 | 736,828,000 | 115 | 48,340,000 | 109 | 17,000 | 214 |
| 1967 | 804,892,000 | 106 | 580,412,000 | 121 | 46,542,000 | 109 | 14,500 | 218 |
| 1966 | 699,308,000 | 116 | 449,347,000 | 135 | 42,924,000 | 116 | 11,600 | 269 |
| 1965 | 447,744,000 | 153 | 356,022,000 | 166 | 31,594,000 | 133 | 7,600 | 367 |

*Source: Fortune* 500 rankings, 1965–1973.

**TABLE 2 ■ MAJOR MERGERS OF ASHLAND OIL, 1930–1972**

| Company | Year | Company | Year | Company | Year |
|---------|------|---------|------|---------|------|
| Tri State Refining | 1930 | Chemical properties of | | Whitehall Canadian Oils | |
| Cumberland Pipe Line | | Archer-Daniels-Mid- | | Ltd. | 1969 |
| Company | 1931 | land Co. | 1967 | Midhurst Oil, Inc. | 1969 |
| Owensboro Oil Company | 1939 | A&P Tires, Inc. | 1967 | Poole's Sure Fire Oil Corp. | 1969 |
| Allied Oil Company | 1948 | OK Rubber Welders, Inc. | 1967 | Sam Finley, Inc. | 1970 |
| Aetna Oil Company | 1949 | Sowerbutt Quarries, Inc. | 1967 | Canadian Gridoil, Ltd. | |
| Anderson Prichard Oil | | James Vandermade, Inc. | 1967 | (New Ashland Oil of | |
| Corporation | 1958 | Sowerbutt Asphalt | 1967 | Canada Ltd.) | 1970 |
| Louisville Refinery | | Pacific Petrochemicals | 1967 | Sold its interest in | |
| Company | 1959 | Cabell Chemical Company | 1967 | American Independent | |
| Produces Pipeline Com- | | Arkhole Companies | 1968 | Oil Company | 1970 |
| pany | 1959 | Tri Star Plastic Moldings, | | Northwest Refinery, Inc. | 1970 |
| United Carbon Company | 1963 | Inc. | 1968 | Gertz Paving Company, | |
| Ja Ro-Chem, Inc. | 1964 | Thomas Petroleum Transit, | | Inc. | 1970 |
| Catalin Corporation | 1966 | Inc. | 1968 | Macasphalt Corp. | 1971 |
| Southern Fiber Glass | | Petroleum Solvents Com- | | Polk Materials, Inc. | 1971 |
| Products | 1966 | pany | 1968 | Eastern Seaboard Petro- | |
| Globe Chemical Company | 1966 | Port of Barkley Lake, Inc. | 1968 | leum, Inc. | 1971 |
| Harry Baumstark & Com- | | Trotte & Thompson & | | Angelo Tomasso, Inc. | 1971 |
| pany | 1966 | Affiliate Companies | 1968 | Union Carbide Petro- | |
| OK Tire & Rubber Com- | | Wanda Petroleum, Inc. | 1968 | leum, Inc. | 1971 |
| pany | 1966 | Jeffersonville Gaso- | | Harrison, Inc. | 1972 |
| Chemical Solvents Com- | | line, Inc. | 1968 | Franklin Stone Company | 1972 |
| pany | 1966 | P. R. Boston, Inc., & | | Star Construction Co. | 1972 |
| Lasp Realty Company | 1966 | Affiliates | 1968 | Reno Construction Com- | |
| Warren Brothers Company | 1966 | New Haven Trap Rock, | | pany | 1972 |
| Fischer Chemical Com- | | Inc. | 1968 | Empire State Oil Com- | |
| pany | 1966 | F. H. Ross, Inc. | 1968 | pany | 1972 |
| Gamma Chemical Com- | | W. B. Bennett Paving & | | Mac's Super Glass Com- | |
| pany | 1966 | Materials Ltd. | 1969 | pany | 1972 |

| | |
|---|---|
| Cleveland Tankers, Inc. | Inland Towing Co. |
| Colmat, Inc. | Lexington Pipe Line Co. |
| Eastern Seaboard Petroleum Co., Inc. | Louisville Refining Co. |
| Equal Opportunity Finance, Inc. | Macasphalt Corp. |
| Frontier Oil Refining Co. Ltd. (Canada) | MacDougald-Warren, Inc. (51 percent) |
| Harrison Construction Co., Inc. | Mac's Super Glass Co., Inc. |

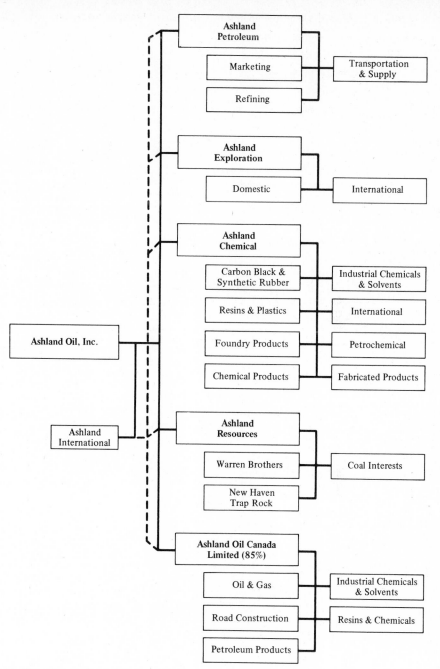

**FIGURE 1** ■ Chart of operations.

Magaw Construction, Inc.

Northwestern Refining Co.

O. K. Tire and Rubber Co., Inc.

O'Neal Paving Co., Inc.

Owensboro-Ashland Co.

Polaris Plastics Corp.

Producers Towing Co.

Reno Construction Co., Inc.

Sam Finley, Inc.

Southern States Asphalt Co.

Thompson-Arthur Paving Co.

Tri-State Plastic Molding Co.

Valvoline Oil Co.[3]

**Other Interests[4]**

Australian Carbon Black Pty., Ltd.

Avebene Products de Fonderie (France)

Ashland-Sued Chemie Giesserein GmbH (Germany)

B. V. Ash-eChemikali Chemikalien GmbH (Germany)

B. V. Ashland Suedchemine V. H. Necof (Holland)

Melamine Chemicals Inc.

Parish Pipe Line Co.

Valvoline (Australia) Pty., Ltd.

Until 1974, Ashland valued 40 percent of its inventories using LIFO. In 1974, it converted to 100 percent LIFO. This reduced net income for 1974 $34,700,000, or $1.48 per share. Ashland's recent financial performance and financial statements are given in Tables 3, 4, and 5.

## Ashland's operations

Fundamentally, Ashland is a firm that operates in most areas of the petroleum industry. Standard and Poor's summed their operations up as follows in June 1974.

Ashland Oil is a complete unit, engaged in all divisions of the oil industry. Petroleum operations accounted for about 62% of revenues in fiscal 1972–3, chemical and petrochemicals 18%, Canadian about 4%, and resources group including highway construction and coal mining most of the balance. Petroleum contributed about 63% of income before unallocated overhead and income taxes, chemicals 15%, resources 17%, Canadian operations 5%, and exploration a loss of less than 1%.

Independent distributors, who usually resell Ashland products under their own name, are the most important marketing factor. Ashland's seven refineries, with a rated capacity of some 377,500 barrels daily, processed an average of 338,211 barrels daily during fiscal 1972–3, up from 327,034 barrels daily in 1971–2. Net production of crude oil and natural gas liquids averaged 50,987 barrels daily, up from 41,745 barrels daily for the prior year. Refined product sales averaged 473,916 barrels daily, up from 452,214 barrels daily. Natural gas production averaged 312,201 Mcf. daily, versus 171,769 Mcf. daily, and coal sales amounted to 11,966,000 tons, compared with 5,807,000 tons a year before. About 44% of the crude production in 1972–3 and 10% of the natural gas output was from the 85%-owned Ashland Oil Canada.

---

[3] In addition to the above, Ashland Oil has numerous other wholly owned consolidated subsidiaries which are omitted above as such subsidiaries, considered in the aggregate as a single subsidiary, would not constitute a significant subsidiary.

[4] Ashland Oil owns a 50 percent interest.

Dividends, paid since *1936,* averaged some 50% of available net in the five years through September 30, 1973.

Employees: *22,000.*     Shareholders: *57,478.*

Ashland has developed an interesting strategy for the petroleum industry. Most successful oil firms produce their own products from their own crude oil and market them through their own outlets. Ashland controls only about 20 percent of the crude it needs. For years, Ashland purchased cheaper crude and was able to undersell competitors. With the OPEC blockade, Ashland was in the position of having competitors with much cheaper foreign and domestic crude than it could buy. Luckily for Ashland, the government instituted a cost equalization program for oil. It assured availability of oil to Ashland and partially offset the price differences. Ashland sells its products primarily through independently owned outlets. More often than not, its customers lease their own stations. Ashland does run some under the Ashland brand.

The firm has tried to develop more of its own crude. It spent $50 million in Togo and Alaska with little or no luck. More recently, it has 25 percent interest in ventures off the shore of Louisiana, on South Marsh Island, where production is expected in 1975. It has interests in the Persian Gulf (Abu Musa) that should provide 120,000 barrels a day. The firm acquired 25 percent interest in an oil shale tract for an investment of $30 million. In conjunction with the Nigerian Natural Oil Company, it is exploring in Nigeria. Up to 50,000 barrels per day, Ashland can take 35 percent of the oil. Above that, it gets 30 percent. Finally, it is negotiating with Iran for crude. In the days of surplus crude, Ashland did quite well. With shortages possible, the results may be more cloudy. As *Forbes* put it (November 1, 1972), Ashland's sales to independents were a good strategy when gasoline was plentiful.

But today they face tougher sledding. When there is refining overcapacity, as there was over the past three years, gasoline is cheap and the independents can prosper with deep discounting. Today, refining overcapacity is at its lowest point in over ten years, and the independents are having to pay more for their gasoline. Moreover, no additional refining capacity is planned for several years to come, in part because of environmental pressures, soaring land costs near major markets and uncertainties over future gasoline quality requirements.

Ashland also operates a large chemical business. This was not especially profitable in the early 1970s. But their gas business was profitable in the past because of less price-conscious areas they operated in and efficient refineries.

*Forbes* labeled them as highly efficient in operations of the refineries and 7000 miles of their own pipeline. Their refineries and crude capacities in 1973 were:

| Location | Crude oil capacity[a] |
|---|---|
| Ashland, Kentucky | 140,000 |
| Canton, Ohio | 66,000 |
| Buffalo, New York | 66,000 |
| Findlay, Ohio (seasonal operation) | 21,000 |
| Louisville, Kentucky | 26,000 |
| Freedom, Pennsylvania | 7,000 |
| St. Paul Park, Minnesota | 68,000 |
| Total | 394,000 |

[a] Barrels of 42 U.S. gallons each.

**TABLE 3 ■ BALANCE SHEET ASHLAND OIL, INC., AND SUBSIDIARIES**
For years ending September 30 (thousands of dollars)

| | 1974 | 1973 | 1972 | 1971 |
|---|---|---|---|---|
| *Assets* | | | | |
| **Current assets** | | | | |
| Cash and short-term securities | $94,376 | $83,858 | $91,381 | $78,663 |
| Accounts and notes receivable, less reserve for doubtful accounts | 428,137 | 289,347 | 233,051 | 207,167 |
| Recoverable advances on leased facilities | 0 | 35,578 | 3,897 | |
| Construction completed and in progress, at contract prices | 27,210 | 28,926 | 21,139 | 14,824 |
| Inventories | 242,072 | 187,567 | 172,183 | 186,752 |
| Prepaid expenses | 29,742 | 15,018 | 14,878 | 13,330 |
| Total current assets | $821,537 | $640,294 | $536,529 | $500,736 |
| **Investments and other assets** | | | | |
| Foreign subsidiaries and affiliates | 33,166 | 27,256 | 23,957 | 23,768 |
| Other companies | 20,961 | 34,020 | 34,491 | 17,532 |
| Notes and accounts receivable | 35,455 | 32,619 | 31,228 | 24,040 |
| Other assets and deferred charges | 13,923 | 14,809 | 17,639 | 15,317 |
| | $103,505 | $108,704 | $107,315 | $80,657 |
| **Property, plant, and equipment—on the basis of cost** | | | | |
| Petroleum | 422,145 | 404,169 | 412,659 | 397,463 |
| Exploration | 347,695 | 303,472 | 260,114 | 138,351 |
| Chemical | 152,790 | 148,751 | 139,223 | 120,346 |
| Resources | 208,788 | 188,683 | 169,542 | 148,332 |
| Canada | 200,640 | 174,699 | 149,790 | 124,876 |
| Other | 58,147 | 16,508 | 14,408 | 12,318 |
| | $1,390,205 | $1,236,282 | $1,145,736 | $941,686 |
| Less accumulated depreciation, depletion, and amortization | 599,486 | 548,028 | 519,924 | 480,546 |
| | $790,719 | $688,254 | $625,812 | $461,140 |
| Total assets | $1,715,761 | $1,437,252 | $1,269,656 | $1,042,533 |
| *Liabilities and stockholders' equity* | | | | |
| **Current liabilities** | | | | |
| Short-term notes payable | | $12,000 | | |
| Trade and other payables | $432,868 | 277,830 | $222,991 | $195,508 |
| Income taxes | 12,032 | 45,391 | 25,656 | 13,152 |
| Current portion of long-term debt | 14,587 | 6,663 | 9,364 | 5,114 |
| Total current liabilities | $459,487 | $341,884 | $258,011 | $213,774 |

**TABLE 3** ▪ *(Continued)*

| | 1974 | 1973 | 1972 | 1971 |
|---|---|---|---|---|
| Production payments and loans to acquire mineral properties | $130,810 | $116,895 | $102,751 | |
| Debentures and notes—less current maturities | 231,361 | 230,462 | 237,040 | $218,641 |
| Convertible subordinated debentures | 100,000 | 100,000 | 80,000 | 80,000 |
| Other long-term liabilities and reserves | 53,184 | 44,005 | 42,614 | 39,410 |
| Deferred income taxes | 56,270 | 31,500 | 30,480 | 18,575 |
| Minority interests in consolidated subsidiaries | 22,821 | 22,990 | 21,225 | 16,799 |
| Stockholders' equity | | | | |
| Capital stock: | | | | |
| Cumulative preferred—without par value | 79,008 | 37,946 | 42,090 | 41,996 |
| Common, par value $1 per share Authorized 60 million shares Outstanding 22,831,336 shares (1973), including shares in treasury | 23,178 | 22,831 | 22,598 | 22,511 |
| Capital surplus | 111,752 | 103,160 | 96,933 | 80,014 |
| Retained earnings | 453,326 | 391,009 | 341,153 | 316,093 |
| | $667,264 | $554,946 | $502,774 | $460,614 |
| Less shares in treasury at cost | 5,436 | 5,430 | 5,239 | 5,280 |
| **Total stockholders' equity** | $661,828 | $549,516 | $497,535 | $455,334 |
| | $1,715,761 | $1,437,252 | $1,269,656 | $1,042,533 |

According to *Moody's* the size of the production through 1972 was:

**CRUDE OIL PROCESSED**
Years ending September 30

| Year | Total | Average per day |
|---|---|---|
| 1974 | 120,373,094 | 329,789 |
| 1973 | 123,446,977 | 338,211 |
| 1972 | 119,694,552 | 327,034 |
| 1971 | 115,178,003 | 315,581 |
| 1970 | 105,405,098 | 288,782 |
| 1969 | 96,386,111 | 264,072 |
| 1968 | 90,510,443 | 247,296 |

**REFINED PRODUCTS PRODUCED**
Years ending September 30 (in thousand barrels)

| Year | Gasoline, etc.[a] | Kerosene distill. | Heavy fuel oil |
|---|---|---|---|
| 1974 | 64,360 | 29,729 | 12,008 |
| 1973 | 64,159 | 32,313 | 11,947 |
| 1972 | 62,764 | 32,329 | 11,853 |
| 1971 | 58,924 | 32,147 | 9,811 |
| 1970 | 52,537 | 29,487 | 10,477 |
| 1969 | 49,536 | 25,978 | 9,486 |
| 1968 | 45,709 | 24,861 | 8,804 |

[a] Gasoline, jet fuel, aromatics, and naphthas.

| Year | Asphalt | Other petroleum products |
|------|---------|--------------------------|
| 1974 | 9,027 | 4,800 |
| 1973 | 9,484 | 4,132 |
| 1972 | 9,414 | 1,593 |
| 1971 | 9,870 | 2,375 |
| 1970 | 8,643 | 1,703 |
| 1969 | 8,192 | 1,089 |
| 1968 | 7,802 | 1,484 |

In addition to the petroleum division, the operating divisions of the company include:

**1** *Ashland Chemical Division* Manufacturing and distribution facilities in 27 states and 11 counties. In the United States, ACD operates 23 plants in 12 states and 53 major distribution centers and sales offices. Major divisions include:

(*a*) *Carbon Black and Synthetic Rubber Division* Manufactures carbon black, synthetic rubber, polymers, and synthetic rubber black master batch for the tire and rubber

**TABLE 4** ■ **STATEMENT OF CONSOLIDATED INCOME**
For years ending September 30 (thousands of dollars)

| | 1974 | 1973 | 1972 | 1971 |
|---|------|------|------|------|
| **Income** | | | | |
| Sales and operating revenues | $3,451,224 | $2,360,454 | $2,045,849 | $1,635,274 |
| Dividends, royalties, foreign and miscellaneous income | 51,043 | 30,573 | 21,178 | 16,739 |
| | $3,502,267 | $2,391,027 | $2,067,027 | $1,652,013 |
| **Cost and expenses** | | | | |
| Cost of sales and operating expenses | $2,722,954 | $1,601,053 | $1,395,898 | $1,297,910 |
| Excise taxes on petroleum products and merchandise | 235,557 | 307,633 | 262,596 | |
| Selling, administrative, and general expenses | 241,006 | 213,100 | 198,190 | 187,832 |
| Provision for depreciation, depletion, and amortization | 80,146 | 73,483 | 65,030 | 54,035 |
| Exploration expenses, including nonproductive wells and amortization of undeveloped leases—note A | 21,329 | 20,220 | 10,314 | 19,859 |
| Interest on debentures, notes, and mineral loans | 29,771 | 25,319 | 20,159 | 19,731 |
| | $3,330,763 | $2,240,808 | $1,952,187 | $1,579,367 |
| **Income before income taxes and extraordinary credit** | $171,504 | $150,219 | $114,840 | $72,646 |
| **Income taxes** | | | | |
| Currently payable, before reduction for investment credit | 53,260 | 68,930 | 41,948 | 29,046 |
| Deferred | 14,300 | 1,020 | 8,408 | 3,141 |
| Investment credit | (9,060) | (4,950) | (3,290) | |
| **Income before extraordinary credit** | $113,004 | $85,219 | $67,774 | $40,459 |
| **Extraordinary credit (net), less related income taxes—note G ($.01 per share)** | | | 283 | (15,417) |
| Net income | $113,004 | $85,219 | $68,057 | $25,042 |

**TABLE 5 ■ SIX-YEAR COMPARISON OF ASHLAND OIL, INC.**
## For years ending September 30

| | 1974 | 1973 | 1972 | 1971 | 1970 | 1969 |
|---|---|---|---|---|---|---|
| **As originally reported to shareholders** | | | | | | |
| Sales and operating revenues | $3,451,224 | $2,360,454 | $2,042,599 | $1,858,141 | $1,585,814 | $1,298,455 |
| Income before extraordinary items | 113,004 | 85,219 | 68,026 | 39,122 | 51,090 | 52,343 |
| Per common share: | | | | | | |
|   Assuming no conversion | $4.45 | $3.37 | $2.65 | $1.47 | $2.09 | $2.30 |
|   Assuming full conversion | $3.83 | $2.98 | $2.40 | $1.43 | $1.97 | $2.15 |
| Net income | 113,004 | 85,219 | 68,309 | 23,805 | 37,769 | 52,343 |
| Per common share: | | | | | | |
|   Assuming no conversion | $4.45 | $3.37 | $2.66 | $.77 | $1.46 | $2.30 |
|   Assuming full conversion | $3.83 | $2.98 | $2.41 | $.82 | $1.42 | $2.15 |
| **Adjusted for poolings of interests and other restatements** | | | | | | |
| Income: | | | | | | |
| Sales and operating revenues | $3,451,224 | $2,360,454 | $2,045,849 | $1,879,389 | $1,620,989 | $1,423,901 |
| Dividends, royalties, foreign and miscellaneous income | 51,043 | 30,573 | 21,178 | 16,739 | 16,070 | 16,405 |
| | $3,502,267 | $2,391,027 | $2,067,027 | $1,896,128 | $1,637,059 | $1,440,306 |
| Costs and expenses: | | | | | | |
| Cost of sales and operating expenses | $2,722,954 | $1,601,053 | $1,395,898 | $1,297,910 | $1,119,427 | $976,288 |
| Excise taxes on petroleum products and merchandise | 235,557 | 307,633 | 262,596 | 244,115 | 178,648 | 146,956 |
| Selling, administrative, and general expenses | 241,006 | 213,100 | 198,190 | 188,432 | 176,547 | 160,207 |
| Provision for depreciation, depletion, and amortization | 80,146 | 73,483 | 65,030 | 53,035 | 48,113 | 43,580 |
| Exploration expenses, including nonproductive wells and amortization of undeveloped leases | 21,329 | 20,220 | 10,314 | 20,859 | 5,085 | 2,926 |
| Interest on debentures, notes, and mineral loans | 29,771 | 25,319 | 20,159 | 19,731 | 18,118 | 13,794 |
| | $3,330,763 | $2,240,808 | $1,952,187 | $1,824,082 | $1,545,938 | $1,343,751 |
| Income before income taxes and extraordinary items | $171,504 | $150,219 | $114,840 | $72,046 | $91,121 | $96,555 |
| Income taxes | 58,500 | 65,000 | 47,066 | 31,887 | 39,441 | 40,123 |
| Income before extraordinary items | 113,004 | 85,219 | 67,774 | 40,159 | 51,680 | 56,432 |
| **Extraordinary items (net), less related income taxes** | | | 283 | (15,417) | (13,321) | |
| Net income | $113,004 | $85,219 | $68,057 | $24,742 | $38,359 | $56,432 |
| **Income per common share before extraordinary items** | | | | | | |
| Assuming no conversion | $4.45 | $3.37 | $2.63 | $1.48 | $2.08 | $2.35 |
| Assuming full conversion | $3.83 | $2.98 | $2.39 | $1.46 | $1.96 | $2.14 |
| **Income per common share after extraordinary items** | | | | | | |
| Assuming no conversion | $4.45 | $3.37 | $2.64 | $.80 | $1.46 | $2.35 |
| Assuming full conversion | $3.83 | $2.98 | $2.40 | $.82 | $1.42 | $2.14 |
| **Assets** | | | | | | |
| Current assets | $821,537 | $640,294 | $536,529 | $501,894 | $481,989 | $407,146 |
| Investments and other assets | 103,505 | 108,704 | 107,315 | 77,099 | 71,287 | 63,384 |
| Property—net | 790,719 | 688,254 | 625,812 | 460,325 | 456,864 | 451,410 |
| Total assets | $1,715,761 | $1,437,252 | $1,269,656 | $1,039,318 | $1,010,140 | $921,940 |
| **Liabilities and stockholders' equity** | | | | | | |
| Current liabilities | $459,487 | $341,884 | $258,011 | $214,024 | $200,029 | $186,029 |
| Production payments and loans to acquire mineral properties | 130,810 | 116,895 | 102,751 | | | |
| Debentures and notes—less current maturities | 231,361 | 230,462 | 237,040 | 221,794 | 226,080 | 188,809 |
| Convertible subordinated debentures | 100,000 | 100,000 | 80,000 | 80,000 | 80,000 | 80,000 |
| Other liabilities, minority interests, and reserves | 132,275 | 98,495 | 94,319 | 77,392 | 63,806 | 45,152 |
| Preferred stocks | 79,008 | 37,946 | 42,090 | 41,995 | 43,500 | 45,048 |
| Common stock | 23,178 | 22,831 | 22,598 | 22,573 | 21,737 | 21,499 |
| Capital surplus and retained earnings | 565,078 | 494,169 | 438,086 | 386,806 | 380,267 | 358,939 |
| Less stock in treasury—at cost | (5,436) | (5,430) | (5,239) | (5,266) | (5,279) | (3,536) |
| Total liabilities and stockholders' equity | $1,715,761 | $1,437,252 | $1,269,656 | $1,039,318 | $1,010,140 | $921,940 |

industry. Carbon black is a petrochemical substance obtained by controlled thermal decomposition of oil. It is used principally as a reinforcing agent for rubber in the manufacture of tires and other rubber products. Ashland is one of the largest domestic manufacturers of reinforcing and tread grade blacks for tire industry. In 1974, Ashland's capacity of carbon black was as follows:

| Plant location | Annual plant capacity (millions of pounds) |
| --- | --- |
| Franklin, Louisiana | 252 |
| Aransas Pass, Texas | 150 |
| Shamrock, Texas | 105 |
| Belpre, Ohio | 100 |
| Mojave, California | 60 |
| Port Jerome, France (100 percent stock ownership) | 106 |
| Speyer, Germany (100 percent stock ownership) | 66 |
| Valencia, Venezuela (40 percent stock ownership) | 50 |
| Melbourne, Australia (50 percent stock ownership) | 90 |
| Bombay, India (40 percent stock ownership) | 110 |
| Swansea, Wales (14½ percent stock ownership) | 85 |
| San Roque, Spain (33⅓ percent stock ownership) | 46 |

(*b*)  *Industrial Chemicals and Solvents Division*  Operates in 57 cities, 27 states, and Puerto Rico and markets solvents and chemicals to paper, auto, and coatings industry. Most sales are Ashland-produced but some are purchased as well.

(*c*)  *Fabricated Products Division*  The division which operates plastics and pipe and petroleum pipe products from Ironton, Henderson, and Cranford plants primarily.

(*d*)  *Resins and Plastics Division*  Plants in Calumet City, Illinois; Valley Park, Missouri; Pensacola, Florida; Los Angeles, California; Newark, New Jersey; Ford, New Jersey. The division markets and manufactures industrial and trade sales coatings of the alkyd, modified oil, copolymer, acrylic, water-soluble and styrenated types; hard resins for adhesives, coatings, chewing gum, and printing inks; polyester resins for the reinforced plastics industry. Specialty resins of the phenolic, urea, resorcinol, cresylic, melamine, and acrylic types are manufactured for a wide range of industrial applications.

(*e*)  *Petrochemical Division*  Refineries in Buffalo and Ashland produce for sale the following products: aromatics, principally benzene, toluene, xylene, cyclohexane, naphthalene, and other aromatic and aliphatic solvents.

(*f*)  *Chemical Products Division*  Manufactures products in Peoria, Illinois; Great Meadows, New Jersey; Oakland, California; Jonesville, Wisconsin; and Donaldsville, Louisiana. The division sells and manufactures antioxidants, fine chemicals including quinoline derivatives and dye intermediates; fatty chemicals including fractionated and whole fatty acids, glycerides, monoglycerides, alcohols, amines, quaternaries, fabric softeners, and other nitrogen-derived intermediates; epoxy and polymeric plasticizers. Its principal customers are in the rubber, plastics, textile, mining, cosmetics, food, pharmaceutical, paint, petroleum, and chemical industries.

(*g*)  *Foundry Products Division*  In manufacturing plants in Cleveland, Ohio, and Hansford, West Virginia, Ashland produces chemicals, coatings, and exothermics for the foundry industry.

The chemical division is supported by an international division, transportation division, and research division. In 1974 Ashland stated that a major company objective was "to see earnings from the chemical operation equal those of the petroleum company within five years." To achieve this, the company said it had a number of projects in early stages of development.

**2**  Ashland Oil Canada, Ltd., which operates the Canadian companies.

**3**  Ashland Exploration Company, which is in charge of domestic and international search for crude and similar products.

**4**  Ashland Resources Company, which is engaged primarily in contract construction, production and sale of construction materials, and production and sale of coal. This division consolidates functions and services of Warren Brothers Co., New Haven Trap Rock Company, and related Ashland subsidiaries engaged primarily in contract construction and construction materials and Arch Mineral Corp., a 44.84 percent owned affiliate, which is engaged in coal production and sales.

Warren Brothers Company is engaged in contract construction, including paving of highways, airports, parking areas, and driveways with asphaltic or portland cement concrete. Warren Brothers owns and operates 140 asphalt plants, 30 aggregate processing plants, 28 concrete plants, and 7 concrete block plants and has 13 quarry locations.

New Haven Trap Rock Company and associated companies produce and sell crushed trap and granite, asphaltic concrete, ready-mixed concrete, and other construction materials in Connecticut, Long Island, northeast New Jersey, and New York City markets. These companies own and operate 13 asphalt plants and 7 aggregate processing plants and have 5 quarry locations.

Arch Mineral Corp. is primarily engaged in exploration, acquisition, and development of coal reserves for sale primarily to electric utilities.

The main division is, of course, Ashland Petroleum Company Division. *Moody's* describes this division as follows:

Historically, Ashland's principal marketing area for gasoline and fuel oils has included most of the region from the Mississippi River to the Appalachians, and from the Great Lakes to central Tennessee. Although sales of such products under Ashland brand names are made primarily through retail outlets in Indiana, Kentucky, western New York, Ohio, Pennsylvania and West Virginia, Ashland has expanded its distribution of unbranded gasoline and fuel oils to include large portions of the eastern seaboard and southeastern United States. In addition, Northwestern Refining Company, wholly-owned Ashland subsidiary, markets gasoline through approximately 400 service stations in Minnesota, Wisconsin, Iowa, Montana, North and South Dakota and northern Illinois.

Ashland markets petroleum products directly through 180 bulk plants, of which 154 are owned and 26 are leased, and also sells petroleum products under Ashland brand names through approximately 2,500 retail outlets. Of these branded outlets, which are operated almost exclusively by lessees and independent dealers, approximately one-third are owned or leased from the landowner by Ashland.

Major portion of Ashland's production of gasoline, kerosene and light fuel oils is sold at wholesale to approximately 1,200 distributors and independent jobbers who resell through several thousand outlets under Ashland's or their own brand names. In addition, Northwestern Refining Co. supplies distributors and independent jobbers in its marketing areas named above, as well as portions of Missouri and Kansas. In connection with its sale of petroleum products, Ashland markets, through its branded stations and through independent jobbers and distributors, a complete line of tires, batteries and automotive accessories manufactured by others.

Ashland's "Valvoline" brand of motor oils and automotive lubricants is sold throughout United States through an estimated 60,000 jobbers and dealers, and is distributed in foreign countries throughout the world. Ashland's "TECTYL" brand of rust preventives is also distributed worldwide. Ashland also manufactures and markets liquefied petroleum gas, asphalt and asphaltic products, rust preventives, industrial lubricants, diesel fuel and jet and ordnance fuels. Through its Allied Oil Company Division and its affiliated companies, Ashland is one of the principal marketers of residual fuel oils to industries in Ohio, western Pennsylvania, western New York, Kentucky, Indiana, Illinois, central Flordia, southern Georgia, and on the Mississippi and Ohio Rivers.

The division accounts for about 60 percent of sales and a slightly larger percentage of the profits. In 1974 the company announced a future emphasis on speciality products, such as lubricating oil and maleic anhydride.

## The energy crisis and energy industry

One of the major factors affecting Ashland and the energy industry has been recent developments in the energy supply. In 1973, the Arabs and other members of the OPEC cut the supply of crude for political and economic reasons. This led to the energy crisis which manifested itself in long lines at gas pumps, great increases in the cost of all energy, and proposals from voluntary restraint to rationing of fuels. The federal government set up an apparatus to coordinate the supply of fuel. Much of this apparatus was manned by petroleum company officials while critics wailed about conflicts of interest.

When crude began flowing again, there were some interesting results.

**1** Partly because of higher prices, conservation, and other factors, the demand for fuel fell. Instead of the surpluses putting price pressure on crude, the producing countries cut production to try to keep the price up.

**2** Although the industry said higher prices would lead to inducements for more exploration and thus greater supply and possibly stable or lower prices, this did not materialize. As the *Wall Street Journal* reported August 22, 1974, the output of petroleum *fell.*

**3** The profits of the oil industry skyrocketed as the data in Table 6 for 1973 show. 1974 figures were expected to be larger. This led some to demand excess profits taxes, others to demand nationalization. Some of the producing countries such as Iran suggested they would lower prices at the well if petroleum companies were required to cut profits.

**4** Doom and gloom were predicted in that the ownership of the world would be transferred to the OPEC countries because of the profits of oil. The monetary system was said to be strained.

**5** In spite of Presidential talk of conservation and Federal Energy Administrators pleading for lower usage, John Sawhill, FEA administrator, felt compelled to speak out on energy companies' hard-sell tactics of marketing of petroleum in August 1974. He wrote a letter to the 20 largest companies (including Ashland). Excerpts include these statements (as quoted in the *Wall Street Journal*).

Mr. Sawhill said "industry efforts to coax the public into buying gasoline that it has indicated it doesn't want or need" could force the agency to take 'strong action' to hold down fuel consumption."

Warning companies against a return to "hard-sell tactics" for gasoline and other petroleum products, Mr. Sawhill said he was concerned that several oil companies recently have urged their dealers to stay open longer and "take other steps to increase gasoline sales." He didn't say what those steps were, but stations around the country

**TABLE 6 ■ ENERGY: YARDSTICKS OF MANAGEMENT PERFORMANCE**

| Company | Profitability | | | | | | Growth | | | | | |
| --- | --- | --- | --- | --- | --- | --- | --- | --- | --- | --- | --- | --- |
| | Return on equity | | | Return on total capital | | | Sales | | | Earnings per share | | |
| | 5-year average | Industry rank | Latest 12 months | 5-year average | Industry rank | Latest 12 months | 1973* vs. 1970–72 | Industry rank | 5-year average | Industry rank | 5-year average | 1973* vs. 1970–1972 |
| Amerada Hess | 20.6% | 1 | 16.1% | 13.1% | 2 | 10.5% | 28.8% | 7 | 14.4% | 9 | 7.4% | −0.9% |
| Tesoro Petroleum | 19.9 | 2 | 20.7 | 13.7 | 1 | 16.3 | 57.3 | 1 | 51.3b | 1 | 37.4b | 78.3 |
| Petrolane | 19.5 | 3 | 15.0 | 12.0 | 5 | 9.1 | 50.9 | 4 | 17.3 | 5 | 9.4 | −5.6 |
| Clark Oil & Refining | 16.8 | 4 | 31.2 | 12.5 | 3 | 19.7 | 33.5 | 8 | 12.9 | 10 | 6.6 | 242.6 |
| American Petrofina | 15.7 | 5 | 16.0 | 12.0 | 4 | 12.6 | 28.6 | 15 | 9.9 | 2 | 15.5 | 31.4 |
| Pittston | 14.8 | 6 | 5.8 | 9.7 | 10 | 4.6 | 11.4 | 14 | 10.9 | 4 | 12.5 | −56.4 |
| Texaco | 14.2 | 7 | 15.4 | 11.0 | 7 | 11.8 | 33.5 | 13 | 11.5 | 14 | 5.0 | 27.1 |
| Charter Company | 14.1c | 8 | 14.7 | 9.3c | 12 | 9.8 | 39.3 | — | d | — | d | 63.3 |
| Exxon | 13.7 | 9 | 17.5 | 11.6 | 6 | 14.3 | 25.5 | 21 | 8.5 | 11 | 5.9 | 47.3 |
| Pennzoil Company | 13.5 | 10 | 13.9 | 7.0 | 26 | 6.5 | 28.7 | 24 | 7.1 | 8 | 7.5 | 29.5 |
| Ashland Oil | 12.3 | 11 | 18.0 | 8.3 | 14 | 9.9 | 50.0 | 3 | 18.4 | 25 | −0.3 | 106.7 |
| Mobil Oil | 11.8 | 12 | 14.1 | 9.9 | 9 | 11.7 | 23.8 | 17 | 9.2 | 6 | 9.1 | 37.1 |
| Marathon Oil | 11.8 | 13 | 13.5 | 9.4 | 11 | 10.4 | 29.3 | 6 | 15.4 | 17 | 4.1 | 38.0 |
| Kerr-McGee | 11.4 | 14 | 11.2 | 8.0 | 17 | 9.3 | 16.4 | 16 | 9.8 | 11 | 5.9 | 27.0 |
| Standard Oil (California) | 11.3 | 15 | 13.5 | 10.1 | 8 | 11.7 | 37.9 | 11 | 11.6 | 13 | 5.5 | 40.0 |
| Standard Oil (Indiana) | 10.6 | 16 | 12.4 | 8.5 | 13 | 9.7 | 19.8 | 20 | 8.5 | 7 | 8.0 | 35.6 |
| Commonwealth Oil Refinery | 10.4 | 17 | 9.7 | 7.4 | 21 | 6.1 | 47.2 | 9 | 12.7 | 29 | −2.9 | 34.0 |
| Eastern Gas & Fuel | 10.4 | 18 | 7.9 | 6.3 | 30 | 4.7 | 7.9 | 19 | 8.8 | 16 | 3.8 | −19.5 |
| Continental Oil | 10.4 | 19 | 12.3 | 8.1 | 16 | 9.2 | 23.3 | 12 | 11.5 | 20 | 4.1 | 38.5 |
| Sun Oil | 10.3 | 20 | 13.1 | 7.7 | 19 | 8.7 | 9.5 | 18 | 4.7 | 23 | 3.5 | 49.2 |
| Gulf Oil | 10.1 | 21 | 12.8 | 8.2 | 15 | 9.6 | 22.1 | 18 | 9.2 | 26 | 0.6 | 58.1 |
| Shell Oil | 10.0 | 22 | 11.4 | 7.8 | 18 | 8.6 | 18.2 | 26 | 6.6 | 24 | −0.4 | 34.9 |
| Union Oil California | 9.7 | 23 | 12.0 | 7.1 | 23 | 7.8 | 18.3 | 23 | 7.3 | 3 | 0.5 | 47.9 |
| Murphy Oil | 9.5 | 24 | 21.3 | 7.2 | 22 | 11.4 | 39.6 | 10 | 12.4 | 21 | 13.5 | 225.3 |
| Occidental Petroleum | 9.2 | 25 | 7.3 | 6.5 | 28 | 5.1 | 23.7 | 2 | 29.9 | 22 | 2.9 | 100.0 |
| Cities Service | 8.7 | 26 | 8.5 | 7.0 | 25 | 7.6 | 16.7 | 27 | 6.5 | 27 | 1.4 | 18.3 |
| Phillips Petroleum | 8.0 | 27 | 9.6 | 6.4 | 29 | 6.9 | 16.2 | 25 | 6.7 | 15 | −0.8 | 35.7 |
| Getty Oil | 8.0 | 28 | 7.4 | 7.4 | 20 | 6.8 | 12.2 | 29 | 4.0 | 18 | 4.7 | 9.7 |
| Atlantic Richfield | 7.8 | 29 | 8.1 | 6.6 | 27 | 6.6 | 16.6 | 22 | 8.4 | 28 | 4.0 | 20.7 |
| Standard Oil (Ohio) | 6.9 | 30 | 5.7 | 7.1 | 24 | 9.3 | 3.8 | 5 | 17.1 | | −2.8 | 34.6 |
| Industry medians | 11.0 | | 13.0 | 8.2 | | 9.3 | 23.8 | | 9.9 | | | 35.4 |

*Latest 12 months. b Three-year average. c Four-year growth. d Not available; not ranked.
*Source: Forbes*, Jan. 1, 1974.

are increasingly posting their prices to try to undercut competitors and some have resumed giving away trading stamps and other items. . . .

In his letter, he told the industry he hopes that "conditions in the petroleum industry will remain favorable enough so that we will be able to keep intrusion into the company-dealer relationship to a minimum.

"The maintenance of those favorable conditions depends in part on your willingness to assist us in holding down demand," he wrote. . . .

Mr. Sawhill wrote that the public's "continued adherence, at our urging, to the principles of conservation has kept gasoline consumption below last year's levels, even though the number of vehicles on the road has risen." Any industry efforts to boost gasoline sales can't "fail to create doubt and confusion in the minds of people regarding the necessity for continued conservation," he said.

Ashland is involved in alternate sources of energy. It owns 48.9 percent of Arch Mineral Corporation which produces 11.6 million tons of coal per year. The company sells coal primarily to electric utilities under long-term contracts.

Ashland is one of four firms investigating the H-coal process of converting coal liquid solvent slurry into concentrated liquid hydrocarbons. The firm also owns 25 percent of a venture in Colorado in oil shale.

## To acquire more crude and/or be bought out

As the supply of crude tightened, Ashland needed to get more crude. As the price of crude went up, the producing countries had more money to invest. One of the countries, Iran, and its shah, saw a chance to match up. When Ashland was seeking more crude from Iran, the shah began discussions of possible relations with Ashland including the possibility of joint ventures and/or purchase of some of Ashland's assets.

In August 1973, in a report to security analysts, Orin Atkins, chairman of the board and chief executive officer of Ashland, described the proposed relationship as follows:

We believe that our expectation of continued profit improvement in refining and marketing was confirmed by the *joint venture* refinery announcement between the National Iranian Oil Company and Ashland.

As many of you may know, Ashland has recently signed *a letter of intent* with the National Iranian Oil Company under which the two companies would form a *joint venture.* The physical assets of this new company would include *Ashland's* 60,000-barrel-a-day refinery at Buffalo, New York, and its related marketing and transportation facilities. NIOC would agree to supply crude oil under a long-term contract to the joint venture at the initial rate of 60,000 barrels a day, escalating to 100,000 barrels a day. NIOC and Ashland are also undertaking joint studies of other projects which would significantly expand the refining and marketing activities of the joint venture into other geographic areas in which Ashland is not currently a major factor.

The theory of the joint venture lies in the expectation that NIOC will find it more profitable to integrate downstream into refining and marketing rather than to remain solely a seller of crude oil. Ashland in turn expects to find added profit by expanding its petroleum activities more rapidly than might otherwise be the case.

The statement was repeated almost word for word in the 1973 Annual Report. The New York State facility which NIOC would become 50 percent owner of included the refinery and petrochemical plant in Buffalo and transportation and marketing facilities for 180 Ashland stations marketing under the Frontier brand in Buffalo and surrounding areas. An Ashland spokesman stated that joint studies were being conducted to extend the activities of the joint venture to other aspects of Ashland's operations. In essence, NIOC would be partially purchasing a division of Ashland with the crude output of NIOC. Whether this ultimately would mean that Ashland would be controlled by NIOC was not clear.

NIOC also let it be known that it was discussing possible joint ventures with other firms in many countries. The thrust of these ventures, however, was for the non-Iranian companies to help finance joint ventures in Iran. Iran's contributions to these ventures would be her crude oil.

Later, difficulties arose in the discussions between Ashland and NIOC. Ashland purchased some Iranian crude but not as part of the joint venture. "Definitive" terms proved difficult to hammer out. As early as January 1974, some spokesmen were saying the venture was "shelved." Ashland sent teams of managers to Iran to try to settle the terms. Alleged stumbling blocks were said to be:

**1** U.S. Rules and Regulations regarding the importation of crude and the prices and allocation program of the Federal Energy Office. These required Ashland to share the crude with other users. This clouds the profitability prospects for the joint venture as does the unclear tax situation with regard to oil.

**2** Other opportunities by Iran for joint ventures with U.S. and other companies, especially West Germany and Japan.

**3** Questions on the part of NIOC and the shah as to how many refineries Iran could supply. The priority problem is closely related. Should Iran emphasize refineries in Iran on a joint venture basis on the "downstream" investments such as Ashland proposed? NIOC wondered about the feasibility of shipping crude to Buffalo and the wisdom of purchasing service stations in 1974's economic conditions.

**4** U.S. antitrust laws, which prevent more than one joint venture within the United States. So Iran might be cautious about which partner it should choose.

In the quarterly report issued by Ashland March 31, 1974, Mr. Atkins stated:

Because of the rapidly changing relations between world oil prices and the impact of United States government regulations on the petroleum business, the possible joint venture with the National Iranian Oil Company covering the company's refining and marketing facilities in New York State has not been consummated. Discussions are continuing with NIOC on this venture, as well as other refining and petrochemical possibilities.

What may never be known is whether the shah really intended to purchase Ashland and the joint venture proposal was simply Ashland's response to that possibility.

## Government-business relations and Ashland

Petroleum companies, because of the nature of their business, must have closer relations with governments than, say, producers of nuts and bolts for the hardware trade. Whether they can buy crude overseas at all depends on their rapport with foreign governments. Whatever their private opinions on Israel, for example, oil executives might have to be very careful about stating their feelings in view of the Arab rulers' views on the subjects. The import policies of U.S. government affecting crude determine if they shall stay in business, grow, or decline. The tax structure, including the depletion allowance, affects their profitability. For all these reasons, petroleum companies are probably more active politically than some business executives. It is likely that executives in oil, banking, maritime, and milk have more political dealings than producers of hardware, flowers, and shoes, if they wish their firm to survive. A few instances which have put Ashland in the news recently will make this point.

### THE NIXON CONTRIBUTION

During the 1972 U.S. national political campaign, a number of executives were approached by those representing the campaign interests of Richard M. Nixon (the Finance Committee to Reelect the President). Maurice Stans, former Commerce secretary for Nixon, telephoned Orin Atkins in March 1972 just before the election financing disclosure act went into effect. He solicited Atkins for a $100,000 contribution. Mr. Atkins responded by giving $100,000 of corporate funds to the committee. Atkins said later he did this without consulting Ashland's board of directors, but did consult some company executives.

In 1973, Atkins revealed the gift, which is illegal under U.S. laws, to the special prosecutor's office and to the public through Senator Ervin's Watergate Investigating Committee.

In his testimony to the Senate committee, Mr. Atkins reconstructed the details of the gift as follows:

Though Mr. Stans didn't specify where the funds should come from, in my mind, it could have come only from one place, the corporation . . . because $100,000 is an awful lot of money.

After consulting with a few fellow officers, but not the company's board of directors, I decided to comply. I viewed the contribution as a "calling card," to assure us of a "forum" within the Executive branch so we could "present our point of view." . . .

Next, I decided to take the money from the "undeveloped leasehold account" of a foreign subsidiary, Ashland Petroleum Gabon Corp., in Africa, because this account is for investment in raw acreage and isn't written off for tax purposes for a long time.

William R. Seaton, vice chairman of Ashland's board of directors, was traveling in Europe on other business, so we asked them to stop by Geneva and pick up the money in the form of a check drawn on the Geneva branch of First National City Bank of New York.

Clyde Webb, an Ashland vice president, subsequently flew to Washington to deliver the money to Mr. Stans. "Mr. Stans took the briefcase and dumped the money in his desk drawer and said 'thank you.' " I don't think Mr. Webb was in Mr. Stans office for more than a minute or two.

Sometime in 1973, when it became apparent that efforts to force the Committee to Re-Elect to disclose the names of contributors would succeed, Mr. Stans tried to convince me to reconstruct a list of individual contributors. "I wasn't about to do that. Soon afterward I decided to cooperate with the office of the special Watergate prosecutor."

The Committee to Reelect the President issued a statement saying it did not know the funds were corporate when it accepted the gift. At Ashland's request, it returned the funds.

Later, Mr. Atkins pleaded no contest (nolo contendere) to violating the law.

He was fined $5000. Mr. Atkins agreed to pay Ashland the interest on the $100,000 gift and out-of-pocket expenses associated with the gift.

The *Wall Street Journal* reported the following about the incident:

For his part, Ashland Oil Chairman Orin E. Atkins expressed bitterness at what he called the "pragmatic problems" created for corporations by the nation's political process.

In a telephone conversation from Ashland, Ky., the company's corporate headquarters, Mr. Atkins said that this process has in the past put corporation in a squeeze. "Those times have come to an end; they'll have to find some other way to finance campaigns," he said.

### ASHLAND AND KENTUCKY SENATE SEAT

In late 1974, Jack Anderson reported on the alleged relationships between Senator Marlow Cook and Clyde Webb, vice president, external affairs, of Ashland. In the Senate Senator Cook represented Kentucky, where Ashland has its home office. Anderson reported that Cook was known in Congress as "the Senator from Ashland." Cook delivered speeches in Congress written by Ashland (according to Anderson) and used Ashland's jets as his own commuter plane. Ashland's vice president, Clyde Webb, has his daughter Betty on the senator's payroll, and Webb spends time at Cook's Florida home. Anderson said:

The record shows, however, that Cook has consistently fought for more incentives for the oil industry and has repeatedly gone to bat for Ashland. When the Canadian government threatened to cut off the crude oil supply to an Ashland refinery, for example, Cook raised an uproar. . . .

Cook has also collected at least $10,950 in campaign contributions from Ashland executives, including $1,000 from company president Orin Atkins and $500 apiece from Webb and his wife. Cook pointed out that Atkins, at least, gave a matching $1,000 to his Senate opponent, Gov. Wendell Ford. . . .

There is no doubt that Ashland Oil has sought out and systematically courted Senator Cook. The situation is an ominous reminder of the days when the robber barons controlled the Senate.

Ashland Oil and Senator Cook denied that they unduly influenced each other. Shortly after, Senator Cook was defeated for his seat by Governor W. Ford.

### ASHLAND AND THE FEDERAL TRADE COMMISSION

In late 1974, Ashland was sued by the Federal Trade Commission. The FTC release indicated that it was suing an Ashland subsidiary for $425,000 civil penalties.

The suit alleges that O.K. Tire & Rubber Co., Ashland, Ky., violated a 1964 cease-and-desist order against its corporate predecessor, O.K. Rubber Welders Inc.

That order required O.K. Tire to stop interfering with the independent choice of its 1,000 franchised dealers concerning the products they sell.

The FTC suit, filed in federal court in Idaho, alleges that O.K. Tire violated the 1964 order in connection with its franchised tire dealers in Idaho, California, Oregon and Washington.

A spokesman for Ashland Oil said the company "is convinced there is no merit to the FTC position."

## ASHLAND AND PRICING

Another recent issue was "excess" profits and pricing of oil during the energy crisis. In August 1974, the Federal Energy Administration took administrative procedures against 14 oil companies, including Ashland, for inflating their prices by $194.4 million.

The FEA found that those four companies passed through, in the form of price increases, their costs in the same month they were incurred, rather than in the next month as the agency's regulations specify. The companies each were ordered to roll back certain prices until the overcharges are made up.

A spokesman for Ashland Oil, questioned in Ashland, said, "We are confident that we haven't been in violation of any pass-through regulations." In July 1975, Ashland was ordered to refund $796,000 in overcharges.

## PETROLEUM COMPANIES AND DIVERSIFICATION

Finally, some oil companies have tried to diversify. This move might spread the risk away from the volatile petroleum industry. One example is the current attempt of Mobil to purchase Marcor. Marcor is itself a merger of Montgomery Ward, the retailer, and a paperboard container firm. Mobil was willing to offer $500 million for 51 percent of Marcor. It proceeded to accept 51 percent but no more of Marcor.

Mobil was criticized by Senator Phillip Hart (D-Mich.), among others, for this move. It would allow a super giant—exceeded only by GM, AT&T, and Exxon—to come into being. It would allow Mobil to control Ward's 600 auto service centers.

Mobil contended it wanted to diversify because of restraints on future investment in the U.S. oil field by Mobil.

Many congressional critics—especially Senators Thomas McIntyre (D-N.H.), Edward Brooke (R-Mass.), and James Abourezk (D-S.Dak.), the Congressman Charles Vanik (D-Ohio)—contended that Mobil's move was simply a way to use up "embarrassing profits" and should be invested in additional capacity for petroleum for U.S. needs.

## ASHLAND AND THE CENTRAL INTELLIGENCE AGENCY

In July 1975, the report Ashland filed with the SEC in response to SEC suits revealed that since 1967, Ashland had received $98,968 in payments from the CIA. It was not clear at the time of this writing if some of the CIA money was used to make political contributions. Why Ashland received the funds from the CIA was not revealed. The board of directors of Ashland Oil, Inc., had not made public any moves it might take concerning Ashland's top executives.

# CASES

# Analyzing environments, resources, and strategic planning

# A pollution-free car?

William F. Glueck

When one says "car" or "automobile," most persons think of an internal-combustion engine fueled by petroleum. This was not always so, nor is it so in all parts of the world for all vehicles. The case writer spent a year in England, where many products such as bread, milk, and soft drinks were delivered to the home in noiseless, exhaustless electric trucks. Had one been observing the horseless carriages at the turn of the century, one would have observed 30,000 electric automobiles and many steam-driven cars—both exceeding by far the number of gasoline-driven autos. The recent pressures of the energy crisis and the growing awareness of ecological problems have raised anew the questions: Why not a nongasoline-driven car? Is it really practical? With the specter of death by noxious fumes or the Arabization of American wealth through the purchase of artificially scarce and/or arbitrarily priced petroleum, perhaps alternatives will be seriously pursued. The pollution threat is real enough. Anyone who has driven across states like Colorado with clear sky and sun visible and has driven into Denver's smog knows the reality. And the reality is there too in Los Angeles, Cleveland, St. Louis, Chicago, and many others. It was estimated as long ago as 1967 that autos, trucks, and buses emitted the following into Cleveland's atmosphere: 41 tons of hydrocarbons, 478 tons of carbon monoxide, and 23 tons of nitrogen oxides, in the business district alone. Probably 80 to 90 percent of air pollution in Los Angeles, where the emissions are *controlled,* and 40 to 50 percent of the pollution in the rest of the country is caused by auto emission. The protest against pollution from industry and utility smokestacks is large and should be. But without action on autos, will this not be in vain?

But is not all this talk of a less polluting car in vain if "the Big Three" do not move on it? The history in the United States has been that the Big Three have the impact. Look at what has happened since 1945:

A new entry by Tucker was stillborn.

There were so many deaths—Studebaker, Packard, Hudson, Nash, and others.

Kaiser failed with a Kaiser, a Frazier, and a Henry J.

The remnant of the deaths—American Motors—barely holds on.

Imports, from time to time, have taken a larger share of market: Volkswagen, Datsun, Toyota, Volvo, British Leyland. But none of them really have addressed this issue either. Surely we know that large companies who dominate a market never lose that dominance—John Kenneth Galbraith has told us that. But he has overlooked a few "exceptions." A&P—the Great A&P Tea Company—and the food business; Curtiss-Wright and the aircraft industry in 1945 and 1975; United States Rubber Company in 1929 and 1969. And all those firms so dominant in the *Fortune* 500s of yesteryear and unknown now—locomotive firms like Baldwin Lima. Surely we know that Parker and Sheaffer, not BIC, dominate the pen market because they used to dominate it.

## The market for electric and steam autos and trucks

It is hard to estimate what the total potential for electric and steam vehicles is. Obviously, in the United States about 9 to 10 million cars are sold yearly. Millions of trucks and buses are also sold. But even a small share of this market could provide an interesting market to many large and small firms.

At a recent conference of electric vehicle makers, three marketing professors at the University of Wisconsin, Whitewater (Gerald Udell, G. Nardin, and George Tesar) predicted that the consumer market could absorb 500,000 to 1,000,000 electric cars at present and could reach 1,600,000 by 1980. These figures would increase if certain technological breakthroughs would come soon. The professors estimated that about 250,000 electrically powered vehicles of all types were sold in the United States in the early 1970s.

The major market at present is for commercial and recreational use of electric vehicles. Some recent illustrations of interest in electrics include:

1 A grant to the city of Lansing, Michigan, by the Department of Transportation for testing electric buses.

2 Yosemite National Park is using electric trucks for regular service.

3 Electric delivery trucks for delivery of pizzas, laundry, flowers.

4 One hundred electric trucks are being tested around the country by utility companies for repair services.

5 The Postal Service has ordered hundreds of the electric delivery vans for delivering the mail.

The 100,000 postal vehicles could be replaced by 5000 electrics a year if the tests in California, Massachusetts, and Pennsylvania prove out. The cities testing the electrics are Lowell, Massachusetts; Allentown and Bethlehem, Pennsylvania; Cupertino and Santa Ana, California.

Detailed date from the Cupertino test may be of interest. Table 1 gives some data on the relative effectiveness of the jeep (gasoline-driven) and electric car.

In Cupertino, the post office plans to go 100 percent electric with 30 electric vans. *Electrical World* described the test vehicles and characteristics (see Table 1).

A combination U.S.-British vehicle will be used for Cupertino's "Electro-Mail" project. Harbilt Electric Vehicle Co. Manchester, England, built the vehicle's electric propulsion system, and the vehicle was completed and assembled by the San Francisco-based Electric Vehicles Inc.

Cupertino Postmaster Alvin R. Carter says the trucks are smog-free, and cost only about one-tenth as much as the conventional type to operate. The electrics can operate for at least two days without recharging the batteries, he says. When a recharging is necessary the batteries are simply connected into an industrial-type charger. The trucks

TABLE 1 ■ CALCULATED VEHICLE AVERAGES, CUPERTINO, CALIFORNIA

| | Harbilt Oct. 1, 1971, to April 14, 1972 | Jeep Nov. 27, 1971, to March 29, 1972 Run #1 | Run #2 |
|---|---|---|---|
| Cost/mile | 2.5¢ | 5.6¢ | 5.2¢ |
| Energy use | 1.3 kwhr/mile (25 mi/gal equivalent) | 6.5 miles/gal (5.1 kwhr/mi equivalent) | 7.0 miles/gal (4.7 kwhr/mi equivalent) |
| Miles/day | 11.1 | 12.4 | 14.4 |
| Cost/day | 27.7¢ | 69.4¢ | 74.9¢ |
| Energy cost | 1.85¢/kwhr | 36.7¢/gal | 36.7¢/gal |

Source: *Electrical World*, Nov. 1, 1973.

are powered by two 36-v lead-acid batteries, and have a top speed of 40 mph on a 2% upgrade. However, they will travel at a maximum of 35 mph to conform with local speed laws.

The almost-silent vehicles produce only a slight hum as they accelerate, insuring quiet early-morning deliveries. And since they draw power only when in motion, pollution from an idling engine is eliminated, and only the power needed to operate the vehicle is used, thus saving critical petroleum products.

The test vehicle has now been in operation at Cupertino for a little over two years and it has been utilized on the same routes as the regular Post Office vehicles. The length of these routes ranges from 8 to 15 miles with 100 to 300 stops.

During the tests, daily mileage, power consumption, the number of stops, and general maintenance readings have been recorded [see Table 1]. In order to give these data some sort of perspective, a control vehicle was selected at random—a jeep powered by a four-cylinder engine—and comparative data were recorded. The overall results of the battery vs ICE comparison proved that four mail-delivery vans powered by batteries could be operated at the cost of operating one ICE vehicle.

Reaction to the vehicles by Cupertino postal carriers who operate them has been generally favorable. One carrier commented that she feels better at the end of the day because the electrics minimize vibration and noise.

The post office said that if the Cupertino test is successful, other "sun belt" cities such as Miami, Los Angeles, Memphis, and Phoenix will be next.

The post office is testing electrics also in Santa Ana. The *Electrical World* article described this test also:

The vehicle being tested in Santa Ana is designed and manufactured in the Stockton (Calif.) Special Vehicle Plant of Otis Elevator Co. The vehicle has been tested by Dynamic Science Laboratories, an independent testing facility in Phoenix, Ariz., which says it meets all specifications set forth by the Postal Service under its electric-vehicle test program.

This van, called the Otis Electric Delivery Vehicle, can travel about 40 miles on a single charge, and has a maximum speed of 43 mph. Sixteen 6-v lead-acid batteries power it.

Since the middle of June, the Otis vehicle has been driven on regular mail routes in the Santa Ana area. Hector Godinex, postmaster of Santa Ana and sectional-center manager of the Orange County Postal Dept., sees the vehicle as the forerunner of the type of vehicle that will eventually be used on all routes in Orange County. Of the 1,500 routes in the county, 1,300 require vehicles to distribute mail.

The tests at Lowell began in late September. An electric delivery van produced by the Transportation Systems Laboratory, a division of Electromotion Inc., Bedford, Massachusetts, is being used.

The vehicle, 2 feet shorter than a Volkswagen sedan, has 75 cubic feet of cargo space for a ⅓-ton payload, and is somewhat bigger than the present Postal Service Jeep. The Electromotion vehicle has a top speed of 45 mph and a range of 35 miles before its pack of 14 6-v batteries have to be recharged.

Maintenance is expected to consist solely of replacing the 950-lb battery pack every 10,000 to 20,000 miles, a once-a-month check on the water level in the batteries and a periodic replacement of the motor brushes.

Costing $6,000 each, the electric vans are about twice as expensive as the conventional Jeeps, but are expected to last 15 years against the six-year life expectancy of a Jeep.

At present average electric rates, the electric van is estimated to operate at a cost of 3½¢ a mile, vs about 21¢ for an ICE-powered vehicle.

## Companies building electric vehicles

A number of companies, mostly small, have jumped into this business. Some of the firms and their products are described below.

**1  Anderson Power Products, Boston**
Plans to market a 750- to 1000-pound-load vehicle for the delivery trade. Its market expectations are based on British dairy, bread, and similar delivery vehicle market. The vehicle will operate at least 40 miles daily.

**2  American Motors, Kenosha, Wisconsin**
The firm has cooperated with Electric Fuel Propulsion Co. (see below) in converting its Hornet to electric power. AMC is not directly involved in electric power cars as yet.

**3  Battronic Truck Corporation, Boyertown, Pennsylvania**
The firm offers a 25-passenger bus, an 11-passenger micro bus, and a 3000-pound delivery van. The firm has been investigating electric cars in its R&D since 1962. The large bus weighs 12,000 pounds and has a 70-mile range at 30 to 35 miles per hour. The delivery van weighs 9500 pounds. The trucks initially cost twice as much as gas-powered trucks, but last twice as long and cost half as much to operate. One truck owned by Battronic has been in service for 55 years. It is building vehicles which are adaptable as cargo vans or passenger vehicles.

**4  Chrysler Corporation, New York and Detroit**
The firm experimented by converting a 1967 Simca, produced by Chrysler's subsidiary, to electric power. According to one report in 1971, Dr. Clayton Lewis, head of Chrysler research, said:

"We had been working long and hard on the subject of electric cars and our calculations just didn't come up to the extravagant claims we had been reading and hearing about. So we developed our own electric car and tested it thoroughly. The extravagant claims didn't always stand up. Our calculations did."

The electric Simca had no heater. "Providing heat in the car comparable to that thrown out by the heater in a conventional car would reduce the driving range by almost one-half. The only heat in the Simca is provided by an electric heating element that runs a windshield defroster. This is needed to meet federal window defogging standards. The device gives off about the same amount of heat as a two-slice toaster," he says.

**5  Club Car Company, Augusta, Georgia**
Produces a utility vehicle called Caroche, retailing for about $2,000. The firms basic business has been golf carts. The Caroche operates up to 53 miles at 26 miles per hour. The Caroche weighs under 1000 pounds. The chassis is composed of two 90-inch

aluminum I beams. The body is fiber glass. The car is slotted for the second-car market. About 60 percent of American driving could be handled with the car. The battery will last 20,000 miles if used for 25-mile-type trips. The electricity charge for these miles was $108 compared with $513 in gas charges (1971 figures). Maintenance costs are much less on the electric. Recently, the car was tested in New York City for 5000 miles. Maintenance was $383. Recreational communities such as Sea Pines–Hilton Head have ordered a number of these cars.

Similar products are available from Electro Dyne Corp. (California) and Vehicle Research (Ontario).

**6  Eagel Pitcher, Cincinnati**
Produces the Silver Eagle, the fastest electric car: 153 miles per hour at Bonneville Salt Flats. It also powered the lunar rover, for the moon landings. Mostly experimental cars, however.

**7  Electromotion, Inc., Bedford, Massachusetts**
Cars ranging from $4000 to $8500. Can travel up to 40 miles per hour for up to 45 miles. Fifty cars or so sold recently.

**8  EVI, Inc., Sterling, Michigan**
Produces the Electric Powered Vehicle: a three-wheeled product costing about $1200 (1974). Can travel up to 25 miles per hour for 45 miles before recharging. This firm has produced bicycle-type two-passenger vehicles. Main market: retirement communities.

**9  Electric Fuel Propulsion, Ferndale, Michigan**
Produces the Thunderbolt, priced at $7500. Can travel up to 75 miles per hour. Can travel up to 90 miles. Costs 1 cent per mile for electricity. Can be completely recharged in 90 minutes. Uses the body and parts of standard Big Three vehicles.

**10  ESB, Inc., Philadelphia**
This firm is the largest battery maker in the United States with sales almost $400 million. Its brand names include Ray-O-Vac and Exide (automotive batteries). It produces the Sundancer, which uses twelve standard 6-volt lead batteries for power and one battery to power the accessories. The car goes 60 mph up to 75 miles before recharging. Firms who might use ESB's systems (ESB does not want to produce cars) include Chrysler, Auto Dynamics (Marblehead, Massachusetts), Transportation Systems Labs (Bedford, Massachusetts), Battronic, and Tork-Link Corp. (Studio City, California).

**11  Ford Motors, Detroit, Michigan**
Designed a two-passenger car and tested it in the United Kingdom. The project was dropped.

**12  General Atomic Division, General Dynamics Corporation, St. Louis, Missouri**
Has done research on zinc-air batteries in San Diego since 1960. Batteries of 50 to 150 kilowatt hours are expected to be the outcome for light trucks (3000 to 4000 pounds).

**13  General Motors Corporation, Detroit and New York**
In general, GM believes that the electric car is not feasible in the near future. One GM executive was quoted as saying that electrics would "simply transfer pollution from the tailpipe of an automobile to the smokestack of an electrical generating facility" (at a recent SAE meeting). GM believes that the additional coal which must be burned in utility power plants to allow for the mandatory nightly recharge of an electric car would emit more pollutants into the air, and potentially more dangerous pollutants than would be emitted by an equal number of cars powered by internal-combustion engines. Further, when the efficiency of electric power generation, transmission and distribution, battery charge and discharge, electric motor and controls is taken into account, the heat value of fuel to be burned at the powerplant is greater than that of gasoline used in the internal-combustion engine on an equivalent basis.

The Detroit Edison Company, in reply to GM, asserted that there is plenty of power for electric cars, that supplying power to electric cars would reduce the cost of electric power to all customers, and that the power for cars from coal would be cleaner than power for other uses. It also pointed out that GM had based its argument on an assumed total switch, or at least a major switch to electric cars. The utility believes that "the best assumption is that the electric car will come into gradual use as continued improvements in electric storage battery systems and electric propulsion systems are developed, and that only a gradual conversion would take place."

GM's position has been stated by Dr. Paul Agarbal, head of their Electric Propulsion Department.

**14  I-Space, Washington**
Distributes British Electric vehicles and the firm concentrates on delivery vehicles in large city areas like Boston, Chicago, and Washington. It markets the products through Eco-Centers, which also sell health foods and natural crafts.

**15  Linear Alpha, Skokie, Illinois**
Manufactures electric trucks on a Dodge Van. Uses lead-acid golf cart batteries. Maximum 55 miles per hour for 40-mile range. Weight of vehicle 6100 pounds. Targeted at telephone companies with lots of stops per day.

**16  Otis Elevator**
The largest producer of electric vehicles in the United States. None produced for highway use. That will require the development of horizontilators—new horizontal transportation systems. Owns Electrobus, Inc. The electric vehicles are still a very small part of the firm's sales. Sales are close to the billion dollar level.

**17  Sebring-Vanguard, Inc., Sebring, Florida**
Produces the Citi-Car with speeds up to 30 miles per hour for a range up to 50 miles. It seats two persons and costs 2½ cents per mile (1974). Cost: about $2000. Essentially an enlarged golf cart. In 1974, expects to produce 2500 cars. As described in *Allstate Motor Club Magazine:*

The Vanguard electric looks a little like a jeep in a ten-gallon hat. It has a body of colored fiber glass, weighs about 980 pounds, and its makers promise a range, between battery charges, of 40 to 60 miles, depending on temperature and terrain. Its charger can be plugged into any household circuit at home or on the road. Recharging its lead-acid batteries takes five to seven hours and costs about 21 cents. The Vanguard's developer, 40-year-old Robert G. Beaumont, used to run an automobile agency. Five years ago, he caught the electric bug, teamed up with a Georgia manufacturer of golf carts and is now turning out the Vanguard's at a price of $1986.

Foreign manufacturers working on electric vehicles include Sony (Japan), Chubu (Japan), Yuan Denchi (Japan), Kobe Steel (Japan), Tokyo Electric Power (Japan), Mitsubishi (Japan), Nissan Motors (Japan), and a consortium in Germany (Messerschmitt-Boelkow-Blohm, Bayer, Bosch, Varta, and others).

## Technological issues in electric vehicles

One of the crucial issues in dealing with the possibility of electric vehicles is the technical practicality of batteries and recharging. Without batteries that allow longer distances the electric won't make it. Without the ability to recharge the batteries in numerous locations, it won't make it either.

What about the power-battery issue? Sony Corporation (Japan) may have the beginning of the answer here. A recent Sony prototype car showed it could travel for 5 hours up to 56 miles per hour without recharging. Density (kilo-

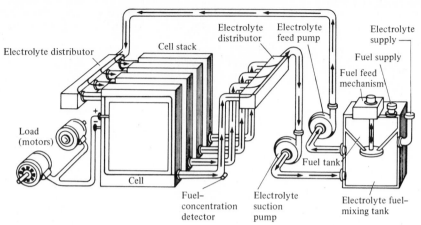

**FIGURE 1** ■ How Sony fuel is mixed and distributed.

watt hours) is the crucial variable. Most lead-acid batteries have a density of 10 watt hours per pound, and recharging is an extended process. The Sony has a density of 42 watt hours per pound in a refuelable zinc-air system. Each of the 256 six- by eight-inch cells in the 6-kilowatt battery has two positive porous-carbon air electrodes with a negative electrode sandwiched between them. Separators prevent the electrodes from touching.

Powdered zinc, suspended in an electrolyte, flows into spaces between the positive and negative electrodes. As the liquid floods the cells, zinc particles become trapped on the negative electrodes.

Air from vents seeps through the porous-carbon electrodes, oxidizing the zinc and liberating electrons. The spent zinc particles are flushed from the electrode plates when fresh fuel is added.

The used-up zinc can be recovered by an electrolytic process. Recycling is fairly efficient: Putting 1 kilowatt hour of energy (fresh zinc) back into the battery takes 3.8 kilowatt hours of line power.

Figure 1 diagrams how the fuel system works. Refueling is easy. Cam-operated distributors operate valves to receive and discharge fuel from storage tanks. The "feeding" period lasts 8 seconds; a 52-second power production period follows.

Since some zinc dissolves in the electrolyte during the power cycle, the concentration must be measured after the fuel is discharged from the cell. The zinc concentration detector linked to the zinc-feed mechanism on the fuel tank maintains the correct zinc level. Sony's production cost is said to be $600 for the car.

Another step forward is the Tri-Polar lead-cobalt battery. Such a battery lasts 50,000 miles, costs $700 (1.4 cents per mile), and can be recharged in 30 minutes up to 80 percent of capacity at night during off-peak hours at lower rates. This battery provides the following characteristics:

Acceleration from 0 to 40 miles per hour in 10 seconds

Sustained top speed of 70 miles per hour, with short-interval overloads over 85 miles per hour

An economical cruising speed of 55 to 60 miles per hour and a corresponding battery range of 125 miles at fixed throttle

A second issue is: Where could one recharge the car? Electric Fuel Propulsion plans to set up about 100 recharging stations across the nation.

The first were set up in Holiday Inns in Chicago and Detroit. Other locations being negotiated include other Holiday Inns, Howard Johnson, Ramada, and Western Inns at strategic expressway locations. Fifteen are expected to be set up in Los Angeles. EFP President Robert Aronson says his company is presently fabricating the charging units. They are described as "essentially a cabinet enclosing a 10 foot cable and plugs, KWH meter and a disconnect switch." Completed cabinets will be sent to electric utility companies in appropriate cities for installation at participating motels.

While the charging stations can service all types of experimental and prototype electric cars now on the road or in the planning stage, they will also provide power assist to experimental models planned by EFP.

## If not electric, what about steam?

The Stanley Steamer returning? Don't laugh: at least six firms are seriously at work on the possibility, and the Environmental Protection Agency is supporting much of the work. Some details on the six firms and their work follow.

### 1  JAY CARTER ENTERPRISES, BURKBURNETT, TEXAS

Jay Carter took a Volkswagen Squareback station wagon and equipped it with its own steam engine. The engine weighs 120 pounds more than the gasoline-powered VW engine, but it fits into the VW engine compartment. Carter's engine was developed without Environmental Protection Agency funds and the engine technology is secret.

The Carter engine runs on a blend of indolene (a special blend of gasoline) and kerosene. It passed the EPA pollution standards for carbon monoxide (less than 1.2 grams per mile in comparison with standards of 3.5 grams per mile), hydrocarbons, and nitrogen oxides.

The fuel consumption was only moderately efficient, however. The car got 15 miles per gallon in town and 17 on the highway. Gasoline-driven VW engines deliver 22 miles per gallon in city driving.

### 2  THERMO ELECTRON CORP., WALTHAM, MASSACHUSETTS

Ford Motors is spending about $4 million in research funds with Thermo Electron Corp., a very small firm. (Sales are $10 million to $19 million.) Thermo Electron is investing $2 million of its own funds in the research and keeps the rights to the engine. Ford would have to pay royalties to use the engine, but it now holds 10,000 shares of Thermo Electron, and gets options on stock that eventually could give it at least a 25 percent holding.

Thermo Electron is designing an engine that would use instead of water a nonaqueous organic fluid to drive it. The fluid does not corrode metal, works at much lower temperatures and pressures, and therefore should cut costs of the engine considerably.

Thermo Electron started in business with Pentagon contracts for development of quiet engines. It has built a 20-horsepower engine. The organic vapor in Thermo Electron's design drives a piston engine. It is condensed and returned to the boiler in a hermetically sealed "closed cycle." As in other steam engines, the fuel heating the boiler is burned continuously with lots of air. This virtually eliminates pollution by unburned hydrocarbons. The low burning temperature also cuts down on nitrogen oxides. Possible products include autos, underground mining vehicles, forklift trucks, and others.

Cost, weight, size, and slow start-up are still problems. The organic vapor may pose problems, too. Thermo Electron is using thiophene (Monsanto's CP-34). William Moore, director of industrial design for Lear Motor Corp., says Lear rejected thiophene because of its "high volatility and toxicity."

To this, Thermo Electron answers that a full-sized prototype of the engine is still a few years away, and a lot—possibly including the working fluid—can change by then.

EPA awarded a recent research grant to Thermo Electron for further development.

### 3 WILLIAMS ENGINE COMPANY, PHILADELPHIA

This firm came into existence in the nineteenth century when the company obtained the first patent for a steam engine. Its current research project has gone on for 30 years. Thomas Williams, president, said of its current engine, "Now we have a product that operates like an internal-combustion engine, even more efficient, while decreasing pollutants by 96 percent, far below the national standards."

The costs of operating are low because no clutch, transmission, carburetor, or distributor is needed. It get 18 miles per gallon on kerosene, fuel oil, diesel fuel, or gasoline. Water must be added every 1600 kilometers.

The Williams design covers a range of 5 to 1000 horsepower in 0.23- to 4.3-liter displacements. With a 0.7-liter engine, the Williams Steamer can do 160 kilometers per hour (100 miles per hour), and with a 1.7-liter engine, it can easily go 210 kilometers per hour. Performances, it is claimed, are better than the internal-combustion engine.

Total weight for the 1000-horsepower engine, plus overall power plant, is only 450 kilograms whereas a diesel engine, of about 500 horsepower, weighs nearly 2250 kilograms. Detroit has shown no interest in the Williams work. EPA may fund the Williams research.

### 4 AUSTRALIAN STEAM ENGINE

Edward Pritchard and Pancoastal, Inc., a Hartford, Connecticut, firm, has acquired the North American rights for the engine which is diagramed in Figure 2.

This engine is closest in style to the late nineteenth- and early twentieth-century steamers, as is the Williams engine. The engine satisfies all EPA standards. The engine averaged 40 miles to a gallon of water, and the fuel consumption was 19 miles per gallon of kerosene.

The engine has an electric blower for the burner and an alternator to

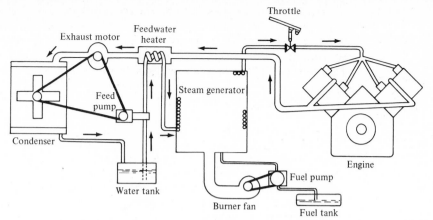

**FIGURE 2** ■ Pritchard steam engine. The steam power system is based on the use of water. A feed pump lifts water from a water tank to a feedwater heater, where it is preheated before entering a monotube steam generator. High-pressure steam is supplied from the generator to a uniflow engine, the amount of steam being regulated by a throttle. Exhaust steam is condensed in an automotive-type radiator, which serves as a condenser.

generate electricity for lights. The water feed pump and condenser fan would be turned by a steam exhaust motor, which would turn the fan much faster than the main engine, called an important factor. Much of the water loss in old-fashioned steam cars was caused by slower fans, Pritchard said.

The entire power plant, including the boiler, fits under the hood. The condenser is no larger than an ordinary auto radiator.

The cost of mass-producing the engine will be comparable to a gasoline engine, since it requires no torque converter and transmission and no starter. The V-2 engine will last about 250,000 miles.

The two firms which have received the most publicity are Steam Engine Systems and Lear.

### 5 STEAM ENGINE SYSTEMS, WATERTOWN, MASSACHUSETTS

EPA has awarded a $2 million contract to develop a 100-horsepower steam engine to SES. Mobil Oil has given some help since they are interested in lubricating the steam engine. SES plans to use kerosene as a fuel, but any fuel will do the job. Kerosene is not exploded inside the cylinder as in current engines. It is burned in an external-combustion chamber at atmospheric pressure. It gives off much lower concentrations of toxic gases than present machines. Because there are no cylinder explosions, the steamer is fairly quiet, merely chattering and hissing instead of roaring like internal-combustion engines.

American Motors has agreed to do an engineering analysis and help in adapting the engine for five-passenger automotive use. The entire propulsion system cannot weigh more than 1600 pounds, compared with 1300 pounds for a conventional medium-size car. The engine system must be able to thrust the car from zero to 60 miles per hour in 13 seconds, drive it up a 5 percent grade at 60 miles per hour, and give it a top speed of 80 miles per hour. To make the engine marketable, the company must also find a way to lessen the danger of freeze-ups in cold weather and to solve the problem of quickly getting up steam to start. SES staffers have only to glance out of their windows for inspiration. Company offices are separated by a small stream from the site of the original Stanley Steamer works. Chrysler Motors now owns 20 percent of SES's stock.

### 6  LEAR MOTORS, RENO, NEVADA

William Lear, inventor of the Lear Jet, car radio, light track tape, says he has spent $17 million to build his steam car. He has employed as many as 165 employees in his plant at Nevada. Although he lost out in recent EPA contracts, he plans to go on. Lear's steam car would be a low polluter, but his fuel economy is still not efficient enough.

Lear entered steam cars as a new mission for his life. He had become bored, then ill, and at one point considered suicide. He still believes he will succeed and has spent most of his fortune trying to achieve that goal.

## Postscript

There are political and social pressures to do something about auto, truck, and bus pollution. Detroit and most major auto and truck manufacturers have approached the problem by trying to "clean up" the internal-combustion engine. This has led to reduction in fuel efficiency. Who knows, one of these electric or steam firms is the IBM or General Motors of the future. It has happened before.

# Avon Products, Inc.

William F. Glueck

Avon employs almost 27,000 persons and has over 750,000 door-to-door saleswomen (305,000 in the United States and Canada, 445,000 overseas). These people have helped make Avon the largest manufacturer of toiletries and cosmetics in the world. Strongest in the United States and Canada (1914)[1] (64 percent of sales and 73 percent of earnings in 1973, for example), Avon also operates in Latin America and Puerto Rico (1954), specifically Argentina (1970), Brazil (1959), Mexico (1958), and Venezuela (1954), where the productivity is comparable with that of the United States and Canada. It does less well in Europe—Belgium (1963), France (1966), Ireland (1968), Italy (1966), Spain (1966), United Kingdom (1959), West Germany (1959), Sweden (1971), the Netherlands (1972), Australia (1963), and Japan (1969). Sales have grown faster there than in the home markets, but profit margins are lower. Major start-up costs in new markets are blamed for lower markets. Avon's almost 35,000 stockholders have received dividends annually since 1919, and these have increased each year since 1953. From 1968 to 1973, the average dividend payout has been 62 percent of earnings.

Avon has come a long way since 1886. David McConnell, a 28-year-old door-to-door book salesman from Oswego, New York, found it easier to sell vials of perfume he offered as "door openers" to potential customers than the books he was selling. He began manufacturing perfumes in New York City, having set up his new firm, the California Perfume Company. That name appealed because of the positive image of California, he believed.

McConnell enlisted the support of Mrs. P. Albee of Winchester, New Hampshire. She made Avon's first call on a farmhouse in New Hampshire. Mrs. Albee was 50 years old then and was the first "Avon lady." She developed the selling network that characterizes Avon and made selling from door to door respectable. She was a neighbor calling on friends, not an itinerant peddler. The founder called Mrs. Albee the "Mother of the California Perfume Company" for her creation of the marketing channel used ever since.

McConnell's philosophy was: *Guarantee* high-quality merchandise and sell it from door to door with part-time salesladies. The firm grew and by the mid-1890s, McConnell's firm had six floors of a building in New York City and a manufacturing lab

---

[1] Year in parentheses is year Avon opened operations there.

**349**

in Suffern. In 1903, he wrote his autobiography *The Greak Oak,* which the firm distributes. He expressed his philosophy in it, and on the front of the 1972 Annual Report, the firm quoted from the book to reemphasize his philosophy. McConnell said (1903):

Our growth only emphasizes what energy and fair dealings with everyone can accomplish. We propose first to be fair with our customers by giving them the very best goods that can be make for the money; we propose to be fair and just, even liberal, with those who form the sinew of our business.

As we have grown in the past, so shall we grow in the future; the limit in this business is measured only by the amount of hard work and energy that is put into it. While we have worked faithfully and loyally in this field, yet if we stop and look over the past and then into the future, we can see that the possibilities are growing greater and greater every day; that we have scarcely begun to reach the proper results from the field we have before us. The millions and millions of people in this country of ours today, who are not using our goods, are the losers, and it is our place and our purpose to see that at least they must be made acquainted with the merits of the goods, the honesty with which they are made and delivered direct from the laboratory to the consumer.

The current philosophy of the firm—an interpretation of McConnell's growth philosophy—was recently given by the firm:

Since the first Avon Representative knocked on the first farmhouse door in New Hampshire in 1886, it has been as steady as that of the "Great Oak" in our founder's autobiography.

What causes such growth? We believe it is Avon's unique method of distribution and a special interplay of people, products and ideals that has survived unchanged for 86 years.

Of first importance to our growth is the earning opportunity offered to the Avon Representative—an excellent way for women to meet their financial objectives with expert guidance and assistance.

Behind this is the atmosphere of mutual trust and respect of the Avon employee toward the Company and toward the Representative and her customer . . . the result of our commitment to the development of people in every area of the organization.

Then, there is Avon's concern for consumers, who welcome the high quality of Avon products, the home-service convenience and personal attention of the Avon Representative.

Another important factor is Avon's unconditional guarantee of satisfaction on every product. Its importance grows as the number and variety of our products increase.

Finally there is Avon's involvement in every community which we enter. This is a natural development of our unique neighbor-to-neighbor method of selling.

Today Avon is a billion-dollar world-wide corporation providing a welcome earning opportunity to over 600,000 independent Representatives in 18 countries on five continents.

The "Great Oak" continues to grow, and to support our founder's belief, "As we have grown in the past, so shall we grow in the future."

By 1905, McConnell had 10,000 Avon ladies and opened his first branch office for sales and distribution (Kansas City). By 1929, Avon had 5000 Avon ladies and sales of $2 million. It was only then that the Avon name began to be used. McConnell believed it evoked Shakespearean images. So he changed the company name to Allied Products. Ten years later (1939) it became Avon Products, Inc.

By 1932, Avon had adopted another of its marketing strategies: 3-week sales promotion campaigns. Each 3-week period pushed specific products often with price reductions. The firm also encouraged regular calls on the same customers. While most firms' sales were declining, Avon increased theirs—almost doubled them by 1936.

In the mid-thirties, the firm elaborated its organization and marketing philosophy even more. Before then, the firm's concentration had been on small towns and rural areas. Now, they divided cities into smaller areas and assigned Avon ladies to specific areas. Company representatives lived in the towns and helped recruit, train, and motivate the Avon ladies in the city. By 1945, there were 25,000 Avon ladies. By 1954, *profits* were almost $5 million. A decade later, *profits* were over $36 million. Avon had come a long way, baby!

## The cosmetics industry

Cosmetics are big business. Government statistics, industry estimates, and analysts' figures place the sales at about $4 billion. The industry composition is about as follows:

| | |
|---|---|
| Small companies (hundreds) | 25% |
| Avon | 25% (depending on source) |
| 15 majors | 50% |

Revlon is the largest of the 15 majors, holding about 10 percent of the market. The next ten have about the same market share.

The sales breakdown in 1973 by product seemed to be as follows:[1]

| | |
|---|---|
| Skin treatment | $225 |
| Eye makeup | 175 |
| Foundation, powder, blusher | 250 |
| Lipstick | 150 |
| Nail enamel and nail care | 75 |
| Fragrance | 425 |

Some industry leaders' recent results are given in Tables 1 and 2.

There have been some major ownership changes in the industry recently which could have some long-range effects on it. Elizabeth Arden was acquired by Eli Lilly in 1971. Squibb Corporation acquired Lanvin and Charles of the

---

[1] Wholesale figures, in thousands. For retail figures, add 40 percent.

**TABLE 1 ■ RESULTS OF COSMETIC INDUSTRY LEADERS (1973)**

| | Earned per share | | | | Divi-dends[a] | Recent price | Yield | P/E ratio[b] |
|---|---|---|---|---|---|---|---|---|
| | Three months | | Annual | | | | | |
| | 1973 | 1972 | 1972 | 1971 | | | | |
| Alberto-Culver | $0.54[c] | $0.46[c] | $1.22 | $1.12 | $0.35 | 18 | 1.9% | 14 |
| Avon Products | 0.35 | 0.29 | 2.16 | 1.89 | 1.40 | 130 | 1.1 | 59 |
| Chesebrough-Pond's | 0.54 | 0.46 | 2.20 | 1.94 | 1.12 | 78 | 1.4 | 34 |
| Faberge Inc. | 0.22 | 0.20 | 1.30 | 1.14 | 0.40 | 9 | 4.5 | 7 |
| Gillette Co. | 0.70 | 0.59 | 2.54 | 2.13 | 1.50 | 58 | 2.6 | 22 |
| Revlon, Inc. | 0.71 | 0.62 | 2.88 | 2.66 | 1.00 | 61 | 1.6 | 21 |

[a] Indicated annual rate.
[b] Based on latest 12 months' earnings.
[c] Six months.
*Source: Financial World,* May 16, 1973.

TABLE 2 ■ RESULTS OF COSMETIC INDUSTRY LEADERS (1972)

| | Earned per share | | | | Divi-dends[a] | Recent price | Yield | P/E ratio[b] |
|---|---|---|---|---|---|---|---|---|
| | Nine months | | Annual | | | | | |
| | 1971 | 1970 | 1970 | 1969 | | | | |
| Alberto-Culver | $1.12[c] | . . . | $1.65 | $1.39 | $0.32 | 22 | 1.5% | 20 |
| Avon Products | 1.01 | $0.94 | 1.72 | 1.46 | 1.30 | 103 | 1.3 | 60 |
| Bristol-Myers | 1.84 | 1.78 | 2.42 | 2.20 | 1.20 | 56 | 2.1 | 23 |
| Chesebrough-Pond's | 1.48 | 1.35 | 1.76 | 1.73 | 1.04 | 59 | 1.8 | 31 |
| Cosmetically Yours | D0.19[d] | 0.05[d] | D1.48[e] | 1.03[e] | . . . | x5 | . . . | . . . |
| Del Laboratories | 0.88 | 0.77 | 0.75 | 0.42 | . . . | 13 | . . . | 15 |
| Faberge, Inc. | 0.58 | 0.02 | 0.41 | 1.67 | 0.40 | 17 | 2.4 | 17 |
| Factor (Max) | 1.07 | 1.10 | 1.60 | 1.56 | s0.60 | 34 | 1.8 | 22 |
| Gillette Company | 1.51 | 1.65 | 2.26 | 2.25 | 1.40 | 39 | 3.6 | 18 |
| Helena Rubinstein | 1.28 | 1.26 | 1.69 | 1.56 | 0.76 | 34 | 2.2 | 20 |
| Helena Curtis Industries | D0.03[d] | 0.18[d] | D0.76[d] | 0.40[e] | . . . | 7 | . . . | . . . |
| International Flavors and Fragrances | 0.71 | 0.65 | 0.87 | 0.78 | s0.42 | 52 | 0.8 | 56 |
| La Maur, Inc. | 0.59 | 0.72 | 1.04 | 1.37 | 0.36 | 14 | 2.6 | 15 |
| MEM Company | 1.10 | 0.84 | 1.83 | 1.72 | 0.72 | 23 | 3.1 | 11 |
| Merle Norman Cosmetics | 0.61[d] | 0.50[d] | 1.00[e] | 1.06[e] | 0.30 | 19 | 1.7 | 17 |
| Noxell Corporation | 0.82 | 0.71 | 0.81 | 0.71 | 0.38 | x41 | 0.9 | 45 |
| Revlon, Inc. | 1.89 | 1.81 | 2.56 | 2.33 | 1.00 | 68 | 1.5 | 24 |

[a] Indicated rate.
[b] Based on latest 12 months' earnings.
[c] Full year.
[d] Six months.
[e] Following year.

s—Plus stock.
x—Over-the-counter.
D—Deficit.

Source: Financial World, Jan. 5, 1972.

Ritz in 1971. Max Factor was purchased by Norton Simon recently, as were Shulton by American Cyanamid and Andrew Jergens by American Brands. Colgate Palmolive purchased Helena Rubinstein in 1972. British American Tobacco purchased Germaine Monteil in the late sixties. Of course, Avon competes with all the companies in the industry for cosmetic sales. But the channels differ. In fact, Revlon's vice president, Lawrence Wechsler, said: "They're not our direct competitor. They are a great distribution machine."

### HOME SALES

The goods and services sold in the home by door-to-door salespersons is estimated to be approximately $5 billion in the United States alone in the 1970s. Jay Van Andel, chairman of Amway, a not disinterested observer, predicted that in-home buying will exceed retail buying in conventional stores by the end of this decade.

Many products are sold in the home. Amway, Fuller Brush, Shaklee, and Stanley Home Products, for example, sell a wide variety of products direct to home purchasers.

Insofar as home sales of cosmetics and toiletries are concerned, Avon has dominated the field. In 1969, for example, the following firms sold the following amounts of *cosmetics and toiletries* in the home:

| | | Total sales |
|---|---|---|
| Avon | $ 463,000,000 | Same |
| Stanley | 29,200,000 | $117,000,000 |
| Fuller | 18,000,000 | 75,000,000 |
| Shaklee | 11,500,000 | 36,000,000 |
| Luzier | 5–10,000,000[a] | . . . |
| Fashion 2–20 | 5–10,000,000[a] | . . . |
| Mary Kay | 5–10,000,000[a] | . . . |
| Viviane Woodard | 5–10,000,000[a] | |

[a] Estimated.

Viviane Woodard was acquired by General Foods in 1969–1970. GF made noises about vast expansion plans for Woodard. Other home sales companies that are part of larger firms include: Luzier (Bristol Myers), Fuller Brush (Consolidated Foods), Vanda Beauty Counselor (Dart Industries), Studio Girl–Hollywood (Helene Curtis).

Fashion 2–20 operates throughout the United States and Canada, advertises in women's magazines, and promotes through the use of in-home shows—not door-to-door sales.

Dart's Vanda division is a result of a merger of Vanda and Beauty Counselors. It advertises in women's magazines and sells from door to door.

Bristol Myers's Luzier division has concentrated in the West, Southwest, and South. They also expanded into the big business in the late sixties.

Mary Kay of Dallas is strongest in the West and Southwest. It expanded next in the South. The firm tends to specialize in skin care products. Its sales in 1974 are close to $20 million. It is the fastest-growing of Avon's competitors.

**TABLE 3 ■ CONSOLIDATED STATEMENT OF FINANCIAL CONDITION, AVON PRODUCTS, INC., AND SUBSIDIARIES**
Year ending December 31

| | 1974 | 1973 | 1972 | 1971 |
|---|---|---|---|---|
| *Assets* | | | | |
| **Current assets** | | | | |
| Cash | $ 23,035,000 | $ 21,528,000 | $ 22,192,000 | $ 16,521,000 |
| Short-term investments | 157,590,000 | 176,983,000 | 161,328,000 | 130,403,000 |
| Accounts receivable (less allowance for doubtful accounts) | 89,926,000 | 83,459,000 | 68,188,000 | 56,416,000 |
| Inventories | | | | |
| Finished goods | 98,210,000 | 86,176,000 | 56,309,000 | 49,039,000 |
| Raw material | 121,685,000 | 91,331,000 | 69,193,000 | 61,075,000 |
| | 219,895,000 | 177,507,000 | 125,502,000 | 110,114,000 |
| Prepaid expenses | 35,943,000 | 32,307,000 | 25,396,000 | 20,263,000 |
| Total current assets | 526,389,000 | 491,784,000 | 402,606,000 | 333,717,000 |
| **Property** | | | | |
| Land | 19,763,000 | 18,873,000 | 18,791,000 | 18,544,000 |
| Buildings | 159,540,000 | 151,999,000 | 132,266,000 | 122,787,000 |
| Equipment | 123,103,000 | 109,768,000 | 92,110,000 | 72,863,000 |
| Construction in progress | 9,947,000 | 14,045,000 | 17,817,000 | 16,048,000 |
| | 312,353,000 | 294,685,000 | 260,984,000 | 230,242,000 |
| Less accumulated depreciation | 98,843,000 | 84,328,000 | 69,831,000 | 60,250,000 |
| | 213,510,000 | 210,357,000 | 191,153,000 | 169,992,000 |
| Deferred charges and other assets | 9,376,000 | 7,047,000 | 4,888,000 | 2,898,000 |
| | $749,275,000 | $709,188,000 | $598,647,000 | $506,607,000 |
| **Current liabilities** | | | | |
| Notes payable | $ 29,023,000 | $ 39,701,000 | $ 16,009,000 | $ 13,294,000 |
| Accounts payable and accrued expenses | 78,483,000 | 72,363,000 | 60,735,000 | 45,975,000 |
| Retail sales and other taxes | 29,973,000 | 24,620,000 | 24,620,000 | 30,919,000 |
| Taxes on earnings | 96,824,000 | 82,752,000 | 73,843,000 | 57,759,000 |
| Total current liabilities | 234,303,000 | 219,436,000 | 175,207,000 | 147,947,000 |
| **Long-term obligations** | | | | |
| Notes payable | 8,962,000 | 7,664,000 | 15,148,000 | 17,597,000 |
| 6¼ percent bonds | 8,820,000 | 10,458,000 | 11,973,000 | 13,494,000 |
| Other | 17,864,000 | 13,574,000 | 10,408,000 | 4,985,000 |
| | 35,646,000 | 31,696,000 | 37,529,000 | 36,076,000 |
| Deferred income taxes | 7,727,000 | 12,130,000 | 6,841,000 | 5,501,000 |
| **Shareholders' equity** | | | | |
| Capital stock, par value $.50 | 28,996,000 | 28,996,000 | 28,923,000 | 28,826,000 |
| Capital surplus | 38,806,000 | 39,061,000 | 25,702,000 | 10,757,000 |
| Retained earnings | 403,797,000 | 377,869,000 | 324,445,000 | 277,500,000 |
| | 471,599,000 | 445,926,000 | 379,070,000 | 317,083,000 |
| | $749,275,000 | $709,188,000 | $598,647,000 | $506,607,000 |

The firm merchandises through the use of in-the-home "parties" rather than door-to-door sales. The home demonstrations stress skin care products such as Magic Masque, Night Cream, Cleansing Creme, and these items equal more than half of the company's sales.

## Financial performance at Avon

Tables 3, 4, and 5 contain the traditional financial statements for Avon. Table 6 gives a multiyear financial overview.

**TABLE 4 ■ CONSOLIDATED STATEMENT OF EARNINGS AND RETAINED EARNINGS, AVON PRODUCTS, INC., AND SUBSIDIARIES**
Year ending December 31

|  | 1974 | 1973 | 1972 | 1971 |
|---|---|---|---|---|
| Net sales | $1,260,292,000 | $1,150,659,000 | $1,005,316,000 | $873,153,000 |
| Less | | | | |
| Cost of goods sold | 499,821,000 | 414,106,000 | 355,886,000 | 315,948,000 |
| Selling and administrative expenses | 521,733,000 | 470,005,000 | 394,603,000 | 336,011,000 |
| Earnings before taxes | 238,738,000 | 266,548,000 | 254,827,000 | 221,194,000 |
| Taxes on earnings | 126,983,000 | 131,398,000 | 129,898,000 | 112,057,000 |
| Net earnings | 111,755,000 | 135,150,000 | 124,929,000 | 109,137,000 |
| Net earnings per share | $1.93 | $2.33 | $2.16 | $1.89 |
| Cash dividends | 85,827,000 | 81,126,000 | 77,984,000 | 72,001,000 |
| Addition to retained earnings | 25,928,000 | 54,024,000 | 46,945,000 | 37,136,000 |
| Retained earnings, January 1 | 377,869,000 | 323,845,000[a] | 277,500,000 | 240,364,000 |
| Retained earnings, December 31 | $ 403,797,000 | $ 377,869,000 | $ 324,445,000 | $277,500,000 |

[a] Between 1973 and 1974, Avon adjusted retained earnings account by deducting $600,000 for research and development expenses.

**TABLE 5 ■ CONSOLIDATED STATEMENT OF CHANGES IN FINANCIAL POSITION, AVON PRODUCTS, INC., AND SUBSIDIARIES**
Year ending December 31

|  | 1974 | 1973 | 1972 | 1971 |
|---|---|---|---|---|
| **Source of working capital** | | | | |
| Net earnings | $111,755,000 | $135,150,000 | $124,929,000 | $109,137,000 |
| *Add* | | | | |
| Depreciation | 16,775,000 | 15,067,000 | 12,819,000 | 11,842,000 |
| Deferred income taxes | (4,403,000) | 5,289,000 | 1,340,000 | 972,000 |
| Working capital provided from operations | 124,127,000 | 155,506,000 | 139,088,000 | 121,951,000 |
| Additional long-term obligations | 3,950,000 | (5,833,000) | 1,453,000 | 1,288,000 |
| Sales of capital stock under options and related tax benefits | 1,255,000 | 13,432,000 | 15,042,000 | 5,671,000 |
| Total | 127,822,000 | 163,105,000 | 155,583,000 | 128,910,000 |
| **Use of working capital** | | | | |
| Cash dividends | 85,827,000 | 81,126,000 | 77,984,000 | 72,001,000 |
| Additions to property | 19,928,000 | 34,271,000 | 33,980,000 | 33,155,000 |
| Deferred charges and other assets | 2,329,000 | 2,159,000 | 1,990,000 | 2,898,000 |
| Decrease (increase) in long-term obligations | . . . | 5,833,000 | (1,453,000) | . . . |
|  | 108,084,000 | 117,556,000 | 112,501,000 | 108,054,000 |
| Total | 19,738,000 | $ 45,549,000 | $ 41,629,000 | $ 20,856,000 |
| **Increase in working capital** | | | | |
| Cash and short-term investments | 17,866,000 | $ 14,991,000 | $ 36,596,000 | $ 36,167,000 |
| Accounts receivable | 6,467,000 | 15,271,000 | 11,772,000 | 7,037,000 |
| Inventories | 42,388,000 | 53,205,000 | 15,388,000 | (4,959,000) |
| Prepaid expenses | 3,636,000 | 6,311,000 | 5,133,000 | 3,311,000 |
| Notes payable | 10,678,000 | (23,692,000) | (2,715,000) | 429,000 |
| Accounts payable and accrued expenses | (6,120,000) | (8,330,000) | (18,058,000) | (7,639,000) |
| Accrued taxes | (19,425,000) | (12,207,000) | (6,487,000) | (13,490,000) |
| Total | $ 19,738,000 | $ 45,549,000 | $ 41,629,000 | $ 20,856,000 |

**TABLE 6 ■ FINANCIAL REVIEW, AVON PRODUCTS, INC., AND SUBSIDIARIES**
(Dollars expressed in thousands except per-share figures)

| | 1974 | 1973 | 1972 | 1971 | 1970 | 1969 | 1968 | 1967 | 1966 | 1965 | 1964 | 1963 |
|---|---|---|---|---|---|---|---|---|---|---|---|---|
| **Net sales** | $1,260,292 | $1,150,659 | $1,005,316 | $873,153 | $759,171 | $656,660 | $558,587 | $474,814 | $408,178 | $351,990 | $299,449 | $248,594 |
| **Earnings before taxes** | 238,738 | 266,548 | 254,827 | 221,194 | 197,144 | 175,258 | 152,734 | 128,410 | 109,246 | 91,576 | 82,276 | 63,039 |
| Percent to net sales | 18.9 | 23.1 | 25.3 | 25.3 | 26.0 | 26.7 | 27.3 | 27.0 | 26.8 | 26.0 | 27.5 | 25.4 |
| **Taxes on earnings** | 126,983 | 131,398 | 129,898 | 112,057 | 98,156 | 90,965 | 81,424 | 63,027 | 53,918 | 44,007 | 42,437 | 33,596 |
| **Net earnings** | 111,755 | 135,150 | 124,929 | 109,137 | 98,988 | 84,293 | 71,310 | 65,383 | 55,328 | 47,569 | 39,839 | 29,443 |
| Percent to net sales | 8.9 | 11.7 | 12.4 | 12.5 | 13.0 | 12.8 | 12.8 | 13.8 | 13.6 | 13.5 | 13.3 | 11.8 |
| **Shares outstanding** (thousands) | 57,991 | 57,949 | 57,766 | 57,600 | 57,525 | 57,488 | 57,460 | 57,414 | 57,394 | 57,383 | 57,370 | 57,347 |
| **Per share of stock** | | | | | | | | | | | | |
| Net earnings | $1.93 | $2.33 | $2.16 | $1.89 | $1.72 | $1.46 | $1.24 | $1.13 | $0.96 | $0.82 | $0.69 | $0.51 |
| Cash dividend | $1.48 | $1.40 | $1.35 | $1.25 | $1.07½ | $0.90 | $0.80 | $0.70 | $0.57 | $0.45 | $0.36 | $0.31 |
| **Working capital** | 292,086 | 272,348 | 227,399 | 185,770 | 164,914 | 132,398 | 124,424 | 100,368 | 87,899 | 72,341 | 59,823 | 53,832 |
| Current ratio | 2.25 | 2.24 | 2.30 | 2.26 | 2.30 | 2.24 | 2.29 | 2.28 | 2.15 | 2.17 | 2.06 | 2.20 |
| **Property—net** | 213,510 | 210,357 | 191,153 | 169,992 | 148,679 | 134,502 | 103,131 | 85,518 | 70,621 | 57,749 | 49,815 | 35,655 |
| **Capital expenditures** | 19,928 | 34,271 | 33,980 | 33,155 | 23,780 | 40,400 | 24,000 | 22,100 | 18,000 | 12,500 | 17,100 | 8,300 |
| **Total assets** | 749,275 | 709,188 | 598,647 | 506,607 | 440,840 | 379,786 | 331,683 | 273,463 | 245,230 | 193,083 | 166,318 | 134,173 |
| **Long-term obligations** | 35,646 | 31,696 | 37,529 | 36,076 | 34,788 | 33,384 | 30,310 | 17,917 | 18,524 | 2,503 | 4,676 | 3,660 |
| **Shareholders' equity** | 471,599 | 445,926 | 379,070 | 317,083 | 274,276 | 235,224 | 201,854 | 175,123 | 149,334 | 126,833 | 104,962 | 85,827 |
| **Shareholders** | 36,000 | 34,800 | 36,700 | 35,700 | 34,000 | 29,100 | 28,500 | 26,800 | 25,200 | 23,800 | 20,000 | 12,800 |
| **Employees** | 26,900 | 27,200 | 25,100 | 23,300 | 22,100 | 20,800 | 18,300 | 15,700 | 13,900 | 12,200 | 11,300 | 9,700 |

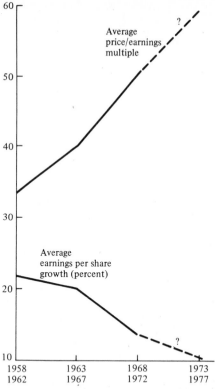

60 ─

Average
price/earnings
multiple

?

50 ─

40 ─

30 ─

Average
earnings per share
growth (percent)

20 ─

?

10 ─

| 1958 | 1963 | 1968 | 1973 |
| 1962 | 1967 | 1972 | 1977 |

**FIGURE 1** ■ Reality gap? Avon's adherents have created a new mathematics. The slower the rate of earnings growth, the higher they push Avon's multiple. Can the new mathematics long endure? From *Financial World*, Jan. 3, 1973.

The firm has been a darling of the stock market for years—a growth stock up there with IBM. Ten percent of the stock is still held by the family and two foundations named for the founder's daughter, Edna McConnell Clark. The founder's son, David McConnell, Jr., was president from 1937 to 1944. Hays Clark, grandson of the founder, is an executive vice president of Avon at present.

Although the firm has been a darling of most investors, in recent years, some investors have begun to ask questions. For example, one analyst recently proposed that there was a reality gap (see Figure 1).

An analyst in the *Wall Street Transcript* (Apr. 10, 1972) concluded his analysis with this comment:

The obvious conclusion is that Avon is well into middle age. A well-preserved middle age to be sure, but the bulges and sags are beginning to show. Looking at Avon with the eyes of a lover (and reluctant to pay capital gains taxes), faithful investors refuse to face this reality. For a while, at least, Avon's growth momentum will keep her admirers happy. But one day they will wake up and face the inescapable facts. If any number try facing them at the same time, the rush out of the stock could easily become a stampede.

*Financial World* (Jan. 3, 1973) pointed out that at that time 70 percent of the stock was owned by the institutions (56 percent), the founding family, the trusts, and directors and executives. One bank, Morgan Guaranty, owned $650 million. The P/E at the time was more than 64, and the article compared P/E ratios of the "glamour" stocks and their stock prices.

| | P/E ratio[a] | 1972[b] | 1973[c] |
|---|---|---|---|
| ARA Services | 33 | 30 | 27 |
| Avon Products | 64 | 61 | 51 |
| Baxter Laboratories | 76 | 68 | 57 |
| Burroughs | 48 | 47 | 39 |
| Chesebrough-Pond's | 39 | 38 | 34 |
| Coca-Cola | 47 | 46 | 41 |
| Disney (Walt) | 78 | 78 | 62 |
| Eastman Kodak | 46 | 45 | 38 |
| IBM | 36 | 35 | 32 |
| International Flavors | 70 | 66 | 54 |
| Johnson & Johnson | 59 | 57 | 46 |
| Kresge | 51 | 48 | 36 |
| Proctor and Gamble | 30 | 29 | 26 |
| Sears, Roebuck | 30 | 29 | 27 |
| Xerox | 47 | 46 | 39 |

[a] P/E ratio based on actual 1971 earnings.
[b] P/E ratio based on 1972 earnings estimate.
[c] P/E ratio based on 1973 earnings estimate.

*Financial World* pointed out that Avon controlled 80 to 90 percent of the direct-sales beauty market; yet because they control about 15 percent of total cosmetic sales, they are less likely to be subject to antitrust pressure. Yet Avon's price (at the time) was 20 times its book value that equaled $7.5 billion. *Financial World* concluded: "It is hard to justify such premium except by the wildest faith in the future."

By Christmas in 1973 it is clear that there were sales problems. The company reacted to less than fantastic sales by shifting to price merchandising.

The company executives explained that earnings declines were due to cost-price squeeze and depressed consumers. Avon's net for the second quarter of 1974 fell 19 percent. Earnings were 40 cents a share when many analysts had predicted 48 cents. Mr. Fusee, chairman and chief executive officer, announced that he doubted 1974 earnings would equal 1973. He stated (July 1974):

This current situation in no way lessens our confidence in Avon's future prospects. We continue to adapt our business to an inflationary climate, and these steps we believe will enable us to regain our traditional profit margins as economic conditions improve.

Earnings for the third quarter were 43 cents a share, down 11 percent from 1973 while sales were rising 12 percent. The nine months' results were down 15 percent from 1973.

## Operations at Avon

Avon's product line consists of 700 products, some of which are shown in Figure 2. The product distribution in the "main line" products is as follows:

**1** Women's fragrance and bath products (perfumes, bath oils and powders, sachets, etc.)    40–45%

(a)

(b)

(c)

(d)

(e)

**FIGURE 2** ■ ■ Some Avon products: *(a)* cologne and bath oil decanters; *(b)* dental products; *(c)* women's products; *(d)* men's products; *(e)* children's products. Photos courtesy of Avon Products, Inc.

**2** Women's makeup and skin care and other women's products (lipstick, eye shadows, eye and face makeup, cleansing creams, nail care products, hair care products, etc.)   25–30%

**3** Men's products (toiletries, shaving lotions, hair and skin care)   10–15%

**4** Other (children's and teen-age products, costume jewelry, and other products)   10–20%

Like many other companies, Avon introduces new products each year. Yet some of its best sellers are old standbys like Skin So Soft Bath Oil. Introduced in 1961, it leads its field and 1974 sold over 23 million units. Some older items like gift items were declining in sales.

Over the last few years, Avon has been diversifying its product lines into the "other" category. Some of these products are:

**1** *Costume jewelry*   This business was entered in 1970. By 1974, Avon's costume jewelry (see Figure 3) made Avon the largest distributor of costume jewelry in the United States. In 1974, the firm decided to build a manufacturing plant in Puerto Rico which will be operating in the latter part of 1975.

**2** *Needlecraft*   In 1972, Avon entered the creative needlecraft business. It offered a limited line of crewel embroidery kits in 1972. The prices were intended to be modest. By 1975, Avon decided to phase out of this business.

**3** *Family fashions*   Avon entered the mail-order men's and women's clothing business in 1973. The firm set up a distribution center in Newport News–Hampton, Virginia.

The first three of these are diversifications in the product line for the Avon sales organization. Two diversifications are away from the group and are considered corporate development.

**4** *Beauty shops*   Avon test-marketed 16 beauty salons in Atlanta, Dallas, and Denver. The test was discontinued in 1974 and Avon decided to continue its participation in the market with the 16 shops.

**5** *Plastic housewares: Genie in the home*   Avon purchased the David Douglas Company of Wisconsin for $5 million in September 1973. It entered the plastics housewares business in Canada. The method of selling the products in the home is similar to Tupperware parties. These parties are not run by Avon ladies, but with Tupperware's own organization.

Although eventually Avon expects to receive profit from these diversifications, these items led directly to a loss of $3 million in 1973 and the firm was expecting a larger loss from them in 1974, costing 7 cents per share in earnings.

One major aspect of marketing products such as Avon's is packaging. Packaging is pragmatic or cost-oriented with some products such as canned corn. But in the cosmetics business, the packaging is an important part of the product image and satisfaction. Avon has been so successful at its packaging that the packages, empty of their contents, are prized as collector's items. They are collected by many and are appearing for sale in antique stores, flea markets, etc.

Another important marketing tool has been the product guarantee, which reads:

### Avon Guarantee

If for any reason whatsoever an Avon product is not found satisfactory, it will be cheerfully exchanged or the full purchase price will be immediately refunded upon its return to us or to your Representative.

**FIGURE 3** ■ Costume jewelry. Photo courtesy of Avon Products, Inc.

The company believes that this has been crucial to its success in door-to-door distribution channels. With regard to labeling requirements, the company said in its recent annual report:

Avon took the lead among cosmetics manufacturers in listing ingredients on product labels. Additional steps were taken not only to inform the public about the Company and our products, but to encourage people to make comments and inquiries. Responding to the consumer right and need to know, our Consumer Information Center answered thousands of questions about the Company and our products.

As far as marketing promotion is concerned, the key is the Avon lady and support for her efforts. Like the other cosmetics companies, Avon supports its marketing efforts by major advertising campaigns. In 1972 Avon spent 1.7 percent of sales on advertising. Revlon spent 10.6 percent of sales. In 1974 Avon plans to spend 33 percent more on TV than in 1973.

But the main marketing effort is directed at the Avon lady. She is provided with sales brochures to use with her customers. In a recent year, Avon printed 250 million brochures. The brochures are well-developed four-color productions about recent economic reversals in 1973. Avon has done some price cutting. Avon issued "mini brochures" every 2 weeks for 8 weeks in 1973. These brochures were tied to sales or incentive programs which Avon called "inflation fighters." This was instituted in September 1973. The company emphasized lower-priced items and heavier discounts through the first quarter of 1974. Then these promotions were dropped.

The company also offers brochures which the Avon lady is urged to leave with her customers before the sale. These she must purchase from Avon for a small charge. They are smaller versions of the large brochures—about 55 pages and in four colors. The sales campaigns are of 2 weeks' duration.

The average territory size for each Avon representative is 200 families.

The firm also experienced trouble in Japan and Germany (among others) in recruiting and motivating women up to the Canadian-American productivity rates. The Japanese division finally made a small profit in 1974.

Like many other large firms, Avon maintains a research and development unit. The unit checks out all products for safety and quality. The National Quality Control Department helps check quality in manufacturing. The IBM 1800 Real Time Computer in the process control department also checks quality. In conjunction with the gas liquid chromatographic analytic instruments, the computer "fingerprints" fragrances to assure consistency in production. Of course, R&D also has a major role in new product development.

The Food and Drug Administration is exerting more influence over the industry, including Avon. Some people have proposed that FDA clear all new products before sale as it does in the case of new drugs. The industry is trying to self-regulate in such areas as controlling raw material quality and microbiological contamination. Avon and the big firms are better able to meet these requirements than the hundreds of small firms in the industry.

One of Avon's strengths has been close control of manufacturing costs. In the 1964 *Fortune* study of Avon, for example, the author pointed to these facts:

1  Cost of goods sold ratio 1964—34.9 percent; 1963—37.3 percent versus Revlon's 45.3 percent.

2  Advertising was 3 percent of sales in 1964 and total marketing promotion expenditure of 6 percent of sales. Competitors were much higher.

3  Very efficient production, including automation in the plants.

4  Lower cost of manufacture because of efficient purchasing of large quantities of raw materials.

Ten years later, Avon was still at cost cutting. Items:

1  Improved purchasing by lengthening planning periods of items. For example, cartons are now planned 16 weeks ahead, not 8.

2  Improved purchasing by better use of the computer to project cost of finished goods and raw materials too.

3  Product specifications now written to include alternative raw materials in case of price increases.

4  Lower costs of production at Monrovia, California, plant because of the use of computerized order assembly line. An order every 4 seconds is assembled into trays for each Avon lady this way. The firm has also purchased automated lipstick manufacturing equipment which automatically supplies lipstick ingredients, fills the lipstick, and labels and packs the product.

## The Avon lady

The early history of the company stresses that Avon treated its Avon ladies and its customers with gallantry and courtesy. Recently, this policy has been questioned, and it is claimed that Avon's system exploits its female employees and its independent businesswomen—the Avon ladies.

Several recent analyses of the Avon lady profiled these women as follows:

Marital status: Married or divorced

Wages and benefits: None. They are paid a commission of 40 percent above $100 sales, 25 percent below that.

Working hours: Average of 15 hours per week, although this is increasing since it is harder to find customers home. More are working themselves.

Job: Calling on customers, writing the order, collecting the funds, delivering the product.

Turnover: Most years 80 to 100 percent; in one recent year it was 126 percent.

Rewards: Commissions vary. One recent report said the average commission was $1460 per year. On the basis of a 15-hour week, this is less than $2 an hour.

Personality: Although this varies, one analyst described her as "having a strong personality and is a very forceful person."

Socioeconomic status: Middle class. Typical husband earns $6000 to $10,000 per year (in 1971).

In 1973–1974 the company had difficulty recruiting new Avon ladies. The person who recruits a new Avon lady is paid a $7.50 referral fee. Part of the problem is that 45 percent of women now work full or part time. When the recruiting got tough, Avon doubled the referral bonus for a short period. In 1975, the company reinstituted its earlier recruiting strategy. It pays Avon ladies $10 per referral, and most new representatives are acquired this way. Others respond to classified advertising, which is a more costly method. By 1975 recruiting was back to normal. At the end of 1974, Avon employed 10,000 more ladies than a year earlier.

The ladies are supervised by about 2300 female district managers. The DM recruits, trains, and motivates the Avon ladies, typically about 150 Avon ladies. They are paid $14,000 to $17,000 a year, which is a result of a small salary plus 3 percent on increase of sales in their territory. The DMs are supervised by over a hundred division managers, who supervise about 15 DMs. About 20 percent of these are women. Above the division managers are region managers, who in turn are supervised by branch managers. In the past, most of these two groups have been men. The typical branch manager makes $50,000 plus bonuses.

In 1974, Avon elected its second woman to the board of directors. In that year, about 65 percent of district managers and up (in management) were women.

Perhaps it would be useful to contrast Avon's policies with those of a competitor, Mary Kay. The firm is run by Mary Kay Ash and her son Richard Rogers. She is the only woman in top management. Mary Kay's representatives are called consultants. These persons run demonstrations in the home and do not sell from door to door. These 16,000 representatives are supervised by about 350 field managers, and both are strictly on commission. Representatives are recruited by referrals. The sponsor gets 4 percent of the wholesale sales of the new rep as long as she stays with the company.

The reps' commissions are: 40 percent of sales between $40 and $100; 45 percent between $100 and $500; and 50 percent over $500. Avon ships merchandise to its ladies on credit. Mary Kay requires cash or money orders (no checks) in advance.

Field managers earn 9 percent of monthly wholesale orders of $1000 for the field manager unit to +12 percent over $6000, plus the 4 percent on their recruits' production.

## Avon's future

Where Avon goes next is subject to interpretation. Where it is trying to go has been spelled out. In the 1973 Annual Report, the company set these objectives:

In order to realize the tremendous opportunities in the United States and internationally, we have established the following two major objectives:

First—to achieve greater penetration of the United States market, with special emphasis on improving the effectiveness of our field organization. It is our goal through better training and new programs for our District Managers to increase the number of customers served by Representatives and thus expand coverage of the country's households.

Second—to pursue the fine potential in foreign markets, which in total are several times larger than the United States. In so doing, it is our objective to improve the marketing programs and operating efficiency of our International operations and to raise their level of profitability to a point comparable with that of the United States.

They described their challenges in the same report as follows:

As we enter 1974, we recognize that many of the uncertainties of 1973 will continue to be with us during the current year and beyond. While we are convinced there are excellent markets for gift-type merchandise, we believe that today's consumer is principally interested in price, value and utility. Therefore, we are placing greater emphasis during 1974 on the promotion of our standard line products with heavy stress on price-value relationships.

The impact of shortages of materials and supplies upon our business is difficult to assess. In designing and developing new products we will be required to take into account the availability of materials such as glass, plastics and chemicals. Another consideration is the availability of paper for promotional communications, such as catalogs and brochures used by Avon Representatives. We are confident we can continue to make and supply attractive high quality products and provide the necessary promotional literature without serious impairment. It is evident, however, that there will be increases in the cost of many of the materials and supplies we use in these areas. To offset these additional costs, we will continue to exercise very close control over the other costs of our business.

As for gasoline shortages, at present our trucking and delivery services are able to transport our products to our distribution branches and to Representatives without major disruption. With regard to Avon Representatives, indications are that in most cases they are able to obtain sufficient gasoline, and they are finding more of their customers at home. However, we are making every effort to obtain fair and equitable treatment for Avon Representatives under any gasoline rationing program that may be imposed.

There are many gloom and doom analysts around. One financial analyst recently observed:

It would be risky, however, to assume that there remains infinite room for growth in so specialized a market. Just consider the implications of projecting Avon's numbers into the future: In the past decade Avon's earnings have grown from $25 million to $125 million, an annual compounded rate of 17.5%. If this rate should continue, Avon would be netting over $600 million a year by 1982, and grossing almost $5 billion. If it could achieve these figures, Avon would be earning somewhere around $11 a share in 1982, a rate of profitability that would justify the recent price of $130 a share.

But Avon's chances of keeping that pace are not very good.

In their enthusiasm, True Believers overlook signs of real trouble in Avon's profit paradise. There are unmistakable signs of maturation in the basic market and of only limited successes in diversification elsewhere.

Still another said (in part):

The simple fact is that Avon is now committed to a rate of growth that it cannot much longer achieve in its basic business. So it is branching out as a matter of necessity—but into areas, such as its catalog mail-order operation, that it may not fully understand. For this central question has yet to be answered: Will the company's management—in spite of its rich hoard of cash—commit the kind of money you need to succeed in the mail-order business? . . .

In any case Avon hasn't a prayer of achieving the kind of dominance—and profit margins—in fields like mail order selling or pottery that it has in door-to-door cosmetics.

But then Avon and others like it have fooled the analysts before and may do so again. Avon has made it clear that its goal in the mail-order fashion business is not to compete equally with Sears or Penney's. It plans to mail to customers seven to nine times a year and achieve a profitable share of market.

# Parkview Symphony

Marcia Blaine
Ichak Adizes

The Parkview Symphony is an established orchestra that has been a part of the community culture for 42 years. It grew out of a group of community people who wanted to get together to make music once a week for the enjoyment of it. Over the years the orchestra grew from 40 to 70 players, and continued to meet regularly. In 1935 a resident conductor was appointed, a man who had been the conductor of one of the German opera houses. After he took over the orchestra, Dr. Carlson used a very personal approach with the musicians, taking time to talk with them and get to know each one. As there was enough money in the growing budget, he saw to it that the musicians, all of whom had played for free up until then, received a small token fee for each concert performed. Many of the musicians developed a deep sense of loyalty to the orchestra and Dr. Carlson.

At this time, Dr. Carlson, now 85 years old, has been asked to retire by the board of directors of the Orchestra Association. The president, Mrs. Jans, remarked at a recent board meeting, "We feel that the orchestra and the community need a younger conductor—one who can spend less time in rehearsals (since our rehearsals cost us so much). We need someone who appreciates more contemporary music, but who wants to be involved with continuing the growth of our orchestra and the musical growth of our community. Dr. Carlson is truly a great person, but it is time for a change. Some of his tempi are getting slower each year. We have designed the current season of concerts to include three guest conductors . . . the best of Dr. Carlson's students from past years. Dr. Carlson was consulted and recommended these three to us. All are promising young conductors who have their own orchestras in surrounding areas, but would like to have a professional orchestra the caliber and size of ours."

At the close of this season, after all three guest conductors have presented their concerts, the board of directors and the manager of the orchestra will have to decide which (if any) of these three will replace Dr. Carlson. There will not be a lot of time to debate the issue, as the publicity and promotion for the next season will have to be started as soon

---

This is a disguised case. That is, the facts in it are based on a real organization. But the names of the persons involved, the location, and the quantitative data have been changed because the organization requested it. It serves no useful purpose to try to determine which organization is the "real" organization.

as the current season of concerts is over. The board has been urged to start thinking about each conductor as he gives his concert, so that when it is time to make a decision, it will be better prepared. A vice president of the board was overheard to say to another board member, "I don't know that much about music, but I know a good conductor when I see one. I don't think the decision will be too difficult to make." Another board member voiced the idea that "the orchestra needs a conductor who will be conscious of our financial situation, and make the most of the limited rehearsal time we can afford. With so many arts organizations going into the red these days, we can't afford to hire a new conductor who will spend our money unwisely."

The board of directors of the Parkview Symphony is made up of 30 community business leaders, society people, and cultural activists. The president of the board is also a board member for three other organizations, all of them nonprofit, but not arts-oriented. She also works as a paid administrative staff member at a hospital and manages a family of seven. Both of the vice presidents are businessmen—one a stockbroker and the other an architect. The treasurer also serves on the City Planning Commission and is an investment counselor. The superintendent of music for the public schools is a board member, as is a church organist, a singer, a woman from a wealthy Parkview family whose main interest is public relations, and several other prominent people. They may serve for two consecutive 3-year terms and then must rotate off the board for at least 3 years.

The season of the Parkview Symphony consists of ten concerts, given at the rate of about one per month for 10 months, excluding July and August. Of these ten, six are regular subscription concerts, one is a choral concert, one is a pops concert, and the other two are youth concerts, given in connection with the Parkview Youth Music Council.

For the last 5 years or so some of the orchestra players have wanted to have an orchestra player sit on the board as a voting member. The board, which is made up of cultural, civic, and business leaders of the community, feels that it has the ability to advise and make the policy of the Orchestra Association because its members can see things more objectively and have business experience. They do not believe the musicians possess these qualities. Mrs. Kinsey, the manager, says, "The orchestra members all know a great deal about music, and many of them have been with the orchestra for a long time . . . some ever since its beginning. . . . Some of them have jobs with various businesses during the day, and are professional musicians in the evenings and on weekends, but there has never been a player on the board. It's just never been done. The board knows what's best for the organization, and thus should satisfy our needs for guidance."

In view of the fact that a new conductor is to be chosen at the end of this season, the old argument about a musician on the board has begun afresh as the orchestra members feel that they want to have a say in who is chosen. At the last rehearsal the principal violist went to the manager and remarked, "I don't know how you feel about it, but we all would like to have something to say about who is chosen. After all, we are the ones who have to play under him, and work with him. If we as musicians aren't happy with the new conductor, we will either quit [the musicians are not on contract], or, you know, if the musicians are dissatisfied it will affect their playing. Many of us have worked with one or many of these conductors before, and we know how effective they are. Why, I've worked with Mr. Langdon for 7 years in other

## TABLE 1 ■ PARKVIEW SYMPHONY BUDGET PER YEAR

### *Receipts*

| | | |
|---|---:|---:|
| Individual memberships | $ 18,000 | |
| Individual contributions | 2,000 | |
| Business and professional contributions | 14,000 | |
| Season ticket sales | 20,000 | |
| Single ticket sales (subscription concerts) | 9,000 | |
| Program advertising | 5,000 | |
| City of Parkview | 24,000 | |
| County | 10,000 | |
| Youth Concert A (3:00 P.M.) | 2,500 | |
| Youth Concert B (4:30 P.M.) | 2,700 | |
| Benefits: | | |
|   Symphony Ball | 10,000 | |
|   Board of Directors' Benefit | 6,000 | |
|   Pops Concert | 3,000 | |
| Endowment fund interest and dividends | 1,300 | |
| | $127,500 | $127,500 |
| Restricted receipts: | | |
|   Student grants | $ 3,500 | |
|   Music library | 500 | |
|   Scholarship funds | 1,000 | |
| | $ 5,000 | |
| Total receipts | | $132,500 |

### *Disbursements*

| | | |
|---|---:|---:|
| Music salaries: | | |
|   Concertmaster | $ 675 | |
|   Conductor | 9,000 | |
|   Accompanist for soloists | 200 | |
|   Librarian | 300 | |
|   Contingency fund | 1,500 | |
| | $11,675 | |
| Orchestra | $48,000 | |
| Soloists | 15,000 | |
| Concert production (symphonic concert): | | |
|   Auditorium rent | $ 6,000 | |
|   Stagehands | 2,400 | |
|   Box office | 400 | |
|   Ticket printing | 600 | |
|   Music charges | 600 | |
|   Instrument rent and transfer | 800 | |
|   Miscellaneous | 100 | |
| | $10,900 | |
| Chamber concerts (all-inclusive costs) | $ 1,925 | |
| Youth concerts (all-inclusive costs) | $ 5,000 | |
| Promotion (for subscription concerts and chamber concert): | | |
|   Advertising | $ 4,000 | |
|   Mailings | 3,000 | |
|   Brochures and fliers | 3,000 | |
|   Posters | 2,000 | |
|   Membership campaign | 1,500 | |
|   Season ticket campaign | 3,000 | |
| | $16,500 | |
| Administrative salaries: | | |
|   Manager | $10,000 | |
|   Secretary | 4,000 | |
| Overhead: | | |
|   Rent (office) | $ 1,400 | |
|   Telephone | 700 | |
|   Supplies | 400 | |
|   Postage | 600 | |
|   Stationery | 200 | |
|   Insurance | 750 | |
|   Taxes (on property) | 200 | |
|   Audit | 100 | |
|   Investment council | 50 | |
|   Miscellaneous | 200 | |
| | $ 4,600 | $127,600 |
| Restricted disbursements: | | |
|   Student grants | $ 3,000 | |
|   Music library | 900 | |
|   Scholarships | 1,000 | |
| | $ 4,900 | |
| Total disbursements | | $132,500 |

orchestras and I know he is the best for our needs. None of them could measure up to Mr. Langdon."

Mrs. Kinsey, the manager, asked the violist, "Do all the other musicians agree with you that Mr. Langdon is the best?"

"No, but they don't know him as well as I do. Some of them prefer Mr. Lear and others have worked with Mr. Borges before. But the fact remains that we'd like to have some say in the choice. How are the board members going to be able to make a choice when they don't know what it is like to play under the man? Most of them haven't even been to a rehearsal of the orchestra."

"The board members have agreed to attend one rehearsal of each conductor so they will see each work. I'll remind them of this." Mrs. Kinsey concluded the conversation.

The next day Mrs. Kinsey called Mrs. Jans, the president of the board, to tell her of the conversation with the principal violist. The president assured the manager that the board was interested in what the orchestra players had to say, and that she herself would personally attend the dress rehearsal and ask for the orchestra's opinions. Then she could relay this to those board members who were unable to attend a rehearsal. When the dress rehearsals came about, very few members of the board attended them. Most board members were busy in their own companies and activities since it was the end of the fiscal year.

Mrs. Kinsey was also concerned about the board making the decision and hiring the right man to be the new conductor. She would have to push for the conductor who could not only keep costs down but make the most of the talent already in the orchestra, keep it growing, and be readily able and willing to stay in close contact with her and to help her coordinate the programs of the orchestra. These kinds of decisions always take so much time. After all, she had her job to do and could not spend all her time listening to musicians and boards. Some musicians, however, expressed their apprehensions over Mrs. Kinsey's desire to almost single-handedly suggest to the board who would be the future conductor. "She does not know much about music," they said. "She confused composers in our concert programs; she suggests combinations of music for concerts which do not make sense. She has no understanding of what is involved in conducting."

Board members, it appeared, were all too willing to rely on Mrs. Kinsey's recommendations since they did not have the time or the knowledge to screen conductors. Mrs. Kinsey, however, did not appear to feel responsible for the decision that was to be made, since it was the board's responsibility to appoint conductors, and if it failed in exercising this responsibility, it was again "another example of the impotency of our artistic boards composed of businessmen who are incompetent in the arts," she said.

Mrs. Kinsey was appointed as the paid manager of the Parkview Symphony after she had been an unpaid member of the board for 6 years. During her membership on the board she was active in fund raising and in social events for the orchestra. When the organization needed a manager, since its expenses had outgrown the abilities of a single secretary to handle them, Mrs. Kinsey was asked by the board whether she would undertake the job of a paid manager on a part-time basis. Being a housewife and having ample time, since her children were already in college, she accepted the position. After 2 years as

TABLE 2 ■ YOUTH CONCERT PRODUCTION COST PER CONCERT

*Orchestra personnel*

60 union members
10 students
―――――
70 musicians

| 2 rehearsals at $20 per musician | 2 rehearsals at $5 per student | |
|---|---|---|
| X 60 musicians | X 10 students | |
| $1200 | $50 | |
| X 2 rehearsals | X 2 rehearsals | |
| $2400 | $100 | |
| | | $2500 |
| 1 concert at $35 per musician | 1 concert at $15 per student | |
| X 60 musicians | X 10 students | |
| $2100 | $150 | |
| | | $2250 |
| | | $4750 |

*Production costs*

| Auditorium rent | $ 200 concert | |
|---|---|---|
| | 300 rehearsals | |
| | $ 500 | |
| Conductor | 1000 | |
| Librarian | 25 | |
| Concertmaster | 35 | |
| | $1560 | $1560 |
| Total cost | | $6310 |

a part-time manager, she became a full-time employee with a $10,000 salary per year.

"She loves the organization," said several board members. "She works hard," said several musicians. "I do the best I can," said Mrs. Kinsey, who knows all the board members on a first-name basis.

During the last 4 months the three guest conductors have each presented their concert with the Parkview Symphony and received praise from the critics. It is the close of the season and the board of directors and the manager have to decide among the three for their future conductor so that publicity and promotional material for the next season can go out and the season ticket campaign can be launched. Most of the planning for the coming season is based on who the new conductor is and promoting his image with that of the orchestra.

The current season included six subscription concerts, performed at the Civic Auditorium, using full orchestra and consisting of the classical works with which Dr. Carlson is most familiar. Of these subscription concerts one was an all-Beethoven program in memory of the composer's 200th birthday. Two youth concerts were given at Christmastime, using a movie star to narrate a musical Christmas Eve story; a dance troupe, including student dancers from the community; and a guest conductor whose specialty is youth concerts. These concerts were very well received by the children and their parents, and drew record crowds, filling the house to 80 percent capacity (attendance for subscription concerts is 60 percent capacity). Each June there is a pops concert given in a park as a benefit for the orchestra. A noted arranger wrote music specifically for this concert and the Parkview Symphony; and there are guest

## TABLE 3 ■ COST OF A SUBSCRIPTION CONCERT

*Orchestra personnel*

60 union musicians
10 students
‾‾‾‾‾‾‾‾‾‾‾‾
70 musicians

| 4 rehearsals at $20 per musician | 4 rehearsals at $5 per student | |
|---|---|---|
| X 60 musicians | X 10 students | |
| $1,200 | $50 | |
| X 4 rehearsals | X 4 rehearsals | |
| $4,800 | $200 | $ 5,000 |

1 1/2 hours overtime at $5 per half hour per union musician
          X 3 half hours
          ‾‾‾‾‾‾‾‾‾‾
          $15
          X 60 musicians
          ‾‾‾‾‾‾‾‾‾‾
          $900                                                          900
                                                                      ‾‾‾‾‾‾‾
                                                                      $5,900

| 1 concert at $35 per musician | 1 concert at $15 per student | |
|---|---|---|
| X 60 musicians | X 10 students | |
| $2,100 | $150 | $2,250 |
| | | ‾‾‾‾‾‾‾ |
| | | $8,150 |

*Production costs*

| Auditorium rent | $ 400 | concert | |
|---|---|---|---|
| | 600 | rehearsals | |
| | ‾‾‾‾‾‾ | | |
| | $1,000 | | |
| Stagehands | 250 | | |
| Box office | 90 | | |
| Conductor | 910 | | |
| Librarian | 50 | | |
| Concertmaster | 75 | | |
| | ‾‾‾‾‾‾ | | |
| | $2,375 | | $2,375 |
| | | | |
| Total cost | | | $10,525 |

artists asked to perform with the orchestra. A choral concert is given once a year in connection with a local chorale, a volunteer group of amateur singers which specializes in oratorios and cantatas. Dr. Carlson has taught them most of the well-known oratorios and performs one each year.

Parkview is far from being isolated culturally. It is a suburb of a large city which has its own prominent orchestra with a 45-week season, and a large Arts Center complex. It is only a 15-minute drive from Parkview to this large city, so that some of the audience that the Parkview Symphony draws is from other communities and the fringes of the large city. The community of Parkview also has a series of chamber music, a large art museum, and several beautiful and well-kept botanical gardens. There is a community Arts Council to coordinate the activities of the various arts organizations. This Council of 15 is made up of representatives of volunteer fund-raising groups, music educators, and business and civic leaders.

The audience that attends the performances of the Parkview Symphony is, for the most part, made up of members of the white upper and wealthy class. The community has an abundance of professional people—doctors and lawyers—who frequent the arts. However, there is a sizable minority community of Chicanos and blacks. None of these people attend the concerts. The average attendance at the subscription concerts is 1800. There is also a group of students who are regular attenders and take advantage of the student-rate tickets available to them. There are approximately 400 students at a performance of the orchestra, in an auditorium which seats 3000. In Parkview and its surrounding communities there are seven colleges, with a total student enrollment of 103,700. The total population of Parkview proper (excluding the students) is 89,000. The tickets at Parkview concerts are priced at $4, $3, $2.50, and $1.50 for students.

Some of the regular attenders have considered the Symphony such a part of their lives that when they passed on, they left bequests to the orchestra in their wills, adding to the Endowment Fund of the orchestra. Some of the gifts are in the form of stocks, cash, real estate, business equipment (typewriters, duplicators, desks, cabinets, etc.), and music.

In order to find more opportunities for the orchestra to perform, the management has tried having the orchestra play concerts in neighboring communities that involve a minimum of travel for the musicians (within 200 miles round trip). However, it does cost more to perform outside Parkview owing to Musicians' Union rules and regulations. Each musician must receive an average additional $28.25 per person ($6.50 to cover the cost of lunch and dinner, 15 cents a mile for transportation, and $3 cartage of his or her instrument) when they travel to another community. In most of the communities outside Parkview the auditoriums have a small capacity, making the possible income from ticket sales less, unless the prices of tickets are raised. The board of directors feels that, although the orchestra is not running a deficit, they cannot take on concerts where there is the possibility of a greater loss by traveling to another community. Therefore, the orchestra has performed only in the various auditoriums and parks of their own community for the last several years. Because the orchestra members are hired by the concert and are not on a yearly contract, it is not allowable by union rules for this orchestra to go on extended tours which would keep them away more than a day or two. Also, some of Parkview's musicians hold other full-time jobs during the week which they could not be away from to go on tour.

Each of the three guest conductors, having been a student of Dr. Carlson's, likes to put at least one classical piece on the concert. They all programmed one such work, along with a more modern piece, and one more obscure composition. None of them chose completely classical programming, as Dr. Carlson does, nor did any one of them program all contemporary music.

Although this orchestra is located in a heavily conservative Republican district, there are some blacks in the orchestra. They would like to see Mr. Lear appointed as the new conductor. Mr. Lear, who is a black himself, was a ghetto musician in New York. Through extensive education and hard work, he now has several offers as a guest conductor all over the country. His beat is easy for the musicians to follow, and his rehearsal technique was well received. He treated the musicians with respect, did not shout and scream when a mistake was made, and ended all of his rehearsals on time, keeping costs to a minimum.

While talking to one of the blacks in the orchestra, Mr. Lear expressed the desire to expand the community services that the orchestra provides if he were appointed as conductor. He also wanted to upgrade the orchestra by providing more outlets for performance and increasing the number of concerts each season, so as to give the musicians more work. One of the board members was

| TABLE 4 ■ MEMBERSHIPS IN THE PARKVIEW SYMPHONY ASSOCIATION | |
| --- | --- |
| 80 at $ 5 | $ 400 |
| 250 at $ 15 | 3,750 |
| 100 at $ 25 | 2,500 |
| 53 at $ 50 | 2,650 |
| 47 at $100 | 4,700 |
| 20 at $200 | 4,000 |
| 550 members | $18,000 |

talking with Mr. Lear backstage at the dress rehearsal for his concert. The board member asked Mr. Lear what he thought of the present policy of having 10 students in the orchestra, training under the professionals. Mr. Lear replied, "I think it is a great beginning, but we should go further. The youth of this generation are the adults of the future. Therefore, we must take music to them and educate them as to its values. You have to go beyond having 10 students in the orchestra, but rather take some of the concerts to the classrooms of the public schools, and to the underprivileged children. There is a lot we could do to serve the needs of the black and underprivileged children of this community."

Mr. Langdon came to his first rehearsal with the Parkview Symphony dressed in splashy sports clothes. He hurried to the podium to begin the rehearsal without speaking to any of the musicians or the manager. After rapping his baton on the side of the music stand to get everyone's attention, he loudly announced the work he would start with. His gestures and cues were exaggerated and showy. He asked the orchestra to play very loud at the end of his large work, "so as to give a display of our strength," he explained.

Mr. Langdon, when he spoke to Mrs. Kinsey, the manager, expressed a different view from that of Mr. Lear in relation to what he would like to do with the orchestra if he were appointed. "As our world gets smaller by virtue of advances in transportation and communications, music of an orchestra will not be unique unto that community. I feel that the Parkview Symphony should begin a touring policy, so that they can take their music to other places, and spread their name in this state and eventually others. After all, how will this ever become a big-name orchestra any other way?"

The third guest conductor brought with him a great deal of experience in setting up and running youth concerts. For many years, while he was getting started as a conductor, he had had to act as manager himself and run the whole orchestra. He founded two orchestras in that manner, and helped two more to expand their operations greatly, often into the educational areas and youth audiences. Yet, he treated the Parkview Symphony with full professional courtesies, and not as an orchestra that has just formed. He recognized the musical ability of the musicians and their desire to make good music.

During the first rehearsal, there were a lot of mumbles from some of the musicians who had played with Mr. Borges before. Mrs. Kinsey, sensing the unrest, asked the principal violist what was causing the distraction. His answer was surprising to Mrs. Kinsey, and to the board members when she relayed it to them. He said, "Many years ago I played in another orchestra that Mr. Borges was conducting. He always fancied the pretty girls in the orchestra, and teased them a lot. I guess he let it get out of hand that year and got involved with one of the cellists in the orchestra. His wife didn't know until the cellist left the orchestra when the other orchestra members all found out. This caused such a commotion in the community that Mr. Borges was asked to resign his position, so as to save the name of the orchestra. I understand that he and his wife separated. Some people never learn their lesson—I noticed him up to his old tricks with one of the violinists in this orchestra at the last rehearsal. I'd watch out for this man. He could cause a lot of trouble."

# Superite Dairies, Inc.

William F. Glueck

Superite Dairies, Inc., is the largest processor of dairy products in the Nashville, Tennessee, area. With over $8 million in sales in 1969, the company claimed about 40 percent of the area market in milk, ice cream, and related products. Its main products are given in Table 1.

## A history of quality

When asked why Superite has been able to maintain such a large share of the market, Mr. C. L. Litney, firm president, replied, "Our success can be summed up in one word: 'quality.' People buy our products because they are superior tasting compared to any others in the area. We've been able to keep national brands out of Nashville because they know they can't top our quality."

Superite's tradition of quality began with the founding of the company in 1929 by Thomas Baker. The former plant manager for a national dairy company, Mr. Baker emphasized efficiency and quality, and was able to keep the company on its feet during the Depression years. In 1938, he decided to get into the more profitable ice cream business, and purchased an existing combination milk and ice cream plant. At the same time, he hired James Hollingsworth, presently executive vice president, as marketing manager. The company grew rapidly in the following years. Mr. Hollingsworth initiated an aggressive marketing program, using methods never employed before in Nashville. Delivery trucks were painted bright colors, route salesmen were put in uniform, and a vigorous advertising campaign was inaugurated. The sales of milk expanded so rapidly that the space needed for the processing of milk crowded out the ice cream facilities. In 1942, Mr. Baker began seeking a new combination milk–ice cream plant. He decided to build a completely new plant, using all the latest features in plant design. Mr. Litney, who had been employed by a national dairy for many years and was thoroughly familiar with the ice cream business, was hired to supervise construction and manage the new plant. After the

This is a disguised case. That is, the facts in it are based on a real company. But the names of the persons involved, the location, and the quantitative data have been changed because the company requested it. It serves no useful purpose to try to determine which company is the "real" company.

**TABLE 1 ■ PERCENT OF SALES OF SUPERITE'S MAIN PRODUCTS**

| Product | Percent of sales |
|---|---|
| Superite milk (homogenized, whole milk) | 36.2 |
| Vita-cal milk (fortified, low-fat milk) | 21.8 |
| Superite ice cream | 14.0 |
| Delite frozen dessert | 8.4 |
| Other assorted products | 19.6 |
| Total | 100.0 |

new plant began operations, sales spiraled upward. The company rapidly passed its competitors in sales. Mr. Baker died suddenly in 1956, leaving Mr. Litney as the new president. Mr. Litney has continued the emphasis on quality and sales growth.

Much of Superite's success can be attributed to the lifelong devotion of its executives. Top management includes the following people.

*President: Charles L. Litney*  Fifty-eight years old, Mr. Litney has worked in dairy operations since graduating from a dairy institution 37 years ago. He has been described by fellow workers as "aggressive" and "hard driving." He has a fierce competitive instinct. He once remarked, "There are no rule books in this game. You kick them (competitors) while they are down, and keep kicking." Mr. Litney is very active in community affairs and recently held a top position in the local Chamber of Commerce.

*Executive Vice President: James D. Hollingsworth*  Mr. Hollingsworth has also spent most of his working life in the dairy business. A capable person, he moves more slowly than Mr. Litney, but seldom makes mistakes. He is regarded as Mr. Litney's closest adviser and confidant. Mr. Hollingsworth is well liked by Superite employees and spends much of his time in employee relations.

*Vice President of Sales and Promotion: Kenneth Baker*  The son of the founder, Thomas Baker, Mr. Baker has been with the company since graduating from high school in 1952. Mr. Baker is in charge of all promotions, but since the company has a contract with an advertising agency, he does little of the actual planning himself. Most of his time is spent in working as a liaison between Superite and the advertising agency.

*General Manager: Chester Hunton*  Mr. Hunton is office manager and head of accounting, finance, and purchasing functions. He has worked for Superite for 15 years. Before that, he was superintendent for a large dairy in Knoxville, Tennessee.

*Marketing Manager: William Starr*  Mr. Starr's main job is to maintain relations with the various retailers who handle Superite products. With Kenneth Baker, he aids in setting up displays, investigates complaints, and in general promotes goodwill between the company and retailers. He has worked for Superite only 2 years. Before that, he had a sales position with a national lumber firm.

*Assistant General Manager: Richard Rodewald*  Mr. Rodewald is in charge of production and quality control, including storage, maintenance, and fleet operations. He has 14 years of supervisory experience in dairy production and processing.

All of Superite's top officials are active in community affairs. Mr. Litney thinks that since Superite is a locally owned and operated business, "We have an obligation to be good citizens and to help Nashville grow and prosper to become a better place to live."

The company's organization is shown in Figure 1.

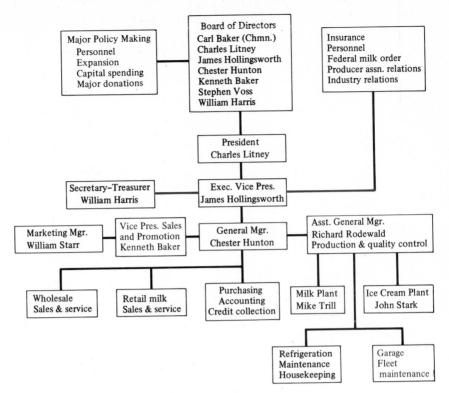

**FIGURE 1** ■ Organization chart.

## The dairy industry

Although 1968 saw the lowest total milk production since 1952 at 117.3 billion pounds, and a corresponding decline in farmers' sales of milk and cream, producer's cash receipts from milk sold to processors were $224 million more in 1968 than in 1967. Income in 1968 was up about $925 million over 1965, an increase of 18 percent in 3 years. Farm returns from marketing milk to processors and distributors have increased every year since 1962.

While milk prices the consumers paid were slightly higher in 1968 than in 1967, milk was the greatest bargain ever in terms of its "real" cost. In 1968, a half gallon of milk could be purchased for what an average production worker earned in 10.7 minutes. Twenty years ago about 6 quarts of milk could be obtained for an hour's wages; in 1968 an hour's earnings would buy more than 11 quarts.

In 1968, fluid milk and cream took 45.7 percent of the total milk supply up from 45.0 percent in 1967. Frozen products, cheese, and "other" products all substantially increased their proportions of the milk supply, while evaporated and condensed milk about held their share. However, butter and farm use lost ground.

Total fluid product sales gained 1.4 percent, whereas sales of milk in all dairy products held at about the 1967 level. Sales of low-fat milk products rose nearly 16 percent, the third year in a row that gains were more than 10 percent.

Total skim and low-fat milk items in 1968 were about 17 percent of the total sales of fluid milk and cream products compared to about 7 percent in 1970. Most of the decrease came from decreased sales of low-fat (2 percent) milk.

Dairy products contribute substantially to the gross national product of the United States, accounting for about 16 percent or $12.9 billion of the total value of food industry shipments in 1967. Fluid milk made up about 60 percent of the dairy product total.

The dairy industry is important to Tennessee as can be seen in Table 2. The milk industry is not equally important to all states, and some must import their

### TABLE 2 ■ MILK COWS, PRODUCTION, AND INCOME BY STATES, 1968 (AS OF JANUARY 1969)

| State | Milk cows[a] (thousands) | Value of cows and heifers Jan. 1, 1968 (1000 dollars) | Milk production (million pounds) | Average production per cow (pounds) | Cash farm income from milk Value (1000 dollars) | Percentage of farm income,[b] % |
|---|---|---|---|---|---|---|
| Alabama | 143 | 25,740 | 808 | 5,650 | 48,910 | 7.7 |
| Alaska | 2 | 665 | 18 | 9,830 | 1,807 | 44.4 |
| Arizona | 51 | 15,950 | 553 | 10,840 | 35,086 | 6.3 |
| Arkansas | 102 | 19,620 | 688 | 6,750 | 36,542 | 3.8 |
| California | 781 | 262,880 | 8,950 | 11,460 | 470,286 | 11.0 |
| Colorado | 99 | 25,300 | 844 | 8,530 | 48,153 | 5.1 |
| Connecticut | 67 | 25,550 | 680 | 10,150 | 45,208 | 28.2 |
| Delaware | 15 | 4,480 | 134 | 8,930 | 8,063 | 6.5 |
| Florida | 182 | 45,360 | 1,554 | 8,540 | 115,123 | 9.4 |
| Georgia | 139 | 28,120 | 1,041 | 7,490 | 64,544 | 6.3 |
| Hawaii | 14 | 6,900 | 134 | 9,930 | 12,619 | 6.1 |
| Idaho | 156 | 44,460 | 1,454 | 9,320 | 60,352 | 11.4 |
| Illinois | 330 | 96,195 | 3,109 | 9,420 | 147,911 | 5.7 |
| Indiana | 252 | 69,870 | 2,434 | 9,660 | 127,731 | 9.3 |
| Iowa | 569 | 157,300 | 5,178 | 9,100 | 215,303 | 6.1 |
| Kansas | 212 | 55,125 | 1,717 | 8,100 | 83,768 | 5.4 |
| Kentucky | 367 | 84,000 | 2,510 | 6,840 | 116,312 | 15.1 |
| Louisiana | 180 | 34,650 | 1,033 | 5,740 | 64,897 | 10.3 |
| Maine | 69 | 22,040 | 598 | 8,670 | 37,506 | 18.1 |
| Maryland | 170 | 53,360 | 1,513 | 8,900 | 91,527 | 26.6 |
| Massachusetts | 69 | 25,125 | 695 | 10,070 | 47,358 | 29.8 |
| Michigan | 473 | 152,195 | 4,588 | 9,700 | 244,928 | 28.3 |
| Minnesota | 1,057 | 303,690 | 10,263 | 9,710 | 425,562 | 23.5 |
| Mississippi | 209 | 37,280 | 1,093 | 5,230 | 59,439 | 7.5 |
| Missouri | 380 | 86,520 | 3,059 | 8,050 | 139,713 | 10.2 |
| Montana | 46 | 11,520 | 356 | 7,740 | 15,589 | 3.3 |
| Nebraska | 210 | 55,590 | 1,659 | 7,900 | 65,540 | 3.9 |
| Nevada | 14 | 4,125 | 137 | 10,020 | 7,425 | 12.6 |
| New Hampshire | 39 | 13,760 | 360 | 9,240 | 22,200 | 38.6 |
| New Jersey | 79 | 29,930 | 810 | 10,250 | 48,886 | 18.9 |
| New Mexico | 38 | 8,385 | 315 | 8,290 | 20,195 | 6.0 |
| New York | 1,039 | 379,220 | 10,203 | 9,820 | 557,058 | 54.1 |
| North Carolina | 193 | 39,035 | 1,475 | 7,640 | 86,182 | 7.2 |
| North Dakota | 156 | 42,000 | 1,164 | 7,460 | 38,431 | 5.3 |
| Ohio | 475 | 135,810 | 4,512 | 9,500 | 144,890 | 19.8 |
| Oklahoma | 155 | 33,200 | 1,283 | 8,280 | 66,969 | 7.9 |
| Oregon | 113 | 27,600 | 971 | 8,590 | 51,448 | 10.2 |
| Pennsylvania | 728 | 277,100 | 6,916 | 9,500 | 407,664 | 44.8 |
| Rhode Island | 8 | 2,760 | 80 | 9,880 | 5,202 | 26.0 |
| South Carolina | 72 | 12,920 | 514 | 7,140 | 33,005 | 8.8 |
| South Dakota | 202 | 55,640 | 1,640 | 8,120 | 64,358 | 6.7 |
| Tennessee | 329 | 65,120 | 2,115 | 6,430 | 106,329 | 17.2 |
| Texas | 365 | 72,930 | 2,982 | 8,170 | 183,660 | 6.8 |
| Utah | 75 | 21,320 | 759 | 10,120 | 38,970 | 20.5 |
| Vermont | 209 | 75,400 | 1,873 | 8,960 | 110,056 | 76.9 |
| Virginia | 231 | 51,865 | 1,763 | 7,630 | 96,366 | 18.9 |
| Washington | 186 | 58,000 | 1,953 | 10,500 | 106,807 | 13.4 |
| West Virginia | 67 | 12,600 | 425 | 6,340 | 21,429 | 21.5 |
| Wisconsin | 1,887 | 628,200 | 18,210 | 9,650 | 807,256 | 54.9 |
| Wyoming | 20 | 4,700 | 158 | 8,110 | 6,954 | 3.3 |
| United States | 13,024 | 3,801,105 | 117,281 | 9,006 | 5,861,517 | 13.5 |

[a] Average number on farms during year, excluding heifers not yet fresh.
[b] Based on data in column 5 and preliminary estimates of total cash receipts from farm marketings.
*Source:* United States Dairy Association.

TABLE 3 ■ PER CAPITA SALES OF FLUID AND MANUFACTURED DAIRY PRODUCTS IN THE UNITED STATES, 1950, 1955, AND 1958 TO 1968[a]

| | Fluid products | | | | | | Butter | Cheese[c] | | | Manufactured products | | | | Frozen desserts |
|---|---|---|---|---|---|---|---|---|---|---|---|---|---|---|---|
| Year | Total fluid milk products | Fresh whole milk | Cream | Skim milk or low-fat items[b] | Condensed whole milk | Evaporated whole milk | | American | Other | Cottage cheese[d] | Dry whole milk | Nonfat dry milk | Evaporated and condensed skim milk[e] | Net milk used[f] | Ice cream product weight |
| | Qt | Qt | Qt | Qt | Lb | Lb | Lb | Lb | Lb | Lb | Lb | Lb | Lb | Lb | Lb |
| 1950 | 141.7 | 129.3 | 5.2 | 7.2 | 2.0 | 18.5 | 9.1 | 5.4 | 2.2 | 3.1 | 0.3 | 3.5 | 5.1 | 45.6 | 17.6 |
| 1955 | 148.7 | 134.9 | 4.5 | 9.3 | 2.0 | 14.5 | 7.5 | 4.8 | 2.5 | 3.9 | .3 | 4.9 | 4.6 | 49.7 | 18.4 |
| 1958 | 147.3 | 133.0 | 4.4 | 9.9 | 2.4 | 12.5 | 7.1 | 4.7 | 2.6 | 4.6 | .3 | 4.7 | 4.2 | 50.6 | 18.2 |
| 1959 | 145.4 | 130.7 | 4.3 | 10.4 | 2.5 | 12.0 | 6.9 | 5.0 | 2.8 | 4.7 | .3 | 5.4 | 4.5 | 53.1 | 19.0 |
| 1960[g,h] | 143.7 | 128.4 | 4.3 | 11.0 | 2.5 | 11.4 | 6.8 | 5.3 | 2.9 | 4.8 | .3 | 5.6 | 4.4 | 52.5 | 18.7 |
| 1961 | 140.7 | 124.7 | 4.1 | 11.9 | 2.6 | 10.8 | 6.4 | 5.5 | 2.9 | 4.6 | .3 | 5.3 | 4.7 | 52.4 | 18.3 |
| 1962 | 140.2 | 123.7 | 4.0 | 12.5 | 2.3 | 10.2 | 6.3 | 5.3 | 3.1 | 4.6 | .3 | 5.1 | 4.8 | 52.4 | 18.2 |
| 1963 | 141.4 | 124.4 | 3.9 | 13.3 | 2.2 | 9.5 | 5.9 | 5.4 | 3.1 | 4.6 | .3 | 4.9 | 4.5 | 52.7 | 18.3 |
| 1964[g] | 141.6 | 123.3 | 3.7 | 14.6 | 2.3 | 9.1 | 5.9 | 5.4 | 3.2 | 4.7 | .3 | 5.1 | 4.7 | 53.6 | 18.5 |
| 1965 | 142.1 | 122.8 | 3.6 | 15.7 | 2.2 | 8.6 | 5.8 | 5.7 | 3.4 | 4.6 | .3 | 4.8 | 5.0 | 54.5 | 18.7 |
| 1966 | 141.8 | 120.9 | 3.4 | 17.5 | 2.0 | 7.9 | 5.4 | 6.2 | 3.6 | 4.6 | .3 | 5.2 | 5.3 | 53.6 | 18.4 |
| 1967 | 138.4 | 115.8 | 3.1 | 19.5 | 1.9 | 7.1 | 4.9 | 6.0 | 3.6 | 4.5 | .3 | 5.0 | 5.0 | 53.2 | 18.1 |
| 1968[g,i] | 138.8 | 113.5 | 3.0 | 22.3 | 1.8 | 6.6 | 4.9 | 6.1 | 4.0 | 4.6 | .2 | 5.2 | 4.7 | 54.6 | 18.8 |

[a] Excludes milk used on farms where produced and distribution from USDA supplies, includes sales to the Armed Services for use in the United States. Based on resident population, except fluid milk product sales are based on estimated population using fluid products from purchased sources.
[b] Includes natural and cultured buttermilk and all skim items, including quantities used in flavored drinks.
[c] Whole and part whole milk cheese (excluding cottage, pot, and bakers').
[d] Includes minor quantities of other skim milk cheese.
[e] Includes evaporated and condensed buttermilk.
[f] Amount of milk (equivalent) used in making ice cream and other frozen products, excluding approximate quantities supplied in the form of butter and condensed whole milk.
[g] Leap year, one additional day of consumption.
[h] Beginning 1960, figures include Alaska and Hawaii.
[i] Preliminary.
Source: U.S. Department of Agriculture.

milk from neighboring areas. Table 2 presents industry data on production and income of the dairy industry in the United States.

Tables 3 and 4 present recent statistics on industry sales and supply for the dairy industry.

In the Nashville area, there are four other processors besides Superite. The largest of these, Hillsdale Dairy, accounts for 22 percent of the area market. Over the years, Superite has steadily increased its market share at the expense of its competitors. In recent years this growth has slowed, and Hillsdale, which markets low- to medium-priced products, has made some gains.

Within the past 8 years two companies have been formed to compete directly with Superite. Soon after the first opened, a mysterious fire destroyed the entire plant. The second plant was closed by a prolonged and extremely violent truck drivers' strike. Neither plant has attempted to reopen. Some store owners, probably not friendly to Superite, implied that Superite had engineered these "misfortunes" by ties with unsavory elements on the fringes of the union movement or even the underworld. Recently, Sealtest, a large national dairy, announced that it would soon begin selling in the Nashville area. At this writing, over one-third of the retail food stores in the area have made preliminary agreements with Sealtest to handle their products.

| Fluid items | 1960 % | 1963 % | 1964 % | 1965 % | 1966 % | 1967 % | 1968 % |
|---|---|---|---|---|---|---|---|
| Whole milk[b] | 87.6 | 85.4 | 84.5 | 83.7 | 82.1 | 80.4 | 78.5 |
| Flavored whole milk | 2.0 | 2.4 | 2.5 | 2.6 | 2.7 | 2.6 | 2.5 |
| Total whole milk items | 89.6 | 87.8 | 87.0 | 86.3 | 84.9 | 83.1 | 81.1 |
| Low-fat (2%) milk | c | c | c | c | 6.5 | 8.3 | 9.9 |
| Plain | c | c | c | c | 1.6 | 2.0 | 2.2 |
| Solids added | c | c | c | c | 5.0 | 6.3 | 7.6 |
| Skim milk | 4.6 | 6.8 | 7.8 | 8.6 | 3.7 | 3.7 | 4.0 |
| Plain | 1.8 | 2.5 | 2.6 | 2.8 | 1.4 | 1.4 | 1.3 |
| Solids added | 2.8 | 4.4 | 5.1 | 5.9 | 2.2 | 2.2 | 2.7 |
| Buttermilk[d] | 2.2 | 1.9 | 1.9 | 2.0 | 2.0 | 2.0 | 2.0 |
| Flavored milk drinks | 0.6 | 0.7 | 0.7 | 0.7 | 0.7 | 0.8 | 0.9 |
| Total skim and low-fat milk items | 7.4 | 9.5 | 10.4 | 11.3 | 12.9 | 14.7 | 16.8 |
| Milk and cream mixtures | 1.7 | 1.6 | 1.5 | 1.3 | 1.3 | 1.2 | 1.2 |
| Light cream | 0.6 | 0.4 | 0.4 | 0.4 | 0.3 | 0.3 | 0.2 |
| Heavy cream | 0.3 | 0.3 | 0.3 | 0.3 | 0.2 | 0.2 | 0.2 |
| Sour cream | 0.2 | 0.3 | 0.3 | 0.3 | 0.3 | 0.3 | 0.3 |
| Total cream items | 1.2 | 1.0 | 0.9 | 0.9 | 0.8 | 0.8 | 0.7 |
| Eggnog | 0.1 | 0.1 | 0.1 | 0.1 | 0.2 | 0.2 | 0.2 |
| Total fluid milk and cream | 100.0 | 100.0 | 100.0 | 100.0 | 100.0 | 100.0 | 100.0 |

[a] Individual items may not add to total; owing to rounding.
[b] Includes whole milk equivalent of small quantity of concentrated milk.
[c] Included with skim milk.
[d] Includes small quantities of yogurt and cultured specialties.

## The human problems at Superite

Most of Superite's 300 employees are engaged in unskilled or semiskilled tasks. Most of the labor hired has had no prior dairy experience, and it is the responsibility of the individual departments to train them through on-the-job training. The more skilled workers and supervisors get some training from nearby colleges and through Superite's own training programs. Employees are sometimes sent to participate in educational programs presented by associations such as the Milk Industry Foundation or the International Association of Ice Cream Manufacturers.

Pay received by Superite employees is consistent with pay scales in the Nashville area. Although not high by national standards, it is deemed "adequate" for this locality. A number of benefits are offered to employees. After 15 years of service, employees are entitled to retire with a pension. Insurance policies are offered to employees on a "half-and-half" basis, meaning that the employees pay half of the insurance premium and Superite pays the remainder. Such policies cover medical and hospitalization expenses for the entire family. The pension plan is funded entirely by Superite.

Superite plant employees do not belong to a union. One attempt has been made to unionize these employees. In this instance, a union, without identifying itself as such, sent out cards to the employees asking them questions such as "Would you like to make more money?" and "Do you want shorter hours, longer vacations?" Later, the union notified the management that it had the signatures of the employees and that they wished to unionize. Mr. Hollingsworth reported that they paid little attention to the union effort, and the employees, upon learning of the union involvement, did not pursue the matter further.

But the drivers are unionized. They have shifted back and forth between the Teamsters Union and a smaller Milk Drivers Union. One individual close to the company told the case writer that at times the management found "ways" to keep labor trouble (slowdowns, strikes, etc.) low by being very friendly with union leaders. One member of management supposedly met the union leader regularly in private to "talk things over." Superite had so little labor trouble that some union members suspected that the manager exchanged more than talk with the labor leader. Of course, Superite had to walk a tightrope when the two unions were battling over representation rights and there had been minor violence, mostly roughing up of drivers at times like that.

It is known that the union would like to get the plant employees to join and may be putting pressure on Superite to "encourage" them to join. When asked if union problems were a major concern of Superite, Mr. Hollingsworth said, "I think union problems are *the* major problem Superite has."

## Processing Superite products

Milk is produced at a rate of about 26,000 gallons per day by Superite. Superite purchases all fresh milk from a dairy co-op (116 producers) at prices set by the Federal Milk Marketing Order. Quality control begins with the purchase of milk. Mr. Hunton said that the best check for quality products is to make sure that only Grade A milk is purchased from the farmers in the first place. All drivers of the tank trucks are licensed milk testers and have the responsibility of checking the milk for quality, smell, and taste.

After the milk is delivered by the company-owned tank trucks, samples are taken for laboratory tests. Then the milk is approved for quality and it goes into giant stainless steel refrigerated storage tanks, where it is held at a temperature of 35°. From there, it is first preheated, and then run through stainless steel pipes to the homogenizer. In the homogenizer, the milk is subjected to high pressures which force the cream to be distributed evenly throughout the milk. After homogenization, the milk is piped to the pasteurizer, where it is heated to a temperature of 163° for 15 seconds. It is then put in bottles or cartons and sent to the cold storage room to await delivery. Mr. Hunton tries to keep a 1-day inventory of milk.

The equipment used to make ice cream is of the latest in design. Fully automatic, it features an electronic quality control device which constantly monitors quality, assuring that all output meets standards for taste, content, and texture. A 3-day inventory of ice cream is carried in the frozen storage vault. Mr. Hunton emphasized that ice cream does not age appreciably and can be kept for up to 3 years if the proper temperatures are maintained.

In addition to milk and ice cream, the company produces a variety of other dairy products, including whipping cream, half and half, cottage cheese, sour cream, and sour-cream party dips. Superite finds it more practical to buy some products from outside than to produce them. Cottage cheese, for example, is imported from Missouri. Milk is used to produce all Superite products. One quart of milk weighs 2.15 pounds.

The quantity of milk actually used to produce 1 pound of each product depends chiefly upon the butterfat test of the milk, and this varies in different sections of the country and, to some extent, with the season.

Milk is presently being produced on an 8-hour shift at about 50 percent of capacity; ice cream production is running nearly 100 percent of capacity on a 14-hour shift. The production volume of each product varies according to the season, with ice cream output reaching a peak in April, May, June, July, and August, and milk output rising in October, November, December, January, and February.

"Our ice cream capacity is actually rather flexible," said Mr. Hunton. "Right now, we could increase our capacity by as much as 35 percent by not changing flavors as often. To change flavors requires 20 minutes of downtime on the freezer so that it may be cleaned. Still, I can see the time, probably within 1.5 years, when we won't be able to produce enough to meet our needs. One way of alleviating this problem would be to add more frozen storage space, so that we could stockpile in the winter months." Presently, about 50 percent of total ice cream production is vanilla-flavored, 11 percent German chocolate, 10 percent chocolate, 9 percent strawberry, and 20 percent in about eight other flavors.

Superite is proud of its quality products. All products exceed the minimum standards set by the government. For example, Superite ice cream contains 12 percent butterfat by weight, whereas the specified minimum is 10 percent. "We could sacrifice just a little quality and obtain great savings in our production costs," said Mr. Litney, "but in the end, we'd just be cutting our own throats. Our quality is our best promotion."

Management is convinced that "the *package* sells the product." Recently, Superite introduced double-coated (inside and out) ice cream cartons. Although more costly than normal cartons, they prevent moisture leakage which gives cartons that "bulging at the sides" look. "All the advertising in the world will do no good if a housewife picks up a carton which is slimy to the touch or unattractive," remarked Mr. Hollingsworth. Ice cream bearing the Superite trademark Princess label is sold in round cartons, which are supposed to add to the quality image.


## The Nashville market

Superite's main sales effort is aimed at the retail grocery market, since this is where management feels that the most profit is. Virtually every major food store in Nashville handles Superite products. "There's simply no one else around here selling Superite quality," said one retailer. Another retailer, when asked why he thought no one was competing with Superite, said, "Everyone knows that someone's looking out for Charles Litney. He's got this town 'sewed up.' People seem to have more than their share of problems if they try to compete with him."

Yet, few retailers are complaining about the situation. They feel that the prices they pay for Superite products are reasonable, and that the products are good. Many retailers said that they would be willing to handle Sealtest products in addition to Superite products, but only because they wanted to give the customers a broader range of selection, not because they were dissatisfied with Superite products. There is only one national chain food store in the city; the rest are locally owned.

In addition to the food stores, Superite sells to hospitals, schools, lunch counters, and various other institutions. Superite bids for the milk contract at the public schools, although there is little profit in this business. The purpose of school sales is to "keep the Superite name in front of the kids." Such sales amount to about $200,000 per year. School accounts are payable 60 to 90 days after delivery. It would be possible for Superite to bid for the milk contract at a nearby military installation, but since profit margins would be slim, and since the inhabitants would not be long-run potential buyers of Superite products, this has not been done.

"Bid business is a ruthless one. You gain or lose a bid on fractions of a cent per carton. At times, we wonder if this business is worth all the effort, time, and grief it involves," said Mr. Baker. "When it's all said and done, we probably lose money on this business. But what with our production situation on milk, we hang on, but we're not sure how long we should."

Another part of the milk business is the home delivery business. This is more competitive than retail store business. Maintenance of the trucks, labor problems with the drivers, and the detailed records involved are factors Superite considers. Again the management feels that it keeps the name before the public and of course it builds volume. About 45 percent of their milk sales are through home delivery, but tend to be much less profitable than retail store business.

Frequently other dairies whose volume is low will try to take some of Superite's home delivery business away from them. They usually do this by offering discounts for an introductory period to the homemakers. Superite drivers usually match these, and so a small milk war can develop. One device Mr. Starr has found effective in stopping a milk war was explained by him.

"In an area where there is a war, I'll go into a large grocery store where I'm not known. I'll fill my basket and take some of the competitor's milk. When I get to the checkout and the clerk starts to ring up the price, I'll say, 'Hey, what's the matter with you? You're charging X cents for a quart of milk. My sister can get that brand delivered at home for 3 cents a quart lower [the price the war has brought it down to].' At this point, I say, 'Well, if that's what you charge for things here, I don't want any' and I stalk out of the store. This usually makes quite a scene for I always pick a busy time. The retailer then puts pressure on the competing dairy wanting to know why they are underselling him with home delivery business. Since the retail business is more profitable, frequently the competition then reduces the fervor of its home delivery expansion plans."

Superite does not have a formal policy for new product development. "We use the old time-honored method of trial and error," said Mr. Litney. "There are four factors that determine whether or not a product will succeed: (1) there must be a demand for that product, (2) it must be conveniently available, (3) the product must be the best, and (4) the public must be made aware of it through advertising." Mr. Litney said that they depended on flavor and ingredient suppliers for new ideas, and that some suggestions came from employees. The company is presently considering the addition of novelty treats, such as ice cream bars and ice cream sandwiches, to its product line. Similar items sold in Nashville are now supplied by an Illinois firm.

A local advertising agency, Miller-Brown Advertising Company, has handled Superite's advertising for many years. Once a week, usually on Wednesday, a member of the Miller-Brown staff meets with Mr. Baker and Mr. Starr to plan promotional activities. Most advertising is done inside the retail stores and includes displays and "flavor-of-the-month" sales. Each month, one flavor of Princess ice cream is selected to be sold at special prices (usually 69 cents per half gallon). A "theme" is selected for the flavor of the month, such as "Hawaiian Holiday," for Superite's Royal Pineapple flavor. This theme is carried through on colorful posters and displays in the frozen goods section of the stores. This sale is popular with the retail store owners, who report increased sales as a result. Their profit margin remains the same on sale products, as Superite gives them discounts to make up for the lower selling price.

Although the flavor-of-the-month sale is a continuous campaign, more intense "saturation" campaigns are conducted about twice yearly. These include extensive radio and television advertising which is designed to convey Superite's "quality message."

One such campaign served to inform the public about the company's new electronic quality control system for ice cream production. Public suspense was first built up by repeated reference to the letters "EQC," without explaining what the letters represented. Radios blared the letters against an echo background, "E . . . Q . . . C . . . ," and newspapers and television emphasized the EQC theme. At the peak of the campaign, EQC was explained to the public in detail. Mr. Baker said that they were not certain whether or not this campaign was successful, since the results were difficult to measure. He did not feel that such advertising had much value.

One of the company's recent advertising successes was a "kiddy auction," in which young children saved Superite bottle caps and labels in order to bid for toys and games. Sales were noticeably increased during this campaign.

Superite has an aggressive promotion campaign for store openings. They usually feature their Princess ice cream and Superite milk. The customer may be offered ½ gallon of ice cream free when purchasing one at the regular 98-cent price. Or Superite can give the retailer a similar "one free with one" offer on milk, but not both at the same opening. These store opening deals are made to all stores likely to carry the Superite line. For some time, stores in the vicinity of the new store have complained to Superite, asking for a special deal at the time of the opening. They don't necessarily want the same deal (for it is quite costly and they had their turn), but feel special arrangements should be made to keep them fairly competitive.

Customers have come to expect specials like this at store openings and stock up to the limit of the sale (usually 2 gallons to a customer). Superite wonders what it should offer competing stores at the time of a nearby opening. Mr. Starr and Mr. Baker worry about this because they want to keep the retailers on their side, especially with Sealtest entering the market.

The case writer asked the marketing executives what their strategy was for the other products (after all it is 20 percent of their business) and home delivery. Mr. Baker replied, "You have us there, I guess. These parts of the business have not been aggressively merchandised. Most of the 'other products' are very profitable and volume has been growing but we've been so busy with milk and ice cream we haven't given them much push. Have you got any ideas on what we should do to merchandise them?"

"Well," the case writer said, "that's an interesting problem and perhaps we can discuss it, but what about the home delivery business?"

"You sure raise questions about things we don't think much about," said Mr. Starr. "I guess we just haven't made exact cost studies on that business. If we did, I suspect profit wouldn't look good on that end of the business, but we'll look into it and think about it."

Recent concern over the company's new competitor, Sealtest, is forcing management to reevaluate its promotional policies. Sealtest is presently conducting an intensive televison and newspaper campaign to acquaint the Nashville residents with its products. Mr. Litney thinks that Superite should step up its own advertising efforts to counter the possible effects of the new competition. The matter was discussed at a meeting between Mr. Litney, Mr. Baker, and Mr. Miller, of the Miller-Brown advertising agency, in which the following conversation took place:

Mr. Litney: "It appears as though they [Sealtest] will be hitting us straight on, up and down the product line. As far as quality is concerned, I think our products are slightly better, but most customers probably won't be able to tell the difference. What we need to do is emphasize the quality difference in our advertising."

Mr. Miller: "That's right. What we can do is emphasize the greater freshness of the locally processed Superite products as compared to those transported from other areas, as Sealtest will be. This is something that the customer can readily understand and relate to quality."

Mr. Baker: "I think we're being slightly paranoid about the situation. Sure, people will try the new brand at first, just to see how they will like it. But after the newness wears off, they'll go back to buying Superite. Why? Because we still have the best products. Oh, we might step up advertising a bit at first, but I think an extended campaign would cost more than it would be worth."

Mr. Litney: "Sure, we can count on a lot of customer loyalty. Our prices are reasonable, and I don't think we'll be undercut. But still, we can't ignore competition. For every sale Sealtest makes, we'll lose a sale. It won't be our present competitors who are hurt—they're not selling in the same market."

Mr. Miller: "What I feel we need to do is to begin an intensive campaign very soon that will firmly implant the Superite quality image in the minds of our customers. This will make them more resistant to the Sealtest sales pitch."

Mr. Litney: "One thing is for certain. We haven't got where we are today just by sitting around and letting it happen. If we're going to maintain our position, we've got to act, and act now."

By the time the case writer had concluded his study, Sealtest had already begun to sell in the Nashville area. Predictably, Superite orders fell off moderately. Management was still uncertain what strategy they would employ to handle the new competition.

## Profit planning and results

The Dairy Processing Industry reports how the average processor allocates his funds (see Figure 2).

Separate accounting procedures are used for retail and wholesale accounts. Wholesale accounts are processed by a small computer, which automatically

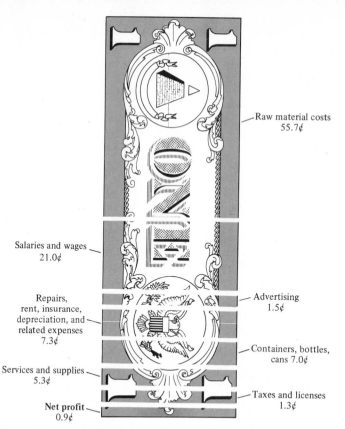

Raw material costs
55.7¢

Salaries and wages
21.0¢

Repairs,
rent, insurance,
depreciation, and
related expenses
7.3¢

Advertising
1.5¢

Containers, bottles,
cans 7.0¢

Services and supplies
5.3¢

Net profit
0.9¢

Taxes and licenses
1.3¢

**FIGURE 2** ■ How the average dairy processor allocates income.

shows sales, accounts receivable, and accounts payable. A weekly printout breaks sales down by products and geographical sales area. This information is then forwarded to Mr. Starr.

The retail (home delivery) system must be processed by hand since the accounts are too small and too frequently changed to be placed on the computer feasibly. Retail route men play an important role in the accounting process. Each day, they bill customers (billing is done at the time of delivery) and calculate sales per customer and total sales for the day. Records prepared by the retail men are given to the accounting department for further processing.

Most wholesale sales are on credit, payable in 30 days; home retail accounts are paid at the end of the month. Bad debts stem mainly from the home retail sales. This is also the least profitable area of operation. Although retail operations account for 22 percent of total sales, they account for only 14 percent of profits. Mr. Hollingsworth attributes the lower profit margin to the cost of salesmen's commissions and the maintenance and upkeep on the company's 150 trucks. Overall, about 75 percent of costs are direct costs, with 50 percent for raw products and 25 percent for wages. Recent financial statements for Superite are given in Tables 5 and 6.

Annual operating budgets are prepared by Mr. Hunton, who was proud to point out that last year's budget proved to be extremely accurate. Predicted

**TABLE 5 ■ SUPERITE DAIRIES INCOME STATEMENT FOR YEARS ENDED DECEMBER 31, 1967 TO 1969**

|  | 1967 | 1968 | 1969 |
|---|---|---|---|
| Sales | $7,023,456 | $7,650,824 | $8,139,174 |
| Cost of sales | 4,675,493 | 5,104,250 | 5,447,439 |
| Gross profit | 2,347,963 | 2,546,574 | 2,691,735 |
| Selling and general expenses | 1,829,653 | 1,988,754 | 2,111,204 |
| Income from operations | 518,310 | 557,820 | 580,531 |
| Other income | 91,604 | 93,646 | 99,732 |
| Total | 609,914 | 651,466 | 680,263 |
| Other income changes | 5,697 | 7,218 | 6,394 |
|  | 604,217 | 644,248 | 673,869 |
| Contributions to pension trust | 167,888 | 170,231 | 172,786 |
|  | 436,329 | 474,017 | 501,083 |
| Federal income taxes | 205,960 | 203,827 | 216,107 |
| Net income | 230,369 | 270,190 | 284,976 |
| Dividends paid | 103,666 | 140,499 | 160,969 |
| Net addition to retained earnings | $126,703 | $129,691 | $124,007 |

sales were within $70,000 of actual sales, with actual selling expenses 3.5 percent under the budget, and general and administrative costs 1 percent under. Manufacturing expenses were 2.5 percent under the budget, and material costs 0.75 percent over.

The company keeps a $5000 standing balance in every bank in each commu-

**TABLE 6 ■ SUPERITE DAIRIES BALANCE SHEET STATEMENT, DECEMBER 31, 1967 TO 1969**

|  | 1967 | 1968 | 1969 |
|---|---|---|---|
| *Current assets* |  |  |  |
| Cash | $ 423,498 | $ 598,766 | $ 590,074 |
| Accounts receivable (less bad debts allowance) | 653,181 | 750,122 | 859,372 |
| Inventories | 112,375 | 130,064 | 150,954 |
| Prepaid expenses | 16,873 | 20,122 | 21,475 |
| Total current assets | 1,205,927 | 1,499,074 | 1,621,875 |
| Land, buildings, and equipment |  |  |  |
| Land | 203,080 | 203,080 | 203,080 |
| Building equipment (less depreciation) | 1,201,161 | 1,301,264 | 1,397,826 |
| Other assets | 13,704 | 11,007 | 3,075 |
| Total assets | $2,623,872 | $3,014,425 | $3,225,856 |
| *Current liabilities* |  |  |  |
| Accounts payable | $ 225,873 | $ 342,154 | $ 372,906 |
| Federal income taxes payable | 64,768 | 82,006 | 88,309 |
| Withholding and social security payable | 21,357 | 29,620 | 36,603 |
| Total current liabilities | 311,998 | 453,780 | 497,818 |
| Stockholder's equity |  |  |  |
| Outstanding capital stock | 1,447,932 | 1,567,012 | 1,610,398 |
| Treasury stock | 71,098 | 73,315 | 73,315 |
| Retained earnings | 863,942 | 993,633 | 1,117,640 |
| Total | 2,382,972 | 2,633,960 | 2,801,353 |
| Less treasury stock | 71,098 | 73,315 | 73,315 |
| Total stockholder's equity | $2,311,874 | $2,560,645 | $2,728,038 |
| Total liabilities and stockholders' equity | $2,623,872 | $3,014,425 | $3,225,856 |

nity in the selling area. Presently this is 60 banks. Mr. Hunton did not approve of the practice, but Mr. Hollingsworth defended it, saying that it helped build their public image and stimulated the economy of the community. He added that if the funds were put in CDs or notes, they would not bring in enough profit after taxes to make it worthwhile.

Mr. Litney, Mr. Hollingsworth, and Mr. Hunton jointly prepare the capital budget. No plant expansion is planned for the near future. In the past, small dairies have been purchased in outlying areas to provide new markets, but the plants proved too costly to operate and were shut down. It is not anticipated that any more such purchases will be made.

Eighty percent of the Superite stock, which is sold over the counter, is owned by four families. These include the Baker, Litney, and Hollingsworth families, and one other family not connected with management. Each family owns between 15 and 20 percent of the stock and 20 percent is held by the general public in smaller amounts.

## Final comments

"All in all, I think we're a profitable and progressive company and will have no problems in the future," Mr. Litney told the case writer as he was ready to leave. "After all, Nashville's our home base and we know how to run a business here," he said. The case writer wondered if Mr. Litney was right about that.

# Holiday Inns, Inc.

William F. Glueck

The lodging industry is a vast enterprise in the United States, Canada, and, increasingly, overseas. In the United States, for example, there are approximately 44,000 lodging properties. Most are independent operators, sometimes linked by reservation systems. Two such systems are Best Western Motels with about 70,000 rooms and Friendship Inns, which list more than 46,000 rooms.

Motels have come a long way from the days when they were a few small cabins next to a farmhouse, many with a reputation that one could stay there with no questions asked about marital status. These questions are rarely asked in the 1970s but often were asked of guests in earlier times.

AAA made an early breakthrough with a listing and rating of motels and hotels for the traveler, but did not market their service as aggressively as some other operators.

If you travel and stay overnight at a hotel or motel, the chances are that you are most familiar with motels operated and/or owned by the 15 major chains in the lodging industry. The leading chains and the approximate number of rooms each offers in 1974 are shown at the top of the following page. But Holiday Inns alone have more rooms than the first two categories (less than 20,999 and from 21,000 to 50,999) and part of Trust Houses combined. Yes, Holiday Inns have about 250,000 rooms for rent each night around the world (1974 figures). Not bad for a company that was incorporated April 30, 1954.

Kemmons Wilson built his first motel, Holiday Inn Hotel Court, in 1952 in Memphis. The price of each room was $4, with children free in the room. Wilson entered the business, he said, because he, his wife, and five children had to pay too much for rooms in Washington, D.C.

The first franchised motel was built in 1954 in Clarksdale, Mississippi. The franchise fee was $116.50. The track record since then:

1958:  50 inns open

1959:  100 inns open

1964:  500 inns open

1967:  100,000 rooms available from Holiday Inns

1968:  1000 inns open

1971:  200,000 Holiday Inn rooms available

The HI stock first began trading over the counter in 1957. The cash on hand on the annual report at the time was $50; sales: hotel, $1,349,299.13; food,

| Less than 20,999 | 21,000 to 50,999 | More than 51,000 |
|---|---|---|
| **1** Club Méditerranee (France)<br>**2** Motel 6, Inc.<br>**3** Rodeway Inns of America<br>**4** Hyatt Corporation<br>**5** Marriott Corporation | **1** Howard Johnson<br>**2** Quality Inns<br>**3** Red Carpet Inns Master Hosts<br>**4** Inter-Continental Hotels<br>**5** Hilton International | **1** Holiday Inns<br>**2** ITT-Sheraton<br>**3** Ramada Inns<br>**4** Hilton Hotels Corporation<br>**5** Trust Houses Forte, Ltd. (United Kingdom) |

$246,518. By 1961, HI had 4,500,000 shares authorized. On September 30, 1962, the Big Board listed a new stock: Holiday Inns. Opening price was $6.06. The first cash dividend was not paid until 1964 (20 cents per share). By 1967, the dividend was up to 50 cents a share. Since 1962, the high price for the stock was 57, the low 4¼ (fourth quarter of 1974).

From the beginning, HI has developed its inns in two ways: company-owned and those owned by franchises. Table 1 gives the distribution of the inns and rooms for the two categories.

By 1974, HI owned 309 of the 1608 inns in the HI system. These company-owned motels offer 59,898 rooms and tend to be located in metropolitan resort areas. The company is expected to concentrate on suburban locations in its future growth in the United States.

Holiday Inns' growth set the pace for the lodging industry. From 1962 to 1972, Howard Johnson more than tripled its rooms to 43,000 and Ramada Inns went from 6700 to 64,000 rooms. Holiday Inns projects 350,000 rooms by 1977. Sheraton is planning to have 120,000 rooms available. Ramada Inns will offer 135,000 rooms by 1977, and Quality Inns will offer 90,000 rooms or so.

In the past, the growth came at the expense of older hotels and nonchain motels. Hotels offer fewer rooms now than 10 years ago, for example. The annual rate of growth in rooms in the late 1960s was about 3 percent yearly. Independent motels have been hurt by chain growth. Some have been taken over by chains who now control almost 30 percent of the rooms. The chains claim they have better locations on busy freeway interchanges, etc. Some observers argue that there is now a shortage of prime sites. Continued growth

**TABLE 1 ■ INNS AND ROOMS: COMPANY-OWNED AND FRANCHISES**

| Year | Company-owned | | Franchise-owned | |
|---|---|---|---|---|
| | Inns | Rooms | Inns | Rooms |
| 1974 | 309 | 59,898 | . . . | . . . |
| 1973 | 305 | 57,940 | 1,286 | 188,973 |
| 1972 | 297 | 54,643 | 1,173 | 166,470 |
| 1971 | 290 | 51,687 | 1,081 | 148,773 |
| 1970 | 286 | 48,800 | 985 | 130,564 |
| 1969 | 270 | 44,728 | 921 | 119,491 |
| 1968 | 173 | 26,635 | 868 | 104,920 |
| 1967 | 139 | 19,436 | 719 | 94,769 |
| 1966 | 120 | 17,842 | 608 | 75,441 |
| 1965 | 92 | 11,299 | 495 | 58,581 |
| 1964 | 81 | 9,217 | 412 | 56,465 |
| 1963 | 71 | 7,910 | 326 | 35,422 |

may lead to diminishing returns. Then, there are locations where the lodging industry has overbuilt, as in Orlando, Florida. The firm had its eye on international growth since early in its history and opened its first non-U.S. inn in 1960. This inn was in Canada. By 1974, there were almost 70 inns in operation or almost in operation in Canada. Since 1960, the firm has opened lodging facilities around the world. It has initially concentrated in Canada and Western Europe. In 1970, for example, the company announced a 10-year program to develop the Western European market, initially concentrating in West Germany and the United Kingdom, but also including Belgium, Spain, Greece, Italy, Sweden, and Switzerland. The firm also operates in Africa (Lesotho, Swaziland, South Africa), West Indies (Antigua, Barbados, Bahamas, Curaçao, Jamaica, Grand Cayman, Saint Kitts, Saint Lucia, Trinidad, Virgin Islands), Mexico, Japan, India, Hong Kong, Australia, Lebanon, Malaysia, Panama, Singapore, Tahiti, and Venezuela. It had problems operating in Morocco and ceased operations there in 1972. In 1970, the firm announced a $72 million venture to operate 32 lodging facilities in Eastern Europe. About 25 percent of its almost 300 international inns (1974) are owned by the parent company.

## HI's management team

The board of directors includes the following persons:

Kemmons Wilson
Chairman of the Board

Roy E. Winegardner
First Vice Chairman of the Board

Wallace E. Johnson
Vice Chairman of the Board

William B. Walton
Vice Chairman of the Board

L. M. Clymer
President

Clyde H. Dixon
Executive Vice President

Frank W. Adams
Senior Vice President

Charles M. Collins
Senior Vice President

E. B. McCool
Senior Vice President

Lewis K. McKee
Chairman, Board of Directors
National Bank of Commerce
Memphis, Tennessee

Allen B. Morgan
Honorary Chairman, Board of Directors
First Tennessee National Corp.
Memphis, Tennessee

John E. Brown
Former Chairman, Board of Directors
Union Planters National Bank
Memphis, Tennessee

William N. Clarke
Partner
Cadwalader, Wickersham and Taft
New York, New York

Frederick G. Currey
President
TCO Industries, Inc.
Dallas, Texas

C. Bennett Harrison
Chairman, Board of Directors
Union Planters National Bank
Memphis, Tennessee

R. A. Lile
President
Transportation Properties, Inc.
Little Rock, Arkansas

Ralph Owen
Board of Directors
American Express
New York, New York

Robert E. Slater
Chairman, Board of Directors
National Liberty Corporation
Frazer, Pennsylvania

The top management includes the following persons:

Kemmons Wilson, the chairman of the board and founder of the firm. He was born in 1913 in Osceola, Arkansas. The *London Times* named Mr. Wilson one of 1000 "makers of the 20th Century and Horatio Alger Award."

Roy Winegardner, first vice chairman of the board, became an officer in 1972. He focuses on development of food and lodging division. Mr. Winegardner opened his first Holiday Inn in 1958 and has helped construct and operate 41 others since then.

Wallace E. Johnson, vice chairman of the board.

William B. Walton, vice chairman of the board, was born in 1920 in Pine Bluff, Arkansas. He holds a law degree from Memphis State University.

L. M. Clymer, president, was born in 1924.

Clyde H. Dixon, executive vice president, joined the firm in 1968. Other top officers include eight senior vice presidents, twelve vice presidents, one treasurer, two assistant treasurers, nineteen assistant vice presidents, and two assistant secretaries. In addition to the corporate officers, each division has its executive team. The Transportation Division has a chairman of the board, and two presidents for TCO and Continental Trailways, and a chairman of the board and president for the Delta Steamship Lines. The other divisions have presidents. The firm directly employs about 45,000 persons (1974).

## Holiday Inns financing

The firm was incorporated in Tennessee April 30, 1954, as Holiday Inns of America, Inc., to continue a partnership which opened the first Holiday Inn in Memphis, Tennessee, on July 20, 1952. On April 22, 1957, the company, which until then had primarily conducted only licensing operations, acquired 17 operating subsidiaries by exchange of stock. Most of these were merged into the parent July 1, 1960. The name Holiday Inns, Inc., was adopted May 22, 1969.

## History

The firm's stock market record is given in Figure 1. Dividends paid in 1973 were 30 cents a share and in 1974 were 31⅞ cents per share. Table 2 contains the income statement, Table 3 the balance sheet, Table 4 the stockholders' equity, and Table 5 a financial review of the firm for the past several years.

## Operations at Holiday Inns

Most of us are familiar with Holiday Inn motels and restaurants. But HI is involved in much more than these. The company operates the following:

1 Food and lodging
2 Franchise sales

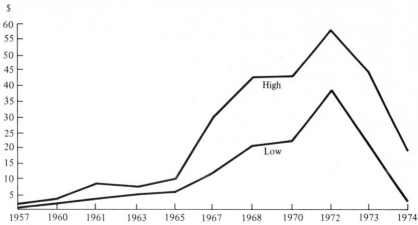

**FIGURE 1** ■ The stock market record of Holiday Inns.

**TABLE 2** ■ HOLIDAY INNS, INC., AND CONSOLIDATED SUBSIDIARIES STATE-MENT OF CONSOLIDATED INCOME (IN THOUSANDS, EXCEPT PER-SHARE AMOUNTS)

| | Year ended | | |
|---|---|---|---|
| | Jan. 3, 1975 | Dec. 28, 1973 | Dec. 29, 1972 |
| Revenues: | | | |
| Food and lodging | $501,792 | $466,244 | $419,349 |
| Products | 198,709 | 195,900 | 157,774 |
| Travel and transportation | 280,613 | 215,884 | 191,395 |
| Other income | 4,976 | 7,651 | 6,692 |
| | $986,090 | $885,679 | $775,210 |
| Operating costs and expenses: | | | |
| Food and lodging | $471,931 | $421,777 | $367,425 |
| Products | 187,252 | 180,066 | 146,409 |
| Travel and transportation | 247,639 | 191,483 | 168,677 |
| General corporate | 21,810 | 17,454 | 14,596 |
| | $928,632 | $810,780 | $697,107 |
| Income before income taxes | $ 57,458 | $ 74,899 | $ 78,103 |
| Provision for income taxes | 24,817 | 28,496 | 36,079 |
| Net income | $ 32,641 | $ 46,403 | $ 42,024 |
| Less dividends on preferred stock | 170 | 297 | 417 |
| Earnings applicable to common and Series A stock | $ 32,471 | $ 46,106 | $ 41,607 |
| Average number of common and common equivalent shares outstanding | 30,678 | 30,818 | 30,297 |
| Earnings per common and common equivalent share | $1.06 | $1.50 | $1.37 |

**TABLE 3 ▪ HOLIDAY INNS, INC., AND CONSOLIDATED SUBSIDIARIES CONSOLIDATED BALANCE SHEET (IN THOUSANDS OF DOLLARS)**

| | Jan. 3, 1975 | Dec. 28, 1973 | Dec. 29, 1972 |
|---|---|---|---|
| *Assets* | | | |
| **Current assets** | | | |
| Cash | $ 24,496 | $ 24,850 | $ 29,543 |
| Certificates of deposit and commercial paper | 21,953 | 8,430 | 20,665 |
| Receivables, less allowance for doubtful accounts of 3,710,000 in 1974, $3,093,000 in 1973, and $2,721,000 in 1972 | 97,175 | 82,338 | 72,211 |
| Inventories, at lower average cost or market | 37,406 | 33,046 | 25,209 |
| Accrued operating differential | . . . | 2,662 | 2,870 |
| Other current assets | 8,019 | 8,002 | 10,158 |
| | 189,049 | 159,328 | 160,656 |
| Less deposits to be made in statutory reserve funds | 10,965 | 7,319 | 5,687 |
| Total current assets | 178,084 | 152,009 | 154,969 |
| Restricted funds (principally statutory reserve funds, including above deposits) | 13,141 | 14,679 | 51,539 |
| **Investments and long-term receivables** | | | |
| Notes receivable and other investments | 16,474 | 11,493 | 9,311 |
| Nonconsolidated subsidiaries and less than majority owned affiliates | 19,146 | 18,832 | 16,884 |
| | 35,620 | 30,325 | 26,195 |
| **Property and equipment, at cost** | | | |
| Land, buildings, improvements, and equipment | 971,332 | 920,049 | 784,723 |
| Less accumulated depreciation and amortization | 284,697 | 250,056 | 223,434 |
| Construction in progress | 10,941 | 11,526 | 40,946 |
| Property held for future use | 7,400 | 5,694 | 4,225 |
| | 704,976 | 687,213 | 606,460 |
| **Deferred charges and other assets** | | | |
| Deferred charges | 13,306 | 13,225 | 10,830 |
| Other assets | 15,985 | 12,239 | 12,140 |
| | 29,291 | 25,464 | 22,970 |
| Total assets | $961,112 | $909,690 | $862,133 |

| | Jan. 3, 1975 | Dec. 28, 1973 | Dec. 29, 1972 |
|---|---|---|---|
| *Liabilities and stockholders' equity* | | | |
| **Current liabilities** | | | |
| Long-term debt due within 1 year | $ 21,133 | $ 16,328 | $ 18,514 |
| Notes payable—banks | 14,356 | 7,554 | 3,822 |
| Accounts payable | 30,203 | 29,040 | 25,570 |
| Accrued federal and state income taxes | 10,739 | 6,096 | 10,473 |
| Accrued expenses and other taxes | 42,199 | 33,897 | 28,974 |
| Dividends payable on common stock | . . . | 2,283 | 1,960 |
| Provision for sinking fund— preferred stock | . . . | 3,015 | 2,422 |
| Other current liabilities | 16,537 | 11,066 | 10,950 |
| Total current liabilities | 135,167 | 109,279 | 102,685 |
| Long-term debt due after 1 year | . . . | 343,937 | 342,003 |
| **Deferred credits** | | | |
| Excess of net assets at acquisition over investment in subsidiary | 8,590 | 9,819 | 11,049 |
| Other (principally unterminated voyage net revenue) | 15,384 | 4,450 | 7,375 |
| | 23,974 | 14,269 | 18,424 |
| Deferred income taxes | 40,627 | 34,457 | 26,846 |
| Minority interest in consolidated subsidiaries | 3 | 1,223 | 1,033 |
| **Stockholders' equity** | | | |
| Capital stock: Preferred; 5% cumulative; $100 per value; authorized 150,000 shares; issued and outstanding 18,964 and 45,513 shares in 1972 and 1973. | . . . | 1,896 | 4,551 |
| Special stock; authorized 5 million shares; Series A; $1.125 par value; issued 761,034 and 1,006,652 shares; convertible into common. | 856 | 865 | 1,133 |
| Common; $1.50 par value; authorized 60 million shares; issued 29,877,812 and 29,295,940 shares | 44,816 | 44,816 | 43,944 |
| Capital surplus | 114,338 | 114,238 | 111,858 |
| Retained earnings | 274,008 | 252,310 | 216,499 |
| Capital stock in treasury, at cost | (6,252) | (4,762) | (4,542) |
| Deferred compensation shares unissued | (2,672) | (2,838) | (2,301) |
| Total stockholders' equity | 425,094 | 406,525 | 371,142 |
| Total liabilities and stockholders' equity | $961,112 | $909,690 | $862,133 |

TABLE 4 ■ STATEMENT OF STOCKHOLDERS' EQUITY (IN THOUSANDS OF DOLLARS)

| | Preferred $100 par value | Common $1.50 par value | Special—Series A $1.125 par value[a] | Capital surplus | Retained earnings |
|---|---|---|---|---|---|
| Balance—December 31, 1971 | $7,301 | $42,270 | $1,271 | $104,813 | $187,704 |
| Prior year tax adjustment | . . . | . . . | . . . | . . . | (3,400) |
| Adjusted balance—December 31, 1971 | 7,301 | 42,270 | 1,271 | 104,813 | 184,304 |
| Net income | . . . | . . . | . . . | . . . | 42,024 |
| Common stock issued in: | | | | | |
| Conversion of 122,966 shares of special stock—Series A for 184,446 shares of common | . . . | 277 | (138) | (139) | . . . |
| Earnout provision of 1969 acquisitions, 587,388 shares | . . . | 881 | . . . | (857) | . . . |
| Exercise of employee stock options, deferred compensation shares, and stock purchase warrants, 283,652 shares | . . . | 425 | . . . | 5,935 | . . . |
| Dividend on special stock—Series A, 40,461 shares | . . . | 61 | . . . | 1,762 | (1,823) |
| Exercise of stock rights on 8% debenture bonds, 9,341 shares | . . . | 14 | . . . | 313 | . . . |
| Acquisitions, 10,515 shares | . . . | 16 | . . . | 72 | 184 |
| Sinking fund requirements, 27,495 shares | (2,750) | . . . | . . . | . . . | . . . |
| Cash dividends declared on: | | | | | |
| Preferred stock | . . . | . . . | . . . | . . . | (417) |
| Common stock, $2.75 per share | . . . | . . . | . . . | . . . | (7,773) |
| Stock issuance expenses | . . . | . . . | . . . | (41) | . . . |
| Balance—December 29, 1972 | 4,551 | 43,944 | 1,133 | 111,858 | 216,499 |
| Net income | . . . | . . . | . . . | . . . | 46,403 |
| Common stock issued in: | | | | | |
| Conversion of 238,072 shares of special stock—Series A for 357,107 shares of Common | . . . | 536 | (268) | (268) | . . . |
| Earnout provision of 1969 acquisitions, 105,946 shares | . . . | 159 | . . . | (142) | . . . |
| Exercise of employee stock options and deferred compensation shares, 58,477 shares | . . . | 87 | . . . | 1,209 | . . . |
| Dividend on special stock—Series A, 59,979 shares | . . . | 90 | . . . | 1,491 | (1,581) |
| Acquisition, 5,238 shares | . . . | . . . | . . . | 169 | . . . |
| Sinking fund requirements, 26,549 shares | (2,655) | . . . | . . . | . . . | . . . |
| Cash dividends declared on: | | | | | |
| Preferred stock | . . . | . . . | . . . | . . . | (297) |
| Common stock, $.30 per share | . . . | . . . | . . . | . . . | (8,714) |
| Stock issuance expenses | . . . | . . . | . . . | (79) | . . . |
| Balance—December 28, 1973 | $1,896 | $44,816 | $ 865 | $114,238 | $252,310 |

[a] Dividends payable in common stock, at the annual rate of $1.70 market value of common.

**TABLE 5 ■ HOLIDAY INNS, INC., AND CONSOLIDATED SUBSIDIARIES FIVE-YEAR FINANCIAL REVIEW (IN THOUSANDS OF DOLLARS, EXCEPT PER-SHARE AMOUNTS)**

| | 1974 | 1973 | 1972 | 1971 | 1970 | 1969 |
|---|---|---|---|---|---|---|
| **Revenues:** | | | | | | |
| Historical | 936,090 | 885,679 | 775,210 | 707,877 | 604,556 | 538,699 |
| Restated for poolings of interests | 936,090 | 885,679 | 775,210 | 707,877 | 604,556 | 539,834 |
| **Income before income taxes:** | | | | | | |
| Historical | 57,458 | 74,899 | 78,103 | 73,644 | 65,613 | 59,592 |
| Restated for poolings of interests | 57,458 | 74,899 | 78,103 | 73,644 | 65,613 | 60,099 |
| **Earnings applicable to common and Series A stock:** | | | | | | |
| Historical | 32,641 | 46,106 | 41,607 | 41,592 | 36,881 | 32,358 |
| Restated for poolings of interests | 32,641 | 46,106 | 41,607 | 41,592 | 36,881 | 32,648 |
| **Earnings per share from operations:[a]** | | | | | | |
| Historical | 1.06 | 1.50 | 1.38 | 1.36 | 1.30 | 1.15 |
| Restated | 1.06 | 1.50 | 1.37 | 1.35 | 1.28 | 1.14 |
| **Cash dividends paid per share:** | | | | | | |
| Historical | 0.31875 | 0.29 | 0.27 | 0.24 | 0.225 | 0.19 |
| Restated | 0.31875 | 0.29 | 0.27 | 0.24 | 0.225 | 0.19 |
| **Depreciation and amortization:[b]** | | | | | | |
| Historical | 59,058 | 58,563 | 47,204 | 39,987 | 37,430 | 31,827 |
| Restated for poolings of interests | 59,058 | 58,563 | 47,204 | 39,987 | 37,430 | 29,009 |
| **Additions to fixed assets:** | | | | | | |
| Historical | 91,954 | 132,176 | 115,654 | 119,394 | 85,658 | 67,321 |
| Restated for poolings of interests | 91,954 | 132,176 | 115,654 | 119,394 | 85,658 | 68,041 |
| **Working capital:[c]** | | | | | | |
| Historical | 42,917 | 42,730 | 55,684 | 33,194 | 38,302 | 19,054 |
| Restated | 42,917 | 42,730 | 52,284 | 33,194 | 38,302 | 18,922 |
| **Total assets:[d]** | | | | | | |
| Historical | 961,112 | 909,690 | 864,434 | 764,229 | 676,350 | 575,267 |
| Restated | 961,112 | 909,690 | 862,133 | 762,577 | 675,731 | 580,770 |
| **Long-term debt:** | | | | | | |
| Historical | 336,250 | 343,937 | 342,003 | 284,634 | 287,271 | 223,793 |
| Restated for poolings of interests | 336,250 | 343,937 | 342,003 | 284,634 | 287,271 | 227,221 |
| **Stockholders' equity:[c,d]** | | | | | | |
| Historical | 425,094 | 406,525 | 376,843 | 338,940 | 358,333 | 214,242 |
| Restated | 425,094 | 406,525 | 371,142 | 333,888 | 254,314 | 211,781 |
| **Average common shares outstanding:[a]** | | | | | | |
| Historical | 30,678 | 30,818 | 30,237 | 29,510 | 28,190 | 27,242 |
| Restated | 30,678 | 30,818 | 30,297 | 29,611 | 28,290 | 27,715 |

[a] Historical figures are as they were reported in HI Annual Reports for respective years, except that amounts have been adjusted for a 2-for-1 stock split effective May 22, 1969, stock dividends, and poolings of interests.
[b] Includes other charges not affecting working capital.
[c] Adjusted to record prior year adjustment relative to income taxes.
[d] Deferred compensation shares unissued was reclassified to stockholders' equity in 1973.

**3**  Transportation Division: Continental Trailways and Delta Steamship Lines, tours and real estate

**4**  Commercial services

**5**  Products Division

Some of the companies in the division were acquired. Others were internally developed.

The revenue distribution in the last few years was as follows:

| Contribution to corporate revenue | 1974 | 1973 | 1972 |
|---|---|---|---|
| Food and Lodging Division | 51% | 53% | 54% |
| Products Division | 20 | 22 | 20 |
| Travel and Transportation | 28 | 25 | 25 |
| Miscellaneous | 1 | 0 | 1 |
| | 100% | 100% | 100% |

Pretax income in 1973 included 52 percent from food and lodging, 29 percent from travel and transportation, and 19 percent from Products Division. In 1974, the pretax revenues in the Food and Lodging and Products Divisions declined from 1973 figures, but Transportation Division figures rose.

For the twenty years prior to 1973, there was continuous growth in revenues and earnings per share. This was not so for 1973. Mr. Wilson attributed the reversal to (1) increases in cost of food, (2) heavy investment in Europe, (3) wage and price controls, (4) energy crisis. He contended that a strength of HI is:

. . . derived from the diversity of services provided for the traveling public. The three principal operating divisions of Holiday Inns, Inc., have been developed as a balanced portfolio of business enterprises.

The inevitable variations in the preferences of leisure travelers have a coincident, but inverse, effect on the profitability of the Food and Lodging and Transportation Divisions. As the business cycle turns downward, for example, some consumers forego leisure travel. But during the same time period, the appeal of intercity bus transportation generally increases.

The Products Division will continue to increase its initial penetration of the vast market for institutional furnishings, equipment and supplies. Consistent growth of the Products Division is facilitated by an organization with the flexibility to respond rapidly to changes in the economic environment and the requirements of the market.

The Food and Lodging Division not only contributes to corporate stability, but also enjoys internal balance. Holiday Inns operated by the Food and Lodging Division serve guests throughout the United States, Europe and the Caribbean in a full range of markets—downtown, suburban, interchange, resort, mid-town, airport and small town. Holiday Inns serve a broad spectrum of the traveling publics—from resort vacationers to the budget-conscious family staying overnight at an economical roadside Holiday Inn. The diversity of markets and broad geographic distribution of Company-owned properties permit the Food and Lodging Division to balance variations that occur in both individual markets and specific geographic areas.

## Products Division

This division offers a series of institutional products and services (of 30 operations) to Holiday Inns and other institutions such as office buildings and apartment houses, hotels and motels, and health care facilities. The principal functional groups within the division are as follows:

1  *Innkeepers Supply Group (IKS):*
   IKS-Dohrmann (West Coast)
   IKS Memphis, Atlanta, Lakeland
   IKS International (Brussels)

2  *Distributor Sales:*
   IMART
   Menumakers Food Service
   Holiday Inn Beverage

3  *Manufacturing:*
   Bianco (chairs, booths)
   International Foam
   Holiday Containers
   Master-Kraft
   Johnson Furniture Co.
   Champion Lighting Co.
   American Woodcraft
   Holiday Woodcraft (furniture, counters, display cases)
   Modern Plastics
   Kitchen Equipment

4  *Food Processing Division:*
   Nat Buring Packing Co. (meats)
   Chambers-Godfrey Mfg. Co.
   R. B. Rice Co.

5  *Holiday Press:*
   Institutional Mart of America
   Holiday Inn Construction (including Teleci, Inc., telephone company)
   HI Air (owns, rents, and sells private aircraft)
   Holiday Industrial Park

6  *Special products:*
   HITSCO (Holiday Inns Timber Sales)

The Products Division provides purchasing and merchandising services for all the groups in the division. The division offers such varied services as developing an industrial park in Memphis (where HI's Holiday Press, Master-Kraft Manufacturing, and Holiday Press Plastics will locate and HI's HI Air will man the Olive Branch Airport) and supplying IKS goods to Japanese lodging institutions. It runs the Institutional Mart in Memphis—127,000 square feet of display space there and in three other locations. The food processing group distributes processed meat to 3000 retail outlets. The 10 manufacturing companies produce equipment, furniture, and fixtures for the IKS group while the Distribution Sales group markets 4000 INN KARE Consumable supplies through 47 distributors in the United States.

## Transportation Division

The Transportation Division of HI includes two major units: Continental Trailways, the second largest intercity bus system in the United States, and Delta Steamship Lines.

Continental Trailways operates over 2500 buses on 70,000 route miles. It increased this mileage to 70,000 with the acquisition of Tamiami Trailways, a Florida bus concern, in 1974.

The Continental system has attempted to improve its services by a number of steps. One is to develop newer and more attractive terminal facilities. Almost 60 percent (in 1974) of the terminals have been built since 1964.

The firm offers tours, charter buses, scheduled buses, and package express service. The company merchandised the energy crisis in 1973 to its advantage. Buses are estimated to get 85 passenger miles per gallon of fuel.

One recent innovation was the Eaglepass. It allows a passenger unlimited-use tickets for the period. The firm also offered Golden Eagle service with reserved seating on the bus, express buses, refreshments served by passenger service personnel, and comfortable seating. Golden Eagle service now operates between 39 U.S. cities.

The tours offered by the company operate in the United States, Canada, and Mexico. The tours tie into Holiday Inn motels, of course.

In 1975, the ICC announced it was investigating numerous complaints about bus service that could require Continental to construct new terminals in some cities and clean up others. ICC is considering requirements to improve baggage handling as well.

Delta provides ship service to Central America, South America, and West Africa. Its latest innovation is LASH (Lighter Aboard Ship) containers. The containers (LASHes) are filled before arrival of the ship. This improves the scheduling of ships. For example, it reduced the South American trip from 70 days to 42 days.

## Food and Lodging Division

The Food and Lodging Division operates the largest food and lodging system in the world. The division owns and operates over 300 inns around the world. The inns offer food, lodging, and even chaplain service at almost 1400 inns. The chaplains are on call for personal advice to the lonely, suicidal, etc.

Some of the inns have fairly plain architecture. Others are going in for the plushness of leisure domes.

The inns not operated by the company are run by independent businessmen and businesswomen; they are called franchises. From time to time, HI has purchased franchises. Recently, for example, the division tried to acquire American Motor Inns, Inc., a franchisee of 53 inns and owner of a Universal Communications System. The proposal fell through.

The details of a franchise change from year to year, of course, but in 1973 some of the requirements were:

1  Payment of a franchise fee of $15,000 (minimum) plus $100 per room over 100 rooms

2  Payment of monthly royalty fees: 3 percent of gross room revenue or 15 cents per room per night (whichever is greater)

3  Payment of operating and service fees:
   (a) Great Sign Lease: $240 per month
   (b) Holiday Reservation Equipment Lease: $3 per room per month

(c) Metropolitan Sales Office Reservation Services: greater of 6 cents per room per night or $\frac{8}{10}$ of 1 percent of gross room revenue

(d) Holiday Inn University Fee: 1 cent per room per night

For this, the franchise is promised 10 to 30 percent net return on equity. Expected revenue is $300,000 from the restaurant (120-room motel size) and a gross of $3500 per room per year.

Occupancy rates are about 72 percent and operating costs run about 52 percent of total sales and income. In 1973, it was costing about $12,000 per room plus land to build a Holiday Inn, put up by franchise.

HI receives about 10,000 franchise requests per year and accepts about 200. The division must approve all plans for constructions of an inn. Before approval, the division runs a market test on such factors as distance to airport, strength of nearby motels, and the road network.

The division has almost 50 investigators who drop in quarterly unannounced. Points are assigned for every aspect of the operation from pool cleanliness to the restaurant. Below 850 points, the inn receives a month to come up to snuff. If it fails again, the franchise contract is canceled (or in the case of a company-owned inn, the manager is fired). As of 1972, 30 franchises had been canceled for low standards.

The division runs Holiday Inn University near Memphis, open since 1958. In 1973, 3500 managerial employees enrolled for introductory and continuing education courses.

One of the keys to the division's success is the Holiday reservation system—the largest nonmilitary on live computer system in the world. It provides the quickest and cheapest reservation service in the industry.

The firm also provides an information retrieval system called Inn Scan. The manager can determine up-to-date information on all phases of the operation. It has been tested in a small number of outlets and will spread to the rest of the system too.

Finally, the division operates about 50 Trav-L-Parks in the United States with about 10,000 rental spaces available to campers in 17 states.

## Current challenges to HI

Most organizations at one time or another appear successful on the surface when they face serious problems. Others appear troubled when they have successfully come through serious problems. Some appear successful and are, others appear troubled and are. The role of the analyst is to determine which organizations are which, which challenges will fade and which will destroy. Top executives are well paid to do this. HI is no exception. At least three recent events seem worth looking at.

### THE LEGAL STATUS OF THE FRANCHISE AGREEMENT

Recently, HI considered merging one of its franchises, American Motor Inns of Roanoke, Virginia, into the parent. It did not work out. One of the resulting problems may have been a court suit by AMI.

One consequence of this suit might be summarized by some statements from the second Quarterly Report issued by HI:

Memphis-Holiday Inns Inc. said its results for the second quarter, ended June 28, will include a provision for a possible loss from litigation growing out of a dispute between it and a licensee. Holiday Inns lost a court decision in the case, but has said it plans to appeal.

The report continues:

The provision is in connection with a ruling by a Newark, N.J., federal district court that Holiday Inns couldn't enforce a clause in its franchise agreement with the licensee, American Motor Inns Inc., Roanoke, Va., prohibiting that concern from having a non-Holiday Inn motel. Additionally, the court awarded American Motor Inns $4 million in damages. Last month American Motor Inns and Holiday Inns ended merger discussions, citing economic conditions.

Holiday Inns, reiterating yesterday that it would appeal the court's decision, said the loss provision was made "in the interest of conservatism."

Other aspects of the franchising agreement with regard to purchase requirements of the franchisee from the parent might also result in a suit.


## The energy crisis

In fall, 1973, there was a shortage of gasoline in the United States. Some alleged it was because of an embargo by Arab states. Others contended that it was a strategy by oil companies to increase their prices and profit margin. This had an effect on the Food and Lodging Division. People who fear they cannot get gasoline travel less and thus use less leisure time in motels. One consequence (from the HI Quarterly Report):

HI occupancy levels at Company-operated inns declined during the first quarter of 1974, compared to the corresponding months of 1973 as shown below:

|  | 1974 Better/(Worse) 1973 |
| --- | --- |
| January | (5.9) Per. Pt. Change |
| February | (4.6) Per. Pt. Change |
| March | (4.2) Per. Pt. Change |
| First Quarter | (4.9) Per. Pt. Change |

Leisure-oriented weekend occupancy levels have declined substantially more than commercially-oriented weekday occupancy levels. Since the removal of the voluntary ban on Sunday Gasoline sales, weekend occupancy levels have improved.

HI did react. To try to reduce gasoline uncertainty, it created a program including the Gasoline Advisory Service to inform guests of the availability of fuel throughout the United States; "mini-vacation" packages for short-distance travel; and vacation packages for longer-distance travel. These vacation packages will combine lodging at participating Holiday Inns with air, bus, and rail transportation and a rental car at the destination.

How serious will this problem be? Standard and Poor's, evaluating HI for 1974, said:

Near Term—Revenues for 1974 are expected to continue trending upward from 1973's record $886 million, aided by additional inns in operation and expansion of travel activities in related fields. However, the gasoline shortage will restrict leisure driving and lower occupancy levels at numerous inns, thus limiting the gain in revenues.

Margins will be under pressure from reduced occupancy levels and rising operating costs. Somewhat offsetting would be greater efficiencies through a realignment of the Products division and continued growth in shipping and bus transportation. On balance, earnings for 1974 are not likely to vary much from 1973's $1.50 a share. Dividends are at $0.07½ quarterly.

Long Term—Included in aggressive expansion plans is the opening of some 500 inns in Europe by 1980. Expansion moves and further integration of travel services should provide greater revenues and profits.

Regarding the energy crisis and HI stock, *Financial World* (Aug. 22, 1973) said:

Holiday Inns was one of the best performing stocks in the 1970. But slower earnings growth in the last few years, fears concerning the energy crisis, and prospects of a slowing in earnings sent the shares into a tailspin this year. But barring gasoline rationing or recessionary conditions, earnings should grow at least moderately well in the oncoming years. At their current depressed level, the shares provide an interesting speculation on the success of the next phase in Holiday Inns development—its expansion into international markets.

## The "budget" motel

With inflation and other factors operating many motels had started charging $20 per night and more. Perhaps it was inevitable then that price competition would rise.

Beginning in the southeastern United States, a series of companies began offering motel rooms for half that price or less. In the early 1970s, prices ranged from $6 per night to $9.90 in the Southeast and West, for example.

Some of the major "budget" chains and headquarters are:

City Investing's Motel 6 (Santa Monica, California)

Scottish Inns of America (Kingston, Tennessee)

Chalet International (Nashua, New Hampshire)

By 1972, it was estimated that there were 10,000 budget rooms available; this was up to 30,000 in 1973, and predictions ranged to 175,000 by 1975.

Apparently Motel 6 was the first major group involved in budget lodging, having begun in the mid-1960s. Some customers were shopping on price.

Perhaps the budget motel entry is one explanation why in 1973 the motel-hotel group of stocks were among the 10 worst-performing groups, dropping 35 percent from January to July 1973.

How do the budgeteers do it? First, they build the hotels cheaper. In fact, many managers in this segment of the industry come from the building industry. It is easier to build them cheaper in the South and West because of the weather. In 1973, the costs were running $5000 per room (compared with $7000 per conventional room at the time). Some observers predict very high maintenance costs after a few years. Typically the budget motels have no meeting or convention rooms, small lobbies, no restaurant, and often no pool.

Ofttimes, the room is somewhat smaller and there are charges for TV (25 cents per hour in some motels). Many times the sites are smaller.

They cut a few corners:

**1** The beds are built close to the floor so that cleaning under the beds is minimal or eliminated.

**2** Bathtubs are rounded to eliminate cleaning the corners.

**3** Advertising is very small—perhaps limited to a bright sign listing rates.

**4** Retired military people are hired to run them in exchange for apartment and small salary with few or no fringe benefits.

**5** To compensate for point 3, ofttimes they try to locate close to the well-advertised motels. Thus Econo Travel tries to locate next to Holiday Inns. This saves them the market research and thus assures a good location, it saves advertising, and the guests may even patronize the Holiday Inn's restaurant.

The budgets present HI with a strategic challenge, however. How do they meet the price competition? Some inns have fought back on price. Thus some HIs advertised: "Sleep Here, Kids Eat Free." Others lowered their base rates.

One strategy would be to ignore the threat. But what if it is the "wave of the future?" *Barron's* does not think so. In an analysis (Sept. 10, 1973) they state:

Nonetheless, the threat to conventional motels may not prove as severe as some observers fear. Despite the rapid growth of budget inns, the 30,000 rooms now in operation are only a fraction of the 1.3 million standard ones. Moreover, as noted, most are concentrated in the Southeast; there is some question whether the idea will spread through the North, where construction costs are higher, unions stronger and winter weather requires sturdier units. Finally, economy types soon may be competing against each other. This could mean that features stripped away will be added back and charges boosted.

Two other adverse developments for the industry—threatened gasoline shortages and the high cost of construction money—could have silver linings. True, scanty gas supplies may inhibit some travel, particularly at night, when some filling stations are closing earlier. However, several motel operators say that motorists who used to travel after dark to avoid heavy traffic and heat now are prone to do so by day, and stop in at an inn at nightfall. Similarly, while high interest rates may curtail some motel building, this could prevent over-expansion, which hurts occupancies in some locales. The Orlando region is a prime example; the proliferation of motels on the roads leading to Disney World has brought occupancies below 50%.

Others have urged HI to create a "No Frills Chain" by HI itself. And there are signs that this is coming. HI is building some units "geared to cost conscious travelers, employing advanced construction techniques and methods aimed at holding down the cost of a night's lodging." Room rates were estimated to be in the $10 to 12 range. The first units were to open in late 1972. "But to cut costs, the company will use modular-construction techniques and do away with such facilities as conference and banquet rooms, which are out of place in a budget establishment. There will be restaurants—but they will offer limited, fast-food menus."

Mr. Wilson does not believe the budget motels will be a significant part of the market. HI's competitors feel they got in too late.

# Winnebago
# Industries, Inc.

Paul Rabinowitz

In 1971 and early 1972, Winnebago was a high-flying glamour issue. Today, the industry's largest manufacturer of motor homes seems to be performing at less exciting altitudes.

Winnebago is the General Motors of the recreational vehicle industry. Based in Forest City, Iowa, it manufactures principally motor homes, travel trailers, and camper trailers. The motor homes account for approximately 88 percent of sales, trailers, campers, and kaps for 7 percent, and parts and panel materials for 5 percent. Winnebago handles sales of recreational vehicles on a wholesale basis to a broadly diversified retailer-dealer organization. There is also a Winnebago Acceptance Corp. subsidiary, which provides dealer financing, and a realty subsidiary which helps to develop dealer sites.

Winnebago is one of 800 recreational vehicle producers. According to the Recreational Vehicle Institute (RVI), the 191 manufacturer members in RVI produce 85 percent of all recreational vehicles and an eventual concentration of manufacturers is a long-run forecast within the industry. "You are going to see a rather severe shake-out in the recreational vehicle industry," predicted John V. Hanson, president of Winnebago.

The recreational vehicle industry covers a wide range of products—from the covers that convert pickup trucks into rough campers for less than $200, to deluxe motor homes retailing for $21,000 and up. In between are slide-in pickup campers, travel trailers, tent trailers, minimotor homes, and converted vans. According to an American Bankers Association's 1972 Installment Credit Survey direct lending for recreational vehicles made up 0.4 percent and indirect lending 0.6 percent of the surveyed banks' loans.

As far as geographic strength of industry goes, a regional rundown of recreational vehicle activity reveals that you have to go west of the Mississippi to find a significant concentration of recreational vehicle financing. The farther west you go, the more voluminous the sales and financing become. One banker in Maine, where there is considerable direct financing but little indirect, said, "People buy recreational vehicles to come here." In California, the recreational vehicle is big. Compare Bank of America's indirect financing through 285 dealers to Marine Midland Bank-Western's ten, or to Union Trust National Bank's one in St. Petersburg, Florida.

## Winnebago and Forest City

Winnebago is based in the small Corn Belt community of Forest City, Iowa, where it was founded. Not only has it become the town's leading employer, but Forest City has the highest per capita ownership of stock of any town in the United States. As Winnebago goes, so does Forest City, and most of its 4400 residents.

The meteoric rise of Winnebago in this corn farming region of northern Iowa created 25 new millionaires with stock market fortunes. Each $1000 put up by early investors was worth nearly $1 million on September 11, 1972. In spite of the new wealth it never surfaced in the way one might expect. Instead of celebrating new wealth by doing the chic thing, many of them who had lived comfortably all their lives did not seem to have the desire to change. Most are descendants of immigrant farm folk from Scandinavia and are firmly tied to the area, its people, and conservative small-town ways. Their attitudes during the most recent crisis are indicative of their prevailing personality. They are, to some degree, worried about the future of the company, which is annually pumping $16 million in salaries into the Forest City area. Most people are convinced, though, that the town and Winnebago will see the hard times through. "If you have an early frost and lose your corn crop, you don't quit farming," said John L. Martin, president of Forest City Bank and Trust Co. "Folks here will put their Winnebago stock in their dresser drawer and wait however long it takes for it to go back up." Even when the stock value was around $5 there was no rush to sell; in fact because of the lower value, buying orders flooded the Des Moines–based brokerage house in Forest City.

Overall, the town's response to wealth has been subdued. Several expensive new homes have been built or planned. A couple dozen Forest Citians got together and chartered a DC-3 for a weeklong fishing trip to northern Canada. It came to be the most talked about event of the year. In general though, the rich here live, work, and play as they always have.

The company started in 1959 with a handful of employees and nearly went broke a couple of times before it began to move in 1965. In September of 1964, when Winnebago was only 5 years old and struggling, the company's entire production facilities were destroyed by fire. In the recession of 1970, the stock tumbled nearly 60 percent before recovering.

The bulk of the market wealth has accrued to the family of 62-year-old John K. Hanson, a former furniture store and funeral parlor owner who founded the company. Mr. Hanson, who is chairman, his wife Luise, and their three children including 33-year-old John V., who is president, own about 58 percent of Winnebago stock. The market value of their holdings, at one time worth over $500 million, slipped to $75 million in the last crisis. John K. had 60 percent of it in his own name. Other Winnebago officers and a number of business and professional men who are friends of John K. and were around in the beginning, round out the major owners. Approximately 900 of the total 3000 company employees owned stock. Some factory workers and secretaries had made up to $100,000 on their investments. Of course, anything made was paper profits.

John K. is not the type of man to sit back with his wealth and relax. He has spurred many projects for community development such as new housing developments, new churches, new parks, and a proposed hospital to replace the old one. He has also given away, mostly unpublicized, hundreds of thousands of dollars to help out the community.

There was an intense loyalty to Winnebago, and the recent crisis has diluted this feeling in part. "We weren't experienced investors and perhaps were blinded by loyalty to the company, but if there are any hard feelings, they're only in ourselves. We should have diversified our holdings and sought professional investment advice all along," said Ben Carter, publisher of the weekly *Forest City Summit,* who "had quite a little chunk" of stock. The town still retains a certain mystique or admiration for John K. Everyone in town knew John K. had been traveling in the Far East for several weeks. "John K. wasn't taking a vacation," said one minister. "He was using his mind as never before." Speculators in town began to imagine some wild schemes.

One speculated, "Winnebago could make small cars in Forest City but, if the stock drops any more, they may go back to making coffins."

In the meantime, life in Forest City goes on unchanged, through booms and busts. Construction of the $2 million hospital has begun on the northeast side of town. A new Catholic church, partly financed by the sale of 1000 Winnebago shares donated by John K., has been completed. The Forest City Council purchased a new diesel generating unit, which, along with other improvements to the town's electrical distribution system, was financed through the sale of $1.7 million of 5.5 percent bonds.

John K. and Winnebago have been the major driving force in Forest City up until this last tailspin. According to Roy Schram, mayor for 26 years and vice president of Kayot Inc.'s Forester Division, a recreational vehicle maker whose 160 workers made it the second-largest employer in town, said, "The town's attitude has been 'Let Winnebago do it.' Now we can't rely on one man and everyone will have to put their shoulder to the wheel and lend a hand."

Despite the moaning there are a lot of new tractors and cars on the farms surrounding this small town. Forest City will not be able to grow as dramatically as before. The Development Commission, for example, temporarily shelved plans to build an 18-hole golf course, a 100-room motel, clubhouse, and a housing development east of town.

The folks in Forest City have handled the ups and downs of Winnebago rather stoically. They never have gone into fits of ecstasy nor have they thought of panic. The attitude has been and will continue to be in the mold of small-town conservatism. The Rev. Owen Gangstead, pastor of Immanuel Lutheran Church, whose congregation includes the Hansons and several ex-millionaires, said, "These are stormy times for Forest City, but it's a storm that will blow itself out." With Winnebago now producing campers on an order basis and stock still at a depressing level perhaps Forest City's greatest test is yet to come.

## Environment of recreation industry

In 1974, the recreational vehicle industry environment is in turmoil. Many questions are facing the industry as a whole, and the final outcome for the industry could be dramatic. Some of these issues will be discussed here.

Whereas the recreational vehicle market has grown by leaps and bounds over the past decade (as of 1971 production was up more than 400 percent since 1961), the campground industry has been much slower to fill the mushrooming demand. Overcrowding of campgrounds is a major problem and has led to the use of such terms as "tenement camping." Some campgrounds just do not measure up to quality standards and their reservation systems are inadequate. Such factors are of importance to a long list of manufacturers ranging from those who make the household appliances carried in most campers, to the major auto firms that supply such products as chassis (as Dodge does for Winnebago), oversize radiators, and brakes to the complete home on wheels. Robert C. Honke, Ford Division recreational vehicle sales manager, said, "A great number of the 200 million of us want to get outdoors but all for different reasons. I want to go fishing—you want to go water skiing. There are times when the two disturb each other. Who has the right of way?"

And critics have recently charged that recreational vehicles "wreck" residential areas. One such critic is Henry Forbes, a retired Air Force colonel living in Santa Barbara, California. Observing his neighbor's motor home he says, "I don't like the looks of it. Everyone takes care of their property here, but to have a bus sitting in the driveway—it's not a very attractive sight." Local groups of owners have banded together in many areas to combat this restrictive mood. Winnebago clubs across the country have sometimes become a political lobbying force. Many RV owners seeking to avoid controversy are keeping their rigs at commercial storage lots. Homebase Inc., which opened 18 months ago on a lot outside Cleveland, now has more than 250 customers who pay $15 to $20 a month to store their RVs at Homebase's lot.

The industry's answer to these problems may be a political response. Lobbying is the word best describing future activity the RV industry is inevitably going to do to defend itself. The campgrounds problem is one area where "political" pressure is likely to continue. Federal and state governments, which traditionally have built and maintained most campgrounds at public parks and forests, have lagged in expanding their facilities. Environmental groups have even pressured that some be closed to all vehicular traffic—things have become so congested. The National Park Service, moreover, plans almost no additions to its camping facilities, and is enthusiastically encouraging private companies to pick up the slack. The message has gotten through, for out of the 16,500 campgrounds in the United States, fewer than 35 percent now are operated by governmental units. Even with approximately 800,000 individual sites capable of handling a travel trailer, there are over 4 million RVs on the road. Demand for space is far beyond existing facilities. Here it will be important to create some impetus to further activity in the establishment of satisfactory campgrounds. The way this problem is being handled is through the major producers acting merely as catalysts. Winnebago has offered any requested assistance to their many local camper clubs, but leaves actions up to them. Getting these people together as a political interest group aids their cause. Another "catalyst" is the Ford Motor Company. With the formation of Outdoor Nation, a loosely knit forum for those interested in the preservation and enjoyment of the out-of-doors, Ford hopes Outdoor Nation will function as an advisory forum to land management branches of the government such as the Bureau of Land Management, the National Park Service, and the Army Corps of Engineers.

The second area of lobbying interest is in fuel conservation measures including restrictive driving periods, higher gas prices, taxes, etc. All have a direct effect on sales of RVs and make the interest here high-pitched. A direct lobby here will be an ongoing expense for the industry until the energy crisis is finally resolved.

### THE QUESTION OF SAFETY

The safety issue has recently jumped to the forefront as the second round of auto safety activity begins to concentrate on recreational vehicles. Basically, motor homes regularly survive collisions with passenger cars without significant injury to motor home passengers. John V. Hanson said, "We are currently in compliance with federal and state laws and will continue to be." However, in collisions with fixed objects, motor homes are more vulnerable than passenger cars because of their inertia.

A National Highway Traffic Safety Administration (NHTSA) spokesman commented that a recent survey of recreational vehicles will lead to some new regulations. One major obstacle to formulating any immediate standards is the lack of vehicles on the highways to draw a sufficient number of statistics to make some reliable conclusions.

Roger Compton, director of engineering systems staff, NHTSA, felt it was unlikely that "regulations will be more severe than those for passenger cars." He believed they would be either less severe or the same.

If trends in passenger car regulations are any indication, the new rules will be written in terms of vehicle-performance standards and legally allowable injury to passengers.

Concern about structural safety considerations, including "crush ability," has caused the National Transportation Safety Board to urge NHTSA to extend vehicle safety standards to cover trailers and pickup campers "as expeditiously as the availability of pertinent accident causation data will permit."

Recently an auto safety group charged that Winnebago motor homes lacked adequate "crash worthiness." The Center for Auto Safety, formerly associated with the consumer advocate Ralph Nader, had challenged the safety of Winnebago's motor homes to John Hanson, himself.

The group cited seven accidents reported to them involving Winnebago motor homes, which closely resemble buslike RVs. The Center charged that in all seven crashes the vehicles "collapsed completely upon impact, with the walls and roofs ripping away from the chassis leaving the occupants totally unprotected."

Furthermore, the group felt, "what appears to be a total lack of 'crash worthiness' in the Winnebago" has been confirmed by the company's own crash tests. The center called on Winnebago to release results of its tests and to recall some 50,000 pre-1973 Winnebagos on the road to install a steel support bar the company has included over the driver's compartment of the 1973 model motor homes.

Hanson said it was "difficult to respond to the letter since we haven't seen a copy of the letter, but statistics prove Winnebago motor homes are safe."

He added, "Available statistics show that the bodily injury rate is six times higher in a car than in a motor home per mile driven. We believe our products have been and are as safe or safer than their contemporaries. Winnebago has been a pacesetter in recreational vehicle safety, meeting or exceeding safety standards set by all governmental bodies."

Both the design and stability of motor homes previously have come under criticism. The National Transportation Safety Board came to the conclusion that some units are "incapable of maintaining structural integrity in a crash," and the NHTSA recently released a report that many motor homes are too heavy for their suspension systems. Naturally, motor home producers have disputed both findings.

Another area under investigation is the question of how seat belt laws pertaining to motor homes should be revised. The NTSB has noted that in many cases motor homes made to sleep six people need only to have seat belts for the driver. All other seating locations can be exempted by placing signs above them which state such seats are "not approved."

Finally, the board has begun to question driver competence. It has been noted that many experts feel "driver error" is the principal factor in recreational motor vehicle accidents. No special certification is needed to take control of a motor home or any other RV with specific design limitations and unusual handling characteristics.

## THE ENERGY CRISIS

In 1973, the Arabs put an embargo on oil. This led to the "energy crisis" with long gas lines, talk of rationing, etc., which had a tremendous impact on the RV industry and Winnebago.

Whether or not there ever really was a shortage of fuel during the recent energy crisis, the sale of recreational vehicles of all types is influenced by the availability of fuel and public opinion about the availability of fuel. Industry people predicted that "even if the energy crisis is a hoax, because so many people believe it anyhow," a turndown in production and sales is inevitable in 1974. William E. Simon, one-time head of the Federal Energy Office, said the largest problem had been, and for the most part still is, convincing the U.S. public that the crisis was real and not an exaggeration manufactured by the government and oil companies—and that it would continue. The energy crisis was the major factor in Winnebago's loss for the year ended on February 23, 1974.

The fears of an unavailability of gas and subsequent increase in prices have made the gasoline crisis for the recreational vehicle industry real. In a June 1974 *Business Week* article the situation is pointedly of major crisis proportions. "Nine months ago, gasoline shortage and fears of rationing wiped out the sales of recreational vehicles almost overnight. By December, 40 of the nearly 300 RV manufacturers in the U.S. were out of business, and nearly all the rest had shut down production. 'From last November until mid-February,' says Robert I. Rubin, marketing director for Open Road Industries, one of the larger markers, 'U.S. business stopped—and I mean stopped.' "

Governmental assurances, particularly by the Federal Energy Office (FEO), are of paramount importance in this problem. However, in December 1973, John Love (then director of the President's Energy Policy Office) declared, after a high-level cabinet meeting with President Nixon:

. . . alternative planning for the rationing of gasoline continues, with additional studies still to be presented for final decision. It is anticipated prior to any implementation of such a program, prospective regulations would be presented for public discussion and evaluation.

It should be understood that while gasoline rationing is a possibility we must face, the absolute necessity of such an action has not been conclusively demonstrated. Whether rationing is needed will depend in substantial measure on the effectiveness of other programs now in place—particularly voluntary and mandatory conservation measures.

On a December 1973 Face the Nation broadcast Simon said, "We have been on a collision course in energy requirements and demands for many years. . . . In 1970 production peaked but energy needs will double between 1973 and 1990." The fact that he stated the energy shortage would not end with resumptions in oil shipments from Arab nations simply encouraged pessimism.

An Atlantic-Richfield Company advertisement in a December 1973 *New York Times* read in part,

Face it: Yesterday's energy shortage is today's energy emergency.

Why? Because oil and gas which provide more than 75% of our Nation's basic energy—are not now available in the quantities we need. . . .

Energy shortages will continue to plague the United States for years to come until we gain the self-sufficiency that means energy independence.

An interesting point should be made though. As the memories of the gasoline shortage faded, somewhat of an upswing in sales occurred. The Recreation Vehicle Industry Association predicted 547,000 units would be shipped in 1974. This is down 27 percent from 1973, but January and February sales were down 70 percent.

The sales of motor homes, travel trailers, truck campers, and pickup truck covers still are reeling from reduced consumer confidence and tight credit.

Champion Home Builders Corp., a major producer, built 12 homes in December 1973. By May 1974, production was up to 733 a month. Yet Champion shipments still were off 62 percent from 1973.

Coinciding with this upswing are warnings to consumers to beware of bargain prices for RVs. Due to buyers' avoiding purchases of RVs, dealers in some areas had to cut prices to move overloaded inventories.

Extreme care is urged in any purchase, especially in that of an "orphan" RV. In the industry, an orphan is an RV whose manufacturer has gone out of business, leaving no reliable supply of replacement parts.

One consumer-oriented journalist suggests, "If you want to buy an RV that has good future trade-in value, get one that is made by a financially strong, national manufacturer and think small. Dealers say that the RVs of the immediate future are going to be small and light—to give better gasoline mileage."

### THE INDUSTRY'S REACTION

When the first signs of fuel problems arose, the sales of recreational vehicles began to soften. And business was not helped by the NTSB's report questioning the safety of many motor homes in collisions or roll-overs. In total though these were just minor blows compared to proposed restrictions on weekend driving (in particular, closing of gas stations on Sunday), higher fuel prices, and the continuing talk of gas rationing to the industry.

Winnebago, the General Motors of the recreational vehicle industry, has felt the severity of the situation. The company's facilities have been designed to provide vertically integrated production line manufacturing of recreational vehicles. The effects of a continued energy shortage could be significant to the utilization of the production facility. Sales of the company's products have increased significantly since the lifting of the oil embargo in March 1974. However, since the magnitude and duration of the shortage are impossible to determine, Winnebago is unable to quantify to what extent, if any, the energy crisis will adversely affect its future operations and the utilization of its manufacturing facilities.

Owing to the uncertainties related to the energy crisis and its subsequent industrywide sales decline, in the latter half of fiscal 1974 Winnebago intensified its efforts in developing new products in the market areas not previously served by Winnebago. The production of new products has been achieved with the use of present production facilities. Winnebago has always felt its facilities are readily adaptable to the manufacture of a variety of nonrecreational vehicle products.

In addition to nonrecreational vehicles, Winnebago's most recent addition to its sagging recreational vehicle line is a low- to middle-priced motor home line called the Itasca model. This new line should be in the $8000 to $15,000 range. Current Winnebago models are priced from $8000 to $25,000.

John K. Hanson said the new line will not be marketed under the Winnebago name and will not have the company's Flying W trademark. He said a separate dealer organization will be developed to handle the new Itasca line.

The new line of motor homes will be built on Chevrolet chassis, he said. Current Winnebago motor homes are built on Dodge chassis. Hanson said an agreement has been signed with GMC's Chevrolet division to purchase type A chassis for initial production.

A type C chassis motor home also is being developed with a Chevrolet chassis and is scheduled for introduction next spring (1975).

Mr. Hanson said, "The new line is intended to attract those potential buyers who for whatever reason haven't wanted to buy a Winnebago brand motor home. We believe the Itasca line won't hurt Winnebago brand sales but will give us overall better market penetration."

As a result of the energy crisis, the company recently had to conduct its first factory-authorized sale. The inventory problem grew out of Winnebago's overoptimistic sales projections, coupled with talk of future gasoline shortages. The price of Winnebago's stock plummeted, and in doing so, it wiped out the fat paper profits of some citizen investors in Forest City. Besides cutbacks in production, "to bring inventories into line with the realities of the marketplace," Winnebago had to cancel plans to build a $20 million RV plant in Reno, Nevada.

On the positive side, the diversification program has placed Winnebago in many opportunistic ventures. Whether these develop and successfully complement Winnebago's product lines remains to be seen.

There is irony in the problem. After the fuel crisis became headlines, many people began predicting the imminent demise of the camper and the motor home. The logic was no fuel, no trips. No trips, no market. No market, no industry.

Then in early January 1974, a small-scale RV show was held in Columbus, Ohio. The turnout was far better than most had hoped for and "they bought plenty," an Ohio Recreational Vehicle Association staff member said.

The stronger than anticipated response has been attributed to a push by the industry throughout the country to publicize shorter trips with smaller fuel requirements, and perhaps, most importantly, the recreational vehicle owner and buyer is not a typical American.

"He's a wanderer," says an Akron area dealer. The average buyer is a man or woman who values a certain kind of freedom, or the illusion of it above just about everything else.

"Some owners would rather have a recreational vehicle than a house. It's a kind of well-upholstered Oakie mentality in the seventies that's really keeping us going," says another dealer.

The irony is that the industry now has a new problem. The problem is far too few RVs to meet a resurgent demand. Owing to short supplies of everything from chassis to labor, many production lines are running at only one-third capacity while inventories have been depleted. John V. Hanson said, "Demand has come back quicker than we could possibly react." The overall effect on the industry was a shake-out of a large number of smaller RV maker operations.

After fiscal 1974, Hanson said, "We can't possibly catch up now. We're looking for a decent fall, but we kind of missed the season." Hanson believes the industry's overall shake-out may have been healthy, and he notes that restored demand indicates that customers are not put off by higher interest rates and gasoline prices. He says, "Once we get through this wild year, I'll be very bullish about the industry."

But the crisis still lurks in the background. In 1973 and 1974 there were significant price increases in gasoline. There was also talk of a 10- to 20-cent tax on gasoline. This certainly has aroused fears further throughout the industry. Although the likelihood of an additional gas tax is slim, there is a possibility and the issue comes down to what is more important when fuel is the commodity. The drive at all governmental levels to conserve fuel is going to be intensified. One industry official said, "Unlike the trucking industry and the agribusiness, which are essential to maintain the economy . . . and will not be drastically constrained by fuel shortages, there undoubtedly will be severe restrictions . . . on recreational activities and recreational vehicles." How should the industry rationalize to the social consciousness of fuel conservation? In last year's national meeting of the Recreational Vehicle Industry (RVI), dealers and manufacturers were provided with information and materials to spread the industry's message "Go 50/50 in an RV." The industry was urging potential and present owners of the vehicles to go no farther than 50 miles from home on a trip and to stay below 50 miles per hour on the highway.

## The RV industry

Before the bottom fell out of the industry, it had been regarded as an "easy-entry industry," particularly since neither technology nor capital requirements were prohibitive. The last several years have seen Ford Motor Company and General Motors finally get into the act after 10 years of sitting back and watching the industry grow.

John V. Hanson acknowledged, "General Motors, by entering this business, adds creditability to the industry. Obviously, it means they are going to bring people into the market who are going to look at the motor home for the first time simply because they (GM) are now in the business."

Underlying the market is the willingness of people to spend whatever surplus money they have. RVs are not necessities and a sluggish or, worse, slumping economy does not make the economic picture bright. Disposable personal income in the United States is expected to reach about $927 billion by 1975, and $1260 billion by 1980. If things regain some normality, recreation spending is expected to be $55 billion in 1975 and $77 billion by 1980.

Winnebago's position in the industry remains one of dominance. Its market share is about 40 percent in the RV industry. It manufactures a broad line of recreational vehicles consisting of motor homes, travel trailers, camper coaches, and kaps. As a result of recent diversification efforts, it also produces modular housing, agricultural products, buses, and cargo vans.

In the 27 weeks ending August 1974, motor homes accounted for 72.4 percent of sales, travel trailers, camper coaches, and kaps 13.5 percent, and other nonrecreational vehicles 14.1 percent. (See Table 1 for Winnebago's net sales by major product areas.) Some 12,041 motor homes (10,127 type A units and 1914 type C units) were sold in 1973–1974 compared with 21,790 homes in fiscal 1972–1973. Type A motor homes, with the exception of appliances, chassis, and power units, are produced completely by Winnebago. Type A motor homes constitute about 90 percent of its current business and are built from a bare chassis. Type C minimotor homes are built on a van-type chassis that includes the driver's compartment. Some 1008 travel trailers were sold (404 conventional units and 604 fifth-wheel units), compared with 1667 in fiscal 1972–1973, and some 404 camper coaches and 22,255 kaps were sold, compared with 1050 and 31,465, respectively, in fiscal 1972–1973.

Sales for the fiscal year ended February 23, 1974, fell 41.6 percent from those of the fiscal 1972–1973 period. Winnebago management believes the sales decline reflects the effects of the gasoline shortage, high interest rates, and

TABLE 1 ■ DISTRIBUTION OF THE COMPANY'S NET SALES BY MAJOR PRODUCT AREAS

| Year ended[a] | Motor homes[b] | Travel trailers and camper coaches[b] | Kaps[b] | Other including parts and service[b] | Totals |
|---|---|---|---|---|---|
| February 28, 1970 | $ 37,407,627 83.2% | $3,684,995 8.2% | $2,745,095 6.1% | $1,122,969 2.5% | $ 44,960,686 100.0% |
| February 27, 1971 | $ 62,364,455 88.0% | $4,838,674 6.8% | $2,430,224 3.4% | $1,232,735 1.8% | $ 70,866,088 100.0% |
| February 26, 1972 | $120,125,124 90.2% | $5,959,321 4.5% | $3,165,894 2.4% | $3,916,099 2.9% | $133,166,438 100.0% |
| February 24, 1973 | $192,029,961 90.6% | $8,210,253 3.9% | $5,180,100 2.4% | $6,615,644 3.1% | $212,035,958 100.0% |
| February 23, 1974 | $108,266,357 87.5% | $5,042,722 4.1% | $3,657,296 3.0% | $6,774,515 5.4% | $123,740,890 100.0% |

[a] The year ended February 28, 1970, contained 53 weeks; all other years included in the table contained 52 weeks.
[b] Optional equipment included in original purchase orders is encompassed in the sales figures for the particular product.

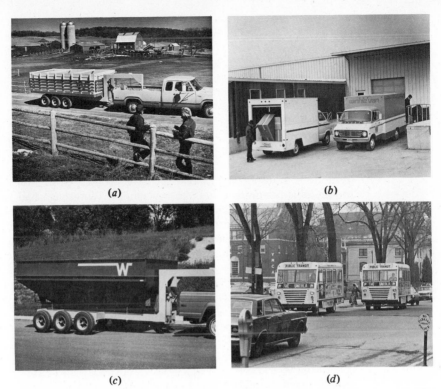

**FIGURE 1** ■ *(a)* A series of fifth-wheel agricultural trailers initiated the company's agricultural product line; *(b)* light-duty panel delivery truck utilizing Winnebago's Thermo-Steel construction; *(c)* gravity box model, featuring fifth-wheel hitch; *(d)* Winnebago's entry into the mass transit field.

production cutbacks to reduce excess motor home inventories. Results were severely affected by increased manufacturing costs, higher advertising, promotional and research and development costs, losses on repurchase of vehicles, provisions for warranty losses, and a loss at Winnebago Acceptance. The net loss was $6.7 million, whereas the net income a year earlier (1972) was $17.3 million. Winnebago's contingent liability on all repurchase agreements at February 23, 1974, was approximately $700,000.

Motor home manufacturers, hard hit by fuel shortages, have tried promoting different uses for the motor home. The promotion has suggested taking fishing, golfing, and swimming trips, and driving it to one location and using it as a vacation home.

Winnebago has embarked on a diversification program. The new products include multifamily modular housing units (developed and to be marketed by Dover Co., Topeka, Kansas), agricultural fifth-wheel grain trailers and gravity boxes (which Winnebago is building for Tasco Inc., Shell Rock, Iowa, and for which the firm has already signed some 230 dealers), 19-passenger intracity buses, and general-purpose cargo van trucks and fifth-wheel cargo vans. (See Figure 1*a* to *d*.) By July 31, 1974, motor home inventories had been reduced and employment at Forest City had reached about 2200, compared with 800 in January 1974 and 3900 in January 1973.

To some manufacturers though, the challenge is to meet the record-high sales of 1972 and 1973. At Coleman Company, Wichita, Kansas, for example, sales of camping trailers (with canvas sides and collapsible tops) reached $5.9 million in 1972; in 1973, sales were $10.2 million. In June 1974, John K. Hanson expressed concern as to "whether we will have enough motor homes available to meet market demand during the balance of this model year, ending in August."

Intensified competition in the market caused by a growing number of established manufacturers and retail dealers has contributed to the partial erosion of Winnebago's position in the industry.

The company's success in the RV market is now threatened by competition from three transporting giants—General Motors, Ford Motor, and White Motor, plus hundreds of less known names. Winnebago had been doubling total dollar sales every 2 years until 1973, when the trend was reversed. There is a tone of considerable confidence when Winnebago talks of competition. Concerning increased competition John K. Hanson said, "When new customers do come in and look at the market, and look at the units, we feel that our value and our convenience in the vehicle will get us our share of the market." He does acknowledge though, "It makes a lot of people more aware. We're proud of Winnebago, but we're not foolish enough to think that more people know about Winnebago than General Motors."

The GM lines, base-priced at $13,500 to $14,500, compare to Winnebago's top line, the Chieftain. The Chieftain line accounts for about 5 percent of the company's sales. Winnebago's greatest sellers have been its middle lines, priced about $10,000. "GM's entry reaches for a portion of the market—the top line," John K. Hanson said.


## Winnebago products

The Chieftain, the Indian, the Brave, and the Minnie-Winnie have made Forest City, Iowa, the recreational vehicle capital of the world. Winnebago has been adept at anticipating consumers' wants in the ideal RV. As a result of this foresight they have been able to maintain adequately a formidable share of the RV market.

One of the great strengths Winnebago has is its customer loyalty. A survey of present owners turned up primarily positive responses. One satisfied customer told the case writer:

Although not an economical way of traveling Winnebago does offer one a special freedom, particularly if you are visiting friends and find it sometimes cumbersome to impose on this person's hospitality. Without a doubt, it "allows an independence I like."

According to John K. Hanson, Winnebago offers 13 "real" models—vehicles of different lengths. By contrast he noted, "Although some of our competitors offer as many as 16 models, this is a little tough to do with two wheelbases." He added that these vehicles often had just slight modifications. With Winnebago's product line they have more than adequately served their market.

The company's products are designed for maximum mobility and are shorter in length and lighter in weight than mobile homes and are used primarily as temporary dwellings during vacation and camping trips. The company's motor home is built directly on a truck chassis and power unit, giving a buslike appearance. In addition to the driver's area, the interior contains a kitchen, dining, sleeping, and bathroom areas, and, in some models, a lounge. The company actually produces 15 motor home models ranging in length from 18 to 29 feet. These units provide complete living accommodations, including cooking, lighting, and refrigeration facilities, for a maximum of four to eight persons and vary primarily in length or capacity and in conveniences and accessories. With the exception of appliances and the chassis and power units, these type A motor homes are produced completely by Winnebago. Four type C, or chopped van, motor home models (including the Winnie Wagon) ranging in length from 18 to 20 feet are also produced. Most are built on Dodge chassis; in fact, 85 percent of *all* motor home chassis now are produced by Dodge.

One of Winnebago's many problems is the rapid growth of the minimotor homes. These particular models compete head-to-head with the lower-priced full-size motor homes—$7000 to $12,000—which have been one of Winnebago's strongholds.

In answer to this problem, Winnebago came up with a new minihome of their own. The Minnie-Winnie is 19 feet long, is built on a Dodge chassis, and will sleep up to five.

The company's motor homes retail from about $6900 to $21,900 depending on size and model. The most recent price increase came in May 1974 when the wholesale base prices on most Winnebago motor homes increased 7 percent. The price increase applied to all travel trailers, camper coaches, fifth-wheel trailers, buses, and commercial vehicles including motor inns and shells, Winnie vans, and cargo vans. Winnie Wagons, agricultural products, and pickup truck covers will not be included in the increase. (See Figure 2a to c for product illustrations.)

An example of the effect of the increase is the popular 23-foot Indian motor home, which would now carry a suggested retail base price of $11,708, up from $10,935.

Travel trailers, which are mounted on a chassis and are designed to be towed behind an automobile or pickup truck, are produced in six models ranging in length from 13 to 23 feet, accommodating four to eight persons with optional equipment and accessories. Two 27-foot and two 31-foot fifth-wheel travel trailer models are made. Camper coaches are produced in two models both 10 feet in length and designed to sleep a maximum of four to six persons. Price ranges from approximately $1300 to $8100 depending on size, model, optional equipment, and delivery charges.

Two other standard products of Winnebago are camper coaches and kaps. A camper coach is a body containing a living area built on a substantial wood underframe, designed to be mounted on a pickup truck by placing or sliding it onto the truck bed. The camper coach can be readily used on all standard domestic pickup models now made. Inexpensive frame jacks are sold as optional equipment to simplify the installing and unloading process and to provide a storage stand when the camper coach is not in use, freeing the pickup for other uses.

The two models of camper coaches presently manufactured by the company are both 10 feet in length, are designed to sleep a maximum of four to six

**FIGURE 2** ■ *(a)* Largest volume line of products is in motor homes, with the Chieftain model a major offering in the line; *(b)* motor home interior; *(c)* Minnie Winnie is one of the company entries in the low-priced economy line of motor homes.

persons, and offer a variety of accessories and accommodations. Prices range from approximately $1400 to $2200, again depending on size, model, optional equipment, and delivery charges.

Kaps are pickup truck bed enclosures, adaptable to all models of pickup trucks, which are designed primarily for sale in the low-cost market for recreational or camping purposes. The company sells finished kaps wholesale and to some extent at retail. In addition, it also manufactures laminated panels together with other components, including windows, screens, doors, and in some cases bunk beds and cabinets, for sale as a package to independent assemblers. (See Figure 3*a* to *d* for products.)

The consumer market for kaps is found largely among persons who own and use pickup trucks in their business and who desire an inexpensive unit to be used as a dwelling for camping and vacation trips. Some of such buyers, when not using the units for camping and vacation trips, use them for limited and incidental protection of cargo, although because of the recreational interior's qualities the cargo usefulness is limited. The retail prices of these units, whose demand is year-round with little seasonal variation, range from approximately $200 to $410, plus optional equipment.

A diversification program by Winnebago includes mass transportation, such as intercity and intracity buses, agricultural products, and the manufacture of original equipment components for other industries. Winnebago has already

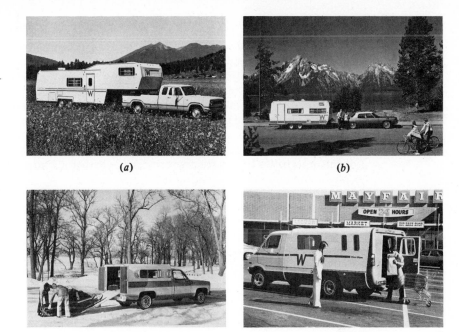

**FIGURE 3** ■ *(a)* A Chieftain fifth-wheel travel trailer; *(b)* traditional travel trailer, the Indian model; *(c)* Winnebago pickup; *(d)* Winnie Wagon, the station wagon for campers.

made some farm grain wagons and sells some aluminum, plastics, and upholstered products to industrial and commercial customers.

Winnebago's 19-passenger bus is expected to be attractive to such businesses as airlines, motels, hotels, and ski resorts. Small communities using the vehicle as a shuttle are another possibility.

The company has also begun making and selling fifth-wheel grain trailers. John K. Hanson said, "We're planning to expand production of these units and exploring other types of farm products, including specialized livestock housing."

Winnebago, which had explored the housing business in the early 1970s, is again entering the field. This time the entrance is with a product totally different.

It is a thermostructural building cell which is part of a building system developed by Victor Loebsack, a Kansas architect, with 30 years' experience in the building design and construction field. The new units, developed and marketed by the Dover Company, Inc., of Topeka, Kansas, are based on the modular building theory and designed for multifamily use. This Living Components Division is part of the Winnebago Realty Division.

Among the many features of this building system is the use of laminated ceiling, floor, and wall panels which combine the strength of box beam construction with the excellent insulating qualities of styrofoam. These units are so strong that as many as five can be stacked on top of each other without additional structural supports to create motels, dormitories, nursing homes, apartments, and other multiunit buildings.

## Marketing at Winnebago

When you talk about Winnebago's marketing management policies, you find yourself looking at a company, a longtime leader in its industry, that has through difficult times become a highly aggressive firm. This aggressiveness is clearly evident in its marketing management policies.

In the particular area of market investigation and research policies they have done quite a remarkable job. They know the market and have for years successfully anticipated and offered to their customers those conveniences asked for. The firm's concern for its products throughout the life of the products is sensitive to constructive criticism, whether it comes from its own people or product safety organizations.

Largely because of potential buyers' uncertainty about the availability of fuel to power the RV and high retail inventory levels of RVs throughout the industry, which resulted in intense competition for the consumer's dollar, the results in the last year of operations were disappointing.

Winnebago points to its hopes in the 1974 annual stockholder's report: "We believe there is a pent-up demand among consumers for good quality recreational vehicles, and with some assurance that fuel will be available for them, more buyers should return to the market place." Their diversification program, especially in the area of new product development, has been ambitious. The product strategy, how it adds to Winnebago's product line, is also well defined.

The most significant market in terms of volume, to date, is the agricultural field. Nearly 190 dealers (over 80 percent not handling other Winnebago products) already have been signed to retail a line of fifth-wheel agricultural trailers. The "fifth-wheel" designation is given to those trailers that may be towed by a pickup truck with a specialized hitch mounted in the bed of the truck over the rear axle, to which the trailer tongue extends over the truck tailgate. The importance of this method is that pickup trucks may tow much larger loads than with conventional trailers.

Presently, it manufactures and sells two types of fifth-wheel trailers to the agricultural market: a gravity box model and a grain hauler box model with hydraulic box tilt for unloading. The latter is capable of hauling farm supplies and livestock.

Another form of fifth-wheel trailer is called a cargo van; it incorporates a closed cargo box on the chassis for a variety of commercial hauling applications. Intended for a similar commercial market, but utilizing a different approach, is the Winnie Van, a commercial light-duty panel delivery truck built on a chassis similar to the type C motor home. Winnebago's diversification has been thorough.

An additional new market for Winnebago is mass transit, specifically buses. The 19-passenger bus has a low initial cost and is expected to be competitive in features and quality offered in the market at which it is aimed. During the product's development, computer stress testing is expected to enable the bus to meet federal TRANSBUS crash-worthiness recommendations regarding both roll-over and side-impact occupant protection. The new bus also meets the motor vehicle safety standards of the Department of Transportation relating to bus construction and operation.

Winnebago is using a specially equipped Dodge chassis that incorporates heavy-duty front disk brakes with special pads, transmission cooling systems, and other components designed to withstand the rigors of start-stop, in-town traffic conditions that normally are not encountered by motor homes in ordinary use.

Finally, to prevent future problems such as the recent overproduction immediately preceding a stagnant market, an interesting research project is under way utilizing a Winnebago motor home. Billings Energy Research Corp., of Provo, Utah, has converted a Winnebago motor home from gasoline and propane power for engine and appliances entirely to liquefied hydrogen. The motor home's 440-cubic-inch engine and also the furnace, cooking range, refrigerator, air conditioner, and 110-volt electric generator can now be operated entirely by hydrogen power. Billings Energy Research staff engineers have proclaimed that hydrogen will be the "fuel of the future," though wide use is not expected for some time to come. Their work has been stimulated by petroleum shortages, which they believe will culminate in eventual conversion to hydrogen as the common fuel for vehicle propulsion. Availability of liquid hydrogen is the chief deterrent to wide-scale conversion at this time.

A key to long-term success in recreational vehicles is service after the sale. A satisfied customer is often a company's best salesperson through word-of-mouth testimonials. Winnebago is a strong advocate of the belief that service that satisfies the customer must be provided by retail dealers. It currently has one of the most comprehensive training programs for dealer service personnel in the industry. Approximately 1000 dealer service people have attended Winnebago service school classes to date.

The company's RVs, with the exception of limited retail kap sales, are sold exclusively on a wholesale basis to a broadly diversified retail dealer organization. This dealer organization includes approximately 350 retail dealers, 44 of whom are dealers for kaps only. No single dealer accounted for as much as 3 percent of the company's net sales in the past fiscal year. Many of the company's dealers are also engaged in another area of business, including approximately 45 percent in the sale of automobiles and/or trucks. The company's dealers (other than kap-only dealers) may be broadly categorized according to the RVs they sell as follows: (1) approximately 45 percent handle only Winnebago's RVs; (2) approximately 40 percent carry recreational products of other manufacturers to complete their line of RVs but do not carry a product competitive with Winnebago's products sold by them; and (3) the remaining 15 percent carry at least one other line competitive with Winnebago's products sold by them. Winnebago is placing increasing emphasis on the capability of its dealers to provide complete servicing for its recreational vehicles. Dealers are obligated to provide full service for owners of Winnebago motor homes or to secure such service at their own expense from other authorized firms.

Winnebago service district managers provide assistance to dealer parts and service departments to aid them in becoming an increasingly profitable part of the dealer's business, while improving service to the customers. Winnebago's dealers are serviced in part directly by home-office sales and service staffs. In the field are three area managers, fourteen district managers, and the fourteen service district managers who are all assigned to various geographic areas. As in the automotive business, parts and accessories are an important feature of sales and service.

The retail market for its products extends to virtually all sections of the United States and Canada. Foreign sales, other than in Canada, have not been material. Winnebago's products are advertised in national magazines and local newspapers, television, and radio, often under local dealer cooperative advertising programs to help expand the total market for recreational vehicles and the dealers' own markets. Only to a limited extent has a national network television and radio program been used.

The company's entrance to national television came in November 1971, kicking off the 1972 model year promotion. Four separate national television campaigns were prepared for the particular phases of the annual selling cycle. These were backed by a promotional package that included newspapers, magazine, and radio advertising and dealer co-op campaigns. The total expenditure came to about $3.5 million during fiscal 1972.

Most Winnebago dealers held retail open houses during that November and were highly successful in stimulating sales.

The Winnebago approach focuses on the concept and the conveniences of "motor homing" rather than the individual advantages of a Winnebago vehicle. Fortunately for Winnebago, programs with magazines, newspapers, television and radio stations, free-lance writers, and outdoor writers have helped Winnebago to maintain a preeminent news coverage position in the industry.

An interesting new promotional device was used by Winnebago soon after the lifting of the most recent oil embargo. Winnebago began its Grand Giveaway, in which buyers received merchandise premiums with their motor home purchases. Under the plan, more than $1 million was spent on additional promotion; Winnebago offered $1000 in merchandise to purchasers of 1973 model motor homes and $300 in merchandise to 1974 model buyers. By spring, this program proved highly successful and all of the 1973 model units in built-up inventory were sold. The question then came to be whether Winnebago could manufacture sufficient quantities of motor homes to keep up with demand.

Probably the most powerful promotional tool Winnebago has is the Winnebago International Travelers. It is a company-sponsored club of Winnebago recreational vehicle owners with many local chapters sponsored by Winnebago dealers. It has passed the 20,000-vehicle and 50,000-person membership level. The 6-year-old club conducts caravans and rallies and generates considerable owner loyalty, tending to produce repeat sales. Membership dues are $15 per year and may in the long run provide a vocal lobbying group for the industry if it becomes threatened by restrictions or other threats to these members' enjoyment of their campers.

The Fifth Grand National Rally of the Winnebago International Travelers club was held at Forest City in August 1974. Its theme was "Circus" and highlights included a minicircus and entertainment by country and western vocal groups. Parades, contests, shows, and games were among other activities held.

Although the industry is still recovering from the slump, and Winnebago is one of those recovering, the strength of its dealer organization is an outstanding advantage in maintaining its position. A measure of its past strength in the dealer organization was Dealer Days (new model introduction) in August 1972, when Winnebago honored eight dealers who had each sold more than $1 million worth of Winnebago vehicles in the previous model year. At Dealer Days in August 1974, the company honored 37 such dealers.

One other consideration is that the market may be reaching saturation. People do not replace motor homes as they do automobiles. Many are sold to retired people, who will take them on one cross-country trip and then turn them in to the used-vehicle market.

Victor J. Raskin of Dean Witter speaks for most of the investment community's current feeling for Winnebago: "With so many other attractive investments around in other industries with companies that haven't had problems, why Winnebago?"

## Dealer relations

Winnebago maintains close tabs on its dealers' businesses. The company has instituted and standardized an accounting system, a business management program for training dealers. While the dealer organization has been considered competent, the standardized accounting system enables Winnebago to spot problems or potential problems and be in a position to more quickly help the dealer recover.

Winnebago has gone greater lengths than most to help finance the development of its entire scope of operations.

The Winnebago Realty Corporation (WRC) was organized to assist in the development of facilities in desirable retail locations. In October 1973 Winnebago announced a program for the construction of 28 sales and service facilities in the next 3 years that were to be leased to independent dealers. To date, however, only one such facility has been built but is not yet leased. Further facility development has been deferred at present. In addition, WRC manages miscellaneous parcels of real estate owned by Winnebago.

On April 23, 1974, WRC executed an agreement with Holiday Hills Recreation Center, Inc., to rent 500 specially built motor homes to serve as lodging for visitors to the Expo '74 world's fair in Spokane, Washington. The fair was held from May 4 to November 4, 1974. WRC was to receive 50 percent of the gross customer charges and was responsible for any maintenance and service covered by Winnebago's standard warranty. Winnebago was not responsible for maid service and cleaning. To finance these rental units, WRC obtained a commitment for back borrowings (guaranteed by Winnebago) to a maximum of approximately $3,900,000 collateralized by title to the units. Winnebago expected to have it paid off before the end of the fair and its due date of December 15, 1974.

Substantially all sales of recreational vehicles to dealers are made on cash terms. Most dealers are financed on a "floor plan" basis on which a bank or finance company lends the dealer all or substantially all of the purchase price, collateralized by a lien upon, or title to, the merchandise purchased. In special cases, upon request of a lending institution financing a dealer's purchases of Winnebago's products and after a complete credit investigation of the dealer, Winnebago will execute its standard form of repurchase agreement. This agreement provides that in the event of default by the dealer on his agreement to pay the lending institution, Winnebago will repurchase the merchandise so financed for the amount due the lending institution. Substantially all the agreements provide that Winnebago's liability will not exceed 100 percent of the dealer's invoice price for 6 months after the original date of payment and 90 percent of such price for an additional 6 months thereafter, and that the merchandise is new and not previously sold or leased. A limited number of agreements executed since January 1, 1974, limit Winnebago's liability to 100 percent of the invoice price for the first 3 months, 90 percent for the next 3 months, and 80 percent and 70 percent, respectively, for the next two successive 3-month periods. Winnebago's contingent liability on all repurchase agreements at February 23, 1974, amounts to approximately $700,000 resulting from the extension of certain agreements beyond their normal expiration date. Winnebago's contingent liability under repurchase agreements will vary and may be substantially greater in the future, depending upon the activities of Winnebago Acceptance Corporation (WAC), seasonal shipments, competition, dealer organization, and other factors.

Winnebago incurred losses of approximately $1,700,000 on repurchases pursuant to agreements and otherwise during the year ended February 23, 1974, including a reserve aggregating approximately $700,000 at that date for possible future losses or repurchases. During the fiscal year ended February 23, 1974, Winnebago repurchased 358 motor homes and 53 other units (including repurchases from WAC) and resold 74 of the motor homes and 5 of the other units. For the most part, losses on repurchases have been insignificant in prior years.

The Winnebago Acceptance Corporation is a wholly owned subsidiary. It was established in 1971 to provide floor plan financing for dealers in Winnebago's recreational vehicles and other products. It also provides an additional source of credit for retail purchases of Winnebago's products. To date, WAC has engaged only in floor plan financing of Winnebago dealers including financing of rental units of Winnebago Motor Homes. Expo '74 is a recent example. WAC currently participates in floor planning solely by WAC. On February 23, 1974, outstanding WAC receivables were $13 million. At the same time in 1973, the figure was $17 million. During the year (1974), Winnebago repurchased 166 repossessed motor homes and 35 other units from WAC at the wholesale value at the time of repurchase.

## Producing Winnebagos

One of the keys to Winnebago's manufacturing management policy has been vertical integration. In vertical integration one company produces a high percentage of components of subassemblies from basic materials, or adds value to components before they become a part of the finished product. In the past, as volume increased, further vertical integration became more economically feasible.

With certain exceptions (principally the chassis and engines which at the present time are purchased from the Dodge Division of the Chrysler Corporation, electric power units, and appliances), Winnebago manufactures all components utilized in its motor homes. Winnebago has consistently invested capital expenditures for equipment to further vertically integrate manufacturing processes or to make existing processes more efficient than they are now.

The company has been extruding its own aluminum components for nearly 4 years. Aluminum extrusions are used in the manufacture of windows, doors, screens, grille moldings, and other parts. Many of Winnebago's extrusions now also go through an anodizing operation which provides a decorative, protective

(a)

(b)

**FIGURE 4** ■ *(a)* Bird's-eye view of Winnebago Industries, Inc.; *(b)* inside production facilities.

coating that is an integral part of the surface of the extrusion. In connection with its extrusion operations, it operates a reclamation facility which includes equipment for melting scrap aluminum and forming it into billets for reuse in the extrusion plant.

The subassembly of the many components before arrival at final assembly aids final assembly of motor homes, fifth-wheel trailers, travel trailers, and pickup covers or kaps, with resulting improvements in capacity and costs.

Uniformity and exactness of fit are all important in the assembly. Cabinets are preassembled and conveyed to the final assembly lines. Complete floor assemblies with wheel well covers, sewage holding tanks, outside steps, gasoline filler access parts, aluminum "skin" to resist weather, and other parts, are brought to the final assembly line intact. Sidewalls and roofs come to the line with wiring and lights already installed. The entire front end assembly comes to the line as a unit with grillwork, dashboard instrumentation, safety padding, and driver's compartment protective sheathing already in place.

The company has instituted a "total quality concept," from inception through production of its products. The technical staff has been increased. The staff has produced quality manuals and training programs as well as new measurements, controls, and action plans to optimize the quality of the products.

The RV industry has been responsible for some technological advances. One of the newest materials concepts is a laminated sandwich wall and floor. This design compresses fireproofed styrofoam between exterior and interior walls. The laminate provides stronger walls and floors, and eliminates the need for studs and exterior screws. Insulation is improved so that exteriors can have a greater range of colors or trim put on them. Sprayed cellulose affords another improved insulation, and improves acoustical qualities and durability.

Other innovations in the RV field include a compact car trailer and hitches; hard-top and soft-top campers; more effective space design; refrigeration, heating, and air conditioning; fiber glass bodies; advances in fire-resistant materials; and more convenience in horsepower and responsiveness in motor homes.

Use of plastics has increased in the construction of RVs because of price increases in wood and steel. By 1980 it is predicted that seat cushions and/or mattresses, cushion covering, insulation coatings, and mechanical goods will be plastic.

Supplying the final assembly lines with the parts and pieces and subassemblies is a complex task. For example, in the main motor home assembly plant, 13 models of motor homes are produced on four assembly lines. Production runs must be scheduled weeks and months ahead of the time the product may be sold, based on product mix inputs from sales and marketing. Once the production run is scheduled, subassemblies, individual components, and a variety of parts peculiar to a particular floor plan or model must also be produced in sufficient time and quantity to be ready to be supplied to the main assembly line at the time the chassis for that model begins its run down the assembly line.

In Forest City, things went from bad to worse in 1973. The motor home production rate, at a level of 600 a week in March and April 1973, slipped to 450, then to 200, and finally to zero in December, when the plant was shut down. Employment plummeted from 3200 to 800, and the company had a field of homes on its lots. And it was borrowing heavily to carry these inventories and operating costs.

Since then, there has been a revival. After production resumed in the late winter of 1974, the company was involved in a diversification program involving various other products.

Winnebago and Forest City have a close relationship. While the recent slump has lessened the closeness somewhat, the community still retains strong support for Winnebago. The center of their strength is their faith that John K. Hanson will steer Winnebago clear of present-day difficulties. This close-knit relationship exists throughout the Winnebago company and is evidenced in employee loyalty. In November 1971, production employees rejected union organizing attempts by a margin of 2½ to 1. In February 1971, independent motor home delivery drivers turned down union representation by about 13 to 1.

Winnebago currently has a qualified contributory profit-sharing plan for all eligible employees. The plan provides for contributions by Winnebago in such amounts as the board of directors may annually determine.

Recent contributions charged to expense were as follows:

| Year ended | Contribution |
|---|---|
| February 22, 1969 | None |
| February 28, 1970 | $ 63,900 |
| February 27, 1971 | 113,542 |
| February 26, 1972 | 327,586 |
| February 24, 1973 | 453,970 |
| February 23, 1974 | None |

Winnebago feels their employees have done a remarkable job. They currently employ approximately 2700 persons. Careful buying and utilization are helping reduce material costs; better engineering leads to products that work better and last longer. Imaginative product development has been coupled with research and development expenditures resulting in competitive products. Their conservative attitude keeps them on top of all activities. Included in their extensive control is an up-to-the-minute accounting and management information service providing management with information needed for the control and planning necessary for optimum profitability and overall growth.

Winnebago has an employee stock purchase plan and option. The Employee Stock Purchase Plan entitles the eligible employee, through payroll deductions which may not exceed 15 percent of his base salary, to purchase shares of common stock on the last business day of February and August of each year. Under the purchase plan the purchase price of the common stock is 85 percent of the closing price on the New York Stock Exchange on that purchase date. Usually, any person who has completed 12 full months of continuous full-time employment with Winnebago can participate in the plan. However, no employee may purchase common stock under the purchase plan if he would own, upon purchase, more than 5 percent of the stock of the company. In addition, no employee may be granted the right to purchase in excess of $25,000 of fair market value of common stock in any calendar year.

Winnebago credits the common stock account with the par value of the stock sold under this plan, and the excess of the sale price over the par value of the stock is credited to additional paid-in capital.

## Money matters at Winnebago

Tables 2, 3, 4, and 5 contain some recent financial data on Winnebago.

Winnebago employs the firm of McGladrey, Hansen, Dunn and Company of Mason City, Iowa, for auditing its books. The board of directors has established an audit committee composed of three nonemployee board members to serve as a liaison with the independent auditors and to supervise the work of the internal audit function. Winnebago's accounting system has also

**TABLE 2 ■ WINNEBAGO INDUSTRIES, INC., AND SUBSIDIARY CONSOLIDATED BALANCE SHEETS**

| | 1969 | 1970 | 1971 | 1972 | 1973 | 1974[a] |
|---|---|---|---|---|---|---|
| *Assets* | | | | | | |
| **Current assets** | | | | | | |
| Cash | $ 2,137,595 | $ 1,624,356 | $ 1,551,953 | $ 4,079,308 | $ 6,038,783 | $ 1,560,998 |
| Marketable securities | 5,700,580 | 530,228 | 541,481 | 16,585,456 | | . . . |
| Trade receivables | | | | | | |
| Less allowance for doubtful accounts | 2,395,542 | 3,449,670 | 6,508,758 | 12,931,907 | 16,892,584 | 1,416,686 |
| Income tax receivable | . . . | . . . | | | | 7,050,000 |
| Interest receivable | 49,786 | 5,852 | 6,534 | . . . | . . . | . . . |
| Inventories | 4,380,751 | 18,716,605 | 12,815,292 | 26,998,994 | 42,765,197 | 40,543,222 |
| Prepaid and deferred expenses | 106,914 | 422,210 | 348,816 | 468,770 | 1,469,248 | 1,628,860 |
| Deferred income tax charges | . . . | . . . | 70,500 | 265,000 | 2,104,800 | 2,315,400 |
| Total current assets | $14,771,168 | $24,748,921 | $21,843,334 | $61,329,435 | $ 69,270,612 | $54,515,166 |
| **Investments** | | | | | | |
| Cash surrender value of life insurance | 14,857 | 15,264 | 17,456 | . . . | . . . | . . . |
| Land, at cost | . . . | 882,750 | 882,750 | 1,115,850 | 1,251,638 | unavailable |
| Employee housing, at cost | . . . | . . . | 99,416 | 910,656 | 823,563 | unavailable |
| Investment in wholly owned WAC | . . . | . . . | . . . | 1,494,698 | 1,528,287 | unavailable |
| Advances to WAC (1974 Inc. Inv.) | . . . | . . . | . . . | . . . | 5,767,101 | 3,209,130 |
| Municipal bonds, at cost | . . . | . . . | . . . | 535,321 | . . . | . . . |
| Other (1974 other assets) | . . . | . . . | . . . | 55,321 | . . . | |
| **Property and equipment** | | | | | | |
| Land and/or improvements | 268,545 | 316,683 | 446,683 | 577,130 | 1,540,761 | 1,447,431 |
| Buildings | 1,786,955 | 4,454,666 | 5,416,332 | 8,218,738 | 19,654,845 | 20,652,669 |
| Machinery and equipment | 870,469 | 2,960,208 | 3,722,753 | 9,509,956 | 16,364,737 | 19,675,265 |
| Transportation equipment | 513,403 | 559,856 | 677,816 | . . . | 4,217,783 | 1,660,348 |
| Dies, jigs, and patterns | 257,303 | 621,594 | 964,538 | . . . | . . . | . . . |
| Construction in progress | 833,053 | 313,555 | 175,820 | . . . | . . . | . . . |
| | $ 4,529,728 | $ 9,226,562 | $11,403,942 | $18,305,824 | $ 41,778,126 | $43,465,713 |
| Less accumulated depreciation | 556,005 | 1,001,467 | 1,660,274 | 2,808,332 | 5,035,874 | 7,351,976 |
| | $ 3,973,723 | $ 8,225,095 | $ 9,743,668 | $15,497,492 | $ 36,742,252 | $36,113,737 |
| Intangibles patents, trademarks, at amortized cost | 12,989 | 15,517 | 23,177 | . . . | . . . | . . . |
| **Other assets** | | | | | | |
| Prepaid and deferred expenses | 5,915 | 5,070 | 4,225 | . . . | . . . | . . . |
| Deposit on land | 55,000 | . . . | . . . | . . . | . . . | . . . |
| Deferred research and development expenses | . . . | . . . | . . . | . . . | 827,941 | . . . |
| Escrowed securities, at cost | . . . | . . . | . . . | . . . | 530,285 | . . . |
| Other | . . . | . . . | . . . | . . . | 242,012 | . . . |
| Total: other assets | 60,915 | 5,070 | 4,225 | . . . | 1,600,238 | 2,735,808 |
| Total assets | $18,833,652 | $33,892,617 | $32,614,026 | $80,938,773 | $116,983,691 | $96,573,841 |
| *Liabilities and stockholders' equity* | | | | | | |
| **Current liabilities** | | | | | | |
| Notes payable | . . . | $11,000,000 | $ 1,000,000 | . . . | $ 11,000,000 | $15,000,000 |
| Current maturities of long-term debt | $ 13,576 | 13,860 | 14,940 | . . . | . . . | . . . |
| Accounts payable, trade | 1,504,323 | 2,965,637 | 5,617,484 | $10,567,385 | 17,489,930 | 3,331,084 |
| Accrued expenses: | | | | | | |
| Advertising and sales incentive | . . . | . . . | . . . | . . . | . . . | 2,576,126 |
| Payroll | 204,854 | 215,826 | 241,269 | 441,267 | 547,083 | 182,954 |
| Property and payroll taxes | 172,402 | 199,372 | 284,833 | 466,240 | 922,425 | 931,943 |
| Insurance, vacation pay, and other expenses | 112,734 | 210,205 | 291,268 | 1,341,045 | 1,318,380 | unavailable |
| Other expenses | . . . | . . . | . . . | . . . | . . . | 383,299 |
| Income taxes payable | 1,233,700 | 428,317 | 1,540,000 | 8,038,542 | 3,492,800 | 151,500 |
| Judgment payable | . . . | . . . | . . . | . . . | 4,000,000 | . . . |
| Provision for estimated future losses on repurchases | . . . | . . . | . . . | . . . | . . . | 700,000 |
| Provision for liability on product warranties | . . . | . . . | . . . | . . . | . . . | 1,600,000 |
| Total current liabilities | $ 3,241,589 | $15,033,217 | $ 8,989,794 | $20,854,479 | $ 38,770,618 | $24,856,906 |
| Long-term debt | 364,142 | 350,337 | 335,044 | . . . | . . . | . . . |
| Deferred income tax credits | . . . | 75,000 | 240,500 | 415,000 | 821,600 | 996,900 |
| **Stockholders' equity** | | | | | | |
| Capital stock | 1,512,100 | 3,024,200 | 6,048,400 | 6,298,400 | 12,603,404 | 12,606,928 |
| Additional paid-in capital | 9,793,006 | 8,280,906 | 5,256,706 | 28,030,480 | 22,150,016 | 22,202,567 |
| Reinvested earnings | 3,922,815 | 7,128,957 | 11,743,582 | 25,340,414 | 42,638,053 | 35,910,540 |
| Total stockholders' equity | $15,227,921 | $18,434,063 | $23,048,688 | $59,669,294 | $ 77,391,473 | $70,720,035 |
| Total liabilities and stockholders' equity | $18,833,652 | $33,892,617 | $32,614,026 | $80,938,773 | $116,983,691 | $96,573,841 |

[a] As of February 1974.

TABLE 3 ■ WINNEBAGO INDUSTRIES CONSOLIDATED STATEMENTS OF OPERATIONS

| | Year ended | | | | |
|---|---|---|---|---|---|
| | February 28, 1970 | February 27, 1971 | February 26, 1972 | February 24, 1973 | February 23, 1974 |
| Net Sales | $44,960,686 | $70,866,088 | $133,166,438 | $212,035,958 | $123,740,890 |
| Cost of goods sold | 35,359,739 | 55,388,292 | 98,394,654 | 162,145,299 | 112,904,485 |
| Gross profit | $ 9,600,947 | $15,477,796 | $ 34,771,784 | $ 49,890,659 | $ 10,836,405 |
| Delivery charges | 793,227 | 1,193,166 | 2,750,861 | 4,807,333 | 3,088,107 |
| | $10,394,174 | $16,670,962 | $ 37,522,645 | $ 54,697,992 | $ 13,924,512 |
| Selling and delivery expenses | $ 2,944,854 | $ 5,939,231 | $ 8,522,381 | $ 14,299,578 | $ 18,126,631 |
| General and administrative expenses | 1,074,531 | 1,461,768 | 3,493,220 | 5,663,360 | 4,881,674 |
| Loss on repurchase and resale of recreational vehicles | | | | | 1,693,773 |
| Interest and other (income) expense, net[a] | 48,647 | 300,117 | (372,287) | (937,925) | 66,759 |
| | $ 4,068,032 | $ 7,701,116 | $ 11,643,314 | $ 19,025,013 | $ 24,768,837 |
| Income (loss) before taxes on income and items shown below | $ 6,326,142 | $ 8,969,846 | $ 25,879,331 | $ 35,672,979 | $ (10,844,325) |
| Provision for federal and state income taxes (credits):[b] | | | | | |
| Current | $ 3,045,000 | $ 4,260,221 | $ 12,297,197 | $ 15,842,252 | $ (5,392,159) |
| Deferred | 75,000 | 95,000 | (20,000) | 493,000 | 362,112 |
| | $ 3,120,000 | $ 4,355,221 | $ 12,277,197 | $ 16,335,252 | $ (5,030,047) |
| Income (loss) before items shown below | $ 3,206,142 | $ 4,614,625 | $ 13,602,134 | $ 19,337,727 | $ (5,814,278) |
| Equity in net income (loss) of Winnebago Acceptance Corporation | $ . . . | $ . . . | $ (5,302) | $ 33,589 | $ (482,706) |
| Income (loss) before extraordinary item and cumulative effect of a change in accounting policy | $ 3,206,142 | $ 4,614,625 | $ 13,596,832 | $ 19,371,316 | $ (6,296,984) |
| Extraordinary item, net of related deferred income tax effect of $1,926,323[c] | . . . | . . . | . . . | (2,073,677) | . . . |
| Cumulative effect on prior years of changing to a policy of expensing research and development expenses, net of related deferred income tax effect of $397,412 | . . . | . . . | . . . | . . . | (430,529) |
| Net income (loss) | $ 3,206,142 | $ 4,614,625 | $ 13,596,832 | $ 17,297,639 | $ (6,727,513) |
| Earnings (loss) per common share:[d] | | | | | |
| Income (loss) before extraordinary item and cumulative effect of a change in accounting policy | $ .13 | $ .19 | $ .56 | $ .77 | $ (.25) |
| Extraordinary item, net of related deferred income tax effect | . . . | . . . | . . . | (.08) | . . . |
| Cumulative effect on prior years of a change in accounting policy, net of related deferred income tax effect | . . . | . . . | . . . | . . . | (.02) |
| Net income (loss) | $ .13 | $ .19 | $ .56 | $ .69 | $ (.27) |
| Weighted average number of shares of common stock outstanding during each period[d] | 24,193,600 | 24,193,600 | 24,336,456 | 25,201,191 | 25,211,422 |

[a] Interest expense for the year ended February 23, 1974, was $944,479. Interest expense was not material in amount for any other year presented.

[b] The company follows the policy of recording the investment credit in the year it arises as a reduction of current tax expense. For the fiscal year ended February 24, 1973, this policy increased net income $835,000 and earnings per common share $.03. This policy has not had a material effect on net income (loss) or earnings (loss) per common share for any other year presented.

Deferred tax expense results from timing differences in the recognition of expense for tax and financial statement purposes. The source of these differences for the year ended February 23, 1974, and the tax effect of each were as follows:

| | |
|---|---|
| Excess of tax over book depreciation | $ 775,600 |
| Out of court settlement charged to expense in a prior year and paid during the current year | 1,926,323 |
| Charges to expense this year but not deductible for income tax purposes until paid: | |
| Advertising and sales incentive programs | (1,219,300) |
| Warranty | (615,300) |
| Estimated future loss on repurchase | (331,300) |
| Other | (173,911) |
| | $ 362,112 |

[c] Related to a $4 million judgment for breach of contract. On May 3, 1973, the judgment was vacated and an out-of-court settlement in the amount of $4 million was paid by the company.

[d] All number of shares and earnings-per-share amounts have been retroactively adjusted to give effect to all stock split-ups. The common stock equivalents (stock option and employee stock purchase plan) have not entered into the earnings-per-share computations because they would not have a dilutive effect.

| | Year ended | | | | |
|---|---|---|---|---|---|
| | February 28, 1970 | February 27, 1971 | February 26, 1972 | February 24, 1973 | February 23, 1974 |
| *Financial resources provided by:* | | | | | |
| Operations: | | | | | |
| Income (loss) before extraordinary item and cumulative effect of a change in accounting policy | $ 3,206,142 | $ 4,614,625 | $13,596,832 | $ 19,371,316 | $ (6,296,984) |
| Depreciation and amortization | 454,940 | 855,370 | 1,322,798 | 2,692,165 | 3,868,267 |
| Deferred income taxes | . . . | . . . | . . . | . . . | 572,712 |
| Equity in net loss of Winnebago Acceptance Corporation | . . . | . . . | . . . | . . . | 482,706 |
| Proceeds from sale of equipment, net of gain included above | . . . | . . . | . . . | . . . | 2,747,759 |
| Other | 75,000 | 165,500 | 179,802 | 373,011 | 282,750 |
| Working capital provided by operations before extraordinary item and cumulative effect of a change in accounting policy | $ 3,736,082 | $ 5,635,495 | $15,099,432 | $ 22,436,492 | $ 1,657,210 |
| Extraordinary item, net of related deferred income tax effect of $1,926,323 | . . . | . . . | . . . | (2,073,677) | . . . |
| Cumulative effect on prior years of changing to a policy of expensing research and development expenses, net of related deferred income tax effect of $397,412 | . . . | . . . | . . . | . . . | (430,529) |
| Total working capital provided by operations | $ 3,736,082 | $ 5,635,495 | $15,099,432 | $ 20,362,815 | $ 1,226,681 |
| Repayments of advances to Winnebago Acceptance Corporation | . . . | . . . | . . . | . . . | 15,522,976 |
| Equity financing, net proceeds from the sale of common stock | . . . | . . . | 23,023,774 | 424,540 | 56,075 |
| Sale of other assets | . . . | . . . | . . . | . . . | 722,500 |
| Other | 32,755 | 34,252 | 90,547 | 181,641 | 144,513 |
| Total | $ 3,768,837 | $ 5,669,747 | $38,213,753 | $ 20,968,996 | $17,672,745 |
| *Financial resources applied to:* | | | | | |
| Acquisition of long-term assets: | | | | | |
| Purchase of property and equipment | $ 4,739,067 | $ 2,408,195 | $ 6,686,581 | $ 24,233,942 | $ 5,920,645 |
| Advances to and investment in Winnebago Acceptance Corporation | . . . | . . . | 1,500,000 | 5,767,101 | 11,919,424 |
| Purchase of other assets | 1,360,068 | 119,676 | 1,529,231 | 942,915 | 568,188 |
| Other | 13,805 | 15,293 | 335,044 | . . . . | 106,222 |
| Total | $ 6,112,940 | $ 2,543,164 | $10,050,856 | $ 30,943,958 | $18,514,479 |
| Increase (decrease) in working capital | $ (2,344,103) | $ 3,126,583 | $28,162,897 | $ (9,974,962) | $ (841,734) |
| Working capital at beginning of year | 11,529,579 | 9,185,476 | 12,312,059 | 40,474,956 | 30,499,994 |
| Working capital at end of year | $ 9,185,476 | $12,312,059 | $40,474,956 | $ 30,499,994 | $29,658,260 |
| *Summary of changes in working capital components:* | | | | | |
| Increase (decrease) in: | | | | | |
| Cash and marketable securities | $ (6,213,819) | $ (72,403) | $19,112,811 | $(14,625,981) | $ (4,477,785) |
| Trade receivables | 1,054,128 | 3,059,088 | 6,423,149 | 3,960,677 | (15,475,898) |
| Income tax refund receivable | . . . | . . . | . . . | . . . | 7,050,000 |
| Inventories | 14,335,854 | (5,901,313) | 14,183,702 | 15,766,203 | (2,221,975) |
| Other | 271,362 | (2,212) | 307,920 | 2,840,278 | 370,212 |
| Decrease (increase) in: | | | | | |
| Current portion of notes payable | (11,000,284) | 9,998,920 | 1,014,940 | (11,000,000) | (4,000,000) |
| Accounts payable and accrued expenses | (1,596,727) | (2,843,814) | (6,381,083) | (7,461,881) | 12,572,412 |
| Income taxes payable | 805,383 | (1,111,683) | (6,498,542) | 4,545,742 | 3,341,300 |
| Other current liabilities | . . . | . . . | . . . | . . . | (2,000,000) |
| Judgment payable | . . . | . . . | . . . | (4,000,000) | 4,000,000 |
| Increase (decrease) in working capital | $ (2,344,103) | $ 3,126,583 | $28,162,897 | $ (9,974,962) | $ (841,734) |

been expanded and formalized for a more mechanized financial reporting
system and to provide better cost center responsibility.

Winnebago's policy is to include subsidiary companies with the parent
company in its consolidated financial statements. Only Winnebago Acceptance
Corporation is excluded, and it is reported separately from the consolidated
statements. All the material intercompany accounts and transactions have
been eliminated.

| | Common shares | | Additional paid-in capital | Reinvested earnings |
|---|---|---|---|---|
| | Number | Amount | | |
| Balance, February 22, 1969 | $ 3,024,200 | $ 1,512,100 | $ 9,793,006 | $ 3,922,815 |
| A 2-for-1 stock split effected as a 100 percent stock dividend | 3,024,200 | 1,512,100 | (1,512,100) | . . . |
| Net income | . . . | . . . | . . . | 3,206,142 |
| Balance, February 28, 1970 | 6,048,400 | 3,024,200 | 8,280,906 | 7,128,957 |
| Net income | . . . | . . . | . . . | 4,614,625 |
| Balance, February 27, 1971 | 6,048,400 | 3,024,200 | 8,280,906 | 11,743,582 |
| A 2-for-1 stock split effected as a 100 percent stock dividend | 6,048,400 | 3,024,200 | (3,024,200) | . . . |
| Proceeds from the sale of 500,000 shares of common stock less issue expenses of $88,726 | 500,000 | 250,000 | 22,773,774 | . . . |
| Net income | . . . | . . . | . . . | 13,596,832 |
| Balance, February 26, 1972 | 12,596,800 | 6,298,400 | 28,030,480 | 25,340,414 |
| A 2-for-1 stock split effected as a 100 percent stock dividend | 12,600,059 | 6,300,029 | (6,300,029) | . . . |
| Proceeds from the sale of common stock to employees and the exercise of the officer stock options | 9,949 | 4,975 | 419,565 | . . . |
| Net income | . . . | . . . | . . . | 17,297,639 |
| Balance, February 24, 1973 | 25,206,808 | 12,603,404 | 22,150,016 | 42,638,053 |
| Proceeds from sale of common stock of employees | 7,049 | 3,524 | 52,551 | . . . |
| Net loss | . . . | . . . | . . . | (6,727,513) |
| Balance, February 23, 1974 | $25,213,857 | $12,606,928 | $22,202,567 | $35,910,540 |

Inventories are valued at the lower of standard cost (first-in, first-out) basis. Deferred income taxes reflect timing differences in reporting the results of operations for income taxes and financial accounting purposes. The principal elements of deferred income taxes are depreciation used for tax purposes in excess of financial accounting depreciation, warranty, and other expenses not currently deductible for income tax purposes. Winnebago utilizes the flow-through method of accounting for investment tax credits.

For financial accounting purposes, depreciation is calculated by the straight-line method. Accelerated depreciation is used for tax purposes. Winnebago's fiscal year ends on the last Saturday of February. Maintenance and repair expenditures are charged to operations, and renewals and betterments are capitalized. When items of property are sold, retired, or otherwise disposed of, they are removed from the asset and accumulated depreciation accounts, and any gains or losses are reflected in income.

During the year ended February 23, 1974, Winnebago commenced charging research and development costs to operations as incurred. Previously such costs had been capitalized and amortized. This change was due to the substantial increase in the amounts being expended. The variety of projects involved together with the uncertainties involved in estimating the future periods to be benefited also led to the change. The effect of the change for the year ended February 23, 1974, was to increase the net loss by approximately $340,000 ($.01 per share). The deferred research and development expenses at February 24, 1973, of $430,529 ($.02 per share), net of related deferred income tax effect,

**TABLE 6 ■ QUARTERLY SALES (MILLIONS OF DOLLARS)**

| Fiscal year begins | May 31 | Aug. 31 | Nov. 31 | Feb. 28 | Full fiscal year |
|---|---|---|---|---|---|
| 1970 | 21.6 | 18.8 | 13.5 | 17.0 | 70.9 |
| 1971 | 32.9 | 29.2 | 35.9 | 35.2 | 133.2 |
| 1972 | 58.9 | 52.8 | 51.8 | 48.5 | 212.0 |
| 1973 | 62.6 | 24.7 | 29.5 | 6.9 | 123.7 |
| 1974 | 30 | 25 | 30 | 25 | 110 |

have been charged to operations to reflect the cumulative effect of the change in the accounting method.

A few comments on recent financial events seem in order. Recovering from the profit-draining effects of the gasoline shortage in 1973, Winnebago reported a profit of $250,000, or a cent a share, for its first fiscal 1974 quarter. It said it is in a "very strong" position to come back from the recent hard times in the RV industry. In all fiscal 1974, it had a $6.7 million loss. In the quarter beginning March 1, 1974, this year's profit gained $827,466 on the sale of RVs repurchased from dealers during the fourth quarter.

With the exception of a $2 million debt by Winnebago Realty, the company was free of debt as of July 31, 1974, having eliminated some short-term debt in 1974.

No cash dividends have ever been paid. The company policy is to conserve cash for investment in its business.

Winnebago's stock performance has been as follows:

| Year | High | Low |
|---|---|---|
| 1968 | 66.00 | 7.75 |
| 1969 | 42.00 | 20.50 |
| 1970 | 22.50 | 10.00 |
| 1971 | 53.38 | 8.50 |
| 1972 | 48.00 | 20.75 |
| 1973 | 27.50 | 2.86 |
| 1974 | 7.625 | 3.125 |

## What now?

Practically all recreational vehicle manufacturers see a great long-term future for RVs once the fuel crisis ends. Peter R. Fink, president of PRF Industries, Inc., of Mount Clemens, Michigan, one of the original builders of motor homes says, "The same growth factors that gave the industry its great years are still there—urbanization and high disposable incomes."

Robert L. Stewart, president of El Dorado Industries, Inc., agrees, "There is going to be an RV industry, a good RV industry." The big question that troubles industry executives though is: Who is going to be around long enough to take advantage of it?

Winnebago itself is trying to diversify. In addition to producing luxuriously decorated motor homes and well-appointed trailers, it is turning out insulated air-conditioned "confinement houses" in which farmers could pamper their calves and baby pigs. This is just one of many projects being undertaken in their diversification.

The fact is that Forest Citians have extraordinary faith in Winnebago, particularly John K. Hanson. Ben Carter, an original stockholder in Winnebago, observed, "Everybody knows old John K. He'd been selling 'em furniture and burying their dead for years. They think he can sell anything. They have faith he'll do it again."

Norm Stromer, a one-time farmer, now an optimistic young broker, says he still carries more than 3000 customers from the Forest City area on his books. He said, "In spite of the layoffs, we handled 25 percent more transactions in January (1974) than we did last year. Why, even some of those laid off were buying Winnebago last week when it went up a little. They have lots of faith in old John K."

"Only today I talked on the telephone with John K.," Mr. Buren, the soft water dealer, said. "He's been through the country, talking to his dealers, and he was on cloud nine. Of course, he's a natural salesman. He can sell you anything. He's certain Winnebago will come back some day."

In the 1974 Annual Report, Winnebago saw itself entering a transition period. Winnebago is moving from a one-market company to a multimarket company that "should better be able to utilize our manufacturing capabilities for diverse products and markets."

Winnebago's brain trust feels that if there is one word characterizing Winnebago Industries, it is *flexibility*. They believe it is flexibility that has enabled them to respond quickly to sudden changes in the RV market, and to search for and take advantage of other opportunities in other related areas.

This particular one-time highflier is confident of making a comeback and regaining a good growth pattern and again becoming profitable.

The entire industry has been turned upside down. The severity of the situation, predicts John V. Hanson, "will be directly proportional to how tough the retail market gets, and I think we're going to see a very rough retail market. . . ." How well is John K., "a natural salesman," going to meet this most crucial challenge?

# CASES

# Choice of strategy and strategic planning

# The Leitch Quality Drug Company

William F. Glueck

## Background of firm

The Leitch Quality Drug Company operates three drugstores in Orlando, Florida. Orlando is a central Florida city having a population of about 100,000. The stores are owned by a partnership of two brothers, Carl and Richard Leitch, Walter Neds, and Norman Henry. All partners except Mr. Henry are registered pharmacists.

The company is an old and well-established firm, having started as the Quality Drug Company in 1926. Carl Leitch began working for the company's store as an assistant pharmacist in 1934. Later, Richard Leitch attended pharmacy school and joined the firm in 1938.

In the early 1940s, the store experienced difficulties because of declining profits. The two Leitch brothers were convinced that they could improve the store's performance and made an offer to buy the store and go into business for themselves. The owners said that they would sell the business, but the price they set was too high for the brothers to afford. They therefore convinced two other men, Keith Steider and Martin Rhodes, to join the partnership. The sale was completed in late 1944, and the Quality Drug Company became known as the Leitch Quality Drug Company. Mr. Steider died in 1953, and his share of the business was sold to Mr. Henry. Mr. Rhodes retired in 1965 and sold his share to Mr. Neds, another registered pharmacist. All partners share equally in the ownership of the firm.

The city of Orlando grew rapidly during the 1950s. In response to this growth Leitch bought out another drug company in 1958 and took over its store, which was only 2 years old at the time. An opportunity for further expansion occurred in 1961, when the owner of a small drugstore in the southern part of the town died. The Leitch Company acquired this store. Currently Leitch owns three stores. No further expansion has been considered. The existing stores have been remodeled from time to time, and in one instance greatly expanded. Two stores, the number one downtown store and the number three "southside" store are rather old-fashioned in design and appearance. All three facilities are leased.

This is a disguised case. That is, the facts in it are based on a real organization. But the names of the persons involved, the location, and the quantitative data have been changed because the organization requested it. It serves no useful purpose to try to determine which organization is the "real" organization.

## TABLE 1 ■ LEITCH QUALITY DRUG COMPANY BALANCE SHEET STATEMENTS AS OF DECEMBER 31

|  | 1969 | 1970 | 1971 |
|---|---|---|---|
| *Assets* | | | |
| **Current assets** | | | |
| Cash on hand | $401,734 | $331,232 | $ 377,388 |
| Accounts receivable | 156,625 | 113,572 | 118,048 |
| Prepaid expenses | 7,001 | 5,388 | 6,792 |
| Inventory | 389,933 | 438,672 | 424,576 |
| Total current assets | $955,293 | $888,864 | $ 926,804 |
| **Fixed assets** | | | |
| Furniture, equipment | $278,562 | $324,908 | $ 331,012 |
| Leasehold improvements | 2,008 | 5,296 | 7,356 |
| | $280,570 | $330,204 | $ 338,368 |
| Less accumulated depreciation | 242,431 | 255,732 | 266,628 |
| Net fixed assets | $ 38,139 | $ 74,472 | $ 71,740 |
| Other assets: stock | 5,200 | 5,200 | 4,200 |
| Total assets | $998,632 | $968,536 | $1,002,744 |
| *Liabilities and net worth* | | | |
| **Current liabilities** | | | |
| Accounts payable | $141,746 | $127,344 | $ 127,280 |
| Notes payable | 2,000 | 2,000 | 2,000 |
| Accrued taxes | 28,211 | 21,620 | 22,968 |
| Other | 13,933 | 4,764 | 5,228 |
| Total current liabilities | $185,890 | $155,728 | $ 157,476 |
| **Partner's accounts** | | | |
| Balance at June 1 | $763,058 | $812,742 | $ 812,808 |
| Add net profit for period | 154,077 | 106,066 | 142,936 |
| Deduct withdrawals | $104,393 | $106,000 | $ 110,476 |
| Balance at end of period | $812,742 | $812,808 | $ 845,268 |
| Total liabilities and net worth | $998,632 | $968,536 | $1,002,744 |

In 1964 the Leitch Quality Drug Company entered into an agreement with Rexall, the national drug manufacturer, to sell Rexall products. The agreement gives Leitch exclusive rights to sell Rexall products within a 25-mile area. In exchange for this privilege, the partners were obligated to buy a small amount of Rexall stock.

For a while after the Rexall agreement, business grew and profits rose. The high point was reached in 1967, when sales exceeded $3 million. Since that time, however, sales have leveled off somewhat. In a conversation with the case writer, Carl Leitch explained why he thought the business was not growing as it should: "It's those new 'supers'—the large discount stores—that have cut into our business," he stated. "Why, I don't even consider them as drugstores. They sell everything—even groceries. Drugs are only a sideline. I can't really understand why people would want to fill their prescriptions at these stores, service is so impersonal. But they're growing and we're not. That's a fact that we have to face."

To illustrate the trend in sales, Mr. Leitch showed the case writer some of his firm's financial statements for the past few years. (See Tables 1, 2, and 3.)

**TABLE 2 ■ LEITCH QUALITY DRUG COMPANY PROFIT AND LOSS STATEMENTS, 1969–1971**

|  | 1969 | 1970 | 1971 |
|---|---|---|---|
| Net sales | $2,913,242 | $2,658,896 | $2,799,124 |
| Cost of sales | 1,700,218 | 1,654,892 | 1,668,296 |
| Gross profit | $1,213,024 | $1,004,004 | $1,130,828 |
| Operating expenses | 860,665 | 803,608 | 852,844 |
| Operating income | $ 352,359 | $ 200,396 | $ 277,984 |
| Federal taxes | 198,282 | 94,330 | 135,148 |
| Net income | $ 154,077 | $ 106,066 | $ 142,836 |

**TABLE 3 ■ LEITCH QUALITY DRUG COMPANY PROFIT AND LOSS STATEMENT FOR STORES, 1971**

|  | Store 1 | Store 2 | Store 3 |
|---|---|---|---|
| *Revenue* |  |  |  |
| Net sales | $646,592 | $1,606,336 | $546,196 |
| Cost of sales | 369,468 | 973,100 | 325,728 |
| Gross profit on sales | $277,124 | $ 633,236 | $220,468 |
| *Operating expenses* |  |  |  |
| Salaries | $134,896 | $ 268,820 | $147,548 |
| Payroll taxes | 4,928 | 8,232 | 3,364 |
| Advertising | 4,692 | 9,970 | 3,896 |
| Trading stamps | 8,400 | 25,600 | 7,600 |
| Depreciation | 6,196 | 8,896 | 2,740 |
| Utilities | 7,420 | 16,192 | 6,916 |
| Repairs | 2,768 | 4,016 | 1,008 |
| Rent | 2,720 | 35,320 | 16,560 |
| Store supplies | 5,352 | 12,676 | 3,884 |
| Bookkeeping services | 6,372 | 9,366 | 6,884 |
| Taxes and insurance | 10,232 | 12,668 | 5,940 |
| Office expenses | 2,812 | 6,388 | 2,620 |
| Other and miscellaneous | 6,720 | 14,688 | 7,544 |
| Total operating expenses | $203,508 | $ 432,832 | $216,504 |
| Operating income | $ 73,616 | $ 200,404 | $ 3,964 |

## Organization and management

Carl Leitch, Richard Leitch, and Walter Neds work as pharmacist-managers at the three stores. Richard Leitch is manager of store 1, the original store; his brother has the responsibility for store 3, and Mr. Neds manages store 2. Mr. Henry is a local factory owner. As a "not-so-silent" financial partner, he frequently offers his advice and helps make major policy or planning decisions.

Carl Leitch explained that each store is managed almost independently of the others. For example, each store orders its own stock and sets its own prices. Nearly all major decisions, including decisions to buy major equipment or redecorate the stores, are made by each store manager. Decisions involving a large capital outlay, such as store expansion, require the joint approval of all three working partners. Also, the stores do join together in some of their promotional efforts. Bookkeeping procedures are standardized, with one accounting firm serving all three stores. "Really, just about the only reason we even have a formal partnership is so we can trade under the Leitch name," Mr. Leitch said. "People know and trust that name."

In 1968 Mr. Henry and Mr. Neds presented a plan to incorporate the business. Convinced of the possibility of tax savings and of the advantages of limited liability, Mr. Henry tried to persuade his partners to follow the plan. The two Leitch brothers strongly opposed such a move, saying that they believed that the four men would lose all control of the company if outside shareholders were brought in. The matter was dropped from any further discussion. Richard Leitch told the case writer that "our present arrangement keeps us out of each other's hair. I'm not sure that we could maintain our present excellent relationship if we incorporated."

## The market and competition

The three stores serve separate market areas within the city. Store 1, located in the downtown area, caters mainly to persons working downtown and to downtown shoppers from other parts of town. Business in the downtown area has tapered off in recent years, partly because of a parking problem and also because of the growth of shopping centers in the outlying districts. Store 2 is in a shopping center at the fringe of a well-to-do residential area. The largest of the three stores, it accounts for 60 percent of total sales. The third store is located directly across the street from one of the city's hospitals. It is in a predominantly low-income area.

All three stores offer basically the same types of products and services. The three main categories are prescription service, fountain service, and sundries. Rexall products are promoted the most vigorously. This is because, according to one of the partners, they have a lower unit cost and higher markup. Other pharmaceutical products are used to supplement the Rexall line, however. Drinks, dairy products, sandwiches, and other snack items are served at the fountain bars. Sundry products include tobacco products, magazines, some cosmetic products, small household items, etc.

Leitch's competition comes from both the small neighborhood-type pharmacies and the large "super" drug discount stores. The services and products offered by the neighborhood pharmacies are usually limited to prescriptions and drugs; few sundry items are carried. There is little price competition from the smaller stores, since they buy in smaller volume and have higher overhead costs.

Leitch's competition mainly comes from four large stores. Two such stores, owned by the O'Shea Drug Company, are located very close to the Leitch stores 1 and 2. Both O'Shea stores, which are operated as franchises for a major retail drug firm, are larger than the Leitch stores. Recently, the O'Shea stores broadened their product lines to include such things as small appliances, school supplies, toys, etc., and began offering discount prices on some proprietary drugs and other items.

Within the past 3 years, two large discount drugstores have been built at suburban shopping center locations in Orlando. One is located three blocks from Leitch store 2. These stores carry a full line of merchandise, including appliances, clothing, a full assortment of household goods, hardware items, and other goods. They do a high-volume discount drug business, with drugs and cosmetics sold at substantially lower prices than those of Leitch's or most of the other drug firms.

The two new discount stores are typical of the new breed of giant discount stores. These stores carry a broad line of merchandise, including many high-margin items (electric hair dryers, etc.), as well as household goods, paper goods, soft goods, toys, photographic equipment, small appliances, records, hardware, and some automotive supplies. The growth of such stores may be explained in several ways. They are usually able to get better sites in the large shopping centers. Also they can price more competitively with supermarkets and other competitors. They generally have more merchandising experience, and enjoy economies in buying.

Another type of competitor is the smaller discount drugstore, averaging 2000 to 3000 square feet in size and featuring fast-moving health and beauty aid products. Markups for such stores are modest, with turnover rapid. At present, there is one such store in Orlando.

In a brief conversation with the case writer, Mr. Neds stated that he was very much concerned about the impact of the new discount stores. He explained that before the new stores were even opened, he told his partners that Leitch would lose sales. At that time, he suggested that they examine their profit margins item by item to see if some prices could be cut to meet the competition. This idea was immediately rejected by the two brothers, who did not want to lose their profit margins. When Leitch sales actually did begin to decline, the Leitches still resisted any move to lower prices. At that time Carl Leitch remarked, "Our main selling point is the personal service we offer. We can't continue to offer this service if margins are cut."

## Promotion

For the most part, advertising is done independently by the three stores. Newspaper ads are run on the average of once a month for each store. Because the stores rarely offer special prices on goods, most of the advertisements mainly promote the store name. A typical ad is headlined: "Thirty Years of Service: You Can Depend on Us."

The Rexall Company furnishes the materials for newspaper insertions and, in addition, pays one-half of the advertising costs. Rexall also runs nationwide ads in many leading magazines, at no cost to the Leitch stores. These advertisements are meant to promote the Rexall name and do not name individual franchises.

Generally speaking, Rexall offers no discounts on its products to druggists. One exception to this policy is the annual summer "one-cent sale." During this sale of Rexall products, the stores offer "two for the price of one plus a penny." The Rexall wholesaler offers sale goods to the individual stores at a reduced price for this sale. Mr. Neds said that this sale is usually successful, but it has not produced the results in recent years that it did in the past.

Although not as low as the prices in discount stores, the prices on Rexall products are, by and large, lower than those for the more famous name brands.

Rexall aspirin, for example, may sell for 15 to 20 cents cheaper per 100 than a better-known brand. Prescription drugs vary less from brand to brand.

The partners proudly point to one aspect of the traditional neighborhood store which remains in their stores: the fountain bar. "This is almost an institution in this country," said Richard Leitch, "but I'm afraid it's dying out. Although we don't realize much in the way of a profit from these bars, we still feel they give our stores a warmer atmosphere. Besides, when the kids come in to get a sundae, their parents often have them buy something else while they're here."

Another aspect of the firm's "personal touch" is the credit given to customers. Most customers, in fact, do business at Leitch stores on credit. Carl Leitch said that the stores did not profit directly from carrying customers on credit (no interest or service fee is charged), but the availability of credit was popular among the "old-timers." Credit applications are rarely checked, since most persons applying for credit are known by the employees. Delivery service is also offered by all three stores.

## Operations

Each store manager is responsible for the purchase and control of all inventory. The department heads assist the managers in buying the goods needed for their own departments. Most purchases are made through salesmen who visit the stores up to twice a week.

Inventories are not kept at fixed levels. Instead, a "short list" is kept in all departments. Thus, when a clerk or department head notices that an item is low or depleted, an entry is made on the list. Whenever a salesman appears, any items that he carries and that are on the short list are ordered. The person doing the ordering decides the quantity. Conceivably, anyone working in the store can order when a salesman visits. Buying trips are made by the three partners about three times per year. At these times, merchandise is selected for the Christmas, summer, and back-to-school seasons.

A physical count of inventory is made for all stores once each year. This occurs between Christmas and the first of the year, before preparation of the financial statements. The permanent records kept on inventory consist of order slips, shipping invoices, and ending inventory listings.

Pricing is done on a cost-plus basis. Three classes of items are marked up by different percentages of costs. All tobacco products are marked up by 25 percent above invoice price. Magazines, books, and periodicals carry a 20 percent markup, and most other items are marked up by one-third of the invoice price. This does not apply to Rexall brand items, which carry a markup of 50 percent above cost. The partners follow "fair trade" practices and do not use price cutting as a tool to increase sales volume. The partners believe that this policy allows them adequate profits and at the same time makes marketing easier.

An accounting firm keeps track of credit sales records. A bookkeeper comes to each of the three stores to record credit slips three times per week. It is possible for an individual to have a separate credit account at all three stores and at the end of the month receive a statement from each. Credit at one store guarantees a person that he may receive credit at the other two.

## Deciding the future

The Leitch brothers, who are both in their mid-sixties, have been thinking about retirement for some time. They were therefore quite receptive to a recent offer by a national food store chain to buy the Leitch Company drugstores. Presently, the food chain operates a chain of discount drugstores, and is anxious to become established in the Orlando area. If it buys the Leitch stores, it plans to remodel them completely and convert them to high-volume discount stores.

According to the terms of the merger proposal, the grocery firm would offer common stock having a book value equivalent to twice the partners' capital accounts in exchange for the Leitch Company's assets. The market value of the stock is presently close to book value. There is no offer for the three Leitch partners to continue in their present capacities, although it was mentioned that "they could probably work as pharmacists at other stores in the chain, if they so desire."

The offer has drawn mixed reactions from the partners. Carl and Richard Leitch both think that it "looks like a good deal," but neither one says that he is quite ready to retire. Mr. Neds, who at 35 is much younger, is bitterly opposed to the sale. Mr. Henry has not expressed his feelings, but it is felt that he would go along with the sale.

In a private conversation, Mr. Neds told the case writer why he opposed the sale of the business: "To begin with, I think we have a lot of potential," he said. "We've already got some of the best locations in town. It's just a matter of tapping into a market that is already there. Oh sure, the new discount stores have hurt us a little, but only because we've let them. We've got to change our image—perhaps do some remodeling. But above all, we must become more competitive price-wise. I'm hoping that you can convince my partners to stick with it a while longer, and perhaps help us lay down some guidelines for the future."

# Lacasse Services Company, Limited

William F. Glueck

Lacasse Services Company, Limited, is a rather small entrepreneurial firm in the sandblasting business in Montreal, Quebec, Canada, founded in 1958 when its owner, Robert Lacasse, set off on his own. He borrowed $800 and set up his own business. Since then, business has boomed and profits have been substantial, as can be seen in Table 1.

The management staff consists of the owner, Mr. Lacasse, and his son-in-law, Mr. Mercier. Mr. Mercier serves as accountant and foreman. He does all the bookkeeping and helps Mr. Lacasse supervise and manage the work. Neither Mr. Lacasse nor Mr. Mercier has received formal schooling beyond the secondary level.

Mr. Mercier keeps all the books and handles the tax calculations. In addition to the yearly financial statements he keeps monthly profit and loss statements and balance sheets. "It takes a lot of time to prepare monthly statements, but it really helps us keep abreast of things," Mr. Mercier pointed out. "This is especially useful in controlling expenses. For example, if wages for a given period exceed 30 percent of revenues, we begin thinking about cutting back employment."

Depreciation charges are calculated on an 8-year straight-line basis for machinery, and a 10-year straight-line basis for the building. No cost accounting or control procedures are used. Both Mr. Lacasse and Mr. Mercier feel that costing methods are impossible, since, as Mr. Mercier put it, "the jobs are too integrated."

The financial condition of the firm can be seen from Mr. Mercier's current balance sheet (Table 2) and income statement (Table 3).

## Operations at Lacasse

Lacasse set up his own business in 1958 in a rented building with leased equipment and three employees—two sandblasters and a helper. Robert Lacasse was the manager and salesman and supplied some of the labor too.

Mr. Lacasse had gained considerable experience in his previous jobs and knew that there was a de-

This is a disguised case. That is, the case is based on a real company situation, but the identity of the company has been disguised. It serves no useful purpose to attempt to ascertain the true name of the company.

| Month | 1968 | 1969 | 1970 | 1971 | 1972 |
|---|---|---|---|---|---|
| January | $ 6,160 | $ 9,217 | $ 6,891 | $ 9,542 | $ 3,226 |
| February | 316 | 739 | 8,966 | 882 | 8,086 |
| March | 10,066 | 5,608 | 7,602 | 6,236 | 8,705 |
| April | 8,870 | 8,004 | 10,539 | 6,686 | 5,580 |
| May | 11,819 | 15,859 | 7,008 | 19,734 | 2,187 |
| June | 8,613 | 11,384 | 12,018 | 12,974 | 5,194 |
| July | 4,334 | 5,989 | 6,244 | 3,659 | 2,578 |
| August | 2,920 | 9,906 | 7,543 | 14,747 | 3,819 |
| September | 4,294 | 10,354 | 7,678 | 5,557 | 8,193 |
| October | 10,023 | 7,378 | 10,685 | 3,470 | 5,572 |
| November | 2,120 | 6,180 | (938) | 451 | 620 |
| December | (2,425) | (2,685) | (12,231) | (6,112) | (3,122) |

mand for good sandblasting service in the Montreal area. He originally intended to do commercial construction cleaning jobs, cleaning buildings during or after construction. Over the years he took on other jobs. With a reputation for expert work and honest dealings, Mr. Lacasse has managed to establish a growing customer list over the years. Revenues for 1972 exceeded $175,000.

Mr. Lacasse owns eight 250 cf/m (cubic feet per minute) compressors purchased at a cost of about $11,000 each, and three 600 cf/m compressors purchased at a cost of about $25,000. All the compressors are portable, but the large ones are rather difficult to transport and are left in the yard for work done at the shop. The eight smaller ones are used for the jobs done on location; they can easily be towed behind one of the trucks.

There are 16 sand pots ($600 each), all of which are portable and can be carried in the bed of a truck. To these are attached one of the hoses with one of the several types of nozzles.

TABLE 2 ■ LACASSE SERVICES COMPANY, LIMITED, BALANCE SHEETS FOR YEARS ENDING DECEMBER 31, 1964–1972

| | 1964 | 1965 | 1966 | 1967 | 1968 | 1969 | 1970 | 1971 | 1972 |
|---|---|---|---|---|---|---|---|---|---|
| *Assets* | | | | | | | | | |
| Cash | $ (913) | $ 2,789 | $ (784) | $ 1,478 | $15,893 | $10,326 | $ 3,430 | $ 25,600 | $13,530 |
| Accounts receivable | 7,548 | 13,066 | 11,612 | 11,459 | 12,070 | 24,144 | 13,384 | 8,192 | 10,575 |
| Supplies and materials | 1,401 | 1,627 | 1,512 | 1,673 | 1,442 | 1,790 | 1,796 | 1,501 | 1,561 |
| Total current assets | 8,036 | 17,482 | 12,340 | 14,610 | 29,405 | 36,260 | 18,610 | 35,293 | 25,666 |
| Machinery and building | 45,660 | 52,808 | 93,084 | 78,389 | 80,937 | 80,937 | 126,050 | 150,010 | 152,558 |
| Office equipment | 994 | 994 | 994 | 994 | 1,238 | 1,238 | 1,238 | 1,238 | 1,238 |
| Total buildings and equipment | 46,654 | 53,802 | 94,078 | 79,383 | 82,175 | 82,175 | 127,288 | 151,248 | 153,796 |
| Less depreciation | (19,267) | (10,780) | (15,772) | (24,270) | (34,208) | (42,384) | (56,216) | (75,746) | (91,210) |
| Prepaid expenses | . . . | . . . | . . . | 2,862 | 3,699 | 1,573 | 4,243 | 3,231 | 2,083 |
| Total assets | $35,423 | $60,504 | $90,646 | $72,585 | $81,071 | $77,624 | $93,925 | $114,026 | $90,335 |
| *Liabilities and net worth* | | | | | | | | | |
| Accounts payable | $ 3,987 | $ 4,656 | $ 4,516 | $11,329 | $ 4,892 | $ 5,244 | $ 2,327 | $ 6,012 | $ 3,461 |
| Taxes payable | 480 | 543 | 851 | 1,999 | 2,573 | 2,472 | 2,652 | 714 | 664 |
| Notes payable | 8,442 | 27,521 | 44,405 | 43,375 | 41,286 | 18,754 | 45,164 | 48,746 | 32,878 |
| Total liabilities | 12,909 | 32,720 | 49,772 | 56,703 | 48,751 | 26,470 | 50,143 | 55,472 | 37,003 |
| Mr. Lacasse's capital | 17,074 | 22,382 | 27,783 | 40,874 | 15,882 | 32,320 | 51,154 | 43,781 | 58,554 |
| Less withdrawals | (10,433) | (10,122) | (17,973) | (53,986) | (30,401) | (39,002) | (47,624) | (32,258) | (42,296) |
| Profit (after tax) | 15,873 | 15,524 | 31,064 | 28,994 | 46,839 | 57,836 | 40,252 | 47,031 | 37,074 |
| Total net worth | 22,514 | 27,784 | 40,874 | 15,882 | 32,320 | 51,154 | 43,782 | 58,554 | 53,332 |
| Total liabilities and net worth | $35,423 | $60,504 | $90,646 | $72,585 | $81,071 | $77,624 | $93,925 | $114,026 | $90,335 |

**TABLE 3 ■ LACASSE SERVICES COMPANY, LIMITED, INCOME STATEMENTS**

| | 1964 | 1965 | 1966 | 1967 | 1968 | 1969 | 1970 | 1971 | 1972 |
|---|---|---|---|---|---|---|---|---|---|
| *Revenue* | | | | | | | | | |
| Outside work | $ 99,994 | $108,494 | $110,413 | $103,316 | $ 98,426 | $125,023 | $135,727 | $165,138 | $ 97,467 |
| Shopwork | . . . | . . . | 51,082 | 73,811 | 112,848 | 122,900 | 111,955 | 103,555 | 78,976 |
| Sand | 862 | 2,940 | 2,610 | 1,824 | 1,422 | 809 | 1,137 | 389 | 1,484 |
| Other | . . . | . . . | . . . | . . . | 2,562 | 602 | . . . | 678 | 15 |
| Total revenue | $100,856 | $111,434 | $164,105 | $178,951 | $215,258 | $249,334 | $248,819 | $269,760 | $177,942 |
| *Expenses* | | | | | | | | | |
| Wages | $ 31,234 | $ 32,458 | $ 49,596 | $ 53,245 | $ 64,800 | $ 66,461 | $ 69,692 | $ 83,840 | $ 60,539 |
| Fuel and transport | 7,305 | 9,064 | 13,784 | 11,684 | 11,270 | 14,966 | 10,632 | 13,927 | 7,653 |
| Depreciation (equipment) | 4,911 | 4,301 | 6,278 | 8,288 | 9,937 | 8,176 | 17,716 | 19,877 | 16,459 |
| Maintenance (equipment) | 4,807 | 2,262 | 3,248 | 2,632 | 2,554 | 7,554 | 5,734 | 7,588 | 3,060 |
| Supplies and materials | 8,588 | 12,300 | 18,701 | 21,389 | 22,123 | 27,698 | 32,413 | 30,363 | 14,197 |
| Contract labor | | 1,260 | | | 3,357 | 5,844 | 4,278 | 742 | 57 |
| Advertising | 9,047 | 10,884 | 11,738 | 8,616 | 7,342 | 7,848 | 10,161 | 8,453 | 7,507 |
| Rent | 2,332 | 2,716 | 3,780 | 3,024 | 3,024 | 3,024 | 3,276 | 3,024 | 2,682 |
| Office and building expenses | 4,102 | 4,452 | 4,567 | 10,318 | 12,160 | 8,826 | 8,484 | 10,987 | 5,513 |
| Taxes | 1,011 | 826 | 1,573 | 1,747 | 4,239 | 4,088 | 3,528 | 3,732 | 3,177 |
| Bad debts | 451 | 1,428 | 1,184 | 941 | 946 | 1,649 | 3,455 | 678 | 459 |
| Equipment rental | 1,584 | 4,018 | 3,822 | 2,349 | 314 | 3,444 | 4,463 | 5,552 | 3,901 |
| Interest | 445 | 199 | 3,212 | 3,996 | 5,169 | 1,823 | 2,982 | 3,181 | 2,100 |
| Other | 3,752 | 1,630 | 2,848 | 1,722 | 913 | . . . | . . . | . . . | . . . |
| Total expenses | $ 79,569 | $ 87,798 | $124,331 | $129,951 | $148,148 | $161,401 | $176,814 | $191,944 | $127,304 |
| Before-tax profit | $ 21,287 | $ 23,636 | $ 39,774 | $ 49,000 | $ 67,110 | $ 87,933 | $ 72,005 | $ 77,816 | $ 50,638 |

In addition to the sandblasting equipment, Mr. Lacasse also has two cement mixers, a forklift, welding and cutting torches, four spray painters, small air compressors for painting, four 1-ton trucks, two ¾-ton pickups, and a ½-ton pickup. This equipment makes it possible for him to be completely portable and capable of performing minor taks in conjunction with sandblasting. This versatility increases the number of jobs which the firm is able to do.

Until 1964 business was conducted in a rented building in an industrial area. In that year, a 10-year lease was signed for another piece of land. Here Mr. Lacasse built a 90 × 60 foot shop and a 60 × 30 foot open shed. The equipment and sand inventory are stored in the main part of the shop; a small office is located in the front. Shopwork is done in the shed.

The landowner is presently trying to lease the property surrounding the Lacasse plant. Many businesses will not rent next to the noise and dirt of a sandblasting establishment, and Mr. Lacasse has been told that he may have to move or pay much higher rent. The building will be written off at the end of the 10-year period.

Basically, Lacasse's service is sandblasting a surface with blasts of sand and compressed air. This cleans and roughs the surface of metal, stone, and many other materials. The applications of sandblasting are numerous. Besides being used to clean large structures, sandblasting may be used on the assembly line to clean parts in preparation for painting or assembly. Even small, delicate items such as electrical components can be sandblasted. Some manufacturing firms do their own sandblasting work. Others subcontract with sandblasting companies such as the Lacasse Company. "A lot of selling still needs to be done to get companies to accept sandblasting as part of their production process," Mr. Lacasse pointed out. "Too many inexperienced and unscrupulous sandblasters have soured manufacturers on the process. You have to be careful in this technique, or you can wind up with a lot of damage. Past experience makes people wary of the process."

The work done by the Lacasse Company is divided into shopwork and outside work. Forty to fifty percent of the revenue comes from shopwork. This includes small jobs brought in by the public, such as automobile bodies and metal furniture, and larger ones from industrial firms. Industrial work includes small electrical components and prepaint assembly items. Mr. Lacasse said that shopwork is not as profitable as outside work, since volume is erratic and the jobs are smaller. Nevertheless, he would like to see this aspect of the business expanded: "We could really reduce the seasonal impact on our workload if we increased our shopwork. Here, we can work in any kind of weather, any time of the year. We just need to sell potential customers on the availability and advantages of the sandblasting technique."

The rest of the company's work is done on location. These are usually large jobs done on a bid basis. One such job consists of cleaning the inside of large tanks for a company which lines such tanks with anticorrosive paint. Lacasse uses sandblasting to clean the large gasoline storage tanks at a local refinery, to clean the internal parts of the steam turbines at a power plant, and to frost glass for a shower door manufacturer. Lacasse also cleans residential and commercial buildings.

Apparently, the firm employs from 10 to 18 men to do the sandblasting work. There is no sandblasters' union in the area. Generally, one sandblaster and a helper are put on each job, while three or four men do the work performed in the shop.

Mr. Lacasse said, "Good experienced sandblasters are hard to find, so we try to keep our men working as steadily as possible. This is pretty hard to do, since our business fluctuates considerably from season to season. We have 10 employees which we consider to be 'permanent.' When our workload increases, we hire additional temporary men, and even Mr. Mercier and I pitch in and help, if necessary. In bad weather, we don't lay off our permanent employees if we can avoid it. The recent business slump may force us to do this, however."

The workers are paid about $2 per hour, plus overtime of time and a half. Much overtime is paid during the peak periods, but Mr. Lacasse feels that it is cheaper to pay an experienced worker overtime than to have the work done by inexperienced temporary help. Table 4 presents a schedule of wages paid out monthly over the last 6 years.

TABLE 4 ■ LACASSE SERVICES COMPANY, LIMITED, MONTHLY WAGES SCHEDULE

| Month | 1967 | 1968 | 1969 | 1970 | 1971 | 1972 |
|---|---|---|---|---|---|---|
| January | $2316 | $4875 | $4536 | $5552 | $5303 | $4721 |
| February | 4077 | 4777 | 4746 | 3987 | 5026 | 4995 |
| March | 7115 | 6006 | 5986 | 4488 | 5715 | 7507 |
| April | 3433 | 5309 | 5180 | 5460 | 9181 | 5214 |
| May | 3086 | 5572 | 7375 | 6034 | 6821 | 4732 |
| June | 4802 | 7210 | 5998 | 5678 | 9066 | 7241 |
| July | 4007 | 5519 | 5891 | 6863 | 9164 | 4841 |
| August | 3805 | 6244 | 6359 | 5281 | 7748 | 6465 |
| September | 4609 | 4894 | 5589 | 5337 | 7610 | 5827 |
| October | 5096 | 5034 | 5762 | 8610 | 5718 | 5337 |
| November | 4707 | 5740 | 5172 | 5104 | 5544 | 4321 |
| December | 5998 | 4903 | 3867 | 7059 | 6941 | 5077 |

| Month | 1967 | 1968 | 1969 | 1970 | 1971 | 1972 |
|-------|------|------|------|------|------|------|
| January | $1490 | $1257 | $1537 | $1047 | $ ·50 | $ 36 |
| February | 2598 | 1571 | 1016 | 2834 | 1898 | 865 |
| March | 5186 | 1464 | 566 | 2932 | 2243 | 1660 |
| April | 1277 | 1072 | 2346 | 2727 | 3044 | 1358 |
| May | 297 | 2971 | 4642 | 1767 | 1464 | 1560 |
| June | 2598 | 2831 | 2503 | 4572 | 4371 | 736 |
| July | 1467 | 944 | 2484 | 3828 | 5169 | 1014 |
| August | 3391 | 2010 | 1826 | 3108 | 2232 | 1963 |
| September | 2078 | 1896 | 2108 | 2002 | 2965 | 630 |
| October | 2946 | 949 | 2755 | 2212 | 1456 | 3268 |
| November | 431 | 1798 | 353 | 2792 | 924 | 602 |
| December | 2108 | 3360 | 5561 | 2596 | 5740 | 4001 |

Like those of most firms, Lacasse's operations include purchasing materials and equipment. Table 5 presents data on the last 6 years' monthly purchases.

Lacasse's major purchases include fuel and sand. The company normally has an inventory of 1 month's sand on hand. Lacasse buys in carload lots (twelve hundred 300-pound bags). The firm normally reorders when the inventory of coarse and fine sand drops below 200 bags. This occurs about every 30 days. Extra-fine sand is normally ordered quarterly or biyearly.

Three grades of washed blasting sand are used: coarse, fine, and extra-fine. The first two are supplied by a firm about 300 miles away, and the third is supplied by another firm about 250 miles away. Most work is done with the coarse and fine grades. Extra-fine is used only on jobs which require special care or a smoother finish. Mr. Mercier usually orders large amounts of sand late in the year so that it can be deducted from the year's revenue and thus decrease the tax payment. The company always takes advantage of a cash discount of 10 cents per ton.

## Marketing Lacasse's services

Lacasse's business has been rather sporadic, as a glance at Table 6 reveals.

Lacasse is an important factor in the construction industry of Montreal. There are very few companies in the Montreal area which specialize in sand-blasting. Construction, painting, housecleaning, and other companies do sand-

TABLE 6 ■ LACASSE SERVICES COMPANY, LIMITED, MONTHLY SALES SCHEDULE

| Month | 1967 | 1968 | 1969 | 1970 | 1971 | 1972 |
|-------|------|------|------|------|------|------|
| January | $13,818 | $14,622 | $15,963 | $16,820 | $18,519 | $12,712 |
| February | 7,344 | 10,472 | 11,525 | 19,337 | 12,390 | 17,505 |
| March | 12,244 | 22,092 | 16,447 | 22,168 | 19,684 | 20,918 |
| April | 13,003 | 19,930 | 21,076 | 24,461 | 24,948 | 12,365 |
| May | 14,126 | 26,664 | 34,838 | 18,108 | 34,468 | 13,409 |
| June | 9,380 | 24,836 | 26,239 | 29,985 | 32,953 | 18,804 |
| July | 31,041 | 15,114 | 19,037 | 21,448 | 24,000 | 11,679 |
| August | 18,127 | 15,324 | 22,254 | 19,785 | 34,217 | 16,677 |
| September | 15,786 | 14,823 | 21,787 | 21,023 | 22,280 | 19,250 |
| October | 21,834 | 23,320 | 24,312 | 28,106 | 17,030 | 18,900 |
| November | 11,516 | 15,901 | 16,847 | 13,686 | 12,370 | 8,328 |
| December | 10,732 | 12,160 | 19,009 | 12,090 | 16,901 | 7,395 |

blasting in conjunction with their specific lines of work, but they are usually limited to these types of jobs. There are only three or four other companies that compete with Lacasse for the large sandblasting jobs. Mr. Lacasse estimates that he has nearly 40 percent of the existing market, not counting those companies engaged in other types of business who do their own sandblasting work.

According to Mr. Lacasse, the sandblasting business has a rather poor reputation. Sandblasters are frequently poor credit risks and are sometimes dishonest in their dealings with customers. Mr. Lacasse said that he "kept his shirt clean" by providing customer satisfaction and by paying debts promptly. He feels that his honest reputation has given him a competitive advantage.

Recently, Lacasse received a merger proposal from Moreau Enterprises, Limited, one of Montreal's largest construction firms. Mr. Lacasse is well acquainted with the Moreau firm, as he has done a large amount of work for that company over the years. In fact, he was not at all surprised that the offer was made, for Moreau officials have talked to him previously about the possibility of a merger. But Mr. Lacasse is uncertain of just how he feels about selling out a company which he has successfully built over the years. In talking it over with the case writer, he said, "I can certainly see some reasons for going along with the merger. For once I would have the capital resources to expand into some areas I've been thinking about for a long time. Also, it may help to even out our workload. As it stands now, we are faced with a sharply fluctuating demand from season to season. Another important consideration is the possibility that we may have to relocate as our lease expires next year. A merger just may not be a bad thing for us right now."

But for other reasons, Mr. Lacasse is not enthusiastic about the proposed merger: "I built this business—it's mine and no one else can tell me what to do with it. There's just a certain amount of satisfaction you get from running your own business that you'll never have working for someone else. Yes, I'll have to think about that offer for a while."

According to the specifications of the proposal, all the assets and goodwill of the Lacasse Company would be turned over to Moreau Enterprises for a cash sum of $100,000 and Moreau stock having a current market value of $150,000. Mr. Lacasse would become a member of the Moreau firm and remain as manager of sandblasting operations.

Mr. Lacasse said that he had built his clientele up through "personal contact and good, honest work." "Our reputation is our most important asset," Mr. Lacasse amplified. "In fact, one of our most difficult selling problems is to overcome the poor reputation other sandblasters have given the business. So much damage has been done by careless firms that sandblasting is now often used as a last resort. Sandblasting can be used cheaply, safely, and effectively in a multitude of industrial and household situations that no one knows about." He added that one of their greatest concerns was the fluctuation in business volume: "If the volume of work was greater and more stable, it could be offered to all at a lower price."

Several new trends are developing in the use of sandblasting techniques. For example, some large structures, such as bridges and gasoline storage tanks, are being sandblasted in preparation for painting. This has become necessary as many of the new paints used on these structures require a very clean, rough surface in order to adhere properly. Also, a modification of the sandblasting technique is now being used to clean and polish natural gas pipelines. Five to eight miles of pipeline can be cleaned at once, increasing transmittability by 8 to 20 percent. Architects and interior designers use sandblasting for artistic and decorative purposes. By placing a rubber template on stone or glass, attractive designs can be etched into the material at a very low cost. Walls, stone fences, tombstones, glass doors, etc., can be so ornamented.

There is considerable seasonality in the sandblasting business, as most sandblasting is done in conjunction with construction and exterior painting. Mr. Lacasse hopes that with new areas of application workloads will even out somewhat.

According to Lacasse, the company has scarcely "scratched the surface" as far as potential applications of the technique are concerned. He stressed that the company's portable equipment and well-trained workers enable them to do almost any job.

Both Mr. Lacasse and Mr. Mercier work on the bids business. For large jobs entailing more than a day outside the shop, they figure that they must receive about $200 for each two-man, 8-hour day in order to make a profit. Bids are frequently higher on the more difficult jobs. For bids on smaller, in-shop jobs, they estimate the number of hours needed and apply an hourly rate of $20. Bids for cleaning the outside of buildings are determined by the outside area of the structure. Painted surfaces are calculated at a rate of $15 per square foot; brick or stone is $10 per square foot.

Mr. Lacasse said that he wins about 75 percent of the contracts on which he bids. Usually, only one or two companies bid against him for a job. Lacasse bids are sometimes 30 to 50 percent higher than the next lowest bid. Until about 5 years ago, Mr. Lacasse bid on jobs outside the local area. He received few of them, however, as travel times and lodging expenses kept him from being competitive. Now, he does work outside the local area only as a special favor to a good customer.

Advertising expenditures were $7500 in 1972 for the firm. Much of the advertising budget is used to pay for a display ad in the phone directory. Mr. Lacasse also distributes promotional gifts such as ashtrays, pencils, calendars, and matchbooks to his customers. Occasionally, he advertises on one of the local radio stations. These radio spots are aimed at noncommercial customers. About once a year, one-page publicity sheets are mailed out to current customers and others who Mr. Lacasse thinks might be able to use his services. All of the advertising stresses the company's portability, its ability to work in bad weather, its versatility, and its competent service. Despite these efforts, there are frequently slack periods in which some of the Lacasse employees are idle.

Mr. Lacasse is unsure just where and how much he wants to expand in the future. "I guess the most important consideration right now is to try and somehow even out our workload," he said at one point. "If this means expanding into other areas, such as painting, then we may be willing to go that route." Mr. Lacasse said that the company presently does some painting work with anticorrosive materials. He sees this as a potential growth avenue, since many new paints (such as epoxy) require sandblasting before application. Lacasse is the only sandblasting firm in the area that does any painting.

Mr. Lacasse would also like to expand the sandblasting technique to a number of new applications. The chief barrier here, he states, is in selling potential customers on the safety and economy of the process. The possibility of hiring a salesman has been considered. As Mr. Mercier expressed it, "I think we need to get out and knock on some doors." He feels that a salesman could increase business as much as 50 percent.

But Mr. Lacasse is not overly enthusiastic about a small or moderate expansion program. "It's getting to the point that for every extra dollar I make, most of it goes to the government," he complained to the case writer. "I'm making a comfortable living now, and sometimes think that I'd like to get away from the office more often and enjoy life with my family. That's another reason why I see a merger as a possibility. But I just haven't committed myself to taking that step."

# Magnavox, Inc.

Walter Newsom

Magnavox was founded in 1911 by Edwin Pridham and Peter Jensen. These men invented the loudspeaker while they were trying to improve the telephone receiver. When they hooked it up to a phonograph and heard the amplified sound, they realized its possibilities. The loudspeaker came into its own with radio broadcasting during the 1920s. "Magnavox" comes from the Latin words for "great voice." The two inventors also developed the electric phonograph, the public address system, and the radio phonograph. They also experimented with air-to-ground communication for World War I planes.

The company was incorporated in Delaware, February 20, 1930, as Magnavox Company, Ltd., to acquire, through exchange of share for share, the stock of Magnavox Company of Arizona and the stock of Amrad Corporation. Seven shares of Magnavox, Ltd., were given for each share of Amrad stock. The Magnavox Company of Arizona was succeeded in 1938 by the Magnavox Company, Inc. (Indiana).

The Depression years and fierce competition ate away the company's earnings, and in 1938, the company went into voluntary bankruptcy. Frank M. Freimann, who had obtained a loan from Magnavox to keep his own sound equipment company going, had a choice of raising $200,000 to pay back to Magnavox or merging with Magnavox and taking an active role in the reorganized company's management. He elected to merge and became vice president and the largest stockholder of a company that was essentially bankrupt.

Freimann, who had a flair for marketing as well as substantial knowledge of complex electronic technology, dominated Magnavox for the next 30 years.

Immediately after becoming a vice president at Magnavox, Freimann felt the company needed a new product. He decided that a high-fidelity phonograph selling for $69.95 was the answer. He built the prototype and also did the marketing. Since there was not another good phonograph on the market at the time, he found ready acceptance for a high-quality phonograph by the dealers. He sold it to the best music dealers and department stores.

On April 1, 1942, the company purchased assets and assumed liabilities of subsidiary Magnavox Company, Inc. (Indiana), which was liquidated in October 1942. The present title was adopted in September 1942. World War II brought Magnavox just enough military contracts to keep the company going.

## The postwar years

In 1946, production of black-and-white televisions began, and 6000 were produced that year. By 1948, 1 million sets were produced. The TV boom was on. Magnavox had neither the capital nor the capacity to rush in on a large scale, so it had to enter the market slowly. However, it was able to pick and choose its retail outlets carefully. Magnavox had a reputation for quality. In addition, Magnavox sold its products directly to the dealer so that it was able to eliminate most of the distributor's markup. More sales dollars could be passed on to the dealer, who got a higher margin from Magnavox than from other brands. When discount houses started cutting margins for most dealers to a little over 1 percent of the gross, dealers retailing the Magnavox line were still remaining profitable. Magnavox sold its quality and service. By selling directly to the dealers, the company could assure them that Magnavox would not be sold in discount stores and that there would be no other dealers in a close proximity selling Magnavox. By the late 1950s, this policy of quality was paying off and new dealers wanted to handle the Magnavox line. Moreover, those that were carrying the line already gave it greater emphasis. Some gave up all other lines except Magnavox.

Magnavox stressed their high quality and customer convenience features in other products also. The company was the first to introduce an automatic changer for long-playing records in 1948. When record makers announced that stereophonic disks would be on the market by 1958, Freimann junked the entire line of Magnavox phonographs and converted completely to stereo models. In both instances, the combination of being first on the market and having high quality paid off very well when customers became interested in these features. Magnavox's Astro-Sonic line of all-transistor phonographs came out more than a year ahead of the rest of the industry as a by-product of military work.

But Magnavox was slow to enter the color TV market. Freimann was quoted as saying, "We don't want to be the biggest, only the best." This philosophy was immensely successful during the early 1960s. Magnavox specialized in high-quality items that were big on design, styling, and customer convenience features.

## Magnavox and mergers

Magnavox's sales grew from its own products. But it also increased sales by merger. The following is a list of the major mergers which Magnavox experienced between 1955 and 1974.

1 December 31, 1955: acquired operating assets and assumed mortgage debt of Sentinel Radio Corporation.

**2**  January 1956: acquired certain assets of Spartan Radio-Television Division of Sparks Withington Company.

**3**  April 1, 1960: acquired 70 percent interest in Collaro Ltd. and remaining 30 percent in March 1962 (now operating as Magnavox Electronics Company, a subsidiary).

**4**  July 1964: acquired Kent-Coffey Manufacturing Company, Lenoir, North Carolina, for over $1 million cash.

**5**  Early in 1965: acquired Carolina Wood Turning Company, Bryson City, North Carolina, and its subsidiary Andrews Furniture Industries, Inc.

**6**  January 1966: acquired Blowing Rock Chair Company.

**7**  December 1966: acquired Spainhour Furniture Company for 545,778 shares.

**8**  December 31, 1966: Blowing Rock Chair Company and Spainhour Furniture Company were consolidated under name of Consolidated Furniture Industries, Inc.

**9**  February 1969: acquired H. & A. Selmer, Inc., and General Atronics Corporation through issuing of 1,096,731 shares of common stock.

**10**  July 1969: acquired Baker Furniture, Inc., Grand Rapids, Michigan.

**11**  May 1970: acquired Holland Furniture Company.

**12**  September 1970: acquired 40 percent interest of Construcciones Electronicas S.A., Naucalpan de Juarez, Mexico; increased interest to 43 percent in 1971.

**13**  November 1970: acquired Craftsman Electronics, Inc., for 231,250 shares of common stock.

**14**  February 1971: acquired La Salle Deitch Company, Inc., for 606,435 common shares.

**15**  May 1971: acquired Instamatic Corporation for 144,992 common shares.

**16**  June 1971: acquired Bristol Laminating Corporation, for 17,200 common shares.

**17**  January 1972: La Salle Deitch Company, Inc., subsidiary, acquired Western Carpet Mills, Inc., for 81,015 company common shares.

**18**  February 1972: La Salle Deitch Company, Inc., subsidiary, acquired Imperial Fabrics and Decor, Inc., for 86,137 common shares.

**19**  March 1972: La Salle Deitch Company, Inc., subsidiary, acquired Groff Supply Company, Inc., for 27,064 common shares.

**20**  La Salle Deitch, subsidiary, acquired Rajan, Inc., for 6,936 common shares.

**21**  September 1972: acquired 41.4 percent interest of Premier Drum Company, Ltd., for 14,167 common shares.

**22**  September 1972: acquired Knapp and Tubbs, Inc., from Armstrong Cork Company for 105,000 common shares.

**23**  1973: acquired 40 percent interest in H. & A. Selmer, Ltd., Toronto, Canada.

**24**  In 1973 Magnavox and Teleprompter Corp. announced they had entered into a cooperative agreement for the development of new equipment for providing premium programming over existing cable television systems.

**25**  In May 1973, Japanese government approved formation of a 50–50 joint venture company by company and Sumitomo Shoji Kaisha, Ltd., a Tokyo trading firm, to be called Japan Magnavox Navigation Equipment Company, Ltd. Japan Magnavox specialized in advanced marine electronic navigation systems and ship's automation electronics. Magnavox Overseas, Ltd., subsidiary, handles the foreign marketing of the joint venture company's products.

## Magnavox's managers

During Freimann's tenure as president, he was referred to as "Mr. Magnavox." Other managers were unknown outside the company, and there was tremendous turnover in this group. Freimann loved to run everything, from product planning to selling. He had an astute awareness of customer interests. His activities in product planning went beyond mere approval. He instigated new products and improvements.

Even though the company was quite decentralized physically, he was apt to drop in without much advance notice to check up personally. He was concerned about being the best. This meant he was most interested in quality, efficiency, and profit. He was a rare combination of marketer and production man.

Freimann hired Robert Platt in 1963 as vice president for finance. Platt became president in 1968. He is still fundamentally a finance man. George H. Fezell, who was president of the Consumer Electronics Group, recommended the go-slow approach in solid state and took an early retirement in 1973. Alfred di Scipio, a highly regarded consumer-electronics marketing man, was hired to replace him. Di Scipio had been a vice president at ITT, a group vice president at Singer (where he turned around its consumer products operation), and just before his hiring by Magnavox, executive vice president of Filmways, Inc.

## Magnavox's market environment

Magnavox operates in several markets, but its central market has been television sales. Table 1 gives the sales of black-and-white television, Table 2 color television, and Figure 1 *Merchandising Week's* estimate of saturation of television sales in the United States.

Historically, the industry has been characterized by tough competition not because of a glut of similar products but rather because of a glut of dissimilar products. The color television set is easily the most complex consumer product manufactured in vast quantity. Engineering a superior model requires huge research and material costs. The strongest, most efficient companies are able to absorb these costs while holding firm on prices, though, to be sure, they suffer tight profit margins. The smaller companies, on the other hand, cannot absorb these costs, yet neither can they boost prices for fear of becoming less competitive. The upshot is that they pile up losses and go out of business, inevitably watching their market share get gobbled up by Zenith and RCA. As a consequence of the recent turmoil both industry giants hope to increase their market share further.

As the industry has moved to solid state, it has been possible to automate and produce high-quality sets much more efficiently, providing you put up the capital. Zenith's president predicts that in 1980 the industry will consist of fewer but stronger companies. Zenith has spent huge sums of money on research and automation so that it is believed to have the lowest manufacturing costs in the industry.

## TABLE 1 ■ NUMBER OF BLACK-AND-WHITE TELEVISION UNITS (000'S OMITTED), PERCENTAGE OF MARKET, AND AVERAGE PRICE, 1946–1972

| Year | Table and portable | | Console | | Combo | | Total | Average price, $ |
|------|------|------|------|------|------|------|------|------|
| 1946 | | | | | | | 6 | |
| 1947 | | | | | | | 179 | |
| 1948 | | | | | | | 975 | 386 |
| 1949 | | | | | | | 3000 | 323 |
| 1950 | 2942 | 40% | 3766 | 50% | 756 | 10% | 7464 | 299 |
| 1951 | 2276 | 42% | 2775 | 52% | 334 | 6% | 5385 | 308 |
| 1952 | 2838 | 46% | 3039 | 50% | 220 | 4% | 6097 | 282 |
| 1953 | 3225 | 45% | 3755 | 52% | 236 | 3% | 7216 | 280 |
| 1954 | 4249 | 58% | 2892 | 39% | 206 | 3% | 7347 | 230 |
| 1955 | 4440 | 57% | 3078 | 40% | 239 | 3% | 7757 | 225 |
| 1956 | 4755 | 64% | 2526 | 34% | 107 | 2% | 7388 | 190 |
| 1957 | 3846 | 60% | 2391 | 37% | 163 | 3% | 6400 | 190 |
| 1958 | 2717 | 55% | 2068 | 42% | 135 | 3% | 4920 | 205 |
| 1959 | 3613 | 57% | 2567 | 40% | 170 | 3% | 6350 | 213 |
| 1960 | 3274 | 57% | 2211 | 39% | 223 | 4% | 5708 | 222 |
| 1961 | 3812 | 62% | 2135 | 34% | 230 | 4% | 6177 | 209 |
| 1962 | 4336 | 67% | 1844 | 29% | 291 | 4% | 6471 | 192 |
| 1963 | 4861 | 68% | 1959 | 28% | 311 | 4% | 7131 | 177 |
| 1964 | 6260 | 77% | 1637 | 20% | 210 | 3% | 8107 | 162 |
| 1965 | 6956 | 83% | 1318 | 16% | 108 | 1% | 8382 | 159 |
| 1966 | 6186 | 85% | 1054 | 14% | 45 | 1% | 7285 | 141 |
| 1967 | 4484 | 88% | 594 | 12% | 26 | | 5104 | 133 |
| 1968 | 5202 | 90% | 586 | 10% | 25 | | 5813 | 132 |
| 1969 | 4855 | 92% | 436 | 8% | 17 | | 5308 | 132 |
| | | | *Console and combo* | | | | | |
| 1970 | 4463 | 92% | 388 | 8% | | | 4851 | 133 |
| 1971 | 4415 | 91% | 433 | 9% | | | 4848 | 129 |
| 1972 | | | | | | | 8200 | 129 |

## TABLE 2 ■ NUMBER OF UNITS (000'S OMITTED), PERCENTAGE OF MARKET, AND AVERAGE PRICE OF COLOR TVS IN THE UNITED STATES, 1954–1972

| Year | Table and portable | | Console | | Combo | | Total | Average price, $ |
|------|------|------|------|------|------|------|------|------|
| 1954 | | | | | | | 5 | |
| 1955 | | | | | | | 20 | |
| 1956 | | | | | | | 100 | |
| 1957 | | | | | | | 85 | |
| 1958 | | | | | | | 80 | |
| 1959 | | | | | | | 90 | |
| 1960 | | | | | | | 120 | |
| 1961 | | | | | | | 147 | 610 |
| 1962 | | | | | | | 438 | 566 |
| 1963 | | | | | | | 747 | 555 |
| 1964 | 157 | 11% | 1182 | 81% | 124 | 8% | 1463 | 551 |
| 1965 | 316 | 12% | 2089 | 79% | 241 | 9% | 2646 | 560 |
| 1966 | 925 | 18% | 3792 | 74% | 402 | 8% | 5119 | 535 |
| 1967 | 1827 | 32% | 3555 | 61% | 395 | 7% | 5777 | 525 |
| 1968 | 2476 | 41% | 3272 | 55% | 233 | 4% | 5981 | 521 |
| 1969 | 2751 | 46% | 3006 | 51% | 205 | 3% | 5962 | 515 |
| 1970 | 2495 | 54% | 2018 | 44% | 119 | 2% | 4632 | 505 |
| 1971 | 3570 | 56% | 2673 | 42% | 106 | 2% | 6349 | 525 |
| 1972 | | | | | | | 8800 | 500 |

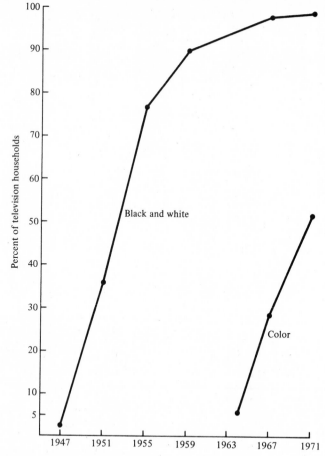

**FIGURE 1** ■ Percentage of U.S. households owning black-and-white and color television, 1947–1971. *Source: Merchandising Week.*

Market share has varied. One-time often-heard names such as Muntz and Capehart are no longer well known.

In 1975, there are only nine domestic producers of television left. American brands are produced in whole or in part in Japan or elsewhere and then sold in the United States. With the import surcharge and dollar devaluation, sales by Japanese manufacturers such as Sony have declined from 28 percent to 10 percent in 1974. But Sony is now building a plant in California. The market shares of the leaders in 1974 are as follows:

| Manufacturer | Market share, in 1974, % |
| --- | --- |
| Zenith | 22 |
| RCA | 22 |
| Motorola (division Matsushita) | 7 |
| Magnavox | 6 |
| Sears (Warwick) | Not known |
| General Electric | Not known |
| Sylvania (division GTE) | Not known |
| Admiral (division Rockwell, Inc.) | Not known |
| Philco Ford (division of GTE) | Not known |

## Operations at Magnavox

Sales at Magnavox have had an up-and-down pattern recently:

| Year | Sales, $ |
|------|----------|
| 1969 | 539,843,000 |
| 1970 | 494,411,000 |
| 1971 | 627,901,000 |
| 1972 | 685,958,000 |
| 1973 | 620,160,000 |

Although it is difficult to piece together, the following seems to be a reasonable summary of recent events. In the later 1960s, especially after Platt succeeded Freimann upon his death, the firm diversified into the home furnishings business and band instruments. Platt had said (about the period just before the diversification): "We don't want to go through another miserable period like that again without a much broader base."

Then came 1969–1970. The recession, modest elsewhere in the economy, was severe in color TV. Magnavox's sales dropped 14 percent to just under $500 million, and earnings slumped almost 40 percent (to $1.56), the lowest in 5 years.

Net income increased in 1971, but a number of factors created problems thereafter. The demand for console TV sets, a Magnavox specialty, was dropping rapidly. While other television manufacturers were rushing to convert from electron tubes to all-solid-state sets, Platt decided that Magnavox should move gradually. He did not think the solid-state sets would catch on quickly with consumers. Moreover, he wanted to wait until a brighter picture tube was available in 1973 before making a full-scale switch to the new devices. However, consumers rushed to buy 100 percent solid-state TV sets because of their greater reliability and ease of service.

In May of 1972, Magnavox introduced a limited line of 25-inch consoles that were 100 percent solid-state. While the competition was gaining sales with full lines of new models, Magnavox's television sales—representing one-third of the company's total volume—were down. They fell to $226 million in 1972, down 2.6 percent from 1971 and 36 percent below the 1968 peak. Magnavox, which was said to to have 10 percent of the television market, dropped to about 6 percent, industry sources contend. Magnavox took drastic action with their older hybrid (part solid-state) sets and substantially reduced prices in order to reduce heavy inventory.

In 1974, sales were down in the first quarter from $156 million in 1973 to $125 million in 1974. Moreover profit was only $805,000 compared to $1,900,000 in 1973. The second quarter sales were approximately the same as a year earlier at $132 million, but Magnavox had a net loss of $93,000 in the second quarter.

## Divisional sales

The results of one recent year might explain the relative importance of various divisions to Magnavox. Sales for the Consumer Electronics Group, which account for 51 percent of sales, were down 9 percent for 1973 and the group had a loss for the year, although the fourth quarter turned profitable.

The Home Furnishings and Music Group contributed 29 percent of the total sales in 1973. The Selmer Music Division increased sales 20 percent and earnings 14 percent over the previous year. The Baker, Knapp & Tubbs Division, a manufacturer and distributor of carpeting, other floor furnishings, plumbing and heating supplies, and accessories primarily for the mobile home and recreational vehicle markets, established record sales and profits with sales up 60 percent and earnings up 39 percent over 1972. Sales of the La Salle Deitch Division increased 5 percent during 1973, but a decline in earnings resulted primarily from a concern for energy and high interest rates, both of which adversely affected the growth of the mobile home market.

The Government and Industrial Group, which accounts for 20 percent of total sales, increased 49 percent over 1972. This was accomplished despite an anticipated 12 percent decrease in volume to $122,500,000. This group makes antisubmarine signal processing equipment, radio communications equipment, electronic warfare systems, radar, sonobuoys, and tactical computer equipment. The decrease in sales was primarily attributable to the completion in mid-year of the long-term Navy contract of product DIFAR (an electronic submarine detection system). The Advanced Products Division is the world's leader in supplying satellite navigation terminals. The Craftsman Electronic Products produces subscriber devices for CATV systems.

The company manufactures its products at the following plant locations:

| | |
|---|---|
| Arden, North Carolina | Jefferson City, Tennessee |
| Barking, England | Johnson City, Tennessee |
| Bristol, Indiana | Manlius, New York |
| Buena Vista, California (2 plants) | Mocksville, North Carolina |
| Cucamonga, California | Morristown, Tennessee |
| Elkhart, Indiana (13 plants) | Moultrie, Georgia |
| Fort Wayne, Indiana | Philadelphia, Pennsylvania |
| Grand Rapids, Michigan | Salisbury, North Carolina |
| Greeneville, Tennessee (3 plants) | Stevensville, Michigan |
| Holland, Michigan (3 plants) | Torrance, California |

## Marketing channel policies

Since 1938, Magnavox has sold directly to dealers and enjoyed great success during the 1950s and 1960s. However, during the 1970s two factors contributed to problems. With only 2500 dealers, compared with upwards of 15,000 each for Zenith and RCA, Magnavox had never tried for mass volume. Instead by fair-trading its products to eliminate price discounting, the company has aimed for fatter profit margins for its dealers. In 1971 under pressure from the Federal Trade Commission, Magnavox agreed not to fix prices in fifteen non-fair-traded states accounting for some 15 percent of its domestic home electronics business, and also in fair trade areas bordering eight nonfair trade areas such as Washington, D.C.

Even more damaging, some of its dealers have been taking on competitive lines to make up for the lack of solid-state Magnavox models. In 1973, for example, a Magnavox dealer in the Southeast added RCA products, mostly to get access to its 100 percent solid-state portables. By 1974, this dealer is selling twice as many RCA sets as Magnavox. Within the last year, Marshall Field, the Chicago department store chain, dropped the Magnavox line and replaced it with Motorola's.

## Some challenges in product line and promotion at Magnavox

In addition, there is growing consumer disenchantment with console TVs. This has been Magnavox's traditional strength. A recent survey indicates that product reliability is the major factor in decisions to purchase television sets. Magnavox is emphasizing the reliability of its color sets to a greater extent than ever. Magnavox built a multimillion-dollar testing facility at Greeneville, Tennessee, where its color television plant is located. At this facility the company is testing all its new 17-, 19-, and 25-inch color sets (representing about 90 percent of its color television sales) for 24 hours. Some 80 percent of set defects usually surface in the first 24 hours of viewing, and it is these that Magnavox hopes to detect. For the industry as a whole, about 10 to 20 percent of new sets contain some defect.

In 1973 Magnavox introduced a new product line with 12-, 14-, 17-, 19-, and 25-inch sizes. The less popular 21- and 23-inch sizes have been eliminated in a move to emphasize portable sets. All the 17- and 19-inch sets contain a new type of picture tube that is supposed to produce more reliable and sharper pictures. The tube is called the in-line tube, and the difference is that the three electron beams in the tube's neck that transmit the picture are arranged in a line and fired out of a single electron gun. In the conventional, or delta, tube the beams are flung out of three separate guns arranged in triangular fashion. These 17- and 19-inch sets also have solid-state transistors instead of tubes. The line as a whole will be 90 percent transistorized, compared with 25 percent in the old line.

Although the company had some changeover problems to solid-state television, the continuing excellence of quality and customer convenience features are apparent. There do not seem to be any major production problems at the present time. The only major question is whether they can continue to maintain the excellence at the cost that will be competitive.

Magnavox has introduced an electronic game center called Odyssey. Twelve different games are included in Odyssey, including football, ski, roulette, table tennis, and hockey. It is easy to install on any television set.

In 1974, Magnavox introduced the first completely random access electronic tuning system for television, via push-button remote control. The STAR (Silent Tuning At Random) viewers have precision tuning and instantaneous, direct access to all 82 VHF and UHF television channels, which are factory-preprogrammed for exact channel frequency. It is one of the largest-scale integrated circuits ever accomplished for any application.

Magnavox also hopes to regain strength through more aggressive advertising. Historically, the company has spent less on advertising than most of its competitors have. For the period of August 1973 through July 1974, the company budgeted $9 million for advertising, up from $4.7 million for the comparable period in 1972–1973. In January 1974, the Magnavox Company signed the baseball superstar Hank Aaron to a long-term promotional contract aimed at further bolstering the television retail merchandising effectiveness in 1974 and the years beyond.

**TABLE 3 ■ MAGNAVOX'S BALANCE SHEETS (000's OMITTED), 1969–1973**

| | 1973 | 1972 | 1971 | 1970[a] | 1969[a] |
|---|---|---|---|---|---|
| *Assets* | | | | | |
| **Current assets** | | | | | |
| Cash | $ 12,070 | $ 10,455 | $ 7,337 | $ 6,024 | $ 7,262 |
| Marketable securities (at cost) | 2,000 | | 1,499 | 3,995 | 5,994 |
| Receivables (net) | 92,960 | 110,798 | 103,421 | 92,668 | 95,017 |
| Inventory | 136,843 | 161,823 | 115,303 | 100,090 | 101,406 |
| Prepayments | 3,337 | 3,116 | 2,045 | 1,540 | 2,089 |
| Total current assets | 247,210 | 286,192 | 229,605 | 204,317 | 211,768 |
| Net property at cost | 64,043 | 72,187 | 70,465 | 69,979 | 66,356 |
| Investments in affiliated companies | 5,106 | 4,683 | 3,140 | 3,019 | |
| Other assets | 6,100 | 1,207 | 1,200 | 1,052 | 2,075 |
| Excess of cost over net assets of acquired companies | 8,261 | 8,289 | 6,825 | 5,061 | 4,624 |
| Total assets | 330,720 | 372,558 | 311,235 | 283,428 | 284,823 |
| *Liabilities* | | | | | |
| **Current liabilities** | | | | | |
| Accounts payable | 50,838 | 54,171 | 40,600 | 39,535 | 30,351 |
| Accruals, etc. | 27,523 | 26,270 | 21,804 | 18,402 | 22,457 |
| Accrued taxes | 1,802 | 4,683 | 13,888 | 14,424 | 17,431 |
| Notes payable | 804 | 56,285 | 1,233 | 1,780 | 12,865 |
| Total current liabilities | 80,967 | 141,409 | 77,525 | 74,141 | 83,104 |
| Debentures 4.75's 1986 | 16,780 | 17,580 | 18,360 | 19,200 | 20,000 |
| Long-term notes | 30,896 | 4,722 | 5,832 | 7,100 | 8,373 |
| Deferred income taxes | | | 2,645 | | |
| Total liabilities | 128,643 | 163,711 | 104,362 | 100,441 | 111,477 |
| Preferred stock | | | | | |
| Common stock $1 par | 17,822 | 17,822 | 17,629 | 16,862 | 16,609 |
| Capital surplus | 20,300 | 20,352 | 17,179 | 14,428 | 14,405 |
| Retained earnings | 165,005 | 171,493 | 179,590 | 160,996 | 152,679 |
| Treasury stock | 1,050 | 820 | 7,524 | 9,299 | 10,346 |
| Net shareholders' equity | 202,077 | 208,847 | 206,874 | 182,987 | 173,347 |
| Total liabilities and equity | 330,720 | 372,558 | 311,236 | 283,428 | 284,824 |

[a] Does not include adjustment for prior years of companies purchased during that year.

**TABLE 4 ■ INCOME STATEMENTS FOR MAGNAVOX (000's OMITTED), 1969–1973**

| | 1973 | 1972 | 1971 | 1970 | 1969 |
|---|---|---|---|---|---|
| Net sales | $620,160 | $685,958 | $627,901 | $494,411 | $539,843 |
| Cost of sales | 504,600 | 540,468 | 468,834 | 366,709 | 385,397 |
| Selling expenses | 100,605 | 101,777 | 88,326 | 73,971 | 72,534 |
| Operating profit | 14,955 | 43,713 | 70,741 | 53,731 | 81,912 |
| Other income (net) | 3,469 | 2,197 | 1,261 | 1,790 | 2,996 |
| Total income | 18,424 | 45,910 | 72,002 | 55,521 | 84,908 |
| Interest expense | 8,403 | 5,024 | 4,021 | 4,381 | 4,471 |
| Income tax | 4,687 | 20,159 | 33,240 | 25,172 | 41,330 |
| Extraordinary items | 531 | (3,082) | (779) | | |
| Net profit | 5,865 | 17,645 | 33,962 | 25,968 | 39,107 |

## Finances at Magnavox

Tables 3 and 4 provide the balance sheets and income statements for Magnavox from 1969 to 1973.

Recent quarterly dividends have been: 30 cents per quarter from 1969 through mid-1973, when the dividend became 15 cents per quarter per share.

Recent stock prices for Magnavox have been as follows:

| Year | High | Low |
|------|------|-----|
| 1969 | 56¾ | 32½ |
| 1970 | 38⅞ | 22¼ |
| 1971 | 55 | 37⅜ |
| 1972 | 52¼ | 25⅝ |
| 1973 | 29⅝ | 6 |
| 1974 | 9⅞ | 3⅞ up to the time of first North American Philips offer on August 28 |

The following is a list of the subsidiaries of Magnavox. (The parent owns the entire capital stock of these subsidiaries.)

**1** Magnavox Company of Tennessee (manufactures television, stereo theaters, radios, tape recorders, clock radios, and cabinets at six plants in Tennessee, two plants in North Carolina, and one plant in Mississippi)

**2** Magnavox Electronics Company, Ltd., formerly Collaro Company (English manufacturer of record changers, tape recording and reproducing machines, and related electronic items)

**3** Magnavox Furniture, Inc.

**4** La Salle Deitch Company, Inc.

**5** Magnavox Overseas

**6** Magnavox International, Inc.

**7** General Atronics Corp.

**8** Magnavision

**9** Sonido de Mexico, S. A. de C. V.

**10** Unimusic, Inc.

Other related companies and affiliates are:

**1** Affiliate: Construcciones Electronicas S.S., Mexico (43.3 percent owned)

**2** Nu-Woods (25 percent owned)

**3** Southern Adhesives (16.7 percent owned)

**4** Premier Drum Company, Ltd. (41.4 percent owned)

**5** Indelec, S.A. (20 percent owned)

**6** Eastern Telecom (14.5 percent owned)

## The merger offer

On August 28, 1974, after the stock market had closed, North American Philips Development Corporation, a subsidiary of N. V. Philips, extended an offer to purchase any and all shares of common stock of the Magnavox Company for cash at $8 per share.

N. V. Philips, a Dutch firm, is the third largest ranking industrial company outside the United States (sales of $8.1 billion in 1973). It is diversified in electronics and pharmaceuticals. Even though N. V. Philips controls 20 percent of the European color television market, North American Philips does not have any share of the American market. North American Philips indicated, at the time of the tender offer, that there have been preliminary talks to explore a relationship with Magnavox since the spring of 1974.

North American Philips said that the offer would be made only by a formal offering document that would be made available after appropriate filing with the SEC. R. H. Platt, president of Magnavox, indicated almost immediately that Magnavox was not happy with the offer. He said the company directors would review the situation to determine what action would be in the best interest of Magnavox stockholders.

Mr. Platt indicated that the book value per share was in excess of $11 and therefore the proposed offer appeared inequitable. It should be noted that the day after the offer was made, Magnavox stock closed at 6⅛, up 2 over the previous close. On August 29, 1974, a statement was released by Magnavox indicating that the directors recommended rejection of the bid and hinted that a better offer might be in the offing. The stock went up another 2¼ the following day.

On September 5, 1974, a decision was made by Philips to amend the offer to $9 per share after talks took place between the two companies. Magnavox said that management had withdrawn objection to the offer and would recommend that its directors accept it. By September 17, North American Philips had acquired 56 percent of the stock and extended its offer to October 1.

# AMMCO Tools, Inc.

Ram Charan

"I have always believed in people. I love to work with creative people regardless of the field they are in. People are an important part of business, and I would like to draw from the best part of these people. Our best man does not have a degree; he has only a seventh grade education; he is long on common sense; he's an inventor," said Mr. Fred G. Wacker, Jr., president of AMMCO Tools, Inc., which was a North Chicago–based, family-owned manufacturer and marketer of engine rebuilding, brake service, and wheel alignment tools and equipment. Under the leadership of Mr. Wacker, Jr., AMMCO enjoyed continued growth, especially since 1960. Sales and profit grew from $4.5 million and $143,000, respectively, to $15.9 million and $1.6 million in 1973. (See Table 1 for selected financial data for the company.)

## The automotive aftermarket industry

The automotive aftermarket industry was, according to Merritt Hursh, vice president of research for *Jobber Topics* (an aftermarket industry trade journal), a very nebulous industry that was "hard to get your arms around." In a general sense it incorporated the entire spectrum of repair and service of cars: engine repair and rebuilding, brake relining, wheel balancing and alignment, exhaust system repairs and replacement, painting, replacement parts, tires, batteries, etc. AMMCO was part of the diverse and individualized tool sector; the latter was composed of many small firms and divisions of larger companies. Competition within the tool sector was hard to pinpoint because numerous firms specialized in only one specific aspect of the industry while others participated in two or three different aspects. For example, one company manufactured one tool to tighten one bolt on a certain type of car, whereas AMMCO produced various tools for engine rebuilding, brake service and repair, and wheel alignment and balancing. Thus, no two firms were in direct competition throughout their entire product lines.

One measure of the aftermarket industry is given in Table 2, which is based on sales by wholesalers. Also shown are the two major categories in which AMMCO competed.

AMMCO's product groups of heavy equipment

# TABLE 1 ■ AMMCO TOOLS, INC., CONSOLIDATED BALANCE SHEETS (THOUSANDS OF DOLLARS)

| | 1960 | 1963 | 1966 | 1967 | 1968 | 1971 | 1972 | 1973 |
|---|---|---|---|---|---|---|---|---|
| **Assets** | | | | | | | | |
| Cash and liquid securities | 312.2 | 65.3 | 117.4 | 225.6 | 1,564.6 | 2,439.3 | 1,215.5 | 528.7 |
| Receivables | 389.2 | 554.6 | 957.7 | 694.3 | 786.9 | 1,037.6 | 1,691.9ᵃ | 1,365.3 |
| Due from LCC | 258.2 | 267.0 | 229.0 | 641.8 | 122.1 | 40.9 | 5.6 | 76.6 |
| Inventories (auto) | 755.3 | 1,102.5 | 1,407.7 | 1,101.5 | 1,292.9 | 1,526.9 | 1,554.7 | 2,202.9 |
| Inventories (meters) | 479.8 | 798.0 | 193.8 | 56.4 | | | | |
| Prepaid expenses | 13.3 | 31.1 | 86.1 | 89.4 | 71.0 | 99.6 | 62.1 | 33.1 |
| Current assets | 2,208.0 | 2,818.5 | 2,991.7 | 2,809.0 | 3,837.5 | 5,144.3 | 4,529.8 | 4,206.6 |
| Investment—LCC | | | 800.0 | 800.0 | 800.0 | 800.0 | 800.0 | 850.0 |
| Other investments | 152.2 | 167.9 | 146.7 | 147.3 | 153.0 | 166.2 | 211.3 | 531.1 |
| Patents and trademarks | 10.6 | 10.0 | 13.1 | 12.9 | 12.3 | 10.8 | 11.2 | 13.1 |
| Property, plant, and equipment | 1,525.9 | 2,007.1 | 2,496.7 | 2,618.6 | 2,684.0 | 4,120.8 | 6,072.7 | 7,408.0 |
| (Accumulated depreciation) | (698.8) | (996.3) | (1,516.0) | (1,686.8) | (1,836.5) | (2,077.0) | (2,429.2) | (2,724.7) |
| Net plant and equipment | 827.1 | 1,010.8 | 980.7 | 931.8 | 847.5 | 2,043.8 | 3,643.5 | 4,683.3 |
| Deferred federal income tax | | | | | | 73.0 | 147.0 | 193.0 |
| Total assets | 3,197.9 | 4,007.2 | 4,932.2 | 4,701.0 | 5,650.3 | 8,238.1 | 9,342.8 | 10,477.1 |
| **Liabilities** | | | | | | | | |
| Payables | 690.6 | 378.3 | 331.8 | 70.9 | 257.1 | 314.1 | 366.2 | 448.8 |
| Accrued expenses | 334.1 | 175.0 | 337.1 | 378.6 | 840.4 | 1,290.9 | 1,060.4 | 879.6 |
| Current liabilities | 1,024.7 | 553.3 | 668.9 | 449.5 | 1,097.5 | 1,605.0 | 1,426.6 | 1,328.4 |
| Long-term debt | | | | | | | | |
| Stockholders and others | 138.0 | 69.0 | | | | 63.6 | 125.3 | 190.0 |
| Prudential | | 805.0 | 1,450.0 | 1,350.0 | 1,250.0 | 950.0 | 850.0 | 750.0 |
| Total liabilities | 1,162.7 | 1,427.3 | 2,118.9 | 1,799.5 | 2,347.5 | 2,618.6 | 2,401.9 | 2,268.4 |
| Equity | 1,891.8 | 2,471.6 | 2,726.6 | 2,813.3 | 2,901.5 | 4,478.5 | 6,519.4 | 6,940.9 |
| Current year earnings | 143.4 | 108.4 | 86.7 | 88.2 | 401.3 | 1,310.8 | 1,661.1 | 1,607.4 |
| (Less dividends) | (—) | (—) | (—) | (—) | (—) | (169.8) | (339.6) | (339.6) |
| (Other) | (—) | (—) | (—) | (—) | (—) | (—) | (900.0) | (—) |
| Total equity | 2,035.2 | 2,579.9 | 2,813.3 | 2,901.5 | 3,302.8 | 5,619.5 | 6,940.9 | 8,208.7 |
| Total liability and equity | 3,197.9 | 4,007.2 | 4,932.2 | 4,701.0 | 5,650.3 | 8,238.1 | 9,342.8 | 10,477.1 |
| **Consolidated income statement** | | | | | | | | |
| Gross shipments | 4,592.9 | 5,279.5 | 6,369.0 | 6,359.4 | 7,780.7 | 12,545.9 | 14,965.5 | 16,206.9 |
| Less: Returns and allowances | 111.8 | 110.1 | 138.4 | 189.9 | 192.1 | 274.0 | 189.3 | 236.9 |
| Net shipments | 4,481.1 | 5,169.4 | 6,230.6 | 6,169.5 | 7,588.6 | 12,271.9 | 14,776.2 | 15,970.0 |
| Cost of sales | 2,206.2 | 2,790.2 | 3,442.4 | 3,447.5 | 3,740.3 | 5,198.7 | 6,301.1 | 7,192.0 |
| Gross profit on sales | 2,274.9 | 2,379.2 | 2,788.2 | 2,722.0 | 3,848.3 | 7,073.2 | 8,475.1 | 8,778.0 |
| Meter incomeᵇ | 41.2 | 44.8 | 145.3 | 81.6 | 29.8 | 3.8 | 2.9 | 4.1 |
| Other costs and expenses | | | | | | | | |
| Commissions | 810.6 | 536.2 | 763.0 | 749.5 | 931.4 | 1,621.4 | 1,963.9 | 2,141.0 |
| Engineering | 206.8 | 214.2 | 289.9 | 193.2 | 244.4 | 188.3 | 215.2 | 332.3 |
| Selling, administrative, general | 952.5 | 1,355.5 | 1,599.3 | 1,569.8 | 1,768.7 | 2,578.2 | 2,962.0 | 3,111.7 |
| Operating income | 346.2 | 318.1 | 281.3 | 291.1 | 933.6 | 2,689.1 | 3,336.9 | 3,197.1 |
| Interest expense | 40.8 | 71.8 | 92.6 | 112.9 | 77.3 | 61.3 | 56.8 | 56.8 |
| Net income | 305.4 | 246.3 | 188.7 | 178.2 | 856.3 | 2,627.8 | 3,280.1 | 3,140.3 |
| Tax provision | 162.0 | 138.0 | 102.0 | 90.0 | 455.0 | 1,317.0 | 1,619.0 | 1,533.0 |
| Net profit | 143.4 | 108.3 | 86.7 | 88.2 | 401.3 | 1,310.8 | 1,661.1 | 1,607.3 |

ᵃ A small tools promotion which encouraged orders by the end of 1972 is the primary cause for the increase in year-end accounts receivable.
ᵇ Minimal subcontracted machining for LCC.

# TABLE 2 ■ SALES BY WHOLESALERS (MILLIONS)

| | 1967 | 1968 | 1969 | 1970 | 1971 | 1972 |
|---|---|---|---|---|---|---|
| Total | $4960 | $5200 | $5442 | $5460 | $5650 | $5933 |
| Equipment (all types) | 274 | 252 | 146 | 127 | 106 | 147 |
| Small hand tools | 82 | 69 | 80 | 101 | 93 | 106 |

(brake lathes and brake shoe grinders), accessories (shop benches, facing sets, silencers, adapters, etc.), parts (replacement parts for the heavy equipment), and wheel service (auto ramp and rack alignment systems) were included in the equipment (all types) category. AMMCO's product groups of small tools (cylinder and brake hones, ridge reamers, torque wrenches, decelerometers, etc.), and stones and cutters (tool bits, stone sets, and abrasive belts) were included in the small hand tools category. A sales summary of AMMCO's products by groups is provided in Table 3.

While not requiring tremendous capital to enter, the industry's tool sector was characterized by a high degree of technology and a need for creative engineering talents. Design was based on ease of operation with a maximum degree of performance. Since the basic structure of the automobile was not subject to frequent, radically new inventions, the automotive aftermarket tool industry had potential for growth but not to the degree associated with the glamour industries of recent years. Thus, it was basically concerned with refining and increasing the efficiency of tools for repairing cars.

Although car sales and servicing were seasonal, the tool sector of the industry was not. The actual market for automotive aftermarket tools was the car, truck, and bus repair industry, which consisted of small operations such

**TABLE 3 ■ AMMCO TOOLS, INC., SALES SUMMARY (IN DOLLARS)**

| | 1960 | 1963 | 1966 | 1967 | 1968 | 1971 | 1972 | 1973 |
|---|---|---|---|---|---|---|---|---|
| *Sales by product group* | | | | | | | | |
| Heavy equipment | 1,948,683 | 2,333,970 | 2,849,866 | 2,568,244 | 3,281,601 | 6,575,378 | 8,274,743 | 9,139,876 |
| Accessories | 391,062 | 464,508 | 654,474 | 745,332 | 823,069 | 1,926,006 | 2,183,295 | 2,279,829 |
| Small tools | 1,049,083 | 1,123,974 | 1,201,324 | 1,294,544 | 1,716,908 | 1,751,667 | 1,903,761 | 1,931,794 |
| Stones and cutters | 721,407 | 879,418 | 934,906 | 966,241 | 1,032,249 | 1,470,178 | 1,697,580 | 1,839,385 |
| Wheel service | | 44,888 | 306,453 | 275,253 | 368,290 | 219,181 | 303,662 | 272,166 |
| Parts | 360,067 | 275,595 | 278,717 | 317,827 | 361,581 | 305,888 | 397,933 | 505,234 |
| Miscellaneous | 10,768 | 47,059 | 4,876 | 2,059 | 4,893 | 23,582 | 15,206 | 1,750 |
| Total | 4,481,070 | 5,169,412 | 6,230,616 | 6,169,500 | 7,588,591 | 12,271,880 | 14,776,180 | 15,970,034 |
| *Cost of sales by group* | | | | | | | | |
| Heavy equipment | 1,009,145 | 1,323,779 | 1,648,859 | 1,518,784 | 1,609,716 | 2,556,467 | 3,143,546 | 3,906,451 |
| Accessories | 202,515 | 223,795 | 344,624 | 399,597 | 359,476 | 702,407 | 817,150 | 918,694 |
| Small tools | 423,861 | 469,495 | 590,935 | 659,098 | 811,252 | 773,748 | 835,642 | 968,781 |
| Stones and cutters | 302,442 | 307,192 | 377,246 | 369,611 | 405,406 | 555,174 | 697,467 | 771,804 |
| Wheel service | | 24,922 | 212,573 | 188,111 | 208,389 | 105,919 | 158,916 | 156,535 |
| Parts | 142,309 | 122,417 | 98,285 | 112,779 | 123,758 | 81,385 | 107,858 | 157,528 |
| Miscellaneous | 7,981 | 25,360 | 4,060 | 442 | 988 | 12,164 | 13,527 | 3,454 |
| Total | 2,088,253 | 2,496,960 | 3,276,582 | 3,248,422 | 3,518,985 | 4,787,264 | 5,774,106 | 6,883,247 |
| *Gross profit by group* | | | | | | | | |
| Heavy equipment | 939,538 | 1,010,191 | 1,201,007 | 1,049,460 | 1,671,885 | 4,018,911 | 5,131,197 | 5,233,425 |
| Accessories | 188,547 | 240,713 | 309,850 | 345,735 | 463,593 | 1,223,599 | 1,366,145 | 1,361,135 |
| Small tools | 625,222 | 654,479 | 610,389 | 635,446 | 905,656 | 977,919 | 1,068,119 | 963,013 |
| Stones and cutters | 418,965 | 572,226 | 557,660 | 596,630 | 626,843 | 915,004 | 1,000,113 | 1,067,581 |
| Wheel service | | 19,966 | 93,880 | 87,142 | 159,901 | 113,262 | 144,746 | 115,631 |
| Parts | 217,758 | 153,178 | 180,432 | 205,048 | 237,823 | 224,503 | 290,075 | 347,706 |
| Miscellaneous | 2,787 | 21,699 | 816 | 1,617 | 3,905 | 11,418 | 1,679 | (1,704) |
| Total | 2,392,817 | 2,672,452 | 2,954,034 | 2,921,078 | 4,069,606 | 7,484,616 | 9,002,074 | 9,086,787 |
| *Sales—domestic and export* | | | | | | | | |
| Territories | 3,877,414 | 4,333,292 | 5,392,349 | 5,343,597 | 6,650,566 | 11,449,851 | 13,774,515 | 15,064,398 |
| House | 104,703 | 131,477 | 352,284 | 384,275 | 398,539 | 180,828 | 125,198 | 56,114 |
| Canada | 154,718 | 125,071 | 153,943 | 127,923 | 171,445 | 286,554 | 319,334 | 326,432 |
| Subtotal | 4,136,835 | 4,589,840 | 5,898,576 | 5,855,795 | 7,220,550 | 11,917,233 | 14,219,047 | 15,446,944 |
| Export | 344,235 | 579,572 | 332,040 | 313,705 | 368,041 | 354,647 | 557,133 | 523,090 |
| Total | 4,481,070 | 5,169,412 | 6,230,616 | 6,169,500 | 7,588,591 | 12,271,880 | 14,776,180 | 15,970,034 |
| Unshipped orders | 43,713 | 63,432 | 207,849 | 527,089 | 880,319 | 441,563 | 1,125,999 | 5,806,606 |

Manufacturer
of
parts, equipment, tools,
paints, supplies

Oil Companies

Engine Rebuilders        Parts Rebuilders

**MANUFACTURER**

**WHOLESALE TRADE**

SIC 5012
Truck body, bus, truck tractor,
trailer wholesalers
3,858 merchant wholesalers

SIC 5014
Tire, tube wholesalers
2,800 merchant wholesalers

SIC 5013
Automotive wholesalers
including
warehouse distributors
redistributing jobbers
jobbers
21,855 merchant wholesalers

SIC 5028
Paint, varnish wholesalers
1,268 merchant wholesalers

SIC 5092
Petroleum bulk stations
and terminals
30,229 establishments
(Some 10,000 involved in automotive)

SIC 5013
Wholesalers with machine shop
6,596 establishments

SIC 5013
Wholesalers without machine shop
13,096 establishments

**DISTRIBUTOR**

**RETAIL TRADE**

SIC 753
Automobile repair shops
109,946 establishments
(55,830 with payroll)

Heavy duty
establishments
Fleets, industrial, contractors,
off-highway equipment
16.3%

SIC 5252
Farm equipment dealers
16,739 establishments
(13,342 with payroll)
2.7%

SIC 5511
Motor vehicle dealers
(New/used)
(32,898 with payroll)
16.8%

SIC 5531
Tire, battery, accessory
dealers
29,189 establishments
(22,521 with payroll)

SIC 5311
Department stores
5,792 establishments
Some with
auto service centers

SIC 5541
Gasoline service
stations
216,059 establishments
(165,190 with payroll)
32.7%

SIC 7538
General automobile
repair shops
57,838 establishments
(28,904 with payroll)

SIC 7531-4-5-9
Specialized
service and repair shops
52,108 establishments
(26,926 with payroll)

SIC 7531
Top and body repair shops
20,828 establishments
(11,298 with payroll)

SIC 7539
Battery and ignition
repair service shops
(1,153 with payroll)

SIC 7539
Exhaust system
service shops
(720 with payroll)

SIC 7539
Wheel, axle, spring
repair shops
(1,095 with payroll)

Miscellaneous
establishments
Government, schools, military,
marine, small engine dealers

Car owners
including
speed enthusiasts,
do-it-yourself owners
12.3%

SIC 7534
Tire retreading and repair
shops
(2,597 with payroll)

SIC 7539
Radiator repair
shops
(1,819 with payroll)

SIC 7539
Automatic transmission
repair shops
(1,789 with payroll)

SIC 7539
Automobile repair shops
N.E.C.
(1,571 with payroll)

SIC 7535
Paint shops
(3,038 with payroll)

SIC 7539
Glass
replacement and repair shops
(1,143 with payroll)
19.2%

SIC 7539
Brake repair
shops
(703 with payroll)

**INSTALLER-USER**

**PERCENTAGE OF ALL SIC 5013 WHOLESALER SALES**

**FIGURE 1** ■ Automotive aftermarket in the 1970s.

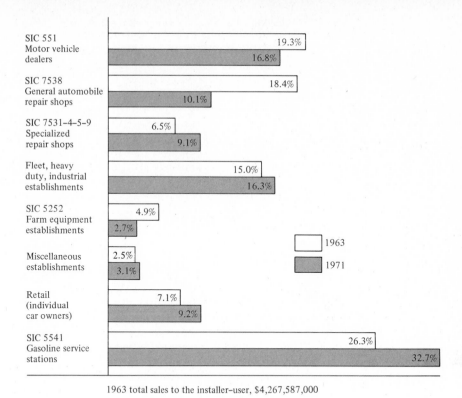

SIC 551
Motor vehicle
dealers — 19.3% / 16.8%

SIC 7538
General automobile
repair shops — 18.4% / 10.1%

SIC 7531–4–5–9
Specialized
repair shops — 6.5% / 9.1%

Fleet, heavy
duty, industrial
establishments — 15.0% / 16.3%

SIC 5252
Farm equipment
establishments — 4.9% / 2.7%

Miscellaneous
establishments — 2.5% / 3.1%

Retail
(individual
car owners) — 7.1% / 9.2%

SIC 5541
Gasoline service
stations — 26.3% / 32.7%

☐ 1963
▨ 1971

1963 total sales to the installer–user, $4,267,587,000
1971 total sales to the installer–user, $5,940,887,000

**FIGURE 2** ■ Changing picture of jobber sales by type of customer.

as auto repair shops and service stations; the auto centers of large chain stores such as Sears and K-Mart; tire stores such as Firestone and Goodyear; the franchised service stations of large oil companies; the federal government; some exports; and auto enthusiasts such as hobbyists and do-it-yourselfers. The structure of the aftermarket and its changing nature are shown in Figures 1 and 2 and Table 4.

## AMMCO Tools, Inc.

Fred G. Wacker, Sr., started AMMCO Tools, Inc., in 1922 (then known as Automotive Maintenance Machine Co.) by purchasing the patent rights for an engine cylinder grinder (a tool used to smooth out the walls of a worn cylinder that had lost its shape, leaving the piston without a complete seal inside the cylinder in an internal-combustion engine). AMMCO started manufacturing hand and machine tools in Chicago with six employees, and by 1929 had a sales volume of $350,000. In 1935 the senior Wacker moved AMMCO to a purchased building in the city of North Chicago. By developing and expanding its line of engine rebuilding tools, the company was able to rebound

| Sales volume | 1971[a] | 1967 | 1963 | 1958 | 1954 | 1948 | 1939 |
|---|---|---|---|---|---|---|---|
| $10,000,000 or more | ... | } 88 | 16 | 11 | ... | ... | ... |
| $5,000,000–$9,999,999 | ... | | 38 | 29 | 25 | 11 | ... |
| $2,000,000–$4,999,999 | ... | 329 | 192 | 112 | 82 | 68 | 6 |
| $1,000,000–$1,999,999 | ... | } 2,650 | 633 | 372 | 240 | 190 | 33 |
| $500,000–$999,999 | ... | | 1,646 | 1,092 | 675 | 573 | 81 |
| Over $500,000 | 4,200 | 3,067 | 2,525 | 1,616 | 1,022 | 842 | 120 |
| $300,000–$499,999 | ... | } 5,807 | 2,307 | 1,480 | 1,126 | 941 | 132 |
| $200,000–$299,999 | ... | | 2,869 | 1,854 | 1,481 | 1,134 | 223 |
| $100,000–$199,999 | ... | 6,075 | 5,949 | 4,080 | 3,418 | 2,778 | 769 |
| $50,000–$99,999 | ... | } 6,381 | } 6,517 | 2,788 | 2,984 | 2,598 | 1,401 |
| Under $50,000 | ... | | | 1,901 | 2,182 | 2,666 | 3,492 |
| Under $500,000 | 17,800 | 18,263 | 17,642 | 12,103 | 11,191 | 10,117 | 6,017 |
| Not operated entire year | 500 | 525 | 885 | 389 | 350 | ... | ... |
| Total establishments | 22,500 | 21,855 | 21,052[b] | 14,108 | 12,563 | 10,959 | 6,137 |

[a] Market PROBE estimate.
[b] Totals based on U.S. Business Census figures published as of given year. Details not available based on adjusted figures reported in later U.S. Business Census Reports.
Source: U.S. Department of Commerce, Bureau of the Census.

from the Depression and reach a $500,000 sales level by 1940. During the war AMMCO produced a small tool room shaper, used for shaping metal, that the government bought in quantity. The company later sold the machine to Delta, a division of Rockwell Manufacturing Company, because AMMCO had decided not to produce any of the complementary machinery to make a complete line (i.e., lathes, milling machines, etc.). Rockwell had sold only a few thousand shapers since the war.

In 1947, when Wacker, Jr., entered the company, there was a stabilization in the demand for engine rebuilding tools because better materials, lubricants, and paved roads increased the time engines could last between repairs; auto owners began taking increasingly complicated engines to centralized engine rebuilders rather than to individual garages or doing their own repairs. This centralization of engine rebuilding reduced the individual garage's demand for tools. Frequently, a tool was used on many jobs continuously in a centralized rebuilding shop rather than on a few jobs in many individual garages. Hence, AMMCO decided to move into brake service tools for the reason that with larger and more powerful cars coming into the market, the brakes were wearing out faster than the engines.

AMMCO pursued brake service tools by purchasing the rights for a brake shoe gauge in 1950 from a West Coast inventor, who, later that year, also sold AMMCO a new design for a brake shoe grinder, something AMMCO had worked on for a year without success. Wacker, Jr., modified the traditional pricing formula to get market acceptance for the new grinder, and the difference between profit and loss in 1950 was due to AMMCO's brake-related business.

In 1952 AMMCO produced its own brake drum lathe. Wacker, Jr., made attempts to buy out two companies already producing lathes, but he was not able to get together with the owners on price. Therefore, AMMCO developed its own lathe, which turned out to be better than the others and became the industry standard. "I was very disappointed when we couldn't buy either of those companies," Wacker, Jr., said, "but the Man upstairs must have been looking out for us."

In 1954, Wacker, Jr., looked to diversify from the company's great dependence on the automobile industry. AMMCO's patent attorney was asked to look for a product that would fit in with AMMCO's production methods and facilities. In the meantime, AMMCO experimented with bicycle engines and food machinery such as orange juicers, but with poor results. The attorney told Wacker, Jr., that the attorney's neighbor, George Richards, had invented a positive displacement meter for measuring heavy fluids such as oil. Wacker, Jr., purchased the Richards patents and formed the Liquid Controls Corporation (LCC). During the 1950s and early 1960s, Wacker, Jr., spent half his time setting up LCC, which took a long while to produce a profit. LCC initially operated from the AMMCO plant, but it was soon moved to a separate facility. Richards, disliking the design of the new plant, refused to carry out Wacker, Jr.'s instructions. There was more trouble when Richards, who was paid a guaranteed minimum and a percentage of yearly sales, wanted a larger percentage, and although Wacker, Jr., talked him out of resigning twice, Richards eventually left in 1967. LCC did not produce attractive profits until 1974 (about 7 percent of sales, after taxes).

Starting in the mid-1950s a number of problems developed in AMMCO. The company became very new-product-oriented, using a scattershot approach, under which products were introduced before they were properly tested. Five or six products had to be recalled and redesigned at great expense. The emphasis on new products resulted in less concentration on AMMCO's old line products, which subsequently declined in quality. At the same time AMMCO's plant and equipment were becoming outdated compared to the rest of the industry, and AMMCO experienced bottlenecks and tie-ups in production. Communications were beginning to break down, and the engineering department began to develop a philosophy different from Wacker, Jr.'s.

Problems were pyramiding in 1967 when cost of goods sold reached 56 percent of sales, profit dropped to 1.4 percent of sales, and Wacker, Jr., felt he might not be able to meet AMMCO's payroll in a few weeks. Appendix A presents quarterly accounting statements for 1967. Also during this time, the lead time for supplies dropped sharply so that AMMCO developed huge inventories of both finished goods and raw materials, and inventories became greater than unfilled orders. The sales prediction for 1967 was for a 10 percent increase in sales, but demand actually dropped. AMMCO's debt to equity ratio reached a high of 70 percent.

Meanwhile, a new computerized inventory system was received with antagonism. Wacker, Jr., asked for changes, but none came—no one seemed to care. Thus in August 1967, Wacker, Jr., with the aid of Wally Mitchell, vice president and director of manufacturing and engineering, and Robert Pranke, treasurer and controller, acted to bail out the company. They devised five steps by which to generate cash and to improve employee morale:

**1** 117 people were fired or left, including the chief engineer. Internal bugs in the basic operation were eliminated, and all new research and development was stopped so that more time could be spent improving the old standard lines.

**2** Bottlenecks were reduced by using new machinery and by redesigning the products so that they were easier to manufacture; overtime, second, and third shifts were eliminated. (The two steps allowed AMMCO to generate enough cash to pay off $800,000 in debt in 6 months and to improve the plant. Wacker, Jr., was no longer "paying bodies." During this time, Wacker, Jr., moved his office into the plant so that he would have a more direct control over the operation.)

**3** Control was enhanced through the use of a computer to monitor the flow of goods through the plant, so that all parts would be ready when needed.

**4** Research and development was reinstituted.

**5** The total operation was refined and expanded.

During this time Wacker, Jr., also began using control charts, produced by the W. C. Heath Company, which graphically showed trends in the company's inventories, accounts receivables, assets, etc. Wacker, Jr., felt that these charts gave the viewer an immediate picture of AMMCO's performance, and the direction in which the company was moving. By 1973 AMMCO had $16 million in sales with 319 people compared to $6 million in sales with 475 people in 1967. This was accomplished with no overtime and using only one shift. By 1973 AMMCO had its cost of goods sold down to 44 percent of sales and its after-tax profit up to 10.6 percent of sales.

## Product policy

"I do not believe in planned obsolescence; I like to produce value for the money the customer pays. We build things by which other people make a living," Wacker, Jr., said. "The company makes and sells the same tool (cylinder grinder) today as my father sold when he started the business in 1922. Nothing that AMMCO Tools manufactures is designed to ever wear out, given reasonable care." Wacker, Jr., was very pleased to show an article written on the first model of AMMCO's brake drum lathe.

●MODEL 1, NUMBER 1 is alive and well. And it's making money everyday in the fabulous world of TBS (tires, brakes, suspension) at Fair's Autocraft, Pontiac, MI.

But Model 1, Number 1 is masquerading as something else. It's birth certificate reads AMMCO Model 3000 Serial No. 201. Twenty years ago it was decided that it might be hard to find a customer anxious to buy the first brake lathe assembled by a manufacturer. So in 1953 the first brake lathe built by AMMCO Tools, Incorporated went into the marketplace with the credentials of a tried and trusted elder citizen. Fortunately, it has lived up to the trouble-free, long-durability image the company hoped to convey.

Ruggedness, and reliability are traits of most quality automotive service equipment. Despite the problems that jobbers and service dealers sometimes experience in their day-to-day business, there are few industries that can match the track record for durability set by automotive equipment.

AMMCO's Model 1, Number 1 still gets a pretty good workout every day, even though its owner specializes in ignition and carburetor work.

Joy Fair, owner of Fair's Autocraft says, "We don't talk about our brake work very much—it's accommodation to our customers—but, we average about 155 brake jobs a year."

The specialty shop also turns drums and faces discs for other shops in his area.

Fair says that his 20-year old brake lathe was field modified in 1971 to resurface disc rotors. He estimates he has earned more than $26,000 turning drums and resurfacing rotors on that one piece of equipment. Except for tool bits and "V" belts, total repair costs during its 20-year life have been less than $15.00, Fair says.

Two separate, and successful careers have been packaged by Joy Fair. And his automotive service equipment plays a part in both of them. One is as a repair specialist, the other is as a builder of modified stock cars which he campaigns on the ARCA circuit. He says the short half-mile oval tracks which dominate that circuit give brakes a real workout.

When he could not get wheels wide enough for some of the racing tires he wanted to use he split regular stock wheels on his lathe and welding them to a "filler" ring to get the correct width.

"I think I got my money's worth—many times over," Fair says with a grin. But, he does not advocate trying to prove a point by running a shop that demands modern service entirely on 20-year equipment.

AMMCO has striven continually for increased product quality while minimizing the operating complexity for the user. For example, a vibration dampener for the lathes was produced to improve the machine finish on the disk brakes. Two nylon pads, used to accomplish the dampening, eventually wore out thereby creating a replacement market. Two years later, a friction material was tried experimentally. This new material extended the life of the dampener pads to such an extent that the replacement market would be eliminated altogether were the design change to be made. Wacker, Jr., made the change regardless of some internal opposition. Also, a very successful double boring bar was introduced, as an accessory, making it possible to machine both faces of a disk brake simultaneously.

This concern for quality often manifested itself in a product's delayed market introduction owing to thorough testing by AMMCO. Also, after a product was released, the company would follow up to see that it still operated correctly.

## Manufacturing

Production at AMMCO basically consisted of machining and assembly operations using bar stock, castings, forgings, and electric motors as basic inventories. Although increasing its dependence on machines, the operation required highly skilled labor. From 1968 to 1973, the number of direct and indirect employees involved in actual production had decreased from 191 to 182.

AMMCO's product line was composed of over 150 items which consisted of 5 to 6000 different parts for each item. Some individual parts required as many as 10 separate operations.

The plant had been expanded in a very piecemeal way. As Fred Wacker, Jr., said, "We did what we had to do at the time. In retrospect it shows poor planning but it worked." (See Figure 3 for layout of present facility.) The current additions or purchases of new machinery were on a pay-as-you-go basis which was best summed up by Wally Mitchell. "I am a believer in the Bohemian plan," he said. "We must earn and have the money before we spend." At Mitchell's recommendation, investments in plant and equipment were made to eliminate production bottlenecks and enhance finished goods turnover.

Considerable emphasis was placed on rationalizing the manufacturing processes to facilitate the flow of materials and reduce scrap losses. Scrap losses were reduced from 6.5 percent of direct material input in 1968 to 1.2 percent in 1973. Wally Mitchell was responsible for product design and manufacturing processing. A recent employee, Lenny Morrison, introduced sophisticated technology in the form of lasers and optical processes to AMMCO's wheel alignment products. Morrison had formerly been associated with the Technological Institute of Northwestern University.

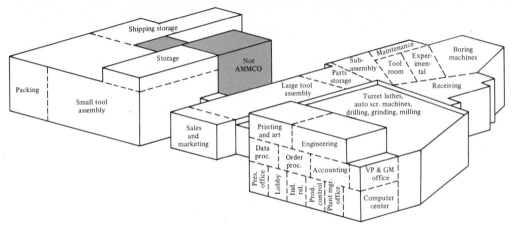

**FIGURE 3** ■ Plant layout.

## Marketing and sales

In sales, AMMCO covered the United States with six regions staffed by 86 district managers under six regional managers. The regional managers were salaried and given bonuses on volume while district managers were paid a straight commission from which they paid their own expenses. Commissions were a percentage of the net invoice amount; the percentage was 10 percent, 15 percent, or 20 percent, depending on the particular item. The district manager in the area, where a product was set up and used, received the commission regardless of whether he took the initial order. Returns necessitated that the district manager in that area forfeit his portion of the commission for those items returned. Sales were highly dependent upon service after the sale. Therefore, the commission system was an incentive not strictly for sales but for high levels of customer service. The district managers' duties included filling orders, installing machines and teaching people to use them, servicing for both dealers and jobbers, and soliciting new orders, which the district managers then sent either to a jobber or to AMMCO directly. House accounts were handled by the home office. Car registrations, counties, and sales volume were used to determine sales areas. As sales volume increased, the areas were trimmed to handle the concentration, allowing AMMCO to take advantage of greater sales at less cost. Initially the salesmen did not like this method, but experience showed that it increased their sales.

By 1973, 20 percent of AMMCO's sales were national accounts such as Sears, Roebuck and Goodyear. This figure was expected to continue to grow.

The company had a strict pricing policy: it marked up each item in the product line at 100 percent above manufacturing cost, and rigidly controlled costs. Price changes were made once a year at most. When an unprofitable item was identified from the computer outputs as making significantly less than 100 percent return on cost, the price of this item was raised, and if the sales volume and higher price did not enhance the item's profitability, it was dropped from the product line by designating the item as discontinued and eventually deleting it from the price list.

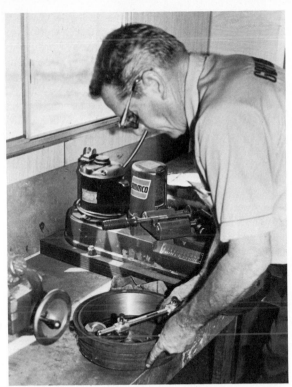

**FIGURE 4** ■ Marvin Panch, field engineer for the Grey-Rock division of Raybestos Manhattan, retired from racing in 1966 after 17 years and 19 major victories. AMMCO drum and disk lathes and brake shoe grinders are used exclusively by Grey-Rock technicians.

The district managers were free to work autonomously in their dealings with customers in implementing programs to increase sales as long as they followed the discount and pricing policies set by the company. The district managers were also free to share commissions when a distributor's area overlapped sales areas. Advertising and marketing vice president Richard Stevenson said the AMMCO sales force was more conscientious than some of its competitors; AMMCO men worked only for AMMCO, whereas in some cases salesmen in the industry represented many companies at the same time. Also, many of AMMCO's salespeople began working in AMMCO's plant so that they knew their product much better. Adding his personal touch at a gathering of the regional managers, Wacker, Jr., was very proud to show the improvements in the work processes at locations where many of the regional managers had begun their careers at AMMCO.

AMMCO did some subcontracting for companies under their brand name (such as Craftsman for Sears, Roebuck), but this was a small part of total sales, as were exports. The company advertised in trade journals either by a straight ad or a placed article (abridged in Figure 4). Twenty direct mailings a year and ads at car races were also used. But AMMCO's biggest publicity was through word of mouth among people using the products in their businesses, which Stevenson said tended to cause the company to minimize field problems.

In 1973, AMMCO spent $300,000 on promotion such as advertising, catalogs, trade shows, etc. The total selling expense for 1973 was $1 million, and AMMCO paid almost $150,000 for sales bonuses, while commissions were about $2.1 million.

For 1973, the top selling item (brake drum lathe) accounted for 38 percent of total sales. The top five and ten selling items accounted for 54 percent and 64 percent of total sales, respectively.

Dick Manning, vice president and general sales manager, felt that the best way to view AMMCO and its competition was to divide AMMCO into three groups: brake equipment, small tools, and wheel alignment equipment. Although few figures were available, Manning referred to a study performed by a competitor in 1970 which showed AMMCO was responsible for about 65 percent of the brake business; the rest of the brake business was divided among five competitors. Manning felt the percentage was presently down to about 55 percent because AMMCO was unable to fill all orders owing to the castings shortage. In small tools, Manning felt that although AMMCO did not produce so diverse a selection of tools as its four competitors, AMMCO was the sales leader (or second highest) in the products it produced. In wheel alignment AMMCO was about ninth in a field of ten competitors. This position was due to AMMCO'S recent entry into the field.

Mr. Yankis, assistant treasurer and controller, felt that AMMCO was the Rolls-Royce of the industry, and that because of this superior quality, AMMCO's prices were higher than the prices of its competitors.

Stevenson suggested that the company diversify from brake equipment by placing more emphasis on hand tools, which would reduce the selling costs of instruction, setup, and service. Stevenson also said he though the company should improve its engineering staff and strengthen its product development.

## Finance

AMMCO made much use of historical data in planning current finances. Monthly estimates were generated from a base of actual performance in previous years. A sales forecast was established and the historical percentages of sales for the various items were used to determine the budgeted amounts, which were used as standards and not as specific authorizations. Expenses continually were compared to sales in order to see if historical percentages were maintained or could be improved. A very modest seasonality was involved, with sales from April 1 to October 1 approximately 53 percent of yearly volume.

Profitability had been hampered during 1973 because of governmental price controls. These controls applied more stringently to AMMCO's products than to some of AMMCO's material and labor inputs. After the price controls were lifted, AMMCO made plans to raise prices where needed.

## Personnel

"We look for two things in a potential employee: attitude and the ability to do the job. With the right attitude you can move mountains," said John

Lauten, industrial relations manager. "We're a shirt-sleeve organization where communication is on a one-to-one basis," he continued. "We don't waste time with memos and notes. We just pick up the phone or go see the guy."

Lauten came from the Chicago Hardware Foundry in North Chicago, that had been taken over by a larger company in 1967. Lauten had been assistant to the personnel manager at the foundry, where he also had much experience in the industry.

AMMCO employed few college graduates. Most of the people in high positions had advanced from within the company, and many of the district managers had started out working in the factory. The company used a registration method for advancement. Everyone could sign up to be considered for any new opening, and 80 to 90 percent of those who registered were advanced. When a man was put ahead, he stayed on a trial basis for a few months, and if he and his supervisor felt he disliked the new position or did poorly, he was given his old job back. The most senior personnel were given the first chance to advance; the decision was made by Lauten, the plant manager, and all the foremen and supervisors involved with the person.

"People working as a team is what makes AMMCO," Lauten said proudly. "We have few rules because everyone knows what's expected of him." As of December 1973 all the foremen were in their late thirties or early forties, except the general foreman, who was in his early fifties, Pranke (50), and Mitchell (69). Half the factory workers had been with the company for more than 5 years. One of the two turnovers in the managerial staff in the past 4 years was due to age.

AMMCO's relationship with the union was generally good, although there had been two strikes within the past 5 years; the most recent strike lasted for 4 months.

Lauten indicated that the company faced the problem of getting good workers for the factory and for the engineering department because the North Chicago area had virtually no unemployment.


## Organization

(See Figure 5 and Table 5 for organizational chart and summary information on principal managers.)

AMMCO was a privately owned corporation whose board of directors was composed of Fred G. Wacker, Jr., his mother, sister, brother, and two bank trustees for Fred G. Wacker, Sr.'s estate. Fred G. Wacker, Jr., was president and chairman of the board; he had held both of these positions since his father's death in 1948.

*Wally Mitchell* Though Mitchell, vice president and director of manufacturing and engineering, had a seventh grade education, he had patented more than 150 inventions. He had previously worked with several companies including Victor Comptometer and Dacor—a manufacturer of scuba diving equipment. For a while, he and two partners had operated their own manufacturing company, Dukes Manufacturing Company.

Mitchell had worked at AMMCO in the 1930s until a difference of opinion with Wacker, Sr., led to his resignation. When Wacker, Jr., entered the company, his father told him to contact Mitchell if he needed help with certain

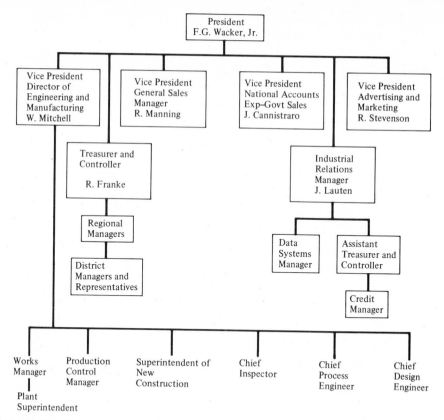

FIGURE 5 ■ Organization chart.

products he had invented. Wacker, Jr., later did hire Mitchell as a consultant.

The friendship between Mitchell and Wacker, Jr., was built on common interests. When Wacker, Jr., was racing with the French auto racing team, he brought Mitchell with him as his chief mechanic. In 1967, Wacker, Jr., had Mitchell survey metalworking firms in Europe and make suggestions for streamlining AMMCO's manufacturing operation. Mitchell had designed some of the company's product line, revamped the production process, and also was responsible for some of AMMCO's literary contributions. He established a research group to develop new AMMCO products to solve problems experienced by the large auto and brake companies in which Wacker, Jr., had contacts. It was Mitchell's feeling that "in U.S. business, most problems are solved by small- to medium-sized firms. The big companies don't solve problems, they overwhelm them."

Mitchell, in his spare time, developed a meter that surpassed all existing meters in accuracy of measurement for LCC. Besides his creative ability, Mitchell always kept in mind that his inventions had to be put together by people. In this vein, he designed AMMCO's products in such a way as to allow them to be assembled as easily and as efficiently as possible. One of AMMCO's executives fondly referred to Mitchell as "the maestro who got the production and engineer people to play the same tune."

Wally Mitchell's philosophy on business centered on manufacturing. "To

TABLE 5 ■ AMMCO TOOLS, INC., PERSONNEL SUMMARY

| Position | Age | Years at AMMCO |
|---|---|---|
| President | 56 | 27 |
| Vice President and Director, Engineering and Manufacturing | 69 | 35 |
| Vice President, General Sales Manager | 53 | 11 |
| Vice President National Accounts, Export, Government Sales | 56 | 20 |
| Vice President Advertising and Marketing | 52 | 28 |
| Treasurer and Controller | 50 | 13 |
| Industrial Relations Manager | 41 | 7 |
| Works Manager | 56 | 15 |
| Product Control Manager | 58 | 16 |
| Superintendent of New Construction | 68 | 15 |
| Chief Inspector | 61 | 40 |
| Chief Process Engineer | 55 | 10 |
| Chief Design Engineer | 39 | 20 |
| Plant Superintendent | 46 | 4 |
| Regional Manager | 65 | 20 |
| Regional Manager | 49 | 18 |
| Regional Manager | 64 | 29 |
| Regional Manager | 61 | 36 |
| Regional Manager | 57 | 37 |
| Regional Manager | 38 | 12 |
| Credit Manager | 42 | 14 |
| Assistant Treasurer and Controller | 37 | 15 |
| Data Systems Manager | 37 | 10 |

increase sales, you first have to increase capacity before the salesmen push sales," he said. He extensively tested products before he would permit market introduction; there was some criticism of Mitchell by those who felt this testing delayed a product's market entry for too long a time. "We need good people to take an idea and pursue it," Mitchell said. "An idea is only as good as what you make it. We must build a better mousetrap; then we'll get the customers."

One thing that was beginning to bother Mitchell was the requirement that every manager affected by a proposed investment sign the request. For example, to spend $31,000 for a machine to handle a new supplier's proposed aluminum castings (to alleviate the shortage of iron castings) required eight signatures.

Mitchell not only was vice president and director of manufacturing and engineering at AMMCO, but filled the same position at LCC. His compensation was in the form of a consultant's fee rather than a fixed salary; generally, Mitchell left work at three o'clock in the afternoon.

*Robert Pranke* Robert Pranke, treasurer and controller, was responsible for pricing policy, forecasts, and budgets. He had developed an early interest in electronic data processing through his past experiences: first with a small company that printed business forms, then later with the Toni Company, a division of Gillette. He came to AMMCO as a controller in 1961, when the company's modest computer system was used for order processing and payroll applications. Two and one-half years later the treasurer resigned because of a nervous condition, and Pranke was promoted to the position of treasurer and controller.

Describing how he came to AMMCO, Pranke said, "I was in Chicago working for Toni, and I wanted to leave; one day, while passing an employment agency, I took a chance and went in. The agency had just received

AMMCO's job listing. I came to visit AMMCO, and I decided to work here. It shows that if you don't take a chance, nothing will ever happen."

"The computer does not necessarily reduce the office staff," he said, "but it halts the growth of the office employees with much more information at the user's disposal." Without an increase in the office staff, AMMCO was able to handle a doubling in sales and the proportional increase in the paperwork volume. Pranke considered the computer "the office man's tool."

Pranke, realizing the feeling of threat that the computer gave many of AMMCO's employees, felt that the only way to get people to accept the computer was to have it supply to foremen and department heads the information they had collected before on their own. This information should be presented in a format identical to the one used by those receiving the information. After this was accomplished, then the computer could provide other information that could be helpful to the foremen and department heads. "You don't have the information user change for the sake of the computer," said Pranke, "but have the computer change for the information user."

Pranke described the interaction between the computer and the manufacturing process at AMMCO: "AMMCO is an industrial engineering textbook case of a metalworking company. For example, the machining operations are all done on an incentive pay plan. The flow of any item is monitored with the computer at each work station to provide payroll information. You have an exact recording of what went on, an accountant's dream. You can't find a better source of information than the measure of activity of 180 people trying to make a buck, and operating our incentive payroll system. Thus, the system automatically provides information on our finished and in-process inventory."

Pranke was also treasurer and controller for LCC.

*Richard Stevenson*  Richard Stevenson, vice president of advertising and marketing, was responsible for all promotional advertising and marketing information. He came to AMMCO in 1946 for a summer job before enrolling at Yale University, but for personal reasons he could not attend Yale, and he has been with AMMCO ever since.

Mr. Stevenson felt that because of the great amount of "word-of-mouth" publicity that AMMCO enjoyed, the marketing department was continually "dragging its feet" before introducing a product, to be sure the product was perfect and did not tarnish AMMCO's reputation.

Besides feeling that AMMCO had "too many eggs in one basket" and that it should diversify more into hand tools, Stevenson said, "I think we are underengineered; our engineers should be younger, travel with the salesmen, and listen more to the salesmen. I don't think our product development is as aggressive as it should be."

*John Lauten*  John Lauten, industrial relations manager, was responsible for personnel and all labor-related matters. "When I came to AMMCO in May of 1967, I thought I was joining a sinking ship," Lauten said. "My secretary told me not to bother her because it was her last day, the chief engineer was fired, and over 100 people left or were fired by December. This place was a mess."

Lauten, having already worked with the union representing AMMCO's employees and having brought many of the better workers over from Chicago Hardware Foundry (including the present union president), was on good terms with the employees and trusted by the union. Lauten felt his job basically consisted of eliminating the barriers that existed between management and labor. "People are the strength of AMMCO; people working as a team is what makes AMMCO," said Lauten.

Lauten felt that he would like to see AMMCO grow to about 500 people but no larger. "After about 500 people," said Lauten, "personal contact begins to die and walls begin to be erected between management and labor."

Although admitting that he enjoyed working at AMMCO and that he had no desire to leave, Lauten had some reservations concerning the future. "Mr. Wacker, through his trust and open door policy, has created the atmosphere here; if he were to die, I don't know what would happen to the company. I don't think his brother or sister would want to run the company, and his mother is too old (84), even though she came to the plant and signed the checks every week until a few years ago. I think Bob Pranke could do a good job of running the company and keeping the same atmosphere. I worry about them selling AMMCO to a larger company. If AMMCO was left alone, it would be fine; but if the new owners brought in their own management, not only would I be out of a job, but AMMCO wouldn't be the same. Those are the risks of working for a privately held company."

*Fred Wacker, Jr.* Wacker, Jr., attended Yale University, where his class-mates were Roy Chapin, who became president of American Motors Company, and Henry Ford II, who became chairman of the board of the Ford Motor Company. After graduating from college in 1940 with a B.A. in English, he worked in the machine shop at the AC spark plug division of General Motors, while also studying at the General Motors Institute. Wacker, Jr., said that "the experience as low man on the totem pole in the machine shop gave me an understanding of the employees' point of view; I learned what it was like to have a six-foot six-inch foreman stand over you all day." Subsequently, he was moved to the time study department of AC. He left General Motors to serve in the Navy from 1943 to 1945, and on his return he formed and conducted the Fred Wacker Swing Band, earning $165 a week.

Greatly involved in auto racing, Wacker drove in the European Grand Prix Circuit as a member of the French racing team after World War II; and in addition, he and Phil Hill (the only American to win the championship on the Grand Prix Circuit) raced as a team in the Le Mans (France) 24-hour race. Wacker, Jr., also, won the first Sebring endurance race (1951). He attempted to break a motorcycle world speed record at the Bonneville Salt Flats in 1972. The impression that "business wasn't very exciting" kept Wacker, Jr., from entering AMMCO, until his father's health was failing in 1947. Drawing on his experience at General Motors, Wacker, Jr., improved company efficiency; and after his father's death in 1948, he became president and chairman of the board of directors.

Wacker, Jr., said his formula for a successful business was a fortuitous combination of men, product, money, and machines; he quoted this equation: (Raw material + human energy) $\times$ tools = man's material welfare. "The multiplying factor is tools, because man has a limited amount of human energy," he said. "And remember always, too, that none of it will be productive unless the entire enterprise is carried out with Christian principles and spiritual guidance throughout."

Wacker, Jr., felt that too many company presidents spent most of their time doing the wrong things—such as going to seminars, arranging financing, having their companies go public, and devoting their attention to advertising, mergers, and acquisitions "But if their manufacturing costs are 65 percent," said Wacker, Jr., "shouldn't they be spending their time on the floor in order to reduce those costs? Furthermore, without the reduction in costs, how can they improve the earnings for the company?" These reductions in costs could only be accomplished by hard work on the president's part, and even then the reductions could only be achieved gradually, according to Wacker, Jr.

Wacker, Jr., in talking of his belief in fair play and in people, pointed out that, even before President Johnson's executive order regarding equal employment, he employed blacks against the advice of his management team. Admitting that he made mistakes concerning certain blacks in his initial recruitment, Wacker, Jr., was very proud of the fact that a black the company hired in 1967 was the union president by 1973. The union was 80 percent white.

Wacker, Jr., felt that it was unfortunate that labor often did not work together with management as in other countries. Wacker, Jr., kept a card catalog that included a photograph of each employee. He would memorize the face and name of every employee and attempt to talk to each one when he was in the plant.

AMMCO had considered going public but resisted. "If the outstanding stock is worth more on the marketplace than the true value of the company, then in a sense we have gulled the stockholders," Wacker, Jr., said. "If it is less, we have gulled the original investors. The Bible says in effect 'Neither a lender or borrower be, or the borrower is the servant of the lender.' It is for this reason, among others, that AMMCO has generated its growth from its own earnings rather than by borrowing. The growth may take longer, but it is slow, solid, and sure."

With a view to the future, Wacker, Jr., said he would like to see AMMCO grow at an annual rate of 10 percent. In the last few years, growth had been around 25 percent per year; over the company's lifetime growth had been about 13 percent per year. Wacker, Jr., felt the growth rate in the past few years had been too fast and was putting pressure on his limited management team since he, Pranke, and Mitchell held the same positions in AMMCO and LCC. AMMCO had not as yet been able to find good management people to alleviate some of the pressure. Because of the castings shortage in 1973, AMMCO was considering purchasing a casting foundry; the company was "feeling out" a few possibilities. AMMCO was experimenting with aluminum castings in their products; however, aluminum was also in tight supply. The fuel crisis caused some concern for AMMCO. However, Wacker, Jr., felt AMMCO would not be too seriously affected. His feeling was that man would find alternative power sources for cars and that wheel alignment and brake repairs would still be needed. Concerning his replacement, Wacker felt there was no need for worry; Pranke and Mitchell, he said, would be able to fill his place with no problem.

"When I came to AMMCO in 1947, things were not up to snuff, and I had no management experience," Wacker, Jr., said. "I've made some mistakes along the way and the company is growing faster than I would like, but we have gone from a day-to-day existence to now being able to plan on a year-to-year basis."

## AMMCO TOOLS, INC., CONSOLIDATED BALANCE SHEETS (THOUSANDS OF DOLLARS)

| | 1Q, 1967 | 2Q, 1967 | 3Q, 1967 | 4Q, 1967 |
|---|---|---|---|---|
| **Assets** | | | | |
| Cash and liquid securities | (240.00)[a] | (124.1)[a] | 140.8 | 225.6 |
| Receivables | 796.0 | 890.7 | 908.5 | 694.3 |
| Due from LCC | 415.7 | 664.0 | 847.4 | 641.8 |
| Inventories (auto) | 1866.0 | 1821.4 | 1485.7 | 1101.5 |
| Inventories (meters) | 278.8 | 234.0 | 160.6 | 56.4 |
| Prepaid expenses | 67.6 | 75.7 | 57.2 | 89.4 |
| Current assets | 3184.1 | 3561.7 | 3600.2 | 2809.0 |
| Investment—LCC | 800.0 | 800.0 | 800.0 | 800.0 |
| Other investments | 146.8 | 141.6 | 141.6 | 147.3 |
| Patents and trademarks | 12.8 | 12.5 | 12.2 | 12.9 |
| Property, plant and equipment | 2540.3 | 2615.4 | 2620.6 | 2618.6 |
| (Accumulated depreciation) | (1570.0) | (1618.0) | (1666.0) | (1686.8) |
| New plant and equipment | 970.3 | 997.4 | 954.6 | 931.8 |
| Total assets | 5114.0 | 5513.2 | 5508.6 | 4701.0 |
| **Liabilities** | | | | |
| Note payable | 400.0 | 700.0 | 700.0 | |
| Payables | 200.1 | 181.2 | 148.3 | 70.9 |
| Accrued expenses | 296.1 | 373.7 | 382.6 | 378.6 |
| Current liabilities | 896.2 | 1254.9 | 1230.9 | 449.5 |
| Long-term debt Stockholders and others Prudential | 1400.0 | 1400.0 | 1350.0 | 1350.0 |
| Total liabilities | 2296.2 | 2654.9 | 2580.9 | 1799.5 |
| Equity | 2813.2 | 2813.2 | 2813.2 | 2813.3 |
| Year to date profit | 4.6 | 45.1 | 114.5 | 88.2 |
| Total equity | 2817.8 | 2858.3 | 2927.7 | 2901.5 |
| Total liability and equity | 5114.0 | 5513.2 | 5508.6 | 4701.0 |
| **Consolidated income statement** | | | | |
| Gross shipments | N.A. | N.A. | 1760.6 | 1586.5 |
| Less: returns and allowances | N.A. | N.A. | 47.9 | 63.3 |
| Net shipments | 1304.8 | 1628.7 | 1712.7 | 1523.2 |
| Cost of sales | 631.3 | 878.8 | 954.2 | 983.1 |
| Gross profit on sales | 673.5 | 749.9 | 758.5 | 540.1 |
| Meter income | 23.4 | 30.5 | 19.4 | 8.3 |
| Other costs and expenses Commissions | 150.2 | 206.9 | 200.8 | 191.6 |
| Engineering | 74.1 | 66.0 | 30.8 | 22.3 |
| Selling, administrative, general | 439.8 | 398.9 | 379.4 | 351.6 |
| Operating income | 32.8 | 108.6 | 166.9 | (17.1) |
| Interest expense | 23.6 | 30.8 | 31.4 | 27.2 |
| Net income | 9.2 | 77.8 | 135.5 | (44.3) |
| Tax provision | 4.6 | 37.3 | 66.1 | (18.0) |
| Net profit | 4.6 | 40.5 | 69.4 | (26.3) |

[a] The balances are negative in these accounts owing to the practice of predating a check for a bill prior to the date on which the check is mailed (a date when the cash reserves covered the amount of the check).

N.A. means "not available."

# A note on
# the American
# soft drink
# industry

William F. Glueck

Although most people identify soft drinks with our modern culture, carbonated beverages have been around for quite a time. Apparently, the ancient Greeks were the first people who drank carbonated beverages. They enjoyed "sparkling water" which was derived from natural springs. As with so many other customs, the Romans imitated the Greeks and sought natural carbonated beverages.

Dr. Joseph Priestley invented artificial carbonated water in the eighteenth century. Townsend Speakman increased the sales of carbonated water in his apothecary shop by adding fruit juices to the water in the later 1800s.

By 1880, there were over 500 firms using hand-operated bottling machines in the United States. Ninety years later, there are almost 2700 bottling plants.

In 1974, 28 percent of Americans chose coffee as their favorite beverage, 27 percent chose water, 10 percent favored soft drinks, and 2 percent beer (according to a Gallup poll). The soft drink has come a long way from Townsend Speakman's drugstore. Per capita consumption in 1974 was over four hundred 8-ounce containers, and the output of the industry is in the $6 billion range.

## Industry sales

Sales of soft drinks vary by quarter. Almost 60 percent of sales are in the second and third quarters of the year. The first and last quarters represent 40 percent of sales. Tables 1 and 2 provide data about sales by company. Table 3 provides some recent sales figures by products.

Recent sales increases have been attributed to increased advertising and marketing and increases in the largest age group in consumption of soft drinks: younger people.

The industry has two major components. The concentrate and syrup makers and the distributors and bottlers. The largest of the concentrate and syrup makers is Coca-Cola. This firm sells its products in 135 countries through 1850 bottlers and 3000 jobbers. It is a diversified firm including other food products. Pepsico has more than 1000 bottlers and sells in almost as many countries as Coke. It also is diversified into foods and nonfoods. Royal Crown has 300 bottlers in the United States and sells in 39 other countries through 90 bottlers. Seven-Up has

| Company | 1954 | 1962 | 1963 | 1965 | 1966 | 1968 |
|---|---|---|---|---|---|---|
| Coca-Cola Company | 705 | 550 | 570 | 790 | 895 | 1685 |
| Pepsico Company | 140 | 400 | 420 | 550 | 595 | 691 |
| Seven-Up Company | 95 | 165 | 185 | 185 | 200 | 249 |
| Dr Pepper Company | 10 | 40 | 55 | 70 | 80 | 127 |
| Royal Crown Company | 60 | 130 | 185 | 230 | 260 | 290 |
| Canada Dry[a] | 95 | 130 | 145 | 160 | 165 | 130 |
| Cott[b] | 10 | 35 | 35 | 60 | 61 | 100 |

[a] Division: Norton Simon.
[b] Division: National Industries; products: Cott, Chiquot Club.

TABLE 2 ■ DOLLAR SALES OF LEADING SOFT DRINK COMPANIES (IN THOUSANDS), 1970–1973

| Company | 1970 | 1971 | 1972 | 1973 |
|---|---|---|---|---|
| Coca-Cola Company | 1606 | 1728 | 1876 | 2144 |
| Pepsico Company | 1122 | 1225 | 1400 | 1697 |
| Seven-Up Company | 100 | 111 | 119 | 146 |
| Dr Pepper Company | 57 | 63 | 77 | 98 |
| Royal Crown Company | 110 | 125 | 191 | 195 |

TABLE 3 ■ TOP 10 SOFT DRINKS, 1971–1972

| | Brand | 1972 | | 1971 | | Percent change |
|---|---|---|---|---|---|---|
| | | Million cases | Market share, % | Million cases | Market share, % | |
| 1 | Coca-Cola | 1,170.0 | 27.9 | 1,105.0 | 28.0 | + 5.9 |
| 2 | Pepsi-Cola | 735.0 | 17.5 | 687.0 | 17.4 | + 7.0 |
| 3 | Seven-Up | 289.6 | 6.9 | 271.4 | 6.9 | + 6.7 |
| 4 | Dr Pepper | 180.0 | 4.3 | 147.7 | 3.7 | +21.9 |
| 5 | Royal Crown | 165.0 | 3.9 | 153.0 | 3.9 | + 7.8 |
| 6 | Sprite (Coke) | 80.0 | 1.9 | 70.0 | 1.8 | +14.3 |
| 7 | Tab (Coke) | 59.5 | 1.4 | 48.0 | 1.2 | +24.0 |
| 8 | Diet Pepsi | 58.0 | 1.4 | 52.0 | 1.3 | +11.5 |
| 9 | Fresca (Coke) | 49.5 | 1.2 | 48.0 | 1.2 | + 3.1 |
| 10 | Diet Rite Cola | 44.0 | 1.0 | 42.0 | 1.1 | + 4.8 |

Source: Sales survey for Beverage Industry by John Maxwell, Jr.

475 bottlers in the United States and 170 in 75 foreign countries. Dr Pepper has over 500 franchised bottlers and sells in the United States, Canada, and Japan. Other syrup and concentrate firms include Canada Dry and Canada's Crush International (Orange Crush, Hires Root Beer).

There are about 2700 bottling plants in the United States. Many of the bottling firms are quite large and their stock trades on major stock exchanges. The largest include:

Allegheny Beverage (Baltimore): sales $68 million, 1974

Beverage Management (Columbus, Ohio): sales $50 million, 1974 (mostly 7UP)

Coca-Cola (Los Angeles): sales $715 million, 1974

Coca-Cola (New York): sales $265 million, 1974

MEI (Minneapolis): sales $55 million, 1974

Pepsi-Cola (Washington, D.C.): sales $35 million, 1974

Associated Coca-Cola (Daytona Beach): sales $100 million, 1974

Sales in 1974 may not be all upward. The largest manufacturer of vending machines shut down because of decreases in soft drink sales due to increased costs. This led to sales declines for vending machines.

International sales of soft drinks have provided major percentage increases for these firms. Coke, Pepsi, and Seven-Up have been strong overseas for some years. Royal Crown is moderately strong. Dr Pepper is just now entering overseas markets. Consumption per capita is very low in Europe and the Far East. Third-world nations have extremely low consumption rates. Coke's overseas sales in 1974 were $925 million. Pepsi's international sales are $225 million. Some of this $225 million is from company-owned bottlers whereas Coke's sales are all in concentrate form. But Pepsi was the first to enter the Soviet Union.

Almost 60 percent of soft drinks sold are colas. Lemon-lime flavors represent 15 percent. Ten percent of the drinks sold are diet beverages. The rest goes to fruit flavors such as root beer, ginger ale, mixers, Dr Pepper, and others. In 1958, the percentages were cola 53 percent; lemon-lime 10 percent; orange 5 percent; and root beer 3 percent.

The diet drinks have been very competitive. The leaders are Tab (Coca-Cola), Sugar Free Pepsi, Fresca (Coca-Cola), and Diet Rite Cola (Royal Crown).

A few of these firms are diversified. Coke has a food division which offers hot chocolate, fruit drinks (Hi C), frozen orange juice, and coffee. It owns Aqua Chem in the water conversion, steam generator, heat exchanger, etc., businesses. Aqua Chem is 4 percent of the sales. Royal Crown owns a home decor company. Pepsico is in snack foods (Frito Lay) and sporting goods among others. Seven-Up has tended toward vertical integration (flavors, lemon production, bottlers). When Seven-Up passed Royal Crown in 1974, Royal Crown made substantial top management and organization changes in an effort to regain its sales position.

## Industry challenges

Like most industries, the soft drink firms have faced many challenges from the environment in the last few years.

### RAW MATERIAL COSTS

The first of these challenges is recent rises, some of them quite dramatic, in the prices of raw materials. Sugar, a major ingredient for soft drinks, has risen 300 percent from 1973 to 1974. And world stocks of sugar have declined drastically. They were at a 10-year low in 1974. Soft drink companies use 20 percent of U.S. sugar sold. By mid-1975, sugar was declining in cost. Some bottlers, such as Coca Cola of New York, were cutting prices accordingly.

The energy crisis and increased cost of oil have affected the price of transportation for the concentrate, the plastic bottles for the concentrate, and other costs. These cost increases have affected the pricing and margins for these firms. Wage and price controls affected the firm's margins in the Nixon administration. Should controls be reimposed, they would affect soft drink firms too.

But the major problem has been sugar. Some analysts were predicting increases of 10 percent in price of soft drinks in the last quarter of 1974. The cost squeeze may force the company profits down, and analysts were recommending against purchase of the stocks. If the public gets more price-conscious, they may increase the trend to cheaper private-label soft drinks. The costs are lower because of lower delivery costs and advertising. These products now represent about 15 percent of the market. Some consumers have shifted to products like Kool Aid.

Up until now, the firms have priced regular and diet drinks the same, taking more profit on diets. Pepsi's president announced that his company would no longer maintain this parity or "level" (in late 1974), and Coca-Cola of New York offered 25 cents off an eight-pack of 12-ounce Fresca or two 48-ounce bottles or three 32-ounce bottles of Tab and Fresca.


NONRETURNABLE CONTAINERS

A second challenge to the soft drink industry is legislation prohibiting the sale of beverages in nonreturnable containers. The use of nonreturnable soft drink containers started with glass and steel containers in the late 1940s. Aluminum cans were added in the late 1950s.

People concerned about the environment oppose the use of nonreturnables because they use more resources and because they contribute to the litter problem. A National Study of Roadside Litter in 1969 estimated that 43 percent of the litter on the national highways in 29 states they studied was disposable packages. Oregon estimated that 75 percent of its litter was nonreturnable beverage containers. It is estimated that it costs from $1 to $5.5 billion in state funds to clean up the litter each year.

The litter problem has led to local, state, and federal legislation about nonreturnable containers. For example, Bowie, Maryland, passed an ordinance requiring deposits on all sales of beverages. Judge Ernest Lovelas recently ruled that this was legal, after three major soft drink manufacturers and local bottlers sued.

Most states have legislation pending on this matter. Vermont and Oregon have outlawed nonreturnable containers. Sales of soft drinks declined after the bill was passed in Oregon. All beverage containers require deposits of from 2 to 5 cents. Since the law was passed, beverage containers in litter have dropped 92 percent in 3 years. The law not only has had an effect on sales; it also affects costs. Returnables cost twice as much to produce. And they must be shipped back to the bottler each time at a cost of about 3.5 cents for each bottle each time.

The state of Washington has taken a different approach to litter. It requires cars and boats to have litter bags or be fined $10. Littering leads to a $250 fine. And a tax of 0.015 percent on gross sales of industries whose products can lead to littering (newspaper publishers, paper manufacturers, supermarket chains, and bottlers) and the fines pay for the cost of picking up litter. An education campaign has been organized to reduce litter. And a department of ecology tries to get citizen drives to reduce litter. These laws have also reduced litter.

At the federal level, there have been hearings regarding a federal law about prohibiting nonreturnables. In hearings before the Senate Environment Subcommittee, N. E. Norton, of the Crusade for Cleaner Environment, and Peter T. Chokola, owner of a small Pennsylvania bottling company, accused the bottlers, supermarkets, and soft drink manufacturers of trying to eliminate returnable bottles. They said that movement to nonreturnable bottles was a result of monopoly power, not consumer demands.

Even industry sources admit the problem is severe. In a recent study of vending and fast food executives, 80 percent of the executives agreed that disposable containers were a major contribution to environmental litter and 67 percent felt that the industry had not dealt with the problem effectively (see Don R. Webb, "Top Management's Perception of the Disposable Packaging and Environmental Litter Issue," University of Missouri, mimeographed). In 1975 the Environmental Protection Agency urged Congress to prohibit plastic soft-drink containers and threatened to sue to prevent the use of these nonreturnable containers.


## THE INGREDIENTS AND NUTRITION ISSUE

Some persons oppose the sale of soft drinks because they believe the product is harmful or not nutritious. The consumer movement is demanding to know the ingredients of soft drinks (other food products must list them) to determine if they are wholesome. In 1971, the Food and Drug Administration limited the use of brominated vegetable oil used to make "cloudy" soft drinks look cloudy (for example, Fresca, Orange Fanta, Mountain Dew). The industry critics want ingredients listed to determine if other additives currently in use are unsafe.

Mary Bralove, writing in *The Wall Street Journal,* January 20, 1972, page 30, also adds:

Angry critics also point to the caffeine in cola drinks. Unknown to many buyers, this caffeine may total as much as 45 to 50 milligrams for a cup of coffee and 110 milligrams in a typical "stay awake" tablet. In a review of caffeine research for a soft drink concern, Dr. Murray E. Jarvick says: "Although caffeinated [soft drinks] provide a lift that refreshes and fights fatique fairly well, they produce a tremor, insomnia, gastro-intestinal disorder and possible cellular damage to the drinker or unborn fetus." Dr. Jarvick, who is professor of pharmacology at New York's Albert Einstein College of Medicine, also contends the caffeine "may play a role in death from cancer or heart stoppage."

Industry executives reply that the research to date is extremely limited and preliminary. They maintain that the caffeine in their drinks is safe at its present levels.

Not all soft drinks contain caffeine; for example, Seven-Up apparently does not contain the caffeine that colas do. In addition, from the beginning, some firms such as Seven-Up had listed the ingredients on the bottle. When the packaging was changed several years ago, the listing was removed. Since there has been renewed interest in this labeling, Seven-Up voluntarily put it back on the label in 1970.

Second, nutritionists accuse soft drinks of providing "empty calories." Michael Jacobson, a consumer advocate, says, "Soft drinks are just tasty garbage." Basically, the argument is that when people consume soft drinks, they forego nutritional food and thus are worse off. A recent study by Ralph Nader's group, "The Food Corporation and the Child," accuses soft drink and snack food manufacturers of producing undesirable products. They would encourage the companies to produce nutritional drinks such as a soybean-based protein drink that Pepsico is testing in Latin America and Coca-Cola's Samson being tested in Surinam.

The industry replies that they never made nutritional claims for their products, which are not intended to replace nutritional food.

Sometimes a contamination problem arises with soft drinks. For example, in January 1972, Coca-Cola of New York recalled 3 million cans of its product which were suspected of chemical contamination (with kerosene). It may have been a problem of defective can lids.

Finally, the issue of the use of sweeteners in low-calorie drinks has come up. In October of 1969, the Food and Drug Administration banned the use of sodium cyclamate, a low-calorie artificial sweetener, in all foods on grounds that heavy doses caused cancer symptoms in lab tests on animals. At this point, soft drink marketers switched from cyclamate to saccharine. By 1971, saccharine was removed from the list of additives "generally regarded as safe" and the FDA placed restrictions on its use. Since the saccharine content in soft drinks is not considered excessive, soft drinks were excluded.

But it is possible that saccharine could be banned by the government, although no one in the industry is really expecting it. There is now better than even chance that the FDA may soon reassess the prohibition of cyclamates. In the meantime, companies such as G. D. Searle are seeking approval of other noncaloric sweeteners. Searle's product "aspartame" is composed of amino acids.

### THE LEGALITY OF THE FRANCHISED BOTTLER

The Federal Trade Commission (FTC) has challenged the franchise system whereby concentrate makers grant monopolies to independent bottlers. In 1972, 7UP's Annual Report stated:

On July 15, 1971, the FTC filed a complaint against the company. The Commission basically contends that the franchising licensing arrangements used by the company, which provide for territorial assignments, are anticompetitive and violate Section 5 of the FTC Act. The relief sought is a cease and desist order. The matter is pending.

The FTC's complaint against the arrangements, whereby concentrate and syrup suppliers grant what amounts to territorial monopolies to bottlers, is felt to be an attempt to hold up the retail price of soft drinks by not encouraging bottlers to compete in each other's markets.

The industry contends that if the FTC wins the case, it will result in a host of smaller franchises overrun by their more powerful bottlers from adjacent markets. Canada Dry's president predicted there would be only 350 bottlers left. The industry feels that it is likely that sales efforts would be concentrated on the chain stores to the detriment of smaller outlets and hence gross sales might suffer.

The industry is readied for a strong defense of the franchise system, and court cases could drag on for years. It is lobbying for legislation to protect the franchise system. Senator James Eastland (D-Mississippi) introduced a bill in 1972 to protect soft drink franchise systems from FTC action, and it passed the Senate.

The last major influence comes from one of the marketer's favorite variables: demographics. During the 1960s, per capita consumption of carbonated beverages in the United States passed such drinks as beer, coffee, and milk. This increase was affected by the big increase of 10- to 24-year-olds. This age group's consumption of soft drinks exceeds the national average by 25 percent. The question is whether these persons will continue their drinking pattern into adulthood. Evidence seems to point to a slowdown in the rate of sales expansion.

If per capita consumption continued to grow at the 1972 rate of 5 to 6 percent, it would double within the next 12 to 14 years. Consumers would be drinking nothing but carbonated beverages. Can marketers hold their maturing customers' loyalty?

The prime market age group (10- to 24-year-olds) will grow by just over 20 percent during the 1970s, down from a 55 percent rate in the 1960s. Historically, per capita consumption drops with advancing age and is lowest among those 45 and over.

## Prospects for the industry

Perhaps one way to sum up the industry's prospects is to cite two analysts with opposite opinions. Fred Weldon, of A. G. Becker and Company, advised against the soft drinks stocks. With regard to recent stock declines, he said (mid-1974):

Rather than being a temporary aberration, in our opinion the decline marks the termination of the group's 16-year relative bull market and the start of a period of below-average performance. [Except for brief respites,] I believe the downtrend may last for several years. . . .

In other words, if the S&P 500 index were to rise 40%, over the next several years, a strong possibility in our judgment, the soft-drink index could probably continue to sell at about the same as it is currently. . . . If the S&P 500 were to make no progress over the next five years, we would expect the soft-drink group to decline about 40% in absolute price during the period. . . .

The companies' long-term growth rates are peaking out. There are a number of potential developments that could result in a slower rate of sales and earnings growth for the industry, at least for the next few years.

The developments he cites to support his opinion are: changes in the population away from growth in younger age groups, increased material costs, the FTC challenge, and the litter challenge.

Taking an opposite position is John Maxwell of First Wheat Securities, a well-known analyst of the industry. Citing the opportunities of foreign sales, per capita consumption records, and others, Maxwell said (January 1974):

I think the industry has less problems than any other industry group I know of. Even if overall corporate profits decline sharply in 1974, I think any company that will grow on its historical trend line will not decline in price that much. And their earnings growth has been 10–15% and this will stand out among the fallen growth companies as unique.

# Dr Pepper Company

Paul Rabinowitz

It was not very long ago that Dr Pepper was practically unknown in many parts of the United States. In spite of its new-found fame, Dr Pepper is far from being a new soft drink. The company has evolved from a small, regional soft drink firm to an international beverage organization.

As Figure 1 reveals, the company's sales have risen 10 years in a row and earnings have been increasing as well.

Recent analyses by *Fortune* have shown Dr Pepper to have one of the highest performances of the 1000 largest manufacturing firms (the first 500 and second 500) as measured by combined return: capital appreciation and dividend yield. As *Fortune* points out (December 1973, pp. 120–124, 128 ff.), the company and its stock has had remarkable performance *without* technological breakthroughs, mergers, or diversification.

## Dr Pepper then and now

The Dr Pepper Company traces its beginning to the 1880s. It is said that a young soda jerk working at an establishment known as the Old Corner Drug Store in Waco, Texas, concocted a new fountain flavor which he named after his father-in-law (Dr Pepper). After undergoing further refinement by a beverage chemist, Robert Lazenby, the drink began to be marketed on a commercial basis in 1885. It was not until 1922 that an extensive sales and distribution program was initiated.

Dr Pepper was still a minor factor in the soft drink industry, even in the early 1960s. The company's volume amounted to about $13 million annually, and distribution covered only three-fourths of the country. Even today, in the $5 billion soft drink industry, Dr Pepper is still a rather small factor. (For further information, see the preceding selection, "A Note on the American Soft Drink Industry.") Total sales volume for 1974 is $120 million, but its recent growth has been so meteoric that it has already overtaken Royal Crown Cola as the fourth largest selling soft drink in the nation behind Coca-Cola, Pepsi, and Seven-Up.

Dr Pepper produces a soft drink marketed under that name and Sugar Free Dr Pepper, a diet soft drink. The industry faced problems when the government banned cyclamate, the ingredient used in Sugar Free Dr Pepper's predecessor, Diet Dr Pepper.

**489**

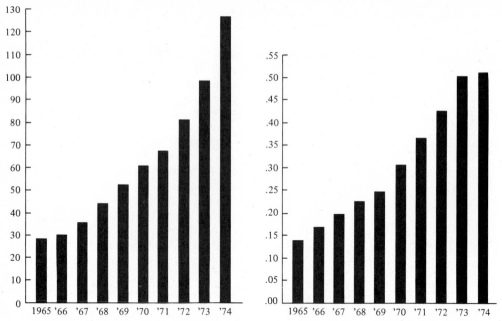

**FIGURE 1** ■ Net sales and earnings per share, 1965–1974.

Dr Pepper is seeking to prevent another major loss and is keeping its diet drink inventories low. It has also prepared several new formulations for replacement. Nevertheless, the psychological impact of a ban on saccharine might cause investors to critically reevaluate the current value of the shares of Dr Pepper or any other soft drink manufacturer's stock. At present, the diet drinks sell about $510 million yearly. Dr Pepper's share is about $10 million per year. Dr Pepper is not diversified. As far as diversification is concerned, W. W. Clements, its president, is leaving that to other companies. "With our untapped potential, it would be criminal to branch off into something else," he said recently.

The company makes and sells concentrate for use in the preparation of the bottled and canned beverage and for fountain drinks. Two syrup manufacturing plants located in Dallas, Texas, and Birmingham, Alabama, produce the concentrate. Company-owned bottling plants are located in Dallas, Waco, Fort Worth, and San Antonio, Texas, and a small cup vending plant (Harry's Fountain Supply Co.) is in Dallas.

The key to its rapid growth has been the company's aggressive marketing strategy. Expansion of its distribution through over 500 franchised bottlers in the United States, Canada, and Puerto Rico (with concentration in the South and Southwest), and intensive advertising and promotional campaigns have enabled Dr Pepper to rise quickly, it appears.

In early December 1973, Dr Pepper launched its first overseas distribution of Dr Pepper through franchise bottling operations in Tokyo and Tone, Japan. This followed the creation of a joint venture (Dr Pepper Japan, Ltd.) with Tokyo Coca-Cola Bottling Co., Ltd. Initial distribution in Okinawa has also begun. It seems safe to assume that entrance to other foreign markets is being contemplated.

# Dr Pepper's management team

Dr Pepper is professionally managed. It has some family control. Virginia Lazenby O'Hara, daughter of the founder, owns approximately 9 percent of the stock. Mrs. O'Hara's late husband was president, then chairman, from 1933 to 1961. He was succeeded by Wesby R. Parker, who joined the firm after some years with General Foods. Three of his top executives died in an airplane crash in 1964, and Parker died in 1967. He was succeeded by Hascal Billingsley. All these presidents came from the financial or operations function.

The current chairman and president is the first with major background in marketing: Woodrow Wilson Clements. "Foots," as Clements likes to be called, studied at Howard College and graduated from the University of Alabama (1935), where he played football. He went from route salesman to sales manager of the Dr Pepper Bottling Co. of Tuscaloosa, 1935 to 1942. He joined the parent Dr Pepper Co. in 1942. He was successively district manager, sales promotion manager, assistant manager of the bottler service, and general sales manager, 1942–1951. He became vice president and general sales manager, 1951–1957; vice president, marketing, 1957–1967; executive vice president and director, 1967–1969; president and chief operating officer, 1969; president and chairman, 1970.

"Foots" Clements reflects his rural Alabama upbringing in his folksy approach to employees and bottlers. He relishes telling tales. Clements is the supersalesman who enjoys drinking the company product hot or cold. He predicts that Dr Pepper will exceed the sales of Coca-Cola, probably within 20 years.

One executive vice president is Joe K. Hughes. Joe Hughes studied at North Texas State and graduated from Southern Methodist University in 1948. He was a writer, then assistant city editor of the *Dallas Times Herald*, 1948–1953; then he was manager of the Dallas office of Harshe-Rotman, Inc., public relations firm, 1953–1955; account executive, vice president, and manager of the Dallas office of Grant Advertising Co., 1956–1964; then he was executive vice president, 1964–1968 (with Grant). He joined Dr Pepper in 1948 as vice president, franchise, 1968–1969; then vice president, marketing services, and then executive vice president.

Other top executives and their ages are as follows: Frederick F. Avery, executive vice president, 44; John R. Albers, vice president, 43; Jerry M. Corbin, vice president, 42; Frank Doran, controller, 38; Hilton Folkes, assistant secretary, 65; Charles P. Grier, vice president, 44; T. C. Hunter, vice president, 56; A. J. Kincaid, vice president, 62; Alvin H. Lane, Jr., vice president, secretary, and treasurer, 32; W. F. Massmann, vice president, 55; C. W. Reeves, vice president, Japan operations, 50; Hal Stockstill, vice president, 48; Robert L. Stone, vice president, 58.

The board of directors of the Dr Pepper Company includes the following persons (1974): H. S. Billingsley, former chairman of the board, Dr Pepper Company, Dallas, Texas; W. W. Clements, chairman of the board, president and chief executive officer, Dr Pepper Company, Dallas, Texas; Edwin L. Cox, oil and gas producer, Dallas, Texas, and chairman of the board, Keebler Company, Elmhurst, Illinois; Robert B. Cullum, chairman of the board, the Cullum Companies, Inc., Dallas, Texas; Raymond H. Cummins, chairman of the board and chief executive officer, Goldsmith's Department Store, Memphis, Tennessee, and vice president, Federated Department Stores, Inc.; J. W. Davis, Dr Pepper Bottling Company, Roanoke, Virginia; E. Burke Giblin, chairman of the board, Warner-Lambert Company, Morris Plains, New Jersey; James A. Gooding, Jr., president and general manager, Dr Pepper Bottling Company, Denver, Colorado; Lamar Hunt, president and owner, Kansas City Chiefs Football Club, Dallas, Texas; W. R. Roberson, Jr., president, Roberson's Beverages, Inc., Washington, North Carolina; John M. Stemmons, president, Industrial Properties Corporation, Dallas, Texas; John P. Thompson, chairman of the board, the Southland Corporation, Dallas, Texas; Jack C. Vaughn, president, Vaughn Petroleum, Inc., and Investments, Dallas, Texas; W. D. White, senior partner, White, McElroy, White & Sides, attorneys at law, Dallas, Texas.

## Merchandising the product

Dr Pepper is different from any brand of soft drink. It is not a cola, nor a root beer, nor any single flavor but a blend of a number of pure fruit flavors. Many attempts have been made to copy the distinctive flavor of the product but none have succeeded. This has become an ever-increasing factor in Dr Pepper's growing success. As most customers say . . . "THERE'S NOTHING QUITE LIKE DR PEPPER . . . IT'S DISTINCTIVELY DIFFERENT."

So states the company in a recent annual report. The company's product is distinctive and is not a cola. It is competing with the colas for the mass market, the consumers who drink two or three bottles a day. Dr Pepper is not a cola, because a judge has so ruled. "When people say it has a cherry taste, I know they are becoming regular Dr Pepper drinkers," says W. W. Clements. "And once we get our taste established with the consumer there is no other drink that can satisfy it." Also as a result of its distinctive taste, the company can franchise with Coke, Pepsi, and Royal Crown bottlers.

Essentially, Dr Pepper's product line includes the following:

6½-ounce glass bottle Dr Pepper (returnable and nonreturnable)

10-ounce glass bottle Dr Pepper (returnable and nonreturnable)

12-ounce glass bottle Dr Pepper (returnable and nonreturnable)

26-ounce glass bottle Dr Pepper (returnable and nonreturnable)

32-ounce glass bottle Dr Pepper (introduced 1974)

48-ounce glass bottle Dr Pepper (introduced 1974)

12-ounce can Dr Pepper

6½-ounce glass bottle Sugar Free Dr Pepper[1]

16-ounce glass bottle Sugar Free Dr Pepper

Salute:[2] six flavors of other soft drinks (introduced 1963)

Waco:[2] fountain syrups—same flavors as Salute

---

[1] Sugar Free Dr Pepper is the saccharine-based product introduced in 1971 to replace the Diet Dr Pepper introduced in 1962 (containing cyclamate). Sugar Free Dr Pepper is estimated to account for 12 percent of dollar sales and is the leading diet drink in many markets.
[2] Salute and Waco are estimated to account for approximately 1 percent of dollar sales. These are distributed in only a few regions.

Dr Pepper offered larger-sized bottles of their product later than their competitors. The company felt the large-size bottles conveyed a low-price image. As yet, their plans to offer 68-ounce or 128-ounce Dr Pepper are unknown. It is estimated that about 50 percent of sales are presently in non-returnable containers.

The firm also distributes (on a limited basis) Pommac (a Swedish cognac-flavored diet soft drink), for which it obtained Western Hemisphere distribution rights in 1963 and Hustle, a high-energy, high-protein drink.

Dr Pepper Company's two entries, Dr Pepper and Sugar Free Dr Pepper, face a tremendous competition. From the Coca-Cola Company they must contend with Coca-Cola, Sprite, Tab, Fresca, Mr. PiBB, Fanta flavors, and Simba. From Pepsico come Pepsi-Cola, Diet Pepsi, Teem, Mountain Dew, Patio flavors, and Tropic Surf. From Royal Crown Cola Company come such soft drinks as Royal Crown Cola, the Diet Rite line, Nehi, and Par-T-Pak. And Seven-Up has its 7UP, Diet 7UP, and Howdy flavors. In addition, many regional and private-label entries help make market share hard to come by.

Dr Pepper is essentially a one-brand domestic company, whereas Coke and Pepsi are multibrand international companies. Dr Pepper is not the leading seller in any major market in the United States. Dr Pepper's president W. W. Clements felt he was already ahead of RC Cola in the United States and Canada and close to 7UP. In 1970, Clements projected, for the next 5 years, annual 15 to 20 percent increases in sales, based on the New York success and untapped overseas markets. So far, he has been on target in his predictions, and if things continue in spite of recent economic troubles, by 1975 Dr Pepper sales will range somewhere between $120 and $150 million and move up to the number four spot in national sales.

One attempt to "extend the product line" was Wesby Parker's promotion of Hot Dr Pepper during the lower sales months of November through March. Hot Dr Pepper has caught on—as witness such sales as 17,000 at a chilly football game—and this has done wonders for business in the normally slow winter season. "We actually can't determine how much Dr Pepper is being consumed hot," said Clements when he was vice president of marketing. "All we know is that our sales have shown phenomenal gains during normally unseasonal soft drink months. We know that our Hot Dr Pepper idea has met with favor among consumers and we know that many like the drink. What actually happens, we suspect, is that housewives buy Dr Pepper with all intentions of serving it hot, but before this happens, someone in the household chills the drink and enjoys it cold."

Dr Pepper pursues an active marketing research program. The company has not been content to have its products used as beverages, exclusively. Work is currently being conducted toward finding new and improved uses in the preparation of food and other culinary applications. A Dr Pepper ice cream topping, which may also be poured over flapjacks, has been developed. The company has been promoting the product as a cooking ingredient and has prepared over 400 recipes for its use in this way.

## Sales trends

Table 1 presents some recent statistics on sales and income of Dr Pepper. Just to give a not-too-distant look back into Dr Pepper's recent past, con-

**TABLE 1 ■ SALES AND INCOME GROWTH (IN MILLIONS OF DOLLARS) OF DR PEPPER**

|      | Net sales | Percent (increase) | Net income | Percent (increase) |
|------|-----------|--------------------|------------|--------------------|
| 1963 | 21.8      | 25                 | 1.4        | 45                 |
| 1964 | 24.6      | 13                 | 1.8        | 30                 |
| 1965 | 27.5      | 12                 | 2.4        | 28                 |
| 1966 | 28.7      | 4                  | 2.9        | 23                 |
| 1967 | 33.8      | 18                 | 3.5        | 21                 |
| 1968 | 41.9      | 24                 | 4.1        | 18                 |
| 1969 | 49.5      | 18                 | 4.6        | 13                 |
| 1970 | 57.5      | 16                 | 5.6        | 21                 |
| 1971 | 63.6      | 11                 | 6.8        | 20                 |
| 1972 | 77.4      | 22                 | 8.1        | 20                 |
| 1973 | 98.6      | 30                 | 9.7        | 19                 |
| 1974 | 128.2     | 30                 | 9.9        | Less than 1%       |

sider the following: (1958) "Dr Pepper announced it was expanding into new markets for 1959. Now distributing in 40 states and Hawaii, the company has bounded out of Texas with its eye on full national distribution by 1960." They had some problems, and national distribution was not reached until late 1970.

For most of its 74 years, Dr Pepper has been a predominantly Southern drink. The company, organized in Texas, has a distribution pattern that has followed a slow-moving franchise bottling plan across the South, Southwest, and Midwest. The Chicago area was not opened until 1948, and New York was not successfully entered until 1970.

One recent trend which may have some long-run impact is the increasing cost consciousness of consumers. The sugar price increases have led to soft drink price increases. The result could be softened demand or a shift to low-cost private-label drinks. Supermarket chains and mass merchandisers are contracting for their own house brands of soft drinks, which now account for approximately 12 to 15 percent of industry volume. During the ever-increasing rise in the cost of living, in particular food costs, cost-conscious consumers have been buying in bulk and looking for the bargain prices. Private-label soft drinks have lower delivery costs and no advertising expense. Supermarket chains' brands can be retailed for adequate profits at far lower prices.

A more direct threat may be the introduction by Coca-Cola of Mr. PiBB. The product's name is similar to Dr Pepper's, and Coke advertises it as cherry-flavored. Coke has been promoting this product heavily in the 70 markets it has entered so far (1974). But there is another problem. In a number of markets, such as New York, Dr Pepper is distributed by the Coke bottler. In 1972, Dr Pepper sued Coca-Cola, charging the company with trademark infringement. A Coca-Cola bottler was introducing a product called Peppo which, Dr Pepper said, had a similarity in flavor and some similarity in name.

Coke test-marketed Mr. PiBB in Temple, Texarkana, and Waco, Texas, and in Starkville and Columbia, Mississippi. Coke contends it did not use the *Fanta* name on their new cherry drink because Fanta drinks are all single flavors, whereas Mr. PiBB is a multiple-flavor drink, including cherry.

Speaking at their annual bottlers meeting, a Dr Pepper official said, "We know that strong efforts and intense pressures have been and will continue to be exerted by our competition [Coke] on certain of the combination Coca-Cola–Dr Pepper bottlers, but despite these pressures and efforts, 25 additional Coca-Cola bottlers have acquired Dr Pepper since our last meeting."

Mr. Clements said recently about Mr. PiBB's impact, "It has had a positive effect on us. They [Coke] have to promote our flavor as a fast-growing one in order to get retailer action. They have to tell it to the consumers, too. They'll offer one free case with every case bought. They spend an awful lot, but in 2 months, we crack it and get our space back on the shelves. We have product loyalty."

He told a *Dun's* reporter (in April 1973):

Now Coke has not said Mr PiBB is an imitation, and they never will, but it is, and I think when the largest company in the industry comes out with a product in the same category as ours, that is the greatest compliment we can receive. It means they recognize the potential of Dr Pepper. . . . In fact, wherever PiBB has done battle with Pepper, Pepper has come out stronger than ever. In those test markets where Mr PiBB has been introduced, our rate of sales growth has increased. The introduction of Mr PiBB has made us work a little harder, and I think it's made more people aware of this type of soft drink.

Dr Pepper has mounted a broad promotional effort. On the subject of developing more Dr Pepper drinkers, Mr. Clements said, "Our prime age target, and therefore our prime area of emphasis, is the youth market. We have said for years 13 to 30, for many years, but I think we now can and should broaden it from 6 to 40. In spite of what we may have heard, the youth market will increase in the United States by more than 25,000,000 by 1980. These are our customers of today and the future. All our surveys show a very high degree of preference for Dr Pepper among this group."

The 1974 advertising program was developed by John Albers, vice president, advertising; Bob Connors, national advertising manager; and Bill Thompson, senior vice president and management supervisor of Young & Rubicam.

The media mix included TV, radio, outdoors, newspapers, and magazines. Dr Pepper is going to sponsor two types of specials—the all-family prestige special and the contemporary music specials for the teen and young adult groups. In 1974, for example, the company sponsored five Dr Pepper TV specials: the Grammy Awards (in March), Emmy Awards (May), Midnight Train to Georgia (June), Chicago (group) with Anne Murry and Charlie Rich (August), and with Olivia Newton John, the Beach Boys, and Doobie Brothers, the New Year's Rocking Eve (December).

No stones are left unturned in their promotional effort. Cuyler Caldwell, national sales promotion manager, described the 1974 promotions as "more package oriented than '73 promotions and more youth oriented." The Sugar Free promotion offers a shape tape, which is also a complete measurement progress chart, free with the purchase of two cartons of Sugar Free Dr Pepper, and a $12 value bathroom scale built as a Sugar Free logo and offered at $5.50. Other sales promotion gimmicks include bicycle safety sets, backpacks, and quick-spurt freeze bottles, inflatable rafts, Calvin Hill footballs, ponchos, stadium cushions, trading cards featuring popular music stars, safety signs, and a toy Saint Bernard puppy called Schuss-Boomer that carries a Dr Pepper coin bank flask around its neck. The typical point of sale material helps promote the drink, too.

Dr Pepper has used advertising for years. The 10–2–4 theme was based on the energy needs of people at those hours as Walter Eddy of Columbia University described them. This theme was used from about 1925 onward.

The 1973 theme, developed by the Young & Rubicam advertising agency, is "All you have to do to like Dr Pepper is to try it." The now-famous trial-conflict situations that have been dramatized over the past 2 years on TV will be continued carrying the copy lines, "Once you try it, you'll love the difference" and "Millions of people love the difference of Dr Pepper." In 1974, the theme became "The most original soft drink ever."

Mr. Clements has said Dr Pepper advertising has had nine objectives over the last 10 years, and selling the product was only ninth. More important objectives, he said, were to impress Dr Pepper's own people, to reach bottlers, to get to prospective bottlers, and to impress the financial world. Dr Pepper also, to borrow an overworked phrase, "put its money where its mouth is." They are heavily involved in co-op advertising, matching bottlers dollar for dollar since 1956. Though this money must be used for local advertising, in approximately 70 markets part of it is directed toward regional advertising, in which several bottlers might participate. For both local and regional campaigns, the favored media are TV, radio, billboards, and newspapers. The advertising agency turning out the advertising that "has been acclaimed by experts and consumers as the most outstanding and effective" in Dr Pepper's history has been New York's Young & Rubicam, which developed the theme, "America's most misunderstood soft drink—but not for long." They also have a house agency, Eagle Advertising, handling coordination and placement of ads in all other markets except New York, which is exclusively handled by Young & Rubicam.

To further develop product identity, Dr Pepper had Sandgren & Murtha, the New York industrial design firm, develop a new logo and color scheme for all their packaging. The "primary object for the change was to give Dr Pepper greater visibility and more dominance in the marketplaces where it is offered for sale," the company said.

In 1972, Dr Pepper spent $8,847,000 for selling and advertising. "Our primary national vehicle will be network television with the emphasis on prime time specials. And again, we're going to have more in 1974," a vice president of advertising at Young & Rubicam said. The specials' impression of prestige and size "makes us appear to be an even bigger brand than we are," he explained.

Outdoor and newspaper ads backing the introduction of 48- and 32-ounce returnable resealable bottles in both single bottles and six-packs have been used to say, "You can love the difference in a big way."

Three Sugar Free Dr Pepper TV commercials have been used to support radio spots in standard, soul, and country and western versions. In addition, magazine ads using the line "one way or another, you'll love Dr. Pepper" were run in *Cosmopolitan, Glamour, Redbook,* and *Weight Watchers* magazines. Outdoor advertising was also used.

Besides cooperative advertising assistance, Dr Pepper every year meets with its bottlers the first week in October to help determine advertising budgets. Matched by Dr Pepper, the budget is set at more or less what the bottler wants to invest in his particular market, unless it exceeds what corporate Dr Pepper feels it can afford.

While the company likes to think it has 100 percent national coverage, *Advertising Age* in a June 18, 1973, issue gives them credit for 99 percent. Dr Pepper still has a relatively limited penetration of many large markets, especially where it has been only recently introduced. Areas such as Chicago, Minneapolis, and New York do not show large market shares of Dr Pepper.

An example of Dr Pepper's aggressiveness is in vending. Mr. Clements has given special attention to it for several years. He claims Dr Pepper spends more money proportionately than any other company to get bottlers to put his drink in their machines. As a result, as of 1970, Dr Pepper was in over 100,000 machines accounting for 20 to 25 percent of Dr Pepper's sales, only a percentage point behind the leader, Coca-Cola. In 1974, the company increased its vending sales by 10 percent.

Dr Pepper has responded to the threat to ecology by sponsoring antilitter campaigns such as the "Pitch In" programs. For example, in 1971 Dr Pepper used Miss Teenage America as spokesperson among youth organizations for antilitter campaigns. The company encouraged recycling centers and litter bags. In 1973, through the bottlers, it provided environmental kits to the schools. A kit included an environmental test set, world ocean globe, and instruction manuals to enable students to discuss pollution and environmental problems.

## Dr Pepper's operations

Before the consumer gets a chance to drink a Dr Pepper, a number of steps must be taken. First, the Dr Pepper Company purchases the ingredients. Then it produces the Dr Pepper concentrate under conditions designed to blend the formula to assure "uniform" and wholesome product. (See Figure 2.)

The firm even produces its own plastic containers for shipping the concentrate (see Figure 3). This takes place at the Dallas, Texas, headquarters (Figure 4). The headquarters is undergoing a major expansion at the present time.

After the concentrate is manufactured, it is shipped to one of the franchised bottlers. There the concentrate which has had sweetener added to it to produce a syrup is combined with carbonated water, and thus Dr. Pepper emerges in bottles (Figure 5) or cans (Figure 6) at the rate of 1000 per minute.

Dr Pepper is very proud of its efficient inventory management policies which recently have seen the days of inventory held drop from over 30 to close to 20 days. Selling the bottlers concentrate rather than syrup has lengthened shelf life and reduced shipping costs. Dr Pepper's concentrate is priced in the same range as Coca-Cola's.

Like many other soft drink firms, the company performs taste tests around the country. Commenting that he has no confidence in taste tests, Mr. Clements said, "Nine out of ten (consumers) won't like it if you tell them what it is. If you tell them it's a 'blend of natural fruit juice' instead of Dr Pepper, seven of nine will like it." He added that consumers are asked what the soft drink tastes like, and if they relate it to something good, "we've gotten through."

From a packaging standpoint, much has changed from the time of 6½-ounce bottles. Some of the industry's success with consumers is its flexible approach to packaging. One-way containers (both cans and bottles) up to 64 ounces in size, someday soon to be 128 ounces, have answered consumers' desires for larger amounts.

Container research in the industry has been extensive. The search for optimal construction materials and design has included the study of glass (with new plastic combinations), plastics (including increased amounts of resin), and

**FIGURE 2** ■ Blending the concentrate.

faster, more versatile systems of mass production in packaging (from filling to containerizing).

Sohio's Vistron Division, which produces the acrylonitrile copolymer (Barex) resin for Pepsi bottles, and Monsanto, the supplier and converter of Coke's methacrylonitrile styrene (Copac bottles), recently arranged to produce the first commercial 210 resin in a project yielding approximately 12 million pounds annually, enough to satisfy Pepsico's plans for the immediate future. Vistron also halved resin price to a 59- to 70-cent per pound range. However, observers have pointed out that more resin capacity and use will be needed to bring the price to the more competitive 30- to 40-cent range. The reason for the slow development in this area and the general secrecy surrounding these programs, aside from the newness of resin-formulating and high-volume molding technology, has been the legislative mood of several states and municipalities. The last 4 years, at least in New York City, have seen the passing of a new law taxing all plastic containers. The banning or taxing of one-way beverage containers is a growing possibility that makes bottlers and the industry itself unsure of what the future will hold.

Automation has continued to expedite packaging. There are presently three new automated systems for basket (carrier) multipacking of beverage bottles. All three systems were designed primarily for nonreturnable bottles, but they also can be adjusted for returnables. The new systems include:

**1** Container Corporation of America's Basket Wrap, an economical hybrid of wrap and basket rated at up to 150 six-packs per minute; installed at Pepsi-Cola Bottling Company of Pennsauken, New Jersey.

**2** Federal Paper Board's Jack-et-Basket, a true basket carrier with output rated at 80 plus, installed at the Coca-Cola Bottling Co., of Paterson, New Jersey.

**3** Mead Packaging's Mastermatic, also a true basket, that the supplier hopes will run 100 or more per minute

While other multipacking methods steadily improved their economics, the design and application of the basket carrying carton for Dr Pepper rested on

**FIGURE 3** ■ Plastic containers used for shipping concentrate.

security, easy bottle removal, replacement, and carrying convenience. But coming under criticism is the basket's physical instability. Its broad expanse of promotional square inches is said to be often wasted because the multipack is too wobbly to display well.

For large bottlers, these machines will have several advantages. First, it will mean an end to hand setup, still surprisingly widespread for baskets. Users can now explore the economies of bulk glass instead of precased bottles. It will also mean the elimination of bottle drop and its attendant glass shock, a major step toward reducing in-plant and in-store bottle breakage. And, for the first time, basket-carrier application is a fast, economical and competitive system. All three systems have been designed to handle the various popular bottle sizes from 7 to 16 ounces.

Another example of the increasing technology in packaging comes from the Gulf Gate plant of Coca-Cola Bottling Co. at Houston, Texas. It has been using a high-speed, continuous-motion, prototype palletizing machine, handling 26,000 cases or more per day of 12-ounce cans since August 1972. The machine is completely controlled by a solid-state programmable controller.

While capable of handling 85 cases or more per minute, the machine is operated at 60 cases per minute (cpm). At speeds of 60 cpm, the use of a solid-state programmable controller is required. Electrical cycling is too fast for conventional relays. They would quickly outrun their useful life. There is no relay failure with the machine's solid-state programmable controller. Other features of the palletizer include (1) first 85-cpm machine to be operational, (2) first high-speed machine to use programmable controller in place of a big

**FIGURE 4** ■ Dallas, Texas headquarters.

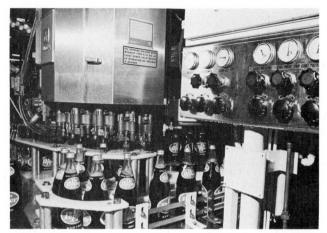

**FIGURE 5** ■ Dr Pepper in bottles. The line operates with automatic monitoring to assure quality.

**FIGURE 6** ■ Dr Pepper in cans. Automatic production facilities speed operation, requiring only a few employees.

**500** ■ Choice of strategy and strategic planning

relay cabinet, and (3) first "continuous" motion palletizer. The programmable controller costs about as much as a relay cabinet, but it takes about one-twentieth the space and is a large improvement in reliability.

One other recent technological development is the control of noise in the bottling plant caused by the clatter of empty cans hitting each other on cable conveyor lines. In some in-plant locations it has been necessary for personnel to wear ear-protective gear. Also, can-to-can contact causes nicks in the lithographic covering.

The solution to this problem came in the way of a modulated-speed, empty can conveyor system which now keeps a constant supply of cans to a 60-valve filler at the Shasta plant in Hayward, California.

Noise level along the cable conveyor line was reduced from a peak 115 decibels to 85 decibels or less by eliminating can-to-can contact. Cans travel with space between them, from depalletizer to filter infeed, to avoid denting and lithographic impairment.

Dr Pepper directly employs about 1150 people. It and its bottlers employ about 695,000 people. For its own employees, the firm offers stock option and an insured noncontributing pension plan for employees. The company expects to maintain the pension plan indefinitely, but has the reserved right to discontinue it at any time. The cost of the plan amounted to $393,000 in 1971 and $374,400 in 1970. Costs of the plan include amounts sufficient to amortize past service costs over the remaining active employment periods of the covered employees, except the additional past service cost resulting from a 1969 amendment. The amendment is applicable to employees scheduled for retirement before 1979 and is being amortized over a 10-year period. The assets of the fund exceeded the actuarially computed vested benefits as of December 31, 1971.

The board can authorize stock options for key executives, normally below the market price of the stock. During 1971, for example, options to purchase 206,000 shares were outstanding, 128,000 exercisable at that time, and 26,250 shares actually were exercised.

## Accounting and finance at Dr Pepper

The company has provided various statements for analysis. Table 2 contains the balance sheets for 1968 through 1974. Table 3 is 1968–1974 income statements. Additional data for analysis are shown in Tables 4 (changes in financial position), 5 (financial position summaries), and 6 (the financial results over the past few years).

Figure 7 presents a recent summary of distribution of revenue at Dr Pepper.

The company's stock is listed on the New York Stock Exchange, symbolized by the letters DOC. It was originally listed on NYSE in 1947. Table 7 provides the high and low prices of the stock for some recent years. Figure 8 plots the stock of the industry against the Value Line industries.

In 1974, for the first time since 1967, the soft drink industries' stocks have failed to outperform the general market for more than 3 months straight. The Value Line Composite Index, which ranks approximately 68 industry groups for year-ahead performance, has dropped soft drinks from 35th to 62d in the last quarter.

**TABLE 2 ■ CONSOLIDATED BALANCE SHEETS**

| | 1974 | 1973 | 1972 | 1971 | 1970 | 1969 | 1968 |
|---|---|---|---|---|---|---|---|
| *Assets* | | | | | | | |
| **Current assets** | | | | | | | |
| Cash, certificates of deposit | $ 364,141 | $ 822,776 | $15,935,367[a] | $11,818,371 | $10,760,891 | $ 8,157,303 | $ 6,934,799 |
| Marketable securities at cost | 4,790,445 | 18,147,335 | | | | | |
| Receivables | 9,114,983 | 6,679,824 | 5,606,732 | 4,676,760 | 3,879,418 | 3,977,290 | 2,720,350 |
| Inventories at lower of cost (first in, first out) or market | 5,728,615 | 3,054,439 | 2,661,848 | 2,155,307 | 1,906,629 | 1,757,371 | 2,158,871 |
| Prepaid expenses | 3,548,258 | 3,314,330 | 2,270,275 | 1,844,082 | 1,046,045 | 1,038,885 | 707,976 |
| Total current assets | 23,546,442 | 32,018,704 | 26,474,222 | 20,494,520 | 17,592,983 | 14,930,849 | 12,521,996 |
| Marketable securities for investment | 8,156,618 | ... | ... | ... | ... | ... | ... |
| Investments (at cost) and notes receivable | 1,260,829 | 1,779,325 | 1,542,978 | 1,153,352 | 470,656 | 352,873 | 426,854 |
| Property, plant, and equipment at cost | 24,531,905 | 20,199,520 | 17,126,101 | 13,469,345 | 12,265,227 | 11,560,331 | 10,748,920 |
| Less accumulated depreciation | 9,171,248 | 8,902,926 | 7,733,128 | 5,594,253 | 5,249,478 | 4,858,193 | 4,490,984 |
| Net property, plant, and equipment | 15,360,657 | 11,296,594 | 9,392,973 | 7,875,092 | 7,015,749 | 6,702,138 | 6,257,936 |
| Formulas, trademarks, and goodwill at cost or nominal value | 270,910 | 272,910 | 272,910 | 272,910 | 272,910 | 272,910 | 272,910 |
| | $48,595,456 | $45,417,533 | $37,683,083 | $29,795,874 | $25,352,298 | $22,258,770 | $19,479,696 |
| *Liabilities and stockholders' equity* | | | | | | | |
| **Current liabilities** | | | | | | | |
| Accounts payable and accrued expenses | $ 4,884,550 | $ 6,006,509 | $ 4,535,029 | $ 3,537,896 | $ 2,859,195 | $ 2,615,148 | $ 1,801,528 |
| Federal and state income taxes | 73,469 | 1,240,930 | 1,541,465 | 996,987 | 715,455 | 800,728 | 1,117,401 |
| Total current liabilities | 4,958,019 | 7,247,439 | 6,076,494 | 4,534,883 | 3,574,650 | 3,415,876 | 2,918,929 |
| **Stockholders' equity** | | | | | | | |
| Common stock | 7,630,732 | 6,717,482 | 5,590,078 | 3,862,860 | 3,538,009 | 3,324,684 | 3,079,029 |
| Retained earnings | 36,006,705 | 31,452,612 | 26,016,511 | 21,398,131 | 18,239,639 | 15,518,210 | 13,481,738 |
| Total stockholders' equity | 43,637,437 | 38,170,094 | 31,606,589 | 25,260,991 | 21,777,648 | 18,842,894 | 16,560,767 |
| | $48,595,456 | $45,417,533 | $37,683,083 | $29,795,874 | $25,352,298 | $22,258,770 | $19,479,696 |

[a] 1972 and previous included marketable securities.

**TABLE 3 ■ CONSOLIDATED EARNINGS AND RETAINED EARNINGS, DECEMBER 31**

| | 1974 | 1973 | 1972 | 1971 | 1970 | 1969 | 1968 |
|---|---|---|---|---|---|---|---|
| Net sales | $128,299,707 | $98,918,466 | $82,037,876 | $63,622,653 | $57,449,749 | $49,514,538 | $41,883,072 |
| Cost of sales | 74,659,678 | 50,791,111 | 38,859,902 | 29,787,613 | 27,428,675 | 24,638,951 | 19,612,383 |
| Gross profit | 53,640,029 | 48,127,355 | 43,177,974 | 33,835,040 | 30,021,074 | 24,875,587 | 22,270,689 |
| Administrative, marketing, and general expenses | 36,297,111 | 31,262,480 | 28,343,000 | 21,991,585 | 19,835,343 | 15,394,624 | 14,027,653 |
| Operating profit | 17,342,918 | 16,864,875 | 14,834,974 | 11,843,455 | 10,185,731 | 9,480,963 | 8,243,036 |
| Miscellaneous income—net | 1,121,634 | 1,502,848 | 847,108 | 894,811 | 899,051 | 301,535 | 416,879 |
| Earnings before income taxes | 18,464,552 | 18,367,723 | 15,682,082 | 12,738,266 | 11,084,782 | 9,782,498 | 8,659,915 |
| Federal and state income taxes | 8,562,853 | 8,632,223 | 7,492,841 | 5,966,125 | 5,455,761 | 5,140,260 | 4,552,229 |
| Net earnings | 9,901,699 | 9,735,500 | 8,189,241 | 6,772,141 | 5,629,021 | 4,642,238 | 4,107,686 |
| Retained earnings, beginning of year | 31,452,612 | 26,016,511 | 21,705,823 | 18,239,639 | 15,518,210 | 13,481,738 | 11,511,918 |
| | 41,354,311 | 35,752,011 | 29,895,064 | 25,011,780 | 21,147,231 | 18,123,976 | 15,619,604 |
| Dividends paid | 5,347,311 | 4,299,399 | 3,878,553 | 3,613,649 | 2,907,592 | 2,605,766 | 2,137,866 |
| Retained earnings, end of year | $ 36,007,000 | $31,452,612 | $26,016,511 | $21,398,131 | $18,239,639 | $15,518,210 | $13,481,738 |

**TABLE 4 ▪ CONSOLIDATED STATEMENTS OF CHANGES IN FINANCIAL POSITION, DECEMBER 31**

| | 1974 | 1973 | 1972 | 1971 | 1970 | 1969 | 1968 |
|---|---|---|---|---|---|---|---|
| **Funds provided** | | | | | | | |
| Net earnings | $ 9,901,699 | $ 9,735,500 | $ 8,189,241 | $6,772,141 | $5,629,021 | $4,642,238 | $4,107,686 |
| Add charge for depreciation which did not require funds | 1,985,629 | 1,649,640 | 1,567,052 | 1,109,447 | 990,225 | 869,489 | 762,889 |
| Funds derived from operations | 11,887,328 | 11,385,140 | 9,756,293 | 7,881,588 | 6,619,246 | 5,511,727 | 4,870,575 |
| Decrease in noncurrent notes receivable | 913,250 | 1,127,404 | 1,667,968 | 324,850 | 213,325 | 73,981 | 356,832 |
| Sale of common stock | | | | | | 245,655 | |
| | 12,800,578 | 12,512,544 | 11,424,261 | 8,206,438 | 6,832,571 | 5,831,363 | 5,227,407 |
| **Uses of working capital** | | | | | | | |
| Dividends on common stock | 5,347,606 | 4,299,399 | 3,878,553 | 3,613,649 | 2,907,592 | 2,605,766 | 2,137,866 |
| Additions to property, plant, and equipment | 6,049,692 | 3,553,261 | 2,149,626 | 1,968,790 | 1,303,836 | 1,313,691 | 1,454,645 |
| Increase in marketable securities | 8,156,618 | . . . | . . . | . . . | . . . | . . . | . . . |
| Increase in investments and non-current notes receivable | . . . | 236,347 | 388,278 | 682,695 | 117,783 | . . . | 175,837 |
| | 19,553,916 | 8,089,007 | 6,416,457 | 6,265,134 | 4,329,211 | 3,919,457 | 3,768,348 |
| Increase (decrease) in working capital | ($ 6,232,842) | $ 4,423,537 | $ 5,007,804 | $1,941,304 | $2,503,360 | $1,911,906 | $1,459,059 |
| **Changes in working capital** | | | | | | | |
| Increase (decrease) in current assets: | | | | | | | |
| Cash and marketable securities | ($13,865,525) | $ 3,084,744 | $ 3,967,678 | $1,057,480 | $2,603,588 | | |
| Receivables | 2,435,159 | 1,073,092 | 634,275 | 797,342 | (97,872) | | |
| Inventories | 2,674,176 | 392,591 | 256,099 | 248,678 | 149,258 | | |
| Prepaid expenses | 233,928 | 1,044,055 | 394,873 | 798,037 | 7,160 | | |
| | (8,522,262) | 5,594,482 | 5,252,925 | 2,901,537 | 2,662,134 | | |
| **Increase (decrease) in current liabilities** | | | | | | | |
| Accounts payable and accrued expenses | (1,121,959) | 1,471,480 | (258,309) | 678,701 | 244,047 | | |
| Federal and state income taxes | (1,167,461) | (300,535) | 503,430 | 281,532 | (85,273) | | |
| | (2,289,420) | 1,170,945 | 245,121 | 960,233 | 158,774 | | |
| Increase (decrease) in working capital | ($ 6,232,842) | $ 4,423,537 | $ 5,007,804 | $ 1,941,304 | $ 2,503,360 | | |

## TABLE 5 ■ FINANCIAL POSITION

| Year | Current assets | Current liabilities | Working capital | Fixed assets net | Other assets | Long-term indebtedness | Stock-holders' equity | Book value per share |
|------|------|------|------|------|------|------|------|------|
| 1974 | $23,546,442 | $4,958,019 | $18,588,423 | $15,360,657 | $9,688,357 | . . . . . . . | $43,637,437 | $2.28 |
| 1973 | 32,068,704 | 7,247,439 | 24,821,265 | 11,296,594 | 2,052,235 | . . . . . . . | 38,170,094 | 2.01 |
| 1972 | 26,474,222 | 6,076,494 | 20,397,728 | 9,392,973 | 1,815,888 | . . . . . . . | 31,606,589 | 1.67 |
| 1971 | 21,221,297 | 5,831,373 | 15,389,924 | 8,810,399 | 1,427,610 | . . . . . . . | 25,627,933 | 1.37 |
| 1970 | 18,449,724 | 5,279,358 | 13,170,366 | 8,055,568 | 805,022 | . . . . . . . | 22,030,956 | 1.18 |
| 1969 | 15,619,602 | 4,568,016 | 11,051,586 | 7,805,838 | 719,103 | . . . . . . . | 19,576,527 | 1.05 |
| 1968 | 13,093,309 | 3,497,143 | 9,596,166 | 6,949,627 | 717,293 | . . . . . . . | 17,263,086 | 0.93 |
| 1967 | 11,790,150 | 3,703,502 | 8,086,648 | 6,221,394 | 543,572 | . . . . . . . | 14,851,614 | 0.81 |
| 1966 | 9,322,130 | 3,453,595 | 5,868,535 | 5,966,646 | 537,800 | . . . . . . . | 12,372,981 | 0.69 |
| 1965 | 7,896,339 | 3,604,954 | 4,291,385 | 5,973,460 | 624,866 | $189,739 | 10,699,972 | 0.60 |

*a* Years 1965 through 1972 restated to give retroactive effect to a pooling-of-interests transaction in 1973.
*b* Adjusted for 2-for-1 stock split March 27, 1968, for 3-for-1 stock split March 25, 1970, and for 2-for-1 stock split October 27, 1972.
*c* Years 1965 and 1966 restated to give retroactive effect to the change during 1967 in method of accounting for returnable containers.

## TABLE 6 ■ FINANCIAL RESULTS

| Year | Net sales | Net earnings | Earnings per share | Dividends | Dividends per share | Shares outstanding |
|------|------|------|------|------|------|------|
| 1974 | $128,299,707 | $9,901,699 | $.52 | $5,347,606 | $.28 | 19,106,034 |
| 1973 | 98,918,466 | 9,735,500 | .51 | 4,299,399 | .22¾ | 18,998,734 |
| 1972 | 82,037,876 | 8,189,241 | .43 | 3,878,553 | .20⅘ | 18,869,934 |
| 1971 | 67,769,898 | 6,884,775 | .37 | 3,613,649 | .19½ | 18,697,860 |
| 1970 | 61,028,665 | 5,733,917 | .31 | 2,916,812 | .15¾ | 18,645,360 |
| 1969 | 52,709,359 | 4,672,571 | .25 | 2,618,966 | .14⅛ | 18,584,460 |
| 1968 | 44,079,937 | 4,197,436 | .23 | 2,142,866 | .11⅔ | 18,490,620 |
| 1967 | 35,614,110 | 3,588,089 | .20 | 1,583,555 | .08⅔ | 18,247,260 |
| 1966 | 30,008,756 | 2,956,213 | .17 | 1,381,856 | .07⅔ | 17,898,060 |
| 1965 | 28,514,655 | 2,493,001 | .14 | 1,154,876 | .06½ | 17,842,860 |

*a* Years 1965 through 1972 restated to give retroactive effect to a pooling-of-interests transaction in 1973.
*b* Adjusted for 2-for-1 stock split March 25, 1964, and for 2-for-1 stock split March 27, 1968.
*c* Years 1965 and 1966 restated to give retroactive effect to the change during 1967 in method of accounting for returnable containers.

## TABLE 7 ■ HIGH AND LOW PRICES FOR DR PEPPER'S STOCK

| Year | High | Low |
|------|------|------|
| 1974 | 22.9 | 6.5 |
| 1973 | 30 | 18.7 |
| 1972 | 27.3 | 18.3 |
| 1971 | 40.3 | 22 |
| 1970 | 24.5 | 13 |
| 1969 | 54 | 43.2 |
| 1968 | 55.3 | 24.3 |
| 1967 | 52 | 30 |

While none of the industry's issues is rated favorable for year-ahead market performance, three are still expected to perform as well as the general market. The three are Dr Pepper, MEI Corp. (reorganized in 1972 by the merging with two Pepsi-Cola bottlers in the Midwest), and the Seven-Up Company.

Industry earnings overall have continued to rise, but the price earnings per share have been suffering. Only in a few cases did earnings experience a decline in either of the last two quarters of 1973. Two companies, Coca-Cola Bottling of New York and Royal Crown had declines exceeding 50 percent. The decline of Coca-Cola Bottling of New York is attributed to acquisition indigestion, narrowing of margins, and, at Igloo Corp. (acquired in 1972), inventory adjustments. At Royal Crown, Phase 4 had a major hand in the decline, especially in its natural citrus juice operations in Texas and Florida. Another profit

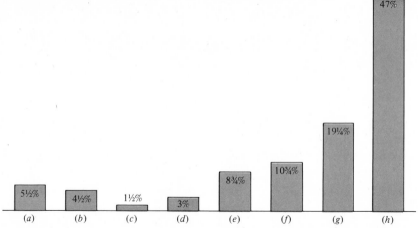

**FIGURE 7** ■ Distribution of revenue, 1973: (*a*) retained in business; (*b*) dividends; (*c*) other operating expenses; (*d*) depreciation and maintenance; (*e*) taxes on income; (*f*) payrolls; (*g*) promotion, advertising, and expansion; (*h*) raw materials and packaging.

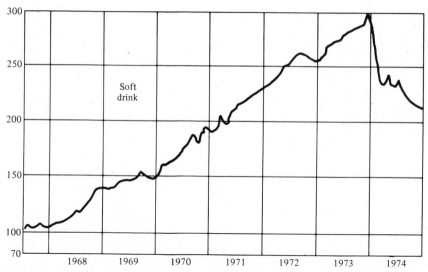

**FIGURE 8** ■ Relative strength: ratio of industry to value line composite index: June 1967 equals 100.

drain was credited to the costs connected with getting the newly formulated Diet Rite Cola on its dealers' shelves.

For most companies, though, earnings are expected to keep growth uninterrupted, and the industry still has many years of substantial growth ahead of it, although the growth rate may have slowed in recent years.

All of Dr Pepper's subsidiaries' results (all of which are wholly owned) are on the statements in the tables provided. All material intercompany accounts, transactions, and profits have been eliminated.

The company and its subsidiaries provide for depreciation of property, plant, and equipment on a straight-line basis for both financial and federal income tax reporting. Annual depreciation rates are:

| | | |
|---|---|---|
| Land improvements | 1⅔ | to 10% |
| Buildings | 1⅔ | to 20% |
| Machines and equipment | 4 | to 25% |
| Steel drums | 8 | to ⅓% |
| Automobiles and trucks | 25–33 | to ⅓% |
| Furniture and fixtures | 5 | to 33⅓% |
| Other trading equipment | 20 | to 25% |

Similarly, there are no significant timing differences between reporting net earnings for financial and for federal income tax purposes. The company uses the inventory method (FIFO, representing a logical flow of goods, and COST, the value of inventory at that point in time) of accounting for returnable containers.

Maintenance and repairs are charged to operations as incurred; renewals and betterments are capitalized and depreciated. The cost and accumulated depreciation of properties sold or disposed of are removed from the accounts. The resultant profit or loss on such transactions is credited or charged to income. The amounts of beginning and ending inventories used in the computation of cost of sales were $1,906,629 and $2,155,307 respectively in 1971, and $2,155,307 and $2,429,672 respectively in 1972.

The company does not amortize the cost of intangible assets because Dr Pepper feels the assets have unlimited terms of existence.

## The future

No one can be sure of the future, of course. But Dr Pepper's executives believe they will be number one in the twenty-first century.

# The Seven-Up Company

William F. Glueck

The Seven-Up Company, International Headquarters, St. Louis, Missouri, is a major factor in the soft drink industry in the United States. 7UP is the third largest selling soft drink in the United States and in the world.

## History of the Seven-Up Company

The Seven-Up Company traces its history to 1920 and the founding of its predecessor company, the Howdy Company. Three men were primarily involved in its founding. C. L. Grigg had operated a small general store in Price's Branch, Missouri. Later he was in the wholesale dry goods business but interested a former coal merchant, E. G. Ridgway, in entering the soft drink business with Howdy orange drink in 1920. In 1921 the third founder, a St. Louis lawyer named F. Y. Gladney, invested in the firm and formed the corporation. Mr. Grigg, whose philosophy had been "sell an idea and the product itself stays sold," had an idea: a new soft drink of highest quality and distinctive taste. He tested eleven formulas before accepting the formula known today as 7UP. It was introduced in mid-October 1929 as "Bib-Label Lithiated Lemon-Lime Soda" in competition with over 600 lemon-based soft drinks. In spite of the inauspicious timing, the company has prospered under a new name for the product, 7UP. The firm franchised at no cost the bottlers who met Mr. Grigg's requirements. All franchises were awarded by 1939, and both Mr. Grigg and Mr. Ridgway died in 1939–1940. Seven-Up is the only major soft drink firm with management related to the founding families.

## Organization and management

The Seven-Up Company is organized with a parent company and seven principal subsidiaries:

1 Seven-Up Services, Inc., which is primarily a canning and services subsidiary, Paul H. Young, Jr., president

2 Seven-Up Canada Limited, which sells 7UP products throughout Canada, John R. Kidwell, president

3 Seven-Up International, Inc., which sells 7UP products in 80 countries, Charles B. Thies, president

4 Dev-Vend Corporation, which finances equipment for bottlers, Paul H. Young, Jr., president

**5** Warner-Jenkinson Company, which manufactures and markets color and flavor ingredients for thousands of consumer food products, O. W. Hickel, Jr., president

**6** Seven-Up Bottling of Phoenix, Inc., which bottles 7UP in the Arizona area, Eugene E. Serres, president

**7** Ventura Costal Corporation, producers of lemons and lemon products, Frank J. Leforgeais, president

Each of these subsidiaries, as well as the parent company, is considered an individual profit center and is required annually to submit a detailed and well-documented plan of action and a budget statement to implement the plan. The plan is used to develop sales and profit targets for the year. The subsidiaries' sales and profit targets are combined with those of the parent company to build a total corporate plan.

The board of directors includes five officers or former officers and six outside directors: Maurice R. Chambers, Fred L. Kuhlmann, Garret F. Meyer, David H. Morey, Harold E. Thayer, and Fred W. Wenzel. They include top executives of St. Louis firms such as Boatmen's Bank, Anheuser-Busch, Kellwood, Mallinckrodt, and Interco. The board meets every 2 months to approve plans of operating management. It includes Executive, Audit, Executive Compensation, and Dividend Policy Committees. The last two are composed entirely of outside directors.

Key top executives include (in 1974):

Ben H. Wells, chairman and chief executive officer, age 68, is a graduate of the University of Michigan. Mr. Wells joined the company in 1938 and served in the marketing department.

William E. Winter, 55, president and chief operating officer, is a graduate of the University of Illinois. He joined the company in 1946 and spent most of his career in the marketing function of 7UP.

Orville J. Roesch, group vice president and director of marketing, is 50 years old. He received a degree from St. Louis University. He entered 7UP in 1956 and has served in the advertising, sales promotion, and marketing departments.

J. Stewart Bakula, vice president and general counsel, 46, is a graduate of Princeton University and the Washington University School of Law. He joined the firm in 1958.

Dr. B. C. Cole, vice president and technical director, is 63 years old. He was educated at Western Kentucky State College (B.S.), the University of Kentucky (M.S.), and Iowa State College (Ph.D.). He joined the company in 1945 and has spent most of his career in the technical services and product department.

Robert W. Simpson, vice president, secretary, and franchise director, joined 7UP in 1942. He is 65 years old. His degree was obtained from Northwestern University. His experience with 7UP was in the sales and franchise departments.

Paul H. Young, Jr., executive vice president and treasurer, is 49 years old. He is a graduate of Washington University and the Wharton Graduate School of Commerce and Finance. He joined 7UP in 1966 and has moved up through the finance function.

David M. Haffner, vice president and director of merchandising, is 31. A Colgate graduate, Haffner has been with 7UP since 1965.

Seven-Up has been significantly influenced by founding families as evidenced by Mr. Grigg's son, H. C. Grigg, chairman emeritus; Mr. Ridgway's son, the late Howard E. Ridgway, also chairman emeritus; and Mr. Gladney's son-in-law, Mr. Wells.

From the subsidiaries' sales and profit targets the parent company devises its total corporate plan. The late Mr. Ridgway explained how this plan is used.

These targets and related information are utilized in the decision-making process to help formulate corporate policy. Two committees play important roles in the decision-making process at Seven-Up. These are the Corporate Development Plans Committee and the Executive Committee.

The Corporate Plans Committee consists of the president, the executive vice-president, and key planning officers. It is the job of this committee to assist the Executive Committee in developing plans for the future growth of the company.

It is also the task of this committee to determine what growth resources can be utilized to meet these goals. In other words . . . they set desirable—but realistic—growth targets, and then they determine how best to reach these targets. They have to take into consideration potential growth through expansion of present business through bottlers and domestic subsidiaries . . . potential growth through Canadian and International operations . . . and potential growth through possible acquisitions.

The Corporate Plans Committee reports through its Chairman directly to the Executive Committee. Plans developed by this Committee are submitted to the Executive Committee for adoption.

The Executive Committee is composed of the Chairman, the President, and the Executive Vice President. The Executive Committee makes recommendations to the Board of Directors for approval. Approved plans are then put into action by the President of the company.

When asked about goals and objectives of the firm, Mr. Ridgway said:

The marketing objectives of The Seven-UP Company are two-fold:

short term, our objective is to make positive advances each year that will result in a growing, increasingly profitable business . . . for 7UP bottlers and The Seven-Up Company.

long term, simply stated, our objective is brand leadership. Our marketing programs are shaped primarily by our obligation to position 7-UP, through creative marketing, as an international brand. The strength of 7-UP is the strength of the brand and all that an international brand suggests.

One can infer something about the Seven-Up Company's managerial philosophy, at least in the past. It is growth-oriented, primarily internal growth, in cooperation with its bottlers. It has taken special steps to protect and encourage its smaller bottlers.

Recently the firm took steps that affect vertical integration. It acquired Ventura Costal Corp. (1973), which provides Seven-Up with some of its lemon oil; and in 1970 Warner-Jenkinson, its source of flavors (vertical integration backward). It also acquired the 7UP bottler in Phoenix, the first company-owned bottling plant in the United States. For several years it has operated the bottling and canning facilities for Toronto and most of southern Ontario.


## Producing 7UP

The Seven-Up Company of St. Louis actually produces very little of the bottled 7UP customers drink. With the exception of Phoenix and the eight company-

---

[1] For an understanding of the challenges facing 7UP and its industry, see "A Note on the American Soft Drink Industry" earlier in this book.

owned subsidiaries of the International Company, 7UP is produced by franchised bottlers in the United States and abroad. Canned 7UP, however, is produced by Seven-Up Services for bottlers who do not have their own canning facilities.

The company's subsidiary Ventura Costal farms 2200 acres in California. It produces some of the lemon oil which is used by Warner-Jenkinson to produce the lemon extract. In addition to the oil, Ventura processes and packs one-third of the frozen concentrate for lemonade in the United States (mostly under private label), fresh lemons, food supplements, and lemon peel.

The Seven-Up Company produces the extract for 7UP through its now wholly owned subsidiary, Warner-Jenkinson. The extract is shipped to the bottlers. The bottlers add sugar to make the syrup and the other ingredients to make the product. In the case of returnable bottles, the bottler also must wash and inspect the bottles. The filling equipment varies in speed up to 1000 units per minute.

This mode of operation differs from Coca-Cola, which adds the sugar to the extract and sells syrup to its bottlers. Since sugar is an important cost, it is difficult to compare sales of 7UP directly to this firm.

The bottlers receive technical advice and supervision from the Seven-Up Company in their bottling operations. A summary of 7UP divisional sales is as follows:

| | Sales of the divisions in 1973 |
|---|---|
| Seven-Up and subsidiaries | $116,349,254 |
| Warner-Jenkinson and subsidiaries | 15,856,965 |
| Ventura Costal | 14,542,143 |
| | $146,748,362 |

### WARNER-JENKINSON

For 50 years, Warner-Jenkinson had produced all the extracts for 7UP products in the United States and about 50 percent for foreign markets. Because of changing legal status of both the Seven-Up Company and Warner-Jenkinson (especially when the Seven-Up Company went public), it was decided that a more formal relationship be developed. So the Seven-Up Company integrated backwards and acquired the company in 1970.

In addition to producing 7UP extract, Warner-Jenkinson is a major supplier of colors and flavors for ice cream and soft drinks. It markets under the Red Seal line of flavors and colors, and Chefmaster and Flavor Mill labels for candies, cereals, bakery goods, snack foods, dentifrices, dairy products, desserts, puddings, processed meats, pet foods, and other products.

Its line includes 3000 flavors, ten basic colors, and over 400 blends for the food industry. Warner-Jenkinson has plants in St. Louis, Santa Ana, Brooklyn, New York City, and Mexico City. The subsidiary maintains its own sales staff and does its own advertising. It expects sales to rise dramatically through such additions as imitation chicken and beef flavor for high-protein food products made from soybeans, and Captain Jimmy's Cosmic Color Poppers. Warner-Jenkinson's share of market has been rising for some years. It has done especially well in the growing market for dry food and beverage bases. It has done this by producing spray-dried flavors and by use of new flavors.

In 1973, the division acquired Creative Perfumers and Flavorists, Salient Flavoring Inc., and United Flavors and United Essential Oils. These strengthened the traditional lines and opened up the fragrance field. Warner-Jenkinson operates in the United States, Europe, and Central and South America, and in Mexico has begun marketing chemical intermediaries to the industrial market.

In 1975, one challenge Warner-Jenkinson faced was whether the Food and Drug Administration will ban the use of Warner-Jenkinson color Red 2. It is a major product of Warner-Jenkinson. Some FDA scientists claim that the widely used Red 2 causes birth defects, abortions, and cancer in animals. The FDA has tried unsuccessfully since March 1971 to ban the product's use and substitute Red 40. Several large manufacturers (Nabisco and General Mills) have recently shifted to Red 40.

## Seven-Up and bottlers

In 1973, 7UP acquired Phoenix 7UP Bottling, its bottler for that territory since 1936. The firm serves approximately 70 percent of Arizona's population with 25 route trucks. It has a modern production plant.

Most 7UP is produced by independent businesses called franchised bottlers. They produce and sell the products in a territory that is exclusively theirs. These firms vary in size. The biggest bottlers of 7UP are in the New York, Chicago, and Los Angeles areas.

Profit is related to relative efficiency of the bottler. More efficient bottlers use larger trucks and new merchandising techniques. For example, 7UP Los Angeles replaced 140 of their 260-case trucks with 400-case trucks. Seven-Up Los Angeles handles principally 7UP products. The bottler who was given the franchise for Los Angeles in 1933 sold the operation to Westinghouse in 1968 for $26 million.

Besides the trucks, 7UP (Los Angeles) owns two bottling plants (242,000 square feet) that produce 40,000 cases per single shift, and a canning plant. They have three 1-story warehouses (103,000 square feet), and so they can deliver to any customer within an hour.

Seven-Up gives an exclusive franchise for a territory, but the bottlers do not distribute 7UP exclusively. Mr. Ridgway explained: "Twenty years ago more than 60 percent of our bottlers carried 7UP exclusively. Lately, because of increased costs, many of our bottlers have felt they had to take on other lines to increase the volume per truck."

As far as Seven-Up bottlers are concerned, about half of them bottle rival soft drink brands. Mr. Ridgway explained that although some of their bottlers handled Coke, Pepsi, or RC, if they did so, they agreed not to distribute Teem, Sprite, or Upper 10.

Employees on the bottling line are normally semiskilled. Pay varies by area, and urban operations are under union contracts. One recent Department of Labor report indicated that productivity in the industry had increased 5.3 percent compared to an all-industry increase of 3.6 percent.

Certain key supplies to Seven-Up and the 7UP bottlers can affect sales and profits. The main supplies are containers. The bottle strike in 1968, for example, led to shortages of bottles and loss of sales. In 1974 the escalating cost of sugar forced bottlers to increase prices frequently with a consequent slowing of sales momentum.

Seven-Up sells vending equipment to its franchised bottlers on the install-ment plan through its Dev-Vend Corp. subsidiary. This subsidiary purchases equipment from manufacturers and basically finances the equipment to the bottlers. In 1974, this amounted to less than 3 percent of consolidated net sales. The sales of this equipment are influenced by interest rates, government tax policies, and weather.

### BOTTLER RELATIONS

Anyone who has purchased soft drinks in several cities recognizes the potential problems a company like Seven-Up has in producing its product through franchised bottlers. Some drinks do not taste the same in various cities because the bottlers have different water supplies to deal with, syrup-water variances, etc. Seven-Up basically has a quality control and consistency challenge to meet.

Mr. Ridgway explained how Seven-Up meets this challenge:

We have a large number of men traveling the country from the Technical Department. These men are not policemen as such. They are there to help the bottlers. The value of the extract is small in total product. So the bottler doesn't try to substitute a cheaper extract.

The problem in quality control is turnover in personnel at bottlers who make the syrup. The Technical Department checks the product in the plant and from the trade on a regular basis. They make tests in plant and samples are sent to the labs in St. Louis to be checked too. They examine the product in his plant to show him there has been a slip up not to "punish" him but to improve his product's sales.

The product is examined for sugar content, taste, purity, clarity, carbonation, and fill. Reports are sent to the bottler. Sometimes, the bottler himself sends samples to St. Louis asking for help in formula problems they are having. As soon as we determine the trouble, a technical man goes out to the bottler to help him.

This is how we maintain quality control over our product and it's a very good system. It is rare we have any serious problem.

In addition to field testing, Seven-Up tries to motivate its bottlers positively by awarding 7UP Quality Awards. In 1974, about half the bottlers qualified for the Outstanding 7UP Quality Award. The bottlers are scored on plant evaluation; trade sample tests; rigorous monthly lab sample tests of purity, carbonation, clarity, acid and sugar content, correct fill, and taste. The tests are performed in the Seven-Up Company labs in St. Louis.

Finally, Seven-Up has improved bottler relations. The company has never terminated a bottler for inadequate sales. It has done so for inadequate finan-cial structure or quality control. It is sometimes difficult to get the bottler to be more aggressive in vending or fountain sales, but aggressive marketing strategies seem to be moving the company ahead.

## Personnel practices

In 1973, Seven-Up employed 772 persons, about half of them overseas. Warner-Jenkinson employs about 350 and Ventura's employment is about 285 persons, though that increases seasonally. Wages and salaries in 1973 were almost $17 million.

The company has pension plans covering most of its employees in the United States and some abroad. The company funds pension costs as accrued. Total expenditures for pensions (including amortization of prior service cost over a period of 10 years) were $714,000 in 1973. Unfunded past service liability was $1,500,000 in 1973.

Employee benefits also include life insurance coverage, health and accident benefits, profit sharing awards, and tuition scholarship grants. In 1973, Seven-Up paid $487,000 out in profit sharing.

The firm has a very low turnover rate of its executives and employees.

The firm is not unionized.

In 1969, the board of directors approved authorization of a stock option plan. It allowed 5-year options to purchase up to 150,000 shares of common stock to key employees, option price being fair market value of stock at date of grant. In 1973, 81,000 shares had options outstanding on them.

The company provides its bottlers, "7UP Developers," with sales and other training.

## Seven-Up International and Seven-Up Canada

In 1974, Seven-Up International supervised 184 franchised bottlers in 77 countries (outside the United States and Canada). It contributed 9 percent of sales. The division opened 10 new plants in 1974, and 12 new bottlers in 1973. Seven-Up Canada has 111 bottlers. Seven-Up is the number two soft drink in all Canada, and number one in some provinces. About 22 percent of Seven-Up's consolidated assets are invested outside the United States.

Seven-Up entered the overseas market in earnest in 1939. At present it operates and runs manufacturing and/or marketing subsidiaries in Argentina, Australia, Brazil, the United Kingdom, Japan, Mexico, and the Netherlands. Earlier it sold off subsidiaries in Pakistan and the Philippines. A recent map of the worldwide bottlers is given in Figure 1.

Worldwide sales have been doing very well, with special gains in Europe (especially Ireland, Norway, Denmark, Belgium, the Netherlands) and South America. Other sales of notable size and increase are in Singapore, Cambodia, Pakistan, Indonesia, Hong Kong, Lebanon, Iran, and the Philippines.

Although overseas operations always sound glamorous and much attention is given to untapped markets, etc., there are special challenges to the Seven-Up international subsidiary. These challenges include money market fluctuations and government requirements regarding balance of payments plus loss in sales of subsidiaries where war or politics affect market conditions.

Marketing cannot be transferred automatically overseas. (See "Advertising in Underdeveloped Countries" by David McIntyre, *Management Review,* May 1974, pp. 13–18.) For example, the "uncola" concept was not introduced to the Canadian market until 1969. Even so, the French-speaking Quebec province citizens did not initially see the point of the uncola since the word does not mean the same in French.

International sales are severely affected by dock strikes which prevent the

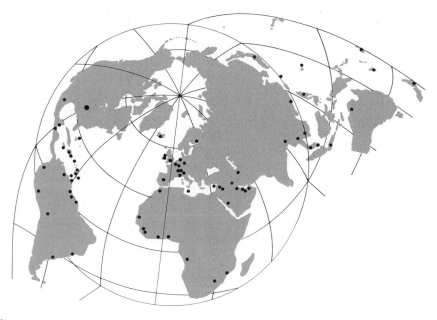

FIGURE 1

shipment of 7UP extract abroad. The dock strikes in the last few years have been especially difficult.

Overseas sales frequently can get quite complicated politically. For example, Seven-Up markets its product through a franchisee in South Africa for that country. Many black African nations wish the company would suspend its operations there. Nevertheless, it is doing very well in Nigeria, where the bottler is adding plants to serve the whole country.

But just as the company operates its business through local business executives in the Unites States, almost all overseas business operates through locally owned bottlers. The only exceptions are the eight export subsidiaries and Canada Seven-Up.

This at once mobilizes the entrepreneurial motivation of home-owned business; it also avoids appropriation difficulties and the feeling of foreign ownership of businesses in other countries.

One potential threat to 7UP is Mexico's recent move to subsidize Mexican brands of soft drinks at the expense of brands like Coke and 7UP. If this spreads to other countries, it can hurt 7UP's sales abroad.

## Finance and accounting

Tables 1, 2, and 3 provide financial information on the Seven-Up Company.

On March 15, 1967, the company went public when certain descendants of the founders sold 423,574 shares of common stock. By February 16, 1968, there were 4100 stockholders all over the United States, Canada, and several foreign countries.

| | 1974 | 1973 | 1972 | 1971 | 1970 |
|---|---|---|---|---|---|
| *Assets* | | | | | |
| **Current assets** | | | | | |
| Cash | $ 2,566,208 | $ 5,012,043 | $ 5,249,627 | $ 3,087,179 | $ 2,212,474 |
| Short-term investments (at cost and accrued interest) | 20,812,739 | 20,710,783 | 18,440,938 | 17,778,924 | 14,180,147 |
| Receivables | | | | | |
| Trade and other accounts | 17,796,492 | 13,575,366 | 12,287,402 | 9,079,169 | 9,333,858 |
| Installment contracts | 1,862,832 | 2,291,970 | 2,244,403 | 2,870,372 | 3,082,587 |
| Allowances for doubtful accounts | (300,000) | (199,000) | (201,000) | (166,000) | (178,000) |
| Inventories | | | | 8,274,020 | 8,131,120 |
| Finished products | 6,930,658 | 5,463,518 | 4,820,198 | . . . . | . . . |
| Extract and raw materials | 15,656,460 | 9,642,462 | 8,203,862 | . . . . | . . . |
| Prepaid expenses and other current assets | 2,005,707 | 2,264,809 | 1,284,358 | 655,577 | 573,399 |
| Total current assets | 67,331,096 | 58,761,951 | 52,329,788 | 41,579,241 | 37,335,585 |
| Other assets | 2,953,990 | 1,800,626 | 2,298,733 | 1,169,741 | 1,133,733 |
| **Property, plant, and equipment (at cost)** | | | | | |
| Land | 6,137,868 | 5,988,722 | 2,957,844 | 1,992,896 | 2,000,573 |
| Orchards | 2,432,364 | 2,317,011 | 1,988,749 | . . . . | . . . |
| Buildings and improvements | 14,127,169 | 12,858,595 | 12,119,728 | 10,541,608 | 10,009,697 |
| Furniture and equipment | 17,015,017 | 13,918,422 | 12,289,779 | 6,881,944 | 6,090,032 |
| Orchards under development | 1,256,728 | 446,972 | 303,922 | . . . | . . . |
| Construction in process (estimated total cost is $2,500,000) | 312,291 | . . . . | . . . . | | |
| Allowance for depreciation | (12,179,869) | (10,903,240) | (10,349,257) | (6,148,588) | (5,811,571) |
| **Intangibles** | | | | | |
| Trademarks at cost | 914,762 | 894,762 | 894,762 | 894,762 | 894,762 |
| Formulas and trademark expense at cost less accumulated amortization | 653,974 | 674,085 | 185,187 | 205,763 | 228,626 |
| Cost in excess of net assets of subsidiaries acquired, less accumulated amortization | 2,727,100 | 2,819,573 | 2,459,461 | 1,399,161 | 1,399,161 |
| Total assets | $103,682,490 | $ 89,577,479 | $ 77,478,696 | $58,516,528 | $53,280,598 |
| *Liabilities and stockholders' equity* | | | | | |
| **Liabilities** | | | | | |
| Notes payable | $ 797,267 | $ 648,631 | $ 2,115,955 | $ 219,176 | $ 537,363 |
| Accounts payable | 12,110,061 | 9,208,615 | 7,186,820 | 6,187,478 | 6,701,547 |
| Employee compensation | 1,131,956 | 738,342 | 794,701 | . . . | . . . |
| Accrued advertising | 3,226,595 | 1,965,722 | 1,784,653 | . . . . | . . . . |
| Other accrued liabilities | 2,753,262 | 2,133,051 | 1,580,668 | 2,691,657 | 2,486,649 |
| Amount due growers for fruit processed | 798,767 | 1,144,326 | 1,282,612 | | |
| Income taxes | 3,072,165 | 3,520,985 | 2,308,492 | 2,691,657 | 2,486,649 |
| Current portion of long-term debt | 743,387 | 694,493 | 657,145 | . . . | 113,756 |
| **Other liabilities and reserves** | | | | | |
| Long-term debt net | 2,652,860 | 3,140,984 | 2,447,818 | . . . | 1,021,424 |
| Reserve for foreign operations | 300,000 | 300,000 | 205,000 | 205,000 | 155,000 |
| Deferred income taxes | 389,399 | 142,043 | 174,122 | 161,466 | 220,777 |
| **Stockholders' equity** | | | | | |
| 6 percent cumulative preferred stock | 3,588,000 | 3,588,000 | 3,588,000 | 3,588,000 | 3,588,000 |
| $5.71 convertible class A preferred stock | 4,615,100 | 4,860,600 | 5,079,900 | 7,307,900 | 7,390,400 |
| Common stock | 10,472,271 | 10,459,701 | 10,449,151 | 5,102,150 | 5,100,392 |
| Additional capital | 5,428,388 | 5,147,092 | 4,910,705 | 98,750 | 18,008 |
| Retained earnings | 51,603,012 | 41,884,894 | 32,912,954 | 30,013,729 | 23,860,019 |
| Total liabilities and net worth | $103,682,490 | $ 89,577,479 | $ 77,478,696 | $58,516,528 | $53,280,598 |

Mr. Ridgway explained that the company went public because of estate and general business taxes. As he put it:

You get to the point where you must either sell out or go public because of expenses of getting big and the needs for capital for expansion. So far, Seven-Up has financed itself entirely from within. There will come a time when we'll have to raise capital. Occasionally in the past, we used bank loans but not on a long term basis. In 1971, there were 8,000 owners of Seven-Up stock.

Before that, on December 19, 1966, the shareholders approved an increase in authorized shares of common stock from 600,000 $10 par shares to 6 million

| | 1974 | 1973 | 1972 | 1971 | 1970 |
|---|---|---|---|---|---|
| Net sales | $190,879,628 | $146,748,362 | $132,519,867 | $111,629,084 | $100,256,825 |
| Cost of products sold | 110,046,723 | 75,783,214 | 69,722,488 | 55,911,234 | 50,613,974 |
| | 80,832,905 | 70,965,148 | 62,797,379 | 55,717,850 | 49,642,851 |
| Selling, administrative, and general expenses | 51,212,637 | 45,164,104 | 40,153,791 | 35,451,519 | 31,459,092 |
| | 29,620,268 | 25,801,044 | 22,643,588 | 20,266,331 | 18,183,759 |
| Other income: | | | | | |
| Interest earned | 2,298,505 | 1,844,231 | 1,069,297 | 905,830 | 946,465 |
| Miscellaneous | 849,207 | 487,169 | 514,138 | 600,388 | 383,561 |
| | 3,147,712 | 2,331,400 | 1,583,435 | 1,506,218 | 1,330,026 |
| | 32,767,980 | 28,132,444 | 24,227,023 | 21,772,549 | 19,513,785 |
| Other deductions: | | | | | |
| Interest expense | 316,243 | 438,406 | 293,604 | 39,118 | 127,774 |
| Miscellaneous | 374,734 | 588,692 | 683,634 | 391,090 | 338,083 |
| | 690,977 | 1,027,098 | 977,238 | 430,208 | 465,857 |
| Income before income taxes | 32,077,003 | 27,105,346 | 23,249,785 | 21,342,341 | 19,047,928 |
| Income taxes: | | | | | |
| Federal and state | 13,496,000 | 11,150,000 | 10,004,265 | 9,243,000 | 8,393,000 |
| Foreign | 1,993,000 | 1,873,000 | 1,201,000 | 1,230,000 | 1,112,000 |
| | 15,489,000 | 13,023,000 | 11,205,265 | 10,473,000 | 9,505,000 |
| Net income | $ 16,588,003 | $ 14,082,346 | $ 12,044,520 | $ 10,869,341 | $ 9,542,928 |

$1 par shares and authorized a 425-for-1 stock split. When these shares were issued, the excess of par (amounting to $2,490,000) was charged to retained earnings and credited to common stock.

In 1968, the descendants of the founders offered 364,008 shares of common to the public. The company then had 5300 shareholders.

On September 24, 1969, the board split the stock 2 for 1, and this was effected by a 100 percent stock dividend. Dividends were raised to 60 cents a share annually; in 1968, 48.8 cents on new stock dividend basis was paid. The board has raised the dividend every year since 1964, when it was 12.5 cents per share.

On January 10, 1972, the board of directors approved a 2-for-1 stock split to holders of record of February 7, 1972, and payable on March 1. It was implemented by a 100 percent stock dividend.

The firm's auditors are Ernst & Ernst.

Inventories were priced at lower of cost (FIFO) or market through 1973. In 1974, the firm began valuing sugar using FIFO because of major price increases. Long-term debt includes a note payable to an insurance company in monthly installments of $14,446 including interest at 5½ percent to July 1984. Depreciation is computed on the basis of its estimated useful life: buildings 40 to 50 years and furniture and equipment 4 to 15 years, using the straight-line method. With regard to long-term leases, the company and its subsidiaries have them for office space expiring between 1974 and 1987; their annual rental is approximately $98,000.

Warner-Jenkinson was merged into the Seven-Up Company December 24, 1969. Seven-Up issued 74,095 shares of new Seven-Up convertible preferred paying an annual dividend of $5.71 per share of $423,100 per year to purchase it.

**TABLE 3 ■ SEVEN-UP AND SUBSIDIARIES, SEVEN-YEAR STATISTICAL SUMMARY, 1968–1974**
Year ended December 31

| | 1974 | 1973 | 1972 | 1971 | 1970 | 1969 | 1968 |
|---|---|---|---|---|---|---|---|
| Net sales | $190,879,628 | $146,748,362 | $132,519,867 | $124,379,262 | $111,648,288 | $103,007,833 | $87,773,071 |
| Cost of products sold | 110,046,723 | 75,783,214 | 69,722,488 | 66,247,562 | 60,047,748 | 55,044,699 | 45,537,947 |
| Gross profit | 80,832,905 | 70,965,148 | 62,797,379 | 58,131,700 | 51,600,540 | 47,963,134 | 42,235,124 |
| Selling, administrative, and general expense | 51,212,637 | 45,164,104 | 40,153,791 | 36,550,453 | 32,461,502 | 30,014,561 | 27,284,671 |
| Operating profit | 29,620,268 | 25,801,044 | 22,643,588 | 21,581,247 | 19,139,038 | 17,948,573 | 14,950,453 |
| Net miscellaneous income | 2,456,835 | 1,304,302 | 606,197 | 661,145 | 457,011 | 228,885 | 44,508 |
| Income before income taxes and extraordinary items | 32,077,103 | 27,105,346 | 23,249,785 | 22,242,392 | 19,596,049 | 18,177,458 | 14,994,961 |
| Federal, state, and foreign income taxes | 15,489,000 | 13,023,000 | 11,205,265 | 10,914,386 | 9,779,390 | 9,587,856 | 8,166,448 |
| Income before extraordinary items | 16,588,103 | 14,082,346 | 12,044,520 | 11,328,006 | 9,816,659 | 8,589,602 | 6,828,513 |
| Extraordinary items (net) | .... | .... | .... | .... | .... | (198,159) | .... |
| Net income | $ 16,588,103 | $ 14,082,346 | $ 12,044,520 | $ 11,328,006 | $ 9,816,659 | $ 8,391,443 | $ 6,828,513 |
| Net income as a percent of sales | 8.7% | 9.6% | 9.1% | 9.1% | 8.8% | 8.1% | 7.8% |
| Per share of common stock: | | | | | | | |
| Net income[a] | $1.54 | $1.30 | $1.10 | $1.03 | $0.89 | $0.75 | $0.60 |
| Dividends[b] | 0.61 | 0.4325 | 0.416 | 0.40 | 0.325 | 0.24 | 0.19 |
| Book value[b] | 6.45 | 5.50 | 4.62 | 3.72 | 3.08 | 2.50 | 1.97 |
| Market price range (OTC) common (high-low bid prices)[b] | 30¾–10½ | 37¼–21¾ | 50⅛–33⅜ | 36⅛–26¾ | 30¾–17¾ | 22¾–14¼ | 14½–7 |
| Depreciation and amortization | $ 2,347,569 | $ 1,750,273 | $ 1,339,384 | $ 1,129,534 | $ 1,189,705 | $ 1,134,413 | [c] |
| Capital expenditures | 6,819,836 | 7,506,958 | 3,086,443 | 2,565,297 | 1,902,143 | 2,892,668 | [c] |
| Working capital: | | | | | | | |
| Current assets | $ 67,331,096 | $ 58,761,951 | $ 52,329,788 | $ 45,845,959 | $ 40,674,266 | $ 35,416,921 | $30,330,674 |
| Current liabilities | 24,633,460 | 20,054,165 | 17,711,046 | 15,944,106 | 15,164,446 | 14,681,230 | 13,152,072 |
| Total working capital | 42,697,636 | 38,707,786 | 34,618,742 | 29,901,853 | 25,509,820 | 20,735,691 | 17,178,602 |
| Current ratio | 2.7 to 1 | 2.9 to 1 | 3.0 to 1 | 2.9 to 1 | 2.7 to 1 | 2.4 to 1 | 2.3 to 1 |

**Other assets:**

| | | | | | | | |
|---|---|---|---|---|---|---|---|
| Land, buildings, and equipment | 29,101,568 | 24,626,482 | 19,310,765 | 17,155,484 | 15,976,359 | 14,805,879 | 13,819,145 |
| Miscellaneous investments | 2,953,990 | 1,800,626 | 2,298,733 | 1,930,319 | 1,926,520 | 2,655,864 | 2,087,373 |
| Intangibles | 4,295,836 | 4,388,420 | 3,539,410 | 2,499,686 | 2,522,549 | 2,494,957 | 2,537,111 |
| Total other assets | 36,351,394 | 30,815,528 | 25,148,908 | 21,585,489 | 20,425,428 | 19,956,700 | 18,443,629 |
| Total | $ 79,049,030 | $ 69,523,314 | $ 59,767,650 | $ 51,487,342 | $ 45,935,248 | $ 40,692,391 | $35,622,231 |

**Capitalization and reserves:**

| | | | | | | | |
|---|---|---|---|---|---|---|---|
| Long-term debt | $ 2,652,860 | $ 3,140,984 | $ 2,447,818 | $ 1,735,063 | $ 2,805,964 | $ 3,249,580 | $ 3,303,579 |
| Reserve for foreign operations | 300,000 | 300,000 | 205,000 | 205,000 | 155,000 | 400,000 | 300,000 |
| Deferred income taxes | 389,399 | 142,043 | 174,122 | 159,788 | 198,440 | 260,662 | 314,153 |
| 6 percent cumulative preferred stock | 3,588,000 | 3,588,000 | 3,588,000 | 3,588,000 | 3,588,000 | 3,588,800 | 4,084,800 |
| $5.71 convertible Class A preferred stock | 4,615,100 | 4,860,600 | 5,079,900 | 7,307,900 | 7,390,400 | 7,408,800 | 7,409,500 |
| Common shareholders' equity | 67,503,671 | 57,491,687 | 48,272,810 | 38,491,591 | 31,796,644 | 25,784,549 | 20,210,199 |
| Total | $ 79,049,030 | $ 69,523,314 | $ 59,767,650 | $ 51,487,342 | $ 45,935,248 | $ 40,692,391 | $35,622,231 |

| | | | | | | | |
|---|---|---|---|---|---|---|---|
| Return on common equity—at end of year | 23.9% | 23.6% | 23.7% | 27.8% | 28.9% | 30.0% | 30.5% |
| Average shares of common stock outstanding[a] | 10,467,739 | 10,457,812 | 10,378,538 | 10,345,034 | 10,335,038 | 10,326,961 | 10,282,192 |

[a] Based on weighted average number of shares outstanding during each year, adjusted to reflect shares issuable upon exercise of stock options and for stock splits in 1969 and 1972.
[b] Adjusted for 2-for-1 stock splits in 1969 and 1972.
[c] Comparable consolidated data not available.
All data have been restated on a pooling-of-interest basis to include the operations of Warner-Jenkinson Co. acquired in 1970, and Ventura Costal Corporation. acquired in 1973.

## Seven-Up's marketing

The sales trend at Seven-Up has been attractive, as a look at Figure 2 will indicate.

7UP is the third largest selling soft drink in the United States and in the world. The largest selling soft drinks are Coca-Cola and Pepsi. These giants compete directly with 7UP with their own lemon-lime drinks.

Coke's lemon-lime drink is Sprite; Pepsi's is Teem. As far as vending sales are concerned, in 1974 7UP was the fourth most preferred brand. The company spends about 17 percent of revenue on marketing.

Mr. Ridgway described the organization and operations of the marketing function as follows:

All of our marketing activities are coordinated to achieve our objectives for the brand. While programs must involve and enthuse the bottler, they must also be structured to the best interest of 7UP. This means that national marketing strategy for the brand must transcend local territory situations.

We go about solving our problems with an exhaustive use of marketing research. This research involves packaging, pricing, promotion, advertising . . . in fact, all of the tools which should be a vital part of any total marketing program. But, we recognize that research is only as good as the people who structure it . . . the people who analyze it . . . and the people who must make high-risk judgment decisions based on the research findings made available to them.

We work against a schedule of tight time limits. We do not lock ourselves into programs that cannot be changed to fit the needs of the marketplace. Admittedly, this usually means more work, but we have seen how this keeps enthusiasm at a high level and ultimately results in more effective programs.

### ORGANIZATION OF THE MARKETING DEPARTMENT

All activities are coordinated under the group vice president and director of marketing. Seven major departments report to the director of marketing. They are Advertising; Promotion; Field Sales; Marketing Planning; Marketing Research; Merchandising; and Fountain Syrup Sales.

The advertising director has responsibility for advertising management and contact with the J. Walter Thompson (Chicago) advertising agency, which handles the 7UP account.

The director of sales has responsibility for supervising activities relating to the personal selling operations of the independent bottlers. The Sales Training division has responsibility for sales training in both the parent company and the bottler organization. For administrative purposes, the country is divided into five sales regions—Northeast, Southeast, East North Central, West Central, and Western, each headed by a regional sales manager who has several district sales managers reporting to him.

District sales managers have responsibility for direct contact with the owners and managers of the various bottling plants. The number of plants assigned to a given district sales manager varies, depending upon the sales contributions of the plants and marketing needs of the area. For example, in some areas, close coordination may be required between a number of bottler organizations in terms of common promotional plans. In such a case, these franchise holders, with overlapping needs, are grouped together and assigned to the same district

**FIGURE 2** ■ Total corporate net sales, in millions, 1969–1974.

| | |
|---|---|
| 1974 | $190.8 |
| 1973 | 146.7 |
| 1972 | 132.5 |
| 1971 | 124.4 |
| 1970 | 111.6 |
| 1969 | 103.0 |

sales manager. Bottling plants vary greatly in size, volume potential, and marketing problems. In general, the amount of contact which a sales manager must maintain with a given operation bears a direct relationship to these factors.

Seven-Up has special representatives who call upon national accounts. Their work is primarily missionary in nature. For example, the grocery trade relations manager calls on chain store headquarters, keeping their beverage merchandisers advised about the details of special promotional programs and obtaining basic approval for store managers to implement those programs. This information is then passed on to the various bottlers throughout the country so that they may follow up in making calls on local supermarkets within the chain. In similar fashion, national account representatives call upon military and airline purchasing agents to obtain an acceptance of various plans, but actual sales to these accounts are made by the independent bottlers.

Fountain 7UP sales are handled by a separate department within the marketing group. Seven-Up did not enter the fountain syrup field until 1960. One reason for this delayed entry centered on the need for stringent quality controls. When the product is to be dispensed through postmix equipment, at such places as fountains and vending machines, special treatment is necessary to filter the water obtained from city water supplies.

Having overcome these technical difficulties, Seven-Up followed most aggressive policies of attempting to increase fountain syrup sales.

The Marketing Planning Department performs a variety of functions, some of which are unique.

### MARKETING PLANNING AT SEVEN-UP

Mr. Ridgway explained how marketing planning worked at Seven-Up.

Marketing planning is best described as a circular process with the consumer as the midpoint of the cycle. All the various elements of marketing are being directed at the consumer—packaging, product, distribution, competition, merchandising, promotion, advertising. The marketing planners stand at the perimeter of the circle evaluating the consumer response to each of these marketing actions. Following their evaluation, they then modify these actions where necessary and redirect them at the consumer, starting the planning process over again.

Inherent in this description of marketing planning is a great dependency—not just upon the creation of innovative marketing action but on a process of review and evaluation of each of these actions.

Marketing planning with The Seven-Up Company is based on the principle of decentralized planning, but centralized coordination of the planning function. All of the departments within the marketing group are expected to contribute to the planning process in their respective areas.

The Advertising Promotion Director is responsible for planning, creating, and scheduling all advertising programs, consistent with analyses made of the market and marketing strategies and objectives approved by the Director of Marketing.

The Director of Sales translates National goals, for 7UP bottle, can, and pre-mix sales into regional and district sales quotas. He plans, creates and executes both short- and long-range sales and merchandising programs to attain sales goals that have been established by the Director of Marketing.

The Fountain 7UP Manager is responsible for planning, creating, and executing sales and merchandising programs to attain sales goals that have been established by the Director of Marketing. Sales and merchandising programs are developed for both 7UP Developer Post-Mix programs and National Accounts.

Obviously, the market planners play a key role in the development of the Annual Marketing Plan. The development of the Annual Marketing Plan follows a process somewhat like the following: The market planners request from field sales, advertising, marketing research and the fountain syrup departments, information which is used to help build the Plan.

The initial draft of the Annual Marketing Plan, which includes sections on problems and opportunities, basic strategy and objectives, is prepared by the marketing planners, again with the active participation of the sales, advertising promotion, and fountain syrup departments. J. Walter Thompson Company also has a prominent role in the review process for each brand. Necessary review, revision and final approval is made by the Director of Marketing.

The various budgets from each of the departments within marketing are submitted to the Marketing Planning Manager. They are accepted without revision and submitted to the Director of Marketing for comparison with profit objectives for the ensuing year. After completion of this review, the budgets are incorporated into the Annual Marketing Plan, or returned to the respective departments for appropriate revisions.

Marketing plans are prepared by the field sales, advertising and promotion and fountain syrup departments, and submitted to the Marketing Planning Manager. They also are accepted without revision and submitted to the Director of Marketing with comments on the effect of the actions on the marketing objectives and strategy for the ensuing year. The Director of Marketing reviews and approves the plans for incorporation into the total marketing plan.

The Seven-Up Annual Marketing Plan has these basic purposes:

1  It brings together in one place all of the essential data needed in identifying the current 7UP position in the market and the problems which must be overcome to improve that position.

2  It states in quantified terms the marketing objectives of the Company for the ensuing year and describes in detailed terms the strategies which will be invoked to attain these objectives.

3  It provides a complete operating guide to all personnel who will play a key role in implementing the plan.

4  It provides a permanent record of marketing decisions and the logical framework within which these decisions were made.

**5**  It establishes quantified criteria against which marketing and advertising accomplishments may be judged.

The Director of Marketing reviews and approves the plans for incorporation into the total marketing plan.

### ADVERTISING 7UP

Perhaps the most important aspect of the total marketing program for a mass consumer product such as 7UP is advertising. The 7UP account for 31 years has been with J. Walter Thompson, Chicago.

Seven-Up has undergone a dramatic change in its advertising program over the last 10 years. In August 1962, *Forbes* related that the soft drink industry as a whole spent $200 million on advertising or about 11 percent of sales. For 7UP itself, *Advertising Age* (Nov. 9, 1964, p. 35) said that 7UP's 1965 advertising budget would be $13,400,000, a 10 percent increase over 1964. The company planned to spend $3.4 million on radio, $2.15 million for TV, $2.75 million on magazines, $1.34 million for posters and billboards, and $3.76 million for special media. For bottler advertising $8 million additional was budgeted. All this was aimed at the young adult with a theme of "Where There's Action."

In the same month, *Broadcasting* indicated that the $8 million was over and above the cooperative advertising with bottlers (additional $5.5 million).

On November 29, 1965, *Advertising Age* reported 7UP's promotional theme for 1966 "Wet and Wild," emphasizing different packages, sizes, etc., available with magazines as a major medium. This campaign was designed to say in three syllables that 7UP was a powerful thirst quencher (Wet) with a unique taste all its own (Wild).

Coupled with the slogan "First against Thirst," the "Wet and Wild" campaign played up the product with such devices as pictures of ice-frosted 7UP bottles, a lively television jingle, and a variety of publicity-getting tie-ins.

In 1967, the company spent $9,300,000 in advertising and the bottlers spent about $6 million.

In 1968, the company introduced its now well-known Uncola theme. The company reported in its 1968 Annual Report:

Early in 1968, the Seven-Up Company unveiled a totally new marketing effort in the United States. It would not only position 7UP as a soft drink fulfilling the same basic needs that colas fulfill, but would also dramatize the fact that 7UP was even better than the colas, having distinctive, thirst-quenching qualities plus an unequalled fresh, clean taste.

The new campaign for 1968 was "7UP, The Uncola."

The result was a total marketing effort designed to help 7UP attain its full potential, deserving a larger share of the total soft drink market, particularly among the heaviest consumers of soft drinks, the 16–24 age group.

*Advertising Age* (Feb. 15, 1969, pp. 48–49) did not think much of the campaign. They called it a "negative pitch." But the journal admitted the campaign was working. The company was happy with its new theme, especially with ads like the "Security Kit." In this ad, the speaker suggests to the user that if he really needs the color of cola for security, perhaps 7UP could provide the color in a kit to be added before drinking 7UP. The firm amplified the theme with "crazy" posters designed to appeal to the young adults and offered them to the public with good response. Seventy-five percent of the ad budget was TV in 1969.

*Advertising Age* reported (Aug. 24, 1970, p. 165) a record ad budget for 7UP of $20 million and additional $6.8 million spent overseas. They also reported 7UP was dropping the use of print media entirely.

Some might wonder how long the company will continue the Uncola theme in its advertising. Mr. Ridgway explained that the theme is not just an advertising gimmick; it is a marketing concept and since sales were still growing, the firm had no present plans to drop it. He explained.

As a result of our finding, we know that many persons did not think of 7UP as a soft drink. How could we deal with this problem?

The solution brought forth by the Company's advertising staff and the J. Walter Thompson Agency was the "Uncola" concept. It was revealed to 7UP bottlers at the annual meeting in Chicago in February, 1968.

"7UP, The Uncola," is more than an advertising theme or slogan that enjoys a wave of popularity and then is replaced by a new phase. The Uncola is a marketing *concept* . . . expressed through a coined word which has become a synonym for 7UP in the minds of the public.

*Advertising Age* (Aug. 26, 1974) contrasted Seven-Up's reported advertising spending with *AA*'s own estimates in 1972 and 1973 (see Tables 4 and 5).

In 1973, Seven-Up introduced a "See the Light" theme to *supplement* the Uncola theme. Other themes were the "Dream Land" theme, use of Ms.

TABLE 4 ■ SEVEN-UP'S FIGURES FOR ADVERTISING EXPENDI-
TURES[a]

|  | 1973 | 1972 |
|---|---|---|
| Magazines | $ 463,950 | $ 380,000 |
| TV (network and spot) | 10,590,445 | 11,620,600 |
| Radio | 3,466,400 | 2,296,600 |
| Outdoor | 2,519,650 | 2,894,250 |
| Total measured | 17,040,445 | 17,191,450 |
| Unmeasured | 10,317,090 | 10,087,000 |
| Estimated total | 27,357,535 | 27,278,450 |

[a] Reported by Seven-Up Co. Includes co-op, p.o.p., newspaper, and marketing services (premiums, pr, sales promotion).

TABLE 5 ■ *ADVERTISING AGE'S* FIGURES FOR ADVERTISING EX-
PENDITURES[a]

|  | 1973 | 1972 |
|---|---|---|
| Newspapers | $ 182,800 | . . . |
| Magazines | 147,300 | $ 11,100 |
| Business press | 42,500 | 52,400 |
| Spot television | 10,286,400 | 9,744,000 |
| Network TV | 1,051,400 | 2,765,400 |
| Spot radio | 1,748,000 | 1,472,000 |
| Network radio | 94,200 | 218,800 |
| Outdoor | 1,469,500 | 1,185,000 |
| Total measured | 15,024,800 | 16,108,700 |
| Unmeasured | 12,333,200 | 11,169,300 |
| Estimated total | 27,358,000 | 27,278,000 |

[a] Based on *Advertising Age's* usual sources. Includes an estimated $3 million in p.o.p. in 1972 and $3,400,000 in 1973, and an estimated $250,000 in newspapers in 1972, when they were not measured.

Goldilocks as a spokesperson, and "Chinese Master" theme tied to the Kung Fu popularity.

In 1974 and 1975, the firm continued its "See the Light" theme. This was tied into new packaging ideas (see next section). In 1974 and 1975, the company offered 50-cent coupons good on the next purchase of ground beef to make "UnBurgers." The recipes for these delights were described on the coupon folder.

### PACKAGING AND THE PRODUCT LINE

In soft drinks, the Seven-Up Company markets the following products:

1  7UP Extract (for 7UP)
2  Sugar Free 7UP Extract
3  7UP Fountain Syrup
4  Sugar Free 7Up Fountain Syrup
5  Howdy Cola
6  Howdy Flavored Drinks

As far as 7UP itself is concerned, it has been sold by bottlers in several sizes, in cans, and very recently in fountain syrups. Unlike Coke and Pepsi, which started in fountains, 7UP only recently entered this business. It is aimed at restaurant and fast food business. In an allied effort, the Seven-Up Company is trying to beef up its military national account and wholesaler-jobber programs for the institution trade. The firm offers 7UP in the following containers: 7-ounce returnable bottle; 10-ounce plastic shield bottle; 10-ounce returnable bottle; 12-ounce returnable bottle; 16-ounce returnable bottle; 32-ounce returnable bottle; 10-ounce nonreturnable bottle; 16-ounce nonreturnable bottle; 32-ounce nonreturnable bottle; 12-ounce can; 12-ounce can (Sugar Free 7UP).

During the last six months of 1971, The Seven-Up Company pioneered in test-marketing an entirely new soft drink container called Plasti-Shield. This glass bottle has a cushion plastic sleeve around the sides and bottom. In selected markets, it is being produced and marketed in 10 oz. and 32 oz. packages.

The Plasti-Shield bottle for 7UP which won Food and Drug Packaging magazine's "Package of the Year" award, is easier to grip, and stays cold longer. Because of these qualities, the new Plasti-Shield bottle is enjoying great consumer acceptance.

Historically, the small returnable bottle had represented as high as 83 percent of the market. By 1964, 50 percent of sales were in 12-ounce containers. By 1970, 44 percent of all soft drinks were sold in nonreturnable containers.

The company pointed out in 1971 that:

Case sales of finished packaged goods sold, reported to the Company by its Developers, indicated that over 55 percent of bottler case sales were made in convenience packaging —either non-returnable bottles or cans. Approximately 25 per cent of the bottler case sales was represented by cans as the most important package size. Bottlers also reported to the Company during 1971 that increasing customer preference for 16-ounce and family-size packages made important contributions to increased sales in their franchise markets.

*Wall Street Journal* (Apr. 22, 1972) reported that top Seven-Up executives would market aggressively the 16-ounce returnable pints. They also reported in 1970, grocery store sales included 30 percent in 16-ounce size (22 percent returnable) whereas 7UP had 24 percent sales in pints, only 14 percent returnable. This was a doubling of 16-ounce sales since 1969. Cents-off promotions will be used to help market the returnable pints. In 1974, the best-selling sizes of 7UP were 12-ounce cans; 16-ounce returnables; 24- through 32-ounce nonreturnables; 24- through 36-ounce returnables in the large returnable category. Forty-two percent of unconverted case sales were in 16-ounce packages or larger in the United States and Canada.

The company has experimented with plastic bottles in cooperation with the container manufacturers. One has been test-marketed and proved satisfactory to customers, but the costs do not make it competitive with glass or cans.

Seven-Up has used green packaging with red and white colors supplementing the green for lemon-lime.

A rather radical change was made in logo and packaging in 1968. Before then, "7UP" appeared in a small red square toward the top of the bottle. The ingredients also were listed on the bottle (at least since 1939). In 1968, the words "7UP" were enlarged greatly, put in white and sideways on the bottle. At that time, the ingredients list was dropped. With increased interest in ingredients the company restored the ingredients on the label in 1970.

In early 1975, Seven-Up became the first major soft drink in the United States to shift to metric measure containers. The firm changed containers and labeling at the same time. The new containers are shorter, squatter bottles which hold more product (see Figure 3).

The logo replaces the 7UP name horizontally surrounded by "theater marquee-like" white dots. On the cartons, 7UP is on a black field outlined by green Day-Glo dots. The dots look like light bulbs and thus tie into the "See the Light" theme. Marketing executives Haffner, Roesch, and others pointed out that the new packaging will allow more product to be stored in smaller space. It will save energy in production and shipment, since it is light. Yet it contains more product for the same price as nonmetric packaging. The new packaging was market-researched in Chicago and Los Angeles on 13- to 19-year-olds and young homemakers who drink soft drinks. Table 6 is a comparison of the old and new packages.

Howdy Orange was the original product for what became the Seven-Up Company. It is now a line of flavors including cola. Mr. Ridgway was questioned about whether Howdy was trying to create competition for Coke or Pepsi. He said:

We are not trying to rival Coke or Pepsi with Howdy. The reason we got into it is because we had a large number of bottlers who do not have Coke or Pepsi but want a cola for their vending machines. We do very little cola fountain business.

The other major flavors of Howdy (in order of sales) are orange and grape.

As far as channels of distribution are concerned, in 1971, *Commercial and Financial Chronicle* (Jan. 7, p. 52) estimated that supermarkets sell 62 percent of soda, vending machines 20 percent. The rest is sold in a variety of outlets from service stations to department stores.

A special problem in the product line has been diet drinks. Initially, 7UP entered the diet business following Coke's strategy: develop a separate diet brand. Pepsi simply brought out Diet Pepsi. Coke promoted Tab and Seven-Up promoted Like. Royal Crown was the leader in diet drinks with its Diet Rite.

**FIGURE 3** ■ Seven-Up's new containers and carton.

Mr. Ridgway was asked why Seven-Up entered the market with Like rather than Diet 7UP. He replied:

We marketed our original product under the "Like" name because we were never really satisfied with the flavor. We tried many formulas with cyclamate and just couldn't get one to come close enough to 7UP. We withdrew most of "Like" sales after the cyclamate ban. We still have several bottlers who sell it (with saccharine) because they had developed a good market for "Like".

Now with saccharine, we went into "Diet 7UP" because most people cannot tell the difference between Diet and regular 7UP.

The cyclamate ban wrecked Like (and hurt others too). Seven-Up decided to reenter the diet market and introduced Diet 7UP in 1970, despite a possible ban on saccharine (the nonsugar ingredient of Diet 7UP) by the Food and Drug Administration. In a report to *Wall Street Journal* (Feb. 23, 1972), Seven-Up executives reported they planned to market Diet 7UP aggressively. It did well. But in 1973, the company developed a better formula without sugar and introduced Sugar Free 7UP. Introduced nationally in April 1974, it outstripped all other soft drinks, diet and regular, in sales increases the rest of the year.

William Winter, president and chief operating officer, has indicated that the number one marketing priority for several years has been fountain sales of

**TABLE 6** ■ METRIC AND CONVENTIONAL BOTTLES

|  | 32 ounce | Liter | 16 ounce | Half-liter |
|---|---|---|---|---|
| *Bottle comparisons* | | | | |
| Capacity (fluid ounces) | 32 oz | 33.82 oz | 16 oz | 16.91 oz |
| Glass weight (ounces) | 28 oz | 23 oz | 16 oz | 13 oz |
| Height (inches) | 11 11/16 in. | 10 1/4 in. | 10 3/4 in. | 8 11/32 in. |
| Diameter (inches) | 3 17/32 in. | 3 47/64 in. | 2 19/32 in. | 2 15/16 in. |
| Headspace (percent liquid volume) | 3% | 2% | 4% | 2% |
| Decoration | 2-color applied color label | 2-color applied color label | 2-color applied color label | 2-color applied color label |
| *Case comparisons* | | | | |
| Full case (weight in pounds) | 55.1 lb | 49 lb | 54 lb | 51 lb |
| Full case (height in inches) | 12 1/6 in. | 10 5/8 in. | 11 1/8 in. | 8 1/2 in. |

7UP. In 1972, the firm's fountain sales were only 2 percent of sales. By 1974, sales were growing twice as fast as overall company sales. The company used 10 million of the Uncola glasses as premiums in 1973 and added thousands of fast food outlets to its customer list.

Seven-Up has changed its marketing indeed. It is using Phyllis Diller endorsing Diet 7UP, and results of marketing change are phenomenal. Recent research indicates 7UP has a much higher percentage of drinkers of their product in the 16 to 24 age group than it did 5 years ago.

For many years, 7UP was perceived by the grocers and trade as being an unaggressive competitor. That has changed now.

Seven-Up's biggest marketing problem has been that it was perceived by the consumer to be what the company euphemistically called a "special occasions beverage." Translated, that means it was used more for liquor mixers, punches, etc., than as a soft drink. Most of its recent marketing efforts have been directed toward changing that image. Sales increases indicate that this has been successful.

The company has also supported its advertising with special promotions such as premiums. In 1969, they ran an "Un of a Kind" sweepstakes giving away Corvette Sting Rays, mink stoles, TV sets, etc. Then "Win Your Un Thing" with youth-oriented prizes, such as ski holidays and wardrobes, was used. These contests had almost 17,000 prizes.

In special activities, the company runs seven 2-day basketball clinics that draw 2500 coaches, and a "special markets" promotion aimed at blacks, giving away black books, backed by the black media, and sponsors auto racing and consumer services through home economics departments in schools. And 7UP has vigorously defended its trademark and image. For example, it won a trademark infringement suit in 1961 against Fizz Up, a soda with similar label, bottle, carton, crown, and case. Seven-Up's market research data indicated considerable consumer confusion.

In 1970, Seven-Up tried to register "The Uncola" as a trademark. The Coca-Cola Company tried to block it because it felt the term could be confused with its trade name. In April 1973 the U.S. Trademark Trial and Appeal Board rejected Coca-Cola's action after 3 years of litigation. The board cited a study by Marketing Research Communications in 1969–1971 which showed 70 to 75 percent of consumers surveyed associated "The Uncola" with 7UP. In July 1974, the Court of Customs and Patent Appeals declared "The Uncola" as registrable.

## Seven-Up and litter

The Seven-Up Company prides itself on its work on the litter problem. It is a member of the Beverage Sub Council of the National Industrial Pollution Control Council and founding member of the National Center for Solid Waste Disposal, Inc. The NCSWD is developing prototype systems for litter and solid waste disposal. When questioned about the litter problem, Mr. Ridgway said:

We are so conscious of the litter problem that we are spending thousands of dollars into every type of program we can to solve the problem. Of all litter, soft drink containers represent only 1%. Have you ever wondered how much of litter in New

York on Monday morning constitutes only the Sunday *New York Times?* No one suggests banning the *New York Times* from publishing. Soft drink containers are visible but only a small part of the litter problem. We have set up an Environmental Affairs Department headed by a Ph.D. He's involved in all programs to induce bottlers to help control litter problems.

We have no control over containers. The public has demanded non-returnable containers. We'd love to do more returnable business because it's more profitable if containers come back. But there is not enough production in the U.S. to do more returnable bottle business, anymore and where we make both returnable and non-returnable available, the public buys more non-returnable.

If the returnable bottle doesn't come back, the bottler makes less money. I don't care what kind of deposit you put on the bottle, they don't come back. For example, before New York City went to complete non-returnable bottles, the bottler would send out 24 bottle cases and get 2 back. The bottles cost 9¢ each. Deposit was 3¢. They raised it to 5¢ deposit and still only 2 per 24 came back.

The litter problem is a people problem, not a container problem. We're making great strides toward solving the litter problem. Where there are litter cans, there is very little litter around. Where there are no cans, litter is all over. In Maryland, an experiment showed that use of litter cans reduced loose litter 40%. When they moved the cans, loose litter went back to where it was before. But as we get more litter cans and more education towards litter and recycling, the litter problem can be solved.

## Recent strategic moves at Seven-Up

The company has diversified in recent years. In May 1973, it purchased Ventura Costal Corporation. The firm owned 2200 acres of lemon groves. Ventura, at the time of purchase, produced one-third of all United States frozen lemonade concentrate, mostly in private-label form. Ventura sells fresh lemons in the United States and overseas. Lemon peel and pectin are also produced.

In November 1974, the Ventura subsidiary purchased Golden Crown Corporation of Evanston, Illinois. Golden Crown produces reconstituted lemon juice and also packs lime and prune juice. It has plants in Evanston and Bridgeton, New Jersey.

Ventura planted 135,000 new lemon trees on 750 acres in 1974 and upped its acreage to 2850 by the end of 1974. Whether the Seven-Up Company will continue to diversify beyond these recent acquisitions is not known in 1975.

# Dictaphone Corporation

## Sally Coltrin

In a few cases, the brand name of a product becomes the generic name for the product. Thus many consumers say they store beer in a Frigidaire and bleach clothes with Clorox although they use different brands. For much of the company's history, such people as John D. Rockefeller, W. C. Fields, Lord Beaverbrook, and John Glenn gave their dictation on a Dictaphone. But recent years have seen severe competition for Dictaphone from IBM and others. Various firms have tried to merge with Dictaphone. Litton made a formal take-over bid and was rebuffed. Dictaphone is a fascinating company in the office equipment industry.

## The office equipment industry

In 1973, the business office equipment machines and supply industry had U.S. sales of over $5.6 billion. In addition to dictating equipment, the industry produces other recording devices and all types of office machines including copying equipment (where Xerox Corporation holds a commanding lead), electronic calculators, typewriters, data terminals, accounting machines, labeling machines, and of course the major machine—the computer—including related hardware and software items. Two other general product lines in the industry are office furniture and all types of business forms.

Business machines quadrupled their sales between 1959 and 1969, and it is projected that they will quadruple again in the 1970s. While some facets of the industry, particularly those products more individually oriented, seem to follow the cyclical patterns of economic trends, others seem able to withstand at least modest downtrends and continue their high-volume sales and profits.

About 66 companies control 85 to 90 percent of the United States business machine production, but about 200 to 300 smaller companies supply related equipment. Foreign competition in the U.S. markets is strong in a few product areas although not considered a threat in most. It is estimated that a $3.4 billion foreign market exists for the office equipment industry. American firms control only 18 percent of this overseas business. The size of the overseas market varies according to analyst commenting.

### DICTATING EQUIPMENT

In 1973, $165 million worth of dictating equipment was sold in the United States. Dictating equipment can be divided into two basic categories: discrete media units and endless loop systems. Discrete media units require the use of belts, cassettes, cartridges, or the like, which must be physically transported from the dictating machine to the transcribing machine. The discrete media systems are of three types: battery-powered portables, desk-top units, and central recording systems which utilize either private wire systems as their connection between dictator and recorder or telephone or PBX systems for connection. An example of a discrete media system is pictured in Figure 1—Dictaphone's 800 Series unit and their portable model.

The other type of dictating equipment is the endless loop system, in which, as the name implies, the dictator and transcriber both work from the continuous loop of magnetic tape without ever physically handling the media.

Endless loop systems can be either individual units (i.e., a tape used by only one executive and his or her secretary) or central units with hookups from many dictating areas including the aforementioned telephone or PBX connectors. Figure 2 is an example of the endless loop dictating system: Dictaphone's Thought Tank model.

The market leaders in dictating equipment in the United States are the following:

| Company | Percent of U.S. business (est. 1973) |
|---|---|
| Dictaphone Corp. | 35% |
| IBM | 35 |
| Phillips (Norelco)<br>Oxford Saviss Industries<br>Lanier (formerly McGraw-Edison)<br>Sony<br>Others | 30 |

## History of the Dictaphone Corporation

In 1888 Charles Sumner Tainter manufactured the first machines for recording and reproducing sound for business purposes. Power for the machines was generated by the old-fashioned sewing machine treadle approach, and the dictator, speaking into a tube, conveyed his voice to a wax cylinder. The cylinders held 10 minutes of dictation each and could be shaved and reused 65 times. The wax cylinder system worked so well that machines were produced using this recording medium from its inception until 1946, when plastic belts were introduced.

Tainter's company evolved into the Columbia Graphophone Company. The company grew, became involved in mergers, and as a result of overexpansion came into financial difficulties in the early 1900s. Dictaphone Corporation was founded in 1923 when Charles "King" Woodbridge persuaded two investment bankers to buy Columbia Graphophone's fledgling dictating machine division for about $1 million. Woodbridge became president and chief executive officer, a position he held for 37 years, from the company's inception until his death in 1960. During the period 1939 to 1956, sales rose from $5 million to over $35 million and Dictaphone became the dominant industry leader, controlling over 50 percent of the market. In 1950 Dictaphone had only two serious competitors, Gray Audograph and McGraw-Edison. Woodbridge was pleased

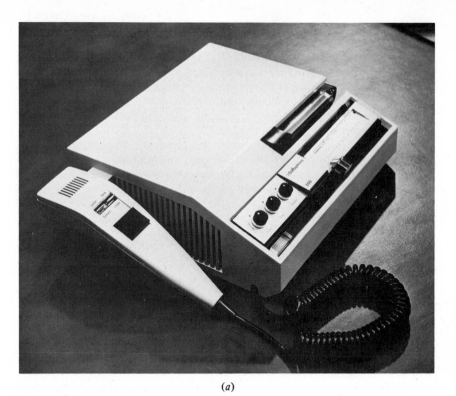

(*a*)

**FIGURE 1** ■ Discrete media units. (*a*) Desk-top model; (*b*) portable model.

by Dictaphone's market lead and its operating profit margins of 15 to 17 percent. Since dictating machines are a highly postponable purchase, the recession of 1958 hit Dictaphone hard at a time when it was spending heavily on new product development to meet the onslaught of competitors who suddenly seemed to appear out of nowhere. Profit margins and earnings per share were halved, a blow from which the company is only recently beginning to recover.

### THE BEGINNING OF THE TURNAROUND

When Woodbridge died in 1960, Lloyd Powell was named chief executive officer with the charge to restore growth and profitability to the troubled company. He began by replacing aging management with much younger men (average age 40 compared with the previous average of 59). He also computerized payroll, inventory, and market research, cautiously expanded Dictaphone's big sales force, and modernized production facilities. Despite these efforts, however, sales of the firm's dictating equipment remained at a standstill. Although the economy was good, the company experienced a decline in earnings per share, to a low of 95 cents by 1963. This occurred just one year after IBM's entry into the field with the third generation of dictating equipment, the erasable magnetic belt. This innovation rather quickly made Dicta-

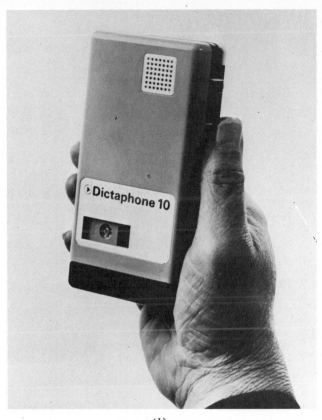

(b)

phone's older one-use, plastic-belt units somewhat outdated. It took IBM 5 years to actually replace Dictaphone as the industry leader, but by 1967, they controlled 35 percent of the $130 million market, while Dictaphone controlled 30 percent.

Perhaps Powell's most important contributions were to persuade Walter Finke of Honeywell Corp. to join the board of Dictaphone in 1963 and, 4 years later, to step aside and allow the hard-driving Finke to become president and chief executive officer. Even before becoming president in 1967, Finke made his presence on the board felt. The Litton bid for take-over apparently shook up Dictaphone. In March 1965, the shareholders approved a new corporate charter that permitted diversification. Finke's philosophy for meeting the barrage of competition, that by 1966 numbered over 30 contenders, thus became to expand through diversification. Finke claimed he came from a background of a systems rather than a product concept. "We are not building a machine, but something that is part of a process," he said. Thus the diversification of Dictaphone was carried out within the loose confines of the "Information Process."

Dictaphone's first effort at diversification was to set up DOT (Dictaphone Office Temporaries) Services in 16 cities to compete with Manpower, Inc., and Kelly Girl Services. Finke felt there was true synergy in this move since

**FIGURE 2** ■ Endless loop system.

Dictaphone's existing widespread sales organization was already there to promote this service. The venture also seemed appealing since at the time the temporary help field was growing at an annual rate of 20 percent, making the market potential of this move appear promising.

The next diversification venture was into the office furniture field through the acquisition of B. L. Marble Furniture Company and the Imperial Desk Company. The amalgamation of these two acquisitions into the company's Marble/Imperial Division offered a line of executive furniture including Centrol, a push-button desk with built-in Dictaphone "appliances" that made it a "management communications center." Thus, Dictaphone now had the capacity to offer furniture and communications equipment in a single package.

In the office supplies field, Dictaphone's first acquisition was American Loose Leaf Corporation. Later in 1968 they acquired Grayarc, a large mail-order company handling a broad range of printed forms and envelopes as well as industrial tape and other disposable items.

As an adjunct to DOT Services, Dictaphone developed the Bryant & Stratton business vocational institutes originally located in Buffalo, Milwaukee, and San Jose. Later the San Jose location was sold, but a new branch was opened in Rochester, New York. The addition of these three areas—furniture and office supplies, temporary help, and vocational education schools—seemed to provide Dictaphone with a broader base of operations, all seemingly at least tangentially related to its original product-service line.

Closer to Dictaphone's new "information appliances" image were two other 1967 acquisitions: Scully Recording Instruments of Bridgeport, Connecticut, maker of tape recorders and reproducers of professional broadcasting quality, and Kinelogic Corporation of Pasadena, which made aerospace industry recording systems. The Recording Automation group was later rounded out with the addition of Metrotech to provide logging recorders used in the broadcasting industry and by police, fire, and other protective agencies.

As yet another means of expansion, Dictaphone began its operations outside the United States in the mid-fifties. The company developed foreign subsidiaries located in Canada, Great Britain, and Switzerland to handle virtually the equivalent of all domestic products and services on an international basis.

While the 1960s were a period of substantial diversification, they were also a period of improving the basic product line of dictating equipment. In its early years Dictaphone had only two or three relatively expensive models which catered primarily to the top-echelon executives. However, during this period the line was increased somewhat in an attempt at giving depth to the product line which would allow broader market penetration in terms of both price ranges and customer needs.

Under Walter Finke's leadership, sales that had long stayed at around $30 million a year soared to nearly $100 million in 1969, and income per common share more than doubled between 1962 and 1969. However, despite the spectacular events at Dictaphone during the 1960s, the Finke era was not without its problems and mistakes. Not all of the large number of acquisitions proved successful. The diversification put added strain on the marketing organization and in fact diluted its efforts in its traditional product lines. Limited expenditures on research and development when competitors were bringing out a wide variety of new products, caused continued loss of market share as the field of competitors grew and giants like IBM took a commanding lead. These and other management and organizational problems brought about the depressed earnings of 1970–1971. This in turn set the stage for a second turnaround recovery period which began in 1972.

### THE TABAT ERA

Although the sharp downturn in the economy in 1970–1971 was certainly not conducive to postponable purchase items, not all of Dictaphone's showing in those years could be attributed to economic trends. In the preceding 5 years Dictaphone had grown like Topsy. Its production plants were geographically widespread, and the inefficiencies of the operations which it acquired were never weeded out. So much of its operating capital went into acquisitions that little was left for R&D and marketing efforts.

Beset with problems and a believer in retirement at age 65, Finke stepped aside 1 year early, and in August 1971 Dictaphone acquired a new president, E. Lawrence Tabat. Before joining Dictaphone, Tabat, age 57, was vice president and general manager of Rockwell Manufacturing Company's Power Tool Division. While this seemed an incongruous background, Tabat was by no means a newcomer to the office equipment business. His first job after graduating from the University of Wisconsin in 1934 was as a duplicating machine salesman with A. B. Dick Company in Chicago, where he became general sales manager during his 19-year career there. He was later an executive at Old Town Corporation, a New York City carbon and ribbon manufacturer, and also for a time marketing vice president of Porter Cable Machine Company of Syracuse, New York.

Tabat was on the job only a month and a half before instigating his "sifting and winnowing," semiretrenchment program which was to be at least a part of the basis of his strategy for bringing the company out of the doldrums it had been in for 2 years. First he talked the board into selling off the entire furniture division, since furniture volume had dropped from $17 million to $13.6 million in 1971, resulting in an operating loss of $3 million. As Tabat said, "That's a lot of potatoes for a company our size."

The thrust of Tabat's second major change was to increase significantly R&D and marketing programs and expenditures. He allocated $1 million to R&D in 1972, doubled that figure in 1973, and budgeted an additional 50 percent increase in 1974. His philosophy was to concentrate efforts in the development of new items in Dictaphone's major product line, dictating equipment. A major breakthrough came in February 1972, when Dictaphone introduced an entirely new concept in dictating equipment, the first real change since belt-style models replaced the wax cylinder.

The product was a large-capacity unit with an endless loop tape that never had to be unloaded and could take as many as six separate inputs. The unit, which Tabat named the Thought Tank (see Figure 2), combines dictating and transcribing functions in a unit that Dictaphone claims eliminates many of the problems (such as "mike fright" and complexity of operation) that make executives shy away from using standard dictating machines.

The machine takes the place of two recording belt machines, one each for dictating and transcribing, and eliminates the need to physically transfer the belts from one machine to another. Instead the central "tank" containing the endless loop tape is concealed anywhere in the building, leaving on desks only a telephonelike instrument for the executive and a small control unit for the secretary. The executive simply picks up the familiar phone and starts talking. A light on the control unit indicates when transcribing is needed, and this can be started as quickly as 12 seconds after dictation has started, or delayed for substantial periods, since the endless loop of magnetic tape holds 60 minutes of recording.

The initial installed price of the Thought Tank was less than the top-of-the-line pair of standard belt machines, and that, in conjunction with the fact that nobody else had any comparable product, made this machine an almost instant success. It began selling so fast that by the end of the year it had boosted Dictaphone's market share, putting it once again about even with IBM.

Other new products resulting from Tabat's beefed up R&D program also showed almost instant success. One is a Swiss-made, hand-sized dictation unit retailing for under $100. Another is a recording unit for courts, already legal in four states, which may eventually replace the court stenographers. A complete list and description of the current dictating equipment product line of Dictaphone and its many competitors are presented in Tables 1 through 6.

Tabat also began putting his years of marketing experience to work. He increased the advertising budget substantially in 1972 and planned an additional increase over that figure for 1973, to eliminate the "too conservative approach" the company had toward marketing. In addition the company

| Firm | Model | Standard cassette | Mini cassette | Magnetic belt | Visible belt | Other | Price, dollars | Weight, ounces | Maximum minutes of recording time |
|---|---|---|---|---|---|---|---|---|---|
| Crown-Japan | CPM-20 | Yes | | | | | 159 | 24 | 60 |
| DeJur-Grundig | Execumate | | Yes | | | | 185 | 19 | 30 |
| DeJur-Grundig | Mark VIII | | | | | Yes | 105 | 13 | 60 |
| Dictaphone | 848 | Yes | | | | | 165 | 27 | 90 |
| Dictaphone | 110 | | Yes | | | | 125 | 10 | 30 |
| Dictaphone | 850 | | | | Yes | | 435 | 64 | 15 |
| Dictran | Doro 701 | Yes | | | | | 125 | 24 | 120 |
| IBM | Portable Input | | | Yes | | | 440 | 30 | 20 |
| Lanier | VIP/C | Yes | | | | | 195 | 24 | 90 |
| Memocord | K70 | | | | | Yes | 179 | 14 | 90 |
| Norelco | 88 | | Yes | | | | 295 | 18 | 30 |
| Norelco | 85 | | Yes | | | | 120 | 12 | 30 |
| Norelco | 95 | | Yes | | | | 175 | 11 | 30 |
| Sony | BM 11 | Yes | | | | | 215[a] | 32 | 90 |

[a] Suggested retail price.
Source: Administrative Management, March 1974, pp. 33–44. "Administrative Management makes no claim as to the complete accuracy of information in the charts . . . except to note that it was, in every case, supplied by the manufacturer or distributor involved. Information . . . was current and timely as of January 28, 1974. Not all models from all companies are included. Chart data and format Copyright © 1974 by Geyer-McAllister Publications, Inc."

switched to a new agency, Scali, McCabe and Sloves, replacing Young and Rubicam, which had handled Dictaphone's advertising for 25 years. The new advertising approach broadened the number and types of media used. Bold new ads such as those depicted in Figure 3 were placed in three basic types of media.

To reach business and professional executives in top and middle management, four ads were placed in the *Wall Street Journal, U.S. News and World Report, Newsweek, Business Week,* and *Time.* Office managers and systems and procedure specialists were the target of ads in *Administrative Management, Modern Office Procedures, Office,* and *Office Products News.* Although the readers of such office publications may not make final decisions about purchases, they are often involved in the decision-making process. A third group

TABLE 2 ■ DISCRETE MEDIA DESK-TOP UNITS

| Firm | Model | Transcribe only | Dictate only | Combination | Standard cassette | Mini cassette | Magnetic belt | Visible belt | Other | Price, dollars | Maximum minutes of recording time |
|---|---|---|---|---|---|---|---|---|---|---|---|
| Crown-Japan | CDM-11 | | | Yes | | | | | | 399 | 90 |
| Crown-Japan | CTM-25 | Yes | | | | | | | | 269 | 90 |
| Crown-Japan | CDM-7 | | | Yes | | | | | | 299 | 90 |
| DeJur-Grundig | Executive | Yes | | | | Yes | | | | 375 | 30 |
| DeJur-Grundig | Executive | | Yes | | | Yes | | | | 390 | 30 |
| DeJur-Grundig | Execumatic | Yes | | | | Yes | | | | 295 | 45 |
| DeJur-Grundig | Execumatic | | Yes | | | Yes | | | | 295 | 45 |
| DeJur-Grundig | Embassy Mark V | Yes | | | | | | | Yes | 365 | 45 |
| DeJur-Grundig | Embassy Mark V | Yes | | | | | | | Yes | 365 | 45 |
| Dictaphone | 241–1 | Yes | | | Yes | | | | | 450 | 90 |
| Dictaphone | 241–2 | | Yes | | Yes | | | | | 450 | 90 |
| Dictaphone | 241–3 | | | Yes | Yes | | | | | 500 | 90 |
| Dictaphone | 111 | Yes | | | | Yes | | | | 325 | 30 |
| Dictaphone | 811 | | Yes | | | | Yes | | | 495 | 12 |
| Dictaphone | 812 | Yes | | | | | Yes | | | 495 | 12 |
| Dictaphone | 851 | | Yes | | | | | Yes | | 525 | 15 |
| Dictaphone | 852 | Yes | | | | | | Yes | | 525 | 15 |
| Dictran | Doro 702 | | | Yes | Yes | | | | | 295 | 120 |
| Fi-Cord | 300A | | | Yes | | | | | Yes | 260 | 48 |
| Fi-Cord | 303A | | | Yes | | | | | Yes | 260 | 24 |
| IBM | Executary Microphone Input | | Yes | | | | Yes | | | 520 | 20 |
| IBM | Executary Transcriber | Yes | | | | | Yes | | | 520 | 20 |
| IBM | Transcriber | Yes | | | | | Yes | | | 430 | 20 |
| IBM | Microphone Input | | Yes | | | | Yes | | | 395 | 20 |
| Lanier | Edisette VIP/E | | Yes | | Yes | | | | | 495 | 90 |
| Lanier | Edisette VIP/S | Yes | | | Yes | | | | | 495 | 90 |
| Lanier | VIP/MCA | Yes | | | | Yes | | | | 544 | |
| Lanier | Edisette 1977 | Yes | | | Yes | | | | | 369 | 90 |
| Lanier | Edisette 1977 | | Yes | | Yes | | | | | 369 | 90 |
| Lanier | Edisette 1977 | | | Yes | Yes | | | | | 409 | 90 |
| Lanier | 1977-MCA | Yes | | | | Yes | | | | 418 | 90 |
| Lanier | Gray MT-1A | Yes | | | | | Yes | | | 395 | 28 |
| Lanier | Gray MD-1A | | Yes | Yes[a] | | | Yes | | | 395 | 28 |
| Lanier | Stenocord 270 | | Yes | Yes[a] | | | Yes | | | 399 | 12 |
| Lanier | Stenocrod 260 | Yes | | | | | Yes | | | 399 | 12 |
| Memocord | AW90DL | | | Yes | | | | | Yes | 349 | 90 |
| Memocord | W100AR | Yes | | | | | | | Yes | 299 | 90 |
| Miles | CC | | | Yes | | | | | Yes | 540 | 180 |

TABLE 2 ■ DISCRETE MEDIA DESK-TOP UNITS (*Continued*)

| Firm | Model | Transcribe only | Dictate only | Combination | Standard cassette | Mini cassette | Magnetic belt | Visible belt | Other | Price, dollars | Maximum minutes of recording time |
|------|-------|:---------------:|:------------:|:-----------:|:-----------------:|:-------------:|:-------------:|:------------:|:-----:|:--------------:|:---------------------------------:|
| | | | | | Type | Medium | | | | | |
| Miles | CCB | | | Yes | | | | | Yes | 560 | 180 |
| Norelco | 96 | | | Yes | Yes | | | | | 395 | 30 |
| Norelco | 98 | | | Yes | Yes | | | | | 495 | 30 |
| Norelco | 86 | Yes | | | Yes | | | | | 320 | 30 |
| Norelco | Uni-Trans CC | Yes | | | Yes | | | | | 395 | 120 |
| Sony | BM 35 | | | Yes | Yes | | | | | 560[b] | 90 |
| Sony | BM 35T | Yes | | | Yes | | | | | 510[b] | 90 |
| Sony | BM 35D | | Yes | | Yes | | | | | 515[b] | 90 |
| Sony | BM 34 | Yes | | | Yes | | | | | 405[b] | 90 |
| Sony | BM 25 | Yes | | | Yes | | | | | 305[b] | 90 |

[a] Dictator can be used as a spare transcriber by adding headset and foot control.
[b] Suggested retail price.

*Source: Administrative Management,* March 1974, pp. 33–44. "*Administrative Management* makes no claims as to the complete accuracy of information in the charts . . . except to note that it was, in every case, supplied by the manufacturer or distributor involved. Information . . . was current and timely as of January 28, 1974. Not all models from all companies are included. Chart data and format Copyright © 1974 by Geyer-McAllister Publications, Inc."

of ads appeared in *ABA Journal, American Medical News, Case & Comment, Government Executive,* and *Medical Record News* to reach doctors, lawyers, and managers responsible for purchases for typing pools. The company's advertising department and its agency also created a 30-minute color film and sales aids for sales meetings. Over $100,000 was spent on two direct-mail campaigns to customers and to a prospect list submitted by salespersons. Finally a new compensation system that will mean more money for the salespersons has already begun to improve the morale of the company's 1200-person sales and service force which had been sagging for years.

Tabat's rejuvenation program continued with a general corporate reorganization, including the closing of several far-flung operating plants and consolidating operations into fewer locations to increase efficiency and reduce the operating costs of duplication of equipment and personnel. In July 1974, Bryant & Stratton was sold back to its original owners. In December 1974, Dictaphone entered the industrial safety surveillance market with a unique new line of equipment for detecting combustible gases.

## Organization and operating group product lines

The corporate headquarters of Dictaphone is located on several parklike acres in Rye, New York. However, only a limited number of the corporate top management operate from this location. (See corporate organization chart in Figure 4.) The expansion and diversification of the 1960s plus Finke's pen-

TABLE 3 ■ DISCRETE MEDIA CENTRAL RECORDING VIA PRIVATE WIRE SYSTEMS

| Firm | Model | Medium | Accessibility | | | Prices, dollars | | | | Selector channels |
| | | | Nonselector | Manual | Automatic | Recorder unit | Hand sets: Installed—I Not installed—N | | | |
| | | | | | | | Mike | Desk phone | Wall mount | |
|---|---|---|---|---|---|---|---|---|---|---|
| Dictaphone | 705 | Visible or magnetic belt | | Yes | | 1115 | | 240-I | 252-I | 6 |
| IBM | Microphone Input | Magnetic belt | Yes | | | 440 | 54 | 128-N[a] | 128-N[a] | |
| Lanier | Tel-Edisette | Standard cassette | Yes | | | 1595 | 195-I | 135-I | 160-I | |
| Lanier | Tel-Edisette | Standard cassette | | Yes | | 1595 | 180-I | 190-I | 215-I | 3 |
| Lanier | Tel-Edisette | Standard cassette | | Yes | | 1595 | 225-I | 250-I | b | 6 |
| Lanier | Tel-Edisette | Standard cassette | | | Yes | 1595 | b | 210-I | 235-I | 3 |
| Lanier | Tel-Edisette | Standard cassette | | | Yes | 1595 | 296-I | 236-I | 261-I | 6 |
| Lanier | Tel-Edisette | Standard cassette | | | Yes | 1595 | 270-I | 210-I | 235-I | 10 |
| Memocord | TDS-100 | Cassette | Yes | | | 1195 | | 100-I | 100-I | |
| Norelco | RMS-10 | Mini cassette | Yes | | | 450 | 125 | | | |
| Norelco | 246 | Mini cassette | | | Yes | 1495 | | 175 | | |

[a] Microphone.
[b] Not available.
*Source: Administrative Management,* March 1974, pp. 33–44. *"Administrative Management* makes no claims as to the complete accuracy of information in the charts . . . except to note that it was, in every case, supplied by the manufacturer or distributor involved. Information . . . was current and timely as of January 28, 1974. Not all models from all companies are included. Chart data and format Copyright © 1974 by Geyer-McAllister Publications, Inc."

chant for decentralization resulted in the formation of six operating groups around which the corporation was structured. Tabat continued this philosophy in principle, but because of the sale of the furniture division, the integration of international operations into their respective product-service groups, and other domestic realignments, the number of operating groups has been reduced to three. Operating groups are set up with a division head and general managers of the various subsections of each division where appropriate.

INFORMATION PRODUCTS AND SYSTEMS GROUP

The largest of the three main operating divisions is the Dictaphone Information Products and Systems Group (DPS). This group is responsible for business machines operations throughout the world. In addition to U.S. operations, it includes the operation of Dictaphone International A.G., a Swiss corporation which operates a factory and engineering center in Killwangen, Switzerland, and is responsible for the sale of all Dictaphone dictating equipment sold throughout the world (except the United States, Puerto Rico and the Caribbean area, Canada, and the United Kingdom); Dictaphone Company

## TABLE 4 ■ DISCRETE MEDIA CENTRAL RECORDING VIA PHONE OR PBX SYSTEMS

| Firm | Model | Medium | Price | Interface supplied | | Features | |
|------|-------|--------|-------|--------------------|---|----------|---|
| | | | | Trunk link price, dollars | Recorder-coupler price, dollars | Voice operated relay price, dollars | Touch tone discrimination price, dollars |
| Dictaphone | 707 | Visible or magnetic belt | 1525 | 550*a* | 210*a* | *b* | 1075*a* |
| IBM | Dial Input | Magnetic belt | 1200 | *c* | | *b* | |
| IBM | Tone Input | Magnetic belt | 2400 | | *c* | *b* | *b* |
| Lanier | Tel-Edisette | Standard cassette | 1595 | 200 | 175 | 100 | 800 |
| Memocord | TDS-100 | Cassette | 1195 | *a,d* | *a,d* | *b* | *b* |
| Memocord | DMC | Cassette | 180 | *a,d* | *a,d* | *b* | |
| Norelco | 2000A | Magnetic cassette | 999 | *c* | *c* | *b* | *c* |
| Norelco | 246 | Magnetic cassette | 1495 | *c* | *c* | *b* | *c* |
| Sony | RD-50 | Standard cassette | *a* | *b* | *b* | *b* | *a,d* |

*a* Optional.
*b* Standard.
*c* Rented from telephone company.
*d* Not available.
*Source: Administrative Management,* March 1974, pp. 33–44. *"Administrative Management* makes no claims as to the complete accuracy of information in the charts . . . except to note that it was, in every case, supplied by the manufacturer or distributor involved. Information . . . was current and timely as of January 28, 1974. Not all models from all companies are included. Chart data and format Copyright © 1974 by Geyer-McAllister Publications, Inc."

## TABLE 5 ■ ENDLESS LOOP INDIVIDUAL SYSTEM

| Firm | Model | Price, dollars | Transcribing stations | | Dictating stations | Telephone interface price | Recording medium in minutes |
|------|-------|----------------|-----------------------|---|--------------------|---------------------------|-----------------------------|
| | | | Number possible | Price of each additional | | | |
| Dictaphone*a* | Thought Tank 191 | 645 | Unlimited | 150 | 6 | 150 | 60 |
| Lanier*a* | Nyematic VIP | 995*b* | No limit*c* | 135*b* | Unlimited input stations 175*b* | | 100*b* |

*a* Also compatible with firm's discrete media central systems.
*b* Includes normal installation, labor, and cable charges.
*c* Usually one nonselect per recorder.
*Source: Administrative Management,* March 1974, pp. 33–44. *"Administrative Management* makes no claims as to the complete accuracy of information in the charts . . . except to note that it was, in every case, supplied by the manufacturer or distributor involved. Information . . . was current and timely as of January 28, 1974. Not all models from all companies are included. Chart data and format Copyright © 1974 by Geyer-McAllister Publications, Inc."

Limited, a British corporation which is responsible for the sale and service of all Dictaphone dictating equipment sold in the United Kingdom; Dictaphone Corporation, Limited, a Canadian corporation which is responsible for the sale and service of all Dictaphone dictating equipment sold in Canada; and a sales and service branch in Puerto Rico.

TABLE 6 ■ ENDLESS LOOP CENTRAL SYSTEM

| Firm | Model | Price, dollars | Record-ing me-dium in minutes | Interface | | Features | |
|------|-------|----------------|-------------------------------|-----------|--|----------|--|
| | | | | Trunk link, dollars | Recorder-coupler, dollars | Voice-operated relay price, dollars | Touch tone price, dollars |
| Dictaphone[a] | 180 | 1220 | 180 | [b] | [c] | [b] | [b] |
| Dictaphone[a] | 181 | 1681 | 180 | [b] | 210[d] | [b] | [b] |
| Dictaphone[a] | 185 | 2036 | 180 | [c] | 210[d] | [c] | 1030[d] |
| Dictaphone[a] | 187 | 1681 | 180 | [b] | 210[d] | [b] | [b] |
| Lanier[a] | Nyematic 100–1 | 1220[e] | 100 | 200 | 175 | 100 | 800 |
| Lanier[a] | Nyematic 108 | 1520[e] | 400 | 200 | 175 | 100 | 800 |
| Lanier[a] | Nyematic 101 | 1605[e] | 100 | 200 | 175 | 100 | 800 |
| Lanier[a] | Nyematic 102 | 1705[e] | 400 | 200 | 175 | 100 | 800 |

[a] Also compatible with firm's discrete media central systems.
[b] Not available.
[c] Standard.
[d] Optional.
[e] Includes normal installation, labor, and cable charges.
*Source: Administrative Management,* March 1974, pp. 33–44. "*Administrative Management* makes no claims as to the complete accuracy of information in the charts . . . except to note that it was, in every case, supplied by the manufacturer or distributor involved. Information . . . was current and timely as of January 28, 1974. Not all models from all companies are included. Chart data and format Copyright © 1974 by Geyer-McAllister Publications, Inc."

The DPS group manufactures, sells, and services a complete line of dictating products and systems. The current major item of the group is the previously described Thought Tank. Recent modifications to the original model include the option of a larger tank with a 3-hour recording capacity, an inexpensive telephone line hookup which allows dictation to be recorded in the "tank" from outside the office, 24 hours per day, and a new Word Monitor system designed to make the Thought Tank a compatible input device for the new "word processing" systems which use output systems such as power typewriters in centralized locations.

The DPS group also markets the Dictaphone 10 dictating machine, a 10-ounce pocket-sized portable cassette dictating machine manufactured by Dictaphone International A.G. in Switzerland. Early in 1973, Dictaphone introduced a new dual-media transcribing unit which permits a secretary to transcribe dictation from either the Thought Tank unit or the Dictaphone 10 machine, thus offering greater dictation flexibility.

In June 1973 the division introduced the Dictasette dictating machine, a desk-top model which uses standard 30-, 60-, or 90-minute cassettes. The unit incorporates several new features, such as an indexing device, that allow secretaries to find their place more quickly.

The DPS group is continuing to produce two types of desk-top dictating and transcribing machines, one using a plastic Dictabelt record, designed and

# Bad News For IBM.

## Dictaphone introduces the Thought Tank.™ A new kind of continuous-flow thought processor that outdates conventional dictating equipment.

The Thought Tank is also bad news for Norelco, Edison, Gray, Stenorette, Stenocord or anyone else who makes conventional dictating equipment.

But it's beautiful news for you, because the Thought Tank can literally cut 38% off the time it used to take to get your correspondence out.

There are no belts or tapes to transfer. There are no separate dictating and transcribing procedures. There is nothing to load or unload.

A small unit that resembles a telephone sits on your desk; a small receiver with a signal light sits on your girl's desk. Somewhere in-between sits the Thought Tank.

The moment you start dictating, the Thought Tank lights the signal on your secretary's desk, and 12 seconds later, she starts typing— while you're still dictating.

So before you've finished dictating a second letter, the first letter is typed and on your desk ready to be signed.

It is the fastest, simplest method of dictating ever devised.

And it is a great deal more than that. You use the Thought Tank as a 24-hour, continuous-flow thought processor.

Any thought—a memo, a letter, a note to yourself, next week's lunch, theater tickets, a BLT with no mayo— any thought you think of, can be put into the Thought Tank.

And you can put your ideas into the Thought Tank from any outside telephone with a simple, inexpensive attachment.

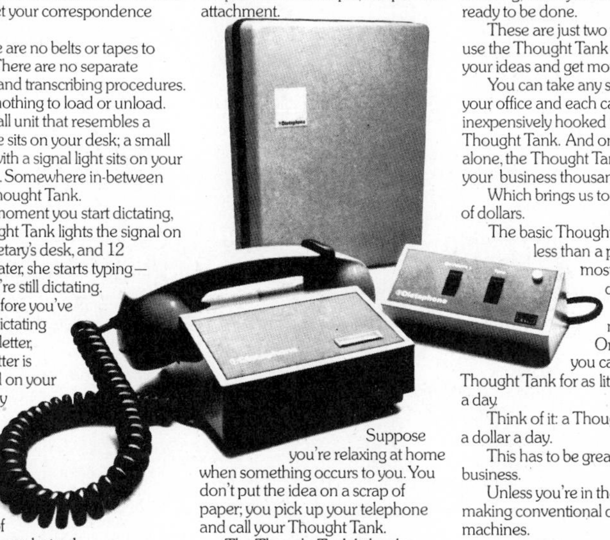

Suppose you're relaxing at home when something occurs to you. You don't put the idea on a scrap of paper; you pick up your telephone and call your Thought Tank.

The Thought Tank lights the signal on your girl's unattended desk, and tells her there's something in the tank. She starts to work on it as soon as she gets to work.

Or say you're at an airport at 7:00 a.m. You have an important memo you want to get out, but your office isn't open.

With the Thought Tank, you simply call it in from a phone booth, and when your office opens in the morning, it's on your secretary's desk, ready to be done.

These are just two ways you can use the Thought Tank to speed up your ideas and get more work done.

You can take any six dictators in your office and each can be inexpensively hooked up to one Thought Tank. And on that basis alone, the Thought Tank could save your business thousands of dollars.

Which brings us to the question of dollars.

The basic Thought Tank costs less than a pair of most conventional dictating and transcribing machines.

Or, if you choose, you can lease a Thought Tank for as little as a dollar a day.

Think of it: a Thought Tank for a dollar a day.

This has to be great news for business.

Unless you're in the business of making conventional dictating machines.

*Call this toll-free number for a free, in-office demonstration of the Thought Tank. 800-243-6000. From Connecticut, call: 1-800-882-6500 or see the Yellow Pages.*

**Dictaphone**

"Dictaphone is one of the family of registered trademarks of Dictaphone Corporation, Rye, New York, U.S.A."

(*a*)

**FIGURE 3** ■ (*a*) and (*b*) Dictaphone's new advertising image.

# Bad News For IBM.

## (CHAPTER 2.)

### Thousands of companies are switching to Dictaphone's Thought Tank™ — the answer to outdated conventional dictating equipment.

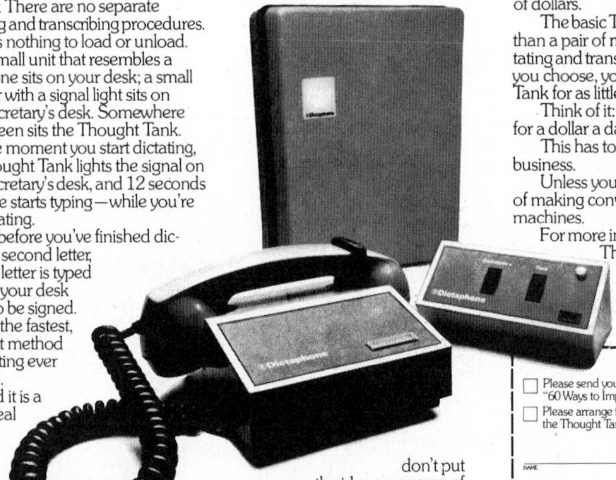

(b)

**FIGURE 3** ■ *(Continued)*

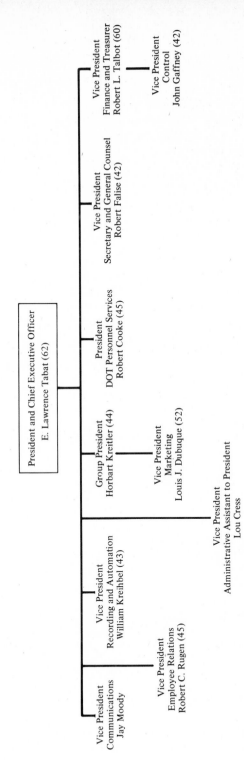

**FIGURE 4** ■ Organization chart. Ages as of 1974.

President and Chief Executive Officer
E. Lawrence Tabat (62)

Vice President
Communications
Jay Moody

Vice President
Recording and Automation
William Kreihbel (43)

Vice President
Employee Relations
Robert C. Rugen (45)

Vice President
Administrative Assistant to President
Lou Cress

Group President
Horbart Kreitler (44)

Vice President
Marketing
Louis J. Dubuque (52)

President
DOT Personnel Services
Robert Cooke (45)

Vice President
Secretary and General Counsel
Robert Falise (42)

Vice President
Finance and Treasurer
Robert L. Talbot (60)

Vice President
Control
John Gaffney (42)

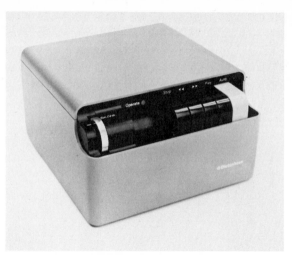

**FIGURE 5** ■ Dictaphone model 610 telephone answering system.

developed by the company, which produces a permanent visible record of dictation, and the other using a reusable magnetic Dictabelt. Standard models of each type include a dictating machine (which can be adapted for use as a telephone recorder), transcriber, and combination dictating-transcribing machine. The group also continues to manufacture Telecord central recording systems which permit a number of persons to record dictation on remote dictating machines for transcription by a secretarial pool. Dictaphone International A.G. continues to manufacture the lower-priced Series 400 dictating and transcribing machines which use a magnetic Sound Sheet as the recording medium.

The division also sells a line of telephone answering machines in the United States under the trademark Ansafone and in Canada under the trademark Dictaphone. (See Figure 5.) Before December 1973 this equipment was marketed only through dealers. In December 1973, a substantial number of U.S. direct-sales offices were also given the opportunity to market these telephone answering machines. In January 1974, the company purchased all the rights to the Trans-A-Call telephone call diverter product line from Electronic Concepts Laboratories Corporation. This acquisition provided the company with additional technology, patents, and prototype products for use in the telecommunications market.

Manufacturing centers for this group are centered at the company's main plant in Bridgeport, Connecticut. In addition, a plant in Concord, New Hampshire, is used for the manufacture of recording belts and assembly of dictating equipment accessories and subassemblies. Production of products for the international markets has been consolidated into the Killwangen, Switzerland, plant after the closing of some marginal production facilities in Great Britain.

The DPS group also has distribution warehouses in El Segundo, California, and Milford, Connecticut, a training center for sales and service personnel at Columbia, South Carolina, and a research and development center in Norwalk, Connecticut, where substantially all the group's dictating products have been conceived, designed, and developed by the firm's own R&D staff.

In 1973, the DPS group accounted for $70,579,000 sales revenue, or approximately 70 percent of the $100,440,000 total revenue for the company. The division's before-tax income for the same period was $9,231,000 or 91 percent of before-tax income.

## RECORDING INSTRUMENTATION GROUP

While clearly not in the dollar volume class of the DPS group, the recording instrumentation group is an important part of the corporate structure. The group, also known as Scully/Metrotech Division, specializes in the development and manufacturing of analog recording equipment for professional applications. Analog recording stores voice or music on straight-line conventional tape of various widths (¼ to 2 inches) for playback when needed. Scully's emphasis is manufacturing recording equipment for broadcast and professional recording studios. Metrotech manufactures equipment for recording communication signals for broadcasting, public safety, and special application markets. The Dictaphone 4000 logger, for instance (see Figure 6), can automatically and simultaneously record radio or telephone messages on up to 40 channels, 24 hours a day on a single tape, and is intended to serve the needs of organizations such as police or fire-fighting units. This product is manufactured by Metrotech but sold and serviced through the DPS group.

In August 1973, the patents and certain prototype products of Hadden Associates, a California-based research organization, were acquired. Now operating as a unit of Scully, this group manufactures Metrotech instruments for the detection of combustible gases.

In anticipation of the future growth of this division, and to reduce past operating inefficiencies, Scully/Metrotech was consolidated in 1972 in a new plant located in Mountain View, California. This facility is used by the Recording Instrumentation Group for both manufacturing and R&D. Expenditures for R&D for this group were $170,000 in 1972 and $743,000 in 1973, and substantial additional increases have been budgeted for 1974.

## OFFICE SUPPLIES AND SERVICES GROUP

The Office Supplies and Services Group consists of Grayarc Company, Inc., DOT Girls temporary and permanent help (U.S.A.), DOT Personnel Services (Canada), and Norma S Kemp Personnel Services Limited (Great Britain).

Grayarc, Dictaphone's mail-order office forms and supplies business headquartered in Brooklyn, New York, had a record year in 1973 in both sales and earnings, and is the backbone of this division. Its product line includes a variety of consumable items used by business, such as letterheads, envelopes, labels, industrial tape for mail room use, and various standard business forms. Its broad customer list provides repeat business at a low selling cost. During 1973 operations were further streamlined through the use of computerized order entry. Plans are also under way to utilize data processing for Grayarc's carefully maintained mailing list, the division's most important asset.

DOT and Kemp provide temporary and permanent personnel trained in all phases of office work, including stenography, typing, business machines operation, key punch operation, bookkeeping, and general clerical skills. This office

**FIGURE 6** ■ Dictaphone 4000 recorder. The New York City Police Department uses this recorder to monitor all emergency calls. The system can log 200 calls simultaneously.

services division continued to show good improvement in 1973, particularly in Canada, where sales and earnings reached record levels, and in Great Britain, where Kemp had its best earnings since it was acquired in 1968. The Canadian DOT Service operation is now the second largest temporary-help organization in that country. The U.S. DOT Services was also profitable; the company operates 13 key markets itself, and licensees run divisions in 16 others. Both the domestic and foreign office service operations are conducted in leased premises in 32 U.S. locations, 12 in Canada, and 1 in England. Therefore these operations do not require substantial investments in fixed assets, although the company does own the office furnishings including machines and equipment.

The contributions to sales and earnings of each division are shown in Table 7.

## Marketing strategy

Sales of equipment in the United States, Puerto Rico, Canada, and the United Kingdom are made, for the most part, directly to ultimate users by company sales personnel.

At the end of 1973, the direct sales organization in the United States consisted of 500 men and women, a 13 percent increase over 1972's year-end total

**TABLE 7 ■ 1972–1974 CONTRIBUTIONS TO SALES AND EARNINGS BY DIVISION**

| Division | 1974 | 1973 | 1972 |
|---|---|---|---|
| *Contributions to sales* | | | |
| Business machines and systems | $ 81,662,000 | $ 70,579,000 | $60,651,000 |
| Office supplies and services | 26,690,000 | 25,723,000 | 22,925,000 |
| Special recording equipment | 3,965,000 | 4,138,000 | 3,115,000 |
| | $112,317,000 | $100,440,000 | $86,691,000 |
| *Earnings and administrative costs and interest before taxes* | | | |
| Business machines and systems | $ 9,229,000 | $ 9,231,000 | $ 5,598,000 |
| Office supplies and services | 3,029,000 | 2,636,000 | 2,487,000 |
| Special recording equipment | 436,000 | | |
| Corporate administrative and interest costs | (2,501,000) | (2,245,000) | (2,473,000) |
| | $ 10,193,000 | $ 10,177,000 | $ 6,035,000 |

of 440. The company also has a group of 730 technicians who provide maintenance service to all Dictaphone's customers.

To facilitate delivery and service to customers, stocks of equipment, accessories, supplies, and service parts are maintained in approximately 220 locations in the United States, 18 locations in Canada, 11 locations in the United Kingdom and the Republic of Ireland, and 1 location in Puerto Rico. Dictaphone Company Limited also maintains a branch in Brussels, Belgium. Sales and service of dictating equipment in more than 70 other foreign countries are made through approximately 150 foreign distributors and agents.

In addition to Tabat's previously discussed marketing changes, he established new Sales and Service Managers' Advisory Councils to further formalize and improve field communications. This selective group of Dictaphone sales managers meets regularly with management to discuss ideas about future products and marketing strategies.

During the fourth quarter of 1973, a change was effected in the marketing management of the DPS group. A new functional activity, Marketing Services, was established with the responsibility for all programs that support the marketing effort, such as product planning, market research, sales education, sales development, and advertising. A new vice president of the DPS group heads this new activity.

In 1973, sales exceeded $100 million for the first time.

## Finance

The consolidated statements of income and retained earnings, balance sheet, sources and uses of funds statement for 1970 through 1974, and a 13-year comparative financial summary are provided in Tables 8 through 11.

In March 1973, the board of directors authorized the company to purchase up to 200,000 shares of its common stock in the open market and in private transactions, to be used in connection with stock option and employee stock purchase plans. Under the program in 1973, 129,279 shares were purchased.

**TABLE 8** ■ CONSOLIDATED STATEMENTS OF INCOME AND RETAINED EARNINGS, DICTA-PHONE CORPORATION AND SUBSIDIARIES
Years ended December 31

|  | 1974 | 1973 | 1972 | 1971 | 1970 |
|---|---|---|---|---|---|
| Revenue: |  |  |  |  |  |
| Sales of products and services | $112,317,000 | $100,440,000 | $86,691,000 | $94,500,000 | $88,621,000 |
| Interest income | 1,056,000 | 1,169,000 | 730,000 | . . . | . . . |
| Miscellaneous income—net | 818,000 | 188,000 | 157,000 | 767,000 | 667,000 |
|  | 144,191,000 | 101,797,000 | 87,578,000 | 95,267,000 | 89,288,000 |
| Costs and expenses: |  |  |  |  |  |
| Cost of products and services sold | 58,325,000 | 51,703,000 | 46,245,000 | 56,044,000 | 54,758,000 |
| Selling and administrative | 45,236,000 | 39,296,000 | 34,199,000 | 36,533,000 | 33,822,000 |
| Interest | 437,000 | 621,000 | 1,099,000 | 1,277,000 | 1,655,000 |
| Depreciation | . . . | . . . | . . . | 1,276,000 | 1,368,000 |
|  | 103,998,000 | 91,620,000 | 81,543,000 | 95,130,000 | 91,603,000 |
| Income (loss) from continuing operations before income taxes | 10,193,000 | 10,177,000 | 6,035,000 | 137,000 | (2,315,000) |
| Provision for income taxes (credits) | 4,567,000 | 4,933,000 | 2,901,000 | 26,000 | (399,000) |
| Income (loss) from continuing operations | 5,626,000 | 5,244,000 | 3,134,000 | 111,000 | (1,916,000) |
| Loss from discontinued operations, less related income tax credit | . . . | . . . | (600,000) | . . . | (982,000) |
| Income (loss) before extraordinary items | 5,626,000 | 5,244,000 | 2,534,000 | 111,000 | (2,898,000) |
| Extraordinary items, less related income tax credit | 148,000 | 402,000 | (1,943,000) | (1,102,000) | . . . |
| Net income (loss) | 5,774,000 | 5,646,000 | 591,000 | (991,000) | (2,898,000) |
| Retained earnings at beginning of year | 24,150,000 | 20,410,000 | 20,120,000 | 21,725,000 | 25,950,000 |
| Less cash dividends on common shares (per share, 1973—$.48; 1972—$.075; 1970—$.36) | 1,997,000 | 1,906,000 | 301,000 | . . . | 1,327,000 |
| Retained earnings at end of year | $ 27,927,000 | $ 24,150,000 | $20,410,000 | $20,734,000 | $21,725,000 |
| Per-share data: |  |  |  |  |  |
| Income (loss) from continuing operations | $1.45 | $1.32 | $.79 | $.03 | $(.51) |
| Loss from discontinued operations | . . . | . . . | (.15) | . . . | (.26) |
| Income loss before extraordinary items | 1.45 | 1.32 | .64 | .03 | (.77) |
| Extraordinary items | .04 | .10 | (.49) | (.28) | . . . |
| Net income (loss) | $1.49 | $1.42 | $.15 | $(.25) | $(.77) |

*Source:* 1974 Corporate Annual Reports.

By April 26, 1974, the repurchase of the entire 200,000 shares was completed.

In September of 1973 the regular quarterly dividend was increased from 7½ to 12 cents per share. In December, in addition to the regular quarterly payment of 12 cents, a year-end extra dividend of 9 cents was paid. This brought the total dividend payment in 1973 to 48 cents, equal to the company's previously high annual payment. At its meeting in February 1974, the board of directors declared a regular quarterly dividend of 12 cents on the common shares, payable March 29, 1974, to shareholders of record on March 1, 1974.

## The take-over bid

In late 1974, Northern Electric Company, 90 percent owned by Bell Telephone Company of Canada, Ltd., attempted to acquire Dictaphone.

This was definitely not the first take-over attempt. Two earlier attempts had been made. In 1965, Litton purchased 20 percent of the stock in the open market. Dictaphone management fought off this merger attempt.

In 1971, Gould Inc. (Chicago) made an offer for Dictaphone. Dictaphone management tentatively agreed to this merger, but later negotiations broke down.

**TABLE 9 ■ CONSOLIDATED STATEMENTS OF FINANCIAL POSITION, DICTAPHONE CORPORATION AND SUBSIDIARIES**
December 31

| | 1974 | 1973 | 1972 | 1971 | 1970 |
|---|---|---|---|---|---|
| Assets—current: | | | | | |
| Cash | $ 3,493,000 | $ 3,123,000 | $ 2,872,000 | $ 3,279,000 | $ 4,775,000 |
| Time deposits and accrued interest | 8,344,000 | 11,647,000 | 12,662,000 | 5,245,000 | 3,573,000 |
| Accounts receivable, less allowance for doubtful accounts, 1973—$858,000; 1972—$718,000; 1971—$732,000; 1970—$661,000 | 18,636,000 | 17,973,000 | 15,302,000 | 17,795,000 | 17,859,000 |
| Refundable federal income tax | . . . | . . . | 1,200,000 | . . . | 2,385,000 |
| Inventories | 24,660,000 | 19,856,000 | 14,907,000 | 22,972,000 | 24,015,000 |
| Income taxes, principally on deferred maintenance income | . . . | . . . | . . . | 1,487,000 | 1,466,000 |
| Total current assets | 55,133,000 | 52,599,000 | 46,943,000 | 50,778,000 | 54,073,000 |
| Property, plant, and equipment } Net 1972, 1973; gross 1970, 1971 | 8,379,000 | 7,628,000 | 6,422,000 | 9,756,000 | 11,095,000 |
| Other assets } | 3,527,000 | 3,815,000 | 3,636,000 | 4,101,000 | 5,607,000 |
| | $67,039,000 | $64,042,000 | $57,001,000 | $64,635,000 | $70,775,000 |
| Liabilities—current: | | | | | |
| Short-term bank borrowings | . . . | . . . | . . . | $ 551,000 | $11,529,000 |
| Current installments on long-term debt | . . . | $ 176,000 | $ 602,000 | 1,032,000 | 633,000 |
| Accounts payable and accrued liabilities | $12,565,000 | 10,588,000 | 7,764,000 | 10,024,000 | 8,260,000 |
| Income taxes payable | 1,245,000 | 3,062,000 | 547,000 | . . . | . . . |
| Deferred income | 5,783,000 | 5,772,000 | 5,855,000 | 5,365,000 | 4,999,000 |
| Deferred gain on foreign currency translation | 697,000 | 399,000 | . . . | . . . | . . . |
| Total current liabilities | 20,290,000 | 19,997,000 | 14,768,000 | 16,972,000 | 25,421,000 |
| Long-term debt | 8,943,000 | 9,461,000 | 10,593,000 | 16,024,000 | 13,269,000 |
| Deferred income taxes | 758,000 | 791,000 | 749,000 | 950,000 | 788,000 |
| Shareholders' equity: | | | | | |
| Common shares | 4,059,000 | 4,010,000 | 4,008,000 | 3,929,000 | 3,842,000 |
| Capital surplus | 6,527,000 | 6,410,000 | 6,473,000 | 6,026,000 | 5,730,000 |
| Retained earnings | 27,947,000 | 24,150,000 | 20,410,000 | 20,734,000 | 21,725,000 |
| Treasury shares, at cost | (1,485,000) | (777,000) | . . . | . . . | . . . |
| Total shareholders' equity | 37,048,000 | 33,793,000 | 30,891,000 | 30,689,000 | 31,297,000 |
| | $67,039,000 | $64,042,000 | $57,001,000 | $64,635,000 | $70,775,000 |

*Source:* 1971, 1973, and 1974 Corporate Annual Reports.

With regard to the Northern Electric take-over bid, between August 7 and September 16, 1974, Northern Electric purchased approximately 137,200 shares of Dictaphone stock for an average price of $7.88 without Dictaphone's knowledge. On August 1 and 2, Mrs. John Lobb, wife of Northern Electric's chairman, purchased 1000 shares of the stock for her own account. She paid approximately $7.43 per share. Mrs. Lobb said later that this purchase was based on articles she read on Dictaphone and without any urging by her husband. She later sold 100 shares for a very small profit.

By mid-September, the Northern Electric management decided to make a tender offer for any and all Dictaphone shares. The decision was made, an NE spokesman later said, "because it is a well run company, and its product lines are complementary to ours."

### SEPTEMBER 24

After only 1 hour's trading of Dictaphone stock, the New York Stock Exchange suspended trading in the stock for the day. NE said it had alerted the NYSE of a forthcoming tender offer. The offer leaked out and became generally known. NE had not had any contacts with the Dictaphone management up until that point.

**TABLE 10 ■ CONSOLIDATED STATEMENTS OF CHANGES IN FINANCIAL POSITION, DICTAPHONE CORPORATION AND SUBSIDIARIES**
Years ended December 31

| | 1974 | 1973 | 1972 | 1971 | 1970 |
|---|---|---|---|---|---|
| Funds provided by: | | | | | |
| Income (loss) from continuing operations | $ 5,626,000 | $ 5,244,000 | $ 3,134,000 | $ 111,000 | $(1,916,000) |
| Add charges to operations not requiring working capital: | | | | | |
| Depreciation and amortization | 894,000 | 822,000 | 916,000 | 1,301,000 | 1,401,000 |
| Deferred taxes on income, noncurrent | (33,000) | 42,000 | 65,000 | 162,000 | (3,000) |
| Loss from discontinued operations, less depreciation and amortization | ... | ... | (522,000) | ... | (899,000) |
| Funds provided from operations | 6,487,000 | 6,108,000 | 3,593,000 | 1,574,000 | (1,417,000) |
| Extraordinary items | 148,000 | 402,000 | (1,943,000) | (1,102,000) | ... |
| Add net charges relating to extraordinary items not requiring working capital, principally loss on sale of property, plant and equipment | ... | ... | 838,000 | 832,000 | ... |
| | 6,635,000 | 6,510,000 | 2,488,000 | 1,304,000 | (1,417,000) |
| Proceeds from disposal of property, plant, and equipment | 102,000 | 197,000 | 2,427,000 | 1,059,000 | 295,000 |
| Common stock issued for business acquired | ... | ... | ... | ... | 2,032,000 |
| Net noncurrent assets of disposed businesses | ... | ... | ... | ... | 597,000 |
| Notes receivable maturing within one year | ... | ... | ... | 750,000 | ... |
| Proceeds of long-term debt | ... | ... | ... | 5,456,000 | ... |
| Proceeds from net noncurrent assets of disposed businesses | 423,000 | ... | ... | ... | ... |
| Proceeds from common stock sold to employees under stock option and stock purchase plans | 506,000 | 501,000 | 502,000 | 542,000 | 382,000 |
| | 7,666,000 | 7,208,000 | 5,417,000 | 9,111,000 | 1,889,000 |
| Funds used for: | | | | | |
| Capital expenditures | 2,211,000 | 2,204,000 | 621,000 | 996,000 | 1,360,000 |
| Reduction of long-term debt | 342,000 | 1,132,000 | 5,431,000 | 2,701,000 | 421,000 |
| Dividends paid on common stock | 1,997,000 | 1,906,000 | 301,000 | ... | 1,327,000 |
| Investment in Echo Science Corp. | ... | ... | ... | 75,000 | 757,000 |
| Net noncurrent assets of acquired businesses | ... | ... | ... | ... | 344,000 |
| Purchases of common stock | 724,000 | 1,339,000 | ... | ... | ... |
| Other, net | 171,000 | 200,000 | (185,000) | 185,000 | (83,000) |
| | 5,445,000 | 6,781,000 | 6,168,000 | 3,957,000 | 4,126,000 |
| Increase (decrease) in working capital | $ 2,221,000 | $ 427,000 | $ (751,000) | $ 5,154,000 | $(2,237,000) |
| Changes in working capital consist of: | | | | | |
| Cash, time deposits, and accrued interest | $(2,933,000) | $ (764,000) | $ 7,010,000 | $ 176,000 | $ 792,000 |
| Receivables | 941,000 | 2,671,000 | (2,493,000) | (64,000) | (3,119,000) |
| Refundable federal income tax | ... | (1,200,000) | 1,200,000 | (2,364,000) | 2,213,000 |
| Inventories | 4,804,000 | 4,949,000 | (8,065,000) | (1,043,000) | (1,304,000) |
| Income taxes payable | ... | (2,515,000) | 66,000 | ... | ... |
| Short-term bank borrowing | ... | ... | ... | 10,978,000 | (2,753,000) |
| Deferred gain on foreign currency translation | (298,000) | (399,000) | ... | ... | ... |
| Other | (293,000) | (2,315,000) | 1,531,000 | (2,529,000) | 1,934,000 |
| | $ 2,221,000 | $ 427,000 | $ (751,000) | $ 5,154,000 | $(2,237,000) |

The trading was halted to allow NE to make a statement. A spokesman for the company said NE planned to make an offer for Dictaphone the next day. NE said it would pay "a substantial premium over recent market price." NE also announced that Lehman Brothers would handle the offer.

Upon the halt in trading, Dictaphone requested the U.S. Securities and Exchange Commission and NYSE to investigate. Robert Falise, vice president, corporate secretary, and general counsel of Dictaphone, said: "We suspect there has been inside trading based on a leak about an impending tender offer."

Mr. Tabat and other executives had been in Europe and rushed to New York when the news began to unfold.

Lehman Brothers had asked Mr. Tabat to a dinner meeting on the twenty-fourth without disclosing the details of the agenda.

Once it became clear that NE was involved, the Dictaphone management requested that the U.S. Justice Department's Antitrust Division investigate possible antitrust implications of such a take-over.

A spokesman for NE admitted NE had purchased some Dictaphone shares on the open market recently: "NE," he said, "had made careful plans to arrange discussions with the management and directors of Dictaphone in advance of the offers. . . . However, action in the Dictaphone stock this morning forced an immediate announcement." The spokesman declined to comment on Dictaphone's request for SEC investigation.

The preceding week, 16,900 shares of Dictaphone's stock had been traded five trading days; 9000 shares had been traded less than an hour before the halt on September 24. Mr. Falise said the company had been concerned over the turnover of 130,000 to 150,000 shares in the stock in recent weeks. The directors held 120,000 shares at that time.

On the evening of September 24, a dinner was held, arranged by Lehman Brothers, the dealer manager for NE. Attending were Mr. Tabat, Fred Sullivan, chairman of the executive committee of Dictaphone, Ross Traphagen, Jr., of Goldman Sacks & Co. (Dictaphone's investment bankers), and Mr. Lobb.

During the meeting, Mr. Lobb disclosed the details of the offer—$12 per share for any and all shares, the offer expiring October 4. Mr. Tabat told Mr. Lobb that $12 was "inadequate." Mr. Lobb refused to negotiate a merger because "in the past, when he (Lobb) had negotiated, he had always been disappointed." Mr. Tabat was told that he and any executives of his choice could stay on with management contracts. Lobb also indicated that his company had take-over plans for other U.S. companies.

When Tabat raised the antitrust issue, Lobb said he was sure that "no serious problem existed" on the idea. He also rejected the idea of a joint study of the matter.

SEPTEMBER 25

Published in many financial journals was the short offer to purchase given in Figure 7 (see p. 556).

The Dictaphone board met and voted unanimously to reject the offer and vigorously fight off NE. The firm issued a letter to all shareholders urging them to resist the offer. Major points in the letter were:

1  NE had not discussed the arrangements before the public announcement.

2  The offer was inadequate—only 8.2 times recent earnings, whereas in 1973 the stock sold at 11.2 times earnings.

3  Recent sales, profit, and dividends increase warranted a higher price and NE was simply taking advantage of the depressed stock market.

4  If successful, NE would receive $12 million cash assets from Dictaphone's treasury.

NE announced that the company had acquired unsecured short-term capital from the Royal Bank of Canada. All the Dictaphone stock at $12 a share would cost $47 million. The firm also said it wished to win the friendship and cooperation of Dictaphone management and directors. It revealed the size of

TABLE 11 ■ 13-YEAR COMPARATIVE FINANCIAL SUMMARY

| | 1974 | 1973 | 1972 | 1971 | 1970 |
|---|---|---|---|---|---|
| **Operating and financial data** | | | | | |
| Sales and services[a] | $112,317,000 | $100,440,000 | $86,691,000 | $94,500,000 | $88,621,000 |
| Income (loss) before taxes[a] | 10,193,000 | 10,177,000 | 6,035,000 | 137,000 | (2,315,000) |
| Income (loss) before extraordinary items[a] | 5,626,000 | 5,244,000[b] | 3,134,000[b] | 111,000[b] | (1,916,000)[c] |
| Depreciation[a] | 834,000 | 801,000 | 889,000 | 1,276,000 | 1,368,000 |
| Common dividends | 1,977,000 | 1,906,000 | 301,000 | . . . | 1,327,000 |
| Preferred dividends | | | | | |
| Capital expenditures | 2,211,000 | 2,204,000 | 621,000 | 996,000 | 1,360,000 |
| Property, plant, and equipment | 8,379,000 | 7,628,000 | 6,422,000 | 9,756,000 | 11,095,000 |
| Net working capital | 34,843,000 | 32,602,000 | 32,175,000 | 33,806,000 | 28,652,000 |
| Common shareholders' equity | 37,048,000 | 33,793,000 | 30,891,000 | 30,689,000 | 31,298,000 |
| Long-term debt | 8,943,000 | 9,461,000 | 10,593,000 | 16,024,000 | 13,269,000 |
| **Per-share data** | | | | | |
| Income (loss) per common share before extraordinary items[a,d] | $1.45 | $1.32[b] | $ .79[b] | $ .03[b] | $(.51)[c] |
| Common equity per share | 9.59 | 8.58 | 7.71 | 7.81 | 8.15 |
| Dividends per common share | .51 | .48 | .075 | . . . | .36 |
| Dividends per preferred share | . . . | . . . | . . . | . . . | . . . |
| **Shares outstanding at year end** | | | | | |
| Common | 3,869,405 | 3,938,798 | 4,008,215 | 3,929,139 | 3,841,996 |
| Preferred | . . . | . . . | . . . | . . . | — |

All data, except dividend data, for the years 1965 through 1968 have been restated to give effect to those businesses subsequently acquired and treated as poolings of interest.

[a] Excludes amounts applicable to businesses disposed of in 1970 and 1968.

[b] Excludes $1,102,000 ($.28 per share) extraordinary loss, net of related income tax credit of $385,000, in 1971 and excludes $336,000 ($.10 per share) extraordinary gain, net of related income taxes of $108,000, in 1968 from sale of division.

[c] The net loss for 1970 has been restated to reflect an increase in the provision for income taxes, $104,000 ($.03 per share), based on the retroactive effect of certain changes in a foreign tax law adopted in 1971.

[d] Based on average shares outstanding during each year, as adjusted for subsequent stock splits and stock dividends.

its prior purchases and said NE wished to acquire at least working control of Dictaphone. The new board would include present directors who would stay on.

Finally the firm spokesman said it did not know of any holdings of Dictaphone stock by its directors, officers, or others associated with NE.

## SEPTEMBER 26

A 2½-page formal offer to purchase was published in the financial journals. The rationale for the offer was explained, as were NE's financial statements. The conditions of the offer included the following statements:

6. *Certain Conditions of this Offer.* The Offeror shall not be required to purchase any Shares tendered if:

(a) there shall have been instituted or threatened any action or proceeding before any court or governmental agency, by any governmental agency or any other person, challenging the acquisition by the Offeror of Shares or otherwise affecting the Offeror or the Company, which is, in the sole judgment of the management of the Offeror, materially adverse; or

(b) the Company shall have (i) issued or authorized or proposed the issuance of additional shares of capital stock of any class or securities convertible into any such shares, (ii) issued or authorized or proposed the issuance of any other securities in respect of, in lieu of, or in substitution for, its now outstanding Shares, or (iii) authorized or proposed any merger, consolidation, acquisition of assets, disposition of assets, or material change in its capitalization, or other comparable event not in the ordinary course of business; or

(c) any change shall have occurred or be threatened in the business, financial condition or results of operations of the Company, which is, in the sole judgment of the management of the Offeror, materially adverse; or

(d) there shall have occurred (i) any suspension of, or limitation of prices for, trading

| 1969 | 1968 | 1967 | 1966 | 1965 | 1964 | 1963 | 1962 |
|---|---|---|---|---|---|---|---|
| $91,012,000 | $77,525,000 | $64,841,000 | $59,172,000 | $50,007,000 | $39,047,000 | $38,238,000 | $37,142,000 |
| 8,241,000 | 7,241,000 | 5,798,000 | 5,919,000 | 4,322,000 | 2,950,000 | 2,367,000 | 2,647,000 |
| 4,314,000 | 3,660,000[b] | 3,166,000 | 3,192,000 | 2,320,000 | 1,467,000 | 1,159,000 | 1,247,000 |
| 1,227,000 | 1,097,000 | 1,138,000 | 1,174,000 | 1,013,000 | 783,000 | 770,000 | 770,000 |
| 1,663,000 | 1,478,000 | 1,234,000 | 1,168,000 | 881,000 | 822,000 | 822,000 | 822,000 |
| | | | 10,000 | 17,000 | 25,000 | 44,000 | 44,000 | 45,000 |
| 2,884,000 | 2,565,000 | 2,357,000 | 2,133,000 | 2,382,000 | 1,032,000 | 806,000 | 1,471,000 |
| 12,282,000 | 10,913,000 | 10,136,000 | 9,043,000 | 7,500,000 | 4,705,000 | 4,429,000 | 4,432,000 |
| 30,889,000 | 29,595,000 | 22,179,000 | 20,770,000 | 20,190,000 | 17,827,000 | 17,688,000 | 17,320,000 |
| 33,046,000 | 30,454,000 | 27,908,000 | 26,059,000 | 23,891,000 | 18,227,000 | 17,615,000 | 17,322,000 |
| 13,905,000 | 12,881,000 | 4,904,000 | 4,186,000 | 4,103,000 | 3,220,000 | 3,480,000 | 3,740,000 |
| $1.20 | $1.03[b] | $ .91 | $ .91 | $ .66 | $ .61 | $ .48 | $ .51 |
| 9.20 | 8.54 | 7.96 | 7.47 | 6.91 | 7.76 | 7.50 | 7.37 |
| .48 | .48 | .45 | .45 | .375 | .35 | .35 | .35 |
| — | — | 4.00 | 4.00 | 4.00 | 4.00 | 4.00 | 4.00 |
| 3,592,042 | 3,565,604 | 3,505,165 | 3,488,229 | 3,459,499 | 2,349,088 | 2,349,088 | 2,349,088 |
| — | — | — | 4,150 | 4,208 | 8,943 | 10,971 | 11,122 |

in securities on the New York Stock Exchange, Inc., (ii) a declaration of a banking moratorium by United States or Canadian authorities, (iii) a commencement of a war, armed hostilities or other international or national calamity directly or indirectly involving the United States or Canada, or (iv) a material change in United States or Canadian currency exchange rates;

which, in the sole judgment of the management of the Offeror in any such case, makes it inadvisable to proceed with the purchase of Shares pursuant to this Offer.

Any determination made in good faith by the Offeror concerning the events described in this Paragraph 6 shall be final and binding upon all parties.

### SEPTEMBER 27–29

During this period, Dictaphone was most active. The company made telephone calls to as many stockholders as they could reach. These calls and the speedy dispatch of the letters were made possible because the company had taken great care to keep their lists of stockholders up to date in case of a take-over attempt. The company enlisted the help of Senators A. Ribicoff (D-Conn.) and L. Weicker (R-Conn.) to get the Justice Department and SEC moving on the case. Senator Weicker was quoted as saying, "I have no desire to see the 700 Dictaphone employees in Bridgeport, Conn., under Canadian management."

Mr. Tabat said that the telephone campaign was desirable since "many of them [stockholders] are getting pressure from their brokers who are desperate for our commissions. But the overwhelming majority of our stockholders told us they don't plan to tender or sell."

### SEPTEMBER 30

Dictaphone stock closes at $12.35 on 80,700 shares traded.

### OCTOBER 1

Dictaphone filed suit in federal court in New York charging NE with fraud in its offer. Dictaphone contends that the secret purchase of 137,200 shares

*This announcement is not an offer to purchase or a solicitation of an offer to sell these securities. The offer is made only by the Offer to Purchase and the related Letter of Transmittal and is not being made to, nor will tenders be accepted from, holders of Shares in any jurisdiction in which the making or acceptance thereof would not be in compliance with the securities laws of such jurisdiction.*

Notice of Offer to Purchase for Cash
Any and All Shares of Common Stock
of

# Dictaphone Corporation

At $12 per Share Net
by

## Northern Electric Company, Limited

Northern Electric Company, Limited (the "Offeror"), is offering to purchase any and all of the outstanding shares of Common Stock (the "Shares") of Dictaphone Corporation (the "Company") at $12, net to the seller, in cash, subject to the terms and conditions set forth in the Offer to Purchase dated September 25, 1974 and in the related Letter of Transmittal. Tendering stockholders will not be obligated to pay brokerage commissions or, subject to Instruction 5 of the Letter of Transmittal, transfer taxes, on the purchase of Shares by the Offeror.

**THE OFFER WILL EXPIRE ON OCTOBER 4, 1974, AT 6:00 P.M., NEW YORK TIME, UNLESS EXTENDED.**

The Offeror will, subject to the terms and conditions set forth in the Offer to Purchase and related Letter of Transmittal, purchase any and all Shares which are duly tendered by 6:00 P.M., New York Time, on October 4, 1974, or, if the Offer is extended, by the time on the date to which the Offer is extended. Shares tendered may be withdrawn at any time prior to October 4, 1974, or, unless theretofore purchased, at any time after November 23, 1974.

The Offeror will pay a solicitation fee of 40 cents per Share purchased pursuant to the Offer to any broker or dealer who is a member of a registered national securities exchange or of the National Association of Securities Dealers, Inc., or to any foreign broker or dealer who agrees to conform to the Rules of Fair Practice of such Association in making solicitations in the United States to the same extent as though it were a member thereof, or to any commercial bank or trust company, whose name appears in the appropriate space in the Letter of Transmittal.

The Offer to Purchase and the Letter of Transmittal contain important information which should be read before any decision is made with respect to the Offer. A tender may be made only by a duly executed Letter of Transmittal.

*Copies of the Offer to Purchase and the Letter of Transmittal may be obtained from the Dealer Manager, the Depositary, any Forwarding Agent or the Soliciting Agent.*

*Depositary*
MONTREAL TRUST COMPANY

*By mail or by hand:*
1 Place Ville Marie
Montreal, Quebec H3B 3L6, Canada

*Forwarding Agents*
BANKERS TRUST COMPANY

| *By mail:* | *By hand:* |
|---|---|
| P.O. Box 396 | 7th Floor |
| Bowling Green Station | Two Broadway |
| New York, New York 10004 | New York, New York |

CONTINENTAL ILLINOIS NATIONAL BANK AND TRUST COMPANY OF CHICAGO

**FIGURE 7**

was part of a conspiracy to get control of Dictaphone by secretive, improper, and illegal means. Dictaphone further argued that the offer to the public was false and misleading in that it omitted pertinent facts. The remedy sought was an injunction to prohibit further purchases (under the tender offer) and to declare void the prior purchases. Failing that, Dictaphone demanded that NE publish the information before any further purchases. Named as codefendants were Lehman Brothers and its officers Peter Peterson and Michael Tarnapol, and Merrill Lynch (which made the purchases for NE).

The pertinent facts not published were the following (according to Dictaphone):

1 The increased dividend of 15 cents per share

2 The $12 million in cash assets that would reduce the cost to NE by $3 per share

3 Possible adverse Canadian tax effects on Dictaphone and nontendering shareholders if NE did not purchase all the stock tendered

Fraud was claimed because by secret open market purchases by Merrill Lynch for NE, NE deprived Dictaphone shareholders of their opportunity to sell at the higher price of the tender offer.

NE directors met in Winnipeg and decided to withdraw its offer. They issued a statement saying that in view of the lack of Dictaphone's desire and in view of the suit filed, it saw no purpose in continuing the offer, which had been made in good faith. It also said it was unaware of any competing offer for the stock and had not decided whether to sell or retain its present holdings in Dictaphone.

Mr. Tabat said: "I personally commend NE's judgment in withdrawing the offer and there isn't any animosity on our part. If the proposal had been presented under more favorable circumstances, it would have been given serious consideration by our board of directors."

Later, a large group of Wall Street firms had purchased between 15 and 20 percent of the stock with a view to tendering it. They purchased the stock at up to $12.375 per share. After NE withdrew its offer, the stock price dropped below $8.

In late October, one of the firms, Neuberger and Berman, sued NE in a class action suit for all those who purchased Dictaphone from September 23 to October 3 (totaling 456,000 shares). The suit claims NE issued "false and misleading material during the tender offer; that it did not reveal that NE would drop the offer if Dictaphone management fought it, or that Dictaphone management did put up opposition." Because of Mrs. Lobb's purchases, Dictaphone had a basis for defeating the tender offer. Finally, Neuberger and Berman said that "if investors had known all the true facts, they wouldn't have bought Dictaphone stock during the tender period and wouldn't have suffered the losses."

## The Sterndent offer

On February 25, 1975, Dictaphone agreed in principle to make Sterndent Corporation a part of Dictaphone. The merger agreement was subject to approval by two-thirds of Sterndent's shareholders. Dictaphone offered $19 for each of the 2.1 million common and common equivalent shares. The offer came shortly after Cable Funding had made an offer for 55 percent of Sterndent's common shares at $14.

After Dictaphone announced its plans to acquire Sterndent, Cable Funding said it favored the Dictaphone merger but would watch its progress before deciding to withdraw its own offer.

Sterndent is in two businesses: dental equipment and supplies and precious metals. Approximately 60 percent of sales and 40 percent of earnings came from the precious metals segment while the dental area accounted for approximately 40 percent of sales and 60 percent of earnings. The Sterndent board unanimously approved Dictaphone's offer and recommended it to Sterndent shareholders. Cable Funding then chose to let its tender offer for Sterndent stock expire.

Dictaphone said most of the money needed to finance the acquisition would come from lending institutions. Although the transactions would have an initial value of $40 million, much of Sterndent's inventories of gold and silver would be sold. The proceeds would go to retire about $15 million of the debt, leaving Dictaphone with about $25 million of long-term debt from the merger.

Dictaphone also said that the merger was subject to certain other conditions, including the approval of Canada's Foreign Investment Review Board (both Sterndent and Dictaphone have Canadian subsidiaries) and the completion of necessary financing arrangements by Dictaphone. The completion of the merger would make Dictaphone a substantially larger company. Combined sales for the companies in 1974 were $225 million, and the net income for Dictaphone would have been in excess of $7 million, or about $1.85 per share if the merger had been in effect for 1974.

Following the announcement of the merger, Sterndent's stock reached a high of $17 per share and closed the day at 16.625, up $3 from the previous trading session. Dictaphone shares fell 50 cents to close at $10.125. On that date the total market value of Dictaphone shares was approximately $39.2 million, or slightly less than the price it had agreed to pay for Sterndent.

## Future outlook

"Word processing systems" seems to be the latest buzz word of the industry. This phrase refers to the automation of both the input and output side of office communications, that is, a system that will combine the functions of dictating, transcribing, editing, and copying. Most analysts believe that IBM will capture substantial portions of the word processing systems market, but IBM will focus its attention on the larger systems where the need for extensive communications and computer know-how prevails. However, there is also general agreement that there will exist a segment of the market where the small systems approach will be needed. Dictaphone with its existing dictating and transcribing capabilities could be in a unique position to capture this market with a carefully conceived acquisition program to give it the necessary typewriter and editing function technology it presently lacks to compete in the total word processing systems arena.

Tabat has repeatedly stated, however, that he plans to keep Dictaphone strictly on the input side of word processing, and that he does not want to make major investments of company funds into automatic typewriter and editing equipment "until the field is shaken out." Dictaphone's input equipment such as the Thought Tank is presently compatible with the output equipment now manufactured by other companies.

In a report delivered to the New York Society of Security Analysts on August 16, 1973, Tabat indicated that he had great confidence in the future for Dictaphone because of "(1) upcoming new products coming from our stepped-up research and development efforts, (2) greater percentages of non-cyclical business than we had before the last recession, (3) a more seasoned management team, (4) better financial controls, and (5) the resources to effect a substantial acquisition." With regard to an acquisition program, Tabat indicated that the company was primarily looking for opportunities that would match their current business capabilities. He said that they were looking at office supply businesses that would complement the Grayarc division, and at possible opportunities to augment the foreign business.

In concluding his report to the analysts' society, he stated that he believed the strengths of Dictaphone to be:

1   A great name, Dictaphone is recognized throughout the world as a leader in the business equipment field.

2   A professional marketing organization with company-owned sales and service offices in the United States, Canada, and the United Kingdom as well as dealer and mail-order outlets for other products.

3   An international base with growing strength in England and on the continent.

4   A dominant position in most of our markets.

5   An excellent balance sheet.

6   An experienced management team.

# A note on the U.S. brewing industry

William F. Glueck

Beer drinking has been with the human race at least since the Mesopotamian cultures that preceded the golden age of Egypt. Beer arrived in the U.S. with the Pilgrims, and the early Virginia colonists were not opposed to ale, either. The U.S. and Canadian brewing industry developed steadily. One interruption in its history was the U.S. Prohibition period in the 1920s and early 1930s.

If one were to use two words that best describe recent trends in the brewing industry, they would be *increasing concentration.* Some data will support this characterization. Table 1 lists the number of breweries operating in the United States by year since 1935. Note that the table lists the number of breweries. By 1974, there were fewer than 60 companies operating in the brewing industry.

Predictions are that the number of firms left in business in 1980 will be 30 or fewer. In 1974, the Big Beer Three (Anheuser-Busch, Schlitz, and Pabst) sold almost 60 percent of the beer in the United States. It is estimated that in 1980 they may sell 70 percent of the beer. Figure 1 indicates the trend in sales of the Big Three and Top Ten up to 1972. Table 2 presents data on the largest breweries' barrel sales and ranking up through 1971.

Table 3 presents data on the share of market of some of the leading brewers, 1950–1968.

## The big get bigger

Each year, a few names once well known drop off. The list of the top ten in 1960 through 1963 included Liebmann (Rheingold beer). No more. Later Ballantine was absorbed by Falstaff, and it disappeared. By 1974, the top firms were:

1 Anheuser-Busch

2 Joseph Schlitz

3 Pabst Brewing

4 Adolph Coors

5 Miller (division of Phillip Morris)

6 Falstaff Brewing

7 F. & M. Schaefer

8 Stroh's

9 G. Heileman Brewing

The industry is concentrated in the north central

TABLE 1 ■ NUMBER OF BREWERIES OPERATING IN THE UNITED STATES

| Year | Number of breweries |
| --- | --- |
| 1935 | 750 (after Prohibition) |
| 1945 | 490 |
| 1949 | 440 |
| 1963 | 211 |
| 1964 | 204 |
| 1965 | 197 |
| 1966 | 187 |
| 1967 | 176 |
| 1968 | 163 |
| 1969 | 158 |
| 1970 | 154 |
| 1971 | 146 |
| 1972 | 139 |

and northeastern part of the United States. There is a chasm between the Big Three and the rest of the Top Ten, much less breweries like Lithia Brewery, West Bend (now Eau Claire), Wisconsin. Lithia, 124 years old (1974), had 22 employees (1972). It is hard for these firms to compete. The chasm is in sales and profits.

### WHY THE CONCENTRATION?

Why have the Big Three grown and the others slowed? That is a question with several answers. One seems to be: economies of scale in production. Generally the argument runs that as bigger and more automated breweries are built, the cost per barrel decreases significantly. Thus Jerry Flum, a securities analyst of some note, estimated that in 1972 Schlitz's production costs per barrel were $1.08, Falstaff's were $4.39. The firm needs large amounts of capital to build its plants. And the Big Three are not standing still. Anheuser-Busch in 1974 planned to spend $540,000,000 for new operations through 1976. Joseph Schlitz is building a new 5,800,000-barrel brewery in Syracuse. Schlitz plans to increase its capacity from 21,700,000 barrels in 1973 to 35 million barrels in 1978. Coors plans to expand its capacity 10 to 15 percent per year in the future. Phillip Morris plans to spend $70 million to build an East Coast brewery for its Miller High Life Division.

Several securities analysts who specialize in the industry discussed it in the *Wall Street Journal* recently in its Heard on the Street column.

"There are two key criteria for success in the brewing industry," says [Lawrence Goldstein, Burnham and Co.]. "You've got to be national, and you've got to have strong finances." If a rainy summer depresses sales in New York, a national brewer can step up its efforts in another part of the country to take up the slack. But New York regionals like F. & M. Schaefer or Rheingold have trouble selling more brew in, say, Los Angeles.

A depressed regional market area makes it difficult to generate the funds to construct large, new and efficient breweries such as the ones the big three have been erecting around the country. In addition, the efficient new breweries of the majors are built closer to their markets, trimming distribution costs.

"The regionals are caught in a very bad position," comments Robert N. Stanton,

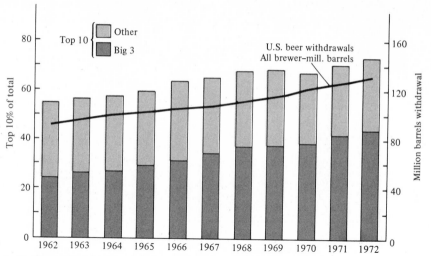

**FIGURE 1** ■ Market position of leading brewers. *Source:* Standard and Poor's, 1974.

an analyst with Dean Witter & Co. New plant efficiencies enable the major brewers to hold the line on prices despite rising costs. Many of the regionals are faced with the choice of raising prices, which narrows price differentials and leads to drinkers switching to national beers, or holding prices, which squeezes profit margins.

"I wouldn't want to own the regional brewers," says Mr. Stanton. His view is seconded by William D. Witter's Mr. Sharpe, and the Burnham analysts, although Mr. Goldstein of Burnham notes that some regional brewers, such as the privately owned, Denver-based Coors, have good growth records.

## Antitrust action?

One factor which could affect the future growth rates of the larger brewers is antitrust action by the Justice Department. In the past, litigation has been primarily in the area of prevention of merger which might lessen competition. Four of the seven cases brought to court between 1957 and 1970 involved Anheuser-Busch, Schlitz, Pabst, and Falstaff. Most of these involved acquisition of a regional or local brewer by a major national firm. The outcome of all cases against the Big Three resulted in court-ordered divestiture.

In addition to antimerger action, the industry may be facing litigation against price and market controls. The U.S. government has expressed concern about practices of territorial pricing and vertical price fixing. Similarly, the Justice Department has scrutinized exclusive dealership and distributor territorialization, where distributors are directed to refrain from handling competitive brands or restricting sales of distributors to specific geographic locations. As major brewers increase their market shares, there will no doubt be further enforcement against "predatory intent." One recent suit was filed by Grain Belt against Schlitz and Anheuser-Busch. The former claims it had to shut its Omaha brewery because of unfair pricing practices of the other two firms.

**TABLE 2 ■ BEER SALES OF THE TOP 20 BREWERS IN THE UNITED STATES AND TOTAL INDUSTRY SALES[a]**

| Brewer | 1971 rank | 1971 sales (thousands of barrels) | 1970 rank | 1970 sales (thousands of barrels) | 1969 rank | 1969 sales (thousands of barrels) | 1968 rank | 1968 sales (thousands of barrels) | 1967 rank | 1967 sales (thousands of barrels) | 1966 rank | 1966 sales (thousands of barrels) |
|---|---|---|---|---|---|---|---|---|---|---|---|---|
| Anheuser-Busch | 1 | 24,309 | 1 | 22,202 | 1 | 18,712 | 1 | 18,400 | 1 | 15,535 | 1 | 13,600 |
| Schlitz | 2 | 16,708 | 2 | 15,129 | 2 | 13,709 | 2 | 11,576 | 2 | 10,220 | 2 | 9,467 |
| Pabst | 3 | 11,797 | 3 | 10,517 | 3 | 10,225 | 3 | 10,910 | 3 | 10,124 | 3 | 9,047 |
| Coors | 4 | 8,525 | 4 | 7,277 | 4 | 6,351 | 5 | 5,333 | 7 | 4,616 | 10 | 3,998 |
| Schaefer | 5 | 5,600 | 5 | 5,749 | 7 | 5,433 | 6 | 5,050 | 6 | 4,714 | 6 | 4,567 |
| Miller | 6 | 5,200 | 7 | 5,150 | 8 | 5,100 | 8 | 4,850 | 8 | 4,584 | 9 | 4,146 |
| Falstaff | 7 | 5,150 | 6 | 5,386 | 5 | 6,200 | 4 | 6,300 | 4 | 6,631 | 4 | 7,010 |
| Carling | 8 | 4,385 | 8 | 4,819 | 6 | 5,440 | 7 | 5,020 | 5 | 4,916 | 5 | 5,125 |
| Hamm | 9 | 4,100 | 9 | 4,470 | 9 | 4,250 | 9 | 4,311 | 9 | 4,311 | 8 | 4,211 |
| Stroh | 10 | 3,676 | 13 | 3,276 | 14 | 2,939 | 15 | 2,536 | 15 | 2,403 | 15 | 2,418 |
| Associated | 11 | 3,582 | 10 | 3,750 | 10 | 3,971 | 10 | 4,000 | 10 | 4,208 | 7 | 4,530 |
| Rheingold | 12 | 3,406 | 11 | 3,417 | 11 | 3,488 | 11 | 3,400 | 11 | 3,582 | 11 | 3,840 |
| C. Schmidt | 13 | 3,162 | 14 | 3,040 | 13 | 2,941 | 14 | 2,816 | 14 | 2,663 | 14 | 2,586 |
| Olympia | 14 | 3,094 | 12 | 3,379 | 12 | 3,375 | 13 | 3,074 | 13 | 2,867 | 13 | 2,677 |
| Heileman | 15 | 2,820 | 15 | 3,000 | 15 | 2,298 | 18 | 1,726 | 19 | 1,218 | 22 | 1,011 |
| Ballantine | 16 | 2,230 | 17 | 2,220 | 17 | 2,000 | 12 | 3,100 | 12 | 3,300 | 12 | 3,776 |
| National | 17 | 2,202 | 16 | 2,262 | 16 | 2,218 | 16 | 2,139 | 16 | 2,083 | 16 | 2,009 |
| Pearl | 18 | 1,656 | 18 | 1,750 | 18 | 1,909 | 17 | 1,827 | 17 | 1,794 | 17 | 1,794 |
| Meister Brau | 19 | 1,580 | 19 | 1,500 | 20 | 1,000 | 25 | 890 | 25 | 898 | 24 | 903 |
| Genesee | 20 | 1,575 | 20 | 1,475 | 19 | 1,445 | 19 | 1,440 | 18 | 1,430 | 19 | 1,370 |
| Total industry sales[a] | | | | 121,360 | | 116,671 | | 111,416 | | 106,974 | | 104,262 |
| Total production | | | | 133,123 | | 127,319 | | 122,408 | | 116,551 | | 113,037 |
| Number of breweries | | 146 | | 154 | | 158 | | 163 | | 176 | | 187 |

[a] Represents tax-paid withdrawals.

| Year | A-B, % | Schlitz, % | Pabst, % | Falstaff, % | Carling, % | Schaefer, % | Ballantine, % | Hamm, % | Miller, % |
|---|---|---|---|---|---|---|---|---|---|
| 1950 | 5.9 | 5.9 | 4.6 | 3.0 | 0.6 | 3.2 | 5.3 | 1.3 | 2.5 |
| 1951 | 6.5 | 6.8 | 4.7 | 2.7 | 0.8 | | 4.8 | 1.4 | 3.1 |
| 1952 | 7.1 | 7.5 | 4.8 | 2.7 | 1.1 | 2.8 | 4.8 | 1.6 | 3.6 |
| 1953 | 7.8 | 6.1 | 4.9 | 3.4 | 1.3 | 3.0 | 4.5 | 2.0 | 2.5 |
| 1954 | 7.0 | 6.5 | 4.2 | 3.9 | 1.6 | 3.2 | 4.5 | 2.7 | 2.5 |
| 1955 | 6.6 | 6.8 | 4.1 | 4.3 | 3.1 | 3.1 | 4.7 | 3.6 | 2.6 |
| 1956 | 6.9 | 7.0 | 3.7 | 4.6 | 3.5 | 3.2 | 4.7 | 3.9 | 2.6 |
| 1957 | 7.0 | 7.1 | 3.2 | 5.1 | 3.7 | 3.5 | 4.7 | 4.0 | 2.6 |
| 1958 | 8.3 | 7.0 | 3.0 | 5.3 | 4.2 | 3.3 | 4.8 | 4.0 | 2.6 |
| 1959 | 9.2 | 6.7 | 5.1 | 5.4 | 5.0 | 3.5 | 4.9 | 4.1 | 2.7 |
| 1960 | 9.6 | 6.5 | 5.0 | 5.6 | 5.5 | 3.6 | 5.0 | 4.4 | 2.7 |
| 1961 | 9.5 | 6.5 | 5.9 | 5.7 | 5.7 | 3.7 | 5.1 | 4.2 | 3.0 |
| 1962 | 9.9 | 7.5 | 6.4 | 5.8 | 5.9 | 4.0 | 5.0 | 4.1 | 3.1 |
| 1963 | 10.0 | 8.4 | 7.1 | 5.9 | 6.1 | 4.1 | 4.8 | 4.1 | 3.1 |
| 1964 | 10.5 | 8.4 | 7.5 | 6.0 | 5.9 | 4.3 | 4.5 | 3.8 | 3.3 |
| 1965 | 11.8 | 8.6 | 8.2 | 6.3 | 5.2 | 4.3 | 4.2 | 3.8 | 3.5 |
| 1966 | 13.0 | 9.1 | 8.7 | 6.7 | 4.9 | 4.4 | 3.6 | 4.0 | 4.0 |
| 1967 | 14.5 | 9.6 | 9.5 | 6.2 | 4.6 | 4.4 | 3.1 | 4.0 | 4.3 |
| 1968ᵃ | 16.5 | 10.5 | 9.7 | 5.9 | 4.5 | 4.6 | 2.8 | 3.9 | 4.4 |

ᵃ Estimate.

*Sources:* Reprinted with permission from the Aug. 6, 1956; Sept. 29, 1958; Jan. 2, 1967; and Sept. 9, 1968, issues of *Advertising Age.*
Copyright 1968 by Advertising Publications Inc.: *Marketing/Communications,* January 1968, p. 28; January 1969, p. 27.

## MARKETING ECONOMICS?

The other major explanation for concentration in the industry is economics of scale in marketing. Greer[1] studied the concentration trend from 1940 to 1968. He cites the data given in Tables 4, 5, 6, and 7.

He compared the marketing and production economics of scale and came to these conclusions:

**1** Economics of scale in production is not a crucial element in the concentration (as of 1968).

**2** Market shares have increased because of the intensity of advertising of the firms on the rise. There is no direct relation: increased advertising equals increased sales and profits, however.

**3** There has been an escalation in advertising by those growing. Much of this may be overkill or wasted advertising.

**4** Once concentration of the industry is moderately high, advertising as a percent of sales will level off, then decline.

Harry McMahon[2] agrees with point 3. He contends that overexpenditure on advertising, frequent changing of agencies, and no continuity in the campaigns hurt Ballantine, Piels, Rheingold, Jax, Rainier, Miller, Hamm's, and Falstaff. With regard to Falstaff, he said:

Falstaff, out in the Midwest, continues to slip as it goes from agency to agency, and each campaign has changed the sales futures to worse. This current campaign is geared, the present agency insists, to the 18–34 market. In view of the fact that Falstaff's longtime market is now all well past 34 and slightly at odds with the youth approach of today's Falstaff advertising, perhaps this suggests further dislocation of the image. What should be a holding operation isn't. . . .

---

[1] Douglas Greer, "Product Differentiation and Concentration in the Brewing Industry," *Journal of Industrial Economics,* **19** (3):201–219, 1971.
[2] Harry McMahon, "Beer is One Industry Where Advertising Can Do Serious Harm," *Advertising Age,* Oct. 8, 1973.

**TABLE 4 ■ THE BREWING INDUSTRY: FIVE-FIRM AND TEN-FIRM CONCENTRATION RATIOS BASED ON QUANTITY OF SALES (barrels), 1940–1968**

| Year | Five-firm concentration ratio, % | Market share of the sixth to tenth ranked firms, % | Ten-firm concentration ratio, % |
|---|---|---|---|
| 1940 | 16.3 | 7.4 | 23.7 |
| 1945 | 18.3 | 8.4 | 26.7 |
| 1950 | 23.4 | 11.7 | 35.1 |
| 1951 | 25.1 | 12.1 | 37.2 |
| 1952 | 26.6 | 11.4 | 38.0 |
| 1953 | 25.4 | 12.7 | 38.1 |
| 1954 | 24.9 | 13.4 | 38.3 |
| 1955 | 25.0 | 15.5 | 40.5 |
| 1956 | 25.5 | 16.1 | 41.6 |
| 1957 | 26.0 | 16.2 | 42.2 |
| 1958 | 28.5 | 16.7 | 45.2 |
| 1959 | 31.5 | 18.4 | 49.9 |
| 1960 | 32.6 | 18.8 | 51.4 |
| 1961 | 33.3 | 19.6 | 52.9 |
| 1962 | 35.4 | 19.6 | 55.0 |
| 1963 | 37.5 | 19.4 | 56.9 |
| 1964 | 38.3 | 19.4 | 57.7 |
| 1965 | 40.1 | 20.6 | 60.7 |
| 1966 | 42.4 | 20.5 | 62.9 |
| 1967 | 44.4 | 20.9 | 65.3 |
| 1968[a] | 47.4 | 21.0 | 68.4 |

[a] Estimate.
*Sources:* Ko Ching Shih and C. Ying Shih, *American Brewing Industry and the Beer Market,* Brookfield, Wisconsin: W. A. Krueger Co., 1958, p. 56; Ira Horowitz and Ann R. Horowitz, "Firms in a Declining Market: The Brewing Case," *Journal of Industrial Economics,* XIII (March, 1965), p. 146; *Advertising Age,* January 2, 1967, p. 42; *Printers' Ink Marketing/Communications,* January 1968, p. 28; January 1969, p. 27.

**TABLE 5 ■ REGIONAL FOUR-FIRM CONCENTRATION RATIOS, BASED ON PRODUCTION,[a] 1950, 1958, AND 1963**

| Region | 1950 | 1958 | 1963 |
|---|---|---|---|
| New England | 61 | 81 | 88 |
| Middle Atlantic | 43 | 50 | 60 |
| East North Central | 42 | 53 | 76 |
| West North Central | 75 | 85 | 84 |
| South Atlantic | 60 | 69 | 80 |
| East South Central | 70 | 100 | 100 |
| West South Central | 66 | 90 | 97 |
| Pacific | 47 | 54 | 60 |

[a] The production basis means that these figures measure the share of regional production by the four largest firms with plants in the designated region. They thus overstate concentration that would be based on sales because there is much interregional sales penetration. For example, in 1950 the four-firm concentration ratio based on sales in Ohio, Michigan, and Wisconsin was 30 percent while the ratio based on production was 50 percent; in the region made up of Arkansas, Louisiana, and Texas these ratios were 53 and 71 percent respectively (limited firm data on sales are available in "1949–1950 Interstate Sales Data on 60 Leading Brewers," Research Company of America, New York, 1951). Despite the discrepancy, trends in the production ratio probably reflect those in sales.
*Sources: Brewing Industry Survey,* Research Company of America, 1951, 1958; U.S. Senate, Subcommittee on Antitrust and Monopoly of the Committee on the Judiciary, *Concentration Ratios in Manufacturing Industry, 1963,* Part 2, Washington, 1967, p. 319.

**TABLE 6 ▪ MEASURED MEDIA ADVERTISING EXPENDITURE (DOLLARS) PER BARREL OF SALES FOR NINE LEADING FIRMS, 1949–1967**
(The media are general magazines, newspapers, and radio, network and spot TV and outdoor.)

| Year | A-B | Schlitz | Pabst | Falstaff | Carling | Schaefer | Ballantine | Hamm | Miller |
|------|-----|---------|-------|----------|---------|----------|------------|------|--------|
| 1949 | $0.26 | $0.33 | $0.48 | $0.21 | n.a. | $0.26 | $0.24 | $0.37 | $0.31 |
| 1950 | 0.30 | 0.34 | 0.63 | 0.17 | n.a. | 0.20 | 0.22 | 0.52 | 0.32 |
| 1951 | 0.34 | 0.41 | 0.72 | 0.10 | n.a. | 0.25 | 0.39 | 0.61 | 0.40 |
| 1952 | 0.28 | 0.37 | 0.73 | 0.34 | n.a. | 0.36 | 0.61 | 0.31 | 0.40 |
| 1953 | 0.45 | 0.71 | 0.73 | 0.41 | n.a. | 0.25 | 0.52 | 0.38 | 0.62 |
| 1954 | 1.17 | 1.35 | 1.18 | 0.83 | n.a. | 0.61 | 0.73 | 0.85 | 1.64 |
| 1955 | 0.98 | 1.29 | 0.97 | 0.71 | $0.16 | 0.58 | 0.40 | 1.17 | 0.77 |
| 1956 | 1.16 | 1.45 | 1.99 | 1.13 | 0.93 | 0.82 | 0.86 | 1.06 | 1.64 |
| 1957 | 1.60 | 1.77 | 1.60 | 1.25 | 0.59 | 0.86 | 0.97 | 1.16 | 1.44 |
| 1958 | 1.47 | 1.31 | 1.26 | 1.16 | 0.83 | 1.19 | 0.83 | 1.19 | 1.45 |
| 1959 | 1.38 | 1.27 | 0.89 | 1.14 | 0.87 | 0.96 | 0.67 | 1.25 | 1.32 |
| 1960 | 1.40 | 1.77 | 1.08 | 1.10 | 0.98 | 0.74 | 0.72 | 1.40 | 1.59 |
| 1961 | 1.47 | 2.21 | 0.99 | 1.11 | 0.99 | 0.68 | 0.79 | 1.08 | 0.88 |
| 1962 | 1.46 | 2.07 | 1.17 | 1.53 | 1.07 | 0.77 | 0.98 | 1.07 | 0.98 |
| 1963 | 1.71 | 2.07 | 1.31 | 1.60 | 1.20 | 0.70 | 0.95 | 1.52 | 1.09 |
| 1964 | 1.59 | 2.22 | 1.29 | 2.00 | 1.98 | 1.02 | 1.29 | 1.59 | 1.68 |
| 1965 | 1.38 | 1.80 | 1.10 | 2.05 | 0.88 | 1.04 | 1.49 | 1.36 | 1.59 |
| 1966 | 0.98 | 1.82 | 1.04 | 1.68 | 1.72 | 1.25 | 1.74 | 1.35 | 1.82 |
| 1967 | 1.09 | 1.59 | 0.84 | 1.25 | 2.02 | 0.91 | 1.40 | 1.71 | 1.09 |

*Source:* Reprinted with permission from the August 6, 1956; September 29, 1958; January 2, 1967; and September 9, 1968, issues of *Advertising Age.* Copyright 1968 by Advertising Publications Inc.

**TABLE 7 ▪ LIQUORS: RATIO OF SHARE OF TOTAL INDUSTRY ADVERTISING EXPENDITURE TO SHARE OF TOTAL INDUSTRY SALES BY LARGEST ASSET SIZE CLASSES, 1947–1966**
Number of firms in parentheses to the left of each ratio

| Year | $100 million or more | $50–$100 million | $25–$50 million | $10–$25 million |
|------|----------------------|------------------|-----------------|-----------------|
| 1947 | . . . . | (3) 0.54 | (19) 1.04 | |
| 1949 | . . . . | (3) 0.59 | (24) 1.09 | |
| 1950 | (1) 0.96 | (2) 0.59 | (27) 1.03 | |
| 1951 | (2) 0.87 | (1) 0.14 | (27) 1.03 | |
| 1952 | n.a. | n.a. | n.a. | |
| 1953 | (2) 0.87 | (1) 0.18 | (33) 1.09 | |
| 1954 | (3) 0.90 | (1) 1.21 | (7) 1.32 | (27) 0.87 |
| 1955 | (2) 1.00 | (2) 1.24 | (10) 1.07 | (21) 0.94 |
| 1956 | (2) 1.02 | (3) 1.30 | (8) 1.02 | (24) 0.90 |
| 1957 | (2) 1.08 | (5) 1.28 | (6) 0.96 | (24) 0.89 |
| 1958 | (3) 1.05 | (4) 1.23 | (7) 0.91 | (22) 0.92 |
| 1959 | (3) 1.12 | (5) 1.27 | (6) 0.87 | (24) 1.03 |
| 1960 | (3) 1.07 | (5) 1.29 | (7) 0.85 | (24) 0.96 |
| 1961 | (3) 1.13 | (6) 1.16 | (5) 0.98 | (24) 1.01 |
| 1962 | n.a. | n.a. | n.a. | n.a. |
| 1963 | (3) 1.15 | (7) 1.13 | (7) 1.07 | (20) 0.98 |
| 1964 | (3) 0.97 | (8) 1.13 | (6) 0.97 | (22) 1.03 |
| 1965 | (5) 0.90 | (7) 1.31 | (9) 1.00 | (21) 1.03 |
| 1966[a] | (5) 0.85 | (6) 1.26 | (8) 1.17 | (20) 0.94 |

[a] Preliminary.
*Source:* U.S. Internal Revenue Service, *Source Book of Statistics of Income.* Note: By their nature these numbers do not greatly diverge from unity, but, because of possible reporting errors little weight should be placed on very small variances on either side of one.

*Advertising Age* has provided us with the advertising costs of the leading beers in Table 8. Despite brewers' protestations (and those of some consumers), most American beers taste pretty much alike. It is the beer's image that sells the product. Research tends to indicate that experienced beer drinkers, with established brand preferences, cannot distinguish among unlabeled

## TABLE 8 ■ ADVERTISING COSTS FOR BEER, ALE, AND MALT LIQUOR[a]

| Brewer and brands | Five-media total[b] | | | | | | | | |
|---|---|---|---|---|---|---|---|---|---|
| | 1972 | 1972 | 1971 | 1970 | 1970 | 1969 | 1968 | 1967 | 1966 |
| *Anheuser-Busch Inc. (Budweiser, Budweiser malt liquor, Michelob, Busch Bavarian)* | | | | | | | | | |
| 1000 barrels sold | 26,522 | 26,522 | 24,309 | 22,202 | 22,202 | 18,700 | 18,400 | 15,500 | 13,600 |
| Ad investment | $25,025,606 | $24,737,600 | $23,715,800 | $18,466,465 | $18,686,798 | $16,057,638 | $14,609,872 | $16,980,767 | $13,366,805 |
| Ad cost per barrel | 94¢ | 93¢ | 98¢ | 83¢ | 84¢ | 86¢ | 79¢ | $1.09 | 98¢ |
| Ad cost per case | 6.7¢ | 6.6¢ | 7¢ | 5.9¢ | 6¢ | 6.1¢ | 5.6¢ | 7.8¢ | 7¢ |
| *Jos. Schlitz Brewing Co. (Schlitz, Schlitz malt liquor, Old Milwaukee, Primo, Encore, Red White & Blue)* | | | | | | | | | |
| 1000 barrels sold | 18,906 | 18,906 | 16,708 | 15,129 | 15,129 | 13,700 | 11,602[c] | 10,220 | 9,450 |
| Ad investment | $20,699,446 | $20,546,600 | $17,165,900 | $16,412,600 | $16,703,792 | $16,423,556 | $17,556,628 | $16,311,026 | $17,162,777 |
| Ad cost per barrel | $1.09 | $1.07 | $1.03 | $1.08 | $1.10 | $1.20 | $1.51 | $1.59 | $1.82 |
| Ad cost per case | 7.8¢ | 7.6¢ | 7.4¢ | 7.7¢ | 7.9¢ | 8.5¢ | 11¢ | 11¢ | 13¢ |
| *Pabst Brewing Co. (Pabst, Blue Ribbon malt liquor, Andeker Supreme, Eastside lager)* | | | | | | | | | |
| 1000 barrels sold | 12,600 | 12,600 | 11,797 | 10,517 | 10,517[d] | 10,225[e] | 10,910 | 10,050 | 9,047 |
| Ad investment | $6,128,132 | $6,053,200 | $6,596,400 | $6,212,740 | $6,426,593 | $5,217,352 | $8,527,808 | $8,473,773 | $9,428,233 |
| Ad cost per barrel | 49¢ | 48¢ | 56¢ | 59¢ | 61¢ | 51¢ | 78¢ | 84¢ | $1.04 |
| Ad cost per case | 3.5¢ | 3.4¢ | 4¢ | 4.2¢ | 4.4¢ | 3.6¢ | 5.6¢ | 6¢ | 7.4¢ |
| *Adolph Coors Co. (Coors)* | | | | | | | | | |
| 1000 barrels sold | 9,785 | 9,785 | 8,525 | 7,277 | 7,277 | 6,350 | 5,333 | 4,600 | 4,005 |
| Ad investment | $1,902,409 | $1,862,800 | $1,862,800 | $1,762,000 | $1,762,000 | $1,021,328 | $786,316 | $1,216,706 | $727,481 |
| Ad cost per barrel | 19¢ | 19¢ | 22¢ | 24¢ | 24¢ | 16¢ | 15¢ | 26¢ | 18.1¢ |
| Ad cost per case | 1.4¢ | 1.4¢ | 1.6¢ | 1.7¢ | 1.7¢ | 1.1¢ | 1.1¢ | 1.9¢ | 1.2¢ |
| *Falstaff Brewing Co. (Falstaff, Krueger, Narragansett, Ballantine ale and beer)* | | | | | | | | | |
| 1000 barrels sold | 6,200[f] | 6,200 | 6,200 | 5,386 | 5,386 | 6,200 | 6,300 | 6,632 | 7,000 |
| Ad investment | $5,135,920 | $4,949,800 | $6,324,300 | $7,889,600 | $8,136,798 | $6,565,067 | $8,466,961 | $8,337,100 | $11,769,198 |
| Ad cost per barrel | 83¢ | 80¢ | $1.23 | $1.46 | $1.48 | $1.06 | $1.34 | $1.25 | $1.68 |
| Ad cost per case | 5.9¢ | 5.7¢ | 8.8¢ | 10.4¢ | 10.6¢ | 7.6¢ | 9.6¢ | 8.9¢ | 12¢ |
| *F. & M. Schaefer Brewing Co. (Schaefer)* | | | | | | | | | |
| 1000 barrels sold | 5,530 | 5,530 | 5,600 | 5,749 | 5,749 | 5,450 | 5,050 | 4,850 | 4,576 |
| Ad investment | $4,884,833 | $4,561,700 | $6,069,300 | $6,583,600 | $6,928,691 | $4,449,433 | $4,796,945 | $4,423,425 | $5,731,248 |
| Ad cost per barrel | 88¢ | 82¢ | $1.08 | $1.15 | $1.20 | 87¢ | 95¢ | 91¢ | $1.25 |
| Ad cost per case | 6.3¢ | 5.9¢ | 7.7¢ | 8.2¢ | 8.6¢ | 6.2¢ | 6.8¢ | 6.5¢ | 8.9¢ |
| *Miller Brewing Co. (Miller High Life, Gettelman, Miller malt liquor, Meister Brau, Lite)* | | | | | | | | | |
| 1000 barrels sold | 5,400[g] | 5,400 | 5,200 | 5,150 | 5,150 | 5,190 | 4,850 | 4,575 | 4,150 |
| Ad investment | $11,079,707 | $11,014,600 | $13,468,300 | $10,850,600 | $10,927,735 | $9,483,172 | $8,901,219 | $8,829,471 | $7,563,713 |
| Ad cost per barrel | $2.05 | $2.04 | $2.59 | $2.11 | $2.12 | $2.12 | $1.83 | $1.92 | $1.82 |
| Ad cost per case | 14.6¢ | 14.6¢ | 18.5¢ | 15.1¢ | 15.1¢ | 13.1¢ | 13¢ | 14¢ | 13¢ |
| *Stroh Brewing Co. (Stroh's)* | | | | | | | | | |
| 1000 barrels sold | 4,231 | 4,231 | 3,676 | 3,276 | 3,276 | 2,939 | 2,536 | 2,403 | 2,440 |
| Ad investment | $4,525,348 | $4,448,300 | $4,407,700 | $3,798,478 | $3,882,200 | $2,465,669 | $3,648,641 | $3,791,655 | $4,521,995 |
| Ad cost per barrel | $1.07 | $1.05 | $1.20 | $1.16 | $1.19 | 84¢ | $1.44 | $1.57 | $1.87 |
| Ad cost per case | 7.6¢ | 6¢ | 8.6¢ | 8.3¢ | 8.5¢ | 6¢ | 10¢ | 11¢ | 13.2¢ |

## TABLE 8 ■ ADVERTISING COSTS FOR BEER, ALE, AND MALT LIQUOR^a (Continued)

| Brewer and brands | Five-media total^b | | | | | | | | |
|---|---|---|---|---|---|---|---|---|---|
| | 1966 | 1967 | 1968 | 1969 | 1970 | 1970 | 1971 | 1972 | 1972 |
| **Carling Brewing Co. (Black Label, Red Cap-ale, Heidelberg beer, ale and light pilsner, Canadian Gold, Carlsberg, Stag, Tuborg)** | | | | | | | | | |
| 1000 barrels sold | 5,100 | 4,900 | 5,020 | 5,440 | 5,000 | 5,000 | 4,535 | 4,200 | 4,200 |
| Ad investment | $8,747,964 | $9,918,132 | $6,703,024 | $5,109,909 | $6,487,200 | $6,384,400 | $8,242,600 | $5,642,325 | $5,868,203 |
| Ad cost per barrel | $1.72 | $2.02 | $1.33 | 94¢ | $1.30 | $1.28 | $1.82 | $1.34 | $1.40 |
| Ad cost per case | 12.2¢ | 14¢ | 9.5¢ | 6.7¢ | 9.3¢ | 9.1¢ | 13¢ | 7.5¢ | 10¢ |
| **Theodore Hamm Co. (Hamm's, Waldech, Burgermeister)** | | | | | | | | | |
| 1000 barrels sold | 4,210 | 4,311 | 4,311 | 4,180 | 4,045 | 4,045 | 3,700 | 3,800 | 3,800 |
| Ad investment | $5,669,322 | $7,402,766 | $4,774,494 | $3,791,764 | $5,976,930 | $5,962,900 | $6,687,500 | $2,737,200 | $2,748,198 |
| Ad cost per barrel | $1.35 | $1.71 | $1.11 | 91¢ | $1.48 | $1.47 | $1.81 | 72¢ | 72¢ |
| Ad cost per case | 9.6¢ | 12¢ | 7.9¢ | 6.5¢ | 10.6¢ | 10.5¢ | 12.9¢ | 5.1¢ | 5.1¢ |
| **G. Heileman Brewing Co. (Blatz, Old Style, Drewry's, Pfeiffer, Sterling, Weidemann, Kingsbury, Mickey's malt liquor, Jacob Schmidt)** | | | | | | | | | |
| 1000 barrels sold | 1,041 | 1,310 | 1,726 | 2,298 | 3,000 | 3,000 | 2,820 | 3,645 | 3,645^h |
| Ad investment | $753,630 | $1,244,400 | $890,800 | $2,854,250 | $3,534,400 | $3,534,400 | $3,710,700 | $5,115,700 | $5,146,090 |
| Ad cost per barrel | 72.4¢ | 94¢ | 52¢ | $1.24 | $1.18 | $1.18 | $1.32 | $1.40 | $1.41 |
| Ad cost per case | 5.2¢ | 6.7¢ | 3.7¢ | 8.8¢ | 8.4¢ | 8.4¢ | 9.4¢ | 10¢ | 10¢ |
| **Olympia Brewing Co. (Olympia)** | | | | | | | | | |
| 1000 barrels sold | 2,660 | 2,866 | 3,074 | 3,350 | 3,379 | 3,379 | 3,094 | 3,330 | 3,330 |
| Ad investment | $3,032,145 | $3,418,707 | $3,483,678 | $3,215,219 | $4,389,710 | $4,317,900 | $4,332,900 | $3,330,900 | $3,417,865 |
| Ad cost per barrel | $1.14 | $1.19 | $1.13 | 96¢ | $1.30 | $1.28 | $1.40 | $1.00 | $1.03 |
| Ad cost per case | 8.1¢ | 8.5¢ | 8.1¢ | 6.8¢ | 9.3¢ | 9.1¢ | 10¢ | 7.1¢ | 7.4¢ |
| **C. Schmidt & Sons (Schmidt's, Prior)** | | | | | | | | | |
| 1000 barrels sold | 2,578 | 2,660 | 2,816 | 2,941 | 3,040 | 3,040 | 3,162 | 3,194 | 3,194 |
| Ad investment | $2,053,430 | $2,079,671 | $2,706,194 | $2,355,563 | $2,936,100 | $2,936,100 | $2,674,700 | $2,143,000 | $2,167,398 |
| Ad cost per barrel | 79.6¢ | 78¢ | 96¢ | 80¢ | 97¢ | 97¢ | 85¢ | 67¢ | 68¢ |
| Ad cost per case | 5.6¢ | 5.5¢ | 6.8¢ | 5.7¢ | 6.9¢ | 6.9¢ | 6.1¢ | 4.8¢ | 4.9¢ |
| **Rheingold Corp. (Rheingold, Knickerbocker, Ruppert, Gablinger's)** | | | | | | | | | |
| 1000 barrels sold | 4,000 | 3,600 | 3,400 | 3,570 | 3,417 | 3,417 | 3,525 | 3,150 | 3,150 |
| Ad investment | $5,176,087 | $6,944,601 | $2,209,107 | $2,818,718 | $3,853,216 | $3,724,200 | $3,829,300 | $2,242,100 | $2,386,537 |
| Ad cost per barrel | $1.29 | $1.92 | 65¢ | 79¢ | $1.07 | $1.09 | $1.09 | 71¢ | 76¢ |
| Ad cost per case | 9.2¢ | 13¢ | 4.6¢ | 5.6¢ | 7.6¢ | 7.8¢ | 7.8¢ | 5.1¢ | 5.4¢ |
| **National Brewing Co. (Altes, National Premium, National Bohemian ale and beer, Regal, A-1, Colt .45 malt liquor, Malt Duck)** | | | | | | | | | |
| 1000 barrels sold | 2,009 | 2,082 | 2,138 | 2,218 | 2,262 | 2,262 | 2,202 | 2,154 | 2,154 |
| Ad investment | $3,286,869 | $3,454,728 | $3,535,689 | $3,055,322 | $3,398,796 | $3,359,400 | $3,678,900 | $3,073,700 | $3,182,992 |
| Ad cost per barrel | $1.64 | $1.65 | $1.65 | $1.38 | $1.50 | $1.49 | $1.67 | $1.43 | $1.48 |
| Ad cost per case | 11.6¢ | 11¢ | 11¢ | 9.8¢ | 10.7¢ | 10.6¢ | 11.9¢ | 10.2¢ | 10.6¢ |

*Genesee Brewing Co. (Genesee beer and ale, Fyfe & Drum)*

| | | | | | | | | |
|---|---|---|---|---|---|---|---|---|
| 1000 barrels sold | 1,370 | 1,430 | 1,440 | 1,445 | 1,475 | 1,575 | 1,725 | 1,725 |
| Ad investment | $1,856,784 | $2,111,866 | $1,359,655 | $1,327,440 | $1,614,500 | $2,185,700 | $2,284,601 | $2,284,601 |
| Ad cost per barrel | $1.35 | $1.47 | 94¢ | 92¢ | $1.09 | $1.39 | $1.32 | $1.32 |
| Ad cost per case | 9.7¢ | 10¢ | 6.7¢ | 6.6¢ | 7.8¢ | 9.9¢ | 9.4¢ | 9.4¢ |

*Pearl Brewing Co. (Pearl Premium, Light, Texas Pride, Country Club malt liquor)*

| | | | | | | | | |
|---|---|---|---|---|---|---|---|---|
| 1000 barrels sold | 1,794 | 1,800 | 1,827 | 1,909 | 1,712 | 1,712 | 1,656 | 1,689 |
| Ad investment | $3,010,424 | $3,411,179 | $2,765,646 | $1,656,902 | $2,671,414 | $2,575,400 | $2,159,700 | $2,921,100 |
| Ad cost per barrel | $1.68 | $1.89 | $1.51 | 87¢ | $1.56 | $1.50 | $1.30 | $1.73 |
| Ad cost per case | 12¢ | 13¢ | 11¢ | 6.2¢ | 11.1¢ | 10.1¢ | 9.3¢ | 12.4¢ |

*General Brewing (Lucky Lager, Draft, Brew 102, Regal Select)*

| | | | | | | | | |
|---|---|---|---|---|---|---|---|---|
| 1000 barrels sold | 1,750 | 1,710 | 1,515 | 1,303 | 1,120 | ... | 1,265ʲ | 1,265 |
| Ad investment | $1,813,783 | $1,622,331 | $1,505,500 | $292,200 | $1,431,754 | ... | $277,816 | $217,300 |
| Ad cost per barrel | $1.04 | 94¢ | 99¢ | 22¢ | $1.28 | ... | 22¢ | 22¢ |
| Ad cost per case | 7.4¢ | 6.7¢ | 7.1¢ | 1.6¢ | 9.1¢ | ... | 1.6¢ | 1.6¢ |

*Grain Belt Breweries (Grain Belt, Storz and Storz tap)*

| | | | | | | | | |
|---|---|---|---|---|---|---|---|---|
| 1000 barrels sold | 1,285 | 1,065 | 1,156 | 1,250 | 1,262 | 1,262 | 1,220 | 1,120 |
| Ad investment | $1,128,514 | $281,345 | $140,300 | $374,200 | $530,600 | $530,600 | $454,100 | $516,900 |
| Ad cost per barrel | 87.8¢ | 26¢ | 12¢ | 30¢ | 42¢ | 42¢ | 37¢ | 46¢ |
| Ad cost per case | 6.3¢ | 1.8¢ | 0.9¢ | 2.1¢ | 3¢ | 3¢ | 2.6¢ | 3.9¢ |

*Lone Star Brewing Co. (Lone Star beer and lager)*

| | | | | | | | | |
|---|---|---|---|---|---|---|---|---|
| 1000 barrels sold | 1,194 | 1,183 | 1,186 | 1,127 | 1,127 | 1,066 | 1,068 | 1,068 |
| Ad investment | $712,389 | $414,011 | $617,972 | $623,862 | $559,000 | $1,000,500 | $648,100 | $648,100 |
| Ad cost per barrel | 59¢ | 35¢ | 52¢ | 55¢ | 50¢ | 94¢ | 61¢ | 61¢ |
| Ad cost per case | 4.2¢ | 2.5¢ | 3.7¢ | 3.9¢ | 3.6¢ | 6.7¢ | 4.4¢ | 4.4¢ |

*Pittsburgh Brewing Co. (Iron City, Hop N Gator beer, DuBois, Cloud 9 malt liquor)*

| | | | | | | | | |
|---|---|---|---|---|---|---|---|---|
| 1000 barrels sold | 1,285 | ... | ... | 1,000 | 1,075 | 1,075 | 1,145 | 1,008 |
| Ad investment | $1,128,514 | ... | ... | $600,791 | $721,747 | $671,800 | $1,064,600 | $644,200 |
| Ad cost per barrel | 87.8¢ | ... | ... | 60¢ | 67¢ | 62¢ | 93¢ | 64¢ |
| Ad cost per case | 6.3¢ | ... | ... | 4.3¢ | 4.8¢ | 4.4¢ | 6.6¢ | 4.6¢ |

a Sales of brewers whose 1972 output exceeded 1 million barrels related to the amount invested by each in general magazines, spot radio, network and spot TV, newspapers and outdoor. These figures are not offered as complete records of expenditures; brewers spent large sums in point of purchase materials and other nonmeasured media (including newspapers, in 1971). Sales figures were taken from *Beer Wholesalers' News*, the monthly bulletin of the National Beer Wholesaler Assn. of America, copyright 1973. Expenditures were compiled from figures supplied by Leading National Advertisers: Radio Expenditure Reports; Broadcast Advertisers Reports; Institute of Outdoor Advertising, and Newspaper Advertising Bureau (compiled by Media Records). Copyright 1973 by Crain Communications Inc.

b Second three columns based on five-media totals, excluding newspaper expenditures, to enable comparison of 1972, 1971, and 1970 ad spendings.

c Excludes sales of Puerto Rico subsidiary, estimated 126,000 barrels, and estimated 175,000 barrels of Spanish subsidiaries.

d Includes Pabst brands only. Blatz brand produced by Pabst (311,000 barrels in 1970) is included in Heileman figures.

e Includes 993,000 barrels Blatz sold prior to Sept. 2, 1969. Sales after that date counted in Heileman totals.

f Includes P. Ballantine & Sons brands.

g Bought Meister Brau Inc. brands in 1971.

h Includes several brands of Associated Brewing.

i Acquired Drewry's in 1965.

j Includes Lucky Lager, Maier brands.

brands of beer.[3] Another study suggests that beer pricing policy connotes images as well (higher price = higher quality).[4] This is one reason why beer producers shy away from launching new brand names of their own. One brewery president indicated that he knew of no new brand introduced since the 1930s that has made money.

Sponsoring sporting events is a typical advertising strategy for the brewers. For years U.S. brewers have looked on the heavy beer drinker as a blue-collar worker in his twenties or thirties, and a sports fan. Nationally Schlitz claims to be the number one sponsor of televised professional baseball. Schaefer, an Eastern U.S. brewer, sponsors a package of sporting events from basketball, hockey, and football to horse racing and Madison Square Garden prizefights.

A significant new trend is the sponsorship of special festivals and concerts, an approach beamed at the young people who are "our most important market, because brand loyalty in this business tends to have a long life." Some firms are running ads directed at women. The U.S. Brewers Association estimates the percentage of women who drink beer is 40 percent compared to 65 percent of men; and women who do drink beer drink far less than men.

### PRICING AND FINANCING

The price of beer varies geographically. It tends to vary with the cost position of those serving the market. Price competition can be sharp, particularly during periods of strikes. Price generally has been used to enter new markets. This has been especially true for the national distributors, who, because of highly automated large plants, have been in a better cost position to use this means with little detriment to overall profits. This territorial pricing without cost justification has come under attack from the federal government as have vertical pricing arrangements whereby firms require distributors to maintain certain price levels. In certain areas, local and regional producers have been able to maintain a lower price position and have successfully kept out new

---

[3] Ralph I. Allison and Kenneth P. Uhl, "Influence of Beer Brand Identification on Taste Perception," *Journal of Marketing Research,* August 1965, pp. 36–39.

[4] J. Douglas McConnell, "An Experimental Examination of the Price-Quality Relationship," *Journal of Business,* October 1968, pp. 439–444.

TABLE 9 ■ WHOLESALE PRICE INDEXES FOR BEER

|  | 12-ounce beer can | Beer bottles | |
|---|---|---|---|
|  |  | Returnable | Nonreturnable |
| 1970 | 111.8 | . . . . | 112.5 |
| 1969 | 107.1 | . . . . | 108.6 |
| 1968 | 102.8 | . . . . | 105.2 |
| 1967 | 100.0 | . . . . | 100.0 |
| 1966 | 99.9 | 89.9 | |
| 1965 | 97.5 | 93.4 | |
| 1964 | 95.5 | 92.6 | |
| 1963 | 95.9 | 94.2 | |
| 1962 | 95.3 | 94.7 | |
| 1961 | 94.6 | 99.6 | |

1967 = 100; 12/66 = 100

competition because of the compactness of their marketing territory. Whole-sale price indexes in the aggregate are presented as Table 9.

Tables 10 and 11 give some recent analyses of some of the leading brewers' financial and stock performance from Standard and Poor's data.

## Ecology and the brewing industry

One factor which may affect the brewing industry in the future is the concern for ecology. The environmental groups feel that the nonreturnable containers used by most brewers as major packaging contribute to litter and damage the environment. Some states and municipalities have passed laws against non-returnables or require deposits on beverage containers (e.g., Oregon, Vermont). The industry commissioned a study to examine the litter problem created by nonrefillable containers. The study indicated that a ban on non-returnable containers would reduce only 1.37 percent of total municipal solid waste, and that a ban would result in a total tax loss of $803 million. This loss would be severe compared to the $209 million cost of pickup and disposal of these containers.

Despite this, brewers continue to be pressured to find suitable containers. Users of aluminum cans assert that these are more suitable owing to relative efficiency of recycling. Proponents of steel containers contend that these are better ecologically because they can be extracted magnetically from solid waste. However, pressure will continue for development and use of biodegrad-able containers. The United States Brewers Association initiated a nationwide antilitter campaign to improve public relations. The main theme for the cam-paign was "Litter Is a Slap in America's Face" with a supporting line en-couraging people to "Pitch In." Firms within the industry may also be affected by pollution problems resulting from operations. The problem is serious to brewers since the packaging machines are set for nonreturnables and cannot handle returnable bottles. It could take 5 years to convert to returnables, one industry specialist has estimated.

The most recent incident is hearings in the U.S. Senate "on a bill which could result in banning the non-returnable container to make a tidier America. This would cost the individual brewers hundreds of millions of dollars. . . . The economic dislocations and unemployment which would result from a switch back to returnable bottles [might be large]. Consumers would pay more. Oregonians, for example, who currently must deposit a nickel on a non-returnable and two-cents on a returnable, also pay 60 to 70 cents a case more than the rest of the nation."

## Beer and cancer?

A study by Dr. James Enstrom, School of Public Health, University of Cali-fornia, Los Angeles, and Dr. Norman Breslow, University of Washington, was released to the press recently. Studying beer consumption and deaths caused

TABLE 10 ■ STATISTICAL POSITION OF COMMON STOCKS IN THE BREWERS INDUSTRY[a]

| | | Interim or annual operating data | | | | | | | | Annual earnings[b] | | | | | $ Divs. per sh. | | | | | |
| | | Gross sales[c] | | | Net income[c] | | | Earns. $ per sh. | | $ per share | | | | | | | | | Price | |
| Brewers | No. of months | 1973 | 1974 | Percent change | 1973 | 1974 | Percent change | 1973 | 1974 | Year ends | 1970 | 1971 | 1972 | 1973 | Paid 1973 | Indic. rate[d] | 1974 price range | 7-18-74 price | earns. ratio[e] | Yields %[f] |
|---|---|---|---|---|---|---|---|---|---|---|---|---|---|---|---|---|---|---|---|---|
| Anheuser-Busch | 3 Mar. | 248.9 | 299.8 | +20.4 | 18.40 | 12.60 | −31.5 | 0.41 | 0.28 | Dec. | 1.40 | 1.60 | 1.70 | 1.46 | 0.60 | 0.60 | 37 3/8 – 27 1/2 | 36 1/2 | 25.0 | 1.6 |
| Falstaff Brewing[g] | 3 Mar. | 39.1 | 39.3 | + 0.5 | 1.14[h] | 0.99[h] | . . . | 0.25[h] | 0.22[h] | Dec. | 0.27 | 0.31 | 1.35[h] | 1.30[h] | Nil | Nil | 3 1/2 – 2 | 2 5/8 | . . . | Nil |
| Heileman (G) Brewing[g] | 3 Mar. | 38.4 | 35.9 | − 6.5 | 1.25 | 0.76 | −39.2 | 0.33 | 0.20 | Dec. | 1.37 | 1.42 | 1.51 | 1.57 | 0.48 | 0.49 | 10 7/8 – 7 1/4 | 7 1/2 | 4.7 | 6.5 |
| Olympia Brewing | 3 Mar. | 28.4 | 33.0 | +16.2 | 0.41 | 0.36 | −12.2 | 0.20 | 0.17 | Dec. | 2.35 | 1.62 | 1.61 | 1.69 | 1.20 | 1.20 | 17 1/4 – 11 3/4 | 14 3/4 | 8.7 | 8.1 |
| Pabst Brewing | 3 Mar. | 109.2 | 107.8 | − 1.3 | 6.49 | 2.61 | −59.8 | 0.68 | 0.28 | Dec. | 2.44 | 2.66 | 2.99 | 2.51 | 0.86 | 0.88 | 24 5/8 – 11 1/4 | 15 | 5.9 | 5.9 |
| Schaefer (F. & M.)[g] | 3 Mar. | 51.2 | 55.3 | + 8.0 | 0.82[h] | 0.74[h] | . . . | 0.44[h] | 0.40[h] | Dec. | 2.21 | 1.75 | 0.55[h] | 0.51 | Nil | Nil | 8 1/4 – 4 | 4 3/8 | 8.5 | Nil |
| Schlitz (Jos.) Brewing[g] | 6 June | 345.1[i] | 401.6[i] | +16.4 | 28.45 | 31.06 | + 9.2 | 0.98 | 1.07 | Dec. | 1.04 | 1.22 | 1.58 | 1.90 | 0.588 | 0.68 | 57 1/2 – 42 1/4 | 46 1/2 | 24.4 | 1.5 |

[a] Adjusted wherever necessary for stock splits and stock dividends.
[b] Based on primary earns.
[c] In millions of dollars.
[d] Based on latest quarterly dividend.
[e] Based on 1972–3 or 1973 earns.

[f] Based on indicated rate.
[g] N.Y.S.E.
[h] Deficit.
[i] Incl. extra.
[j] Plus stk.

Note: Net income and earnings per share are shown before special credits and special charges. Information has been obtained from sources believed to be reliable, but its accuracy and completeness, and that of the opinions based thereon, are not guaranteed.

**TABLE 11 ■ COMPOSITE INDUSTRY DATA**
Per share data based on Standard and Poor's group stock price indexes[a]

| | 1965 | 1966 | 1967 | 1968 | 1969 | 1970 | 1971 | 1972 |
|---|---|---|---|---|---|---|---|---|
| Sales | 113.1 | 120.8 | 65.01 | 68.49 | 77.47 | 82.82 | 91.82 | 101.97 |
| Operating income | 9.47 | 10.12 | 6.16 | 8.01 | 9.16 | 10.50 | 10.93 | 10.96 |
| Profit margins percent | 8.37 | 8.38 | 9.48 | 11.70 | 11.82 | 12.68 | 11.90 | 10.75 |
| Depreciation | 3.13 | 3.73 | 1.99 | 2.01 | 1.94 | 2.06 | 2.33 | 2.95 |
| Taxes | 2.03 | 2.15 | 2.04 | 3.26 | 3.65 | 3.74 | 3.63 | 3.39 |
| Earnings | 3.10 | 3.15 | 1.96 | 2.57 | 3.03 | 3.51 | 3.70 | 3.42 |
| Dividends | 1.28 | 1.34 | 1.27 | 1.26 | 1.38 | 1.23 | 1.32 | 1.42 |
| Earnings as a percent of sales | 2.74 | 2.61 | 3.01 | 3.75 | 3.91 | 4.24 | 4.03 | 3.35 |
| Dividends as a percent of earnings | 41.29 | 42.54 | 64.80 | 49.03 | 45.54 | 35.04 | 35.68 | 41.52 |
| Price (1941–43 = 10) | | | | | | | | |
| —high | 74.32 | 57.95 | 51.82 | 70.75 | 84.87 | 88.76 | 99.47 | 164.02 |
| —low | 48.37 | 36.85 | 39.38 | 43.64 | 59.19 | 60.60 | 70.17 | 97.50 |
| Price-earning ratios | | | | | | | | |
| —high | 23.97 | 18.40 | 26.44 | 27.53 | 28.01 | 25.29 | 26.88 | 47.96 |
| —low | 15.60 | 11.70 | 20.09 | 16.98 | 19.53 | 17.26 | 18.96 | 28.51 |
| Dividend yield percent | | | | | | | | |
| —high | 2.65 | 3.64 | 3.22 | 2.89 | 2.33 | 2.03 | 1.88 | 1.46 |
| —low | 1.72 | 2.31 | 2.45 | 1.78 | 1.63 | 1.39 | 1.33 | 0.87 |
| Book value | 29.43 | 27.44 | 24.66 | 25.41 | 26.82 | 24.19 | 26.33 | 27.03 |
| Return on book value, percent | 10.53 | 11.48 | 7.95 | 10.11 | 11.30 | 14.51 | 14.05 | 12.65 |
| Working capital[b] | 14.72 | 14.75 | 9.55 | 7.52 | 9.38 | 9.14 | 8.77 | 10.95 |
| Capital expenditures | 11.87 | 4.18 | 2.38 | 3.84 | R5.92 | 8.10 | 7.90 | 4.51 |

The companies used for this series of per share data are: Falstaff Brewing; Heileman (added 6–20–73); Schaefer (F. & M.) Corp. (added 3–18–70); and Schlitz (Jos.) Brewing. Associated Brewing was deleted 3–18–70. Rheingold was dropped 6–20–73.

[a] Per share data are expressed in terms of the S & P Stock Price Index, i.e., stock prices, 1941–43 = 10. Each of the items shown is first computed on a true per share basis for each company. Totals for each company are then reconstructed using the same number of shares outstanding as was used to compute our stock price index as of December 31. This is done because the shares used on December 31, although the latest known at the time, may differ from those reported in the annual reports which are not available for 6 or 8 weeks after the end of the year. The sum of these reconstructed totals is then related to the base period value used to compute the stock price index. As a double check, we relate the various items to the dividends as these are the most stable series. So, for example, if total sales amount to 15 times the total dividend payments, then with per share dividends at 3.50 the indicated per share sales will be (15 × 3.50) 52.50 in terms of the S & P Stock Price Index. For comparability between the various groups, all data are on a calendar year basis, corporate data being posted in the year in which most months fall. Fiscal years ending June 30 are posted in the calendar year in which the fiscal year ends.

[b] Current assets less current liabilities, without allowance for long-term debt.

by cancer in 41 states, they found a correlation between beer consumption and cancer. The strongest correlation was between beer consumption and cancer of the large intestine and rectum in men and women. Other correlations included cancer of the stomach and kidney in men and women, cancer of the bladder in men, and cancer of the small intestine, liver, and breast in women.

At this time, it is not known what effect, if any, this report will have on beer sales. Earlier publicized links between cancer and use or consumption of products have produced different sales effects. For example, on November 9, 1959, Secretary of Health, Education and Welfare Fleming announced that some cranberries grown in the states of Oregon and Washington had been sprayed with an insecticide which had been shown to cause cancer of the thyroid in rats. Even though this statement indicated that only some cranberries were affected, many stores halted sales of all cranberries and several states banned the sales of cranberries. As a result, by January 1960, the growers had sold only 381,000 barrels of their 1,252,000-barrel crop. The federal government purchased many of these barrels for school lunch, military, and similar programs and helped the industry merchandise its product. This it did in response to political and threatened legal action by the growers. It was several years before the cranberry industry returned to its "normal" sales trend.

Cigarettes are another product which has been affected by cancer correlations. Up until the surgeon general's report linking cigarettes and cancer in 1964, sales were increasing about 3 percent per year. Sales fell off after the report, and then began a slow rise in the late 1960s. Additional evidence in the late sixties led to sales declines again until 1971. During this period, TV stations were required to run "cigarettes cause cancer" ads in proportion to cigarette ad revenue. When the government banned the advertising, the "public service ads" stopped too. Total unit sales for cigarettes rose 2.5 percent in 1971 and have been rising at about that rate since. By 1974, cigarette sales per capita had returned to the pre-surgeon-general level.

## Production cost in brewing beer

Several factors have been affecting the production costs of beer. One is the cost of materials. Among the raw materials used, malt is the most important, and its price follows that of barley, the principal grain used in making malt. In the past, the price of barley and malt has been fairly stable. From 1964 until 1973, malt prices were less than in 1963, but they doubled from early 1973 to 1974. Some brewers produce their own malt.

Corn and corn products are next in importance to malt. The cost of corn grits went from 74 cents a barrel of beer in early 1973 to $1.43 in 1974. Brewers' rice also doubled during the period. Some of the causes of these price rises were U.S. dollar devaluation, harvest, and railcar problems. Thus, brewers may have high agricultural costs at least through 1975. Emmanuel Goldman, analyst at Sanford C. Bernstein Company, estimates the influence of agricultural cost on the costs and profits of brewers as follows (1974):

Every 50-cents per bushel rise in the price of malt, if it isn't recovered by a beer price increase, would affect per-share net of Anheuser-Busch 14.1 cents, Schlitz by 13.3 cents and Pabst by 24.8 cents. The price increases needed to offset this: 1.17% at Anheuser-Busch, 1.29% at Schlitz and 1.37% at Pabst.

Each $1 per-100-pound increase in rice costs would mean 6.5 cents a share at Anheuser-Busch which uses rice instead of corn; this could be neutralized by a 0.46% beer-price boost.

Every 50-cent-per-bushel increase in corn prices would mean 8.5 cents a share to Schlitz and 16.9 cents a share to Pabst; Schlitz would need a 0.64% price increase and Pabst a 0.68% boost as an offset.

Each 1% boost in can prices would mean 4.7 cents a share at Anheuser-Busch, 4.9 cents at Schlitz and 7.2 cents at Pabst. Beer-price increases of 0.33%, 0.37% and 0.29%, respectively, would make up those amounts.

Figure 2 charts the recent rises in grain prices.

Water has not been a problem for brewers as yet, but environmental factors may affect this in the future. Another item affecting the price of beer is

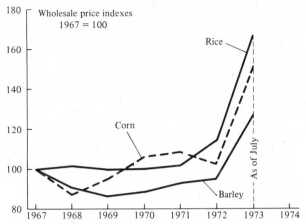

**FIGURE 2** ■ Wholesale grain prices. *Source:* Standard and Poor's, 1974.

containers. Figure 3 charts recent prices of the containers used most frequently by brewers.

In 1973 and 1974, nonreturnable glass bottles increased 10 percent and can prices are up 25 percent. Cans now cost more than bottles. Also going up is linerboard. Some brewers are trying to offset this by making their own cans. This can save a brewer $5 to $8 per thousand cans.

Two of the big three brewers are currently involved in manufacturing their own containers. Schlitz bought some of the front-running technical expertise of Coors. . . . Schlitz expects to supply . . . [80 percent] of its own can requirements within . . . ten years. Anheuser-Busch is using Jeffco, among others, as a supplier for its aluminum containers; Jeffco was the only other buyer of the Coors expertise.

Busch expects to be 50 percent self-sufficient in containers by 1980.

About 90 percent of beer is now sold in packages and only 10 percent is draft. Of this 90 percent, about 56 percent is sold in cans and 25 percent in returnable bottles. The rest is sold in nonreturnable bottles.

Packaging innovations over the past few years may have stimulated beer consumption. Disposable bottles, soft-top aluminum cans, tab-open cans, and small kegs of draught beer designed to fit into the home refrigerator are examples. A composite plastic-glass bottle may become a commercial reality. This is less likely to break and will allow brewers to double the speed of beer bottling lines which are now running at up to 700 to 800 bottles a minute.

Differentiation in packaging may sell beer too. Hamm's is striving to get its beer known as the one in the two-piece aluminum can. Carling introduced a squat, keg-shaped bottle. It was successful.

The final cost factor is the efficiency of the production process itself. Because beer production is basically a chemical process, labor costs are relatively low. Direct wages and salaries of the Big Three brewers amounted to roughly 20 percent of sales in 1969, making the industry capital-intensive. With industry concentration continuing to rely on highly automated plants, the labor-cost ratio for the leading brewers could decline somewhat despite rising wage rates.

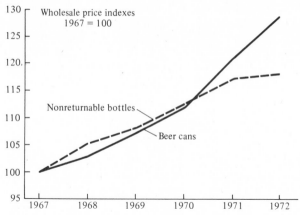

**FIGURE 3** ■ Beer container prices. *Source:* Standard and Poor's, 1974.

Some costs of production by various brewers are:

Schlitz—$1.08, industry's lowest

Anheuser-Busch—$3.08

Falstaff—$4.39 (1972)

There are some measurable differences in the cost of production. One estimate is that a firm must produce at least 1,500,000 barrels a year to be minimally effective. The brewers that are producing the most efficiently are closing older facilities and building large plants with the latest equipment. For example, in some of the newer Schlitz plants, the firm produces 1200 cans or 900 bottles per minutes. Older machinery produces 800 cans or 500 bottles per minute. The machinery allows lower labor costs, too. Thus in 1972, the new Schlitz breweries in Memphis and Winston-Salem had a capacity to produce 4,400,000 barrels per year each. Each employed 483 production workers.

This contrasts with Falstaff, in four older factories with a total capacity of 4,100,000 barrels, employing 1800 workers. The brewery workers are paid more per hour than any other workers except some in construction trades.

Another major cost differential is the length of time it takes to produce a barrel of beer. Budweiser takes 42 days to produce. Pabst takes 31 days. Falstaff's production time is close to Pabst's. Schlitz is 10 days shorter than Pabst, and this increases the capacity of the brewery and thus cuts unit costs. Busch is trying to cut its production time by 2 days.

Schlitz has led Anheuser-Busch both in speeding up its brewing cycle and in placing more emphasis on its own metal container manufacturing capability. Savings from self-manufacture in this area run about $3 to $4 a barrel. Schlitz is presently studying the return on investment provided by a single furnace at certain of its breweries with glass production geared to first- and fourth-quarter needs, supplemented by purchases during the second and fourth quarters. In this way, the furnace would operate at capacity throughout the year.

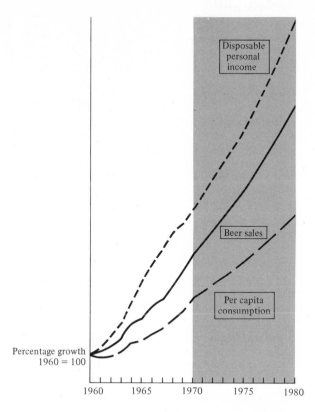

Percentage growth
1960 = 100

| | Beer sales millions of barrels) | Disposable personal income (billions of 1969 dollars) | Per capita consumption (gallons) |
|---|---|---|---|
| 1960 | 87.9 | 420.1 | 15.1 |
| 1961 | 89.0 | 433.0 | 15.0 |
| 1962 | 91.2 | 453.5 | 15.1 |
| 1963 | 93.8 | 470.8 | 15.4 |
| 1964 | 98.6 | 503.7 | 15.9 |
| 1965 | 100.4 | 537.1 | 16.0 |
| 1966 | 104.3 | 566.6 | 16.4 |
| 1967 | 107.0 | 589.6 | 16.7 |
| 1968 | 111.4 | 616.2 | 17.2 |
| 1969 | 116.3 | 631.6 | 17.7 |
| 1970 | 122.0 | 654.0 | 18.4 |
| 1975 | 143.0 | 780.0 | 20.5 |
| 1980 | 172.0 | 960.0 | 23.2 |

**FIGURE 4** ■ Industry projections for beer through 1980. *Source: Industry Week,* Dec. 14, 1970.

The return from this type of project is enhanced by the elimination of quantity discounts on bottles which appears possible in the future.

Most brewers are not diversified. Busch runs Busch Gardens and owns the St. Louis Cardinals baseball team. Schlitz runs an animal feed company and wine subsidiary.

# Demographics and beer consumption pattern

In the last few years, the industry has shipped the following amounts of beer, according to the U.S. Brewers Association:

**BEER SHIPMENTS, MILLION BARRELS**

| 1972 | 1973 | 1974 |
|---|---|---|
| 8.62 | 9.67 | 10.97 |
| 9.09 | 9.43 | 9.87 |
| 11.69 | 12.01 | 11.82 |
| 11.09 | 11.65 | 11.74 |
| 12.41 | 12.87 | 13.65 |
| 13.12 | 12.55 | |
| 12.22 | 12.77 | |
| 12.89 | 13.68 | |
| 10.88 | 11.50 | |
| 10.60 | 11.54 | |
| 9.91 | 10.73 | |
| 9.26 | 10.08 | |
| 131.78 | 138.48 | |

From 1947 through 1961, consumption of beer showed little net change, primarily because of shift in the age composition of the population. Beginning in 1962, growth accelerated and barrel sales have risen without interruption, increasing by a compound annual rate of about 3.5 percent thereafter.

With the resumption of growth in aggregate beer sales, per capita consumption has also increased. This is largely attributable to the increase in the 21-to-39 age group which consumes some 70 percent of all beer. Some feel that a change in legal age to drink may change consumption habits from beer to other forms of alcoholic beverages. Figure 4 projects consumption and production through 1980.

There are regional consumption patterns in beer. In 1969, 10 states consumed 60 percent of beer sold. They were Texas, New Jersey, Wisconsin, Florida, New York, California, Illinois, Pennsylvania, Ohio, and Michigan. Nevada led the nation in per capita consumption in 1972 (30.1 gallons per person). Alabama was lowest with 12.2 gallons. The nationwide average was 19.4 gallons per capita in 1972.

There are major variations in seasonal consumption of beer, of course. The summer months see 50 percent of the beer consumed, when the weather is warm. The convenience of packaging and good economic conditions have contributed to sales increases, as well as demographics, of course.

The brewing industry has had its ups and downs in its long history. It will be interesting to observe its future fluctuations.

# Falstaff Brewing Corporation

## William F. Glueck

Falstaff is one of the largest brewers in the United States. In 1974, the firm manufactured and marketed beer and ale under the following labels:

1 Ballantine Ale, Beer, Bock Beer, Draft Beer, India Pale Ale (45 states and overseas)

2 Falstaff Beer, Draft Beer, Griesedieck Malt Liquor (48 states and overseas)

3 Narragansett Ale, Bock Beer, Lager Beer, and Porter Ale (New England states)

4 Boh Beer; Croft Ale; Haffenreffer (Beer, Malt Liquor); Hanley Lager Beer; Krueger (Ale, Pilsner Beer); Munich Beer; Pickwichs Ale

Falstaff ships from seven breweries with total capacity of 8,300,000 barrels annually. The breweries are located in California, Texas, Louisiana, Nebraska, Missouri, and Rhode Island. The firm employs slightly less than 3000 employees (1974).

Data about the brewing industry are contained in "A Note on the U.S. Brewing Industry."

## Falstaff in history

The founding family at Falstaff is the Griesediecks. They trace their interest in beer to John Henry Griesedieck, a brewmaster of German beer 200 years ago. The founder of Falstaff, Joseph "Papa Joe," was one of America's first graduate brewmasters. In 1917, he bought a 125-barrel brew kettle from the Forest Park Brewery Company of St. Louis. His capacity was 10,000 barrels per year. He entered the business in spite of threats of Prohibition.

During that period, Papa Joe acquired the Falstaff name from a closed brewery, and the family waited out Prohibition producing soft drinks, near beer, and ham and bacon.

Papa Joe was first in line for federal permits in 1933. The firm was innovative in many ways. Falstaff was the first company (in 1935) to brew its beer in more than one location, having purchased a brewery in Omaha in 1935. Many followed this practice later. Falstaff was listed on NYSE in 1948—one of the first brewers to do this and the first brewer to allow a stock purchase by payroll deduction. For many years, Falstaff was a one-name beer house. Only through acquisition did it acquire more beer brands.

Falstaff showed itself a sharp trader. For example,

**FIGURE 1** ■ Some Falstaff products.

it leased, then purchased the Fort Wayne facility (245,000-barrel capacity) for $10 a barrel after modernization while rivals were spending $30 per barrel. Falstaff acquired Narragansett in 1965 and Ballantine in 1972. Falstaff, in agreement with Burgermeister Brewing, also purchased the former Schlitz-Burgermeister brewery in San Francisco in 1972. This brewery was sold in 1974.

Some Falstaff products are shown in Figure 1.

In 1965, Joseph Griesedieck, Jr., described the corporate strategy of Falstaff in *Forbes*. The firm, Mr. Griesedieck said, grew because it had to. He felt local and regionals would not survive—only nationals. Falstaff did not have the capital to build breweries like Schlitz or its cross-city rival Busch. So it bought out faltering locals and regionals. It bought two Texas breweries (Galveston and El Paso) for $1,500,000 in debentures and some cash. Up until that point, Falstaff had not diluted the stock by these mergers. National brewers can offset bad weather, Mr. Griesedieck said. But mergers also forced a change on the earlier single brand marketing strategy at Falstaff. The firm tried to buy breweries with good distribution systems since this is a key to success in the beer business. And he believes multiple products might help Falstaff give distributors enough beer so they will not need to take on competitors to fill out their line.

He made no bones about why distribution is so important. "All beers taste alike. Advertising alone isn't going to get a guy to change his beer permanently. You've got to get the dealers behind you."

## Some legal hurdles for Falstaff

The U.S. federal government has become concerned about brewery concentrations. One major response has been to contest mergers. This has affected

Falstaff. It may have been part of the reason Falstaff's attempted merger with Liebman (Rheingold Beer) fell through in 1963.

When Falstaff acquired Narragansett in 1965 for $19 million, it got a modern plant in Rhode Island and the largest beer in New England. The Antitrust Division of the U.S. Justice Department sued to prevent the merger. Arguing as it did in the Procter and Gamble–Clorox case, the division contended that the merger would decrease competition; that if Falstaff entered New England with its own beer, it might reduce the concentration of 81 percent of beer sales made by eight companies. The district court dismissed the suit, saying the government had failed to prove that Falstaff was a potential independent entrant in the New England market. It said the evidence showed Falstaff's management had decided not to enter the market unless it could acquire a strong brewer.

The decision, appealed directly to the Supreme Court by the Justice Department, was a sharp setback for the Department's "potential competition" theory. In urging Supreme Court review, the Department said the district court "relied exclusively on its evaluation of the subjective intent" of Falstaff's management. The Department insisted that, if it had to prove in all "potential competition" cases management's subjective intent to enter a market independently before it decided to enter by acquisition, it would "seriously undermine the effectiveness of the Clayton Act in preserving competition in the beer and other industries." Moreover, the Department said the high court had "never required subjective evidence in potential competition cases."

In March 1973, the Supreme Court ordered the lower court to reconsider its rejection of the government's suit. Without deciding whether the transaction violates antitrust law, the Court reinforced its position that mergers may be illegal if one of the merger parties is eliminated as a potential competitor in the area affected by the transaction. The Falstaff decision came on a 5 to 2 vote, but with four separate written opinions dealing partly with how potential anticompetitive impact is proved.

The Court, in sending the case back, said the lower court should have considered whether Falstaff was a potential competitor simply because it operated on the fringe of the New England market and this "exerted beneficial influence on competitive conditions in that market." The lower court should have considered such things as Falstaff's financial capabilities and the business conditions of the market, and then decided whether it was reasonable to consider the company as a potential entrant. In St. Louis, Falstaff's president Gutting said that if Falstaff were required to divest itself of Narragansett, the impact on Falstaff would be severe.

In buying Ballantine beer in 1972, Falstaff took a calculated risk of another antitrust suit to improve its financial prospects according to Joseph Griesedieck, Jr., then president. Ballantine is a long-established brand in New York and other Eastern metropolitan markets. The purchase, said Griesedieck, would be defended from any challenge by the federal government on the grounds that Ballantine was a failing company. Ballantine lost $8 million in 1971 and was expected to lose $4 million in 1972. Sales had stabilized in recent years after a long decline.

Ballantine trademarks, brand names, and trade names were sold for $4 million plus 50 cents a barrel on all Ballantine sales during the next 6 years, and the assumption by Falstaff of certain liabilities. Ballantine beer was to be produced by Falstaff's seven breweries throughout the United States. Ballantine's 1971 sales totaled 2,230,000 barrels. Falstaff also purchased up to $9.5

million of Ballantine accounts receivable, and included items of inventory and certain equipment at cost. The former owner of Ballantine retained ownership of the Newark, New Jersey, plant and its interest in the Boston Celtics Basketball Club. Ballantine had reported substantial losses in the previous few years with loss of $3.3 million for the 9 months ended September 30, 1971. The antitrust case was still pending in 1974.

## Falstaff and marketing beer

Table 1 gives the sales data on Falstaff. As can be seen from these figures, Falstaff is clearly one of the nation's leading brewery companies.

In some recent years, notably 1973, the Falstaff brand has been increasing in sales volume which partially offsets some declines in the Ballantine and Narragansett brands. For example in 1972, Ballantine and Narragansett sales declined by 323,000 barrels from 1971 sales. Another explanation given for some sales declines is the reduction in size of the U.S. military forces in recent years. Falstaff has derived many sales from military outlets, especially in the Far East. Another explanation has been strong price competition. In some cases, "premium" beers such as Budweiser and Schlitz have priced themselves lower than Falstaff's standard beer pricing.

Before the acquisitions in 1965 and 1973, Falstaff was a strong regional brewer. It was strong in the South, Southwest, and Midwest. Market shares of some typical areas in the mid-1960s were Texas (20 percent), St. Louis (45 percent), New Orleans (40 percent). The acquisitions provided access to Eastern and Western markets. Thus Falstaff entered the New York market in June 1966—the last of the big five beers at the time to do so. New Yorkers purchased 10 million barrels of beer in 1966. Thus Falstaff's sales strategy had been to expand by purchasing troubled and smaller breweries. That is harder to do in the 1970s. Falstaff lost its fourth place in the big brew leagues to Coors (Denver) for the first time in 1969.

One approach Falstaff has tried to increase efficiency, cut costs, and increase effectiveness as measured by increased profitable sales of beer has been to reorganize and strengthen its marketing organization. This has included bringing in outside executives to head the marketing department (e.g., Edward Fitzmaurice from American Bakeries and General Foods). Almost each year, the company announced reorganization, streamlining, etc., the marketing or-

TABLE 1 ■ FALSTAFF BEER SALES (BARRELS)

| 1963 | 5,548,000 | |
|------|-----------|---|
| 1964 | 5,820,000 | |
| 1965 | 6,336,000 | Purchased Narragansett |
| 1966 | 7,010,218 | |
| 1967 | 6,631,082 | |
| 1968 | 6,289,111 | |
| 1969 | 6,192,000 | |
| 1970 | 5,386,133 | |
| 1971 | 5,134,871 | |
| 1972 | 6,167,718 | Purchased Ballantine |
| 1973 | 6,009,318 | |
| 1974 | 5,789,766 | |

ganization (and the corporate offices and staff as well). For example, in 1969, the company instituted the Brand Management organization for Falstaff's various products.

In 1970, the company established regional profit centers. The president said:

> Big problems are most readily solved by reducing them to smaller, manageable parts and assigning good, confident people to work on those parts. We have employed this method of attacking our problems in marketing.

Subsequently, he appointed three general managers to assume full responsibility for profitable sales and production in the Central, Pacific, and Northeast regions. General managers for other regions are to be named in 1971.

The purpose of this decentralization was to increase sales. Within certain guidelines, the regional managers were given authority for decision making in their regions. In 1972, a reorganization of the regional concept of production and marketing being combined was made to enable regional managers to devote their full efforts to sales. The position of director of marketing was reestablished.

The acquisition of Ballantine, which contributed to heavy losses in 1972, was expected to be beneficial in the long run after "complete integration into our distribution system under well administered cost controls." These brands were also expected to provide additional volume and permit plants to operate closer to capacity.


MARKET CHANNELS FOR BEER

Beer can be purchased at many locations: taverns, restaurants, sporting events, and millions of retail outlets such as beverage stores, groceries, gas stations, and many others. For example, Falstaff's beers are available in over 200,000 outlets in the United States and overseas.

Falstaff ships its beer from the breweries to distribution centers or to its wholesalers. In 1972, Falstaff opened new distribution centers. In May, Ballantine beer and ale deliveries were initiated from a 125,000-square-foot distribution center in North Bergen, New Jersey. The 300,000-case, 8000-half-barrel capacity facility served as the hub of the Atlantic region sales and distribution activities.

Earlier in the year, company-operated distribution centers were established in Oklahoma and in Dallas–Fort Worth (Arlington), Texas. The Oklahoma City facility will add Ballantine beer to its product line in May of 1973. Dallas–Fort Worth distributes Falstaff, Krueger Pilsner, Ballantine beer and ale, and Hanley brands.

The key intermediary is the wholesaler. Falstaff had 600 wholesalers in 1966 and now has over 1000. These independent firms purchase the beer and resell it to the outlets. They may carry Falstaff's brands exclusively or carry Falstaff and other beers. About 25 percent carry the Falstaff beers exclusively. The percentage of beer sold through taverns dropped from a high of 70 percent to 35 percent in 1964 and is now less than half of that.

In recent years, the firm formalized its contracts with its wholesale distributors. Falstaff offers a 1-year nonterminable contract. Notice must be given if Falstaff wishes to make a change. At times, Falstaff tries to increase sales by use of incentive programs with its distributors. For example, in 1971, incentive programs and awards were tried to improve the sales efforts of distributors. Market planning was brought to the distributor level under a system whereby each market is analyzed and projects for increased volume are jointly adopted by distributors and Falstaff's district managers. The field sales organization was expanded to better service, coordinate, and plan the success of the distributors and Falstaff in that year.

Falstaff has waited to enter markets until it has lined up the best distributors. This was true in Chicago and San Diego. The best recent example was its entrance into the largest market: New York. The company did not feel the market would yield to a frontal attack by an unknown brand, so it slipped in via Narragansett. The warehouse of Liebman Sales Corp., New York distributor of "Gansett's" Krueger brand, began to store Falstaff as well in 1966, and moved into New York supermarkets. Within a month, Falstaff could be purchased in Westchester County, some beer depots on Long Island, over the bar at Manhattan's plush Carlyle Hotel, and in the Diamond Club at the Mets' Shea Stadium. The initial goal was a modest 1 percent of market share, or just about what the brand achieved in Chicago in the 2 years after its introduction there. According to Alvin Griesedieck, Jr., then vice president for marketing, "We don't expect to be a factor in New York overnight. You don't just get people to decide their usual beer isn't any good anymore."

Falstaff was not unknown in New York, as it made a special point of penetrating military PXs and canteens, and New York has plenty of ex-GIs who took their basic training in the South and Southwest, where Falstaff has its greatest strength. "The market is so large, we figure we can get 0.5% just from people who moved in from an area where we sell."

In smaller markets the tactic of matching leading local brands dollar for dollar and salesperson for salesperson allowed Falstaff to slug it out with entrenched competition, trying to reach a profitable sales level quickly. In large markets, the cost of such an approach is risky and prohibitive. In New York, Falstaff followed the pay-as-you-go tactic whereby the whole of gross margin on sales is plowed back into promotions. As barrel sales grow, promotion expenditures also rise, and per-barrel costs decline until they reach the company's national average. At that point, Falstaff would consider the market established and start taking profit out of it.

### PRODUCT PLANNING AND DEVELOPMENT

Essentially, Falstaff markets beer, ale, and malt liquor using the following labels: Falstaff, Ballantine, and Narragansett (primary labels), and India Pale, Griesedieck, Porter, Boh, Croft, Haffenreffer, Hanley, Krueger, Ambassador, Munich, and Pickwich (minor labels). In recent years, there has been some attempt to eliminate some less well-known labels such as Ambassador and Pickwich.

The beers sold by Falstaff are intended to appeal to the typical beer drinkers. In recent years, several breweries have attempted to appeal to the diet-conscious and younger beer drinkers with "lite beers" or diet beers. In 1971, Falstaff changed its products to attempt to reach the young adults with a "lighter tasting" beer. The firm does extensive independent taste tests of its beer.

In 1969, Falstaff was emphasizing that it sold draft-type beer in bottle form.

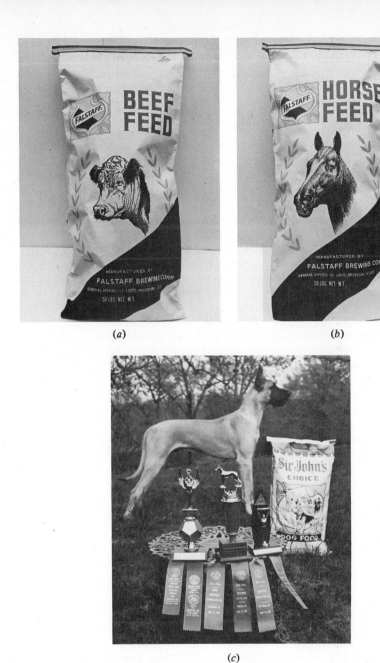

**FIGURE 2** ■ Some of Falstaff's nonbrewery products. (*a*) Beef feed; (*b*) horse feed; (*c*) dog food.

This became technically feasible when Falstaff began using a new filter process which allowed the beer to be bottled without pasteurization.

Falstaff also offers Griesedieck Malt Liquor and Haffenreffer Malt Liquor in that segment of the market. It is said to represent about 5 percent of beer barrelage. Colt 45 is a leader, as are Budweiser Malt Liquor and Schlitz's Malt

Liquor. Falstaff has not penetrated this market very deeply. Malt liquor is growing. It has a higher alcoholic content than beer. Some firms have offered flavored malt liquor such as National Brewings (Colt 45) Apple Malt Duck.

Falstaff also markets high-protein animal feed supplements, by-products of the brewing process, in 26 states and several foreign countries. These feeds are formulated to provide additional nutrition for beef cattle, dairy cattle, horses, and a variety of other animals. This has been Falstaff's main diversification effort, though the firm has seriously considered pet foods and beverages other than beer. In 1970, the firm changed to corporate charter to make it easier to diversify. Some of its feed products are shown in Figure 2.

### PRICING AND PACKAGING

Essentially, Falstaff has priced its products at "popular beer" prices—below "premium beers" such as Budweiser, Schlitz, and Pabst, for example. At one time, some wholesalers promoted only premium beers. In the 1950s, many added popular beers to their lines. Thus came such beers as Busch Bavarian from Anheuser-Busch.

In the late 1960s, some of the premium beers began to cut their prices to "popular" or even lower prices as marketing devices, especially when they entered new markets. Falstaff resists price cutting, though they did go along with some cuts for competitive reasons in 1972.

With the wage and price controls in the early 1970s, some firms including Falstaff were caught in a price squeeze. The costs (of wages and materials) were going up. But they could not raise their prices. Schlitz, with the lowest costs, was prohibited from raising prices and this kept industry prices down. It also depressed profits.

From January through August of 1974, however, beer prices at wholesale rose 6.6 percent. For the 10 preceding years, the rise was 1.5 percent yearly. Retailers tack on still more. The companies also reduced price discounts severely. In earlier years, orders of over 50 or 100 cases led to quantity discounts. The note on the industry explains the details of cost pressures. Thus far (late 1974) the price increases have not dampened sales. The theories are that sales are not down because beer is still the best buy for the money. Even soft drinks can cost as much as beer, some executives point out.

Packaging has been considered an important part of the marketing effort. Recently, clubs which save beer cans have sprung up. Thirty-five hundred persons belong to these clubs. Cans for beer began in 1935, and since then 12,000 U.S. beer labels have been produced. Some of the rarer cans have been appraised as high as $250 (1974). From time to time, Falstaff has been a leader in packaging. In 1969, it introduced the 2¼-gallon "tapper"—an aluminum keg. It wound up being sued by Maier Brewing over it and took a write-off over the affair.

In 1970, the firm introduced the 12-ounce "slender" nonreturnable can. The 12-ounce is the most frequently sold size. In 1974, more firms are introducing 7-ounce canned beers. These cans are aimed at the women beer drinkers. Women buy 57 percent of beer, but drink only 37 percent of it. New entries have included Anheuser-Busch (Mich VII, 7-ounce of Michelob), Miller High Life, and others. One brewery, Latrobe Brewery in Pennsylvania, has sold half its beer in 7-ounce "Rolley Rock" cans since 1939. With as many brands as

Falstaff now has, choice of size and type of containers is an important inventory challenge. The largest Falstaff brands are sold in the following sizes of bottles and cans:

|  | Cans | Bottles | |
|---|---|---|---|
| Falstaff | 12 ounces | 12 ounces | 32 ounces |
| Ballantine | 12 ounces | 12 ounces | 32 ounces |
| Narragansett | 12 ounces | 12 ounces | 32 ounces |

## ADVERTISING AND SALES PROMOTION

For some years, Falstaff has advertised heavily to support its distributors in the sales of their beers. The firm has tended to spend $8 to $10 million yearly, though some years, such as 1970 and 1971, the budget was cut on advertising. A series of advertising themes has been used recently.

In 1967 and 1968, Narragansett's theme was "The Good Beer for All Hours." This was changed in 1969 to "Your First One Is Never Your Last One." By 1973, the theme was "Our Own New England Beer."

Ballantine came on board in 1972, and its theme has been "The Only Answer."

Krueger was selling "Brewed Slowly: A Little at a Time" in 1968. In 1969 the theme was "Tastes Lighter than Other Premium Beers."

The Falstaff beer has had several themes:

1967–1968: Falstaff—The Thirst Slaker
1969: The Choicest Product of the Brewer's Art
1970: Falstaff Revolution for the Fun of It

In the early 1970s, a theme was pushed about Papa Joe and his good beer. The most recent theme has involved two cowboys—Gabe and Walker (see Figure 3)—and why they drink Falstaff. Later a third cowboy was added (a black).

The firm has changed advertising agencies several times: to Foote Cone and Belding in 1968 and to Needham, Harper and Steers (Los Angeles) in 1970 for all the beers. The company also pressed for Falstaff as "The Racing Beer" in the late sixties and early seventies.

Falstaff has been criticized for a lack of continuity in its advertising. President Ford Gutting said in 1972:

It is my opinion that the company has lacked continuity and consistency in its advertising and marketing approaches. While we cannot turn back the clock, we are doing all possible to avoid further drastic changes in these important matters. We have worked closely with our advertising agency to build and develop our product themes into harder selling messages. We also are employing more advertising media weight where it is most needed.

Apparently, some stockholders feel the company's advertising is not optimal. At the annual meeting of April 23, 1974, President Gutting defended the company's Falstaff advertising campaign that features the cowboys, Gabe and Walker, from sharp criticism. The advertising theme was continued primarily because Falstaff's themes had been changed too often in the last 7 or 8 years, he explained. These changes confused consumers and damaged the image of

**FIGURE 3** ■ Falstaff's latest advertising theme.

the brand. He noted, however, that more product identification was built into the newer advertising.

Sales promotion usually supports the advertising campaign with such items as point of purchase material, merchandising, and incentive programs. For example, recently Falstaff has provided a simple, do-it-yourself consumer research kit for independent retailers and small chains, who appreciate an inexpensive way to survey their customers' wants, habits, and complaints. Falstaff also considers packaging a promotional tool and has adopted several innovations early enough to capitalize on them.

Another example in the late 1960s was the Rail of Heritage. This simulated wood display piece could be used to display Falstaff promotional materials or mugs.

Typical of merchandising and sales promotion activities are several ideas used by Falstaff. Falstaff decided to sponsor the sports as most other brewers do, especially since they are located in St. Louis, where August Busch owns the Cardinals baseball team and sells Anheuser-Busch products at the games. Falstaff, which had long sponsored basketball and the baseball game of the week, wanted a tie-in with sports like Busch. Falstaff bought a 10 percent interest in the Chicago Cardinals football team and got them to move to St. Louis in the early 1960s. Now Busch sells in the summer, and Falstaff in the fall. Falstaff also sponsors Chicago White Sox games (TV) and Kansas City

Royals games (radio). Falstaff's Ballantine sponsors the radio broadcasts of the New York Mets. Narragansett sponsors the radio broadcasts of the Boston Red Sox.

Two new major promotional activities were sponsored in 1972. One was sponsorship of a fair. In the 1904 World's Fair St. Louis's Forest Park became the focal point for recreational and cultural activities around the country. Falstaff and the St. Louis Visitors Center wanted the same reaction, even if on a smaller scale, for Fair '72 St. Louis. They got it. The 3-day event included sky diving by the Army's Golden Knights, beer gardens with lots of Falstaff, a variety of sporting events, and an international area where food, singing, dancing, and crafts were provided by the many ethnic groups from the St. Louis area. Falstaff employees volunteered their time to sell balloons and beer steins and work in many of the booths.

For the second event, Falstaff was awarded national recognition for sponsorship of the nationally televised "Will Rogers' U.S.A." show. The company was cited by the American Council for Better Broadcasts for "taking sole responsibility for a significant special television program which makes a valuable contribution to our society."

## Finances at Falstaff

The financial statements for Falstaff are given in Tables 2, 3, and 4. In 1974, the company had 4,496,625 shares outstanding. The stock is traded on the New York Stock Exchange (FAL). Its high and low in 10 years (1964–1974) have been high 43¾ and low 1⅞.

A summary of significant accounting policies is as follows:

**1**  All subsidiaries are wholly owned and are included in the consolidations. All significant intercompany transactions have been eliminated.

**2**  The corporation, with minor exceptions, uses the straight-line method of computing depreciation for financial reporting purposes. Depreciation rates are based on the estimated useful lives of assets. Leasehold improvements are amortized over the terms of the leases including renewal option periods, or the life of the asset, whichever is shorter.

Average composite rates of depreciation for financial reporting purposes are as follows:

| | |
|---|---|
| Buildings | 3.36% |
| Machinery and equipment | 6.88% |
| Cooperage, bottles, and pallets | 9.78% |

**3**  Inventories are stated at the lower of average cost or market.

**4**  The corporation follows the practice of reducing its provision for current income taxes by the full amount of its investment tax credits. Deferred income taxes are provided for amounts which affect financial and taxable income in different periods.

**5**  Pension costs include charges applicable to current service and amortization of unfunded prior service costs, wherever applicable, generally over periods ranging from 12 to 30 years. It is the policy to fund pension costs accrued.

**6**  Licenses and trademarks are amortized over the life of the related royalty agreement.

TABLE 2 ■ FALSTAFF BREWING COMPANY AND SUBSIDIARIES, CONSOLIDATED BALANCE SHEET AT DECEMBER 31

| Assets | 1974 | 1973 | 1972 | 1971 | 1970 | 1969 | 1968 | 1967 | 1966 |
|---|---|---|---|---|---|---|---|---|---|
| **Current assets** | | | | | | | | | |
| Cash (and C.D.'s) | $ 3,093,551 | $ 2,465,777 | $ 5,009,854 | $ 5,723,605 | $ 3,546,440 | $ 4,009,095 | $ 4,149,582 | $ 6,128,028 | $ 4,889,297 |
| Marketable securities, at cost not in excess of market | .... | .... | 110,465 | .... | .... | .... | .... | .... | .... |
| Accounts receivable: | | | | | | | | | |
| Trade accounts receivable | 14,214,718 | 16,907,591 | 17,090,035 | 10,568,745 | 10,882,002 | 11,312,439 | 10,577,038 | 10,935,497 | 12,271,663 |
| Other | 1,354,950 | 1,122,015 | 904,810 | 1,202,215 | 1,830,916 | 1,236,798 | 1,127,288 | 1,167,246 | 1,487,528 |
| Allowance for doubtful receivables (credit) | (738,227) | (1,159,563) | (1,148,687) | (556,086) | (829,175) | (771,751) | (596,613) | (567,533) | (547,776) |
| Refundable federal income taxes | .... | .... | 2,961,913 | .... | .... | .... | .... | .... | .... |
| Inventories (at average cost, not in excess of market): | | | | | | | | | |
| Finished goods | 5,779,931 | 5,461,859 | 4,354,611 | 3,183,906 | 2,768,206 | 3,164,837 | 2,892,263 | 2,766,728 | 3,160,376 |
| Products in process, materials, and supplies | 12,023,883 | 13,272,517 | 10,062,146 | 9,848,759 | 9,359,239 | 8,032,207 | 9,113,283 | 10,038,354 | 9,377,825 |
| Other current assets | 1,082,327 | 1,339,973 | 1,473,659 | 1,606,197 | 1,061,503 | 913,552 | 1,160,595 | 1,144,253 | 2,257,151 |
| Total current assets | 36,831,133 | 39,410,169 | 40,818,906 | 35,956,639 | 35,269,673 | 37,895,910 | 37,630,222 | 35,576,185 | 35,874,601 |
| **Investments, deferred charges, and misc. assets** (at cost, less allowance for possible loss on investments) | 5,388,284 | 2,248,715 | 1,169,191 | 1,067,886 | 1,109,672 | 1,186,738 | 790,270 | 429,142 | 325,989 |
| **Property—at cost:** | | | | | | | | | |
| Land | 2,656,872 | 3,367,122 | 3,547,234 | 2,823,056 | 2,823,056 | 2,569,711 | 2,573,261 | 3,166,694 | 3,162,067 |
| Buildings | 30,394,757 | 31,475,317 | 31,629,330 | 30,967,529 | 27,836,835 | 27,604,228 | 27,676,177 | 30,114,217 | 29,589,150 |
| Machinery and equipment | 42,757,111 | 46,474,187 | 48,961,816 | 47,973,596 | 46,058,064 | 44,616,866 | 46,987,041 | 52,667,386 | 51,560,917 |
| Cooperage, bottles, and pallets | 8,695,234 | 9,278,332 | 24,183,221 | 21,352,701 | 22,601,655 | 23,444,417 | 23,409,320 | 23,573,419 | 23,333,748 |
| Construction in progress | 116,137 | 115,923 | 2,448,577 | 944,448 | 3,020,231 | 1,869,219 | .... | .... | .... |
| Total | 84,620,111 | 90,710,881 | 110,770,178 | 104,061,330 | 102,339,841 | 100,104,441 | 100,645,799 | 109,521,716 | 107,645,882 |
| Less accumulated depreciation and other reserves | 39,277,255 | 37,734,228 | 52,119,184 | 49,685,857 | 49,922,041 | 44,932,587 | 42,880,937 | 40,134,433 | 32,172,349 |
| Total | 45,342,856 | 52,976,653 | 58,650,994 | 54,375,473 | 52,417,800 | 55,171,854 | 57,764,862 | 69,387,283 | 75,473,533 |
| Leasehold improvement—unamortized portion | 907,841 | 925,733 | 956,410 | 567,405 | 543,777 | 545,856 | 557,960 | 497,576 | 512,802 |
| Property—net | 46,250,697 | 53,902,386 | 59,607,404 | 54,942,878 | 55,961,577 | 55,717,710 | 58,322,822 | 69,884,859 | 75,986,335 |
| Licenses and trademarks—unamortized portion | 533,193 | 697,253 | 1,050,037 | .... | .... | .... | .... | .... | .... |
| Total assets | $88,983,307 | $96,258,523 | $102,645,438 | $91,967,403 | $92,340,922 | $94,800,358 | $96,743,284 | $105,890,186 | $112,186,925 |

## Liabilities and shareowners' equity

| | | | | | | | | | |
|---|--:|--:|--:|--:|--:|--:|--:|--:|--:|
| **Current liabilities** | | | | | | | | | |
| Accounts payable and accruals | $10,900,601 | $10,878,589 | $11,682,135 | $7,889,326 | $10,369,982 | $9,256,597 | $8,733,562 | $11,611,677 | $12,822,005 |
| Current maturities of long-term debt | 3,000,000 | 3,100,000 | 3,100,000 | 1,500,000 | 1,914,100 | 3,846,000 | 3,269,200 | 995,600 | 81,500 |
| Short-term bank borrowing (due on demand) | 5,000,000 | 5,000,000 | | | | | | | |
| Dividend payable | | | | | | 449,663 | 450,163 | 855,955 | 856,506 |
| Income taxes payable—net | 45,605 | 66,506 | 316,014 | 2,564,131 | 1,500,204 | 1,761,113 | 1,226,984 | 121,138 | 114,688 |
| Other taxes (principally excise) | 3,615,667 | 3,629,185 | 4,672,120 | 2,706,067 | | | | | |
| Estimated expenses to be incurred in connection with closed plants | | | | | | | | 219,296 | |
| Total current liabilities | 22,661,873 | 22,674,280 | 19,770,269 | 14,659,524 | 13,784,286 | 15,313,373 | 13,679,909 | 13,803,666 | 13,874,699 |
| **Deposits on containers expected to be replaced or to remain with customers** | 1,668,145 | 1,744,538 | 1,487,183 | 1,361,499 | 1,356,339 | 1,556,964 | 1,884,877 | 2,253,919 | 2,379,181 |
| **Other liabilities and deferred credits:** | | | | | | | | | |
| Deferred income taxes | 2,230,456 | 2,284,356 | 2,695,056 | 3,844,463 | 4,414,763 | 4,256,863 | 3,306,767 | 5,868,467 | 6,763,082 |
| Unfunded past service costs | 724,176 | 839,376 | 954,576 | 1,069,776 | 1,184,976 | 1,300,576 | 1,415,776 | 1,531,176 | 1,646,561 |
| Other | 242,603 | 289,884 | 374,200 | | | | | | |
| Total | 3,197,235 | 3,413,516 | 4,023,832 | 4,914,239 | 5,599,739 | 5,557,439 | 4,722,543 | 7,399,643 | 8,409,643 |
| **Long-term debt** | 23,515,000 | 26,615,000 | 29,715,000 | 17,315,000 | 18,815,000 | 20,805,400 | 24,656,500 | 27,933,800 | 28,961,900 |
| **Shareowners' equity:** | | | | | | | | | |
| Capital stock: | | | | | | | | | |
| Preferred—authorized: 500,000 shares; par value $20 a share; issued and outstanding—none | | | | | | | | | |
| Common—authorized: 6 million shares; par value $1 a share; issued (including shares held in treasury) | 4,530,025 | 4,530,025 | 4,530,025 | 4,530,025 | 4,530,025 | 4,530,025 | 4,530,025 | 4,530,025 | 4,530,025 |
| Additional paid-in capital | 9,885,001 | 9,885,001 | 9,885,001 | 9,885,001 | 9,885,001 | 9,885,001 | 9,885,001 | 9,885,001 | 9,885,001 |
| Retained earnings | 23,961,385 | 27,831,520 | 33,669,485 | 39,737,472 | 38,805,889 | 37,577,523 | 37,764,999 | 40,427,302 | 44,489,646 |
| Common capital stock held in treasury (at cost—(deduction) | (435,357) | (435,357) | (435,357) | (435,357) | (435,357) | (435,357) | (380,570) | (343,170) | (343,170) |
| Shareowners' equity | 37,941,044 | 41,811,195 | 47,649,154 | 53,717,141 | 52,785,558 | 51,557,182 | 51,799,455 | 54,499,158 | 58,561,502 |
| Total | $88,983,307 | $96,258,523 | $102,645,438 | $91,967,403 | $92,340,922 | $94,800,358 | $96,743,284 | $105,890,186 | $112,186,925 |

**TABLE 3 ■ FALSTAFF BREWING CORPORATION AND SUBSIDIARIES, STATEMENT OF CONSOLIDATED INCOME AND RETAINED EARNINGS FOR THE YEARS ENDED DECEMBER 31**

| | 1974 | 1973 | 1972 | 1971 | 1970 | 1969 | 1968 | 1967 | 1966 |
|---|---|---|---|---|---|---|---|---|---|
| Sales | $254,858,267 | $242,950,024 | $242,061,818 | $202,157,465 | $205,476,860 | $227,879,278 | $225,051,886 | $237,572,093 | $250,892,397 |
| Less federal and state excise taxes | 66,478,023 | 69,229,179 | 72,204,702 | 60,721,246 | 61,864,229 | 71,481,481 | 71,245,743 | 77,637,983 | 82,761,220 |
| Net sales | 188,380,244 | 173,720,845 | 169,857,116 | 141,436,219 | 143,612,631 | 156,397,797 | 153,806,143 | 159,934,110 | 168,131,177 |
| Cost of goods sold | 157,205,611 | 142,650,258 | 138,768,129 | 110,386,012 | 110,206,898 | 117,890,417 | 112,880,083 | 117,430,946 | 117,849,327 |
| Gross profit | 31,174,633 | 31,070,587 | 31,088,987 | 31,050,207 | 33,405,733 | 38,507,380 | 40,926,060 | 42,503,164 | 50,281,850 |
| Marketing, general, and administrative expenses | 32,873,044 | 34,267,132 | 38,653,959 | 27,748,520 | 30,974,973 | 34,653,320 | 35,720,836 | 38,545,850 | 42,348,907 |
| Profit (loss) from operations | (1,698,411) | (3,196,545) | (7,564,972) | 3,301,687 | 2,430,760 | 3,854,060 | 5,205,224 | 3,957,314 | 7,932,943 |
| Other income | 796,582 | 239,912 | 283,744 | 571,185 | 874,192 | 1,122,070 | 1,685,643 | 1,017,137 | 864,954 |
| Total | (901,829) | (2,956,633) | (7,281,228) | 3,872,872 | 3,304,952 | 4,976,130 | 6,890,867 | 4,974,451 | 8,797,897 |
| Income charges: | | | | | | | | | |
| Interest | 2,924,275 | 2,463,768 | 1,587,760 | 1,021,680 | 1,176,830 | 1,324,565 | 1,433,228 | 1,433,722 | 1,440,640 |
| Other | 21,041 | 539,564 | 63,599 | 135,946 | 139,746 | 394,515 | 743,499 | 404,254 | 232,119 |
| Total income charges | 2,945,316 | 3,003,332 | 1,651,359 | 1,157,626 | 1,316,576 | 1,719,080 | 2,176,727 | 1,837,976 | 1,672,759 |
| Income (loss) before provision for taxes | (3,847,145) | (5,959,965) | (8,932,587) | 2,715,246 | 1,988,376 | 3,257,050 | 4,714,140 | 3,126,475 | 7,125,138 |
| Provision for income taxes (credit): | | | | | | | | | |
| Current | 132,000 | 288,800 | (2,278,600) | 1,284,000 | 657,300 | 1,798,600 | 1,591,500 | 652,000 | 722,000 |
| Deferred | 109,000 | (410,800) | (586,000) | 50,000 | 102,700 | 20,000 | 886,000 | 920,000 | 2,041,000 |
| Total provision | 23,000 | (122,000) | (2,864,600) | 1,334,000 | 760,000 | 1,818,600 | 2,477,500 | 1,572,000 | 2,763,000 |
| Income (loss) before extraordinary items | (3,870,145) | (5,837,965) | (6,067,987) | 1,381,246 | 1,228,376 | 1,438,450 | 2,236,640 | 1,554,475 | 4,362,138 |
| Extraordinary items. less applicable income tax | | | | | | 173,714 | (3,097,953) | (2,193,000) | |
| Net income (loss) for the year | (3,870,145) | (5,837,965) | (6,067,987) | 1,381,246 | 1,228,376 | 1,612,164 | (861,313) | (638,525) | 4,362,138 |
| Retained income at beginning of year | 27,831,520 | 33,669,485 | 39,737,472 | 38,805,889 | 37,577,513 | 37,764,999 | 40,427,302 | 44,489,646 | 43,564,968 |
| Remainder | 23,961,375 | 27,831,520 | 33,669,485 | 40,187,135 | 38,805,889 | 39,377,163 | 39,565,989 | 43,851,121 | 47,927,106 |
| Deduct cash dividends declared | | | | 449,663 | | 1,799,650 | 1,800,990 | 3,423,819 | 3,437,460 |
| Retained earnings at end of year | $23,961,375 | $27,831,520 | $33,669,485 | $39,737,472 | $38,805,889 | $37,577,513 | $37,764,999 | $40,427,302 | $44,489,646 |
| Per share of common stock: | | | | | | | | | |
| Income (loss) before extraordinary items($.86) | ($.86) | ($1.30) | ($1.35) | $.31 | $.27 | $.32 | $.50 | $.35 | $.97 |
| Extraordinary items. net of tax | | | | | | .04 | (.69) | (.49) | |
| Net income (loss) | ($.86) | ($1.30) | ($1.35) | $.31 | $.27 | $.36 | ($.19) | ($.14) | $.97 |

TABLE 4 ■ FALSTAFF BREWING CORPORATION, CHANGES IN WORKING CAPITAL AND SOURCE AND USE OF FINANCIAL RESOURCES, FOR THE YEARS ENDED DECEMBER 31

| | 1974 | 1973 | 1972 | 1971 | 1970 | 1969 | 1968 | 1967 | 1966 |
|---|---|---|---|---|---|---|---|---|---|
| *Sources derived from:* | | | | | | | | | |
| Net income (loss) | ($5,441,587) | ($5,837,965) | ($6,067,987) | $1,381,246 | $1,228,376 | $1,612,164 | ($ 861,313) | ($ 638,525) | $ 4,362,138 |
| Charges (credits) to income which did not require current expenditures of working capital: | | | | | | | | | |
| Depreciation and amortization | 5,978,601 | 6,501,351 | 6,827,863 | 6,097,120 | 6,105,772 | 6,165,056 | 6,439,525 | 6,870,652 | 7,314,595 |
| Provision for deferred federal income taxes (credit) | 109,000 | (410,800) | (586,000) | 50,000 | 102,700 | 20,000 | 886,000 | 920,000 | 2,041,000 |
| Other (deductions) | 3,122,285 | 708,061 | 158,733 | (92,220) | (170,724) | (96,031) | 3,140,811 | 1,501,313 | |
| Miscellaneous—net | 676,752 | 388,447 | 495,892 | 221,539 | 182,604 | 1,111,563 | 1,442,959 | 114,204 | 627,766 |
| Long-term debt | ... | ... | 15,500,000 | ... | | | | | ... |
| Total | 4,445,051 | 1,349,094 | 16,328,501 | 7,657,685 | 7,448,728 | 8,812,752 | 11,047,982 | 8,767,644 | 14,345,499 |
| *Resources used for:* | | | | | | | | | |
| Additions to property | 1,249,207 | 2,362,226 | 12,629,056 | 5,078,843 | 6,387,745 | 3,664,580 | 2,959,622 | 4,024,693 | 7,329,818 |
| Reduction of long-term debt | 3,100,000 | 3,100,000 | 3,100,000 | 1,500,000 | 1,990,400 | 3,851,100 | 3,277,300 | 1,028,100 | 103,100 |
| Reduction of other noncurrent liabilities and miscellaneous | 162,481 | 199,516 | 229,416 | 141,951 | 157,733 | 820,381 | 794,906 | 518,415 | 752,365 |
| Payment of dividends | ... | ... | ... | 449,663 | ... | 1,799,650 | 1,800,990 | 3,423,819 | 3,437,460 |
| Purchase of common stock for treasury | | | | | | 54,787 | 37,400 | | 343,170 |
| Settlement of income tax issues charged to deferred liability account | ... | ... | 618,607 | 675,500 | | | | | ... |
| Total | 7,011,688 | 5,661,742 | 16,577,079 | 7,845,957 | 8,535,878 | 10,190,498 | 8,870,218 | 8,995,027 | 11,965,913 |
| Increase (decrease) in working capital | ($2,566,629) | ($4,312,648) | ($248,578) | ($ 188,272) | ($1,087,150) | ($1,377,746) | $2,177,764 | ($ 227,383) | $ 2,379,586 |

The company has certain dividend restrictions. The agreements relating to long-term debt contain restrictions on payment of cash dividends and the purchase or retirement of the corporation's capital stock. Under the most restrictive agreement, there were no consolidated retained earnings available for the payment of cash dividends or the purchase or retirement of the corporation's capital stock at December 31, 1972. Payments per share in other years were as follows: 1971—10 cents; 1969—40 cents; 1968—40 cents; 1967—76 cents; 1966—76 cents.

With regard to contingent liabilities, Falstaff's executive office building in St. Louis is rented under a 25-year lease from the Falstaff Foundation (a nonprofit charitable foundation) at an annual rental of $135,000. The company pays real estate taxes and provides for insurance, maintenance, and upkeep of the building.

The corporation has a number of noncancelable lease agreements covering office and warehouse space and data processing equipment, primarily expiring before 1983. The annual rentals, exclusive of real estate taxes, insurance, and normal maintenance, for the 5 years ending December 31, 1977, are as follows:

| 1973 | $978,000 |
| 1974 | 974,000 |
| 1975 | 881,000 |
| 1976 | 812,000 |
| 1977 | 761,000 |

The corporation also leases, under agreements which generally are cancelable within periods of less than 1 year, automobiles, trucks, and other equipment, and such warehouse and other office space as is required in connection with their operations. Annual expense under these leases is approximately $1,050,000.

With regard to the Ballantine acquisition in 1972, Falstaff agreed to pay $4 million for Ballantine's trade names, trademarks, brand names, vehicles, cooperage, bottles, pallets, and advertising promotional signs and materials.

The allocation of such cost to the various types of assets acquired has been recorded in the accompanying financial statements, as follows:

| Machinery and equipment (vehicles) | $ 202,200 |
| Cooperage, bottles, and pallets | 2,279,288 |
| Licenses and trademarks | 1,193,952 |
| Cartons and signs (expensed in 1972) | 324,560 |
| Total | $4,000,000 |

The corporation also is required to pay a royalty of 50 cents per barrel on Ballantine products sold during the succeeding 6 years, or $1,100,000 per annum over the remainder of the 6-year period in the event that the distribution of beer under the brand name Ballantine is substantially discontinued by the corporation. The agreement also provided, among other things, for the corporation to purchase Ballantine's inventory and supplies at cost and certain of its receivables and assume certain obligations and commitments of Ballantine as of March 31, 1972.

# The human side of Falstaff

Falstaff employs about 3000 people. This figure has been about the same for about 10 years (ending in 1974). The two mergers did not increase the work force substantially.

The brewery industry's blue-collar work force is unionized. The wages paid are the highest of unionized groups with the exception of some construction workers and a few others.

The industry has not been free from strikes from the Brewery Workers or the Teamsters. These strikes have hurt Falstaff. For example, in May of 1964, Falstaff's California plants were shut down because of a teamsters' strike. During that strike, big breweries shipped in beer from other states, hurting Falstaff's share of the market there. Also, higher costs were encountered owing to inventory stockpiling in anticipation of the strike.

By effectively using early retirement programs, management in 1970 was able to eliminate some restrictive labor contract provisions and operate plants more efficiently.

In 1971, without work stoppages, major labor contract settlements of 3 years' duration were achieved with Brewery Worker production unions at Galveston, Omaha, and Fort Wayne, while a 2-year agreement was obtained at the Chicago malting plant. These settlements highlight the use of pension and early retirement to increase work force efficiencies without employee termination.

Major 1972 negotiations were centered upon wage reopener negotiations in St. Louis for production and craft contracts expiring between January 1 and March 1, 1972, and Cranston production contracts expiring June 1. The company again achieved labor contract settlements at these breweries without work stoppages in 1972. Major contracts with production employees and craft unions expired in 1973.

In November 1973 the United Brewery Workers Union voted to leave the AFL-CIO and merge with the International Brotherhood of Teamsters effective at the end of 1974.

Falstaff has pension and retirement plans for substantially all its employees. Under some of the plans in effect for hourly employees, Falstaff has no liability for current or prior service costs other than to pay fixed amounts per hour or per day worked by covered employees, as negotiated under union contracts.

Salaried employees are covered principally under a noncontributory retirement plan that provides benefits through company contributions to a pension trust fund. Some of the pension plans for hourly paid employees provide for employee contributions as well as employer contributions. The normal retirement age under the plans is 65 years.

The total pension expense was as follows for the following years:

| | |
|------|------------|
| 1966 | $1,800,000 |
| 1967 | 1,800,000 |
| 1968 | 1,750,000 |
| 1969 | 1,650,000 |
| 1970 | 1,600,000 |
| 1971 | 1,915,000 |
| 1972 | 2,561,000 |
| 1973 | 2,759,000 |
| 1974 | 2,630,000 |

These figures do not include $115,000 per year for unfunded past services of some employees.

Falstaff has a stock option plan as an incentive for certain key persons. As of December 1974, 246,600 shares were reserved for option grants at prices from $8.50 to $9.75 per share. In 1974 none of the employees exercised their rights to shares of Falstaff stock.

In 1970 Falstaff designed and implemented Affirmative Action programs for both the corporation and individual plants. "Falstaff traditionally has been an equal opportunity employer," said Harry J. Pettery, vice president, administration. "Re-affirming this long standing voluntary policy and practice, we also have complied with recent government regulations by developing and publicizing techniques and programs to increase minority opportunities wherever possible." The company successfully met federal requirements in five compliance reviews held in 1971 by the Department of Agriculture.

Affirmative Action programs at the corporate and region levels, each with specific goals and timetables, continued in 1972, when the company successfully met federal requirements in another compliance review.

In addition, late in 1972, Falstaff's board of directors approved the implementation of a stepped-up minority relations program encompassing placement of capital formation and short-term tax deposits in minority financial institutions, encouraging the establishment of minority owned and/or operated beer distributorships; channeling larger portions of the company's material and supply purchases to minority enterprises; aiding minority educational activities and institutions; and providing philanthropic support to worthy minority endeavors.

In January 1974, the following executives provide leadership for Falstaff.

Fred Gutting, age 64, is chairman of the board, president, and chief executive officer. He is the first nonfamily president of Falstaff. He became president in 1972, replacing Joseph Griesedieck, who had been president from 1953 to 1972. In 1973 Gutting also became chairman. He had formerly served as controller of the firm and also worked in planning since joining Falstaff in 1958. Prior to that he worked for another St. Louis brewery, Griesedieck Brothers Co., whose owners were cousins of Falstaff's founders.

Other executive officers are (in 1974): Harvey Beffa, Jr., vice president of malting and feed; John C. Calhoun, controller; Charles W. Dependahl, Jr., vice president and director of marketing; Edward J. Griesedieck, Jr., vice president of corporate relations; William J. Healy, vice president and secretary-treasurer; John Strauss, vice president and technical director; and Arthur J. Tonna, vice president of brewery operations.

Harvey Beffa, Jr., and Edward J. Griesedieck, Jr., also serve on the Falstaff board.

The 1973 salaries paid to the executives, as revealed at the stockholders' meetings were J. Griesedieck, $56,505; Fred Gutting, $70,487; Charles Dependahl, $47,451; E. Griesedieck, Jr., $35,000; William Healy, $47,451; John Strauss, $47,853; Arthur Tonna, $45,156.

## Operations

As a close look at "A Note on the U.S. Brewing Industry" will indicate, operating a brewery the last few years was not the easiest way to make a living. There were major increases in the cost of materials and labor. There were demands that the industry label the ingredients of the product. Environmentalists attacked the nonreturnable containers, the most frequently purchased form of beer. Falstaff reported that it took the following steps to deal with this issue:

1 Conducted and expanded container collection and recycling programs. The New England "Yes We Can" project has been particularly successful and has already resulted in the reprocessing of more than 1,370,000 cans.

In 1972, a pilot program called Operation Buyback for recycling cans and nonreturnable bottles was being tried in St. Louis. Falstaff pays 10 cents a case for 12-ounce or 16-ounce cans and 15 cents a case for 12-ounce nonreturnable bottles or twelve 32-ounce bottles for the return of its packages. In a 5-week period 4440 pounds of cans were reclaimed at the recycling center adjacent to the St. Louis brewery.

Operation Buyback is intended to promote recycling by making it worthwhile for wide participation by individuals and organizations. It is also hoped that Operation Buyback will stimulate and encourage recycling, not only through the Falstaff center, but also through the many recycling centers run by municipal governments and organizations.

2 Participated in the massive "Pitch In" public education program, an anti-litter effort sponsored by the USBA. In 1972, the company tried educating the littering public through programs such as the United States Brewers Association's Pitch In! and in encouraging large scale clean-up and recycling activities under the Falstaff banner of Operation Clean America.

3 Followed through with our own anti-litter programs under the banner of Operation Clean America. These environmental action events involve local citizen groups and have brought us special recognition from Keep America Beautiful.

4 Continued our anti-pollution programs related to our production operations. These include not only effluent controls but also recycling of waste products such as paper and metal.

The last step resulted in substantial expenditures for installation of equipment at breweries which helps to protect the environment but does not necessarily increase operating efficiencies.

With costs increasing, Falstaff tried to cut its costs. In 1973, for example, Falstaff cut costs by $6 million, mostly in the general and administrative expenses area. There were major cuts in staff and executive costs. In 1974 through August, Falstaff reported cutting $1,800,000 in marketing, administrative, and general expenses.

Many companies have tried to cut costs by vertical integrations. Falstaff produces its own malt, for example. Other firms are increasingly manufacturing their own cans. Falstaff reported negatively with can companies to lease and operate Falstaff-owned can plants near its New Orleans, Fort Wayne, and Galveston breweries.

### PRODUCTION PROCESS

The person who supervises the production process is John Strauss, the brewmaster. He has held this type of job for nearly 45 years.

To make good beer, one starts with quality ingredients. The barley buyers must purchase the best of each crop.

From this premium barley Falstaff makes its own malt to rigid specifications. The Chicago malting plant's "weather factory," for example, provides precisely controlled humidity and temperature to assure barley germination to a perfection of mellowness. The temperatures vary from 29 to 215°F. Falstaff also buys only the finest-quality, seedless virgin hops, and the water used in brewing is conditioned to absolute standards. The famous Falstaff yeast culture has been passed down from generation to generation. Measuring, cooking, mashing, straining, cooling, fermenting, aging, and packaging—all carefully monitored, with 286 separate quality checks in all—are completed under the scrutiny of the company's skilled brewmasters and quality-control technicians.

Brewing of beer is essentially a chemical process. In making beer, hops are added to a mixture of malt, corn and/or rice, and water, and the product is boiled and fermented with yeast. This process takes place in brewery kettles.

Twice each day, taste testers in St. Louis sample-test the beer produced at all the Falstaff breweries for quality; 7681 taste comparisons by consumers have been made to check the quality of Falstaff's beer compared with other beers.

Beer is measured in 31-gallon barrels. Three hundred and thirty 12-ounce servings or 55 six-packs result from each barrel of beer. The cost of producing premium beer is one-half and more per bottle or can than popular-priced beer.

After the sale of the San Francisco brewery, Falstaff's capacity was 6,800,000 barrels at its six branches (St. Louis, Omaha, New Orleans, Fort Wayne, Galveston, and Cranston). In addition to the sale of the brewery in San Francisco, Falstaff closed smaller breweries in El Paso, St. Louis, and San Jose in recent years.

In 1972, Mr. Gutting told the stockholders:

Much has been written by various analysts on the importance of the newly built "superplant" breweries. We believe that we can produce and sell our beers profitably by maintaining established brewing facilities in a modern up-to-date condition through installation of automated equipment and high speed production lines. Many of the nation's brewers, be they national, regional or local, are doing exactly that today. At Falstaff, this is evidenced by our expenditure of over $29.5 million in the past five years to enhance efficiency and increase capacities of our brewery operations.

The firm distributes beer from three regional distribution centers: Arlington, Texas; North Bergen, New Jersey; and Oklahoma City, Oklahoma. The New Jersey center is 125,000 square feet and holds 300,000 cases and 8000 half barrels of beer. The others are similar in size.

The company runs its own malt plant in Chicago, Illinois, which ships the malt by special container cars to the breweries. The Chicago malting plant processed over 6 million bushels of malt during 1974. The plant supplies malt to the company's brewing operations as well as to other brewers, distillers, and industrial customers.

Feed sales, while still a small part of total corporate dollar volume, increased by 10 percent in 1974. The division produces more than 50 formulated feed products. The primary products are horse, beef, and dairy feeds.

Even though dollar investment is limited, the higher rate of return on sales of formulated feeds, compared with dried spent grain, makes this enterprise attractive and one with considerable potential. In order to take advantage of this potential, the feed division maintains production facilities at St. Louis, Chicago, Cranston, La Grange, Galveston, and New Orleans.

During 1972, Falstaff acquired the La Grange, Texas, feed mill, which had been leased for Feed Division production since 1969. Distribution warehouses are at St. Louis and Sarasota, Florida. Falstaff-formulated feeds are registered for sale in 32 states.

Development of pet food formulations is proceeding at a measured pace with products being tested in the marketplace on a limited basis.

## The future

It is hard to speculate what the future holds for Falstaff. The firm has a long history and is proud of its accomplishments. The Falstaff management are doing their utmost to make sure many future generations can enjoy a refreshing glass of one of Falstaff's fine beers.

# CASES

# Implementation and evaluation of strategic planning

# Shuckman Interiors, Inc.

William F. Glueck

Shuckman Interiors, Incorporated, is a small firm in Milwaukee, Wisconsin. Its business at present involves the installation of flooring, walls, and ceilings in commercial buildings.

The company historically has been well run and profitable. Founded by the late John Shuckman, Sr., in 1955, the company then concentrated on installation and sales of floor tile. Shuckman, Sr., would approach potential buyers, acquire installation contracts, and then hire workers to install the tile.

Noting the increased interest in acoustical tile, Mr. Shuckman diversified his business by adding it to his product-service mix in 1957. This decision was wise, for by 1965, the new product exceeded the sales of floor tiles.

Always on the alert for new products that would fit into the company's line, Shuckman added wall partition products to its list of installation services in 1964.

## A family firm

John Shuckman, Sr., had been a tile salesman for another firm, but he longed for the pleasures and pains of his own business. Psychologists have not often studied the motives of people to form their own firms. This decision often means that they will work longer hours for less money and with high risk that they will lose all their investments and have no job at all. The failure rate of small new businesses is high. William Henry, analyzing the thematic apperception tests of successful entrepreneurs, concluded that the firms were mother substitutes for men with oedipal complexes.[1] But some people do have desire for independence and success that entrepreneurship can bring, and Shuckman seems to be one of them. He knew the construction business and by watching cash contracts and careful bidding for jobs, he avoided the bankruptcy that most similar businesses experience.

In 1970, he became ill, and he died in June 1971, after a lengthy illness. He was succeeded in the presi-

This is a disguised case. That is, the case is based on a real company situation, but the identity of the company has been disguised. It serves no useful purpose to attempt to ascertain the true name of the company.
[1] See Orvis Collins and Daniel Moore, *Enterprising Man,* East Lansing: Michigan State University Press, 1965.

dency by his 26-year-old son, John. The younger Shuckman had received a bachelor of education degree from Wisconsin State University at Whitewater, and spent three years in the Air Force before entering the business during his father's illness. His experience in the business was limited to part-time work while in high school and college.

The case writer interviewed young Shuckman and asked him what the outlook was for his business. He replied:

This has always been a profitable business, but in the last few years we've suffered setbacks in sales and profits. But some of this is due to slowdown in the construction industry in the last 5 years. I think we're just about over the slump period. We should see a reversal in the sales situation over the next few years.

I'm more concerned about other aspects of our operations. It seems like a lot of inefficiencies and poor practices have crept into our work in recent years. Dad was in poor health much of that time, and I guess he just didn't realize what was happening.

One main problem is that our jobs are poorly coordinated. We usually have three crews working on large projects: a floor crew, a wall crew, and a ceiling crew. Changes in work procedures and work schedules for one crew can completely wreck the plans of the other crews. Yet, in most instances, none of the crews know what each of the other crews is doing. Sometimes it's like we're three different companies working on the same job.

Another problem is a lack of good supervision. Often times I find workers just loafing around, waiting for some types of material or just waiting for further instructions. Invariably, the supervisor in charge is up to his elbows in another job—doing things that the foremen should be doing. This sort of thing may have been permitted in the past, but we're simply too big now. We need supervisors who will be supervisors.

Yes, I'm anxious to get a few things straightened out—to really shake things up around here. The trouble is, any time I mention changes, I meet with resistance. For example, I met with the supervisors last week to try and iron out the problem I was just telling you about. They agreed to do a better job of supervision, but the last on-site visit I made revealed that the problem is worse, if anything.

At first I thought that such resistance was due to the fact that I am fairly young and inexperienced. People seem to resent being told what to do by a newcomer. But now I'm beginning to think that some people around here are just plain stubborn. I can tell you one thing: a few heads are going to roll unless things improve pretty soon!

The case writer then asked Mr. Shuckman to describe briefly the business as he saw it in view of its history and possible future. He described it as follows:

For the past, Shuckman served both residential and commercial customers. Presently, the company limits its business to commercial customers. You see, it is difficult to compete in the residential market, since the small contractors selling in that market are not unionized and are therefore able to do the job cheaper. And we didn't want to spread ourselves too thin. Typically, we lay the floor, put up wall and ceiling work for medium-to-large stores and office buildings. We try to work out a "package" deal with our customers. That is, we prefer to do all the basic interior work—floors, walls, and ceilings—ourselves. These three jobs require a certain amount of coordination, and it is usually better to have one outfit doing them rather than many. We do, on occasion, contract to do just a portion of the interior work. Profit-wise, these jobs have not been as satisfactory.

Mr. Shuckman continued:

We offer a total interior service, you see. The floor line consists of vinyl tile, carpeting, and other resilient coverings. The ceiling line includes acoustical board material, illumination panels, and suspension hardware. We do some plastering work, but most of its wall work involves installation of drywalls. The company has developed its own line of drywalls, which features metal studs and channels rather than the more common wood studs and bases. These light and nonpermanent wall partitions have been especially popular for us in remodeling.

## How Shuckman evolved

When the company began, Mr. Shuckman, Sr., performed a wide range of tasks himself. He did all the selling, ordered materials, scheduled and supervised operations, and handled all bookkeeping and accounting routines. He employed a secretary and four or five workers. More workers were added as the business grew. Then, as the company began taking on simultaneous projects, it became necessary to hire foremen for each project, and supervisors to supervise the foremen. Salespeople were hired to help Mr. Shuckman find new business.

Presently, the organization consists of about 110 employees, 65 of whom are skilled or semiskilled laborers. At the management level there are two vice presidents, an accountant, and three production supervisors. Figure 1 shows what the organization presently looks like.

Mr. Thomas Oslin is the vice president in charge of production and also serves as general manager. Forty-eight years old, Mr. Oslin began working for Shuckman Interiors in 1961. Before that, he worked for a firm which manufactures acoustical ceiling material. Besides having responsibility for all production activity, Mr. Oslin is in charge of the main office and accounting department. Mr. Howard reports directly to him.

Reporting to Mr. Oslin are three production supervisors. One is in charge of drywall construction, another supervises ceiling operations, and the third is responsible for floor installation. These persons schedule and control all production activity. Each supervisor assigns work crews to their jobs, ensures that needed supplies are on hand at the work sites, and coordinates work activities with the other two supervisors. The foremen working on specific projects report to these men. All three supervisors have worked for Shuckman for many years and have "risen through the ranks."

The vice president of sales is Glynn Rickers. Mr. Rickers worked in the construction business for 18 years before coming to Shuckman. He started as a sales estimator and was promoted to vice president in 1968. Mr. Rickers is knowledgeable in all aspects of the company's business and works closely with Mr. Oslin in planning and scheduling jobs.

Four sales estimators work directly under Mr. Rickers. These men are responsible for locating new business and for preparing price estimates for bids. They also assist customers in selecting materials and color schemes. All four have had considerable experience in the interior finishing business. One man previously owned an acoustical tile company.

## The Shuckman operation

Jobs at Shuckman Interiors are obtained either by bids or negotiated sales. Most Shuckman business is a result of bid jobs. Typically, a job is announced

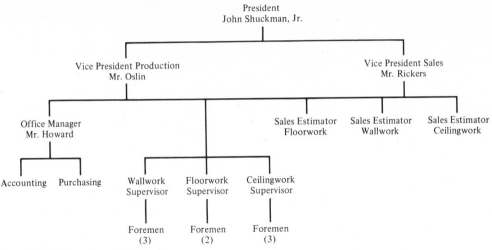

President
John Shuckman, Jr.

Vice President Production
Mr. Oslin

Vice President Sales
Mr. Rickers

Office Manager
Mr. Howard

Sales Estimator
Floorwork

Sales Estimator
Wallwork

Sales Estimator
Ceilingwork

Accounting    Purchasing

Wallwork
Supervisor

Floorwork
Supervisor

Ceilingwork
Supervisor

Foremen
(3)

Foremen
(2)

Foremen
(3)

**FIGURE 1** ■ Organization chart

in a trade magazine, or in a construction service bulletin to which the company subscribes. When a potential job is announced, Mr. Rickers sends sales estimators to review the plans with the building owners and architects. Guided by the blueprint plans, the sales estimators compute the costs for materials and labor. Estimates of costs are made as close as possible to actual direct costs, with overhead, error allowance, and profit margin added on.

Mr. Rickers emphasized the importance of accurate cost estimation: "Most firms lose their shirts because they underestimate costs," he said. "A good estimator can determine almost exactly what the labor and materials needs will be from a good set of plans. A poor set of plans can throw estimates off seriously. We give ourselves a large error margin if plans are not specific. Overall, we've done a pretty good job of bidding most projects. Sometimes we're caught off guard by unforeseen hikes in wages or materials prices, but this is unusual."

Mr. Rickers said that they try to make a 13 percent operating margin on most projects. He added that it was not always possible to obtain such a margin, particularly if a number of other firms are anxious to obtain a given project. Profits for most companies have been generally lower during the construction decline of recent years.

A small proportion of jobs are obtained through direct negotiation with general contractors. In most such instances, contractors have worked with Shuckman in the past, or desire a specific skill or material available only from Shuckman. Some interior materials businesses have salespeople who solicit sales by calling on architects and contractors. Mr. Rickers does not feel that this marketing approach is worthwhile, particularly since most of Shuckman's work involves rather large projects for which bids are necessary.

There are dozens of firms in the Milwaukee area that install floor, wall, or ceiling material. However, only four firms engage in all three types of activities on a large commercial scale. Mr. Shuckman said that his company has about 25 percent of the commercial market, and that this market percentage has remained fairly constant for the past 5 years. Shuckman presently limits its market to the immediate Milwaukee area.

The other three firms are Bischoff Construction Company, Arrighi Services, Incorporated, and Pulaski Interiors. Bischoff is the leading firm, having about 35 percent of the commercial market. But in addition, it has as much residential business as commercial. An old well-established and respected firm (founded in 1920), it originated as a family concern but is no longer dominated by the family. Its bids are always competitive, yet it stresses quality workmanship as well. It does not do as much wall business as Shuckman.

The third firm, Pulaski Interiors, was founded in the Depression and has about 20 percent of the commercial business. Its share of market has been declining. Mr. Pulaski, whose son was killed in the Korean War, seems to have lost interest in the business as he nears retirement in about 1976. Pulaski's business is about the same size as Shuckman.

The newest entry is Arrighi Services. At present it gets only 5 percent of the commercial business, but it has a fairly large residential business. It also offers wider services, including painting and decorating. The business is about two-thirds the size of Shuckman but growing fast. Shuckman feels Arrighi cuts a few corners and has been getting more bids than he should of late.

Like other firms tied to the construction business, these firms find that their business fluctuates considerably. Construction activity is both seasonal and cyclical. Seasonability does not affect firms doing interior work as much as it does firms doing outside work, since workers inside are afforded protection from the elements. Nevertheless, most companies such as Shuckman do a greater amount of work during the warm months. All construction activity is dependent upon a number of political and economic variables, including interest rates, rate of business growth, employment rates, etc. Recessions in construction activity are often rather prolonged, and marginal companies are sometimes forced to go out of business during such periods. The level of manpower in this labor-intensive industry fluctuates in proportion to the level of construction activity.

Once the job is obtained, a sales ticket and work ticket are filled out. The sales ticket is sent to the accounting office, and the work ticket is sent to the production department. As soon as the production supervisors receive the work ticket, they begin planning operations. Materials for the job are ordered, and manpower assignments are tentatively made. The production supervisor must keep in close contact with the general contractor to determine the exact date when the job will begin. When the job is ready for Shuckman to begin operations, the material is sent to the job site from the warehouse and labor is scheduled.

The accounting office records job expenses as they accrue. Actual material costs and labor costs are compared to bid cost estimates on a weekly basis. Wide variances between bid and actual costs are reported immediately to Mr. Oslin, who investigates the discrepancy and takes corrective action, if necessary.

To explain more about his operations, Mr. Shuckman took the case writer on a visit of several work sites. He explained what he considers the production problems to be. He said:

For one thing, our work crews can never seem to follow schedules. You see, work crews for the three basic operations—wall work, ceiling work, and floor work—are scheduled so that the needed workers are available for each successive phase of a project. But if one crew gets behind, this delays the starting time for the next crew. For example, if the wall crew is delayed in finishing a job, the ceiling crew cannot begin on time.

Since there is often no more work for the ceiling crew to do, they are temporarily idle. This is not because of a lack of planning, but subsequent changes in work assignments throw projects off schedule. What happens is that the wall superintendent sees that he's getting a little behind on one project, so he shifts men over from another. This delays work on the other project, and throws everything off schedule. Mr. Oslin and I have talked over the problem a great deal, but haven't come up with any workable solutions. He claims that you just have to expect so much slack in the work schedule.

On a later day, the case writer visited with the production vice president, Mr. Oslin. Earlier a worker had told the case writer that he should talk to Mr. Oslin, since "he ran the whole place, anyway."

The case writer asked Mr. Oslin about the production problem mentioned by Mr. Shuckman. He replied rather sharply:

No, I don't think we have poor supervision or poor work conditions. John seems to think that something is wrong when every single man is not working every single minute of the day. But this just isn't always possible. Things happen which upset even the most carefully planned schedules. I try to keep in touch with the production supervisors about scheduling and work assignment changes. We work things out the best way we can.

But I'll tell you one thing, we do have a supervisor problem. Our three supervisors are spread too thinly. Right now, for instance, we have four major projects under way. It's impossible for each supervisor to be everywhere at once, although sometimes it's almost necessary for him to do so. We need more supervisors. That's the only solution.

The case writer asked several other questions and at one point commented that a worker had said he really ran the Shuckman company. Mr. Oslin replied:

Oh, sure, I guess you might say that I did run the place for quite a while. Mr. Shuckman, Sr., became so sick that he even stopped coming to work. He left everything in my hands. The business would have gone to pieces if someone hadn't taken over. But now that John, Jr., is here, things are different. There's only room for one man at the top, and right now that's him. I'm careful not to infringe on his authority. Sometimes that's difficult, because many people still look to me for instructions and guidance. I discourage this. I'm trying to help John, Jr., all I can.

Asked to comment on Mr. Shuckman's abilities as president, he said:

Well, you can't learn everything there is to know about this business overnight, but John is working hard and learning fast. He's interested in the business. Sometimes, though, I think that there could be better communication between John and the rest of us. He makes a lot of decisions without talking them over with anyone. Some guys resent this. But I'm not going to say anything. As I said before, he's running this show, not me.

## Financial management

Mr. Howard, the company's accountant, told the case writer about the financial problems that are unique to the business.

For one thing, we must pay for materials and labor long before we receive payment from the customer. Furthermore, the customers retain a certain amount to assure the completion of a job. Usually, 10 to 15 percent of our accounts receivable consists of such funds. Because of these factors, we must manage our money more carefully. This

| | 1965 | 1966 | 1967 | 1968 | 1969 | 1970 | 1971 |
|---|---|---|---|---|---|---|---|
| *Assets* | | | | | | | |
| Current assets: | | | | | | | |
| Cash | $ 9,024 | $ 35,818 | $ 10,782 | $ 456 | $ 50,400 | $ 37,608 | $ 32,285 |
| Accounts receivable | 174,122 | 166,893 | 165,906 | 178,086 | 108,288 | 91,425 | 131,632 |
| Inventory | 42,207 | 47,648 | 50,205 | 84,535 | 71,886 | 106,333 | 78,436 |
| Total current assets | 225,353 | 250,359 | 226,893 | 263,077 | 230,574 | 235,366 | 242,353 |
| Fixed assets: | | | | | | | |
| Furniture and fixtures (net of depreciation) | 4,070 | 4,280 | 5,010 | 3,417 | 2,309 | 2,540 | 3,016 |
| Equipment | 13,953 | 30,335 | 22,651 | 24,912 | 35,936 | 40,122 | 42,895 |
| Less reserve for depreciation | 8,544 | 19,171 | 15,409 | 16,232 | 22,523 | 27,455 | 28,371 |
| Net equipment | 5,409 | 11,164 | 7,242 | 8,680 | 13,413 | 12,667 | 14,524 |
| Total fixed assets | 9,479 | 15,444 | 12,252 | 12,097 | 15,722 | 15,207 | 17,540 |
| Other assets | 15,801 | 17,528 | 19,433 | 19,041 | 15,318 | 16,455 | 12,968 |
| Total assets | 250,633 | 283,331 | 258,578 | 294,215 | 261,614 | 267,028 | 272,861 |
| *Liabilities and net worth* | | | | | | | |
| Current liabilities: | | | | | | | |
| Accrued payroll taxes | 3,872 | 6,650 | 5,500 | 8,402 | 12,885 | 12,891 | 27,632 |
| Accrued interest | . . . | 309 | . . . | | | 155 | |
| Accounts payable | 69,342 | 27,122 | 26,214 | 16,379 | 41,693 | 50,155 | 58,496 |
| Accruals | 26,045 | 21,735 | 35,926 | 54,150 | . . . | 21,000 | 23,846 |
| Income tax payable | 8,222 | 12,064 | 14,805 | 14,397 | 3,359 | 12,962 | 26,864 |
| Total current liabilities | 107,481 | 67,880 | 82,445 | 93,328 | 57,937 | 97,163 | 136,838 |
| Long-term debt | 37,500 | 67,500 | . . . | . . . | . . . | 21,114 | 6,000 |
| Total liabilities | 144,981 | 135,380 | 82,445 | 93,328 | 57,937 | 118,277 | 142,838 |
| Capital stock | 75,000 | 100,000 | 100,000 | 100,000 | 100,000 | 100,000 | 100,000 |
| Surplus (after withdrawals) | 30,652 | 47,951 | 76,133 | 100,887 | 103,677 | 48,751 | 30,023 |
| Total net worth | 105,652 | 147,951 | 176,133 | 200,887 | 203,677 | 148,751 | 130,023 |
| Total liabilities and net worth | $250,633 | $283,331 | $258,578 | $294,215 | $261,614 | $267,028 | $272,861 |

involves sound financial planning. Also, it's imperative that we maintain a good relationship with the bank. Since there are relatively few fixed assets to serve as collateral in this business, most banks want prompt payment. Yes, many firms in this business fail because they lack financial management capabilities.

Mr. Howard stressed the importance of using accurate accounting and control procedures. The Internal Revenue Service permits two types of accounting methods for businesses that operate on a long-term contract basis. These are the completed-contract and the percentage-of-completion methods. Shuckman is presently using the completed-contract method, with its fiscal year ending March 31. Mr. Howard said that this method was more appropriate for the company when it had smaller and shorter jobs, but that since Shuckman has been taking on larger jobs, a change to the percentage-of-completion method is being considered. Presently, a quarterly inventory of

TABLE 2 ■ SHUCKMAN INTERIORS, INCORPORATED, INCOME STATEMENTS FOR YEARS ENDED MARCH 31

| | 1965 | 1966 | 1967 | 1968 | 1969 | 1970 | 1971 |
|---|---|---|---|---|---|---|---|
| Sales | $908,000 | $1,261,396 | $1,368,434 | $1,508,643 | $1,347,740 | $806,431 | $941,775 |
| Cost of operations | 783,768 | 1,105,596 | 1,201,473 | 1,320,772 | 1,159,713 | 714,799 | 830,645 |
| Gross margin | 124,232 | 155,800 | 166,961 | 187,871 | 188,027 | 91,632 | 111,130 |
| Selling and building costs | 37,425 | 39,616 | 44,811 | 47,310 | 56,800 | 45,812 | 46,444 |
| Administrative costs | 43,801 | 51,911 | 50,714 | 58,289 | 67,327 | 74,818 | 79,722 |
| Total selling and administrative costs | 81,226 | 91,527 | 95,525 | 105,599 | 124,127 | 120,630 | 126,166 |
| Gross profit | 43,006 | 64,273 | 71,436 | 82,272 | 63,900 | (28,998) | (15,036) |
| Federal taxes | 21,324 | 30,678 | 35,142 | 40,898 | 31,421 | | |
| Net profit | $ 21,682 | $ 33,595 | $ 36,294 | $ 41,374 | $ 32,479 | $ 28,998 | $ 15,036 |

materials is taken. Mr. Howard plans to have a monthly inventory count and prepare monthly income statements and balance sheets in the near future.

Shuckman recently investigated the possibility of computerizing such operations as accounting, inventory control, cost estimation, and profit planning. Mr. Shuckman decided that there is not enough work to justify the purchase of a computer but feels that it may be worthwhile to contract with an outside computer service in the future. Presently, the office force handles the bookkeeping, payroll, and job-cost records. Mr. Howard personally keeps track of delinquent accounts receivable. Entries to all accounts are made by hand and checked by machine.

Mr. Howard's department also handles purchasing functions. Purchases are made for inventory and in response to specific job requests. All materials are stored in a new warehouse building having rail access. Mr. Howard explained that since there is ample storage space, he usually goes ahead and orders materials as soon as he finds out that they will be needed.

Sometimes we have all the materials for a job as much as 3 months in advance of the time they are needed. This way we avoid the possibility of work stoppage due to the late arrival of materials.

I think we've done a good job managing our assets. You're welcome to look at our financial records if you wish.

Tables 1 and 2 are the company's balance sheet and income statements for the last 7 years.

## Some final comments

As the case writer was getting ready to leave, he was pondering the challenges and problems at Shuckman. Running through his mind were some of John Shuckman's earlier comments about his dream for the firm. He had said:

I want to get things shaped up around here first—make the most of what we have now. But my real hopes are far beyond that period. I dream of a firm that is growing and expanding. We've entrenched ourselves—cut out our share of the pie. But we've been standing still—we still think of ourselves as a small outfit. It's about time our managerial thinking caught up to our size and do some long-range thinking instead of operating only on a day-to-day basis.

The case writer wondered if Shuckman Interiors was capable of fulfilling those dreams.

# Seattle Opera Association

Ichak Adizes

The year 1962 was a landmark for Seattle. In that year Seattle held its World Fair, which left the city with an acoustically excellent renovated auditorium holding 3167 seats. Civic-minded people felt that the auditorium should be used in some way that would enhance Seattle's name. The Seattle Symphony undertook some presentation of opera, which had always had very limited production in Seattle. Operas are costly and at this period the Symphony was already $160,000 in the red. To pay off the debt, and assist artistic organizations in raising funds, an organization called Poncho was established and a sum exceeding the $160,000 was obtained by a fund-raising campaign which included an auction of a commando airplane and $35,000 houses. Poncho, whose board of directors includes members of all the arts organizations, continues to operate as a social function organization in the northwestern United States and now serves as a united fund-raising organization for any branch of the arts.

Some members of the symphony board of directors were most interested in opera. Until 1962 there was only a small organization presenting opera productions. This organization, the Western Opera Association, had accumulated losses over the years.

In 1963, Glynn Ross was offered the position of director of the Seattle Opera Association, a new organization then established. Ross accepted the position. The newly established Seattle Opera merged with the Western Opera Association and undertook its losses. The initiating board was composed of members of the Seattle Symphony board who were interested in opera more than in symphony orchestra. It appeared to the researcher who interviewed some of the initiating members of the board that some of the younger members of the symphony board were looking for new avenues of activity and new challenges. The old Seattle Symphony establishment could not offer these opportunities to them, but they could be found in the opera.

In the spring of 1964, the first shakedown season of operations for the Seattle Opera Association, 6000 people bought tickets and two performances each were held for *Tosca* and *Carmen*. Four years later, five performances each of five operas, *Otello, Fidelio, The Crucible, Romeo et Juliette,* and *Don Giovanni,* were produced, and they fetched 70,000 seats. In 1969 there were 15,000 season subscribers, 1500 of them students. Sixty-five percent resubscribed for the 1968–1969 season before the schedule was even announced. Response has also been excellent for the company's National Series, in which young American artists take on the major roles in place of international stars in productions that are otherwise identical, but with sharply reduced admission prices.

What is the reason for the opera's growing attendance in Seattle? A student interviewed for the local newspapers answered this question categorically: "Because it's exciting. With Ross running the show, you never know what to expect next" (*Seattle Post-Intelligencer,* Nov. 15, 1968). In 5 years Ross has changed a city struggling to put on two performances a year into one that was surpassed in the United States by only two or three cities in the 1967–1968 season.

This Nebraska-born impresario is an accomplished linguist, fluent in four languages. When interviewed by the researcher as to his training, his reply was, "My background is in farming." However, the story of his life as depicted in news releases reads as follows: As a youth he first tried his hand at acting. He left this field and at age 26 took charge of the new opera department at the New England Conservatory of Music in Boston. As an army sergeant in World War II, Ross ran rest and recreation centers in the Mediterranean. While serving in Naples, he helped reopen the 225-year-old Teatro San Carlo, where he made his debut in 1945. In 1953 and 1954 he participated in the Wagner Festival in Bayreuth, Germany, where he was enthusiastically accepted. Ross has also staged operas throughout the United States, including San Francisco, Los Angeles, Fort Worth, Philadelphia, and New Orleans. Later he became the resident stage director for the San Francisco Opera. He staged the American debuts of Tito Gobbi, Birgit Nilsson, Regina Resnik, and Gianna d'Angelo. Many others made their San Francisco debuts under his direction. In 1963 Glynn Ross became general manager of the Seattle Opera.

For the future, Seattle Opera plans to create "bush league" opera companies to present its productions in the adjoining areas in the Northwest. A secondary plan (diversification of productions from grand opera to light opera and new forms) will present difficulties since, on the one hand, operatic singers might find it difficult to perform in musicals, and, on the other, light opera singers might find it impossible to perform in grand opera. In 1968 Seattle Opera did not have its permanent singing staff operating on a year-to-year contractual basis. The plans for growing might mean the need of establishing a permanent staff of singers. However, the plans for diversified productions might also create difficulties of casting and thus difficulties of staffing the ensemble.

In order to develop its future markets, Seattle Opera needs $250,000 which it will use for performances in areas where opera has not been performed. Audiences have to be developed and until that happens, touring costs need to be subsidized. To secure funds for its existence and future expansion, Seattle Opera is considering raising an endowment fund of $1 million.

Seattle Opera's future expansion plans have generated several decisions which the Association will have to make. It has reached the point where it needs a permanent stage director, since the number of productions has been increased to a point beyond the control of the existent staff. Until now, stage directors have been brought from outside. However, both the general director, Ross, and the music assistant, Henry Holt, prepared everything possible for the guest director, thus making the work facing him upon arrival relatively easy. The work of both Ross and Holt expanded as the number of productions grew and the portion of work involved in stage directing had to be delegated to a new person. Since Ross is the producer (which implies his being both the artistic and administrative director), the questions which had to be considered were the authority that should be granted to the stage director and the qualifications of individuals who were to be appointed.

Seattle Opera performs at the Opera House, which serves the opera, the Seattle Symphony, and various touring shows. Since the seasons of the two resident organizations are spread throughout the year, during the writing of this case, no conflict was noted between them over the bookings—that is, for use of the hall.[1] This problem will intensify, especially if the long-term goals of the Seattle Opera—to perform 22 weeks each year as the Metropolitan does in New York—are achieved.

## Production

### INTERNATIONAL AND NATIONAL OPERA

The company operates two opera series concurrently—the International and the National Series. There are five productions each season, each of which has five performances, four for the International and one for the National Series. The International performances are produced in the original language and feature the "big names" of international stars together with an international cast. They come to Seattle a few days before the performance, and only a few rehearsals are held. The National Series performances differ from the International in that (1) they have a national cast composed of the singers associated with the Seattle Opera that year, (2) they are always sung in English, (3) they have no big-name stars, and (4) they are offered at a lower price. The International Series is the *stagione,* with stars following the Italian school (stand and sing); the National features the ensemble (German school). The ensemble at Seattle Opera is composed of singers who are associated with the company for a year only. (One singer in 1969 was contracted from among the ensemble of 1968. Two of the 1968 ensemble moved to the New York City Opera at the end of the season.) Most of the singers in the ensemble are National Artist Fellows. The stage decor is the same for both productions, which run in a sequence.

In the star system most performers are brought in for a specific show, as are the director, the designer, etc. They work independently and the director coordinates them. The ensemble approach, generally speaking, fosters an esprit de corps—the director, designers, performers, etc., are all resident members who work together in an institutional manner. Like the star system, the ensemble also needs stars. Its distinguishing features are the length of time people work together in one company, their long-term orientation and interest in it, and the greater control of the director. There are more rehearsals and the dramatic content is emphasized more since group cohesiveness and interaction (which distinguish the ensemble from the star system) have to reach their full expression.

The ideal operation is to have an excellent ensemble and bring in the special

---

[1] However, there was constant conflict between the traveling shows and the rehearsals needed by the opera. As the Opera House is primarily a civic auditorium, the opera company gets no priorities with regard to time needed in the theater.

stars necessary for specific, star-oriented operas such as *Tosca*. Certain operas are performed better with ensembles; others are star-oriented and require several stars to be performed well. Few ensembles can afford to have as permanent members of their company all the best stars (with all the particular characteristics required for specific roles) necessary for major operations.

Seattle Opera attempts to have both an ensemble and a star production. The National Series performances are performed by the resident ensemble. Guest stars are brought in for the same production in the International Series, and those singers from the ensemble who played leading roles in the National Series take minor roles in the International. Here they have an opportunity to perform with the "big names," hopefully learning from the "masters" and thus developing their talents further.

Seattle Opera's season is spread over 8 months from September to April. Thus, each opera receives distinct recognition. Concentrating all their performances into one short period of time, as is usually done, would mean that the interested audience would have to see opera night after night for a limited period, and then no opera at all for the rest of the year. Furthermore, this spreading of the season over most of the year creates the opportunity to concentrate more closely on the production, and to pay more attention to the artistic quality.

The young singers of the Seattle Opera's National Artists Program work daily with Henry Holt, a young American operatic conductor, who is Ross's musical assistant. The National Artists Program allows the National Series to have five singers and a coach in the company. Musicians for both series are contracted on a yearly basis from the Seattle Symphony. Henry Holt conducts the National Series. Ballet dancers and the choreographer are contracted according to the needs of the specific production only, and there are no permanent dancers on the staff.

### SELECTING A REPERTOIRE FOR A SEASON

Over the years from 1964 to 1970, the repertoire has shown a gradual expansion.

1964–1965: 2 performances each of 2 productions

1965–1966: 2 performances each of 4 productions

1966–1967: 3 performances each of 4 productions

1967–1968: 5 performances each of 5 productions

1968–1969: 5 performances each of 5 productions[2]

1969–1970: 5 performances each of 5 productions[2]

1970–1971: 5 performances each of 5 productions[3]

In its first season in Seattle in 1964, the Opera presented a total of four performances. The total in the 1968–1969 season was 25. During that season the company presented *Aida* (with Cossotto), *Andrea Chenier* (with Corelli), *Der Rosenkavalier* (with Crespin), *Tosca* (with Kirsten), *L'Elisir d'Amore*

---

[2] Four International and one National.

[3] One extra National performance added with second production for school students.

(with Costa). The 1969–1970 season was rather more venturesome in repertoire: *Die Fledermaus, Turandot, Of Mice and Men, La Forza del Destino,* and *Salome.* Each of these operas has four International Series performances and one National Series performance.

### CRITERIA FOR SELECTION OF REPERTOIRE

In spite of the Seattle Opera's bent for the new and the unusual, it is still the old and established operas that attract the biggest audiences and pay the major portion of the bills, which in the 1969 season amounted to approximately $750,000. "We have to strike a balance between popular appeal and innovative production," says the general director. "In other words, to get our audience we have to do some old warhorses, but to keep the opera alive we have to give them swinging productions" (*Seattle Times,* August 1969).

However, the organization does not want to have more than two popular operas in a repertoire of five productions. A popular opera can be repeated too much with the result of being overexposed. The popular works are balanced—one Italian and one French (not more than one Puccini). A choice of opera is considered in light of the particular organization of artists on hand; for example, the ensemble would be an asset for *Figaro* or *La Bohème* but a liability for *The Barber of Seville* or *Tosca* since these were written for virtuosi. Other variables considered in choosing a popular opera are its dramatic content and the number of rehearsals it will require.

The organization follows up newspaper reports of what is happening in the opera field both in the United States and internationally. It takes a number of factors into consideration: What has not been done? What is available? What is it able to do? For a rarely performed opera, is there a star who has built his or her name on one of its roles? Should a particular star be desired, what is the best opera for maximizing his or her ability? (*Turandot* was chosen since the company wanted Birgit Nilsson. She was willing to come and she was known to excel in this role.)

Specific examples of the selection criteria for the 1969–1970 repertoire will serve by way of presenting the decision-making process. *Die Fledermaus:* This was the preference of Henry Holt, musical assistant to the general manager. He considered this opera to be strong in impact but light in content, and therefore an "in-between opera." He felt that it would be accepted in English and would draw the growing opera audience. *Aida,* which has the same qualities as *Die Fledermaus* and which was considered a standard opera, had already opened the 1968–1969 season. *Turandot:* For this popular Italian opera, written for virtuosi, the company wanted Birgit Nilsson to take the leading role and therefore her excellence in this production determined its choice. The "scenery" for this Puccini opera was highly unusual. It consisted of 108 minutes of moving images on film played against receding arches, resembling the images seen in "2001—A Space Odyssey," when the spacecraft approached its destination. The film was prepared by two young Seattle film makers, and the opera was staged on kidney-shaped, interlocking platforms. *Of Mice and Men:* This opera, written by Carlyle Floyd, was chosen because it was experimental and new. It was to be a world premiere production under American leadership. *La Forza del Destino:* Since an unusual presentation was planned for *Turandot,* a counterbalance was sought. This consideration partly determined the choice of the traditional *Forza.* Other possible choices could have been *Rigoletto* and *La Traviata.* Compared with *Rigoletto, Forza* needs far more "good" performers and is more difficult. Because of its quality and the challenge involved, *Forza* was chosen for the repertoire. *Salome:* This German opera is a "giant." Its great overpowering music has strong emotional appeal. The production could use the sets of the Vancouver Opera. The alternative could have been a French opera, but *Salome* was considered to be far more effective as a work with which to end the season.


PRESENTATION

For a production, either the sets are rented or someone is hired to make them. A set for *Tales of Hoffmann* will be built and used in San Diego, Houston, Vancouver, Edmonton, and Seattle; thus an excellent set is obtained at a smaller price. Budgets are revised monthly and according to the officers of the company it never goes above its budget. Scenery is based to some extent on past experience. Scenery for a production is budgeted at $10,000, for example, and it is then presented to a builder who is told that he has a $6000 limit. The limit is then extended. The person in charge of scenery usually accepts Ross's judgment as to how much a set should cost. The reason apparently is that Ross has been a stage director and is familiar with the ins and outs of opera production. For something quite novel and experimental, this normal procedure of budgeting is modified. For the film set of the 1969–1970 production of *Turandot,* for example, the company received a grant which covered part of the cost.

Seattle Opera takes its work seriously. The content of opera is sacred, but the organization is not afraid of new trends. Ross has promoted opera as a lively art, as a "now, cosmic happening of sight and sound," and so he presents it on those terms. "An opera that has to do with a mouldy Spanish castle isn't going to be real to most people today. They think of that as a 'fairytale,' " he says (*Wall Street Journal,* Apr. 16, 1968).

In the 1967–1968 season, the company presented Beethoven's *Fidelio,* and sets made of junk sculpture were used. For the settings of the 1969–1970 *Turandot* production, Birgit Nilsson, the leading artist, commented on the scheme: "Never. It's just too wild. I tell you, it just can't work. . . . OK, We'll do it" (*New York Times,* May 18, 1969). Way-out scenery coupled with operatic staples and superstars like Corelli and Sutherland is part of the Opera's attempt to "be everything to everybody."

Experimentation is a keynote. According to Seattle Opera's executives, the boundaries between grand opera, light opera, and speaking musicals are breaking down. In May 1969, the company produced a show called "The Lively Arts—A Trip in Multi-Media." All the pieces but one were prepared originally by the Seattle Opera for programs for schoolchildren funded by Title III of the Federal Elementary and Secondary Education Act of 1965. *Mantra,* the final piece in the show, was a highly imaginative work combining dance, kinetic sculpture technique, and music of different styles—jazz, rock, electronic, contemporary symphonic, and operatic. Audiences and critics alike hailed it enthusiastically as a first-rate, "swinging" show.

Seattle Opera is in a good position, having a monopoly on a culturally hungry, developing community. Critics' reviews of the company's productions represent a more or less unbroken chain of enthusiasm.

Of the 1968–1969 production of *Andrea Chenier* (with Corelli), the *Seattle Post-Intelligencer* (Nov. 14, 1968) commented:

This is a sophisticated, skillfully crafted production, a masterly blending of elements that result in spectacle. . . . Infrequently does a setting so completely match the tone of the opera itself.

The production was a big step forward for the Seattle Opera because never before had local singers constituted so large a percentage of the cast.

Of the 1968–1969 *Der Rosenkavalier,* the *Seattle Times* (Jan. 23, 1969) said that this production

. . . is certainly the best the Seattle Opera has mounted this season and another happy indication of the growing artistic maturity of the relatively young organization. Only a couple of years ago, a good *Rosenkavalier* would have been beyond the grasp of the Seattle Opera. Now it has one.

A critic for the *Seattle Post-Intelligencer* expressed his dismay at the fact that opera audiences tend to be negatively conditioned toward this art. They make up their minds to be bored, and these attitudes are such that nothing the performers can do can change them. Praising both the opera itself and the production, he commented that in spite of these positive features,

Bravos in the Opera House are infrequent and faint. One can never conceive of a Seattle audience standing and cheering. The attitudes get in the way . . . [Nov. 18, 1968].

Only months later, in May of 1969, the same critic said of *Mantra:*

The performance is about as close to a complete artistic experience as the Opera House has ever undergone. . . . It is, in brief, exciting, enthralling and wholly absorbing. It is an experience. . . . The audience (about two-thirds capacity of the Opera House) gave the work and the performance a standing ovation, and well it should [*Seattle Post-Intelligencer,* May 20, 1969].

Evidently these "traditional" attitudes to opera are becoming more flexible. Seattle's young audiences seem to be just as lively as its artists. Commenting on one concert, a boy wrote, "I liked the man that played the drum. He was cool and I like the lady that played the harp and I liked the violins and strumpets [sic]" (*New York Times,* May 18, 1969).

More experienced critics are not altogether categorical in their praise and have reservations. Commenting on the 1968–1969 production of *Andrea Chenier,* the *Seattle Times* (Nov. 14, 1968) said the following in an article entitled "Opera Stages Boring 'Chenier' ":

Last year the Seattle Opera took a third-rate opera—written by a Frenchman and set in Italy—and, with the most impressive production in the local Opera's history, made it look like a first-rate work.

Last night in the Opera House, the Seattle Opera presented another third-rate opera—this one written by an Italian and set in France—and it came off looking decidedly third-rate.

The common factor in both productions—Gounod's *Romeo and Juliet* last year and Giordano's *Andrea Chenier* last night—was Franco Corelli, who is now without question the world's leading Italian tenor. Corelli was also the reason the two operas were presented; they were the lures with which he was attracted to the Opera House stage.

It is obviously a treat for Seattleites to be able to see and hear Corelli. But if the price they have to pay for the treat is *Andrea Chenier,* then the whole experience may be too expensive.

In opera-poor Seattle, where the local Opera presents only five different operas a year, there hardly seems room in the schedule for a yawning bore like *Andrea Chenier*—even with Corelli.

The choice of the opera might have been justified if the work had been given the kind of production *Romeo and Juliet* received here. The *Romeo* production was so skillfully mounted and so visually stunning that the audience never had a chance to wool-gather and to notice that the opera was musically and dramatically thin.

The *Chenier* production is insistently old-fashioned. The new sets (by Enzo Deho of Milan) look 50 years old; they're the kind of flimsy, flown sets in which apparently solid stone walls flap in the breeze when they're accidentally hit by a chorister's elbow. The rented costumes look as if they were originally from productions of *Naughty Marietta* and *The Three Musketeers.* The so-called acting is of the arm-waving, stand-up-and-belt-it-out variety, and the collective and individual actions of the chorus are embarassing when they're not ludicrous enough to be actively funny.

It must be said, however, in fairness to the stage director, Riccardo Moresco, that *Andrea Chenier* didn't give him much to work with.

Of the 1968–1969 National Series production of *Der Rosenkavalier,* the *Seattle Post-Intelligencer* (Feb. 1, 1969) comments:

There were some awkward spots in last night's performance, and a lack of adequate rehearsal time was one factor. Another was by and large the cast's unfamiliarity with *Der Rosenkavalier,* and a lot of time was spent assiduously watching the conductor. . . . This failing apart, *Der Rosenkavalier* was once again completely charming, captivating and light-hearted. This is altogether so gay and so lovely an opera that it's hard to fault at all.

Another critique on the same production of the International version commented:

The whole work is absolutely stunning, despite some minor irritations that can easily be ironed out later. . . . If there are blots on the production it comes with the mounting. For example, silhouetted figures off stage can be seen in the Marschallin's window at the boudoir, this is disturbing [*Seattle Post-Intelligencer,* date unavailable].

The *Seattle Times* (Jan. 23, 1969) summed up its view of the performance in the following words:

The production is not perfect (is one ever?) but it is clearly one of the most ambitious and most successful in the Seattle Opera's history.

The *Seattle Times* (Feb. 20, 1969) had the following comments in its article entitled "*Tosca,* Competent, Not Great":

The Seattle Opera Association's *Tosca,* which opened last night at the Opera House had good singing and good to poor acting. Although the production was at least competent throughout, it fell short of being genuinely memorable. . . . Last night's *Tosca* spun its dramatic wheels for an uncomfortably long time before it finally started moving. . . . Although the production took on dramatic life when Miss Kirsten and MacNeil came on stage, it never really quite recovered from its molasses-slow beginning.

The critique concluded with the following comments:

This production of *Tosca* was directed by Malcolm Black, a highly regarded stage director who for three years was the director of the Vancouver, B.C., Playhouse Theater

Company and who now is a visiting professor at the University of Washington. This *Tosca* was Black's first fling at operatic directing, and he is probably now pulling out his hair over the irritating differences between directing an opera and directing a play.

What does a director do by way of creating a fresh new production when he is saddled with insistently old-fashioned sets (by Ercole Sormani of Milan)? What does he do to create dramatic tension and believability when he has only a few hours rehearsal with the imported stars, who, moreover, arrive with their set notions of how their role should be played?

Black's directorial skill was clearly apparent in his crisp staging of the crowd scene at the end of the first act and the scene in which Scarpia is murdered. If he had had more time, he probably would have been able to solve the dramatic problems of the first scene and to have devised a more convincing staging of the opera's final melodramatic spasm, when Tosca leaps to her death.

Of the same performance, the *Seattle Post-Intelligencer* (Feb. 20, 1969) says:

. . . But what troubled the Seattle Opera Association's production was a sad diversity of purpose on stage, and a lack of life especially in the first act. . . . Regrettably, the principals retain the flamboyant, overdone, "operatically" dramatic gestures that don't serve well anymore. . . . The orchestra, directed by Milton Katims, drowned out the singers a few times in Act I and II. Otherwise it was sensitive and sensible.

The *Seattle Times* (Sept. 29, 1969) comments on the production of the National Series performance of Johann Strauss's *Die Fledermaus:*

Friday's *Fledermaus* had most of the virtues of the International Series performances —and most of its deficiencies as well. It was a big, splashy, colorful show which was generally well sung and funny, but it also strained hard for comic effects, achieving a style that fell somewhere between camp and merely cute. The Seattle Opera apparently felt that it had to spice up *Fledermaus* with eye-winking vaudeville business and topical references. But, in fact, the opera works better when it is simply played straight without being cluttered with gimmicky effects. It is more charming and certainly funnier if the characters don't indulge themselves in blatant foolishness.

Not everyone in the audience likes Ross's innovations. The multimedia approach, according to some interviewed, disrupts the opera. They like the music, and when movies and sculptures attract attention, they feel that the effect of the music is diminished. One symphony fan who attended the opera swore never to come again. He was highly alienated by their attempt to generate audience participation by guiding the audience to clap hands along with the music.

In New York, Seattle Opera is looked down upon by some self-acclaimed experts. "They have no permanent ensemble, musicians, ballet," they said. "It is merely a well-managed production organization." They are also not excited about the innovations which they consider to be degrading tricks of merchandising unfit for opera.

## Organization

The board of directors is composed of 60 members whose average age is young. Several informal, unspoken values appear to guide the members of the board. All board members must be subscribers. One of the criteria for eligibility to the board is either ability to give money or to raise it. The subscription and fund-raising activity appears to be a test of commitment to the organization.

Everyone on the board is supposed to raise at least $500 and if he or she cannot fulfill this function, the alternative is to provide professional services, for example, attorney-legal or advertising-consulting services. The following professions are represented by board members (among others): attorneys, advertising executives, labor relations experts, and media representatives. Care is taken to select people who have a family tradition of serving the arts and who are unselfishly dedicated to them. Potential members are avoided if viewed as using the organization as a social and financial ladder. Once selected, if a board member offers neither money nor a productive service in committee work, he is tactfully eased out. This easing-out process is made possible by the general social values governing the board, by which noncommitted members are ostracized.

The board of directors has an executive committee of 20 people, made up of the chairman of the board and the vice chairmen. Each vice chairman heads one of the board's committees, such as subscription sales, the "Divas and Diamonds" fund-raising activity, etc.

The board and its executive committee meet alternately once a month, affording Ross the opportunity to meet monthly with his board members. Discussions range from the routine approval of the season as proposed by Ross to serious and somewhat heated arguments about the future of the company.

Seattle Opera follows its administrative activities closely. In its offices every visitor sees numerous charts which are kept up to date. One indicates ticket sales on an accumulative basis, updated weekly and compared with ticket sales of the past year. Another indicates budget requirements for the coming season—ticket sales goals, and the fund-raising requirements that must be met. An additional chart shows funds raised as compared to the previous year. To the walls are fastened newspaper reviews of the productions, letters from subscribers, and pictures of smiling people wearing the famous Seattle Opera button, "Opera Lives." Goals for ticket sales are set on a 90 percent occupancy rate. (In the 1968–69 season they sold beyond this goal.) The fund-raising goal is set as the difference between what their projected expenses will be and what the ticket sales plus the United Fund will allocate. Variables which are thus being controlled at Seattle Opera include (1) the subscription rate which is recorded daily on an accumulative basis; (2) single ticket sales, also recorded on a daily basis for each show; and (3) the money expropriated for children's performances. The corrective action taken for subscription sales includes increasing the number of performances per show when subscription exceeds 80 percent of the occupancy rate. The organization is audited by a CPA firm which designed and maintains its charts of accounts. One girl does the bookkeeping within the organization, but as a part-time job only.

The public relations department is composed of one woman and her assistant. They are aided by work-study students from the University of Washington. Seattle Opera pays only part of the salary for these student aids; the remainder is paid by the federal government. (The researcher was told that this arrangement is available to any nonprofit cultural organization.) The Seattle Opera organization presently has about 10 music or drama students who find working at the Opera most exciting. Some work as key punchers, utilizing the data processing equipment of the University; part of the data processed is a record of those who have contributed to the Seattle Opera over the years, their latest addresses, the sums they have donated, etc.

Seattle Opera has a radio-television committee composed of volunteers, usually young women, whose average age is 25. They contact radio-television personalities and obtain spots for the Opera. Press releases are delivered personally by any one of these women. They work closely with the hostesses assigned to artists performing with the company in order to bring in interviews. They initiate and select music appropriate to the current program to be played on popular music stations. They attempt (often successfully) to persuade disk jockeys to play parts of arias of famous operas which are going to be performed in the near future.

From an administrative point of view, what distinguishes the operations of the Seattle Opera is the personal touch given to its handling of customers. For example, typed letters (MTST machine) rather than brochures are circulated. Volunteers who do not have pleasant voices and who cannot adopt friendly tones are not given the task of telephoning during subscription campaigns or answering the phones at the cashier's office.

No staff meetings are held, but constant communication occurs among the members of the organization since they are all crammed into a single large office. Ross is the only person who has something of a semiprivate office. His room has a large open doorway which leads into the staff room. The permanent staff organization is composed of:

```
11 members on the payroll
10 work-study students
 8 volunteers (full-time)
29 total
```

Glynn Ross, presently general director, was formerly both the artistic and business director. This was a source of potential misinterpretation, since newspaper criticism of stage direction was interpreted as an attack on the organization. A different director is now contracted for each production of the International Series. A graduate music student on a work-study basis assists in directing rehearsals and at the time of writing, Ross is entertaining the idea of a permanent director for the National Series. A young American opera director who has spent several years directing in Switzerland, Germany, and Italy was being considered for this purpose, if funds could be found to finance him. The conductor, chorus master, choreographer, orchestra, chorus, ballet rehearsal accompanist, etc., are all contracted per show.

Henry Holt, the music director, does all the music preparation for the visiting directors. Holt was the music director of the Portland Opera. When invited to join Seattle Opera, he accepted, expressing his belief that "Working under Ross is most exciting, and Seattle Opera is innovative and striving." He interacts with people, asks opinions of the musicians, and acknowledges individuals and their respective successes in performances. He holds production meetings of all people involved in technical aspects.

Glynn Ross considers himself the producer. He sees to casting, appoints directors and set designers, does the budgets, and hires his staff. He chooses the productions that are to make up a series. There is a production scheduling committee with which he works in order to choose the repertoire. This committee is composed of Ross, Holt, and Lloyd Yunker, the administrative assistant.

Ross's management philosophy can be identified from the following notes which the researcher found placed under the glass top of his desk:

Carefully plan your change before you present it. Outline it in writing. Anticipate questions. Be ready with solutions to possible obstacles. Discuss it with others who will be concerned. Try to see its effects from your boss's viewpoint.

Time your presentation with care. There's a right and a wrong time to spring a new idea on your superior. Many excellent ideas die because they were presented at a wrong time.

Gradually prepare your boss for the idea you will present. Avoid suddenly dropping it on him out of the blue.

Make the change a cooperative enterprise. Face the problems and difficulties the change will bring honestly with your co-workers. Help to make it their change, not yours.

Set clearly defined goals and performance standards. By doing so, each person affected by the change will know what is expected of him.

Keep all policies, manuals, organizational charts, and job descriptions current. Revise them regularly.

Clearly spell out the lines of authority and responsibility.

Clarify fuzzy policies; give the official interpretation.

Have a simple and clear organizational structure.

Smoke out duplication . . . unnecessary procedures . . . excessive reviews . . . any staff encroachment on line functions.

Finally, pick your management personnel carefully, and keep them abreast of all decision-making.

Ross works in close conjunction with the Opera Guild and the volunteers' association, whose services form much of the backbone of the operating organization. The organization chart in 1970 is given in Figure 1.

ORGANIZATIONAL PHILOSOPHY

The general director of the Seattle Opera has been highly commended by several art critics. Of his ideas, the *Seattle Post-Intelligencer* (June 4, 1969) comments: "Some are profound. Others are startling. Invariably they have merit. Usually Ross, the General Director of the thriving opera, is years ahead of his time."

The organization's philosophy and plans are best summed up in the words of the general director himself, in speaking to members at the annual meeting in June 1969: "We are not custodians of the old order. We are not curators of establishment art. We must be oriented towards the future" (*Seattle Times,* June 4, 1969). He urged the bridging of the gap between generations with presentations that are meaningful to young people, and that utilize new concepts in theater arts. One of the most important operatic goals is to communicate.

The organization is most aware of the youth of society—its receptiveness to new and revolutionary ideas, its buying power and ability to influence the older generation. The Seattle Opera's marketing approach appears to create an aura of excitement that attracts young people. Publicity is flamboyant. Ross prefers to call it "merchandising" and he does not regard "merchandising strategy" as degrading. He says that it is giving opera its place as a lively art. The idea behind the National Series in English was to lure people to the Opera House. A special series of performances starting in the fall of 1967 was initiated, priced sufficiently low ($2 for a balcony seat) in order to compete with the movies.

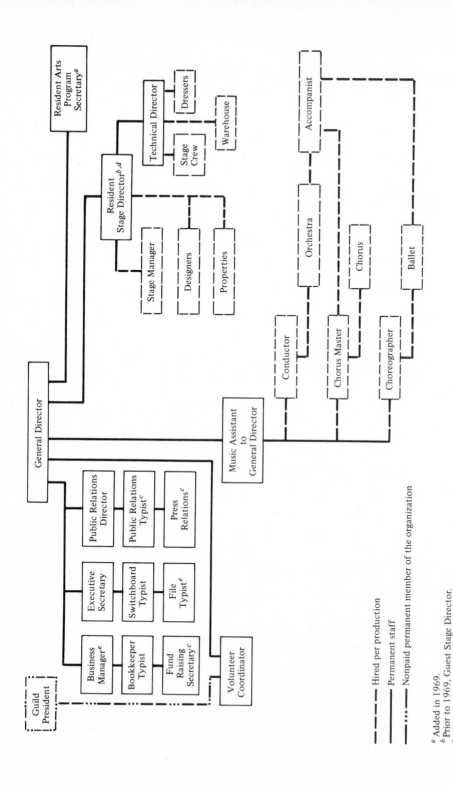

a Added in 1969.
b Prior to 1969, Guest Stage Director.
c Added in 1969.
d 1969 separate stage manager existed for National and International performances.
e Added in 1967.

------ Hired per production
───── Permanent staff
·····  Nonpaid permanent member of the organization

**FIGURE 1 ■** Organization chart, 1970.

At the same time the Seattle Opera Association made history in that it is probably the only one in the country which distributed bumper stickers. These are brilliant red in color and say "Bravo Opera." Cashing in on the current button craze, the Association also issues large buttons proclaiming "Opera Lives."

After introducing the popular-priced series, Ross, aided by six college students (at the time of writing this number has increased to ten), launched a promotional campaign to attract youth by projecting opera as a "now, cosmic happening of sight and sound." The students produced a display of giant antiwar junk sculpture at the 1967 Seattle Teen Spectacular. In addition to the bumper stickers and buttons, they turned out pamphlets with op-art drawings. These talented Opera Whiz Kids wrote a barrage of radio spots in current hippie dialect; a full-page news picture was issued portraying two college swingers walking from their Ford GTO into the Opera House; an entire series of ads in cartoon style appeared, patterned after the drawings of the popular Jules Feiffer. In one ad a girl derides her boy friend for never having attended an opera. "Incredible," she says. "Someone like you . . . Not even once? But why? Why? I know you're cheap, but it costs less than the movies. . . . You don't have to study—it's on weekends! I know you're dumb in languages, but it's in English." In another ad, a dejected male who has "always failed in that one vital area" decides to take his girl to the opera. "A season ticket to the opera is a powerful thing," he rationalizes. "Now I'm irresistible."

Art critics themselves are taken up with the *nouvelle vogue* of the Seattle Opera, as is indicated in the tone and style of one typical report, entitled "It's Like, Man, Wow: Seattle Opera House Sells It Like It Is" (*Wall Street Journal,* Apr. 16, 1968):

Want to hear the story of "four old-time hippies . . . one of the real old-time happenings?" Or the tale of "two kids in real, real trouble with their families?" Try the Opera House. A one-time Golden Gloves boxer is selling opera here the way Madison Avenue sells beer, soap, and autos. Those four hippies are the main characters of Puccini's *La Boheme.* And the real troubled kids? They're better known as Romeo and Juliet.

The campaign has had an impact. In 1968 about 1500 people purchased season tickets and, on the nights of the special series, youngsters fill from two-thirds to three-quarters of the auditorium. Within the world of the University of Washington, opera going is a "kind of prestige thing to do," comments one student, who adds that out of fifty girls in her dormitory hall, six bought season tickets. "It doesn't seem in," she said, "but it doesn't seem out either" (*Wall Street Journal,* Apr. 16, 1968).

### VOLUNTEERS' ASSISTANCE

The Opera Guild is made up of women only, with an average age of 35. Its membership is 700. It provides time and money. It has social parties, holds fund-raising events to promote the opera in different ways (in addition to other things, it provides donations and scholarships for singers), meets artists at the airport, and staffs the ticket office and subscription department at Seattle Opera, which estimates savings of $16,000 annually. The head of the ticket and subscription department is an elderly woman who is a member of the Guild board. This ex officio function means being vice chairman of the Opera board and thus a member of the executive board as well. The woman who holds this position volunteered to work for the Symphony and moved to the Opera Association when it was established. She is assisted by others, but has a full-time job running her department, selecting new volunteers, guiding them, and supervising them. While she is not very wealthy herself, she helps in raising money for the opera through the sale of special tickets which are especially high in price, and thus qualify as donations. Ross has nominated her for ticket chairman, and she was honored at the Women's Press Club.

### RECRUITMENT OF VOLUNTEERS

The Opera Guild recruits a number of volunteers. They plan the printing of tickets, call up people on the telephone, and see to the selling of the tickets. The policy is to give volunteers those functions which encourage deep personal involvement. Ticket selling was chosen especially for them since the responsible nature of this job is such that the volunteers will feel their contribution to the organization and the significance of what they do. Chiefly in charge of the ticket office, they are able to see the difference between their approach and the more impersonal approach of the profit-oriented booking agent. The researcher's impression was that motivation appeared to be at its highest. The women work in groups whose combination seldom changes. They are used to communal working conditions and appear to like being together. Volunteers are invited to all opera celebrations, and Ross sees to it that their work is given the appropriate credit.

All volunteers must be subscribers. The researcher was told that on "all sold out" evenings, several volunteers donate their subscription tickets to the organization and stand during the performance.

The Guild tries to avoid people who might be volunteering predominantly for prestige purposes. Selection is made with extreme care, and potential volunteers' backgrounds are investigated thoroughly. Checks are made on the following points: the sincere love of opera and performance in other volunteer jobs. (References are sought from the organization where the applicant previously worked. Such information as "She is good only for check spots—one-shot jobs" or "She completes her assignment, is able to endure hardship," etc., is acquired and evaluated.) Further information is obtained on whether the prospective volunteer likes people; on her ability to conduct telephone conversations patiently and well (much time is devoted to this activity); on her typing ability; on whether or not she can soft-sell, etc. All information is recorded and considered before a volunteer is accepted.

The volunteer is accepted initially on a trial basis. If she does not appear to cooperate sufficiently, or if she does not appear to be responsible, a process of easing out takes place by way of allocating her a boring routine job (obviously a volunteer cannot be fired) such as typing, until she leaves. A "responsible" volunteer at Seattle Opera means a volunteer that asks questions, shows interest, generates new ideas, asks for new tasks, initiates new activities, etc. Unlike an agency, the volunteer when accepted is informed of how much of her time the job will consume and since it is a demanding job, women with young children are usually not accepted. Most of the volunteers are not selected from the "Blue Ribbon class" of the wealthy families. They are mostly young professors' wives, teachers, and career women.

Once recruited, volunteers are handled with tender care. The office in which they work adjoins the large room of the permanent staff and is just across from Ross's easily accessible office. If tickets are left over on the day of a performance, volunteers are asked if they want to see the opera a second time. The development of factions within the group of volunteers appears to be rare. They entertain one another and there is a strong sense of esprit de corps within which close friendships evolve. They seem to like coming down to work as they have some say in determining with whom they are going to work and can therefore be with friends. The idea of being part of the corps is highly attractive to the newcomer in town who is looking for company, social integration, and acceptance, plus a feeling of being needed and useful in her new social environment. Thus, new volunteers are usually being sought among newcomers.

### VOLUNTEERS' ACTIVITIES

In addition to the radio-television committee activities, the Guild organizes first-night dinners on the opening night of each production. For the price of $5, subscribers, single-ticket buyers, and anyone else, as a matter of fact, can receive an invitation. For National performances, the Guild asks a different local organization to hold the party under its auspices. The Rotary Club and the Navy Club, for example, were among those that hosted the National cast and purchased the invitations. It is a practice that the hosting clubs become subscribers to the opera. The opera singers come to the dinner and interact with their audience and the volunteers, thus giving the latter a feeling of being part of the organization. For one of the operas of the season in progress at the time of our interview, the party after the opening performance was sponsored by the Navy Club. Many Navy people who had never before been to the opera attended the occasion and met the stars of the show. The wives of members of the Navy Club bought a block of 50 tickets which was financed from the club's treasury.

For the International productions, no organization other than the Opera Guild makes the party at the Opera House. This practice is adhered to for two reasons: first, it discourages an undesirable competition which might develop among local organizations with regard to this activity; and second, it minimizes inconvenience to the international stars who might otherwise be put off by the bother of having to travel. On the whole, most stars enjoy this activity as it brings them into closer contact with the audiences and their comments. Some, though, resent it and do not appear.

When the Opera Guild has such a party for the International Series, it picks up the tab of losses after the $5 invitation fee. It charges only $5 in order to encourage maximum participation. "The people who give us $5 are as important as those who give $50, since $50 can be foundation money," said one of the volunteers.

# Other activities

The Opera House and its environs have a scarcity of parking facilities. Thus the Opera Association had to deal with this factor which evidently limited a desire to come to the performances.

The solution to the problem was found in providing transport to the Opera House by buses leaving from various points in town to which patrons would come in their own cars. Free parking space is provided at each of the points from which a special opera bus leaves for the Opera House.

One of the pickup points is a music store where a volunteer hostess welcomes the waiting patrons and serves coffee. If it is their first ride, they get champagne. In the period between arrival at the store and departure by bus for the opera, the store familiarizes the crowd with the music of the opera they are to attend. The music store benefits from this arrangement, as people purchase records while strolling along the aisles waiting for their departure. Bus tickets cost $1.25; free tickets were issued to those who used the bus on its very first trip.

Another pickup point is a famous restaurant in town. There is ample parking space there and members of the audience can dine there before the show. Usually a member of the Opera Association will be there for dinner to give a talk or explanation about the opera they are going to see. Attending also are hostesses from the Opera Guild, who regard it as their function to facilitate social interaction, thereby adding to the communal spirit shared by all who avail themselves of the opera's transport system. (At the time of writing, a possibility of free advertisements for the restaurant was being considered.)

## TICKET SALES

In 1968, Seattle Opera had 15,000 subscribers. Four thousand telephone calls were made by the volunteers to those who did not resubscribe for the new season; 36 percent of the subscribers had to be phoned. Fifty percent of those called resubscribed on the first call, and on the second and third calls 20 percent of the 2000 remaining resubscribed. The end result was that 1600 out of 15,000 were lost. A record is kept of the reasons given for refusals to resubscribe.[4] The most common reason is the cost of tickets, which as a portion of personal income becomes too much for families that have expanded or undertaken new financial burdens. Others do not resubscribe because they have moved out of the city.

For opening nights, the center box seats (104) are sold at $125 a ticket. On nonopening nights these tickets are sold at $50 each. The price of these tickets is tax-deductible. As the demand for them exceeds the supply, the center box seats are "stretched" to offer more seats at this price.

Subscribers have their seats permanently as long as they subscribe. If seats are freed from one season to another, subscribers are offered better seats

---

[4] No record is kept of tickets sold per price per year, nor are records kept of the number of tickets unsold.

**TABLE 1 ■ SEATTLE OPERA TICKET PRICES, 1964–1971**

| | Season tickets | Single tickets | | | Season tickets | | Single tickets |
|---|---|---|---|---|---|---|---|
| 1964 | | 6.00[a] | 1967–1968 | International series | 37.50 | 41.25 | 12.00 |
| | | 5.00 | | | 32.65 | 36.25 | 10.00 |
| | | 4.00 | | | 27.00 | 30.00 | 8.00 |
| | | 3.00 | | | 18.00 | 20.00 | 6.00 |
| | | 2.50 | | National series | 22.50 | 25.00 | 6.00 |
| 1964–1965 | 30.00 | 7.50 | | | 17.50 | 20.00 | 5.00 |
| | 24.00 | 6.00 | | | 15.00 | 17.50 | 4.00 |
| | 20.00 | 5.00 | | | 10.00 | 12.50 | 3.00 |
| | 12.00 | 3.00 | 1968–1971 | International series | 39.00 | 45.00 | 12.00 |
| 1965–1967 | 34.50 | 7.50 | | | 37.00 | 40.00 | 10.00 |
| | 29.90 | 6.50 | | | 27.00 | 30.00 | 8.00 |
| | 27.60 | 6.00 | | | 20.00 | 25.00 | 6.00 |
| | 25.30 | 5.00 | | National series | 20.00 | 25.00 | 6.00 |
| | 16.10 | 3.50 | | | 17.50 | 20.00 | 5.00 |
| | | | | | 15.00 | 17.50 | 4.00 |
| | | | | | 10.00 | 12.50 | 3.00 |
| | | | | | * 7.00 for boxes | | |

[a] Prices of tickets vary. The "best" tickets cost the most, the poorest the least, and the rest are in between.

according to their seniority as subscribers. If a subscriber does not want to change his seat, the words "never move" are written next to his name on the list and the opportunity of moving is not offered him again. The allocation of seats is done by the volunteers. Ticket prices are given in Table 1. Percentages of subscriptions were: 1967–1968, 75 percent; 1968–1969, 92 percent; 1969–1970, 59 percent; 1970–1971, 75 percent.

### FUND RAISING

Seattle Opera received a $100,000 grant from the Ford Foundation for 5 years. In addition to this grant, it is supported by Seattle's United Fund (see financial statements). It has its own sustaining fund-raising activities as well. One of these is the "Divas and Diamonds" fashion show. "Divas" stands for the opera stars and "Diamonds" for the jewelry fashion show. The timing of the event is such that no other nonprofit organization is in the midst of or at the beginning of its own campaign.

## Plans for future expansion

Speaking of the organization's progress and development, its general director said in August 1969: "We've never had to force-feed our audience, never had to tell them that they'd better take opera because it's good for them" (*Seattle Times*, August 1969). He felt that the organization had reached a "healthy plateau" in the Seattle area and that it was ready to move on to a regional basis.

Concerning his management approach, Mr. Ross has three rules: (1) to make the product as good as he can; (2) to spread his market; and (3) "to use

## TABLE 2 ■ SEATTLE OPERA ASSOCIATION'S BUDGETS

| | 1969–1970[a] | 1970–1971 | 1971–1972 |
|---|---|---|---|
| *Income* | | | |
| International productions | $360,588 | $350,000 | $350,000 |
| National productions | 46,447 | 46,255 | 46,255 |
| National Artists | 119,702 | 64,200 | 68,694 |
| Ford Foundation | 52,500 | 20,000 | . . . |
| Rentals | 4,000 | 5,500 | 6,000 |
| Libretti | 3,400 | 1,700 | 1,700 |
| Interest and dividends | 6,000 | 6,500 | 6,500 |
| Other | 2,683 | 20,000 | 30,000 |
| Operating income | 595,320 | 514,155 | 509,149 |
| Sustaining fund | 96.590 | 106,249 | 116,874 |
| U.A.C. | 66,821 | 134,825 | 230,132 |
| Total | $758,731 | $755,229 | $856,155 |
| *Expense* | | | |
| International productions | $400,800 | $453,790 | $521,858 |
| National productions | 52,268 | 49,493 | 52,957 |
| National Artists | 118,932 | 64,200 | 68,694 |
| Fund-raising | 5,000 | 5,350 | 5,725 |
| Salaries | 102,309 | 106,162 | 113,594 |
| Office | 46,169 | 49,934 | 54,927 |
| Warehouse | 4,200 | 6,300 | 8,400 |
| Other | 3,095 | . . . | . . . |
| Contingency | 20,000 | 20,000 | 30,000 |
| Total | $752,773 | $755,229 | $856,155 |

[a] 5,958 surplus.

the budget almost totally for performance, as little as possible for paper work" (*Christian Science Monitor,* Feb. 12, 1969).

The Seattle Opera began its market spreading, its regional expansion, in the spring of 1969, when it took its production of *Tosca* to Spokane, Washington, and Missoula, Montana. The company took the principals, the scenery, and the costumes. Spokane furnished the orchestra and chorus. In Spokane, a daytime performance for schoolchildren was presented, underwritten by funds from the Federal Title III program.

In both cities there were evening performances sponsored by local residents. The children's performance was packed, but more significant is the fact that both of the evening performances were fully sold out well in advance. Ross comments that "We were successful beyond our dreams in involving these communities in the whole idea of opera. . . . The best indication of our success is that both want us back next year—and for more performances" (*Seattle Times,* August 1969). The opera is also planning to perform in many more Washington State communities and to increase its Montana exposure by performing in Butte, Billings, Bozeman, and Great Falls.

At the time of writing, Seattle Opera was locating halls in different places and securing commitments for future performances. It was planned to offer *Salome* on weekdays for school children, as well as 17 performances of the special multimedia show. Such plans are represented graphically on a large wall map of the northwestern region of the United States which hangs on a wall of Mr. Yunker's office. Different-colored pins indicate the Seattle Opera's expansion program, noting its plans for touring through 1974. Various marks indicate availability of halls and the sizes of the various communities.

For 1969 the company wanted $250,000 for touring and for developing other markets. It had already had some experience with touring, having performed in about 10 places in 1968–1969. Seattle Opera would like to have a touring company and a 22-week season like the Metropolitan Opera to provide for such expansion.

*Seattle Post-Intelligencer* (June 4, 1969) reported comprehensively the major points made by the Seattle Opera's general director in his speech at the annual meeting of the Opera Association.

If there's one thing Glynn Ross of the Seattle Opera doesn't lack, it's ideas. Ross has called for the following:

Bridging the gap between the generations—or, as he phrased it, between the Opera House and Eagles Auditorium (site of rock and light shows)—with presentations that are meaningful to young people and that utilize the new concepts in theater arts.

Supplementing the current volunteer plan of bringing the poor to performances by taking operas to the people through works designed to be shown in churches; continuation and expansion of the present program of cooperating with other population centers (Spokane is an example) in staging operas using local talent.

Establishing a summer music festival—to be called Music in the Forest—supported by the lumber industry and creating a strong national attraction for all generations, and establishing a new and strong relationship with the two other Northwest opera companies (Portland and Vancouver), leading to the sharing of sets and costumes, which would result in more quality at less cost.

Echoing *The Post-Intelligencer* in its lead editorial on page 10 today, Ross summoned the city, the county, and the state governments to support the arts, citing the fact that the Seattle Opera is the only major opera company in the nation not to be financially aided by government.

He asked that the city modernize the lighting facilities in the Opera House and pointed out that the opera needs a home to keep administration, rehearsals, scenery and props under one roof. The way things are now, scattered with the Opera House only sparingly available, the opera is penalized beyond belief.

Just to think that, after all these years at the Seattle Center, the Opera, the Symphony, the Repertory are isolated from the facilities they are compelled to use, with offices and scant rehearsal space all around town. And the opera just cannot survive without the Opera House. No other major opera suffers this way.

This city makes a big to-do about the arts until it comes to support them with cold, hard cash. Then, we grow noticeably reluctant. In this sort of a situation words don't help a great deal. Not even these.

Seattle Opera wants to achieve a level of artistic reputation and financial stability that will enable it to have on its permanent staff singers of world reputation. For the time being, it prides itself on the fact that members of its ensemble are invited to join the well-established opera houses such as New York City Opera. Furthermore, it is succeeding in bringing back some excellent American opera singers who had had to join opera houses in Germany and France because they could not find employment in the United States.

In its 6 years of operation, Seattle Opera has succeeded in creating excitement for opera, in building an audience and an organization which is able not only to break even, but to generate a surplus as well. The local newspapers have given excellent reviews of its artistic achievement.

The questions facing Seattle Opera are where to go next and how to go about it.

In his interviews, the researcher recorded several comments made by Mr. Ross about his financial policy. In his opinion, "Every artistic organization should pay its own way." International productions should carry all the cost of the production including sets, designs, etc. National performances then are budgeted on incremental basis: How much more will it cost to have a National performance, and will it pay for itself?

In forecasting revenues, the occupancy of the hall is estimated to be 90 percent. Season tickets are sold at 25 percent discount price. The season subscription in 1968 was 63 percent of total tickets sold. Subscription is sold according to the strategy that the only way for a customer to secure a seat for a performance with a well-known star will be by buying a subscription for the whole season in advance.

Ross believes in making budgets as accurate as possible and then sticking to them. According to the Seattle Opera executives, Ross does not allow budget deviations if they can be prevented in any way. The *Wall Street Journal* (Apr. 16, 1968) gives certain information about Seattle Opera's financial conditions: the company's budget for the first year (1964) was $165,363; for the 1968–1969 season, the general director planned to spend close to $850,000.

**TABLE 3 ■ BALANCE SHEETS OF SEATTLE OPERA ASSOCIATION, 1966–1970**

|  | 1966 | 1967 | 1968 | 1969 | 1970 |
|---|---|---|---|---|---|
| *Assets* | | | | | |
| Current assets: | | | | | |
| Cash | $ 100 | $ 100 | $ 100 | $ 1,205 | $ 28,658 |
| Overdraft in checking account | (1,709) | . . . | . . . | . . . | . . . |
| Savings and cDs | 153,644 | 161,088 | 45,007 | . . . | 112,851 |
| Treasury bills | . . . | . . . | . . . | 35,000 | 35,000 |
| Prepaid expenses | . . . | . . . | 744 | . . . | 27,934 |
| Securities | | | | | |
| (value date of donation) | 1,313 | 1,364 | 1,226 | 347 | . . . |
| Accounts receivable | 33,867 | 7,414 | 72,553 | 70,187 | 17,822 |
| Miscellaneous receivables | 771 | . . . | . . . | . . . | . . . |
| Total current assets | 187,986 | 169,966 | 119,630 | 106,739 | 222,265 |
| Properties and fixed assets: | | | | | |
| Furniture and fixtures net of | | | | | |
| depreciation | 3,900 | 9,135 | 8,820 | 11,073 | 15,250 |
| Costumes net of depreciation | 3,908 | 6,510 | 8,821 | 11,072 | 15,316 |
| Total assets | $195,794 | $185,611 | $137,271 | $128,884 | $252,831 |
| *Liabilities and surplus* | | | | | |
| Accounts payable | $ 3,828 | $ 6,704 | $ 1,885 | $ 4,648 | $ 2,186 |
| Advance receipts: | | | | | |
| Ticket receipts | 114,604 | 89,334 | 86,967 | 64,965 | 198,669 |
| Contributions received | 36,094 | 53,610 | 24,864 | 53,529 | 16,568 |
| Less expenditures incurred for | | | | | |
| upcoming season | 4,268 | 13,882 | 10,288 | 29,103 | . . . |
| Total receipts | 146,430 | 129,062 | 101,543 | 89,391 | 215,237 |
| Surplus: | | | | | |
| Balance last year | 1,227 | 45,536 | 49,845 | 33,843 | 34,845 |
| Net income (loss) this year | 44,309 | 4,309 | (16,002) | 1,002 | 563 |
| Total liabilities and surplus | $195,794 | $185,611 | $137,271 | $128,884 | $252,831 |

**TABLE 4 ■ SEATTLE OPERA ASSOCIATION, COMPARATIVE FINANCIAL FIGURES, 1965–1969**

| | 1965–1966 | 1966–1967 | 1967–1968 | 1968–1969 |
|---|---|---|---|---|
| **Revenue:** | | | | |
| Tickets | $197,097 | $314,952 | $378,863 | $444,307 |
| Title III | 33,867 | 90,128 | 93,635 | 133,618 |
| Direct revenue, performances | 230,964 | 405,080 | 472,498 | 577,925 |
| Other operating revenue[a] | 8,798 | 18,867 | 14,240 | 10,405 |
| Total operating revenue | 239,762 | 423,947 | 486,738 | 588,330 |
| Contributions[b] | 59,452 | 89,704 | 138,682 | 184,272 |
| Total income | 299,214 | 513,651 | 625,420 | 772,602 |
| **Expenses:** | | | | |
| Direct productions | 207,634[c] | 376,974[d] | 484,415[e] | 581,273[f] |
| Indirect[g] | 47,271 | 112,368 | 157,007 | 145,018 |
| Others[h] | | | | 45,309 |
| Total expenses | 254,905 | 489,342 | 641,422 | 771,600 |
| Overoperating revenue[i] (loss) | (15,143) | (65,395) | (154,684) | (137,961)[j] |
| Net revenue[k] | 44,309 | 24,309 | (16,002) | 1,002 |
| Total assets | $195,794 | $185,611 | $137,271 | $128,884 |
| Total operating revenue / Total assets | 1.22 | 2.28 | 3.55 | 4.57 |

[a] Interest earned, program advertising, etc., which are related to the performances but are not derived from direct ticket selling.
[b] Net, i.e., less direct fund-raising expenses.

[c] Direct production costs:

| | |
|---|---|
| La Bohème | $ 34,775 |
| Samson | 35,246 |
| Lohengrin | 31,911 |
| Il Trovatore | 42,555 |
| Madame Butterfly | 32,153 |
| La Bohème, Title III | 30,994 |
| | $207,634 |

[d] Direct production costs:

| | |
|---|---|
| Lakme | $ 91,136 |
| La Traviata | 31,116 |
| La Bohème | 7,883 |
| Turandot | 53,351 |
| Barber of Seville | 53,914 |
| Cav-Pag | 56,370 |
| Stravinsky | 23,028 |
| Title III performances | 60,176 |
| | $376,974 |

[e] Direct production costs:

| | |
|---|---|
| Othello | $ 83,036 |
| Romeo and Juliet | 106,176 |
| The Crucible | 53,792 |
| Fidelio | 63,935 |
| Don Giovanni | 97,883 |
| Title III | 79,593 |
| | $484,415 |

[f] Direct production costs:

| | |
|---|---|
| Aida | $109,150 |
| Andrea Chenier | 102,543 |
| Der Rosenkavalier | 100,668 |
| Tosca | 77,498 |
| Tosca tour | 16,439 |
| L'elisir d'amore | 65,464 |
| Title III | 109,511 |
| | $581,273 |

[g] Overhead, insurance, office rent, salary of director and administrative staff.
[h] United Artist program.
[i] Overoperating revenue = total operating revenue − total expenses.
[j] Not including United Artist program.
[k] Including contributions, funds, grants, etc.

(In 1971 he earns a salary of $22,000; in 1964 his salary was $13,000.) In 1967 the Ford Foundation gave the Seattle Opera a $100,000 grant to be spread over 5 years, and the federal government supports special performances for schoolchildren ($105,000 was expected in the 1968–1969 season).

Those contributions combined with season ticket sales should account for 75 to 80 percent of the opera's budget. Outright contributions will make up the balance. But even the percentage of gifts needed is below what most opera companies have to solicit.

Currently, Ross has a drawer full of projects and ideas which would bring

**TABLE 5 ▪ JUNE 30, 1970, STATEMENT OF REVENUE AND EXPENSES, SEATTLE OPERA ASSOCIATION**

*Operating revenue*

| | |
|---|---:|
| Ticket sales for regular season performances | $ 403,282 |
| Cultural Enrichment performances | 64,630 |
| Cultural Enrichment—*La Bohème* tour | 10,000 |
| *Tosca* tour | 15,639 |
| Sale of libretti and program advertising—net | 5,875 |
| Miscellaneous income—net | 6,029 |
| Total revenue | $ 505,455 |

*Operating expenses*

| | | |
|---|---:|---:|
| Direct production: | | |
| Regular season performances | $438,317 | |
| Cultural Enrichment performances | 42,182 | |
| Cultural Enrichment—*La Bohème* tour | 6,592 | |
| Tosca tour | 16,096 | 503,187 |
| Indirect expenses | | 176,300 |
| Total expenses | | $ 679,487 |
| Excess of operating expenses over income | | $(174,032) |

*Other revenue (expense)*

| | | |
|---|---:|---:|
| Contributions, less fund-raising expenses of $3,756 | $111,167 | |
| Ford Foundation | 52,500 | |
| National Artists Program: | | |
| Poncho grant | 15,000 | |
| Other grants | 18,630 | |
| Salaries and expenses applicable thereto | (32,235) | |
| Interest income | 9,533 | 174,595 |
| Net revenue to surplus | | $      563 |

Seattle Opera into close relationship with the community. The Work-Study program gives part-time employment to students and is already in operation. A community Performing Arts Combine would involve the cooperation of performing arts groups throughout the state and, ultimately, the country.

One of the ideas closest to Ross's heart is the formation of a nationwide opera community through which computers sort repertory, ticket sales, tours, finances, box office, schedules group-owned sets and costumes, everything but the singing. One small stepping-stone of this dream is already under way. The first sessions of a planned Northwest Opera Workshop were held between November 20 and 22, 1970. By means of this workshop voice students from participating colleges and universities in the Northwest were brought to Seattle to join in seminars given by professionals. Ross, Holt, and Robert DeSimone, the resident stage director, each presented discussions about professionalism and the professional theater. Coaching sessions and the presentation of various operatic scenes were included in the program. It is hoped that the workshop can expand into a regular contributing part of the opera business and in the Northwest and become an exciting means by which young singers can be exposed to professional situations that are otherwise hard to come by.

Seattle Opera's 1970–1971 season has proved most unusual in that all indications are that the company is having its most successful year to date. Harold

| | 1967 | 1968 | 1969[a] | 1970 |
|---|---|---|---|---|
| Annual meeting | $ 570 | $ . . . | $ 876 | $ 494 |
| Administrative, travel, and entertainment | 6,453 | 5,726 | 7,021 | 5,851 |
| Professional services | 1,454 | 1,100 | 1,150 | 1,500 |
| Auto expense | 600 | 1,200 | 1,200 | 1,200 |
| Postage | 6,255 | 11,123 | 8,113 | 8,307 |
| General publicity | 9,106 | 23,536 | 3,155 | 6,576 |
| Office supplies and expense | 7,880 | 8,075 | 5,021 | 8,788 |
| Office rent | 1,200 | 1,880 | 1,920 | 1,920 |
| Warehouse rent and expense | 3,350 | 3,465 | 4,166 | 4,798 |
| Programs | 5,584 | . . . | . . . | |
| Telephone and telegraph | 5,016 | 5,781 | 8,131 | 10,640 |
| Insurance | 1,070 | 1,808 | 2,157 | 6,020 |
| Salaries | 50,846 | 80,488 | 87,497 | 97,630 |
| Payroll taxes and medical | 4,583 | 3,930 | 3,717 | 5,348 |
| Dues and subscriptions | 372 | 461 | 662 | 660 |
| Rentals | 1,696 | . . . | . . . | 1,536[b] |
| Central Area Project | 226 | . . . | . . . | |
| Business taxes | 66 | 41 | . . . | 1,099[c] |
| Depreciation not charged to productions (straight-line method) | 4,989 | 4,299 | 4,737 | 5,844 |
| Other expense | 1,052 | 494 | 114 | 1,589 |
| Contribution to retirement plan | . . . | 3,600 | 3,600 | 6,500 |
| Lecture series | . . . | . . . | 1,781 | . . . |
| Total indirect expenses | $112,368 | $157,007 | $145,018 | $176,300 |

[a] These statements are presented on the accrual basis. It should be noted, however, that accounting procedures have been adapted to suit your particular circumstances. Revenue from ticket sales for the future 1969–1970 season is shown on the balance sheet as advance receipts, and applicable incurred direct expenses have been deducted therefrom. Similarly, contributions received which can be attributed to the Spring Campaign are defined as revenue for the 1969–1970 season and deferred. Other contributions are current revenue. Unpaid pledges are not included in the statements. Administrative or indirect expense has not been divided between seasons notwithstanding that a portion of the expense has been incurred for the 1969–1970 season. Assets or revenue of the Seattle Opera Association Endowment Fund, a separate trust, are not reflected in the attached financial statements.

[b] Office machine rent.

[c] City and state taxes.

Schonberg, music critic for the *New York Times,* said in a recent article in that newspaper (Nov. 22, 1970):

Seattle at the moment is having trouble. Its economy is closely allied with Boeing, and Boeing is suffering from cutbacks. The rate of unemployment in Seattle is much higher than the national average. Yet people continue to support the opera, money comes in, and Ross is not crying poor. Far from that.

Ticket subscriptions are up and general ticket sales have increased. The first two productions have played to standing room only capacity. When questioned about the apparent success of the season, Ross replied that the economic downturn had been planned for when the season was planned 2 years previously. For that reason, the five operas composing the 1970–1971 season reflect an intended emphasis on popular opera. The five operas are *Madame Butterfly, The Tales of Hoffmann, The Marriage of Figaro, Don Carlos,* and *Carmen.* Within this structure, the company was able to maintain its balance of Puccini, Verdi, and French opera. *Carmen* and *Butterfly* are two of the most popular of all operas; *Figaro* is also on the popular list. Although not as popular, both *Don Carlos* and *Hoffmann* are traditional works and fall into the category of the tried-and-true.

Ross has a theory about the opera's success so far despite the economic environment. He maintains that opera in Seattle serves as an entertainment-oriented escape for people who are continually faced with difficulties in the world around them. By attending the opera, they are able to enter a world of make-believe which provides the necessary respite from their economic troubles.

Tables 2, 3, 4, 5, and 6 contain some recent financial data.

# St. Luke's Episcopal Hospital

Richard M. Grimes
William A. Russell

## Introduction

St. Luke's Episcopal Hospital is a 773-bed institution located in Houston, Texas (see Figure 1). It is known internationally for the high-quality research, teaching, and patient care which it provides to society.

St. Luke's opened in 1954. A general, adult hospital, it shares many facilities, services, and departments with Texas Children's Hospital, and supports research in cardiovascular (heart and circulatory system) disease through the Texas Heart Institute, the third corporation of the St. Luke's complex. Each corporation has its separate governing board, but the three share a chief executive officer, Mr. Newell E. France, a nationally known figure in hospital circles. The chart of administrative organization for this three-corporation management arrangement is shown in Figure 2. Affiliated with Baylor College of Medicine, St. Luke's emphasizes clinical programs in cardiac surgery, cardiology, neurology, obstetrics and gynecology, orthopedic surgery, urology, and, although otherwise an adult hospital, premature and stress infant care. Specialized facilities include coronary and medical intensive-care units, a 25-bassinet premature nursery, heart catheterization laboratories, and a urodynamics laboratory. The hospital employs 1800 people. It treats 26,000 inpatients, and nearly as many outpatients, annually.

By being located in Houston, St. Luke's is both the beneficiary and the victim of several interesting crosscurrents. Houston is the fastest-growing city in the United States, increasing in population from 385,000 in 1940, to 596,000 in 1950, to 938,000 in 1960, and to 1,233,000 in 1970. Estimated 1980 population is 1,600,000. Located 50 miles from the Gulf of Mexico, Houston gives access, by ship channel, to a commerce which is third in tonnage among seaports of the nation. The city is diversified in commerce, and its industry includes petrochemicals, cotton exporting, the Johnson Space Center, and oil-oriented manufacturing and distribution.

## The Houston hospital community

Medical care is also a significant Houston industry. Attracting patients from both hemispheres and all

**635**

**FIGURE 1** ■ St. Luke's Episcopal Hospital, Houston, Texas.

compass points, the city's largest medical-industry grouping is in and around the Texas Medical Center. This research, education, and treatment campus is composed of 27 public and private institutions and organizations, compactly situated on 189.5 acres. The Texas Medical Center is interrelated with and complemented by the University of Texas Health Science Center at Houston, which separately has an additional 100 acres of property. Building value in the medical center in 1974 was approximately $283 million, and was increasing by millions. Annual operating expenditures of the center's institutions totaled $226 million. About 5000 are enrolled in education programs which include two medical schools, six nursing schools, a dental school, a school of public health, and several allied health schools. Institutions within the center treat 118,000 inpatients a year, and more than 1,100,000 outpatients. Spin-off industry is nearly as big as that of the medical center itself; it includes several

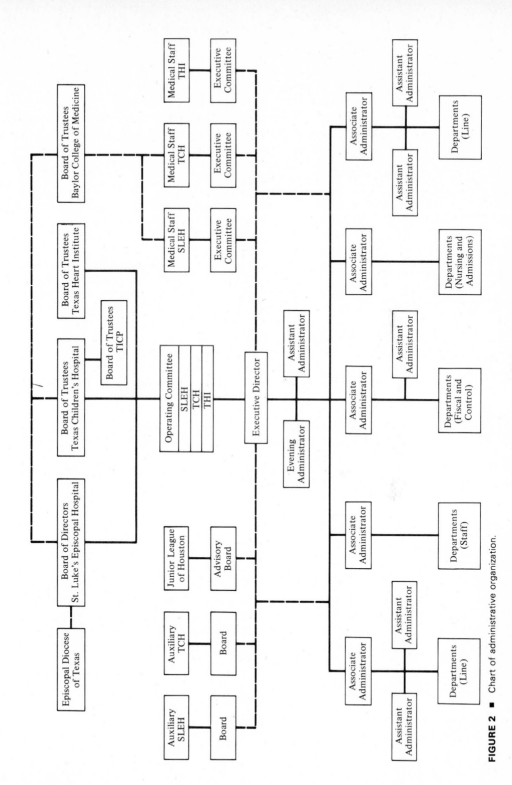

**FIGURE 2** ■ Chart of administrative organization.

637

hospitals and many office buildings for doctors. Within the center there are 3600 patient beds, including the 773 operated by St. Luke's. An additional 1000 beds are within a mile or two of the medical center.

The growth of hospitals in the Houston area has surpassed the rate of population growth. From approximately 6300 general hospital beds in 1966, the number of beds had grown to more than 9000 in 1973. A study prepared for the local health planning agency suggested that the number of beds in 1974 was sufficient to meet Houston's hospital needs through 1980. However, more than 4000 new hospital beds were either planned or under construction in Houston in 1974.

The sizable 1974 excess of beds (estimated to be 1366 by the State Health Department) and the enormous potential excess was a grave concern to hospital administrators because of the unique operating characteristics of hospitals. For most hospitals, about 70 percent of expenses are fixed costs. This highly levered situation means that any substantial reduction in the percentage of occupancy (occupied beds divided by total beds) has dire financial consequences. The 1974 occupancy rate of all Houston hospitals was approximately 70 percent (a marginally profitable level for most hospitals). If the planned hospitals were constructed, the average occupancy rate would be about 50 percent, a level which could raise the specter of bankruptcy for many institutions. The direction of such an occupancy shift is suggested by Table 1. This was particularly true for those institutions without substantial reserves, those that have heavy debt loads with their attendant repayment schedules, and those without a patient referral base beyond the five-county region.

These circumstances indicate a substantial competition for patients over the next several years from 1974 as beds under construction are completed. However, public policy and ethics prevent hospitals from advertising or using other means, conventional for most businesses, of attracting clients. In addition, a hospital does not market its services directly to patients, but rather to doctors who, in general, determine in which hospital a particular patient will receive treatment. The usual mechanism for a hospital to arrange for physicians to admit patients is to extend "privileges" to physicians. This means that, as long as the doctor obeys the rules of the hospital, he will be allowed to admit his patients to the hospital and to treat them to the degree that his privileges allow. (That is, the physician may admit and treat patients with certain types of diseases, but not patients with other diseases. These latter patients must be referred to a physician who may admit and treat patients with this disease. For example, an obstetrician might have privileges to deliver babies, but not to perform brain surgery.)

The wise physician obtains privileges at several hospitals so that, for example, if one hospital's rules becomes onerous, or if one hospital becomes too full to admit his patients, he can take his patients elsewhere. However, a physician usually has one hospital where he sends the majority of his patients. This reduces the physician's travel time in seeing his hospitalized patients, and it allows him to become highly familiar with the staff and facilities at one hospital. However, he will use a secondary hospital, when necessary, to obtain a bed for his patient, or because of special personnel or equipment that is available at that hospital and not at his primary hospital.

Most hospital administrators recognize that not only the well-being of patients is at stake when they are dealing with physicians, but also the financial well-being of the hospital.

| Year | Admissions | Patient days per hospital bed |
|------|-----------|-------------------------------|
| 1972 | 272,548 | 216 |
| 1971 | 264,923 | 241 |
| 1970 | 271,760 | 249 |
| 1969 | 241,723 | 243 |
| 1968 | 236,323 | 271 |
| 1967 | 215,966 | 250 |

Source: Texas: 1974 (and 1971) State Plan for the Construction and Modernization of Hospitals and Related Medical Facilities, Texas State Department of Health, Austin.

## St. Luke's conditions

St. Luke's was licensed to operate a 330-bed hospital in 1954. By 1958, after 4 years of operation, St. Luke's average occupancy was 88.3 percent. Critical bed shortages for the entire hospital were seasonal; but since the patient was admitted to a nursing unit based on his diagnosis—units designated as medicine, urology, obstetrics, gynecology, general surgery, and orthopedics—bed shortages also tended to vary by such nursing units. Bed shortage problems were not general, and the medical staff opposed directly limiting admissions. When bed space problems occurred, the practice was for emergency cases to be given preference; elective cases were admitted by the order in which they were scheduled.

In 1962, St. Luke's average occupancy was 90 percent. On occasions, the hospital was filled to capacity, and the average length of stay for all patients had increased from 6.6 days in 1958 to 6.9 days in 1961.

By 1970, St. Luke's had built a high-rise hospital, containing a patient care tower, which reaches 28 stories, and the structural foundation for a second such tower. This $50 million construction project was financed by gifts and a $23 million loan.

In connection with the loan, by 1974, St. Luke's and its physically related institutions—Texas Children's Hospital and the Texas Heart Institute—were jointly and severally liable under an 8¼ percent mortgage loan in the amount of $22,080,000, secured by a first lien on the land owned by St. Luke's and Texas Children's and on their building, equipment, and personal property. This loan was due in quarterly installments of $230,000 plus interest through 1998; accordingly, $920,000 of the principal amount due was classified as a current liability, as of June 30, 1974. Another part of long-term debts related to a 1970 transaction in which the institutions issued $6,600,000 of their notes payable and refinanced $5 million of these notes in 1971, and $4,200,000 in 1972. During 1973, the institutions completed the refinancing of $3,200,000 of these notes at a discount rate of 8¾ percent. These notes in 1974 were secured by bank letters of credit, which were further protected by surety and credit agreements covering the institutions' accounts receivable and certain pledges of future contributors. Pursuant to the agreement on the $6,600,000, it was expected in 1974 that portions of the notes would be refinanced over 1975 and 1976 in decreasing amounts. At June 30, 1974, St. Luke's and her

**TABLE 2 ■ COMBINED BALANCE SHEET FOR THE ST. LUKE'S COMPLEX, JUNE 1974, AND SELECTED YEARS**

| | 1962 | 1963 | 1964 | 1972 | 1973 | 6 months ending March 31, 1974 |
|---|---|---|---|---|---|---|
| *Assets* | | | | | | |
| Operating funds: | | | | | | |
| Current assets | $ 1,253,104 | $ 1,460,258 | $ 1,618,934 | $ 6,394,636 | $ 7,451,990 | $ 9,021,637 |
| Investments | . . . | . . . | . . . | 1,022,858 | 860,610 | 831,986 |
| Pledges receivable | 131,171 | 111,366 | 59,165 | 333,333 | . . . . | . . . . |
| Deferred pledge expense | . . . | . . . | . . . | 380,000 | 320,000 | 300,000 |
| Property plant and equipment | 10,380,961 | 9,942,350 | 10,498,504 | 60,983,317 | 61,803,023 | 62,396,289 |
| Less: depreciation | (2,218,405) | (2,521,949) | (2,842,103) | (8,203,607) | (9,802,854) | (10,806,566) |
| | 8,162,556 | 7,420,401 | 7,656,401 | 52,779,710 | 52,000,169 | 51,589,723 |
| Total operating fund assets | 9,546,831 | 8,992,025 | 9,334,500 | 60,910,537 | 60,632,769 | 61,743,346 |
| Assets restricted for capital improvements | 413,860 | 1,285,503 | 2,042,333 | 4,429,161 | 4,331,932 | 3,804,009 |
| Assets restricted for endowments and other: | | | | | | |
| Endowments | 671,341 | 815,464 | 961,633 | 6,313,192 | 6,432,745 | 11,265,981 |
| Other | 186,544 | 241,530 | 272,138 | 969,608 | 2,656,389 | . . . . |
| Total assets | $10,818,576 | $11,334,522 | $12,610,604 | $72,622,498 | $74,053,835 | $76,813,336 |
| *Liabilities* | | | | | | |
| Operating funds: | | | | | | |
| Current liabilities | $ 331,674 | $ 171,172 | $ 208,697 | $ 5,636,655 | $ 4,843,328 | $ 5,364,930 |
| Deferred Medicare reimbursement | . . . | . . . | . . . | 376,000 | 578,000 | 675,200 |
| Pledge payment | . . . | . . . | . . . | 380,000 | 320,000 | 300,000 |
| Uncollected contribution pledge | 131,171 | 111,366 | 59,165 | | | |
| Long-term debt | 201,639 | . . . | . . . | 26,944,970 | 24,794,970 | 24,212,282 |
| Total operating fund liabilities | 664,484 | 282,538 | 267,862 | 33,337,625 | 30,536,298 | 30,552,412 |
| Due to operating funds | 164,408 | 97,982 | 145,731 | 15,419 . | 287,375 | 300,808 |
| Uncollected contribution pledges (plant fund) | 249,353 | 204,965 | 152,584 | . . . | . . . | . . . |
| Fund balance | 9,740,331 | 10,749,037 | 12,044,427 | 39,269,454 | 43,230,162 | 45,960,116 |
| Total liabilities—fund balances | $10,818,576 | $11,334,522 | $12,610,604 | $72,622,498 | $74,053,835 | $76,813,336 |

two sister institutions had funded $475,000 toward the retirement of a portion of these notes and, accordingly, this amount had been offset against the balance due, then classified as long-term indebtedness. The loan agreements and letters covering the long-term debt provided for various restrictions, including (1) the restriction of certain installment purchases, (2) a limitation on the incurrence

**TABLE 3 ■ COMBINED INCOME AND EXPENSE STATEMENT FOR THE ST. LUKE'S COMPLEX, JUNE 1974, AND SELECTED YEARS**

| | 1962 | 1963 | 1964 | 1972 | 1973 | 6 months ending March 31, 1974 |
|---|---|---|---|---|---|---|
| Patient service revenue | $5,961,470 | $6,217,341 | $6,724,116 | $30,480,407 | $36,617,539 | $20,514,304 |
| Less: Allowances | (521,626) | (447,068) | (492,693) | (1,851,253) | (1,634,352) | (1,163,644) |
| Net patient revenue | 5,439,844 | 5,770,273 | 6,231,423 | 28,629,154 | 34,983,187 | 19,350,660 |
| Other operating revenue | 604,333 | 454,991 | 326,799 | 1,194,998 | 1,840,185 | 168,215 |
| Total operating revenue | 6,044,177 | 6,225,264 | 6,558,222 | 29,824,152 | 36,823,372 | 19,518,875 |
| Operating expenses | 5,315,729 | 5,583,447 | 6,072,546 | 28,118,648 | 32,589,771 | 16,769,783 |
| Depreciation expense | 306,113 | 313,035 | 343,798 | 1,729,284 | 1,956,701 | 1,040,937 |
| Interest expense | 18,451 | 6,733 | . . . | 2,159,425 | 2,306,609 | 1,104,002 |
| Operating income (loss) | 403,884 | 322,049 | 141,878 | (2,183,205) | (29,709) | 604,153 |
| Unrestricted gifts | 468,063 | 686,657 | 1,153,512 | 1,967,196 | 676,870 | 471,605 |
| Loss on sale of power plant | . . . | . . . | . . . | . . . | (299,775) | . . . |
| Settlement, prior year's Medicare report | . . . | . . . | . . . | 287,740 | . . . | . . . |
| Excess (deficit) | $871,947 | $1,008,706 | $1,295,390 | $ 71,731 | $ 347,386 | $ 1,075,758 |

| Year | Licensed bed capacity | St. Luke's beds available and in use | Other beds in use | Percentage occupancy[a] |
|---|---|---|---|---|
| 1975 | 773 | | | |
| 1974 | 794 | 765 | . . . | 81 |
| 1973 | 732 | 773 | | |
| 1972 | 732 | 699 | | |
| 1971 | 355 | 548 | 89 | |
| 1970 | 340 | 295 | 131 | |
| 1969 | 340 | 295 | 31 | |
| 1968 | 340 | 295 | | |
| 1967 | 340 | 295 | | |
| 1966 | 340 | 295 | | |
| 1965 | 340 | 295 | | |
| 1964 | 340 | 295 | . . . | 92 |
| 1963 | 340 | 295 | | |
| 1962 | 340 | 295 | . . . | 90 |
| 1961 | 340 | 295 | | |
| 1960 | 340 | 295 | | |
| 1959 | 330 | 295 | | |
| 1958 | 330 | 295 | . . . | 88 |
| 1957 | 330 | 295 | | |
| 1956 | 330 | 295 | | |
| 1955 | 330 | 295 | | |
| 1954 | 330 | 295 | | |

[a] Computed as follows: Number of patient days over beds open and staffed expressed as a percent. Where percentages are not given, the occupancy was never computed.

of additional indebtedness, and (3) a requirement that not more than $300,000 of accounts payable remain unpaid for more than 120 days. The June 30, 1974, balance sheet and income and expense statement for the three institutions are shown in Tables 2 and 3, which incorporate similar financial information for other selected years.

In addition to the 1974 beds, shelled-in space was available for future expansion of the number of beds at St. Luke's. Table 4 provides historical bed use data for St. Luke's; Figure 3 illustrates the 1974 use pattern of the facility and suggests the growth and auxiliary use pattern for the following several years.

## The 1962 problem[1]

Among St. Luke's medical staff members is the illustrious heart surgeon Denton A. Cooley, M.D., who attracts patient referrals from all parts of the globe. The resulting and associated large volume of cardiovascular patients posed particular problems in the 1960s, even before the heart-transplant era.

Many of the cardiovascular patients were emergency admissions. Large numbers were from out of Houston, and when they were not emergencies, they were referred to nearby hotels and motels to await admission, creating a backlog of patients. Among the latter group, emergencies arose daily. In order

---

[1] This section, the 1962 solution, and certain other parts of this report are based in part on an unpublished manuscript of John E. Creighton, associate administrator in the St. Luke's complex, and are supplemented with the assistance of Mrs. Emma Foreman, secretary for trustee affairs.

| Texas Children's Hospital: North | Texas Children's Hospital: South | South Tower | St. Luke's Episcopal Hospital: South | St. Luke's Episcopal Hospital: North |
|---|---|---|---|---|
| | | Mechanical | | |
| | | 27 Open; future nuclear medicine | | |
| | | 26 Baylor College of Medicine | | |
| | | 25 Baylor College of Medicine | | |
| | | 24 Baylor College of Medicine | | |
| | | 23 Open; future patient floor | | |
| | | 22 Open; future patient floor | | |
| | | 21 Open; future patient floor | | |
| | | 20 Mechanical | | |
| | | 19 Cardiology | | |
| | | 18 Medicine | | |
| | | 17 Medicine and orthopedics | | |
| | | 16 Cardiology | | |
| | | 15 Urology | | |
| | | 14 General surgery | | |
| | | 12 Gynecology | | |
| | | 11 General surgery | | |
| | | 10 Cardiovascular surgery | | |
| | | 9 Mechanical | | |
| Medicine | Medicine | 8 Cardiovascular surgery | | |
| Medicine | Cardiovascular surgery | 7 Cardiovascular surgery | V.I.P. suites | |
| General surgery | General surgery | 6 Orthopedics | Neurology | Orthopedics |
| Medicine | Urology | 5 Orthopedics | Orthopedics | General surgery |
| Child development center | Clinical research center | 4 Infant care, nurseries, obstetrics | | |
| Pediatric intensive care | (Patient services) | 3 Operating rooms, surgical recovery rooms, intensive care | | Neurointensive and progressive care |
| | (Street level) | 2 Offices, services, and outpatient clinics | | |
| | | 1 Emergency center, other services | | |
| | | Basement: Mechanical | | |

**FIGURE 3** ■ St. Luke's floor use plan in 1974.

to alleviate the problems with these patients in particular, the admitting officers tended to give priority to the cardiovascular patient, although he may not have been an emergency at the time.

These circumstances caused several problems. (1) Surgical patients were being admitted to nonsurgical nursing units. The nursing units assigned to internal medicine felt the admitting practice particularly, because it became difficult to admit patients for elective or diagnostic purposes, and medical emergencies were occasionally referred to other hospitals. (2) The number of declared emergencies increased, the designation being used by many physicians in order to obtain a bed. (3) Postings for elective surgery were being canceled and reset, with a resulting procedural inefficiency and inconvenience to patients. The admissions were either canceled because of the lack of a bed, or because juggling the surgery schedule was necessary to accommodate the large number of surgical emergencies. (4) Balancing beds among the services was difficult, and the nursing units often had internal medicine and surgery patients mixed together. The results were a less efficient use of nurse specialists and inconveniences to physicians because of the dispersion of their patients. Beds were often available on the obstetrics and gynecology units, but because of the extreme danger of infection, there was hesitancy in putting other types of patients on these units. Never could any but a noninfectious case be housed in an obstetrics unit. Also, it was desirable to move patients not belonging to the service when a bed became available on a unit more appropriate to the patient's diagnosis. These patient transfers resulted in much confusion and higher costs. (5) Many medical staff members expressed alarm, and several began taking most of their patients to other hospitals. Each service felt it was being encroached upon. Most of them blamed the large cardiovascular load for the problem.

Alternatives included (1) expanding on-site bed capacity, which usually requires about 5 to 10 years, (2) expanding bed capacity by using part of another underutilized hospital, (3) earlier discharge or transfer of patients, as to a convalescence center, (4) limiting the range of privileges of physicians, (5) removing physicians from the medical staff, on the basis of such criteria as quality of patient care, nonparticipation in medical staff affairs, or limited use of the hospital—that is, a low patient admitting rate, (6) the elimination of services which might provide deficit or low financial returns, such as obstetrics or psychiatry, (7) limiting the admission of additional (new) members to the medical staff, and (8) setting patient condition or diagnosis priorities on the admission of patients. The administrator of the hospital insisted on the exclusion of housing patients in corridors as an alternative, and steadfastly held for control of the surgery schedule by the nurse-director of operating rooms.

## The 1962 solution

In 1962, a newly commissioned admissions committee began a study of the occupancy problem. The committee reached the following conclusions: (1) Because of the fame of the cardiovascular service, there was some feeling that it would be unwise to limit this service. (2) It did not seem wise to limit arbitrarily the number of admissions either by service or by the then 806 positions on the medical staff. It was felt this would reduce the possibility for admissions for each staff member and satisfy none. (3) While the medical staff was composed predominantly of specialists, Houston was largely a general practice town. Thus, general practitioners controlled the medical society and often referred patients to St. Luke's specialists. It did not seem wise to risk the good working relationship between the hospital and the medical society and its general practitioner element by taking action which would be specifically to the detriment of this sector. Some argued that such a move would be correct neither ethically nor morally. (4) A major expansion of St. Luke's was planned. While completion was scheduled for about 1970, it seemed unwise to alienate the medical community to the extent that they might be unwilling to use the hospital after the new facilities were completed. (5) The medical education programs required consideration and preference for those physicians who were on the faculty at Baylor and who were directly related to such programs by way of an affiliation agreement between Baylor and St. Luke's. (6) It appeared not to be in the interest of the medical staff of the hospital to curtail privileges of all courtesy staff members or to close the staff. Many of the future leaders of the medical staff were still unquestionably in the courtesy category; some potentially outstanding, usually young physicians would be applying for privileges. A staff selection process appeared necessary which would assure continuity of a technically highly qualified, age-distributed staff.

Considering the problem in the light of the above-mentioned obstacles, there seem to be valid objections to all the proposals. It was decided, nevertheless, that a priority system of privileges might incorporate the good points of several of the proposals, and it seemed to be the least objectionable course.

In keeping with this option, each chief of service was requested to submit a priority list to the admissions committee. With the request, the chief of service was given the following data by medical staff members on his service: (1) number of patients admitted within the year (thus, Is this his primary hospital?); (2) participation in medical staff affairs, such as meetings attended (thus, Is he interested in what is going on?). Each service was requested to reduce by 10 percent its number of admissions by the designation of staff members who lacked priority. Received and passed on by the admissions committee, the lists were sanctioned by the medical executive committee. The lists were returned to the chiefs of service, and members of the medical staff were sent a letter on the action, although individuals were not notified of their priority status. The effect of the latter detail was that a staff member without a preference for beds would not be aware of his secondary priority, only that a bed was not available on high census days. By this mechanism it was felt that negative connotations were avoided.

The priority system for limiting admissions was reviewed by the admissions committee in October of 1963, 1 year after it had been put into effect, with the recommendation that the system be continued as it has since that time, serving in connection with annual reappointments and promotions of medical staff members. It was noted that a better relationship between the admitting office and this regular staff developed and that admissions planning became easier. The immediate result in 1964 was an occupancy rate of 92 percent. An improved attitude and morale on the part of the internal medicine service physicians was sensed and expressed by the chief of that service.

Across the street from the Texas Medical Center, about one block away

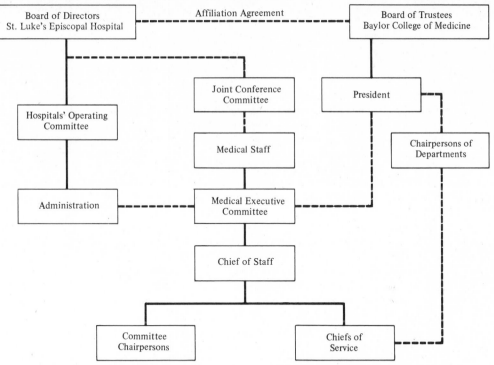

**FIGURE 4** ■ Chart of organization, St. Luke's medical staff. A typical medical staff organization for a teaching and research hospital is essentially achieved, with designated chiefs of service and representatives of the college of medicine constituting the medical executive committee chaired by an elected chief of staff. The clinical services are divided into active (attending, associate, and assistant), consulting, and courtesy categories with privileges, duties, and responsibilities assigned accordingly by the chiefs of service. An elaborate medical staff committee structure functions to mold the academic and nonacademic interests and permit balance of the service, teaching, and research facets of the hospital program.

from St. Luke's Episcopal Hospital, the Center Pavilion Hospital was being established in 1965 in what was formerly a high-rise apartment building. On August 16 of that year, St. Luke's utilization committee had arranged a meeting in the office of the Center Pavilion administrator, Mr. David De-Backer. The committee said the demand for beds in St. Luke's far exceeded supply, with the shortage growing more serious every day. The committee saw a number of aggravating factors on the horizon. Medicare, then soon to become active, was expected to greatly increase the demand for hospital beds. During the planned construction, some beds, then in use, would be sacrificed temporarily to facilitate construction. The committee saw a serious discrepancy between the supply of beds and the demand for them, with the prospect of these effects worsening seriously unless immediate steps were taken to provide more beds. Detrimental effects were seen in external relations of St. Luke's, a loss of potential revenue, a loss of potential friends and benefactors, and the continued inability to provide for the needs of new physicians who would be the medical staff of the future. Several problems internal to St. Luke's were cited: (1) valued members of the medical staff were lost when, because of their own need to work, they had gone to other hospitals where they could admit patients; (2) the destructive pressures relating to the competition for beds were being felt with increasing severity; (3) overloaded facilities were resulting in a loss of valuable personnel, particularly in nursing; and (4) the overcrowding of St. Luke's facilities had the potential of endangering patients.

The committee observed that the Texas Medical Center hospitals, during periods of rapid growth, used ingenious temporary measures to facilitate patients' needs. The M. D. Anderson Hospital, for example, while expanding facilities, had constructed temporary steel buildings on the grounds, and had leased the second floor of the new Center Pavilion Hospital for offices and laboratories. The Methodist Hospital, although it had added 350 beds during the last 2 or 3 years and then had under construction another 100, had leased a convalescent home to be operated as an extension of the Methodist facilities. Hermann Hospital also had expressed interest in using a part of the facilities of the Center Pavilion. It was obvious to St. Luke's utilization committee that these other institutions in the medical center continued to grow faster than their ability to establish new facilities.

The utilization committee concluded that every reasonable step had been taken to assure continued maximum use of facilities in St. Luke's. No significant relief from the bed shortage could be expected from more efficient use of the facilities occupied there. It was the expressed feeling of the administration and of the medical staff that St. Luke's was getting from its facilities all that could be expected. An opportunity was seen in Center Pavilion to expand temporarily services and facilities and effectively to increase bed capacity as much as 23 percent. The proposal was that the beds be operated as an extension of St. Luke's, so that St. Luke's quality of care remained under its control. The patients placed in the unit might be those who had advanced malignant disease, a selected group of convalescent surgical patients who needed less than full general hospital care but were not ready for discharge, or a selected group of ambulatory patients whose problems of diagnosis made facilities of a general hospital necessary. The director of nursing service and the laboratory director agreed it was feasible for St. Luke's services to be provided in a unit at such a remote location. It was the committee consensus that the space could be made available quickly, at low costs. Center Pavilion recognized the nature of St. Luke's problems and agreed to provide the facilities on a lease basis.

The utilization committee recommended to the board of directors an expansion of St. Luke's program into Center Pavilion's space, commenting that such action would accelerate and contribute to the continued development of the large staff that would be necessary to serve an expanded permanent facility. The committee recommended an arrangement for the use of beds in Center Pavilion, to be concluded as soon as possible. The report was signed by Dr. Bold (pseudonym), a surgeon and one of the influential members of the St. Luke's medical staff, whose name is carried in the firm name of Houston's largest group practice.

The utilization committee's recommendation was accepted by the board of directors, and effected. Medical staff members, however, wanted others to put their patients in Center Pavilion—St. Luke's was more convenient. Fewer problems occurred in temporarily using space in the Texas Children's Hospital, which then adjoined and still physically adjoins St. Luke's. Table 4 covers the usage data during this period and continuing into the 1970s.

# The solution in 1973

In early September 1973, a female applicant for general surgery privileges asked about the status of her application for medical staff appointment. Mrs. Lucille McCutcheon, administrative secretary for medical staff affairs, knew from her control system the location of the pending application. On inquiry, Dr. Bold, who had chaired the 1965 utilization committee, a former president of the St. Luke's medical staff and chief of the surgery service, affirmed he had the application, as well as others he was holding because he felt the hospital had enough surgeons, as was reflected in the difficulty in scheduling surgery cases in the operating room.

At the September 19 meeting of the medical executive committee (a committee composed of the elected chiefs of certain physician specialties; see Table 5 for the composition), Dr. Bold responded to the situation and proposed an institutional policy regarding medical staff appointments. He said the rate of growth of the hospital had resulted in a shortage of certain kinds of beds and of operating rooms. He said new appointments to the medical staff should be

TABLE 5 ■ ST. LUKE'S MEDICAL STAFF, MEMBERSHIP BY POSITION OF SELECTED COMMITTEES, 1974

**Medical executive committee**
Chiefs of the following services:

Anesthesiology, Cardiovascular Surgery, Dentistry (appointed by dean of the University of Texas Dental Branch), Family Practice, Medicine (chairman and chief of staff), Neurology, Nuclear Medicine, Obstetrics and Gynecology, Orthopedic Surgery, Pathology, Radiology (vice chairman and vice chief of staff), Surgery, and Urology

Plus the following representatives by medical staff rank:

Consulting: Surgery (president of the Baylor College of Medicine)

Attending: Medicine (4, including secretary of the medical staff, chairman of the medical education, research, and publications committee, and a representative of Texas Heart Institute), Orthopedic Surgery, and Otolaryngology

Associate: Medicine

Executive Director (secretary)

Associate Administrator—Nursing

**Credentials committee**
Chiefs of the following services:

Medicine (ex officio) (chief of staff), Neurology

Plus the following representatives by medical staff rank:

Attending: Family Practice, Medicine (chairman), Obstetrics and Gynecology, Orthopedic Surgery, Surgery, and Urology

Executive Director

**Bylaws revision committee**
Chiefs of the following services:

Family Practice, Medicine (ex officio) (chief of staff), and Pathology (chairman)

Plus the following representatives by medical staff rank:

Attending: Medicine and Obstetrics and Gynecology

Associate: Surgery

Executive Director

Associate Administrator

limited until more operating rooms and beds were available. Mr. France responded that, as of the end of August, there had been a net gain for 1973 of only 15 members to the medical staff (see Tables 6, 7, and 8). It was Mr. France's view that increased use of the hospital by the courtesy staff (physicians whose primary hospital was elsewhere and who used St. Luke's only occasionally) was a major factor in the occupancy buildup. The committee chairman, Dr. Arman (pseudonym), a leading internist and president in his second term of the St. Luke's medical staff, offered to appoint an ad hoc committee to study a policy regarding medical staff appointments. Quickly, Dr. Bold moved that the chairman be so authorized, and the motion was seconded and carried.

At the November 14 meeting of the credentials committee (the committee which recommends privileges), a proposal was approved that each chief of service (surgery, internal medicine, etc.) be charged to develop criteria for the delineation of privileges for physicians on, or to be appointed to, his service. These criteria would be subject to the approval of the medical executive committee. This report was approved at the medical executive committee on November 21, and preceded a report from the ad hoc committee on an institutional policy regarding medical staff appointments. Dr. Bold had been appointed chairman, and he presented five recommendations intended to regulate the appointment of applicants to the medical staff. They were as follows:

**1** With the current occupancy rate in the hospital of less than 70% and a projected occupancy of 73.3% for the Fiscal Year 1974, there should not be a limitation of medical staff membership at this time.

TABLE 6 ■ NUMBER OF MEDICAL STAFF MEMBERS BY SERVICES JANUARY 1973 AND JANUARY 1974

| Service | January 1973 | January 1974 | Gain or loss |
|---|---|---|---|
| Anesthesiology | 21 | 22 | 1 |
| Dentistry | 22 | 19 | −3 |
| Family practice | 58 | 58 | |
| Medicine | 226[a] | 242[a] | 16[a] |
|   Dermatology section | 12 | 12 | |
|   Psychiatry section | 18 | 16 | −2 |
| Neurology | 17 | 22[a] | 5[a] |
| Neurophysiology | . . . | 1 | 1 |
| Neurosurgery | 15 | 17 | 2 |
| Newborn and premature | 98 | 103 | 5 |
| Nuclear medicine | 4 | 3 | −1 |
| Obstetrics and gynecology | 75 | 75 | |
| Ophthalmology | 27 | 31 | 4 |
| Orthopedic surgery | 45 | 47 | 2 |
| Otolaryngology | 28 | 31 | 3 |
| Pathology | 11 | 12 | 1 |
| Physical medicine | 11 | 9 | −2 |
| Plastic surgery | 16 | 17 | 1 |
| Radiology | 12 | 12 | |
| Surgery | 94 | 94 | |
|   Proctology section | 4 | 6 | 2 |
|   Thoracic surgery section | 4 | 3 | −1 |
| Urology | 38 | 34 | −4 |
| Total | 824[b] | 850[b] | 26 |

[a] Including dual appointments. Total dual appointments January 1973: 36. Total dual appointments January 1974: 42.
[b] Dual appointments deducted from total staff.

TABLE 7 ■ INCREASE IN THE NUMBER OF SUR-
GEONS BY SUBSPECIALTY, JANUARY
1973 TO JANUARY 1974

| | |
|---|---|
| Neurosurgery | 2 |
| Ophthalmology | 4 |
| Orthopedic surgery | 2 |
| Otolaryngology | 3 |
| Plastic surgery | 1 |
| Proctology | 2 |
| Total | 14 |

TABLE 8 ■ INCREASE IN PHYSICIANS BY SERV-
ICES, JANUARY 1973 TO JANUARY
1974

| | |
|---|---|
| Anesthesiology | 1 |
| Internal medicine | 6[a] |
| Neurology | 4[b] |
| Newborn and premature | 5 |
| Pathology | 1 |
| Total | 17 |

[a] 10 dual appointments deducted.
[b] 1 dual appointment deducted.

2   Because the census (number of patients in the hospital) changes rapidly and could cause certain areas of the hospital to become over-utilized, it is recommended that the composition of the medical staff and its growth be evaluated at least every six months.

3   At a time when the hospital occupancy rate reaches 85%, limitation of staff appointments will be considered by the Medical Executive Committee. Also with an occupancy rate of 85%, appointments of new members to the medical staff should be made only when formerly active members leave the staff. In addition, when an occupancy rate of 85% is achieved, priority privileges will be given for scheduling and admitting patients by members of the active staff.

4   Before January, 1974 and annually thereafter, there should be a review of courtesy staff utilization of the hospital and those using the facilities very infrequently will be asked to indicate in writing their interest in continued membership. A positive response will be necessary for continued staff appointment.

5   For all future appointments to staff membership there would be an indication from the applicant regarding his plans for use of the hospital. This indication can be in the form of a letter to or an interview with the chief of his clinical service. This letter or memo regarding the interview will accompany the application for medical staff appointment.

Mr. France questioned the validity of the figures used for the occupancy report. He pointed out that beds in obstetrics, premature nursery, coronary care, and intensive care, if used in the computation, would distort percentages. The issue was addressed by Dr. Kauldon (pseudonym), who holds the chair in obstetrics and gynecology at Baylor College of Medicine, which is funded by St. Luke's. He is also chief of the St. Luke's obstetrics and gynecology service. Dr. Kauldon said that the percentage of occupancy should not be the criterion for admitting candidates to the medical staff. Rather, whether the service wants the applicant and feels the facilities are adequate to accommodate him is the criterion that should be used. The committee chairman, Dr. Arman, noted that a privileges or admitting-limiting procedure might need to be specific for each service because, for example, the operating rooms (and consequently the surgery service) might be at peak utilization at a time when the medicine and obstetrics services are not. Dr. Bold moved that his ad hoc committee's report be accepted subject to the validity of the figures upon which the occupancy percentages were based. The motion was seconded and carried.

At the January 16, 1974, meeting of the executive committee, however, Dr. Bold recommended that point 2 of the November 21 guidelines be revised to read "monthly" instead of "at least every six months."

Mr. France, as before, questioned the basis for the percentage computations. Dr. Bold responded that the figures used did not include the beds in the nursery, and that the proposed policy would not affect the newborn and premature service. He said the beds in the intensive-care unit, however, as well as those in the coronary-care unit and obstetrics and gynecology were included. (These are traditionally low-occupancy areas.)

Dr. Arman observed that the Joint Commission on Accreditation of Hospitals recommends that staff applications be processed within 100 days. He questioned if this could be accomplished if an application were presented at a time when there was an atypical, seasonally high 90 percent occupancy. Dr. Bold moved that his recommendation be approved, and the motion was seconded and carried.

When the medical executive committee met in February, 11 candidates were recommended for appointment to the medical staff. Dr. Arman called attention to the policy recommendation which had been acted upon at the previous committee meeting. He said if the policy were observed, none of the candidates could be added because the percentage occupancy was at 85 percent, where it had been for some time. Noting paragraph 3, as amended, of the policy recommendation adopted in November, it was observed that deferred applications would accumulate and the list would grow monthly. It was the consensus of the committee that the policy as proposed could not be implemented, because it was based on an occupancy rate which fluctuated. (Such fluctuations are suggested by Table 9 on the number of patient days by month for selected years; also, seasonal and weekly fluctuations are suggested by Figure 5.) Dr. Kauldon pointed out that the problem with such a blanket policy is that certain

TABLE 9 ■ PATIENT DAYS,[a] ST. LUKE'S EPISCOPAL HOSPITAL, BY MONTH, SELECTED YEARS

| Month | 1972 | 1973 | 1974 | 1975 budget |
|---|---|---|---|---|
| October | 13,011 | 14,448 | 16,800 | 18,400 |
| November | 11,799 | 13,786 | 15,755 | 17,500 |
| December | 9,558 | 10,950 | 13,014 | 14,830 |
| January | 14,017 | 15,162 | 16,889 | 18,400 |
| February | 13,291 | 15,029 | 16,707 | 18,000 |
| March | 14,541 | 17,085 | 18,553 | 19,900 |
| April | 14,067 | 15,698 | 18,170 | 19,500 |
| May | 14,267 | 15,420 | 18,061 | 19,500 |
| June | 13,912 | 15,765 | 18,150 | 19,500 |
| July | 12,793 | 16,137 | 18,480 | 19,100 |
| August | 12,727 | 16,391 | 16,800 | 18,700 |
| September | 13,477 | 15,798 | 16,800 | 18,700 |
| Total | 157,460 | 181,669 | 204,179 | 222,030 |

[a] The convention for counting patient days in American hospitals is such that the day of admission, but not the day of discharge, is included.

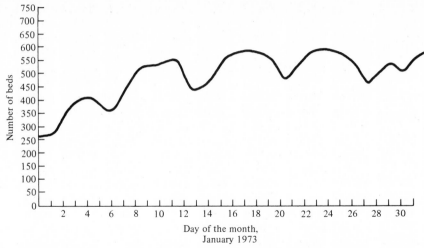

FIGURE 5 ■ Graph of St. Luke's patient census following the seasonal low at Christmas and suggesting the weekly fluctuations associated with heavy admissions at the beginning of a week followed by discharges as the weekend approaches. St. Luke's bed complement was 732.

services may not have a high occupancy while others may have. He said if no additional obstetricians, for example, could be appointed, the obstetrics service could not grow. Mr. France said that the policy would be difficult to administer, and suggested a priority system which had worked well in the past when the occupancy rate was much higher and other circumstances more acute. He suggested that the priority system such as that used in 1962 should be reactivated; then, when a new physician comes onto the courtesy staff, he could be told that the hospital is quite full and that chances for his admitting patients may be limited unless beds are available. It was Mr. France's view that the occupancy problem was created by the increased orientation to St. Luke's of not new, but rather, of long-standing staff members. Dr. Find (pseudonym), a past president of the St. Luke's medical staff and chief of the pathology service, concurred, pointing out the number of physicians, by rank, who discharged patients and those who discharged no patients, as listed in Table 10. He said about 10 percent of the admissions were from courtesy staff members who admitted periodically. Another committee member pointed out that it was with great effort and expense that services had been developed in the past, and that the medical executive committee should not wish to see these services crowded out, as had happened before. Dr. Kauldon moved that paragraph 3 of the November policy be amended to read, "When an occupancy

TABLE 10 ■ NUMBER OF MEDICAL STAFF MEMBERS BY RANK, AND NUMBER DISCHARGING NO PATIENTS

| Rank | Total number | Number not active |
|---|---|---|
| Attending | 111 | 43 |
| Associate | 69 | 23 |
| Assistant | 68 | 31 |
| Courtesy | 481 | 380 |

rate of 85 percent is achieved, privileges for scheduling and admitting patients by members of the active and courtesy staff should be given by each service." As the committee continued its discussion of the credentials committee report, the committee chairman noted the policy that physicians not be appointed initially to the active staff except under special circumstances. He observed that, in contrast with this policy, one of the candidates was recommended for appointment to the active staff of the obstetrics and gynecology service. Dr. Find moved that all candidates be approved for appointment to the courtesy staff. This was passed.

When the bylaws revision committee, chaired by Dr. Find, met in May, procedures for appointment and reappointment to the medical staff were discussed. It was felt that the rules for a 1-year initial appointment followed by an annual reappointment should be maintained. There was discussion about adding a category called "provisional courtesy." This category was envisioned as the first category of staff appointment, and a physician in this category would be expected to demonstrate that he will, in fact, work in St. Luke's; otherwise he would not be moved to courtesy or active status.

# Kellwood Company

Archibald D. Cameron

The Kellwood Company produces apparel, recreational equipment, and home furnishings. Its home office is in St. Louis, Missouri.

In 1974 *Fortune* listed Kellwood as number 424 in the top 500 U.S. industrial companies. At that time, Kellwood had sales of $326 million, assets of $235 million, a net income of $7 million, and stockholders' equity of $52 million. Kellwood has been growing at a fast rate for this particular industry, and its growth is a result of internal expansion and aquisitions. Between 1961 and 1971 sales increased 225 percent, while profits increased 215 percent.

Approximately 80 percent of Kellwood's sales are purchased by Sears, Roebuck and Company. Kellwood is second only to Whirlpool Corporation in dollar sales as a Sears supplier. Kellwood is now one of the 10 largest apparel producers in the United States, and in 1974 was 50 percent larger in size than Bobbie Brooks, twice the size of Farah, and four times the size of Henry I. Siegal. In addition Kellwood is the recognized industry leader in the specialized area of supplying mass merchandisers such as Sears, Roebuck and J. C. Penney. The industry is a risky one in which financial stability, quality control, production efficiency, computerized scheduling, and large capacity are all equally critical, if not more critical, than for the marketers of advertised brands of apparel.

Kellwood's quality, style, and price are aimed at a major segment of the consumer's market, the middle-income group which accounts for 70 percent of disposable income.

## History of the company

Kellwood was founded in 1961. The company name was derived from the names of two former Sears, Roebuck and Company board chairmen, C. H. Kellstedt and R. E. Wood.

The company resulted from a merger of 15 firms. These firms all owned sewing equipment, they sold the majority of their products to Sears, Roebuck,

This case study was prepared by Archibald D. Cameron under the supervision of Professor William F. Glueck. It has been prepared as a mechanism for analysis and not as an example of either good or poor administrative practice. The author wishes to thank the officers of the Kellwood Company for their cooperation in this endeavor.

TABLE 1 ■ CORPORATIONS MERGED TO FORM KELLWOOD COMPANY AND KELLWOOD STOCK ISSUED TO EACH

**TABLE 1 ■ CORPORATIONS MERGED TO FORM KELLWOOD COMPANY AND KELLWOOD STOCK ISSUED TO EACH**

| | |
|---|---:|
| Ahoskie Manufacturing Company | 26,400 shares |
| Albert of Arizona, Inc. | 32,301 shares |
| Biltmore Mfg. Co., Inc. | 74,239 shares |
| Calhoun Garment Company | 62,315 shares |
| Garver Manufacturing Corporation | 30,741 shares |
| Greenfield Manufacturing Co., Inc. | 94,285 shares |
| Hawthorn Finishing Company | 143,629 shares |
| McComb Manufacturing Company | 194,811 shares |
| Monticello Manufacturing Company | 113,830 shares |
| Ottenheimer Bros. Mfg. Co., Inc. | 158,552 shares |
| Oxford Manufacturing Company | 4,065 shares |
| Rutherford Garment Company | 93,339 shares |
| Siler City Manufacturing Co., Inc. | 76,799 shares |
| Southern Foundations, Inc. | 95,400 shares |
| Spencer Mfg. Co. | 49,288 shares |
| | 1,249,994 shares |

Subsidiaries of merged corporations:
Georgia Decor, Inc.
Liberty Mills, Inc.
Pramco, Inc.

and Sears, Roebuck had financial interest in each firm. Sears thus was better assured of a continuity of supply from one stronger firm than from 15 smaller firms. Combined sales at the time were $86 million.

On September 25, 1961, Kellwood issued 1,249,994 shares of its common stock in exchange for all the outstanding common and preferred equital stock of the merged companies. The excess of the aggregate stated value of the shares issued by Kellwood over the total par value of the capital stock of the merged corporations of $307,080 was changed to retained earnings. Kellwood also issued 50 shares of its common stock to Sears in September 1961 for $1000 in order to qualify the company to commence business. There were no significant intercompany transactions between the merged corporations. All intercompany balances and transactions with subsidiaries were eliminated in consolidation. The 15 merged corporations and 3 subsidiaries and the number of shares of stock issued by Kellwood are given in Table 1.

Kellwood's equity in the three wholly owned subsidiaries (formerly subsidiaries of the merged corporations) exceeded its investment therein by $298,726, representing accumulated earnings of these companies since acquisition by the merged companies. Kellwood was formed to give the shareholders of the 15 original companies the advantage of trading in closed corporate stock in return for a marketable security and still maintaining operating control.

From 1961 until 1973 Kellwood was traded on the over-the-counter market under the symbol KLWD. In November 1973 Kellwood began trading on the New York Stock Exchange under the symbol KWD.

Table 2 provides a list of the plant locations, size, and the major products produced by the merged corporations in 1961.

## The apparel industry

The apparel industry is affected by many variables, each of which is of some consequence to the individual companies, in particular the smaller firms.

| Location | Approximate building size in square feet, including warehouse areas | Principal products |
|---|---|---|
| Ahoskie, North Carolina | 77,000 | Children's outer apparel |
| Alamo, Tennessee | 64,000 | Women's foundation garments |
| Asheville, North Carolina | 60,000 | Women's and girls' sportswear |
| Calhoun City, Mississippi | 57,300 | Boys' pants |
| Dresden, Tennessee | 31,000 | Women's and girls' outerwear |
| Glasgow, Missouri | 61,000 | Camping and sporting equipment |
| Greenfield, Tennessee | 87,000 | Women's and girls' coats |
| Liberty, Mississippi | 28,000 | Women's, girls', and infants' lingerie |
| Little Rock, Arkansas | 161,000 | Women's dresses, robes, and blouses |
| Mesa, Arizona | 60,000 | Girls' and women's lingerie |
| McComb, Mississippi | 125,000 | Tricot lingerie |
| Milton, Delaware | 20,600 | Women's and girls' hosiery and leotards |
| Monticello, Mississippi | 71,000 | Men's work pants |
| New Haven, Missouri | 175,000 | Camping and sporting equipment |
| Oxford, Mississippi | 30,000 | Little boys' suspender pants and shorts |
| Perry, Georgia | 62,000 | Bedding products |
| Punxsutawney, Pennsylvania | 61,500 | Women's blouses, slacks, and skirts |
| Rutherford, Tennessee | 70,250 | Men's and boys' outerwear |
| Siler City, North Carolina | 78,000 | Women's and girls' hosiery and leotards |
| Spencer, West Virginia | 89,600 | Men's, women's, and children's sweaters |
| Summit, Mississippi | 63,000 | Bedding products |
| Wilmington, North Carolina | 71,500 | Men's sport shirts and swimwear |

Developments in the major markets and market segments, the firm's managerial abilities (financial and production controls, and its flexibility in judging styles and trends), the firm's financial resources, and the available distribution channels (chains, discount stores, department and specialty stores, and branded or unbranded lines) are all critical to the success or failure of the firm. Of particular importance is the effectiveness of management in controls and fabric purchasing.

The apparel manufacturing business is labor-intensive, and because wages have risen rapidly, so have costs. Industry payroll costs were 25 percent of sales in 1963 and 33 percent of sales in 1973. When these costs are combined with the difficulty of automating, the result is increased prices.

Many of the individual firms in the industry will be in a critical position in the coming years because costs are increasing and not all of these costs can be passed on to the consumer. In addition, tighter fabric supplies are pushing apparel manufacturers into greater exposure than they would normally assume. They are being forced to make commitments for fabric much further in advance and in greater quantities than they normally would. Wrong guesses could be costly, and because the retailer may be playing it safe, many manufacturers may have to hold inventory for the retailer and hence take more than the usual risk at a time when consumer spending could be very low.

The apparel industry is not a very stable one, particularly for small companies. There are more failures in this industry than in any other manufacturing group. It is usually the small firms with little initial capital that fail, and a large percentage of the industry is made up of small firms. In 1972, 28 percent of the firms employed between 20 and 49 people, 24 percent employed 18 to 19 people, and 19 percent employed 1 to 3 people.

Men's apparel firms have been less subject to fashion changes than women's. In the first quarter of 1972, there were 424 failed firms compared to 382 and 309 in the first quarters of 1971 and 1970 respectively. Manufacturing and wholesaling bankruptcies also were up from 80 to 102 in this period. The highest failure rate of all was in the women's and misses' ready-to-wear stores. The firms with the status of prime resources were the least vulnerable. The effect of foreign competition on the industry has been reduced in the last few years owing to new textile import restrictions.

The industrial organization of the apparel industry in the United States is given in Table 3.

The apparel industry sales pattern is responsive to nationwide trends such as market changes, inventory policies, imports, cost and availability of raw materials, increases in wages, and changing consumption patterns. Industry sales have been growing irregularly, as have profits (see Table 4), and in the next 5 to 10 years the apparel industry might evolve into a more mature steadily growing industry composed of larger companies. At the moment, however, individual companies are still small and their operations are volatile.

Several factors have contributed to the recent growth of the apparel business, one of which is the increased demand for sportswear. This demand is

TABLE 3 ■ PERCENTAGE OF APPAREL INDUSTRY BY PRODUCT GROUPS IN THE UNITED STATES

| | |
|---|---|
| Children's outerwear | 5% |
| Miscellaneous fabrics and textiles | 15 |
| Women's and children's undergarments | 9 |
| Miscellaneous apparel | 8 |
| Men's and boys' suits and coats | 10 |
| Men's and boys' furnishings | 22 |
| Women's and misses' outerwear and sportswear | 31 |
| | 100% |

TABLE 4 ■ SALES AND PROFITS IN THE UNITED STATES APPAREL INDUSTRY

| | Sales | | Net profits | |
|---|---|---|---|---|
| | Billions | Percent change | Millions | Percent change |
| 1973 | 27 | 8 | 835 | 25 |
| 1972 | 25 | 5.5 | 670 | 20 |
| 1971 | 23.7 | 7.5 | 559 | 31 |
| 1970 | 22 | −3 | 426 | −18.5 |
| 1969 | 22.7 | 9.5 | 523 | 3 |
| 1968 | 20.7 | 13.5 | 507 | 20.5 |
| 1967 | 18.2 | 0.5 | 420 | − 3 |
| 1966 | 18.1 | 11 | 432 | 14.5 |

Source: Wall Street Transcript, Feb. 2, 1973.

**TABLE 5** ■ *FORBES* YARDSTICKS OF MANAGEMENT PERFORMANCE: APPAREL, JANUARY 1974

| Company | Profitability | | | | | | Growth | | | | | |
|---|---|---|---|---|---|---|---|---|---|---|---|---|
| | Return on equity | | | Return on total capital | | | Sales | | | Earnings per share | | |
| | 5-year average | Industry rank | Latest 12 months | 5-year average | Industry rank | Latest 12 months | 5-year average | Industry rank | 1973 vs. 1970–1972 | 5-year average | Industry rank | 1973 vs. 1970–1972 |
| Rapid American | 25.2 | 2 | 17.7 | 9.7 | 13 | 7.7 | 26.7 | 1 | 12.0 | 7.6 | 8 | 64.4% |
| Levi Strauss | 17.3ª | 3 | 13.9 | 15.5ª | 2 | 12.0 | 25.0ª | 2 | 46.6 | 17.3ª | 1 | 7.4 |
| Manhattan Ind. | 9.1 | 21 | 10.1 | 7.2 | 18 | 7.5 | 21.9 | 3 | 16.9 | 2.3 | 17 | 25.6 |
| Blue Bell | 15.3 | 9 | 13.2 | 12.7 | 5 | 11.4 | 18.6ᵇ | 4 | 41.0 | 12.4 | 4 | 10.1 |
| VF Corp. | 16.2 | 6 | 17.1 | 14.1 | 3 | 14.5 | 15.8ᵇ | 6 | 23.0 | 16.1ᵇ | 2 | 30.0 |
| Warnaco | 9.5 | 20 | 12.7 | 7.4 | 17 | 9.1 | 13.3 | 9 | 17.0 | -3.7 | 26 | 81.4 |
| Hart Schaffner and Marx | 9.6 | 16 | 10.0 | 8.1 | 16 | 8.4 | 12.9 | 10 | 18.7 | 0.9 | 19 | 32.0 |
| Phillips–Van Heusen | 8.6 | 23 | 9.4 | 6.7 | 24 | 7.3 | 12.1 | 11 | 14.8 | 5.2 | 14 | 28.7 |
| Collins & Aikman | 15.9 | 7 | 12.7 | 13.2 | 4 | 9.7 | 11.8 | 13 | 20.7 | 8.0 | 7 | -8.5 |
| Kellwood | 13.8 | 11 | 15.8 | 10.6 | 10 | 12.7 | 11.6 | 14 | 16.8 | 4.3 | 15 | 37.6 |

ª 3-year average.
ᵇ 3-year growth.

the result of changing life styles in America (a move from cosmopolitan to suburban), the advent of early retirement, the 4-day workweek and an associated increase in leisure time, and the changing attitude of buyers who now seek new styles and colors. In addition to the increased demand for sportswear, men have become more style-conscious, and personal income has risen and is expected to rise 50 percent in the next decade. As personal income rises, so does disposable income, and it is with disposable income that clothing is purchased. In 1970, a little over 6 percent of disposable personal income was spent on apparel, a level of spending which is projected to last through 1980. The accompanying expenditure for clothes on an industrywide basis is expected to rise from $43.7 billion in 1970 to $64.8 billion in 1975 and to $88 billion in 1980.

Although the rate of consumer spending is supposed to slow down in 1974, the durable rather than the nondurable goods should suffer. Industry analysts see a 1974 sales growth similar to that in 1973 of about 9 percent. Of the total apparel sales, about 15 percent result from imports. Imports are more noticeable in the less fashionable lines, where they constitute 30 to 40 percent of sales, as compared to only 5 percent of rapidly changing fashions.

The apparel industry aims its sales mainly at the fastest-growing consumer age group, the 20- to 34-year-old group. These persons are the most fashion-conscious and have the most income. Families which are headed by 25- to 34-year-old persons and with incomes in excess of $15,000 are expected to grow from 15.5 percent to 24 percent of all families by 1976.

Although a long-term growth pattern is projected for the apparel industry, analysts are pessimistic about the immediate future. Apparel companies may be hard hit by the effects of a recession in 1974 and 1975. Consumers may be reluctant to spend on postponable items such as clothing, while food, rent, and utility bills are increasing. In addition the threat of increasing gas prices may cut mobility and with it the spur-of-the-moment shopping trips.

*Forbes* analyzed the apparel industry leaders, and Table 5 presents some relevant excerpts.

## Organization and management

The basic organization of Kellwood Company is shown in the organization chart (Figure 1). Kellwood strives to improve its marketing capabilities, and current and future customer needs are important to the company. In an attempt to optimize its efficiency, Kellwood has combined its fifty-one marketing facilities into 8 semiautonomous consumer-oriented groups. Each group's president is also a corporate vice president of Kellwood.

Each of the eight groups has its own women's furnishings, men's and boys' furnishings, men's and boys' apparel, and recreational goods. Each group also has its own accounting, employee relations, and engineering departments, merchandising, and sales staffs. The home office in St. Louis provides general policy direction and financial, engineering, and personnel and legal assistance. Basically, however, each group operates on a decentralized basis, and in this way it is felt that the individual group can concentrate on its own marketing capabilities which in turn results in larger sales and profits. Table 6 gives the operating organization of the company.

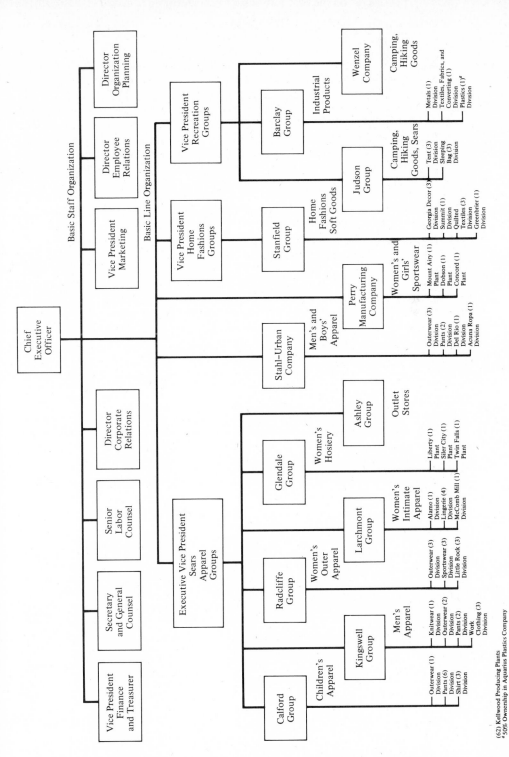

Basic Staff Organization

Basic Line Organization

**FIGURE 1** ■ Organization chart, 1974.

(62) Kellwood Producing Plants
[a] 50% Ownership in Aquarius Plastics Company

TABLE 6 ■ OPERATING GROUPS AT KELLWOOD, 1974

**Calford group**
Children's apparel
Executive office: St. Louis, Missouri
Plants in:
Sunbright and Trenton, Tennessee
Albany, Kentucky
Calhoun City, Coffeeville, Grenada, and Oxford, Mississippi
Frederick, Oklahoma
Phil Campbell, Alabama
President: Eugene D. Johnson

**Glendale group**
Women's, girls', and children's hosiery
Executive office: Siler City, North Carolina
Merchandising office: New York, New York
Plants in:
Siler City and Liberty, North Carolina
Twin Falls, Idaho
President: Robert B. McKinley

**Kingswell group**
Men's apparel
Executive office: St. Louis, Missouri
Merchandising office: New York, New York
Plants in:
Independence, Louisiana
Wesson and Monticello, Mississippi
Fairbury, Nebraska
Idabel and Pauls Valley, Oklahoma
Rutherford, Tennessee
Spencer, West Virginia
President: Mack A. Gale

**Larchmont group**
Intimate apparel
Executive office: St. Louis, Missouri
Merchandising office: New York, New York
Plants in:
Fernwood, Liberty, and McComb, Mississippi
Altus, Oklahoma
Mesa, Arizona
Alamo, Tennessee
President: H. Eugene Trotter

**Radcliffe group**
Women's and girls' apparel

Executive office: Little Rock, Arkansas
Merchandising office: New York, New York
Plants in:
Little Rock (3) and Lonoke, Arkansas
Asheville and Charlotte, North Carolina
Dresden and Greenfield, Tennessee
Morgantown, Kentucky
President: Norwood M. L. Jones

**Recreation market**
Recreation goods and services
Executive office: New Haven, Missouri
Corporation Vice President: William N. Kelley

*American Waterproofing Corp.*
Subsidiary
Industrial products and finishing services
Executive office: New Haven, Missouri
President: William N. Kelley

*Arvid's of Norway*
Subsidiary
Recreation goods
Executive office: Troy, Michigan
President: H. Arvid Henriken

*Judson group*
Recreation goods
Executive office: New Haven, Missouri
Plants in:
Bland, New Haven (3), Glasgow, and Nevada, Missouri
Lyons, New York
St. George (2), Utah
President: Thomas M. Nolan

*The Wenzel Company*
Subsidiary
Recreation goods
Executive office: St. Louis, Missouri
Sales office: Lyons, New York, and Los Angeles, California
President: William H. Wenzel

*Aquarius Plastics, Inc.*
Affiliate
Custom injection molding
Plant and executive office: Washington, Missouri
President: J. H. Klenke

**Stanfield group**
Home fashions
Executive office: St. Louis, Missouri
Plants in:
Perry (2) and Cuthbert, Georgia
Clinton (2), Oklahoma
Summit (2), Mississippi
Lewisburg, West Virginia
Corporation Vice President: John R. Barsanti, Jr.

**Stahl-Urban Company**
Subsidiary
Men's and boys' apparel
Executive office: Brookhaven, Mississippi, and New York, New York
Plants in:
Ackerman, Booneville, and Brookhaven, Mississippi
Shelbyville, Tennessee
Winnsboro, Louisiana
Del Rio, Texas
Ciudad Acuna, Coahuila, Mexico
President: Norville E. Wilson

**Perry Manufacturing Company**
Subsidiary
Women's and girls' apparel
Executive office: Mount Airy, North Carolina, and New York, New York
Plants in:
Mount Airy and Dobson, North Carolina
President: William K. Woltz

**Ashley group**
Retail outlet stores (40)
Executive office: St. Louis, Missouri
President: Frank L. Prins, Jr.

**Kellwood International, Ltd.**
Importing and marketing
Office: Hong Kong
President: William N. Kelley

**Research and development**
Shelbyville, Tennessee
General manager: William R. Conner, Jr.

The top executives and directors of the company include the following persons:

Fred W. Wenzel is the chairman of the board and president of Kellwood. He is 58 years old and graduated from the University of Wisconsin. Mr. Wenzel was vice president of the Wenzel Tent and Duck Company for 15 years, was the founder of the Hawthorn Company, and was its president for 12 years. He was a founder of Kellwood Company and served as its vice president and director for 3 years. Mr. Wenzel has been president and chairman of Kellwood for 10 years.

Robert A. Collett is the vice president of finance, and treasurer and a director. He is 52 years old and graduated from Beloit College and Northwestern University. Mr. Collett had 15 years of experience in industry before joining Kellwood; 14 of those years were with Sears, Roebuck and Company. Mr. Collett died suddenly in late 1974.

Frank L. Prins is a corporate vice president and president of the Ashley Group and a director in corporate relations. He is 59 years old and graduated from Harvard University. Mr. Prins had 21 years of experience in industry before joining Kellwood and was a founder of Kellwood.

Stanley M. Guthunz is executive vice president and a director. He is 64 years old and for 9 years was president of a manufacturing company before joining Kellwood. Mr. Guthunz was a founder of Kellwood Company.

William N. Kelley is corporate vice president, recreation market, and a director. He is 56 years old and graduated from Princeton University. Mr. Kelley had 23 years of experience in industry before joining Kellwood, mostly with the Hawthorn Finishing Company, one of the corporations which merged to form Kellwood.

John R. Barsanti is president of the Stanfield Group, corporate vice president of the Home Fashions Market, and a director. He is 46 years old and received an undergraduate and a law degree from Washington University. Mr. Barsanti had 15 years of experience in law before joining Kellwood.

Other directors of Kellwood are Sidney L. Bayar, who has worked for Sears for 40 years and who is also a member of the Sears Board of Directors; William L. Davis, who was previously president of Emerson Electric Company and was appointed to the Kellwood board of directors in 1973; Edward M. Cummings, who was president of the Continental Illinois National Bank of Chicago for 4 years and joined the Kellwood board in 1971; Eugene M. Adler, who worked for Sears for 31 years and was a Kellwood founding director; John F. Gallagher, who has worked for Sears for 23 years and was appointed to the Kellwood board of directors in 1973; James S. Marcus, who has been a partner with Goldman Sachs for 19 years and joined Kellwood's board in 1965; and John F. Hutcheson, Jr., who was chairman of the board of Happy Valley Farm and appointed to Kellwood's board in 1961.

Other Kellwood officers are as follows:

Mack A. Gale is corporate vice president and president of the Kingswell Group. He is 48 years old and attended Arkansas A&M and Texas Christian University. Mr. Gale had experience in industry before joining Kellwood.

H. Eugene Trotter is corporate vice president and president of the Larchmont and Radcliffe Groups. He is 48 years old and attended the University of South Carolina. Mr. Trotter had 12 years of experience in industry before joining Kellwood.

Eugene D. Johnson is corporate vice president and president of the Calford Group. He is 49 years old and graduated from Northwestern University. Mr. Johnson had 18 years of experience in industry before joining Kellwood.

Robert B. McKinley is corporate vice president and president of the Glendale Group. He attended Northwestern University and worked for Sears for 15 years before joining Kellwood.

Dale S. Dickman is the controller. He is 43 years old, graduated from the University of Missouri, and worked as assistant to the controller for Sears for 11 years before joining Kellwood.

Robert A. Maddocks is general counsel and secretary. He is 41 years old, graduated from Drake University, and had 12 years of experience in law before joining Kellwood.

George B. Smolen is corporate vice president of merchandising. He is 56 years old, graduated from the University of Virginia, and was president of Ahoskie Manufacturing Company (later merged to form Kellwood) before joining Kellwood.

Lorenz J. Koerber, Jr., is assistant secretary. He is 53 years old, received his law degree from the University of Chicago, and had 23 years of experience in law before joining Kellwood.

When Kellwood acquires companies, it usually allows them to operate as wholly owned subsidiaries. For example, Kellwood acquired the H. Wenzel Tent and Duck Company and related companies, the American Waterproofing Company, and the Wenzel Company West. These companies were encouraged to maintain the same executives, personnel, sales, and marketing policies.

## Financing Kellwood

Although Kellwood is a fast-moving company of substantial size, there has been little public interest in its affairs to date. This could have been because Kellwood was only recently listed on the New York Stock Exchange. Or it could have been the result of a lagging interest in apparel companies. Or, finally, it is less well known because, until it was NYSE listed, many of its operating figures were not made public.

Kellwood has 3967 stockholders and in January of 1974 had 3,337,678 shares outstanding. At one time Sears, Roebuck and Company owned 21 percent of the stock. However, owing to stock offerings, Sears now owns 16.1 percent of the stock of 535,476 common shares. Kellwood has no preferred stock outstanding. Officers and directors of Kellwood own 12.9 percent of the stock. The original owners of the 15 corporations owned 70 percent of Kellwood's stock when it went public. In 1974, only 40 percent is now in the hands of the original owners; the other 60 percent is in the market. Kellwood rarely issues new stock now, reserving that prerogative for acquiring new companies.

Kellwood makes its acquisitions with equity, thereby giving stock to companies who could not go public and could never have the market to do so alone. The amount of equity offered depends on the acquisition as measured against its own industry and against Kellwood. A decision is made whether to pay a premium for the company or to buy it at a discount. Kellwood looks at the proposed acquisition's book value, earnings, and earnings multiple. The most important factor is projected earnings per share and whether or not to give the company some leverage. Kellwood may give an acquisition some leverage if it is well managed and an industry leader. If the acquisition is marginal, then Kellwood tries to purchase it at a discount.

Less than 5 percent of Kellwood's buildings are owned by them. Ninety-five percent are leased on long-term agreements. Many of the arrangements are industrial revenue bond financing, 20-year leases with renewal options at substantially reduced rent. Thus shareowners' equity and borrowings are invested in much more liquid assets with a much faster turnover, resulting in high return on equity.

The apparel industry is highly sensitive to changing conditions. In 1963 and 1969, Kellwood had two bad years which were the result of higher interest costs, lower than expected volume, losses from its Alladin Knit Mills operations, and start-up costs. Alladin has since been closed and completely written off. Premature expansion in 1968 and 1969 resulted in a decrease in earnings per share in 1971. Kellwood had invested $16.5 million in production equipment in 1968 and 1969, and in addition increased leased facilities by 50 percent for another $10 million. They followed these procedures because both they and Sears thought business would increase. However, growth was only half of that expected.

While Kellwood has a more secure source of income from its borrowings as long as the Sears repurchase agreement is valid than it would have from attempting to float new stock, there are heavy costs involved with borrowing. Interest rates are quite high now, and in bad years, Kellwood receives a sizable interest bill, large enough to cause some problems should sales drop. This is one reason why Kellwood's dividend payments, which have been at a 20-cent quarterly rate, are likely to remain conservative. For example, the company was required each year to make prepayments on its debt in an aggregate amount equal to 50 percent of new earnings over $2 million through 1968.

Merchandising agreements, with Sears's obligation for its purchase of Kellwood's inventory of goods produced for Sears, are the basis for Kellwood's borrowing capacity and leverage. Kellwood's operations are financed through a revolving line of credit. The lending bank has an agreement from Sears to purchase the inventory on demand, thus providing inventory liquidity. Sears's ability to finance Kellwood's growth thus makes Sears's strength and future plans very important for Kellwood. From an investment point of view, an affiliation with Sears tends to upgrade Kellwood's stock in comparison with equities of competitors which do not enjoy this relationship.

As a result of the merchandise agreements with Sears and their purchasing agreement with the lending bank, Kellwood is presently highly leveraged with short-term borrowings. Kellwood has adapted its basic marketing model to be able to show the effects of various business levels and methods of financing. The result is a series of "what if" financial models. Kellwood is attempting to make contingencies in the event of Sears's growth ever slowing.

TABLE 7 ■ AVERAGE BORROWINGS AND STOCK-HOLDERS' EQUITY AT KELLWOOD, 1962–1968

|  | Stockholders' equity | Borrowings[a] | Ratio |
|---|---|---|---|
| 1962 | 14,413 | 24,129 | 1.7 |
| 1963 | 16,123 | 29,732 | 1.8 |
| 1964 | 16,830 | 36,758 | 2.2 |
| 1965 | 18,948 | 36,872 | 1.9 |
| 1966 | 26,429 | 43,888 | 1.7 |
| 1967 | 28,578 | 50,423 | 1.8 |
| 1968 | 34,758 | 45,992 | 1.3 |

[a] Thousands of dollars.
*Source: Wall Street Transcript,* Jan. 20, 1969.

TABLE 8 ■ KELLWOOD BALANCE SHEETS (IN DOLLARS)

| | April 30, 1974 | April 30,[a] 1973 | October 31, 1973 | October 31, 1972 | October 31, 1971 | October 31, 1970 |
|---|---|---|---|---|---|---|
| *Assets* | | | | | | |
| **Current assets:** | | | | | | |
| Cash | 11,748,000 | 9,948,000 | 5,450,000 | 9,046,001 | 9,825,950 | 11,289,646 |
| Receivables: | | | | | | |
| Sears, Roebuck and Company | 20,808,000 | 14,869,000 | 26,801,000 | 26,849,326 | 22,087,245 | 20,424,930 |
| Other | 16,601,000 | 16,824,000 | 16,885,000[b] | 12,728,658 | 10,807,121 | 11,225,085 |
| | 37,409,000 | 31,693,000 | 43,686,000 | 39,577,984 | 32,894,366 | 31,650,015 |
| Inventories: | | | | | | |
| Raw materials | 69,547,000 | 59,031,000 | 58,867,000[c] | 49,400,696 | 41,384,488 | 32,944,178 |
| Work in process | 14,547,000 | 12,155,000 | 12,625,000[c] | 11,499,332 | 10,558,588 | 10,494,905 |
| Finished goods | 95,433,000 | 83,348,000 | 85,583,000[c] | 62,115,616 | 61,633,553 | 57,073,337 |
| | 179,527,000 | 154,534,000 | 157,075,000 | 123,015,644 | 113,576,629 | 100,512,420 |
| Prepaid expenses | 863,000 | 942,000 | 1,143,000 | 493,795 | 464,497 | 849,762 |
| Total current assets | 229,547,000 | 197,117,000 | 207,354,000 | 172,133,424 | 156,761,442 | 144,301,843 |
| **Property, plant, and equipment, at cost:** | | | | | | |
| Land | 354,000 | 363,000 | 363,000 | 1,553,669 | 356,472 | 352,787 |
| Buildings | 2,325,000 | 2,254,000 | 8,562,000 | 2,387,336 | 2,181,670 | 1,993,782 |
| Leasehold improvements | 7,093,000 | 5,688,000 | | 5,656,401 | 4,958,569 | 4,693,934 |
| Machinery and equipment | 46,819,000 | 42,197,000 | 43,683,000 | 40,917,820 | 36,562,866 | 34,932,407 |
| | 56,591,000 | 50,502,000 | 52,608,000 | 50,515,226 | 44,059,577 | 41,972,910 |
| Less accumulated depreciation and amortization | 34,260,000 | 30,038,000 | 31,941,000 | 28,338,904 | 24,719,687 | 21,438,104 |
| | 22,331,000 | 20,464,000 | 20,667,000 | 22,176,322 | 19,339,890 | 20,534,806 |
| Capitalized facility leases, less accumulated amortization of $3,022,000— 1973 | 17,315,000 | 14,420,000 | 14,096,000 | 14,334,343 | 11,387,950 | 11,203,850 |
| | 39,646,000 | 34,884,000 | 34,763,000 | 36,510,665 | 30,727,840 | 31,738,656 |
| Other assets | 2,319,000 | 3,326,000 | 4,780,000 | 2,211,835 | 2,446,194 | 4,454,734 |
| Total assets | 271,958,000 | 235,327,000 | 246,897,000 | 210,855,924 | 189,935,476 | 180,495,233 |
| *Liabilities and shareowners' equity* | | | | | | |
| **Current liabilities:** | | | | | | |
| Short-term notes payable— banks | 126,113,000 | 108,450,000 | 113,800,000 | 93,355,000 | 82,285,000 | 78,725,000 |
| Accounts payable and miscellaneous accruals: | | | | | | |
| Sears, Roebuck and Company | 28,655,000 | 22,604,000 | 13,288,005 | 14,088,353 | 12,232,086 | 14,161,691 |
| Other | 20,134,000 | 19,026,000 | 24,750,995 | 16,963,007 | 15,992,003 | 11,193,607 |
| | 48,789,000 | 41,630,000 | 38,039,000 | 31,051,360 | 28,224,089 | 25,355,298 |
| Accrued employees' compensation and other expenses | 13,362,000 | 9,781,000 | 3,899,000 | 10,169,176 | 9,452,101 | 10,336,392 |
| Federal and state income taxes | 514,000 | 1,677,000 | 2,256,000 | 3,957,778 | 3,444,917 | 1,966,694 |
| Dividends payable | 668,000 | 601,000 | 668,000 | 598,542 | 569,219 | 573,075 |
| Current portion of long-term debt | 49,000 | 26,000 | 11,000 | 160,907 | 193,232 | 226,762 |
| Current portion of capitalized lease obligations | 1,632,000 | 1,344,000 | 1,411,000 | 1,360,180 | 1,240,582 | 1,155,957 |
| Short-term notes payable—others | -0- | -0- | 10,000,000 | -0- | -0- | -0- |
| Total current liabilities | 191,127,000 | 163,509,000 | 171,562,000 | 140,652,943 | 125,409,140 | 118,339,178 |
| **Deferred items:** | | | | | | |
| Federal income taxes | -0- | -0- | -0- | | 519,923 | 1,431,903 |
| Investment tax credit | 882,000 | 752,000 | 682,000 | 754,965 | 723,016 | 897,404 |
| Incentive stock credits | 442,000 | 245,000 | 397,000 | 298,890 | 282,000 | 177,120 |
| Self-insurance reserves | -0- | -0- | 1,010,000 | -0- | -0- | -0- |
| | 1,324,000 | 997,000 | 2,089,000 | 1,053,855 | 1,524,939 | 2,506,427 |
| **Long-term debt, less portion due within one year:** | | | | | | |
| Capitalized lease obligations | 20,651,000 | 18,096,000 | 17,354,000 | 18,325,651 | 16,196,660 | 16,914,717 |
| Other | 438,000 | 264,000 | 269,000 | 281,000 | 442,452 | 389,462 |
| | 21,089,000 | 18,360,000 | 17,623,000 | 18,607,198 | 16,639,112 | 17,304,179 |

**TABLE 8** ■ **KELLWOOD BALANCE SHEETS** *(Continued)*

| | April 30, 1974 | April 30,[a] 1973 | October 31, 1973 | October 31, 1972 | October 31, 1971 | October 31, 1970 |
|---|---|---|---|---|---|---|
| Shareowners' equity: | | | | | | |
| Preferred stock—without par value; authorized 200,000 shares | | | | | | |
| Common stock—without par value; authorized 6 million shares; issued and outstanding shares, 1973—3,337,673 | 7,283,000 | 7,284,000 | 7,287,000 | 7,059,563 | 6,652,967 | 5,828,926 |
| Retained earnings | 51,135,000 | 45,177,000 | 48,336,000 | 43,482,365 | 39,709,318 | 36,516,523 |
| | 58,418,000 | 52,461,000 | 55,623,000 | 50,541,928 | 46,362,285 | 42,345,449 |
| Total liabilities and shareowners' equity | 271,958,000 | 235,327,000 | 246,897,000 | 210,855,924 | 189,935,476 | 180,495,233 |

[a] Change in accounting year from October 31 to April 30.
[b] Less allowance for doubtful accounts.
[c] Inventories at lower of cost (first in, first out) or market.

The repurchase agreement is directly related to the Sears business; if other business grows faster, then it becomes necessary to change the financing system. When Kellwood was developing its model, it found that there had to be a certain ratio of Sears to non-Sears business in order to maintain the right financial position with sufficient collateral. Sears's business has grown historically about 11 percent a year and could conceivably grow as much as 15 percent a year without disrupting the financing. However, under these circumstances, outside business can grow only about 6 or 7 percent, and this is opposed to Kellwood's goal of following optimum growth under favorable conditions.

As an attempt to cover themselves more in financing the non-Sears operations, Kellwood varies the inputs for its models, changing such things as dividend policy and setting options. By working with the basic marketing model, the company can change the variables for present and proposed acquisitions. It can consider divestment and start-up costs in Sears and non-Sears business. (Sears may agree to pay part of this for the Sears business, but Kellwood has to carry a portion of that money for a period of time.) Start-up losses must also be taken into account. In sum, Kellwood does not consider sales growth alone. It will take a lower sales growth for a better profit growth. In order to realize this intention, the company uses the basic marketing model as the basic tool in financial strategy.

Kellwood's finance committee is presently working on a new alternative method of funding non-Sears business. It is unlikely that Kellwood would sell equity, as they have always been opposed to that and prefer to retain that alternative for purchasing acquisitions. Long-term debt may be one possibility open to the company, but even so with borrowing over a long period of time, accomplished perhaps through several installments, this alone would not meet all of Kellwood's requirements.

Kellwood does not have an even year-round sales pattern. However, usually the fourth quarter of August, September, and October provides one-third of the total sales and 40 percent of total earnings. The first quarter provides only 12 percent of the earnings. (Kellwood changed its fiscal year to one ending April 30, from October 31 in 1973.)

**TABLE 9 ■ KELLWOOD COMPANY AND SUBSIDIARIES STATEMENT OF CONSOLIDATED EARNINGS**

| | Year ended April 30, 1975 | Year ended April 30, 1974 | Six months ended April 30, 1973 | Year ended October 31, 1972 | Year ended October 31, 1971 | Year ended October 31, 1970 |
|---|---|---|---|---|---|---|
| **Net sales:** | | | | | | |
| Sears, Roebuck and Company | $307,513,000 | $287,548,000 | $113,157,000 | $241,212,141 | $223,975,152 | $215,998,069 |
| Other | 76,047,000 | 79,931,000 | 29,232,000 | 66,130,244 | 58,752,479 | 54,203,750 |
| | 383,560,000 | 367,479,000 | 142,389,000 | 307,342,385 | 282,727,631 | 270,201,819 |
| **Cost and expenses:** | | | | | | |
| Cost of products sold | $358,945,000[a] | $307,753,000 | $120,676,000 | $263,826,795 | $243,401,424 | $232,265,720 |
| Selling, general, and administrative expenses | . . . | 30,633,000 | 12,280,000 | 24,514,817 | 21,527,132 | 19,148,234 |
| Interest expense | 18,290,000 | 12,271,000 | 3,184,000 | 5,908,217 | 6,469,564 | 8,367,516 |
| | 377,235,000 | 350,657,000 | 136,140,000 | 294,249,829 | 271,398,120 | 259,781,470 |
| Earnings before income taxes[b] | . . . | $ 16,822,000 | $ 6,249,000 | $ 13,092,556 | $ 11,329,511 | $ 10,420,349 |
| Federal and state income taxes | 138,000 | 8,260,000 | 3,059,000 | 6,420,727 | 5,394,595 | 5,192,765 |
| Earnings before extraordinary charge | 418,000 | 8,562,000 | 3,190,000 | 6,671,829 | . . . | . . . |
| Extraordinary charge—Brownsville, net of applicable income taxes | . . . | –0– | 294,000 | 479,000 | . . . | . . . |
| Net earnings | $ 418,000 | $ 8,562,000 | $ 2,896,000 | $ 6,192,829 | $ 5,934,916 | $ 5,227,584 |
| Weighted average shares outstanding | 3,349,680 | 3,337,640 | 3,332,575 | 3,318,092 | 3,275,821 | 3,235,319 |

[a] 1975 cost and expenses are the total of cost of products plus administrative expenses.
[b] 1975 not given.

Recent Kellwood financial statements and allied data are given in Tables 8 through 11.

## Kellwood operations

In 1974, the Kellwood Company employed approximately 18,500 persons in 55 locations in the United States.

In 1972, Kellwood grouped its manufacturing facilities into consumer-oriented groups. These included eight groups, six of which were to manufacture for Sears. These six groups were realigned to fit Sears's categories (men's wear, children's wear, and women's wear). Figure 2 provides a list of the groups and the locations of Kellwood's 54 manufacturing plants. As can be seen from this figure, the plants are located in the following states: Alabama (1), Arizona (1), Arkansas (4), Georgia (3), Idaho (1), Kentucky (2), Louisiana (1), Mississippi (14), Missouri (4), New York (1), North Carolina (6), Oklahoma (6), Tennessee (7), Utah (2), and West Virginia (1).

The breakdown of Kellwood's sales by product category is given in Table 12. The home fashions group produces bedspreads, draperies, covers, quilts, and mattress pads. The group has established a marketing plan for the sale of products to the "open market" (all non-Sears business).

The apparel group, which accounted for over 78 percent of 1972 sales, plans to expand its existing products. The lines of women's wear produced include lingerie, dresses, uniforms, robes, blouses, slacks, skirts, hosiery, underwear, coats, and jackets. Men's apparel includes sport shirts, swimwear, jackets and coats, work trousers, slacks, outer coats, and insulated innerwear. The children's line includes boys' and girls' jackets and coats, trousers and shorts, and sweaters. Kellwood also produces a variety of infants' wear.

## TABLE 10 ■ STATEMENT OF CONSOLIDATED SHAREOWNERS' EQUITY

| | Number of shares | Amount | Retained earnings |
|---|---|---|---|
| **Balance, October 31, 1969** | | | |
| Kellwood Company and subsidiaries (common stock balances exclusive of $202,293 cost of 40,296 shares in treasury) | 3,135,337 | $4,866,826 | $33,420,151 |
| Acquisitions | 241,662 | 457,611 | 200,107 |
| Less treasury shares acquired | (101,662) | (18,544) | |
| Balance, October 31, 1969, restated | 3,275,337 | 5,305,893 | 33,620,258 |
| Incentive stock granted | 6,520 | 163,000 | |
| Stock options exercised | 28,842 | 360,033 | |
| Escrowed shares and dividends returned to company by Perry Manufacturing Company selling shareowners | (56,000) | | 110,860 |
| Net earnings | | | 5,227,584 |
| Cash dividends declared: | | | |
| Kellwood Company ($.72 per share) | | | (2,285,032) |
| Pooled companies less imputed taxes | | | (157,147) |
| **Balance, October 31, 1970** | | | |
| Kellwood Company and subsidiaries (common stock balances exclusive of $220,837 cost of 141,958 shares in treasury) | 3,251,699 | 5,828,926 | 36,516,523 |
| Incentive stock granted | 6,451 | 174,505 | |
| Stock options exercised | 43,297 | 649,536 | |
| Net earnings | | | 5,934,916 |
| Cash dividends declared: | | | |
| Kellwood Company ($.72 per share) | | | (2,268,155) |
| Pooled companies less imputed taxes | | | (473,966) |
| Balance, October 31, 1971 | 3,301,447 | 6,652,967 | 39,709,318 |
| **Balance, November 1, 1971** | | | |
| (Common stock balances exclusive of $220,837 cost of 141,958 shares in treasury) | 3,301,447 | 6,652,967 | 39,709,318 |
| Acquisition | 3,000 | 5,000 | (2,577) |
| Incentive stock granted | 5,283 | 173,853 | |
| Stock options exercised | 15,635 | 227,743 | |
| Net earnings | | | 6,192,829 |
| Cash dividends declared: $.72 per share | | | (2,417,205) |
| Balance, October 31, 1972 | 3,325,365 | 7,059,563 | 43,482,365 |

The recreation group produces camping and sporting equipment including such items as tents, tarpaulins, sleeping bags, life jackets, and boat covers. The tents and sleeping bags were added in 1972, and at that time Kellwood was also considering entry to the cross-country skiing market. The recently acquired Wenzel companies have established lines of distribution through which Kellwood hopes to sell new products.

**TABLE 11 ■ KELLWOOD COMPANY 10-YEAR SUMMARY OF OPERATIONS**
Years ended October 31[a]

| | 1973[b] | 1972 | 1971 | 1970 | 1969[c] | 1968 | 1967 | 1966 | 1965 | 1964 |
|---|---|---|---|---|---|---|---|---|---|---|
| *Operations* | | | | | | | | | | |
| Sales | $325,652 | $307,342 | $282,728 | $266,332 | $243,218 | $220,143 | $182,076 | $164,964 | $136,059 | $123,908 |
| Earnings before income taxes | 14,890 | 13,093 | 11,330 | 10,107 | 9,568 | 13,087 | 9,250 | 8,174 | 6,709 | 4,753 |
| Earnings before extraordinary charge | 7,679 | 6,672 | 5,935 | 5,069 | 4,644 | 6,350 | 4,835 | 4,292 | 3,419 | 2,343 |
| Extraordinary charge | 773 | 479 | | | 720 | | | | | |
| Net earnings | $ 6,906 | $ 6,193 | $ 5,935 | $ 5,069 | 3,924 | 6,350 | 4,835 | 4,292 | 3,419 | 2,343 |
| Shares outstanding | 3,328 | 3,318 | 3,276 | 3,095 | 3,111 | 3,061 | 2,924 | 2,918 | 2,535 | 2,510 |
| Per share: | | | | | | | | | | |
| Earnings before extraordinary charge | $ 2.31 | $ 2.01 | $ 1.81 | $ 1.64 | $ 1.49 | $ 2.08 | $ 1.66 | $ 1.47 | $ 1.35 | $ .94 |
| Extraordinary charge | .23 | .14 | | | .23 | | | | | |
| Net earnings | 2.08 | 1.87 | 1.81 | 1.64 | 1.26 | 2.08 | 1.66 | 1.47 | 1.35 | .94 |
| Cash dividends per share—Kellwood Company | .72 | .72 | .72 | .72 | .72 | .63 | .56 | .54 | .45 | .40 |
| *Financial* | | | | | | | | | | |
| Net working capital | $ 33,608 | $ 31,480 | $ 31,352 | $ 25,868 | $ 22,401 | $ 29,565 | $ 28,644 | $ 26,278 | $ 17,894 | $ 17,295 |
| Property, plant, and equipment (net) | 20,464 | 22,176 | 19,340 | 20,446 | 19,502 | 14,029 | 8,311 | 8,139 | 6,883 | 6,187 |
| Shareowners' equity | 52,461 | 50,542 | 46,362 | 41,705 | 38,287 | 35,969 | 30,507 | 27,231 | 20,138 | 17,528 |
| Shareowners' equity per share | 15.72 | 15.20 | 14.04 | 13.40 | 12.21 | 11.66 | 10.43 | 9.33 | 7.95 | 6.98 |

Shown below are the comparative sales and earnings for the years 1969 through 1973 which have been restated, when applicable, to include pooled companies for years prior to their affiliation with Kellwood Company

| | 1973[b] | 1972 | 1971 | 1970 | 1969[c] |
|---|---|---|---|---|---|
| Net sales | $325,652 | $307,342 | $282,728 | $270,202 | $246,173 |
| Earnings before extraordinary charge | 7,679 | 6,672 | 5,935 | 5,228 | 4,732 |
| Per share | 2.31 | 2.01 | 1.81 | 1.62 | 1.48 |
| Net earnings | 6,906 | 6,193 | 5,935 | 5,228 | 4,012 |
| Per share | 2.08 | 1.87 | 1.81 | 1.62 | 1.25 |

[a] As reported in the respective annual reports to shareowners.
[b] A pro forma 12-month-year ended April 30, 1973.
[c] Per-share data and shares outstanding have been adjusted to reflect the 2-for-1 stock split of February 25, 1969.

| Home fashions | Apparel | Recreation |
|---|---|---|
| Bedspreads—<br>quilted and unquilted | **Intimate**<br>Brassieres and girdles | Back packs |
| Canopies | Hosiery and pantyhose<br>Leotards and tights | Boat covers |
| Coverlets | Lingerie and sleepwear | Canvas products |
| Curtains | **Men and Boys**<br>Coats and jackets | Inflatable rafts |
| Draperies | Dress and sport shirts<br>Jeans, shorts, and slacks | Injection-molded plastics |
| Dust ruffles | Sweaters and tops<br>Work shirts and pants | Sleeping bags |
| Mattress pads | **Women and Girls**<br>Blouses and sweaters | Skis and accessories |
| Pillow covers | Dresses and shifts<br>Jeans, pants, shorts, and | Tarpaulins |
| Slumber bags | slacks<br>Jumpers, pantsuits, and skirts | Tents and accessories |
|  |  | Trailer accessories |

- • Apparel
- ■ Recreation
- ▲ Home fashion
- ○ Same city
- ★ Headquarters

**FIGURE 2** ■ Kellwood's eight operating groups and their plant locations.

## Producing Kellwood products

In general Kellwood's manufacturing process is labor-intensive, mechanized, and integrated; that is, most of the final products are generated from the basic raw materials. The processes used are different for clothing, household furnishings, and recreation goods.

In the manufacture of clothing, all sewing, pressing, and hanging are done by machine, although human labor is required to operate all the machines. Ovens are utilized for remnant press goods, and all products are prepared for

**TABLE 12 ■ KELLWOOD'S SALES BY PRODUCT CATEGORY**

| Product category | Percent of 1972 sales |
|---|---|
| Apparel (women's and girls' 45%, men's and boys' 33.1%) | 78.1 |
| Home furnishings | 10.7 |
| Recreation goods | 11.2 |
| | 100.0 |

*Source:* Standard and Poor's Over the Counter Reports, Oct. 10, 1973.

shipment either by boxes or hangers. The raw materials are received in the apparel plants and then cut to fit the required designs. Kellwood may not design the product. Both hosiery and lingerie are knit from scratch. Product design for special sections of apparel (outerwear and all-weather lines, women's and girls' clothes) comes from 50 people in New York who watch the fashion trends and adapt the new styles to Kellwood's products. Product design and research and development for the simple lines such as underwear and work pants are practically nonexistent.

The most basic product that Kellwood makes is boys' pants, and these are made in assembly fashion 250 days per year with no layoffs and no slowdowns. Kellwood has a special subsidiary company, ARK, engaged in "de-skilling operations," that is, designing new equipment. Kellwood has one single-plant division and one with six plants. Of the company's thirteen divisions, six are vertically integrated (they produce all or most of their raw materials from fibers or perform major finishing functions on purchased material). The other seven divisions are primarily fabricators that piece goods and cut, sew, and finish apparel or furnishing items.

Sears has yearly renewable contracts with Kellwood that range from 8 percent to 90 percent of production, depending on the item. Kellwood can schedule production evenly throughout the year because Sears places orders in advance. This allows Kellwood to purchase raw materials at advantageous times (several items are placed in inventory until their selling season). Inventory losses are nonexistent because each contract states that the selling price to Sears is agreed upon in advance of production on the basis of estimated manufacturing costs. Sears is therefore obligated to take the finished inventory and any unused piece goods.

In the production of household furnishings a couple of the units are totally integrated; that is, Kellwood manufactures its own filler, operates its own bonding machines, and does its own quilting. In the recreation goods division, Kellwood works with all raw unfinished duck and does all its own finishing. All tubing for its tents is made in the company aluminum tubing mill. Research and development for the camping equipment division is done at the plant level.

Kellwood introduced its own electronic data processing system 4 years ago in Memphis, Tennessee. One of its original developments was a corporation-wide entry and billing system for the Sears business. The system was developed with Sears and involves teletype order entry direct from the stores to Kellwood's computers. It includes a billing system which can reduce carrying time on Sears's receivables by 40 percent. Kellwood is now developing remote input and output devices (teleprocessing) so that each plant can use the computer.

In 1973, Kellwood built two new plants, one to manufacture men's work shirts for Sears, and the other to produce inflatable rafts for sale to Sears and other recreational companies. Kellwood also announced plans to begin building a new aluminum tubing mill (tubing for tents) in 1974, as well as a new corporate headquarters building in St. Louis. Kellwood also began building two new plants to produce boy's jackets, and acquired a 50 percent *overship* of Aquarius Plastics Corporation (Missouri). Aquarius Plastics manufactures molded plastic products and recreation products. Kellwood estimated that all of its new plants begun in 1973 would contribute $30 million to sales annually.

Kellwood has acquired many companies, some to generate non-Sears business and some to supplement the Sears business. In 1966, Kellwood acquired the Stahl-Urban Company (manufacturers of men's and boys' clothes) and the Perry Manufacturing Company (women's sportswear and robes). Both of these companies were to boost the non-Sears business. In 1966, Kellwood also acquired the Quilted Textiles Corporation of Georgia, which made quilted fabrics and linings.

In 1972, Kellwood entered a joint venture development program with North American Rockwell to produce warp knit for men's and women's outerwear. Kellwood is using the produced material for apparel manufacture at its other facilities. In the same year, Kellwood spent $1.5 million to expand its camping equipment and home fashions plants. Kellwood also sold its Brownsville, Kentucky, plant, which had been losing money, to Fairfield-Noble (makers of women's apparel).

In January of 1974, Kellwood announced that it would enter the carpeting market for the first time. Kellwood was seeking companies which would want to take part in Kellwood's entry either through acquisition, merger, a joint venture, or other agreement. Fred Wenzel had said "we will achieve the greatest growth from the addition of entirely new products." Kellwood had indicated that home fashions was its fastest-growing market, expanding at a compounded annual rate of more than 19 percent since 1961.

Only three of Kellwood's plants are unionized. Kellwood has two retirement plans, one for the office workers and one for the rank and file (the 66 plan). The company also provides all employees with life and health insurance, seven paid holidays a year, and 3 weeks' paid vacation after 10 years of service.

## Kellwood and Sears, Roebuck

At the present time and very probably in the future, Kellwood sells approximately 80 percent of its products to Sears, Roebuck and Company.

Kellwood gains at least four advantages from their relationship with Sears:

**1** The economics of large-scale production.

**2** Low selling, general, and administrative expenses. The low expenses are a result of nearly all production being gauged for one customer. In 1968, these expenses were 5 to 7 percent of sales volume for Kellwood compared to 20.6 percent for Kayser-Roth and 13.6 percent for Henry I. Siegal.

**3** Kellwood does not face the large risks of costly inventory write-off with Sears because everything produced for them is presold.

**4** Kellwood receives a good borrowing capability. The return on stockholders' equity due to leverage was 17.7 percent in 1968 compared to 12.2 percent for Kayser-Roth and 10.2 percent for Henry I. Siegal.

Over the years, Kellwood has been able to improve and use its organization, marketing people, designers, engineers, and production management to enhance the Sears relationship and to provide quality merchandise, on-schedule deliveries, and other services. Vital to the success of this relationship has been the company's ability to expand and diversify its capabilities in tune with and in time with Sears's own dynamic growth and changing needs.

Kellwood's share of Sears business varies depending upon the type of product and Kellwood's ability, facilities, and capacity. In some cases the company acts almost as a contractor; in others—for example, lingerie and hosiery—it is very integrated. In the latter, it begins with the yarn and completes the finished product.

Apparel has always been Kellwood's major business, although household furnishings and recreation goods are now accounting for a substantial part of sales. Broken down by category as a percentage of total sales, household furnishings account for 13 percent, recreation goods 12 percent, and apparel 75 percent (45 percent on women's apparel). Kellwood has, therefore, generated new sales by diversifying.

Sales to Sears have increased steadily. For example, they were $139.5 million in 1966 and $220 million in 1971. The company's share of Sears sales ranges from 10 to 50 percent, except for women's hosiery, which is 100 percent. Table 13 presents a recent breakdown of sales to Sears. Later sales were allocated similarly.

Kellwood seeks to account for up to 50 percent of Sears's projected needs in each product category. This allows Sears to buy a large proportion of its projected needs advantageously with close control on quality and delivery. At the same time, it gives Sears the flexibility to augment its selection and inventories in response to changing fashion trends and economic conditions. Occasionally, Sears asks that Kellwood design and take on the responsibility of supplying a new product, for example, men's knit shirts.

Sears has not wanted Kellwood to be 100 percent Sears-oriented. There were some problems with Sears representatives visiting various plants. The fact that Kellwood has now developed separate Sears-oriented and non-Sears-oriented operating groups has improved the relationship. In this way, Sears representatives can go through the plants without seeing products being made for other department stores and non-Sears customers can go through the other plants without seeing Sears products.

**TABLE 13 ■ KELLWOOD SALES TO SEARS, ROEBUCK AND COMPANY, 1972**

| Kellwood group | Sears market served | 1972 sales volume (in millions) |
|---|---|---|
| Calford | Children's and youth apparel | $ 41.2 |
| Glendale | Hosiery and related products | 29.4 |
| Judson | Recreation | 16.5 |
| Kingswell | Men's apparel | 35.0 |
| Larchmont | Women's intimate apparel | 34.6 |
| Radcliffe | Women's apparel | 52.5 |
| Stanfield | Home fashions | 32.0 |
| | | $241.2 |

Kellwood feels sure that Sears will continue to grow, a feeling which is based on projected growth trends and the recent announcement of Sears's expansion plans. Sears intends to build 40 additional stores every year. In 1974, Sears has 840 stores, 680 of which are full-line stores which carry all Kellwood products. An increase of 40 stores a year beyond the present 680 full-line stores is a potential growth for Kellwood products, of more than 10 percent. In addition a Sears study on general merchandise sales indicated that department stores such as Sears got 21.6 percent of total business in 1960, got 32.9 percent in 1970, and will have a projected 38 percent in 1980.

Kellwood feels, therefore, that Sears is going to experience real growth as a result of both an increased number of stores and a larger market. Sears has its own specific goals of reaching $20 billion in sales by certain dates, and Kellwood can put these goals into its own models. Kellwood also plans on a push-pull basis, which entails recognizing the profitable areas, the better lines, and the efficient management teams, and adding and deleting where appropriate. Although Kellwood's computer is used mainly for repetitive supportive operations, the company does use some computer facilities for planning.

Kellwood has many competitors in supplying Sears, but is not overly concerned about them. Kellwood has no desire to take 75 percent of Sears's business in any one product, because if Sears's market falls, then so does Kellwood's business. Kellwood wishes to provide about 50 percent of Sears's business; then if that total business drops, Sears can take away from some of its fringe market sources and keep Kellwood level. If Kellwood is too dominant in one area, then Sears has nothing to cushion Kellwood with.

## SEARS'S CONTRACTS WITH KELLWOOD

Sears has bought from Kellwood's Rutherford Division for 27 years. Each of the divisions has a firm contract committing Sears to buy a certain percentage of their needs from the division, which in turn results in economical manufacturing. Sears benefits from this by getting good sources capable of handling orders throughout 840 stores and 1600 catalog and telephone ordering offices.

The contracts between Sears and Kellwood commit Sears to purchase specified quantities of merchandise at specified prices. The contracts are on a 1-year basis and can be canceled by either party with a year's notice. If Sears does not want to take delivery at the specified dates, it adjusts the contract prices to cover Kellwood's inventory carrying costs.

Sears wants its suppliers to be able to ship goods practically overnight. Therefore, computers are being used more to get the orders in and shipped out again. Shipping is done on an allocation basis and decisions are premade; in the event of a backup, a program puts the orders in line and ships out the most critical. Usually there is only a 1-day turnaround on a normal order.

Products manufactured for Sears are scheduled for production quarterly to meet Sears's reasonable delivery requirements. Sears furnishes Kellwood, a specified number of days before the beginning of each quarter, a written estimate of their requirements of product for such quarter. Kellwood then provides an estimated manufacturing cost of the product for Sears. This estimated cost is agreed upon between Kellwood and Sears in order to set billing prices. An appropriate profit margin on the costs is added to meet Kellwood's target rate of return on investment. Kellwood can exceed this margin by continuing effective management. The firm production order for the quarter at billing price is then placed by Sears.

These contractual agreements also recognize start-up costs in new operations or expansions and are included as a reimbursable cost subject to profit. Thus, actual manufacturing costs will be higher in the early stages than later on, and Sears recognizes this. Whenever Sears is hit by a fashion change, it still buys the contracted merchandise; thus Kellwood's profits are not subject to fluctuations in the Sears business. Kellwood can, therefore, project on a lower profit rate for Sears but with guaranteed good performance.

Although Sears allows Kellwood a margin on contracts, it will not protect Kellwood from the consequences of management mistakes such as the expansion in 1969 and the purchase of an unprofitable and unmanageable knitting operation. These experiences resulted in a 28 percent dip in earnings per share in fiscal 1969 from $2.08 per share to $1.49 per share.

If an item for Sears does not sell, Sears must dispose of it, but goods are frequently not shipped until the following year. Kellwood does not record gross profit until the goods are shipped; thus inventory carry-over results in lower profit levels until Sears takes delivery. Carry-overs result in reduced demand by Sears and thus lower plant utilization rates. Kellwood and Sears recently adopted a new inventory system whereby Sears orders smaller amounts at more frequent rates throughout the year, thereby reducing the amount of time that Kellwood must hold Sears inventory.

Sears has encouraged Kellwood to obtain leading members of the apparel industry, and to add them to the management team. Kellwood's groups and subsidiary companies which operate as self-contained semiautonomous profit centers all rely on the executives at Kellwood's headquarters for general policy direction, advice, and counsel. The corporate headquarters determines objectives, strategies, and structure. It also allocates resources and coordinates the individual units in an effort to achieve the corporate goals. Planning is an organized function with executives at the headquarters and within each operating unit regularly meeting to develop plans and review results.

The two Sears members on Kellwood's board have no more weight than any other two members. However, they do sometimes bring good advice from Sears. As a result of the amount of business Sears takes, Kellwood listens to that advice.

## Strategic planning

Strategic planning takes place at corporate headquarters and at the operating group headquarters. Each has established long-range objectives and strategic plans. These are reviewed and revised continuously, for strategic planning is a dynamic process subject to changing conditions.

Kellwood really began to emphasize strategic planning about in 1970 and has now developed a series of "what if" models to make assumptions with and to choose between alternative paths for growth. These models are flexible and allow the replacement of various accounting units. Kellwood has a basic marketing model which it developed itself and in which it is possible to substitute a different growth plan, a total Sears plan, and an outside growth plan.

Kellwood's projections show the company growing at 18.7 percent a year with Sears business, that is, with inflation of 8 percent, and 9.8 percent in units, and the non-Sears business growing at 21 percent a year (12 percent after inflation). Kellwood is, therefore, growing at different rates in different areas and accordingly feels the need for a highly flexible strategy for growth.

Kellwood has no fixed goals for its Sears/non-Sears business ratio; it prefers to maintain a flexible and dynamic outlook. If Kellwood has a goal to attain a certain position in a specific market or product, they will decide on a specific approach. The company's general rule, however, is to take whatever action generates the greatest return.

### ACQUISITION STRATEGY

Kellwood previously acquired companies on an opportunistic basis. Recently, it has developed specific criteria for acquisitions. In addition to typical financial requirements (equity, debt, ROI, inventory amount, and turnover) there are other criteria.

The potential acquisition must fit the marketing plans and Kellwood's basic market such as apparel, home furnishings, and recreation. The proposal must have real growth potential. The marketing division makes its own studies and proposals, which are then in turn evaluated from a financial point of view.

Geographic location is important to Kellwood. It does not want to locate in an area where there is so much business that employees leave at the first sign of conflict. The company produces heavy items; therefore, it wants to be roughly in the center of the country and near to its major markets, thereby facilitating shipment at minimum cost. In addition, Kellwood never makes an acquisition without considering the prospective company's position, facilities, and management.

Kellwood has developed several acquisition models. These are industry models, derived by examining specific industries. When Kellwood looks at a prospective acquisition, it can measure that company against its industry, and determine where that company is stronger and weaker than the industry. One of Kellwood's long-range plans includes five potential acquisitions doing a projected total business of $144 million in sales by 1978.

Kellwood also has a model of its own company. So, when a potential acquisition is considered, the industry and company can be simulated with Kellwood's models. For example, Kellwood has a model of the carpeting industry based on previous 5-year figures. It is possible to tell what a typical carpeting company's balance sheet and profit and loss statement look like by examining the model. By weighing the years to get a trend, Kellwood can determine the industry's average figures for equity, long-term debt, return, borrowing, amount of inventory, and inventory turnover. This was developed in conjunction with its decision to enter the carpet industry.

Kellwood considers two types of acquisitions. The first type of acquisition is a result of Kellwood's need for more plant capacity. In this case, Kellwood might buy a business run by one person who has a plant, machinery, and employees, trained about 75 percent up to Kellwood's standards. Here the company is buying just for the facility and the machinery, not the management, and is taking this action in lieu of finding a new location and building a plant. In this type of acquisition Kellwood is not concerned with the continuity of management and markets. Kellwood has acquired five such plants between 1970 and 1974.

In this type of acquisition Kellwood always puts in its own management and runs things its own way. Overcoming the employee problems is accomplished by offering better benefits and by handling many of the problems (OSHA, EEOC, and other federal requirements) that a small business may have some difficulty with. Kellwood feels that it must maintain close control of these kinds of acquisitions because it needs consistent quality. In addition, Kellwood must support the areas that Sears is promoting, such as equal employment opportunity, because the company is listed as a subsidiary in the Sears annual report. Sears looks to Kellwood to uphold the company image.

The second kind of acquisition is to diversify into new businesses. In this type of acquisition, the company is buying a total business in effect and would like to see the original management stay in, to retain the same marketing, and to continue to sell to the present customers. For example, the company acquisitions for new products, such as the Stahl-Urban, Wenzel, and Perry Manufacturing companies. Any acquisition for the proposed entry to the carpet business will be a total acquisition.

Kellwood is now hoping to enter the carpet business. They would not, however, acquire a carpet mill that does all of its business with Sears. Kellwood wants to get into the business, build up new outside sales, and then gradually bring the Sears business in. In this way they hope to develop a synergistic effect with the management and facilities they have.

## The 20 percent non-Sears business

Acquisitions have helped to boost Kellwood's strategic expansion independently of Sears, and Sears has encouraged the diversification. Kellwood entered the non-Sears field in 1966 by acquiring Stahl-Urban Company (producer of men's and boys' apparel). They also acquired Perry Manufacturing Company in 1968 (producer of women's apparel). Since then the Wenzel Company (recreation equipment) has also been acquired.

Non-Sears business accounts for around 20 percent of Kellwood's business. In the last 10 years this volume has risen from $4.8 million. Sears encourages this action by its suppliers because through these outside relationships the suppliers remain competitive in product line and price.

Kellwood's Stahl-Urban Company and the Perry Manufacturing Company are both wholly owned subsidiaries. The Wenzel group, also wholly owned, is concentrating its sales effort on the open market. In addition Kellwood has 32 retail outlet stores, and it plans 200 more in the next 5 years (the stores sell all irregular sizes, odd lots, and out of season goods). These retail outlet stores are grouped under the Ashley division.

Table 14 presents the data for sales of the 20 percent of Kellwood's output. The sales percentage by group was much the same in 1974. Each of these non-Sears groups is structured like the Sears-oriented groups, and each is a profit center. Each group has a charter and pursues the same long- and

**TABLE 14 ■ KELLWOOD'S NON-SEARS BUSINESS, 1972**

| Group or subsidiary | Market | 1972 sales volume (in thousands) |
|---|---|---|
| Stahl-Urban Company | Men's and boys' wear | $29.5 |
| Wenzel Company | Recreation | 17.7 |
| Perry Manufacturing Company | Women's and girls' sportswear | 11.8 |
| Ashley | Retail outlet stores | 6.0 |
| Various | . . . . . . . | 1.1 |
| Total | | $66.1 |

short-range planning, uses the same monitoring and controls, and makes use of the same merchandising and styling expertise.

For the non-Sears business, Kellwood must build in a factor of 2 or 3 percent extra for the goods that will not sell when these people are hit by a fashion change. Kellwood has different less secure contracts with its non-Sears customers. If these customers do not want to take the goods, then Kellwood has to negotiate with them. Kellwood has to take the markdowns on this business; therefore, it charges a higher price to its non-Sears business. As a result, profits will fluctuate with non-Sears customers, whereas they will be smooth with Sears. Kellwood feels the two blend well together; 75 percent of their business is stable and so they can afford fluctuations in the rest of their business.

Kellwood can use its basic model to determine which areas of its present business are doing well, which acquisitions to leave alone, and which ones to push. The company ceases to expand certain areas once they become too expensive. Kellwood's marketing staff, its group executives, and Sears to some extent, all contribute to Kellwood's strategy by determining what is needed at which locations and in which time periods. Kellwood then adjusts the strategy to allow for its own goals and its desires to be independent in some areas.

### SEARS, SEARS'S SUPPLIERS, AND STRATEGY

Sears sometimes has a direct effect on Kellwood's strategic planning. Sears will get involved when Kellwood must take some action to meet Sears's requirements. If, for example, Sears wants to double its market penetration in one area and wants Kellwood to be the source, then Kellwood will need new plants. In order that the plants will not be empty until Sears achieves its desired market penetration, Sears will take business away from its market sources and give it to Kellwood. When the plants are up to capacity, Sears will phase out the excess business back into the market sources.

Sears does not get directly involved in Kellwood's acquisitions of new products, plants, or executives in the non-Sears business. Generally, however, Kellwood would not make an acquisition that Sears would not be happy with, even if it was for non-Sears business.

Kellwood does get together with other major Sears suppliers such as Whirlpool, DeSoto, Roper, and Universal to discuss functional efficiencies. Kellwood does observe Whirlpool's operations in an informal way to see whether help is needed or operations should be improved.

## The future

Kellwood appears to have great growth potential both with Sears and in its non-Sears business. For the latter, Kellwood has chosen businesses with growth potential. With regard to the Sears business, Sears has not penetrated the soft goods business nearly as deeply as it has the hard goods business. Thus, the potential for this penetration with Sears is great. The future looks bright at Kellwood.

# Hawaii Best Company

Ram Charan

Gradually rising from his chair in his third-floor plush office overlooking Waikiki Beach in Honolulu, James Lind, president of Hawaii Best Company (HBC), greeted Charles Carson, vice president and general manager of the company's Islands Division, and invited him to take the seat across from his desk.

"Charlie, I am sure that something has gone wrong," he said as Carson remained standing. "You have many fine qualities—I was the one who recognized them when I promoted you to vice president—but I have been reviewing your progress these past few months and—and the results have not met our expectations."

Carson fidgeted at the window, watching the October morning across the harbor. His face reddened, his pulse quickened, and he waited for Lind to continue.

"The costs in your division are higher than budgeted, the morale is low, and your branch managers are unhappy with your stewardship," Lind said. "And your cooperation with Gil Harris has fallen short of satisfactory."

Carson grew angrier at the mention of Harris, a young aggressive man with a master's degree from a well-known eastern business school. Harris was a latecomer to HBC, but Carson knew that everyone was pleased with his performance.

"Charles, at the country club last week, I was speaking to one of our vendors. He intimated that your dealings with him had not been entirely clean. This is what hurts me the most.

"I know you are 49, that your son is only 8, that this is a difficult time for you and your family," Lind concluded as Carson stared out of the window. "You have spent almost all your life in Hawaii; it would be difficult for you to move to the mainland. It will be even harder for you to find a similar position in the Honolulu community. But I must ask for your resignation, and I will do my best to help you find a more suitable opportunity."

"Jim, I can't believe it," Carson finally replied. "It's just all wrong." He turned slowly from the window, his face bloodred.

"I have been with this company for 10 years. I built this division. Sure, this year's results are not quite what you expect, but my division is still the

---

This is a disguised case. That is, the case is based on a real company situation, but the identity of the company has been changed. It serves no useful purpose to attempt to ascertain the true name of the company.

largest contributor to corporate profits. I'll bet your friend Gil has been telling you about the vendor deals. Well, it's a damned lie, and I won't stand for it! That boy will stop at nothing to grab power."

There was a long silence as Lind and Carson stared at opposite corners of the large office. "I will not resign," Carson suddenly declared, and he left the president's office coughing, his face flushed and his heart pounding.

Lind stood motionless as he watched the door close. He was uncertain about what to do; it never had occurred to him that Carson might refuse to resign. He decided to proceed as he had planned, but with one modification.

"Janice, please take a memo," he said to his secretary, and he dictated a note to Charles Carson informing him that his employment with HBC was terminated as of that afternoon, October 10, 1972.

After sending out a general release memo informing all division heads that Carson had resigned and that Joseph Ward, a promising young executive, presently employed as the manager of planning in the Operations Division, would assume the position of acting general manager of the Islands Division, Lind hurriedly left the office. He had less than an hour to catch the 12:30 plane, intending to visit each of the seven branch heads on the outer islands, to tell them about the change and their new acting general manager.

While Lind was having his memos sent out, Carson was trying to contact his previous boss and old friend, Roy North, past president of HBC and presently an influential member of the company's board of directors and its powerful executive committee. Carson intended to have the matter taken to the board for deliberation.

## Background

Mr. North was one of five members of the board's executive committee, which customarily approved the appointments, promotions, stock options, and salary adjustments of personnel earning over $10,000. This included department heads, division managers, and vice presidents. The committee held at least one meeting a month, and these, like the regular monthly meetings of all 12 board members, were well-attended. (Table 1 shows selected data about the directors.)

Several of the directors were descendants or close friends of the founders of the Hawaii Best Company, but only James Lind and Thomas Johnson were HBC employees. Board members held 5 percent of outstanding stock; the rest was widely owned by the people and business concerns in Hawaii. No one outside the board represented more than 1 percent of the HBC stock.

In 1971, with $30 million in sales and an e.p.s. of $1, the Hawaii Best Company was a manufacturer and marketer of a special formula. The company was listed on the Pacific Coast stock exchange with 1 million shares outstanding which yielded a stable dividend of $1 per share over the last 5 years. It sold its line of special formula X to industrial, commercial, and residential customers in the state of Hawaii. Its manufacturing facilities and three sales branches were strategically located in Honolulu, and seven other sales branches were spread over the outer islands. The company usually negotiated hard for its basic raw material K, used in the manufacture of special formula X, from its only locally available long-term supplier. Imports of the

TABLE 1 ■ HAWAII BEST COMPANY BOARD OF DIRECTORS, 1972

| Name | Age, place most of life spent | Background | Current activity | Previous association in years | | Number of shares represented |
|------|------|------|------|------|------|------|
| | | | | Industry | Company | |
| Choy, Eduardo | 65, Hawaii | No academic degree, financial | Entrepreneur, corporate chairman, banker | 0 | 15 as director | 3,000 |
| Donahue, John | 70, Hawaii | Engineer, retired | Retired corporate executive of the company, vice president of a property management company | 40 with company | 8 as director | 500 |
| Eichi, Ishi | 40, Hawaii | Legal, attorney | Practicing attorney | 0 | 2 as director | 0 |
| Fields, J. B.[a] | 54, Hawaii | M.B.A. (Harvard), finance | Executive vice president of a very large multinational company headquartered in Honolulu | 0 | 15 as director | 2,500 plus 4% owned by his company |
| Fong, Charles | 40, Hawaii | M.B.A. (Harvard), finance | Executive vice president of a real estate development and investment firm | 0 | 2 as director | 500 |
| Hanley, Don[a] | 70, Hawaii | Secretary | Retired | 19 | 19 as director | 10,000 |
| Johnson, T.[b] | 48, Hawaii | Accounting | Corporate treasurer of the company | 15 | 2 as director | 1,000 |
| Lind, James[a,b] | 53, mainland U.S.A. | Engineer, alumnus of Columbia Business School | Corporate president | 28 | 2 as president and director | 4,000 |
| North, Roy[a] | 56, mainland and 16 years in Hawaii | Engineer, financial analyst | Executive vice president of a conglomerate headquartered in Honolulu | 16 | 10 as director | 1,500 |
| Rusk, Dean[a] | 52, Hawaii | Accounting and finance insurance, alumnus of Harvard Business School | Executive vice president of a local large company operating in insurance, sugar, real estate, and merchandising business | 0 | 5 as director | 0 |
| Simon, A. F.[a] | 65, Hawaii | Contractor, entrepreneur | Corporate chairman and president, entrepreneur | 0 | 20 as director | 30,000 |
| Vogel, Lawrence | 63, Hawaii | Finance, fiduciary | Corporate president; fiduciary agent representing a large local trust | 0 | 10 as director | 0 |

[a] Member of the board's executive committee.
[b] HBC employee.

raw material were deemed uneconomical for HBC, and a second source of local supply did not appear on the horizon.

The company also sold special formula Y but only in the outer island branches and not in Honolulu. It was purchased in finished packaged form from several vendors within and outside the state of Hawaii, but the company was in no way involved in its manufacture.

Over the past 5 years the company's sales grew at an average annual rate of 4 percent, but its market share remained constant. Relative to the competition, HBC's profit performance had declined and, according to one competitor, "it was only through some 'creative' accounting that the company barely made its dividend in 1971."

HBC had two rivals in its industry: the larger company had annual sales of $60 million, the smaller sales of $15 million a year. It was a fiercely competitive industry, and special favors or discounts, although illegal, were sometimes granted to woo customers from another company. And customers were precious; just 10 clients accounted for one-quarter of HBC sales.

## HBC's organization structure

Figure 1 shows HBC's skeletal organizational structure. The president, James Lind, was responsible to the board of directors. Thomas Johnson, vice president finance and secretary, and president James Lind regularly attended the monthly board meetings, and other vice presidents were also invited frequently to keep the board informed on matters of importance in the area of their specialty. According to Andrew Simon, chairman of the board of directors, "This practice gives us an opportunity to know what we have underneath the first layer."

In addition to managing five divisions and attending to the normal duties of the president, Lind took a special interest in the negotiations involving labor contracts and purchasing of raw material K and special formula Y. The specific responsibility for negotiating labor contracts rested with the vice president of industrial relations, John Wyle. Control of the purchase of raw material K lay with the senior vice president of operations. The vice president and general manager, Islands Division, was responsible for buying special formula Y.

In all these negotiations, however, it was not uncommon for Johnson to get involved as well.

Among the corporate vice presidents in 1971, John Wyle, 51, had been the longest with the company. However, he had suffered two serious heart attacks since joining the company in 1945—one in 1959 and the other in 1968. According to the former HBC president North, "Wyle is the best industrial relations man we can find and he is a good personal friend of ours [their wives played cards together] but, frankly, his health concerns me and several of the directors."

Since joining the company in 1947 as a clerk, Thomas Johnson had risen to the position of vice president finance by 1968. In 1970 at the age of 46, he was elected to the company's board of directors at the suggestion of president Lind. Johnson had been actively under consideration for the presidency when Roy North vacated the position in December 1969. One member of the selection committee put it this way: "Johnson is quite happy in his present position. He is a little lazy. He never wanted the top job."

Gil Harris, 33, joined the company in March 1970 as vice president for marketing and general manager of the Honolulu Division, responsible for the conduct and performance of the three Honolulu branches and for the companywide market research, market planning, and advertising campaigns.

As vice president and general manager of the Islands Division, Charles Carson had controlled the conduct and profit performance of all the branches in the state outside Honolulu. Carson also participated in the marketing decisions such as advertising and promotions, and his division was charged a pro rata share of expenses on the basis of divisional sales.

According to the highly summarized report distributed quarterly to the

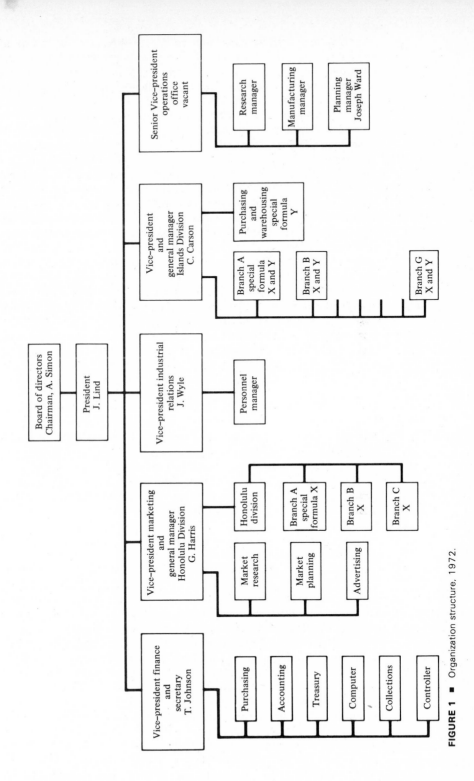

**FIGURE 1** ■ Organization structure, 1972.

board of directors, the Islands Division for the first half of 1972 had not met the budget expectations, although its performance was better than it had been the previous year.

The Islands Division and the Honolulu Division were created by Lind in February 1970, after the sudden death of vice president sales Robert Gellerman, 46. Gellerman had been responsible for the companywide sales and advertising throughout the state. Before the establishment of the two divisions, Lind consulted chairman Simon, former HBC president North, and other members of the executive committee, and received their unanimous support. Also included in the restructuring were the functions of market planning and market research, which were consolidated under the new vice president for marketing and general manager, Honolulu Division.

The position of senior vice president operations had been vacant since May 1970, when Lind asked for the resignation of the man who had held that office. The three managers within the division—manufacturing, planning, and research—had since been reporting directly to Lind. They constantly vied for the attentions of the president and the corporate vice presidents in the hope that one of them could assume the vice presidency. Three key members of the board were acquainted with Donald May, the research manager, but the other two were virtually unknown to the board.

## Arrival of James Lind

On January 1, 1970, James Lind replaced Roy North as president of Hawaii Best Company when the latter left the company to become an executive vice president of a multinational conglomerate headquartered in Honolulu. North, under whose control HBC had prospered for 7 years, recommended Lind for the presidency after an unfruitful search for a candidate within the company and the Hawaiian community. The board of directors accepted Lind, then a top executive in a trade association in New York, and he soon proved to be a man of integrity, dedication, and charm.

Although the business community in Hawaii, according to some observers, was tight-knit and nearly impervious to outsiders, Lind was readily admitted and liked. The morale at HBC soared during the early months of his presidency, because he was a man who was both extraordinarily hardworking—he put in up to 70 hours a week—and "human." He was one of the best fund raisers for community projects in Hawaii.

Financially, however, the company was not performing well under Lind's leadership. Rising labor and material costs, and the combination of the inflationary spiral and the fierce competition, put pressure on the profit margins. Lind began to make changes in key personnel in an effort to offset the problem.

In February, he promoted Charles Carson, a man who had been with the company for over 8 years, to vice president and general manager of the newly created Islands Division.

Three months later he asked for the resignation of Frank Adams, senior vice president for operations. Lind felt that Adams, after 27 years at HBC, was "utterly lacking in an ability to negotiate for key raw materials," and brought his grievance to the board of directors. Before Adams was asked to resign, a severance package was worked out and approved by the board.

Adams, then 53, was utterly shaken. He became an estimator for a local construction firm at one-quarter of his former salary. This was the first such severance in the history of the company, and as one director put it: "The event was extremely painful; it left deep scars on us and our families."

Lind's final major organizational change was to bring in an old friend of his who he hoped could develop new marketing strategies for the entire company. Gil Harris, from the Global Chemical Company of New York, was made vice president for marketing and general manager of the newly formed Honolulu Division.

## Lunch at the club

"Jason, thank you for meeting me here, and for canceling your other engagement to see me. I'm sorry, but I had to talk to you; something has happened that I think you should know about."

Charles Carson leaned heavily on the table in the restaurant of Honolulu's only country club. The man across from him curiously fingered the stem of his martini glass. Jason Fields, the executive vice president of the third largest international company based in Hawaii, was a busy and important man. An illustrious graduate of the Harvard Business School, Fields was one of the three most influential members of the company's board and its executive committee. Field's employer controlled 4 percent of the HBC's outstanding stock. He did not have too much time to spend with Carson, his golf buddy and a vice president of one of the two companies of which Fields was a director. (The other company was a major buyer from Carson's division at HBC.)

"I'll try to be brief," Carson said. "Jim called me to his office this morning and asked me to submit my resignation. I refused. But before he left for his bloodsucking trip, he terminated my association with the company as of this afternoon."

Fields raised his eyes briefly.

"I control the company's three largest customers, you know," Carson continued. "I can easily take them to the competition. But he still has the gall to accuse me of taking a kickback, with absolutely no proof! I think Harris has put him up to it. He's been charging a substantial proportion of his division's expenses to my division. I have been arguing with him about these expenses during the last several weeks, and he finally told me he'd have my head if I went to Lind about it.

"Not even a note of thanks. Not even a mention of it to the board," Carson murmured. "I wonder how long the board will allow Lind to destroy the very people who built this company.

"I don't know what to do."

"Neither do I, Charlie," Fields answered. "I'm truly sorry to hear about this. This is strange. I had no idea this was even being considered. The executive committee met this morning and Jim, of course, was there, but this was never mentioned. I'd like to help in any way I can, Charlie. All I can say is wait and see what happens at the next board meeting. It's scheduled for October 17."

"Well," said Carson, "I just hope the board takes this chance to finally straighten up the organization. Its relationship to the company, the delegation of responsibility, the criteria for employee evaluation—there are a lot of things that have remained garbled and unclear ever since Frank Adams was asked to resign. The morale of the executive staff is low. Earnings are not improving. Everyone is concerned about his own skin. Who will be axed next?"

## Lind's turbulent ride

Lind was deeply shaken over Carson's refusal to resign, and on the plane to Maui he tried to analyze the situation. He realized that he had made a mistake in promoting Carson a year and a half ago, although the psychological tests that he had had administered to all executives at the time pointed strongly to Carson as the man for the job. Lind remembered too the annual physical checkup the company executives were required to undergo, and recalled sadly the high blood pressure and excessive cholesterol level that Carson's exams revealed.

"I must stick to my guns," Lind mused. "I refuse to be blackmailed by the three powerful customers Charlie has in his pocket. I cannot let my authority be challenged, especially by a man who I believe has taken kickbacks."

After a sleepless night, Lind telephoned Andrew Simon to inform him of Carson's resignation.

"Yes, Jim, Jason Fields called me yesterday to tell me," Simon relayed. "He was quite upset. And I saw Roy North at a cocktail party last night. He, too, knew about the event, and he appeared visibly disturbed. This is a sad situation. I am a little more than concerned, but you are the boss. We'll try to handle the matter appropriately at the board meeting next week."

Simon returned the receiver to the cradle thoughtfully. For the first time in his 20 years as chairman of the board, he felt that there was a conflict between the management of company affairs and the way he thought they ought to be managed.

Approaching 65, Simon was still active and healthy, and never missed a board meeting. He was once the caretaker president of HBC for 1 year, in 1956. His deep concern for the company was reflected in the way he usually helped in its decision-making process—carefully—after long consideration and debate. He had discussed the matter of Adams's resignation privately first with Lind, then with the executive committee, and then with the entire board before Simon had been fully convinced that Adams should go. Similarly, he had spent long hours deciding on Lind's appointment, consulted extensively with several members of the board individually. Both Mr. and Mrs. Lind were interviewed thoroughly before the board selected him for the presidency.

## Meeting of the board

The board of directors of the Hawaii Best Company met at 7:30 A.M. on October 17 and, as usual, the meeting promptly came to order. The items on the agenda were: the company's performance for the third quarter; the long-term lease on the HBC building; the anticipated state of the nation's economy for the upcoming year; the contributions that HBC made annually to three local charities.

Lind's announcement was the last item.

"Mr. Chairman, members of the board," he said, "I regret to inform you that as of October 10, 1972, Charles Carson resigned from our company. . . ."